# THE SELF IN
# SOCIAL PSYCHOLOGY

**Key Readings in Social Psychology**
General Editor: ARIE W. KRUGLANSKI, University of Maryland at College Park

The aim of this series is to make available to senior undergraduate and graduate students key articles in each area of social psychology in an attractive, user-friendly format. Many professors want to encourage their students to engage directly with research in their fields, yet this can often be daunting for students coming to detailed study of a topic for the first time. Moreover, declining library budgets mean that articles are not always readily available, and course packs can be expensive and time-consuming to produce. **Key Readings in Social Psychology** aims to address this need by providing comprehensive volumes, each one of which will be edited by a senior and active researcher in the field. Articles will be carefully chosen to illustrate the way the field has developed historically as well as current issues and research directions. Each volume will have a similar structure to include:

- An overview chapter, as well as introduction to sections and articles
- Questions for class discussion
- Annotated bibliographies
- Full author and subject indexes

**Titles in preparation:**

| | |
|---|---|
| Social Psychology | *Arie Kruglanski and E. Tory Higgins* |
| Social Cognition | *David Hamilton* |
| Motivation and Cognition | *Arie Kruglanski and E. Tory Higgins* |
| Close Relationships | *Harry Reis and Caryl Rusbult* |
| Group Processes | *John Levine and Richard Moreland* |
| Intergroup Relations | *Michael Hogg and Dominic Abrams* |
| Stereotypes and Prejudice | *Charles Stangor* |
| Language and Communication | *Gün R. Semin* |
| Attitudes and Persuasion | *Richard E. Petty and Shelly Chaiken* |
| Social Psychology of Emotions | *W. Gerrod Parrott* |
| Social Psychology of Culture | *Hazel Markus and Shinobu Kitayama* |
| Social Psychology of Health | *Peter Salovey and Alexander J. Rothman* |

# THE SELF IN
# SOCIAL PSYCHOLOGY

Edited by

## Roy F. Baumeister
*Case Western Reserve University*
*Cleveland, OH*

| USA | Publishing Office | Psychology Press |
| | | A member of the Taylor & Francis Group |
| | | 325 Chestnut Street, Suite 800 |
| | | Philadelphia, PA 19106 |
| | | Tel: (215) 625-8900 |
| | | Fax: (215) 625-2940 |
| | Distribution Center | Psychology Press |
| | | A member of the Taylor & Francis Group |
| | | 7625 Empire Drive |
| | | Florence, KY 41042 |
| | | Tel: (800) 634-7064 |
| | | Fax: (800) 248-4724 |
| UK | | Brunner/Mazel |
| | | A member of the Taylor & Francis Group |
| | | 27 Church Road |
| | | Hove, E. Sussex, BN3 2FA |
| | | Tel: +44 (0) 1273 207411 |
| | | Fax: +44 (0) 1273 205612 |

## THE SELF IN SOCIAL PSYCHOLOGY

2 3 4 5 6 7 8 9 0

Printed by Edwards Brother, Ann Arbor, MI, 1999.

A CIP catalog record for this book is available from the British Library.
♾ The paper in this publication meets the requirements of the ANSI Standard Z39.48-1984 (Permanence of Paper)

### Library of Congress Cataloging-in-Publication Data

Available by request from publisher

CIP

ISBN: 0-86377-573-X (paper)
ISBN: 0-86377-572-1 (hardcover)

# Contents

# About the Editor

**Roy F. Baumeister** holds the Elsie B. Smith Chair in the Liberal Arts at Case Western Reserve University. He received his Ph.D. in 1978 from Princeton and then had a postdoctoral fellowship at the University of Virginia, the University of Texas, and the Max-Planck-Institute in Munich, Germany. Roy F. Baumeister has authored over 200 scientific publications. His research and writing span a a range of topics in social psychology, including self-esteem, self-control, performance under pressure, reactions in emergencies, guilt, sexuality, emotion, decision-making, taking risks, and trying to make a good impression.

# The Nature and Structure of the Self:
# An Overview

Roy F. Baumeister

**N**o topic is more interesting to people than people. For most people, moreover, the most interesting person is the self. Psychology is a large and popular department in almost every university because it promises to teach students something about people and, indeed, something about themselves. Other sources that promise self-knowledge, from fortunetellers and astrology to magazine articles to medical tests to religion, likewise find a steady stream of interested seekers. Yet what is this "self" about which so many people are so curious?

Providing a satisfactory definition of the self has proven fiendishly difficult. It is what you mean when you say "I". Most people use "I" and "self" many times each day, and so most people have a secure understanding of what the self is—but articulating that understanding is not easy. This conceptual elusiveness is one reason that the study of self has so many sides and subtopics: self-awareness, self-monitoring, self-presentation, self-concept, self-esteem, self-actualization, self-verification, self-schema, self-enhancement, self-regulation, and more.

Writing in 1943, Gordon Allport predicted that the psychology of self would expand and flourish over the coming decades. His prediction has been amply confirmed. Ashmore and Jussim (1997) searched a major psychological database and found over 31,000 publications on self over two recent decades. The self is one of the most actively researched topics in all of psychology. Part of the popularity of self as a topic, however, is that the many subtopics of self guarantee that there will be plenty of questions to keep researchers busy. When ideas or methods cease to produce new findings on one aspect of self, another area takes up the slack.

## Nature of the Self

The fact that everyone can use the term "self" with such ease and familiarity suggests that the concept of selfhood is rooted in some simple, universal human experience. I have spent considerable time and effort trying to formulate just what this was. The first thing to consider is the fact of having a physical body. To a child, and to many adults in less psychologically minded cultures, self is body. It would make no more sense to speak of trying to

1

"find yourself" than it would make sense to talk of having misplaced your body. Everywhere in the world, self starts with body.

Soon, however, self encompasses more than body. When adults in Western civilized countries speak about the self, they generally are referring to a psychological rather than a physical being, and it is one that contains thoughts, feelings, and attitudes, one that is socially validated and holds down multiple places in the matrix of social relationships. It is often regarded as having a vast hidden component, so that other people cannot perceive or understand your "self" unless you reveal it to them, and indeed even you may have to struggle and work hard in order to know your own self. Thus, there is something more than the body that must be consulted when seeking the foundations or origins of selfhood.

Three major human experiences form the basis of selfhood. These three appear to be universal, in that people all over the world experience them. They are also broad enough to integrate almost everything that psychology knows about the self. I have elaborated these in a considerably longer work (Baumeister, 1998), but a brief overview here is in order to furnish a point of departure for thinking and reading about the self.

First, there is the experience of *reflexive consciousness.* The conscious human mind can turn its inquiring attention back toward its own source and seek the self. In plain terms, people are self-aware. The self is not known directly but either observed in action or inferred from social events, which is why the self is harder to know and understand than, say, a table or spoon. In any case, the very concept of self would be meaningless if we were not able to become aware of ourselves.

In psychology, reflexive consciousness encompasses a broad set of research. There is the study of self-awareness per se, as well as the study of how knowledge about the self is acquired, stored, transformed, and used. Self-esteem involves the evaluative dimension of self-knowledge (e.g., "am I good at this?"). In everyday experience, thinking about yourself, feeling self-conscious, experiencing a rise or drop in self-esteem, and trying to learn about yourself are all encompassed under this aspect of the self.

Second, there is *interpersonal being.* The self is a member of groups and relationships, and indeed one of the crucial functions of the self is to enable people to relate to others. The self is not created nor discovered in social isolation, through looking inward. Instead, the first things that the child learns about its self involve its connections to others (as in being a member of a certain family) and about how its traits set it apart from others (as in being male or female).

In psychology, the interpersonal dimension of selfhood encompasses the study of how the self is involved in interacting with others. This features the study of self-presentation, which involves how people communicate images of themselves to others and alter their behavior when others are watching. It also includes the study of how interpersonal interactions alter self-perceptions, as well as how views of self shape interactions and relationships. In everyday life, the interpersonal aspect of selfhood includes explaining one's acts to others, performing for an audience, taking pride or shame in the actions of partners and family members, and the like.

Third, the self has an *executive function.* This enables the self to make choices, initiate action, and exert control over self and world. Without this, the self might still be something that could be known and could relate to other people—but it could not *do* anything. Terms such as "agent" and "origin" express this important aspect of the self.

The executive function is least studied and least well understood of the three aspects of the self, but it still has received attention (which is steadily growing). This aspect of self encompasses research on autonomy and volition, self-regulation, self-defeating behavior, choice and decision-making, the quest for control, and other volition. In daily life, the executive function is experienced when one weighs options and makes a decision, forces oneself to do something, restrains an impulse, and similar phenomena.

## How the Self Became a Problem

Thus, the self has somehow evolved from a banal, obvious, everyday phenomenon into an intricate and challenging problem that continues to elicit a flood of research articles. The rising interest among psychologists in the self is itself part of a broader social trend in which the individual self has become a fascinating problem, and this in turn is a result of how the self has actually changed in recent history to become more difficult, challenging, and important to explore.

In previous work (Baumeister, 1986, 1987), I provided a rather detailed explanation of how the self took its modern, problematic form in Western history, moving from the relatively straightforward and untroubled way that selfhood was understood in medieval Europe to the complex, conflicted selfhood found in Western culture today. That analysis was organized around four main problems of the self, and the relevant changes can be only briefly summarized here.

The first problem is that of self-knowledge. Medieval Europeans did not recognize the self as particularly difficult or interesting to know, and the self was equated with visible manifestations and actions. Self-knowledge became more complex when the culture began to think of the self as something inner and hidden. A greatly expanded awareness of self-deception made self-knowledge suspect. These changes occurred around the early modern period (1500–1800), and they escalated until around the early 20th century, by which time the self was viewed as a vast inner continent that could only be explored with considerable difficult and possibly with expert help (e.g., in psychoanalysis). Thus, the self went from being supposedly one of the easiest to one of the hardest things to know.

The second problem is that of human potential and fulfillment. In medieval society, the dominance of Christian views meant that by and large people viewed life on earth as a preamble to the afterlife, which would involve eternal fulfillment (salvation) or damnation. The secularization of society in the early modern period instigated a quest for fulfillment that could be achieved during life on earth. Artistic creation, the work ethic, and the idealization of romantic love all represented partial answers to this new problem. Furthermore, the view emerged during the Romantic period that each person had a unique, special destiny and potential, instead of the older (e.g., soteriological) view that held out the same goal of human life for everyone. Discovering one's unique potential and achieving fulfillment came to be understood in the 19th and 20th centuries as starting with inner exploration of the self and then cultivating its special gifts. Even in the case of modern psychology's notions of individuation and self-actualization, however, the means to achieve fulfillment remain largely unspecified, and the goals themselves are hazy and elusive. Furthermore, human fulfillment tends to be short-lived, and as a result, few people manage to resolve this problem successfully.

The third problem is the relation between the individual and society. In medieval thought, the social order was fixed and stable—and, being a product of God's will, was considered supremely legitimate. People were not supposed to want to change their station in society. With the Industrial Revolution, the population explosion, and other social changes, social mobility became the norm, and people abandoned the view that mankind should not question God's ordering of the world. The American and French revolutions repudiated age-old understandings about the social order and introduced radical new ideas such as individual freedom and equality.

The newly secular and open-minded understanding of the relation between individual and society progressed through stages of escalating pessimism. Early 18th century social reformers believed that the ideal society was just around the corner, and in the mean time escapists (such as Rousseau and Thoreau) believed that going back to nature for a little while would enable the individual to find fulfillment and undo the harmful effects of civilization. By 1900, urbanization made such escapes less thinkable, and the dark view predominated that alienated masses of humanity were helpless, exploited victims of an uncaring social order. In the latter half of the 20th century, new ideas about how people could possibly live in the world of mass media and mass production, while yet finding individuality and satisfaction, began to point the way toward a less dismal view.

The fourth problem is that of self-definition. In the Middle Ages, identity was largely defined by very stable, visible, ascribed attributes, such as family membership, social rank, adult vs. child, place of birth, and gender. Over the centuries, liberal reforms and other factors have tried to free human life from being dictated by such factors, so that everyone can be free to become whatever he or she wants. Therefore, modern self-definition has come to depend on a changing, uncertain mixture of choices and accomplishments, and the self is assumed (perhaps unrealistically) to contain the values and other bases on which these choices are made.

Taken together, these trends provide the basis for the fascination with self that pervades modern Western thought and culture. The self is at once something obvious, immediate— and deeply problematic. To know the individual self, to ascertain and fulfill its potential, to work out its proper relationship to society at large, and to be able to define it despite shifting, fluid criteria constitute a source of endless concerns and difficulties, and these difficulties have become increasingly acute over the past few centuries. The self is likely to continue to be a problem for the foreseeable future!

## Knowledge and Awareness of Self

Human selfhood depends on the capacity for reflexive consciousness, which is to say that the human mind is remarkably able to turn attention toward itself and construct extensive knowledge of itself. The self does not seem able to be directly aware of itself in the same way it can be aware of a tree or a pork chop or even of another human being. Self-awareness and, hence, self-knowledge remain incomplete and depend on inference.

### Self-Awareness

The topic of self-awareness was introduced to social psychology by Duval and Wicklund (1972). They proposed that self-awareness generally involved focusing on some aspect or property of the self and comparing it to some ideal, goal, or other standard. Because people are generally imperfect, the result of this comparison is normally a recognition that the self is flawed or deficient in some way. Motivational and emotional consequences follow from this recognition. The awareness of the self's shortcomings produces various forms of unpleasant emotions along with the desire to remedy the shortcoming and bring the self closer to its ideal standard. Unreasonable or inconsistent behavior, poor performance, socially undesirable acts, and the like are all recognized by self-awareness, and the emotional distress that accompanies these recognitions makes the person want to improve.

Not all self-awareness is aversive, of course, as other researchers quickly recognized (e.g., Carver & Scheier, 1981; Greenberg & Musham, 1981). When one has just enjoyed a major success or other good outcome, self-awareness can be quite pleasant, and people may enjoy thinking about how wonderful they are. Also, not all standards are as daunting as ideals of perfection. When people compare themselves to the average person or to someone less fortunate than themselves, they generally feel good, because they regard themselves as relatively capable, attractive, likeable, and virtuous (e.g., Taylor & Brown, 1988; Wills, 1981).

At times, people may seek to escape from self-awareness, such as when recent events cast the self in an unflattering or undesirable light, or simply because continuous self-awareness can become stressful and aversive (Baumeister, 1991). Part of the appeal of consuming alcohol is that it reduces self-awareness, thereby enabling people to forget their troubles or to enter with fewer inhibitions into a celebrative party (Hull, 1981). More aggressive means of escaping self-awareness include suicidal behavior, sexual masochism, binge eating, and meditation (Baumeister, 1988, 1990, 1991; Heatherton & Baumeister, 1991).

Self-awareness also has several interesting direct effects. It can improve introspection, at least in the sense that people's attitude self-reports match their behavior more closely when their self-awareness is high (Pryor, Gibbons, Wicklund, Fazio, & Hood, 1977). Some emotional reactions are intensified, possibly due to the fact that the self's inner states are all the more salient when attention is focused inward (Scheier & Carver, 1977). Performance on controllable, effort-sensitive tasks is improved by self-awareness (Wicklund & Duval, 1971), but skilled performance is impaired (a phenomenon commonly described as "choking under pressure") insofar as attending to inner processes disrupts the smooth execution of automatic or overlearned responses (Baumeister, 1984). Last, highly self-aware people tend to overestimate the degree to which external events are directed at them, a pattern analogous to paranoid thinking (Fenigstein, 1984).

## Self-Knowledge

A generation ago, it was common to speak of "the self-concept" as the main term that encompassed what people know and believe about themselves. That term implies, however, that all self-knowledge is integrated into a single concept, and most theorists have come to reject that assumption as false. Instead, it may be more appropriate to speak of a large stock of self-knowledge, of which only a small part (the *phenomenal self,* in Jones & Gerard's, 1967, term) is conscious at any given time. The conscious part may tend to resemble a self-concept in that it is largely coherent and integrated. The full stock of self-knowledge, however, is free to contain gaps, contradictions, inconsistencies, and plenty of material that is at best very loosely connected together.

Hence, a more appropriate unit of analysis may be the self-schema, which is to say an individual piece of information or a specific belief about the self (Markus, 1977). Moreover, by activating different self-schemas, people may regard themselves in quite different ways. Indeed, research such as that by Fazio, Effrein, and Falender (1981) managed to induce people to think of themselves and behave in substantially different ways simply by asking loaded questions that induced them to search through their stock of self-knowledge for information that portrayed the self in a different light.

Beyond question, people have a high desire to gain self-knowledge. The quest for information about the self, whether from learning test scores, to getting feedback from social interactions, to consulting astrology and other scientifically dubious sources of information, is widespread, familiar, and seemingly relentless.

Yet people are not equally motivated to seek all manner of self-knowledge. They have clear preferences for certain kinds of information about themselves, and of course when people learn about themselves they are sometimes dismayed at what they find. Social psychology has identified three main motives that dominate the human quest for self-knowledge.

The first of these can be called the appraisal motive: It seeks accurate information that is diagnostic of the self's traits, whether good or bad. Trope (1983, 1986) has provided solid evidence of the simple quest for valid, useful information about the self.

The second motive that shapes self-knowledge is the quest for consistency. People seek information that confirms what they already believe. Once people have formed an opinion of themselves, whether favorable or unfavorable, they are reluctant to discard it. Swann (1985, 1987) has provided good evidence for the preference for consistent information, which he calls *self-verification* processes.

The third motive is the desire for information that casts the self in a favorable light. It can be called the *self-enhancement* motive: It entails seeking new, favorable knowledge about the self as well as finding ways to reject or revise preexisting, but unfavorable, views of the self. Many authors have documented these self-enhancement biases (see Greenwald, 1980; Taylor & Brown, 1988).

In principle, accurate information should be the most useful and adaptive, and so the appraisal motive should be the dominant one. In a series of studies that pit the three motives against each other, however, Sedikides (1993) found that the self-enhancement motive tended to be the strongest, with consistency (self-verification) a distant second, and appraisal an even more distant third. The desire to think well of oneself is apparently stronger than the desire to have one's beliefs confirmed or the desire to learn the truth about oneself.

Thus, the human quest for self-knowledge is shaped to a substantial extent by a preference for learning favorable, flattering things. Paulhus and Levitt (1987) showed that people have a pattern of automatic egotism that causes people to become simply, widely favorable about themselves when threatened or distracted. Taylor and Brown (1988) proposed that the tendency to overestimate the self's good qualities, along with a tendency to overestimate the self's control over outcomes and a general pattern of unwarranted, exaggerated optimism, is a common ingredient in mental health and good psychological adjustment.

In view of the pervasive motivation to think well of oneself, it is not surprising that people have developed many strategies for doing so. Many of the defense mechanisms proposed by Freud actually operate quite successfully to protect self-esteem against threatening, undesired information (see Baumeister, Dale, and Sommer, 1998, for review). Alongside these, modern researchers in personality and social psychology have identified multiple patterns of self-deception that protect the self against unwelcome information or help inflate self-esteem. Although space precludes a full summary of these (see Goleman, 1985, for a thorough if by now slightly dated review; for a more recent summary, Baumeister, 1998), it is useful to list major ones briefly.

Self-deceptive mechanisms that bolster self-esteem include the self-serving bias, by which people take credit for successes but deny blame for failures (Zuckerman, 1979). People selectively forget failure feedback more readily than success or praise (Mischel, Ebbesen, & Zeiss, 1976; Crary, 1966). They accept praise uncritically but receive criticism skeptically, with a view toward finding reasons to dismiss it (Kunda, 1990; Wyer & Frey, 1983), and if possible they dismiss interpersonal criticism as motivated by prejudice (Crocker & Major, 1989). They search their stock of self-knowledge and memories in a biased fashion that increases the likelihood of finding agreeable results (Kunda & Sanitioso, 1989). They shift the meaning of ambiguous traits so that the criteria they choose make them look best (Dunning, Meyerowitz, & Holzberg, 1989). They persuade themselves that their good traits are exceptional while their flaws are common and shared by many other people, so that as a result they stand out only in good ways (Campbell, 1986; Marks, 1984; Suls & Wan, 1987).

No doubt more findings about different strategies for protecting or boosting self-esteem will be coming in future years. The three motives underlying self-knowledge guarantee a rich, productive source of motivational conflict and ensure that the topic of self-knowledge remains as important to individuals as it does to researchers.

## Self-Esteem

Trait self-esteem has been one of the most studied individual differences in personality over the past several decades. Part of the interest stems from the belief that low self-esteem is responsible for a broad assortment of personal and social problems, so that raising self-esteem could bring about dramatic improvements on the American social scene (e.g., California Task Force, 1990). Recent evidence has cast severe doubt on that view, however, and there continues to be a dearth of evidence that school programs (for example) aimed at raising children's self-esteem will produce reductions in crime, delinquency, drug abuse, unwanted pregnancy, underachievement in school, or the like.

More generally, it does not appear that low self-esteem is a widespread problem in the United States. As already noted, the average person already tends to regard himself or herself as above average. In nearly every research sample, self-esteem scores range from the high end of the scale to around the midpoint, with very few people scoring substantially below the middle (Baumeister, Tice, & Hutton, 1989). The "low" self-esteem in a typical research sample is therefore low only in a relative sense.

Research has gradually provided a well-founded picture of what high vs. low self-esteem yields. High self-esteem is generally associated with greater persistence in the face of failure, suggesting that self-esteem facilitates resilience (Shrauger & Rosenberg, 1970; Shrauger & Sorman, 1977). People with low self-esteem are more vulnerable to the psychological impact of everyday events, as indicated by wider mood swings and affective reactions (Campbell, Chew, & Scratchley, 1991). People with low self-esteem are also more flexible and malleable, and so they are more strongly affected (than people with high self-esteem) by persuasion and influence (Brockner, 1984). People with low self-esteem suffer from a motivational conflict, such that they want success and approval but are often skeptical of it (Brown, 1993), and there is even evidence that happy, desirable life events can have adverse effects on their physical health (unlike people with high self-esteem, who are healthier when life goes well) (Brown & McGill, 1989).

Two main underlying differences are associated with trait self-esteem. One is self-concept confusion: People with low self-esteem are less likely to have a thorough, consistent, stable stock of self-knowledge than people with high self-esteem (Campbell, 1990; Campbell & Lavallee, 1993). People with high self-esteem know more about themselves (although their beliefs are not necessarily more accurate). This knowledge is more stable over time and less marred by internal contradictions, and they express more certainty about this knowledge, than people with low self-esteem (Campbell, 1990).

The other difference is in motivational orientation (Baumeister, Tice, & Hutton, 1989). People with high self-esteem have a self-enhancing orientation, in that they seek to capitalize on their good traits and pursue successes even under risky conditions. In contrast, people with low self-esteem have a self-protective orientation, which means that they seek to remedy their shortcomings and to avoid failures and other setbacks.

## Self as Interpersonal Being

The self develops amid a network of interpersonal relationships, starting with family and then extending to peer groups and various organizations. To regard the self as merely a knowledge structure or information processor is to overlook its crucial interpersonal function. Selves are tools that help people interact with others and forge lasting relationships. Even such features as self-esteem may serve interpersonal functions, such as operating as a meter that keeps track of whether the self has sufficient qualities to make it a desirable interaction and relationship partner for other people (Leary, Tambor, Terdal, & Downs, 1995).

### Self-Presentation

Self-presentation consists of the self's effort to convey a particular image of itself, or information about itself, to other people. An influential early work by Goffman (1959) analyzed social behavior in terms of theater and drama, suggesting that people play roles for audiences. The view that people change their behavior when others are watching, in order to make an impression on those others, has been well supported. In hundreds of studies, people have been found to behave differently depending on whether they believe their acts are private and anonymous, as opposed to publicly identified and known to others (for reviews, see Baumeister, 1982; Leary, 1995; Schlenker, 1980).

Motives for self-presentation can be classified into two groups: strategic and expressive. The strategic ones aim to manipulate the audience, often for ulterior ends. A taxonomy of five strategic motives was provided by Jones and Pittman (1982). They noted that you may seek to persuade others that you are competent (which they called self-promotion), to induce others to like you (ingratiation), to get them to regard you as dangerous (intimidation), to view you as a morally respectable individual (exemplification), or to take pity on you as helpless and needy (supplication). These motives suggest ways that people may seek to manipulate others. Thus, they are more likely to hire you if you succeed at self-promotion, more likely to spend time and form relationships with you if you succeed at ingratiation, more likely to help and support you if you succeed at supplication, and so forth, than if you fail. In such cases, self-presentation is guided by the audience's beliefs and standards, and the self-presenter strategically seeks to secure some benefit by making the optimal impression.

Expressive motives for self-presentation involve claiming desired identities for the self (Baumeister, 1982; Schlenker, 1980; Wicklund & Gollwitzer, 1982). In this case, self-presentation is based more on the self-presenter's own standards and values than on the audience's. Sometimes people will seek to prove to others that they are not what the other people want or expect, that they refuse to go along with what others want them to do, that they hold opinions and values that differ from those of others, and so forth.

These expressive motives reflect the facts that identity requires social validation. One cannot really "be" a great artist or successful entrepreneur or hero or genius unless some other people recognize one as such. Hence, an important step in claiming a desired identity is having one's claim validated by others. Even if the other people do not share the same values, it is sometimes desirable to have them validate your identity claims. For example, the sometimes outrageous behaviors of musicians and other artists may scandalize the witnesses, but that scandalized reaction helps validate the artist's identity as notorious, rebellious, or iconoclastic.

Generally, though, people seek to make favorable impressions, and so self-presentation deals primarily in trying to make various positive impressions, particularly when meeting people for the first time. The main limits to the favorability of impressions people try to make are plausibility: People are reluctant to make overly favorable claims that could be discredited, such as if they claim to be highly competent at something but then will have to demonstrate their alleged proficiency by performing well (Schlenker, 1975). Self-presentation is thus often the result of a tradeoff between favorability and plausibility (Schlenker, 1980).

Self-presentation, like most forms of social interaction, has mainly been studied in the context of strangers meeting for the first time (such as in a laboratory experiment), but everyday life is mainly lived in interaction with people with whom one has ongoing social relationships, such as family, friends, and colleagues. Self-presentation continues to be important when one is interacting with friends, and in some respects people care more about what their friends think of them than about how strangers evaluate them (Brown & Garland, 1971). Yet the rules for self-presentation may change among friends. In particular, boastful favorability may be appropriate with strangers, but among friends people tend to be modest and self-deprecating (Tice, Butler, Muraven, & Stillwell, 1995). Even the pattern of automatic egotism (e.g., Paulhus & Levitt, 1987) is reversed when among friends—the automatic response among friends is modest and self-effacing (Tice et al., 1995).

The change in self-presentation when one moves from strangers to friends is revealing about the interpersonal self. To attract others, it is often necessary to showcase one's best and most favorable traits, because these qualities are presumably what will attract the other person to want to form a more lasting relationship with you. Once the relationship is formed, however, self-enhancing egotism may be disruptive. People resent egotistical others, partly because an egotistical person is often difficult to get along with (Colvin, Block, & Funder, 1995). In long-term relationships, fairness may become an issue, and egotistical people may overestimate how much they deserve, which puts a burden on others (see Ross & Sicoly, 1979, on overestimation).

## Selves and Cultural Context

Across different cultures, the nature of selfhood varies. This chapter already noted that the independent, autonomous, highly complex self is historically relative, emerging in Western history over the last few centuries. Apparently, society changed in some way that led to the gradual production of the modern form of selfhood.

Cultural differences in selfhood confirm the relativity of the self. An influential work by Triandis (1989) distinguished individualistic from collectivistic societies. Individualistic societies support diversity, self-expression, and individual rights, whereas collectivistic ones promote conformity, obligation to the group, and the welfare of the group as the supreme good. Societies also vary in the degree to which they put pressure on individuals to conform to the group's values, norms, and role definitions, as opposed to letting people do whatever they want.

Markus and Kitayama (1991) carried this argument a step further by arguing that the basic difference between selfhood in (collectivistic) Asian cultures and (individualistic) Western ones concerns the dimension of independence versus interdependence. In their view, Westerners seek to distinguish themselves from others, supporting their independence by establishing unique positive traits, whereas Asian selves are defined in interdependence with the group and, hence, are far less likely to seek to be distinctive.

Why would cultures differ in this way? In my view, a decisive difference that sets the modern Western cultures apart from collectivistic ones (both in earlier Western history and in modern Asia) is the instability of social relations. Social, occupational, and geographical mobility has made social relationships highly unstable in the modern West, as reflected in recent statistics of high divorce rates, high occupational turnover and mobility, and the like. To illustrate, if a modern American surveys his close relationships, he may recognize that most of them will be gone in ten years and replaced by others. In contrast, in a collectivistic society, a person may feel confident that most or all of her relationships are likely to still be in place ten years from now.

The stability or instability of social relationships changes the demands on the self. Where relationships are unstable, the self must constantly act to attract new partners, or at least to persuade existing partners to stick around. Showing others your independent uniqueness, autonomy, and other qualities may be useful for this, and indeed the findings on self-presentational favorability by Tice et al. (1995) showed that people commonly present themselves favorably when they interact with new partners—but not when they interact with known friends. Where relationships are stable, maintaining group or relationship harmony becomes the overriding goal, and so an interdependent self that is persistently modest and self-effacing will be most conducive to such harmony.

## Influence of Interpersonal Processes on the Self

An important theory about the origins and development of selfhood was proposed in symbolic interactionist theory (Cooley, 1902; Mead, 1984). In this view, the inner self starts off nearly empty or blank and gradually fills up with information attained from other people.

The newborn baby has no set stock of self-schemas but gradually accumulates them as parents, teachers, peers, and others inform the child about itself: what gender, age, family membership, personality traits, motivations, and goals it has.

One simple way to test this theory is to see how well people's beliefs about themselves correlate with what their friends and acquaintances think of them. If the inner self derives directly from information communicated in social interaction, these correlations should be high. Unfortunately for symbolic interactionist theory, the correlations tend to be weak or negligible. In a well-known review of the research findings, Shrauger and Schoeneman (1979) found that people's self-ratings did not match up well with how other people rated them.

On the other hand, people's self-ratings did match up well with how they *believed* other people rated them. Beliefs about self could thus derive from the feedback one believes that one gets from others. The discrepancy appears to be between how people believe others perceive them and how the others actually perceive them. Two factors produce this discrepancy. First, other people do not always tell you honestly what they think of you. Social communication is diluted by norms of politeness and simple reluctance to communicate bad news. Second, even when people do tell you frankly what they think of you, you may not accept this information. As noted earlier in this chapter, people use many self-deception processes to help them avoid facing disagreeable facts about themselves.

Thus, the inner self may well be shaped by social communication, but the self is far from a passive accepter of feedback. Instead, the self actively processes and selects (and sometimes distorts) information from the social world. A similar conclusion has been reached in research on expectancy effects. People are affected by what others expect of them, especially when they are interacting with the people who hold the expectancies (e.g., Snyder, Tanke, & Berscheid, 1977). But they only internalize these expectancies and exhibit lasting self change under certain circumstances, which may require some active participation of the self (Snyder & Swann, 1978). People are quite capable of not living up to others' expectancies and indeed of rejecting the views of themselves that are implicit in those expectancies.

The active participation of the self in the social process brings up an issue that was already raised, namely the quest for social validation of desired identities. The fact that people are able to dismiss social feedback under some circumstances does not mean that they can dispense with others' opinions altogether. (Remember, Shrauger & Schoeneman, 1979, did conclude that people's self-concepts were closely linked to how they believed others perceived them.) It may still be true that people can only regard themselves as having some desired trait or quality if they can secure some social feedback to confirm it. Self-presentation thus becomes an important step in the process of building the inner self.

Research on self-concept change confirms the importance of social validation for constructing the inner self. When people present themselves as being a certain kind of person, they can internalize that view of self and gradually become that sort of person (Jones, Rhodewalt, Berglas, & Skelton, 1981). The social validation is crucial, however. If people perform the same behaviors either publicly or privately, only the public behaviors (i.e., those witnessed by others) are internalized (Tice, 1992). Inner processes of perceiving the self a certain way do not seem to mediate this effect so much as getting others to perceive the self that way (Schlenker, Dlugolecki, & Doherty, 1994).

## Influence of Self on Perceiving Others

The previous section emphasized how social interactions shape the self, but the relationship is two-way: the self also affects social interactions. That is, people's views of themselves shape how they perceive and relate to others.

The idea that the self's traits affect perceptions of others is far from new. The popular

Freudian concept of *projection* suggests that people perceive their own traits in other people, especially their bad or undesirable traits. Despite the popular appeal of the idea of projection, however, research has not confirmed a broad or simple process of defensively projecting one's own traits (Holmes, 1968, 1978, 1981). (There is however a tendency to assume that other people agree with your values and opinions, which is called the *false consensus effect*; Ross, Greene, & House, 1977). Newman, Duff, and Baumeister (1997) found that when people tried to suppress thoughts about some bad trait they supposedly had, they became highly attuned to that trait, and so they were more likely to interpret other people's ambiguous behavior as indicating that trait. Still, in that case projection was a side effect of thought suppression (see Wegner & Erber, 1992; Wegner, Schneider, Carter, & White, 1987), not a general tendency.

Another broad idea is that having a self-schema for a particular trait will make people perceive others as likewise having that trait. This idea likewise is too broad. Instead, it appears that having a self-schema for a particular trait makes people act like an expert on that trait: They pay more attention to behaviors relevant to that trait and process information about it more closely and integratively than other traits. The net result is not necessarily to increase or decrease the likelihood of seeing others as having that trait—but one does make a more informed, sophisticated judgment about others.

Yet another variation is the self-image bias, which entails that people judge others mainly on dimensions on which they themselves score well (Lewicki, 1983, 1984). Thus, beautiful people will judge others by their appearance, whereas smart people will focus on others' intelligence. This is in some ways the opposite of the Freudian concept of projection, which suggests that the dimensions on which the self looks bad will be the ones used most prominently to judge others. Yet the self-image bias does help bolster a favorable view of self. By focusing on domains where the self stands out in a positive dimension, and especially by judging others on those domains, one can get ample confirmation that oneself is a worthy, superior person.

All these effects appear to revolve around accessibility. The attributes that the self wants to emphasize, as well as the ones the self wants most earnestly to deny, operate as highly accessible categories for interpreting others' behavior (Higgins, King, & Mavin, 1982). In other words, those are the dimensions that come to mind most readily and are found most useful for perceiving others.

## Self-Evaluation Maintenance

People's self-concepts become intertwined with those of their close friends and relationship partners. Indeed, some research by Aron, Aron, Tudor, and Nelson (1991) suggests that the boundary lines between self and others become blurred in the mind, at least for long-term relationship partners, so that people cannot always keep straight whether they themselves or a relationship partner has a certain trait, behavior, or preference.

Yet people may experience an approach-avoidance conflict when it comes to linking their self-esteem with a relationship partner's achievements. This conflict and its many implications have been elucidated by Tesser (1988) in his self-evaluation maintenance (SEM) theory. According to this theory, two main processes predominate, but they pull the individual in opposite directions, and so the effects of self on relationship and vice versa depend on the interplay of these two forces.

The first process is *reflection*, which means that the partner's successes or failures reflect on the self. A highly successful partner brings credit and esteem to the self, just as a partner's failure or disgrace reflects badly on the self. Hence, people try to associate themselves with star performers and other successes. For example, university students identify more strongly with their university when its sports teams win than when they lose (Cialdini et al., 1976; Cialdini & Richardson, 1980).

The second process is *comparison,* which entails judging the self in terms of how well you stack up against your partner. On this process, a partner's successes and achievements can take esteem away from the self instead of conferring it. For example, if your partner is a successful, acclaimed musician, the reflection process may help you feel proud of being connected to such a widely admired person, but the comparison process means that your own musical efforts may look all the more feeble and second-rate because everyone will compare them to your partner's. Hence, people may ironically distance themselves from a friend or partner who performs well, especially when the performance is in a domain that is important to the people's self-concepts, because the partner's success would make them look bad in comparison (Pleban & Tesser, 1981).

## Self as Agent: The Executive Function

The previous section highlighted that the self is not a mere passive recipient of feedback from the social world but rather actively chooses, selects, and controls. In fact, the active role of the self goes far beyond processing information selectively: The self often seeks to exert control over the environment, to initiate action, and to pursue its various goals. This active, controlling aspect of the self is sometimes called the *agent* or the *executive function.*

It is generally accepted among researchers in the area of self that the executive function is the least well understood aspect of self. Self-knowledge and self-awareness have been extensively researched, and the interpersonal aspects of selfhood have received less but still considerable attention. In contrast, the study of how the self exerts control has languished until recently. It is therefore one of the most promising and exciting topics for new researchers to take up.

The importance of this aspect of self is much higher than the relative lack of research would imply. Making choices, taking responsibility, and exerting control are extremely important features of normal social life. Recent distinctions between automatic and controlled processes (e.g., Bargh, 1982, 1997) are also relevant, because the self is the controller of controlled processes. Furthermore, controlling the external world is only one side of things: The self also regulates itself, such as by trying to change its emotional states, to improve task performance, and to resist impulses to eat, drink, smoke, or aggress. These self-regulation processes are central to the nature of the self.

### Choice and Control

The nature of the self includes a strong desire for control and choice. The motive to control is as pervasive and as well established as the motivation to achieve positive self-esteem (described earlier). Moreover, the desire to achieve control is more beneficial and adaptive than the desire for esteem, which makes it all the more plausible that it is innate. If Freud were alive today, his view of human nature would probably rest on at least three major instincts rather than two: He would likely add control to the pair of instincts (sex and aggression) that he featured when he developed his theories early in the 20th century.

The motivation to attain control has been proposed and supported in many contexts. An early formulation was White's (1959) theory of effectance motivation. At that time, most motivation theories were based on some lack or deficit in the organism, such as a need for food. Although those theories had much to offer, White proposed that they were inadequate for explaining several varieties of important behavior, such as curiosity, exploration, strivings for competence, and the pursuit of mastery seemingly for its own sake.

Subsequent work has continued to confirm the striving for control. Research on stress has shown that people suffer greater harm and distress when deprived of control than when they have control, even if the outcomes are similar (e.g., Glass & Singer, 1972; Seligman, 1975). When deprived of control, they often seek to reassert control, and in some cases the deprivation of control causes people to aggress against whoever has curtailed their freedom (Brehm, 1966). When actual control is elusive, people sometimes cultivate illusions of control, which are appealing and comforting (Langer, 1975). Recovery from trauma and misfortune is facilitated by achieving a sense of control, even if it is based on illusion (Taylor, 1983). People who believe they have a high degree of control over their lives are significantly happier than other people (Campbell, 1981; Campbell, Converse, & Rodgers, 1976).

The link between the self and control motivation is most explicit in Bandura's (1977) theory of self-efficacy. He proposed that the self's belief that it can produce the optimal or requisite responses is a powerful source of confidence from which flows a broad set of positive outcomes. Hence, one centrally important aspect of the self is a broad sense of its degree of efficacy. Particular experiences that involve effectively exerting control—or signally failing to do so—can have powerful reverberations because they alter self-efficacy.

Self-determination theory (Deci & Ryan, 1991, 1995) provides another way to look at the vital links between selfhood and control. Deci and Ryan separate the quest for competence from the need for autonomy, and they argue that both motives are intrinsic to the self. The need for competence is similar to Bandura's self-efficacy motive, in that it is based on learning to master the environment, achieving particular tasks, and generally coming to regard the self as capable and effective. The need for autonomy is a motivation to act in ways that originate within the self. Failing to fulfill the need for competence leaves the self feeling helpless, useless, and incompetent, whereas failing to fulfill the need for autonomy leaves the self feeling that its actions are dictated by external forces. (A third need, for relatedness, is postulated by Deci and Ryan as also intrinsic to the self.)

Happiness, self-esteem, and well-being depend crucially on satisfying these intrinsic needs, according to Deci and Ryan. Their research findings (e.g., Kasser & Ryan, 1993, 1996) show that people who orient their lives toward extrinsic goals such as money and fame end up worse off than people who orient themselves around the intrinsic needs. The differences can be found in measures of anxiety, depression, social functioning, vitality, and self-actualization, among others. Although high self-esteem can be achieved based on extrinsic motivations (such as by the person who successfully pursues wealth and fame), Deci and Ryan regard that as a relatively hollow success, and they distinguish such self-esteem from what they consider true self-esteem—which has to be based on the intrinsic strivings for competence, autonomy, and meaningful relationships.

Thus, a variety of theoretical perspectives has emphasized how the self is deeply motivated to achieve control. Although the motivation to seek control is important, pervasive, and powerful, it does have exceptions. A thought-provoking review by Burger (1989) elucidated ways and circumstances in which people desire to relinquish control. Sometimes people are better off letting someone else (especially someone more competent, such as the designated driver) take control. Sometimes control brings pressure, anxiety, and responsibility but does not necessarily pay off in producing favorable outcomes for the self, and so any rational person would relinquish control. Sometimes people simply want to avoid being blamed for bad things that they expect might happen. In such cases, people cede control to others. Still, these are exceptions, and in general the quest for control is a basic theme of the psychology of self.

## Ego Depletion

An apparent paradox has emerged surrounding the self's motivations pertaining to control. On the one hand, as already noted, the self has a strong and pervasive motive to acquire, maintain, and exert control. On the other hand, sometimes people avoid control, and moreover many behaviors reflect automatic, passive, habitual, or other processes in which the self does not exert control. Why might the self both relinquish control and seek it?

A possible answer is that it is costly to exert control. In cognitive processes, researchers distinguish between automatic and controlled ones (e.g., Bargh, 1982, 1994). Controlled processes are more flexible, but they are costly and strenuous, and while engaged in a controlled process the mind is not free to do much else simultaneously (unlike automatic processes).

My own colleagues and I have recently found, somewhat to our surprise, that the costs of control seem to involve depleting a very limited resource. It appears that the executive function operates rather like a muscle that becomes tired after being used. As a result, it will be most rational and adaptive to use it sparingly, so as to conserve the resource for important decisions and events.

This research began by examining the consequences of exerting self-control. When people attempted to control their emotions, thoughts, or impulses, they later exhibited decrements on other tasks that required control (Baumeister, Bratslavsky, Muraven, & Tice, 1998; Muraven, Tice, & Baumeister, 1998). Later we extended these studies to include other operations of the executive function, such as making choices or responding in an active rather than passive mode, and similar effects obtained (Baumeister et al., 1998).

Converging evidence can be found in other work. Mischel (1996) suggests that the term *willpower* be revived, because it accurately reflects how the self exerts energy in its regulatory operations. Pennebaker and Chew (1985) found that arousal occurred when people attempted to suppress certain nonverbal behaviors, indicating that some exertion is involved. Glass and Singer (1972) showed that people who cope with stress show various decrements afterward, suggesting again that some resource becomes depleted by the coping process. Self-control breaks down when people must devote their resources to coping with stress or other exertions, or after people have already exerted self-control recently (see Baumeister, Heatherton, & Tice, 1994, for review).

Thus, the executive function seems to operate on the basis of some resource that resembles an energy or strength. Two facts about this resource are noteworthy. First, the same resource appears to be involved in quite different acts of control and self-control, which means that this stock of energy must be regarded as a highly important feature of the self. Second, it appears to be quite limited, so that even a brief exertion depletes it (e.g., Baumeister et al., 1998). Most likely, these brief exertions in laboratory experiments do not deplete the resource entirely, but rather they deplete it enough so that the self tries to conserve what it has left, presumably in case an important decision had to be made or some vital act of self-control became necessary.

The self's reliance on habit, automatic processes, routines, and stable values may thus be understood in the context of the self's need to conserve its limited resources for important acts of volition. A person cannot afford to exercise free, deliberate choice at every possible point, starting with putting on socks in the morning, because that would deplete it and render it unable to cope with important decisions and demands. Free, deliberate choice and control over self are quite limited in what they can do, and to be fully effective the self must manage this limited resource carefully.

## Self-Regulation

The capacity of the organism to monitor and alter itself is far more advanced and sophisticated in human beings than in other organisms, especially if one does not count the body's homeostatic mechanisms (which are remarkable in humans but exist in animals too). People are able to resist their own impulses and motivations, to make themselves do things they do not want to do, and to alter their behavior on the basis of a broad assortment of standards and prescriptions ranging from recent, changing laws to long-standing codes of honor to ancient religious commandments. They are also able to change their current behavior so as to pursue an outcome or goal that could be many years away.

These patterns suggest that the capacity for self-regulation is one of the most felicitous and adaptive aspects of the human psyche. Research confirms that it is. Effective self-control is beneficial in terms of work, relationships, health, well-being, and other positive outcomes. It also appears to be a durable, central aspect of personality. Research findings have shown that children who performed better at delaying gratification at age 4 were also better off than others over a decade later, both in terms of academic performance and social competence (e.g., popularity) (Mischel, Shoda, & Peake, 1988; Shoda, Mischel, & Peake, 1990).

Self-regulation depends vitally on having the self monitor itself. Monitoring includes keeping track of the activities and states of the self as well as comparing these to standards of proper, desired behavior. The most influential formulation of these ideas can be found in the work by Carver and Scheier (1981, 1982), who applied cybernetic theory (e.g., Powers, 1973) to self-regulation. In Carver and Scheier's account, self-regulation operates based on a feedback loop summarized by the acronym TOTE, which stands for test, operate, test, exit. That is, the self first tests by comparing itself to its goals, rules, ideals, obligations, or other standards. If it finds that it is falling short, it operates on itself to bring about a change. Then another test is performed. If deficiencies remain, the operations are continued, but if they have been resolved, then the self can exit the feedback loop and move on to other things.

The usual analogy is to how a thermostat regulates the temperature of a room by testing the current degree of warmth against a set standard, operating by turning on the furnace or air conditioner, and then continuing to test until the desired conditions are achieved, whereupon it turns the furnace off. In human behavior, self-regulation operates on several spheres. These include impulses and appetites such as how much to eat (dieting), aggression, sex, smoking, drugs and alcohol, and shopping or spending money. They also include control over thoughts and feelings, to the extent that people try to focus their thoughts on or away from particular topics (e.g., trying to concentrate) or to alter their moods and emotional states (e.g., trying to cheer up). Finally, self-regulation also operates in many performance settings, such as when people try to perform at their best or to keep trying when they are tired and discouraged. In all these, the operation of the feedback loop can be observed or inferred, insofar as the person compares the current status against the standards and tries to operate to resolve deficiencies.

Recent work has begun to explore how the "operate" phase of the TOTE loop functions—that is, precisely how do people change themselves? The research findings on ego depletion (described above) suggest that some quantity of strength or energy is expended in many efforts to alter the self. Hence, a major cause of self-regulatory failure would be ego depletion; that is, a deficit in energy caused by prior exertions or other demands.

Indeed, if people become efficient at regulating themselves, they may fare all the worse when they are tired, depleted, or simply when they stop exerting self-regulation, because the monitoring process continues to function. Thus, a dieter may learn to scan the world for warning signs of fattening foods so that willpower can be marshalled to resist their temptations—but when the person stops trying to resist these, the mind continues to scan the environment for fattening foods, and so the temptations become all the more salient and influential (Wegner, 1994).

Self-regulation can fail for a variety of reasons (see Baumeister et al., 1994, for review). Emotional distress is a common cause, and people often lose their self-control when they are upset (e.g., Heatherton, Herman, & Polivy, 1991; Heatherton & Polivy, 1991; Kirschenbaum, 1987). If their standards are confused or conflicting, self-regulation is difficult. Alcohol consumption impairs self-control in nearly every sphere, possibly because it lowers self-awareness and thereby impairs the self's capacity to monitor its own behavior (e.g., Hull, 1981). People may sometimes fail at self-regulation simply because they are too lazy or unmotivated to try to control themselves. In other cases, people may lack the proper knowledge to regulate themselves effectively, and so their efforts at self-regulation may backfire, as in the example of the person who responds to depressed feelings by getting drunk, only to find that the intoxication makes the depressed mood get worse rather than better.

## Self-Defeating Behavior

Psychology has a long-standing interest in self-defeating behaviors, partly because they show the bounds of rational thought. After all, the pursuit of enlightened self-interest is the hallmark of rationality, and so when people thwart their own self-interest, their behavior is irrational by definition. Such irrationality suggests that bias, error, and other factors intrude into the human decision-making process, often aided by strong motivations.

For present purposes, interest in self-defeating behavior arises because it suggests some impairment of the executive function. When people have a clear understanding of their own best interest, they nearly always choose to pursue it, and even if their first response would not be optimal, the executive function would try to override that response and pursue the best outcome. That is, after all, probably why the executive function exists and operates as it does—to ensure that the person's actions lead toward the best outcomes in the long run, even if short-term distractions or temptations try to interfere.

This view does contradict some theories about self-defeating behavior, such as the view that people have self-destructive motivations (e.g., Menninger, 1938/1966) or may seek punishment when they feel guilty (e.g., Piers & Singer, 1953). A review by Baumeister and Scher (1988) failed to find any evidence that people seek bad outcomes for themselves, at least in the research literature in social psychology. There was plenty of evidence of self-defeating behavior, but none of it proved that people want to suffer or try to fail (except when some positive, desirable outcome accompanies the suffering or failure).

Instead, the causes of self-defeating behavior fall into two main categories. One of these is tradeoffs, in which the person pursues some positive, desirable goal and accepts risks, costs, or suffering that comes with it. For example, people may consume alcohol, drugs, and tobacco despite the long-term health risks associated with them, because the short-term yield of pleasure is highly appealing. Cigarette smoking alone causes several hundred thousand deaths each year in the United States, and so smoking cigarettes is self-destructive—but people smoke for the pleasure or image, not in order to kill themselves with lung cancer.

A common feature of self-defeating tradeoffs is that the anticipated gains are fairly immediate, salient, and definite, whereas the costs are delayed, hidden, or uncertain. To pursue the example of cigarette smoking, the pleasure of the cigarette is immediate and reliable, whereas lung cancer may not develop (many smokers die of causes unrelated to smoking), and even if it does come, it will not ensue for many years,

The second cause of self-defeating behavior is self-regulatory failure. In general, the person is generally pursuing some positive, desirable outcome, but the person chooses some strategy that is counterproductive. The earlier example of drinking alcohol while depressed is an example of this because intoxication does not reliably banish depressed feelings and in fact can make them worse. Persisting in an unproductive endeavor (such as squandering precious time and resources in pursuing a hopeless love affair or unreachable career goal) can be costly and self-destructive, but again such fruitless persistence is usually motivated by (misguided) hopes that success will eventually be achieved. The executive function is thus not intentionally self-destructive; it is simply misinformed.

## Conclusion

It is safe to predict that the self will continue to be one of the most heavily studied topics in social psychology for the foreseeable future. Part of the self's vitality as a research topic, however, is that it contains multiple facets and topics, and so just when one aspect of the self has been studied seemingly to the limits of available methods and ideas, another emerges to challenge and fascinate researchers. Self-awareness, self-schemas, self-presentation, self-regulation, and self-esteem have enjoyed different periods of being the focus of widespread interest. For the vitality of research on the topic of self, this diversity is very good news.

## About this Volume

The chapters in this volume represent many of the most important and influential contributions to the study of self. With the exception of this introductory overview, all the works have been published previously. They were chosen by means of a lengthy ballot mailed to over 100 experts in the field (in fact, the entire membership of the International Society for Self and Identity). The majority of the articles represent the top vote-getters from that poll. That core of articles has been augmented by adding a few other articles based on two criteria. First, it was desirable to get some more recent papers; the experts in the field tend to agree on what are the "classic" papers from past decades, but current work takes longer to command consensus. Hence, several recent papers were added. Second, there was some need to round out the topics to cover the full area of self. The high vote-getters tended to cluster in certain topics, and so to make a broader, fuller coverage I added some papers from other areas. Still, by and large, this list of papers represents the collective judgment of a broad and large assortment of expert opinions. Enjoy them!

The topic of self has seen more than its share of important, influential articles, and so any selection is bound to omit a few favorites. This reader, compiled on the basis of a broad survey, is probably more inclusive than any single expert's list would be. But that raises the opposite problem: how to keep the size of the volume down? To address this, it has been necessary to edit some of the papers. To keep the core contributions of the various papers full and clear, the editing was done chiefly by trimming sections (usually near the end) of some of the longer articles, particularly ones in which the authors compare their theory to previous works, offer loose speculations about possible implications, and present evidence about the most subtle distinctions and nuances of their theory. Some of the papers still no doubt run long, but, by and large, this procedure has made it possible to include a broad selection of important works, with their main points still fully explained.

## REFERENCES

Allport, G. W. (1943). The ego in contemporary psychology. *Psychological Review, 50,* 451–478.

Aron, A., Aron, E. N., Tudor, M., & Nelson, G. (1991). Close relationships as including other in the self. *Journal of Personality and Social Psychology, 60,* 241–253.

Ashmore, R. D., & Jussim, L. (1997). Toward a second century of the scientific analysis of self and identity. In R. Ashmore & L. Jussim (Eds.), *Self and identity: Fundamental issues* (pp. 3–19). New York: Oxford University Press.

Bandura, A. (1977). Self-efficacy: Toward a unifying theory of behavior change. *Psychological Review, 84,* 191–215.

Bargh, J. (1982). Attention and automaticity in the processing of self-relevant information. *Journal of Personality and Social Psychology 43,* 425–436.

Bargh, J. A. (1994). The four horsemen of automaticity: Awareness, intention, efficiency, and control in social cognition. In R. S. Wyer, Jr., & T. K. Srull (Eds.), *Handbook of social cognition* (pp. 1–40). Hillsdale, NJ: Lawrence Erlbaum Associates.

Bargh, J. A. (1997). The automaticity of everyday life. In R. S. Wyer (Ed.), *The automaticity of everyday life: Advances in social cognition* (Vol. 10, pp. 1–61). Mahwah, NJ: Erlbaum.

Baumeister, R. F. (1982). A self-presentational view of social phenomena. *Psychological Bulletin, 91*, 3–26.

Baumeister, R. F. (1984). Choking under pressure: Self-consciousness and paradoxical effects of incentives on skillful performance. *Journal of Personality and Social Psychology, 46*, 610–620.

Baumeister, R. F. (1986). *Identity: Cultural change and the struggle for self.* New York: Oxford University Press.

Baumeister, R. F (1987). How the self became a problem: A psychological review of historical research. *Journal of Personality and Social Psychology, 52*, 163–176.

Baumeister, R. F. (1988). Masochism as escape from self. *Journal of Sex Research, 25*, 28–59.

Baumeister, R. F. (1990). Suicide as escape from self. *Psychological Review, 97*, 90–113.

Baumeister, R. F. (1991). *Escaping the self: Alcoholism, spirituality, masochism, and other flights from the burden of selfhood.* New York: Basic Books.

Baumeister, R. F. (1998). The self. In D. T. Gilbert, S. T. Fiske, & G. Lindzey (Eds.), *Handbook of social psychology* (4th ed., pp. 680–740). New York: McGraw-Hill.

Baumeister, R. F., Bratslavsky, E., Muraven, M., & Tice, D. M. (1998). Ego depletion: Is the active self a limited resource? *Journal of Personality and Social Psychology, 74*, 1252–1265.

Baumeister, R. F., Dale, K., & Sommer, K. L. (1998). Freudian defense mechanisms and empirical findings in modern social psychology: Reaction formation, projection, displacement, undoing, isolation, sublimation, and denial. *Journal of Personality, 66*, 1081–1124.

Baumeister, R. F., Heatherton, T. F., & Tice, D. M. (1994). *Losing control: How and why people fail at self-regulation.* San Diego, CA: Academic Press.

Baumeister, R. F., & Scher, S. J. (1988). Self-defeating behavior patterns among normal individuals: Review and analysis of common self-destructive tendencies. *Psychological Bulletin, 104*, 3–22.

Baumeister, R. F., Tice, D. M., & Hutton, D. G. (1989). Self-presentational motivations and personality differences in self-esteem. *Journal of Personality, 57*, 547–579.

Brehm, J. (1966). *A theory of psychological reactance.* New York: Academic Press.

Brockner, J. (1984). Low self-esteem and behavioral plasticity: Some implications for personality and social psychology. In L. Wheeler (Ed.), *Review of personality and social psychology* (Vol. 4, pp. 237–271). Beverly Hills, CA: Sage.

Brown, B. R., & Garland, H. (1971). The effects of incompetency, audience acquaintanceship, and anticipated evaluative feedback on face-saving behavior. *Journal of Experimental Social Psychology, 7*, 490–502.

Brown, J. D. (1993). Motivational conflict and the self: The double-bind of low self-esteem. In R. Baumeister (Ed.), *Self-esteem: The puzzle of low self-regard* (pp. 117–130). New York: Plenum.

Brown, J. D., & McGill, K. L. (1989). The cost of good fortune: When positive life events produce negative health consequences. *Journal of Personality and Social Psychology, 57*, 1103–1110.

Burger, J. M. (1989). Negative reactions to increases in perceived personal control. *Journal of Personality and Social Psychology, 56*, 246–256.

California Task Force to Promote Self-esteem and Personal and Social Responsibility (1990). *Toward a state of self-esteem.* Sacramento, CA: California State Department of Education.

Campbell, A. (1981). *The sense of well-being in America.* New York: McGraw-Hill.

Campbell, A., Converse, P. E., & Rodgers, W. L. ( 1976). *The quality of American life: Perceptions, evaluations, and satisfactions.* New York: Russell Sage.

Campbell, J. D. (1986). Similarity and uniqueness: The effects of attribute type, relevance, and individual differences in self-esteem and depression. *Journal of Personality and Social Psychology, 50*, 281–294.

Campbell, J. D. (1990). Self-esteem and clarity of the self-concept. *Journal of Personality and Social Psychology, 59*, 538–549.

Campbell, J. D., Chew, B., & Scratchley, L. S. (1991). Cognitive and emotional reactions to daily events: The effects of self-esteem and self-complexity. *Journal of Personality, 59*, 473–505.

Campbell, J. D., & Lavallee, L. F. (1993). Who am I? The role of self-concept confusion in understanding the behavior of people with low self-esteem. In R. Baumeister (Ed.), *Self-esteem: The puzzle of low self-regard* (pp. 3–20). New York: Plenum.

Carver, C. S., & Scheier, M. F. (1981). *Attention and self-regulation: A control theory approach to human behavior.* New York: Springer-Verlag.

Carver, C. S. & Scheier, M. F. (1982). Control theory: A useful conceptual framework for personality-social, clinical and health psychology. *Psychological Bulletin, 92*, 111–135.

Cialdini, R. B., Borden, R. J., Thorne, A., Walker, M. R., Freeman, S., & Sloan, L. R. (1976). Basking in reflected glory: Three (football) field studies. *Journal of Personality and Social Psychology, 34*, 366–375.

Cialdini, R. B., & Richardson, K. D. (1980). Two indirect tactics of image management: Basking and blasting. *Journal of Personality and Social Psychology, 39*, 406–415.

Colvin, C. R., Block, J., & Funder, D. C. (1995). Overly positive evaluations and personality: Negative implications for mental health. *Journal of Personality and Social Psychology*, 1152–1162.

Cooley, C. H. (1902). *Human nature and the social order.* New York: Scribner's.

Crary, W. G. (1966). Reactions to incongruent self-experiences. *Journal of Consulting Psychology, 30*, 246–252.

Crocker, J., & Major, B. (1989). Social stigma and self-esteem: The self-protective properties of stigma. *Psychological Review, 96*, 608–630.

Deci, E. L., & Ryan, R. M. (1991). A motivational approach to self: Integration in personality. In R. Dienstbier (Ed.), *Nebraska symposium on motivation* (Vol. 38, pp. 237–288). Lincoln, NE: University of Nebraska Press.

Deci, E. L., & Ryan, R. M. (1995). Human autonomy: The basis for true self-esteem. In M. Kernis (Ed.), *Efficacy, agency, and self-esteem* (pp. 31–49). New York: Plenum.

Dunning, D., Meyerowitz, J. A., & Holzberg, A. (1989). Ambiguity and self-evaluation: The role of idiosyncratic trait definitions in self-serving assessments of ability. *Journal of Personality and Social Psychology 57*, 1082–1090.

Duval, S., & Wicklund, R. A. (1972). *A theory of objective self-awareness.* New York: Academic Press.

Fazio, R. H., Effrein, E. A., & Falender, V. J. (1981). Self-perceptions following social interactions. *Journal of Personality and Social Psychology, 41*, 232–242.

Fenigstein, A. (1984). Self-consciousness and the overperception of self as a target. *Journal of Personality and Social Psychology, 47*, 860–870.

Glass, D. C., & Singer, J. E. (1972). *Urban stress: Experiments on noise and social stressors.* New York: Academic Press.

Goffman, E. (1959). *The presentation of self in everyday life.* New York: Anchor Books.

Goleman, D. (1985). *Vital lies, simple truths.* New York: Simon & Schuster.

Greenberg, J., & Musham, C. (1981). Avoiding and seeking self-focused attention. *Journal of Research in Personality, 15,* 191–200.

Greenwald, A. G. (1980). The totalitarian ego: Fabrication and revision of personal history. *American Psychologist, 35,* 603–618.

Heatherton, T. F., & Baumeister, R. F. (1991). Binge eating as escape from self-awareness. *Psychological Bulletin, 110,* 86–108.

Heatherton, T. F., Herman, C. P., & Polivy, J. (1991). Effects of physical threat and ego threat on eating. *Journal of Personality and Social Psychology, 60,* 138–143.

Heatherton, T. F., & Polivy, J. (1991). Development and validation of a scale for measuring state self-esteem. *Journal of Personality and Social Psychology, 60,* 895–910.

Higgins, E. T., King, G. A., & Mavin, G. H. (1982). Individual construct accessibility and subjective impressions and recall. *Journal of Personality and Social Psychology, 43,* 35–47.

Holmes, D. S. (1968). Dimensions of projection. *Psychological Bulletin, 69,* 248–268.

Holmes, D. S. (1978). Projection as a defense mechanism. *Psychological Bulletin, 85,* 677–688.

Holmes, D. S. (1981). Existence of classical projection and the stress-reducing function of attributive projection: A reply to Sherwood. *Psychological Bulletin, 90,* 460–466.

Hull, J. G. (1981). A self-awareness model of the causes and effects of alcohol consumption. *Journal of Abnormal Psychology, 90,* 586–600.

Jones, E. E., & Gerard, H. B. (1967). *Foundations of social psychology.* New York: Wiley.

Jones, E. E., & Pittman, T. S. (1982). Toward a general theory of strategic self-presentation. In J. Suls (Ed.), *Psychological perspectives on the self* (Vol. 1, pp. 231–262). Hillsdale, NJ: Erlbaum.

Jones, E. E., Rhodewalt, F., Berglas, S. C., & Skelton, A. (1981). Effects of strategic self-presentation on subsequent self-esteem. *Journal of Personality and Social Psychology, 41,* 407–421.

Kasser, T., & Ryan, R. M. (1993). A dark side of the American dream: Correlates of financial success as a central life aspiration. *Journal of Personality and Social Psychology, 65,* 410–422.

Kasser, T., & Ryan, R. M. (1996). Further examining the American dream: Differential correlates of intrinsic and extrinsic goals. *Personality and Social Psychology Bulletin, 22,* 280–287.

Kirschenbaum, D. S. (1987). Self-regulatory failure: A review with clinical implications. *Clinical Psychology Review, 7,* 77–104.

Kunda, Z. (1990). The case for motivated reasoning. *Psychological Bulletin, 108,* 480–498.

Kunda, Z., & Sanitioso, R. (1989). Motivated changes in the self-concept. *Journal of Experimental Social Psychology, 25,* 272–285.

Langer, E. J. (1975). The illusion of control. *Journal of Personality and Social Psychology, 32,* 311–328.

Leary, M. R. (1995). *Self-presentation: Impression management and interpersonal behavior.* Madison, WI: Brown & Benchmark.

Leary, M. R., Tambor, E. S., Terdal, S. K., & Downs, D. L. (1995). Self-esteem as an interpersonal monitor: The sociometer hypothesis. *Journal of Personality and Social Psychology, 68,* 518–530.

Lewicki, P. (1983). Self-image bias in person perception. *Journal of Personality and Social Psychology, 45,* 384–393.

Lewicki, P. (1984). Self-schema and social information processing. *Journal of Personality and Social Psychology, 47,* 1177–1190.

Marks, G. (1984). Thinking one's abilities are unique and one's opinions are common. *Personality and Social Psychology Bulletin, 10,* 203–208.

Markus, H. R. (1977). Self-schemata and processing information about the self. *Journal of Personality and Social Psychology, 35,* 63–78.

Markus, H. R., & Kitayama, S. (1991). Culture and the self: Implications for cognition, emotion, and motivation. *Psychological Review, 98,* 224–253.

Mead, G. H. (1934). *Mind, self, and society.* Chicago, IL: University of Chicago Press.

Menninger, K. (1938/1966). *Man against himself.* New York: Harcourt, Brace, & World.

Mischel, W. (1996). From good intentions to willpower. In P. Gollwitzer & J. Bargh (Eds.), *The psychology of action* (pp. 197–218). New York: Guilford.

Mischel, W., Ebbesen, E. B., & Zeiss, A. R. (1976). Determinants of selective memory about the self. *Journal of Consulting and Clinical Psychology, 44,* 92–103.

Mischel, W., Shoda, Y., & Peake, P. K. (1988). The nature of adolescent competencies predicted by preschool delay of gratification. *Journal of Personality and Social Psychology, 54,* 687–696.

Muraven, M., Tice, D. M., & Baumeister, R. F. (1998). Self-control as limited resource: Regulatory depletion patterns. *Journal of Personality and Social Psychology, 74,* 774–789.

Newman, L. S., Duff, K., & Baumeister, R. F. (1997). A new look at defensive projection: Suppression, accessibility, and biased person perception. *Journal of Personality and Social Psychology, 72,* 980–1001.

Paulhus, D. L., & Levitt, K. (1987). Desirable responding triggered by affect: Automatic egotism? *Journal of Personality and Social Psychology, 52,* 245–259.

Pennebaker, J. W., & Chew, C. H. (1985). Behavioral inhibition and electrodermal activity during deception. *Journal of Personality and Social Psychology, 49,* 1427–1433.

Piers, G., & Singer, M. (1953). *Shame and guilt: A psychoanalytic and cultural study.* New York: Norton.

Pleban, R., & Tesser, A. (1981). The effects of relevance and quality of another's performance on interpersonal closeness. *Social Psychology Quarterly, 44,* 278–285.

Powers, W. T. (1973). *Behavior: The control of perception.* Chicago, IL: Aldine.

Pryer, J. B., Gibbons, F. X., Wicklund, R. A., Fazio, R. H., & Hood, R. (1977). Self-focused attention and self-report validity. *Journal of Personality, 45,* 514–527.

Ross, L., Greene, D., & House, P. (1977). The "false consensus effect": An egocentric bias in social perception and attribution processes. *Journal of Experimental Social Psychology, 13,* 279–301.

Ross, M., & Sicoly, E. (1979). Egocentric biases in availability and attribution. *Journal of Personality and Social Psychology, 37,* 322–336.

Scheier, M. F., & Carver, C. S. (1977). Self-focused attention and the experience of emotion: Attraction, repulsion, elation, and depression. *Journal of Personality and Social Psychology, 35,* 625–636.

Schlenker, B. R. (1975). Self-presentation: Managing the impression of consistency when reality interferes with self-enhancement. *Journal of Personality and Social Psychology 32,* 1030–1037.

Schlenker, B. R. (1980). *Impression management: The self-concept, social identity, and interpersonal relations.* Monterey, CA: Brooks/Cole.

Schlenker, B. R., Dlugolecki, D. W., & Doherty, K. (1994). The impact of self-presentations on self-appraisals and behavior: The roles of commitment and biased scanning. *Personality and Social Psychology Bulletin, 20,* 20–33.

Sedikides, C. (1993). Assessment, enhancement, and verification determinants of the self-evaluation process. *Journal of Personality and Social Psychology, 65,* 317–338.

Seligman, M. E. P. (1975). *Helplessness: On depression, development, and death.* San Francisco, CA: Freeman.

Shoda, Y., Mischel, W., & Peake, P. K. (1990). Predicting adolescent cognitive and self-regulatory competencies from preschool delay of gratification: Identifying diagnostic conditions. *Developmental Psychology, 26,* 978–986.

Shrauger, J. S., & Rosenberg, S. E. (1970). Self-esteem and the effects of success and failure feedback on performance. *Journal of Personality, 38,* 404–417.

Shrauger, J. S., & Schoeneman, T. J. (1979). Symbolic interactionist view of self-concept: Through the looking glass darkly. *Psychological Bulletin, 86,* 549–573.

Shrauger, J. S., & Sorman, P. B. (1977). Self-evaluations, initial success and failure, and improvement as determinants of persistence. *Journal of Consulting and Clinical Psychology, 45,* 784–795.

Snyder, M., & Swann, W. B. (1978). Behavioral confirmation in social interaction: From social perception to social reality. *Journal of Experimental Social Psychology 14,* 148–162.

Snyder, M., Tanke, E. D., & Berscheid, E. (1977). Social perception and interpersonal behavior: On the self-fulfilling nature of social stereotypes. *Journal of Personality and Social Psychology 35,* 656–666.

Suls, J., & Wan, C. K. (1987). In search of the false-uniqueness phenomenon: Fear and estimates of social consensus. *Journal of Personality and Social Psychology, 52,* 211–217.

Swann, W. B. (1985). The self as architect of social reality. In

B. R. Schlenker (Ed.), *The self and social life* (pp. 100–125). New York: McGraw-Hill.

Swann, W. B. (1987). Identity negotiation: Where two roads meet. *Journal of Personality and Social Psychology 53,* 1038–1051.

Taylor, S. E. (1983). Adjustment to threatening events: A theory of cognitive adaptation. *American Psychologist, 38,* 1161–1173.

Taylor, S. E., & Brown, J. D. (1988). Illusion and well-being: A social psychological perspective on mental health. *Psychological Bulletin, 103,* 193–210.

Tesser, A. (1988). Toward a self-evaluation maintenance model of social behavior. In L. Berkowitz (Ed.), *Advances in experimental social psychology* (Vol. 21, pp. 181–227). San Diego, CA: Academic Press.

Tice, D. M. (1992). Self-presentation and self-concept change: The looking glass self as magnifying glass. *Journal of Personality and Social Psychology, 63,* 435–451.

Tice, D. M., Butler, J. L., Muraven, M. B., & Stillwell, A. M. (1995). When modesty prevails: Differential favorability of self-presentation to friends and strangers. *Journal of Personality and Social Psychology, 69,* 1120–1138.

Trope, Y. (1983). Self-assessment in achievement behavior. In J. Suls & A. Greenwald (Eds.), *Psychological perspectives on the self* (Vol. 2, pp. 93–121). Hillsdale, NJ: Erlbaum.

Trope, Y. (1986). Self-enhancement and self-assessment in achievement behavior. In R. Sorrentino & E. T. Higgins (Eds.), *Handbook of motivation and cognition* (Vol. 2, pp. 350–378). New York: Guilford.

Wegner, D. M. (1994). Ironic processes of mental control. *Psychological Review, 101,* 34–52.

Wegner, D. M., & Erber, R. (1992). The hyperaccessibility of suppressed thoughts. *Journal of Personality and Social Psychology, 63,* 297–333.

Wegner, D. M., Schneider, D. J., Carter, S. R., & White, T. L. (1987). Paradoxical effects of thought suppression. *Journal of Personality and Social Psychology, 53,* 5–13.

White, R. (1959). Motivation reconsidered: The concept of competence. *Psychological Review, 66,* 297–333.

Wicklund, R. A., & Duval, S. (1971). Opinion change and performance facilitation as a result of objective self-awareness. *Journal of Experimental Social Psychology, 7,* 319–342.

Wicklund, R. A., & Gollwitzer, P. M. (1982). *Symbolic self-completion.* Hillsdale, NJ: Erlbaum.

Wills, T. A. (1981). Downward comparison principles in social psychology. *Psychological Bulletin, 90,* 245–271.

Wyer, R. S., & Frey, D. (1983). The effects of feedback about self and others on the recall and judgments of feedback-relevant information. *Journal of Experimental Social Psychology 19,* 540–559.

Zuckerman, M. (1979). Attribution of success and failure revisited, or: The motivational bias is alive and well in attribution theory. *Journal of Personality, 47,* 245–287.

# Self-Knowledge

Across the ten centuries of the Middle Ages, the Western world produced scarcely any autobiographical writing. When people began to write about themselves after that, some of them felt they needed to justify the practice. Michel de Montaigne (1533–1592) wrote an autobiography that was published in the 1580s and he provided just such a justification for devoting so many pages to such a seemingly trivial topic as himself. With tongue presumably in cheek, he admitted that his topic was less important than the topics chosen by other authors, but he hoped his work would make up for that deficiency by the fact that Montaigne knew his topic much better than another writer could know any topic, because Montaigne was writing about himself. The implication was that self-knowledge was the most complete and perfect form of knowledge.

That easy confidence in the completeness and perfection of self-knowledge is a thing of the past. Recognition that self-knowledge is frequently marred by self-deception spread through much of the culture. In psychology, Freud proposed that each person has a great stock of unconscious knowledge, particularly about the self, and the conscious self is barred from access to that knowledge. He listed a variety of defense mechanisms that supposedly helped people avoid unsavory truths about themselves, especially impulses or desires that were deemed unacceptable. Although research has failed to support some of these defense mechanisms, others have stood the test of time and data very well, although the goal of the defenses seems to have more to do with protecting self-esteem than with denying unacceptable impulses (see Baumeister, Dale, & Sommer, 1998).

Modern personality and social psychology has done its share to question self-knowledge. An influential paper by Anthony Greenwald (1980) compared the self to a totalitarian government that rewrites history and edits the news so as to make itself look powerful, benevolent, and successful. As Greenwald explained, the self distorts information (both new and from memory) so as to make itself look good. Another blow to self-knowledge came from Nisbett and Wilson (1977), who contended that people are not able to know and report on much that happens inside their own minds. People may know their attitudes and opinions, but they do not know how they arrived at these. And if they think about their attitudes too long, especially by trying to assess the reasons and bases for their attitudes, they end up confusing themselves about the attitudes too (Wilson, Dunn, Bybee, Hyman, & Rotondo, 1984).

Two papers on self-knowledge are reproduced here. The first, by Shrauger and Schoeneman (1979), tackles one of the core ideas of symbolic interactionism. According to that idea, people learn about themselves from others, through social interaction. If self-knowledge derives from how others know the person, then a person's self-ratings ought to be strongly correlated with how the others rate him or her. But Shrauger and Schoeneman found that such correlations have typically been very weak. Instead, they found that people's self-ratings were highly correlated with how they thought others viewed them. But they are often wrong about how others view them.

Subsequent studies have found somewhat higher correlations between self-ratings and other-ratings than Shrauger and Schoeneman found, but they are still far from strong. Thus, Shrauger and Schoeneman's conclusion remains largely correct. The gap seems to be between how people think they are viewed and how others actually view them. Two factors produce this gap (see Felson, 1989). One is that people do not communicate all their perceptions accurately, particularly when it comes to telling someone what you dislike about him or her. The other is that people distort information (as Greenwald, 1980 argued) as it comes in, especially disagreeable evaluations. Thus, when it comes to one person holding an unflattering opinion of another, the first person is reluctant to say it and the other is reluctant to hear it, so its chances for being incorporated into the latter's self-knowledge are slim.

The distortion and selective suppression of disagreeable information about the self plays a big role in the second paper in this section, by Taylor and Brown (1988). From reviewing the literature on self-knowledge, they concluded that normal people show three patterns of systematic distortion: they overestimate their good points, they overestimate their degree of control over events, and they are unrealistically optimistic. Further, people who suffer from depression and some other forms of mental illness fail to exhibit these biases, and so they conclude that these "positive illusions" are integral to mental health and adjustment. In other words, being mentally healthy means viewing the world (and particularly the self) through rose-colored glasses.

The linking of mental health with distorted perception of reality has troubled some, although the weight of evidence and opinion continues to favor Taylor and Brown's conclusions about the existence of such distortions and illusions. Colvin and Block (1994) questioned Taylor and Brown's interpretations of evidence and argued against the view that distorting is healthy. They have a certain logic on their side, in that one can presumably make the best, most effective and optimal decisions if one uses accurate rather than distorted information. How can this seeming advantage of accuracy be reconciled with the pervasive evidence of bias that Taylor and Brown showed?

Two answers have been suggested. The simpler one is that people's illusions tend to remain small, so that they produce some benefits in terms of confidence and good feelings but do not grossly distort the calculations necessary to make good decisions (Baumeister, 1989). The other is that people simply manage to suspend their illusions when it comes time to make a decision (Gollwitzer & Kinney, 1989). In the latter view, people go through life carrying a pleasantly enhanced view of how capable and effective they are, until it is necessary to make a decision—whereupon they sober up and briefly face the cold facts as they are. Once the decision is made, they return to their comfortable illusions.

## REFERENCES

Baumeister, R. F. (1989). The optimal margin of illusion. *Journal of Social and Clinical Psychology, 8,* 176–189.

Baumeister, R. F., Dale, K., & Sommer, K. L. (1998). Freudian defense mechanisms and empirical findings in modern social psychology: Reaction formation, projection, displacement, undoing, isolation, sublimation, and denial. *Journal of Personality, 66,* 1081–1124.

Colvin, C. R., & Block, J. (1994). Do positive illusions foster mental health? An examination of the Taylor and Brown formulation. *Psychological Bulletin, 116,* 3–20.

Felson, R. B. (1989). Parents and the reflected appraisal process: A longitudinal analysis. *Journal of Personality and Social Psychology, 56,* 965–971.

Gollwitzer, P. M., & Kinney, R. F. (1989). Effects of deliberative and implemental mind-sets on illusion of control. *Journal of Personality and Social Psychology, 56,* 531–542.

Greenwald, A. G. (1980). The totalitarian ego: Fabrication and revision of personal history. *American Psychologist, 35,* 603–618.

Nisbett, R., & Wilson, T. D. (1977). Telling more than we can know: Verbal reports on mental processes. *Psychological Review, 84,* 231–259.

Shrauger, J. S., & Schoeneman, T. J. (1979). Symbolic interactionist view of self-concept: Through the looking glass darkly. *Psychological Bulletin, 86,* 549–573.

Taylor, S. E., & Brown, J. D. (1988). Illusion and well-being: A social psychological perspective on mental health. *Psychological Bulletin, 103,* 193–210.

Wilson, T. D., Dunn, D. S., Bybee, J. A., Hyman, D. B., & Rotondo, J. A. (1984). Effects of analyzing reasons on attitude-behavior consistency. *Journal of Personality and Social Psychology, 44,* 5–16.

# Discussion Questions

1. What are the most important sources of self-knowledge?
2. If self-knowledge is derived from social interactions, how could anyone ever reply "No, I'm not" when told that "You are _____" (e.g., friendly, stupid, paranoid, hot-tempered, unhappy)?
3. What possible dangers could arise from overestimating your good qualities or your degree of control over events?
4. Why are people so reluctant to face the truth about themselves, especially when it involves not being as wonderful and competent as they might have wished?
5. Shrauger and Schoeneman concluded that certain pitfalls prevent reflected appraisals from creating fully accurate self-concepts. How might these pitfalls operate in the case of very powerful individuals, such as kings, presidents, and corporate CEOs?
6. Suppose you had to communicate some critical, negative feedback to someone. How might you increase the chances that the person would actually accept and incorporate it into his or her self-concept?
7. Is it easy or difficult to change people's beliefs about themselves? What circumstances might make it especially easy or difficult?

# Suggested Readings

Nisbett, R., & Wilson, T. D. (1977). Telling more than we can know: Verbal reports on mental processes. *Psychological Review, 84*, 231–259. This influential article questioned the accuracy of introspection and proposed that people often lack an understanding of their own mental processes.

Greenwald, A. G. (1980). The totalitarian ego: Fabrication and revision of personal history. *American Psychologist, 35*, 603–618. A memorable article that compared the self to a totalitarian regime. It seeks to control information and re-write history so as to make itself look benevolent and competent.

Goleman, D. (1985). *Vital lies, simple truths*. New York: Simon & Schuster. An easy-to-read and informative book on self-deception, written by the author of *Emotional intelligence*. Goleman mixes amusing stories, news events, and research findings.

Felson, R. B. (1989). Parents and the reflected appraisal process: A longitudinal analysis. *Journal of Personality and Social Psychology, 56*, 965–971. Felson reports an impressive, long-term investigation of communication and self-concept in families.

Colvin, C. R., & Block, J. (1994). Do positive illusions foster mental health? An examination of the Taylor and Brown formulation. *Psychological Bulletin, 116*, 3–20. Colvin and Block challenge Taylor and Brown's conclusions and seek to limit generalizations about the benefits of positive illusions. The article is followed by a response from Taylor and Brown and then another comment by Colvin and Block, so readers can follow the debate among these influential experts.

Taylor, S. E. (1989). *Positive illusions: Creative self-deception and the healthy mind*. New York: Basic Books. Taylor re-phrases her views and conclusions in an entertaining book written for the general public.

Bem, D. J. (1965). An experimental analysis of self-persuasion. *Journal of Experimental Social Psychology, 1*, 199–218. (OR) Bem, D. J. (1972). Self-perception theory. In L. Berkowitz (Ed.), *Advances in experimental social psychology* (Vol. 6, pp. 1–62). New York: Academic Press. These early papers laid out an influential theory holding that people learn about themselves in ways similar to how they learn about other people—by observing actions and making appropriate inferences.

# Symbolic Interactionist View of Self-Concept: Through the Looking Glass Darkly

J. Sidney Shrauger and Thomas J. Schoeneman
• State University of New York at Buffalo

Research on the relationship between self-perceptions and evaluations from other people is reviewed. Studies of naturalistic interactions indicate that people's self-perceptions agree substantially with the way they perceive themselves as being viewed by others. However, there is no consistent agreement between people's self-perceptions and how they are actually viewed by others. There is no clear indication that self-evaluations are influenced by the feedback received from others in naturally occurring situations. When feedback from others is manipulated experimentally, self-perceptions are usually changed. However, methodological limitations such as the questionable external validity and strong demand characteristics of the experimental situations employed make the significance of these findings unclear. The available evidence is examined within a framework that considers the transmission, processing, and evaluation of judgments from others. Other means by which interaction may influence self-perceptions aside from direct evaluative feedback are considered.

O wad some power the giftie gie us
Te see oursels as others see us!
  Robert Burns, *To a Louse*

**B**urns's couplet expresses a concern about self-knowledge and its origins that is ancient and contemporary. Recently, a resurgence of interest in the self has flourished in many areas of psychology, especially in psychotherapeutic formulations that view cognitions about oneself as vital mediators in the maintenance of modification of behavior and in social psychological theories involving attribution, cognitive dissonance, and self-awareness. Understanding how attitudes about the self are developed and maintained has thus become increasingly important.

When people are asked how they know that they possess certain characteristics, a typical answer is that they have learned about them from other people. A more formal theoretical statement of this view has been articulated by the influential school of thought known as symbolic interactionism. This theory proffers the idea of a "looking glass self" and asserts that one's self-concept is a reflection of one's perceptions about how one appears to others. This assertion has received widespread professional acceptance and is intoned with catechistic regularity in many leading texts on social behavior (e.g., Raven & Rubin, 1976; D. J. Schneider, 1976; Secord & Backman, 1974).

Social philosophers and psychologists of the late 19th century such as Peirce (1868), James (1890), and Baldwin (1897) were precursors of symbolic interactionism in their emphasis on the self as a product and reflection of social life (Gordon & Gergen, 1968; Ziller, 1973). Cooley (1902), generally credited as the first interactionist, developed the idea of the looking glass self. He posited that the self is inseparable from social life and necessarily involves some reference to others. This process of social reference results in the looking glass self: "A self idea of this sort seems to have three principal elements: the imagination of our appearance to the other person; the imagination of his judgment of that appearance, and some sort of self-feeling, such as pride or mortification" (Cooley, 1902, p. 152). According to Cooley, from early childhood our concepts of self develop from seeing how others respond to us: "In the presence of one whom we feel to be of importance, there is a tendency to enter into and adopt, by sympathy, his judgment of ourself" (p. 175). Mead (1934), the major theorist of symbolic interactionism, amplified and expanded the view of the self as a product of social interaction: "The individual experiences himself as such, not directly, but only indirectly, from the particular standpoints of other individuals of the same social group, or from the generalized standpoint of the social group as a whole to which he belongs" (p. 138). Essential to the genesis of the self is the development of the ability to take the role of the other and particularly to perceive the attitude of the other toward the perceiver. Mead's looking glass self is reflective not only of significant others, as Cooley suggested, but of a generalized other, that is, one's whole sociocultural environment. More recently, Kinch (1963) has summarized and systematized symbolic interactionist self theory by noting that it basically involves an interrelation of four components: our self-concept, our perception of others' attitudes and responses to us, the actual attitudes and responses of others to us, and our behavior.

In recent years, self theories have been proposed that do not insist on the primacy of social others as sources of information about the self. Bem (1967, 1972) has asserted that self-perception is a special case of person perception:

Self-descriptive attitude statements can be based on the individual's observations of his own overt behavior and the external stimulus conditions under which it occurs. . . . As such, his statements are functionally similar to those that any outside observer could make about him. (1967, pp. 185–186)

Jones and Nisbett (1971) have qualified Bem's analysis somewhat by proposing that "actors tend to attribute the causes of their behavior to stimuli inherent in the situation, while observers tend to attribute behavior to stable dispositions of the actor" (p. 93). Duval and Wicklund's (1972) objective self-awareness theory also emphasizes the potential of the individual for active self-appraisal. Objective self-awareness is a state of consciousness in which attention is focused inward on the self, making the individual an object to his or her consciousness. The assumption that self-awareness is dependent on the imagination of another's views is minimized. Although these self-perception theories have stimulated considerable research, the initial justification for each view was mainly on theoretical rather than empirical grounds. Thus, some attention is given to the relevance of the data presented here to self-perception theories, although the main objective is to evaluate the evidence relevant to the looking glass self.

Information concerning the looking glass self derives from several lines of inquiry, not all of them explicitly related to this theory. Even work that has been done within the framework of symbolic interactionism suffers from a severe case of "ahistoricity," so that there is little sense of cumulative development of information. This article attempts to examine thoroughly the studies done under the auspices of symbolic interactionism. An exhaustive review of relevant studies outside of this framework cannot be claimed, however, since these come from many divergent bodies of literature.

The research presented is divided into two sections. First, studies are reported that examine feedback given in uncontrolled, naturally occurring interactions. Next, investigations of the effects of controlled feedback in structured situations are considered, with attention given to work in which feedback is purportedly based either on objective information or on more subjective judgments. Some restrictions on the types of research reviewed here should be noted. The main dependent variable examined is expressed self-perceptions. Studies exploring the impact of self-relevant feedback on other aspects of behavior are typically not covered, since it is debatable whether such changes are necessarily mediated by changes in self-perceptions. Also, although it may be argued that studies of attitude change on any topic involve some implied reappraisal of self-evaluations, the focus here is limited to changes in attitudes about the self, since there is evidence that reactions to feedback about the self differ from those about other attitudes (e.g., Eagly, 1967). A final restriction involves the area of self-presentation. Expressing one's self-perceptions in any public fashion inevitably has some potential instrumental value, and numerous investigations have focused on the functional impact of such self-statements. These studies, however, address issues that are not central to our discussion. The focus of this article is on investigations in which self-statements are perceived as fairly accurate estimates of the individual's actual attitudes and external incentives to a particular type of self-presentation are minimized.

## Naturalistic Studies

Many investigations have sought support for the idea of the looking glass self in naturally occurring interactions. One group of studies has focused on the proposition that individuals' self-perceptions should be highly congruent with the way they see themselves as being perceived by others. These studies vary widely along a number of different dimensions. Most analyses were correlational, some involved statistical comparisons, and some of the earlier studies relied on nonstatistical "eyeballing" of the data (e.g., Miyamoto & Dornbusch, 1956, Quarantelli & Cooper, 1966, Reeder, Donohue, & Biblarz, 1960). Samples have been drawn from all levels of the educational system and from a variety of other populations. Evaluations by self and others have most often centered on global measures of self-concept, although some investigations have examined more specific aspects of personality and behavior. Overall, these studies show modest to strong correlations between individuals' perceptions of themselves and the way they assume others perceive them. Nonsignificant relationships have occurred in situations in which deviant groups, such as delinquents (Teichman, 1972), learning disabled students (Swanson, 1969),

and sociometrically rejected students (Goslin, 1962), have been studied. The only exception to this pattern is Swanson's finding that for 11 emotionally disturbed children there was congruence between self-acceptance and perceived parental acceptance, and that for 35 normal children this congruence was absent.

In addition to postulating concordance between self-evaluation and the perceived evaluations of *significant* others, Mead (1934) contended that self-concept is reflective of the perceived evaluation of a *generalized* other. Relatively few studies have examined this facet of symbolic interactionism. There is some evidence that individuals' self-perceptions are similar to their perceptions of how they are viewed by others in general (Miyamoto & Dornbusch, 1956; Quarantelli & Cooper, 1966; Reeder et al., 1960). The evidence on whether self-perceptions are more strongly related to the perceived impressions of specific others or to the perceived impressions of the generalized other, however, is contradictory (Miyamoto & Dornbusch, 1956; Quarantelli & Cooper, 1966).

The demonstration of a relationship between people's self-perceptions and how they feel others see them is not sufficient in validating the symbolic interactionist position. It is necessary, in addition, to demonstrate congruence between (a) self-perceptions and others' actual perceptions of the person and (b) perceived other-evaluations and actual other-evaluations. A large number of studies have examined the former relationship. Although many of these studies are of questionable statistical and conceptual significance (Wylie, 1974), the overall pattern of the conclusions drawn by these investigations suggests much less agreement between self-judgments and actual judgments by others than between self-judgments and perceived judgments. Approximately half the studies reviewed show no significant correlations between self-perceptions and others' actual evaluations. The majority of the remaining investigations have reported either significant but low correlations or ambiguous results. There are no easily distinguishable factors that account for the presence or absence of positive associations. A wide range of subjects and evaluators were used, and comparisons were made on many attributes, most frequently self-esteem or task competence. Also, a number of studies have shown that perceived reactions of others are closer to self-concept than are actual reactions (Miyamoto & Dornbusch, 1956; Orpen & Bush, 1974; Quarantelli & Cooper, 1966; Sherwood, 1965; Walhood & Klopfer, 1971). The minimal associations between self-perceptions and others' actual evaluations suggest that people do not accurately perceive others' opinions of them, that these opinions minimally influence self-judgments, or, as indicated by a study by Reese (1961), that these two variables may be curvilinearly related, thus explaining why significant linear correlations do not often emerge (Hartup, 1970). Studies assessing degree of influence are infrequent and are discussed below.

The issue of accuracy in perceiving others' opinions has also been examined by the consideration of the relationship between individuals' perceptions of others' views of them and others' actual views. Of the studies assessing this relationship, some show congruence (Ausubel & Schiff, 1955; Ausubel, Schiff, & Gasser, 1952; De Jung & Gardner, 1962), some indicate partial or ambiguous relationships (Goslin, 1962; Israel, 1958; Reeder et al., 1960; Tagiuri, Blake, & Bruner, 1953; Walhood & Klopfer, 1971), and others demonstrate no association (Ausubel, 1955; Fey, 1955; Kelman & Parloff, 1957; Orpen & Bush, 1974). Most of the studies showing congruence have involved judgments of highly evaluative characteristics, such as liking by the other person, whereas those showing minimal associations have typically involved more content-specific judgments. Ability to predict peers' liking increases with age, at least from the lower grades through high school (Ausubel & Schiff, 1955; Ausubel et al., 1952; De Jung & Gardner, 1962), reflecting perhaps a more extensive interaction with those judged, more frequent expression of interpersonal preferences, or greater sensitivity to interpersonal cues. Also, whether one is predicting positive or negative feelings may be important; people seem to be better able to predict who likes them best as opposed to who likes them least (Tagiuri et al., 1953). That self-perceptions are consistently more strongly correlated with people's perceptions of how they think others view them than with how others actually view them suggests that the tendency to assume greater similarity between one's own and others' attitudes than actually exists (e.g., Newcomb, 1961) extends into the area of attitudes toward oneself. Thus, subjects' self-evaluations may be weakly related to others' opinions of them

because they frequently do not know what others' opinions are.

Since the studies reported thus far show no direction of causality or change over time, it is impossible to decide whether the actual or perceived evaluations of people by others are a cause or effect of how they perceive themselves. If one is to infer that others' judgments influence self-perception, assessments must be made at different times to see if self-perceptions change in the direction of others' earlier evaluations. Almost all of the relevant investigations have examined short-term changes in self-evaluation in relation to actual or perceived evaluations by others. Sherwood (1965) had sensitivity training participants rate themselves on a set of bipolar trait scales during the second day of a 2-week program. At the end of the program they rated themselves again, rated how they felt other group members would rate them, and rated other group members on the same set of dimensions. The ratings of a person by others were more similar to his or her self-ratings at the end of the program than to initial self-ratings. Since others' ratings were not obtained at the outset, one cannot infer that they actually influenced self-ratings. Instead, both the subject and other group members may have observed and responded to changes in subjects' presentation of themselves as the sessions continued.

Rosengren (1961), in a study of 10 institutionalized pre-adolescent boys with emotional disturbances, obtained self-ratings and ratings by peers over a 1-year interval. He found that for the post- as compared with the pre-ratings, self-ratings were more similar to both subjects' perceptions of others' ratings of them and others' actual ratings of them. Although these subjects did see themselves more similarly to the way they were seen by others, the critical comparison showing that self-ratings in the second evaluation became more similar to others' initial evaluations of them was not made.

The most sophisticated naturalistic investigation to date remains an early study by Manis (1955). Male undergraduates assigned as dormitory roommates rated themselves, their ideal selves, and their roommates at the beginning of a semester and after 6 weeks. Based on sociometric choices at the beginning of the first sessions, a friend and a nonfriend were designated for each subject. Subjects' self-perceptions and their friends' perceptions of them were more similar after their final rating than after their first. The most important finding was that subjects' final self-ratings were more similar to others' initial judgments of them than were their initial self-ratings. Furthermore, others' second ratings of a subject were no more similar to the subject's initial self-perceptions than were their first ratings, suggesting that others' impressions were not substantially influenced by the subject's initial self-evaluation.

Although these data suggest that individuals do change their self-perceptions in the direction of others' opinions about them, methodological limitations make this conclusion equivocal. Most significantly, subjects' self-perceptions changed in the direction of friends' initial judgments of them only when the designated friend had initially described them more favorably than subjects had described themselves. When their designated friend described them less positively than their own self-perceptions, there were no increases in the similarity of their self-descriptions. A friend who views subjects more positively than the subjects view themselves would be likely to reciprocate the subjects' friendship more than someone who views them less favorably than they view themselves. Learning that they have chosen as a friend someone who also likes them may enhance people's feelings of interpersonal perceptiveness and social competence and cause them to raise their self-evaluation.

Even if Manis's results indicate that a friend who describes a peer positively influences the peer's self-perceptions, the nature of the changes generated remains unclear. Subjects may either change the overall favorableness of their self-ratings to more closely match that of their evaluators, or they may change their assessments on specific dimensions so that the pattern of their self-descriptions across dimensions becomes more similar to that of their evaluators. This distinction raises the issue of whether the influence of others' assessments extends beyond the general evaluative level to more specific elements of the dimension being assessed. Perhaps when people are reacting to others' evaluations of them, the principal or even exclusive information that they process is whether they are being perceived in some globally positive, negative, or neutral way.

The only long-term longitudinal study that has been reported involved self-ratings and ratings by peers and teachers of children in the first and second grades who were later reassessed in the fifth and sixth grades (Trickett, 1969). Neither peer nor teacher ratings from the initial assessment were significantly correlated with self-ratings in the second assessment. Children's perceptions of how peers saw them in the initial assessment were uncorrelated with their self-perceptions in the second measurement. Although the author implied some causal influence of others' ratings (particularly those of teachers) on later self-perception, this is difficult to detect in the data. The absence of such an effect is not surprising in light of the fact that by the time subjects were in the later grades they had been exposed to a number of different peers and teachers, whose influence was impossible to gauge.

The numerous naturalistic studies that have been undertaken have not, by and large, contributed substantially to an understanding of the extent to which others' perceptions influence self-judgments. Currently, there is little evidence that in their ongoing social interactions people's views of themselves are shaped by the opinions of others. This is due primarily to the lack of repeated assessments of self-perceptions and others' perceptions whereby movements of one toward the position of the other could be determined.

Other issues are also important in evaluating the naturalistic data. Many investigations may not have examined situations in which the input of other people was maximal. For instance, most studies have used late adolescents and adults as subjects. If these individuals are in stable life situations, they may be more likely to maintain relatively solidified self-images. The impact of others' opinions could possibly be enhanced and more pronounced if adults were studied in unfamiliar situations in which their norms for self-evaluation and the behavior patterns that they displayed were in a state of flux, as in Manis's (1955) study of incoming college freshmen in dormitories. It also seems likely that younger people are more susceptible to external influence in developing their self-concept than are older individuals.

A final consideration in assessing the work reviewed above concerns the individuals who are sources of feedback and their relationship to the subjects studied. Although peers are the most commonly used and are, in many cases, perhaps the most appropriate sources of evaluations, more attention should be given to the actual degree of interaction between them and the people whose self-perceptions are being assessed. Membership as a peer in a group of students or workers does not necessarily demand that colleagues offer appraisals to one another. For both children and adults, a relatively small number of people may serve as significant sources of evaluative feedback. In most studies it is the researcher who decides who the subjects' significant others are, and in many cases this designation may be off the mark. Investigations that attempt to identify the significant others of a given population (e.g., Denzin, 1966) would be useful preliminary steps in future naturalistic investigations.

## Studies of Controlled Feedback from Others

Although researchers have employed a wide range of specific procedures for assessing the role of controlled feedback on judgments of others, most studies have followed one of two paradigms, which differ mainly in the extent to which the evaluator's judgments are based on objective data. In the first type of study the feedback received is purportedly based on tests of personality or competence. Typically, subjects describe themselves on the attributes assessed by the tests, then take the tests, receive feedback about their performance either immediately or within a week or two, and finally reappraise themselves. This procedure has been employed not only in specific efforts to assess the symbolic interactionist position but also in studies examining the effects of change in self-evaluation on other aspects of behavior, with change in self-evaluation often examined principally as a manipulation check. In the second type of study, feedback is based on the subjective impressions of other individuals who have no specific knowledge of objective assessment results. These studies have varied in the extent to which the other person is presented as having expertise in the topics considered.

The most elementary question typically asked in this research is, "Will individuals modify their self-descriptions in the direction of the feedback they receive?" The most elementary answer is, "usually." Such changes have been shown for numerous populations and for many different attributes, from competence in public speaking

(Videbeck, 1960) and physical skills (Haas & Maehr, 1965) to a variety of personality traits (e.g., Backman, Secord, & Pierce, 1963; Binderman, Fretz, Scott, & Abrams, 1972; Cooper & Duncan, 1971; Eagly, 1967; Evans, 1962; Harvey & Clapp, 1965; Harvey, Kelley, & Shapiro, 1957; Regan, Gosselink, Hubsch, & Ulsh, 1975; Shrauger & Lund, 1975; Snyder & Shenkel, 1976; Steiner, 1968). In almost all cases changes in self-perception have been judged by modifications in verbal self-descriptions made immediately following others' evaluations and in the presence of the evaluator.

Although controlled feedback from others typically produces some changes in people's self-description, several factors influence the extent of such changes. These include the discrepancy of feedback from subjects' self-perceptions, favorableness of feedback, characteristics of the evaluator, consensual validation of the judgments given, and attributes of those evaluated. After these factors have been examined, some general observations on the significance and limitations of studies employing manipulated feedback are considered.

### Discrepancy of Feedback from Self-Perceptions

The amount of discrepancy between others' evaluations and one's own self-perceptions has been examined in several studies. Bergin (1962) found that the credibility of feedback influenced the relationship between discrepancy and self-perception changes. With a high-credibility source, increases in discrepancy resulted in greater changes in self-relevant attitudes, whereas for a low-credibility source, the tendency was for greater credibility to produce less change. Although not wholly consistent, other results have suggested that when others' evaluations are purportedly based on objective test data, self-perceptions change more as the discrepancy from initial perceptions increases (Binderman et al., 1972; Eagly, 1967; Gerard, 1961: Johnson, 1966). However, Gerard found that this occurred only when subjects felt that the feedback they had received would be made public, and Eagly found that changes increased from low to moderate but not from moderate to high levels of discrepancy. Johnson found a curvilinear trend, with attitude change first increasing with increased discrepancy and then decreasing. In contrast with the findings based on objective test data, when feedback was based on subjective ratings of a personality dimension made by subjects' classmates, changes in self-evaluations were not enhanced by increased discrepancy between their judgments and subjects' initial self-perceptions (Harvey & Clapp, 1965; Harvey et al., 1957). Although many factors may differentiate these studies from one another, they are generally consistent with Bergin's argument about the role of credibility and suggest that for feedback that diverges substantially from one's views to have a strong effect on self-evaluations, it must be perceived as being based on clear objective information.

## Favorableness

Several studies have examined amount of change in self-perceptions as a function of feedback favorableness. Some of these studies involved the "Barnum effect," that is, the acceptance of bogus personality feedback (Meehl, 1956). Most such investigations indicate that favorable information is more readily accepted than unfavorable information (Sundberg, 1955; Halperin, Snyder, Shenkel, & Houston, 1976; Mosher, 1965; Weisberg, 1970), with a few showing no differential acceptance (Dmitruk, Collins, & Clinger, 1973; Evans, 1962). These studies' significance is questionable, however, since they involved no preassessments of subjects' self-evaluations and may have reflected the greater comparability between positive information and initial self-perception than between negative information and initial self-perceptions.

A few studies have attempted to control for the discrepancy between feedback and initial impressions. Steiner (1968) examined changes in self-ratings on bipolar traits and found that positive feedback produced greater changes than negative feedback, when feedback was based on upper level undergraduates' interpretations of self-report tests. Another study (Snyder & Shenkel, 1976) attempted to control for the "initial truthfulness" of the information evaluated and found no differences in the acceptance of positive or negative feedback given by the graduate student and based on projective tests.

Turning to studies in which feedback was not based on personality test results, we find that most were not designed to assess differences in reactions to equally discrepant positive and negative

evaluations (Haas & Maehr, 1965; Jones, Gergen, & Davis: 1962; Maehr, Mensing, & Nafzger, 1962; Papageorgis & McCann, 1965; Videbeck, 1960). Two careful investigations that did examine initial self-perceptions produced inconsistent findings similar to those of Steiner and Snyder and Shenkel just discussed. Eagly (1967) found no differential acceptance of feedback from a trained rater with regard to subjects' assertiveness or submissiveness. Harvey and Clapp (1965), however, found that students changed their self-ratings on a set of bipolar adjectives more when they had received positive feedback than when they had received negative feedback from classmates. The evaluators in Eagly's study may have had more legitimized expertise than those in Harvey and Clapp's study, and the same may have been true in the Barnum effect study of Snyder and Shenkel (1976) versus that of Steiner (1968). These results may suggest that subjects are reluctant to accept unflattering information about themselves unless they feel that the source of that information has a particularly strong basis for judgment. The inconsistency of these findings, however, suggests that the differential acceptance of positive versus negative information may depend on a variety of parameters. Eagly and her colleagues have shown, for example, that positive information is readily accepted if the recipients of the information do not expect to be evaluated again (Eagly & Acksen, 1971) and if they have no choice over the information they have received (Eagly & Whitehead, 1972). Other factors such as the strength of the subject's initial self-perceptions and the attributes on which feedback was given may also be relevant here.

## Evaluator Characteristics

The most systematic investigation of factors affecting the influence of an information source involved several studies by Webster and Sobieszek (1974), who examined subjects' responses to evaluations of their ability on a perceptual task. Each subject worked with a partner, and both subjects' initial performance was judged by an evaluator whose apparent competence on the task was varied. The impact of the evaluator's assessment on subjects' self-perceptions was not measured directly, but was inferred from the extent to which subjects acquiesced to their partners' judgments on a subsequent set of items. The evaluator's judgments had more effect on rate of acquiescence when the evaluator was presented as very competent as opposed to moderately competent and had no effect when he was presented as incompetent. Manipulation of more general aspects of the evaluator's competence by presenting him to high school subjects as either a college junior or an eighth grader produced no differential changes in acquiescence level.

Other investigators have also examined the effects of manipulating general competence. Whether a test evaluator was a Ph.D. or a counseling practicum student influenced the degree of acceptance of bogus personality feedback if that information was highly discrepant from the subject's initial self-perception, but not if it was less discrepant (Binderman et al., 1972). Whether a person received ratings on adjective dimensions from an acquaintance or from a stranger in his or her class had no effect on the degree of change in subsequent self-ratings (Harvey et al., 1957). Although it is difficult to develop generalizations from such scattered findings these data suggest that others' expertise or competence has an impact on the acceptance of their evaluations only when that competence is specifically relevant to the judgment being made.

## Consensual Validation

Another aspect of the credibility of information received involves the extent to which it is validated by others. Presumably, as a larger number of individuals reject a particular perception to the subject, the likelihood that the subject will incorporate that perception is increased. Following this assumption, Backman et al. (1963) found that bogus personality feedback had less effect on college students' self-ratings as a greater number of significant others were viewed as agreeing with the subject's initial self-perception. The specific relevance of the number of others who hold an opinion is unclear, however, since neither the salience of the dimensions to the subjects themselves nor the strength of their own self-perceptions was assessed. In another study, junior high school boys were given feedback about their physical skills by either one or two experts (Hass & Maehr, 1965). Initial postfeedback ratings did not differ as a function of the number of raters, but self-ratings made 6 weeks after the experts' judgments showed greater changes on the attributes evaluated for the

group judged by two experts. Since there was no condition in which consistent feedback was repeated by a single judge, it is not certain that it was a second person as opposed to a repetition of the communication that was the critical factor in enhancing feedback. This is an important issue, since there is some evidence that the repetition of an evaluation by the same evaluators enhances changes in self-evaluations (Kinch, 1968). Thus, there is no clear evidence that increasing the number of people who make an evaluation enhances the likelihood that it will be accepted.

The consistency of feedback across different evaluators has also been examined. Although there has been some suggestion that people respond more strongly to feedback that is consistent than to feedback that varies from evaluator to evaluator (Sherwood, 1967), other findings offer little support for this view (Kinch, 1968; Sobieszek & Webster, 1973). Because of the wide variation in the methodology of these studies, it is impossible to determine which differences among them account for the inconsistency in findings. However, given the ambiguous nature of these results, plus the fact that multiple and inconsistent evaluations may be frequent in real-life interactions, more careful examination of how evaluative information is combined and integrated seems warranted.

## Self-Evaluator Characteristics

There is some evidence that individuals differ in their receptivity to information about themselves. The main characteristic that has been examined in this regard is level of self-esteem, perhaps because most of the work on response to others' feedback has focused on highly evaluative information. There is some consistency in the finding that individuals who have generally low self-esteem are more influenced by negative feedback from others and less by positive feedback than are individuals with high self-esteem. This has been shown even when subjects' initial self-perceptions about the specific attributes evaluated were comparable, and it has been demonstrated for judgments of assertiveness–submissiveness (Eagly, 1967), social sensitivity (Shrauger & Rosenberg, 1970), and several other personality traits (Harvey & Clapp, 1965). The only instance in which such a differential acceptance was not demonstrated was for self-awareness (Shrauger & Lund, 1975).

Studies of other individual differences in recipients have been more episodic. Gerard (1961) found that a self-report measure of susceptibility to social influence predicted degree of change in self-perception, but only when the evaluation from others was supposed to be made public. People who had a less well-developed sense of self or a lower level of ego identity (Erikson, 1956) changed their self-evaluations more following success or failure feedback on an intellectual task than did those at higher levels of ego identity (Marcia, 1967). Harvey, Hunt, and Schroder (1961) reported that levels of concreteness–abstractness in cognitive processes predicted the extent of changes in self-descriptions following personality test feedback. These data indicate that in the future, precise appraisals of the impact of others' judgments on self-perceptions will require acknowledging the association between subject characteristics and the nature of the judgments given.

## Significance of Manipulated Feedback

Having considered some factors that can affect the impact of others' ratings, we turn to an examination of the broader significance of feedback manipulation studies, particularly the degree of influence that feedback in such studies has been shown to have. Issues to be considered here are how long feedback effects last, their situational specificity, and the influence of feedback about a specific attribute for self-appraisal on other attributes.

One important but relatively neglected issue is the longevity of the impact of others' evaluations. Only two studies have examined the effect of others' appraisals over time. In one investigation, subjects were given positive or negative feedback about physical skills by an expert, and their self-perceptions were reassessed immediately, after 1 day, 6 days, and 6 weeks (Haas & Maehr, 1965). Both positive and negative evaluations affected self-perceptions, and these effects were maintained over the 6-week period, although they appeared to diminish over time. Changes in dimensions not specifically evaluated were evident immediately after the evaluation, but were insignificant thereafter. Hicks (1962) gave subjects feedback that classmates judged them more favorably than their own self-perceptions on a group of personality traits. Two days after the initial evaluation, subjects were more likely to have raised their self-judgments on the elevated traits than on the con-

trol traits, although this difference did not hold after a week. Thus, the minimal evidence available on this issue suggests that the impact of others' judgments on self-perceptions holds over short periods of time but tends to diminish as time passes.

Also relevant in assessing the importance of feedback from others is the extent to which the effect of feedback generalizes from focal attributes to other characteristics. The three studies that have examined this effect used expert sources and systematically varied the relatedness of secondary attributes to the focal dimension (Haas & Maehr, 1965; Maehr et al., 1962; Videbeck, 1960). They found, not surprisingly, that judgments changed more on the dimension that was evaluated than on the one that was not (Maehr et al., 1962) and that those changes that did occur in other dimensions dissipated over time (Haas & Maehr, 1965). Therefore, relatively little information exists regarding the manner and extent to which content-focused evaluations are generalized to other characteristics of oneself.

Situational factors may also influence the degree of acceptance of others' self-evaluations, since the functional utility of accepting or rejecting others' impressions may vary from situation to situation. When college students feel that evaluations of their performance on a test are going to be made public, for example, they change their self-perceptions regarding that attitude more than do subjects who feel their responses will be known only to themselves (Gerard, 1961). Eagly and Acksen (1971) found that individuals changed their self-perceptions more in the direction of negative information and less in the direction of positive information when they felt that they would be retested on the attribute on which their performance was assessed, as compared with when they felt no retesting would occur. Positive attributes may be accepted and negative attributes may be fended off if there is no immediate prospect that the accuracy of these self-enhancing beliefs will be challenged. Other potential costs and gains of accepting or rejecting others' evaluations might also be envisioned. For instance, acknowledgment of certain positive attributes might be accompanied by the anticipation of favorable future outcomes or of increased demands from others. Similarly, the endorsement of negative attributes might lead to the anticipation of social rejection or loss of other favorable outcomes. In examining such problems, it is important to distinguish between self-presentation and self-perception, since certain external factors might influence the manner in which people present themselves without affecting their actual self-perceptions.

The factors that most limit the interpretation of these manipulated feedback studies are the demand characteristics of the situation in which changes in self-perception are assessed. Invariably the appraisal of changes in self-evaluation was made in the presence of the evaluator or experimenter. When the evaluator is present, subjects who do not change their self-perceptions directly discredit the evaluator's appraisal, which may be difficult, particularly if the evaluator is presented as an expert. Even when evaluators are absent, experimenters may be perceived as being likely to communicate with them. Very rarely are there clearly reported efforts to disguise the postmanipulation self-appraisal process (Shrauger & Rosenberg, 1970).

One major way that the significance of manipulated feedback studies might be enhanced would involve making the assessment of change less reactive and more subtle. For example, the appraisal might be woven into some other aspect of the experiment supposedly unrelated to the portion in which feedback was given, as has been done in counterattitudinal advocacy studies (e.g., Rosenberg, 1965; Hendrick & Seyfried, 1974). Another possibility is to have the final self-evaluation made after an initial "debriefing," with the evaluation presented in the context of an appraisal of the effects of psychological experiments on individuals' attitudes and feelings.

A final issue in manipulated feedback studies is whether changes in self-evaluation are specific only to the self or can reflect modifications in judgments of others as well. There is evidence (Bramel, 1962; Edlow & Kiesler, 1966; Steiner, 1968) that when people are confronted with information discrepant from their self-evaluations, they not only change their self-evaluations but also modify their evaluations of others on the attribute judged. This may reflect a process of defensive projection or simply a change in the criteria they use for evaluating the attribute in question. Unfortunately, most studies have looked only at shifts in the absolute level of self-judgments and not at changes in judgments of self relative to others. Such relative appraisals may be at least as significant as absolute judgments. Therefore, the effect of feedback on judgments of others as well as of oneself should be evaluated.

## Discussion and Conclusions

The numerous studies of naturalistic and manipulated feedback that we have reviewed have had much to say about the relationship between others' judgments and self-appraisals; it is unfortunate that the flaws and limitations of these investigations have rendered the significance and validity of their findings questionable. Although there is evidence that individuals' self-perceptions and their views of others' perceptions of them are quite congruent, there is less evidence that self-perceptions are related to or influenced by others' actual perceptions. None of the studies of naturally occurring interactions were designed so that they would demonstrate unequivocally that receiving content-focused feedback from others leads to corresponding changes in one's own self-perceptions. In contrast, there is ample evidence of changes in self-perceptions following controlled feedback in laboratory settings. However, the importance of these findings is unclear because of the short-term nature of most assessments and the potential effects of demand characteristics. In evaluating the contributions and limitations of the available research, we give some attention to how information from others about the self is transmitted, received, interpreted, and acted upon. These are aspects of social self-perception that have for the most part been neglected by researchers in this area.

### Availability of Evaluative Information

That there is minimal agreement between individuals' judgments of others' perceptions of them and their actual perceptions suggests that the communication of feedback to others may often be infrequent or ambiguous. Although norms regarding the evaluation of other people's behavior probably vary widely across different subcultures and situations, strong sanctions are often maintained against making direct appraisals, particularly when they are negative. In some of the only research on the communication of evaluations, Blumberg (1972) found that people report inhibiting the direct communication of all types of evaluations to others, particularly if it is negative or if the recipient is not known well. Barriers to direct expression can be found in intimate relationships as well as in more impersonal social interactions. This "not-even-your-best-friend-will-tell-you" phenomenon has been noted by Goffman (1955), who pointed out that unfavorable evaluations of close associates are typically given only when directly solicited, and that in such a situation, chances are that the asker has already made some negative self-appraisal. Perhaps this accounts in part for the popularity of sensitivity training, in which people have the privilege of finding out what others really think of them, and of assertiveness training, in which they can learn to communicate their true feelings about others.

To understand the real impact of others' opinions, one must determine how frequently such opinions are communicated directly in people's everyday social interactions. Who gives evaluations? On what dimensions? Under what circumstances? How often and how explicitly? The answers to such questions would facilitate an assessment of the relative influence of others' judgments on self-perceptions, as opposed to the opposite influence of self-perceptions on the perception of others' judgments. When information from others is not explicit, its interpretation may depend substantially on one's own self-perception on the attribute being assessed. In clinical contexts, for example, if people have concerns about what others think of them, it is frequently assumed that their inferences about others' feelings reflect a projection of their own self-evaluations.

It is quite likely that direct feedback occurs extensively in the socialization of young children by parents and other adults. During the process of language development, for instance, it seems certain that children come to model the construct system of those around them and to apply these constructs to themselves. Symbolic interactionists (Cooley, 1902; Mead, 1934) and self-perception theorists (Bem, 1967, 1972; Duval & Wicklund, 1972) alike have discussed the importance of preschool interactions in the development of a concept of self. It is surprising, however, that an empirical literature substantiating these arguments is nonexistent. Naturalistic studies of self-concept and perceived or actual assessments by others pick up developing selves as they enter the captive environment of elementary school. The subjects in these studies are typically in at least third or fourth grade; only two studies have used first graders (Alberti, 1971; Trickett, 1969). Studies of con-

trolled feedback almost exclusively use undergraduates. Since the preschool years are so vital to theories of the development of self-concept, it seems imperative that this period be attended to empirically. However, this may be easier to recommend than to implement. Trickett, for example, has noted the difficulties encountered in assessing the self-concept of first graders, which means that new and imaginative methods are necessary in this regard. Furthermore, recent work raises questions about whether young children possess the abstract concepts necessary to process information from others and use it in forming perceptions of themselves (Herzberger, 1978). A naturalistic study of parent–child evaluative interactions might be a desirable first step in determining just what kind of feedback is given in the earliest stages of life.

Finally, in considering the availability of information from others it is important to recognize that people who are evaluated may help to determine how much evaluative information they receive. People's frequency of social interaction, how directly they ask for information, and how much they behave in ways that might elicit others' comments may all affect the amount of evaluative feedback received.

## Interpretation of Information from Others

Although it is likely that people differ in their interpretations of others' feedback, particularly if that feedback is not explicit, these differences have not been explored extensively. People may disagree about what cues from others constitute an evaluation. And even when cues have been identified, people may differ in the inferences or conclusions they draw from these cues about others' judgments of them. For instance, it might be important to examine the extent to which information is considered principally for its specific content or for its evaluative meaning. To date, the evidence suggests that content specific feedback changes self-descriptions principally for those attributes on which feedback is given and only minimally on other attributes (Haas & Maehr, 1965; Videbeck, 1960). However, the nature of the situation in which these data were obtained may have maximized the impersonal, objective quality of evaluations and minimized the generalization that can occur in other contexts.

Characteristics of the evaluator may also be significant in determining the extent to which information is accepted. To date, examinations of evaluator competence (Webster & Sobieszek, 1974) imply that only competence relevant to the attribute being judged has real impact on the acceptance of information. Expertise of the evaluator may be more complex, however, when the attributes judged do not involve specific, clearly defined skills. In these more subjective judgments, evaluators' competence may be judged more on global indices of status or, on the extent to which they are perceived, to hold norms similar to one's own on the dimensions in question.

A more situational aspect of the evaluator's competence involves whether or not the evaluator has a sufficient sample of one's behavior to make an adequate appraisal. Even if an appraiser is viewed as a good judge, his or her evaluation may be discounted if it is based on a limited or unrepresentative sample of behavior. Wyer, Henninger, and Wolfson (1975) showed, for example, that observers were much more likely to base their judgments on the limited behavior sample that they observed than were actors, whose self-appraisals were based less on that specific behavior sample and more on previous experiences.

Finally, the interpretation of the evaluation may depend on a perception of how candid other people are being. If one believes that there is some ulterior motive in making the evaluation (e.g., ingratiation or one-upmanship), it may not have as much effect on one's self-perception as a communication interpreted as more genuine.

## Comparison With Self-Evaluations

An important aspect of others' judgments is how closely they agree with one's initial self-appraisal. Although judgments that match an initial self-perception may do little more than fortify this perception, judgments that are at variance frequently set up some dissonance or tension that requires cognitive reappraisal. There is an implicit disagreement between symbolic interactionist and self-attribution theories as to how such discrepancies are resolved. The symbolic interactionist view implies that such discrepancies are typically dealt with by changing one's self-perceptions, whereas self-attribution theories suggest that people have a reasonably clear and stable picture of themselves and may not readily conform to the discrepant appraisal of another individual.

The extent to which self-perception is maintained in the face of contradicting information from others presumably depends on the certainty of an individual's initial self-perceptions. Several factors may influence people's assuredness about their self-perceptions, all of which are related to opportunities for examining their own behavior. One factor is the salience of the dimension on which a judgment is made. Individuals are expected to have more clearly developed opinions about themselves on dimensions that are more important to them. A second aspect regarding the opportunity for observation may be the degree to which the person can compare his or her behavior with that of other people (cf. Festinger, 1954). Impressions may be more firmly established if people have the chance to compare themselves with other individuals. However, the opportunity for such comparisons may vary depending on the dimension being judged. A final determinant of assuredness may be the clarity of the criteria against which attributes are judged. A person is more likely to have a firmly established self-appraisal on an attribute that has a very clear public definition. One reason for children's potential susceptibility to self-concept molding may be their lack of clear criteria for defining particular characteristics. This may also account for the clinical observation that negative global self-perceptions (e.g., "I am rotten" or "I am a total failure") are resistant to change without exploration of what those attributes actually entail.

One complication in assessing the impact of others' feedback is that some changes in self-perception might be attributed to input from others when in fact they really reflect changes in individuals' independent appraisals of themselves. In the naturalistic studies cited previously, changes toward others' perceptions could be accounted for by the individuals having changed or reappraised their own behavior. Certainly there is little in this literature that would negate the potential significance of the claim of self-perception theories that most self-knowledge comes from direct observation of one's own actions.

## Maintenance of Changes

As previously mentioned, there is little evidence of the long-term effects of others' judgments on self-appraisals, and more adequate investigations of these effects are clearly required. Although these investigations would ideally involve naturally occurring interactions, manipulated feedback designs could also be employed. The use of negative feedback in such studies would, of course, be unacceptable ethically, but the effects of positive feedback could feasibly be investigated.

Long-term investigations are particularly important, since at least three processes may mitigate the impact of others' evaluations over time. First, discrepant feedback tends to be distorted so that it becomes more congruent with one's own initial self-perceptions (Harvey et al., 1957; Steiner, 1968; Suinn, Osborne, & Page, 1962). This tendency toward distortion has been demonstrated in experimental situations, although it is unclear how extensively such distortions occur in real-life settings.

A second mitigating factor may be that evaluations from another person may sometimes induce people to change their behavior in an opposite direction. If, for instance, an individual were evaluated as being self-centered but did not like that attribute, he or she might expend a special effort to be more altruistic and accordingly strengthen this perception of altruism. It has been shown that when subjects are told that they are making shorter or slower responses than those of other individuals, they lengthen and speed up their subsequent responses (Burnstein & Zajonc, 1965; Kleinke, 1975). Thus, the long-range impact of others' judgments may sometimes be to produce either no change in self-ratings or even changes in the opposite direction.

A third long-term effect of others' feedback may be that people change their social interactions so that they minimize their exposure to evaluators or to situations in which such feedback is likely to occur. Conceivably these mitigating long-term effects could be offset by an opposing tendency for people to change their behavior and also their self-perceptions to conform to others' role expectations. Unfortunately, there are yet no investigations that have sorted out these potential outcomes.

## Some Neglected Aspects of Others' Influence

It should be noted that empirical investigations of Mead and Cooley's looking-glass-self hypothesis have explored almost exclusively the impact of direct feedback from others. There may, however, be several less direct but equally important effects of others' judgments on self-perception. Simply being in the presence of others may influence the manner in which people behave (Goffman, 1959) and presumably come to evaluate their own behavior. At a conscious level one might deliberately enhance socially desirable and minimize socially undesirable behaviors when in the presence of others, and such changes could influence how one saw oneself. Less deliberately controlled aspects of behavior may also be affected by others' presence, as suggested in studies of audience effects on performance (e.g., Zajonc, 1965) and on self-evaluations of competence (Shrauger, 1972). Also, as Mead's (1934) notion of the generalized other implies, the physical presence of others is not imperative, so long as the perceiver can manage a mental impression of them.

Other individuals may also influence one's self-judgments by the manner in which they interact with people. Whether or not one receives help from a co-worker, for example, has been shown to affect one's subsequent self-esteem (Fisher & Nadler, 1974, 1976). In certain role relationships, such as that between a boss and subordinate, many interpersonal behaviors become quite clearly prescribed. The nature of these interactions may convey to the individuals involved a certain degree of competence, or self-worth, without any explicit communication of these qualities over occurring. Although such processes have been described often in role theory (Goffman, 1955, 1959; Scheff, 1966), they have much less frequently been explored empirically, particularly with reference to their effects on people's self-perceptions.

A third indirect way that social interaction may influence self-perceptions is by affording the opportunity for people to compare their behavior with that of other people. Social comparison obviously requires the presence of other people at some point. It does not, however, prevent people from being active, reflective observers of their own behavior. The observance of others' behavior provides relative standards against which one's own actions and attributes may be judged. Although the significance of such comparison processes has long been recognized, few studies have explored how attributes of those against whom one compares oneself influence self-evaluation (Fontaine, 1974; Morse & Gergen, 1970; Strong & Gray, 1972). Morse and Gergen's investigation found that job applicants' judgments of themselves were substantially influenced by the apparent competence and appearance of other potential applicants. Perhaps even in situations that do not pull so explicitly for social comparisons, the observation of others' actions affects one's self-perceptions.

Finally, other people may indirectly affect one's self-perceptions when they are observed making evaluations of other individuals. Even if people do not receive feedback directly, observing someone make a judgment of another individual may provide indirect information about how they are viewed by the evaluator. How much this actually occurs depends of course on how explicit the criteria for evaluating the other person's behavior are and on the degree to which one sees similarity or dissimilarity between one's own behavior and that of the person being evaluated.

In sum, it may be that the aspect of the looking-glass-self hypothesis that has been most frequently examined, the effect of direct feedback from other people, reflects only one of the ways that interaction with others has an impact on self-judgments. Furthermore, this means of influence may well be of no greater importance than the others. The relative ease with which direct evaluation can be explored ought not to preclude the examination of other viable aspects of social interaction that may also lead to the modification of self-evaluations.

## REFERENCES

Alberti, J. M. (1971). Self-perception-in-school: Validation of an instrument and a study of the structure of children's self-perception-in-school, and its relationship to school achievement, behavior and popularity (Doctoral dissertation, State University of New York at Buffalo, 1970). *Dissertation Abstracts International, 31*, 4535A-4536A. (University Microfilms No. 71-6048)

Amatora, M. (1956). Validity in self-evaluation. *Educational and Psychological Measurement, 16*, 119–126.

Ausubel, D. P. (1955). Socioempathy as a function of sociometric status in an adolescent group. *Human Relations, 8*, 75–84.

Ausubel, D. P., & Schiff, H. M. (1955). Some intrapersonal and interpersonal determinants of individual differences in socioempathic ability among adolescents. *Journal of Social Psychology, 41*, 39–56.

Ausubel, D. P., Schiff, H. M., & Gasser, E. B. (1952). A preliminary study of developmental trends in socioempathy: Accuracy of perception of own and others' sociometric status. *Child Development, 23*, 111–128.

Backman, D., Secord, P., & Pierce, J. (1963). Resistance to change in the self-concept as a function of consensus among significant others. *Sociometry, 26*, 102–111.

Baldwin, J. M. (1897). *Social and ethical interpretations in mental development: A study in social psychology*. New York: Macmillan.

Bem, D. J. (1967). Self-perception: An alternative interpreta-

tion of cognitive dissonance phenomena. *Psychological Review, 74*, 183–200.

Bem, D. J. (1972). Self-perception theory. In I. Berkowitz (Ed.), *Advances in experimental social psychology* (Vol. 6). New York: Academic Press.

Bergin, A. E. (1962). The effect of dissonant persuasive communications upon changes in a self-referring attitude. *Journal of Personality, 30*, 423–438.

Binderman, R. M., Fretz, B. R., Scott, N. A., & Abrams, M. H. (1972). Effects of interpreter credibility and discrepancy level of results on responses to test results. *Journal of Counseling Psychology, 19*, 399–403.

Bishop, J. B. (1971). Another look at counselor, client and supervisor ratings of counselor effectiveness. *Counselor Education and Supervision, 10*, 319–323.

Bledsoe, J. C., & Wiggins, R. G. (1973). Congruence of adolescents' self-concepts and parents' perceptions of adolescents' self-concepts. *Journal of Psychology, 83*, 131–136.

Blumberg, H. H. (1972). Communication of interpersonal evaluations. *Journal of Personality and Social Psychology, 23*, 157–162.

Bramel, D. A. (1962). A dissonance theory approach to defensive projection. *Journal of Abnormal Social Psychology, 69*, 121–129.

Brams, J. (1961). Counselor characteristics and effective communication in counseling. *Journal of Counseling Psychology, 8*, 25–30.

Breslin, H. B. (1968). The relationship between the physically handicapped child's self-concept and his peer reputation (Doctoral dissertation, Oregon State University, 1968). *Dissertation Abstracts International, 29*, 1493B. (University Microfilms No. 68-14,871).

Buckley, E. F. (1970). The relationship between student teacher perceptions and pupil perceptions of the student-teacher (Doctoral dissertation, North Texas State University, 1970). *Dissertation Abstracts International, 30*, 4672A–4673A. (University Microfilms No. 70-9121)

Burke, P. J. (1969). Some preliminary data on the use of self-evaluations and peer ratings in assigning university grades. *Journal of Educational Research, 62*, 444–448.

Burns, R. (1965). To a louse. In, *Poems*. New York: Heritage Press.

Burnstein, E., & Zajonc, R. B. (1965). Individual task performance in a changing social structure. *Sociometry, 28*, 16–29.

Carroll, J. B. (1952). Ratings on traits measured by a factored personality inventory. *Journal of Abnormal and Social Psychology, 47*, 626–632.

Cogan, L. C., Conklin, A. M., & Hollingworth, H. L. (1915). An experimental study of self-analysis, estimates of associates, and the results of tests. *School and Society, 2*, 171–179.

Cooley, C. H. (1902). *Human nature and the social order*. New York: Scribner's.

Cooper, J., & Duncan, B. L. (1971). Cognitive dissonance as a function of self-esteem and logical inconsistency. *Journal of Personality, 39*, 289–302.

Davidson, H. H., & Lang, C. (1960). Children's perceptions of their teachers' feelings toward them related to self-perception, school adjustment and behavior. *Journal of Experimental Education, 29*, 107–118.

De Jung, J. E., &. Gardner, E. F. (1962). The accuracy of self-role perceptions: A developmental study. *Journal of Experimental Education, 31*, 27–41.

Denzin, N. K. (1966). The significant others of a college population. *Sociological Quarterly, 7,* 298–310.

Douce, P. D. M. (1970). Selected aspects of personality related to social acceptance and clothing-oriented variables (Doctoral dissertation, Utah State University, 1969). *Dissertation Abstracts International, 30,* 3730B. (University Microfilms No. 70-2392)

Duval, S., & Wicklund, R. A. (1972). *A theory of objective self-awareness.* New York: Academic Press.

Dmitruk, V. M., Collins, R. W., & Clinger, D. L. (1973). The "Barnum effect" and acceptance of negative personal evaluation. *Journal of Consulting and Clinical Psychology, 41,* 192–194.

Eagly, A. H. (1967). Involvement as a determinant of response to favorable and unfavorable information. *Journal of Personality and Social Psychology Monograph, 7*(3, Pt. 2).

Eagly, A. H., & Acksen, B. A. (1971). The effect of expecting to be evaluated on change toward favorable and unfavorable information about oneself. *Sociometry, 34,* 411-422.

Eagly, A. H., & Whitehead, G. I. (1972). Effect of choice on receptivity to favorable and unfavorable evaluations of oneself. *Journal of Personality and Social Psychology, 22,* 223-230.

Edlow, D. W. & Kiesler, C. A. (1966). Ease of denial and defensive projection. *Journal of Experimental Social Psychology, 2,* 56-69.

Eisenmann, R. & Robinson, N. (1968). Peer-, self- and test-ratings of creativity. *Psychological Reports, 23,* 471–474.

Erikson, E. H. (1956). The problem of ego identity. *Journal of the American Psychoanalytic Association, 4,* 56–121.

Evans, G. C. (1962). The influence of "fake" personality evaluations on self-descriptions. *Journal of Psychology, 53,* 457–463.

Festinger, L. (1954). A theory of social comparison processes. *Human Relations, 7,* 117–140.

Fey, W. F. (1955). Acceptance by others and its relation to acceptance of self and others. A revaluation. *Journal of Abnormal and Social Psychology, 50,* 244–276.

Fisher, J. D., & Nadler, A. (1977). The effect of similarity between donor and recipient on recipient's reactions to aid. *Journal of Applied Social Psychology, 4,* 230–243.

Fisher, J. D., & Nadler, A. (1976). Effect of donor resources on recipient self-esteem and self-help. *Journal of Experimental Social Psychology, 12,* 139–150.

Fontaine, G. (1974). Social comparison and some determinants of expected personal control and expected performance in a novel task situation. *Journal of Personality and Social Psychology, 29,* 487–496.

Friedsam, H. J., & Martin, H. W. (1963). A comparison of self and physicians' health ratings in an older population. *Journal of Health and Human Behavior, 4,* 179–183.

Gerard, H. B. (1961). Some determinants of self-evaluation. *Journal of Abnormal and Social Psychology, 62,* 288–293.

Goffman, E. (1955). On face-work: An analysis of ritual elements in social interaction. *Psychiatry: Journal for the Study of Interpersonal Processes, 18,* 213–231.

Goffman, E. (1959). *The presentation of self in everyday life.* New York: Anchor Books.

Goldings, H. J. (1954). On the avowal and projection of happiness. *Journal of Personality, 23,* 30–47.

Goodman, S. A. (1973). A further exploration of the relationship between self-concept and sociometric status (Doctoral dissertation, University of North Carolina at Chapel Hill,

1973). *Dissertation Abstracts International, 34,* 170A. (University Microfilms No. 73-16,476)

Gordon, C., & Gergen, K. J. (Eds.). (1968). *The self in social interaction* (Vol. 1). New York: Wiley.

Goslin, P. A. (1962). Accuracy of self-perception and social acceptance. *Sociometry, 25,* 283–296.

Gray, D. F., & Gaier, E. L. (1974). The congruency of adolescent self-perceptions with those of parents and best friends. *Adolescence, 9,* 299–304.

Green, G. H. (1948). Insight and group adjustment. *Journal of Abnormal and Social Psychology, 43,* 49–61.

Haas, H. I., & Maehr, M. L. (1965). Two experiments on the concept of self and the reaction of others. *Journal of Personality and Social Psychology, 1,* 100–105.

Halperin, K., Snyder, C. R., Shenkel, R. J., & Houston, B. K. (1976). Effects of source status and message favorability on acceptance of personality feedback. *Journal of Applied Psychology, 61,* 85–88.

Hamilton, D. L. (1969). Measures of self-esteem, dominance, and dogmatism: Convergent and discriminant validity. *Proceedings of the 77th Annual Convention of the American Psychological Association, 4,* 127–128. (Summary)

Hartup, W. W. (1970). Peer interactions and social organization. In P. H. Mussen (Ed.), *Carmichael's manual of child psychology.* New York: Wiley.

Harvey, O. J., & Clapp, W. F. (1965). Hope, expectancy, and reactions to the unexpected. *Journal of Personality and Social Psychology, 2,* 45–52.

Harvey, O. J., Hunt, D. E., & Schroder, H. M. (1961). *Conceptual systems and personality organization.* New York: Wiley.

Harvey, O. J., Kelley, H. H., & Shapiro, M. M. (1957). Reactions to unfavorable evaluations of the self made by other persons. *Journal of Personality, 25,* 393–411.

Hase, H. D., & Goldberg, L. R. (1967). Comparative validity of different strategies of constructing personality inventory scales. *Psychological Bulletin, 67,* 231–248.

Helper, M. M. (1958). Parental evaluations of children and children's self-evaluations. *Journal of Abnormal and Social Psychology, 56,* 190–194.

Hendrick, C., & Seyfried, B. A. (1974). Assessing the validity of laboratory-produced attitude change. *Journal of Personality and Social Behavior, 29,* 865–870.

Herzberger, S. (1978). The development of social self-perception. In J. Chevalier & R. Wolfe (Chairs), *Through a lens clearly: Enhancing a dim view of person perception.* Symposium presented at the State University of New York College at Geneseo.

Hicks, J. (1962). The influence of group flattery upon self-evaluation. *Journal of Social Psychology, 58,* 147–151.

Horowitz, F. D. (1962). The relationship of anxiety, self-concept, and sociometric status among fourth, fifth, and sixth grade children. *Journal of Abnormal and Social Psychology, 65,* 212–214.

Israel, J. (1958). Self-evaluation in groups. *Acta Sociologica, 3,* 29–47.

James, W. (1890). *The principles of psychology.* New York: Holt.

Jansen, D. G., Robb, G. P., & Bonk, E. C. (1973). Peer ratings and self-ratings on twelve bipolar items of practicum counselors ranked high and low in competence by their peers. *Journal of Counseling Psychology, 20,* 419–424.

Jones, E. E., Gergen, K. J., & Davis, K. (1962). Some determinants of reactions to being approved or disapproved as a person. *Psychological Monographs, 76*(2, Whole No. 521).

Jones, E. E., & Nisbett. R. E. (1971). *The actor and the observer: Divergent perceptions of the causes of behavior.* Morristown, NJ: General Learning Press.

Johnson, H. H. (1966). Some effects of discrepancy level on responses to negative information about one's self. *Sociometry, 29,* 52–66.

Jorgenson, G. Q. (1967). Relationships among self, peer and teacher evaluations of motivational dispositions and behaviors in third grade (Doctoral dissertation, University of Utah, 1967). *Dissertation Abstracts, 27,* 3314A–3315A. (University Microfilms No. 67-3132)

Jourard, S. M., & Remy, R. M. (1955). Perceived parental attitudes, the self, and security. *Journal of Consulting Psychology, 19,* 364–366.

Kelman, H. C., & Parloff, M. B. (1957). Interrelations among three criteria of improvement in group therapy: Comfort, effectiveness, and self-awareness. *Journal of Abnormal and Social Psychology, 54,* 281–288.

Kemper, T. D. (1966). Self-conceptions and the expectations of significant others. *Sociological Quarterly, 7,* 323–343.

Kinch, J. W. (1963). A formalized theory of the self-concept. *American Journal of Sociology, 68,* 481–486.

Kinch, J. W. (1968). Experiments on factors related to self-concept change. *Journal of Social Psychology, 74,* 251–258.

Kleinke, C. L. (1975). Effects of false feedback about response length on subjects' perception of an interview. *Journal of Social Psychology, 95,* 99–104.

Klimoski, P. J., & London, M. J. (1974). Role of the rater in performance appraisal. *Journal of Applied Psychology, 59,* 445–451.

Lomont, J. F. (1966). Repressors and sensitizers as described by themselves and their peers. *Journal of Personality, 34,* 224–240.

Maehr, M. L., Mensing, J., & Nafzger, S. (1962). Concept of self and the reactions of others. *Sociometry, 25,* 353–357.

Manis, M. (1955). Social interaction and the self-concept. *Journal of Abnormal and Social Psychology, 51,* 362–370.

Marcia, J. (1967). Ego-identity status: Relationship to change in self-esteem "general maladjustment" and authoritarianism. *Journal of Personality, 35,* 119–133.

Mayo, G. D., & Manning, W. H. (1961). Motivation measurement. *Educational and Psychological Measurement, 21,* 73–83.

McConnell, G. (1959). Questions about you. *Education, 80,* 112–114.

McIntyre, C. J. (1952). Acceptance by others and its relation to acceptance of self and others. *Journal of Abnormal and Social Psychology, 47,* 624–625.

Mead, G. H. (1934). *Mind, self and society.* Chicago: University of Chicago Press.

Meehl, P. E. (1956). Wanted—A good cookbook. *American Psychologist, 11,* 263–272.

Miyamoto, S. F., & Dornbusch, S. (1956). A test of the symbolic interactionist hypotheses of self-conception. *American Journal of Sociology, 61,* 399–403.

Morse, S., & Gergen, K. J. (1970). Social comparison, self-consistency, and the concept of self. *Journal of Personality and Social Psychology, 16,* 148–156.

Mosher, D. L. (1965). Approval motive and acceptance of "fake" personality test interpretations which differ in favorability. *Psychological Reports, 17,* 395–402.

Mote, F. B. (1967). The relationship between child self-concept in school and parental attitudes and behaviors in child rearing (Doctoral dissertation, Stanford University, 1966). *Dissertation Abstracts, 27,* 3319A. (University Microfilms No. 67-4309)

Newcomb, T. M. (1961). *The acquaintance process.* New York: Holt, Rinehart & Winston.

Orpen, C., & Bush, R. (1974). The lack of congruence between self-concept and public image. *Journal of Social Psychology, 93,* 145–146.

Papageorgis, D., & McCann, B. M. (1965). Effect of discrepant communications on self-perception. *Journal of Social Psychology, 67,* 227–237.

Peirce, C. S. (1868). Questions concerning certain faculties claimed for man. *Journal of Speculative Philosophy, 2,* 103–114.

Perkins, H. V. (1958). Teachers' and peers' perception of children's self-concepts. *Child Development, 29,* 203–220.

Peterson, D. R. (1965). Scope and generality of verbally defined personality factors. *Psychological Review, 72,* 48–59.

Phillips, B. N. (1963). Age changes in accuracy of self-perception. *Child Development, 64,* 1041–1046.

Powell, M. G. (1948). Comparison of self-rating, peer-ratings, and experts'-ratings of personality adjustment. *Educational and Psychological Measurement, 8,* 225–234.

Quarantelli, E. L., & Cooper, J. (1966). Self-conceptions and others: A further test of the Meadian hypothesis. *Sociological Quarterly, 7,* 281–297.

Raven, B. H., & Rubin, J. Z. (1976). *Social psychology: People in groups.* New York: Wiley.

Reeder, L. G., Donohue, G. A., & Biblarz, A. (1960). Conceptions of self and others. *American Journal of Sociology, 66,* 153–159.

Reese, H. W. (1961). Relationship between self-acceptance and sociometric choice. *Journal of Abnormal and Social Psychology, 62,* 472–474.

Regan, J. W., Gosselink, H., Hubsch, J., & Ulsh, E. (1975). Do people have inflated views of their own ability? *Journal of Personality and Social Psychology, 31,* 295–301.

Rokeach, M. (1945). Studies in beauty: II Some determiners of the perception of beauty in women. *Journal of Social Psychology, 22,* 155–169.

Rosenberg, M. J. (1965). When dissonance fails: On eliminating evaluation apprehension from attitude measurement. *Journal of Personality and Social Psychology, 1,* 28–42.

Rosengren, W. R. (1961). The self in the emotionally disturbed. *American Journal of Sociology, 66,* 454–462.

Scheff, T. J. (1966). *Being mentally ill: A sociological theory.* Chicago: Aldine.

Schneider, B. (1970). Relationship between various criteria of leadership in small groups. *Journal of Social Psychology, 82,* 253–261.

Schneider, D. J. (1976). *Social psychology.* Reading, MA: Addison-Wesley.

Scott, W. A., & Johnson, R. C. (1972). Comparative validity of direct and indirect personality tests. *Journal of Consulting and Clinical Psychology, 38,* 301–318.

Secord, P. F., & Backman, C. W. (1974). *Social psychology.* New York: McGraw-Hill.

Sherwood, J. J. (1965). Self-identity and referent others. *Sociometry, 28,* 66–81.

Sherwood, J. J. (1967). Increased self-evaluation as function of ambiguous evaluations by referent others. *Sociometry, 30,* 404–409.

Shrauger, J. S. (1972). Self-esteem and relations to being observed by others. *Journal of Personality and Social Psychology, 23,* 192–200.

Shrauger, J. S., & Lund, A. (1975). Self-evaluation and reactions to evaluations from others. *Journal of Personality, 43,* 94–108.

Shrauger, J. S., & Rosenberg, S. E. (1970). Self-esteem and the effects of success and failure feedback on performance. *Journal of Personality, 38,* 404–417.

Snyder, C. R., & Shenkel, R. J. (1976). Effects of "favorability," modality, and relevance on acceptance of general personality interpretations prior to and after receiving diagnostic feedback. *Journal of Consulting and Clinical Psychology, 44,* 34–41.

Sobieszek, B. I., & Webster, M. (1973). Conflicting sources of evaluations. *Sociometry, 36,* 550–560.

Steiner, I. D. (1968). Reactions to adverse and favorable evaluations of one's self. *Journal of Personality, 36,* 553–563.

Strong, S. R., & Gray, B. L. (1972). Social comparison, self-evaluation, and influence in counseling. *Journal of Counseling Psychology, 19,* 178–183.

Suinn, R. M., Osborne, D., & Page, W. (1962). The self-concept and accuracy of recall of inconsistent self-related information. *Journal of Clinical Psychology, 18,* 473–474.

Sundberg, N. D. (1955). The acceptability of "fake" versus "bona fide" personality test interpretations. *Journal of Abnormal and Social Psychology, 50,* 145–147.

Swanson, B. M. (1969). Parent-child relations: A child's acceptance by others, of others and of self (Doctoral dissertation, University of Oklahoma, 1969). *Dissertation Abstracts International, 30,* 1890B. (University Microfilms No. 69-16,576)

Tagiuri, R., Blake, R. R., & Brunet, J. S. (1953). Some determinants of the perception of positive and negative feelings in others. *Journal of Abnormal and Social Psychology, 38,* 585–592.

Teichman, M. (1972). Cognitive differentiation between self-concept and image of self ascribed to parents in boys on the verge of delinquency. *Perceptual and Motor Skills, 34,* 573–574.

Todorosky, N. R. (1972). Self-acceptance and acceptance by peers (Doctoral dissertation, Michigan State University, 1972). *Dissertation Abstracts International, 33,* 2359B–2360B. (University Microfilms No. 72-30,054)

Trickett, H. V. (1969). Stability and predictability of children's self-concept and perception by others: A developmental study (Doctoral dissertation, Stanford University, 1968). *Dissertation Abstracts International, 29,* 2577A. (University Microfilms No. 69-306)

Tschechtelin, S. M. A. (1945). Self-appraisal of children. *Journal of Educational Research, 39,* 25–32.

Videbeck, R. (1960). Self-conception and the reactions of others. *Sociometry, 23,* 351–359.

Walhood, D. S., & Klopfer, W. G. (1971). Congruence between self-concept and public image. *Journal of Consulting and Clinical Psychology, 37,* 148–150.

Webb, W. B. (1955). Self-evaluations, group evaluations, and objective measures. *Journal of Consulting Psychology, 19,* 210–212.

Webster, M., & Sobieszek, B. I. (1974). *Sources of self evaluation: A formal theory of significant others and social influence.* New York: Wiley.

Weisberg, P. (1970). Student acceptance of bogus personality interpretations differing in level of social desirability. *Psychological Reports, 27,* 743–746.

Werdelin, I. (1969). A study of the relationship between teacher rating, peer ratings and self ratings of behavior in school. *Scandinavian Journal of Educational Research, 13,* 147–169.

Winthrop, H. (1959). Self-images of personal adjustment vs. the estimates of friends. *Journal of Social Psychology, 50,* 87–99.

Wyer, R. S., Henninger M., & Wolfson, M. (1975). Informational determinants of females' self-attributions and observers' judgments of them in an achievement situation. *Journal of Personality and Social Psychology, 32,* 556–570.

Wylie, R. C. (1974). *The self-concept* (Vol. 1, Rev. ed.). Lincoln: University of Nebraska Press.

Zajonc, R. B. (1965). Social facilitation. *Science, 149,* 269–274.

Ziller, R. C. (1973). *The social self.* New York: Pergamon Press.

# Appendix 1

Investigations of the Relationship Between Subject's Self-Descriptions and Subjects' Perceptions of How Others Describe Them

**Study**

Davidson & Lang (1960)

Goodman (1973)

Goslin (1962)

Jourard & Remy (1955)

Kemper (1966)

Miyamoto & Dornbusch (1956)

**Study**

Orpen & Bush (1974)

Quarantelli & Cooper (1966)

Reeder, Donohue, & Biblarz (1960)

Swanson (1969)

Teichman (1972)

Walhood & Klopfer (1971)

## Appendix 2

Investigations of the Relationship Between Subjects' Self-Descriptions and Actual Descriptions of Them by Significant Others

**Study**

Alberti (1971)
Amatora (1956)
Bishop (1971)
Bledsoe & Wiggins (1973)
Brams (1961)
Breslin (1968)
Buckley (1970)
Burke (1969)
Carroll (1952)
Cogan, Conklin, & Hollingworth (1915)
Douce (1970)
Eisenmann & Robinson (1968)
Fey (1955)
Friedsam & Martin (1963)
Goldings (1954)
Goodman (1973)
Goslin (1962)
Gray & Gaier (1974)
Green (1948)
Hamilton (1969)
Hase & Goldberg (1967)
Helper (1958)
Horowitz (1962)
Israel (1958)
Jansen, Robb, & Bonk (1973)

**Study**

Jorgenson (1967)
Kelman & Parloff (1957)
Klimoski & London (1974)
Lomont (1966)
Mayo & Manning (1961)
McConnell (1959)
McIntyre (1952)
Miyamoto & Dornbusch (1956)
Mote (1967)
Orpen & Bush (1974)
Perkins (1958)
Phillips (1963)
Powell (1948)
Reeder, Donohue, & Biblarz (1960)
Reese (1961)
Rokeach (1945)
B. Schneider (1970)
Scott & Johnson (1972)
Todorosky (1972)
Tschechtelin (1945)
Walhood & Klopfer (1971)
Webb (1955)
Werdelin (1969)
Wetzel (cited in Peterson, 1965)
Winthrop (1959)

# Illusion and Well-Being: A Social Psychological Perspective on Mental Health

Shelley E. Taylor • University of California, Los Angeles
Jonathon D. Brown • Southern Methodist University

Many prominent theorists have argued that accurate perceptions of the self, the world, and the future are essential for mental health. Yet considerable research evidence suggests that overly positive self-evaluations, exaggerated perceptions of control or mastery, and unrealistic optimism are characteristics of normal human thought. Moreover, these illusions appear to promote other criteria of mental health, including the ability to care about others, the ability to be happy or contented, and the ability to engage in productive and creative work. These strategies may succeed, in large part, because both the social world and cognitive-processing mechanisms impose filters on incoming information that distort it in a positive direction; negative information may be isolated and represented in as unthreatening a manner as possible. These positive illusions may be especially adaptive under these circumstances.

**D**ecades of psychological wisdom have established contact with reality as a hallmark of mental health. In this view, the well-adjusted person is thought to engage in accurate reality testing, whereas the individual whose vision is clouded by illusion is regarded as vulnerable to, if not already a victim of, mental illness. Despite its plausibility, this viewpoint is increasingly difficult to maintain (cf. Lazarus, 1983). A substantial amount of research testifies to the prevalence of illusion in normal human cognition (see Fiske & Taylor 1984; Greenwald, 1980; Nisbett & Ross, 1980; Sackeim, 1983; Taylor, 1983). Moreover, these illusions often involve central aspects of the self and

the environment and, therefore, cannot be dismissed as inconsequential.

In this article, we review research suggesting that certain illusions may be adaptive for mental health and well-being. In particular, we examine evidence that a set of interrelated positive illusions—namely, unrealistically positive self-evaluations, exaggerated perceptions of control or mastery, and unrealistic optimism—can serve a wide variety of cognitive, affective, and social functions. We also attempt to resolve the following paradox: How can positive misperceptions of one's self and the environment be adaptive when accurate information processing seems to be essential for learning and successful functioning in the world? Our primary goal is to weave a theoretical context for thinking about mental health. A secondary goal is to create an integrative framework for a voluminous literature in social cognition concerning perceptions of the self and the environment.

## Mental Health as Contact with Reality

Throughout psychological history, a variety of views of mental health have been proffered, some idiosyncratic and others widely shared. Within this theoretical diversity, a dominant position has maintained that the psychologically healthy person is one who maintains close contact with reality. For example, in her distillation of the dominant views of mental health at the time, Jahoda (1958) noted that the majority of theories considered contact with reality to be a critical component of mental health. This theme is prominent in the writings of Allport (1943), Erikson (1950), Menninger (1930), and Fromm (1955), among others. For example, concerning his self-actualized individuals, Maslow (1950) wrote,

> Our healthy individuals find it possible to accept themselves and their own nature without chagrin or complaint. . . . They can accept their own human nature with all of its discrepancies from the ideal image without feeling real concern. It would convey the wrong impression to say that they are self-satisfied. What we must rather say is that they can take the frailties and sins, weaknesses and evils of human nature in the same unquestioning spirit that one takes or accepts the characteristics of nature. (p. 54)

On the basis of her review, Jahoda concluded,

> The perception of reality is called mentally healthy when what the individual sees corresponds to what is actually there. (1958, p. 6)

> Mentally healthy perception means a process of viewing the world so that one is able to take in matters one wishes were different without distorting them to fit these wishes. (1953, p. 349)

Since Jahoda's report, the position that the mentally healthy person perceives reality accurately has been put forth in major works by Haan (1977) and Vaillant (1977), and it has also been incorporated into textbooks on adjustment (e.g., Jourard & Landsman, 1980; Schulz, 1977). For example, after reviewing a large number of theories of the healthy personality, Jourard and Landsman (1980) noted, "The ability to perceive reality as it 'really is' is fundamental to executive functioning. It is considered one of the two preconditions to the development of [the healthy personality]" (p. 75).

To summarize, then, although it is not the only theoretical perspective on the mentally healthy person, the view that psychological health depends on accurate perceptions of reality has been widely promulgated and widely shared in the literature on mental health.

## Social Cognition, Reality, and Illusion

Early theorists in social cognition adapted a view of the person's information-processing capabilities that is quite similar to the viewpoint just described. These theorists maintained that the social perceiver monitors and interacts with the world like a naive scientist (see Fischhoff, 1976; Fiske & Taylor, 1984; Nisbett & Ross, 1980, for discussions). According to this view, the person gathers data in an unbiased manner; combines it in some logical, identifiable fashion; and reaches generally good, accurate inferences and decisions. Theories of the causal attribution process (e.g., Kelley, 1967), prediction (see Kahneman & Tversky, 1973), judgments of covariation, and other tasks of social inference (see Fiske & Taylor, 1984; Nisbett & Ross, 1980) incorporated the assumptions of the naive scientist as normative guidelines with which actual behavior could be compared.

It rapidly became evident, however, that the social perceiver's actual inferential work and decision making looked little like these normative models. Rather, information processing is full of incomplete data gathering, shortcuts, errors, and biases (see Fiske & Taylor, 1984; Nisbett & Ross, 1980, for reviews). In particular, prior expectations and self-serving interpretations weigh heavily into the social judgment process. In summarizing this work, Fiske and Taylor (1984) noted, "Instead of a naive scientist entering the environment in search of the truth, we find the rather unflattering picture of a charlatan trying to make the data come out in a manner most advantageous to his or her already-held theories" (p. 88). The implications of these conclusions for cognitive functioning have been widely debated and discussed (see Fiske & Taylor, 1984; Greenwald, 1980; Nisbett & Ross, 1980). But these findings also seem to have implications for the understanding of mental health, inasmuch as they appear to contradict a dominant conception of its attributes: How can the normal, healthy individual perceive reality accurately if his or her perceptions are so evidently biased and self-serving? Before considering this issue, a note concerning terminology is required.

At this point, we exchange the terms *error* and *bias* for a broader term, *illusion*. There are several reasons for this change in terminology. *Error* and *bias* imply short-term mistakes and distortions, respectively, that might be caused by careless oversight or other temporary negligences (cf. Funder, 1987). *Illusion*, in contrast, implies a more general, enduring pattern of error, bias, or both that assumes a particular direction or shape. As the evidence will show, the illusions to be considered (unrealistically positive self-evaluations, exaggerated perceptions of control, and unrealistic optimism) do indeed seem to be pervasive, enduring, and systematic. Illusion is defined as

> a perception that represents what is perceived in a way different from the way it is in reality. An illusion is a false mental image or conception which may be a misinterpretation of a real appearance or may be something imagined. It may be pleasing, harmless, or even useful. (Stein, 1982, p. 662)

The definition of an illusion as a belief that departs from reality presupposes an objective grasp of reality. This point puts us on the perilous brink of philosophical debate concerning whether one can ever know reality. Fortunately, at least to some degree, the methodologies of social psychology spare us this frustrating conundrum by providing operational definitions. In some cases, evidence for illusions comes from experimental work that manipulates feedback provided to a person (e.g., whether the person succeeded or failed on a task) and measures the individual's perceptions or recall of that feedback; this paradigm can provide estimates of an individual's accuracy as well as information about the direction (positive or negative) of any distortions. As will be seen, people typically distort such feedback in a self-serving manner. More subjective self-evaluations (e.g., how happy or well-adjusted one is) do not have these same objective standards of comparison. In such cases, an illusion is implied if the majority of people report that they are more (or less) likely than the majority of people to hold a particular belief. For example, if most people believe that

they are happier, better adjusted, and more skilled on a variety of tasks than most other people, such perceptions provide evidence suggestive of an illusion. Illusions about the future are operationally difficult to establish because no one knows what the future will bring. If it can be shown, however, that most people believe that their future is more positive than that of most other people or more positive than objective baserate data can support, then evidence suggestive of illusions about the future is provided. We now turn to the evidence for these illusions.

## Positive Illusions and Social Cognition

Any taxonomy of illusions is, to some extent, arbitrary. Many researchers have studied biases in the processing of self-relevant information and have given their similar phenomena different names. There is, however, considerable overlap in findings, and three that consistently emerge can be labeled *unrealistically positive views of the self, exaggerated perceptions of personal control,* and *unrealistic optimism.* Those familiar with the research evidence will recognize that much of the evidence for these positive illusions comes from experimental studies and from research with college students. We will have more to say about potential biases in the experimental literature later in this article. At present, it is important to note that all three of the illusions to be discussed have been documented in noncollege populations as well.

### Unrealistically Positive Views of the Self

As indicated earlier, a traditional conception of mental health asserts that the well-adjusted individual possesses a view of the self that includes an awareness and acceptance of both the positive and negative aspects of self. In contrast to this portrayal, evidence indicates that most individuals possess a very positive view of the self (see Greenwald, 1980, for a review). When asked to indicate how accurately positive and negative personality adjectives describe the self, normal subjects judged positive traits to be overwhelmingly more characteristic of self than negative attributes (Alicke, 1985; Brown, 1986). Additionally, for most individuals, positive personality information is efficiently processed and easily recalled, whereas negative personality information is poorly processed and difficult to recall (Kuiper & Derry, 1982; Kuiper & MacDonald, 1982; Kuiper, Olinger, MacDonald, & Shaw, 1985). Most individuals also show poorer recall for information related to failure than to success (Silverman, 1964) and tend to recall their task performance as more positive than it actually was (Crary, 1966). Research on the self-serving bias in causal attribution documents that most individuals are more likely to attribute positive than negative outcomes to the self (see Bradley, 1978; Miller & Ross, 1975; Ross & Fletcher, 1985; Zuckerman, 1979, for reviews).[1]

*Evidence for (+)*

Even when negative aspects of the self are acknowledged, they tend to be dismissed as inconsequential. One's poor abilities tend to be perceived as common, but one's favored abilities are seen as rare and distinctive (Campbell, 1986; G. Marks, 1984). Furthermore, the things that people are not proficient at are perceived as less important than the things that they are proficient at (e.g., Campbell, 1986, Harackiewicz, Sansone, & Manderlink, 1985; Lewicki, 1984; Rosenberg 1979). And people perceive that they have improved on abilities that are important to them even when their performance has remained unchanged (Conway & Ross, 1984).

In sum, far from being balanced between the positive and the negative, the perception of self that most individuals hold is heavily weighted toward the positive end of the scale. Of course, this imbalance does not in and of itself provide evidence that such views are unrealistic or illusory. Evidence of this nature is, however, available.

First, there exists a pervasive tendency to see the self as better than others. Individuals judge positive personality attributes to be more descriptive of themselves than of the average person but see negative personality attributes as less descriptive of themselves than of the average person (Alicke, 1985; Brown, 1986). This effect has been documented for a wide range of traits (Brown, 1986) and abilities (Campbell, 1986; Larwood & Whittaker, 1977); individuals even believe that their driving ability is superior to others' (Svenson, 1981). Because it is logically impossible for most people to be better than the average person, these highly skewed, positive views of the self can be regarded as evidence for their unrealistic and illusory nature. People also tend to use their positive

qualities when appraising others, thereby virtually assuring a favorable self–other comparison (Lewicki, 1983). And people give others less credit for success and more blame for failure than they ascribe to themselves (Forsyth & Schlenker, 1977; Green & Gross, 1979; Mirels, 1980; Schlenker & Miller, 1977; Taylor & Koivumaki, 1976).

Although the tendency to see the self as better than others is attenuated somewhat when the others being evaluated are close friends or relatives (Brown, 1986), a corresponding tendency exists for individuals to see their intimates as better than average. One's friends are evaluated more positively and less negatively than the average person (Brown, 1986), and, compared with others, close friends and relatives receive more credit for success and less blame for failure (Hall & Taylor, 1976; Taylor & Koivumaki, 1976). Moreover, these effects at the individual level also occur at the group level: Research using the minimal intergroup paradigm has established that even under the most minimal of social conditions, a pervasive tendency exists for individuals to see their own group as better than other groups (see Tajfel & Turner, 1986, for a review). Thus, although research demonstrates a general person-positivity bias (Schneider, Hastorf, & Ellsworth, 1979; Sears, 1983), individuals are inclined to appraise themselves and their close associates in far more positive and less negative terms than they appraise most other people.

A second source of evidence pertaining to the illusory quality of positive self-perceptions comes from investigations in which self-ratings have been compared with judgments made by observers. Lewinsohn, Mischel, Chaplin, and Barton (1980) had observers watch college-student subjects complete a group-interaction task. Observers then rated each subject along a number of personality dimen-

---

[1]Despite a general pattern indicating that people accept more responsibility for positive outcomes than for negative outcomes, some evidence suggests that people may exaggerate their own causal role in the occurrence of highly negative events (e.g., Bulman & Wortman, 1977; Janoff-Bulman, 1979; Taylor, Lichtman, & Wood, 1984). These data might appear to be at odds with a general pattern of self-serving attributions, but they may not be. Self-attribution does not imply personal responsibility or self-blame (Shaver & Drown, 1986) and therefore may not produce any blow to self-esteem. Moreover, some have suggested that self-attribution may enable people to begin to achieve mastery over an adverse event, helping to maintain a sense of personal control (Bulman & Wortman, 1977; Taylor, 1983).

sions (e.g., friendly, warm, and assertive). Subjects also rated themselves on each attribute. The results showed that self-ratings were significantly more positive than the observers' ratings. In other words, individuals saw themselves in more flattering terms than they were seen in by others.

In sum, the perception of self that most individuals hold is not as well-balanced as traditional models of mental health suggest. Rather than being attentive to both the favorable and unfavorable aspects of self, normal individuals appear to be very cognizant of their strengths and assets and considerably less aware of their weaknesses and faults. Evidence that these flattering self-portrayals are illusory comes from studies in which researchers have found that (a) most individuals see themselves as better than the average person and (b) most individuals see themselves as better than others see them. For these reasons, overly positive views of the self appear to be illusory.[2]

Does there exist a group of individuals that is accepting of both the good and the bad aspects of themselves as many views of mental health maintain the normal person is? Suggestive evidence indicates that individuals who are low in self-esteem, moderately depressed, or both are more balanced in self-perceptions (see Coyne & Gotlieb, 1983; Ruehlman, West, & Pasahow, 1985; Watson & Clark, 1984, for reviews). These individuals tend to (a) recall positive and negative self-relevant information with equal frequency (e.g., Kuiper & Derry, 1982; Kuiper & MacDonald, 1982), (b) show greater evenhandedness in their attributions of responsibility for balanced outcomes (e.g., Campbell & Fairey, 1985; Kuiper, 1978; Rizley, 1978), (c) display greater congruence between self-evaluations and evaluations of others (e.g., Brown, 1986), and (d) offer self-appraisals that coincide more closely with appraisals by objective observers (e.g., Lewinsohn et al., 1980). In short, it appears to be not the well-adjusted individual but the individual who experiences subjective distress who is more likely to process self-relevant information in a relatively unbiased and balanced fashion. These findings are inconsistent with the notion that realistic and evenhanded perceptions of self are characteristic of mental health.

## Illusions of Control

A second domain in which most individuals' perceptions appear to be less than realistic concerns beliefs about personal control over environmental occurrences. Many theorists, including social psychologists (e.g., Heider, 1958), developmental psychologists (e.g., White, 1959), learning theorists (Bandura, 1977; deCharms, 1968), and psychoanalytic theorists (Fenichel, 1945; Hendrick, 1942) have maintained that a sense of personal control is integral to the self-concept and self-esteem. Research evidence, however, suggests that people's beliefs in personal control are sometimes greater than can be justified.

In a series of studies adopting gambling formats, Langer and her associates (Langer, 1975; Langer & Roth, 1975) found that people often act as if they have control in situations that are actually determined by chance. When manipulations suggestive of skill, such as competition, choice, familiarity, and involvement, are introduced into chance situations, people behave as if the situations were determined by skill and, thus, were ones over which they could exert some control (see also Goffman, 1967). For example, people infer that they have greater control if they personally throw dice than if someone else does it for them (Fleming & Darley, 1986; Langer, 1975). Similarly, a large literature on covariation estimation indicates that people substantially overestimate their degree of control over heavily chance-determined events (see Crocker, 1982, for a review). When people expect to produce a certain outcome and the outcome then occurs, they often overestimate the degree to which they were instrumental in bringing it about (see Miller & Ross, 1975).

Is there any group in which this illusion of control appears to be absent? Mildly and severely depressed individuals appear to be less vulnerable to the illusion of control (Abramson & Alloy, 1981;

---

[2]One might argue that overly positive self-descriptions reflect public posturing rather than privately held beliefs. Several factors, however, argue against the plausibility of a strict self-presentational interpretation of this phenomenon. For example, Greenwald and Breckler (1985) reviewed evidence indicating that (a) self-evaluations are at least as favorable under private conditions as they are under public conditions; (b) favorable self-evaluations occur even when strong constraints to be honest are present; (c) favorable self-referent judgments are made very rapidly, suggesting that people are not engaging in deliberate (time consuming) fabrication; and (d) self-enhancing judgments are acted on. For these as well as other reasons, a consensus is emerging at the theoretical level that individuals do not offer flattering self-evaluations merely as a means of managing a public impression of competency (see Schlenker, 1980; Tesser & Moon, 1986; Tetlock & Manstead, 1985).

Golin, Terrell, & Johnson, 1977; Golin, Terrell, Weitz, & Drost, 1979; M. S. Greenberg, Vazquez & Alloy, 1988). When skill cues are introduced into a chance-related task or when outcomes occur as predicted, depressed individuals provide more accurate estimates of their degree of personal control than do nondepressed people. Similarly, relative to nondepressed people, those in whom a negative mood has been induced show more realistic perceptions of personal control (Alloy, Abramson, & Viscusi, 1981; see also Shrauger & Terbovic, 1976). This is not to suggest that depressed people or those in whom a negative mood has been induced are always more accurate than nondepressed subjects in their estimates of personal control (e.g., Abramson, Alloy, & Rosoff, 1981; Benassi & Mahler, 1985), but that the preponderance of evidence lies in this direction. Realistic perceptions of personal control thus appear to be more characteristic of individuals in a depressed affective state than individuals in a nondepressed affective state.

## Unrealistic Optimism

Research suggests that most people are future oriented. In one survey (Gonzales & Zimbardo, 1985), the majority of respondents rated themselves as oriented toward the present and the future (57%) or primarily toward the future (33%) rather than toward the present only (9%) or toward the past (1%). Optimism pervades people's thinking about the future (Tiger, 1979). Research suggests that most people believe that the present is better than the past and that the future will be even better (Brickman, Coates, & Janoff-Bulman, 1978). Questionnaires that survey Americans about the future have found the majority to be hopeful and confident that things can only improve (Free & Cantril, 1968). When asked what they thought was possible for them in the future, college students reported more than four times as many positive as negative possibilities (Markus & Nurius, 1986).

Is there any evidence, however, that such optimism is actually unrealistic? Although the future may well hold more subjectively positive events than negative ones for most individuals, as with excessively positive views of the self, evidence for the illusory nature of optimism comes from studies comparing judgments of self with judgments of others. The evidence indicates that although the

warm and generous vision of the future that individuals entertain extends to all people, it is decidedly more in evidence for the self. People estimate the likelihood that they will experience a wide variety of pleasant events, such as liking their first job, getting a good salary, or having a gifted child, as higher than those of their peers (Weinstein, 1980). Conversely, when asked their chances of experiencing a wide variety of negative events, including having an automobile accident (Robertson, 1977), being a crime victim (Perloff & Fetter, 1986), having trouble finding a job (Weinstein, 1980), or becoming ill (Perloff & Fetter, 1986) or depressed (Kuiper, MacDonald, & Derry, 1983), most people believe that they are less likely than their peers to experience such negative events. In effect, most people seem to be saying "The future will be great, especially for me." Because not everyone's future can be rosier than their peers', the extreme optimism that individuals display appears to be illusory.

Other evidence also suggests that individuals hold unrealistically positive views of the future. Over a wide variety of tasks, subjects' predictions of what will occur correspond closely to what they would like to see happen or to what is socially desirable rather than to what is objectively likely (Cantril, 1938; Lund, 1975; McGuire, 1960; Pruitt & Hoge, 1965; Sherman, 1980). Both children and adults overestimate the degree to which they will do well on future tasks (e.g., Crandall, Solomon, & Kelleway, 1955; Irwin, 1944, 1953; R. W. Marks, 1951), and they are more likely to provide such overestimates the more personally important the task is (Frank, 1953). Unrealistic optimism has even been documented for events that are entirely chance determined (Irwin, 1953; Langer & Roth, 1975; R. W. Marks, 1951).

In contrast to the extremely positive view of the future displayed by normal individuals, mildly depressed people and those with low self-esteem appear to entertain more balanced assessments of their likely future circumstances (see Ruehlman et al., 1985, for a review). Relative to judgments concerning others, these individuals fail to exhibit the self-enhancing tendency to see positive events as more likely for self and negative events as less likely for self (Alloy & Ahrens, 1987; Brown, 1985; Pietromonaco & Markus, 1985; Pyszczynski, Holt, & Greenberg, 1987). Thus, although in some cases such tendencies may reflect pessimism on the part of depressed people, it appears to be

*Future*

individuals who are high, not low, in subjective well-being who evince more biased perceptions of the future.

## Summary

To summarize, traditional conceptions of mental health assert that well-adjusted individuals possess relatively accurate perceptions of themselves, their capacity to control important events in their lives, and their future. In contrast to this portrayal, a great deal of research in social, personality, clinical, and developmental psychology documents that normal individuals possess unrealistically positive views of themselves, an exaggerated belief in their ability to control their environment, and a view of the future that maintains that their future will be far better than the average person's. Furthermore, individuals who are moderately depressed or low in self-esteem consistently display an absence of such enhancing illusions. Together, these findings appear inconsistent with the notion that accurate self-knowledge is the hallmark of mental health.

Two other literatures also suggest that accurate self-knowledge may not always be positively related to psychological well-being. Consider, first, research on the correlates of private self-consciousness as assessed by the Self-Consciousness Scale (Fenigstein, Scheier, & Buss, 1975). Private self-consciousness refers to the degree to which a person characteristically attends to the private, covert aspects of the self (e.g., "I'm always trying to figure myself out"). People scoring high on this measure have been shown to possess more detailed and accurate self-knowledge than those who are less attentive to this aspect of the self (Franzoi, 1983; Turner, 1978). Additionally, researchers have found that private self-consciousness is positively related to depression (Ingram & Smith, 1984; Smith & Greenberg, 1981; Smith, Ingram, & Roth, 1985). Although the relation between these variables is correlational, experimental research also suggests that under some circumstances focusing attention on the self may engender negative emotional states (Duval & Wicklund, 1972).

Additional support for the argument that accurate self-knowledge may be negatively related to psychological health comes from research on the correlates of self-deception. Specifically, scores on the Self-Deception Questionnaire (Sackeim & Gur, 1979), a measure of the degree to which individuals typically deny psychologically threatening but universal feelings and behaviors (e.g., "Do you ever feel guilty?") have been found to be inversely related to depression (Roth & Ingram, 1985; see Sackeim, 1983, for a review). The fact that individuals who are most apt to engage in self-deception also score lowest on measures of psychopathology further suggests that accurate self-knowledge may not be a *sine qua non* of mental health.

## Mental-Health-Promoting Aspects of Illusion

It is one thing to say that positive illusions about the self, personal control, and the future exist and are true for normal people. It is another to identify how these illusions contribute to mental health. To do so, one first needs to establish criteria of mental health and then determine whether the consequences of the preceding positive illusions fit those criteria. One dilemma that immediately arises is that, as noted earlier, many formal definitions of mental health incorporate accurate self-perceptions as one criterion (see Jahoda, 1958; Jourard & Landsman, 1980). In establishing criteria for mental health, then, we must subtract this particular one.

When we do so, what is left? The ability to be happy or, at least, relatively contented, has been one central criterion of mental health and well-being adopted by a variety of researchers and theorists (e.g., Menninger, 1930; see E. Diener, 1984; Jahoda, 1958 for reviews). In her landmark work, Jahoda (1958) identified five additional criteria of positive mental health: positive attitudes toward the self; the ability to grow, develop, and self-actualize; autonomy; environmental mastery in work and social relationships; and integration (i.e., the balance of psychic forces of the id, ego, and superego). Reviewing both older and more recent formulations, Jourard and Landsman (1980, p. 131) distilled very similar criteria: positive self-regard, the ability to care about others and for the natural world, openness to new ideas and to people, creativity, the ability to do productive work, the ability to love, and the ubiquitous realistic self-perceptions. Because positive self-regard has already been considered in our section on exaggeratedly positive self-perceptions, we will not review it here. Thus, the common elements in these criteria that we examine in the next section are happiness or contentment, the ability to care for and about others, and the capacity for productive and creative work.

## Happiness or Contentment

Most people report being happy most of the time. In surveys of mood, 70% to 80% of respondents report that they are moderately to very happy. Whereas most respondents believe that others are average in happiness, 60% believe that they are happier than most people (Freedman, 1978). Positive illusions have been tied to reports of happiness. People who have high self-esteem and self-confidence, who report that they have a lot of control in their lives, and who believe that the future will bring them happiness are more likely than people who lack these perceptions to indicate that they are happy at the present (Freedman, 1978).

As alluded to earlier, when the perceptions of happy people are compared with those of people who are relatively more distressed, happy people have higher opinions of themselves (e.g., Beck, 1967; Kuiper & Derry, 1982; Kuiper & MacDonald, 1982; Kuiper et al., 1985; Lewinsohn et al., 1980; see Shrauger & Terbovic, 1976), are more likely to evince self-serving causal attributions (Kuiper, 1978; Rizley, 1978), show exaggerated beliefs in their ability to control what goes on around them (Abramson & Alloy, 1981; Golin et al., 1977; Golin et al., 1979; M. S. Greenberg, Vazquez, & Alloy, 1988), and are more likely to be unrealistically optimistic (Alloy & Ahrens, 1987).

The association between illusions and positive mood appears to be a consistent one, but the evidence is largely correlational rather than causal. Some evidence that illusions directly influence mood has, however, been reported. For example, we noted earlier that individuals are more inclined to attribute success than failure to the self. MacFarland and Boss (1982) tested whether such a self-serving pattern promotes positive mood states. These investigators had subjects perform a laboratory task in which they manipulated success and failure. Some subjects were led to attribute success (failure) to the self, whereas other subjects were led to attribute success (failure) to the task. Mood measures were then gathered. In line with the hypothesis that the self-serving attributional bias causally influences positive mood states, subjects led to attribute success to the self

and failure to the task reported more positive mood after success and less negative mood after failure. More recently, Gibbons (1986) found evidence that another self-enhancing illusion—the tendency to see the self as better off than others—also improves mood states among depressed people. Thus, although these investigations do not rule out the possibility that positive mood may also cause illusions, that is, that these variables may be reciprocally related (Brown, 1984; Brown & Taylor, 1986), they do provide evidence that illusions promote happiness.

## Ability to Care for Others

The ability to care for others has been considered an important criterion of mental health, and evidence suggests that positive illusions are associated with certain aspects of social bonding. For example, research with children indicates that high self-evaluations are linked to both perceived and actual popularity among peers (Bohrnstedt & Felson, 1983; Felson, 1981). Optimism may also improve social functioning. One study found that people with high self-esteem and an optimistic view of the future were better able to cope with loneliness at college than were individuals who displayed an absence of these tendencies (Cutrona, 1982).

Illusions may also affect the ability to care for and about others indirectly by means of their capacity to create positive mood. Research indicates that when a positive (as opposed to negative or neutral) mood has been induced, people are generally more likely to help others (e.g., Batson, Coke, Chard, Smith, & Taliaferro, 1979; Cialdini, Kenrick, & Baumann, 1982; Moore, Underwood, & Rosenhan, 1973), to initiate conversations with others (Batson et al., 1979; Isen, 1970), to express liking for others and positive evaluations of people in general (Gouaux, 1971; Griffith, 1970; Veitch & Griffith, 1976), and to reduce the use of contentious strategies and increase joint benefit in bargaining situations (Carnevale & Isen, 1986). Summarizing the research evidence, Isen (1984) concluded, "Positive affect is associated with increased sociability and benevolence" (p. 189; see also E. Diener, 1984).

Overall, then, there is evidence associating positive illusions with certain aspects of social bonding. This relation may also be facilitated indirectly by means of positive mood.

## Capacity for Creative, Productive Work

Positive illusions may promote the capacity for creative, productive work in two ways: First, these illusions may facilitate intellectually creative functioning itself; second, they enhance motivation, persistence, and performance.

### FACILITATION OF INTELLECTUAL FUNCTIONING

The evidence for direct effects of positive illusions on intellective functioning is sparse. Whether unrealistic optimism or exaggerated beliefs in personal control affect intellectual functioning directly is unknown. There may, however, be intellectual benefits to self-enhancement. Memory tends to be organized egocentrically, such that people are able to recall self-relevant information well. Greenwald (1980) suggested that there are cognitive benefits to an egocentrically organized memory: The self as a well-known, highly complex, densely organized system allows for rapid retrieval of information and extensive links among elements in the system. As yet, it is unclear, however, whether self-enhancement biases directly facilitate egocentrically organized memory.

Positive illusions may also facilitate some aspects of intellectual functioning by means of positive mood, although this possibility has not been tested directly. Positive affect is an effective retrieval cue, especially for positive information (e.g., Isen, Shalker, Clark, & Karp, 1978); positive affect can facilitate the use of efficient, rapid problem-solving strategies (Isen & Means, 1983); positive affect appears to facilitate the association of multiple cues with encoded information, thus creating a more cognitively complex mental environment for making judgments and decisions (Isen & Daubman, 1984); and positive affect facilitates unusual and diverse associations that may produce more creative problem solving (Isen, Daubman, & Nowicki, 1987; Isen, Johnson, Mertz, & Robinson, 1985).

Is the impact of positive affect on mental functioning always positive? Some research suggests that positive affect may lead people to use simple, rapid, problem-solving strategies that may be inappropriate for complex decision-making tasks (Isen et al., 1985). More recent work (Isen et al., 1987), however, suggests that positive affect does not reduce cognitive capacity or lead to lazy or inefficient problem solving. Thus, positive affect appears to have a largely positive impact on intellectual functioning.

### MOTIVATION, PERSISTENCE, AND PERFORMANCE

Self-enhancing perceptions, a belief in personal control, and optimism appear to foster motivation, persistence at tasks, and ultimately, more effective performance.

Evidence for the impact of self-enhancing perceptions on motivation, persistence, and performance comes from several sources. Positive conceptions of the self are associated with working harder and longer on tasks (Felson, 1984); perseverance, in turn, produces more effective performance and a greater likelihood of goal attainment (Bandura, 1977; Baumeister, Hamilton, & Tice, 1985; see also Feather, 1966, 1968, 1969). People with high, as compared to low, self-esteem also evaluate their performance more positively (Vasta & Brockner, 1979), even when it is equivalent to that of low-self-esteem people (Shrauger & Terbovic, 1976). These perceptions then feed back into enhanced motivation. People with high self-esteem have higher estimations of their ability for future performance and higher predictions of future performance, even when prior performance on the task would counterindicate those positive estimations (McFarlin & Blascovich, 1981).

Evidence relating beliefs in personal control to motivation, persistence, and performance comes from a variety of sources. Research on motivation has demonstrated repeatedly that beliefs in personal efficacy (a concept akin to control) are associated with higher motivation and more efforts to succeed (Bandura, 1977; see also Brunstein & Olbrich, 1985; Dweck & Licht, 1980). In a series of studies, Burger (1985) found that individuals high in the desire for control responded more vigorously to a challenging task and persisted longer. They also had higher (and, in this case, more realistic) levels of aspiration and higher expectations for their performance than did individuals low in desire for control.

Individual-difference research on mastery also indicates the value of believing that one has control. C. I. Diener and Dweck (1978, 1980) found differences between mastery-oriented and helpless children in their interpretations of success and failure. Even when their performance was equivalent to that of helpless children, mastery-oriented children (i.e., those with a sense of control over the task) remembered their success better, were more likely to see success as indicative of ability, expected successes in the future, and were less daunted by failure. Following failure, mastery-oriented children chose to focus on ways to overcome the failure. In fact, they seemed not to recognize that they had failed (C. I. Diener & Dweck, 1978).

Several lines of research suggest that optimism is associated with enhanced motivation and performance. High expectations of success prompt people to work longer and harder on tasks than do low expectations of success (Atkinson, 1964; Mischel, 1973; Weiner, 1979). Gonzales and Zimbardo (1985) found that a self-reported orientation toward the future was associated with self-reports of higher income, higher motivation to work, more goal seeking, more pragmatic action, more daily planning and less fatalism. Indirect evidence for the relation of optimism to effort, perseverance, and ultimately, goal attainment comes from studies of depression and studies of learned helplessness. Beck (1967) maintained that pessimism is one of the central attributes of depression,[3] and it is also prominent in learned helplessness (Seligman, 1975). One of the chief symptoms of depression is inactivity, and researchers in learned helplessness have also noted the centrality of generalized deficits of motivation in this syndrome (Seligman, 1975). Negative mood, then, depresses activity level, perhaps because it facili-

tates seeing the negative consequences attached to any action. This pessimism may then reduce motivation and consequent activity toward a goal.

Overall, then, research evidence indicates that self-enhancement, exaggerated beliefs in control, and unrealistic optimism can be associated with higher motivation, greater persistence, more effective performance, and ultimately, greater success. A chief value of these illusions may be that they can create self-fulfilling prophecies. They may help people try harder in situations with objectively poor probabilities of success; although some failure is inevitable, ultimately these illusions will pay off more often than will lack of persistence (cf. Greenwald, 1980).[4]

## Summary and Implications

To summarize, we return to the criteria of mental health offered earlier and relate them systematically to positive illusions. Those criteria include happiness or contentment, caring for and about others, and the capacity for creative, productive work. Although research does not systematically address the role of each of the three positive illusions with respect to each criterion of mental health, the evidence is suggestive in all cases. Happy people are more likely to have positive conceptions of themselves, a belief in their ability to control what goes on around them, and optimism about the future. They also typically have high self-esteem. The ability to care for others appears to be associated with positive illusions in that illusions are associated with certain aspects of social bond-

---

[3]Positive mood provides a potential secondary route whereby illusions may foster motivation and persistence. Manipulated positive mood enhances perceived probability of success and the tendency to attribute success to personal stable factors (Brown, 1984). By way of perpetuating the cycle of positive mood–perserverence–success, people in a naturally occurring or experimentally induced positive mood are also more likely to believe that they have succeeded and to reward themselves accordingly (Mischel, Coates, & Raskoff, 1968; Wright & Mischel, 1982). Their performance also increases more in response to increases in incentives than does that of people in a negative mood (Weinstein, 1982). Manipulated negative mood is associated with lower expectations for future success, with attributions of success to unstable factors (Brown, 1984), and with less self-reward (Mischel et al., 1968; Wright & Mischel, 1982). Motivation and positive mood appear to influence each other reciprocally: Involvement in activity elevates mood, and elevated mood increases involvement in activity (E. Diener, 1984). Overall, the links between

being happy and being active are so well established that one of our earliest psychologists, Aristotle, maintained that happiness is a by-product of human activity (Freedman, 1978).

[4]We have assumed that the relation between illusions and persistence generally results in positive outcomes. Perseverance may sometimes be maladaptive, however, as when an individual persists endlessly at a task that is truly intractable (see Janoff-Bulman & Brickman, 1982). Although some evidence (e.g., McFarlin, Baumeister, & Blascovich, 1984) suggests that such nonproductive perseverance may be most prevalent among people with high self-esteem (i.e., those who are most apt to display self-enhancing illusions), other studies (e.g., Baumeister & Tice, 1985; McFarlin, 1985) suggest that people with high self-esteem may be most apt to desist from persisting endlessly at an unsolvable task when they are given the opportunity to do so. Thus, the nature of the relation between unproductive persistence and self-enhancing illusions is unclear and needs further empirical clarification.

ing. The capacity for creative, productive work is fostered both by enhanced intellectual functioning, which may be an outgrowth of positive illusions, and by the increased motivation, activity level, and persistence that are clearly fostered by a positive sense of self, a sense of control, and optimism.

## Accommodating Illusions to Reality

The previous analysis presents some theoretical and practical dilemmas. On the one hand, we have an established view of mental health coming largely from the fields of psychiatry and clinical psychology that stresses the importance of accurate perceptions of the self, one's circumstances, and the future. On the other hand, we have a sharply different portrait from cognitive and social psychology of the normal individual as one who evidences substantial biases in these perceptions. Moreover, these biases fall in a predictable direction, namely, a positive one. How are we to reconcile these viewpoints?

A second dilemma concerns the functional value of illusions. On the one hand, positive illusions appear to be common and, more important, appear to be associated with positive outcomes that promote good mental health. On the other hand, this evidence flies in the face of much clinical wisdom as well as commonsense notions that people must monitor reality accurately to survive. Thus, it is important to consider how positive illusions can be maintained and, more important, can be functional in the face of realistic and often contradictory evidence from the environment.

### Reconciling Contradictory Views of Mental Health

In addressing the first dilemma, a useful point of departure in a reconciliation is to examine the potential flaws in the data-gathering methods of the relevant clinical and social psychological literatures in deriving their respective portraits. Historically, clinical constructions of mental health have been dominated by therapy with and research on abnormal people. Many psychologists and psychiatrists who have written about mental health devote their research and clinical endeavors to individuals whose perceptions are disturbed in a variety of ways. How might an understanding of

mental health be influenced when abnormality is an implicit yardstick? Contrasts between pathological and normal functioning are likely to loom large. Because an attribute of many psychologically disturbed people is an inability to monitor reality effectively, the healthy individual may be portrayed as one who maintains very close contact with reality. More subtle deviations in perceptions and cognitions from objectively accurate standards may well go unnoticed.

But just as a strict clinical view of mental health may result in an overemphasis on rationality, a view of mental health derived solely from social cognition research may be skewed to reveal an overemphasis on illusions. Much research in social cognition extricates individuals from the normal settings in which they interact for the purpose of providing them with experimentally manipulated information and feedback. Yet social and cognitive research on the prevalence and usefulness of schemata makes clear that people rely heavily on their prior expectations for processing incoming data (see Fiske & Taylor, 1984; Hastie, 1981; Taylor & Crocker, 1981, for reviews). To the extent that manipulated information and feedback are similar to the information and feedback that people normally encounter in their chosen environments, one might expect to see perceptions similar to those that people usually develop in their normal world. However, to the extent that the information and feedback that are provided experimentally deviate from the usual information and feedback that an individual might encounter in the real world, the implications of any errors and biases in perception and cognition are unclear. Within social cognition, these experimentally documented errors and biases are often interpreted as evidence for news in human information processing strategies. Another interpretation, however, is at least as tenable. Individuals may merely assimilate unfamiliar or unexpected data to their prior beliefs with relatively little processing at all. If prior beliefs include generally positive views of the self, personal efficacy, and the future, then interpretation of any negative feedback may appear, falsely, to be error prone in a positive direction.

Taking these respective flaws of the social and clinical portraits into account, what kind of reconciliation can we develop? First, a certain degree of contact with reality seems to be essential to accomplish the tasks of everyday life. If the errors and biases identified by social cognition dominated all inferential tasks, it would be difficult to understand how the human organism could learn. On the other hand, it is also evident that when errors and biases do occur, they are not evenly distributed. They consistently stray in a positive direction, toward the aggrandizement of the self and the world in which one must function. The key to an integration of the two views of mental health may, then, lie in understanding those circumstances under which positive illusions about the self and the world may be most obvious and useful. The nature of these circumstances is suggested both by social cognition research itself and by research on victims of misfortune.

If one assumes either that people's prior beliefs about themselves, their efficacy, and their future are positive or that their information-processing strategies bias them to interpret information in this way, then it follows that errors and biases will be most obvious when feedback from the real world is negative. In fact, in experimental circumstances examining positive biases, research reveals that positive biases are more apparent as threats to the self increase (Greenwald, 1981). The importance of information may also alter the prevalence of positive biases. Greenwald (1981) found self-enhancing biases to be more in evidence as the importance of the situation increased. Thus, for example, the self-serving causal attribution bias is more likely to occur for behaviors that are important to an individual than for personally trivial events (e.g., Miller, 1976).

Consistent with both points, research with victims of misfortune, such as cancer patients, suggests that illusions about the self, one's efficacy, and the future are in evidence in dealing with these potentially tragic events (Taylor, 1983). For example, a study of patients with breast cancer found that the belief that one's coping abilities were extraordinary (Wood, Taylor, & Lichtman, 1985) and the belief that one could personally prevent the cancer from coming back, even in the face of a likely recurrence, were quite common (Taylor, Lichtman, & Wood, 1984). More to the point, they were associated with successful psychological adjustment to the cancer.

In a recent review of the literature on personality factors as buffers of the stress–disorder relation, Cohen and Edwards (1989) found only scattered evidence for stress-buffering effects across a large number of personality variables; they sug-

gested that this may occur because only a few superordinate mechanisms actually buffer stress successfully. Significantly, they offered as possible superordinate mechanisms feelings of personal control, self-efficacy or self-esteem, optimism, and effort or ability. At present, the evidence is strongest for sense of personal control. Their analysis provides converging evidence for the potential functional value of self-enhancement, personal control, optimism, and their concomitants under conditions of threat. Becker (1973) made a related point in his Pulitzer-Prize winning book, *The Denial of Death*. He argued that because the world is an uncertain and frightening place to live in, people create positive, life-affirming illusions to enable them to cope with their existential terror (cf. J. Greenberg, Pyszczynski, & Solomon, 1986).

To summarize then, evidence from converging sources suggests that positive illusions about the self, one's control, and the future may be especially apparent and adaptive under circumstances of adversity; that is, circumstances that might be expected to produce depression or lack of motivation. Under these circumstances, the belief in one's self as a competent, efficacious actor behaving in a world with a generally positive future may be especially helpful in overcoming setbacks, potential blows to self-esteem, and potential erosions in one's view of the future.

## Management of Negative Feedback

If illusions are particularly functional when a person encounters negative feedback, we must consider, first, how the process of rejecting versus accommodating negative feedback occurs and, second, how people negotiate the world successfully and learn from experience without the full benefit of negative feedback. To anticipate the forthcoming argument, we maintain that a series of social and cognitive filters make information disproportionately positive and that the negative information that escapes these filters is represented in as unthreatening a manner as possible.

### SOCIAL CONSTRUCTION OF SOCIAL FEEDBACK

A variety of social norms and strategies of social interaction conspire to protect the individual from the harsher side of reality. Research indicates that, although people are generally unwilling to give feedback (Blumberg, 1972), when it is given, it is overwhelmingly likely to be positive (Blumberg, 1972; Parducci, 1968; Tesser & Rosen, 1975). Evaluators who must communicate negative feedback may mute it or put it in euphemistic terms (Goffman, 1955), thus rendering it ambiguous. In a similar vein, studies of opinion moderation (Cialdini, Levy, Herman, & Evenbeck, 1973; McGuire, 1985; M. Snyder & Swann, 1976; Tetlock, 1983) reveal that when people expect that others will disagree with them, they often moderate their opinions in advance to be less extreme and thereby more similar to what they perceive to be the attitudes of their audience. If a person holds negative beliefs about another, he or she is highly likely to discontinue interaction with the person, rather than communicate the negative feedback (Darley & Fazio, 1980). Implicitly, then, people collectively subscribe to norms, ensuring that they both give and receive predominantly positive feedback (see also Goffman, 1955).

The interaction strategies that people adopt in social situations also tend to confirm preexisting self-conceptions (see Swann, 1983, 1984, for reviews). People implicitly signal how they want to be treated by adopting physical identity cues (such as clothing or buttons that express political beliefs), by taking on social roles that communicate their self-perceptions (such as mother or radical), and by using methods of communication that preferentially solicit self-confirming feedback (Swann, 1983). In this last category, people actively seek to disconfirm others' mistaken impressions of them (Swann & Hill, 1982) and are more likely to seek social feedback if they believe it will confirm their self-conceptions (Swann & Read, 1981a, 1981b). Because most individuals have favorable self-views, such strategies lead to a tendency to seek feedback primarily when feedback is likely to be positive (Brown, 1987).

The construction of social relationships with friends and intimates also facilitates positive self-impressions. People select friends and intimates who are relatively similar to themselves on physical resources, nearly equal on ability and achievement, similar in attitudes, and similar in background characteristics (Eckland, 1968; Hill, Rubin, & Peplau, 1976; Richardson, 1939; Spuhler, 1968; see Swann, 1984, for a review). This selection process reinforces one's beliefs that one's attitudes and attributes are correct. People form relationships with people who see them as they see them-

selves (Secord & Backman, 1965; Swann, 1983) and tend to be unhappy in relationships in which they are not seen as they want to be seen (Laing, Phillipson, & Lee, 1966). Tesser and his associates (Tesser, 1980; Tesser & Campbell, 1980; Tesser, Campbell, & Smith, 1984; Tesser & Paulhus, 1983) have suggested that people select friends whose abilities on tasks central to the self are somewhat inferior to their own but whose abilities on tasks less relevant to the self are the same or superior. In this way, individuals can achieve the best of both worlds: They can value their friends for exceptional qualities irrelevant to the self (thereby enhancing the self by means of association) without detracting from their own positive self-evaluations.

Some negative feedback, such as losing a job or being abandoned by a spouse, is difficult to rebut, and under such circumstances, one's friends and family may help in the esteem-restoring process by selectively focusing on one's positive qualities, on the positive aspects of the unpleasant situation, and on the negative aspects of the former situation. In analyses of the social support process, researchers have uniformly regarded the maintenance of self-esteem as a major benefit of social support (e.g., Cobb, 1976; House, 1981; Pinneau, 1975; Schaefer, Coyne, & Lazarus, 1981), and research indicates that social support buffers people from physical and emotional distress during periods of high stress (Cobb, 1976; Cohen & Hoberman, 1983; Cohen & McKay, 1983; Kaplan, Cassel, & Gore, 1977; LaRocco, House, & French, 1980). Experimental studies are consistent with this conclusion (e.g., Backman, Secord, & Peirce, 1963; Swann & Predmore, 1985) by showing that friends' agreement on one's personal attributes can act as a buffer against disconfirming feedback.

Overall, then, norms and strategies of social interaction generally enhance positive self-evaluations and protect against negative ones. One caveat, however, deserves mention. A considerable amount of the research cited demonstrates that people solicit and receive self-confirming feedback, not necessarily positive feedback. For example, a woman who thinks of herself as shy may seek and receive feedback that she is (see Swann, 1983). At first, these results may seem contradictory with the position that social feedback fosters positive self-conceptions, but in fact, they are not. Because most people think well of themselves on

Implicit reinforcement

*Self-verification as self-enhancement*

most attributes, confirming feedback is typically positive feedback.

## BIASES IN ENCODING, INTERPRETATION, AND RETRIEVAL

Social interaction itself, then, is one filter that biases the information an individual receives in a positive direction. Another set of filters is engaged as the cognitive system encodes, interprets, or retrieves information. People generally select, interpret, and recall information to be consistent with their prior beliefs or theories (see Fiske & Taylor, 1984; Greenwald, 1980; Taylor & Crocker, 1981, for reviews).[5] Consequently, if a person's prior beliefs are positive, cognitive biases that favor conservatism generally will maintain positive illusions more specifically.

Some potentially contradictory information never gets into the cognitive system. Preexisting theories strongly guide the perception of information as relevant (Howard & Rothbart, 1980; Rothbart, Evans, & Fulero, 1979; see Fiske & Taylor, 1984; Nisbett & Ross, 1980). Ambiguous information tends to be interpreted as consistent with prior beliefs (see Taylor & Crocker, 1981, for a review); thus, a behavior that is neither clearly a success nor clearly a failure is likely to be seen as positive by most individuals. In particular, ambiguous feedback from others may be perceived as more favorable than it really is (Jacobs, Berscheid, & Walster, 1971).

If feedback is not positive, it may simply be ignored. In their review of approximately 50 studies, Shrauger and Schoeneman (1979) examined the evidence relating self-perceptions to evaluations by significant others in natural settings. They found little evidence that self-evaluations are consistently influenced by others' feedback, nor did they find evidence of congruence between self-perceptions and evaluations by others (see also Shrauger, 1982). They did, however, find substantial evidence that people's views of themselves and their perceptions of others' evaluations of them were correlated. People who thought well of themselves believed that they were well-thought-of, and people who thought poorly of themselves believed that others did as well (see also Schafer & Keith, 1985).

Interpretational biases also mute the impact of incoming information. Generally speaking, discrepant self-relevant feedback is more likely to be perceived as inaccurate or uninformative than is feedback that is consistent with the self (Markus, 1977; Swann & Read, 1981a, 1981b). It is scrutinized more closely than is confirmatory information in terms of the evaluator's motives and credibility, with the result that it is likely to be discounted (Halperin, Snyder, Shenkel, & Houston, 1976; Shavit & Shouval, 1980; Shrauger, 1982). One manifestation of this tendency is that, because self-perceptions are generally positive, negative feedback is seen as less credible than positive feedback (C. R. Snyder, Shenkel, & Lowery, 1977), especially by people with high self-esteem (Shrauger & Kelly, 1981; Shrauger & Rosenberg, 1970; see Shrauger, 1975, for a review). When all else fails, discrepant behaviors may be explained away by excuses that offer situational explanations for the behavior (C. R. Snyder, Higgins, & Stucky, 1983). In those cases in which personal responsibility for failure cannot be denied, one can maintain that the attributes on which one is successful are important, whereas the attributes on which one fails are not (e.g., Tesser & Paulhus, 1983).

Finally, information that is consistent with a prior theory is, generally speaking, more likely to be recalled (e.g., Anderson & Pichert, 1978; Owens, Bower, & Black, 1979; Zadny & Gerard, 1974). People are better able to remember information that fits their self-conceptions than information that contradicts their self-conceptions (see Shrauger, 1982; Silverman, 1964; Suinn, Osborne, & Page, 1962; Swann, 1984; Swann & Read, 1981a, 1981b, for reviews). When social feedback is mixed in its implications for the self, people preferentially recall what confirms their self-conceptions (Swann & Read, 1981a, 1981b). Typically, these self-conceptions are positive.

## COGNITIVE DRIFT

If negative or otherwise contradictory information succeeds in surmounting the social and cognitive filters just described, its effects may still be only

---

[5]Hastie and Kumar (1979) and others (see Higgins & Bargh, 1987, for a review) have found that under certain circumstances, inconsistent information is better recalled than consistent information. This finding appears to occur primarily under impression-formation conditions, however, which are unlikely to characterize self-inference.

*cognitive drift*

temporary. Research demonstrates that beliefs may change radically in response to temporary conditions and then drift back again to their original state (e.g., Walster & Berscheid, 1968). This characteristic, cognitive drift can act as another method of absorbing negative feedback. For example, a dramatic change in self-perception may occur following a negative experience, such as failing a test or being accused of insensitivity by a friend. But, with time, any single encounter with negative feedback may fade into the context of other so-called evidence bolstering positive self-conceptions (cf. Swann, 1983).

Some direct evidence for cognitive drift exists in the literature on-serving attributions. In a series of experiments, Burger and Huntzinger (1985) found that initially modest attributions for successful and failed performance became more self-serving over time. Similarly, in research on attributions for joint performance, Burger and Rodman (1983, Experiment 2) found people that gave a partner more credit than the self for a joint task immediately following the task (an attribution that may have considerable social value) but later gave themselves more credit for the joint product, as the self-centered bias predicts. Markus and Nurius (1986) made a similar point in noting that the working self-concept is highly responsive to the social environment, whereas the stable self-concept is more robust and less reactive. Cognitive drift, then, is a conservative mechanism that can protect against change in the cognitive system. To the extent that beliefs about one's self and the environment are positive, cognitive drift also maintains positive self-conceptions.

## ACKNOWLEDGED POCKETS OF INCOMPETENCE

Certain kinds of negative feedback recur repeatedly and, therefore, elude the social and cognitive filters just described. Presumably this negative information has validity and therefore must be dealt with in some way that acknowledges its existence without undermining generally positive conceptions of the self and the world. One such method is accepting a limitation in order to avoid situations that would require it. In essence, one creates an acknowledged pocket of incompetence. Each person may have a few areas of life (e.g., finances, tennis, artistic or musical ability, fashion sense, or ability to dance) in which he or she

readily acknowledges a hopeless lack of talent. People may relegate such behaviors to others and avoid getting themselves into circumstances in which their talents would be tested.

We know of no research that directly addresses these acknowledged pockets of incompetence, but we venture a few speculations on their attributes. *Pocket of Incompetence* First, one might expect that people actually exaggerate their incompetence in these areas to justify their total avoidance of and nonparticipation in the activities. Second, people may admit to these incompetencies, in part, to lend credibility to their positive self-assessments in other areas. Third, to protect self-esteem, people may downgrade the importance or significance of the domains in which they lack skill. For this last point, there is considerable supportive evidence (e.g., Campbell, 1986; Harackiewicz, Manderlink, & Sansone, 1984; Lewicki, 1984, 1985; Rosenberg, 1979).

Despite the absence of research on them, psychological theory provides ample mechanisms whereby such pockets of incompetence might develop. Punishment, in which a behavior is followed by a noxious stimulus, leads to avoidance, and performance declines in that domain in the future (Hilgard & Bower, 1966). "Helplessness training," in which one's efforts to control repeatedly come to naught, produces affective, cognitive, and motivational deficits in both the initial situation in which helplessness occurred and in similar situations, i.e., learned helplessness (Seligman, 1975). Avoidance of a task or its consistent delegation to another person may act as cues that lead one to assume that one is not good at something, an example of what Langer and Benevento (1978) called self-induced dependence.

Research that has adopted the punishment, learned helplessness, or self-induced dependence research models has uniformly stressed the liabilities of assumed incompetence: low self-esteem, poor performance, low motivation, and the like. These adverse effects occur, however, only when a person must actually perform a task relevant to the doubted skill. In real life, except under unusual circumstances, a person may well avoid the domain. Paradoxically, then, the effects of punishment, learned helplessness, or self-induced dependence may actually be quite positive. By allowing the person to avoid the area of incompetence, they permit self-esteem, motivation, and performance to be left largely intact (cf. Frankel & Snyder, 1978; Rothbaum, Weisz, & Snyder, 1982).

## NEGATIVE SELF-SCHEMATA

Avoiding situations in which one lacks skill or talent is one method of compartmentalizing negative self-relevant information. For some attributes, however, negative self-relevant information or situations cannot be avoided. For example, if the negative attribute is a physical one that a person unavoidably carries around (e.g., obesity) or if the negative attribute figures prominently into many situations (e.g., shyness), avoidance is an impractical solution. Under these circumstances, a person may develop a negative self-schema (Markus, 1977). A self-schema is a knowledge structure that summarizes information about the self in a particular domain and facilitates the processing of information about the self in that domain. Like positive self-schemata, negative self-schemata enable people to identify schema-relevant information as self-descriptive and to do so with greater speed and confidence than is true for information not related to a self-schema (Wurf & Markus, 1983).

Negative self-schemata have not been widely studied, and consequently, whatever self-protective functions they may serve are speculative. A negative self-schema may enable a person to label and cordon off an area of weakness, so that it need not permeate all aspects of identity (Wurf & Markus, 1983). The fact that schema-relevant situations can be easily identified may make it possible for an individual to anticipate, prepare for, or avoid situations in which he or she will be at a disadvantage (Wurf & Markus, 1983). A negative self-schema may act as a convenient attribution for any failure (e.g., "I didn't get the job because of my weight") that mitigates other, more threatening attributions (e.g., "I didn't get the job because I'm not good enough"; Wurf & Markus, 1983). Future research can address these and other potential self-protective functions.

To summarize, then, an individual's social and cognitive environments may not only fail to undermine positive illusions but may help maintain or even enhance them through a variety of mechanisms. Thus, each person is able to live out positive illusions relatively immune to negative feedback because, individually and collectively, people construct a social world that is as self-enhancing as the private, internal one and a cognitive system that maintains it. In those cases in which negative feedback cannot be eluded, it may be isolated as much as possible from the rest of the self-concept and come to provide guidelines for avoiding or managing situations relevant to negative attributes.

## Summary and Conclusions

Evidence from social cognition research suggests that, contrary to much traditional, psychological wisdom, the mentally healthy person may not be fully cognizant of the day-to-day flotsam and jetsam of life. Rather, the mentally healthy person appears to have the enviable capacity to distort reality in a direction that enhances self-esteem, maintains beliefs in personal efficacy, and promotes an optimistic view of the future. These three illusions, as we have called them, appear to foster traditional criteria of mental health, including the ability to care about the self and others, the ability to be happy or contented, and the ability to engage in productive and creative work.

An analysis of the possible mechanisms whereby these illusions may operate suggests that people may simply assimilate contradictory, negative, or ambiguous information to preexisting positive schemata about the self and the world with little processing at all. Positive illusions may also be maintained by a series of social and cognitive filters that discard or distort negative information. Negative information that eludes these filters may be cordoned off from having general implications for the self and one's world through such mechanisms as acknowledged pockets of incompetence or negative self-schemata.

Despite empirical support for this analysis, our perspective has some intrinsic limitations both as a theory and as a delineation of a functional system. The first theoretical weakness is that some links are not well established and require further empirical documentation. Chief among these are the direct links between illusions and positive affect, illusions and social skills, and illusions and intellectual functioning. The evidence for all three links is sparse, largely correlational, or both, and experimental studies are needed. Further research is especially necessary regarding the link between illusions and positive affect, because, as noted earlier, affect represents a potential route by which illusions may indirectly affect other criteria of mental health.

A second limitation is that the model does not speak persuasively to another common criterion of mental health, namely, the capacity for personal growth and change (Jahoda, 1958). Indeed, one might speculate that the present approach is actually antithetical to growth and change. That is, if people are so able to maintain positive self-conceptions and buttress their decisions even in the face of negative feedback, where is the impetus for growth and change? This criticism implicitly assumes that growth and change necessarily emerge from negative experiences. We suggest that change is often provoked by positive experiences, such as the perception that a new career direction will be even more rewarding than a current one. Unrealistic optimism, an exaggerated sense of mastery, and excessive self-confidence may inspire people to make changes that might be avoided if the uphill battle ahead was fully appreciated. Growth and change may also occur when a person is faced with a negative event such as being fired from a job or developing a serious illness. In this case, the existence of the negative event is given, but the capacity to alter its meaning in positive ways may produce growth and change. Thus, we argue that, far from undermining personal growth and change, positive illusions may actually help people, first, to seek change by minimizing awareness of the potential costs of change initially and, second, to profit from negative events that are unavoidable by enabling them to put those events in the best light (cf. Taylor, 1983). Research evidence on these points is needed.

A third issue concerning the viability of the present perspective concerns the experimental nature of much of the evidence. We have already noted several potential biases in experimental evidence, such as the tendency to extract people from their customary environments, expose them to unfamiliar stimuli, and draw far-reaching conclusions about human behavior that may in part be a response to novelty. Another problem with experimental evidence is that the time perspective is short, so the long-term consequences of any observed biases cannot easily be ascertained.

This criticism leads directly to a fourth major question: Are positive illusions always adaptive? Might there not be long-term limitations to positive illusions? Indeed, each of the positive illusions described would seem to have inherent risks. For example, a falsely positive sense of accomplishment may lead people to pursue careers and interests for which they are ill-suited. Faith in one's capacity to master situations may lead people to persevere at tasks that may, in fact, be uncontrollable; knowing when to abandon a task may be as important as knowing when to pursue it (Janoff-Bulman & Brickman, 1982). Unrealistic optimism may lead people to ignore legitimate risks in their environments and to fail to take measures to offset those risks. False optimism may, for example, lead people to ignore important health habits (Weinstein, 1982) or to fail to prepare for a likely catastrophic event, such as a flood or an earthquake (Lehman & Taylor, 1987). Faith in the inherent goodness of one's beliefs and actions may lead a person to trample on the rights and values of others; centuries of atrocities committed in the name of religious and political values bear witness to the liabilities of such faith. If positive illusions foster the use of shortcuts and heuristics for making judgments and decisions (Isen & Means, 1983), this may lead people to oversimplify complex intellectual tasks and to ignore important sources of information.

It is not clear that the preceding points are limits of positive illusions, only that they are possible candidates. It is important to remember that people's self-evaluations are only one aspect of judgments about any situation, and there may be non-ego-related information inherent in situations that offsets the effects of illusions and leads people to amend their behavior. For example, a man who does poorly at a job may fail to correctly interpret negative feedback as evidence that he is doing a poor job, but he may come to feel that he does not like the job, his boss, or his co-workers very much; consequently, he may leave. The certitude that one is right may lead to discrimination against or hatred of others who hold different beliefs. People may be dissuaded, however, from committing certain actions, such as murder or incarceration of others, in service of their beliefs because they believe the means are wrong or because they know they will be punished; this recognition may, nevertheless, leave their beliefs intact. Potential liabilities associated with one illusion may be canceled out by another. For example, false optimism may lead people to underestimate their vulnerability to cancer, but mastery needs may lead people to control their smoking, diet, or other risk factors. The preceding argument is not meant to suggest that positive illusions are without liabilities. Indeed, there may be many. One should not, however, leap to any obvious conclusions regarding potential liabilities of positive illusions without an appreciation of possible countervailing forces that may help offset those liabilities.

In conclusion, the overriding implication that we draw from our analysis of this literature is that certain biases in perception that have previously been thought of as amusing peccadillos at best and serious flaws in information processing at worst may actually be highly adaptive under many circumstances. The individual who responds to negative, ambiguous, or unsupportive feedback with a positive sense of self, a belief in personal efficacy, and an optimistic sense of the future will, we maintain, be happier, more caring, and more productive than the individual who perceives this same information accurately and integrates it into his or her view of the self, the world, and the future. In this sense, the capacity to develop and maintain positive illusions may be thought of as a valuable human resource to be nurtured and promoted, rather than an error-prone processing system to be corrected. In any case, these illusions help make each individual's world a warmer and more active and beneficent place in which to live.

## REFERENCES

Abramson, L. Y., & Alloy, L. B. (1981). Depression, non-depression, and cognitive illusions: A reply to Schwartz. *Journal of Experimental Psychology, 110*, 436–447.

Abramson, L. Y., Alloy, L. B., & Rosoff, R. (1981). Depression and the generation of complex hypotheses in the judgment of contingency. *Behaviour Research and Therapy, 19*, 35–45.

Alicke, M. D. (1985). Global self-evaluation as determined by the desirability and controllability of trait adjectives. *Journal of Personality and Social Psychology, 49*, 1621–1630.

Alloy, L. B., Abramson, L. Y, & Viscusi, D. (1981). Induced mood and the illusion of control. *Journal of Personality and Social Psychology, 41*,1129–1140.

Alloy, L. B., & Ahrens, A. H. (1987). Depression and pessimism for the future: Biased use of statistically relevant information in predictions for self versus others. *Journal of Personality and Social Psychology, 52*, 366–378.

Allport, G. W. (1943). *Becoming: Basic considerations for a psychology of personality*. New Haven, CT. Yale University Press.

Anderson, R. C., & Pichert, J. W. (1978). Recall of previously unrecallable information following a shift in perspective. *Journal of Verbal Learning and Verbal Behavior, 17*, 1–12.

Atkinson, J. W. (1964). *An introduction to motivation*. Princeton, NJ: Van Nostrand.

Backman, C. W., Secord, C. F., & Peirce, J. R. (1963). Resistance to change in the self-concept as a function of consensus among significant others. *Sociometry, 26*, 102–111.

Bandura, A. (1977). *Social learning theory*. Englewood Cliffs, NJ: Prentice-Hall.

Batson, C. D., Coke, J. S., Chard, F., Smith, D., & Taliaferro, A. (1979). Generality of the "glow of good will": Effects of mood on helping and information acquisition. *Social Psychology Quarterly, 42*, 176–179.

Baumeister, R. F., Hamilton, J. C., & Tice, D. M. (1985). Public versus private expectancy of success: Confidence booster or performance pressure? *Journal of Personality and Social Psychology, 48*, 1447–1457.

Baumeister, R. F., & Tice, D. M. (1985). Self-esteem and responses to success and failure: Subsequent performance and intrinsic motivation. *Journal of Personality, 53*, 450–467.

Beck, A. T. (1967). *Depression: Clinical, experimental and theoretical aspects*. New York: Harper & Row.

Becker, E. (1973). *The denial of death*. New York: Free Press.

Benassi, V. A., & Mahler, H. I. M. (1985). Contingency judgments by depressed college students: Sadder but not always wiser. *Journal of Personality and Social Psychology, 49*, 1323–1329.

Blumberg, H. H. (1972). Communication of interpersonal evaluations. *Journal of Personality and Social Psychology, 23*, 157–162.

Bohrnstedt, G. W., & Felson, R. B. (1983). Explaining the relations among children's actual and perceived performances and self-esteem: A comparison of several causal models. *Journal of Personality and Social Psychology, 45*, 43–56.

Bradley, G. W. (1978). Self-serving biases in the attribution process: A reexamination of the fact or fiction question. *Journal of Personality and Social Psychology, 36*, 56–7 I.

Brickman, P., Coates, D., & Janoff-Bulman, R. (1978). Lottery winners and accident victims: Is happiness relative? *Journal of Personality and Social Psychology, 35*, 917–927.

Brown, J. D. (1984). Effects of induced mood on causal attributions for success and failure. *Motivation and Emotion, 8*, 343–353.

Brown, J. D. (1985). [Self-esteem and unrealistic optimism about the future]. Unpublished data, University of California, Los Angeles.

Brown, J. D. (1986). Evaluations of self and others: Self-enhancement biases in social judgments. *Social Cognition, 4*, 353–376.

Brown, J. D. (1990). Evaluating one's abilities: The self-assessment versus self-enhancement debate revisited. *Journal of Experimental Social Psychology, 26*, 149–167.

Brown, J. D., & Taylor, S. E. (1986). Affect and the processing of personal information: Evidence for mood-activated self-schemata. *Journal of Experimental Social Psychology, 22*, 436–452.

Brunstein, J. C., & Olbrich, E. (1985). Personal helplessness and action control: Analysis of achievement-related cognitions, self-assessments, and performance. *Journal of Personality and Social Psychology, 48*, 1540–1551.

Bulman, R. J., & Wortman, C. B. (1977). Attributions of blame and coping in the "real world": Severe accident victims react to their lot. *Journal of Personality and Social Psychology, 35*, 351–363.

Burger, J. M. (1985). Desire for control and achievement-related behaviors. *Journal of Personality and Social Psychology, 48*, 1520–1533.

Burger, J. M., & Huntzinger, R. M. (1985). Temporal effects on attributions for one's own behavior: The role of task outcome. *Journal of Experimental Social Psychology, 21*, 247–261.

Burger, J. M., & Rodman, J. L. (1983). Attributions of responsibility for group tasks: The egocentric bias and the actor-observer difference. *Journal of Personality and Social Psychology, 45*, 1232–1242.

Campbell, J. D. (1986). Similarity and uniqueness: The effects of attribute type, relevance, and individual differences in self-esteem and depression. *Journal of Personality and Social Psychology, 50*, 281–294.

Campbell, J. D., & Fairey, P. J. (1985). Effects of self-esteem, hypothetical explanations, and verbalization of expectancies on future performance. *Journal of Personality and Social Psychology, 48*, 1097–1111.

Cantril, H. (1938). The prediction of social events. *Journal of Abnormal and Social Psychology, 33*, 364–389.

Carnevale, P. J. D., & Isen, A. M. (1986). The influence of positive affect and visual access on the discovery of integrative solutions in bilateral negotiation. *Organizational Behavior and Human Decision Processes, 37*, 1–13.

Cialdini, R. B., Kenrick, D. T, & Baumann, D. J. (1982). Effects of mood on prosocial behavior in children and adults. In N. Eisenberg (Ed.), *The development of prosocial behavior* (pp. 339–359). New York: Academic Press.

Cialdini, R. B., Levy, A., Herman, C. P, & Evenbeck, S. (1973). Attitudinal politics: The strategy of moderation. *Journal of Personality and Social Psychology, 25*, 100–108.

Cobb, S. (1976). Social support as a moderator of life stress. *Psychosomatic Medicine, 38*, 300–314.

Cohen, S., & Edwards, J. R. (1989). Personality characteristics as moderators of the relationship between stress and disorder. In R. W. J. Neufeld (Ed.), *Advances in the investigation of psychological stress* (pp. 235–283). New York: Wiley.

Cohen, S., & Hoberman, H. M. (1983). Positive events and social supports as buffers of life change stress. *Journal of Applied Social Psychology, 13*, 99–125.

Cohen, S., & McKay, G. (1983). Social support, stress, and the buffering hypothesis: A theoretical analysis. In A. Baum, S. E. Taylor, & J. Singer (Eds.), *Handbook of psychology and health* (Vol. 4, pp. 253–267). Hillsdale, NJ: Erlbaum.

Conway, M., & Ross, M. (1984). Getting what you want by revising what you had. *Journal of Personality and Social Psychology, 47*, 738–748.

Coyne, J. C., & Gotlieb, I. H. (1983). The role of cognition in depression: A critical appraisal. *Psychological Bulletin, 94*, 472–505.

Crandall, V. J., Solomon, D., & Kelleway, R. (1955). Expectancy statements and decision times as functions of objective probabilities and reinforcement values. *Journal of Personality, 24*, 192–203.

Crary, W. G. (1966). Reactions to incongruent self-experiences. *Journal of Consulting Psychology, 30*, 246–252.

Crocker, J. (1982). Biased questions in judgment of covariation studies. *Personality and Social Psychology Bulletin, 8*, 214–220.

Cutrona, C. E. (1982). Transition to college: Loneliness and the process of social adjustment. In L. A. Peplau & D. Perlman (Eds.), *Loneliness: A sourcebook of current theory, research and therapy* (pp. 291–309). New York: Wiley

Darley, J. M., & Fazio, R. H. (1980). Expectancy confirmation processes arising in the social interaction sequence. *American Psychologist, 35*, 867–881.

deCharms, R. (1968). *Personal causation: The internal affective determinants of behavior.* New York: Academic Press.

Diener, C. I., & Dweck, C. S. (1978). An analysis of learned helplessness: Continuous changes in performance, strategy, and achievement cognitions following failure. *Journal of Personality and Social Psychology, 36*, 451–462.

Diener, C. I., & Dweck, C. S. (1980). An analysis of learned helplessness: II. The processing of success. *Journal Personality and Social Psychology, 39*, 940–952.

Diener, E. (1984). Subjective well-being. *Psychological Bulletin, 95*, 542–575.

Duval, S., & Wicklund, R. A. (1972). *A theory of objective self-awareness.* New York: Academic Press.

Dweck, C. S., & Licht, B. G. (1980). Learned helplessness and intellectual achievement. In M. E. P Seligman & J. Garber (Eds.), *Human helplessness: Theory and applications* (pp. 197–222). New York: Academic Press.

Eckland, B. K. (1968). Theories of mate selection. *Eugenics Quarterly, 15*, 71–84.

Erikson, E. H. (1950). *Childhood and society* (2nd ed.). New York: Norton.

Feather, N. T. (1966). Effects of prior success and failure on expectations of success and subsequent performance. *Journal of Personality and Social Psychology, 3*, 287–298.

Feather, N. T. (1968). Change in confidence following success or failure as a predictor of subsequent performance. *Journal of Personality and Social Psychology, 9*, 38–46.

Feather, N. T. (1969). Attribution of responsibility and valence of success and failure in relation to initial confidence and task performance. *Journal of Personality and Social Psychology, 13*, 129–144.

Felson, R. B. (1981). Ambiguity and bias in the self-concept. *Social Psychology Quarterly, 44*, 64–69.

Felson, R. B. (1984). The effect of self-appraisals of ability on academic performance. *Journal of Personality and Social Psychology, 47*, 944–952.

Fenichel, O. (1945). *The psychoanalytic theory of neurosis.* New York: Norton.

Fenigstein, A., Scheier, M. F., & Buss, A. H. (1975). Public and private self-consciousness: Assessment and theory. *Journal of Consulting and Clinical Psychology, 43*, 522–528.

Fischhoff, B. (1976). Attribution theory and judgment under uncertainty. In J. H. Harvey, W. J. Ickes, & R. F. Kidd (Eds.), *New directions in attribution research* (Vol. 1, pp. 421–452). Hillsdale, NJ: Erlbaum.

Fiske, S. T., & Taylor, S. E. (1984). *Social cognition.* Reading, MA: Addison-Wesley.

Fleming J., & Darley, J. M. (1986). *Perceiving intention in constrained behavior: The role of purposeful and constrained action cues in correspondence bias effects.* Unpublished manuscript, Princeton University, Princeton, NJ.

Forsyth, D. R., & Schlenker, B. R. (1977). Attributing the causes of group performance: Effects of performance quality, task importance, and future testing. *Journal of Personality, 45*, 220–236.

Frank, J. D. (1953). Some psychological determinants of the level of aspiration. *American Journal of Psychology, 47*, 285–293.

Frankel, A., & Snyder, M. L. (1978). Poor performance following unsolvable problems: Learned helplessness or egotism? *Journal of Personality and Social Psychology, 36*, 1415–1423.

Franzoi, S. L. (1983). Self-concept differences as a function of private self-consciousness and social anxiety. *Journal of Research in Personality, 17*, 272–287.

Free, L. A., & Cantril, H. (1968). *The political beliefs of Americans: A study of public opinion.* New York: Clarion.

Freedman, J. (1978). *Happy people: What happiness is, who has it, and why.* New York: Harcourt Brace Jovanovich.

Fromm, E. (1955). *The sane society.* New York: Rinehart.

Funder, D. C. (1987). Errors and mistakes: Evaluating the accuracy of social judgment. *Psychological Bulletin, 101,* 75–90.

Gibbons, F. X. (1986). Social comparison and depression: Company's effect on misery. *Journal of Personality and Social Psychology, 51,* 140–149.

Goffman, E. (1955). On face-work: An analysis of ritual elements in social interaction. *Psychiatry: Journal for the Study of Interpersonal Processes, 18,* 213–231.

Goffman, E. (1967). *Interaction ritual.* Newport Beach, CA: Westcliff.

Golin, S., Terrell, T., & Johnson, B. (1977). Depression and the illusion of control. *Journal of Abnormal Psychology, 86,* 440–442.

Golin, S., Terrell. T., Weitz, J., & Drost, P. L. (1979). The illusion of control among depressed patients. *Journal of Abnormal Psychology, 88,* 454–457.

Gonzales, A., & Zimbardo, P. G. (1985, March). Time in perspective. *Psychology Today,* pp. 21–26.

Gouaux, C. (1971). Induced affective states and interpersonal attraction. *Journal of Personality and Social Psychology , 20,* 37–43.

Green, S. K., & Gross, A. E. (1979). Self-serving biases in implicit evaluations. *Personality and Social Psychology Bulletin, 5,* 214–217.

Greenberg, J., Pysznynski, T., & Solomon, S. (1986). The causes and consequences of a need for self-esteem: A terror management theory. In R. R. Baumeister (Ed.), *Public self and private life* (pp. 189–212). New York: Springer-Verlag.

Greenberg, M. S., Vazquez, C. V., & Alloy, L. B. (1988). Depression versus anxiety: Differences in self-and-other schemata. In L. B. Alloy (Ed.), *Cognitive processes in depression* (pp. 109–142). New York: Guilford Press.

Greenwald, A. G. (1980). The totalitarian ego: Fabrication and revision of personal history. *American Psychologist, 35,* 603–618.

Greenwald, A. G. (1981). Self and memory. In G. H. Bower (Ed.), *The psychology of learning and motivation* (Vol. 15, pp. 201–236). New York: Academic Press.

Greenwald, A. G., & Breckler, S. J. (1985). To whom is the self presented? In B. Schlenker (Ed.), *The self and social life* (pp. 126–145). New York: McGraw-Hill.

Griffith, W. B. (1970). Environmental effects on interpersonal affective behavior: Ambient temperature and attraction. *Journal of Personality and Social Psychology, 15,* 240–244.

Haan, N. (1977). *Coping and defending.* New York: Academic Press.

Hall, J., & Taylor, S. E. (1976). When love is blind. *Human Relations, 29,* 751–761.

Halperin, K., Snyder, C. R., Shenkel, R. J., & Houston, B. K. (1976). Effects of source status and message favorability on acceptance of personality feedback. *Journal of Applied Psychology, 61,* 85–88

Harackiewicz, J. M., Manderlink, G., & Sansone, C. (1984). Rewarding pinball wizardry: Effects of evaluation and cue value on intrinsic interest. *Journal of Personality and Social Psychology, 47,* 287–300.

Harackiewicz, J. M., Sansone, C., & Manderlink, G. (1985). Competence, achievement orientation, and intrinsic motivation: A process analysis. *Journal of Personality and Social Psychology, 48,* 493–508.

Hastie, R. (1981). Schematic principles in human memory. In E. T. Higgins, C. P. Herman, & M. P. Zanna (Eds.), *Social cognition: The Ontario Symposium* (Vol. 1, pp. 39–88). Hillsdale, NJ: Erlbaum.

Hastie, R., & Kumar, P. (1979). Person memory: Personality traits as organizing principles in memory for behaviors. *Journal of Personality and Social Psychology, 37,* 25–38.

Heider, F. (1958). *The psychology of interpersonal relations.* New York: Wiley.

Hendrick, I. (1942). Instinct and the ego during infancy. *Psychoanalytic Quarterly, 11,* 33–58.

Higgins, E. T., & Bargh, J. A. (1987). Social cognition and social perception. *Annual Review of Psychology, 38,* 369–425.

Hilgard, E. R., & Bower, G. H. (1966). *Theories of learning.* New York: Appleton-Century-Crofts.

Hill, C. T, Rubin, Z., & Peplau, L. A. (1976). Breakups before marriage: The end of 103 affairs. *Journal of Social Issues, 32,* 147–168.

House, J. A. (1981). *Work stress and social support.* Reading, MA: Addison-Wesley.

Howard, J. W., & Rothbart, M. (1980). Social categorization and memory for ingroup and outgroup behavior. *Journal of Personality and Social Psychology, 38,* 301–310.

Ingram, R. E., & Smith, T. W. (1984). Depression and internal versus external focus of attention. *Cognitive Therapy and Research, 8,* 139–151.

Irwin, F. W. (1944). The realism of expectations. *Psychological Review, 51,* 120–126.

Irwin, F. W. (1953). Stated expectations as functions of probability and desirability of outcomes. *Journal of Personality, 21,* 329–335.

Isen, A. M. (1970). Success, failure, attention, and reactions to others: The warm glow of success. *Journal of Personality and Social Psychology, 36,* 1–12.

Isen, A. M. (1984). Toward understanding the role of affect in cognition. In R. Wyer & T. Srull (Eds.), *Handbook of social cognition* (pp. 174–236). Hillsdale, NJ: Erlbaum.

Isen, A. M., & Daubman, K. A. (1984). The influence of affect on categorization. *Journal of Personality and Social Psychology, 47,* 1206–1217.

Isen, A. M., Daubman, K. A., & Nowicki, G. P. (1987). Positive affect facilitates creative problem solving. *Journal of Personality and Social Psychology, 52,* 1122–1131.

Isen, A. M., Johnson, M. M. S., Mertz, E., & Robinson, G. (1985). The influence of positive affect on the unusualness of word association. *Journal of Personality and Social Psychology, 48,* 1413–1426.

Isen, A. M., & Means, B. (1983). The influence of positive affect on decision-making strategy. *Social Cognition, 2,* 18–31.

Isen, A. M., Shalker, T., Clark, M., & Karp, L. (1978). Affect, accessibility of material in memory, and behavior: A cognitive loop? *Journal of Personality and Social Psychology, 36,* 1–12.

Jacobs, L., Berscheid, E., & Walster, E. (1971). Self-esteem and attraction. *Journal of Personality and Social Psychology 17,* 84–91.

Jahoda, M. (1953). The meaning of psychological health. *Social Casework, 34,* 349.

Jahoda, M. (1958). *Current concepts of positive mental health.* New York: Basic Books.

Janoff-Bulman, R. (1979). Characterological versus behavioral self-blame: Inquiries into depression and rape. *Journal of Personality and Social Psychology, 37,* 1798–1809.

Janoff-Bulman, R., & Brickman, P. (1982). Expectations and what people learn from failure. In N. T. Feather (Ed.), *Expectations and action: Expectancy-value models in psychology* (pp. 207–272). Hillsdale, NJ: Erlbaum.

Jourard, S. M., & Landsman, T. (1980). *Healthy personality: An approach from the viewpoint of humanistic psychology* (4th ed.). New York: Macmillan.

Kahneman, D., & Tversky, A. (1973). On the psychology of prediction. *Psychological Review, 80,* 237–251.

Kaplan, B. H., Cassel, J. C., & Gore, S. (1977). Social support and health. *Medical Care, 15* (Suppl. 1), 47–58.

Kelley, H. H. (1967). Attribution theory in social psychology. In D. Levine (Ed.), *Nebraska Symposium on Motivation* (Vol. 15, pp. 192–240). Lincoln: University of Nebraska Press.

Kuiper, N. A. (1978). Depression and causal attributions for success and failure. *Journal of Personality and Social Psychology, 36,* 236–246.

Kuiper, N. A., & Derry, P. A. (1982). Depressed and nondepressed content self-reference in mild depression. *Journal of Personality, 50,* 67–79.

Kuiper, N. A., & MacDonald, M. R. (1982). Self and other perception in mild depressives. *Social Cognition, 1,* 233–239.

Kuiper, N. A., MacDonald, M. R., & Derry, P. A. (1983). Parameters of a depressive self-schema. In J. Suls & A. G. Greenwald (Eds.), *Psychological perspectives on the self* (Vol. 2, pp. 191–217). Hillsdale, NJ: Erlbaum.

Kuiper, N. A., Olinger, L. J., MacDonald, M. R., & Shaw, B. F. (1985). Self-schema processing of depressed and nondepressed content: The effects of vulnerability on depression. *Social Cognition, 3,* 77–93.

Laing, R. D., Phillipson, H., & Lee, A. R. (1966). *Interpersonal perception: A theory and a method of research.* New York: Springer Publishing.

Langer, E. J. (1975). The illusion of control. *Journal of Personality and Social Psychology, 32,* 311–328.

Langer, E. J., & Benevento, A. (1978). Self-induced dependence. *Journal of Personality and Social Psychology, 36,* 886–893.

Langer, E. J., & Roth, J. (1975). Heads I win, tails it's chance: The illusion of control as a function of the sequence of outcomes in a purely chance task. *Journal of Personality and Social Psychology, 32,* 951–955.

LaRocco, J. M., House. J. S., & French, J. R. P., Jr. (1980). Social support, occupational stress, and health. *Journal of Health and Social Behavior, 21,* 202–218.

Larwood, L., & Whittaker, W. (1977). Managerial myopia: Self-serving biases in organizational planning. *Journal of Applied Psychology, 62,* 194–198.

Lazarus, R. S. (1983). The costs and benefits of denial. In S. Breznitz (Ed.), *Denial of stress* (pp. 1–30). New York: International Universities Press.

Lehman, D. R., & Taylor, S. E. (1987). Date with an earthquake: Coping with a probable, unpredictable disaster. *Personality and Social Psychology Bulletin, 13,* 546–555.

Lewicki, P. (1983). Self-image bias in person perception. *Journal of Personality and Social Psychology, 45,* 384–393.

Lewicki, P. (1984). Self-schema and social information processing. *Journal of Personality and Social Psychology, 47,* 1177–1190.

Lewicki, P. (1985). Nonconscious biasing effects of single instances on subsequent judgments. *Journal of Personality and Social Psychology, 48,* 563–574.

Lewinsohn. P. M., Mischel, W., Chaplin, W., & Barton, R. (1980). Social competence and depression: The role of illusory self-perceptions. *Journal of Abnormal Psychology, 89,* 203–212.

Lund, F. H. (1975). The psychology of belief: A study of its emotional and volitional determinants. *Journal of Abnormal and Social Psychology, 20,* 63–81.

MacFarland, C., & Ross, M. (1982). The impact of causal attributions on affective reactions to success and failure. *Journal of Personality and Social Psychology, 43,* 937–946.

Marks, G. (1984). Thinking one's abilities are unique and one's opinions are common. *Personality and Social Psychological Bulletin, 10,* 203–208.

Marks, R. W. (1951). The effect of probability, desirability, and "privilege" on the stated expectations of children. *Journal of Personality, 19,* 332–351.

Markus H. (1977). Self-schemata and processing information about the self. *Journal of Personality and Social Psychology, 35,* 63–78.

Markus, H., & Nurius, P. (1986). Possible selves. *American Psychologist, 41,* 954–969.

Maslow, A. H. (1950). Self-actualizing people: A study of psychological health. *Personality,* Symposium No. 1, 11–34.

McFarlin, D. B. (1985). Persistence in the face of failure: The impact of self-esteem and contingency information. *Personality and Social Psychology Bulletin, 11,* 153–163.

McFarlin, D. B., & Baumeister, R. F., & Blascovich, J. (1984). On knowing when to quit: Task failure, self-esteem, advice, and nonproductive assistance. *Journal of Personality, 52,* 138–155.

McFarlin, D. B., & Blascovich, J. (1981). Effects of self-esteem and performance feedback on future affective preferences and cognitive expectations. *Journal of Personality and Social Psychology, 40,* 521–531.

McGuire, W. (1960). A syllogistic analysis of cognitive relationships. In M. Rosenberg, C. Hovland, W. McGuire, R. Abelson, & J. Brehm (Eds.), *Attitude organization and change* (pp. 65–111). New Haven, CT: Yale University Press.

McGuire, W J. (1985). Attitudes and attitude change. In G. Lindzey & E. Aronson (Eds.), *Handbook of social psychology* (3rd ed., Vol. 2, pp. 233–346). New York: Random House.

Menninger, K. A. (1930). What is a healthy mind? In N. A. Crawford & K. A. Menninger (Eds.), *The healthy-minded child.* New York: Coward-McCann.

Miller, D. T. (1976). Ego involvement and attributions for success and failure. *Journal of Personality and Social Psychology, 34,* 901–906.

Miller, D. T., & Ross, M. (1975). Self-serving biases in attribution of causality: Fact or fiction? *Psychological Bulletin, 82,* 213–225.

Mirels, H. L. (1980). The avowal of responsibility for good

and bad outcomes: The effects of generalized self-serving biases. *Personality and Social Psychology Bulletin, 6,* 299–306.

Mischel, W. (1973). Toward a cognitive–social learning reconceptualization of personality. *Psychological Review, 80,* 252–283.

Mischel, W, Coates, B., & Raskoff, A. (1968). Effects of success and failure on self-gratification. *Journal of Personality and Social Psychology, 10,* 381–390.

Moore, B. S., Underwood, B., & Rosenhan, D. L. (1973). Affect and altruism. *Developmental Psychology, 8,* 99–104.

Nisbett, R. E., & Ross, L. (1980). *Human inference: Strategies and shortcomings of social judgment.* Englewood Cliffs, NJ: Prentice-Hall.

Owens, J., Bower, G. H., & Black, J. B. (1979). The "soap-opera" effect in story recall. *Memory and Cognition, 7,* 185–191.

Parducci, A. (1968). The relativism of absolute judgments. *Scientific American, 219,* 518–528.

Perloff, L. S., & Fetter, B. K. (1986). Self–other judgments and perceived vulnerability of victimization. *Journal of Personality and Social Psychology, 50,* 502–510.

Pietromonaco, P. R., & Markus, H. (1985). The nature of negative thoughts in depression. *Journal of Personality and Social Psychology, 48,* 799–807.

Pinneau, S. R., Jr. (1975). *Effects of social support on psychological and physiological stress.* Unpublished doctoral dissertation, University of Michigan, Ann Arbor.

Pruitt, D. G., & Hoge, R. D. (1965). Strength of the relationship between the value of an event and its subjective probability as a function of method of measurement. *Journal of Experimental Psychology, 5,* 483–489.

Pysznynski, T., Holt, K., & Greenberg, J. (1987). Depression, self-focused attention, and expectancies for positive and negative future life events for self and others. *Journal of Personality and Social Psychology, 52,* 994–1001.

Richardson, H. M. (1939). Studies of mental resemblance between husbands and wives and between friends. *Psychological Bulletin, 36,* 104–120.

Rizley, R. (1978). Depression and distortion in the attribution of causality. *Journal of Abnormal Psychology, 87,* 32–48.

Robertson, L. S. (1977). Car crashes: perceived vulnerability and willingness to pay for crash protection. *Journal of Community Health, 3,* 136–141.

Rosenberg, M. (1979). *Conceiving the self.* New York: Basic Books.

Ross, M., & Fletcher, G. J. O. (1985). Attribution and social perception. In G. Lindzey & E. Aronson (Eds.), *The handbook of social psychology* (3rd ed., pp. 73–122). Reading, MA: Addison-Wesley.

Roth, D. L., & Ingram, R. E. (1985). Factors in the Self-Deception Questionnaire: Associations with depression. *Journal of Personality and Social Psychology, 48,* 243–251.

Rothbart, M., Evans, M., & Fulero, S. (1979). Recall for confirming events: Memory processes and the maintenance of social stereotyping. *Journal of Experimental Social Psychology, 15,* 343–355.

Rothbaum, E, Weisz, J. B., & Snyder, S. S. (1982). Changing the world and changing the self :A two-process model of perceived control. *Journal of Personality and Social Psychology, 42,* 5–37.

Ruehlman, L. S., West, S. G., & Pasahow, R. J. (1985). De-

pression and evaluative schemata. *Journal of Personality, 53,* 46–92.

Sackeim, H. A. (1983). Self-deception, self-esteem, and depression: The adaptive value of lying to oneself. In J. Masling (Ed.), *Empirical studies of psychoanalytical theories* (Vol. 1, pp. 101–157). Hillsdale, NJ: Analytic Press.

Sackeim, H. A., & Gur, B. C. (1979). Self-deception, other deception, and self-reported psychopathology. *Journal of Consulting and Clinical Psychology, 47,* 213–215.

Schaefer, C., Coyne, J. C., & Lazarus, R. S. (1981). The health-related functions of social support. *Journal of Behavioral Medicine, 4,* 381–406.

Schafer, B. B., & Keith, P. M. (1985). A causal model approach to the symbolic interactionist view of the self-concept. *Journal of Personality and Social Psychology, 48,* 963–969.

Schlenker, B. R. (1980). *Impression management.* Monterey, CA: Brooks/Cole.

Schlenker, B. R., & Miller, R. S. (1977). Egocentrism in groups: Self-serving biases or logical information processing? *Journal of Personality and Social Psychology, 35,* 755–764.

Schneider, D. J., Hastorf, A. H., & Ellsworth, P. C. (1979). *Person perception.* Reading, MA: Addison-Wesley.

Schulz, D. (1977). *Growth psychology: Models of the healthy personality.* New York: Van Nostrand Reinhold.

Sears, D. O. (1983). The person-positivity bias. *Journal of Personality and Social Psychology, 44,* 233–250.

Secord, P. F., & Backman, C. W. (1965). An interpersonal approach to personality. In B. A. Maher (Ed.), *Progress in experimental personality research* (Vol. 2, pp. 91–125). New York: Academic Press.

Seligman, M. E. P. (1975). *Helplessness: On depression, development and death.* San Francisco: Freeman.

Shaver, K. G., & Drown, D. (1986). On causality, responsibility, and self-blame: A theoretical note. *Journal of Personality and Social Psychology, 4,* 697–702.

Shavit, H., & Shouval, R. (1980). Self-esteem and cognitive consistency effects on self–other evaluation. *Journal of Experimental Social Psychology, 16,* 417–425.

Sherman, S. J. (1980). On the self-erasing nature of errors of prediction. *Journal of Personality and Social Psychology, 39,* 211–221.

Shrauger, J. S. (1975). Responses to evaluation as a function of initial self-perception. *Psychological Bulletin, 82,* 581–596.

Shrauger, J. S. (1982). Selection and processing of self-evaluative information: Experimental evidence and clinical implications. In G. Weary & H. L. Mirels (Eds.), *Integrations of clinical and social psychology* (pp. 128–153). New York: Oxford University Press.

Shrauger, J. S., & Kelly, R. J. (1981). *Self-confidence and endorsement of external evaluations.* Unpublished manuscript.

Shrauger, J. S., & Rosenberg, J. E. (1970). Self-esteem and the effects of success and failure feedback on performance. *Journal of Personality, 38,* 404–417.

Shrauger, J. S., & Schoeneman, T. J. (1979). Symbolic interactionist view of self-concept: Through the looking glass darkly. *Psychological Bulletin, 86,* 549–573.

Shrauger, J. S., & Terbovic, M. L. (1976). Self-evaluation and assessments of performance by self and others. *Journal of Consulting and Clinical Psychology, 44,* 564–572.

Silverman, I. (1964). Self-esteem and differential responsiveness to success and failure. *Journal of Abnormal and Social Psychology, 69*, 115–119.

Smith, T. W., & Greenberg, J. (1981). Depression and self-focused attention. *Motivation and Emotion, 5*, 323–331.

Smith, T. W., Ingram, R. E., & Roth, D. L. (1985). Self-focused attention and depression: Self-evaluation, affect, and life stress. *Motivation and Emotion, 9*, 381–389.

Snyder, C. R., Higgins, R. L., & Stucky, R. J. (1983). *Excuses: Masquerades in search of grace.* New York: Wiley.

Snyder, C. R., Shenkel, R. J., & Lowery, C. R. (1977). Acceptance of personality interpretations: The "Barnum effect" and beyond. *Journal of Consulting and Clinical Psychology, 45*, 104–114.

Snyder, M., & Swann, W. B. (1976). When actions reflect attitudes: The politics of impression management. *Journal of Personality and Social Psychology, 34*, 1034–1042.

Spuhler, J. N. (1968). Assortative mating with respect to physical characteristics. *Eugenics Quarterly, 15*, 128–140.

Stein, J. (Ed.). (1982). *The Random House dictionary of the English language* (unabridged ed.). New York: Random House.

Suinn, R. M., Osborne, D., & Page, W. (1962). The self-concept and accuracy of recall of inconsistent self-related information. *Journal of Clinical Psychology, 18*, 473–474.

Svenson, O. (1981). Are we all less risky and more skillful than our fellow drivers? *Acta Psychologica, 47*, 143–148.

Swann, W. B., Jr. (1983). Self-verification: Bringing social reality into harmony with the self. In J. Suls & A. G. Greenwald (Eds.), *Social psychology perspectives* (Vol. 2, pp. 33–66). Hillsdale, NJ: Erlbaum.

Swann, W. B., Jr. (1984). Quest for accuracy in person perception: A matter of pragmatics. *Psychological Review, 91*, 457–477.

Swann, W. B., Jr., & Hill, C. A. (1982). When our identities are mistaken: Reaffirming self-conceptions through social interaction. *Journal of Personality and Social Psychology, 43*, 59–66.

Swann, W. B., Jr., & Predmore, S. C. (1985). Intimates as agents of social support: Sources of consolation or despair? *Journal of Personality and Social Psychology, 49*, 1609–1617.

Swann, W. B., Jr., & Read, S. J. (1981a). Acquiring self-knowledge: The search for feedback that fits. *Journal of Personality and Social Psychology, 41*, 1119–1128.

Swann, W. B., Jr., & Read, S. J. (1981b). Self-verification processes: How we sustain our self-conceptions. *Journal of Experimental Social Psychology, 17*, 351–370.

Tajfel, H., & Turner, J. C. (1986). The social identity theory of intergroup behavior. In S. Worchel & W. Austin (Eds.), *Psychology of intergroup relations* (pp. 7–24). Chicago: Nelson-Hall.

Taylor, S. E. (1983). Adjustment to threatening events: A theory of cognitive adaptation. *American Psychologist, 38*, 1161–1173.

Taylor, S. E., & Crocker, J. (1981). Schematic bans of social information processing. In E. T. Higgins, C. P. Herman, & M. P. Zanna (Eds.), *Social cognition: The Ontario Symposium* (Vol. 1, pp. 89–134). Hillsdale, NJ: Erlbaum.

Taylor, S. E., & Koivumaki, J. H. (1976). The perception of self and others: Acquaintanceship, affect, and actor–observer differences. *Journal of Personality and Social Psychology, 33*, 403–408.

Taylor, S. E., Lichtman, R. R., & Wood, J. V. (1984). Attributions, beliefs about control, and adjustment to breast cancer. *Journal of Personality and Social Psychology, 46*, 489–502.

Tesser, A. (1980). Self-esteem maintenance in family dynamics. *Journal of Personality and Social Psychology, 39*, 77–91.

Tesser, A., & Campbell, J. (1980). Self-definition: The impact of the relative performance and similarity of others. *Social Psychology Quarterly, 43*, 341–347.

Tesser, A., Campbell, J., & Smith, M. (1984). Friendship, choice and performance: Self-evaluation maintenance in children. *Journal of Personality and Social Psychology, 46*, 561–574.

Tesser, A., & Moore, J. (1986). On the convergence of public and private aspects of self. In R. F. Baumeister (Ed.), *Public self and private life* (pp. 99–116). New York: Springer-Verlag.

Tesser, A., & Paulhus, D. (1983). The definition of self: Private and public self-evaluation management strategies. *Journal of Personality and Social Psychology, 44*, 672–682.

Tesser, A., & Rosen, S. (1975). The reluctance to transmit bad news. In L. Berkowitz (Ed.), *Advances in experimental psychology* (Vol. 8, pp. 193–232). New York: Academic Press.

Tetlock, P. E. (1983). Accountability and complexity of thought. *Journal of Personality and Social Psychology, 45*, 74–83.

Tetlock, P. E., & Manstead, A. S. R. (1985). Impression management versus intrapsychic explanations in social psychology: A useful dichotomy? *Psychological Review, 92*, 59–77.

Tiger, L. (1979). *Optimism: The biology of hope.* New York: Simon & Schuster.

Turner, R. G. (1978). Effects of differential request procedures and self-consciousness on trait attributions. *Journal of Research in Personality, 12*, 431–438.

Vaillant, G. (1977). *Adaptation to life.* Boston: Little, Brown.

Vasta, R., & Brockner, J. (1979). Self-esteem and self-evaluation covert statements. *Journal of Consulting and Clinical Psychology, 47*, 776–777.

Veitch, R., & Griffitt, W. (1976). Good news–bad news: Affective and interpersonal effects. *Journal of Applied Social Psychology, 6*, 69–75.

Walster, E., & Berscheid, E. (1968). The effects of time on cognitive consistency. In R. P. Abelson, E. Aronson, W. J. McGuire, T. M. Newcomb, M. J. Rosenberg, & P. H. Tannenbaum (Eds.), *Theories of cognitive consistency: A sourcebook* (pp. 599–608). Chicago: Rand McNally.

Watson, D., & Clark, L. A. (1984). Negative affectivity: The disposition to experience aversive emotional states. *Psychological Bulletin, 96*, 465–490.

Weiner, B. (1979). A theory of motivation for some classroom experiences. *Journal of Educational Psychology, 71*, 3–25.

Weinstein, N. D. (1980). Unrealistic optimism about future life events. *Journal of Personality and Social Psychology, 39*, 806–820.

Weinstein, N. D. (1982). Unrealistic optimism about susceptibility to health problems. *Journal of Behavioral Medicine, 5*, 441–460.

White, R. W. (1959). Motivation reconsidered: The concept of competence. *Psychological Review, 66*, 297–335.

Wood, J. V., Taylor, S. E., & Lichtman, R. R. (1985). Social comparison in adjustment to breast cancer. *Journal of Personality and Social Psychology, 49,* 1169–1183.

Wright, J., & Mischel, W. (1982). Influence of affect on cognitive social learning person variables. *Journal of Personality and Social Psychology, 43,* 901–914.

Wurf, E., & Markus, H. (1983, August). *Cognitive consequences of the negative self.* Paper presented at the annual convention of the American Psychological Association, Anaheim, CA.

Zadny, J., & Gerard, H. B. (1974). Attributed intentions and informational selectivity. *Journal of Experimental Social Psychology, 10,* 34–52.

Zuckerman, M. (1979). Attribution of success and failure revisited, or: The motivational bias is alive and well in attribution theory. *Journal of Personality, 47,* 245–287.

# Self-Conceptions

What exactly is the self? Two classic papers on the true basis of selfhood are presented in this section.

William James is generally recognized as the father of American psychology. In this excerpt from his classic work *Principles of Psychology*, he articulates a distinction between the "I" and the "Me" that has influenced theories about the self ever since. The "I" is the knower, and the "Me" is the known; the self consists of both.

Meanwhile, what version of the self is the real and true one? The quest for true self has been a perennial theme in the psychological life of modern America, featured in its books, movies, research, therapies, and in the lives of individuals. A well-known sociological paper by Turner (1976) proposed that there are two very different versions of what is the true or real self, and at different times and places one or the other of the two predominates. One of these is the inner self of feelings and impulses; the other is the institutional self of public roles and social obligations. Neither is inherently more real or true than the other, but different social eras will emphasize one or the other. For example, is a successful marriage based on love as a spontaneous feeling that continuously bubbles up from inside each person (the impulse view)—or is it the result of commitment and work to treat each other in a loving fashion, consistent with the wedding vows?

## REFERENCES

James, W. (1892/1948). *Principles of Psychology*. Cleveland, OH: World Publishing.

Turner, R. H. (1976). The real self: From institution to impulse. *American Journal of Sociology, 81*, 989–1016.

# Discussion Questions

1. Which topic do you suppose has proven easier for researchers to study: The "I" or the "Me"?
2. James says, "A man has as many social selves as there are individuals who recognize him"—is this plausible? How different are these different selves likely to be?
3. Explain Turner's concepts of impulsive and institutional selves in terms of James' "I" and "Me."
4. Is there any sense to the concept of having a "true self' or is the term merely relative and socially constructed? How would you know whether some trait pertains to your true self or a false self? How would someone else know this about you?
5. Are any aspects of self not readily translatable into "I" and "Me"?
6. Would you rather live among people who identify with impulse or institution? Which type of self would you prefer to have?

# Suggested Readings

Brewer, M. B., & Gardner, W. (1996). Who is this "we"? Levels of collective identity and self representations. *Journal of Personality and Social Psychology, 71*, 83–93. Is the self only "I" and "me"—or is there also an element of "we"? Brewer and Gardner show how people's concepts of self incorporate belonging to groups and categories. Their paper offers an important corrective to views of self as something that is all about one's unique individuality. Note: this paper involves some complex and technical discussions and is better suited to advanced students.

Markus, H., & Nurius, P. S. (1986). Possible selves. *American Psychologist, 41*, 954–969. In this popular and delightful paper, Markus and Nurius argue that people maintain clear concepts not only of who they are but also of "possible" future or alternative versions of self—the famous me, the me as overweight, me in prison, me as a parent of a large family, and so forth. They discuss the motivational power that these views of self have.

Baumeister, R. F. (1986). *Identity: Cultural change and the struggle for self.* New York: Oxford University Press. This work discusses how people come to know and construct the self, as well as considering how historical change and social progress have made the self increasingly complex.

Epstein, S. (1973). The self-concept revisited: Or a theory of a theory. *American Psychologist, 28,* 404–416. In this popular article, Epstein argues that information about the self more closely resembles a theory than a concept.

# The Self

W. James

Whatever I may be thinking of, I am always at the same time more or less aware of *myself,* of my *personal existence.* At the same time it is *I* who am aware; so that the total self of me, being as it were duplex, partly known and partly knower, partly object and partly subject, must have two aspects discriminated in it, of which for shortness we may call one the *Me* and the other the *I.* I call these 'discriminated aspects,' and not separate things, because the identity of *I* with *me,* even in the very act of their discrimination, is perhaps the most ineradicable dictum of common-sense, and must not be undermined by our terminology here at the outset, whatever we may come to think of its validity at our inquiry's end.

I shall therefore treat successively of the self as known, or the *me,* the 'empirical ego' as it is sometimes called; and of the self as knower, or the I, the 'pure ego' of certain authors.

## The Self as Known

### The Empirical Self or Me

Between what a man calls *me* and what he simply calls *mine* the line is difficult to draw. We feel and act about certain things that are ours very much as we feel and act about ourselves. Our fame, our children, the work of our hands, may be as dear to us as our bodies are, and arouse the same feelings and the same acts of reprisal if attacked. And our bodies themselves, are they simply ours, or are they *us*? Certainly men have been ready to disown their very bodies and to regard them as mere vestures, or even as prisons of clay from which they should some day be glad to escape.

We see then that we are dealing with a fluctuating material; the same object being sometimes treated as a part of me, at other times as simply mine, and then again as if I had nothing to do with it at all. *In its widest possible sense,* however, *a man's Me is the sum total of all that he* CAN *call his,* not only his body and his psychic powers, but his clothes and his house, his wife and children, his ancestors and friends, his reputation and works, his lands and horses, and yacht and bank-account. All these things give him the same emotions. If they wax and prosper, he feels triumphant; if they dwindle and die away, he feels cast down—not necessarily in the same degree for each thing, but in much the same way for all. Understanding the Me in this widest sense, we may begin by dividing the history of it into three parts, relating respectively to—

a. Its constituents;
b. The feelings and emotions they arouse,—*self-appreciation;*
c. The acts to which they prompt,—*self-seeking and self-reservation.*

a. *The constituents of the Me* may be divided into two classes, those which make up respectively—

The material me;
The social me; and
The spiritual me.

## The Material Me

The *body* is the innermost part of the material me in each of us; and certain parts of the body seem more intimately ours than the rest. The clothes come next. The old saying that human person is composed of three parts—soul, body and clothes—is more than a joke. We so appropriate our clothes and identify ourselves with them that there are few of us who, if asked to choose between having a beautiful body clad in raiment perpetually shabby and unclean, and having an ugly and blemished form always spotlessly attired, would not hesitate a moment before making a decisive reply. Next, our immediate family is a part of ourselves. Our father and mother, our wife and babes, are bone of our bone and flesh of our flesh. When they die, a part of our very selves is gone. If they do anything wrong, it is our shame. If they are insulted, our anger flashes forth as readily as if we stood in their place. Our home comes next. Its scenes are part of our life; its aspects awaken the tenderest feelings of affection; and we do not easily forgive the stranger who, in visiting it, finds fault with its arrangements or treats it with contempt. All these different things are the objects of instinctive preferences coupled with the most important practical interests of life. We all have a blind impulse to watch over our body, to deck it with clothing of an ornamental sort, to cherish parents, wife, and babes, and to find for ourselves a house of our own which we may live in and 'improve.'

An equally instinctive impulse drives us to collect property; and the collections thus made become, with different degrees of intimacy, parts of our empirical selves. The parts of our wealth most intimately ours are those which are saturated with our labor. There are few men who would not feel personally annihilated if a life-long construction of their hands or brains—say an entomological collection or an extensive work in manuscript—were suddenly swept away. The miser feels similarly towards his gold; and although it is true that a part of our depression at the loss of possessions is due to our feeling that we must now go without certain goods that we expected the possessions to bring in their train, yet in every case there remains,

over and above this, a sense of the shrinkage of our personality, a partial conversion of ourselves to nothingness, which is a psychological phenomenon by itself. We are all at once assimilated to the tramps and poor devils whom we so despise, and at the same time removed farther than ever away from the happy sons of earth who lord it over land and sea and men in the full-blown lustihood that wealth and power can give, and before whom, stiffen ourselves as we will by appealing to anti-snobbish first principles, we cannot escape an emotion, open or sneaking, of respect and dread.

## The Social Me

A man's social me is the recognition which he gets from his mates. We are not only gregarious animals, liking to be in sight of our fellows, but we have an innate propensity to get ourselves noticed, and noticed favorably, by our kind. No more fiendish punishment could be devised, were such a thing physically possible, than that one should be turned loose in society and remain absolutely unnoticed by all the members thereof. If no one turned round when we entered, answered when we spoke, or minded what we did, but if every person we met 'cut us dead,' and acted as if we were non-existing things, a kind of rage and impotent despair would ere long well up in us, from which the cruelest bodily tortures would be a relief; for these would make us feel that, however bad might be our plight, we had not sunk to such a depth as to be unworthy of attention at all.

Properly speaking, *a man has as many social selves as there are individuals who recognize him,* and carry an image of him in their mind. To wound any one of these his images is to wound him. But as the individuals who carry the images fall naturally into classes, we may practically say that he has as many different social selves as there are distinct *groups* of persons about whose opinion he cares. He generally shows a different side of himself to each of these different groups. Many a youth who is demure enough before his parents and teachers, swears and swaggers like a pirate among his 'tough' young friends. We do not show ourselves to our children as to our club companions, to our customers as to the laborers we employ, to our own masters and employers as to our intimate friends. From this there results what practically is a division of the man into several selves;

and this may be a discordant splitting, as where one is afraid to let one set of his acquaintances know him as he is elsewhere; or it may be a perfectly harmonious division of labor, as where one tender to his children is stern to the soldiers or prisoners under his command.

The most peculiar social self which one is apt to have is in the mind of the person one is in love with. The good or bad fortunes of this self cause the most intense elation and dejection—unreasonable enough as measured by every other standard than that of the organic feeling of the individual. To his own consciousness he *is* not, so long as this particular social self fails to get recognition, and when it is recognized his contentment passes all bounds.

A man's *fame*, good or bad, and his *honor* or dishonor are names for one of his social selves. The particular social self of a man called his honor is usually the result of one of those splittings of which we have spoken. It is his image in the eyes of his own 'set,' which exalts or condemns him as he conforms or not to certain requirements that may not by made of one in another walk of life. Thus a layman may abandon a city infected with cholera; but a priest or a doctor would think such an act incompatible with his honor. A soldier's honor requires him to fight or to die under circumstances where another man can apologize or run away with no stain upon his social self. A judge, a statesman, are in like manner debarred by the honor of their cloth from entering into pecuniary relations perfectly honorable to persons in private life. Nothing is commoner than to hear people discriminate between their different selves of this sort: "As a man I pity you, but as an official I must show you no mercy"; "As a politician I regard him as an ally, but as a moralist I loathe him"; etc., etc. What may be called 'club-opinion' is one of the very strongest forces in life. The thief must not steal from other thieves; the gambler must pay his gambling-debts, though he pay no other debts in the world. The code of honor of fashionable society has throughout history been full of permissions as well as of vetoes, the only reason for following either of which is that so we best serve one of our social selves. You must not lie in general, but you may lie as much as you please if asked about your relations with a lady; you must accept a challenge from an equal, but if challenged by an inferior you may laugh him to scorn: these are examples of what is meant.

## The Spiritual Me

By the 'spiritual me,' so far as it belongs to the empirical self, I mean no one of my passing states of consciousness. I mean rather the entire collection of my states of consciousness, my psychic faculties and dispositions taken concretely. This collection can at any moment become an object to my thought at that moment and awaken emotions like those awakened by any of the other portions of the Me. When we *think of ourselves as thinkers,* all the other ingredients of our Me seem relatively external possessions. Even within the spiritual *Me* some ingredients seem more external than others. Our capacities for sensation, for example, are less intimate possessions, so to speak, than our emotions and desires; our intellectual processes are less intimate than our volitional decisions. The more *active-feeling* states of consciousness are thus the more central portions of the spiritual Me. The very core and nucleus of our self, as we know it, the very sanctuary of our life, is the sense of activity which certain inner states possess. This sense of activity is often held to be a direct revelation of the living substance of our Soul. Whether this be so or not is an ulterior question. I wish now only to lay down the peculiar *internality* of whatever states possess this quality of seeming to be active. It is as if they *went out to meet* all the other elements of our experience. In thus feeling about them probably all men agree.

b. *The feelings and emotions of self* come after the constituents.

## Self-appreciation

This is of two sorts, *self-complacency* and *self-dissatisfaction*. 'Self-love' more properly belongs under the division *C,* of *acts,* since what men mean by that name is rather a set of motor tendencies than a kind of feeling properly so called.

Language has synonyms enough for both kinds of self-appreciation. Thus pride, conceit, vanity, self-esteem, arrogance, vainglory, on the one hand; and on the other modesty, humility, confusion, diffidence, shame, mortification, contrition, the sense of obloquy, and personal despair. These two opposite classes of affection seem to be direct and elementary endowments of our nature. Associationists would have it that they are, on the other hand, secondary phenomena arising from a rapid computation of the sensible pleasures or pains to which our prosperous or debased personal predicament is likely to lead, the sum of the represented pleasures forming the self-satisfaction, and the sum of the represented pains forming the opposite feeling of shame. No doubt, when we are self-satisfied, we do fondly rehearse all possible rewards for our desert, and when in a fit of self-despair we forebode evil. But the mere expectation of reward is not the self-satisfaction, and the mere apprehension of the evil is not the self-despair; for there is a certain average tone of self-feeling which each one of us carries about with him, and which is independent of the objective reasons we may have for satisfaction or discontent. That is, a very meanly-conditioned man may abound in unfaltering conceit, and one whose success in life is secure, and who is esteemed by all, may remain diffident of his powers to the end.

One may say, however, that the normal *provocative* of self-feeling is one's actual success or failure, and the good or bad actual position one holds in the world. "He put in his thumb and pulled out a plum, and said, 'What a good boy am I!'" A man with a broadly extended empirical Ego, with powers that have uniformly brought him success, with place and wealth and friends and fame, is not likely to be visited by the morbid diffidences and doubts about himself which he had when he was a boy. "Is not this great Babylon, which I have planted?" Whereas he who has made one blunder after another, and still lies in middle life among the failures at the foot of the hill, is liable to grow all sicklied o'er with self-distrust, and to shrink from trials with which his powers can really cope.

The emotions themselves of self-satisfaction and abasement are of a unique sort, each as worthy to be classed as a primitive emotional species as are, for example, rage or pain. Each has its own peculiar physiognomical expression. In self-satisfaction the extensor muscles are innervated, the eye is strong and glorious, the gait rolling and elastic, the nostril dilated, and a peculiar smile plays upon the lips. This whole complex of symptoms is seen in an exquisite way in lunatic asylums, which always contain some patients who are literally mad with conceit, and whose fatuous expression and absurdly strutting or swaggering gait is in tragic contrast with their lack of any valuable personal quality. It is in these same castles of despair that we find the strongest examples of the opposite physiognomy, in good people who think they have committed 'the unpardonable sin' and are lost forever, who crouch and cringe and slink from notice, and are unable to speak aloud or look us in the eye. Like fear and like anger, in similar morbid conditions, these opposite feelings of Self may be aroused with no adequate exciting cause. And in fact we ourselves know how the barometer of our self-esteem and confidence rises and falls from one day to another through causes that seem to be visceral and organic rather than rational, and which certainly answer to no corresponding variations in the esteem in which we are held by our friends.

c. *Self-seeking and self-preservation* come next.

These words cover a large number of our fundamental instinctive impulses. We have those of *bodily self-seeking,* those of *social self-seeking,* and those of *spiritual self-seeking.*

## Bodily Self-seeking

All the ordinary useful reflex actions and movements of alimentation and defence are acts of bodily self-preservation. Fear and anger prompt to acts that are useful in the same way. Whilst if by self-seeking we mean the providing for the future as distinguished from maintaining the present, we must class both anger and fear, together with the hunting, the acquisitive, the home-constructing and the tool-constructing instincts, as impulses to self-seeking of the bodily kind. Really, however, these latter instincts, with amativeness, parental fondness, curiosity and emulation, seek not only the development of the bodily Me, but that of the material Me in the widest possible sense of the word.

Our social self-seeking, in turn, is carried on directly through our amativeness and friendliness, our desire to please and attract notice and admiration, our emulation and jealousy, our love of glory, influence, and power, and indirectly through whichever of the material self-seeking impulses prove serviceable as means to social ends. That the direct social self-seeking impulses are probably pure instincts is easily seen. The noteworthy thing about the desire to be 'recognized' by others is that its strength has so little to do with the worth of the recognition computed in sensational or rational terms. We are crazy to get a visiting-list which shall be large, to be able to say when any one is mentioned, "Oh! I know him well," and to be bowed to in the street by half the people we meet. Of course distinguished friends and admiring recognition are the most desirable—Thackeray somewhere asks his readers to confess whether it would not give each of them an exquisite pleasure to be met walking down Pall Mall with a duke on either arm. But in default of dukes and envious salutations almost anything will do for some of us; and there is a whole race of beings today whose passion is to keep their names in the newspapers, no matter under what heading, 'arrivals and departures,' 'personal paragraphs,' 'interviews,'—gossip, even scandal, will suit them if nothing better is to be had. Guiteau, Garfield's assassin, is an example of the extremity to which this sort of craving for the notoriety of print may go in a pathological case. The newspapers bounded his mental horizon; and in the poor wretch's prayer on the scaffold, one of the most heart-felt expressions was: "The newspaper press of this land has a big bill to settle with thee, O Lord!"

Not only the people but the places and things I know enlarge my Self in a sort of metaphoric social way. *'Ca me connaît,'* as the French workman says of the implement he can use well. So that it comes about that persons for whose *opinion* we care nothing are nevertheless persons whose notice we woo; and that many a man truly great, many a woman truly fastidious in most respects, will take a deal of trouble to dazzle some insignificant cad whose whole personality they heartily despise.

Under the head of spiritual self-seeking ought to be included every impulse towards psychic progress, whether intellectual, moral, or spiritual in the narrow sense of the term. It must be admitted, however, that much that commonly passes for spiritual self-seeking in this narrow sense is only material and social self-seeking beyond the grave. In the Mohammedan desire for paradise and the Christian aspiration not to be damned in hell, the materiality of the goods sought is undisguised. In the more positive and refined view of heaven, many of its goods, the fellowship of the saints and of our dead ones, and the presence of God, are but social goods of the most exalted kind. It is only the search of the redeemed inward nature, the spotlessness from sin, whether here or hereafter, that can count as spiritual self-seeking pure and undefiled.

But this broad external review of the facts of the life of the Me will be incomplete without some account of the . . .

## Rivalry and Conflict of the Different Mes

With most objects of desire, physical nature restricts our choice to but one of many represented goods, and even so it is here. I am often confronted by the necessity of standing by one of my empirical selves and relinquishing the rest. Not that I would not, if I could be both handsome and fat and well dressed, and a great athlete, and make a million a year, be a wit, a *bon-vivant,* and a lady-killer, as well as a philosopher; a philanthropist, statesman, warrior, and African explorer, as well as a 'tone-poet' and saint. But the thing is simply impossible. The millionaire's work would run counter to the saint's; the *bon-vivant* and the philanthropist would trip each other up. [. . .] Such different characters may conceivably at the outset of life be alike *possible* to a man. But to make any one of them actual, the rest must more or less be suppressed. So the seeker [. . .] must review the list carefully, and pick out the one on which to stake his salvation. All other selves thereupon become unreal, but the fortunes of this self are real. Its failures are real failures, its triumphs real triumphs, carrying shame and gladness with them. This is as strong an example as there is of that selective industry of the mind on which I insisted some pages back. Our thought, incessantly deciding, among many things of a kind, which ones for it shall be realities, here chooses one of many possible selves or characters, and forthwith reckons it no shame to fail in any of those not adopted expressly as its own.

So we have the paradox of a man shamed to death because he is only the second pugilist or the second oarsman in the world. That he is able to beat the whole population of the globe minus one is nothing; he has 'pitted' himself to beat that one; and as long as he doesn't do that nothing else counts. He is to his own regard as if he were not, indeed he is not. Yonder puny fellow, however, whom every one can beat, suffers no chagrin about it, for he has long ago abandoned the attempt to 'carry that line,' as the merchants say, of self at all. With no attempt there can be no failure; with no failure, no humiliation. So our self-feeling in this world depends entirely on what we back ourselves to be and do. It is determined by the ratio of our actualities to our supposed potentialities; a fraction of which our pretensions are the denominator and the numerator our success: thus,

$$\text{Self-esteem} = \frac{\text{Success}}{\text{Pretensions}}$$

Such a fraction may be increased as well by diminishing the denominator as by increasing the numerator. To give up pretensions is as blessed a relief as to get them gratified; and where disappointment is incessant and the struggle unending, this is what men will always do. The history of evangelical theology, with its conviction of sin, its self-despair, and its abandonment of salvation by works, is the deepest of possible examples, but we meet others in every walk of life. There is the strangest lightness about the heart when one's nothingness in a particular line is once accepted in good faith. *All* is not bitterness in the lot of the lover sent away by the final inexorable 'No.' Many Bostonians, *crede experto* (and inhabitants of other cities, too, I fear), would be happier women and men today, if they could once for all abandon the notion of keeping up a Musical Self, and without shame let people hear them call a symphony a nuisance. How pleasant is the day when we give up striving to be young,—or slender! Thank God! we say, *those* illusions are gone. Everything added to the Self is a burden as well as a pride. A certain man who lost every penny during our civil war went and actually rolled in the dust, saying he had not felt so free and happy since he was born.

Once more, then, our self-feeling is in our power. As Carlyle says: "Make thy claim of wages a zero, then hast thou the world under thy feet. Well did the wisest of our time write, it is only with *renunciation* that life, properly speaking, can be said to begin."

Neither threats nor pleading can move a man unless they touch some one of his potential or actual selves. Only thus can we, as a rule, get a 'purchase' on another's will. The first care of diplomatists and monarchs and all who wish to rule or influence is, accordingly, to find out their victim's strongest principle of self-regard, so as to make that the fulcrum of all appeals. But if a man has given up those things which are subject to foreign fate, and ceased to regard them as parts of himself at all, we are well-nigh powerless over him. [. . .]

## Summary

The following table may serve for summary of what has been said thus far. The empirical life of Self is divided, as below.

## The Self as Knower

The I, or 'pure ego,' is a very much more difficult subject of inquiry than the Me. It is that which at any given moment *is* conscious, whereas the Me is only one of the things which it is conscious *of.* In other words, it is the *Thinker*; and the question immediately comes up *what* is the thinker? Is it the passing state of consciousness itself, or is it something deeper and less mutable? The passing state we have seen to be the very embodiment of change. Yet each of us spontaneously considers that by 'I,' he means something always the same. This has led most philosophers to postulate behind the passing state of consciousness a permanent Substance or Agent whose modification or act it is. This Agent is the thinker; the 'state' is only its instrument or means. 'Soul' 'transcendental Ego,' 'Spirit,' are so many names for this more permanent sort of Thinker. [. . .]

## Distinct Mental States Cannot 'Fuse'

But not only is the notion that our ideas are combinations of smaller ideas improbable, it is logically unintelligible; it leaves out the essential features of all the 'combinations' which we actually know. [. . .]

### Divisions of the Empirical Life of Self

| | Material | Social | Spiritual |
|---|---|---|---|
| Self-Seeking | Bodily Appetites and Instincts. Love of Adornment, Foppery Acquisitiveness, Constructiveness. Love of Home, etc. | Desire to Please, be Noticed, Admired, etc. Sociability, Emulation, Envy, Love, Pursuit of Honor, Ambition, etc. | Intellectual, Moral and Religious Aspirations, Consciousness. |
| Self-Estimation | Personal Vanity, Modesty, etc. Pride of Wealth, Fear of Poverty | Social and Family Pride, Vainglory, Snobbery, Humility, Shame, etc. | Sence of Moral or Mental Superiority, Purity, etc. Sense of Inferiority or of Guilt. |

## The Soul as a Combining Medium

The spiritualists in philosophy have been prompt to see that things which are known together are known by one *something,* but that something, they say, is no mere passing thought, but a simple and permanent spiritual being on which many ideas combine their effects. It makes no difference in this connection whether this being be called Soul, Ego, or Spirit, in either case its chief function is that of a combining medium. This is a different vehicle of knowledge from that in which we just said that the mystery of knowing things together might be most simply lodged. Which is the real knower, this permanent being, or our passing state? If we had other grounds, not yet considered, for admitting the Soul into our psychology, then getting there on those grounds, she might turn out to be the knower too. But if there be no *other* grounds for admitting the Soul, we had better cling to our passing 'states' as the exclusive agents of knowledge; for we have to assume their existence anyhow in psychology, and the knowing of many things together is just as well accounted for when we call it one of their functions as when we call it a reaction of the Soul. *Explained* it is not by either conception, and has to figure in psychology as a datum that is ultimate.

But there are other alleged grounds for admitting the Soul into psychology, and the chief of them is. . .

## The Sense of Personal Identity

It was stated [earlier] that the thoughts which we actually know to exist do not fly about loose, but seem each to belong to some one thinker and not to another. Each thought, out of a multitude of other thoughts of which it may think, is able to distinguish those which belong to it from those which do not. The former have a warmth and intimacy about them of which the latter are completely devoid, and the result is a Me of yesterday, judged to be in some peculiarly subtle sense the *same* with the I who now make the judgment. As a mere subjective phenomenon the judgment presents no special mystery. It belongs to the great class of judgments of sameness; and there is nothing more remarkable in making a judgment of sameness in the first person than in the second or the third. The intellectual operations seem essentially alike, whether I say 'I am the same as I was' or whether I say 'the pen is the same as it was yesterday.' It is as easy to think this as to think the opposite and say 'neither of us is the same.' The only question which we have to consider is whether it be a right judgment. *Is the sameness predicated really there?*

## Sameness in the Self as Known

If in the sentence 'I am the same that I was yesterday,' we take the 'I' broadly, it is evident that in many ways I am *not* the same. As a concrete Me, I am somewhat different from what I was: then hungry, now full; then walking, now at rest; then poorer, now richer; then younger, now older; etc. And yet in other ways I *am* the same, and we may call these the essential ways. My name and profession and relations to the world are identical, my face, my faculties and store of memories, are practically indistinguishable, now and then. Moreover the Me of now and the Me of then are *continuous:* the alterations were gradual and never affected the whole of me at once. So far, then, my personal identity is just like the sameness predicated of any other aggregate thing. It is a conclusion grounded either on the resemblance in essential respects or on the continuity of the phenomena compared. And it must not be taken to mean more than these grounds warrant or treated as a sort of metaphysical or absolute Unity in which all differences are overwhelmed. The past and present selves compared are the same just so far as they *are* the same, and no farther. They are the same in *kind.* But this generic sameness coexists with generic differences just as real; and if from the one point of view I am one self, from another I am quite as truly many. Similarly of the attribute of continuity: it gives to the self the unity of mere connectedness, or unbrokenness, a perfectly definite phenomenal thing—but it gives not a jot or tittle more.

## Sameness in the Self as Knower

But all this is said only of the Me, or Self as known. In the judgment 'I am the same,' etc., the 'I' was taken broadly as the concrete person. Suppose, however, that we take it narrowly as the *Thinker,* as *'that to which'* all the concrete determinations of the Me belong and are known: does there not then appear an absolute identity at different times? That something which at every moment goes out and knowingly appropriates the *Me* of the past, and discards the non-Me as foreign, is it not a permanent abiding principle of spiritual activity identical with itself wherever found?

That it is such a principle is the reigning doctrine both of philosophy and common-sense, and yet reflection finds it difficult to justify the idea. *If there were no passing states of consciousness,* then indeed we might suppose an abiding principle, absolutely one with itself, to be the ceaseless thinker in each one of us. But if the states of consciousness be accorded as realities, no such 'substantial' identity in the thinker need be supposed. Yesterday's and today's states of consciousness have no *substantial* identity, for when one is here the other is irrevocably dead and gone. But they have a *functional* identity, for both know the same objects, and so far as the by-gone me is one of those objects, they react upon it in an identical way, greeting it and calling it *mine,* and opposing it to all the other things they know. This functional identity seems really the only sort of identity in the thinker which the facts require us to suppose. Successive thinkers, numerically distinct, but all aware of the same past in the same way, form an adequate vehicle for all the experience of personal unity and sameness which we actually have. And just such a train of successive thinkers is the stream of mental states (each with its complex object cognized and emotional and selective reaction thereupon) which psychology treated as a natural science has to assume.

The logical conclusion seems then to be that *the states of consciousness are all that psychology needs to do her work with. Metaphysics or theology may prove the Soul to exist; but for psychology the hypothesis of such a substantial principle of unity is superfluous.*

## How the I Appropriates the Me

But *why* should each successive mental state appropriate the same past Me? I spoke a while ago of my own past experiences appearing to me with a 'warmth and intimacy' that the experiences thought of by me as having occurred to other people lack. This leads us to the answer sought. My present Me is felt with warmth and intimacy. The heavy warm mass of my body is there, and the nucleus of the 'spiritual me,' the sense of intimate activity, is there. We cannot realize our present self without simultaneously feeling one or other of these two things. Any other object of

thought that brings these two things with it into consciousness will be thought with a warmth and an intimacy like those which cling to the present me.

Any *distant* object that fulfills this condition will be thought with such warmth and intimacy. But which distant objects *do* fulfill the condition, when represented?

Obviously those, and only those, that fulfilled it when they were alive. *Them* we shall still represent with the animal warmth upon them; to them may possibly still cling the flavor of the inner activity taken in the act. And by a natural consequence, we shall assimilate them to each other and to the warm and intimate self we now feel within us as we think, and separate them as a collection from whatever objects have not this mark, much as out of a herd of cattle let loose for the winter on some wide Western prairie the owner picks out and sorts together, when the round-up comes in the spring, all the beasts on which he finds his own particular brand. Well, just such objects are the past experiences which I now call mine. Other men's experiences, no matter how much I may know about them, never bear this vivid, peculiar brand. This is why Peter, awakening in the same bed with Paul, and recalling what both had in mind before they went to sleep, reidentifies and appropriates the 'warm' ideas as his, and is never tempted to confuse them with those cold and pale-appearing ones which he ascribes to Paul. As well might he confound Paul's body, which he only sees, with his own body, which he sees but also feels. Each of us when he awakens says, "Here's the same old Me again," just as he says, "Here's the same old bed, the same old room, the same old world."

And similarly in our waking hours, though each pulse of consciousness dies away and is replaced by another, yet that other, among the things it knows, knows its own predecessor, and finding it 'warm,' in the way we have described, greets it, saying: "Thou art *mine,* and part of the same self with me." Each later thought, knowing and including thus the thoughts that went before, is the final receptacle—and appropriating them is the final owner—of all that they contain and own. As Kant says, it is as if elastic balls were to have not only motion but knowledge of it, and a first ball were to transmit both its motion and *its* consciousness to a second, which took both up into its consciousness and passed them to a third, until the last ball held all that the other balls had held, and realized it as its own. It is this trick which the nascent thought has of immediately taking up the expiring thought and 'adopting' it, which leads to the appropriation of most of the remoter constituents of the self. Who owns the last self owns the self before the last, for what possesses the possessor possesses the possessed. It is impossible to discover any *verifiable* features in personal identity that this sketch does not contain, impossible to imagine how any transcendent principle of Unity (were such a principle there) could shape matters to any other result, or be known by any other fruit, than just this production of a stream of consciousness each successive part of which should know, and knowing, hug to itself and adopt, all those that went before,—thus standing as the *representative* of an entire past stream with which it is in no wise to be identified. [. . .]

## Review, and Psychological Conclusion

To sum up this long chapter:—The consciousness of Self involves a stream of thought, each part of which as 'I' can remember those which went before, know the things they knew, and care paramountly for certain ones among them as '*Me*,' and *appropriate to these* the rest. This Me is an empirical aggregate of things objectively known. The *I* which knows them cannot itself be an aggregate; neither for psychological purposes need it be an unchanging metaphysical entity like the Soul, or a principle like the transcendental Ego, viewed as 'out of time.' It is a *thought*, at each moment different from that of the last moment,

but *appropriative* of the latter, together with all that the latter called its own. All the experiential facts find their place in this description, unencumbered with any hypothesis save that of the existence of passing thoughts or states of mind.

If passing thoughts be the directly verifiable existents which no school has hitherto doubted them to be, then they are the only 'Knower' of which Psychology, treated as a natural science, need take any account. The only pathway that I can discover for bringing in a more transcendental Thinker would be to deny that we have any such *direct* knowledge of the existence of our 'states of consciousness' as common-sense supposes us to possess. The existence of the 'states' in question would then be a mere hypothesis, or one way of asserting that there *must* be a knower correlative to all this known; but the problem *who that knower is* would have become a metaphysical problem. With the question once stated in these terms, the notion either of a Spirit of the world that thinks through us, or that of a set of individual substantial souls, must be considered as *primâ facie* on a par with our own 'psychological' solution and discussed impartially. I myself believe that room for much future inquiry lies in this direction. The 'states of mind' which every psychologist believes in are by no means clearly apprehensible, if distinguished from their objects. But to doubt them lies beyond the scope of our natural-science point of view. And in this book the provisional solution which we have reached must be the final word: the thoughts themselves are the thinkers.

# The Real Self:
# From Institution to Impulse

Ralph H. Turner • University of California, Los Angeles

It is proposed that people variously recognize their real selves either in feelings and actions of an institutional and volitional nature, such as ambition, morality, and altruism, or in the experience of impulse, such as undisciplined desire and the wish to make intimate revelations to other people. A shift toward the impulse pole seems to be under way and might be plausibly explained by changing cultural definitions of reality, modified terms of social integration, shifting patterns of deprivation, or new opportunities and consequences. Many standard sociological assumptions about social control are incompatible with the new pattern of self-identification.

The [. . .] idea of a self-as-object permits me to distinguish among the various feelings and actions that emanate from my person. Some emanations I recognize as expressions of my real self; others seem foreign to the real me. I take little credit and assume little blame for the sensations and actions that are peripheral to my real self (Turner, 1968). Others are of great significance, because they embody my true self, good or bad. The articulation of *real selves* with social structure should be a major link in the functioning and change of societies. This approach to linking person and social structure is especially compatible with symbolic interactionist and phenomenological perspectives that stress the ongoing creation of reality by each member of society.

The aim of this paper is to elaborate a dimension of self-conception that may have important implications for sociological theories of social control and other aspects of societal functioning. To varying degrees, people accept as evidence of their real selves either feelings and actions with an *institutional* focus or ones they identify as strictly *impulse*. There are suggestive signs that recent decades have witnessed a shift in the locus of self away from the institutional pole and toward that of impulse. This shift may have altered substantially the world of experience in which people orient themselves, setting it apart from the one that much established sociological theory describes. [. . .]

## Institution and Impulse of Loci of Self

The self-conception is most frequently described sociologically by naming the roles that are preeminent in it. In a good example of this approach, Wellman (1971) finds that the self-conceptions of both black and white adolescents can be characterized on the basis of the same set of identities—namely, their age, gender, family, religion, race, ethnic heritage, and their roles as students, athletes, and friends. Studies comparing the place of occupation and work in the life organizations of various groups of workers (Dubin, 1956; Wilensky,

1964) likewise relate the self-conception to particular roles in society.

Self-conceptions can also be compared on the basis of distinctions at a more abstract level. The relationship between self and social order is put in more comprehensive terms when we distinguish between self as anchored in *institutions* and self as anchored in *impulse.*

To one person, an angry outburst or the excitement of extramarital desire comes as an alien impetus that superficially beclouds or even dangerously threatens the true self. The experience is real enough and may even be persistent and gratifying, but it is still not felt as signifying the real self. The true self is recognized in acts of volition, in the pursuit of institutionalized goals, and not in the satisfaction of impulses outside institutional frameworks. To another person, the outburst or desire is recognized—fearfully or enthusiastically—as an indication that the real self is breaking through a deceptive crust of institutional behavior. Institutional motivations are external, artificial constraints and superimpositions that bridle manifestations of the real self. One plays the institutional game when he must, but only at the expense of the true self. The true self consists of deep, unsocialized, inner impulses. Mad desire and errant fancy are exquisite expressions of the self.

Again, conscientious acceptance of group obligations and unswerving loyalty can mean that the real self has assumed firm control and overcome the alien forces. But for those who find out who they really are by listening to the voice of impulse, the same behavior is a meaningless submission to institutional regimens and authoritarianism. A mother's self-sacrifice for her child is the measure of her real self when seen through institutional eyes, and it is a senseless betrayal of the parent's true being to those who find personal reality in the world of impulse.

It is no accident that this polarity parallels Freud's classic distinction between id and superego. To Freud, the id was more truly the person and the superego merely an external imposition. As he turned to examinations of society, he expressed the same conviction when he wrote, "Our civilization is entirely based upon the suppression of instincts" (1931, p. 13), and when he proposed a relaxation of social norms and standards as a solution to the discontents of modern civilization (1930). This position sharply contrasts with a view shared by many writers and exemplified in Park's assertion that "the role we are striving to live up to—this mask is our truer self" (1927, p. 139). Although in other writings Park sometimes expressed a different conviction, his statement epitomized the institutional locus of self, while Freud located the self chiefly in the world of impulse— until his belated concessions to ego.

## The Key Differences

Several crucial differences between the two contrasting loci of self can be briefly stated.

1. Under the institution locus, the real self is revealed when an individual adheres to a high standard, especially in the face of serious temptation to fall away. A person shows his true mettle under fire. Under the impulse locus, the real self is revealed when a person does something solely because he wants to—not because it is good or bad or noble or courageous or self-sacrificing, but because he spontaneously wishes to do so.

2. To *impulsives*, the true self is something to be discovered. A young person drops out of school or out of the labor force in order to reflect upon and discover who he really is. To the *institutional*, waiting around for self-discovery to occur is ridiculous. The self is something attained, created, achieved, not something discovered. If vocational counseling to help the individual find his peculiar niche has elements of the impulse conception of self, the idea that a person can make of himself what he will, that one chooses a task and then works at it, is the view of institutionals. The contrast is well stated in a contemporary prescription for effective living, written from the institutional perspective:

So if we reach a point of insight at which we become disgustedly aware of how we stage ourselves, play games, and ingratiate others, to say nothing of using defense mechanisms and strategies, and if at this point we want to enrich life by finding honest, deeply felt, loving interactions with others, it is tempting to believe that we can change simply by opening a door and letting out our "true" unsullied impulses. Change is never so simple. What is really involved is not the releasing of a true self but the making of a new self, one that gradually transcends the limitations and pettiness of the old. (White, 1972, p. 387)

3. Under the institution locus, the real self is revealed only when the individual is in full control of his faculties and behaviors. Allport (1955) locates the self in planning and volition, in contrast to impulse. "When the individual is dominated by segmental drives, by compulsions, or by the winds of circumstances, he has lost the integrity that comes only from maintaining major directions of striving" (pp. 50–51). When control is impaired by fatigue, stress, alcohol, or drugs, an alien self displaces the true self. The danger of any of these conditions is that after repeated experiences the individual may lose the capacity to distinguish between the true self and the counterfeit and become progressively less able to resume control and reinstate the true self. If use of alcohol is viewed with favor, it is only on condition that the user is able to practice moderation or "hold his liquor," maintaining control in spite of alcohol.

But under the impulse locus, the true self is revealed only when inhibitions are lowered or abandoned. In a magnificent statement of an institutional perspective, Wordsworth (1807) called upon Duty, "stern daughter of the voice of God," for relief from the "weight of chance-desires" and for "a repose that ever is the same." But let the barest suspicion arise that a good deed has been motivated by a sense of duty, and it loses all value as a clue to self in the eyes of the impulsive. For some impulsives drugs and alcohol are aids—often indispensable—to the discovery of self, for without them socially instilled inhibitions irresistibly overpower the true self. A participant in a Los Angeles "love-in" in 1971 said: "It's a place where people can get out, get smashed, get stoned, or whatever. A love-in is a place to get away from the apartment. It's like being out and touching people for a change, rather than working with paper and working with inanimate objects. It's like being out in the real world for a change."

4. Hypocrisy is a concern of both types, but the word means different things to each. For the institutionals, hypocrisy consists of failing to live up to one's standards. The remedy is not to lower standards but to make amends and adhere to the standards the next time. If one's failings persist, he ceases to represent himself as what he cannot be, so that he at least escapes the charge of hypocrisy by presenting himself only as what he is. For the impulsives, hypocrisy consists of asserting standards and adhering to them even if the behavior in question is not what the individual wants to do and enjoys doing. One who sets exacting standards for himself and by dint of dedicated effort succeeds in living up to them is still a hypocrite if he must suppress a desire to escape from these strict demands. Altruism, in the traditional sense of responding to duty and setting one's own interests aside, is a penultimate hypocrisy, compounded by the probability that it is a dissimulated self-seeking and manipulation. The institutional goal is correspondence between *prescription and behavior;* the goal of impulsives is correspondence between *impulse and behavior:* hypocrisy in either instance is a lack of the appropriate correspondence.

5. In the light of the foregoing differences, the qualities that make a performance admirable differ. The polished, error-free performance, in which the audience forgets the actor and sees only the role being played, is the most admired by institutionals. Whatever the task, perfection is both the goal and the means by which the real self finds expression. But impulsives find technical perfection repelling and admire instead a performance that reveals the actor's human frailties. They are in harmony with the motion picture star system, in which Gregory Peck, John Wayne, and Gina Lollobrigida, rather than the characters they play in a given picture, are the centers of attention. Ed Sullivan's popular appeal, generally attributed to his very awkwardness and ineptitude, is incomprehensible to the institutionals. Of course, the specific cues for spontaneity have changed, so a younger generation of impulsives no longer responds to these stars as did an older generation.

6. The difference between discovery and achievement also suggests a difference in time perspective. The self as impulse means a present time perspective, while the self as institution means a future time perspective. Institutionals, who

build themselves a real world by making commitments, have difficulty retaining a vital sense of self when the future perspective is no longer tenable. The *malaise* of retirement is a common indication of this pattern. In contrast, freedom from past commitments is heralded poetically in the popular song "Gentle on My Mind," by John Hartford.

7. Just as hypocrisy takes on different meanings within the two patterns, individualism is found in both settings with different implications. The individualist is one who rejects some kind of social pressure that threatens his true identity. But there are different kinds of pressure. In one view, social pressures can divert a person from achievement, from adherence to ethical standards, and from other institutional goals. The rugged individualists of 19th-century America thought in these terms. Children were imbued with an individualistic ethic in order to protect them from peer group pressures toward mediocrity or compromise of principle, either of which meant failure to realize the potential that was the true self. But individualism can also be a repudiation of the institutional and interindividual claims that compete with impulse. The individualist may be protecting himself against a conspiracy to force him into institutional molds, to make him do his duty, or to aspire. Both types would agree that one must resist the blandishments of friends and the threats of enemies in order to be true to himself. But the institutional individualist is most attentive to pernicious pressures on the side of mediocrity and abandonment of principle; the impulsive individualist sees clearly the social pressures in league with a system of arbitrary rules and false goals.

Both institution and impulse loci allow for individualistic and nonindividualistic orientations. We have found it useful to employ a crosscutting distinction between *individual* and *social* anchorages for the self. Institutionals stress either achievement, a relatively individual goal, or altruism, a social aim, as the road to self-discovery. Somewhere between the two lies adherence to an ethical code which will vary according to whether ethics is viewed as applied altruism or a forum for individual achievement. Impulsives may stress the simple disregard of duties and inhibitions in order

to gratify spontaneous impulses; this is essentially an individual route to self-discovery. Or they may seek self-discovery through expressing potentially tabooed feelings to other persons and thereby attain a state of interpersonal intimacy that transcends the normal barriers between people.

It is essential not to confuse these alternative anchorages with the question of whether people are preoccupied with maintaining appearances or conforming instead of "being themselves." Describing a mass gathering of youths, a student wrote, "People tend to forget how they would hope to come across, and instead act as their true selves." This is a terse statement of how participants felt in the situation and expresses the point of view of an impulse self-anchorage. But from an institutional perspective, the same youths appear to be tumbling over one another in their anxiety to comply with the latest youthful fad and to avoid any appearance of being square. The institutional hopes that after passing through this stage the youths will "find themselves," discovering their special niches in the institutional system. The self-anchorage determines which kinds of behavior seem genuine and which are concessions to appearances. [. . .]

Concerning this initial statement of the two loci of self, the reader should bear in mind that specifying polar types such as these is merely a way to start thinking about variation in the sense of self. Except on the fringes of society, we are unlikely to find the extremes. Elements of both anchorages probably coexist comfortably in the average person. Yet differences among groups of people in key facets of self may be of sufficient importance that their experience of each other is noncongruent, and little true communication can occur.

## A Contemporary Trend

It is my speculative hypothesis that over the past several decades substantial shifts have occurred away from an institution and toward an impulse emphasis. Accounts of the "new sensibility" in American culture (Bell, 1970, p. 59) or of "consciousness III" (Reich, 1970) already associate many of the same features with the youthful protest of the 1960s. But it would be shortsighted not to see the shift in a more extended historical context or to overlook the possibility of rural–urban differences, class differences, and differences among national cultures, as well as generational differences. A revolutionary consciousness often unwittingly adopts perspectives that have been growing in established society, frees them from accommodation to other aspects of that society, and applies them to a contemporary crisis.

There is nothing novel in attending to changing values over the last few generations. But I suggest that the changes be viewed as a shift in what are conceived as valid indications of what is real about ourselves and our associates, telling us whether we really know a person or not. Distinguishing the real from the unreal is a matter of intuition, not of logic. Faultless logic that concerns unreal objects falls on deaf ears. A shifting locus of self means that successive generations are talking about different worlds of reality. At the heart of each are the shared and socially produced intuitions through which people identify their true selves.

Literary themes often presage shifts in popular consciousness. Examining the writings of James Frazer, Friedrich Nietzsche, Joseph Conrad, Thomas Mann, and Sigmund Freud, Lionel Trilling (1961) traces the theme that we must accept the reality of those human impulses that were judged unacceptable by an artificial and unreal civilization. He identifies "a certain theme which appears frequently in modern literature—so frequently, indeed, and in so striking a manner, that it may be said to constitute one of the shaping and controlling ideas of our epoch. I can identify it by calling it the disenchantment of our culture with culture itself—it seems to me that the characteristic element of modern literature, or at least of the most highly developed modern literature, is the bitter line of hostility to civilization which runs through it" (p. 26).

I have already noted Freud's penchant for the impulse perspective. Perhaps the greatest impact Freud had on the modern world was to discredit normative behavior and conscience as manifestations of our true selves and to elevate impulses to that position. Under his aegis, guilt has ceased to be the redemptive experience through which the real self reasserts itself and has become an external impediment to personal autonomy. Lynd (1958) exemplifies this newer intuition of reality when she writes, "Living in terms of guilt and righteousness is living in terms of the sanctions and taboos of one immediate culture. To some extent such living is necessary for everyone. Living in terms of the confronting of shame—and allowing shame

to become a revelation of oneself and one's society—makes way for living beyond the conventions of a particular culture. It makes possible the discovery of an integrity that is peculiarly one's own and of those characteristically human qualities that are at the same time most individualizing and most universal" (p. 257).

Concern with discovery of the true self, vaguely identified as a set of impulses that have been repressed or dissipated under institutional constraint, turns up as a novel element in the political process of recent years. It became a prominent theme in youth movements, minority movements, and women's movements during the 1960s (Turner, 1969). Miller (1973) traces the "politics of the true self" back to the poet William Blake and shows that violence is conceived of as the ultimate form of self-expression and self-discovery in the writings of Fanon and Sartre.

The term "soul" has often been used in much the same sense as our term "true self." It can be found in the work of poets as different as Richard Lovelace and William Wordsworth. But its meaning has changed to suit prevailing conceptions of personal reality. A century ago the soul was essentially a moral force. As secular psychology brought the term into disrepute, it disappeared, sank into obscurity, reemerging to describe a special quality attributed to blacks. It retains its character as a dynamic force, but a supposed lack of inhibition is a crucial criterion of "soul."

Miller and Swanson (1958) documented changing conceptions of child rearing as new middle-class parents evinced less concern about internalized controls and more about social adjustment than did parents from the old middle class. In studies of another stage in life, students, as they progressed through college or university, were found to look more favorably on the expression of impulses (Feldman and Newcomb, 1969, p. 34). If the inner-directed person of Riesman et al. (1950) has much in common with our institutionals, the other-directed person may have been a transitional type, clinging to the institutional framework for his identity but finding a way to accept constant change. Perhaps the total repudiation of institutional identities is the product of a growing sense of unreality in *all* roles that comes from the other-directed person's efforts to *be* all his roles. In the world of business, the shift is from the view that human relations take care of themselves when tasks are effectively managed to the position that human-relations engineering is essential to effective production. In education the progressive movement promoted a conception of the child in terms of his impulses, and not merely his learning and conduct. Rieff's (1966) depiction of cultural change as "the shifting balance of controls and releases" (p. 233) and his account of the "triumph of the therapeutic" describe a historical change toward greater impulsiveness.

Lifton (1970) has described a type of personality he believes is becoming much more common throughout the developed world. His "protean man" has no true shape of his own but assumes varied shapes according to circumstance. Except for the fact that Riesman et al. describe other-direction as a mode of conformity, "protean man" may be a new name for the same kind of person. But the idea that rapid social change makes fixed identities unworkable has also inspired Zurcher (1972, 1973) to identify the "mutable self" as a phenomenon unique to the present generation. Zurcher cites as evidence for the "mutable self" his discovery that students no longer answer Kuhn's TST as they used to. Early use of the procedure produced mostly "B mode" responses, meaning that the subject identified himself with various institutionalized roles and statuses. Now students give principally "C mode" responses, which specify characteristic modes of acting, feeling, and responding.

"C mode" responses clearly attenuate the linkage between self and institutional anchorage. The real self is marked by characteristic orientations–attitudes, feelings, desires—rather than characteristic placement in social organization. Young people find self-realization in patterns that are viewed apart from their institutional settings. Consistent with this evidence is the contemporary view that, on meeting a stranger, it is inappropriate to ask where he comes from, what he does, and whether he is married, or to categorize him in other ways. Instead, one seeks to know him through his tastes and his feelings. [. . .]

## Sentiments

Much of the spontaneous joy that lubricates the functioning of social orders resides in the social sentiments. Love is of paramount importance among the sentiments. Because sentiment seems to express the inner person, in contrast to external behavior that may be contrived, people seek agreement on signs by which to tell genuine from false sentiment. The choice of cues reflects the anchorage of self. Self-as-impulse can feel love as genuine, as a true reflection of self, only when it arises and persists as a spontaneous attachment, untrammeled by promises, covenants, and codes of behavior. Sentiment is not helped along by a facilitative social order: it erupts in spite of the order and threatens it. The less organization and preparation, the more easily can the individual discover his true sentiments. Institutionals, on the other hand, understand love as something that requires effort to attain and preserve. The infatuation that explodes impulsively is undependable and unreal. The institutional seeks to learn how to achieve true love and turns for guidance to such documents as Paul's chapter on love in the New Testament (1 Cor. 13). The contrasting perspectives are represented in the analysis of popular sex manuals by Lewis and Brissett (1967). Manuals popular with married middle-class people in the 1940s and 1950s are institutional in orientation. They offer readers an opportunity to enhance the vitality and mutuality of sexual experience, leading to a deeper union of the two selves. But Lewis and Brissett read the manuals from the impulsive perspective. Stripped of the institutional perspective, the quest for mutual self-attainment becomes sheer, meaningless "work." Thus, they write of "sex as work." To the extent to which the self-locus has moved away from institutions, the correlations found by Burgess and Cottrell (1939), Burgess and Wallin (1953), and Locke (1951) with persistence and love in marriage may become increasingly invalid, and new and different indicators may become relevant.

## The Meaning of Ritual

In 1930, an article entitled "Ritual the Conserver" (Cressman) appeared in the *American Journal of Sociology.* It elaborated the crucial part played by ritual in sustaining the Catholic church and its doctrines. To a contemporary reader, the paper seems peculiarly unconvincing. To those who find not only religious ritual but also marriage ceremonies, funeral and memorial services, initiation ceremonies, and graduation exercises devoid of meaning, it is unclear how ritual could add vitality and reality to anything. Yet plainly many people have been, and continue to be, moved deeply by participation in collective ritual, and for many people dedication to institutional goals and forms is strengthened in this way. The locus of self must be closely intertwined with the ability to gain a vital experience from engaging in collective rituals. It would be premature to label one cause and the other effect, but the impulsive's self-fulfilling prophecy that he will not experience his real self thought participation in institutional ritual contrasts with the equally self-fulfilling prophecy from the institutional.

But the matter cannot be reduced to a differential receptivity to ritual. Writing on the "collective search for identity," Klapp (1969) describes the contemporary poverty of ritual, then insists that "ritual is the prime symbolic vehicle for experiencing emotions and mystiques together with others—including a sense of oneself as sharing such emotions . . ." (p. 118). In the place of traditional forms, there have arisen new rituals that participants experience as spontaneous outpourings instead of institutional routines. Sitting on the floor in a circle and singing to the accompaniment of guitars takes the place of sitting in rows on pews and listening to an organ. Rock festivals and love-ins are only the more dramatic rituals, for even the conventional partying rituals of middle-class establishmentarians are experienced as a welcome contrast to institutional routine. Here, then, is another set of rituals that have meaning and vitality as opportunities for experiencing a self that contains more impulse than institution.

Ritual is commonly viewed as a support of the institutional order, and Klapp's "poverty of ritual" does indeed characterize many of the forms that have been employed to strengthen a collective sense of institutional commitment. But it is doubtful that there is any poverty of ritual today in those forms that increase the vitality of an impulsive view of self.

## REFERENCES

Allport, G. W. (1955). *Becoming: Basic considerations for a psychology of personality*. New Haven, CT: Yale University Press.

Bell, D. (1910). Quo warranto. *Public Interest, 19*, 53–68.

Burgess, E. W., & Cottrell, L S. Jr. (1939). *Predicting success or failure in marriage*. Englewood Cliffs, NJ: Prentice-Hall.

Burgess, E. W., & Wallin, P. (1953). *Engagement and marriage*. Chicago: Lippincott.

Cressman, L. S. (1930). Ritual the conserver. *American Journal of Sociology, 35*, 564–572.

Dubin, R. (1956). Industrial workers' world. *Social Problems, 3*, 131–142.

Feldman, K. A., & Newcomb, T. M. (1969). *The impact of college on students*. Vol. 1. San Francisco: Jossey-Bass.

Freud, S. (1930). *Civilization and its discontents*. London: Hogarth.

Freud, S. (1931). *Modern sexual morality and modern nervousness*. New York: Eugenics.

Klapp, O. E. (1969). *Collective search for identity*. New York: Holt, Rinehart & Winston.

Lewis, L. S., & Brissett, D. (1967). Sex as work: A study of avocational counselling. *Social Problems, 15*, 8–17.

Lifton, R. J. (1970). *Boundaries: Psychological man in revolution*. New York: Random House.

Locke, H. J. (1951). *Predicting adjustment in marriage*. New York: Holt.

Lynd, H. M. (1958). *On shame and the search for identity*. New York: Harcourt, Brace.

Miller, D. R., & Swanson, G. E. (1958). *The changing American parent*. New York: Wiley.

Miller, S. (1973). The politics of the 'True Self.' *Dissent, 20*, 93–98.

Park, R. E. (1927). Human nature and collective behavior. *American Journal of Sociology, 32*, 733–741.

Reich, C. A. (1970). *The greening of America*. New York: Random House.

Rieff, P. (1966). *The triumph of the therapeutic*. New York: Harper & Row.

Riesman, D., Glazer, N., & Denney, R. (1950). *The lonely crowd*. New Haven, CT: Yale University Press.

Trilling, L. (1961). The modern element in modern literature. *Partisan Review, 28*, 9–25.

Turner, R. H. (1968). The self in social interaction. In C. Gordon and K. Gergen (Eds.), *The self in social interaction* (pp. 93–106). New York: Wiley.

Turner, R. H. (1969). The theme of contemporary social movements. *British Journal of Sociology, 20*, 390–405.

Wellman, B. (1971). Social identities in black and white. *Sociological Inquiry, 41*, 57–66.

White, R. W. (1972). *The enterprise of living: Growth and organization in personality*. New York: Holt, Rinehart & Winston.

Wilensky, H. L. (1964). Varieties of work experiences. In H. Borow (Ed.), *Man in a world at work* (pp. 125–154). Boston: Houghton Mifflin.

Wordsworth, W. (1807). *Ode to Duty*.

Zurcher, L. A. (1972). The mutable self: An adaptation to accelerated sociocultural change. *Et al, 3*, 3–15.

Zurcher, L. A. (1973). Alternative institutions and the mutable self: An overview. *Journal of Applied Behavioral Sciences, 9*, 369–380.

# Motivational Roots

We know that people want to think well of themselves, but why? A simple answer is that it feels good. Undoubtedly, people who hold favorable opinions of themselves are happier than people who hold low opinions of themselves (e.g., Campbell, 1981). Yet this is not a satisfactory answer. Why should emotions and overall well-being be linked to having high self-esteem—especially given that self-esteem does not seem to cause very many adaptive advantages for the individual?

Two intriguing answers have been put forward in recent years. The first was proposed in 1986 by Greenberg, Pyszczynski, and Solomon, and it is further elaborated (with data) in the article reproduced here by the same authors and some colleagues. Based on the work of Ernest Becker (1973), these authors propose that the knowledge of death is the most fundamental threat and most fundamentally motivating fact in human life. Self-esteem, they propose, is part of a defense against that threat. By holding high self-esteem, one can in some way escape from the anxiety that would arise from recognizing that one will die. Thus, the drive for self-esteem is rooted in the terror of death.

A different answer has been proposed by Leary and his colleagues in the paper reproduced here. In their view, the basic driving force is the need to belong rather than the fear of death. Leary and I reviewed evidence that people are widely, pervasively driven by a need to form and maintain a handful of close social relationships (Baumeister & Leary, 1995). Leary has extended this view to propose that self-esteem is a person's inner monitor for how well one is satisfying this basic need. Leary has noted in other work that self-esteem is correlated quite strongly (around −.50 across multiple studies) with anxiety over social rejection and exclusion, whereas it shows no correlation with death anxiety (Leary & Kowalski, 1995; Leary, Saltzman, & Bednarski, 1995). In his view, it seems illogical to argue that high self-esteem means one has conquered the threat of death; rather, it means that one has conquered the threat of loneliness and social rejection.

## REFERENCES

Baumeister, R. F., & Leary, M. R. (1995). The need to belong: Desire for interpersonal attachments as a fundamental human motivation. *Psychological Bulletin, 117,* 497–529.

Becker, E. (1973). *The denial of death.* New York: Free Press.

Campbell, A. (1981). *The sense of well-being in America.* New York: McGraw-Hill.

Greenberg, J., Pyszczynski, T., & Solomon, S. (1986). The causes and consequences of self-esteem: A terror management theory. In R. Baumeister (Ed.), *Public self and private self* (pp. 189–212). New York: Springer-Verlag.

Greenberg, J., Solomon, S., Pyszczynski, T., Rosenblatt, A., Burling, J., Lyon, D., Simon, L., & Pinel, E. (1992). Why do people need self-esteem? Converging evidence that self-esteem serves an anxiety-buffering function. *Journal of Personality and Social Psychology, 63,* 913–922.

Leary, M. R., & Kowalski, R. (1995). *Social anxiety.* New York: Guilford.

Leary, M. R., Saltzman, J. L., & Bednarski, R. F. (1995). *Does high self-esteem buffer people against fear of death?* Unpublished manuscript/under editorial review, Wake Forest University, Winston-Salem, NC.

# Discussion Questions

1. What are people more often worried about: death or social exclusion?
2. How might the authors of these two articles interpret each other's findings?
3. Are there occasions when people are unconcerned about losing self-esteem?
4. Can social rejection ever lead to a boost in self-esteem, instead of a loss?
5. Do *you* try to maintain a favorable opinion of yourself? If so, why? How do your reasons compare with those suggested in these two articles?

# Suggested Readings

Maslow, A. H. (1968). *Toward a psychology of being.* New York: Van Nostrand. In this classic work, Maslow expounds his theory of the basic motivations in human nature. Self-preservation and belongingness both take precedence over esteem.

Baumeister, R. F., & Leary, M. R. (1995). The need to belong: Desire for interpersonal attachments as a fundamental human motivation. *Psychological Bulletin, 117,* 497–529. This review of published studies amasses evidence that one of the most important and basic motivations in life is the need to belong. The self may therefore be a tool for satisfying this need.

Ogilvie, D. M. (1987). The undesired self: A neglected variable in personality research. *Journal of Personality and Social Psychology, 52,* 379–385. Ogilvie proposes that people are often motivated by the wish to distance themselves from an unwanted view of self.

Becker, E. (1973). *The denial of death.* New York: Free Press. This is the work that formed the basis for terror management theory. Becker argues that culture, self-esteem, and other constructions are efforts to avoid recognition of human death and mortality.

Baumeister, R. F., & Tice, D. M. (1990). Anxiety and social exclusion. *Journal of Social and Clinical Psychology, 9,* 165–195. A review of published studies on anxiety examines the causal role of fears about injury and death as well as the role of social rejection and exclusion.

# Self-Esteem as an Interpersonal Monitor: The Sociometer Hypothesis

Mark R. Leary • Wake Forest University
Ellen S. Tambor • Johns Hopkins University
Sonja K. Terdal • Northwestern Michigan College
Deborah L. Downs • Ohio State University

Five studies tested hypotheses derived from the sociometer model of self-esteem according to which the self-esteem system monitors others' reactions and alerts the individual to the possibility of social exclusion. Study I showed that the effects of events on participants' state self-esteem paralleled their assumptions about whether such events would lead others to accept or reject them. In Study 2, participants' ratings of how included they felt in a real social situation correlated highly with their self-esteem feelings. In Studies 3 and 4, social exclusion caused decreases in self-esteem when respondents were excluded from a group for personal reasons, but not when exclusion was random, but this effect was not mediated by self-presentation. Study 5 showed that trait self-esteem correlated highly with the degree to which respondents generally felt included versus excluded by other people. Overall, results provided converging evidence for the sociometer model.

The proposition that people have a fundamental need to maintain their self-esteem has provided the cornerstone for a great deal of work in personality, social, developmental, clinical, and counseling psychology. In the century since William James (1890) first referred to self-esteem as an "elementary endowment of human nature," many classic theories of personality have addressed the importance of self-esteem needs, many emotional and behavioral problems have been attributed to unfulfilled needs for self-esteem, and many psychotherapeutic approaches have focused in one way or another on the client's feelings about himself or herself (Adler, 1930; Allport, 1937; Bednar, Wells, & Peterson, 1989; Horney, 1937; Maslow, 1968; Rogers, 1959). Among social psychologists, the self-esteem motive has been offered as an explanation of a wide array of phenomena, including self-serving attributions (Blaine & Crocker, 1993), reactions to evaluation (S. C. Jones, 1973), self-handicapping (E. E. Jones & Berglas, 1978), downward social comparison (Wills, 1981), attitude change (Steele, 1988), and in-group/out-group perceptions (Crocker, Thompson, McGraw, & Ingerman, 1987).

Despite the fact that the self-esteem motive has been invoked to explain so many phenomena, little attention has been paid to the source or functions of the self-esteem motive itself. The field has taken it for granted that people have a motive to protect their self-esteem without adequately addressing the question of why they should have such a motive or what function it might serve. In five studies we evaluated the hypothesis that the self-esteem system functions as a *sociometer* that monitors the degree to which the individual is being included versus excluded by other people and that motivates the person to behave in ways that minimize the probability of rejection or exclusion.

## Explanations of the Self-Esteem Motive

Although few efforts have been made to systematically address the functions of the self-esteem motive, at least three general explanations of the motive can be gleaned from the literature.

The most widely acknowledged explanation is that people strive for self-esteem because high self-esteem promotes positive affect by buffering the person against stress and other negative emotions and by enhancing personal adjustment, whereas low self-esteem is associated with depression, anxiety, and maladjustment. Research findings attest that people with low self-esteem experience virtually every negative emotion more commonly than those with high self-esteem (e.g., Cutrona, 1982; Goswick & Jones, 1981; Leary, 1983; Taylor & Brown, 1988; White, 1981). Furthermore, high self-esteem appears to buffer people against feelings of anxiety, enhance coping, and promote physical health (Baumeister, 1993; Greenberg et al., 1992; Taylor & Brown, 1988).

Although the link between self-esteem, affect, adjustment, and health is undisputed, it is less clear why self-esteem should produce these effects. One possibility is that, because self-esteem is associated with confidence and high expectations of success, high self-esteem is associated with optimism and lowered anxiety. In a variation on this theme, Greenberg, Pyszczynski, and Solomon (1986) suggested that high self-esteem serves as a buffer against the existential anxiety people experience when they contemplate their own fragility and mortality. However it is unclear why such a psychological system for buffering people against anxiety and uncertainty should have developed. Indeed, from an evolutionary perspective, we might expect that people who worried about possible misfortunes (including death) would have been more likely to survive and reproduce.

A second set of explanations emphasizes the role of high self-esteem in promoting goal achievement. The motive to seek self-esteem may have developed because high self-esteem enhances people's willingness to strive toward desired goals and to persist in the face of obstacles and setbacks (Bandura, 1977; Greenwald, 1980; Kernis, 1995). In a related vein, Tedeschi and Norman (1985) suggested that people seek self-esteem because self-esteem is associated with feelings of control over one's environment.

In support of explanations that implicate goal accomplishment, people with high self-esteem often work harder and perform better after an initial failure than people with low self-esteem (Perez, 1973; Shrauger & Sorman, 1977). However, it is also true that high self-esteem may lead to nonproductive persistence when tasks prove to be insurmountable (McFarlin, Baumeister, & Blascovich, 1984). Although self-efficacious cognitions can undoubtedly facilitate achievement, this explanation cannot explain why self-esteem is inherently affectively laden (Brown, 1993). Although we concur that it may often be useful for people to think that they possess certain favorable attributes or abilities (i.e., to have high self-efficacy), this does not explain why self-esteem is intimately linked to strong self-relevant emotions.

A third set of explanations of the self-esteem motive involves the possibility that people seek self-esteem for its own sake. Many writers have implicitly assumed the existence of a self-system that maintains a sense of integrity or adequacy (e.g., Epstein, 1973; James, 1890; Steele, 1988). One difficulty with this assumption is that it fails to explain why a motive to behave in ways that promote self-esteem should exist at all. It also does not adequately explain why certain events pose threats to self-integrity and others do not. In fact, to the extent that, over the long run, rewarding encounters and the attainment of one's goals depends on accurate knowledge of oneself, a self-system that functioned purely to elevate one's sense of self may actually be less adaptive than one that sought accurate self-knowledge (Heatherton & Ambady, 1993).

## Properties of the Self-Esteem System

Although each of these explanations can explain why people prefer to evaluate themselves positively under certain circumstances, none clearly and fully explains why people appear generally to need self-esteem and regularly behave in ways to maintain and enhance it. Before offering an alternative explanation of the self-esteem motive that we believe parsimoniously explains the properties of the self-esteem system, we must clarify precisely what we mean by the term *self-esteem*.

Self-esteem has often been described as an attitude, specifically an attitude toward oneself (Coopersmith, 1967; Rosenberg, 1965). Like all attitudes, self-esteem has cognitive and affective components. A distinction can be drawn between the self-concept (beliefs about the self) and self-esteem (evaluation of oneself in light of those beliefs). Although self-esteem is often based on self-relevant cognitions, not all cognitions about the self, even evaluatively laden ones, are relevant to a person's self-esteem. Each person has many self-beliefs that have no affective quality. People may believe firmly that they are very good or very bad at certain mundane tasks, for example, yet experience no corresponding increase or decrease in their self-esteem.

Self-esteem includes an essential affective quality that "cold" cognitions about the self do not. Brown (1993) persuasively argued that self-esteem is fundamentally based in affective processes, specifically positive and negative feelings about oneself. People do not simply think favorable or unfavorable self-relevant thoughts; they *feel* good or bad about themselves. Furthermore, they fiercely desire to feel good rather than bad. Most previous explanations of the self-esteem motive have difficulty explaining the inherent emotional and motivational qualities of self-esteem. We return to this point shortly.

Although people can be characterized as having some average level of self-esteem over situations and time (trait self-esteem), self-esteem inevitably fluctuates as people move about their daily lives (state self-esteem). To our knowledge, researchers have not previously addressed the question of whether people are motivated to maintain state self-esteem, trait self-esteem, or both. However, we think it is reasonable to assume that people want both to feel good about themselves in the present moment as well as maintain positive self-feelings over time. As will become clear, *state self-esteem* is of paramount importance in the explanation of the self-esteem system we describe.

## Self-Esteem System as a Sociometer

The hypothesis to be considered in this article is that the self-esteem system is a sociometer that is involved in the maintenance of interpersonal relations (Leary, 1990; Leary & Downs, 1995). Specifically, a person's feelings of state self-esteem are an internal, subjective index or marker of the degree to which the individual is being included versus excluded by other people (the person's *inclusionary status*) and the motive to maintain self-esteem functions to protect the person against social rejection and exclusion. We believe that this perspective on self-esteem more parsimoniously explains the emotional and motivational aspects of self-esteem than other explanations.

Many writers have observed that human beings possess a fundamental motive to seek inclusion and to avoid exclusion from important social groups and that such a motive to promote gregariousness and social bonding may have evolved because of its survival value (Ainsworth, 1989; Barash, 1977; Baumeister & Leary, 1995; Baumeister & Tice, 1990; Bowlby, 1969; Hogan, 1982; Hogan, Jones, & Cheek, 1985). Because solitary human beings in a primitive state are unlikely to survive and reproduce, psychological systems evolved that motivated people to develop and maintain some minimum level of inclusion in social relationships and groups.

Successfully maintaining one's connections to other people requires a system for monitoring others' reactions, specifically the degree to which other people are likely to reject or exclude the individual. Such a system must monitor one's inclusionary status more or less continuously for cues that connote disapproval, rejection, or exclusion (i.e., it must be capable of functioning preconsciously), it must alert the individual to changes in his or her inclusionary status (particularly decrements in social acceptance), and it must motivate behavior to restore his or her status when threatened. In our view, the self-esteem system serves precisely the functions of such a sociometer.

From this perspective, what have previously been viewed as threats to self-esteem are, at a more basic level, events that make the possibility of social exclusion salient. Events that lower self-esteem appear to be those that the person believes may jeopardize his or her social bonds. Ego-threatening events are aversive because they signal a possible deterioration in one's social relationships.

Strictly speaking, then, people do not have a need to maintain self-esteem per se. Self-esteem is simply an indicator of the quality of one's social relations vis-à-vis inclusion and exclusion. To use an analogy, a behavioral researcher from another planet might conclude that Earthlings who drive automobiles are motivated to keep the indicator on their fuel gauges from touching the E (empty); every time the indicator approaches E, Earthlings behave in ways that move the indicator back toward F (full). However, the fuel gauge is simply a monitor to help people avoid running out of gas, just as self-esteem is a monitor to help people avoid social exclusion. Thus, our analysis departs sharply from explanations that impute people with an inherent need to maintain self-esteem.

As noted earlier, self-esteem is closely tied to affective processes (Brown, 1993). Self-esteem involves how people feel about themselves; high self-esteem "feels" good, whereas low self-esteem does not (Scheff, Retzinger, & Ryan, 1989). Most motivational and drive systems elicit aversive affect when potential threats to the organism's well-being are detected (i.e., when needs are not being met). People experience unpleasant affect when they are hungry, thirsty, sleepy, or in physical danger, for example, but feel better when they are well fed, hydrated, rested, and safe. In the case of self-esteem, negative emotions arise when cues that connote disapproval, rejection, or exclusion are detected. It is for this reason that "some of the best evidence for changes in self-esteem can be inferred from self-reports of mood" ( Heatherton & Polivy, 1991, p. 896).

The affective reactions to changes in self-esteem tend to center around the "self-relevant" emotions, such as feelings of pride and shame. In particular, losses of self-esteem are associated with feeling foolish, ashamed, inadequate, or awkward, whereas increased self-esteem is associated with pride, self-satisfaction, and confidence ( Scheff et al., 1989).

Real or potential threats to self-esteem also elicit anxiety. Not only does state self-esteem correlate highly with state anxiety but trait self-esteem and trait anxiety correlate as well (Spivey, 1989). According to the sociometer model, lowered self-esteem and anxiety are coeffects of perceived exclusion (Leary, 1990). Baumeister and Tice (1990)

argued that anxiety is a natural consequence of perceived threats to one's social bonds. Viewed from this perspective, social anxiety, which originates from people's concerns with others' impressions of them (Leary & Kowalski, 1995; Schlenker & Leary, 1982), is also a product of the sociometer. Concerns about other people's impressions raise the specter of disapproval and rejection.

This is not to say that self-esteem is nothing more than mood (see Heatherton & Polivy, 1991). Changes in mood occur for a wide variety of reasons that have nothing to do with social exclusion or with self-esteem. Even so, decreases in self-esteem are invariably accompanied by negative affect.

Our conceptualization offers a functional perspective on the self-esteem motive and explains several facts about self-esteem. Although space does not permit a full discussion of the implications of this explanation (see Leary & Downs, 1995), we offer a few examples that demonstrate its applicability as a general model of self-esteem. For example, viewing the self-esteem system as a sociometer explains Cooley's (1902) observation that people's feelings about themselves are highly sensitive to how they think they are being regarded by other people. The more support and approval people receive, the higher their self-esteem tends to be (Harter, 1993). Such feelings are a direct reflection of one's inclusionary status, with deflations of self-esteem alerting the individual to the possibility that their standing in important groups or relationships is in jeopardy.

The sociometer model also explains why people place varying degrees of importance on different domains of the self (e.g., intellectual, athletic, social), as well as why the importance people place on these domains correlates highly with the importance they think others place on them. It also explains why self-esteem correlates highly with the individual's performance in domains judged important to others (Harter & Marold, 1991). People strive to excel in domains that will enhance their inclusion by certain other people. As a result, they adopt others' standards, and their self-esteem is affected by performance in domains that others value. People's self-evaluations are also differentially affected when they visualize different significant others (Baldwin & Holmes, 1987), presumably because the sociometer is sensitive to the idiosyncratic standards of particular people.

What may not jeopardize one's image in one person's eyes may lead to rejection by another.

This perspective also helps us understand why people with lower self-esteem are more sensitive to socially relevant cues than those with high self-esteem (Brockner, 1983). People who already feel included, accepted, and socially integrated need not be as concerned with fitting in as people who feel less so (Moreland & Levine, 1989; Snodgrass, 1985).

The sociometer hypothesis also answers the seemingly paradoxical question of why, if people possess a system for maintaining self-esteem, some people have low self-esteem (Baumeister, 1993). The answer is that people do not have a system for maintaining self-esteem per se but a system for avoiding social exclusion. To function properly, the system must lead the person who faces potential exclusion or ostracism to feel badly about it. Over time, people who experience real or imagined rejection repeatedly will have lower trait self-esteem than people who feel warmly included.

## Overview of Our Research

In brief, conceptualizing the self-esteem system as a sociometer that monitors one's standing with others helps to explain most of its central properties. In addition, it confers an essential function on self-esteem that helps to explain why the need for self-esteem appears to be innate and universal.

Empirical validation of the sociometer conceptualization of state self-esteem requires the evaluation of at least three general theoretical implications. Most fundamentally, the theory stipulates that changes in self-esteem should be closely associated with changes in the degree to which people perceive they are being included versus excluded by other people (perceived inclusionary status). Second, research must show that the sociometer model accounts for such changes better than alternative conceptualizations of self-esteem. Third, research must demonstrate that behavioral reactions to what have been viewed as threats to self-esteem are in fact responses to real, potential, or imagined social exclusion.

Obviously, fully testing these three general implications of the theory will require much research. In this article we report the results of five studies that focused on the first (and most fundamental)

theoretical implication just described: that self-esteem is highly sensitive to changes in perceived inclusionary status. Failure to demonstrate an integral link between perceived inclusion–exclusion and self-esteem would provide disconfirmatory evidence for the sociometer perspective. On the other hand, converging support from these five studies would lend credence to the notion that the self-esteem system is involved in the monitoring of the quality of one's social bonds vis-à-vis inclusion–exclusion.

## Study 1: Self-Feelings and Anticipated Inclusion–Exclusion

At minimum, the sociometer model of self-esteem predicts that the effects of people's own behavior on their self-feelings should closely parallel the degree to which they expect those behaviors may result in rejection or exclusion. Casual observation suggests that this is the case: Events that raise self-esteem (e.g., achievement, recognition, compliments, being helpful, being loved) tend to be associated with improvement in the individual's chances of being accepted and included, whereas events that lower self-esteem (e.g., failure, moral violations, possession of socially undesirable attributes, rejection) are associated with decreased inclusion likelihood.

To test this fundamental prediction, participants in Study 1 indicated how they would expect other people to react to each of several behaviors. In addition, they rated how they would feel about themselves if they had personally performed each of these actions. The sociometer model predicts that these sets of ratings should be positively correlated.

### Method

#### PARTICIPANTS

Seventy-five male and 75 female undergraduate students served as participants in fulfillment of a course research requirement.

#### PROCEDURE

Participants completed two questionnaires that were embedded in a much longer instrument. Each questionnaire described 16 behaviors that varied in social desirability (e.g., I lost my temper; I cheated on a final exam; I donated blood; I saved a drowning child). One questionnaire asked respondents to indicate on 5-point scales how they thought others would react toward them if they had performed each behavior (1 = *many other people would reject or avoid me*, 5 = *many other people would accept or include me*).

The second questionnaire asked respondents to rate on four 7-point bipolar adjective scales how they personally would feel about themselves if they performed each behavior (i.e., good–bad, proud–ashamed, valuable–worthless, happy–dejected). Ratings on these adjectives were summed to provide an index of self-esteem feelings resulting from each behavior; higher ratings indicated more positive self-feelings.

To minimize the extent to which participants' might try to be consistent in their responses to the two questionnaires, (a) the items were presented in a different random order on each questionnaire, (b) different response formats were used (5-point vs. 7-point scales), and (c) the questionnaires were separated by several unrelated instruments that took approximately 30 minutes to complete. One half of the respondents completed the inclusion–exclusion ratings first, whereas the others completed the self-feelings ratings first.

## Results

Each of the four-item self-feelings scales demonstrated an adequate degree of interitem reliability (Cronbach's alpha was greater than .70 for all 16 behaviors). Also, considerable agreement was obtained across participants regarding the relative orderings of the 16 situations. Kendall's coefficient of concordance was .79 for ratings of inclusion–exclusion and .87 for self-reported self-feelings.

The canonical correlation between respondents' ratings of others' reactions (inclusion–exclusion) and their own feelings of resultant self-esteem across all 16 situations was .70. That is, expectations of the degree to which one's behaviors would result in social inclusion–exclusion correlated highly with the impact of those behaviors on feelings of self-esteem.

On an item-by-item basis, the correlations between expectations of social inclusion–exclusion

and state self-esteem across the 16 situations ranged from .14 to .47, with an average of .32. The order of respondents' ratings was virtually identical on the two sets of questions. Thus, the effects of performing the 16 behaviors on self-esteem closely mirrored their effects on others' expected reactions.

## Discussion

Participants' ratings of their self-feelings after performing 16 behaviors mirrored their expectations regarding how others would respond to these behaviors. Across all 16 situations, ratings of others' expected reactions accounted for nearly 50% of the variance in self-feelings. The correlations for each of the 16 situations ranged from small to moderate, but it must be remembered that they were based on single-item measures of unknown reliability. These data are open to alternative explanations but are consistent with the proposition that self-esteem feelings serve as an internal index of the degree to which one's behavior is likely to result in inclusion versus exclusion.

## Study 2: Personal Experiences Involving Reactions to Exclusion

One weakness inherent in Study 1 is that participants responded to hypothetical target behaviors. As a result, some respondents would not have experienced many of these behaviors, either as a participant or as an observer. In the absence of direct experience, respondents may have relied on their personal assumptions about how people would react to such behaviors. To the extent that these assumptions may have been based on their own personal evaluations of the actions, we would obtain a spurious correlation between respondents' ratings of how others would react and their own self-feelings. As a first step in counteracting this alternative interpretation of the findings, Study 2 examined the relationship between exclusion and self-esteem in situations that respondents had actually experienced.

To avoid producing demand characteristics that would focus respondents' attention on inclusion and exclusion specifically, we asked the respondents to write essays describing the last time they experienced situations that involved either positive or negative emotions. They then answered questions concerning their reactions to the occasion they described; embedded in these questions were ratings involving perceived exclusion and self-feelings. We predicted that their ratings of how included versus excluded they felt in the situations they described would correlate highly with their self-esteem feelings in these situations.

## Method

### PARTICIPANTS

Eighty male and 80 female undergraduates enrolled in introductory psychology courses received credit toward a class requirement for their participation.

### PROCEDURE

Participants were randomly assigned to write a paragraph about the last occasion on which they experienced one of four negative emotional responses (i.e., social anxiety, loneliness, jealousy, or depression) or the opposite, positive pole of one of these responses—"feeling particularly at ease in a social situation" (nonanxious), "satisfied about having as many close friends and family as desired" (nonlonely), "particularly secure in a relationship" (nonjealous), or "particularly happy in response to a social situation or relationship" (nondepressed). We felt that writing about interpersonal situations that produced negative and positive affect would lead participants to write about situations that varied in inclusion–exclusion (without cuing participants into the fact that this was the focus of the study ). Each respondent wrote an essay about one of these eight types of experiences.

After completing the paragraph, participants rated how they felt on five 7-point scales intended to measure how included or excluded they felt in the situation (i.e., accepted, excluded, welcomed, rejected, included); higher ratings were associated with greater feelings of social exclusion. A second set of 15 unipolar scales asked respondents how they felt about themselves on the occasion they described (i.e., good, adequate, attractive, inferior, ashamed, bad, socially desirable, popular, likable, proud, worthless, superior, confident, valuable, and competent, each paired with its op-

posite); higher numbers reflected more positive self-feelings.

Participants were also asked to state in a phrase the primary reason why they felt as they did in the situation they described. This phrase was later coded to determine the extent to which it involved factors relevant to inclusion and exclusion (1 = clear evidence of inclusion, 2 = probable inclusion, 3 = unclear or not relevant to inclusion–exclusion, 4 = probable exclusion, 5 = clear evidence of exclusion).

Respondents also rated their emotional reactions on 7-point scales intended to measure anxiety (i.e., relaxed, tense, anxious, calm, nervous), loneliness (i.e., lonely, popular, involved, lonesome, isolated), jealousy (i.e., trusting, jealous, secure, possessive, suspicious), and depression (i.e., cheerful, happy, sad, depressed, gloomy).

## Results

Cronbach's alpha for the measure of perceived exclusion was .94, and alpha for the index of self-feelings was .95. The Pearson product–moment correlation between ratings of perceived exclusion and self-feelings was calculated separately for participants who wrote each of the kinds of essays ( i.e., social anxiety, loneliness, jealousy, and depression). As can be seen in Table 5.1, their ratings of how excluded they felt in the situation correlated highly with how they felt about themselves in that situation ($-.68 < rs < -.92$, $ps < .001$). In addition, their attributions for their feelings clearly reflected the effect of exclusion. Attributions relevant to exclusion, coded from answers to the open-ended question, correlated as expected with self-feelings ($-.38 < r < -.68$, $ps < .01$).

Cronbach's alphas for the four affective measures each exceeded .84. Respondents' affective

**TABLE 5.1. Study 2: Correlations Between Situational Self-Feelings and Perceived Exclusion**

| Essay type | Perceived exclusion | Attribution to exclusion |
|---|---|---|
| Social anxiety | −.68** | −.38* |
| Loneliness | −.92** | −.68** |
| Jealousy | −.83** | −.64** |
| Depression | −.80** | −.45* |

*$p < .01$.   **$p < .001$.

ratings (scored so that higher numbers indicated negative affect) also correlated highly with perceived exclusion ($.52 < r < .97$, $ps < .001$) and with attributions to exclusion ($.23 < r < .76$, $ps < .08$). These data show that changes in inclusionary status were accompanied by affective changes as well.

## Discussion

Respondents' retrospective accounts of personal experiences involving positive or negative affect again showed a strong relationship between perceived exclusion and self-feelings. The more excluded respondents reported they felt in each type of situation, the less positively they indicated they felt about themselves in that setting. Importantly, in each instance, the magnitude of the correlation approached the reliability of the scales. For all practical purposes, self-feelings were a proxy for perceived exclusion.

Furthermore, their reports of why they felt as they did corroborated this finding. Attributions that invoked interpersonal exclusion as an explanation correlated with participants' self-feelings in each type of situation.

## Study 3: State Self-Esteem in Reaction to Exclusion From a Group

The first two studies showed clearly that self-esteem feelings are strongly tied to perceived social exclusion. However, the correlational nature of both of these studies leaves open alternative explanations other than that perceived exclusion causes self-esteem to decrease. In particular, both studies are open to the explanation that people who evaluate themselves positively may assume that others will like and accept them, whereas those with lower self-esteem are primed to perceive others' behaviors as rejecting (Alloy, 1988; Beck. 1967).

To directly examine the causal effects of exclusion on self-esteem, we experimentally manipulated social inclusion–exclusion in a third study. In this experiment, respondents were informed that they were either included or excluded from a laboratory work group. In addition, respondents were told that this selection was based either on a random procedure or on the preferences of other group members. According to the sociometer hypothesis,

when the selection is based on others' preferences, and thus reflects personally on the individual, respondents should demonstrate increased self-esteem when they are included and decreased self-esteem when they are excluded, compared with random inclusion and exclusion.

## Method

### PARTICIPANTS

One hundred twelve male and female undergraduates recruited from introductory psychology courses served as participants and received required credit for their participation.

### PROCEDURE

Five respondents participated in each experimental session, but they reported to separate locations and were brought individually to separate cubicles in the same laboratory to limit interaction among them throughout the study. (Data from 3 respondents were discarded to create equal cell sizes.)

Respondents were told that the study involved group and individual decision making. To begin, participants completed a brief "information exchange questionnaire" that they were told would be shown to the other 4 participants. This questionnaire asked them to rate themselves on thirteen 7-point scales (e.g., open–closed, tense–relaxed, athletic–nonathletic) and to write two short essays on "what it means to be me" and "the kind of person I would most like to be." These questions were designed to provide participants with information that would provide the basis for their subsequent evaluations of one another. After they finished, the researcher circulated each participant's questionnaire to all of the other participants.

After viewing the other participants' responses, each participant completed a form on which he or she rated the other 4 respondents. They also indicated which 2 of the other participants they would most want to work with and which 2 could be most relied on in time of trouble, and they rank ordered the other participants in terms of who they would most want to work with later in the study.

After taking time to ostensibly collate respondents' ratings of one another, the researcher distributed sheets that made task assignments. First, respondents were told that 3 of the 5 participants would work together on the decision-making problems as a group and that the other 2 participants would work on the same problems individually. They were then told that (a) they either would work as a member of the 3-person group (included condition) or would work alone (excluded condition) and (b) this selection was based either on the other members' preferences (based on the rating sheets that respondents completed earlier) or on a random procedure. (The random procedure was justified by noting that the researcher wanted to assign participants to groups irrespective of their preferences.) Thus, the experimental design was a 2 (included in vs. excluded from the group) × 2 (assignment based on others' preferences or random procedure) randomized factorial.

Respondents then completed a questionnaire that assessed their reactions and rated how they currently felt about themselves on twelve 7-point bipolar adjective scales. The adjectives, which were drawn from McFarland and Ross's (1982) low and high self-esteem feelings factors, were as follows: good, competent, proud, adequate, useful, superior, smart, confident, valuable, important, effective, and satisfied, each paired with its opposite. On half of the items, the positive pole was on the left end of the scale, and on half it was on the right. Participants also rated how excluded they felt on three 7-point scales (i.e., included–excluded, rejected–accepted, welcomed–avoided).

Respondents were also asked to rate the other respondents (as a group) on seven 7-point scales (i.e., good, competent, adequate, useful, smart, valuable, and likable, each paired with its opposite) and to indicate how much they had wanted to be selected for the 3-person group.

Finally, manipulation check questions asked (a) how the assignments to the experimental tasks were made and (b) whether the participant was assigned to work alone or with the group. Respondents were then fully debriefed, and the rationale for the study and all deceptions were explained.

## Results

### MANIPULATION CHECKS

All but 3 of the 112 participants accurately reported whether they were assigned to work with the 3-person group or alone. Thus, the manipulation of task assignment was apparently effective.

Twelve participants incorrectly answered the question that asked how assignments to the group were made. Examination of the pattern of errors revealed a roughly equal number of errors across

conditions. Analyses conducted with and without these 12 participants did not produce different findings.

### SELF-FEELINGS

Cronbach's alpha for the self-feelings scale was .84. A 2 × 2 × 2 (Inclusion–Exclusion × Mode of Assignment × Gender) analysis of variance (ANOVA) performed on the mean of participants' self-ratings revealed a significant main effect of inclusion–exclusion, $F(1, 104) = 9.36, p < .01$, that was qualified by a significant Inclusion–Exclusion x Mode of Assignment interaction, $F(1, 104) = 9.60, p < .01$. Tests of simple main effects showed that inclusion–exclusion affected participants' self-esteem feelings only if it was attributable to acceptance or rejection by the group, $F(1, 104) = 18.55, p < .05$ (see Table 5.2).

Furthermore, the pattern of data suggests that this effect was attributable to the effects of exclusion rather than inclusion. Whereas participants felt no better about themselves when the group included them than when they were included randomly, $F(1, 104) = 1.42, p > .20$, respondents who thought they were excluded on the basis of the group's preferences rated themselves significantly more negatively than those who believed they had been randomly excluded, $F(1, 104) = 10.00, p < .01$.

A main effect of participant sex, $F(1, 104) = 4.01, p < .05$, and an Inclusion–Exclusion × Sex interaction were also obtained on participants' self-ratings, $F(1, 104) = 6.63, p < .01$. Tests of simple effects revealed that, although men ($M = 5.6$) and women ($M = 5.6$) rated themselves identically when they were included in the group, women ($M = 4.8$) rated themselves significantly less positively than did men ($M = 5.5$) following exclusion ($p < .05$). Interestingly, this effect was not qualified by mode of assignment. Finally, participants' feelings about themselves correlated strongly with their feelings of being excluded ($r = -.75, p < .001$).

### RATINGS OF THE OTHER PARTICIPANTS

Ratings of the other 4 respondents also showed a main effect of inclusion–exclusion, $F(1, 104) = 14.18$, which was qualified by the two-way Inclusion–Exclusion × Mode of Assignment interaction, $F(1, 104) = 7.96, ps < .01$. As shown in the second line of Table 5.2, respondents rated one another significantly less positively when they believed

**TABLE 5.2. Study 3: Effects of Exclusion and Mode of Assignment**

| | Mode of assignment | | | |
| | Random | | Group choice | |
| Variable | Included | Excluded | Included | Excluded |
|---|---|---|---|---|
| Self-feelings | 5.5 | 5.5$_a$ | 5.7$_b$ | 4.8$_{ab}$ |
| Ratings of other participants | 5.6 | 5.5$_a$ | 5.9$_b$ | 4.9$_{ab}$ |
| Desire to be included | 5.1 | 5.6 | 6.5$_a$ | 4.9$_b$ |

*Note.* Means in a single row tht share a common subscript differ significantly by tests of simple main effects, $p < .05$.

they had been excluded by the group rather than when the group had included them, $F(1, 104) = 23.41$, $p < .001$. When the assignment was random, participants' ratings of one another were unaffected by whether they were assigned to work with the group, $F(1, 104) = 0.47$, $p > .40$. In addition, participants derogated one another more when exclusion was based on group members' preferences rather than on a random selection procedure, $F(1, 104) = 8.67$, $p < .01$. The more excluded respondents felt, the more negatively they rated the other participants ($r = -.52$, $p < .001$).

RETROSPECTIVE INCLUSION MOTIVATION

An Inclusion–Exclusion × Mode of Assignment interaction was also obtained on the item that asked respondents, "How much did you want to be selected for the 3-person 'central' group?," although the effect just failed to reach the .05 level of significance, $F(1, 104) = 3.61$, $p < .06$. As can be seen in the third line of Table 5.2, a sour-grapes effect was obtained: Participants who thought the group had included them retrospectively indicated a greater desire to be included than those who thought the group had excluded them, $F(1, 104) = 4.74$, $p < .03$. The simple effect of inclusion–exclusion was not significant when selection was ostensibly random, $F(1, 104) = 0.24$, $p > .60$.

Discussion

The central conclusion to be drawn from the findings of Study 3 is that exclusion that reflects rejection by others produces strong effects on self-feelings and social perceptions. Compared with respondents who thought their peers had selected them to participate in the group, those who thought the group had excluded them rated themselves more negatively, more strongly derogated the other

group members, and claimed less interest in being a member of the group. By contrast, inclusion and exclusion had no discernible effect on respondents' responses when they were based on a random selection procedure. Furthermore, the data showed that exclusion had a stronger effect in lowering respondents' self-feelings than inclusion had in raising them.

These data suggest that exclusion that implies disapproval or rejection results in lowered self-esteem even in contexts in which social inclusion has no identifiable implications for people's well-being (e.g., survival, assistance, or comfort). In fact, given the experimental situation, we were surprised that respondents responded as strongly as they did to being excluded by the group. Participants had neither a history of previous experience nor expectations of future interaction (beyond this study) with other group members: they did not even know who the other members were. In addition, it was not clear that working on the decision-making problems with the group was in any way more desirable than working alone, and the basis on which respondents were excluded was limited and superficial. Yet, those who were rejected by the group suffered a decrease in state self-esteem. These findings attest to the strength of people's desire to avoid disapproval and rejection in the absence of any tangible benefits of being accepted.

They may also shed light on people's motivation to maintain and foster their connections to seemingly meaningless groups. As research using the minimal in-group paradigm shows, even when people are "members" of a group in name only, they come to identify with the group and its members (e.g., Tajfel, 1981). Given that the motivation toward social inclusion and away from social exclusion is potent, maintained by an inner sociometer that monitors inclusionary status, even a minimal sense of "belongingness" may be rewarding.

The effects of exclusion on ratings of the other group members comes as no surprise, but it deserves attention from the perspective of the sociometer hypothesis. Traditional approaches to self-esteem would explain that, by derogating those who rejected them, individuals could minimize the importance or validity of the others' evaluations and thereby protect their own self-esteem. People's self-esteem is less likely to be damaged if they can convince themselves that those who rejected them were socially undesirable people they did not want to associate with anyway. We have no complaints with this explanation as far as it goes. Given that perceived exclusion is anxiety producing, once permanent rejection is detected, people may indeed try to reduce their distress through cognitive means, such as by derogating the rejector or minimizing the importance of acceptance.

However, the sociometer model suggests two additional explanations. First, the derogation of sources of rejection may reflect an interpersonal tactic aimed at others who are present. Being rejected calls one's social acceptability into question in the eyes of others who are privy to the rejection. By lambasting the rejector, the individual may lead others to ignore or discount the rejection. (If a person who was recently rejected by a romantic partner praises the ex-partner's judgment and social qualities, new acquaintances may conclude that such a wonderful person had good reasons for dumping him or her.) Other evidence on self-serving reactions to failure and negative evaluation shows that such reactions are sometimes for the benefit of others (Leary & Forsyth, 1987; Schlenker, 1980). In Study 3, rejected participants might have derogated the other group members to convince the researcher that they did not deserve to be excluded.

Second, from a practical standpoint, continuing to seek inclusion by those who have excluded the individual is not an optimal strategy. When rejection is permanent and irreversible, as it was in this study, the person should turn his or her attention away from the rejectors and toward those who may be more accepting. Focusing on the desirability of being included by a rejecting group may actually impede the person's general success in establishing and maintaining connections with other people. Thus, derogating the group and minimizing the importance of its acceptance may be adaptive in terms of facilitating one's ability to

move on to other groups and relationships. All three of these processes operate to produce the derogation effect obtained here, and we have no way to choose among them. However, they provide a ripe source of hypotheses for future research.

Overall, male and female respondents reacted similarly to the experimental manipulations. The only gender difference obtained showed that women who were excluded rated themselves less positively than did men irrespective of whether they were excluded randomly or because of other respondents' preferences. Although obtained on only a single measure, this finding suggests that women may be more sensitive than men to cues that connote exclusion, possibly because typical patterns of socialization in American culture lead them to be more attuned to others' reactions (Snodgrass, 1985) or more motivated to emphasize communal relationships (Eagly & Wood, 1991). If, indeed, this is a general finding, research is needed to explore the sources of gender differences in reactions to exclusion.

## Study 4: Interpersonal Exclusion and Self-Esteem Feelings

Study 3 provided concrete evidence that social exclusion results in lowered self-esteem, at least when the exclusion was based on others' personal evaluations and preferences, and this effect occurred even when exclusion has no notable implications for the individual. The purpose of Study 4 was to conceptually replicate and extend these findings using a somewhat different paradigm and different measures.

In this experiment, participants provided information about themselves via an intercom to an anonymous participant in another room. They then received feedback from the other participant that connoted either inclusion and acceptance or exclusion and rejection, or else they received no feedback relevant to inclusion–exclusion. Participants then rated their feelings about themselves on a questionnaire that they believed would be seen by either the same participant who had listened to them previously (and who, in two conditions, had ostensibly provided his or her feedback) or to a new participant.

This latter manipulation was included to examine the possibility that the effects of inclusion–exclusion on self-ratings were mediated by self-presentational rather than self-esteem processes. If respondents know their self-ratings will be seen by someone who is aware of the fact they were previously included or excluded, they may use their self-ratings as a self-presentational strategy in an attempt to support or counteract the prior effects of inclusion or exclusion on their social image. This possibility would be detected if participants' self-ratings after inclusion or exclusion differed as a function of who would be seeing their ratings.

## Method

### PARTICIPANTS

Forty-five male and 45 female undergraduates served as subjects in return for required credit in an introductory psychology course.

### PRETESTING

As part of a large mass testing procedure conducted early in the semester, all participants rated themselves on 12 evaluatively laden adjectives: cheerful, absent-minded, honest, clear thinking, deceitful, friendly, forgetful, dependable, arrogant, intelligent, prejudiced, and irresponsible. Ratings were done on 12-point scales with five equally spaced scale labels (not at all, slightly, moderately, very, and extremely ). These ratings were used as a pretest measure of self-feelings.

### EXPERIMENTAL SESSION

Each session used a mixed-sex pair of participants who went to different locations to maintain anonymity. They were informed that the study was concerned with how people form impressions of others. They would be asked to talk into a microphone about themselves while another respondent of the other sex listened. After the participant signed an informed consent form, the researcher gave each participant a personal information sheet ostensibly completed by the other participant in the session. This information was provided to convince the respondent of the presence of the other respondent and involved innocuous demographic information.

Participants then spoke into a microphone for 5 minutes about topics drawn from a standard list, believing that the other participant was listening. These topics were intended to be moderately disclosing so that the participant would discuss enough personal information for the other person to ostensibly make a personal appraisal. For example, one question asked participants to describe aspects of themselves they liked best and least.

After the 5-minute verbal presentation, participants were randomly assigned to receive feedback indicating that the other person either liked, accepted, and wanted to interact with them (inclusion condition); to receive feedback indicating that the other participant did not particularly like, accept, or want to interact with them (exclusion condition); or to receive no feedback from the other participant (no-feedback condition). In the inclusion and exclusion conditions, the feedback sheet participants received contained ratings on a number of dimensions that connoted inclusion and exclusion. For example, one question asked whether the listener would want to continue a conversation with the participant, and another asked whether the listener would want to introduce the participant to a friend. In response to each question, the other participant had ostensibly marked "yes," "no," or "unsure."

It should be noted that although respondents in the inclusion condition received predominately accepting feedback (with a couple of "unsure" responses marked), those in the exclusion condition received predominately "unsure" responses (with a couple of rejecting answers) to minimize the aversiveness of the manipulation. We felt that uncertain and ambivalent responses would connote sufficient rejection for purposes of the study. To preserve the illusion that the researcher was ignorant of the ratings, this feedback was provided in an envelope, and participants were told not to read the ratings until the researcher left the room.

After reading the feedback, participants were asked to complete a questionnaire about themselves that would ostensibly be shown to either the participant who had heard and evaluated them or to another participant. Participants rated themselves on the same 12 self-relevant adjectives they had provided during mass testing several weeks earlier using 12-point scales.

On a questionnaire that respondents were told only the researcher would see, they indicated the degree to which the other respondents' perceptions of them were accurate (1 = *not at all,* 12 = *extremely*). To assess the effectiveness of the feedback manipulation, they also indicated how positively or negatively the other respondent regarded them (1 = *extremely negative,* 12 = *extremely posi-*

*tive*). After completing the experimental questionnaires, participants were fully debriefed, with all deceptions explained in detail.

## Results

### MANIPULATION CHECK

An ANOVA conducted on participants' ratings of the feedback they received revealed that the manipulation of inclusion–exclusion was highly successful, $F(1, 86) = 8.76$, $p < .01$. A Tukey's test revealed that participants who received positive feedback reported that they were perceived most positively ($M = 11.4$), followed by participants receiving no feedback ($M = 7.9$) and those who received rejecting feedback ($M = 2.4$; all $ps < .05$).

### SELF-FEELINGS

Examination of the interitem reliability of the 12 self-ratings revealed that one item (intelligent) had an unacceptably low item–total correlation. After this item was dropped, Cronbach's alpha coefficient for the remaining 11 items was .79.

A 3 (feedback: acceptance, rejection, none) × 2 (target: same vs. other respondent) ANOVA was conducted on the sum of the 11 self-ratings after reverse scoring the negatively worded items. This revealed only a significant main effect of feedback, $F(2, 90) = 4.93$, $p < .01$. Inspection of condition means revealed that respondents receiving accepting feedback subsequently rated themselves more positively ($M = 106.5$) than did those who received no feedback ($M = 103.2$) and rejecting feedback ($M = 104.4$).

To explore the extent to which respondents' self-esteem deviated from their "typical" self-feelings following inclusion and exclusion, difference scores were calculated between the sum of the self-ratings obtained during mass testing and the sum of the self-ratings obtained during the experiment itself. A 3 × 2 ANOVA indicated a significant main effect of feedback, $F(2, 91) = 5.95$, $p < .01$. A Tukey's test revealed that rejected participants' self-feelings were significantly more negative relative to the ratings they gave during mass testing (mean difference = –5.9) compared with accepted participants (mean difference = 2.0, $p < .05$). Participants who received no feedback did not differ from the other two groups (mean difference = –1.4, $ps > .05$).

The *t* tests comparing the mean difference score in each feedback condition with a score of zero (which would reflect "no change" from mass testing) indicated that although participants who were rejected rated themselves significantly more negatively than they rated themselves during mass testing, $t(32) = 3.64$, $p < .05$, the ratings of accepted and no-feedback participants did not differ from their mass testing ratings ($ps > .10$). Thus, rejection significantly lowered self-feelings, but acceptance did not significantly raise them.

### ACCURACY RATINGS

Respondents' ratings of the accuracy of the other respondents' perceptions of them were also significantly affected by the feedback they received, $F(2, 86) = 4.60$, $p < .01$. A Tukey's test showed that accepted respondents believed the other respondent to be significantly more accurate ($M = 8.2$) compared with respondents who were rejected ($M = 3.6$) and those who received no feedback ($M = 5.5$, $ps < .05$). However, the rejected and no-feedback conditions did not differ significantly ($p > .05$).

## Discussion

The results of Study 4 provide a conceptual replication of the primary findings of Study 3 using a different paradigm, cover story, and measures: Those who were accepted on the basis of personal reasons subsequently felt more positively about themselves than did those who were excluded. Furthermore, as in Study 3, exclusion had a notably stronger effect in lowering participants' self-esteem than inclusion had in enhancing their self-feelings. As we discuss in the General Discussion section, these findings suggest that the self-esteem system may be more sensitive to decrements than increments in inclusionary status.

The effects of feedback on self-feelings described earlier were obtained even though participants in the exclusion condition explicitly dismissed the feedback. Respondents who were rejected rated the other person's perceptions as highly inaccurate, but their feelings about themselves were affected nonetheless. This finding suggests that people need not view exclusion as warranted in order for it to affect self-esteem. Although it stands to reason that self-esteem would suffer when people are rejected because of their actual transgressions and shortcomings, the fact that self-esteem fell even when respondents dismissed the feedback as inaccurate provides further support that self-esteem is sensitive to others' reactions per se.

The fact that the identity of the target for whom respondents rated themselves did not moderate the effects of exclusion on self-feelings suggests that the findings of Studies 3 and 4 are unlikely to be attributable to participants' attempts to convey certain impressions of themselves to those who had accepted or rejected them. Although it is impossible to prove the null hypothesis, the failure to find an effect of target at least renders such an interpretation implausible.

## Study 5: Individual Differences in Self-Esteem

In each of the first four studies, we were interested in the effects of social inclusion and exclusion on people's state self-esteem in a given social setting. However, a corollary of the sociometer model is that individual differences in trait self-esteem should be related to *individual differences* in the extent to which people generally feel that they are socially included versus excluded. On one hand, a history of real or perceived exclusion may ultimately result in lowered trait self-esteem (Harter, 1993; Shrauger & Schoeneman, 1979). Furthermore, once formed, self-esteem may color people's perceptions of others' reactions. People with low self-esteem may be more likely to perceive others' reactions as rejecting than people with high self-esteem.

### Method

#### PARTICIPANTS

Two hundred twenty male and female undergraduates participated in the study to fulfill a requirement for their introductory psychology course.

#### PERCEIVED INCLUSIONARY STATUS

A scale to measure individual differences in perceived inclusionary status was constructed and pilot tested on a sample of 150 respondents. This measure consisted of nine items that assessed the extent to which individuals feel they are generally included versus excluded by others. Examples in-

cluded, "People often seek out my company," "I often feel like an outsider in social gatherings," and "If I want to socialize with my friends, I am generally the one who must seek them out." Cronbach's alpha was .77 in pilot testing. Although unpublished, this scale has demonstrated usefulness in previous research (Miller, 1995).

#### SELF-ESTEEM

General self-esteem was measured with two scales. Rosenberg's (1965) Self-Esteem Scale is a 10-item scale that has high internal consistency ($\alpha = .85$) and test–retest reliability (.85) and is perhaps the most widely used measure of dispositional self-esteem.

In a factor analysis of self-relevant mood items, McFarland and Ross (1982) found that the following items loaded on a self-esteem feelings factor: proud, competent, confident, smart, resourceful, effective, efficient, inadequate, incompetent, stupid, worthless, and shameful. Thus, the sum of these items (after reverse scoring negatively worded items) was used as a second measure of self-esteem.

#### PROCEDURE

Each of the scales just described was administered during two separate sessions. Regardless of the original response format, participants answered all items on 5-point scales.

### Results

Cronbach's alpha was acceptable for all three measures: perceived inclusionary status (.80), Rosenberg self-esteem (.88), and McFarland and Ross self-feelings scale (.91). The two measures of self-esteem correlated .75.

The Pearson product–moment correlation between perceived exclusionary status and Rosenberg self-esteem scores was $-.55$ ($p < .001$). The correlation between perceived exclusionary status and the McFarland and Ross measure of self-feelings was $-.51$ ($p < .001$).

### Discussion

As predicted by the sociometer model, the degree to which people think they are generally excluded versus included correlated moderately with two different measures of trait self-esteem. Whereas Rosenberg's (1965) measure asks respondents to indicate their agreement or disagreement with 10 statements about their self-perceived worth, McFarland and Ross's (1982) items consist of self-descriptive adjectives. Although the correlational nature of the data does not rule out the possibility that self-esteem feelings mediate perceptions of inclusion rather than vice versa, the data further support the hypothesized link between perceived exclusion and self-esteem.

To extend our analogy of a fuel gauge, trait self-esteem may be conceptualized as the typical or average resting position of the "indicator needle" on the person's sociometer. This position reflects the person's perception of his or her inclusionary status in the absence of explicit cues connoting inclusion or exclusion. As noted, the relationship between perceived exclusion and trait self-esteem is probably reciprocal. A history of exclusion may lead to low trait self-esteem, and having low trait self-esteem predisposes the person to perceive rejection more readily. Because their sociometers are calibrated differently, people with very low trait self-esteem may perceive others as rejecting most of the time, whereas those with higher self-esteem generally feel they are being accepted.

## General Discussion

Taken together, these five studies provide converging evidence for the hypothesized relationship between perceived social exclusion and self-esteem. In Study 1, we found that participants' self-feelings varied with how they thought others would react to various behaviors vis à vis inclusion–exclusion. Study 2 showed that respondents' retrospective reports of how they felt about themselves in recent social encounters correlated highly with how included versus excluded they felt in those situations. Studies 3 and 4 used experimental designs to demonstrate that exclusion by other people results in lower state self-esteem than inclusion. Study 5 showed that the degree to which people generally believe that others include versus exclude them correlated negatively with two different measures of trait self-esteem. Although alternative explanations may be offered for some of these findings, we believe that the consistency of our findings across widely disparate studies,

using different paradigms and measures of self-feelings, provides converging support for the hypothesized link between perceived social exclusion and self-esteem.

Of course, an empirical demonstration of this relationship does not necessarily indicate that the function of the self-esteem system is to monitor social exclusion; such a functional explanation is difficult to test directly. Even so, we believe that the sociometer model provides a parsimonious explanation of both our results and previous findings. State self-esteem appears to function as a subjective marker that reflects, in summary fashion, the individual's social standing in a particular social setting and thus serves to apprise the individual of changes in his or her inclusionary status (Leary, 1990; Leary & Downs, 1995). In essence, one function of self-esteem may be to provide a relatively fast and automatic assessment of others' reactions vis-à-vis inclusion and exclusion. Such an ongoing inclusion assessment mechanism would enhance the individual's likelihood of establishing and maintaining supportive social relationships and of avoiding social exclusion (Baumeister & Tice, 1990).

From the earliest days of psychology and sociology, theorists interested in the self have suggested that people's self-images, as well as their self-esteem, are based heavily on their perceptions of the evaluative reactions of other people. In particular, symbolic interactionists have long maintained that one's self-perceptions reflect others' perceptions of and reactions to the individual (Cooley, 1902; Mead, 1932; see Shrauger & Schoeneman, 1979). The sociometer perspective shows clearly why this is the case. The self-esteem system serves its primary function only if it is sensitive to others' reactions.

In everyday life, inclusion–exclusion and interpersonal evaluations are highly confounded. We tend to associate with those we regard positively while avoiding those we regard negatively. To the extent that social evaluations are closely related to inclusion and exclusion (Baumeister & Tice, 1990), people's self-esteem is often affected by evaluative feedback. Yet, we believe that the degree to which others appear to include versus exclude the individual, rather than the nature of others' evaluations per se, is the most important determinant of self-esteem. Furthermore, we believe that, in behaving in ways that promote self-esteem, people are striving to enhance their inclusionary status rather than to be evaluated positively per se. We find it easy to understand why a potent mechanism to increase inclusion would have evolved among humans but more difficult to understand why a motive to be perceived positively would have developed.

Throughout this article we have alternated between referring to self-esteem as a means of enhancing inclusion and as a means of avoiding exclusion. Although the data on this point are only suggestive, we believe that the sociometer system responds primarily, if not exclusively, to exclusion rather than to inclusion. First, at a conceptual level, most motivation and drive systems, both physiological and psychological, respond to deprivation states rather than to less-than-complete satiation. For example, people are far more motivated to avoid being hungry than they are to remain full. Just as there is little merit in a system that constantly motivated a person to maintain a full stomach, there would be little reason for a psychological system to evolve that pushed a person toward greater and greater inclusion by increasing numbers of people. In fact, the excessive social responsibilities associated with multiple group memberships may be disadvantageous. The sociometer system would serve its purpose if it simply assured that the person maintained sufficient social connections with a relatively small set of personally significant people (Baumeister & Leary, 1995).

Second, in both Study 3 and Study 4, respondents who thought they were excluded showed a decrement in self-esteem, but those who were included showed no corresponding increment. Similarly, previous writers have discussed the asymmetry of positive and negative feedback. Although receiving positive reactions may be mildly pleasant, negative reactions carry far more weight. Not only does a slightly negative reaction have a much greater impact on most people than even a strongly positive one, but a single negative reaction can counteract and undo a plethora of accolades. Although other explanations are possible (e.g., because most interactions range from neutral to positive, positive responses from others lack the saliency and diagnosticity of negative ones), the sociometer hypothesis provides a parsimonious explanation of this pattern. Specifically, our psychological systems are designed to detect and place greater emphasis on reactions that connote exclusion than reactions that connote inclusion.

Kernis and his colleagues have recently shown that people's reactions to esteem-threatening events are moderated not only by their level of self-esteem but by its stability. Some people show little variation in self-esteem across situations and time, whereas other people's self-esteem is exceptionally labile. People with unstable self-esteem, whether low or high, show more extreme emotional and behavioral reactions to events involving negative evaluations by other people and other threats to self-esteem (for a review, see Kernis, 1993). In our view, people with unstable self-esteem essentially have an unstable sociometer that overresponds to cues that connote acceptance and rejection. For such people, minor changes in inclusion or exclusion result in large changes in the sociometer (and self-esteem). In extreme cases of unstable self-esteem, the fluctuations of the sociometer may be only minimally tied to real changes in inclusionary status, much like a faulty gas gauge that registers "full" one minute, "half full" a few minutes later, then "three-quarters full" after that.

Several theorists have conceptualized the self as having at least two distinct facets, which are commonly labeled *public* and *private* (Baumeister, 1986; Buss, 1980; Carver & Scheier, 1981; Fenigstein, 1987; Greenwald & Breckler, 1985; Schlenker, 1985). For example, ego-task analysis theory (Greenwald, 1982; Greenwald & Breckler, 1985) suggests that different aspects of the self are sensitive to different aspects of self-evaluation and perform different "tasks" in the service of protecting the ego. Whereas the public self "is sensitive to the evaluation of others and seeks to win the approval of significant outer audiences" (Greenwald & Breckler, 1985, pp. 132–133), the private self evaluates oneself on the basis of the individual's internalized standards. We concur that, once the self develops in childhood, people are able to evaluate themselves from the perspectives of both themselves and various other people.

However, we propose that this ability to perceive and evaluate oneself from varying perspectives does not necessarily involve the sociometer mechanism that we have described in this article. After all, people are able to evaluate all manner of stimuli, including themselves, and some of their self-judgments are irrelevant to their feelings of self-esteem. As we have argued, the self-esteem system appears specifically designed to detect real or potential changes in the individual's inclusionary status and to elicit emotional and motivational processes in response to threats to one's connections with other people. Some events to which the sociometer responds are "private" ones involving thoughts and feelings that, if known by others, might jeopardize their inclusion in important groups and relationships, whereas other such events are "public" ones that others may easily observe. Even so, the sociometer responds to both private and public events in terms of their potential effects on inclusion–exclusion. Thus, the sociometer and the self-esteem feelings it mediates are responsive to both private and public self-relevant events.

In summary, the self-esteem system appears to function as a sociometer designed to detect possible deleterious changes in people's inclusionary status. Furthermore, rather than serving primarily to maintain one's inner sense of self, the self-esteem motive prompts people to behave in ways that maintain their connections with other people.

## REFERENCES

Adler, A. (1930). *Understanding human nature.* New York: Greenberg.

Ainsworth, M. D. S. (1989). Attachments beyond infancy. *American Psychologist, 44,* 709–716.

Alloy, L. (1988). *Cognitive processes in depression.* New York: Guilford Press.

Allport, G. W. (1937). *Personality: A psychological interpretation.* New York: Holt.

Baldwin, M. W., & Holmes, J. G. (1987). Salient private audiences and awareness of self. *Journal of Personality and Social Psychology, 52,* 1087–1098.

Bandura, A. (1977). Self-efficacy: Toward a unifying theory of behavioral change. *Psychological Review, 84,* 191–215.

Barash, D. P. (1977). *Sociobiology and behavior.* New York: Elsevier.

Baumeister, R. F. (1986). *Public self and private self.* New York: Springer-Verlag.

Baumeister, R. F. (Ed.). (1993). *Self-esteem: The puzzle of low self-regard.* New York: Plenum.

Baumeister, R. F. & Leary, M. R. (1995). The need to belong: Desire for interpersonal attachments as a fundamental human motivation. *Psychological Bulletin, 117,* 497–529.

Baumeister, R. F., & Tice, D. M. (1990). Anxiety and social exclusion. *Journal of Social and Clinical Psychology, 9,* 165–195.

Beck, A. (1967). *Depression: Clinical, experimental, and theoretical aspects.* Philadelphia: University of Pennsylvania Press.

Bednar. R. L., Wells, M. G., & Peterson, S. R. (1989). *Self-esteem: Paradoxes and innovations in clinical theory and practice.* Washington, DC: American Psychological Association.

Blaine, B., & Crocker, J. (1993). Self-esteem and self-serving biases in reactions to positive and negative events: An integrative review. In R. F. Baumeister (Ed.), *Self-esteem:*

*The puzzle of low self-regard* (pp. 55–85). New York: Plenum.

Bowlby, J. (1969). *Attachment and loss: Vol. I. Attachment.* New York: Basic Books.

Brockner, J. (1983). Low self-esteem and behavioral plasticity: Some implications. *Review of Personality and Social Psychology, 4,* 237–271.

Brown, J. D. (1993). Self-esteem and self-evaluations: Feeling is believing. In J. Suls (Ed.), *Psychological perspectives on the self* (Vol. 4, pp. 27–58). Hillsdale, NJ: Erlbaum.

Buss, A. H. (1980). *Self-consciousness and social anxiety.* San Francisco: Freeman.

Carver, C. S., & Scheier, M. F. (1981). *Attention and self-regulation: A control-theory approach to human behavior.* New York: Springer-Verlag.

Cooley, C. H. (1902). *Human nature and the social order.* New York: Scribner.

Coopersmith, S. (1967). *The antecedents of self-esteem.* San Francisco: Freeman.

Crocker, J., Thompson, L., McGraw, K., & Ingerman, C. (1987). Downward comparison, prejudice, and evaluations of others: Effects of self-esteem and threat. *Journal of Personality and Social Psychology, 52,* 907–916.

Cutrona, C. E. (1982). Transition to college: Loneliness and the process of social adjustment. In L. A. Peplau & D. Perlman (Eds.), *Loneliness: A sourcebook of current theory, research, and therapy* (pp. 291–309). New York: Wiley.

Eagly, A. H., & Wood, W. (1991). Explaining sex differences in social behavior: A meta-analytic perspective. *Personality and Social Psychology Bulletin, 17,* 306–315.

Epstein, S. (1973). The self-concept revisited: Or a theory of a theory. *American Psychologist, 28,* 404–416.

Fenigstein, A. (1987). On the nature of public and private self-consciousness. *Journal of Personality, 55,* 543–554.

Goswick, R. A., & Jones, W. H. (1981). Loneliness, self-concept, and adjustment. *Journal of Psychology, 107,* 237–240.

Greenberg, J., Pyszczynski, T., & Solomon, S. (1986). The causes and consequences of a need for self-esteem: A terror management theory. In R. F. Baumeister (Ed.). *Public self and private self* (pp. 189–207). New York: Springer-Verlag.

Greenberg, J., Solomon, S., Pyszczynski, T., Rosenblatt, A., Burling, J., Lyon, D., Simon, L., & Pinel, E. (1992). Why do people need self-esteem? Converging evidence that self-esteem serves an anxiety buffering function. *Journal of Personality and Social Psychology, 63,* 913–922.

Greenwald, A. G. (1980). The totalitarian ego: Fabrication and revision of personal history. *American Psychologist, 35,* 603–613.

Greenwald, A. G. (1982). Ego task analysis: An integration of research on ego-involvement and awareness. In A. H. Hastorf & A. M. Isen (Eds.), *Cognitive social psychology* (pp. 109–147). New York: Elsevier.

Greenwald, A. G., & Breckler, S. (1985). To whom is the self presented? In B. R. Schlenker (Ed.), *The self and social life* (pp. 126–145). New York: McGraw-Hill.

Harter, S. (1993). Causes and consequences of low self-esteem in children and adolescents. In R. F. Baumeister (Ed.), *Self-esteem: The puzzle of low self-regard* (pp. 87–116). New York: Plenum.

Harter, S., & Marold, D. B. (1991). A model of the determinants and mediational role of self-worth: Implications for adolescent depression and suicidal ideation. In G. Goethals

& J. Strauss (Eds.), *The self: An interdisciplinary approach.* New York: Springer-Verlag.

Heatherton, T. F., & Ambady, N. (1993). Self-esteem, self-prediction, and living up to commitments. In R. F. Baumeister (Ed.), *Self-esteem: The puzzle of low self-regard* (pp. 131–145). New York: Plenum.

Heatherton, T. F., & Polivy, J. (1991). Development and validation of a scale for measuring state self-esteem. *Journal of Personality and Social Psychology, 60,* 895–910.

Hogan, R. (1982). A socioanalytic theory of personality. In M. Page (Ed.), *Nebraska Symposium on Motivation* (pp. 55–89). Lincoln: University of Nebraska Press.

Hogan, R., Jones, W. H., & Cheek, J. M. (1985). Socioanalytic theory: An alternative to armadillo psychology. In B. R. Schlenker (Ed.), *The self and social life* (pp. 175–198). New York: McGraw-Hill.

Horney, K. (1937). *The neurotic personality of our time.* New York: Norton.

James, W. (1890). *Principles of psychology.* New York: Dover.

Jones, E. E., & Berglas, S. (1978). Control of attributions about the self through self-handicapping strategies: The appeal of alcohol and the role of underachievement. *Personality and Social Psychology Bulletin, 4,* 200–206.

Jones, S. C. (1973). Self- and interpersonal evaluations: Esteem theories versus consistency theories. *Psychological Bulletin, 79,* 185–199.

Kernis. M. (1993). The roles of stability and level of self-esteem in psychological functioning. In R. F. Baumeister (Ed.), *Self-esteem: The puzzle of low self-regard* (pp. 167–182). New York: Plenum.

Kernis, M. (1995). *Efficacy, agency, and self-esteem.* New York: Plenum.

Leary, M. R. (1983). *Understanding social anxiety: Social personality and clinical perspectives.* Newbury Park, CA: Sage.

Leary, M. R. (1990). Responses to social exclusion: Social anxiety, jealousy, loneliness, depression, and low self-esteem. *Journal of Social and Clinical Psychology, 9,* 221–229.

Leary, M. R., & Downs, D. (1995). Interpersonal functions of the self-esteem motive: The self-esteem system as a sociometer. In M. Kernis (Ed.), *Efficacy, agency, and self-esteem.* New York: Plenum.

Leary, M. R., & Forsyth, D. R. (1987). Attributions of responsibility for collective endeavors. In C. Hendrick (Ed.), *Group processes* (pp. 167–188). Newbury Park, CA: Sage.

Leary, M. R., & Kowalski, R. M. (1995). *Butterflies, blushes, and bashfulness: Social anxiety and interpersonal behavior.* New York: Guilford.

Maslow, A. H. (1968). *Motivation and personality.* New York: Harper & Row.

McFarland, C., & Ross, M. (1982). Impact of causal attributions on affective reactions to success and failure. *Journal of Personality and Social Psychology, 43,* 937–946.

McFarlin, D. B., Baumeister, R. F., & Blascovich, J. (1984). On knowing when to quit: Task failure, self-esteem, advice, and nonproductive persistence. *Journal of Personality, 52,* 138–155.

Mead. G. H. (1932). *Mind, self, and society.* Chicago: University of Chicago Press.

Miller, R. S. (1995). On the nature of embarrassability: Shyness, social-evaluation, and social skill. *Journal of Personality, 63,* 315–339.

Moreland, R., & Levine, J. (1989). Newcomers and oldtimers in small groups. In P. Paulus (Ed.), *Psychology of group influence* (Vol. 2, pp. 143–186). Hillsdale, NJ: Erlbaum.

Perez, R. C. (1973). The effect of experimentally-induced failure, self-esteem, and sex on cognitive differentiation. *Journal of Abnormal Psychology, 81,* 74–79.

Rogers, C. (1959). A theory of therapy, personality and interpersonal relationships, as developed in the client-centered framework. In S. Koch (Ed.), *Psychology: A study of a science* (Vol. 3, pp. 184–256). New York: McGraw-Hill.

Rosenberg, M. (1965). *Society and the adolescent self-image.* Princeton, NJ: Princeton University Press.

Scheff, T. J., Retzinger, S. M., & Ryan, M. T. (1989). Crime, violence, and self-esteem: Review and proposals. In A. M. Mecca, N. J. Smelser, & J. Vasconcellos (Eds.), *The social importance of self-esteem* (pp. 165–199). Berkeley: University of California Press.

Schlenker, B. R. (1980). *Impression management.* Monterey, CA: Brooks/Cole.

Schlenker, B. R. (1985). Identity and self-identification. In B. R. Schlenker (Ed.), *The self social life* (pp. 65–99). New York: McGraw-Hill.

Schlenker, B. R., & Leary, M. R. (1982). Social anxiety and self-presentation: A conceptualization and model. *Psychological Bulletin, 92,* 641–669.

Shrauger, J. S., & Schoeneman, T. J. (1979). Symbolic interactionist view of self-concept: Through the looking glass darkly. *Psychological Bulletin, 86,* 549–573.

Shrauger, J. S., & Sorman, P. B. (1977). Self-evaluations, initial success and failure, and improvement as determinants of persistence. *Journal of Consulting and Clinical Psychology, 45,* 784–795.

Snodgrass, S. E. (1985). Women's intuition: The effect of subordinate role on interpersonal sensitivity. *Journal of Personality and Social Psychology, 49,* 146–155.

Spivey, E. (1989). *Social exclusion as a common factor in social anxiety, loneliness, jealousy, and social depression: Testing an integrative model.* Unpublished master's thesis, Wake Forest University, Winston-Salem, NC.

Steele, C. M. (1988). The psychology of self-affirmation: Sustaining the integrity of the self. *Advances in Experimental Social Psychology, 21,* 261–302.

Tajfel, H. (1981). *Human groups and social categories.* Cambridge, England: Cambridge University Press.

Taylor S. E., & Brown, J. D. (1988). Illusion and well-being: A social psychological perspective on mental health. *Psychological Bulletin, 103,* 193–210.

Tedeschi, J. T., & Norman, N. (1985). Social power, self-presentation, and the self. In B. R. Schlenker (Ed.), *The self and social life* (pp. 293–322). New York: McGraw-Hill.

White, G. L. (1981). Some correlates of romantic jealousy. *Journal of Personality, 49,* 129–147.

Wills, T. A. (1981). Downward comparison principles in social psychology. *Psychological Bulletin, 90,* 245–271.

# Why Do People Need Self-Esteem? Converging Evidence That Self-Esteem Serves an Anxiety-Buffering Function

Jeff Greenberg • University of Arizona

Sheldon Solomon • Skidmore College

Tom Pyszczynski • University of Colorado at Colorado Springs

Abraham Rosenblatt • University of California, San Francisco

John Burling • University of Montevallo

Deborah Lyon • University of Arizona

Linda Simon • University of Arizona

Elizabeth Pinel • University of Colorado at Colorado Springs

Three studies were conducted to assess the proposition that self-esteem serves an anxiety-buffering function. In Study 1, it was hypothesized that raising self-esteem would reduce anxiety in response to vivid images of death. In support of this hypothesis, subjects who received positive personality feedback reported less anxiety in response to a video about death than did neutral feedback subjects. In Studies 2 and 3, it was hypothesized that increasing self-esteem would reduce anxiety among individuals anticipating painful shock. Consistent with this hypothesis, both success and positive personality feedback reduced subjects' physiological arousal in response to subsequent threat of shock. Thus, converging evidence of an anxiety-buffering function of self-esteem was obtained.

A diverse array of classic and contemporary psychological theories converge on the notion that people have a strong and pervasive need for self-esteem (e.g., Allport, 1961; Becker, 1962, 1973; Horney, 1937; Rogers, 1959; Snyder, Stephan, & Rosenfield, 1976; Steele, 1988; Tesser & Campbell, 1983). From William James's *Principles of Psychology* to the most recent issues of scholarly journals, one can find a multitude of conceptual analyses and empirical studies in which a need for self-esteem has been used to explain various forms of behavior. Indeed, Scheff (1990) has noted that there are over 10,000 published studies concerning self-esteem and its correlates.

Given this consensus that self-esteem is a vital human need, it is important to understand why people need self-esteem; unfortunately, this question has been all but ignored by contemporary social scientists. We recently proposed a *terror management* theory of social behavior, which posits that people are motivated to maintain a positive self-image because self-esteem protects them from anxiety. The three experiments reported in this article tested this proposition.

## Terror Management Theory

Terror management theory (Greenberg, Pyszczynski, & Solomon, 1986; Solomon, Greenberg, & Pyszczynski, 1991b), which is based largely on the writings of Ernest Becker (1962, 1973, 1975), was developed to address a variety of interrelated questions concerning what self-esteem is, what psychological function it serves, and how it is related to other aspects of the individual's conception of reality. The theory proposes that self-esteem is the feeling that one is an object of primary value in a meaningful universe. Individuals sustain self-esteem by maintaining faith in a culturally derived conception of reality (the cultural worldview) and living up to the standards of value that are prescribed by that worldview. From the perspective of terror management theory, people need self-esteem because it is the central psychological mechanism for protecting individuals from the anxiety that awareness of their vulnerability and mortality would otherwise create.

The roots of this connection between self-esteem and protection from anxiety reside in the individual's early interactions with his or her parents and other socializing agents of the culture. As a variety of theorists have noted, in early childhood, the need fulfillment, love, and protection afforded by the parents comprise the virtually helpless child's primary basis of security (e.g., Bowlby, 1969; Horney, 1937; Rogers, 1959; Sullivan, 1953). Over the course of childhood, these commodities become increasingly contingent on meeting parental standards of goodness and value. As these standards become internalized, this contingency leads to an association between the perception that one is meeting internalized standards of value (self-esteem) and feelings of safety and security. This association is reinforced throughout life, both directly, through the responses of others to one's behavior, and vicariously, through cultural teachings and myths in which the virtuous are rewarded and the evil are punished. The basic message that is transmitted through such teachings is that the world is a just place where aversive events can be avoided by being a good, valuable person (cf. Lerner, 1980). Beyond

that, societal standards of value also serve as requirements for death transcendence through literal and symbolic immortality (e.g., afterlife, prosperous children, and cultural achievements).[1] Self-esteem thus provides protection from anxiety because it is the prerequisite for feeling loved, safe, and secure (see Solomon et al., 1991b, for a more extensive discussion of how self-esteem acquires its anxiety-buffering function).

The initial research concerning terror management focused on the worldview component of the cultural anxiety buffer. The general strategy taken in this research was to test the proposition that if one's worldview serves an anxiety-buffering function, then reminding subjects of the source of their anxiety should increase their need for the buffer and thus intensify their reactions to anyone or anything that impinges on it. In support of this notion, 13 experiments have shown that reminding subjects of their mortality leads them to respond especially favorably to those who bolster their worldviews and especially unfavorably to those who threaten them (Greenberg, Pyszczynski, Solomon, Rosenblatt, et al. 1990; Greenberg, Simon, Solomon, Pyszczynski, & Lyon, 1992; Greenberg, Simon, Pyszczynski, Solomon, & Chatel, 1992; Rosenblatt, Greenberg, Solomon, Pyszczynski, & Lyon, 1989). For example, Greenberg et al. (1990) found that for Christian subjects, mortality salience increased liking for a fellow Christian and decreased liking for a Jew. These studies have also ruled out a variety of alternative explanations for these findings. In addition, Greenberg, Simon, Pyszczynski, et al. (1992) found evidence that mortality salience

---

[1]Although the specific modes of immortality vary from culture to culture and across historical periods (see e.g., Rank, 1931/1961), most cultures promise literal immortality to those who qualify, through souls or spirits that continue to exist in some form after physical death. These spiritual or collective modes of immortality are often supplemented by symbolic forms of immortality striving, ways of feeling that one is making some permanent mark on reality. In modern western culture, these modes include children, accumulated wealth, estates, socially valued accomplishments, awards, memorials, and so forth. It is important to keep in mind that cultural worldviews are structured so that all of these paths to immortality involve meeting the requirements of goodness or value prescribed by the particular worldview. Being a good, valuable person is the required qualification for immortality in whatever cultural forms it takes; self-esteem is thus the belief that makes one feel immortal.

Attachment + society

differential Parenting styles

tie to religion " " IQ

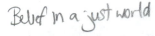

Belief in a just world

motivates adherence to the values prescribed by one's worldview as well as defense of that worldview. None of this research has, however, directly assessed the role of self-esteem in buffering anxiety.

## Empirical Evidence Consistent With the Anxiety-Buffer Proposition

Although we know of no previous experimental studies of the psychological functions of self-esteem, there are two huge literatures, one correlational and one experimental, that are generally consistent with the proposition that self-esteem functions to buffer anxiety. Although even a cursory review of these literatures would be beyond the scope of this article (for reviews, see Solomon et al., 1991a, 1991b), several findings are especially relevant to present concerns.

The correlational literature is replete with evidence of positive associations between self-esteem and various indexes of mental and physical well-being (e.g., Antonucci & Jackson, 1983; Hobfoll & Leiberman, 1987; Lester, 1986) and negative associations between self-esteem and anxiety and anxiety-related problems (e.g., French, 1968; Lipsitt, 1958; Rosenberg & Simmons, 1972). Although the correlational nature of these findings precludes causal inference, they are consistent with the notion that self-esteem serves an anxiety-buffering function.

The experimental literature on threats to self-esteem is also generally consistent with this idea. If self-esteem protects people from anxiety, then threats to self-esteem should produce anxiety; research using both self-report and physiological indexes has shown that they do (e.g., Bennett & Holmes, 1975; Burish & Houston, 1979). In addition, when threatened, people should engage in strategies to defend or restore self-esteem. There is a large body of evidence demonstrating that threats to self-esteem do indeed produce defensive reactions to either defuse the specific threat or to restore a more general sense of self-worth (see Greenberg et al., 1986, for a review).

It also seems fairly clear that these defensive maneuvers are mediated by the negative affect produced by threats to self-esteem. Research has shown that (a) high levels of arousal in response to failure are associated with self-serving external attributions (Brown & Rogers, 1991), (b) encouraging subjects to attribute any arousal they experience after failure to a neutral source reduces their tendency to engage in such defenses (Fries & Frey, 1980; Stephan & Gollwitzer, 1981), (c) increasing subjects' perceived level of arousal increases their tendency to engage in such defenses (Gollwitzer, Earle, & Stephan, 1982; Stephan & Gollwitzer, 1981), and (d) anxiety is reduced when threatened individuals defend their self-esteem (e.g., Bennett & Holmes, 1975; Hakmiller, 1966; Mehlman & Snyder, 1985).

The correlational and experimental findings just noted are all consistent with the proposition that self-esteem protects individuals from anxiety: People low in self-esteem tend to be anxious, threats to self-esteem cause anxiety, and defense of self-esteem reduces anxiety. However, to directly assess whether self-esteem buffers anxiety, it would be necessary to manipulate self-esteem, expose subjects to threat, and then measure anxiety. If self-esteem serves an anxiety-buffering function, then when exposed to threatening stimuli subjects whose self-esteem has been bolstered should exhibit less anxiety than subjects whose self-esteem has not been altered. The research reported in this article was designed to provide several converging tests of this general hypothesis.

## Study 1

Study 1 was designed to test the hypothesis that increasing self-esteem reduces anxiety in response to threat. Because terror management theory views concern about vulnerability and mortality to be the ultimate basis of all anxiety (for an extended discussion of this relationship, see Pyszczynski, Greenberg, Solomon, & Hamilton, 1990; Solomon et al., 1991b), we chose to manipulate threat by exposing half of our subjects to a graphic video depiction of death-related scenes and the remainder to a neutral video. Before this threat induction, self-esteem was manipulated by providing subjects with either highly positive or neutral feedback on a bogus personality test. If self-esteem provides protection from anxiety, then increased-self-esteem subjects should experience less anxiety in response to the threatening film than neutral self-esteem subjects.

## Method

### SUBJECTS

Subjects were 52 male students who participated in partial fulfillment of a course requirement and who had previously participated in a mass testing session. Male subjects were selected for the study because during pilot sessions, female subjects expressed great discomfort with the death video; although male subjects also expressed some discomfort during debriefings, none of them objected to seeing the film or seemed excessively distressed.

### PROCEDURE

Experimental sessions were conducted in groups of 3 to 5 subjects per session. Subjects were randomly assigned to self-esteem and threat conditions. The experimenter was unaware of the self-esteem manipulation.

On arrival, subjects were told that the study concerned the relationship between personality traits and reactions to emotionally arousing stimuli; this cover story provided a rationale for the death video. They were then given a consent form, which stated that they would view scenes from a video, after which their reactions would be assessed. The video constituted the threat manipulation. Threat subjects were informed in the consent statement that the video included scenes of an autopsy and an electrocution so that they were truly informed regarding the most impactful aspect of the study before consenting to participate.

The experimenter then explained that subjects' personality characteristics had already been measured in the previous mass testing session and that she was required to give them individual reports on the results of these tests. This feedback constituted the self-esteem manipulation. Subjects then read the bogus personality feedback in individual cubicles and filled out a questionnaire regarding the feedback. They then returned to the main room to view the video and were given the dependent measure and a check on the self-esteem manipulation. When everyone finished, subjects were probed for their reactions to the study and thoroughly debriefed.

### SELF-ESTEEM AND THREAT MANIPULATIONS

The self-esteem manipulation was presented in the form of a psychological assessment report that had the subjects' names at the top of the page. On the basis of previous research on the Barnum effect (e.g., Forer, 1949) the feedback was highly general in nature so that it could plausibly apply to all subjects. It was designed to convey either a positive or neutral evaluation of the subject's personality. For example, in the neutral feedback condition it was stated "While you have some personality weaknesses, you are generally able to compensate for them" and "Some of your aspirations may be a bit unrealistic." Similarly, in the positive feedback condition, it was stated "While you may feel that you have some personality weaknesses, your personality is fundamentally strong" and "Most of your aspirations tend to be pretty realistic." With the exception of such minor changes in wording to convey different meaning, the two forms of feedback were similar with respect to content and length.

The threat manipulation was created by selecting scenes from the video documentary *Faces of Death, Volume 1*. This video graphically presents various ways in which individuals die.[2] The scenes selected for the threat condition included actual footage of an autopsy and an electrocution of an inmate on death row. The neutral scenes selected for the nonthreat condition of the study were from the same video but did not include graphic depictions of death. The overall length of the video segments used for the two conditions were the same (approximately 7 minutes).

### MEASURES

After receiving the personality feedback, and before the video, subjects were asked a series of questions regarding their reactions to the feedback. Following the video, subjects filled out the primary dependent measure, the A-State form of the State–Trait Anxiety Inventory (Spielberger, Gorsuch, & Lushene, 1970). Finally, following this

---

[2] We gave careful consideration to the ethical issues surrounding the use of this video as a threat induction and decided that it was acceptable for several reasons. First, the video from which we took our threatening excerpts is widely available in video stores and is very popular. At the time this study was conducted, one clerk told us that the video is rented almost every night. Second, none of the male subjects who participated in pilot sessions objected to being shown the video (nor did any of the subjects in the actual experimental sessions). Finally our consent statement informed subjects of exactly what the video would depict and that they were free to withdraw at any time.

anxiety measure, subjects filled out the Rosenberg Self-Esteem Scale (Rosenberg, 1965) as a check on the self-esteem manipulation.

## Results and Discussion

Separate 2(threat) × 2(self-esteem) analyses of variance (ANOVAs) were conducted on each measure.

### SELF-ESTEEM MANIPULATION CHECK

As expected, the ANOVA on the self-esteem measure revealed only a main effect of the self-esteem manipulation, $F(1, 48) = 4.20$, $p < .05$. Subjects in the increased-self-esteem condition exhibited higher self-esteem ($M = 33.04$) than those in the neutral self-esteem condition ($M = 30.73$), thus demonstrating that the personality feedback successfully manipulated self-esteem.

### THE DEPENDENT MEASURE: ANXIETY

The ANOVA on the anxiety measure revealed the predicted Threat × Self-Esteem interaction, $F(1, 48) = 4.55$, $p < .04$. As the cell means in Table 1 suggest, pairwise comparisons revealed that anxiety was higher in the neutral self-esteem threat condition than in any of the other conditions (all $t$s > 2.10, all $p$s < .05); cell means for anxiety were virtually identical in the other three conditions (all $t$s < 1). Thus, although the death video led to increased anxiety among neutral self-esteem subjects, it had no effect on increased-self-esteem subjects. In addition, increased-self-esteem subjects exhibited less anxiety in response to the film than did neutral self-esteem subjects.

### SUBSIDIARY MEASURES

Following the personality feedback and before the video, subjects filled out a 15-item questionnaire concerning the feedback. Across all conditions, the

**TABLE 6.1. Mean Anxiety Scores for Interaction Between Mortality Salience and Level of Self-Esteem: Study 1**

| Personality feedback | Neutral | Positive |
|---|---|---|
| Neutral video | 43.46 | 44.93 |
| Death video | 54.15 | 43.09 |

*Note.* Scores on the anxiety measure could range from 20 (low anxiety) to 80 (high anxiety).

personality feedback was rated as describing subjects very well ($M = 7.47$, with 9 = *extremely well*). Four of the items that assessed subjects' perceptions of the accuracy and usefulness of the feedback were summed to form a composite measure of the perceived quality of the feedback. Four other items that assessed how much they liked and enjoyed reading their feedback were summed to form a composite measure of liking for the feedback. No effects were found on either of these composites (all $p$s > .10). In debriefings it seemed that the subjects uniformly liked the feedback because it was so "accurate." One item assessed the extent to which the subjects felt self-confident; no effects were found on this item ($p > .10$). Six items concerned the extent to which the subjects were feeling negative emotions (disgusted, disturbed, anxious, angry, insecure, or fearful) and were summed to form a composite measure of negative affect. Only a main effect of self-esteem emerged on this composite, $F(1, 48) = 11.84$, $p < .001$. Increased-self-esteem subjects exhibited less negative affect than neutral self-esteem subjects ($M$s = 1.76 and 2.84, respectively, on a scale from 1 = *not at all* to 9 = *extremely*).

The results of Study 1 support the hypothesis that self-esteem reduces susceptibility to anxiety in response to threat. Although the death video led to a clear increase in anxiety in the neutral feedback condition, it had no effect whatsoever on the levels of anxiety exhibited by subjects whose self-esteem had been experimentally enhanced. Viewed differently increased self-esteem subjects showed less anxiety in response to threat than did neutral self-esteem subjects. This study provides the first direct evidence that self-esteem serves an anxiety-buffering function.

## Study 2

Although the finding that increasing self-esteem reduces anxiety in response to death-related stimuli is consistent with terror management theory, the theory also posits that self-esteem provides protection from anxiety in response to other types of threat. According to the theory, people experience anxiety in response to two major types of threat: (a) direct threats to their physical well-being and continued existence and (b) threats to the psychological structures (i.e., self-esteem and worldview) that protect them from this basic anxiety. Beck,

Laude, and Bohnert's (1974) observation that anxiety reactions generally stem from threats to either one's physical well-being or one's social value is consistent with this proposition.

Study 2 was designed to assess the generality of the anxiety buffering effect of self-esteem to other types of threat by determining whether increasing self-esteem reduces anxiety in response to the threat of painful electric shocks. To provide converging evidence that self-esteem is indeed the conceptual variable affecting anxiety, we manipulated self-esteem with a different operationalization, specifically, feedback on a supposed test of verbal intelligence. Given the extent to which intelligence is valued in American culture, positive feedback concerning one's intelligence should increase self-esteem. To provide converging evidence that anxiety-proneness is indeed being affected by our self-esteem induction, we used a different measure of anxiety, physiological arousal (i.e., skin conductance) in response to threat. This measure also has the advantage of being less prone to reporting biases. We hypothesized that increasing self-esteem would reduce arousal in response to the threat of shock.

## Method

### SUBJECTS AND LABORATORY/FACILITIES

Forty-four male undergraduates volunteered to participate in return for course credit. Subjects were randomly assigned to conditions in a 2 (increased vs. neutral self-esteem) × 2 (threat vs. no threat) factorial design. Four subjects were subsequently excluded, 2 before assignment to conditions because we could not get stable physiological baseline measures and 2 because they expressed suspicion about the threat manipulation. Throughout the experiment, subjects were seated at a desk in a straight-backed chair in a sound-attenuated room. A control room directly adjoining the experimental room contained a Grass Instrument Company physiograph that was used to record subjects' skin resistance and a tape recorder that was used to administer experimental instructions.

### PROCEDURE

On arriving for their individual sessions, subjects were given a brief tour of the control room, were shown the physiograph, and were told that we would be measuring skin resistance, which was described as a measure of general physiological activity. Subjects were also shown the tape recorder and were informed that most of the instructions for the study would be recorded so that the experimenters could be in a different room while the physiological measures were being taken.

Subjects were then escorted into the adjacent room and read an informed-consent statement that described the study as concerned with the relationship between mood, cognitive and physical stimulation, and physiological responses. After signing the consent form, Beekman skin resistance electrodes were attached to the second and fourth fingers of the subjects' nondominant hand, and a dummy electric shock plate was attached to the subjects' nondominant wrist (to lend credence to the threat manipulation described later).

The experimenters returned to the control room and started the tape-recorded instructions, which reiterated the general purpose of the study and instructed the subject to sit back and rest for 5 minutes. This adaptation period enabled physiological responses to come to a resting level and stabilize. At the end of this period, subjects completed a self-report measure of anxiety that used adjectives from the Affect Adjective Check List (AACL; Zuckerman, 1960). For each adjective, subjects marked a 4-point scale (1 = *not at all* to 4 = *a great deal*) that reflected the degree to which that word described how they felt at that time. This measure has been used successfully in previous research (e.g., Bennett & Holmes, 1975).

After completing the anxiety measure, subjects were told that the cognitive stimulation we were studying would be provided by a version of the Thorndike Anagram Test, which was described as a highly accurate measure of verbal intelligence. The bogus test consisted of 20 anagrams that were designed such that the average subject would solve 16–18 problems correctly in the 5-minute period. Subjects were asked to take the anagram test while we ostensibly recorded their physiological responses. While subjects were taking the test, the experimenter randomly assigned them to either the neutral or increased self-esteem condition. After the test was completed, the experimenter returned to the room and told subjects in the neutral self-esteem condition that because we were primarily interested in physiological responses to taking the test rather than performance, we would not score or look at the test. Subjects assigned to the increased-self-esteem condition were told that we were especially interested in how well people performed on the anagram test and that, consequently, the test would be scored, and they would receive feedback on their performance. The test was then scored by the experimenter, and subjects were told that they got $N$ right (where $N$ = the actual number of anagrams solved correctly), that no one in the experiment thus far had gotten more than $N - 2$ right, and that their score was in the 90th percentile.

The experimenters then returned to the control room and randomly assigned the subject to a physical stimulation condition. The tape then informed subjects that after the instructions were completed there would be a 90-second anticipation period during which a yellow light mounted in front of them would come on, at which time their physiological responses would be measured in the absence of physical stimulation.[3] There would then be a 90-second experimental period during which a red light mounted in front of them would come on, at which time subjects would be exposed to physical stimulation while their physiological responses were recorded.

Subjects assigned to the threat condition were told that the physical stimulation would be provided by mildly painful electrical shocks administered randomly during the experimental period through the electrodes on their wrists. Subjects in the no threat condition were told that the physical stimulation would be provided by the light waves given off by the red light that would be turned on during that period. These subjects were informed that we were interested in how people respond to lights at different points of the color spectrum. The anticipation and experimental periods then occurred as described, except that no shocks were administered to any subjects. Following the experimental period, subjects completed a second AACL in which they were asked to describe how they felt during the experimental period. The session was then concluded, and subjects were thoroughly debriefed.

## Results and Discussion

### SKIN RESISTANCE[4]

Skin resistance was scored for seven 30-second periods. The first period was the last 30-seconds of the adaptation period that preceded any of the experimental manipulations. The highest skin resistance (lowest arousal) from this period was used

as an indication of subjects' initial level of arousal. The second, third, and fourth periods were the three 30-second periods within the 90-second anticipation period, and the fifth, sixth, and seventh periods were the three 30-second periods within the confrontation period. Skin resistance was scored during these periods by determining the lowest skin resistance (highest arousal). Skin resistance scores (in K-ohms) were then transformed to skin conductance scores (in siemens) using a reciprocal transformation as prescribed by Dawson, Schell, and Filion (1990; see this article for a discussion of the distinction between skin resistance and skin conductance, including a conceptual rationale for the use of conductance rather than resistance).

The logarithm of each skin conductance score was then computed to reduce skew and kurtosis (as recommended by Venables & Christie, 1990). Finally, the logarithm of skin conductance scores for 30-second periods within the anticipation and confrontation periods were averaged to obtain separate scores for anticipation and confrontation that were subsequently used as the primary dependent measures.[5] To eliminate the influence of initial levels on subsequent arousal (i.e., "law of initial values," Lacey, 1956; Wilder, 1962) skin conductance scores during the adaptation period were used as a covariate for the major analyses.[6]

---

[3]The inclusion of an anticipation period before the experimental period permitted an evaluation of subjects' responses during different phases of the coping process during which there may be important differences (Lazarus, 1966).

[4]We chose to measure skin resistance because electrodermal activity is known to be related to anxiety (see Dawson et al., 1990, for a review of this literature) and is commonly used as an indication of anxiety in contemporary social psychophysiological research. In addition, pilot testing indicated that our threat manipulation produced decreases in skin resistance (increased arousal) and would thus allow us to assess the hypothesis that self-esteem enhancement would attenuate this effect. We also measured heart rate at that time but did not obtain an effect for the threat manipulation.

[5]Initial analyses in which the three 30-second segments of each period were included in the ANCOVA revealed no effects involving either factor. Consequently, skin resistance scores for these periods were averaged to obtain one score for each period.

[6]The assumption of homogeneity of regression slopes necessary for analysis of covariance (ANCOVA) was met for this analysis as well as for the ANCOVAs conducted for Study 3. In addition, in both studies, there were no premanipulation differences on the covariates, and the covariates were significant in the ANCOVAs (all $p$s < .05). For the sake of brevity and simplicity of presentation, only adjusted means are reported for the ANCOVAs.

A 2(self-esteem) × 2(threat) × 2(time: anticipation vs. confrontation) analysis of covariance (ANCOVA) performed on the transformed skin conductance scores, using the adaptation period score as a covariate, revealed a main effect for threat, $F(1, 35) = 11.56$, $p < .002$; a marginal main effect for self-esteem, $F(1, 35) = 3.43$, $p < .07$; a main effect for time, $F(1, 36) = 6.59$, $p < .01$; and a significant Self-Esteem × Threat × Time interaction, $F(1, 36) = 5.48$, $p < .02$. The main effect for threat resulted from threat subjects being generally more aroused than no threat subjects ($M$s = 1.3290 vs. 1.2253); this suggests that the threat manipulation successfully produced differential levels of arousal. The marginal main effect for self-esteem reflects the fact that increased self-esteem subjects were generally less aroused than neutral self-esteem subjects ($M$s = 1.2471 vs. 1.3042). The main effect for time reflects the fact that subjects were more aroused during the confrontation period than during the anticipation period ($M$s = 1.2800 vs. 1.2706). Mean skin conductance scores for each condition are presented in Table 6.2.

Pairwise comparisons conducted to explicate the nature of the Self-Esteem × Threat × Time interaction revealed that the predicted pattern of lower arousal in response to threat of shock among increased self-esteem subjects than among neutral self-esteem subjects emerged in both the anticipation and confrontation periods but was stronger in the confrontation period. Specifically, during the anticipation period, increased self-esteem threat subjects were marginally less aroused than neutral self-esteem threat subjects, $t(17) = 1.81$, $p < .10$. During the confrontation period, increased-self-esteem threat subjects were significantly less aroused than neutral self-esteem threat subjects, $t(17) = 2.38$, $p < .05$.

In addition, in the anticipation period, neutral self-esteem threat subjects were significantly more aroused than neutral self-esteem no threat subjects, $t(19) = 3.17$, $p < .01$, whereas increased-self-esteem threat subjects were only marginally more aroused than their nonthreatened counterparts, $t(17) = 1.81$, $p < .10$. During the confrontation period, neutral self-esteem threat subjects were significantly more aroused than neutral self-esteem no threat subjects, $t(19) = 3.60$, $p < .002$, whereas there was no difference in arousal in the increased self-esteem condition between threat and no threat subjects, $t(17) = 1.31$, $ns$. These results indicate that increasing self-esteem reduced physiological

arousal in response to a threatening event and that this effect was more pronounced during the confrontation period than the anticipation period.

## SELF-REPORTED AFFECT

A 2(self-esteem) × 2(threat) ANCOVA was performed on the self-report anxiety measure, using the score from the adaptation period as a covariate. Mean self-reported anxiety scores for each condition are presented in Table 6.3. This analysis revealed only a main effect for threat, $F(1, 35) = 18.24$, $p < .0001$. Subjects in the threat condition reported higher anxiety than subjects in the no threat condition ($M$s 16.1 vs. 7.09, respectively). This suggests that the threat manipulation successfully produced different levels of self-reported anxiety. Although the individual cell means are clearly in the predicted direction (i.e., increased self-esteem threat subjects tended to report less anxiety than neutral self-esteem threat subjects), the interaction was not statistically significant.

In sum, the physiological data from Study 2 suggest that the anxiety-buffering effect of self-esteem observed in Study 1 extends to measures of physiological arousal and generalizes to threats not explicitly linked to death. Increased self-esteem subjects exhibited less arousal in response to threat of shock than neutral self-esteem subjects, particularly during the period when shocks were actually expected. Furthermore, whereas the threat of shock led to clear increases in arousal in the neutral self-esteem condition, it had less effect on arousal among subjects in the increased-self-esteem condition. The boost to self-esteem apparently reduced subjects' susceptibility to anxiety in response to the threat of electric shock. Whereas Study 1 demonstrated the anxiety-buffering effect on reports of anxiety in response to death-related stimuli, the present study demon-

**TABLE 6.2. Adjusted Cell Means for the Three-Way Interaction of Self-Esteem, Threat, and Time on Transformed Skin Conductance Scores: Study 2**

| Measure | Anticipation | | Confrontation | |
| --- | --- | --- | --- | --- |
| | SE raised | SE neutral | SE raised | SE neutral |
| Threat | 1.2813 | 1.3606 | 1.2800 | 1.3846 |
| No threat | 1.2052 | 1.2343 | 1.2220 | 1.2375 |

Note. Cell means are logarithms of skin conductance scores in siemens. A higher number is indicative of higher arousal. SE = self-esteem.

Mind was on something else, didn't realize/notice

strated a parallel effect of a different self-esteem manipulation on physiological arousal in response to a different type of threat, thus providing converging evidence for the anxiety-buffer hypothesis.

Although the means on the self-report measure of anxiety in Study 2 were in the predicted direction, the lack of a reliable effect on that measure is puzzling. Perhaps the retrospective nature of the measure reduced its sensitivity; the measure came after the threat of shock was over. Alternatively, it may be that subjects threatened with electric shocks that have been described as painful feel some demand to report anxiety.

Although these two studies show that increasing self-esteem can reduce anxiety in response to threat, there is a plausible alternative explanation for these results. Perhaps positive affect engendered by the self-esteem boost rather than self-esteem per se provides the protection against anxiety. We think this is unlikely because recent research suggests that positive and negative affective states are largely independent of each other (e.g., Watson, Clark, & Tellegen, 1988). Thus, even if the positive feedback created positive affect, it is not clear why that would inhibit anxiety in response to subsequent threat. Nevertheless, the possible role of positive affect in mediating the effects of the self-esteem manipulation is examined in Study 3.

## Study 3

Study 3 was designed to provide further evidence concerning the anxiety-buffering effect of self-esteem and to assess the possible role of positive affect in mediating this effect. To this end, the basic design of Study 2 was replicated and the self-report anxiety measure was replaced with the Positive and Negative Affect Schedule (PANAS; Watson et al., 1988). To assess the generality of the effect on physiological arousal demonstrated in Study 2, we returned to the personality feedback manipulation of self-esteem that was effective in Study 1. Other than that, the design of Study 3 was essentially the same as Study 2. We hypothesized that increasing self-esteem by using positive personality feedback would reduce arousal in response to the threat of shock and that this reduction in arousal would not covary with any effect the personality feedback might have on positive affect.

## Method

### SUBJECTS AND LABORATORY FACILITIES

Fifty male undergraduates participated individually as part of a research requirement. All subjects had previously participated in a mass testing session in which they completed a variety of personality assessments, the results of which supposedly provided the basis for the personality profiles used to manipulate self-esteem. Subjects were randomly assigned to conditions in a 2(increased vs. neutral self-esteem) × 2(threat vs. no threat) factorial design. Three subjects were excluded from data analyses because of suspicion. Laboratory facilities and equipment were the same as in Study 2.

### PROCEDURE

Procedures were the same as in Study 2, with the following exceptions:

1. At the conclusion of the 5-minute adaptation period, during which baseline levels of arousal were recorded, subjects completed an initial PANAS, which served as the baseline measure of affect.
2. Self-esteem was manipulated with the same personality feedback that was used in Study 1 rather than the feedback on the bogus intelligence test used in Study 2. Subjects were randomly assigned to receive either positive or neutral feedback supposedly based on a set of personality tests they had taken during a mass testing session. This feedback was given after subjects completed the initial PANAS.
3. The procedures used for the threat manipulation were identical to those used in Study 2, including the assessment of arousal during separate anticipation and confrontation periods, with two exceptions. Because we did not want suspicions aroused by the absence of actual

TABLE 6.3. Adjusted Means for the Self-Report Anxiety Measure: Study 2

| Measure | Self-esteem | |
| --- | --- | --- |
| | Increased | Neutral |
| Threat | 13.40 | 18.16 |
| No threat | 6.30 | 7.81 |

Note. A higher number is indicative of higher anxiety.

shocks during the confrontation period, threat subjects were told they would receive between zero and six shocks on a random basis. In addition, the anticipation and confrontation periods were shortened to 60 seconds each. After the confrontation period, subjects filled out a second PANAS, which enabled us to assess possible effects of the self-esteem and threat manipulations on positive and negative affect and the likelihood that the effects on arousal could have been mediated by positive affect.

4. After finishing the second PANAS, subjects completed a final questionnaire containing manipulation checks and probes for suspicion. To check on the self-esteem manipulation, subjects were asked to report on 9-point scales how well the personality feedback described them (1 = *not at all* to 9 = *completely*) and how good the personality feedback made them feel about themselves (1 = *very good* to 9 = *very bad*). After completing this questionnaire, subjects were thoroughly debriefed and dismissed.

## Results and Discussion

### MANIPULATION CHECKS

Individual 2(self-esteem) × 2(threat) ANOVAs were conducted on responses to the self-esteem manipulation check questions. On the question regarding how well the personality feedback described them, subjects rated the personality feedback as describing them very well (grand $M$ = 7.21), with no differences across conditions (all $p$s > .25). The ANOVA on the question about how good the feedback made subjects feel about themselves produced main effects for self-esteem, $F(1, 43)$ = 17.13, $p$ < .0002, and threat, $F(1, 43)$ = 4.30, $p$ < .05. Specifically, increased-self-esteem subjects reported that the personality feedback made them feel better about themselves than did neutral self-esteem subjects ($M$s = 2.83 and 4.48, respectively); lower values indicate better feelings, and no threat subjects reported that the personality feedback made them feel better about themselves than did threat subjects ($M$s = 3.25 and 4.0, respectively). This latter effect was most likely due to the measure being taken after the threat manipulation. Consistent with this notion, there was no hint of an interaction between self-esteem and threat, $F(1, 43)$ = .13. These findings suggest that self-esteem was again successfully manipulated.

### SKIN CONDUCTANCE

Procedures for scoring, transforming to conductance, and analyzing skin resistance were identical to those used in Study 2. A 2(self-esteem) × 2(threat) × 2(time) ANCOVA performed on transformed skin conductance scores, using adaptation period scores as a covariate, produced main effects for threat, $F(1, 43)$ = 5.00, $p$ < .03, self-esteem, $F(1, 43)$ = 4.27, $p$ < .05, and time, $F(1, 43)$ = 9.90, $p$ < .005; a Threat × Time interaction, $F(1, 43)$ = 12.06, $p$ < .001; and the predicted Self-Esteem × Threat interaction, $F(1, 43)$ = 8.59, $p$ < .006. The main effect for threat reflects the fact that the threat manipulation successfully produced more arousal among threatened than nonthreatened subjects ($M$s = 1.3270 and 1.2126, respectively; higher values indicate greater arousal). The main effect for self-esteem indicates that increased self-esteem subjects were less aroused than neutral self-esteem subjects ($M$s = 1.2118 and 1.3266, respectively). The main effect for time was due to subjects being more aroused during confrontation than during anticipation ($M$s = 1.2882 and 1.2578, respectively). The Threat × Time interaction reflects the fact that there was no increase in arousal over time for no threat subjects ($M$s of 1.2082 and 1.2050, respectively) but a significant increase in arousal between anticipation and confrontation periods for threat subjects ($M$s = 1.3070 and 1.3713, respectively), $t(22)$ = 6.25, $p$ < .001.

Of most relevance to present concerns, mean skin conductance scores for the Self-Esteem × Threat interaction are presented in Table 6.4. Pairwise comparisons revealed that, as predicted, among threatened subjects, those in the increased-self-esteem condition were significantly less aroused than those in the neutral self-esteem condition, $t(22)$ = 3.49, $p$ < .01. Also as predicted, whereas threatened neutral self-esteem subjects exhibited significantly greater arousal than

**TABLE 6.4. Adjusted Cell Means for the Two-Way Interaction of Self-Esteem and Threat on Transformed Skin Conductance Scores: Study 3**

| Measure | Self-esteem | |
| --- | --- | --- |
| | Increased | Neutral |
| Threat | 1.1932 | 1.4851 |
| No threat | 1.2319 | 1.1813 |

*Note.* Cell means are logarithms of skin conductance scores in siemens. A higher number is indicative of higher anxiety.

nonthreatened neutral self-esteem subjects, $t(21)$ = 3.57, $p < .01$, no difference in arousal as a function of threat was found in the increased self-esteem condition ($t < 1$). Unlike Study 2, this effect was consistent across the anticipation and confrontation periods; time did not moderate the interaction of self-esteem and threat.

## SELF-REPORTED AFFECT

Separate 2(self-esteem) × 2(threat) ANCOVAs were performed on the Positive and Negative Affect subscales from the PANAS, using the appropriate subscale score from the adaptation period as a covariate. No effects of any kind were found on either subscale ($ps > .20$). To assess whether some effect of the manipulations on anxiety could be detected, we formed a scale using the three items from the Negative Affect subscale of the PANAS that are identical to items from the A-State form of the State-Trait Anxiety Inventory (Spielberger et al., 1970; nervous, upset, and jittery). We then conducted an ANCOVA on this crude measure of anxiety using a composite measure of the same items from the baseline PANAS as covariate, which produced only a main effect for threat, $F(1, 42) = 4.18$, $p < .05$. As in Study 2, subjects in the threat condition reported higher levels of anxiety on this measure than subjects in the control condition, ($Ms = 2.01$ and 1.78, respectively) indicating that the threat manipulation was successful. As in Study 2, the self-esteem manipulation did not moderate this effect on self-reported anxiety.

## ASSESSING THE POSITIVE AFFECT ALTERNATIVE

The fact that the manipulation did not seem to be confounded with positive affect casts doubt on positive affect as an explanation for the moderating effect of the self-esteem manipulation on arousal. We also conducted a multiple regression analysis with arousal as the dependent variable, entering the premeasure and postmeasure of positive affect before the baseline, main effect, and interaction terms. Neither positive affect measure contributed significantly to the equation (both $Fs < 1$). As in the ANCOVA, the predicted interaction term still contributed significantly $F(1, 41) = 6.02$, $p < .025$. Thus, there was no indication that the interaction resulted from an effect of the manipulation on positive affect.

In sum, the findings of Study 3 replicate those of Study 2 in showing that the anxiety-buffering effect of self-esteem generalizes to threats not explicitly linked to death. Whereas the threat of painful electric shock led to clear increases in arousal in the neutral self-esteem condition, it had no effect on arousal among subjects in the increased-self-esteem condition. Thus, the boost to self-esteem reduced subjects' susceptibility to anxiety in response to the threat of electric shock.

The findings of Study 3 are also consistent with those of Study 2 in demonstrating an effect of increased self-esteem on physiological arousal in response to threat of shock in the absence of a parallel effect on self-reported anxiety-related items. Although the absence of parallel effects on self-reports are somewhat puzzling, the fact that reliable effects on self-reported anxiety were found in Study 1 suggests that self-esteem inductions can affect both types of measures. Perhaps the difference in threat manipulations between Study 1 and Studies 2 and 3 might account for the different effects on self-report. As noted earlier with regard to Study 2, subjects may have felt a demand to report symptoms of anxiety when threatened with shock. In addition, in both shock studies, because we did not want the self-report measures to interfere with our physiological readings, the self-report measures came after the threat of shock was over, rendering the measures retrospective and perhaps insensitive to an effect of the earlier self-esteem manipulation in the threat condition.

## General Discussion

The three studies reported in this article provide converging support for the proposition that self-esteem provides a buffer against anxiety. Study 1 demonstrated that a boost to self-esteem makes subjects less prone to experience anxiety in response to threatening images of death; in fact, although control subjects reported significantly more anxiety in response to the threatening than neutral video increased-self-esteem subjects' levels of anxiety were unaffected by this presentation. Studies 2 and 3 demonstrated that the anxiety-buffering effect of self-esteem extends to events not directly associated with death and can be detected with a physiological indicator of anxiety. In these studies, increased-self-esteem subjects exhibited less arousal in response to the threat of electric shock than did control subjects.

These findings are generally consistent with those of previous studies that have shown self-esteem to be negatively correlated with anxiety and other signs of psychological and physical distress. They are also consistent with the experimental literature that has shown threats to self-esteem produce anxiety, that this anxiety motivates defense of self-esteem, and that defensive maneuvers reduce anxiety resulting from such threats. The present findings go beyond those of previous studies by demonstrating a causal relationship between self-esteem and anxiety.

From the perspective of terror management theory, all of the previous findings can be explained by positing an anxiety-buffering function for self-esteem. The present research provides direct support for this proposition by showing that increasing self-esteem reduces self-reported anxiety in response to death images and physiological arousal in response to the threat of pain. Although when taken individually each study has limitations, by using two operationalizations of self-esteem and finding effects on two indicators of anxiety, the present research provides converging support for the anxiety-buffer proposition.[7] [ . . . ]

## Conclusion

In our view, the most compelling explanation for the present set of findings is that self-esteem—the feeling that one is valuable—provides protection against anxiety in response to threat. From the perspective of terror management theory, this feeling of personal value reduces one's susceptibility to anxiety because of the primitive affective and cognitive linkages between valued behavior and parental protection that are reinforced throughout one's life by cultural institutions and teachings. Clearly, all aspects of terror management theory cannot be unequivocally confirmed or disconfirmed by any single study or small set of studies. The theory is very broad and can be used to deduce hypotheses about a wide variety of psychological phenomena. The studies presented were focused exclusively on our analysis of the anxiety-buffering function posited for the self-esteem motive; they do not bear on a variety of other propositions and hypotheses that can be derived from the theory (some of which have been assessed by the research cited earlier).

Although these studies support one of the theory's most central propositions, their most important contribution may be that they raise a variety of intriguing questions for future inquiry. For example, it will be important to explore the precise processes through which self-esteem acquires and produces its anxiety-buffering effects. In addition, further inquiry should be directed toward investigating the types of anxiety-producing events for which self-esteem provides protection.

Because the need for self-esteem is usually taken as a fundamental, irreducible psychological need, or, more commonly, as an unexplained postulate, there has been little, if any, discussion of why the need exists or what functions self-esteem might serve for the individual. Although it might be possible to derive functions for this widely recognized need from other theoretical orientations, empirically oriented social scientists have rarely attempted to do so. This is unfortunate because the answer to a question as basic as this is bound to have profound implications for understanding human nature.

The idea that self-esteem is primarily a defensive structure has implications for any theory that posits the need for self-esteem as a central explanatory process. If self-esteem is primarily a means of insulating oneself from one's deeply rooted fears, the whole concept of a self-esteem motive must be viewed in a very different light. Conceptualizing the pursuit of personal value as a defensive avoidance of basic human fears draws one to consider the possibility of alternative means of serving this superordinate function. Although such a defensive conception of self-esteem may at first glance seem to be an unpleasant way of thinking about the human condition, it may ultimately have the liberating quality of leading to the consideration of alternative means of addressing our most basic human problems.

---

[7]It should be noted that the anxiety-buffer proposition could be derived from other theoretical perspectives that share some commonalities with terror management theory, such as Bowlby's (1969), Sullivan's (1953), and Horney's (1937).

REFERENCES

Allport, G. W. (1961). *Pattern and growth in personality.* New York: Holt, Rinehart & Winston.
Antonucci, T., & Jackson, J. (1983). Physical health and self-esteem. *Family and Community Health, 6,* 1–9.
Beck, A., Laude, R., & Bohnert, M. (1974). Ideational com-

ponents of anxiety neurosis. *Archives of General Psychiatry, 31,* 319–325.

Becker, E. (1962). *The birth and death of meaning.* New York: Free Press.

Becker, E. (1973). *The denial of death.* New York: Free Press.

Becker, E. (1975). *Escape from evil.* New York: Free Press.

Bennett, D. H., & Holmes, D. S. (1975). Influences of denial (situational redefinition) and projection on anxiety associated with threat to self-esteem. *Journal of Personality and Social Psychology, 32,* 915–921.

Bowlby, J. (1969). *Attachment and loss: Vol. I. Attachment.* New York: Basic Books.

Brown, J. D., & Rogers, R. J. (1991). Self-serving attributions: The role of physiological arousal. *Personality and Social Psychology Bulletin, 17,* 501–506.

Burish, T. G., & Houston, B. K. (1979). Causal projection, similarity projection, and coping with threat to self-esteem. *Journal of Personality, 47,* 57–70.

Dawson, M. E., Schell, A. M., & Filion, D. L. (1990). The electrodermal system. In J. T. Cacioppo & L. G. Tassinary (Eds.), *Principles of psychophysiology: Physical, social and inferential elements* (pp. 295–324). Cambridge, England: Cambridge University Press.

Forer, B. R. (1949). The fallacy of personal validation: A classroom demonstration of gullibility. *Journal of Abnormal and Social Psychology, 44,* 118–123.

French, J. R. P. (1968). The conceptualization and measurement of mental health in terms of self-identity theory. In S. B. Bells (Ed.), *The definition and measurement of mental health.* Washington, DC: U.S. Department of Health, Education, and Welfare.

Fries, A., & Frey, D. (1980). Misattribution of arousal and the effects of self-threatening information. *Journal of Experimental Social Psychology, 16,* 405–416.

Gollwitzer, P. M., Earle, W. B., & Stephan, W. G. (1982). Affect as a determinant of egotism: Residual excitation and performance attributions. *Journal of Personality and Social Psychology, 43,* 702–709.

Greenberg, J., Pyszczynski, T., & Solomon, S. (1986). The causes and consequences of a need for self-esteem: A terror management theory. In R. F. Baumeister (Ed.), *Public self and private self* (pp. 189–207). New York: Springer-Verlag.

Greenberg, J., Pyszczynski, T., Solomon, S., Rosenblatt, A., Veeder, M., Kirkland, S., & Lyon, D. (1990). Evidence for terror management theory II: The effects of mortality salience on reactions to those who threaten or bolster the cultural worldview. *Journal of Personality and Social Psychology, 58,* 308–318.

Greenberg, J., Simon, L., Pyszczynski, T., Solomon, S., & Chatel, D. (1992). Terror management and tolerance: Does mortality salience always intensify negative reactions to others who threaten one's worldview? *Journal of Personality and Social Psychology, 63,* 212–220.

Greenberg, J., Simon, L., Solomon, S., Pyszczynski, T., & Lyon, D. (1992). *Exploring the nature of mortality salience effects: Terror management, value accessibility, or aversive thought.* Unpublished manuscript, University of Arizona, Tucson.

Hakmiller, K. L. (1966). Threat as a determinant of downward comparison. *Journal of Experimental Social Psychology, 2,* 32–39.

Hobfoll, S., & Leiberman, J. (1987). Personality and social

resources in immediate and continued stress resistance among women. *Journal of Personality and Social Psychology, 52,* 18–26.

Horney, K. (1937). *The neurotic personality of our time.* New York: Norton.

Lacey, J. (1956). The evaluation of autonomic responses: Toward a general solution. *Annals of the New York Academy of Science, 67,* 123–164.

Lazarus, R. S. (1966). *Psychological stress and the coping process.* New York: McGraw-Hill.

Lerner, M. J. (1980). *The belief in a just world: A fundamental delusion.* New York: Plenum Press.

Lester, D. (1986). Subjective distress and self-esteem of police officers. *Perceptual and Motor Skills, 63,* 1334.

Lipsitt, L. P. (1958). A self-concept scale for children and its relationship to the children's form of the Manifest Anxiety Scale. *Child Development, 29,* 463–472.

Mehlman, R. C., & Snyder, C. R. (1985). Excuse theory: A test of the self-protective role of attributions. *Journal of Personality and Social Psychology, 49,* 994–1001.

Pyszczynski, T., Greenberg, J., Solomon, S., & Hamilton, J. (1990). A terror management analysis of self-awareness and anxiety: The hierarchy of terror. *Anxiety Research, 2,* 177–195.

Rank, 0. (1961). *Psychology and the soul.* New York: Perpetual Books. (Original work published 1931)

Rogers, C. R. (1959). A theory of therapy, personality, and interpersonal relationships, as developed in the client-centered framework. In S. Koch (Eds.), *Psychology: A study of a science* (Vol. 3, pp. 184–256). New York: McGraw-Hill.

Rosenberg, M. (1965). *Society and the adolescent self-image.* Princeton, NJ: Princeton University Press.

Rosenberg, M., & Simmons, R. G. (1972). *Black and white self-esteem: The urban school child.* Washington, DC: American Sociological Association.

Rosenblatt, A., Greenberg, J., Solomon, S, Pyszczynski, T., & Lyon, D. (1989). Evidence for terror management theory I: The effects of mortality salience on reactions to those who violate or uphold cultural values. *Journal of Personality and Social Psychology, 57,* 681–690.

Scheff, T. (1990). *Crisis in the academic system: Is the emperor wearing clothes?* Unpublished manuscript, University of California, Santa Barbara.

Snyder, M. L., Stephan, W. G., & Rosenfield, D. (1976). Egotism and attribution. *Journal of Personality and Social Psychology 33,* 435–441.

Solomon, S., Greenberg, J., & Pyszczynski, T. (1991a). Terror management theory of self-esteem. In C. R. Snyder & D. Forsyth (Eds.), *Handbook of social and clinical psychology: The health perspective* (pp. 21–40). New York: Pergamon Press.

Solomon, S., Greenberg, J., & Pyszczynski, T. (1991b). A terror management theory of social behavior: The psychological functions of self-esteem and cultural worldviews. In M. P. Zanna (Ed.), *Advances in experimental social psychology* (Vol. 24, pp. 93–159). San Diego, CA: Academic Press.

Spielberger, C. D., Gorsuch, R. L., & Lushene, R. E. (1970). *Trait anxiety inventory (self-evaluation questionnaire).* Palo Alto, CA: Consulting Psychologists Press.

Steele, C. M. (1988). The psychology of self-affirmation: Sustaining the integrity of the self. In L. Berkowitz (Ed.),

*Advances in experimental social psychology* (Vol. 21, pp. 261–302). San Diego, CA: Academic Press.

Stephan, W. G., & Gollwitzer, P. M. (1981). Affect as a mediator of attributional egotism. *Journal of Experimental Social Psychology, 17,* 443–458.

Sullivan, H. S. (1953). *The interpersonal theory of psychiatry.* New York: Norton.

Tesser, A., & Campbell, J. (1983). Self-definition and self-evaluation maintenance. In J. Suls & A. G. Greenwald (Eds.), *Psychological perspectives on the self* (Vol. 2, pp. 1–31). Hillsdale, NJ: Erlbaum.

Venables, P. H., & Christie, M. J. (1990). Electrodermal activity. In I. Martin & P. H. Venables (Eds.), *Techniques in psychophysiology* (pp. 3–67). Chichester, England: Wiley.

Watson, D., Clark, L. A., & Tellegen, A. (1988). Development and validation of brief measures of positive and negative affect: The PANAS scales. *Journal of Personality and Social Psychology, 53,* 1063–1070.

Wilder, J. (1962). Basimetric approach (law of initial values) to biological rhythms. *Annals of the New York Academy of Science, 98,* 1211–1220.

Zuckerman, M. (1960). The development of an affective adjective checklist from the measurement of anxiety. *Journal of Consulting Psychology, 24,* 457–462.

# Self and Informational Processing

Psychology's prevailing view of human nature changed fundamentally during the so-called cognitive revolution of the 1970s and 1980s. Prior to that, psychologists had been largely divided into two main camps. Psychodynamic psychologists were the heirs of Freud and regarded human nature as a complex mixture of dark, instinctual forces, including sex and aggression, which provided the central motivations that had to be channeled and transformed into everyday behavior, or else consigned to lurk in the unconscious. Behaviorists, in contrast, clung to the far simpler theories that were heavily based on conditioning research done with rats and other animals, and human beings were regarded as merely complex products of reinforcement histories, copycat modeling, and other simple learning processes.

The cognitive revolution introduced a new model: The human being is similar to a computer, in that it takes in information from the environment, stores it and uses it in calculations, and formulates its own behavioral responses based on its memories and social calculations.

Not surprisingly, the cognitive revolution changed the way psychologists thought about the self. Psychodynamic theory depicted the ego as the agent trying to serve the powerful forces of instinctive cravings and internalized prohibitions (the superego) while dealing with the practical constraints of the external world. Learning theory sometimes considered the self a mere epiphenomenon that falsely believes it makes free choices while actually being no more than a linguistic quirk. Social cognition, however, came to regard the self as an important and autonomous player that both actively intervenes in the processing of information and is itself a knowledge structure resulting from information processing.

The first two papers included here reflect these two cognitive functions of the self. Rogers, Kuiper, and Kirker (1977) made the simple but profound point that information relevant to the self gets processed more extensively and thoroughly, and is therefore remembered better than other information. In an elegant experimental procedure, they gave people words to read and asked them one of several questions about each word. If the question caused the person to think about the word in relation to the self, the person was more likely to remember the word later than any other question. The self is thus a source of cognitive power that endows information with added force, thereby earning extra processing and leaving a stronger memory trace. We remember things that bear on ourselves much better than we remember other information, even if no pragmatic consequences are involved.

A radical paper by Markus (1977) sought to replace the time-worn notion of a self-concept with the newer notion of self-schemas. Schemas organize information, but one can have multiple, even conflicting schemas about the self, and in that respect self-schemas represent an important advance over the notion of a single, global, unitary self-concept. Moreover, thinking in terms of schemas offered the novel characterization of being "aschematic." That is, a person may simply not have formed an opinion of himself or herself on a particular dimension. The older notion of a self-concept was typically approached by asking people whether they regard themselves, for example, as independent or dependent, or somewhere in between; Markus's approach suggested a fourth alternative, which is "none of the above"—which may be translated as not having any clear opinion on the matter.

The self-schema approach was adopted with enthusi-asm by researchers interested in person perception, and debates raged as to whether someone who was aschematic vs. schematic on a trait would be more likely to see another person as having that same trait. The eventual result did not resolve itself in simple projection or other mechanisms, however. Rather, the point seemed to be that having a self-schema for some trait makes one act more like an expert on that trait: The schematic person makes more subtle distinctions about others on that trait, attends more to details, spots relevant information more quickly, and integrates relevant information more effectively (Fong & Markus, 1982; Markus, Smith, & Moreland, 1985).

Of course, the self does not live by cognition alone: Emotion is also relevant. Yet emotion too may depend on how information is processed. The link between self and emotion was addressed in an influential work by Higgins (1987). He proposes that people compare themselves with two types of self-guides, one involving ideals, the other involving "oughts." The notion that self-evaluation involves two elements—how you are, and what you are comparing yourself to—goes back to James's formula that self-esteem equals successes divided by aspirations ("pretensions" in James's term), but Higgins elaborates this traditional view by suggesting that emotional responses differ depending on what type of self-guide is involved. The comparison of self with standards is found by many researchers to be important, but the idea that people really have two different kinds of self-guides, linked to different emotions, has been more controversial (cf. Tangney, Niedenthal, Covert, & Barlow, 1998). Regardless of how that controversy is resolved, Higgins will have advanced the field by focusing study on the vitally important question of the link between self and emotion.

## REFERENCES

Fong, G. T., & Markus, H. (1982). Self-schemas and judgements about others. *Social Cognition, 1,* 191–204.

Higgins, E. T. (1987). Self-discrepancy: A theory relating self and affect. *Psychological Review, 94,* 319–340.

James, W. (1892/1948). *Principles of Psychology.* Cleveland, OH: World Publishing.

Markus, H. R. (1977). Self-schemata and processing information about the self. *Journal of Personality and Social Psychology, 35,* 63–78.

Markus, H., Smith, J., & Moreland, R. (1985). Role of the self-concept in the perception of others. *Journal of Personality and Social Psychology, 49,* 1494–1512.

Rogers, T. B., Kuiper, N. A., & Kirker, W. S. (1977). Self-reference and the encoding of personal information. *Journal of Personality and Social Psychology, 35,* 677–688.

Tangney, J. P., Niedenthal, P. M., Covert, M. V., & Barlow, D. H. (1998). Are shame and guilt related to distinct self-discrepancies? A test of Higgins's (1987) hypotheses. *Journal of Personality and Social Psychology, 75,* 256–268.

# Discussion Questions

1. Which is more central to the nature of the self: thinking or feeling?
2. Why do you suppose people remember information relevant to the self better than other information?
3. Name some traits for which you know people who are clearly "aschematic."
4. Are some people "aschematic" on more traits than other people? What causes a person to become generally aschematic?
5. Is the ideal or the ought self more relevant to each of these emotions: fear, guilt, love, grief, panic/anxiety, anger, satisfaction, embarrassment?

# Suggested Readings

Bargh, J. (1982). Attention and automaticity in the processing of self-relevant information. *Journal of Personality and Social Psychology, 43,* 425–436. An influential paper that linked the self with two kinds of information processing: automatic and controlled.

Tangney, J. P., Niedenthal, P. M., Covert, M. V., & Barlow, D. H. (1998). Are shame and guilt related to distinct self-discrepancies? A test of Higgins's (1987) hypotheses. *Journal of Personality and Social Psychology, 75,* 256–268. A critique (with data) of self-discrepancy theory, focusing especially on the linking of two types of emotions with two self-guides.

Lewicki, P. (1983). Self-image bias in person perception. *Journal of Personality and Social Psychology, 45,* 384–393. (ALSO) Lewicki, P. (1984). Self-schema and social information processing. *Journal of Personality and Social Psychology, 47,* 1177–1190. These papers show how views of self can influence views of others: People form impressions of others using traits on which they themselves score well.

Andersen, S. M., & Ross, L. (1984). Self-knowledge and social inference: I. The impact of cognitive/affective and behavioral data. *Journal of Personality and Social Psychology, 46,* 280–293. (ALSO) Andersen, S. M. (1984). Self-knowledge and social inference: II. The diagnosticity of cognitive/affective and behavioral data. *Journal of Personality and Social Psychology, 46,* 294–307. These papers examine the relative weight people put on different types of information in knowing themselves: Inner processes such as thoughts and feelings count for far more than actual behavior, despite what psychologists have learned.

Wicklund, R. A., & Duval, S. (1971). Opinion change and performance facilitation as a result of objective self-awareness. *Journal of Experimental Social Psychology, 7,* 319–342. (ALSO) Carver, C. S., & Scheier, M. F. (1981). *Attention and self-regulation: A control theory approach to human behavior.* New York: Springer-Verlag. These works focus on self-awareness, which is another important dimension of the cognitive self. Wicklund and Duval's paper was the first to examine self-awareness in a laboratory, experimental context. Carver and Scheier's book a decade later summed up a large number of studies that had appeared on that topic.

# Self-Schemata and Processing Information about the Self

Hazel Markus • The University of Michigan

Attempts to organize, summarize, or explain one's own behavior in a particular domain result in the formation of cognitive structures about the self or *self-schemata*. Self-schemata are cognitive generalizations about the self, derived from past experience, that organize and guide the processing of the self-related information contained in an individual's social experience. The role of schemata in processing information about the self is examined by linking self-schemata to a number of specific empirical referents. Female students with schemata in a particular domain and those without schemata are selected and their performance on a variety of cognitive tasks is compared. The results indicate that self-schemata facilitate the processing of information about the self (judgments and decisions about the self), contain easily retrievable behavioral evidence, provide a basis for the confident self-prediction of behavior on schema-related dimensions, and make individuals resistant to counterschematic information. The relationship of self-schemata to cross-situational consistency in behavior and the implications of self-schemata for attribution theory are discussed.

The quantity and variety of social stimulation available at any time is vastly greater than a person can process or even attend to. Therefore, individuals are necessarily selective in what they notice, learn, remember, or infer in any situation. These selective tendencies, of course, are not random but depend on some internal cognitive structures that allow the individual to process the incoming information with some degree of efficiency. Recently, these structures for encoding and representing information have been called *frames* (Minsky, 1975), *scripts* (Abelson, 1975), and *schemata* (Bobrow & Norman, 1975; Stotland & Canon, 1972; Tesser & Conlee, 1975).

The influence of cognitive structures on the selection and organization of information is probably most apparent when we process information about ourselves. A substantial amount of information processed by an individual (some might even argue a majority of information) is information about the self, and a variety of cognitive structures are necessarily involved in processing this information. Yet in research on the self, in the personality area for example, there has been a notable lack of attention to the structures used in encoding one's own behavior and in the processing of information about one's own behavior. Research on self-perception (Bem, 1967, 1972) and research on self-monitoring (Snyder, 1974; Snyder & Monson, 1975) clearly suggests that the individual is an active, constructive information processor, but no specific cognitive structures have yet been implicated in this theorizing and research.

It is proposed here that attempts to organize,

summarize, or explain one's own behavior in a particular domain will result in the formation of cognitive structures about the self or what might be called self-schemata. *Self-schemata are cognitive generalizations about the self, derived from past experience, that organize and guide the processing of self-related information contained in the individual's social experiences.* The main purpose of the studies is to examine some functions of self-schemata in the processing of information about the self.

Self-schemata include cognitive representations derived from *specific* events and situations involving the individual (e.g., "I hesitated before speaking in yesterday's discussion because I wasn't sure I was right, only to hear someone else make the same point") as well as more *general* representations derived from the repeated categorization and subsequent evaluation of the person's behavior by himself and by others around him (e.g., "I am very talkative in groups of three or four, but shy in large gatherings," "I am generous," "I am creative," or "I am independent").

Self-schemata are constructed from information processed by the individual in the past and influence both input and output of information related to the self. They represent the way the self has been differentiated and articulated in memory. Once established, these schemata function as selective mechanisms that determine whether information is attended to, how it is structured, how much importance is attached to it, and what happens to it subsequently. As individuals accumulate repeated experiences of a certain type, their self-schemata become increasingly resistant to inconsistent or contradictory information, although they are never totally invulnerable to it.

Self-schemata can be viewed as a reflection of the invariances people have discovered in their own social behavior. They represent patterns of behavior that have been observed repeatedly, to the point where a framework is generated that allows one to make inferences from scant information or to quickly streamline and interpret complex sequences of events. To the extent that our own behavior exhibits some regularity or redundancy, self-schemata will be generated because they are useful in understanding intentions and feelings and in identifying likely or appropriate patterns of behavior. While a self-schema is an organization of the representations of past behavior, it is more than

a "depository." It serves an important processing function and allows an individual to go beyond the information currently available. The concept of self-schema implies that information about the self in some area has been categorized or organized and that the result of this organization is a discernible pattern which may be used as a basis for future judgments, decisions, inferences, or predictions about the self.

There is substantial historical precedent for the schema term and for schemalike concepts, and it would entail a very lengthy discussion to trace the history of the term (cf. Bartlett, 1932; Kelley, 1972; Kelly, 1955; Piaget, 1951). In social psychology, schema-like concepts (e.g., causal schemata, scripts, implicit personality theories) have been vaguely defined heuristics with no real empirical moorings. Despite their assumed cognitive consequences, they have been viewed primarily as epiphenomena, inferred on the basis of behavior or invoked in various post hoc explanations. The investigation of self-schemata requires examining the hypothesized functions of schemata for their particular empirical implications. To date this has not been done.

Recent work in the general area of cognition suggests a number of ways of investigating self-schemata. This work provides models of information processing (e.g., Anderson & Bower, 1973; Atkinson & Shiffrin, 1968; Erdelyi, 1974), indicates the possible functions of cognitive structures, and makes use of a variety of measures (recognition, recall, response latency, etc.) and techniques (signal detection, chronometric descriptions of information flow, etc.) capable of empirically identifying these functions. The experimental work in this area, however, has concentrated largely on the processing of neutral or nonsense material. With the exception of some work (Mischel, Ebbesen, & Zeiss, 1976), there has been little empirical work on the influence of cognitive structures on the selective processing of significant *social* information (e.g., information about important aspects of one's self).

The idea of self-schemata as cognitive generalizations about the self has a number of implications for the empirical work on personality and cross-situational consistency. For example, an endorsement of a trait adjective as self-descriptive or an endorsement of an item on a self-rating scale *may* reflect an underlying, well-articulated self-schema. It is equally possible, however, that the mark on the self-rating scale is not the product of a well-specified schema, but is instead the result of the favorability of the trait term, the context of the situation, the necessity for a response, or other experimental demands. *Only when a self-description derives from a well-articulated generalization about the self can it be expected to converge and form a consistent pattern with the individual's other judgments, decisions, and actions.* Thus, a person who does not really think about herself as conscientious, yet would not object to labeling herself as such, cannot be expected to react to being late for an appointment in the same way as one who actively conceives of herself as conscientious, who can readily describe numerous displays of conscientiousness in the past, and who can enumerate the way she insures future conscientious behavior on her part.

To demonstrate the construct validity of the concept of self-schemata, a number of empirical referents can be specified. If self-schemata are built up from cognitive representations of past experiences, individual differences in self-schemata should be readily discovered because individuals clearly differ in their past experiences. If a person has a developed self-schema, he should be readily able to (a) process information about the self in the given domain (e.g., make judgments or decisions) with relative ease, (b) retrieve behavioral evidence from the domain, (c) predict his own future behavior in the domain, and (d) resist counterschematic information about himself. If a person has had relatively little experience in a given domain of social behavior, or has not attended to behavior in this domain, then it is unlikely that he will have developed an articulated self-schema.

Consistency in patterns of response on a number of self-description tasks, as well as convergence in results from a number of diverse cognitive tasks involving self-judgments, should provide evidence for the existence of an organization of knowledge about the self on a particular dimension of behavior, or a self-schema. To the extent that individuals do not possess an articulated self-schema on a particular dimension of behavior, they will not exhibit consistency in response. Nor will they display the discrimination necessary for the efficient processing of information and the prediction of future behavior along this dimension.

The procedure of the first study is to select a dimension of behavior, to identify individuals with schemata and those without schemata on this dimension, and then to compare their performance on a variety of cognitive tasks. Several tasks utilizing self-rating, self-description, and prediction of behavior are combined to determine whether the processing of information about one's self varies systematically as a function of self-schemata. The second study investigates the selective influence of self-schemata on the interpretation of information about one's own behavior. Individuals with articulated self-schemata (along a specific behavioral dimension identified in the first study) and individuals without such schemata are induced to engage in behavior that is potentially diagnostic of this dimension. The impact of this information is evaluated for both groups.

## Study 1

This study is concerned with the impact of self-schemata on the selection and processing of information about the self. Individuals with self-schemata along a particular dimension of behavior are compared with individuals without such self-schemata. Also compared are individuals with different self-schemata along the same dimension of behavior. Specifically, it is hypothesized that a self-schema will determine the type of self-judgments that are made, and that these judgments will vary in latency depending on the presence and content of self-schemata. Also, individuals with self-schemata should find it easier to describe specific behavior that is related to their schema and should be relatively more certain about prediction of their behavior along this dimension than individuals without schemata.

### Method

To gain a preliminary idea of each subject's self-schema on various dimensions, a number of self-rating scales were administered in introductory psychology classes. The most appropriate pattern of variation in self-ratings was found on the independence–dependence dimension and thus it was selected as the dimension for further study. From among the individuals completing this questionnaire, 48 were selected to participate individually in the laboratory sessions.

The first laboratory session consisted of three separate cognitive tasks designed to assess the influence of self-schemata about independence on the processing of information about the self. These included:

### CONTENT AND LATENCY OF SELF-DESCRIPTION

Subjects were given a number of trait adjectives associated with independence and dependence and were asked to indicate for each whether it was self-descriptive or not. Response latency was recorded for each judgment.

### SUPPLYING BEHAVIORAL EVIDENCE FOR SELF-DESCRIPTION

Subjects were asked to select trait adjectives that were self-descriptive and then to cite instances from their own past behavior to support their endorsement of a particular adjective as self-descriptive.

### PREDICTING THE LIKELIHOOD OF BEHAVIOR

Subjects were given a series of descriptions of independent and dependent behavior and were asked to judge how likely it was they would behave in these ways.

## Subjects

For the questionnaire phase of the experiment, subjects were 101 female students in introductory psychology classes at a large university. Subjects for the first laboratory sessions were 48 students selected from this group. Only female students were used in this study because the distribution of self-ratings on various dimensions appears to differ with sex. Using male and female students would have required selecting more dimensions.

## Materials and Procedures

### INITIAL QUESTIONNAIRE

Individuals in introductory psychology classes were asked to rate themselves on the Gough-Heilbrun Adjective Check List (Gough & Heilbrun, 1965) and on several semantic differential scales describing a variety of behavioral domains. On the latter measure, subjects were also asked to rate the importance of each semantic dimension to their self-description. From these re-

spondents, three groups of 16 subjects each were selected to participate in the experimental sessions.

### INDEPENDENTS

Individuals who rated themselves at the extreme end (points 8–11 on an 11-point scale) on at least two of the following semantic differential scales: Independent–Dependent, Individualist–Conformist, or Leader–Follower, and who rated these dimensions as important (points 8–11 on an 11-point scale), and who checked themselves as "independent" on the adjective check list were termed *Independents*.[1]

### DEPENDENTS

Individuals who rated themselves at the opposite end (points 1–4) on at least two of these scales, and who rated these dimensions as important (points 8–11 on an 11-point scale), and who checked themselves as "dependent" on the adjective check list were termed Dependents.

### ASCHEMATICS

Individuals who rated themselves in the middle range (points 5–7) on at least two of these three scales, and fell in the lower portion of the distribution on the importance scale, and did not check themselves as either "independent" or "dependent" on the adjective check list were termed Aschematics. The term aschematic is used here to mean without schema on this particular dimension.[2]

Invoking the importance criterion conjointly with the extremity criterion made it possible to avoid confusing Aschematics with persons who act (and think of themselves) as independent in some

---

[1] Although subjects were selected on the basis of their "extreme" scores on these self-rating scales, only 2 subjects of the 48 actually used the endpoints 11 or 1 in their self ratings on the semantic differential scales.

[2] Another indicator of a subject's self-schema about independence was her score on the Autonomy scale of the Gough-Heilbrun Adjective Check List (ACL). The Autonomy scale is one of the ACL's 24 empirically derived scales designed to correspond to dimensions of the California Psychological Inventory and Murray's need-press system. Autonomy is defined as the tendency to act independently of others or of social values and expectations. Subjects selected as Independents in this study were among the 25 with highest scores on this measure, and those selected as Dependents were among the 25 with lowest scores. Aschematics scored in the

classes of situations and as dependent in other classes of situations, and do so consistently. Making such fine discriminations would lead these individuals to develop a fairly well-articulated conception of the independence domain of social behavior, and thus it would be incorrect to classify them as Aschematics. However, if these people had a well-articulated conception of themselves as both dependent and independent, they would no doubt be quite sensitive to social behavior in the domain of independence and would consider it to be a significant and important area. Hence, they would not be classified as Aschematics according to our criteria. Among the Aschematics, the average importance rating on the three semantic differential scales was 6.4, while among the Schematics it was 9.5.

Three to four weeks after the questionnaire was administered, the 48 subjects were called individually to the laboratory and received identical treatment. They were not informed of a connection between this session and the questionnaire, and it is unlikely that they could have inferred such a connection since different experimenters were used.

## TASK 1: CONTENT AND LATENCY OF SELF-DESCRIPTION

Sixty-nine trait adjectives were prepared on 2 × 2 inch (5 × 5 cm) slides; 15 had been previously judged (by another group of 50 subjects) to be related to independence and nonconformity (independent words) and 15 were judged to be related to dependence and conformity (dependent words). These 30 words were the critical schema-related stimuli.[3] Thirty other words, included for comparison with the schema-related adjectives, clustered around the notions of creativity and noncreativity and were used as control words. In each group of 30 words, 10 were negatively rated, 10 were positively rated, and 10 neutral, according to Anderson's (1968) list of the likableness of 555 trait adjectives. The words were either of high frequency or moderate frequency (according to the

norms of Carroll, Davies, & Richman, 1971). The remaining 9 words were 3 practice adjectives, 3 adjectives that nearly all subjects had indicated were self-descriptive on the initial questionnaire (honest, intelligent, friendly), and 3 adjectives that nearly all subjects had indicated were not self-descriptive (rude, obnoxious, unscrupulous).

Each of these 69 adjectives was presented on the screen for 2 seconds by a slide projector activated by the experimenter. Following the presentation of a word, the subject was required to respond by pushing a *me* button if the word was self-descriptive, or a *not me* button if the word was not self-descriptive. The response stopped an electronic clock that began with the presentation of the stimulus. The subject had to respond with one of the two buttons before the next stimulus would appear. For each word the experimenter recorded both response latency and the choice of *me* or *not me*. Subjects were not aware that response latency was being measured. Four different randomly determined orders of presentations were used for the slides, with 12 subjects in each order. In addition, for half of the subjects the *me* button was on the right side of the panel and for the remaining half on the left side. To insure that individuals were associating similar types of behaviors to the trait adjectives, a particular context was specified for the self-judgments. The instructions were:

> When you are making these decisions about yourself, try to imagine yourself in a typical group situation, one that might occur for example, in a classroom, in the dorm lounge, or at a meeting in a friend's home. You are together to discuss an important and controversial issue and to make some decisions about it. Many of the people in the group you know or are familiar to you, while others are not.

## TASK 2: SUPPLYING BEHAVIORAL EVIDENCE FOR SELF-DESCRIPTIONS

After the categorization task, each subject received a booklet containing 16 words (1 on each page)

---

middle range on this measure. It is important to note that all of the subjects who would be labeled autonomous on the basis of this measure (that is, they were among the 25 highest scorers) also rated themselves extremely (points 8–11) on at least two of the semantic differential scales. Those who would be labeled nonautonomous or dependent on the basis of this measure also rated themselves extremely (points 1–5) on the three semantic differential scales.

[3]The *independent* adjectives were: individualistic, independent, ambitious, adventurous, self-confident, dominating, argumentative, aloof, arrogant, egotistical, unconventional, outspoken, aggressive, assertive, uninhibited. The *dependent* adjectives were: dependable, cooperative, tactful, tolerant, unselfish, impressionable, conforming, dependent, timid, submissive, conventional, moderate, obliging, self-denying, cautious.

from the set described in Task 1. Seven of these words were from the set of independent words and 7 were from the set of dependent words. Two additional words were from the creative/noncreative set. Of the 16 words, 4 were positively rated for likableness, 4 were negatively rated, and 8 were neutral. The order of the adjectives in each booklet was randomly determined. Subjects were given written instructions to circle each adjective they considered to be self-descriptive and were also asked the following:

> Immediately after you circle an adjective, list the reasons you feel this adjective is self-descriptive. Give specific evidence from your *own* past behavior to indicate why you feel a particular trait is self-descriptive. . . . List the first kinds of behaviors that come to your mind. Do not worry about how other people might interpret a particular behavior; use your own frame of reference. (Several examples were given.)

### TASK 3: PREDICTING THE LIKELIHOOD OF BEHAVIOR

The third task utilized a series of specific behavioral descriptions taken from a large number of descriptions that had been rated by a separate group of 40 introductory psychology students as characterizing either independence and nonconformity or dependence and conformity. This outside group of subjects was asked to decide how they would label or categorize each act if they saw it or if they heard someone describe themselves in these terms. The final list included 10 pairs of behavioral descriptions matched in content but differing in the way the behavior would be categorized, for example, "You hesitate before commenting, only to hear someone else make the point you had in mind" (rated dependent) and "You speak up as soon as you have some comments on the issue being discussed" (rated independent). Several filler items also were included. A context for the behavioral descriptions similar to the one in Task 1 was provided and then the subjects were given written instructions which read:

> Listed below are a number of behaviors and reactions that might be true of you in a gathering like this. For each one, indicate how likely or how probable it is that you would behave or react in this way. You may assign each item any number from 0 to 100. A 0 means that this could not be true of you, that it is extremely unlikely that you

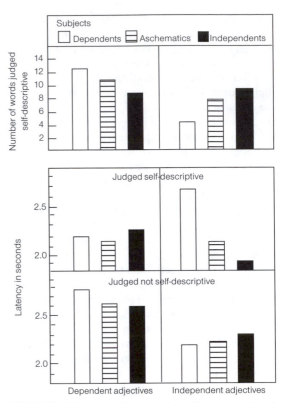

**FIGURE 7.1** ■ Top panel: Mean number of independent and dependent adjectives judged as self-descriptive. Bottom panel: Mean response latency for independent and dependent adjectives judged as self-descriptive and as not self-descriptive.

would act or feel this way. A 100 means that this could very well be true of you, that it is likely that you would act or feel this way.

## Results

For the purpose of analysis, subjects were divided into three groups labeled Independents, Dependents, and Aschematics, as described in the Procedure section.

### TASK 1: CONTENT AND LATENCY OF SELF-DESCRIPTION

As shown in the top panel of Figure 7.1, the three groups of subjects clearly differed in the average number of the 15 dependent words judged as self-descriptive, $F(2, 45) = 14.89$, $p < .001$. The three groups also differed in the average number of the 15 independent adjectives judged as self-descriptive, $F(2, 45) = 9.27, p < .001$. Using $p < .05$ as a criterion, Newman-Keuls comparisons showed that Dependents judged significantly more dependent words as self-descriptive than did Independents, and conversely, Independents judged significantly more independent words as self-descriptive than did Dependents.

The bottom panel of Figure 7.1 presents the average response latencies for self-descriptive judgments (*me*) and for not self-descriptive judgments (*not me*) for the independent and dependent adjectives. Dependent subjects were reliably faster at making *me* judgments for dependent words than for independent words, $t(15) = 2.63, p < .01$.[4] Congruently, Independent subjects were reliably faster at making *me* judgments for independent adjectives than for dependent adjectives, $t(15) = 2.72$, $p < .01$. The Aschematics, however, did not differ in response latency for independent and dependent words.

When the top and bottom panels of Figure 7.1 are considered together, a number of other points about the self-categorization of these three groups of subjects can be made. A *me* response to a particular adjective may be the result of an individual labeling her behavior or reactions in this way or thinking about herself in these terms. But it may also be the result of several other considerations, such as the positivity or social desirability of a particular adjective. Looking within groups, it can be seen from the top panel that Dependent subjects responded *me* to significantly more dependent words than independent words; there is a clear differentiation here, $t(15) = 10.55, p < .001$. Independent subjects however, although responding *me* to more independent words than either of the other two groups of subjects, found nearly as many dependent adjectives to be self-descriptive, $t(15) < 1$. On the basis of these findings alone, one might conclude that this group does not use independent or dependent words differentially or that independence is not a meaningful dimension for these subjects. The bottom panel indicates that this is not the case, however. Independent subjects respond much faster to the independent words than they do to the dependent words. The faster processing times for the independent words suggest that it is indeed easier for Independent subjects to think about themselves in these terms or that they are used to thinking about themselves in these terms.

The latency measure is also useful in interpreting the results of the Aschematic group. From the top panel it can be seen that Aschematics respond *me* to more dependent words than independent words, $t(15) = 2.42, p < .05$. If the response latencies for these judgments are ignored, one might take this to mean that these subjects are similar to the Dependents. It is evident, however, that Aschematic subjects do not really use these two sets of words differentially in describing themselves in the same way Dependent subjects do. There is no difference among Aschematic subjects in processing time for the two sets of words. Even though they were constrained to think of a specific social situation, Aschematics appear to be equally at ease labeling their behavior with independent or dependent adjectives.[5]

Response latency for self-categorization appears to be a sensitive measure that reveals variations in judgments that rating scales and check lists cannot. Endorsements that result from the positivity or desirability of a stimulus can potentially be separated from responses that reflect more valid self-characterizations. This is clearly demonstrated in Figure 7.2. The top panel shows the responses of three groups of subjects to the three control words that were included in the list of presented adjectives. The number of subjects out of the total 16 that responded *me* to each word is shown beneath the bar. Not surprisingly, nearly all subjects viewed themselves as honest, intelligent, and friendly. And there are no differences among the three groups in the processing time for these adjectives. The overall average latency for these three words was much shorter (1.67 seconds) than the overall average latency for all words (2.23 seconds). These adjectives appear to be synonymous with general "goodness" and do not convey unique information about an individual. The three groups of subjects also

---

[4]Except where specified, all *t* tests are two-tailed.

[5]Overall, subjects find more dependent words than independent words to be self-descriptive, despite the fact that the two sets of words were initially matched for positivity and frequency. In fact, across all subjects an average of 7.4 independent words were judged to be self-descriptive compared to an average of 10.9 dependent words. This may also explain the relatively longer response times for *not me* judgments of dependent words obtained in all three groups of subjects. Across all subjects the average latency for a *not me* response to dependent words was 2.63 seconds compared with 2.22 seconds for independent words. It is possible that within the set of our 69 words (Anderson's subjects rated a set of 555 adjectives), the dependent words appeared as more positive or desirable, and thus it was difficult for subjects to respond *not me* to them.

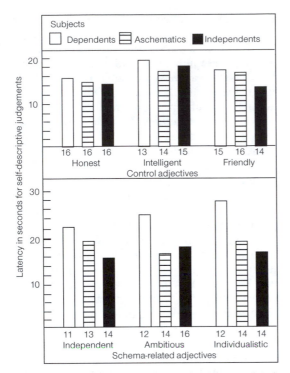

did not differ in processing time for *not me* judgments to the negatively rated adjectives rude, obnoxious, and unscrupulous.

This was not true, however, for other adjectives that presumably are tied to more specifically defined behaviors. The bottom panel of Figure 7.2 shows the responses of the three groups of subjects to three schema-related words; that is, three words from the set of independent words shown to subjects. Here again, just on the basis of their overt responses, it would appear that these subjects did not differ in their characterization of themselves, as the clear majority of subjects also responded *me* to these three schema-related words. The latency measures exhibited a much different pattern, however. Dependent subjects, for the most part, indicated that they were independent, ambitious, and individualistic, but it took them significantly longer to make this judgment than it did for Independent subjects. Separate analyses of variance performed on the response latencies for these three words yielded significant differences among the three groups of subjects: ambitious, $F(2, 35) = 6.59, p < .01$; independent, $F(2, 35) = 6.59, p < .01$; individualistic, $F(2, 37) = 4.56, p < .01$. It is

probable that Dependent subjects would like to label themselves with these words and subsequently do, but they experience some difficulty endorsing the words; a difficulty they do not experience with the dependent words. This result cannot be explained by assuming that Dependent subjects just take longer to make self-judgments, for on the control adjectives the latencies of the Dependents did not differ from those of the other groups of subjects. The faster processing times of the Independent subjects on schema-related words may be indicative of schemata that contain information about independence and individualism. Dependent subjects do not have information about themselves that might be reasonably labeled in this way, and their hesitation in making unsubstantiated judgments about themselves is reflected in relatively longer latencies.

The lack of differentiation in response latency to the schema-related adjectives shown by the Aschematics relative to the other two groups of subjects has been interpreted as evidence for the absence of a schema on this dimension. There is an alternative explanation, however. It may be that a clear self-definition in terms of one set of adjectives or another is not a result of past behavior that has been categorized or labeled in this way, but rather a function of general cognitive differentiation or articulation. Independents and Dependents might be individuals who generally prefer to have things compartmentalized along a number of different dimensions. Aschematics, in contrast, may have global or undifferentiated cognitive styles. A direct test of this possibility cannot be made given the present data. However, as an indirect test, an index which reflected the articulation of the schema for each subject was calculated on the basis of the number of independent and dependent words judged *me* and *not me*. The measure was the Kendall $\tau_b$, and it reflected a subject's departure from the standard of responding *me* to all 15 independent words and *not me* to all 15 dependent words. The closer the value to 1 or −1, the more clearly the subject defines herself on this dimension. This measure was also calculated for each subject on the basis of her *me* responses to the 30 creative/noncreative adjectives which were included in the list presented to subjects. A cognitive style explanation would predict that subjects with high $\tau_b$ values (either positive or negative) on the independent/dependent adjectives would also be the subjects with high absolute values of $\tau_b$ on the creative/noncreative words, reflecting a general tendency toward differentiation or articulation. In fact, there was no association between the sets of $\tau_b$ absolute values for Independents ($r = .00$), Dependents ($r = -.07$), or Aschematics ($r = -.14$).

The fact that subjects with schemata on independence–dependence do not necessarily have schemata on creativity–noncreativity and vice versa indicates that differences in self-categorizations may be the result of an individual's behavior and its subsequent cognitive interpretation rather than a reflection of differences in the general complexity of cognitive structure. It is also consistent with the idea that individuals develop schemata on dimensions they choose to attend to and do not develop schemata on others.

## TASK 2: SUPPLYING BEHAVIORAL EVIDENCE FOR SELF-DESCRIPTION

In this task, it was hypothesized that if one has a schema that is a reflection of past behavior, then one should be readily able to provide specific behavioral evidence related to it; that is, to generate specific instances of behavior that were labeled or categorized by oneself or others in a particular way.

This task appeared to be generally meaningful to subjects and they performed it with little difficulty. For example, the dependent adjective conforming elicited responses such as "I didn't go to any of the rallies about the teaching-fellow strike because my friends didn't" or "I watched a television show I couldn't stand last night just to save a hassle with my roommates" or "I pierced my ears because all my friends did."

Independent subjects wrote more behavioral descriptions for Independent words than did either of the other two groups of subjects. The differences in the mean number of behavioral examples written for each independent adjective for the three groups were significant, $F(2, 45) = 4.91$, $p < .005$. Across all of the seven independent adjectives, the Independent subjects supplied almost one specific example of behavior for each word (.93 behavioral descriptions per adjective) compared to .56 for the Aschematics and .36 for the Dependent subjects. A significant opposite pattern occurred for the dependent words, $F(2, 45) = 3.59$, $p < .05$.

Across all the adjectives, the subjects with schemata (the Dependents and the Independents) and

the Aschematics did not differ in the average number of words that were judged as self-descriptive, but they did differ in the average number of behavioral descriptions that were written for each word, $t(46) = 1.78$, $p < .05$,[6] with the Aschematics supplying somewhat fewer examples of behavior than subjects with schemata. This result is consistent with the expectation that individuals without schemata on this dimension probably have not used many independent or dependent adjectives to label their behavior, and thus it should be more difficult for them to supply specific behavioral descriptions.

A more detailed analysis of the individual words revealed that the smaller number of behavioral examples supplied by the Aschematics was primarily the result of these subjects producing fewer examples for the four negatively rated adjectives. It is interesting in this respect that for the Aschematics there was a substantial relationship between the percentage of individuals judging a word as self-descriptive and the positivity of the word ($r = .53$, $p < .05$). This relationship was not evident for the other two groups of subjects (Dependents, $r = .11$; Independents, $r = .21$). As a group, then, the Aschematics appear to be relatively more affected by the positivity of the adjective and may use this attribute to decide whether a particular word is self-descriptive. Independent and Dependent subjects are relatively more willing to use negative labels for their behavior. It may be that an individual with a schema about her behavior on a particular dimension is aware of both the positive and negative aspects of it and has evidence for both.

This task employed 14 of the same adjectives used in Task 1 and thus it is possible to evaluate the consistency of self-descriptive responses for the three groups of subjects. For the Independents, the correlation between me responses on the two tasks was .64 ($p < .01$), for the Dependents .56 ($p < .05$), and for the Aschematics it was .20. Of the 14 adjectives employed in this task, independent subjects exhibited the shortest processing time for the words independent, self-confident, and cooperative in Task 1. In the present task, these were the 3 words that were most likely to be judged self-descriptive by Independent subjects, and in

---

[6]One-tailed test of the hypothesis that individuals with schemata are able to provide more specific behavioral evidence for their self-judgments than Aschematics.

addition, these were the 3 words that elicited the largest number of behavioral descriptions. Dependent subjects responded fastest to the adjectives *cooperative, cautious,* and *moderate* in Task 1. Again, in this task these were the words that were the most likely to be judged self-descriptive by the Dependent subjects and also the words for which they gave the greatest number of behavioral descriptions. This pattern, however, was not found for the Aschematic subjects; the adjectives requiring the least processing times were not those most likely to be judged self-descriptive. The lack of congruence between these two judgments suggests either that Aschematics were fluctuating from Task 1 to Task 2 on which adjectives they considered to be self-descriptive or that different types of considerations were mediating the two judgments. For the Independents and the Dependents, the two judgments appear to be mediated by a similar type of consideration, presumably whether or not they have previously characterized or labeled their own behavior in this way.

## TASK 3: PREDICTING THE LIKELIHOOD OF BEHAVIOR

In this task, it was expected that people with self-schemata on the independence–dependence dimension would assign either relatively higher or lower probabilities to independent and dependent behaviors than individuals who do not have a self-schema on this dimension of behavior. It was assumed that subjects with self-schemata would be relatively more aware or more certain of what behaviors would be elicited from them in these situations and could make more confident predictions of their behavior.

Dependent subjects assigned a significantly higher likelihood to dependent behaviors than to independent behaviors, $t(15) = 3.30$, $p < .01$. In contrast, Independent subjects assigned a reliably higher likelihood to independent behaviors than they did to dependent behaviors, $t(15) = 3.31$, $p < .01$. For the Aschematics, however, there was no difference between the likelihood assigned to independent behaviors and the likelihood assigned dependent behaviors, $t(15) < 1$.

It was evident that the Independent and the Dependent subjects differ in the actions they think likely of themselves, although some items were better than others in differentiating among the groups. The average subjective likelihood assigned to the dependent behaviors was 35.7 for Independent subjects, 45.9 for the Aschematic subjects, and 54.4 for Dependent subjects, $F(2, 45) = 5.57$, $p < .01$. The average likelihood assigned to the independent behaviors was 53.8 for Independent subjects, 45.7 for Aschematic subjects, and 37.1 for Dependent subjects, $F(2, 45) = 7.40$, $p < .001$.

Overall, the Independent and the Dependent subjects differ markedly from the Aschematic subjects. The former two groups are relatively polarized in their estimations of the probabilities of these behaviors occurring, indicating that they are more certain about what types of behavior might be characteristic of them in particular settings. For the independent behaviors, the average deviation from the mean likelihood rating was 7.60 for Independents, and –9.12 for Dependents. For the dependent behaviors the average deviation from the mean likelihood was –9.63 for the Independents and 8.99 for the Dependents. Aschematics, however, do not show this polarization in their judgments. For the independent behaviors, the average deviation was .45, for dependent behaviors it was –.05. For these individuals there appears to be little difference in the subjective likelihood of independent and dependent behaviors; they are equally likely to occur or not to occur. Recall again in this respect that the subjects were constrained to think of a fairly specific context. These data suggest, therefore, that the Aschematics have no articulated cognitive generalizations or self-schemata along the dimension of independence–dependence.

One possible alternative explanation for the lack of difference in the mean ratings of independent and dependent behaviors for Aschematics is that Aschematics are really a heterogeneous collection composed of approximately equal numbers of subjects responding like Independents and Dependents. However, inspection of the distributions of likelihood ratings yielded no evidence to support this possibility. The distributions of likelihood ratings for all three groups of subjects with respect to both independent and dependent behaviors are unimodal and fairly symmetric about the mean.

The consistent pattern of responses observed for the Independents and Dependents across these diverse tasks argues for the existence of a prevailing self-schema which facilitates the processing of social information. Individuals assumed to have schemata clearly performed differently on these tasks than did individuals assumed not to have schemata.

Aschematics did not discriminate among the independent and dependent stimuli on any of the tasks. It seems that for these individuals, independence–dependence was not a meaningful dimension of behavior; that is, they did not categorize or make distinctions on the basis of the independence or dependence of their actions.

The pattern of findings describing the Aschematics clearly indicates why self-characterizations such as adjective self-descriptions may often be misleading as indicators of future behavior. For those individuals who had a self-schema about their independence or dependence, the responses to the self-categorization task were highly consistent with their responses to the other two tasks and would most likely be consistent with behavior along this dimension. The responses of the Aschematics to the self-categorization task, however, could not be generalized even to the other self-description tasks. It would be surprising, therefore, if these responses were consistent with observable behavior.

## Study 2

This study focuses on how self-schemata may produce differences in the selection and interpretation of information about the self. If self-schemata produce differences in judgments about the self, in description of past behavior, and in prediction of future behavior, it is reasonable that they should also produce differences in interpreting new information about the self. Thus, it is hypothesized that a self-schema along a particular dimension of behavior will make an individual resistant to counterschematic information about his or her behavior. This study employed the same individuals who took part in Study 1, provided them with information about themselves (a rigged score on a test of suggestibility) which was incongruent with their assumed schema, and then evaluated the impact of this information. Subjects with definite schemata should be unwilling to accept or believe the incongruent information produced by this measure, while Aschematic subjects should find the test results relatively more credible. Following the suggestibility test and a subsequent ques-

tionnaire, content and latencies of self-descriptions (Task 1 from Study 1) were again assessed.

## Method

### SUBJECTS

Forty-seven of the 48 subjects who participated in Experiment 1 also participated in this experiment.

### MATERIALS AND PROCEDURES

Three weeks after completion of the laboratory session in Study 1, subjects were scheduled for a second experiment. They were given the QPAT Suggestibility Test, a fictitious test prepared especially so that the experimenter could provide feedback that was incongruent with the subject's self-schema. Independents were given information that stated they were not independent at all but rather very suggestible and good followers. Dependents were given information indicating that they were very independent and not at all suggestible. The Aschematics were randomly assigned to one feedback condition or another.

Upon arriving at the laboratory, subjects were told:

> Before beginning today's experiment, I wonder if you would like to take part in a Psychology Department project. They are in the process of validating a new test . . . that involves measuring physiological changes by attaching these [electrodes] to your fingers.

After subjects agreed to take part, electrodes were attached to two of their fingers. Standard galvanic skin response apparatus was in clear view. Subjects were then given the QPAT Suggestibility Test. In this task subjects were asked to relax and then to perform a number of simple movements such as standing up and squeezing hands together. In addition, they were asked to imagine a number of specific scenes and were asked questions about these images. The test took about 10 minutes. The experimenter then removed the electrodes and ostensibly calculated the subject's score. The subject was told:

> This is a test of suggestibility in everyday life. It has been found to be a quick and reasonably accurate way to measure suggestibility. Your physiological data, the responses you made, as well as the time it took you to answer, indicate that you

are highly suggestible (not at all suggestible). . . . This sheet will tell you what this score means.

Subjects were then handed one of the two descriptions, depending on their experimental condition. Independents and the Aschematics assigned to this condition were given the following description:

> For individuals who score 55–65: Individuals who receive a score in this range are generally quite susceptible to social influence. They are quite likely to be influenced by others. Because they are open-minded and receptive to the suggestions of others . . . they are generally good team members. . . . Individuals in this range are not usually concerned with making their own point or standing up for a particular issue. . . . This score also suggests that one is quite sensitive and able to see things from the other person's point of view.

Dependents and the Aschematics assigned to this condition were given a description that was very similar in form, but written to describe an individual who is not suggestible and not likely to be influenced by the ideas of others.[7]

None of the words used in these descriptions were the same as words used in any of the tasks in Study 1, although suggestibility is dearly related to the general independence–dependence dimension. After subjects finished reading their description, acceptance of the incongruent information was assessed by means of a brief questionnaire. Following the completion of this questionnaire, subjects were asked to put their questionnaire in a campus mail envelope addressed to the Psychology Department and were given a name and number to call in case they wanted to find out more about the tests.

Following this procedure, subjects were told that the experiment they were called for would begin. Subjects were given Task 1 (content and latency of self-description) from Study 1 again. The task was identical using the same 69 adjectives and requiring a subject to respond either *me* or *not me*. Each subject was randomly assigned to one of the four orders of presentation, with the exception that no subject received the same order she received in Study 1.

## Results

In the analysis of these results individuals assumed to have schemata on the independence–dependence

dimension were compared with individuals assumed not to have schemata on this dimension.

## SUGGESTIBILITY TEST

Reactions to the suggestibility test support the expectation that individuals with schemata are less willing than Aschematics to accept incongruent or counterschematic information as self-diagnostic. When asked, "How accurately does this test describe you?" Aschematics felt that the suggestibility test described them more accurately than did the other two groups of subjects, $t(45) = p < .05$. In addition, a larger proportion of Independents and Dependents indicated some disagreement or disbelief about their score than did Aschematics, $t(45) = 2.11$, $p < .05$. More of the Aschematics were also willing to take the test again, although this difference was not reliable.

The degree to which subjects accepted test feedback is indicated by how distant from the neutral point of the 11-point scale of suggestibility they placed themselves following the manipulation. The Independents and the Dependents placed themselves on the average 2.17 points away from the neutral point in the direction indicated by the suggestibility information they received. The Aschematics, however, placed themselves 2.83 points away from the neutral point in the direction indicated by the suggestibility information, $t(45) = 1.86$, $p < .05$.[8]

## SELF-DESCRIPTION TASK

For each of the three groups, there were no significant differences between number of endorsements at time$_1$ and endorsements at time$_2$ (which

---

[7]The two descriptions were written with the intention of making the independent and the dependent feedback convey different types of information, but give equally favorable overall impressions. To test for this, the two descriptions were given to female students in several introductory psychology classes not participating in this experiment. These students were asked to rate the two descriptions for "How much would you like an individual who fits this description?" on a 7-point Like–Dislike scale. Half of the respondents received one description first and the other half received the alternative description. The Dependent, or suggestible description, received an average rating of 4.55 and the Independent, or not suggestible description, received an average rating of 4.45, a nonsignificant difference.

[8]One-tailed test of the hypothesis that Aschematics are relatively more accepting of the information provided by the suggestibility test.

immediately followed the suggestibility test) on any of the four judgments (*me*-dependent words, *not me*-dependent words, *me*-independent words, *not me*-independent words). Aschematics, however, exhibited relatively more inconsistency in their pattern of *me/not me* responses than did the Independents and Dependents. A correlation between the Kendall $\tau_b$ for each subject at time$_1$ and time$_2$ for the pooled Independents and Dependents was .82 compared to .41 for the Aschematics. While the overall number of independent and dependent words that were endorsed by the Aschematics as a group did not change, there was substantially less stability in their responses over time. This type of inconsistency was also noted in the Aschematics between the two self-characterizations tasks of Study 1.

As for processing times, the pattern is very similar to that shown in Figure 7.1, with Dependents again responding faster to dependent words than to independent words, $t(15) = 3.53$, $p < .01$, and Independents again responding faster to independent words than to dependent words, $t(15) = 2.61$, $p < .05$. Aschematics again showed no differences in processing times between the two types of judgments. Subjects with schemata (Independents and Dependents), however, showed significantly longer average latencies for these self-judgments on this second task than on the first, $t(31) = 2.05$, $p < .05$. The Aschematics, however, did not evidence longer processing times for these judgments on the second task, $t(15) < 1$.

The longer response latencies at time$_2$ for the self-judgments of individuals with schemata may have been the result of these subjects trying to be consistent from time$_1$ to time$_2$. This, however, should also have been the case for the control adjectives, the creativity/noncreativity words, but these judgments did not evidence longer latencies in the second self-categorization task; in fact, they generally became shorter. It appears, then, that the longer processing times for the independent/dependent words may well have been due to the counterschematic information provided by the suggestibility test. Subjects with schemata appear to realize that they have received information about themselves that does not fit with their current self-conception on this dimension. While this realization is not sufficient to warrant a change in self-characterization (and thus no change in adjective endorsement is observed), it probably caused these subjects to reflect slightly longer to check this information against their schemata before making a judgment.

Like the Independents and the Dependents, the Aschematics did not change their self-characterizations in the direction of the feedback. However, unlike subjects with schemata, their processing times for the independent/dependent words remained unchanged following the suggestibility information. The most plausible explanation for this finding is that individuals without schemata on a particular dimension of behavior may indeed not see the relationship or the convergence among the suggestibility information and independent/dependent adjectives used in the self-description task. For Aschematics the suggestibility test score may have been just an isolated fact about a noncentral dimension. It should be recalled here that the suggestibility test feedback was carefully worded to avoid any of the words used in this self-categorization task. Thus, telling someone that she is very suggestible may not imply anything at all about whether or not she is conforming or dependent, if she does not categorize her behavior along an independence–dependence dimension. It should, and in this study did, influence her assessment of her relative suggestibility, however. Generalizations across various chunks of information about the self may only occur if individuals possess schemata relating them. Because the Aschematics did not have an integrated picture of themselves on the independence–dependence dimension, the suggestibility information was not perceived as relevant to the judgments being made. The self-judgments and latencies for these judgments were, therefore, not affected.

## General Discussion

These studies provide converging evidence for the concept of self-schemata, or cognitive generalizations about the self, which organize, summarize, and explain behavior along a particular dimension. Systematic differences were observed among the three groups of subjects in the selection and processing of information about the self. Thus, the group of individuals who thought of themselves as "independent" endorsed significantly more adjectives associated with the concept of independence than did individuals who did not characterize themselves this way. Additionally, these people required shorter processing times for *me* judgments to words concerned with independence than to other types of words, were able to supply relatively more specific examples of independent behavior, thought they were likely to engage in future independent behavior, and were resistant to the acceptance of information that implied they were not independent. A parallel pattern of results was found with dependent stimuli for those individuals who thought of themselves as "dependent" people.

In clear contrast to the Independents and Dependents were the Aschematics who did not differ in their processing times for independent and dependent words, had relatively greater difficulty in providing behavioral evidence of independence and dependence, thought they were as likely to engage in independent as dependent behavior, and were relatively accepting of information about themselves on this dimension. Aschematics did not appear to view themselves along an independence–dependence dimension at all.

There are, of course, a number of alternative explanations for some of these findings which are taken as evidence for the self-schema concept. One of the major findings of these studies was that the group of Aschematics did not respond differentially to the independent and dependent stimuli. This lack of selectivity was interpreted as indicating that these individuals do not categorize their behavior according to its independence or dependence and that this is not a meaningful dimension for them. It could be argued, however, that these people are not really aschematic with regard to independence and dependence, but instead have a schema about themselves that encompasses elements of both independent and dependent behavior. Aschematics may simply have monitored their behavior (Snyder, 1974) on the independence–dependence dimension and have found a mixed pattern. Some of the Aschematics, for example, may have felt that they were independent from social influence but not at all aggressive or assertive. It might be argued, then, that there are no substantial differences between subjects with schemata and those without schemata in the types of cognitive structures that mediate information about the self. Both groups may simply be offering accurate reports of their behavior in the independence–dependence domain.

A number of results, however, argue against this alternative. First, if the underlying cognitive structures were equally articulated among the groups, the same consistency among the tasks should be found for the Aschematics that was found for the Independents and Dependents. Yet, considerable inconsistency was exhibited by the Aschematics between the two self-description tasks of Study 1, as well as between the self-categorization task in Study 1 and its identical counterpart in Study 2. Second, if there were no differences in the articulation and precision of the underlying cognitive structures between Schematic and Aschematic subjects, there should have been no differences in their readiness to make predictions about their future behavior in the domain of independence–dependence. All subjects would be expected, under these circumstances, to be equally polarized in the likelihood they assigned to future behaviors, even though they may have differed in the specific behaviors they considered likely. For example, a subject who monitors her past behavior and recalls that she has always been quite active in group discussions and shows no hesitation in giving advice and opinions, but generally stops short of starting an argument to defend a point, may see herself in the middle of the independence–dependence dimension. Nevertheless, this subject, when asked, should be quite ready to predict the manner of her future participation in group discussion. The present results on behavioral predictions, however, clearly indicate that Aschematics do not assign extreme likelihoods to any of the behaviors and report that they are as likely to engage in dependent as in independent behavior. It would appear, therefore, that subjects who have been categorized as Aschematics do not have clear and precise cognitive structures about the self in the domain of independence, for if they did, these structures would allow them to generate relatively unambiguous judgments about their future behavior.

There is, of course, the more remote possibility that Aschematics are individuals who are truly inconsistent in their behavior, such that one day they may be timid and shy in a discussion and the next day surly and aggressive. In this case, inconsistency in self description from one time to another might be expected if individuals think about themselves as highly variable or inconsistent in a particular domain. But one should also expect longer latencies for self-judgments, reflecting uncertainty or conflict over which trait labels are most appropriate, or at least more variance in judgments. None of these results was found, however.

The results of these studies have a number of implications for research on personality and the search for cross-situational consistency in behavior. It seems likely that those individuals who have schemata about themselves on a particular behavioral dimension are those most likely to display a correspondence between self-description and behavior and to exhibit cross-situational consistency on that dimension. In contrast, those individuals who have no clear schema about themselves are unlikely to exhibit such consistency in behavior. For example, Bem and Allen (1974) were able to identify a group of individuals who displayed substantial cross-situational consistency in behavior. Individuals who identified themselves as consistent on a particular trait dimension (claiming that they did not vary on this dimension across situations) exhibited substantial correspondence between self-description and behavior and were also cross-situationally consistent in their behavior. The subjects in Bem and Allen's studies who claimed they were consistent on a particular dimension may have been acknowledging a self-schema on this dimension. And the cross-situational consistency that was subsequently noted for these consistent individuals may have resulted from these individuals engaging in behavior that was motivated from a desire to be consistent with their self-schemata. Differences in the ways individuals generalize and interpret their own behavior may thus be a significant source of individual differences, and such differences may actually predict differential behavior.

These studies give empirical substance to the idea that not all people have a subjective position on every dimension of behavior. It is entirely possible that systematic effects in social behavior depend less on people having some amount of a particular substantive attribute, such as independence or dependence, and more on the readiness or ability to categorize behavior along certain dimensions. This, of course, was the notion behind Kelly's (1955) methodology of allowing the individual to generate his own constructs for categorizing himself and the social environment and is pertinent to Bem and Allen's (1974) call for an idiographic approach to personality. If the dimensions under study are not the ones an individual characteristically attends to, he cannot be expected to make corresponding conceptual and behavioral discriminations along that dimension.

The concept of self-schemata that function as selective mechanisms resulting in differential attention and processing of information about the self also has implications for self-perception and attribution theory. In the study of social attribution, there are a number of well-known studies (e.g., Davison & Valins, 1969; Schachter & Wheeler, 1962; Valins & Ray, 1967; Weick, 1967; Zimbardo, 1969) that reveal behavior changes in the absence of subsequent change in self-categorizations (how one says he thinks, feels, or is). These studies are discrepant with the model of self-attribution that assumes that inferences about internal states, dispositions, or attitudes follow from behavior and thus have been something of a puzzle for attribution theorists. Valins and Ray (1967), for example, gave snake phobic subjects false feedback about their fear of snakes. These subjects were able to approach a snake more closely than controls without false feedback. They did not, however, report themselves as any less fearful as a result of their experience. In view of the present results, this finding is perhaps not surprising. A correspondence between self-categorization and overt behavior depends on the mediating self-schemata. For example, snake phobic individuals probably have a fairly well-articulated self-schema about how they feel toward snakes. The elements of this generalization include cognitive representations of specific encounters with snakes and the subsequent evaluation of these encounters. If such an individual is induced to handle snakes, it does not follow that he will immediately perceive himself as no longer afraid of snakes. This type of dispositional attributions would be (a) based on only one isolated experience and (b) contradict a well-established schema. However, individuals with no particular generalizations about their attitudes towards snakes may readily interpret their positive experience with a snake as unambiguously self-diagnostic—as indicative that they don't mind snakes and are not afraid of them. If this argument is correct, it implies that individuals will use information about their own behavior to make an inference about their own internal state, disposition, or attitude only when the behavior appears to the individual to be related to the self-characterization to be made and when it does not run counter to a prevailing generalization about the self. Within an attribution theory framework, self-schemata can be viewed as implicit theories used by individuals to make sense of their own past behavior and to direct the course of future behavior. And a given chunk of behavioral information has decidedly different self-attribution consequences for an individual with an implicit theory or self-schema than it does for one without such a schema.

## REFERENCES

Abelson, R. P. (1975, April 24–26). *Script processing in attitude formation and decision making.* Paper presented at the Eleventh Carnegie-Mellon Symposium on Cognition.

Anderson, J. R., & Bower, G. H. (1973). *Human associative memory.* Washington: V. H. Winston.

Anderson, N. H. (1968). Likeableness ratings of 555 personality-trait words. *Journal of Personality and Social Psychology, 9,* 272–279.

Atkinson, R. C., & Shiffrin, R. M. (1968). Human memory: A proposed system and its control processes. In K. W. Spence & J. T. Spence (Eds.), *Advances in the psychology of learning and motivation research and theory* (Vol. 2). New York: Academic Press.

Bartlett, F. C. (1932). *Remembering.* London: Cambridge University Press.

Bem, D. J. (1967). Self-perception: An alternative interpretation of cognitive dissonance phenomena. *Psychological Review, 74,* 183–200.

Bem, D. J. (1972). Self-perception theory. In L. Berkowitz (Ed.), *Advances in experimental social psychology* (Vol. 6). New York: Academic Press.

Bem, D. J., & Allen, A. (1974). On predicting some of the people some of the time: The search for cross-situational consistencies in behavior. *Psychological Review, 81,* 506–520.

Bobrow, D. G., & Norman, D. A. (1975). Some principles of memory schemata. In D. G. Bobrow & A. Collins (Eds.), *Representation and understanding: Studies in cognitive science.* New York: Academic Press.

Carroll, J. B., Davies, P., & Richman, B. (1971). *Word frequency book.* New York: American Heritage.

Davison, G. C., & Valins, S. (1969). Maintenance of self-attributed and drug-attributed behavior change. *Journal of Personality and Social Psychology, 11,* 25–33.

Erdelyi, M. H. (1974). A new look at the New Look: Perceptual defense and vigilance. *Psychological Review, 81,* 1–25.

Gough, H. G., & Heilbrun, A. B. (1965). *The Adjective Check List Manual.* Palo Alto, CA: Consulting Psychologists Press.

Kelley, H. H. (1972). Causal schemata and the attribution process. In E. E. Jones, D. E. Kanouse, H. H. Kelley, R. E. Nisbett, S. Valins, & B. Weiner (Eds.), *Attribution: Perceiving the causes of behavior.* New York: General Learning Press.

Kelly, G. A. (1955). *The psychology of personal constructs.* New York: Norton.

Minsky, M. (1975). A framework for representing knowledge. In P. Winston (Ed.), *The psychology of computer vision.* New York: McGraw-Hill.

Mischel, W., Ebbesen, E. B., & Zeiss, A. M. (1976). Determinants of selective memory about the self. *Journal of Consulting and Clinical Psychology, 44,* 92–103.

Piaget, J. (1951). *The child's conception of the world.* New York: Humanities Press.

Schachter, S., & Wheeler, L. (1962). Epinephrine, chlorpromazine, and amusement. *Journal of Abnormal and Social Psychology, 65,* 212–218.

Snyder, M. (1974). Self-monitoring of expressive behavior. *Journal of Personality and Social Psychology, 30,* 526–537.

Snyder, M., & Monson, T. C. (1975). Persons, situations, and the control of social behavior. *Journal of Personality and Social Psychology, 32,* 637–644.

Stotland, E., & Canon, L. K. (1972). *Social psychology: A cognitive approach.* Philadelphia: Saunders.

Tesser, A., & Conlee, M. C. (1975). Some effects of time and thought on attitude polarization. *Journal of Personality and Social Psychology, 31,* 262–270.

Valins, S., & Ray, A. A. (1967). Effects of cognitive desensitization of avoidance behavior. *Journal of Personality and Social Psychology, 7,* 345–350.

Weick, K. E. (1967). Dissonance and task enhancement: A problem for compensation theory? *Organizational Behavior and Human Performance, 2,* 175–216.

Zimbardo, P. G. (Ed.). (1969). *The cognitive control of motivation.* Glenview, IL: Scott, Foresman.

# Self-Reference and the Encoding of Personal Information

T. B. Rogers, N. A. Kuiper, and W. S. Kirker
• University of Calgary, Canada

The degree to which the self is implicated in processing personal information was investigated. Subjects rated adjectives on four tasks designed to force varying kinds of encoding: structural, phonemic, semantic, and self-reference. In two experiments, incidental recall of the rated words indicated that adjectives rated under the self-reference task were recalled the best. These results indicate that self-reference is a rich and powerful encoding process. As an aspect of the human information-processing system, the self appears to function as a superordinate schema that is deeply involved in the processing, interpretation, and memory of personal information.

Present research and theory in personality appear to be placing more and more emphasis on how a person has organized his or her psychological world. Starting with Kelly's (1955) formulation of personal constructs, we see a gradual emergence of a number of avenues of inquiry that use this as their focal point. In person perception, the concept of lay personality theory stresses that the observer's analytic network of expected trait covariations is an integral part of how he processes (and generates) interpersonal data (Hastorf, Schneider, & Polefka, 1970). Bem and Allen (1974), in their embellishment of Allport's (1937) idiographic position, argue that an important determinant of predictive utility of trait measurement is the manner in which the respondent has organized his or her view of the trait being measured. These authors see the overlap between the respondent's and the experimenter's concept of the trait as a necessary prerequisite of prediction. Attribution theory (Jones et al., 1972) is another example of this increased accent on personal organi-

zation. Here the emphasis is on how the subject explains past behavior and how these explanations are organized in an attributional network. The common thread in all of these contemporary research areas is the notion that the cognitions of a person, particularly their manner of organization, should be an integral part of our attempts to explain personality and behavior.

Of concern in the present article is the construct of self and how it is implicated in the organization of personal data. Our general position is that the self is an extremely active and powerful agent in the organization of the person's world. More specifically, the present research was designed to determine if self-reference serves a meaningful function in the processing of certain kinds of information. That is, we attempted to determine the relative strength of self-reference as an agent in the processing of people-related information.

The self is defined as an abstract representation of past experience with personal data. Phenomenologically, it is a kind of vague idea about who

139

the person thinks he or she is. It probably develops to help the person keep track of the vast amounts of self-relevant information encountered over a lifetime. The self, then, represents the abstracted essence of a person's perception of him or herself. A more formal definition of self is to view it as a list of terms or features that have been derived from a lifetime of experience with personal data. More than likely a portion of the list consists of general terms—not unlike traits—that represent the abstracted essentials of a person's view of self. In addition to these general terms, there are also some more specific entries in the self. These relate to less salient and more situation-specific aspects of self-perception as well as to specific behaviors. This definition is supported by Jones, Sensenig, and Haley (1974). They simply asked subjects to describe their "most significant characteristics." The most frequent entries in the obtained response protocols were positively worded terms such as *sensitive, intelligent,* and *friendly.* These appear to be the general terms in the self and appear to resemble traits. Jones et al. (1974, p. 38) also present a single response protocol. Of interest here is the tendency for conditionals (e.g., such situational hedges as *sometimes*) to emerge later in the protocol. Furthermore, as the protocol develops, the entries tend to relate to more specific situations than did the earlier terms (e.g., "have a hang-up about authority figures"). These latter entries appear to be the specific terms in the self.

One of the main functions of the self is to help the individual process personal data. When a person encounters a situation involving personal information, this structure is activated and becomes part of the available information-processing system. For example, when students encounter a list of characteristics of a psychopathological state (e.g., in an introductory psychology lecture), they tend to interpret (and attempt to remember) these by referring them to their own views of self. Such a strategy could lead to the "medical student syndrome," where students begin to see themselves in the varying states described by the lecturer. In extreme cases, some students can be convinced they are raving lunatics—despite repeated warnings of the instructor. Other examples of this self-reference phenomenon can occur in situations involving personal feedback, expressive behaviors, and the processing of information about other people.

The central aspect of self-reference is that the self acts as a background or setting against which incoming data are interpreted or coded. This process involves an interaction between the previous experience of the individual (in the form of the abstract structure of self) and the incoming materials. The involvement of the self in the interpretation of new stimuli imparts a degree of richness and fullness to the input because of the availability of the immense amounts of previous experience embodied in the self.

The interaction between new input and previous experience, postulated to be central to self-reference, has been modeled in the cognitive literature under the concept of schema or prototype (Bartlett, 1932; Posner & Keele, 1968). For example, subjects shown a series of dot patterns tend to abstract a prototypical visual pattern and use it as a standard in a memory task (Posner & Keele, 1970). In personality, several recent papers have suggested that personal data are processed using schemata or prototypes. Markus (1977), using a series of measurements, categorized subjects by whether dependence was part of their self. Schematics, or those with dependence as part of their self, were those who rated themselves as extreme on several dependence items, as well as indicating that they viewed dependence as important. Aschematics were midrange on dependence and low on importance ratings, representing subjects who did not have dependence in their general concept of self. On the basis of impressive convergent evidence, Markus (1977) found that schematics and aschematics showed differences in how they processed personal data. For example, schematics were more resistant to incorrect personal information than were the aschematics. These data suggest that the traits, such as those found in the self, serve an important function in processing certain kinds of information.

Cantor and Mischel (1977) tested the proposition that traits function as prototypes using a recognition memory task. Subjects were shown a series of statements that represented an introvert. When faced with a task requiring recognition of these statements from among some new introvert statements, subjects tended to misidentify some of the new items as having been original statements. This suggests that the concept of introvert mediated subjects' processing of the initial set of statements. This mediation was postulated to be in the form of a prototype, which represents an abstraction of the concept of introvert from the initial items. The observed memory bias for new, yet conceptually related items reflected the involvement of this abstraction.

The Markus (1977) and Cantor and Mischel (1977) data indicate that traits are implicated in information-processing functions. They appear to be involved in the organization, storage, and retrieval of personality-related information. Our view of self places these traitlike schemata or prototypes as general terms in the feature list making up the self.

Rogers, Rogers, and Kuiper (1977) explored the manner in which this set of schemata is involved in processing personal data. They hypothesized that the self functions like a grand or superordinate schema. If the self is a schema, it should be possible to observe the kinds of memory biases documented by Cantor and Mischel (1977). In one study (Rogers et al., 1977, Experiment 2), subjects filled out self-ratings on 84 adjectives. Two and a half months later, these same subjects participated in a recognition memory study involving these same adjectives. They first saw a randomly selected set of 42 of the words, and then had to recognize these from among the total set of 84. If the self was involved as a schema, subjects should tend to falsely recognize new items that were rated as self-descriptive (i.e., Posner & Keele, 1970). Each subject's recognition protocol was divided into high, neutral, and low self-descriptive categories on the basis of their self-ratings. Performance for the 42 items initially shown in the recognition study was not affected by degree of self-reference. However, performance on the new or distracter items (correct rejects) became poorer as degree of self-reference increased. In other words, more false alarms occurred as the adjectives became more self-descriptive. This clearly confirms the prediction derived from viewing the self as a schema.

To review, self-reference can be seen as a process involving the schema of self. This process involves the interaction between previous experience with personal data and new stimulus input. When self-reference is involved, it should provide a useful device for encoding or interpreting incoming information by virtue of accessing the extensive past experience abstracted in the self. Contact with the reservoir of history embodied in the self should provide considerable embellishment and richness to an incoming stimulus. Rogers (1977) explored this possibility using recognition memory for personality items. Subjects instructed to "read the item, decide if it describes you, and use this to help your memory" performed significantly better than subjects receiving either no or different (i.e., imagery) instructions. These data, in combination with some older research (e.g., Cartwright, 1956), indicate that explicit instructions to use the self in a memory task increase performance, which supports the claim that self-reference serves to enrich input.

This enriching aspect of self-reference is the focal point of the present article. Our major concern is how powerful self-reference is as an encoding device. More specifically, self-reference is compared to several other encoding processes in an effort to determine the relative degree of richness and embellishment that self-reference imparts to the encoding of adjectives.

The experimental manipulation used in the present context is an incidental recall paradigm, in which subjects make different kinds of ratings on a set of words. For example, a subject rates whether a given word means the same as a target word. This would be a *semantic rating,* as the subject must extract the meaning of the word to perform the task. The same subject rates whether another word is written in big letters. This is a *structural* coding task, since all the subject has to do is inspect the structure of the stimulus item rather than extract the meaning of the word. Other words are rated on a *phonemic* task, which involves deciding whether a word rhymes with a target. The *self-reference* rating, which subjects perform on some of the words, involves the respondent's deciding whether the word describes him or her. When the rating task is completed, each subject has rated one fourth of the words on each of the four rating tasks. These four tasks are thought to vary in depth, or semantic richness, from the structural task as the most shallow to the semantic and/or self-rating task as the deepest. The test of coding strength comes when the subjects are given a surprise recall task at the conclusion of the ratings. According to Craik and Lockhart (1972), words that have been deeply coded during the rating task should be recalled better than words with shallow coding. This manipulation permits us to determine the relative deepness of self-reference as a coding device.

Craik and Tulving (1975) have done a series of studies using this methodology. They have restricted their efforts to the structural, phonemic, and semantic types of tasks. Their results indicate that recall (or recognition) is best for semantic tasks and poorest for structural ratings, with phonemic in the middle. These data are interpreted as support for the position that the strength of the memory trace is "a positive function of 'depth' of processing, where depth refers to greater degrees of semantic involvement" (Craik & Tulving, 1975, p. 268). Presumably the rating tasks (structural, phonemic, etc.) force the subject to code the word to a specific level, and the incidental recall is a function of the depth of these tasks. These kinds of results have emerged quite consistently in the cognitive literature (e.g., D'Agostino, O'Neill, & Paivio, 1977; Klein & Saltz, 1976; Schulman, 1974; Walsh & Jenkins, 1973).

Of particular concern in the present study is the comparison between incidental recall for words rated under the semantic and self-reference tasks. Both of these tasks involve semantic encoding, but there is an important difference between them. The self-reference task forces the subject to use the self in the rating task, whereas the semantic task does not. The self-reference/semantic comparison permits assessment of the degree to which the self aids in producing a stronger trace, in contrast to usual semantic encoding. If the self is an active agent in the encoding of personal data, we predicted that the self-reference rating would produce good incidental recall in this depth-of-processing paradigm. If incidental recall of the self-reference words is superior to that for semantic words, the hypothesis that the self serves an active and powerful role in processing personal data would be supported.

The present article offers two experiments that examine this proposition. The first study involves a close replication of Craik and Tulving's (1975) initial experiments, with the self-reference task included. The second experiment replicates and extends the first study by using a different technique and different semantic rating task.

## Experiment 1

This experiment is intended to determine the relative position of self-reference in Craik's (Craik & Lockart, 1972) depth hierarchy. The procedural details have been chosen to closely approximate Craik and Tulving's (1975) initial experiments in an effort to maximize the degree of comparability of the present results.

### Method

The study has two main parts. First, subjects rated 40 adjectives on one of four tasks. This involved presenting a cue question, followed by 1 of the 40 adjectives. Subjects answered yes or no to the cue question as it applied to the adjective. The cue questions, along with the manipulations for each task, are presented in Table 8.1. After completing the ratings, subjects attempted to recall the adjectives in the second part of the study.

#### MATERIALS

The main items for this study were 40 adjectives that were deemed appropriate for a self-description task. They were chosen to represent a broad spectrum of possible characteristics and were selected from all of the trait descriptions found in Jackson's (1967) *Personality Research Form A Manual.* Thirty-eight of the adjectives, selected to be familiar to the subject population, came from this source. Two other adjectives (shy and outgoing) were added to make up the total of 40.

**TABLE 8.1. Examples of the Rating Tasks**

| Task | Cue question | Manipulation |
|------|-------------|--------------|
| Structural | Big letters? | The adjective was either presented in the same size type as the question or twice as large. |
| Phonemic | Rhymes with xxxx? | xxxx was a word that either rhymed or did not rhyme with the adjective. |
| Semantic | Means same as yyyy? | yyyy was either a synonym or unrelated word to the presented adjective. |
| Self-reference | Describes you? | Subjects simply responded *yes* or *no* to indicate the self-reference quality of the presented adjective. |

We used *Roget's Thesaurus* to construct a further set of 40 synonyms for the semantic tasks. The final synonyms chosen represented consensus among the three authors.

The phonemic task dictated a second supplementary list of 40 words that rhymed with the main adjective set. The authors generated a set of possible rhyming words, and consensus among ourselves was the final criterion for selection. Most (90%) of these words were adjectives.

A third supplementary list of nonsynonym, nonrhyming words was also required, so that one half of the cue questions could result in a *no* rating. Kirby and Gardner's (1972) set of adjectives was consulted to derive this list. Again, author consensus regarding the nonrhyming and nonsynonym quality of the adjectives dictated the final list.

A set of eight further adjectives and supplementary words was generated to provide buffer items of four ratings each at the beginning and end of the list. These items, which were constant across lists, were not included in the data analysis. This was intended to minimize the effects of primacy and recency in the incidental recall task.

Four lists of adjectives were constructed, such that 10 adjectives in each list were rated under each cue question, and over the four lists, each adjective was rated under each cue question.

To guard against the possibility that *no*-rated words are recalled differently than *yes*-rated words, each of the four lists was reversed to generate eight lists in total. For example, if in a given list, under the structural task, a word appeared in small letters (generating a *no* response), the reversed list would have the word presented in big letters (generating a *yes* response). The one exception to this counterbalancing was the self-reference task. Here it was impossible to have experimental control over *yes* and *no* responses, since the person's view of self would dictate his or her response.

In all lists, order of the cue questions was randomly assigned in blocks of eight trials, such that each combination of cue question and expected response was represented once every eight trials.

PROCEDURE

Subjects were tested individually. Initial instructions did not indicate that recall was expected. All stimuli were displayed on a television monitor driven by a PDP8/1 computer, which also recorded the ratings and rating times. Including the four buffer items at the end and beginning of the list, there were 48 rating trials. Each of these consisted of (a) a 3-second presentation of the cue question, (b) a 500-millisecond blank interval, (c) presentation of the target adjective, which was terminated by the subject's response, indicated on a two-button response panel placed comfortably in front of the subject, and (d) a 2-second intertrial interval before the next cue question was presented. After the rating task, the subject was given a piece of paper and was asked to recall, in any order, the adjectives he or she had rated. Three minutes were allowed for recall.

SUBJECTS

Volunteers from the introductory psychology subject pool served as subjects. There were 32 subjects (16 female and 16 male) with an average age of 20.2 years. Each was paid $1.50 for participating. Subjects were randomly assigned to the eight list conditions, yielding 4 subjects per order.

Results and Discussion

For each subject, the number of adjectives recalled as a function of rating task (structural, phonemic, etc.) and observed *yes* or *no* rating was calculated. The means of these figures are presented in the top panel of Table 8.2. A 4 (rating tasks) × 2 (*yes/no* rating) two-way analysis of variance revealed a significant main effect of rating task, $F(3, 93) = 29.01$, $p < .001$. Newman-Keuls tests indicated meaningful differences ($p < .05$ or better) in the recall for all points in this main effect except for the structural-phonemic comparison. The main effect of rating was also significant, $F(1, 31) = 4.22$, $p < .05$, indicating superior recall for words given a *yes* rating. The Rating Task × Rating interaction was also significant, $F(3, 93) = 3.47$, $p < .05$. Post hoc tests of this interaction revealed a meaningful *yes/no* difference for the self-reference rating, $t(31) = 2.62$, $p < .05$.

The overall pattern of these results is similar to that typically found in the literature (e.g., Experiments 1, 2, and 3 in Craik & Tulving, 1975). The main effect of rating task is used to suggest that the depth to which items are processed during the rating task determines the strength of the memory trace. As recall is a function of trace strength, the present results support this position.

**TABLE 8.2. Recall, Rating Time, and Adjusted Recall as a Function of Rating Task and Rating for Experiment 1**

| Rating | Structural | Phonemic | Semantic | Self-reference | Total |
|---|---|---|---|---|---|
| | | | Rating task | | |
| | *Mean recall* | | | | Total |
| *yes* | .28 | .34 | .65 | 1.78 | 3.05 |
| *no* | .06 | .34 | .68 | 1.06 | 2.14 |
| Total | .34 | .68 | 1.33 | 2.84 | 5.19 |
| | *Mean rating time (msec)* | | | | *M* |
| *yes* | 1,267 | 2,177 | 2,255 | 3,194 | 2,223 |
| *no* | 1,474 | 2,104 | 3,006 | 2,689 | 2,318 |
| Total | 1,371 | 2,141 | 2,631 | 2,941 | 2,271 |
| | *Mean adjusted recall* | | | | *M* |
| *yes* | .05[a] | .08 | .14 | .30 | .14 |
| *no* | .01 | .06 | .12 | .29 | .13 |
| *M* | .03 | .07 | .13 | .30 | .13 |

[a] This figure represents the mean (over 32 subjects) of the number of recalled *yes*-rated structural items divided by the number of *yes* ratings made on the structural task.

Of central interest is the finding that the self-reference task develops a stronger trace than the semantic task, as shown by the significant recall differences between these two conditions. This result clearly supports the idea that self-reference functions as a powerful coding device. In the case of self-reference ratings, the subject uses his or her concept of self to respond to the adjective. The self-ratings involve comparison of the incoming adjective with the terms and schemata that are part of the self (see Rogers, 1974). This comparison culminates in the subject's *yes/no* response, which leads to a strong and specific encoding of the rated item. During the recall phase of the study, items with this detailed and specific encoding are easily retrieved, producing good recall performance.

In the semantic rating task it is unnecessary for an elaborate structure such as the self to be involved. Rather, the subject accesses his associative memory (e.g., Estes, 1976) for the target adjective and makes his synonymity judgment from this. The resulting trace is not as specific or detailed as that involved with self-reference. Clearly, the access of associative memory produces a more detailed trace than either the structural or phonemic tasks. However, when compared to self-reference, the trace derived from a synonymity judgment is relatively weak. This difference in the specificity of the self-reference and semantic tasks seems to be the major reason for the inferior incidental recall of the semantically rated words.

The time required to make the ratings is typically used to monitor the effectiveness of the experimental manipulations in this paradigm. Further, these reaction time (RT) data provide convergent evidence for self-reference as a useful encoding task. The RTs from the present study were sorted separately for each subject into *yes/no* by rating-task categories. The means are presented in the middle panel of Table 8.2. Only the main effect of rating task was significant in this analysis, $F(3, 93) = 10.35$, $p < .001$. A clear linear trend in RTs is evident in these data, indicating maximal RT for the self-reference rating task.[1] This analysis replicates Craik and Tulving (1975) and is clearly compatible with the recall data presented above, supporting the involvement of the self as a coding device.

The finding that *yes*-rated words are recalled better than *no*-rated words occurs in other studies and has a number of interesting implications. Craik

[1] It is possible that items with large RTs are better recalled, calling into question this interpretation. If study time is the important factor, its effects should be observable *within* each task as well as across tasks. Thus, within a given rating task, the items with the longer study times should be recalled better. To explore this, the 10 RTs under each of the four rating tasks were subdivided separately for each subject into a fast and a slow subset (5 RTs in each). The recall for these subsets was analyzed in a 4 (rating tasks) × 2 (fast and slow study times) two-way analysis of variance. The study-time hypothesis predicts significant effects for the terms involving study time. The analysis indicated only the expected main effect of rating task, $F(3, 93) = 30.85$, $p < .001$. This analysis weakens the study-time interpretation and reinforces the interpretation that the recall data are due to the qualitative nature of the various encoding tasks.

explains these data by arguing that in the case of *yes*-rated words, the "encoding questions or context forms an integrated unit with the target word" (Craik & Tulving, 1975, p. 291). Presumably this integrated unit forms a stronger trace than less integrated ones (*no*-rated words), thereby augmenting recall. The interaction observed in the present data indicates that this *yes/no* difference occurred only for the self-reference case, which suggests that items viewed as self-descriptive (*yes*-rated words) form a "more integrated unit" than do non-self-descriptive terms. These results strengthen even more our view of self, as it appears that terms that match the subject's self-view become more integrated than those that do not match. This finding is consonant with both Markus's (1977) and Cantor and Mischel's (1977) finding that personal data are processed using schemalike structures.

There are several aspects of these data that require examination before the previous conclusions are fully warranted. The *yes/no* difference in recall for self-reference words could be due to a differential number of *yes* responses as a function of rating task. Since experimental control over the number of *yes* responses was not possible for the self-reference task, this is a distinct possibility. For each subject, the number of *yes* responses made under each rating task (maximum = 10) was calculated. The means were 5.00, 4.34, 4.06, and 6.13 for the structural, phonemic, semantic and self-reference tasks, respectively. A simple analysis of variance on these figures revealed a significant effect, $F(3, 93) = 16.99$, $p < .001$, indicating that number of *yes* responses is related to rating task. The deviations from 50% *yes* responses for the phonemic and semantic tasks are due to the difficulty of constructing exact rhymes and synonyms for the adjectives.

More important than the significant variation in number of *yes* responses is the possible effect this might have on the recall data. Since it is already known that *yes*-rated words are better recalled (e.g., Craik & Tulving, 1975), it is possible that self-reference recall was superior because subjects made more *yes* responses in the self-reference task. To assess this, the recall data were transformed to a proportion score that adjusts for differential numbers of *yes* responses. Specifically, a particular subject's recall of *yes*-rated words under a specific rating task was divided by the number of *yes* ratings the subject made while doing

the task. This transformed score represents the proportion of recalled words the subject rated as *yes*. Similarly, the *no*-rated word recall under a given rating task can be divided by the number of *no* responses made on this rating task to provide a score representing the proportion of recalled words rated as *no*. Note that this is a subject-specific correction that reflects recall corrected for differential numbers of *yes* and *no* ratings. The means of the adjusted recall scores are presented in the bottom panel of Table 8.2. An analysis of variance of these data revealed only a main effect of rating task, $F(3, 93) = 31.63$, $p < .001$. The important recall difference between semantic and self-reference survived this adjustment ($p < .01$), but the *yes/no* difference for the self-reference task did not. This analysis reaffirms self-reference as a coding tool but questions the possibility that *yes*-rated items form a more integrated unit.

In summary, the data from Experiment 1 provide evidence that self-reference is a powerful encoding device. The superior incidental recall of adjectives rated under the self-reference task, in combination with the RT data, suggests that self-reference provides a rich and powerful encoding. The involvement of self in the rating task provides a good encoding unit, which functions effectively as a memory cue.

## Experiment 2

It is possible that the superiority of self-reference encoding documented in Experiment 1 is specific to synonymity ratings. Maybe other kinds of semantic tasks would produce equally powerful results. Semantic tasks can be thought of as a family of judgments, all of which involve the extraction (and possibly some elaboration) of the meaning of the target item. Such tasks as synonymity ratings, judgments of semantic specificity, and deciding whether a word fits into a sentence frame can be considered members of this semantic family. Experiment 2 employed meaningfulness ratings as the semantic task. Since recall is a function of meaningfulness (see Noble, 1952; Paivio, Yuille, & Rogers, 1969), this encoding task should be very beneficial for recall, particularly for words given a *yes* rating. If self-reference emerges as superior to meaningfulness ratings, evidence confirming the strength and reliability of self-reference as an encoding device will be provided.

**TABLE 8.3. Rating Tasks and Mean Adjusted Recall for Experiment 2**

| Rating task | Cue question | Definition | Yes rating | No rating | M |
|---|---|---|---|---|---|
| | | | Mean adjusted recall | | |
| Structural | Long? | Rate whether you feel the word is long or short. | .21 | .18 | .20 |
| Phonemic | Rhythmic? | Rate whether you feel the word has a rhythmic or lyrical sound. | .20 | .18 | .20 |
| Semantic | Meaningful? | Rate whether you feel the word is meaningful to you. | .23 | .15 | .19 |
| Self-reference | Describes you? | Indicate whether the word describes you. | .33 | .31 | .32 |
| M | | | .24 | .21 | .23 |

A second purpose of this experiment is to explore the robustness of the self-reference findings. Experiment 1 was performed using fairly tight experimental controls. The present experiment deviates from this by using a group testing procedure. Craik and Tulving (1975) and Klein and Saltz (1976) have used similar procedures and replicated the findings from more rigorous paradigms, suggesting that the self-reference finding should stand up in this group procedure.

## Method

The four rating tasks used for this experiment are outlined in Table 8.3. Subjects were given a rating sheet which indicated which of the four tasks they were to perform on a given word; this was indicated by the cue questions from Table 8.3. After the subjects had read the task cue to themselves, an adjective was read aloud by the experimenter, and the subjects made their *yes* or *no* responses on the sheet. After the ratings, subjects turned over their rating sheets and attempted to recall the adjectives.

### MATERIALS

The 40 adjectives used in Experiment 1 made up the target items in this study. Four different task orders were generated, such that each adjective was rated under each task considered across the four orders, and within each order one fourth of the words were rated under each task. Within each list the order of tasks was randomized in blocks of four, such that each task was represented once in every four trials.

### PROCEDURE

Subjects were run in one group. After instructions, the experimenter read the item number, said the word *task* (which cued the subjects to read the cue question), and then read out the adjective. After 40 such trials, subjects were given 3 minutes to recall, in any order, as many of the adjectives as they could. Subjects were not expecting this free-recall task.

### SUBJECTS

Twenty-seven students in a fourth-year summer class served as subjects. The mean age was 27.7 years.

## Results and Discussion

For each subject, recall as a function of rating task and rating was calculated. These figures were converted to adjusted recall scores following the procedures for Experiment 1. The means of the adjusted recall scores are presented in the far right columns of Table 8.3. Analysis of variance of the adjusted recall scores produced a lone significant main effect of rating task, $F(3, 78) = 4.20, p < .01$, and a meaningful semantic/self-reference recall difference ($p < .05$).

Experiment 2 demonstrates self-reference recall superiority when a meaningful rating task is used. This kind of task has been previously implicated in recall, resulting in a seemingly powerful semantic encoding task. However, the present results indicate that self-reference still is the more useful encoding task in this paradigm.[2]

Taken in total, the results of these experiments indicate that self-reference induces superior incidental recall compared to a diversity of strictly semantic rating tasks. The important thing is that self-reference appears to produce recall that is superior to any other task ever used in the incidental recall paradigm. This by itself attests to the power of self-reference.

## General Discussion

As a test of encoding strength, the depth-of-processing paradigm forces the subject to process stimuli to a specific depth by having the subject rate the words on different tasks. During the rating task a memory trace of the rated word is created. Tasks that are deep or semantically rich produce strong traces, which in turn serve as useful cues in the incidental recall of the rated words. The relative power of an encoding device is correlated with incidental recall in this paradigm. The present data indicate unequivocally that words rated under the self-reference task show superior recall. This indicates that self-reference represents a powerful and rich encoding device. Clearly, self-reference produces a rich encoding unit that can function effectively during information processing (see also Markus, 1977; Rogers, 1977; Rogers et al., 1977).

The major difference between the semantic and self-reference encoding tasks lies in the involvement of self in the latter rating. The self is a superordinate schema that contains an abstracted record of a person's past experience with personal data. The richness of self-reference encoding shown in the present article is due to the access of this schema. The semantic rating task does not force involvement of a powerful schema, and hence fails to induce as powerful and rich an encoding unit. The mere act of making a self-referent decision produces such powerful internal reactions that the attending memory trace is stronger than any observed in the present experimental situation.

In order for self-reference to be such a useful encoding process, the self must be a uniform, well-structured concept. During the recall phase of the study, subjects probably use the self as a retrieval cue (e.g., Moscovitch & Craik, 1976). In order for this to be functional, the self must be a consistent and uniform schema. This property of the self is also shown by Rogers et al. (1977), who were able to predict memory performance with a measure of self taken 2½-months earlier. The present data support the contention that the self is a well-structured and powerful schema. Presumably the self-referent decision activates the superordinate schema of self as well as the salient sub-schemata. The strength of the trace developed from this activation suggests that a consistent and well-structured schema underlies these decisions. This consistency produces a rich and effective encoding unit, which accounts for the present data.

The present data permit some further statements about the schema properties of the self. Considering the four experiments reported here (including the two supplementary studies in Footnote 2), it has been consistently found that *yes*-rated items are better recalled than *no*-rated items in the self-reference task.[3] These data support the schema view, since *yes*-rated items would fit more easily into the schema, and thereby form a more integrated encoding unit (Schulman, 1974). Such a pattern of results is compatible with Markus (1977) and Cantor and Mischel (1977) and further reinforces a view of the self as a schema.

The data indicating that the self is a schema prompt consideration of how the various traits (i.e., subschemata) and specific elements (i.e., individual behaviors) are organized within this structure. The terms of the self are organized in an hierarchical fashion, with the most central traits represented initially. At first blush, it seems reasonable to think that this hierarchy relates to extremity. That is, the initial trait in the self would be a person's most extreme trait, followed by the second most extreme, and so on, until meaningful

---

[2]The same pattern of results has been replicated twice for this group procedure using different semantic rating tasks. Typically this group procedure fails to replicate Craik and Tulving's (1975) findings for the structural, phonemic, and semantic tasks used (see Table 8.2). This is probably due to the rating tasks used. For example, in the structural task some subjects may have rated whether the word was a "big" word (rather than long), which would be a semantic task. Regardless of this problem, the important semantic/self-reference difference clearly emerged in all studies using the group procedure.

[3]Statistical significance for this difference tends to disappear in the adjusted recall analyses. However, the consistent emergence of the effect across this series of experiments (even in the adjusted recall data) suggests a substantial effect.

traits for the person were exhausted. This simple extremity organization may hold for some persons, but another aspect of the traits must also be considered. Specifically, the salience of a trait for a person also adds to the organization of self. For example, a person who views him or herself in the midrange on "friendly," may perceive this characteristic as exceptionally important, and thereby have it included in the self. Markus (1977) included this consideration when she used importance ratings in her definition of schematics. This aspect of traits or constructs has also been discussed under the labels of centrality (Snygg & Combs, 1949) and salience (Jackson, 1968). The important thing to note is that the traits involved in a person's self are not necessarily the most extreme ones. Rather, they represent a mix of salience and extremity.

The inclusion of specific behaviors in the self derives from the work in cognition. Posner and Keele (1968) postulate that a person stores both the prototype and some indication of how a given stimulus deviates from this norm. This means that a schema, by virtue of its abstract property, must also contain specific data indicating aspects of the previous input that do not conform to the abstracted structure.

In sum, the self contains a set of ordered features. The ordering appears to be from general to specific, with the general terms (e.g., traits) ordered by a combination of salience and extremity. The general terms can serve as schemata when studied independently of a person's idiographic view of self (e.g., Cantor & Mischel, 1977; Markus, 1977).

The present data stress how the self can become involved in the encoding of personal data. Focusing on the organizational properties of the self is by no means new (e.g., Bertocci, 1945; Gergen, 1971). In fact, as early as James (1890) the self has been postulated to be an active agent in the overall human cognitive apparatus. The present research adds to this tradition by providing a strong empirical test of a proposition deriving from such a view of self. Our emphasis is upon the information-processing functions of the self, specifically relating to self-reference as an encoding device. This represents a *neo-mentalistic* approach (Paivio, 1975) to the self. While behavioral evidence (i.e., memory performance) is the key element in this approach, the focal concern is upon the inferred construct—in this case, the self.

It should be noted that there are certain classes of information likely to receive self-reference encoding. Only after certain contextual information indicates that the self may be a functional aid to processing will the schema be activated. In the present context, we forced this process with the encoding task. In real life situations, it seems likely that the self would be functional in a number of situations involving feedback of personal data, such as conversations, expressive behaviors, and attempts to assess personal impact on others. The kinds of situations that activate this schema or possible individual differences in the frequency and intensity of the involvement of self in data processing may prove to be very useful extensions of the present formulation.

Probably the main advantage of the process-oriented view of information processing underlying our approach to self is the opportunity to move toward less descriptive models of social behavior. If we understand the processes and mechanisms underlying the processing of personal information, we will have a real opportunity to construct substantive models based on hard experimental findings (see Sechrest, 1976). For example, the finding that the self induces certain biases during the processing of personal data (Cantor & Mischel, 1977; Markus, 1977) can be related to the cross-situational consistency issue. As noted by Bem and Allen (1974), our intuitions tell us that there are cross-situational consistencies in behavior, even though the research data do not tend to confirm this. Our process approach would interpret this as follows: (a) Personal data are processed using the self (e.g., Experiment 1). (b) The self induces people to view novel but self-relevant data as having been previously experienced (Rogers et al., 1977). (c) Therefore new personal data will appear to conform to expectation (i.e., fit into the scheme), which could produce a perception of consistency. This interpretation focuses upon the organizational and biasing aspects of the human information processor, which provides an alternate construction of these important data. Although the utility of this interpretation rests on further empirical tests, the amenability of such a model to direct experimental scrutiny argues in its favor.

In summary, the present article offers data to suggest that self-reference is a very potent encoding device. The pattern of results indicates that the use of self during the encoding of adjectives produces as elaborate and integrated a memory trace as has been found using the present experimental paragm. These data suggest the self is an extremely important aspect of the processing of personal information. In the realm of human information processing it is difficult to conceive of an encoding device that carries more potential for the rich embellishment of stimulus input than does self-reference.

## REFERENCES

Allport, G. W. (1937). *Personality: A psychological interpretation.* New York: Holt,

Bartlett, F. C. (1932). *Remembering.* Cambridge, England: Cambridge University Press.

Bem, D. J., & Allen, A. (1974). On predicting some of the people some of the time: The search for cross-situational consistencies in behavior. *Psychological Review, 81,* 506–520.

Bertocci, P. A. (1945). The psychological self, the ego, and personality. *Psychological Review, 52,* 91–99.

Cantor, N., & Mischel, W. (1977). Traits as prototypes: Effects on recognition memory. *Journal of Personality and Social Psychology, 35,* 38–48.

Cartwright, D. (1956). Self-consistency as a factor affecting immediate recall. *Journal of Abnormal and Social Psychology, 52,* 212–219.

Craik, F. I. M., & Lockart, R. S. (1972). Levels of processing: A framework for memory research. *Journal of Verbal Learning and Verbal Behavior, 11,* 671–684.

Craik, F. I. M., & Tulving, E. (1975). Depth of processing and the retention of words in episodic memory. *Journal of Experimental Psychology: General, 104,* 268–294.

D'Agostino, P. R., O'Neill, B. J., & Paivio, A. (1977). Memory for pictures and words as a function of levels of processing: Depth or dual coding? *Memory & Cognition, 5,* 252–256.

Estes, W. K. (1976). Structural aspects of associative models for memory. In C. N. Cofer (Ed.), *The structure of human memory.* San Francisco: Freeman.

Gergen, R. J. (1971). *The concept of self.* New York: Holt, Rinehart & Winston.

Hastorf, A. H., Schneider, D. J., & Polefka,, J. (1970). *Person perception.* Don Mills, Ontario: Addison-Wesley.

Jackson, D. N. (1967). *A manual for the Personality Research Form.* Goshen, NY: Research Psychologists Press.

Jackson, D. N. (1968). *A threshold model for stylistic responding.* Paper presented at the meeting of the American Psychological Association, San Francisco.

James, W. (1890). *Principles of psychology.* New York: Holt.

Jones, E. E., Kanouse, D. E., Kelley, H. H., Nisbett, R. E., Valins, S., & Weiner, B. (Eds.). (1972). *Attribution: Perceiving the causes of behavior.* Morristown, NJ: General Learning Press.

Jones, R. A., Sensenig, J., & Haley, J. V. (1974). Self-descriptions: Configurations of content and order effects. *Journal of Personality and Social Psychology, 30,* 36–45.

Kelly, G. A. (1955). *Psychology of personal constructs.* New York: Norton.

Kirby, D. M., & Gardner, R. C. (1972). Ethnic stereotypes: Norms on 208 words typically used in their assessment. *Canadian Journal of Psychology, 26,* 140–154.

Klein, K., & Salts, E. (1976). Specifying the mechanisms in a levels-of-processing approach to memory. *Journal of Experimental Psychology: Human Learning and Memory, 2,* 671–679.

Markus, H. (1977). Self-schemata and processing information about the self. *Journal of Personality and Social Psychology, 35,* 63–78.

Moscovitch, M., & Craik, F. I. M. (1976). Depth of processing, retrieval cues, and uniqueness of encoding as a factor in recall. *Journal of Verbal Learning and Verbal Behavior, 15,* 447–458.

Noble, C. E. (1952). An analysis of meaning. *Psychological Review, 59,* 421–430.

Paivio, A. (1975). Neomentalism. *Canadian Journal of Psychology, 29,* 263–291.

Paivio, A., Yuille, J. C., & Rogers, T. B. (1969). Noun imagery and meaningfulness in free and serial recall. *Journal of Experimental Psychology, 79,* 509–514.

Posner, M. I., & Keele, S. W. (1968). On the genesis of abstract ideas. *Journal of Experimental Psychology, 77,* 353–363.

Posner, M. I., & Keele, S. W. (1970). Retention of abstract ideas. *Journal of Experimental Psychology, 83,* 304–308.

Rogers, T. B. (1974). An analysis of two central stages underlying responding to personality items: The self-referent decision and response selection. *Journal of Research in Personality, 8,* 128–138.

Rogers, T. B. (1977). Self-reference in memory: Recognition of personality items. *Journal of Research in Personality, 11,* 295–305.

Rogers, T. B., Rogers, P. J., & Kuiper, N. A. (1977). *Recognition memory for personal adjectives:. Some evidence for self-reference or an aspect of memory.* Unpublished manuscript, University of Calgary.

Schulman, A. I. (1974). Memory for words recently classified. *Memory & Cognition, 2,* 47–52.

Sechrest, L. (1976). Personality. In M. R. Rosenzweig & L. W. Porter (Eds.), *Annual review of psychology.* Palo Alto: Annual Reviews.

Snygg, D., & Combs, A. W. (1949). *Individual behavior.* New York: Harper.

Walsh, D. A., & Jenkins, J. J. (1973). Effects of orienting tasks on free recall in incidental learning: "Difficulty," "effort," and "process" explanations. *Journal of Verbal Learning and Verbal Behavior, 12,* 481–488.

# Self-Discrepancy:
# A Theory Relating Self and Affect

*Possibly relate to Michaelangelo phen? →*

E. Tory Higgins • New York University

This article presents a theory of how different types of discrepancies between self-state representations are related to different kinds of emotional vulnerabilities. One domain of the self (actual; ideal; ought) and one standpoint on the self (own; significant other) constitute each type of self-state representation. It is proposed that different types of self-discrepancies represent different types of negative psychological situations that are associated with different kinds of discomfort. Discrepancies between the actual/own self-state (i.e., the self-concept) and ideal self-states (i.e., representations of an individual's beliefs about his or her own or a significant other's hopes, wishes, or aspirations for the individual) signify the absence of positive outcomes, which is associated with dejection-related emotions (e.g., disappointment, dissatisfaction, sadness). In contrast, discrepancies between the actual/own self-state and ought self-states (i.e., representations of an individual's beliefs about his or her own or a significant other's beliefs about the individual's duties, responsibilities, or obligations) signify the presence of negative outcomes, which is associated with agitation-related emotions (e.g., fear, threat, restlessness). Differences in both the relative magnitude and the accessibility of individuals' available types of self-discrepancies are predicted to be related to differences in the kinds of discomfort people are likely to experience. Correlational and experimental evidence supports the predictions of the model. Differences between self-discrepancy theory and (a) other theories of incompatible self-beliefs and (b) actual self negativity (e.g., low self-esteem) are discussed.

The notion that people who hold conflicting or incompatible beliefs are likely to experience discomfort has had a long history in psychology. In social psychology, for example, various early theories proposed a relation between discomfort and specific kinds of "inconsistency" among a person's beliefs (e.g., Abelson & Rosenberg, 1958; Festinger, 1957; Heider, 1958; McGuire, 1968; Newcomb, 1968; Osgood & Tannenbaum, 1955). And various classic theories relating self and affect proposed that self-conflicts or self-inconsistencies produce emotional problems (e.g., Adler,

1964; Allport, 1955; Cooley, 1902/1964; Freud, 1923/1961; Horney, 1939, 1946; James, 1890/1948; Lecky, 1961; Mead, 1934; Rogers, 1961). The theory to be presented here, self-discrepancy theory, has close ties to this historical tradition. But its construction was guided by a distinct set of aims: (a) to distinguish among different kinds of discomfort that people holding incompatible beliefs may experience, (b) to relate different kinds of emotional vulnerabilities systematically to different types of discrepancies that people may possess among their self-beliefs, and (c) to consider the role of both the availability and the accessibility of different discrepancies people may possess in determining the kind of discomfort they are most likely to suffer.

Although many different types of belief incompatibility have been described in the literature—for example, dissonance (e.g., Aronson, 1969; Festinger 1957), imbalance (e.g., Heider, 1958; Newcomb, 1968), incongruity (e.g., Osgood & Tannenbaum, 1955), and self-inconsistency (e.g., Epstein, 1980; Lecky, 1961)—the emotional consequences have typically been described only in very general terms, such as tension, unpleasantness, pressure, conflict, stress, or discomfort. And yet it is clear from the general psychological literature that distinct emotional clusters or syndromes exist. From factor analysis, cluster analysis, and circular scaling, researchers have reported that dissatisfaction, feeling discouraged, feeling pitiful, feeling sad, feeling gloomy, and feeling miserable tend to cluster (e.g., Cattell, 1973; DeRivera, 1977; Ewert, 1970; Kemper, 1978; Zuckerman & Lubin, 1965), whereas guilt, anxiety, worry, fear, feeling tense, feeling alarmed, and feeling threatened form another cluster (Ausubel, 1955; Bibring, 1953; Cattell, 1973; DeRivera, 1977; Ewert, 1970; Kemper, 1978; Russell, 1980; Zuckerman & Lubin, 1965). This basic distinction between dejection-related emotions and agitation-related emotions has also been made frequently in the clinical literature, not only to distinguish between depression and anxiety but also to distinguish between different kinds of depression (see, e.g., Beck, 1967, 1983; Cameron, 1963; White, 1964).

Thus previous theories of belief incompatibility are limited in that they do not consider that distinct kinds of discomfort may be associated with belief incompatibility. These theories, then, cannot predict *which* kind of discomfort or emotional problem will be induced by a particular type of belief incompatibility. In addition, the possibility does not arise that chronic individual differences in type of belief incompatibility may be related to individual differences in emotional vulnerability. Indeed, among theories concerned with self-evaluation, theories of vulnerability to generally positive or negative emotions are relatively common, such as theories of achievement motivation (e.g., Atkinson, 1964; McClelland, 1961), but theories of vulnerability to *different kinds of negative emotions* are rare. And those that have been proposed tend to describe emotional vulnerability in terms of problem areas, such as interpersonal dependency problems versus achievement or self-efficacy problems, rather than to relate emotional vulnerability to specific types of incompatible beliefs (e.g., Beck, 1983; Blatt, D'Afflitti, & Quinlan, 1976). A primary purpose of self-discrepancy theory, then, is to predict which types of incompatible beliefs will induce which kinds of negative emotions.

Another purpose is to consider whether the availability and accessibility of different types of incompatible beliefs induce different kinds of discomfort. Incompatible beliefs are cognitive constructs, and as such they can vary in both their availability and their accessibility. Construct *availability* refers to the particular kinds of constructs that are actually present (i.e., available) in memory to be used to process new information, whereas construct *accessibility* refers to the readiness with which each stored construct is used in information processing (see Higgins & Bargh, 1987; Higgins, King, & Mavin, 1982; Tulving & Pearlstone, 1966). Individual differences can arise either because people have different types of constructs available or because they have the same types available but their relative accessibilities differ.

Common to theories of belief incompatibility is the assumption that the incompatibility reflects a particular type of psychological situation that influences its possessor's responses. Thus, these theories compare persons who do or do not possess the particular belief incompatibility (e.g., cognitive dissonance, imbalance) and thus are or are not likely to respond in terms of the psychological situation associated with it. These theories, then, compare only whether a particular (negative) psychological situation is or is not available and thus are limited by considering only the absence or presence of one basic type of psychological situation.

In contrast, Kelly's (1955) theory of personal constructs proposed that individuals vary widely in the particular types of psychological situations available to them; that is, there is a wide variety of personal viewpoints or ways of construing the world (see also Lewin, 1935). But Kelly did not relate different types of available constructs to different types of emotional vulnerability. And neither Kelly's nor any other theory of belief incompatibility distinguished between individual differences in construct availability and individual differences in construct accessibility. Following Kelly, individual differences in personal constructs have been commonly conceived as differences in the nature and content of people's constructs, in the viewpoint people have of social objects and events (e.g., Markus, 1977; Sarbin, Taft, & Bailey, 1960; Tagiuri, 1969). Such differences constitute differences in the availability of social constructs. Higgins et al. (1982) proposed that the accessibility of social constructs can also differ, momentarily or chronically.

Considerable evidence indicates that various contextual factors, such as prior exposure to construct-related stimuli (i.e., priming), can produce temporary individual differences in the accessibility of generally available social constructs (e.g., common trait constructs, such as "stubborn" or "hostile") and that these differences in turn can produce differences in subsequent responses to social stimuli (for reviews, see Higgins, Bargh, & Lombardi, 1985; Higgins & King, 1981; Wyer & Srull, 1981). There is also evidence that chronic individual differences in construct accessibility can influence social information processing (e.g., Bargh & Thein, 1985; Gotlib & McCann, 1984; Higgins et al., 1982). Another important purpose of self-discrepancy theory, then, is to introduce construct accessibility as a predictor of when available types of incompatible beliefs (and which of the available types) will induce discomfort.

## Self-Discrepancy Theory

Over the years many different facets of the self or self-images have been identified. One finds descriptions of two "actual" selves—the kind of person an individual believes he or she actually is and the kind of person an individual believes that others think he or she actually is. The "others" can be significant others or the generalized other (see Erikson, 1950/1963; Lecky, 1961; Mead, 1934; Wylie, 1979). In addition to these actual selves, a variety of different potential selves have been identified (e.g., Markus & Nurius, 1987).

James (1890/1948), for example, distinguished between the "spiritual" self, which included one's own moral sensibility and conscience, and the "social" self, which included the self that is worthy

of being approved by the highest social judge. Rogers (1961) distinguished between what others believe a person should or ought to be (i.e., the normative standard) and a person's own belief about what he or she would "ideally" like to be. Elaborating on Freud's (1923/1961) basic "superego"/"ego ideal" conceptions, Schafer (1967) and Piers and Singer (1971) distinguished between the superego representing the moral conscience and the ideal self representing hopes and goals (see also Cameron, 1963). Cooley (1902/1964) also described a social "ideal self" built up by imagining how a "better I" of aspiration would appear in the minds of persons we look up to. In his programmable theory of cognition and affect, Colby (1968) distinguished between "wish-beliefs," such as "I want to marry Tom," and "value-beliefs," such as "I ought to help my father." Although a variety of aspects of the self have been distinguished across different theories (see Greenwald & Pratkanis, 1984), there has been no systematic framework for revealing the interrelations among the different self-states. In an attempt to do so, self-discrepancy theory postulates two cognitive dimensions underlying the various self-state representations: domains of the self and standpoints on the self.

### Domains of the Self

There are three basic domains of the self: (a) the *actual* self, which is your representation of the attributes that someone (yourself or another) believes you actually possess; (b) the *ideal* self, which is your representation of the attributes that someone (yourself or another) would like you, ideally, to possess (i.e., representation of someone's hopes, aspirations, or wishes for you); and (c) the *ought* self, which is your representation of the attributes that someone (yourself or another) believes you should or ought to possess (i.e., a representation of someone's sense of your duty, obligations, or responsibilities).

The distinction proposed here between the ideal self and the ought self is reflected in various distinctions suggested in the literature (e.g., Colby, 1968; James, 1890/1948; Piers & Singer, 1971; Rogers, 1961; Schafer, 1967). In an extensive discussion of the difference between moral conscience and personal ideals, Schafer (1967) cogently argued that "ideals and superego morality have been confined together when each should long ago have had a place of its own" (p. 131). A classic literary example of the difference between the ideal self and the ought self is the conflict between a hero's "personal wishes" and his or her "sense of duty." A current real-world example is the conflict some women have between their own wishes to be successful professionals and some other persons' beliefs that they ought to be housewives and mothers.

## Standpoints on the Self

It is not enough to distinguish among different domains of self if one wishes systematically to relate self and affect. One must also discriminate among self-state representations by considering whose perspective on the self is involved. There are two basic standpoints on the self, where a standpoint on the self is defined as a point of view from which you can be judged that reflects a set of attitudes or values (see Turner, 1956): (a) your *own* personal standpoint, and (b) the standpoint of some significant *other* (e.g., mother, father, sibling, spouse, closest friend). A person can have self-state representations for each of a number of significant others.

Except for theories focusing solely on the actual self, previous theories of the self have not systematically considered the different domains of self in terms of the different standpoints on those domains (e.g., your beliefs concerning the attributes you would personally like ideally to possess versus your beliefs concerning the attributes that some significant other person, such as your mother, would like you ideally to possess). In fact, this failure to be explicit about which standpoint on the self is involved in a particular self-concept has led to confusions in the literature. For example, although most measures of "low self-esteem" have involved comparing a person's actual self and his or her *own* ideal self, some measures have involved comparing a person's actual self and his or her beliefs about *others'* ideals for him or her (often referred to as the "social ideal self" in the literature), and other measures have been ambiguous concerning whose ideal standpoint is involved (see Wylie, 1979).

In addition to Turner's (1956) work, the concept of standpoint is found in some writings on the impact of reference groups on self-judgment, where a "normative reference group" is described as a source of a person's values or perspectives (see Kelley, 1952). In discussing "level of aspira-

tion" Lewin (1935) distinguished between the expectations of adult authority figures that can raise a child's level of aspiration (i.e., "other" standpoints) and a child's own hopes and personal goals (i.e., "own" standpoint). The notion of standpoint is also implicit in Mead's (1934) discussion of the development of the self, where a person's own recognition of self as distinct from others develops from the viewpoint of significant others (usually a child's mother and father). Mead, however, did not make clear to what extent the different standpoints on self remain distinct, and, in fact, suggested that in later development a person's self-concept becomes based on the viewpoint of "generalized others" rather than particular others.

In contrast to the relatively rare use of the distinction between "own" versus "other" standpoints in classifying different types of self-state representations, the distinction between "own" versus "other" has frequently been used as a critical feature in various systems for classifying emotions (e.g., Dahl, 1979; DeRivera, 1977; Freud, 1915/1957; Kemper, 1978; Roseman, 1984) and distinguishing among motivations (e.g., Breckler & Greenwald, 1986; Buss, 1980; Scheier & Carver, 1983; Snyder, 1979). By incorporating the distinction between "own" and "other" as a feature for classifying self-state representations, we can relate different emotional/motivational conditions to different self-state conditions (as described later).

## Self-State Representations and Their Motivational Significance

Combining each of the domains of the self with each of the standpoints on the self yields six basic types of self-state representations: actual/own, actual/other, ideal/own, ideal/other, ought/own, and ought/other. The first two self-state representations (particularly actual/own) constitute what is typically meant by a person's *self-concept* (see Wylie, 1979). The four remaining self-state representations are self-directive standards or acquired guides for being—in brief, *self-guides* (see Higgins, Strauman, & Klein, 1986, for a review of different kinds of standards). Self-discrepancy theory proposes that people differ as to which self-guide they are especially motivated to meet. Not everyone is expected to possess all of the self-guides—some may possess only ought self-guides, whereas others may possess only ideal self-guides.

Self-discrepancy theory postulates that we are

motivated to reach a condition where our self-concept matches our personally relevant self-guides. The notion that standards, particularly ideal and ought standards, are motivating has a long history. James (1890/1948) pointed out that standards both directly prompt action and, through their use in self-evaluation, arouse emotions that are themselves motivating. Theories of level of aspiration, although focusing on the relation between performance and standard setting (see Festinger, 1942; Lewin, 1935; Rotter, 1942), have traditionally assumed that people need high "ideal" goals or aspiration levels in order to motivate performance. Control theory or cybernetics (see Miller, Galanter & Pribram, 1960; Wiener, 1948) assumes that people self-regulate through a discrepancy-reducing negative feedback process whose function is to minimize differences between one sensed value (which could be a self-concept) and some other reference value or standard of comparison (which could be a self-guide). Duval and Wicklund's (1972) theory of objective self-awareness argues that increasing self-focused attention increases our awareness of discrepancies between our real self and personal standards of correctness, subsequently inducing a motivation to reduce the discrepancy (see also Wicklund & Gollwitzer, 1982). And Carver and Scheier's control-theory approach to behavioral self-regulation (e.g., Carver & Scheier, 1981; Scheier & Carver, 1982), which integrates both of these latter two perspectives, emphasizes the motivational significance of matching to standards.

Self-discrepancy theory differs from these other theories in proposing that different types of chronic discrepancies between the self-concept and different self-guides, as well as between different self-guides, are associated with different motivational predispositions. It is not possible in this article to consider all of the possible types of self-discrepancies (e.g., ideal/own vs. ought/other).[1] An especially important set of self-discrepancies is the set that reflects a discrepancy between an individual's self-concept and his or her self-guides. This set of self-discrepancies has also received the most empirical attention. In this article, therefore, we focus on the following four types of discrepancies: actual/own:ideal/own, actual/own:ideal/other,

actual/own: ought/own, and actual/own:ought/other.

## Types of Self-Discrepancies and Quality of Discomfort

Although self-discrepancies might be considered to constitute a form of belief inconsistency, the source of discrepancy-induced discomfort is not assumed to be simply a failure to achieve internal consistency or a "good Gestalt fit." Indeed, if this was assumed to be the only source of the discomfort, then self-discrepancy theory, like previous inconsistency theories, would not predict that different types of discrepancies induce different kinds of discomfort. But as Abelson (1983) has pointed out with respect to Heider's (1958) balance theory and Festinger's (1957) cognitive dissonance theory, inconsistencies among cognitions reflect personal costs and problems—not simply cognitive experiences. Self-discrepancy theory shares this perspective (see also Holt, 1976; Kemper, 1978; Plutchik, 1962; Schlenker, 1985) by assuming that each type of discrepancy reflects a particular type of negative psychological situation that is associated with specific emotional/motivational problems.

When people believe that they have lost or will never obtain some desired goal, they feel sad or disappointed. When people believe that something terrible is going to happen they feel apprehensive or threatened. More generally, there are two basic kinds of negative psychological situations that are associated with different kinds of emotional states (see, for example, Jacobs, 1971; Lazarus, 1968; Mowrer, 1960; Roseman, 1984; Stein & Jewett, 1982): (a) the *absence of positive outcomes* (actual or expected), which is associated with dejection-related emotions (e.g., dissatisfaction, disappointment, sadness); and (b) the *presence of negative outcomes* (actual or expected), which is associated with agitation-related emotions (e.g., fear, threat, edginess). It has been understood for many years that psychological situations are a function of both the nature of external events and people's interpretations of those events (see, for example, Asch, 1952; Lewin, 1951; Merton, 1957), and that there are individual differences in how external events are interpreted (see, for example, Kelly, 1955; G. S. Klein, 1970; Murray, 1938; see also Coyne & Lazarus, 1980). Self-discrepancy theory proposes that individual differences in types

---

[1]The Self-Discrepancies and Self-Concept Negativity section includes a brief description of the kind of discomfort that is associated with a discrepancy between two self-guides.

of self-discrepancies are associated with differences in the specific types of negative psychological situations their possessors are likely to experience.

Just as your emotional response to your performance is not determined by the properties of the performance per se, but by its significance or meaning to you, self-discrepancy theory assumes that the motivational or emotional effects of your actual/own attributes, or self-concept, are determined by the significance to you of possessing such attributes. And the significance is assumed to depend on the *relation* between the self-concept and your self-guides, with different types of relations representing different types of negative psychological situations, as described next:

1. Actual/own versus ideal/own: If a person possesses this discrepancy, the current state of his or her actual attributes, from the person's own standpoint, does not match the ideal state that he or she personally hopes or wishes to attain. This discrepancy then represents the general psychological situation of the absence of positive outcomes (i.e., nonobtainment of own hopes and desires), and thus the person is predicted to be vulnerable to *dejection-related emotions.*

   More specifically, the person is predicted to be vulnerable to *disappointment* and *dissatisfaction* because these emotions are associated with people believing that their personal hopes or wishes have been unfulfilled. Most psychological analyses of these emotions have described them as being associated with (a) the individual's *own* standpoint or agency (e.g., James, 1890/ 1948; Kemper, 1978; Roseman, 1984; Wierzbicka, 1972) and (b) a discrepancy from his or her hopes, desires, or ideals (e.g., Abelson, 1983; Carver & Ganellen, 1983; Durkheim, 1951; Duval & Wicklund, 1972; Horney, 1950; James, 1890/1948; Kemper, 1978; Rogers, 1961; Wierzbicka, 1972). The motivational nature of this discrepancy also suggests that it might be associated with *frustration* from unfulfilled desires.

2. Actual/own versus ideal/other: If a person possesses this discrepancy, the current state of his or her actual attributes, from the person's own standpoint, does not match the ideal state that the person believes some significant other person hopes or wishes that he or she would attain. This discrepancy, then, again represents the general psychological situation of the absence of positive outcomes (i.e., nonobtainment of a significant other's hopes or wishes), and thus the person is again predicted to be vulnerable to *dejection-related emotions.*

More specifically, because people who believe that they have failed to obtain some significant other's hopes or wishes are likely to believe that the significant other is disappointed and dissatisfied with them, self-discrepancy theory predicts that they will be vulnerable to *shame, embarrassment,* or *feeling downcast,* because these emotions are associated with people believing that they have lost standing or esteem in the opinion of others. Most psychological analyses of "shame" and related emotions have described them as being associated with (a) the standpoint or agency of one or more *other* people (e.g., Ausubel, 1955; Cooley, 1902/1964; DeRivera, 1977; Lewis, 1979; Piers & Singer, 1971; Wierzbicka, 1972) and (b) a discrepancy from achievement or status standards (e.g., Cooley, 1902/1964; DeRivera, 1977; Erikson, 1950/1963; Kemper, 1978; Piers & Singer, 1971). Some analyses describe shame as being associated discrepancy from both moral and nonmoral standards (e.g., Ausubel, 1955; Lewis, 1979). The motivational nature of this discrepancy suggests that it might also be associated with concern over losing the affection or esteem of others.

3. Actual/own versus ought/other: If a person possesses this discrepancy, the current state of his or her actual attributes, from the person's own standpoint, does not match the state that person believes some significant other person considers to be his or her duty or obligation to attain. Because violation of prescribed duties and obligations is associated with sanctions (e.g., punishment), this discrepancy represents the general psychological situation of the presence of negative outcomes (i.e., expectation of punishment), and thus the person is predicted to be vulnerable to *agitation-related emotions.*

More specifically, the person is predicted to be vulnerable to *fear* and *feeling threatened,* because these emotions occur when danger or harm is anticipated or impending. Most psychological analyses of these emotions have described them as associated with (a) external agents, in particular the standpoint or agency of one or more *other* people (e.g., Abelson, 1983; Ausubel, 1955; DeRivera, 1977; Freud, 1923/1961; Kemper, 1978; Piers & Singer, 1971; Sullivan, 1953), and (b) a discrepancy from norms or moral standards (e.g., Ausubel, 1955; Dahl, 1979; Freud, 1923/1961; Kemper, 1978; Piers & Singer, 1971; Sullivan, 1953). The motivational nature of this discrepancy suggests that it might also be associated with feelings of *resentment* (i.e., resentment of the anticipated pain to be inflicted by others).

4. Actual/own versus ought/own: If a person possesses this discrepancy, the current state of his or her attributes, from the person's own standpoint, does not match the state that the person believes it is his or her duty or obligation to attain. This discrepancy, then, again represents the general psychological situation of the presence of negative outcomes (i.e., a readiness for self-punishment), and thus self-discrepancy theory predicts that the person is vulnerable to *agitation-related emotions.*

More specifically, the person is predicted to be vulnerable to *guilt, self-contempt,* and *uneasiness,* because these feelings occur when people believe they have transgressed a personally accepted (i.e., legitimate) moral standard. Most psychological analyses of guilt have described it as associated with (a) a person's *own* standpoint or agency (e.g., Ausubel, 1955; Erikson, 1950/1963; Freud, 1923/1961; James, 1890/1948; Kemper, 1978; Lewis, 1979; Piers & Singer, 1971) and (b) a discrepancy from his or her sense of morality or justice (e.g., Ausubel, 1955; Erikson, 1950/1963; Freud, 1923/1961; Horney, 1939; James, 1890/1948; Kemper, 1978; Lewis, 1979; Piers & Singer, 1971). The motivational nature of this discrepancy suggests that it may be associated with feelings of moral worthlessness or weakness.

The distinction between shame and guilt suggested here is that shame involves feeling that one has been lowered in the esteem of others because one has disappointed them by failing to accomplish their hopes and wishes for one, whereas guilt involves feeling that one has broken one's own rules concerning how one ought to conduct one's life. This distinction is consistent with previous discussions of the difference between shame and guilt (e.g., Erikson, 1950/1963; James, 1890/

1948). It is also evident from the preceding descriptions of psychological analyses of these two emotions that most theories consider shame to involve the "other" standpoint and guilt to involve the "own" standpoint, and that most theories consider shame to involve the "ideal" domain and guilt to involve the "ought" domain. Nevertheless, there are some theories that consider guilt to involve the "other" standpoint as well (e.g., Horney, 1939; Piers & Singer, 1971) and shame to involve the "ought" domain as well (e.g., Ausubel, 1955; Lewis, 1979). These theories, then, would predict that discrepancies in addition to those postulated by self-discrepancy theory can induce shame and guilt. But all of the theories would agree that the discrepancies postulated by self-discrepancy theory to induce shame and guilt should do so.

The distinction between fear and guilt suggested here is that fear involves anticipating sanctions from others for having violated their rules, whereas guilt involves chastising oneself for having broken one's own rules of conduct. This distinction between fear and guilt is consistent with those previously made in the psychological literature on emotions (e.g., Ausubel, 1955; Freud, 1923/1961; Kemper, 1978).

As I mentioned earlier, self-discrepancy theory does not assume that people possess only one or the other of these types of self-discrepancies. Particular individuals can possess none of them, all of them, or any combination of them. Thus, one can have no emotional vulnerability, only one (i.e., a pure case), or a number of different kinds of emotional vulnerabilities. Moreover, even if a person possesses more than one type of self-discrepancy, and thus more than one kind of emotional vulnerability, the discrepancies are not necessarily equally active and equally likely to induce discomfort. In order to determine which types of discrepancies a person possesses and which are likely to be active and induce their associated emotions at any point, we must consider the next feature of self-discrepancy theory: distinguishing between the availability and the accessibility of self-discrepancies.

## Availability and Accessibility of Self-Discrepancies

The *availability* of any particular type of self-discrepancy is assumed to depend on the extent to which the attributes of the two conflicting self-state representations diverge for the person in question. Each attribute in one of the self-state representations (e.g., actual/own) is compared to each attribute in the other self-state representation (e.g., ideal/own). Each pair of attributes is coded as either a match (i.e., synonymous attributes of the same or similar degree) or a mismatch (i.e., antonymous attributes, such as actual/own: "unattractive" vs. ideal/own: "attractive," and synonymous attributes of very different degrees, such as actual/own: "slightly attractive" vs. ideal/own: "extremely attractive").

The greater the difference between the number of mismatches and the number of matches (i.e., the greater the divergence of attributes between the two self-state representations), the greater is the magnitude of that type of self-discrepancy available to the subject. And the greater the magnitude of a particular type of discrepancy, the greater will be the *intensity* of the kind of discomfort associated with the discrepancy when it is activated. The likelihood that an available self-discrepancy will be activated in turn depends on its accessibility.

The *accessibility* of an available self-discrepancy is assumed to depend on the same factors that determine the accessibility of any stored construct (for reviews, see Higgins & King, 1981; Higgins, Bargh, & Lombardi, 1985; Wyer & Srull, 1981). One factor is how recently the construct has been activated. For example, it has been demonstrated that exposure to trait labels in a prior "unrelated" task (a *priming* manipulation) increases the likelihood that subjects will subsequently interpret a target person's ambiguous behaviors in terms of the particular constructs activated by the labels (e.g., Higgins, Rholes, & Jones, 1977; Srull & Wyer, 1979; see also Bargh & Pietromonaco, 1982). As Abelson (1959) pointed out, there are numerous inconsistencies in anyone's belief system that may lie dormant, and it is plausible to assume that pressure operates only when the issue is salient (e.g., when the self-discrepancy has been contextually primed).

It has also been shown that the more frequently a construct is activated, the more likely it will be used subsequently to interpret social events (e.g., Higgins, Bargh, & Lombardi, 1985; Srull & Wyer, 1979, 1980). The influence of frequency of activation is also reflected in the effects of chronic individual differences in construct accessibility on social interpretation and memory (e.g., Bargh & Thein, 1985; Higgins et al., 1982).

The accessibility, or likelihood of activation, of a stored construct also depends on the relation between its "meaning" and the properties of the stimulus event. A stored construct will not be used to interpret an event unless it is applicable to the event (see Higgins & Bargh, 1987; Higgins et al., 1977). Thus, the negative psychological situation represented in a self-discrepancy (i.e., the "meaning" of the discrepancy) will not be activated by an unambiguously positive event. And a self-discrepancy need not have high prior accessibility in order to be used to interpret a negative event if the event instantiates the discrepancy's "meaning" clearly enough. In sum, the accessibility of a self-discrepancy is determined by its *recency of activation,* its *frequency of activation,* and its *applicability* to the stimulus event.

I should note that self-discrepancy theory does not assume that people are aware of either the availability or the accessibility of their self-discrepancies. It is clear that the availability and accessibility of stored social constructs can influence social information processing automatically and without awareness (see Bargh, 1984; Bargh, Bond, Lombardi, & Tota, 1986; Bargh & Pietromonaco, 1982; Higgins & Bargh, 1987; Higgins & King, 1981; Kelly, 1955). Thus, self-discrepancy theory assumes that the available and accessible negative psychological situations embodied in one's self-discrepancies can be used to assign meaning to events without one's being aware of either the discrepancies or their impact on processing. The measure of self-discrepancies requires only that one be able to retrieve attributes of specific self-state representations when asked to do so. It does *not* require that one be aware of the relations among these attributes or of their significance.

## General Hypothesis of Self-Discrepancy Theory

A number of implications follow from the set of assumptions above:

1. Individual differences in which types of self-discrepancies are available will be associated with individual differences in the kinds of dis-

comfort that people will suffer (i.e., individual differences in emotional vulnerability).

2. The greater the magnitude of a particular type of self-discrepancy, the more intensely its possessor will suffer the kind of discomfort associated with that type of discrepancy.

3. If a person possesses more than one type of self-discrepancy (i.e., has more than one type of self-discrepancy available), he or she is likely to suffer most intensely the kind of discomfort associated with whichever type of discrepancy has the greatest magnitude.

4. Individual differences in whichever type of self-discrepancy is temporarily most accessible will be associated with momentary individual differences in the kinds of discomfort that people will suffer (i.e., individual differences in emotional episodes).

5. The greater the accessibility of a particular type of self-discrepancy, the greater the likelihood that its possessor will suffer the kind of discomfort associated with that type of discrepancy.

6. If a person possesses more than one type of self-discrepancy, he or she is most likely to suffer momentarily the kind of discomfort associated with whichever type of discrepancy has the greatest temporary accessibility.

These implications of self-discrepancy theory are captured in the following general hypothesis: The greater the magnitude and accessibility of a particular type of self-discrepancy possessed by an individual, the more the individual will suffer the kind of discomfort associated with that type of self-discrepancy.

## Evidence for Self-Discrepancy Theory

In this section, I will review evidence for the preceding hypothesis of self-discrepancy theory. First, I will discuss observational and correlational evidence supporting the hypothesized distinct associations between particular types of self-discrepancies and particular kinds of discomfort. Next, I will present experimental evidence for the causal assumptions in the theory. Then I will describe some additional evidence of the relations between self-discrepancies and more general emotional problems (i.e., dejected depression vs. agitated depression or anxiety).

## Evidence of Distinct Self-Discrepancy–Discomfort Associations

Although the previous literature relating self and affect does not contain studies that directly tested self-discrepancy theory, there is some evidence of distinct relations between particular types of discrepant self-beliefs and particular kinds of discomfort that is relevant to, and generally supports, the proposed hypothesis.

James (1890/1948) stated that when success does not match our pretensions or aspirations (an actual/own:ideal/own discrepancy), we will feel disappointed. Duval and Wicklund (1972) also reported that when we focus on our own "real self: ideal self" discrepancy, as a consequence of being objectively self-aware, we become increasingly dissatisfied and disappointed. Various other researchers have observed that a felt discrepancy between what one actually is and what one wants or hopes to be, once again reflecting an actual/own:ideal/own discrepancy, leads to disappointment and dissatisfaction (e.g., Durkheim, 1951; Fenichel, 1945; Jacobson, 1946; Rogers, 1961).

Cooley (1902/1964) stated that if people have a sense of the difference between their current self and their social ideal self (an actual/own:ideal/other discrepancy), they are plunged into feelings of shame or unworthiness. Similarly, James (1890/1948) said that when self-estimation does not match the social ideal self, a person experiences shame. Piers and Singer (1971) observed that when people fail to reach the goals and hopes for them that are associated with their parents (i.e., their ideal/other), they feel shame, which can include an expectation of loss of love. As discussed earlier, an actual/own:ideal/other discrepancy reflects our belief that we have failed to obtain some significant other's goals for us, which is associated with believing that the significant other is disappointed in or dissatisfied with us. It has frequently been noted that shame associated with failure to meet a significant other's goals or wishes involves loss of face and presumed exposure to the dissatisfaction of others (e.g., Ausubel, 1955; Mead, 1934; Tompkins, 1984).

A discrepancy between one's actual behavior and the behavior prescribed by significant others (an actual/own:ought/other discrepancy) has often been said to create fear and anxiety because of apprehension over anticipated sanctions or negative responses by others (e.g., Freud, 1923/1961;

Scheier & Carver, 1977; Sullivan, 1953). In contrast, transgression of one's own internalized moral and religious standards (actual/own:ought/own discrepancy) has been associated with guilt and self-criticism (e.g., Ausubel, 1955; Bibring, 1953; Freud, 1923/1961; James, 1890/1948; Piers & Singer, 1971; Tompkins, 1984). Weiner, Russell, and Lerman (1979) reported that when people attribute their failures to a lack of sufficient effort on their part (i.e., not trying as hard as they know they should have), which perhaps reflects an actual/own:ought/own discrepancy, they feel guilty.

There is also some evidence of distinct relations discernible in previous self-conflict theories of depression. A review of these theories reveals a basic similarity: Each theory proposes that the emotions associated with depression arise from a discrepancy between a person's perceived self and some standard. It has not been noted, however, that there are two different self-conflict theories of depression as a function of the type of standard that is emphasized. One set of theories, which could be described as the "actual:ought" theories, emphasizes the ought standard. These theories propose that depression is caused by discrepancy between a person's actual self and his or her superego or moral conscience (e.g., Cameron, 1963; Fenichel, 1945; Freud, 1917/1959, 1923/1961; Rado, 1927/1956). Freud, for example, suggested that depression results from a felt disparity between the ego as object and the superego or conscience. Another set of theories, which could be described as the "actual:ideal" theories, emphasizes the ideal standard. These theories propose that depression is caused by a discrepancy between a person's actual self and his or her goals, aspirations, or ideal self (e.g., Bibring, 1953; Jacobson, 1946; Sandler & Joffe, 1965). Bibring, for example, suggested that depression results from an inner-systemic conflict involving a discrepancy between a person's actual self and his or her goals and aspirations.

According to self-discrepancy theory, these two different types of self-conflicts or discrepancies should induce different kinds of depression—an actual:ought discrepancy should induce agitated depression, whereas an actual:ideal discrepancy should induce dejected depression. Indeed, the depressive symptoms emphasized by the "actual:ought" conflict theorists have been guilt, apprehension, anxiety, and fear (i.e., agitated depression), whereas the depressive symptoms emphasized by the "actual:ideal" conflict theorists

have been feelings of failure, disappointment, devaluation, and shame (i.e., dejected depression). It is also interesting in this regard that people who develop involutional melancholia tend to be highly moralistic (i.e., high ought standard), and their illness usually involves agitated depression (Mendels, 1970).

With regard to standpoint, the importance of distinguishing between performance:ought/own discrepancies and performance:ought/other discrepancies is suggested in the moral socialization findings of Hoffman (e.g., 1971, 1975). In one study involving elementary school children and adults, Hoffman (1975) found that moral transgression was associated with guilt for females but with fear and anticipation of punishment for males (especially for the adults). Hoffman suggested that males may represent moral standards mostly in terms of external sanctions, whereas females may internalize moral standards. If so, then the results of his study are consistent with the distinction between the actual/own:ought/own discrepancy (for females) and the actual/own:ought/other discrepancy (for males) proposed in the model. Moreover, fear and anticipation of punishment were uncorrelated with expressions of guilt, consistent with the model's proposal that these emotions have distinct underlying causes. In another study, Hoffman (1971) also found that emphasis on an ought/other standard (as measured by identification with one's parents' moral standards) was not associated with guilt or moral confession but was associated with conformity to rules (presumably because of anticipation of punishment).

In a direct test of self-discrepancy theory, my colleagues and I (Higgins, Klein, & Strauman, 1985) had undergraduates fill out a questionnaire designed to measure their self-discrepancies (the Selves questionnaire) as well as a variety of questionnaires that measured different kinds of chronic discomfort and emotional symptoms. The Selves questionnaire asked respondents to list up to 10 traits or attributes for each of a number of different self-states. It was administered in two sections, the first involving the respondent's own standpoint and the second involving the standpoints of the respondent's father, mother, and closest friend. In the beginning of the questionnaire the actual, ideal, and ought self-states were defined (as described earlier). Each page of the questionnaire concerned a particular self-state: for example, "Please list the attributes of the type of person *you* think you ac-

*tually* are" or "Please list the attributes of the type of person your *Mother* believes you *should* or ought to be." By having subjects spontaneously list the attributes associated with each of their self-states (as opposed to a constrained, checklist procedure), we increased the likelihood that the attributes obtained would be important and accessible to each subject.

The subjects were also instructed to rate the overall extent to which a particular standpoint (self, mother, etc.) on a particular domain of self (actual, ideal, ought) was relevant or meaningful to them as a source of information. This was done because self-discrepancy theory assumes that only *relevant standpoints* are motivationally or emotionally significant. Indeed, a study by R. Klein and Higgins (1984) found preliminary support for this assumption. Undergraduates filled out a questionnaire containing some questions that measured the relevance of the standpoint of different significant others designated by their role relationship to the subject (e.g., mother, father, best friend) with respect to different domains (e.g., for the ought domain, "Whose viewpoint on the type of person you should or ought to be matters most to you?"; "Whose viewpoint matters least to you?"). A few weeks later, as part of a different study, the subjects were asked to imagine different types of performance: guide discrepancies involving the standpoints of different significant others, and they reported how the event would make them feel. As expected, the magnitude of discomfort reported was significantly greater ($p < .05$) when the "other" standpoint was the most relevant to the domain than when it was the least relevant.

This effect of standpoint relevance is consistent with Newcomb's (1968) conclusion concerning the discomfort associated with incompatible beliefs:

> An individual's most salient concern, in dealing with such multiple cognitions, is the suitability of the other person as a source of information, or support, or of influence concerning the object cognized by each of them. Insofar as the other person is devalued in this context, he will be indifferent to the latter's cognitions. (p. 50)

Newcomb's research suggests that standpoint relevance is critical for whether self-state incompatibility will induce discomfort (see also Rogers, 1961; Rosenberg, 1979).

Thus in the Higgins, Klein, and Strauman (1985) study, subjects' ratings of the relevance of the different significant others were used to select for each domain that "other" who was most relevant to the subject. Four different types of self-discrepancies were then calculated: actual/own:ideal/own; actual/own:ideal/other; actual/own:ought/other; and actual/own:ought/own. First, for each self-discrepancy the attributes in one self-state were compared to the attributes in the other self-state to determine which attributes *matched* (i.e., both self-states listed the same attribute; synonyms were considered to be the same attribute) and which attributes *mismatched* (i.e., an attribute in one self-state was an antonym of an attribute in the other self-state). Second, the self-discrepancy score for the two self-states was calculated by subtracting the total number of matches from the total number of mismatches.

In order to measure chronic discomfort and emotional symptoms, the following measures were used (for more details about these measures, see Higgins, Klein, & Strauman, 1985): the Beck Depression Inventory (Beck, Ward, Mendelson, Mock, & Erbaugh, 1961), the Blatt Depressive Experiences Questionnaire (Blatt et al., 1976), the Hopkins Symptom Checklist (Derogatis, Lipman, Rickels, Uhlenhuth, & Covi, 1974), and the Emotions Questionnaire (Higgins, Klein, & Strauman, 1985).

Because the published results of our study did not consider all four possible types of actual/own:guide discrepancies, the data from this study were reanalyzed to compare all four types of discrepancies. To test the hypothesis of self-discrepancy theory, partial correlations between each of the discrepancies and each of the items were calculated, partialing out the contribution to each correlation deriving from their common relation to all the other discrepancies (*all* significant partial correlations are reported):

1. Actual/own versus ideal/own: We predicted this discrepancy would be associated with feelings of disappointment and dissatisfaction in particular and with dejection in general. As predicted, the actual/own:ideal/own discrepancy was uniquely associated ($p < .05$) with subjects' feeling "disappointed," "dissatisfied," *not* feeling "effective," feeling "blameworthy," and "feeling no interest in things."

   The actual/own:ideal/own discrepancy was also uniquely associated ($p < .05$) with the Introjection subscale of the Blatt Depressive Experiences Questionnaire, which consists mostly of items measuring general discrepancy with standards, especially ideal standards (e.g., "I often find that I don't live up to my own standards or ideals") and general dejection (e.g., "There are times when I feel empty inside"). In general, then, the results of this study suggest that the actual/own:ideal/own discrepancy is associated with *dejection from perceived lack of effectiveness or self-fulfillment.*

2. Actual/own versus ideal/other. We predicted this discrepancy would be associated with feeling shame and embarrassment in particular and with dejection in general. As predicted, the actual/own:ideal/other discrepancy was uniquely associated ($p < .05$) with subjects' feeling lack of "pride," lack of feeling "sure of self and goals," "feeling lonely," "feeling blue," and "feeling no interest in things."

The actual/own:ideal/other discrepancy was also uniquely associated ($p < .05$) with the Blatt Introjection subscale as well as with the Blatt Anaclitic subscale, which mostly measures beliefs concerning dependency on others and sensitivity to others' expectations (e.g., "If I fail to live up to expectations, I feel unworthy," "I am very sensitive to others for signs of rejection"). In general, then, the results of this study suggest that the actual/own:ideal/other discrepancy is associated with *dejection from perceived or anticipated loss of social action or esteem.*

3. Actual/own versus ought/other: This discrepancy was predicted to be associated with fear and feeling threatened in particular and with agitation in general. The actual/own:ought/other discrepancy was uniquely associated ($p < .05$) with subjects' suffering "spells of terror or panic," feeling "suddenly scared for no reason," feeling "so concerned with how or what I feel that it's hard to think of much else," and feeling "shame." The association between feeling "shame" or "lack of pride" and possessing a discrepancy from either a significant other's ought standard or a significant other's ideal standard supports the position, discussed earlier, that shame is associated with "other" standpoints on either moral or nonmoral domains (e.g., Ausubel, 1955; Lewis, 1979). In general, the results of this study suggest that the actual/own:ought/other discrepancy is associated with *agitation from fear and threat.*

4. Actual/own versus ought/own: This discrepancy was predicted to be associated with feelings of guilt and self-contempt in particular and with agitation in general. As predicted, the actual/own:ought/own discrepancy was associated with "feelings of worthlessness" and was the only type of discrepancy that was uniquely associated with feelings of "guilt." But the latter correlation was *negative,* partial $r(49) = -.27$, $p < .05$. In a later study (Strauman & Higgins, 1987), we also found that the actual/own:ought/own discrepancy was uniquely but negatively associated with "anxiety over transgressions of rules," partial $r(59) = -.26$, $p < .05$. Although the direction of these results was not expected, the overall pattern is consistent with an analysis of "guilt" provided by Horney (1939) and others (e.g., Cameron, 1963). Horney suggested that the more people's feelings of guilt or self-recrimination for moral transgression are genuine, the more they may refrain from expressing them. Indeed, it has been suggested that "guilty" neurotics tend to deny their feelings of guilt and instead express them as feelings of worthlessness that less directly imply sinfulness.

There was also evidence that the actual/own:ought/own discrepancy was uniquely associated ($p < .05$) with the following emotional symptoms: "feeling irritated all the time," "feeling low in energy or slowed down," "feeling no interest in things," and "feeling everything is an effort." This cluster of emotional symptoms is consistent with the classic description of "guilty" or "anxiety" neurotics as suffering from irritability and fatigue (see Cameron, 1963). In general, then, the results of this study tentatively suggest that the actual/own:ought/own discrepancy is associated with *agitation from self-criticism.* Further research on this discrepancy is clearly needed, however, to test this hypothesis.

We also found evidence of distinct self-discrepancy–discomfort associations in a study by Strauman and Higgins (1987) that extended and refined the Higgins, Klein, and Strauman (1985) study in a number of respects. First, the method for calculating the magnitude of self-discrepancies was improved. In the Selves questionnaire, after respondents listed the attributes for each self-state, they were asked to rate the extent to which the standpoint person (self or other) either believed they actually possessed or ought to possess or wanted them ideally to possess each attribute they listed. The 4-point rating scale ranged from *slightly* (1) to *extremely* (4). These ratings permitted a new distinction to be made—between "true" matches, where synonymous attributes across two self-states also had ratings that varied by no more than 1 scale point, and synonymous "mismatches," where synonymous attributes across two self-states had ratings that varied by 2 or more scale points (e.g., actual/own: "slightly attractive" versus ideal/own: "extremely attractive"). Antonymous attributes across two self-states continued to be coded as mismatches. This new measure of the magnitude of self-discrepancy, then, reserves the "match" classification to cases of true overlap and takes into account the severity of a mismatch.

The second improvement in the study was the collection of the various measures of discomfort and emotional symptoms approximately *2 months after* subjects filled out the Selves questionnaire. The delay both reduced the likelihood that subjects would respond to the discomfort measures by trying to relate them to their answers on the Selves questionnaire and permitted a test of the stability of the self-discrepancy–discomfort associations over a period of time. The final improvement was the development of subscales reflecting distinctive kinds of discomfort that could be used as multi-item measures to replace the item-by-item analyses performed in our 1985 study. We accomplished this refinement by performing a series of factor analyses on subjects' responses to the unambiguously dejection-related and agitation-related items in the Beck Depression Inventory (BDI), the Blatt Depressive Experiences Questionnaire (BDEQ), the Hopkins Symptom Checklist (HSCL), and the Emotions Questionnaire (EQ).

These analyses identified two distinct sets of items (i.e., high within-set intercorrelations and low between-set intercorrelations), which reflected a "disappointment/dissatisfaction" emotional syndrome and a "fear/restlessness" syndrome, as follows:

1. *Disappointment/dissatisfaction*: (a) "disappointed in yourself" (EQ); (b) "I am very satisfied with myself and my accomplishments" (BDEQ, reversed scoring); (c) "I feel I am always making full use of my potential abilities" (BDEQ, reversed scoring); (d) "uncertain over ability to achieve goals" (EQ); and (e) "blam-

ing yourself for failure to achieve goals" (EQ).
2. *Fear/restlessness*: (a) "feeling you are or will be punished" (BDI); (b) "feeling afraid to go out of your house alone" (HSCL); (c) "feeling afraid to travel on buses, subways or trains" (HSCL); (d) "sleep that is restless or disturbed" (HSCL); and (e) "feeling so restless you couldn't sit still" (HSCL).

According to self-discrepancy theory, the actual/own:ideal/own discrepancy should be related to the disappointment/dissatisfaction cluster, whereas the actual/own:ought/other discrepancy should be related to the fear/restlessness cluster. And indeed they were: the actual/own:ideal/own discrepancy was significantly related to the disappointment/dissatisfaction subscale (as measured 2 months later), $r(70) = .38$, $p < .001$, and the actual/own:ought/other discrepancy was significantly related to the fear/restlessness subscale, $r(70) = .42$, $p < .001$. But the critical question is whether these associations are unique. To test this, each of the self-discrepancies was related to each of the kinds of discomfort, with the contribution to the association between each pair of variables from their associations to the alternative variables being statistically removed. The partial correlational analysis revealed, as predicted, that the actual/own:ideal/own discrepancy was uniquely related to the disappointment/dissatisfaction cluster (as measured 2 months later), partial $r(66) = .30$, $p = .01$, but was unrelated to the fear/restlessness cluster, partial $r(66) = -.08$, $p > .35$. The actual/own:ought/other discrepancy was uniquely related to the fear/restlessness cluster, partial $r(66) = .35$, $p < .01$, but was unrelated to the disappointment/dissatisfaction cluster, partial $r(66) = .04$, $p > .50$.

It should be noted that, as predicted by self-discrepancy theory, it was the actual/own discrepancy from the self-guide as defined by both domain *and* standpoint that was critical for predicting each distinctive kind of emotional syndrome. Consistent with the theory's predictions concerning which specific type of self-discrepancy would be associated with which particular kind of discomfort, the disappointment/dissatisfaction cluster was significantly correlated with the actual/own:ideal/own discrepancy but *not* with the actual/own:ideal/other discrepancy ($p > .10$), and the fear/restlessness cluster was significantly correlated with the actual/own:ought/other discrepancy but *not* with the actual/own:ought/own discrepancy ($p > .5$).

This study also tested the theory's prediction that the actual/own:ideal/own discrepancy and the actual/own:ought/other discrepancy are associated with two different kinds of anger—frustration and resentment, respectively. The partial correlational analysis revealed, as expected, that the actual/own:ideal/own discrepancy was uniquely related to "frustration" (as measured 2 months later), partial $r(66) = .36$, $p < .01$, but not with "resentment" ($p > .15$), whereas the actual/own:ought/other discrepancy was uniquely associated with "resentment," partial $r = .39$, $p < .01$, but not with "frustration" ($p > .2$).

## Evidence That Magnitude and Accessibility of Different Types of Self-Discrepancy Determine Kind of Discomfort

Self-discrepancy theory proposes that the greater the magnitude and accessibility of a particular type of self-discrepancy, the more its possessor will experience the kind of discomfort associated with it. That is, the theory proposes that discomfort is influenced by two factors: (a) The magnitude of one's available types of self-discrepancies—the greater the discrepancy, the more intensely its possessor will experience the kind of discomfort associated with it. Thus, everything else being equal, one will experience most intensely the kind of discomfort associated with the greatest self-discrepancy. (b) The accessibility of one's available types of self-discrepancies—the greater the accessibility of a particular type of discrepancy, the more likely its possessor will experience the kind of discomfort associated with it. Thus, everything else being equal, one is most likely to experience the kind of discomfort associated with the most accessible self-discrepancy. These implications of the central hypothesis of the theory were directly tested in a couple of experimental studies (Higgins, Bond, Klein, & Strauman, 1986).

The first study tested whether the kind of discomfort that resulted from focusing on a negative event would vary depending on the type of self-discrepancy that was predominant for an individual (i.e., the type of self-discrepancy with the greatest magnitude). Undergraduates were asked to imagine either a positive event in which performance matches a common standard (e.g., receiving a grade of A in a course) or a negative event in which performance fails to match a common standard (e.g., receiving a grade of D in a course that is

necessary for obtaining an important job). For the "negative event" condition, we expected that subjects with a predominant actual:ideal discrepancy would show an increase in dejection-related emotions, whereas subjects with a predominant actual:ought discrepancy would show an increase in agitation-related emotions. For the "positive event" condition, we expected that the subjects' predominant self-discrepancies would produce less effect on their emotions because the negative psychological situations associated with the discrepancies would not be applicable to positive events (see Higgins & King 1981; see also Mischel, 1984, for a similar argument).

Subjects filled out the Selves questionnaire a few weeks before the experimental session. They were divided into high and low actual:ideal discrepancy groups at the median of their actual/own:ideal/own discrepancy scores, and into high and low actual:ought discrepancy groups at the median of their actual/own:ought/own discrepancy scores. We then used these divisions to create two distinct groups of subjects varying on which type of discrepancy was predominant—a high actual:ideal discrepancy/low actual:ought discrepancy group and a high actual:ought discrepancy/low actual:ideal discrepancy group. When the subjects arrived at the experimental session, they first completed a semantic differential questionnaire that assessed their general mood prior to the experimental manipulation. They also performed a simple writing-speed task. Writing speed scores have been found to decrease following a "sad" mood induction (Natale & Hantas, 1982). Subjects then received either the positive or negative guided-imagery task, modeled after a procedure used by Wright and Mischel (1982). Following the guided-imagery task, subjects were given the writing-speed test for the second time. They then filled out the Multiple Affect Adjective Checklist (MAACL; Zuckerman & Lubin, 1965) to measure their current feelings.

The MAACL was used to create a summary score for dejection-related emotions (e.g., blue, discouraged, low, happy [reversed for scoring], satisfied [reversed for scoring]) and a summary score for agitation-related emotions (e.g., afraid, agitated, desperate, calm [reversed for scoring], quiet [reversed for scoring]). A Type of Self-Discrepancy (predominant actual:ideal discrepancy; predominant actual:ought discrepancy) × Event Focus (positive event; negative event) × Kind of

Discomfort (dejection-related; agitation-related) analysis of variance (ANOVA) was performed on the postmanipulation mood scores, with subjects' premanipulation mood (as measured by the semantic differential) as a covariate. We found a significant three-way interaction. As predicted, there was no difference between predominant actual:ideal discrepancy subjects and predominant actual:ought discrepancy subjects in their dejection-related and agitation-related mood scores when they were exposed to a positive event; but when they were exposed to a negative event, predominant actual:ideal discrepancy subjects felt significantly more dejected than did predominant actual:ought discrepancy subjects, whereas the latter tended to feel more agitated than their counterparts.

We also tested the hypothesis by performing a Type of Self Discrepancy × Event Focus ANOVA on the percentage of increase in subjects' writing speed, again using subjects' premanipulation mood as a covariate. We found a two-way interaction. As predicted, the predominant actual:ideal discrepancy subjects were slower following the negative event focus as compared to the positive event focus, whereas the predominant actual:ought discrepancy subjects were, if anything, faster.

The results of this first study indicated that both the intensity and the quality of emotional change induced by focusing on an event that was likely to be experienced as negative varied as a function of the magnitude and type of self-discrepancy that was predominant for a subject (as measured weeks earlier). Thus we verified the hypothesized relation between the relative magnitude of different types of discrepancies and differences in emotional change.

The purpose of the second study was to demonstrate our second hypothesized relation, between the relative accessibility of different types of self-discrepancies and differences in emotional change. Four to six weeks before the experimental session, undergraduates completed the Selves questionnaire. Two groups of subjects were recruited for the experiment (for further procedural details, see Higgins, Bond, Klein, & Strauman, 1986)—subjects who were relatively high on both actual:ideal discrepancy (i.e., actual/own:ideal/own discrepancy and actual/own:ideal/other discrepancy combined) and actual:ought discrepancy (i.e., actual/own:ought/own discrepancy and actual/own:ought/other discrepancy combined) and subjects who were relatively low on both discrepancies. The ostensible purpose of the study was to obtain the self-reflections of a youth sample for a life-span developmental study. The subjects were told that their mood during the study would be checked because previous research indicated that mood can sometimes influence people's self-reflections. This cover story provided the rationale for obtaining mood measures both before and after the experimental manipulation.

Half of the subjects in each discrepancy group were randomly assigned to an ideal priming condition, and the other half were assigned to an ought priming condition. In the ideal priming condition, the subjects were asked (a) to describe the kind of person that they and their parents would ideally like them to be and the attributes that they and their parents hoped they would have, and (b) to discuss whether there had been any change over the years in these hopes and aims. In the ought priming condition, subjects were asked (a) to describe the kind of person that they and their parents believed they ought to be and the attributes that they and their parents believed it was their duty or obligation to have, and (b) to discuss whether there had been any change over the years in these beliefs. Both before and after this priming manipulation, subjects filled out a mood questionnaire that identified both dejection-related emotions (e.g., sad, disappointed, and enthusiastic [reversed for scoring]) and agitation-related emotions (e.g., tense, nervous, and calm [reversed for scoring]). The subjects were asked to rate the extent to which they *now* were feeling each emotion on a 6-point scale that ranged from *not at all* (0) to *a great deal* (5). The scores for the dejection-related emotions were combined to create a dejection measure, and the scores for the agitation-related emotions were combined to create an agitation measure.

For the subjects who were high in both types of self-discrepancies, we predicted the kind of discomfort associated with the type of self-discrepancy whose accessibility was temporarily increased by the priming manipulation—an increase in dejection-related emotions in the ideal priming condition and an increase in agitation-related emotions in the ought priming condition. In contrast, for the subjects who were low in both types of self-discrepancies, we predicted that the priming manipulation would, if anything, decrease the kind of discomfort associated with the primed discrepancy (i.e., make them feel better by reminding them of goals or obligations they have met)—a slight decrease in dejection-related emotions in the ideal priming condition and a slight decrease in agitation-related emotions in the ought priming condition. To test these predictions, a Level of Self-Discrepancy (high actual:ideal and high actual: ought; low actual:ideal and low actual:ought) × Type of Priming (ideal priming; ought priming) × Kind of Discomfort (dejection-related; agitation-related) ANOVA was performed on subjects' mood change scores (i.e., the postpriming score minus the prepriming score).

As Table 9.1 shows, we found a significant three-way interaction. As predicted, ideal priming increased high-discrepancy subjects' dejection and slightly decreased low-discrepancy subjects' dejection, whereas ought priming increased high-discrepancy subjects' agitation and slightly decreased low-discrepancy subjects' agitation. Thus, this study demonstrates that increasing the accessibility of different types of self-discrepancies increases different kinds of discomfort, but only for subjects whose magnitude of discrepancy is high (i.e., individuals for whom the self-discrepancies are available). And this occurs even for those who possess *both* types of self-discrepancies. The fact that people with both types of self-discrepancies can experience either an increase in dejection or an increase in agitation depending on which type of discrepancy is made temporarily more accessible by the momentary context explains why some people suffer from dejection and agitation at different moments in their lives.

The results of these studies indicate that activating self-discrepancies by having people think about negative events or their own personal guides (i.e., their hopes and goals or duties and obligations) will induce the kind of discomfort that is associated with the activated self-discrepancy. But if a self-discrepancy is a cognitive structure composed of the relation between two self-state representations (e.g., the relations between a person's actual/own attributes and his or her ought/other attributes), then it should be possible to *automatically* activate this structure, and thus induce its associated discomfort, by simply activating a single component of the structure. Moreover, given that the attributes in people's self-guides are inherently positive, activating even a *positive* attribute should induce discomfort if the attribute is a component of a person's self-guide and the person's actual/own value on the attribute is discrepant from his or her self-guide value on that attribute. And if it were possible to activate the self-discrepant structure and induce its associated discomfort with a task that did not even involve self-focused attention (i.e., a non-self-referential task), the notion that self-discrepancies are emotionally significant cognitive structures would be especially compelling. These possibilities were tested in a study by Strauman and Higgins (1987).

New York University undergraduates were asked to participate in a study on "physiological effects of perceiving others" in which they were given phrases of the form, "An *x* person is"_____ (where *x* would be a trait adjective such as "friendly" or "intelligent") and were asked to complete each sentence as quickly as possible. For each sentence, each subject's total verbalization time and skin conductance amplitude were recorded. In addition, subjects reported their mood at the beginning and end of the session. The subjects were either predominantly actual:ideal discrepant or predominantly actual:ought discrepant as measured at least 4 weeks earlier. Each of these groups of subjects was randomly assigned to one of three priming conditions: (a) "nonmatching" priming, where the trait adjectives were attributes in a subject's self-guide but the attributes did not ap-

**TABLE 9.1. Mean Change in Dejection Emotions and Agitation Emotions as a Function of Level of Self-Discrepancies and Type of Priming**

| Level of self-discrepancies | Ideal priming | | Ought priming | |
|---|---|---|---|---|
| | Dejection emotions | Agitation emotions | Dejection emotions | Agitation emotions |
| High actual:ideal and actual:ought discrepancies | 3.2 | −0.8 | 0.9 | 5.1 |
| Low actual:ideal and actual:ought discrepancies | −1.2 | 0.9 | 0.3 | −2.6 |

*Note.* Each of the eight dejection emotions and eight agitation emotions was measured on a 6-point scale from *not at all* to *a great deal*. The more positive the number, the greater the increase in discomfort.

pear in the subject's actual/own self-concept; (b) "mismatching" priming, where the trait adjectives were attributes in a subject's self-guide and the value of these attributes in the subject's actual/own self-concept was discrepant from the value in the self-guide; and (c) "yoked (mismatching)" priming, where the trait adjectives were attributes that did *not* appear in either a subject's self-guide or actual/own self-concept but were the *same* attributes that appeared as the trait adjectives for some other subject in the "mismatching" priming condition. In addition to these trait adjectives that defined the three subject-related priming conditions, all subjects received the same set of "subject-unrelated" trait adjectives, which were attributes that did not appear in any of the subjects' self-guides or actual/own self-concepts.

The basic prediction was that priming mismatching attributes would induce a dejection-related syndrome (i.e., mood, physiology, and behavior) in ideal-discrepant subjects but would induce an agitation-related syndrome in ought-discrepant subjects. The results were consistent with this predic-

tion. The greatest increase in dejection-related emotions (from the beginning to the end of the session) occurred for ideal-discrepant subjects in the "mismatching" priming condition, and the greatest increase in agitation-related emotions occurred for ought-discrepant subjects in the "mismatching" priming conditions ($p < .05$). The same basic pattern of results was also found on the physiological and behavioral measures. As shown in Table 9.2, in the "mismatching" priming condition, ideal-discrepant subjects' mean skin conductance amplitudes and total verbalization time *decreased* (for subject-related attributes as compared with subject-unrelated attributes), whereas ought-discrepant subjects' mean skin conductance amplitudes and total verbalization time *increased* (both $p$s < .05). As predicted, for the subject-related attributes in the mismatching priming condition, the differences between actual:ideal discrepant subjects and actual:ought discrepant subjects in mean skin conductance amplitude and mean total verbalization time were quite striking (both $p$s < .01).

**TABLE 9.2. Mean Standardized Skin Conductance Amplitude and Mean Total Verbalization Time as a Function of Type of Self-Discrepancy and Type of Priming for Subject-Related and Subject-Unrelated Attributes**

| Type of self-discrepancy and type of priming | Subject-unrelated attributes | Subject-related attributes |
|---|---|---|
| Mean standardized skin conductance amplitude[a] | | |
| Actual:ideal discrepancy | | |
| Mismatching | −0.10 | −0.30 |
| Nonmatching | −0.21 | 0.19 |
| Yoked (mismatching) | −0.02 | 0.24 |
| Actual:ought discrepancy | | |
| Mismatching | −0.14 | 0.26 |
| Nonmatching | −0.25 | 0.09 |
| Yoked (mismatching) | −0.09 | 0.14 |
| Mean total verbalization time[b] | | |
| Actual:ideal discrepancy | | |
| Mismatching | 1.59 | 1.31 |
| Nonmatching | 1.89 | 1.97 |
| Yoked (mismatching) | 2.15 | 2.26 |
| Actual:ought discrepancy | | |
| Mismatching | 1.99 | 2.47 |
| Nonmatching | 1.60 | 1.65 |
| Yoked (mismatching) | 1.40 | 1.42 |

[a]All values standardized using the mean and standard deviation skin conductance amplitude from each subject's priming trials (subject-related and unrelated attributes).
[b]The length in seconds of each subject's total verbal response to each attribute phrase.

## Self-Discrepancies and Emotional Problems

The results of these various correlational and experimental studies provide considerable support for the central hypothesis of self-discrepancy theory. Further support is provided by some additional evidence that also raises an important question: Given that people can suffer greatly from discrepancies between their actual self-state and their self-guides, why do they not simply lower or change their self-guides to reduce the discrepancy?

It is socialization factors in the etiology of self-discrepancies, I believe, that provide the answer both to why they do not and to why self-discrepancies can be so painful. Perhaps people possessing actual:ought discrepancies had an early history of parental interactions that involved the presence of negative outcomes—for example, parents who criticized, punished, or rejected them for not being the type of child their parents believed they ought to be; parents who were intrusive or controlling in order to make them become the type of child the parents believed they ought to be; parents who communicated to them their worries about them or their own fear and dread of the world in general. In contrast, people possessing actual:ideal discrepancies may have had an early history of parental interactions that involved the absence of positive outcomes—for example, parents who withdrew from them, abandoned them, or paid little attention to them whenever they were not the type of child the parents wanted or hoped for, parents who did not or could not satisfy the child's needs for love, nurturance, or approval; parents who communicated to them their disappointment in them or their own feelings of hopelessness, sadness, and discouragement about life. People possessing both types of self-discrepancies may have experienced both kinds of negative interactions with their parents.

It is likely that children are motivated to avoid the negative psychological situation associated with their parents' negative interactions with them. To do so, children must learn to anticipate these events and discover how their own responses and attributes increase or decrease the likelihood that these events will occur. This learning process ultimately leads to the acquisition of mental representations of their parents' ideal guides for them (to avoid the absence of positive outcomes) and/or their parents' ought guides for them (to avoid the presence of negative outcomes). It also causes children to acquire beliefs about the negative consequences of failing to meet their parents' guides. It is well known, for example, that depressed people often grow up believing that their parents' care, affection, and approval are dependent on their living up to and pursuing their parents' standards for them (see Arieti & Bemporad, 1978; Beck, 1967; Guidano & Liotti, 1983).

If children believe that it is essential to meet their parents' guides to avoid experiencing a negative psychological situation, then a failure to do so (as reflected in a discrepancy between their current state and the end-state represented by their parents' guides for them) is likely to induce intense emotional discomfort. In order to avoid this intense pain, the child must attempt to meet the parents' guides, which requires in turn that the child monitor his or her progress toward meeting the guide. Such monitoring involves comparing a current performance or attribute to the standard represented by the guide. This means that the current level of the attribute is interpreted in reference to the guide rather than in reference to some factual standard, such as the child's previous level of the attribute (see Higgins, Strauman, & Klein, 1986). Over time, then, the child's actual/own self may be constructed, at least in part, in reference to his or her guides. Thus to the extent that children believe it is essential to meet the guides for them, they are more likely to acquire actual:guide discrepancies, they are more likely to suffer intensely from any discrepancy they do possess, and they are more likely to resist any attempt to modify their guides.

We have argued (Higgins, Klein, & Strauman, 1985) that in order for self-discrepancy theory to be maximally useful as an approach for understanding, and eventually treating, emotional problems, it must be extended to include variables that reflect personal beliefs about the interpersonal consequences of possessing the discrepancy. Therefore, a measure of beliefs in such contingencies was included in Strauman and Higgins's (1987) study described earlier. Part of a general Socialization Questionnaire asked the subjects the following kinds of questions: (a) "Have you ever felt unloved because you didn't live up to your parents *ideals* for you? To what extent?" (b) "Have you ever felt you would be emotionally abandoned if you didn't live up to your parents' ideals for you? To what extent?" (c) "Did you ever believe that your parents would reject you if you didn't live up to their *oughts* for you? To what extent?" Subjects' scores for the three ideal questions were averaged to form an overall ideal outcome contingency score, and their scores for the three ought questions were averaged to form an overall ought-outcome contingency score.

As described earlier, subjects' self-discrepancies were obtained weeks before they answered the questionnaires measuring their emotional problems. Using tertiary splits, we divided the subjects into three levels—high, medium, and low—with regard to both actual:ideal discrepancy (i.e., actual/own:ideal/own discrepancy and actual/own:ideal/other discrepancy combined) and actual:ought discrepancy (i.e., actual/own:ought/own discrepancy and actual/own:ought/other discrepancy combined). Using median splits, we also divided the subjects into two levels of ideal-outcome contingency and two levels of ought-outcome contingency. We then performed a Level of Actual:Ideal Discrepancy × Level of Ideal-Outcome Contingency ANOVA and a Level of Actual:Ought Discrepancy × Level of Ought-Outcome Contingency ANOVA for each of a set of general measures of emotional problems.

Our most important prediction was that the intensity of the subjects' emotional problems would be related to both their level of self-discrepancy and their level of outcome contingency and that the quality of their emotional problems would depend on the type of self-guide involved (i.e., ideal vs. ought). Table 9.3 shows the results. As predicted, an actual:ideal discrepancy combined with an ideal-outcome contingency was strongly associated with depressive (i.e., dejection-related) symptoms but had a relatively weak association with anxiety/paranoid (i.e., agitation-related) symptoms, whereas the reverse was true for an actual:ought discrepancy combined with an ought-outcome contingency. (For other results of this study, see Higgins, Klein, & Strauman, 1987.)

The results in Table 9.3 suggest that there is some relation (although weak) between an actual/own:ideal/own discrepancy and agitation-related symptoms and some relation between an actual/own:ought/other discrepancy and dejection-related symptoms. This apparent weak relation, however, could be due to the intercorrelation between the two types of self-discrepancies. In order to control statistically for this potential factor, analyses of covariance were performed in which level of actual:ought discrepancy was the covariate for the analyses involving the ideal domain, and level of actual:ideal discrepancy was the covariate for the analyses involving the ought domain. These analyses replicated the significant relation between ideal domain and depressive symptoms and the significant relation between ought domain and anxiety/paranoid symptoms, but both the relation between ideal domain and anxiety and the relation between ought domain and depression were no longer significant ($p > .20$).

The ability of self-discrepancy theory to discriminate between people vulnerable to mild depression and those susceptible to anxiety was retested in a subsequent study by Strauman and Higgins (1987). We used a latent variable analysis to evaluate simultaneously the validity of the predicted constructs (see Bentler, 1980). Introductory psychology students first filled out the Selves questionnaire as part of a battery of measures they received at the beginning of the semester. Approximately 1 month later they filled out another battery of measures that comprised both the latent variable for *depression*—the Beck Depression Inven-

---

**TABLE 9.3. Squared Multiple Correlations Between Domain of Self-Discrepancy Plus Outcome Contingency and Type of Emotional Problem**

| Domain of self-discrepancy and outcome contingency | BDI depression | HSCL depression | HSCL anxiety | HSCL paranoid |
|---|---|---|---|---|
| Ideal | .39*** | .27*** | .18* | .11 |
| Ought | .11 | .17* | .22** | .24** |

*Note.* BDI = Beck Depression Inventory; HSCL = Hopkins Symptom Checklist. *N* = 70.
*$p < .05$. **$p < .01$. ***$p < .001$.

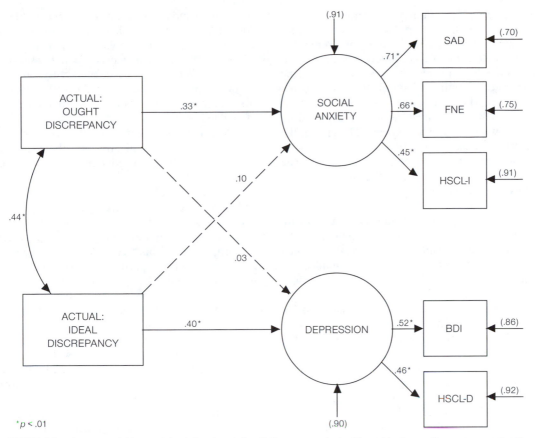

**FIGURE 9.1** ■ Latent-variable model relating type of self-discrepancy (actual/own:ideal:own discrepancy; actual/own:ought/other discrepancy) to kind of emotional problem (depression, social anxiety). (SAD = Social Avoidance and Distress Scale; FNE = Fear of Negative Evaluation Scale; HSCL = Hopkins Symptom Checklist, I = Interpersonal Sensitivity subscale, D = Depression subscale; BDI = Beck Depression Inventory.)

tory (BDI) and the Hopkins Symptom Checklist Depression subscale (HSCL-D)—and the latent variable for *social anxiety*—the Fear of Negative Evaluation Scale (FNE; Watson & Friend, 1969), the Social Avoidance and Distress Scale (SAD; Watson & Friend, 1969), and the Hopkins Symptom Checklist Interpersonal Sensitivity subscale (HSCL-I).

The hypothesized causal structure—the validity of both the depression construct and the social anxiety construct, a relation between actual/own:ideal/own discrepancy and depression that is independent of a relation between actual/own:ought/other discrepancy and social anxiety, and vice versa—was the only model to provide an acceptable fit to the sample data, $\chi^2$ (11, $N$ = 163) = 16.70, $p$ > .15. (For further discussion of the comparison of the hypothesized causal structure

with alternative models, see Strauman & Higgins, 1987.) As Figure 9.1 shows, actual/own:ideal/own discrepancy was uniquely associated with depression but not with anxiety, whereas actual/own:ought/other discrepancy was uniquely associated with social anxiety but not with depression. The results of this study, then, strongly support the predictions of self-discrepancy theory. [. . .]

## General Discussion and Conclusions

Self-discrepancy theory shares a long tradition in psychology of models proposing that incompatible beliefs, and particularly self-beliefs, induce discomfort. Self-discrepancy theory, however, has some distinctive features. First, it systematically relates different types of discrepancies between self-state representations to vulnerability to different kinds of discomfort. Second, not only does it consider whether particular types of discrepancy are available to people as a function of the magnitude of the discrepancies, but it also considers the relative accessibility of individuals' available discrepancies. The various assumptions and implications of self-discrepancy theory are captured by the following general hypothesis: The greater the magnitude and accessibility of a particular type of self-discrepancy possessed by an individual, the more the individual will suffer the kind of discomfort associated with that type of self-discrepancy.

This hypothesis was tested in a series of correlational and experimental studies. Consistent with the hypothesis, when either the magnitude or the accessibility of the subjects' discrepancy between their self-concepts and their ideal self-guides was greater, the subjects suffered more from dejection-related emotions (e.g., disappointment, dissatisfaction, sadness). When either the magnitude or the accessibility of discrepancy between their self-concepts and their ought self-guides was greater, the subjects suffered more from agitation-related emotions (e.g., fear, restlessness, tension).

The present article has presented the basic assumptions of self-discrepancy theory in the context of related theories and described initial empirical support for the theory's major hypothesis. Future research will need to consider a number of other important issues: (a) how the theory could be used to predict *positive* emotions (e.g., we have found that the absence of an actual/own:ideal/own discrepancy is associated with feeling "happy" and "satisfied," whereas the absence of an actual/own: ought/other discrepancy is associated with feeling "calm" and "secure"); (b) the conditions under which self-guides initiate and direct action as well as being used as standards for self-evaluation; (c) the role of people's beliefs concerning the likelihood that they will ever meet their guides in moderating the motivational and emotional consequences of possessing self-discrepancies (e.g., the role of perceived self-efficacy; see Bandura, 1986); and (d) whether different regions of life should be distinguished when measuring discrepancies in order to predict more accurately emotional vulnerabilities in each region (e.g., achievement vs. interpersonal).

Even in its current form, however, self-discrepancy theory has implications for other areas of psychology. For example, self-discrepancy theory has some implications for treating emotional problems. Although it is not possible to review these implications in detail, it is interesting to note that each of the major alternative ways of reducing self-discrepancies is currently associated with some important approach to treatment. According to self-discrepancy theory, emotional problems are associated with accessible discrepancies between people's actual/ own self-concept and one or more of their self-guides. Logically, then, there are three general alternatives for reducing emotional problems induced by self-discrepancies.

First, one could change a client's actual/own self-concept to be less discrepant from the client's self-guides. Behavioral therapeutic approaches accomplish this by modifying clients' persistent performance, and both cognitive and psychodynamic therapeutic approaches accomplish it by modifying clients' interpretations of their performance. Second, one could change the client's self-guides to be less discrepant from the client's actual/own self-concept. Both cognitive and psychodynamic therapeutic approaches accomplish this by lowering either the level or the perceived relevance of a self-guide (e.g., by leading clients to question its fairness, legitimacy, reasonableness, or utility). Third, one could change the accessibility of the discrepancies. Behavioral and environmental intervention approaches accomplish this by reducing clients' exposure to situations and social interactions that are associated with their problems (i.e., that are likely to prime the discrepancy). Cognitive approaches accomplish this by having clients actively rehearse positive thoughts and attitudes, which then function as active sets that inhibit passive accessibility effects (see Higgins & King, 1981). Thus, self-discrepancy theory potentially provides a single, unified framework for understanding the functional consequences of different kinds of therapeutic approaches—what they do and do not accomplish.

This article has focused on the implications of self-concept discrepancy theory for self-evaluations and personal emotional responses. Nevertheless, the theory also has more general implications for motivation, evaluations of others, and interpersonal relations. People's emotional reactions to their performance, for example, can influence their subsequent motivations to achieve (for a review, see Weiner, 1986). Moreover, individual differences in achievement motivation may reflect individual differences in which self-guides are accessible and used at different stages of the process of self-evaluation (Higgins, Strauman, & Klein, 1986). The differences, for instance, between low- and high-resultant achievers described in the literature (e.g., Atkinson, 1964; Kuhl, 1978; Kukla, 1978; Weiner, 1972) could be due to low achievers' having a tendency to interpret their performance as a success or a failure on the basis of whether it is above or below their high ought/other standard, in contrast to high achievers' having a tendency to interpret their performance as a success or a failure on the basis of a more moderate factual comparison standard (e.g., their own past performance or the average performance) and appraising it in relation to their ideal/own standard.

Thus, low achievers would tend to judge their performance as a failure and subsequently feel apprehensive and anxious, whereas high achievers would tend to judge their performance as a success, thereby increasing their self-confidence, but they would also feel dissatisfied because they had not yet fulfilled their personal aspirations. This, in turn, would cause low achievers to avoid subsequent achievement tasks and high achievers to increase their efforts.

Self-discrepancy theory may also have implications for individual differences in evaluating others. There is considerable evidence that people's self-concepts and chronic personal constructs can influence their judgments and memory of others (e.g., Hastorf, Richardson, & Dornbusch, 1958; Higgins, King & Mavin, 1982; Kelly, 1955; Kuiper & Derry, 1981; Markus & Smith, 1981; Shrauger & Patterson, 1974). If individuals' self-guides are also used in evaluating others, then self-discrepancy theory could predict not only whether the judgment is likely to be positive or negative (i.e., depending on how high are the perceiver's self guides), but also what the perceiver's specific emotional response to the target's behavior is likely to be. For example, a target's behavior that was discrepant from a perceiver's ideal standards could cause the perceiver to feel dissatisfied and disappointed with the target or to feel sad for the target, whereas a target's behavior that was discrepant from a perceiver's ought standards could cause the perceiver to feel resentful or critical toward the target or to worry about the target.

Similarity between partners in the guides they use to evaluate themselves and others could promote positive relationships because it would increase the likelihood of the partners' responding similarly to social events, which in turn is associated with balanced relationships (e.g., Heider, 1958; Newcomb, 1961). On the other hand, similarity between partners in their self-discrepancies could increase the likelihood that both partners would be emotionally vulnerable to the same events, which would reduce the ability of each partner to serve as a "safety zone" for the other. Perhaps similarity of social evaluative guides but dissimilarity in regions of vulnerability (e.g., achievement vs. interpersonal) would provide the most balanced relationship.

Finally, people's emotions in relationships may be influenced by the role their partner plays in their self-discrepancy system. In some cases, the partner (e.g., parent, spouse, boss) may be represented directly as the significant other in an actual:ideal/other or actual:ought/other discrepancy. In such cases, self-discrepancy theory would predict that the intensity and kind of emotion a person would be vulnerable to experiencing in the relationship would be a function of the magnitude and type of his or her available self-discrepancy involving the partner as significant other. (See McCann & Higgins, 1988, for evidence supporting this prediction.) In other cases the partner may not be represented directly as a significant other in an available self-discrepancy, but the partner may have characteristics (e.g., physical and personality attributes; opinions and attitudes; interaction style) that are subjectively similar to a significant other whose standpoint on their self is involved in a preestablished "other" discrepancy, and thus exposure to the partner could activate the discrepancy and its associated discomfort. If someone attempts to resolve a prior discrepancy through a relationship with a new person, then we have the makings for a classic neurotic relationship (i.e., "The relationship makes me miserable, but I feel somehow that I'm getting a lot out of it"). Moreover, because the dynamic source of emotional reactions is the preestablished self-discrepancy and not the partner's actual behavior per se, it explains why the person overreacts to the situation.

With the exception of such neurotic relationships, one might predict more generally that people would seek out relationships that decrease the magnitude or accessibility of their self-discrepancies by modifying their self-concept and that they would avoid relationships that modify their self-concept in a way that increases the magnitude or accessibility of their self-discrepancies. Indeed, even in neurotic relationships, such as those described by Horney (1939) in her discussion of narcissism, the relationship may be maintained because it reduces a self-discrepancy or supports an essential nondiscrepancy.

If support for these additional implications of self-discrepancy theory is found in future research, then the theory would have the potential of providing a unified model for addressing central issues that fall on the interface of social, personality, and abnormal psychology.

## REFERENCES

Abelson, R. P. (1959). Modes of resolution of belief dilemmas. *Journal of Conflict Resolution, 3,* 343–352.

Abelson, R. P. (1983). Whatever became of consistency theory? *Personality and Social Psychology Bulletin, 9,* 37–54.

Abelson, R. P., & Rosenberg, M. J. (1958). Symbolic psychologic: A model of attitudinal cognition. *Behavioral Science, 3,* 1–13.

Adler, A. (1964). *Problems of neurosis.* New York: Harper & Row.

Allport, G. W. (1955). *Becoming.* New Haven, CT: Yale University Press.

Anderson, N. H. (1968). Likableness ratings of 555 personality-trait words. *Journal of Personality and Social Psychology, 9,* 272–279.

Arieti, S., & Bemporad, J. (1978). *Severe and mild depression: The psychotherapeutic approach.* New York: Basic Books.

Aronson, E. (1969). The theory of cognitive dissonance: A current perspective. In L. Berkowitz (Ed.), *Advances in experimental social psychology* (Vol. 4, pp. 1–34). New York: Academic Press.

Asch, S. E. (1952). *Social psychology.* Englewood Cliffs, NJ: Prentice-Hall.

Atkinson, J. W. (1964). *An introduction to motivation.* Princeton, NJ: Van Nostrand.

Ausubel, D. P. (1955). Relationships between shame and guilt in the socializing process. *Psychological Review, 62,* 378–390.

Bandura, A. (1986). *Social foundations of thought and action: A social cognition theory.* Englewood Cliffs, NJ: Prentice-Hall.

Bargh, J. A. (1984). Automatic and conscious processing of social information. In R. S. Wyer, Jr., & T. K. Srull (Eds.), *Handbook of social cognition* (Vol. 3, pp. 1–43). Hillsdale, NJ: Erlbaum.

Bargh, J. A., Bond, R. N., Lombardi, W. J., & Tota, M. E. (1986). The additive nature of chronic and temporary sources of construct accessibility. *Journal of Personality and Social Psychology, 50,* 869–878.

Bargh, J. A., & Pietromonaco, P. (1982). Automatic information processing and social perception: The influence of trait information presented outside of conscious awareness on impression formation. *Journal of Personality and Social Psychology, 43,* 437–449.

Bargh, J. A., & Thein, R. D. (1985). Individual construct accessibility, person memory, and the recall-judgment link: The case of information overload. *Journal of Personality and Social Psychology, 49,* 1129–1146.

Beck, A. T. (1967). *Depression: Causes and treatment.* Philadelphia: University of Pennsylvania Press.

Beck, A. T. (1983). Cognitive therapy of depression: New perspectives. In P. J. Clayton & J. E. Barrett (Eds.), *Treatment of depression: Old controversies and new approaches* (pp. 315–350). New York: Raven Press.

Beck, A. T., Ward, C. H., Mendelson, M., Mock, J., & Erbaugh, J. (1961). An inventory for measuring depression. *Archives of General Psychiatry, 4,* 561–571.

Bentler, P. M. (1980). Multivariate analysis with latent variables: Causal modeling. *Annual Review of Psychology, 31,* 419–456.

Bibring, E. (1953). The mechanism of depression. In P. Greenacre (Ed.), *Affective disorders* (pp. 13–48). New York: International Universities Press.

Blatt, S. J., D'Afflitti, J. P., & Quinlan, D. M. (1976). Experiences of depression in normal young adults. *Journal of Abnormal Psychology, 86,* 203–223.

Breckler, S. J., & Greenwald, A. G. (1986). Motivational facets of the self. In R. M. Sorentino & E. T. Higgins (Eds.), *Handbook of motivation and cognition: Foundations of social behavior* (pp. 145–164). New York: Guilford Press.

Buss, A. H. (1980). *Self-consciousness and social anxiety.* San Francisco: Freeman.

Cameron, N. (1963). *Personality development and psychopathology.* Boston: Houghton Mifflin.

Carver, C. S., & Ganellen, R. J. (1983). Depression and components of self-punitiveness: High standards, self-criticism, and overgeneralization. *Journal of Abnormal Psychology, 92,* 330–337.

Carver, C. S., & Scheier, M. E. (1978). Self-focusing effects of dispositional self-consciousness, mirror presence, and audience presence. *Journal of Personality and Social Psychology, 36,* 324–332.

Carver, C. S., & Scheier, M. E. (1981). *Attention and self-regulation: A control-theory approach to human behavior.* New York: Springer-Verlag.

Cattell, R. B. (1973). *Personality and mood by questionnaire.* San Francisco: Jossey-Bass.

Colby, K. M. (1968). A programmable theory of cognition and affect in individual personal belief systems. In R. P. Abelson, E. Aronson, W. J. McGuire, T. M. Newcomb, M. J. Rosenberg, & P. H. Tannenbaum (Eds.), *Theories of cognitive consistency: A source book* (pp. 520–525). Chicago: Rand McNally.

Cooley, C. H. (1964). *Human nature and the social order.* New York: Schocken Books. (Original work published 1902)

Coyne, J. C., & Lazarus, R. S. (1980). Cognitive style, stress perception, and coping. In I. Kutash & L. Schlesinger (Eds.), *Handbook on stress and anxiety: Contemporary knowledge, theory and treatment.* San Francisco: Jossey-Bass.

Dahl, H. (1979). The appetite hypothesis of emotions: A new psychoanalytic model of motivation. In C. E. Izard (Ed.), *Emotions in personality and psychopathology* (pp. 201–225). New York: Plenum Press.

DeRivera, J. (1977). A structural theory of the emotions. *Psychological Issues, 10*(4), Monograph 40.

Derogatis, L. R., Lipman, R. S., Rickels, K., Uhlenhuth, E. H., & Covi, L. (1974). The Hopkins Symptom Checklist

(HSCL): A self-report symptom inventory. *Behavioral Science, 19,* 1–15.

Durkheim, E. (1951). *Suicide: A study in sociology.* New York: Free Press.

Duval, S., & Wicklund, R. A. (1972). *A theory of objective self-awareness.* New York: Academic Press.

Epstein, S. (1980). The self-concept: A review and the proposal of an integrated theory of personality. In E. Staub (Ed.), *Personality: Basic aspects and current research* (pp. 82–132). Englewood Cliffs, NJ: Prentice-Hall.

Erikson, E. H. (1963). *Childhood and society* (2nd ed.). New York: Norton. (Original work published 1950)

Erikson, E. H. (1968). *Identity: Youth and crisis.* New York: Norton.

Ewert, O. (1970). The attitudinal character of emotion. In M. B. Arnold (Ed.), *Feelings and emotions: The Loyola Symposium* (pp. 233–240). New York: Academic Press.

Fenichel, O. (1945). *The psychoanalytic theory of neurosis.* New York: Norton.

Festinger, L. (1942). A theoretical interpretation of shifts in level of aspiration. *Psychological Review. 49,* 235–250.

Festinger, L. (1957). *A theory cognitive dissonance.* Evanston, IL: Row, Peterson.

Freud, S. (1957). Instincts and their vicissitudes. In J. Strachey (Ed. and Trans.), *The standard edition of the complete psychological works of Sigmund Freud* (Vol. 14, pp. 109–140). London: Hogarth Press. (Original work published 1915)

Freud, S. (1959). Mourning and melancholia. In E. Jones (Ed.), *Sigmund Freud Collected Papers* (Vol. 4, pp. 152–170). New York: Basic Books. (Original work published 1917)

Freud, S. (1961). The ego and the id. In J. Strachey (Ed. and Trans.), *The standard edition of the complete psychological works of Sigmund Freud* (Vol. 19, pp. 3–66). London: Hogarth Press. (Original work published 1923)

Gotlib, I. H., & McCann, C. D. (1984). Construct accessibility and depression: An examination of cognitive and affective factors. *Journal of Personality and Social Psychology, 47,* 427–439.

Greenwald, A. G., & Pratkanis, A. R. (1984). The self. In R. S. Wyer & T. K. Srull (Eds.), *Handbook of social cognition* (Vol. 3, pp. 129–178). Hillsdale, NJ: Erlbaum.

Guidano, V. E., & Liotti, G. (1983). *Cognitive processes and emotional disorders.* New York: Guilford Press.

Hastorf, A. H., Richardson, S. A., & Dornbusch, S. M. (1958). The problem of relevance in the study of person perception and interpersonal behavior. In R. Tagiuri & L. Petrullo (Eds.), *Person perception and interpersonal behavior* (pp. 54–62). Stanford, CA: Stanford University Press.

Heider, F. (1958). *The psychology of interpersonal relations.* New York: Wiley.

Higgins, E. T., & Bargh, J. A. (1987). Social cognition and social perception. *Annual Review of Psychology, 38,* 369–425.

Higgins, E. T., Bargh, J. A., & Lombardi, W. (1985). The nature of priming effects on categorization. *Journal of Experimental Psychology: Learning, Memory and Cognition, 11,* 59–69.

Higgins, E. T., Bond, R. N., Klein, R., & Strauman, T. (1986). Self-discrepancies and emotional vulnerability: How magnitude, accessibility, and type of discrepancy influence affect. *Journal of Personality and Social Psychology, 51,* 5–15.

Higgins, E. T., & King, G. (1981). Accessibility of social constructs: Information processing consequences of individual and contextual variability. In N. Cantor & J. Kihlstrom (Eds.), *Personality, cognition, and social interaction* (pp. 69–121). Hillsdale, NJ: Erlbaum.

Higgins, E. T., King G. A., & Mavin, G. H. (1982). Individual construct accessibility and subjective impressions and recall. *Journal of Personality and Social Psychology, 43,* 35–47.

Higgins, E. T., Klein, R., & Strauman, T. (1985). Self-concept discrepancy theory: A psychological model for distinguishing among different aspects of depression and anxiety. *Social Cognition, 3,* 51–76.

Higgins, E. T., Klein, R., & Strauman, T. (1987). Self-discrepancies: Distinguishing among self-states, self-state conflicts, and emotional vulnerabilities. In K. M. Yardley & T. M. Honess (Eds.), *Self and identity: Psychosocial perspectives* (pp. 173-186). New York: Wiley.

Higgins, E. T., Rholes, W. S., & Jones, C. R. (1977). Category accessibility and impression formation. *Journal of Experimental Social Psychology, 13,* 141–154.

Higgins, E. T., Strauman, T., & Klein, R. (1986). Standards and the process of self-evaluation: Multiple affects from multiple stages. In R. M. Sorrentino & E. T. Higgins (Eds.), *Handbook of motivation and cognition: Foundations of social behavior* (pp. 23–63). New York: Guilford Press.

Hoffman, M. L. (1971). Identification and conscience development. *Child Development, 42,* 1071–1082.

Hoffman, M. L. (1975). Sex differences in moral internalization. *Journal of Personality and Social Psychology, 32,* 720–729.

Holt, R. R. (1976). Drive or wish? A reconsideration of the psychoanalytic theory of motivation. In M. M. Gill & P. S. Holzman (Eds.), Psychology versus metapsychology: Psychoanalytic essays in memory of George S. Klein [Special issue]. *Psychological Issues, 9,* 158–197.

Horney, K. (1939). *New ways in psychoanalysis.* New York: Norton.

Horney, K. (1946). *Our inner conflicts: A constructive theory of neurosis.* London: Routledge & Kegan Paul.

Horney, K. (1950). *Neurosis and human growth.* New York: Norton.

Jacobs. D. (1971). Moods-emotion-affect: The nature of and manipulation of affective states with particular reference to positive affective states and emotional illness. In A. Jacobs & L. B. Sachs (Eds.), *The psychology of private events* (pp. 118–142). New York: Academic Press.

Jacobson, E. (1946). The effect of disappointment on ego and superego formation in normal and depressive development. *Psychoanalytic Review, 33,* 129–147.

James, W. (1948). *Psychology.* New York: World. (Original work published 1890)

Kelley, H. H. (1952). Two functions of reference groups. In G. E. Swanson, T. M. Newcomb, & E. L. Hartley (Eds.), *Readings in social psychology* (2nd ed., pp. 410–414). New York: Holt, Rinehart & Winston.

Kelly, G. A. (1955). *The psychology of personal constructs.* New York: Norton.

Kemper, T. D. (1978). *A social interactional theory of emotions.* New York: Wiley.

Klein, G. S. (1970). *Perception, motives and personality.* New York: Knopf.

Klein, R., & Higgins, E. T. (1984). *Standpoint relevance as a determinant of the magnitude of discomfort from discrep-*

*ant self-concepts.* Unpublished manuscript, New York University.

Kuhl, J. (1978). Standard setting and risk preference: An elaboration of the theory of achievement motivation and an empirical test. *Psychological Review, 85,* 239–248.

Kuiper, N. A., & Derry, P. A. (1981). The self as a cognitive prototype: An application to person perception and depression. In N. Cantor & J. F. Kihlstrom (Eds.), *Personality cognition and social interaction* (pp. 215–232). Hillsdale, NJ: Erlbaum.

Kukla, A. (1978). An attributional theory of choice. In L. Berkowitz (Ed.), *Advances in experimental social psychology* (Vol. 11, pp. 113–144). New York: Academic Press.

Lazarus, A. A. (1968). Learning theory and the treatment of depression. *Behavior Research and Therapy, 6,* 83–89.

Lecky, P. (1961). *Self-consistency: A theory of personality.* New York: Shoe String Press.

Lewin, K. (1935). *A dynamic theory of personality.* New York: McGraw-Hill.

Lewin, K. (1951). *Field theory in social science.* New York: Harper.

Lewis, H. B. (1979). Shame in depression and hysteria. In C. E. Izard (Ed.), *Emotions in personality and psychopathology* (pp. 371–396). New York: Plenum Press.

Markus, H. (1977). Self-schemata and processing information about the self. *Journal of Personality and Social Psychology, 35,* 63–78.

Markus, H., & Nurius, P. (1987). Possible selves. In K. M. Yardley & T. M. Honess (Eds.), *Self and identity: Psychosocial perspectives* (pp. 157–172). New York: Wiley.

Markus, H., & Smith, J. (1981). The influence of self-schema on the perception of others. In N. Cantor & J. F. Kihlstrom (Eds.), *Personality, cognition and social interaction* (pp. 233–262). Hillsdale, NJ: Erlbaum.

McCann, C. D., & Higgins, E. T. (1988). Motivation and affect in interpersonal relations: The role of personal orientations and discrepancies. In L. Donohew, H. E. Sypher, & E. T. Higgins (Eds.), *Communication, social cognition, and affect* (pp. 53–79). Beverly Hills, CA: Sage.

McClelland, D. C. (1961). *The achieving society.* Princeton, NJ: Van Nostrand.

McGuire, W. J. (1968). Theory of the structure of human thought. In R. P. Abelson, E. Aronson, W. J. McGuire, T. M. Newcomb, M. J. Rosenberg, & P. H. Tannenbaum (Eds.), *Theories of cognitive consistency: A source book* (pp. 140–162). Chicago: Rand McNally.

Mead, G. H. (1934). *Mind, self, and society.* Chicago: University of Chicago Press.

Mendels, J. (1970). *Concepts of depression.* New York: Wiley.

Merton, R. K. (1957). *Social theory and social structure.* Glencoe, IL: Free Press.

Miller, G. A., Galanter, E., & Pribram, K. H. (1960). *Plans and the structure of behavior.* New York: Holt, Rinehart, & Winston.

Mischel, W. (1984). Convergences and challenges in the search for consistency. *American Psychologist, 39,* 351–364.

Mowrer, O. H. (1960). *Learning theory and behavior.* New York: Wiley.

Murray, H. A. (1938). *Exploration in personality.* New York: Oxford University Press.

Natale, M., & Hantas, M. (1982). Effect of temporary mood states on selective memory about the self. *Journal of Personality and Social Psychology, 42,* 927–934.

Newcomb, T. M. (1961). *The acquaintance process.* New York: Holt, Rinehart, & Winston.

Newcomb, T. M. (1968). Interpersonal balance. In R. P. Abelson, E. Aronson, W. J. McGuire, T. M. Newcomb, M. J. Rosenberg, & P. H. Tannenbaum (Eds.), *Theories of cognitive consistency: A sourcebook* (pp. 28–51). Chicago: Rand McNally.

Osgood, C. E., & Tannenbaum, P. H. (1955). The principle of congruity in the prediction of attitude change. *Psychological Review, 62,* 42–55.

Piers, G., & Singer, M. B. (1971). *Shame and guilt.* New York: Norton.

Plutchik, R. (1962). *The emotions: Facts, theories, and a new model.* New York: Random House.

Rado, S. (1956). The problem of melancholia. In S. Rado, *Collected papers* (Vol. 1, pp. 220–246). New York: Grune & Stratton. (Original work published 1927)

Rogers, C. R. (1961). *On becoming a person.* Boston: Houghton Mifflin.

Roseman, I. J. (1984). Cognitive determinants of emotion: A structural theory. *Review of Personality and Social Psychology, 5,* 11–36.

Rosenberg, M. (1979). *Conceiving the self.* New York: Basic Books.

Rotter, J. B. (1942). Level of aspiration as a method of studying personality: 1. A critical review of methodology. *Psychological Review, 49,* 463–474.

Russell, J. A. (1980). A circumplex model of affect. *Journal of Personality and Social Psychology, 39,* 1161–1178.

Sandler, J., & Joffe, W. G. (1965). Notes on childhood depression. *International Journal of Psychoanalysis, 46,* 88–96.

Sarbin, T. R., Taft, R., & Bailey, D. E. (1960). *Clinical inference and cognitive theory.* New York: Holt, Rinehart, & Winston.

Schafer, R. (1967). Ideals; the ego ideal, and the ideal self. In R. R. Holt (Ed.), Motives and thought: Psychoanalytic essays in honor of David Rapaport [Special issue]. *Psychological Issues, 5*(2–3), 131–174.

Scheier, M. F., & Carver, C. S. (1982). Cognition, affect, and self-regulation. In M. S. Clark & S. T. Fiske (Eds.), *Affect and cognition: The seventeenth annual Carnegie Symposium on cognition* (pp. 157–183). Hillsdale, NJ: Erlbaum.

Scheier, M. F., & Carver, C. S. (1983). Two sides of the self: One for you and one for me. In J. Suls & A. G. Greenwald (Eds.), *Psychological perspectives on the self* (pp. 123–157). Hillsdale, NJ: Erlbaum.

Schlenker, B. R. (1985). Identity and self-identification. In B. R. Schlenker (Ed.), *The self and social life* (pp. 65–100). New York: McGraw-Hill.

Shrauger, J. S., & Patterson, M. B. (1974). Self-evaluation and the selection of dimensions for evaluating others. *Journal of Personality, 42,* 569–585.

Snyder, M. (1979). Self-monitoring processes. In L. Berkowitz (Ed.), *Advances in experimental social psychology* (Vol. 12). New York: Academic Press.

Srull, T. K., & Wyer, R. S., Jr. (1979). The role of category accessibility in the interpretation of information about persons: Some determinants and implications. *Journal of Personality and Social Psychology, 37,* 1660–1672.

Srull, T. K., & Wyer, R. S., Jr. (1980). Category accessibility and social perception: Some implications for the study of person memory and interpersonal judgments. *Journal of Personality and Social Psychology, 38,* 841–856.

Stein, N. L., & Jewett, J. L. (1982). A conceptual analysis of the meaning of negative emotions: Implications for a theory of development. In C. E. Izard (Ed.), *Measuring emotions in infants and children* (pp. 401–443). New York: Cambridge University Press.

Strauman, T. J., & Higgins, E. T. (1987). Automatic activation of self-discrepancies and emotional syndromes: When cognitive structures influence affect. *Journal of Personality and Social Psychology, 53,* 1004–1014.

Strauman, T. J., & Higgins, E. T. (1987). *Vulnerability to specific kinds of chronic emotional problems as a function of self-discrepancies.* Unpublished manuscript, New York University.

Sullivan, H. S. (1953). *The collected works of Harry Stack Sullivan* (Vol. 1, H. S. Perry & M. L. Gawel, Eds.). New York: Norton.

Tagiuri, R. (1969). Person perception. In G. Lindzey & E. Aronson (Eds.), *The handbook of social psychology* (2nd ed., Vol. 3, pp. 395–449). Reading, MA: Addison-Wesley.

Tompkins, S. S. (1984). Affect theory. In K. R. Scherer & P. Ekman (Eds.), *Approaches to emotion* (pp. 163–195). Hillsdale, NJ: Erlbaum.

Tulving, E., & Pearlstone, Z. (1966). Availability versus accessibility of information in memory for words. *Journal of Verbal Learning and Verbal Behavior, 5,* 381–391.

Turner, R. H. (1956). Role-taking, role standpoint, and reference-group behavior. *American Journal of Sociology, 61,* 316–328.

Watson, D., & Friend, R. (1969). Measurement of social-evaluative anxiety. *Journal of Consulting and Clinical Psychology, 33,* 448–457.

Weiner, B. (1972). *Theories of motivation: From mechanism to cognition.* Chicago: Rand McNally.

Weiner, B. (1986). Cognition, emotion, and action. In R. M. Sorrentino & E. T. Higgins (Eds.), *Handbook of motivation and cognition: Foundations of social behavior* (pp. 281–312). New York: Guilford Press.

Weiner, B., Russell, D., & Lerman, D. (1979). The cognition-emotion process in achievement-related contexts. *Journal of Personality and Social Psychology, 37,* 1211–1220.

White, R. W. (1964). *The abnormal personality* (3rd ed.). New York: Ronald Press.

Wicklund, R. A., & Gollwitzer, P. M. (1982). *Symbolic self-completion.* Hillsdale, NJ: Erlbaum.

Wiener, N. (1948). *Cybernetics: Control and communication in the animal and the machine.* Cambridge, MA: M.I.T. Press.

Wierzbicka, A. (1972). *Semantic primitives.* Frankfurt, West Germany: Athenaum.

Wright, J., & Mischel, W. (1982). Influence of affect on cognitive social learning person variables. *Journal of Personality and Social Psychology, 43,* 901–914.

Wyer, R. S., & Srull, T. K. (1981). Category accessibility: Some theoretical and empirical issues concerning the processing of social stimulus information. In E. T. Higgins, C. P. Herman, & M. P. Zanna (Eds.), *Social cognition: The Ontario Symposium.* Hillsdale, NJ: Erlbaum.

Wylie, R. C. (1979). *The self-concept* (rev. ed.). Lincoln: University of Nebraska Press.

Zuckerman, M., & Lubin, B. (1965). *Manual for the Multiple Affect Adjective Check List.* San Diego, CA: Educational and Industrial Testing Service.

# Self-Presentation

Everyone knows that people change their behavior when others are watching, such as to make a good impression. The term self-presentation was introduced by Goffman (1959) as part of a broader depiction of human social life as theatre: People play roles, follow scripts, tailor their performances to the audience, and change their behavior "backstage" (i.e., when the audience is absent).

Experimental psychologists began to adapt Goffman's ideas to the laboratory in the ensuing decades. A controversial, attention-getting work charged that cognitive dissonance was really a matter of self-presentation: Tedeschi, Schlenker, and Bonoma (1971) contended that people did not really change their attitudes in dissonance experiments but simply tried to appear consistent so as to make a good impression on the experimenter. Because dissonance phenomena had been the bread and butter for many social psychologists, the interest in self-presentation rose sharply in response to the critique, although many researchers regarded self-presentation as the enemy. Later work gradually concluded that dissonance effects are in fact real attitude change, although self-presentation plays an important role (e.g., Baumeister & Tice, 1984; Schlenker, 1982).

The controversy over dissonance helped lend self-presentation a distinctive laboratory method, which involved comparing public versus private versions of the same procedure in order to see whether people acted differently when they knew others were watching. An influential early study by Schlenker (1975) showed that many consistency effects depend on self-presentation. Specifically, he gave people bogus feedback about their alleged ability on a new trait and measured whether they described themselves to others consistently with their feedback. The crucial

177

moderator was whether the feedback information was likely to become public. If people believed no one would find out their true level of ability, they tended to exaggerate their ability and describe themselves to others in favorable terms, but if their performance was likely to become public, they stayed consistent with the feedback.

Many researchers began using public-vs.-private methods, and soon a broad spectrum of phenomena had been shown to be influenced by self-presentation. A literature review by Baumeister (1982) summarized work showing that attitude change, helping, receiving help, reactance, aggression, attributions, conformity, and several other categories of behavior changed between public and private behaviors and were therefore influenced by self-presentational motives. It was necessary however to expand self-presentational theory beyond the simple motivation to make a good impression. Two classes of motives were proposed: One involves doing what the audience likes and prefers, and the other involves constructing one's identity by publicly claiming desired attributes. Wicklund and Gollwitzer (1982) emphasized the latter, even showing that people will do things that the audience will dislike or reject when doing so will help the person claim a desired identity. For example, if you feel strongly about certain political or religious ideas, you may assert them dramatically even to people who you know will disagree.

Up to about 1985, self-presentation research remained focused on the question of whether any particular phenomenon resulted from public, interpersonal motives or intrapsychic processes. Thus, for example, researchers debated whether research findings on cognitive dissonance and reactance represented true inner changes or simply an effort to make a particular impression. Gradually, however, the field came to recognize that self-presentation involved inner processes too. An influential

paper by Tetlock and Manstead (1985) proposed that the field should begin integrating self-presentational and intrapsychic theories rather than simply pitting them against each other.

This section offers a pair of recent works offering creative new directions for self-presentation research. The first, by Leary, Tchvidjian, and Kraxberger (1994), reviews literature on the dangers to health caused by people's pursuit of self-presentational goals. Clearly, people are willing to take risks to their well-being and even slight risks to their lives in order to make favorable impressions on others.

One important implication of Leary et al.'s work has to do with the question of basic motives. Earlier in this volume, we covered Greenberg et al.'s (1986) terror management theory contending that the fear of death is the root of concern with self-esteem and many other factors. Indeed, a more recent work by the same authors (Pyszczynski et al., 1997) proposes that fear of death and the resulting desire for self-preservation is the "master motive" from which all other motives can be derived. I have argued that that position overstates the case severely and that people are more fundamentally concerned with a need to belong (as well as perhaps several other goals) than with avoiding death (e.g., Baumeister & Leary, 1995; Baumeister & Tice, 1990). The health psychology paper by Leary et al. establishes that people will often give priority to making a good impression over avoiding harm and the risk of death, which suggests that they are willing to sacrifice the self-preservation motive for the sake of interpersonal connection. Self-preservation cannot therefore be taken as the master motive, in my view.

The second paper in this section presents a series of experiments on just how interpersonal behavior affects the inner self. The question of how self-concepts change has posed long-standing difficulties for social psychologists, partly because it seems unethical to cause long-term change in the self as part of a laboratory experiment, and partly because it is difficult to show actual change in laboratory work. Still, several interesting contributions were made. Jones, Rhodewalt, Berglas, and Skelton (1981) showed that people sometimes internalize their self-presentations: That is, acting a certain way can sometimes cause the person to perceive himself or herself as being that way. Based on studies by Fazio, Effrein, and Falender (1981), these authors proposed a *biased scanning* theory. People scan their memories for information about themselves that is relevant to the immediate situation, and the resulting mass of information may furnish a biased view of the self that can, in time, shape how the person thinks of himself or herself. Fazio et al. (1981) asked people loaded questions that induced them to think about themselves as either extraverts or introverts, and they found that later people's self-ratings and even their interpersonal behavior had shifted toward believing these randomly induced views of self.

Tice's (1992) paper addresses a contradiction in that literature about self-concept change: Although the theories such as the biased scanning hypothesis emphasized intrapsychic processes, the procedures for the experiments were largely interpersonal. Her findings show that people internalize public but not private behavior. Hence, just as Wicklund and Gollwitzer (1982) emphasized the need for social validation of one's identity claims, Tice's findings show that a given behavior only has an impact on the self-concept if it is witnessed by other people.

Although Tice interprets her findings as potentially consistent with a revised version of biased scanning behavior, converging evidence from another source has mounted a more serious challenge to biased scanning. Schlenker, Dlugolecki, and Doherty (1994) induced biased scanning without self-presentation and found no evidence of self-concept change. Meanwhile, they had people present themselves one way (e.g., extraverted) and then engage in biased scanning for the opposite trait (e.g., introversion), to pit self-presentation against biased scanning, and they found no support for biased scanning. Although some researchers continue to believe that biased scanning is important, the current state of knowledge appears to be that interpersonal recognition and self-presentation are the decisive keys to self-concept change.

## REFERENCES

Baumeister, R. F. (1982). A self-presentational view of social phenomena. *Psychological Bulletin, 91,* 3–26.

Baumeister, R. F., & Leary, M.R. (1995). The need to belong: Desire for interpersonal attachments as a fundamental human motivation. *Psychological Bulletin, 117,* 497–529.

Baumeister, R. F., & Tice, D. M. (1990). Anxiety and social exclusion. *Journal of Social and Clinical Psychology, 9,* 165–195.

Baumeister, R. F., & Tice, D. M. (1984). Role of self-presentation and choice in cognitive dissonance under forced compliance: Necessary or sufficient causes? *Journal of Personality and Social Psychology, 46,* 5–13.

Fazio, R. H., Effrein, E. A., & Falender, V. J. (1981). Self-perceptions following social interactions. *Journal of Personality and Social Psychology, 41,* 232–242.

Goffman, E. (1959). *The presentation of self in everyday life.* New York: Anchor Books.

Greenberg, J., Pyszczynski, T., & Solomon, S. (1986). The causes and consequences of self-esteem: A terror management theory. In R. Baumeister (Ed.), *Public self and private self* (pp. 189–212). New York: Springer-Verlag.

Jones, E. E., Rhodewalt, F., Berglas, S. C., & Skelton, A. (1981). Effects of strategic self-presentation on subsequent self-esteem. *Journal of Personality and Social Psychology, 41,* 407–421.

Leary, M. R., Tchividjian, L. R., & Kraxberger, B. E. (1994). Self-presentation can be hazardous to your health: Impression management and health risk. *Health Psychology, 13,* 461–470.

Pyszczynski, T., Greenberg, J., & Solomon, S. (1997). Why do we need what we need? A terror management perspective on the roots of human social motivation. *Psychological Inquiry, 8,* 1–20.

Schlenker, B. R. (1975). Self-presentation: Managing the

impression of consistency when reality interferes with self-enhancement. *Journal of Personality and Social Psychology, 32,* 1030–1037.

Schlenker, B. R. (1982). Translating actions into attitudes: An identity-analytic approach to the explanation of social conduct. In L. Berkowitz (Ed.), *Advances in experimental social psychology* (Vol. 15, pp. 193–246). San Diego, CA: Academic Press.

Schlenker, B. R., Dlugolecki, D. W., & Doherty, K. (1994). The impact of self-presentations on self-appraisals and behavior: The roles of commitment and biased scanning. *Personality and Social Psychology Bulletin, 20,* 20–33.

Tedeschi, J. T., Schlenker, B. R., & Bonoma, T. V. (1971). Cognitive dissonance: Private ratiocination or public spectacle? *American Psychologist, 26,* 685–695.

Tetlock, P. E., & Manstead, A. S. (1985) Impression management versus intrapsychic explanations in social psychology: A useful dichotomy? *Psychological Review, 92,* 59–77.

Tice, D. M. (1992). Self-presentation and self-concept change: The looking glass self as magnifying glass. *Journal of Personality and Social Psychology, 63,* 435–451.

Wicklund, R. A., & Gollwitzer, P. M. (1982). *Symbolic self-completion.* Hillsdale, NJ: Erlbaum.

# Discussion Questions

1. How much do people really act differently in public than in private situations?
2. Is self-presentation necessarily or inherently deceptive? Is it always an obstacle when perceiving the true or inner self?
3. Is it fair to conclude that Leary et al.'s review of health risks shows people to be self-destructive?
4. Describe the last time you changed in an important, meaningful way. Were other people part of the process?
5. Research finds that people are most likely to change in personal ways at times when they graduate from high school or college or switch to a new job. How might Tice's findings explain this pattern?

# Suggested Readings

Schlenker, B. R. (1975). Self-presentation: Managing the impression of consistency when reality interferes with self-enhancement. *Journal of Personality and Social Psychology, 32,* 1030–1037. This influential experiment helped stimulate the great mass of research on self-presentation over the subsequent decade.

Goffman, E. (1959). *The presentation of self in everyday life.* New York: Anchor Books. A sociologist given to quietly observing people going about their lives, Goffman created a sensation by invoking a dramaturgical model: People are like actors who perform for others but act quite differently "backstage" when the public cannot see them.

Baumeister, R. F. (1982). A self-presentational view of social phenomena. *Psychological Bulletin, 91,* 3–26. A review of published research studies showing how many different patterns of behavior are affected by self-presentational motives.

Tetlock, P. E., & Manstead, A. S. (1985) Impression management versus intrapsychic explanations in social psychology: A useful dichotomy? *Psychological Review, 92,* 59–77. This work challenged the tradition of pitting self-presentation explanations against other theories that invoked inner processes to explain behavior. It helped lead to a reconciliation between these two approaches, including an appreciation of how inner processes accompany self-presentations.

Schlenker, B. R., Dlugolecki, D. W., & Doherty, K. (1994). The impact of self-presentations on self-appraisals and behavior: The roles of commitment and biased scanning.
*Personality and Social Psychology Bulletin, 20,* 20–33. This paper converges with Tice's
to emphasize the role of self-presentation in changing the self-concept. Schlenker and
his colleagues go farther than Tice, however, in questioning whether "biased scanning"
plays any part in the process.

Leary, M. R. (1995). *Self-presentation: Impression management and interpersonal behavior.* Madison, WI: Brown & Benchmark. This is a recent and entertaining summary of
the field of self-presentation, written especially for students. By comparing it with
Goffman's (1959) book, one can appreciate how much the field has progressed in the
intervening decades.

# Self-Presentation Can Be Hazardous to Your Health: Impression Management and Health Risk

Mark R. Leary, Lydia R. Tchividjian, and Brook E. Kraxberger

• Department of Psychology, Wake Forest University

People's concerns with how others perceive and evaluate them can lead to behaviors that increase the risk of illness and injury. This article reviews evidence that self-presentational motives play a role in several health problems, including HIV infection; skin cancer; malnutrition and eating disorders; alcohol, tobacco, and drug use; injuries and accidental death; failure to exercise; and acne. The implications of a self-presentational perspective for research in health psychology, the promotion of healthful behaviors, and health care delivery are discussed.

The first step in promoting healthy behavior is to understand why people do not take adequate care of their health. Most research on this question has focused on people's health-relevant cognitions, such as their estimates of the likelihood that they will experience a certain medical problem, their perceptions of the severity of the problem, and their expectations regarding whether behavioral change will improve their health (e.g., DiClemente, 1986; Janz & Becker, 1984; Rosenstock, 1974).

In contrast, relatively little attention has been devoted to interpersonal motives that affect health-related behaviors. Such processes are sometimes included in cognitively oriented models of health behavior as factors related to health values, outcomes, or barriers, but their role in health has rarely been studied in its own right. The focus of this article is on the role of self-presentational motives in health-relevant behaviors. The premise is that several patterns of behavior that increase the risk of illness and injury arise from people's concerns with how they are regarded by others.

## Self-Presentation: An Overview

Self-presentation (also called *impression management*) refers to the processes by which people control how they are perceived and evaluated by others (Goffman, 1959; Leary, 1994; Leary & Kowalski, 1990; Schlenker, 1980). Because many of people's material, social, and personal outcomes in life depend in part on how others regard them, people are understandably concerned that others perceive them in desired ways. The impressions others form have implications for their friendships and social lives, job success, romantic involvements, and casual interactions, as well as for their self-evaluations and mood (Baumeister, 1982; Schlenker, 1980).

Although the notion of self-presentation sometimes evokes images of Machiavellian deceit, most self-presentational behaviors are not deceptive. Rather, people tactically control the inferences that others draw about them by selectively presenting sides of themselves that will result in the outcomes they desire while concealing information that is inconsistent with the impressions they want others to form (Schlenker & Weigold, 1992). Of course, people sometimes do lie about themselves, presenting images that they know are not accurate, but self-presentational dissimulation is the exception rather than the rule (Leary, 1993). Not only do most people view self-presentational deceit as wrong, but fabrication carries interpersonal risks (Baumeister & Jones, 1978; Goffman, 1959; Schlenker, 1980).

Although the impressions people try to make are often positive and socially desirable, self-presentation is motivated by more than pure approval seeking. People sometimes present undesirable images of themselves and sacrifice others' good will when they think negative self-presentations will help them achieve important social goals (E. E. Jones & Pittman, 1982).

Regardless of how hard people try to enhance and protect their public images, self-presentational failures inevitably befall them. Projecting undesired impressions results in aversive feelings that people typically call *embarrassment* and in behavioral efforts to repair the damage to one's social image (R. S. Miller, 1986; R. S. Miller & Leary, 1992). Because embarrassment is distressing, people try to avoid self-presentational failures; some health-relevant behaviors discussed below involve attempts to avoid embarrassment.

Self-presentation is essential for smooth interpersonal relations and for the accomplishment of people's social goals (Goffman, 1959; Schlenker, 1980). People would have much difficulty negotiating social encounters if others did not purposefully convey information regarding their personal characteristics, attitudes, preferences, emotional states, and intentions. Likewise, people would find it difficult to pursue their social goals without regulating the amount and type of information others have about them. Unfortunately, the motive to convey certain social images can lead to behaviors that are deleterious for the individual, if not for others as well. Self-presentational motives are often so strong that they lead people to engage in impression-creating behaviors that are, in the long term, dangerous to themselves or to others.

The focus in this article is on ways in which self-presentational processes affect health-related behaviors. People's concerns with their social images can increase health risks as diverse as cancer, HIV infection, and substance abuse. It must be emphasized that this does not suggest that the health-related behaviors described in this article arise solely from people's concerns with others' impressions. Yet research evidence suggests that self-presentational motives play an important role in these behaviors and that the self-presentational perspective has implications for understanding, preventing, and treating a diverse array of health problems.

## Condom Use and the Risk of AIDS

Although health professionals have long advocated using condoms to prevent pregnancy and sexually transmitted diseases (STDs), the impetus for condom use increased markedly with the spread of AIDS during the past 10 years. Recent data suggest, however, that many people continue to take inadequate precautions against pregnancy and STDs. Approximately 1 million teenage girls in the United States become pregnant each year (Fielding & Williams, 1991), and over 12 million Americans contract some form of STD ("Sexually Transmitted Diseases Up", 1993). Less than 20% of the sexually active college students surveyed in one American study reported using condoms regularly ("Safer Sex", 1991; see also Hanna, 1989).

Although younger teens might not fully understand the implications of sexual behavior for pregnancy and health, for most people the failure to use condoms is not due to lack of information about pregnancy, STDs, or condoms (M. A. Bruch & Hynes, 1987; Markova, Wilkie, Naji, & Forbes, 1990; "Safer Sex", 1991). Rather, one primary reason people fail to use condoms seems self-presentational: People are concerned about how they will be perceived by others if they obtain condoms or discuss condoms with their sexual partners.

Self-presentational concern about obtaining condoms seems a primary barrier to their use. Studies have shown that between 30% and 63% of sexually active respondents reported being embarrassed when buying condoms (Hanna, 1989; Herold, 1981). Teenagers in particular are deterred from obtaining condoms and other forms of contraception by concerns about others' perceptions of them (Clinkscales & Gallo, 1977; Herold, 1981; Sorenson, 1973; Zabin, Stark, & Emerson, 1991).

One study of embarrassment arising from obtaining contraception from a physician or pharmacist showed that young women were more embarrassed about getting condoms than other forms of contraception such as contraceptive pills or foam, which, of course, do not protect against AIDS and other STDs (Herold, 1981). This may be because they think that others view it as more acceptable for women to purchase oral contraceptives or contraceptive foam than condoms. Not only do many people associate condoms with casual sex, STDs, and promiscuity (Lees, 1986), but, unlike using condoms, being on the pill does not necessarily imply that a woman is sexually active (e.g., she may be taking the pill because of menstrual problems; Herold, 1981).

Even if a person acquires condoms, self-presentational concerns may deter him or her from using them in a sexual encounter (Herold, 1981). Leary has talked to college students who had unprotected sexual intercourse even though they had a condom in their possession at the time. With a new sexual partner, people may worry that having a condom will imply that they had anticipated having sex, or worse, had actively worked to seduce the other person. In a study of adolescents in five American cities, teenagers of both sexes indicated that making plans to use a contraceptive would be perceived as too calculating unless they were involved in a stable, ongoing relationship (Kisker, 1985). Similarly, a recent study of Scottish teenagers concluded that "perceived barriers, particularly awareness of impression-management processes, were important predictors of teenagers' endorsement of HIV-preventive intentions" (Abraham, Sheeran, Spears, & Abrams, 1992, p. 369). Women in particular may be reluctant to carry condoms because they are afraid that their partners will perceive them as very sexually experienced (if not promiscuous) and as too bold (Abraham et al., 1992; Lees, 1986).

Among gay men, a primary justification for having unprotected anal intercourse was a fear of making a negative impression on one's partner (e.g., "He'll think I'm a wimp. Real men should be willing to take a risk") (Gold, Skinner, Grant, & Plummer, 1991). Over one third of the respondents indicated that concerns with their partners' impressions of them had led them to have unprotected anal intercourse (see Catania et al., 1991).

Other people seem to think that insisting on using a condom will lead sexual partners to conclude that they have an STD. This is a particular concern for people who do, in fact, have an STD. In one study of hemophiliacs, the primary reason for not using a condom was anxiety about being rejected if others learned they were HIV positive. Thus, those who have the greatest need to use a condom may not do so because they fear that insisting on a condom will cause their STD to be detected (Markova et al., 1990)!

Given the effects of self-presentational worries on condom use, one might expect people who are highly concerned about others' impressions of them to be particularly unlikely to discuss safe sex with their partners. One study showed that socially anxious women, who are more concerned about others' impressions of them (Schlenker & Leary, 1982), were less likely to discuss contraception with their partners before having intercourse (M. A. Bruch & Hynes, 1987; see also Leary & Dobbins, 1983). In contrast, high self-esteem, which is associated with self-presentational confidence and low need for social approval, is associated with more effective contraceptive use (Herold, Goodwin, & Lero, 1979).

The effects of self-presentational concerns on condom use are perhaps the most important discussed in this article. Not only is the potential risk involved with failure to use a condom exceptionally serious, but the failure to use a condom poses a health risk not only for oneself but for others as well.

## Sunbathing and Skin Cancer

The incidence of skin cancer has increased markedly in the United States during the past 30 years. The risk of basal cell carcinoma (the most common but least dangerous form) has been increasing at a rate of about 3% per year, whereas malignant melanoma (which is most likely to be fatal) has quadrupled since 1960 (Fears & Scotto, 1982). This increase is due to the convergence of several factors, including increased time spent sunbathing, increased vacationing in southern latitudes, and the popularity of tanning salons (Elwood, Whitehead, & Gallagher, 1989). Whatever the specific cause, the predominant cause of skin cancer is excessive exposure to ultraviolet radiation.

Sometimes people receive excessive exposure to the sun incidentally while engaging in outdoor work or recreational activities. However, many people purposefully expose themselves to the sun to obtain a tan. Because people tend to judge tanned people more positively than untanned people (Broadstock, Borland, & Gason, 1992; A. G. Miller, Ashton, McHoskey, & Gimbel, 1990), many people think (perhaps correctly) that being tanned will help them make a better impression.

To the extent that this is true, people who are most interested in enhancing others' impressions of them may be at an increased risk for skin cancer. Leary and Jones (1993) found that the best predictors of engaging in behaviors that increase one's risk for skin cancer involve concerns with others' impressions generally or with one's appearance specifically. The best single predictor of risk behaviors was the belief that being tan enhanced one's physical appearance. Similarly, people who scored high in public and body self-consciousness, characteristics associated with a concern about others' impressions, were more likely to engage in behaviors that put them at risk for skin cancer (see also Mermelstein & Riesenberg, 1992).

Given that much tanning behavior is motivated by a desire to make better impressions on others, J. L. Jones and Leary (1994) reasoned that messages that emphasize the negative effects of tanning on appearance (e.g., wrinkling, aging, and scarring) might be more effective in promoting safe sun attitudes than messages that emphasize the cancer risk. Their findings showed that overall this was true, although appearance-based warnings were less effective for people high in appearance motivation.

A self-presentational approach suggests that the most direct way to deter voluntary tanning is to alter the positive stereotype of the tanned individual (A. G. Miller et al., 1990). During the 19th century, pale skin was prized because being tanned was associated with manual outdoor labor. Only after the industrial revolution, when much of the working class began to work indoors, did being tan become associated with leisure and healthfulness (Keesling & Friedman, 1987). Efforts could be made to change contemporary American stereotypes of tanned people. For example, under-

mining the image that tanned people are healthier (Broadstock et al., 1992) may stigmatize tanning in much the same way that stressing the negative effects of smoking has led many to view smoking as a stigma (Jeffrey, 1989). Well-regarded celebrities who are seen as attractive and fashionable without being tan would further reinforce a more positive stereotype of untanned people (see Borland, Hill, & Noy, 1990).

## Nutrition, Weight, and Eating Disorders

People tend to draw more favorable inferences about attractive people than unattractive people, inferring that attractive people are more sociable, warm, intelligent, socially skilled, and so on (Feingold, 1992). In light of this, people are understandably concerned with maintaining an attractive appearance or at least with not being perceived as unattractive.

In contemporary America, physical attractiveness involves not only facial appearance but also having an appropriate body weight and, often, being in good physical shape (Hayes & Ross, 1987). Besides the fact that being overweight is generally viewed as aesthetically unappealing, people tend to draw negative inferences about overweight people—that they are lazy and self-indulgent and lack self-control. Put simply, being fat is a stigma (Allon, 1982; Crocker, Cornwell, & Major, 1993; Millman, 1980). In contrast, being thin is viewed as a sign of status, discipline, and healthfulness. As Brownell (1991b) observed, "the body therefore becomes a visible means to project these qualities for all to see" (p. 307). In short, people may regulate their weight as a self-presentational strategy.

Self-presentational concerns involving weight can have both positive and negative effects on health. On the one hand, people try to eat nutritionally and to control their weight as much out of a concern for their appearance to others as for healthfulness per se (Hayes & Ross, 1987). If everyone suddenly lost their motivation to be regarded positively, most people might soon gain weight.

On the negative side, excessive concerns with weight can lead to a range of unhealthy behaviors. At the mild end, over twice as many people diet as need to diet for health reasons (see Brownell, 1991b). This excessive rate of dieting is fueled by the fact that Americans' perceptions of the ideal weight is actually below the average weight for healthy, normal-weight individuals (Brownell, 1991a). Rather than improving health, unnecessary dieting leads to problems including mild malnutrition, lowered resistance to illness and infection, insufficient energy, and decreased performance.

Furthermore, certain kinds of diet regimens are hazardous to one's health. People, particularly women, may come to rely on diet pills, amphetamines, and even cigarette smoking to control their weight (e.g., Camp, Klesges, & Relyea, 1993; Gritz & Crane, 1991). In more extreme cases, the excessive use of laxatives or purposeful vomiting to control weight can affect one's digestive system and heart.

Furthermore, yo-yo dieting (also called *weight cycling*) can have negative implications for health. Chronic on-again–off-again dieters develop an increasing preference for fat and sugar (Drewnowski, Kurth, & Rahaim, 1990), and recent research also suggests a link between yo-yo dieting and the risk of coronary heart disease (Hamm, Shekelle, & Stamler, 1989; Lissner et al., 1991).

The most serious consequences of insufficient eating are life-threatening eating disorders. Eating disorders represent a diverse set of problems with a variety of antecedents, some of which have little to do with self-presentation. Nevertheless, excessive concerns about one's social image lead certain people, particularly women, to starve or to purge themselves in an attempt to be thin (Hayes & Ross, 1987). Women with eating disorders tend to have a high need for social approval and an intense fear of rejection, particularly by men (Dunn & Ondercin, 1981; Katzman & Wolchik, 1984; Weinstein & Richman, 1984). Anorexics, for example, have been described as highly motivated to fulfill others' expectations (H. Bruch, 1978), and bulimics indicate that they "live to please others— family, friends, even strangers" (Weinstein & Richman, 1984, p. 211).

One experimental study showed that women with anorexic tendencies reduced how much they ate when they were unsuccessful at controlling how much attention another person paid to them (Rezek & Leary, 1991). Although this research did not study self-presentation directly, its results are consistent with the idea that perceived self-presentational failures can affect the eating behavior of women predisposed to eating disorders. Women with eating disorders also tend to have lower self-esteem and higher social anxiety than women of normal weight (Gross & Rosen, 1988; Katzman & Wolchik, 1984), which are factors associated with self-presentational concerns (Leary, 1983).

It is interesting that women with eating disorders often manifest a discrepancy between how they think they truly are and their public presentation. For the most part, for example, bulimics are as successful, attractive, and socially active as anyone else, and they are often regarded quite favorably by other people. Yet they believe that their public persona is but a ruse to hide their true, inner selves from others. Because of their concerns with others' reactions, bulimics are often dutifully good, passive, and nonassertive (Weinstein & Richman, 1984).

Direct evidence for the role of self-presentational factors in eating was provided by the finding that female subjects ate less with a socially desirable male confederate than with a less desirable man or with a woman (Mori, Chaiken, & Pliner, 1987; Pliner & Chaiken, 1990). Women also ate less when they were motivated to convey an impression of being feminine to the male confederate (Mori et al., 1987).

The fact that eating disorders are far more common among women than among men may reflect the fact that appearance, eating behaviors, and body weight are more important in others' impressions of women than of men (Freedman, 1984; Hayes & Ross, 1987; Nasser, 1988; Rodin, Silberstein, & Striegel-Moore, 1985; Rolls, Fedoroff, & Guthrie, 1991). Studies showed that subjects' perceptions of women were affected by how much they ate (women who ate less were viewed as more feminine and less masculine), whereas perceptions of men were not affected by their eating (Chaiken & Pliner, 1987; Pliner & Chaiken, 1990). Furthermore, Guy, Rankin, and Norvell (1980) found that subjects judged unusually thin female silhouettes as *most feminine* but judged normal-weight male silhouettes as *most masculine*. These findings suggest that cultural views of femininity may contribute to eating disorders in women by prescribing unrealistically thin body shapes and sizes (Brownell, 1991a). Even among women without eating disorders, feeling that oneself is fat is associated with perceiving that friends and family exert pressure for one to be thin (Striegel-Moore, McAvay, & Rodin, 1986), and decisions to lose weight are often based on perceived social pressure to be thin and the stigma of obesity (Rosen, Gross, & Vara, 1987).

Although cultural standards for men's weight are more lenient than standards for women's weight, men also experience pressure to be fit and trim. In one study, 17% of male college students indicated that their greatest fear in life was becoming fat (Collier, Stallings, Wolman, & Cullen, 1990), suggesting that researchers should pay greater attention to the weight concerns of men.

Some researchers have suggested that the increase in anorexia nervosa and bulimia in the past 30 years has resulted from the idealization of thinness in American culture (Nasser, 1988). Eating disorders of the sort common in the United States are almost nonexistent in cultures that prize plumpness (Nasser, 1988). As other cultures adopt American values about weight, dieting, and their implications for others' impressions of the individual, an increase in eating disorders should be observed.

## Alcohol, Tobacco, and Illegal Drug Use

The cumulative effects of excessive alcohol, tobacco, and illegal drug use are staggering. Hundreds of thousands of people die of illnesses and injuries each year as a result of alcohol, tobacco, and other drugs. Tobacco use alone is the single most preventable cause of death in the United States; approximately 500,000 people die of smoking-related illnesses each year in the United States (U.S. Department of Health and Human Services, 1990). In this section we examine evidence that drug use and abuse is initiated and maintained in part by self-presentational processes.

Self-presentational motives are strongly involved in the decision to use alcohol, tobacco, and illicit drugs. Few people sneak off alone for their first experiences with any of these substances. Indeed, one study found that only 11% of adolescents reported that they first smoked cigarettes alone (L. S. Friedman, Lichtenstein, & Biglan, 1985). Rather, most people first try alcohol, tobacco, and other drugs in an interpersonal context in which they want others to perceive them as adventuresome, sociable, or unrepressed.

Although laypeople often speak of adolescents succumbing to peer pressure in such contexts, the so-called pressure is typically implied rather than explicit. Adolescents and young adults often believe, sometimes correctly, that the use of alcohol and other drugs can facilitate their social image

and, thus, peer acceptance (Kandel, 1980). As Shute (1975) noted,

> the influences of peers related to the individual's felt needs to be "cool," to respond to challenges or dares, to prove one's openness and flexibility, and to demonstrate one's maturity and emotional depth are thought to be quite powerful motivators toward (or away from) experimentation with drugs. (p. 233)

The use of alcohol, tobacco, and other drugs depends in part on the belief that such behavior is tolerated, if not condoned, by important reference groups. People are unlikely to drink, smoke, or use drugs when they know that such behaviors seriously undermine the impressions that important people in their lives have of them. For example, boys who smoke indicate that smoking "makes you feel part of the gang" (Clayton, 1991, p. 119), presumably because one has conveyed the impression of being the right kind of person for group membership. Adolescents associate images of toughness, independence, and maturity with cigarette smoking (Camp et al., 1993; Chassin, Presson, Sherman, Corty, & Olshavsky, 1981; Covington & Omelich, 1988).

In addition, a study of the reasons why people drink alcohol revealed two primary factors, one of which involved drinking as a means toward attaining goals such as peer acceptance and social approval (Farber, Khavari, & Douglass, 1980). Among adolescents, those who drink are perceived as tougher, more precocious, and more rebellious than those who do not drink. Furthermore, many adolescent boys believe that their peers admire the attributes that characterize one who drinks alcohol and aspire to that image (Chassin, Tetzloff, & Hershey, 1985).

The effect of image concerns on substance abuse is also seen in the case of smokeless tobacco. Smokeless tobacco (oral snuff and chewing tobacco) is currently quite popular among adolescent and young adult males. Risks associated with smokeless tobacco include cancer of the mouth, noncancerous oral pathologies (recession of the gums, dental carries, and leukoplakia—white lesions of the oral mucosa), loss of bone mass in the jaw, and nicotine dependence (Boyd & Glover, 1989; White, 1990). The current popularity of smokeless tobacco can be traced in part to the fact that it is associated with a professional athlete image (Strauss, 1991). In one survey of over 1,000 minor- and major-league baseball players and coaches, 39% reported that they had used smoke-less tobacco in the week before the study (White, 1990)! Apparently some boys and men begin using smokeless tobacco as a self-presentational tactic so they will be seen as athletic and tough.

Studies of personality predictors of drug and alcohol use also support the role of self-presentation in these behaviors. Wolfe, Lennox, and Cutler (1986) showed that college students who scored high on a measure of concern for appropriateness reported that they used drugs because of the influence of other people. In addition, drug abusers tend to score higher on measures related to self-presentational concern, such as social anxiety, than nonabusers (Lindquist, Lindsay, & White, 1979).

In addition to serving as a means of conveying desired images of oneself to one's peers, drug use can serve self-presentational goals in at least four other ways. First, adolescents may use alcohol, tobacco, or drugs as a means of conveying their autonomy or rebelliousness to parents and other adults (see Clayton, 1991). Second, people who are socially insecure may use alcohol or other drugs to reduce their anxiety in interpersonal contexts or because they think doing so will produce positive changes in their social behavior (Leonard & Blane, 1988).

Third, people may use alcohol or other drugs as self-handicapping strategies. By getting drunk or stoned before important evaluative events (e.g., tests), people who doubt their ability to perform well can create a viable excuse for poor performance (Berglas, 1986; E. E. Jones & Berglas, 1978). Although self-handicapping has sometimes been described as a tactic for preserving one's self-esteem, research shows clearly that it is also used for self-presentational purposes (Kolditz & Arkin, 1982).

Finally, some substances may be used because they have a secondary effect on a person's image. For example, many adolescent girls and adult women say they smoke because it is a good way to control their weight (Charlton, 1984; Gritz & Crane, 1991; Page & Gold, 1983; Pirie, Murray, & Leupker, 1991). Such people smoke not because they think smoking per se projects a desired image but because smoking has other self-presentational benefits.

Although to our knowledge no controlled studies have been conducted on the effects of self-presentational processes on actual tobacco, alcohol, or drug use, Shute (1975) demonstrated that col-lege students readily conform to the expressed attitudes of their peers regarding drugs in laboratory group discussions. This occurred even when the peers were strangers with whom the subject had no previous contact. Clearly, subjects were motivated to convey an accepting attitude toward drugs to others whom they thought were in favor of drugs. If such effects occurred with complete strangers, one can only imagine the power of natural peer groups to induce self-presentational compliance.

Self-presentational motives can also facilitate and impede people's attempts to stop their use of alcohol, tobacco, and other drugs. On the positive side, people often decide to stop unhealthy habits because of what other people think. The stigmatization of smoking in the United States during the past 25 years has been credited with the steadily decreasing number of adult smokers (Jeffrey, 1989).

On the other hand, self-presentational concerns can interfere with people's willingness to stop using certain substances. The most clear-cut example involves people who are unwilling to stop smoking because they are afraid they will gain weight (Klesges & Klesges, 1988). Such concerns are not unfounded; smokers have been found to gain an average of 4.5 to 7.5 lb after they stop smoking (e.g., Klesges, Meyers, Klesges, & LaVasque, 1989). That people are willing to risk very serious health consequences (such as cardiovascular disease, emphysema, and lung cancer) because they fear gaining 5 or 6 lbs. demonstrates the potency of the self-presentational motive.

An evaluation of one school-based drug prevention program showed that the most potent mediator of the program's effects involved perceived changes in friends' tolerance of drug use (MacKinnon et al., 1991). Analyses showed that 66% of the program's effect on drug use and 45% of its effect on smoking was explained by changes in friends' reactions to drug use. Although this is but a single study, it suggests that large-scale efforts to reduce alcohol, tobacco, or drug use should include a component that attempts to change the prevailing impressions of people who use such substances.

## Accidental Injury and Death

Although data on this point do not exist, we suspect that a high percentage of injuries and accidental deaths result from self-presentational motives. Many injuries result from reckless behaviors that are performed primarily, if not solely, for self-presentational reasons. Because the image of being fearless and risk taking is often valued (Finney, 1978; Hong, 1978), people sometimes engage in dangerous behaviors to convey an impression of bring brave or adventuresome (or, conversely, so as not to be regarded as a wimp). For instance, many people (adolescents and young adults in particular) drive at excessive and unsafe speeds to convey an impression of bravery or recklessness. In the extreme case, the game of "chicken"—in which two drivers speed toward one another to see who swerves first—is essentially a self-presentational game in which the competitors play for the right to claim certain social identities (i.e., brave vs. cowardly). Russian roulette is a similar example. People sometimes try risky activities that they do not have the experience or ability to perform safely (e.g., spelunking, white water canoeing, and repelling) because they do not want to be perceived as cowardly or as a poor sport. Adolescents appear particularly prone to engage in dangerous activities because of concerns with what other people think (H. L. Friedman, 1989; Jonah, 1990).

In addition, injuries sometimes occur when people do not take adequate precautions with everyday activities. Although some such injuries occur because of pure carelessness or misfortune, others happen because the person did not want others to perceive him or her as too careful. For example, many people seem to avoid wearing seat belts in automobiles, helmets on bicycles and motorcycles, and life preservers in boats because such devices convey an impression of excessive cautiousness. In addition, many people seem reluctant to wear protective gear (e.g., safety goggles, gloves, and helmets) when operating power tools or dangerous machinery because they will be viewed as neurotic or extremely careful. This concern emerges at a young age; anecdotally, children as young as 6 or 7 years old are sometimes reluctant to wear knee pads and helmets when rollerskating because of what other children will think of them.

We know of no research that has investigated the role of self-presentational motives in accidental injury and death. If our theory is correct, such motives are a leading cause of injuries and deserve greater research attention. We also suspect that men are more likely than women to suffer self-presentationally caused injuries because men are more motivated to be perceived as brave, adventuresome, and reckless than women (Doyle, 1989).

## Steroid Use

Steroids cause a number of health problems including acne, early balding, changes in the reproductive organs, stunted growth, heart problems, and possibly brain cancer. Undesirable behavioral changes, including aggressiveness and depression, are also common. Unfortunately, black market steroid use is increasing in the United States. It is estimated that 1 million Americans use steroids, one-half of whom are adolescents. Although steroid use is often associated with competitive athletes, such as weight lifters and football players, approximately one third of the male adolescents who use steroids are not involved in competitive athletics (Schrof, 1992). For these young men, the motivation is primarily self-presentational—to have a muscular physique that will enhance their social image and bring about desired rewards such as attention, respect, romantic involvements, and increased self-esteem.

## Failure to Exercise

Similar to weight control, physical exercise is sometimes motivated by self-presentation. People often get in and stay in shape not to be healthier but to make better impressions on other people. In this regard, self-presentational motives can facilitate good health.

Yet we suspect that there are certain people who need and want to exercise but do not do so because of concerns with the impressions they make while exercising. People who perceive themselves to be overweight, scrawny, or disproportioned may be reluctant to be seen bouncing around in an aerobics class, swimming at the local pool, jogging in public, or lifting weights. Such concerns are likely to be particularly acute among those who are high in physique anxiety (Hart, Leary, & Rejeski, 1989).

A study of overweight women's reactions to exercise programs showed that self-presentational concerns were quite salient. "Although factors such as safety, comfort, and quality of instruction affected the women's exercise behaviors, the most powerful influences seemed to be the social circumstances of the exercise setting, especially concerns about visibility, embarrassment, and judgment by others" (Bain, Wilson, & Chaikind, 1989, p. 139). For example, these women reported that they preferred exercise classes that included only overweight women. Sport psychologists and fitness professionals should begin to pay increased attention to the effects of self-presentational concerns on people's willingness to exercise (Leary, 1992).

## Acne

In American culture, many girls and women use makeup as a way of enhancing others' impressions of them. Furthermore, those most attuned to others' impressions are more likely to wear makeup to enhance their appearance (L. C. Miller & Cox, 1982). Unfortunately, frequent use of cosmetics can have negative consequences for health. It is estimated that one third of adolescent girls who regularly use cosmetics develop facial blemishes caused solely by the cosmetics, and this can occur even in girls who are not otherwise prone to acne (Freedman, 1984). This problem can become cyclical when women apply additional makeup to cover their blemishes, which further exacerbates the skin problem, leading to more covering makeup, then to more acne, and so on.

Although admittedly a minor affliction compared with AIDS, drug abuse, or skin cancer, acne creates a great deal of distress for many people. *Acne cosmetica* is an example of a condition for which people seek medical attention that is precipitated solely by attempts to manage one's impressions.

## Cosmetic Surgery

When people think of medicine, they generally think of a field that deals with illness and injury. However, at least one medical specialty provides services that are primarily self-presentational rather than medical. Over 1.5 million people underwent cosmetic surgery in 1988 (Findlay, 1989), a substantial increase during the past decade. Between 1981 and 1989, the number of face lifts increased from 39,000 to 75,000, breast augmentation from 72,000 to 100,000, and liposuction from 1,000 to 250,000. Historically, women have sought cosmetic surgery at a higher rate than men, but an increasing number of men are now seeking plastic surgery (Yoffe, 1990).

Although some cosmetic surgery is conducted to repair disfigurements resulting from birth defects, accidents, or disease, the majority involves elective surgery intended to enhance appearance (Schouten, 1991). For example, the primary reason women give for seeking breast augmentation is to reduce their self-consciousness and embarrassment over the size of their breasts, a purely self-presentational motive (Birtchnell, Whitfield, & Lacey, 1990). Similarly, 80% of people who seek orthodontic treatment do so solely for cosmetic reasons (Giddon, 1983). Permanent modification of the body for self-presentational purposes is by no means new. Cultures throughout history have relied on various methods of mutilation (e.g., scarring, piercing, and stretching) to achieve cultural standards of beauty (Freedman, 1984).

Although safer than ever, cosmetic surgery is not risk free. Infection, abnormal bleeding, and pain are risks with all types of cosmetic surgery, and more serious consequences, including muscle damage, blood and fat clots, and death, can result (Findlay, 1989; Yoffe, 1990). The serious problems associated with silicone breast implants have recently become well-known (Podolsky, 1991). Breast augmentation carries the additional risk of obscuring breast tissue on standard mammograms, thereby reducing the early detection of breast cancer (Podolsky, 1991). Complications of liposuction occur in roughly 10% of patients (Henig, 1989).

Given the degree to which others' impressions are influenced by physical appearance, the desire to use surgical procedures to enhance one's appearance is understandable, and we should not be interpreted as criticizing cosmetic surgery. Yet these procedures, which are most often performed for self-presentational rather than for medical reasons, can constitute a health risk.

## Implications of the Self-Presentation Perspective

We have reviewed several ways in which people's self-presentational motives can be hazardous to their health. In some cases, such as with sun-induced skin cancer or *acne cosmetica,* self-presentation may be the most important factor that places the person at risk. In other instances, such as contracting HIV through unsafe sex or using steroids, self-presentation is but one of many factors that lead to unhealthy behaviors. In either case, our review suggests that interpersonal motives, which have been largely neglected by health researchers and practitioners, deserve greater attention.[1]

Traditionally, health educators have tried to promote healthy lifestyles by warning people of the unhealthy consequences of certain behaviors. Our review suggests that, for certain health problems, increased attention should be devoted to the self-presentational motives that maintain unhealthy patterns of behavior. For example, one way to promote safe sex practices is to destigmatize condom use. If people come to believe that not using a condom will make a bad impression—connoting to a sexual partner that the individual is irresponsible, immature, or sexually repressed—condom use should increase. Similarly, getting people to regard a suntan as a sign of poor health should reduce purposeful tanning, and changing attitudes about the attractiveness of excessive thinness should reduce the prevalence of eating disorders. In each case, widespread changes in behavior are unlikely as long as people believe that their public images (and others' reactions to them) are enhanced by unhealthy behaviors.

Furthermore, people may be induced to behave more heathfully if they see the negative consequences of doing so for the impressions others form. For example, Klohn and Rogers (1991) showed that stressing the visibility of osteoporosis strengthened women's intentions to engage in behaviors that prevent the disorder. Similarly, stressing the negative effects of tanning on appearance increased safe sun intentions (J. L. Jones & Leary, 1994). In particular, when problems have consequences for both health and physical appear-ance, people may be more likely to be persuaded to change unhealthy behaviors when the risks to appearance are emphasized.

Unfortunately, efforts to minimize the unhealthy effects of self-presentational motives on health wrestle against two facts of interpersonal life: (a) The impressions that people make often do have important consequences for their relationships with others, and (b) people's assumptions about how others will regard them if they engage in certain unhealthy behaviors are often correct. At the present time, there are many people who really do frown on women who carry condoms, rate tanned individuals positively, view extreme thinness as attractive, advocate that women use cosmetics, reward risky behaviors, and so forth. The big question for health researchers and professionals is how to lead people to pay more attention to their health and less attention to their public image when health and self-presentation collide.

## REFERENCES

Abraham. C., Sheeran, P., Spears, R., & Abrams, D. (1992). Health beliefs and promotion of HIV-preventive intentions among teenagers: A Scottish perspective. *Health Psychology, 11*, 363–370.

Allon, N. (1982). The stigma of overweight in everyday life. In B. B. Wolman (Ed.), *Psychological aspects of obesity* (pp. 130–174). New York: Van Nostrand Reinhold.

Bain, L. L., Wilson, T., & Chaikind, E. (1989). Participant perceptions of exercise programs for overweight women. *Research Quarterly for Exercise and Sport, 60*, 134–143.

Baumeister, R. F. (1982). A self-presentational view of social phenomena. *Psychological Bulletin, 91*, 3–26.

Baumeister, R. F., & Jones, E. E. (1978). When self-presentation is constrained by the target's knowledge: Consistency and compensation. *Journal of Personality and Social Psychology, 36*, 608–618.

Berglas, S. (1986). A typology of self-handicapping alcohol abusers. In M. J. Saks & L. Saxe (Eds.), *Advances in applied social psychology* (Vol. 3, pp. 29–56). Hillsdale, NJ: Erlbaum.

Birtchnell, S., Whitfield, P., & Lacey, J. H. (1990). Motivational factors in women requesting augmentation and reduction mammaplasty. *Journal of Psychosomatic Research, 34*, 509–514.

Borland, R., Hill, D., & Noy, S. (1990). Being Sun Smart: Changes in community awareness and reported behavior following a primary prevention program for skin cancer control. *Behavior Change, 7*, 126–135.

Boyd, G. M., & Glover, E. D. (1989). Smokeless tobacco use by youth in the U.S. *Journal of School Health, 59*, 189–194.

Broadstock, M., Borland, R., & Gason, R. (1992). Effects of suntan on judgments of healthiness and attractiveness by adolescents. *Journal of Applied Social Psychology, 22*, 157–172.

---

[1] In addition to contributing to unhealthy behaviors, self-presentational concerns can interfere with obtaining adequate medical care. For example, self-presentational concerns regarding the nature of one's problem (as in the case of STDs or alcoholism) or about the medical exam itself (as in the case of cervical screening or mammograms; e.g., Kowalski & Brown, 1994) may deter people from seeking treatment. Furthermore, people may fail to disclose medically relevant information to medical practitioners if they believe they will convey an undesired image by doing so. People may even hesitate to follow prescribed medical regimens if doing so may affect others' impressions of them. Leary and Kowalski (1995) discuss ways in which self-presentation may interfere with health care.

Brownell, K. D. (1991a). Dieting and the search for the perfect body: Where physiology and culture collide. *Behavior Therapy, 22,* 1–12.

Brownell, K. D. (1991b). Personal responsibility and control over our bodies: When expectation exceeds reality. *Health Psychology, 10,* 303–310.

Bruch, H. (1978). *The golden cage: The enigma of anorexia nervosa.* New York: Vintage.

Bruch, M. A., & Hynes, M. J. (1987). Heterosexual anxiety and contraceptive use. *Journal of Research in Personality, 21,* 343–360.

Camp, D. E., Klesges, R. C., & Relyea, G. (1993). The relationship between body weight concerns and adolescent smoking. *Health Psychology, 12,* 24–32.

Catania, J. A., Coates, T. J., Stall, R., Bye, L., Kegeles, S. M., Capell, F., Henne, J., McKusick, L., Morin, S., Turner, H., & Pollack, L. (1991). Changes in condom use among homosexual men in San Francisco. *Health Psychology, 10,* 190–199.

Chaiken, S., & Pliner, P. (1987). Women, but not men, are what they eat: The effect of meal size and gender on perceived femininity and masculinity. *Personality and Social Psychology Bulletin, 13,* 166–176.

Charlton, A. (1984). Smoking and weight control in teenagers. *Public Health, 98,* 277–281.

Chassin, L., Presson, C. C., Sherman, S. J., Corty, E., & Olshavsky, R. W. (1981). Self-images and cigarette smoking in adolescence. *Personality and Social Psychology Bulletin, 7,* 670–676.

Chassin, L., Tetzloff, C., & Hershey, M. (1985). Self-image and social-image factors in adolescent alcohol use. *Journal of Studies on Alcohol, 46,* 39–47.

Clayton, S. (1991). Gender differences in psychosocial determinants of adolescent smoking. *Journal of School Health, 61,* 115–120.

Clinkscales, K., & Gallo, J. (1977). How teens see it. In D. J. Bogue (Ed.), *Adolescent fertility* (pp. 134–134). Chicago: University of Chicago Press.

Collier, S. N., Stallings, S. F., Wolman, P. G., & Cullen, R. W. (1990). Assessment of attitudes about weight and dieting among college-aged individuals. *Journal of the American Diabetic Association, 90,* 276–279.

Covington, M. V., & Omelich, C. L. (1988). I can resist anything but temptation: Adolescent expectations for smoking cigarettes. *Journal of Applied Social Psychology, 18,* 203–227.

Crocker, J., Cornwell, B., & Major, B. (1993). The stigma of overweight: Affective consequences of attributional ambiguity. *Journal of Personality and Social Psychology, 64,* 60–70.

DiClemente, C. C. (1986). Self-efficacy and the addictive behaviors. *Journal of Social and Clinical Psychology, 4,* 302–315.

Doyle, J. A. (1989). *The male experience* (2nd ed.). Dubuque, IA: Wm. C. Brown.

Drewnowsky, A., Kurth, C. L., & Rahaim, J. (1990). *Human obesity and sensory preferences for sugar and fat: Age at onset and history of weight cycling.* Unpublished manuscript.

Dunn, P. K., & Ondercin, P. (1981). Personality variables related to compulsive eating in college women. *Journal of Clinical Psychology, 37,* 43–49.

Elwood, J. M., Whitehead, S. M., & Gallagher, R. P. (1989).

Epidemiology of human malignant skin tumors with special reference to natural and artificial ultraviolet radiation exposures. In C. J. Conti, T. J. Slaga, & A. J. P. Klein-Szanto (Eds.), *Skin tumors: Experimental and clinical aspects* (pp. 55–84). New York: Raven Press.

Farber, P. D., Khavari, K. A., & Douglass, F. M., IV. (1980). A factor analytic study of reasons for drinking: Empirical validation of positive and negative reinforcement dimensions. *Journal of Consulting and Clinical Psychology, 48,* 780–781.

Fears, T. R., & Scotto, J. (1982). Changes in skin cancer morbidity between 1971–72 and 1977–78. *Journal of the National Cancer Institute, 69,* 365–370.

Feingold, A. (1992). Good-looking people are not what we think. *Psychological Bulletin, 111,* 304–341.

Fielding, J. E., & Williams, C. A. (1991). Adolescent pregnancy in the United States: A review and recommendations for clinicians and research needs. *American Journal of Preventive Medicine, 7,* 47–52.

Findlay, S. (1989, May 1). Buying the perfect body. *U.S. News and World Report,* pp. 68–75.

Finney, P. D. (1978). Personality traits attributed to risky and conservative decision-making: Culture values more than risk. *Journal of Psychology, 99,* 187–197.

Freedman, R. J. (1984). Reflections on beauty as it relates to health in adolescent females. *Women and Health, 9,* 29–45.

Friedman, H. L. (1989). The health of adolescents: Beliefs and behavior. *Social Science and Medicine, 29,* 309–315.

Friedman, L. S., Lichtenstein, E., & Biglan, A. (1985). Smoking onset among teens: An empirical analysis of initial situations. *Addictive Behaviors, 10,* 1–13.

Giddon, D. B. (1983). Through the looking glasses of physicians, dentists, and patients. *Perspectives in Biology and Medicine, 26,* 451–458.

Goffman. E. (1959). *The presentation of self in everyday life.* New York: Doubleday.

Gold, R. S., Skinner, M. J., Grant, P. J., & Plummer, D. C. (1991). Situational factors and thought processes associated with unprotected intercourse in gay men. *Psychology and Health, 5,* 259–278.

Gritz, E. R., & Crane, L. A. (1991). Use of diet pills and ampethamines to lose weight among smoking and nonsmoking high school seniors. *Health Psychology, 10,* 330–335.

Gross, J., & Rosen, J. C. (1988). Bulimia in adolescents: Prevalence and psychological correlates. *International Journal of Eating Disorders, 7,* 51–61.

Guy, F., Rankin, B., & Norvell, M. (1980). The relation of sex-role stereotyping to body image. *Journal of Psychology, 105,* 167–173.

Hamm, P., Shekelle, R. B., & Stamler, J. (1989). Large fluctuations in body weight during young adulthood and twenty-five-year risk of coronary death in men. *American Journal of Epidemiology, 129,* 312–318.

Hanna, J. (1989, September 25). Sexual abandon: The condom is unpopular on the campus. *Maclean's,* p. 48.

Hart, E. A., Leary, M. R., & Rejeski, W. J. (1989). The measurement of social physique anxiety. *Journal of Sport and Exercise Psychology, 11,* 94–104.

Hayes. D., & Ross, C. E. (1987). Concern with appearance, health beliefs, and eating habits. *Journal of Health and Social Behavior, 28,* 120–130.

Henig, R. M. (1989, October). Health. *Vogue, 179,* p. 294.

Herold, E. S. (1981). Contraceptive embarrassment and contraceptive behavior among young single women. *Journal of Youth and Adolescence, 10,* 233–242.

Herold, E. S., Goodwin, M. S., & Lero, D. S. (1979). Self-esteem, locus of control, and adolescent contraception. *Journal of Psychology, 101,* 83–88.

Hong, L. K. (1978). Risky shift and cautious shift: Some direct evidence on the culture-value theory, *Journal of Social Psychology, 41,* 342–346.

Janz. N. K., & Becker, H. M. (1984). The health belief model: A decade later. *Health Education Quarterly, 11,* 1–47.

Jeffrey, R. W. (1989). Risk behaviors and health: Contrasting individual and population perspectives. *American Psychologist, 44,* 1194–1202.

Jonah, B. A. (1990). Age differences in risky driving. *Health Education Research, 5,* 139–149.

Jones, E. E., & Berglas, S. (1978). Control of attributions about the self through self-handicapping strategies: The appeal of alcohol and the role of underachievement. *Personality and Social Psychology Bulletin, 4,* 200–206.

Jones, E. E., & Pittman, T. S. (1982). Toward a general theory of strategic self-presentation. In J. Suls (Ed.), *Psychological perspectives on the self* (Vol. 1, pp. 231–262). Hillsdale, NJ: Erlbaum.

Jones, J. L., & Leary, M. R. (1994). Effects of appearance-based admonitions against sun exposure on tanning intentions in young adults. *Health Psychology, 13,* 86–90.

Kandel, D. B. (1980). Drug and drinking behavior among youth. *Annual Review of Sociology, 6,* 235–285.

Katzman, M. A., & Wolchik, S. A. (1984). Bulimia and binge eating in college women: A comparison of personality and behavioral characteristics. *Journal of Consulting and Clinical Psychology, 52,* 423–428.

Keesling, B., & Friedman, H. S. (1987). Psychosocial factors in sunbathing and sunscreen use. *Health Psychology, 6,* 417–428.

Kisker, E. E. (1985). Teenagers talk about sex, pregnancy, and contraception. *Family Planning Perspectives, 17,* 83–90.

Klesges, R. C., & Klesges, L. M. (1988). Cigarette smoking as a dietary strategy in a university population. *International Journal of Eating Disorders, 7,* 413–417.

Klesges, R. C., Meyers, A. W., Klesges, L. M., & LaVasque, M. E. (1989). Smoking, body weight, and their effects on smoking behavior: A comprehensive review of the literature. *Psychological Bulletin, 106,* 204–230.

Klohn, L. S., & Rogers, R. W. (1991). Dimensions of the severity of a health threat: The persuasive effects of visibility, time of onset, and rate of onset on young women's intentions to prevent osteoporosis. *Health Psychology, 10,* 323–329.

Kolditz, T. A., & Arkin, R. M. (1982). An impression management interpretation of the self-handicapping strategy. *Journal of Personality and Social Psychology, 43,* 492–502.

Kowalski, R. M., & Brown, K. (1994). Psychosocial barriers to cervical cancer screening: Effects of self-presentation and social evaluation. *Journal of Applied Social Psychology, 24,* 941–958.

Leary, M. R. (1983). *Understanding social anxiety: Social, personality, and clinical perspectives.* Beverly Hills, CA: Sage.

Leary, M. R. (1992). Self-presentational processes in exercise and sport. *Journal of Sport and Exercise Psychology, 14,* 339–351.

Leary, M. R. (1993). The interplay of private self-processes and interpersonal factors in self-presentation. In J. Suls (Ed.), *Psychological perspectives on the self* (Vol. 4, pp. 127–155). Hillsdale, NJ: Erlbaum.

Leary, M. R. (1994). *Self-presentation: Impression management and social behavior.* Dubuque, IA: Brown & Benchmark.

Leary, M. R., & Dobbins, S. E. (1983). Social anxiety, sexual behavior, and contraceptive use. *Journal of Personality and Social Psychology, 45,* 1347–1354.

Leary, M. R., & Jones, J. L. (1993). The social psychology of tanning and sunscreen use: Self-presentational motives as a predictor of health risk. *Journal of Applied Social Psychology, 23,* 1390–1406.

Leary, M. R., & Kowalski, R. M. (1990). Impression management: A literature review and two-component model. *Psychological Bulletin, 107,* 34–47.

Leary, M. R., & Kowalski, R. M. (1995). *Social anxiety.* New York: Guilford Press.

Lees, S. (1986). *Losing out: Sexuality and adolescent girls.* London: Hutchinson.

Leonard, K. E., & Blane, H. T. (1988). Alcohol expectancies and personality characteristics in young men. *Addictive Behaviors, 13,* 353–357.

Lindquist, C. U., Lindsay, J. S., & White, G. D. (1979). Assessment of assertiveness in drug abusers. *Journal of Clinical Psychology, 35,* 676–679.

Lissner, L., Odell, P. M., D'Agostino, R. B., Stores, J., Kreger, B. E., Belanger, A. J., & Brownell, K. D. (1991). Variability in body weight and health outcomes in the Framingham population. *New England Journal of Medicine, 324,* 1839–1844.

MacKinnon, D. P., Johnson, C. A., Pentz, M. A., Dwyer, J. H., Hansen, W. B., Flay, B. R., & Wang, E. Y. (1991). Mediating mechanisms in a school-based drug prevention program: First-year effects of the Midwestern Prevention Project. *Health Psychology, 10,* 164–172.

Markova, I., Wilkie, P. A., Naji, S. A., & Forbes, C. D. (1990). Knowledge of HIV/AIDS and behavioural change of people with haemophilia. *Psychology and Health, 4,* 125–133.

Mermelstein, R. J., & Riesenberg, L. A. (1992). Changing knowledge and attitudes about skin cancer risk factors in adolescents. *Health Psychology, 11,* 371–376.

Miller, A. G., Ashton, W. A., McHoskey, J. W., & Gimbel, J. (1990). What price attractiveness? Stereotype and risk factors in suntanning behavior. *Journal of Applied Social Psychology, 24,* 1212–1300.

Miller, L. C., & Cox, C. L. (1982). For appearances' sake: Public self-consciousness and make-up use. *Personality and Social Psychology Bulletin, 8,* 748–751.

Miller, R. S. (1986). Embarrassment: Causes and consequences. In W. H. Jones, I. M. Cheek, & S. R. Briggs (Eds.), *Shyness: Perspectives on research and treatment* (pp. 295–311). New York: Plenum Press.

Miller, R. S., & Leary, M. R. (1992). Social sources and interaction functions of emotion: The case of embarrassment. In M. S. Clark (Ed.), *Emotion and social behavior* (pp. 202–221). Beverly Hills, CA: Sage.

Millman, M. (1980). *Such a pretty face: Being fat in America.* New York: Berkley Press.

Mori, D., Chaiken, S., & Pliner, P. (1987). "Eating lightly" and the self-presentation of femininity. *Journal of Personality and Social Psychology, 53,* 693–702.

Nasser, M. (1988). Eating disorders: The cultural dimension. *Social Psychiatry and Psychiatric Epidemiology, 23,* 184–187.

Page, R. M., & Gold, R. S. (1983). Assessing gender differences in college cigarette smoking intenders and nonintenders. *Journal of School Health, 53,* 531–535.

Pirie, P. L., Murray, D. M., & Leupker, R. V. (1991). Gender differences in cigarette smoking and quitting in a cohort of young adults. *American Journal of Public Health, 81,* 324–327.

Pliner, P., & Chaiken, S. (1990). Eating, social motives, and self-presentation in women and men. *Journal of Experimental Social Psychology, 26,* 240–254.

Podolsky, D. (1991, March). Breast implants: What price vanity? *American Health, 14,* 70–75.

Rezek, P. J., & Leary, M. R. (1991). Perceived control, drive for thinness, and food consumption: Anorexic tendencies as displaced reactance. *Journal of Personality, 59,* 129–142.

Rodin, J., Silberstein, L., & Striegel-Moore, R. (1985). Women and weight: A normative discontent? In T. B. Sonderregger (Ed.), *Nebraska Symposium on Motivation: Psychology and gender* (pp. 267–307). Lincoln: University of Nebraska Press.

Rolls, B. J., Fedoroff, I. C., & Guthrie, J. F. (1991). Gender differences in eating behavior and body weight regulation. *Health Psychology, 10,* 133–142.

Rosen, J. C., Gross, J., & Vara, L. (1987). Psychological adjustment of adolescents attempting to lose or gain weight. *Journal of Consulting and Clinical Psychology, 55,* 742–747.

Rosenstock, I. M. (1974). The health belief model and preventive health behavior. *Health Education Monographs, 2,* 354–386.

Safer sex (1991, December 9). *Newsweek,* pp. 52–56.

Schlenker, B. R. (1980). *Impression management: The self-concept, social identity, and interpersonal relations.* Monterey, CA: Brooks/ Cole.

Schlenker, B. R., & Leary, M. R. (1982). Social anxiety and self-presentation: A conceptualization and model. *Psychological Bulletin, 92,* 641–669.

Schlenker, B. R., & Weigold, M. F. (1992). Interpersonal processes involving impression regulation and management. *Annual Review of Psychology, 13,* 133–168.

Schouten, J. W. (1991). Selves in transition: Symbolic consumption in personal rites of passage and identity reconstruction. *Journal of Consumer Research, 17,* 412–425.

Schrof, J. M. (1992, June 1). Pumped up. *U.S. News and World Report,* pp. 55–63.

Sexually transmitted diseases up. (1993, April 1). *The Winston-Salem Journal,* p. 20.

Shute, R. E. (1975). The impact of peer pressure on the verbally expressed drug attitudes of male college students. *American Journal of Drug and Alcohol Abuse, 2,* 231–243.

Sorenson, R. C. (1973). *Adolescent sexuality in contemporary America.* New York: World.

Strauss, R. H. (1991). Spittin' image: Breaking the sports–tobacco connection. *The Physician and Sportsmedicine, 19,* 46.

Striegel-Moore, R., McAvay, G., & Rodin, J. (1986). Psychological and behavioral correlates of feeling fat in women. *International Journal of Eating Disorders, 5,* 935–947.

U.S. Department of Health and Human Services. (1990). *The health benefits of smoking cessation: A report of the Surgeon General* (DHHS Publication No. CDC 90-8416). Washington, DC: U.S. Government Printing Office.

Weinstein, H. M., & Richman, A. (1984). The group treatment of bulimia. *Journal of American College Health, 32,* 208–215.

White, J. (1990). Smokeless tobacco snuffs out oral health. *The Physician and Sportsmedicine, 18,* 15–16.

Wolfe, R. N., Lennox, R. D., & Cutler, B. L. (1986). Getting along and getting ahead: Empirical support for a theory of protective and acquisitive self-presentation. *Journal of Personality and Social Psychology, 50,* 356–361.

Yoffe, E. (1990, November 26). Valley of the silicone dolls. *Newsweek,* p. 72.

Zabin, L. S., Stark. H. A., & Emerson, M. R. (1991). Reasons for delay in contraceptive clinic utilization. *Journal of Adolescent Health, 12,* 225–232.

# Self-Concept Change and Self-Presentation: The Looking Glass Self Is Also a Magnifying Glass

Dianne M. Tice • Case Western Reserve University

Studies 1 and 2 showed that identical behaviors had greater impact on the self-concept when performed publicly rather than privately. That is, the self-concept is more likely to change by internalizing public behavior than by internalizing behavior that is identical but lacks the interpersonal context. The self-concept change extends even to behavioral changes and occurs even when participants are unaware of being observed. In addition, those who are high in self-monitoring are more likely to internalize their behavior than those who are low in self-monitoring. Study 3 provided evidence about what components of a public situation affect the internalization of behavior. Choice about making the self-portrayal, drawing on episodes from one's own past rather than relying on a yoked script, and expecting future interaction with the audience all increased the internalization of a public behavior.

How do people change their views about themselves? Psychological theory and evidence have provided ample evidence that self-concepts resist change and maintain stability (e.g., Maracek & Mettee, 1972; McFarlin & Blascovich, 1981; Sullivan, 1953; Swann, 1983, 1987; Swann & Ely, 1984; Swann & Hill, 1982; Swann & Predmore, 1985; Swann & Read, 1981). Yet occasionally people do change; indeed, such change is considered desirable in some settings, including psychotherapy and assertiveness training.

Research by social psychologists has recently produced one paradigm for studying and analyzing self-concept change. In this paradigm, people are induced to behave in a particular way, and their subsequent self-ratings show that they come to regard themselves as having the traits implied by their overt behavior (e.g., Fazio, Effrein, & Falender, 1981; Gergen, 1965; Jones, Rhodewalt, Berglas, & Skelton, 1981; Kulik, Sledge, & Mahler, 1986; Rhodewalt & Agustsdottir, 1986; Schlenker & Trudeau, 1990; Tice, 1987). This tradition is partially an outgrowth of research on cognitive dissonance, which showed that people who are induced to make initially counterattitudinal opinions come to hold those opinions (e.g., Collins & Hoyt, 1972; Cooper & Fazio, 1984; Kiesler, 1971; Riess & Schlenker, 1977; Schlenker, 1982; Schlenker & Goldman, 1982; Schlenker & Schlenker, 1975; Wicklund & Brehm, 1976), especially if the person is publicly identified with the behavior (e.g., Baumeister & Tice, 1984; Carlsmith, Collins, & Helmreich, 1966; Helmreich & Collins, 1968; Paulhus, 1982).

Theories about the mechanism behind self-concept change have been focused on intrapsychic processes, particularly biased scanning (see especially Jones et al., 1981). Biased scanning is a self-perception process in which behavior calls the individual's attention to certain aspects or potentialities of the self, which are then highly accessible and therefore exert a powerful influence on subsequent self-assessment. In principle, this pattern of self-perception occurs inside the individual and does not involve other people, but the experiments designed to test the theory have invariably included the presence of other people to create public, interpersonal contexts. This discrepancy between private, intrapsychic processes in theory and public, interpersonal settings in empirical practice stimulated the present investigation. More precisely, the purpose of this article was to examine whether performing an action publicly has any impact on the self-concept over and above the effects of performing the same behavior privately. The core hypothesis was that interpersonal factors provide the motivating force that makes self-concept change work. This work is not intended to discredit biased scanning theory but rather to revise and extend it.

## Biased Scanning and Internalization

The term *internalization* can be used to refer to the act of bringing one's private concept of self into agreement with one's recent behavior (e.g., Festinger & Carlsmith, 1959). Internalization is thus a potentially important mechanism for self-concept change.

Research on internalization has been guided by theorizing about cognitive processes set in motion by one's own behavior. For example, Jones et al. (1981) and Rhodewalt and Agustsdottir (1986) found that induced behavior caused self-concepts to shift so as to reflect an internalization of the overt behavior, and they suggested two cognitive mechanisms for these self-concept shifts. First, cognitive dissonance (which arose from behaving in a manner inconsistent with one's beliefs about oneself) was reduced by changing the beliefs about the self. Second, in *biased scanning,* the induced behavior directs attention toward certain aspects of the self-concept, and so self-evaluations shift in the direction of the salient cognitions. For ex-

ample, inducing generous behavior may make the self's trait of generosity salient.

Likewise, Fazio et al. (1981) found that responding to situational constraints, such as answering loaded questions that pulled for introverted or extraverted responses, affected their subjects' self-concepts. When their subjects were subsequently asked to think of themselves on an introversion–extraversion dimension and were given a chance to behave in a manner consistent with their self-concepts, subjects' self-concepts came to include the traits implied by their publicly presented behavior. These researchers also explained their findings in cognitive terms, specifically self-perception. They suggested the loaded questions asked in the public interview made the subjects consider their own introverted or extraverted behavior in a biased manner. If the loaded questions pulled for extraverted responses, extraverted behavior was more salient to the subjects; whereas if the questions pulled for introverted responses, introverted behavior was more salient. As a result, subjects' self-concepts shifted toward agreement with their behavior.

Similarly, Markus and Kunda (1986) induced subjects to label themselves as very unique or very similar to others; afterward, subjects' self-concepts were subtly affected by the label. Like Jones et al. (1981) and Fazio et al. (1981), Markus and Kunda provided a cognitive explanation, asserting that these effects "resulted from a change in the accessibility of particular self-conceptions" as a result of the prior social interaction (p. 865).

Thus, researchers have generally explained evidence of internalization in terms of accessibility or salience of information to the self. Internalization was interpreted as occurring because subjects focused their attention on instances of their past behavior that supported their self-presentation. For example, an individual who just presented himself or herself positively to an audience was described as having more positive than negative information about the self immediately accessible in memory (Jones et al., 1981). A person who was induced to respond to loaded questions in an introverted manner was described as having more instances of past introverted behavior available to be incorporated into the working self-concept (Fazio et al., 1981). Given the weight of the evidence just described, there appears to be some support for the assertion that biased scanning leads to self-concept shifts. However, a full explanation may involve further complexities beyond these purely cognitive analyses. Salience and accessibility may be responsive to interpersonal cues.

## Self-Presentation and Social Reality

Although the phenomenon of the self-concept shift has often been explained in terms of intrapsychic changes (e.g., in accessibility), the experimental procedures eliciting self-concept change have typically involved interpersonal events. Indeed, most studies demonstrating internalization have used public self-presentations or social interactions to instigate the self-concept shift, even though the biased scanning theories seemingly would operate just as well on private behavior. The importance of an interpersonal context was not specified in these versions of the biased scanning model of self-concept change, but if the empirical findings were indeed dependent on that context, then the biased scanning model would need to be extended to encompass the role of interpersonal factors. The present investigation was specifically concerned with establishing whether interpersonal factors do indeed play an important role in self-concept change.

To study interpersonal factors, I relied heavily on the subjective distinction between public and private behavior. Public behavior is known to other people, and in fact the performing individual knows or expects that his or her behavior will be both known to others and linked by them to his or her identity. Private behavior can be defined as behavior that is exempt from those criteria; thus, it is behavior that is not known to others or, if it is known, cannot be linked to the individual's identity. Anonymous or confidential acts are prototypes of private behavior. To be sure, in a laboratory setting, no behavior is truly private (as Tetlock & Manstead, 1985, argued), because the subject may think that it will potentially be observed by others, as it usually is. However, it is possible to convince subjects that their behavior will be effectively anonymous or untraceable to their identities, such as (in the present case) by having subjects furnish anonymous responses and put them in sealed envelopes. In such cases of private behavior, interpersonal motivations, such as to conform to others' expectations or to make a good impres-

sion, become irrelevant. [. . .] I shall attempt to examine the effects of self-presentation on the self-concept by testing the hypothesis that the publicness of one's actions can increase the impact of behavior on the self-concept.

Research has suggested that public events can have more impact on self-evaluations than private events. For example, Baumeister and Tice (1984) found that subjects in a cognitive dissonance paradigm who had publicly performed the counterattitudinal behavior internalized the presented attitude to a greater degree than subjects whose presentations were private. Baumeister and Jones (1978) found that public evaluations had greater impact on the self-concept (in the domain of the evaluation) than did private evaluations, and Greenberg and Pyszczynski (1985) found this to be true even when the self-regard measures were considered to be private (although both of these studies were concerned with the effects of evaluations on the self-concept, rather than self-concept changes resulting from internalization of behavior as in the present study). If public behavior does have a greater impact on the self-concept than private behavior, then the internalization of a behavior may be more effective and powerful if the behavior is public than if it is private.

Social interactions provide additional impact that may supplement the internalization that occurs as a result of biased scanning. In keeping with a long tradition (e.g., Cooley, 1902; James, 1890; Mead, 1934), most researchers of the self acknowledge the importance of social interaction in constructing and modifying the self-concept (e.g., Baumeister, 1982, 1986; Gollwitzer, 1986; Rhodewalt, 1986; Schlenker, 1986; Wicklund & Gollwitzer, 1982). Because the self is publicly constructed and exists in relation to others, public events should have greater impact on the self-concept than private events. Public behavior implicates the self more than private behavior: Private behavior can be canceled, ignored, or forgotten, but public behavior cannot, because other people know about it. Public behavior may be more carefully monitored and processed than private behavior, resulting in greater internalization.

Hence, in the studies that follow, greater internalization was predicted after public acts than after private acts. If public behavior does indeed produce greater self-concept changes than private behavior, several possible mechanisms can be suggested. At one extreme, one might suggest that the internalization effects are superficial or insincere responses to social situations, or are the result of some labeling process by which the person simply applies a verbal label to the self and continues to use it later. Such effects would presumably be found mainly on verbal measures rather than on behavioral ones. On the other hand, if public events are experienced and regarded as being more important than private ones, internalization may be greater in public than in private. Public events may simply increase the power of the mechanisms of biased scanning and altered accessibility.

One could conceivably make the opposite prediction, namely that private behavior would have more impact than public behavior. Public behavior, after all, is elicited partly by external, situational demands, and so a thoughtful person might discount it (see Kelley, 1971, on discounting) and regard private behavior as more truly diagnostic of inner traits. My own analysis, however, would emphasize subjective importance rather than diagnosticity, and there seems to be little doubt but that public behavior is subjectively more important than private behavior. Issues of reputation, accountability and social relationships make it imperative that people keep track of how their actions are perceived by others, whereas private behavior does not carry that additional weight. Moreover, in public situations people may be attending to other people, leaving fewer cognitive resources available for analyzing the attributional implications of their own actions (Baumeister, Hutton, & Tice, 1989), and so they may fail to discount their own actions as being externally manded. Hence, it seemed likely that the increased subjective importance of public behavior would outweigh the attributional advantages of private behavior and result in the greater degree of internalization.

Study 1 sought to verify that self-concept change is greater after public than after private behavior. Study 2 replicated the findings of Study 1 using a different self-concept dimension (i.e., a different trait) and also sought to determine whether the impact is limited to transient shifts in verbal self-ratings or is reflected in behavior as well. Study 3 sought to determine whether some components of a public situation, such as expectation of future interaction, self-referenced (vs. yoked) presentation, and choice influenced the internalization of behavior.

## Study 1: Publicness and Internalization

The purpose of Study 1 was to establish that public circumstances increase internalization and self-concept change following from a person's behavior. To do this, it was necessary to elicit identical behaviors in public and private settings and measure the degree of internalization of the behavior.

Individuals were asked to portray themselves as either emotionally stable or as emotionally responsive. Control groups were added that requested that participants portray themselves in a manner that was irrelevant to the subsequent dependent variable. Participants were asked to portray themselves in the requested manner either publicly to another person who could identify them, or (relatively) privately and anonymously. To ensure that behavior was identical in both public and private conditions, participants' self-portrayals were rated for extensiveness of self-presentation. If no differences emerged between public and private groups on extensiveness of presentation ratings, then the assumption can be made that self-presentations were not more detailed or extensive in public than in private (or vice versa).

An interaction between publicness and self-presentation was predicted for the main dependent variables, in which participants in the public condition would internalize their behavior to a greater extent than participants in the private condition. Participants in the public conditions were expected to rate themselves as being more similar to their previous presentations than participants in the private conditions.

### Method

PARTICIPANTS AND DESIGN

Ninety introductory psychology students volunteered to participate. (Four additional participants were excluded because of equipment failure or other failure to complete the procedure.) The 57 women and 33 men were distributed approximately equally across the four conditions. The experiment consisted of a 2 (public vs. private) × 3 (emotionally stable self-portrayal vs. emotionally responsive self-portrayal vs. irrelevant self-portrayal) design.

## THE COVER STORY AND OVERVIEW

Participants were told that the study involved the detection of personality traits in others' self-descriptions, and participants were requested to serve as stimulus persons for judgments made by other students. Participants were told that graduate students in training for degrees in clinical psychology would view participants' self-portrayals to test whether they could detect which participants really possessed the trait they claimed to possess. Participants were asked to portray themselves as possessing a given personality trait for the purposes of the study, regardless of whether they actually possessed that trait. One third of the participants were instructed to portray themselves as having high emotional stability and one third were instructed to portray themselves as having high emotional responsiveness to situations. The remaining one third of participants served as a control group and portrayed themselves in a manner irrelevant to the subsequently assessed trait (they portrayed themselves as exceptionally athletic). Half of the participants in each group performed the behavior in a highly identifiable, public manner, whereas the other half of the participants in each group performed the behavior under relatively anonymous conditions. After portrayal of the behavior, participants were asked to rate their "true selves" on emotional stability–responsiveness dimensions.

In all three self-portrayal descriptions (emotionally responsive, emotionally stable, and athletic), the trait the participant was asked to portray was described positively. Participants in the emotionally responsive conditions were asked to present themselves as the type of person who reacts to situations with fairly strong (although appropriate) emotional responses and as someone who is responsive to the different aspects of different situations and reacts with appropriate emotional responses—not as someone who is depressed all the time or angry all the time or optimistic all the time, but rather as someone who responds distinctly and differently to different emotion-producing situations. Participants in the emotionally stable conditions were asked to present themselves as the type of person who maintains a degree of emotional stability in the face of the ups and downs of everyday life, and does not experience extremely intense moods or wild emotional fluctuations (as opposed to a highly moody person with intense and unpredictable emotional responses). Participants in the athletic conditions were asked to present themselves as the type of person who enjoys participating in athletic events and activities and often does so. Participants were asked to draw on examples of their own past behavior in answering the questions for the self-portrayal. They were instructed that, rather than lying or making up responses to the questions, they should focus their responses to the questions on selected examples from their past behavior that supported the portrayal they were trying to make (even if those few examples were not representative of their true nature).

## PROCEDURE

Participants came to the laboratory individually, were given a detailed description of the cover story, and were told they could choose not to participate if they felt they were completely unable to portray themselves in the prescribed manner (participants were either asked to portray themselves as emotionally stable, as emotionally responsive, or, in the control condition, as athletic). [. . .] All participants chose to continue in the experiment (perhaps because the traits they were asked to portray were all described as positive characteristics, all participants may have felt that they had some instances of the trait in their backgrounds to draw on for the self-portrayal).

Participants were given a list of questions and were told that their opportunity for self-portrayal would consist of providing answers to those questions. The questions asked about past relationships with same-sex and opposite-sex friends, family plans, extracurricular activities, and the most important thing learned in college. They were then asked to sign a consent form agreeing to allow their responses to the questions to be tape recorded for future analysis. All participants agreed to the recording of their responses. They were told they would have a few minutes to look over the questions and compose their responses on the basis of incidents from their past.

All participants were shown into a room with a one-way mirror. For participants in the public condition, the experimenter indicated that the graduate student would be interviewing the participant from the room behind the mirror. The experimenter

what if not (+)

indicated that the graduate student was already in the room and thus could see the participant. She told the participant to wave to the graduate student (so that the participant would feel highly visually identifiable) before she pulled the curtain closed. She then pulled the curtain closed completely so that the participant would not be subject to the self-focusing effects of the mirror during the interview and self-portrayal.[1] For participants in the private condition, the experimenter indicated that, although the room contained a one-way mirror, participants would not be observed while they responded to the questions. The experimenter emphasized that participants would remain anonymous and insisted on drawing the curtain to assure participants that they had complete confidentiality. After drawing the participant's attention and gaze to the mirror (to equal any mirror-induced self-focusing effects of the public condition), the experimenter closed the curtain completely.

Participants were told that they would be answering questions over an intercom system. The experimenter demonstrated how to operate the intercom. Participants in the public condition were told that when the tone sounded, they were to identify themselves to the graduate student. They were instructed to provide their names, ages, majors, hometowns, and dormitories to the graduate assistant. They were told that this information helped the graduate student "get to know them better" before beginning the interview. They were told that the graduate student would hear their responses; their responses would also be tape recorded for future coding. Participants in the private condition were told that, because of the personal nature of the questions, it was essential that they avoid any identifying information in their self-portrayals. They were told that when the tone sounded, they were to identify themselves only by providing their subject number, age, and gender. Participants in the private condition were led to believe that the graduate student who would evaluate their responses to the questions would do so at a different time by listening to the tape recording of their responses. All participants were told that only the graduate student who was being evaluated would listen to the participant's responses; in particular,

the experimenter would not listen to their responses. This was done to help reduce the desire on the part of the participants to appear consistent to the experimenter. They were instructed to push a button signaling the experimenter when they finished responding.

After responding to the five interview questions over the intercom system, all participants were told that the experimenter wanted them to rate themselves on a couple of questionnaires so that the experimenter would have a measure of their "true" personalities to compare with the graduate student's ratings. At this point, participants completed a single-item rating of their own level of emotional responsiveness–stability (the main dependent measure). Participants rated themselves in response to the following: "Thank you very much for your cooperation and for helping us by presenting yourself as the type of person with [either high emotional responsiveness or high emotional stability]. In order for us to best understand our data, it would also be helpful to us to know how emotionally [responsive–stable] you really are, as that may have affected your ability to portray a person with high emotional [responsiveness–stability]. On a scale of 1–25, how would you rate your own degree of emotional [responsiveness–stability]? Please circle the X that best represents your self-rating (your own beliefs about your true emotional [responsiveness–stability])." Endpoints were labeled *highly emotionally stable (unresponsive)* and *highly emotionally responsive (unstable)*. Participants in the control condition were thanked for their presentations and were requested to fill out the self-rating forms to provide the experimenter with a measure of their personalities. [. . .]

All self-ratings were done in private; participants did not put their names on the measures. (Measures were identified only by subject number.) Ratings were made privately to reduce the participants' desires to appear consistent in front of the experimenter, which might be especially salient if they were in the public condition. Subsequent to filling out the emotion questionnaires, participants completed a postexperimental manipulation check questionnaire in which they responded to the probe "To what extent do you think your presentation in this experiment is publicly identifiable? Do you think anyone might recognize you or know what you said during your presentation (including the graduate student interviewer)?" on a 5-point scale with endpoints labeled

---

[1]Mirrors have been commonly used to cause a state of self-focused attention; see Duval and Wicklund (1972), and Carver and Scheier (1981).

*highly publicly identifiable* (I) and *not at all publicly identifiable* (5).

Participants were then carefully debriefed using a process debriefing to eliminate any lasting effects of experimental manipulations on the self-concepts of the participants. The initial phases of the debriefing included describing all conditions and hypotheses of the study and explaining the effects that the independent variables were expected to have on participants' self-images. The process debriefing consisted of asking participants to remember three times when they had behaved in a manner opposite to the manner they had portrayed in the experiment and emphasized that behavior and self-ratings in the laboratory did not reflect the true state of the participants' personality. After further discussion of the effects of the manipulations on the participants' self-images, the experimenter explained the concept of perseverance (Ross, Lepper, & Hubbard, 1975) and discussed how the perseverance of the manipulations could further affect participants' self-images.

## Results

### MANIPULATION CHECK

A postexperimental questionnaire confirmed that participants in the public condition were significantly more likely than participants in the private condition to believe that their behavior (their self-portrayal) could be publicly identified by others, $F(1, 89) = 160.58, p < .001$.

### MAIN ANALYSES: SELF-RATINGS

The main dependent measure was the single item asking participants to rate their level of emotional stability–responsiveness. The data for overall self-ratings of emotional stability–responsiveness are in Table 11.1. A 2 (public vs. private) × 3 (emotionally stable self-portrayal vs. emotionally responsive self-portrayal vs. irrelevant self-portrayal) analysis of variance (ANOVA) revealed a main effect for valence of self-portrayal, indicating that self-reports were significantly affected by self-portrayal, $F(2, 84) = 28.14, p < .001$. Thus, regardless of whether the participants were in the public or private condition, those who described themselves as emotionally stable later rated their true selves as more emotionally stable than those who described themselves as emotionally respon-

**TABLE 11.1.** Mean Self-Ratings of Emotional Responsiveness or Stability and of Emotional Intensity (AIM): Study 1

| Valence of self-protrayal | Public condition | | Private condition | |
|---|---|---|---|---|
| | M | SD | M | SD |
| Emotionally stable | | | | |
| Main self-rating | 6.9 | 2.6 | 10.1 | 3.7 |
| Emotionally responsive | | | | |
| Main self-rating | 19.1 | 4.11 | 4.9 | 4.3 |
| Control | | | | |
| Main self-rating | 12.3 | 5.5 | 3.3 | 5.4 |

*Note.* Higher numbers reflect more emotionally responsive self-ratings. For each cell, $n = 15$.

sive. This main effect was modified by a significant interaction between valence of self-portrayal and publicness of portrayal, $F(2, 84) = 5.65, p < .01$. Thus, participants who portrayed themselves under public conditions rated themselves as being more similar to the presented behavior than participants who portrayed themselves under less identifiable conditions. In other words, there was more internalization of the behavior in the public condition than in the private condition. In the public conditions, all planned comparisons were significant. Participants who had publicly described themselves as emotionally responsive rated themselves as actually more emotionally responsive ($M = 19.1$) than participants who had privately described themselves as emotionally responsive ($M = 14.9$), $t(28) = 2.73, p < .02$. Participants who had publicly described themselves as emotionally stable rated themselves as actually more stable ($M = 6.9$) than participants who had privately described themselves as emotionally stable ($M = 10.1$, where higher numbers represent lower stability), $t(28) = 2.74, p < .02$.

Planned comparisons between the experimental and control groups also supported the conclusion that public self-portrayals had greater impact on self-ratings than private self-portrayals. Participants who publicly portrayed themselves as emotionally responsive rated themselves as actually being more emotionally responsive ($M = 19.1$) than participants in the control group who had publicly portrayed themselves as athletic ($M = 12.3$), $t(28) = 3.81, p < .001$. Participants who publicly portrayed themselves as emotionally stable rated themselves as actually being more emotionally stable ($M = 6.9$) than participants in the control group who had publicly portrayed themselves as athletic ($M = 12.3$, where higher scores indicate lower stability), $t(28) = 3.42$, $p < .01$. Thus, in the public conditions there were significant differences between the experimental and control groups in the emotional stability or responsiveness ratings.

In the private conditions, however, no significant differences were found between either the emotionally responsive portrayers ($M = 14.9$) and the private control group ($M = 13.3$, $t < 1$, ns) or between the emotionally stable portrayers ($M = 10.1$) and the private control group ($M = 13.3$, $t = 1.94$, ns). In other words, the emotional responsiveness self-ratings of participants who privately described themselves as emotionally responsive were no different from the emotional responsiveness self-ratings of participants in the control group. Likewise, the emotional stability self-ratings of participants who privately described themselves as emotionally stable were no different from the emotional stability self-ratings of participants in the control group.

Although there were no differences between either of the private experimental groups and the private control group as described above, a significant difference emerged if the two private experimental groups were compared with each other. Participants who privately described themselves as emotionally responsive were more likely to rate themselves as emotionally responsive ($M = 14.9$) than were participants who privately described themselves as emotionally stable ($M = 10.1$), $t(28) = 3.28$, $p < .01$. Thus, even in the private condition there was some support for internalization of behavior. [. . .]

## RATINGS OF INTERVIEW RESPONSES

If participants in the public conditions gave more detailed or extensive self-portrayals than participants in the private conditions, that could result in the findings that internalization was greater in public than in private. To test this hypothesis, ratings of each participant's responses to the interview questions (the requested self-portrayal) were coded on a scale of 1–10 for the extensiveness of emotional stability–responsiveness. The rater was blind to the experimental condition of the participant. If participants in the public conditions gave more detailed or extensive self-portrayals (presentations) than participants in the private conditions,

then there should be significant differences in the ratings made of the presentations.

The data for the ratings of participants' portrayals of emotional stability and responsiveness are reported below. A highly significant main effect for valence of self-portrayal (emotionally responsive vs. stable) was found, $F(1, 56) = 178$, $p < .001$, suggesting that participants in the emotionally responsive portrayal conditions presented themselves as much more emotionally responsive than participants in the emotionally stable portrayal conditions. In other words, participants portrayed themselves in a manner consistent with the experimental request. Participants who had been asked to portray themselves as emotionally responsive did so and participants who had been asked to portray themselves as emotionally stable did so. No main effect for publicness or interaction between publicness and valence of self-portrayal was found (both $F$s $< 1$, ns), suggesting that participants' self-portrayals did not differ depending on whether they were in the public or private condition. The ratings of participants portraying themselves as emotionally responsive in the public condition ($M = 7.60$) did not differ from the ratings of participants portraying themselves as emotionally responsive in the private condition ($M = 7.53$), $t(28) < 1$, ns. Likewise, the ratings of participants portraying themselves as emotionally stable in the public condition ($M = 2.53$) did not differ from the ratings of participants portraying themselves as emotionally stable in the private condition ($M = 2.27$), $t(28) < 1$, ns.

Apparently, the self-portrayals of participants portraying themselves publicly did not differ from the self-portrayals of participants portraying themselves privately (in fact, the means were nearly identical; the nonsignificant trend is in the opposite direction). Thus, the difference in self-ratings subsequent to the self-portrayals cannot be accounted for by the explanation that participants in the public conditions gave more detailed or extensive self-portrayals than participants in the private conditions. No main effects or interactions involving gender of participant were significant (all $F$s $< 1$, ns).

## Discussion

Portraying a role in front of others elicited greater internalization of the behavior than portraying a role in more anonymous settings. Despite all participants drawing on past experiences of their own behavior in answering the questions, participants who portrayed themselves to another in a highly identified, public manner showed more internalization than participants who portrayed themselves anonymonsly. There was some evidence of internalization in the private condition on the single-item measure, but the interaction reflected significantly greater internalization in the public conditions.

Internalization of behavior was measured only by self-report measures in Study 1, however. After portraying themselves in the desired manner either publicly or privately, participants were asked to rate their "true selves" for the experimenter. It is possible that the effects found in Study 1 were simply a result of verbal cues or demand characteristics and do not represent any real self-concept change. Perhaps participants were simply saying that they were emotionally stable (or responsive) without really regarding themselves as stable. Behavioral evidence would be necessary to show that the apparent shifts in self-concept found in Study 1 went beyond verbal cues. If self-concepts really changed, then trait-linked behaviors should change as well. To address this issue, in Study 2, I measured internalization of behavior by both self-report measures and unobtrusive behavioral measures of which the participants were unaware.

## Study 2: Internalization and Behavior

Study 2 was a replication and extension of Study 1. To increase the generalizability of the findings, I used a different self-concept dimension: Individuals were asked to portray themselves as either introverted or extraverted (rather than as emotionally stable vs. responsive as in Study 1). Participants were asked to portray themselves in the requested manner either publicly to another person who could identify them, or (relatively) privately and anonymously. Along with self-report variables assessing internalization of behavior as in Study 1, behavioral dependent variables were added to the design of Study 2. Participants were put in an unstructured situation in which they had the opportunity to act in either an introverted fashion or an extraverted fashion (as in Fazio et al., 1981). As in Study 1, an interaction between publicness and valence of self-portrayal was predicted, in which participants in the public condition would internalize their behavior to a greater extent than participants in the private condition.

In addition, although group means in Study 1 showed that in general, participants, especially those in the public conditions, were likely to internalize their behavior, an examination of the raw data showed that this effect was much stronger for some participants in each cell than for others. Snyder has shown that the concept of self-monitoring is relevant to individual differences in sensitivity to audiences (e.g., Snyder, 1974; Snyder & Gangestad, 1986); therefore, individual differences in self-monitoring were measured in Study 2 in an effort to determine which participants were most likely to internalize their behavior within each group. Self-monitoring is a personality construct designed to differentiate between individuals who "are thought to regulate their expressive self-presentation for the sake of desired appearances, and thus be highly responsive to social and interpersonal cues of situationally appropriate performances" and those who "are thought to lack the ability or the motivation to so regulate their expressive self-presentations" (Snyder & Gangestad, 1986, p. 125). High self-monitors are thought to process situational cues and events more carefully and to be more responsive to those cues. It was predicted that self-monitoring would moderate the internalization effect. High self-monitors might internalize more because they monitor their own performance more closely than low self-monitors and therefore are more likely to be "taken in" by their own performance. Alternatively, low self-monitors might internalize more because high self-monitors, in paying more attention to the situational cues in the experiment, would be more likely to recognize the situational constraints on their behavior.

### Method

#### PARTICIPANTS AND DESIGN

Eighty introductory psychology students volunteered to participate. (Three additional participants were not tested because they were friends of the confederates or because of equipment failure.) The 36 women and 44 men were distributed approximately equally across the four conditions. The design consisted of a 2 (public vs. private) × 2 (introverted self-portrayal vs. extraverted self-portrayal) × 2 (high vs. low self-monitor) ANOVA.

## PROCEDURE

The cover story and procedure are similar to those used in Study 1, except that in Study 2 participants were asked to portray themselves as either introverted or extraverted instead of as emotionally stable or responsive as in Study 1. In addition, participants rated themselves on the Self-Monitoring Scale (Snyder, 1974) in a large group pretesting session at the beginning of the semester before attending the laboratory session. Participants came to the laboratory individually and were given a detailed explanation of the same cover story used in Study 1 (in which they were asked to portray themselves in a given way as a stimulus person to be rated by a clinical graduate student). Participants were asked to portray themselves as possessing a given personality trait for the purposes of the study, whether or not they actually possessed that trait. One half of the participants were asked to portray themselves as introverts, and the other half of the participants were asked to portray themselves as extraverts in response to the same set of interview questions used in Study 1. The five questions were general enough to allow both introvert versus extravert responses in Study 2 as well as emotionally responsive versus emotionally stable responses in Study 1. Participants were given a brief definition of the term (either *introvert* or *extravert*) that was specifically designed to create a positive impression of the trait they were to portray. Participants in the extravert-portrayal condition were asked to portray themselves as extraverted, outgoing, socially skilled, a "people person," eager to tackle new situations and meet new people, able to handle leadership, and enthusiastic about being with people. Participants in the introvert-portrayal condition were asked to portray themselves as introverted, shy, thoughtful, sensitive, and quiet, and not pushy, bossy, or demanding of attention. Participants were told that they could choose not to participate if they felt they were completely unable to portray themselves in the prescribed manner; all participants chose to continue in the experiment. (As in Study 1, this may have been because the trait they were asked to portray was always described as a positive characteristic.)

The public versus private manipulation was manipulated in exactly the same manner as in Study 1 (see Study 1 for a more complete description). For participants in the public condition, the experimenter indicated that the graduate student was in the next room behind the mirror, and participants were asked to identify themselves in some detail into the intercom–tape recorder. For participants in the private condition, the experimenter emphasized that participants must remain anonymous.

After taking a few minutes to prepare their responses, participants responded to the five interview questions over the intercom system. All participants were then told that the experimenter wanted them to rate themselves on a questionnaire so that she would have a measure of their "true" personalities to compare with the graduate student's ratings. At this point participants completed the self-rating questionnaire used by Fazio et al. (1981), which consisted of 10 trait terms. Participants were requested to rate their "true" selves on the ten 11-point scales (rather than the 7-point scales used by Fazio et al., 1981) with instructions similar to those given for Study 1. All self-ratings were done privately; participants did not put their names (only their subject numbers) on the measures.

When participants had completed the self-rating form, the experimenter asked them to seal it in an envelope and put the envelope in a box entitled "Self-Rating Forms." Thus, participants were assured the confidentiality of their self-ratings. After they had deposited their forms, the experimenter told participants that she needed to get one more short form for them to fill out and asked them to wait in the waiting room until she returned with the form. The experimenter checked in the waiting room and then asked the participants to bring the chair they were sitting on along with them to the waiting room, because "for some reason all the chairs but one were taken out of this room, and there is a student waiting for a different study sitting in the one chair that is in the waiting room." The confederate was already seated in the chair in the far corner of the waiting room and was reading a book; participants brought their chairs in and the distance between the participant's chair and the confederate's chair was later recorded. Male participants were paired with the male confederate and female participants were paired with the female confederate. All participants were left alone with the confederate for exactly 3 minutes; all conversation between participants and the confederates was tape recorded and subsequently timed by the confederates. Both confederates were instructed and trained to be nonresponsive to conversation attempted by participants (without being blatantly rude). As in the Fazio et al., (1981), study, extraverted behavior was operationalized as speaking to and sitting relatively close to the confederate; introverted behavior was operationalized as sitting far from and not speaking to the confederate.

After 3 minutes had passed, the experimenter returned with the manipulation check sheet and escorted the participant back to the experimental room. The manipulation check consisted of a 5-point scale asking participants to rate the degree of public identifiability versus anonymity of their responses to the interview questions. Participants were subsequently debriefed with an extensive process debriefing similar to that described in Study 1.

## Results

### MANIPULATION CHECK

A postexperimental questionnaire confirmed that participants in the public condition were significantly more likely than participants in the private condition to believe that their behavior (their self-portrayal) could be publicly identified by others, $F(1, 79) = 1807.2, p < .0001$.

### SELF-RATING MEASURE

The main self-rating measure was the 10-item scale used by Fazio et al. (1981), in which participants rated themselves on 11-point bipolar scales on the following dimensions: *talkative–quiet, unsociable–sociable, friendly–unfriendly, poised–awkward, extroverted–introverted, enthusiastic–apathetic, outgoing–shy, energetic–relaxed, warm–cold,* and *confident–unconfident.* The data for the self-ratings are in Table 11.2. A $2 \times 2 \times 2$ ANOVA revealed a main effect for valence of self-portrayal, indicating that self-reports were significantly affected by self-portrayal, $F(1, 72) = 24.20$, $p < .001$. Thus, across both public and private conditions, those who described themselves as introverted later rated their true selves as more introverted than those who described themselves as extraverted. This main effect was modified by two

significant interactions. Replicating the results of Study 1, an interaction between publicness and valence of self-portrayal was also revealed, in which participants answering the interview questions publicly internalized their behavior to a greater extent than did participants answering the questions in a relatively private and anonymous fashion, $F(1, 72) = 9.46, p < .01$.

Planned comparisons between the introvert-portrayal group and extravert-portrayal group also supported the conclusion that public self-portrayal had greater impact on self-ratings than private self-portrayal. Participants who publicly portrayed themselves as extraverted rated themselves as actually being more extraverted ($M = 77.6$) than participants who had publicly portrayed themselves as introverts ($M = 50.75$), $F(38) = 23.91, p < .001$. Thus, in the public conditions there were significant differences between the self-ratings of extraversion made by participants who had portrayed themselves as introverts compared with those who had portrayed themselves as extraverts.

In the private conditions, however, no significant differences were found between the introvert-portrayal group ($M = 61.35$) and the extravert-portrayal group ($M = 67.55$), $F = 2.04$, *ns.* In other words, the extraversion self-ratings of participants who privately described themselves as extraverted were no different from the extraversion self-ratings of participants who privately described themselves as introverted. Thus, there was evidence for

**TABLE 11.2. Mean Self-Rating of Extraversion and Mean Distance (in Centimeters) Participants Sat From the Conferate: Study 2**

| Valence of self-portrayal | Public condition | | Private condition | |
|---|---|---|---|---|
| | *M* | *SD* | *M* | *SD* |
| Introverted | | | | |
|   Self-rating of extraversion | 50.75 | 15.96 | 61.35 | 14.55 |
|   Distance from confederate | 168.85 | 29.55 | 158.75 | 20.94 |
| Extraverted | | | | |
|   Self-rating of extraversion | 77.60 | 18.67 | 67.55 | 12.87 |
|   Distance from confederate | 146.00 | 28.68 | 159.45 | 20.43 |

*Note.* Higher self-rating numbers reflect higher extraverted self-ratings, based on the scale used by Fazio, Effrein, and Falender (1981). For each cell, $n = 20$.

the internalization of behavior in the public but not in the private conditions.

An interaction between self-monitoring and valence of portrayal was revealed, in which high self-monitors internalized their behavior (portraying themselves as introverts or as extraverts) to a greater extent than did low self-monitors, $F(1, 72)$ = 7.47, $p < .01$. A three-way interaction among self-monitoring, publicness, and valence of self-portrayal did not attain traditional levels of statistical significance, $F(1, 72) = 2.76$, $p = .10$.

## BEHAVIORAL MEASURES

*Sitting distance.* As in the Fazio et al. (1981) study, extraverted behavior was operationalized as sitting relatively close to the confederate; introverted behavior was operationalized as sitting far from the confederate (under the assumption that shy or introverted people prefer to remain at a distance from strangers and highly social or extraverted people prefer to minimize the distance between themselves and others). After the participant had left the waiting room and was filling out the manipulation checks, the confederate measured the distance separating the two nearest legs of their respective chairs. The data for the sitting distance variable are in Table 11.2. A 2 × 2 × 2 ANOVA revealed a main effect for valence of self-portrayal, indicating that participants who had described themselves as introverted during the interview later sat farther from the confederate than those who had described themselves as extraverted, $F(1, 72)$ = 4.12, $p < .05$. This main effect was modified by two significant interactions. An interaction between self-monitoring and valence of self-portrayal was revealed, in which high self-monitors internalized their behavior (with those who had portrayed themselves as introverted in the interview sitting further from the confederate than those who had portrayed themselves as extraverts) to a greater extent than did low self-monitors, $F(1, 72) = 6.09$, $p < .05$. An interaction between publicness and valence of self-portrayal was also revealed, in which participants answering the interview questions publicly internalized their behavior to a greater extent than did participants answering the questions in a relatively private and anonymous fashion, $F(1, 72)$ = 4.65, $p < .05$. A three-way interaction between self-monitoring, publicness, and valence of self-portrayal attained only marginal levels of statistical significance, $F(1, 72) = 3.01$, $p = .0869$.

Planned comparisons between the public groups (comparing the introvert-portrayal group and extravert-portrayal group) also supported the conclusion that public self-descriptions had greater impact on the behavioral measures than private self-descriptions. Participants who publicly portrayed themselves as extraverted sat closer to the confederate ($M = 146.0$ cm) than participants who had publicly portrayed themselves as introverts ($M = 168.85$), $F(38) = 6.16$, $p < .02$.

In the private conditions, however, no significant differences were found between the introvert-portrayal group ($M = 158.75$) and extravert-portrayal group ($M = 159.45$), $F < 1$, *ns*. In other words, participants who had privately described themselves as extraverted were no more likely to sit near the confederate than were participants who privately described themselves as introverted. Thus, again, there was evidence for the internalization of behavior in the public but not in the private conditions.

*Speaking to confederate.* As in the Fazio et al. (1981) study, extraverted behavior was operationalized as speaking extensively to the confederate; introverted behavior was operationalized as not speaking to or speaking only briefly with the confederate (under the assumption that highly social or extraverted people prefer to chat or socialize with others whereas shy or introverted people may be less likely to make conversation with strangers). The proportions of participants in each condition who initiated conversation with the confederate were compared using arcsine transformation analysis (cf. Fazio et al., 1981; Langer & Abelson, 1972; collapsing across the self-monitoring variable). A significant interaction between publicness and valence of self-portrayal was revealed ($z = 3.35$, $p < .05$), suggesting that participants who had portrayed themselves publicly were more likely to have acted in accordance with their self-portrayals than were participants who had portrayed themselves more anonymously. Subsequent arcsine transformation analyses revealed that the difference between proportions of participants initiating conversations comparing participants who had portrayed themselves as introverts versus those who had portrayed themselves as extraverts was significant in the public conditions ($z = 1.927$, $p < .05$). In other words, participants who had publicly portrayed themselves as extraverts were more likely (65%) to initiate a conversation than were participants who had publicly portrayed themselves as introverts (35%). In the private conditions, however, there was no difference, and, in fact, the proportion of participants initiating a conversation was identical regardless of whether the participants had portrayed themselves as introverts (55%) or extraverts (55%, $z = 0$, $ns$). Thus, as in the measures reported above, participants were likely to act in accordance with their previous self portrayals if those self-portrayals were public, but not if those self-portrayals were relatively private and anonymous.

Further comparisons of proportions of participants speaking with the confederate using arcsine transformation analyses revealed that high self-monitors were likely to act in accordance with their previous self-portrayals if those self-portrayals were public (with participants who had portrayed themselves as extraverts being significantly more likely to speak than participants who had portrayed themselves as introverts, 30% vs. 70%; $z = 3.65$, $p < .05$), but not if their self-portrayals were private ($z = 0.45$, $ns$). Low self-monitors were not likely to act in accordance with either their public self-portrayals ($z = .90$, $ns$) or with their private self-portrayals ($z = 0$, $ns$).

The duration of speech was also measured, but the data had high variance and were highly skewed (47.5% of the participants never spoke to the confederate at all during the waiting room situation; skewedness = .68). Even after the data were transformed using the transformations recommended by Fazio et al. (1981), no significant effects were obtained.

## RATING OF SELF-PORTRAYALS

To evaluate the alternative, artifactual interpretation of the data suggesting that participants in the public conditions gave more extreme self-portrayals than participants in the private conditions, each participant's responses to the interview questions (the requested self-portrayal) were rated on a scale of 1–5 for the extremity of introversion or extraversion. A highly significant main effect for valence of self-portrayal (introversion vs. extraversion) was found, $F(1, 72) = 1,075.9$, $p < .001$, suggesting that participants in the introversion-portrayal conditions portrayed themselves as much more introverted than participants in the extraversion-portrayal conditions. In other words, participants portrayed themselves in a manner consistent with the experimental request, as in Study 1.

Participants who had been asked to portray themselves as introverted did so, and participants who had been asked to portray themselves as extraverted did so.

No main effect for publicness or interaction between publicness and valence of self-portrayal was found (both $F$s < 1, $ns$), suggesting that participants' self-portrayals did not differ depending on whether they were in the public or private condition. The presentations of participants portraying themselves publicly did not differ from the presentations of participants portraying themselves privately. Thus, the difference in self-ratings subsequent to the self-portrayals cannot be accounted for by the explanation that participants in the public conditions gave more extreme self-portrayals than participants in the private conditions.

No main effects or interactions for self-portrayal ratings involving self-monitoring were significant, although an interaction between self-monitoring and valence of self-portrayal did suggest a non-significant trend for high self-monitors' self-portrayals to be somewhat more extreme than low self-monitors' self-portrayals, $F(1, 72) = 2.80$, $p = .10$. Because the interaction failed to reach conventional levels of significance, however, insufficient evidence exists to conclude that the self-portrayals of high self-monitors differed conclusively from the self-portrayals of low self-monitors.

To examine the hypothesis that high self-monitors internalize their behavior more than low self-monitors, I computed correlations between extremity of initial behavior and subsequent self-ratings and behavior. The correlations between self-portrayal extremity ratings and subsequent behaviors were significant for high self-monitors, $r(38) = -.61$, $p < .001$, for self-ratings and $rs(38) = .45$, $p < .01$, for distance participants sat from confederate, but not for low self-monitors, $rs(38) = .22$ and $-.07$, respectively. This suggests that high self-monitors' self-portrayals significantly affected their subsequent behavior, but low self-monitors' self-ratings and behavior were not systematically related to their prior behavior.

## GENDER

The only gender effect uncovered by the analyses was a main effect for gender on the sitting distance variable. Male participants chose to sit significantly farther from the male confederate ($M = 163.0$) than female participants chose to sit from the female confederate ($M = 152.4$), $F(1, 64) = 4.62$, $p < .05$.

## Discussion

Study 2 replicated the self-report findings of Study 1 and supplemented the self-report measures with behavioral measures collected without the participants' awareness. An interaction between publicness and valence of self-portrayal was found: Consistent with the main finding of Study 1, public behavior led to more internalization than private behavior. On both self-report measures and behavioral measures, there was more self-concept change in the public condition than in the private condition. Subjects who were led to describe themselves publicly as extraverted later sat closer to the confederate and spoke to the confederate more than subjects who had been led to describe themselves as introverted. But similar self-descriptions given privately and anonymously had no effect on subsequent behavior.

Study 2 suggests that the internalization of behavior findings from Study 1 were not simply a superficial or deliberate repetition of verbal labels but rather a true alteration in self-concept that was strong enough to produce changes in behavior in a subsequent situation without the participant's awareness.

Study 2 also suggested that high self-monitors internalized their behavior to a greater extent than did low self-monitors. High self-monitors process situational cues and events more carefully and are more responsive to those cues; this suggests that self-observation and self-regulation (guided by situational and social cues) can contribute to the internalization of behavior. Participants who were more likely to monitor themselves, their actions, and their surroundings (i.e., high self-monitors) were more likely to act in accordance with their previously portrayed behavior than were low self-monitors. High self-monitors showed a significant relationship between the extremity of their self-portrayals and their subsequent behavior, with participants who gave more extreme self-portrayals showing more internalization than participants who gave less extreme presentations. Low self-monitors, on the other hand, demonstrated little relationship between their initial self-portrayals and their subsequent behavior.

It is somewhat ironic that high self-monitors internalized their behavior more than low self-monitors. High self-monitors are thought to regulate their expressive behavior for strategic impression management reasons, that is, to produce desired public appearances, but the high self-monitors seem as influenced by their own behaviors as they wanted their audience to be. High self-monitors are the behavioral chameleons, but perhaps their strategic public self-presentations are not just hypocritical staged acts. High self-monitor themselves seem to come to believe some of their own presentations.

Both Study 1 and Study 2 gave participants a high degree of choice about presenting themselves in the requested manner and asked participants to supply self-referenced anecdotes to support their presentations. Study 3 was an attempt to determine whether choice and self-referenced presentations affect participants' internalization of their public presentations.

## Study 3: Choice, Self-Reference, and Future Interaction

Study 3 investigated some of the process variables associated with the internalization of behavior. Studies 1 and 2 suggested that public behavior was internalized to a greater extent than private behavior; Study 3 attempted to determine some of the components of a public situation that might cause behavior to carry over into another situation and some of the limiting conditions for the internalization effect.

Self-presentational effects are often studied by examining the differences between public and private conditions as in Studies 1 and 2, but that is not the only method available for increasing our understanding of the process of self-presentation. By varying some of the situational factors present during self-presentation, we can better understand the components of the situation affecting self-presentations or their outcomes (see, for example, Baumeister et al., 1989).

Both Study 1 and Study 2 asked participants to draw on examples from their own past behavior to support their public presentations, and both gave participants a high degree of choice about whether they would present themselves in the requested fashion for the experiment. Both self-referencing and choice have been shown to affect internalization of behavior in past work under some conditions. Jones et al. (1981) found that when their subjects portrayed themselves in a self-enhancing manner, they raised their self-evaluations in the self-referencing condition (i.e., internalized their behavior) but not in the non-self-referencing condition; choice had no effect on self-evaluations. In contrast, when their subjects portrayed themselves in a self-deprecating manner, they lowered their self-evaluations in the high-choice condition but not in the low-choice condition; self-referencing had no effect on self-evaluations. The authors suggested that biased scanning was engaged after self-enhancement, whereas dissonance was produced by self-deprecation (see also Rhodewalt & Agustsdottir, 1986, for replication and extension of the Jones et al., 1981, findings).

The present study attempts to build on the Jones et al. (1981) and Rhodewalt and Agustsdottir (1986) findings and determine what variables affect the internalization of more evaluatively neutral traits. In everyday life, some self-presentations may entail portraying oneself extremely positively or extremely negatively, but many self-presentations may involve portraying the self in a less highly evaluative manner. If one portrays oneself in a relatively evaluatively neutral manner, perhaps both choice and self-referencing may affect the internalization process. This may be especially true of public behavior. In public, as compared with the privacy of one's own thoughts, one may be constrained from portraying oneself in an extreme manner (either extremely positively or extremely negatively, as in Jones et al., 1981), because others may doubt one's presentation, or because one may be forced to live up (or down) to one's claims. Thus, both choice and self-referencing may play a greater role in affecting the internalization of public behavior than of private behavior. In addition, public situations may contain pressures for truthfulness that are absent in private situations (see Baumeister & Ilko, 1991), because one's presentation could be challenged or one might be compelled to act consistently with one's presentation or other norms in public to a greater extent than in private.

In addition to choice and self-referencing, the expectation of future interaction may affect the internalization of behavior. Individuals might feel more committed to their behavior in a public situation than they do in a relatively private and anonymous situation because of the increased opportunity for future interaction with the audience of the public presentation. Portraying oneself publicly carries with it the risk of meeting the audience in the future and possibly disconfirming one's earlier self-portrayal; in other words, the expectation of future interaction contributes to the increased subjective importance of public behavior, leading to greater internalization. Hence, in Study 3, participants expecting future interaction with their audience were predicted to show more internalization than participants not expecting future interaction.

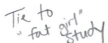

Tie to "fat girl" study

## Method

### PARTICIPANTS AND DESIGN

Eighty introductory psychology students volunteered to participate. The experiment consisted of a 2 (own responses vs. yoked responses) × 2 (expectancy of future interaction vs. no interaction) × 2 (high vs. low choice) design.

### PROCEDURE

The cover story and procedure are similar to those used in Study 2, except that in Study 3 all participants were asked to portray themselves as introverts in a public, highly identifiable manner (as in the public condition of Studies 1 and 2). Participants came to the laboratory individually and were given a detailed explanation of the same cover story used in Studies 1 and 2, in which they were asked to portray themselves in a given way as a stimulus person to be rated by a clinical graduate student. Participants were asked to portray themselves as introverts in response to the same set of questions used in the previous studies for the purposes of the experiment, regardless of whether they actually felt they were introverted. Participants were given a brief definition of the term *introvert* that was specifically designed to create a neutral, nonevaluative impression of the trait (unlike in Study 2, in which the definition was specifically designed to create a positive impression of the term). Introverted behavior was defined as being "shy, quiet . . . more likely to stand back and take everything in rather than trying to run everything or be a part of everything."

*Yoked versus self-referencing manipulation.* One half of the participants were instructed to draw on their own past experiences for examples of introversion to use in response to the five questions and were given exactly the same instructions as the participants in Studies 1 and 2, except that they were requested to write their answers down. The other half of the participants were yoked to the responses of the other group; that is, each participant in the yoked group was paired with a (same gender) participant in the own-experiences group and read the same responses that the self-referencing group participant had generated. Instructions to participants in the yoked conditions were similar to those reported by Jones et al. (1981, Experiment 3). Thus, participants in the self-referencing conditions and in the yoked conditions reported identical responses to the questions, but only for the self-referencing group were these responses likely to access self-information.

*Future interaction manipulation.* One half of the participants were led to expect that they would have a variety of future interactions with the graduate student who heard their self-portrayals. These participants were told that the graduate student was going to meet them afterward to talk about the experience of participating in psychology experiments and that this graduate student was also just beginning an assignment as the teaching assistant for their section of their psychology lecture class, so they would be seeing her on a regular basis until the end of the semester. The other half of the participants were led to believe that the graduate student who heard their self-portrayals was a student at another university and, although she would have a great deal of identifying information about them, they were not likely to ever see her or come into contact with her.

*High-choice versus low-choice manipulation.* One half of the participants were put in the same high-choice condition as participants in Studies 1 and 2, in which they were told that they could choose not to participate if they felt they were completely unable to portray themselves as introverts; as in Studies 1 and 2, all participants chose to continue in the experiment. The other half of the participants were told that although participants usually got to choose whether they wanted to make the presentation or not, enough people had chosen the other option, so the participants had no choice but to portray themselves as introverts. Thus, it was emphasized that participants usually had a choice but that this freedom was diminished for these participants.

After participants had responded to the interview questions over the intercom system, they were told that the experimenter wanted them to rate

themselves on a questionnaire so that she would have a measure of their "true" personalities to compare with the graduate student's ratings. At this point participants completed the self-rating questionnaire used in Study 2. All self-ratings were done in private; participants did not put their names (only their subject numbers) on the measure.

After making the self-ratings, the participants filled out a sheet of manipulation checks that consisted of three 5-point scales asking them to rate to what degree the responses to the interview questions represented experiences actually drawn from their own past, to what degree did they expect to meet the graduate students who heard their presentations, and how much choice did they feel they had about participating in the study as requested. Participants were subsequently debriefed with an extensive process debriefing similar to that described in Study 1.

## Results

### MANIPULATION CHECK

A postexperimental questionnaire confirmed that participants in the yoked conditions were significantly less likely than participants in the self-referencing conditions to rate their presentations as containing samples from their own life experiences, $F(1, 79) = 3,128, p < .0001$. Participants in the future-interaction conditions were significantly more likely than participants in the no-future-interaction conditions to report expecting to meet the graduate student who heard their presentations, $F(1, 79) = 12,482, p < .0001$. Participants in the high choice conditions were significantly more likely than participants in the low-choice conditions to report a high degree of choice regarding making the introverted presentation, $F(1, 79) = 460.2, p < .0001$.

### MAIN ANALYSIS: SELF-RATINGS

The main dependent measure was the 10-item scale used in Study 2. The data for the self-ratings are in Table 11.3. A $2 \times 2 \times 2$ ANOVA revealed three main effects and no interactions. A main effect for self-referencing suggested that participants who drew on their own past experiences to portray themselves as introverts to the audience were significantly more likely to internalize their behavior and rate themselves as introverts ($M = 55.5$) than were yoked participants who simply read someone else's experiences to the audience ($M = 65.7$), $F(1, 72) = 21.5$, $p < .001$. A main effect for future-interaction conditions suggested that participants who expected to meet the graduate student who had heard their introverted self-presentations were significantly more likely to internalize their behavior and rate themselves as introverts ($M = 56.9$) than were participants who were not led to expect to meet the graduate student ($M = 64.3$), $F(1, 72) = 11.4$, $p = .001$. A main effect for choice conditions suggested that participants who were led to believe that they had a high degree of choice about portraying themselves as introverts were significantly more likely to internalize their behavior and rate themselves as introverts ($M = 58.05$) than were participants who were led to believe that they had a low degree of choice about how they portrayed themselves ($M = 63.15$), $F(1, 72) = 5.42$, $p < .05$.

One additional question was whether the effects of the three independent variables are additive; that is, does the presence of expecting future interaction, self-referencing, and choice produce more internalization than any one of those factors in the absence of the others? This possibility was explored with a post hoc $t$ test comparing the cell that combined all three factors against the pooled mean of the three cells that each contained only one of the three factors (i.e., from Table 11.3, 49.0 against the pooled means 67.0, 64.8, and 61.5). This difference was significant, $t(72) = 4.30$, $p < .001$, supporting the additivity hypothesis.

## Discussion

Study 3 was an attempt to begin to deconstruct the public self-presentational situation to determine which components of the situation influenced the internalization of behavior. Results suggested that high choice as compared with low choice, self-referenced presentation as compared with non-self-referenced (yoked) presentation, and expectation of future interaction with the audience of one's self-presentation as compared with no expectation of future interaction all increased the internalization of the self-presentation,

Jones et al. (1981) found (in their third study) that choice affected a self-deprecating presentation but not a self-enhancing presentation, whereas self-referencing affected a self-enhancing presentation but not a self-deprecating presentation. When an evaluatively neutral trait is portrayed (as

**TABLE 11.3. Mean Self-Rating of Extraversion: Study 3**

| Future interaction | High choice | | Low choice | |
|---|---|---|---|---|
| | M | SD | M | SD |
| Self-referenced group | | | | |
| Expect future interaction | 49.0 | 9.7 | 54.6 | 10.2 |
| Expect no future interaction | 57.0 | 9.6 | 61.5 | 8.1 |
| Yoked group | | | | |
| Expect future interaction | 59.2 | 10.9 | 64.8 | 11.1 |
| Expect no future interaction | 67.0 | 10.0 | 71.7 | 8.3 |

*Note.* Lower numbers reflect greater internalization of behavior, based on scale used by Fazio et al. (1981). For each cell, $n = 10$.

in Study 3), both choice and self-referencing, as well as the expectancy of future interaction with the audience, can affect the internalization of the self-presentation.

Thus, Study 3 shows that the internalization of public behavior can be increased by several factors that all strengthen the link between one's public behavior and one's inner self. When self-presentation is based on searching one's own memory rather than just playing an assigned role, the behavior is internalized more strongly. Likewise, when the individual's free consent to engage in the self-presentation is made salient, the behavior is internalized more strongly. Last, when the audience to one's public behavior is someone with whom future interaction is expected, internalization again increases. These effects appear to be additive, insofar as their combination produced more internalization than any one of them alone. A proper theoretical understanding of self-concept change must therefore take the form of a continuum. That is, identical behaviors can be internalized to various degrees depending on several different, independent factors that raise or lower the impact of the interpersonal context.

## General Discussion

The results of these three studies attest to the high importance of public circumstances and interpersonal context for producing self-concept change. A pattern of significant interactions showed that identical behaviors produced consistently stronger impact on the self-concept when they had been performed publicly rather than privately. Public behaviors led to substantial shifts in self-descriptions and even to consistent behavioral change, found even on unobtrusive measures in subsequent situations. The internalization effects of the public conditions were robust, unlike the effects in the private conditions.

In fact, evidence of self-concept change in private conditions was weak and inconsistent, and one may question whether internalization occurs reliably under private circumstances. If only the private conditions in these studies had been tested, the present investigation would not have found sufficient evidence to assert that internalization occurs reliably at all. In the private condition of Study 1, one self-report measure found no effect, and the other measure found a difference between two opposite conditions, neither of which differed from the control group condition. In the private condition of Study 2, the self-report measure showed only a trend that was far from significant, and the behavioral measures failed to yield even a slight trend. In other words, out of five measures, only one found significant evidence of internalization in the private condition, whereas public circumstances produced significant effects on all five measures.

Moreover, Tetlock and Manstead (1985) have pointed out that private conditions in laboratory experiments are not truly private and may therefore contain some vestiges of interpersonal, self-presentational motivations. The vestiges of internalization could conceivably be linked to the vestiges of publicness in the private conditions. It therefore remains uncertain whether self-concept change caused by internalization of behavior can occur in the absence of an interpersonal context.

As noted in the introduction, previous theorizing about self-concept change has emphasized intrapsychic processing, most notably biased scanning. Biased scanning is indeed assumed to be the process responsible for the present effects, and some of my results are quite consistent with that assumption. Thus, the largest single effect found in Experiment 3 was for the self-reference manipulation, which is the one most directly relevant to biased scanning (because it entails generating answers by scanning one's own self-concept rather than giving someone else's answers).

The present results do, however, suggest that biased scanning theory needs to be extended to

assign an important role to interpersonal factors and context. To put it simply, biased scanning apparently occurs more powerfully, or is more effective at altering the self-concept, when one's behavior is known to others than when it is private and secret. Behavior is much more likely to be internalized, leading to self-concept change, if it is observed by others, as opposed to being anonymous or confidential. Self-observation alone is at best weak and at worst wholly inadequate for internalization; some degree of observation by others appears to be an important and powerful factor for producing internalization.

## Possible Causal Processes

Although this article is essentially concerned with demonstrating the effect of interpersonal processes rather than with elucidating cognitive processes, it is instructive to consider possible links between the interpersonal and the cognitive processes. It appears that both cognitive and interpersonal factors operate to produce self-concept change.

One simple explanation might be that public situations raise motivations to please others, and so the person casually says whatever will satisfy those who happen to be present. Thus, as one anonymous reviewer suggested, the results of Study 1 could have been obtained because the subject wanted to help the experimenter by providing useful, confirming data. This explanation is contradicted by the results of Experiment 2, however, which found that self-concept change extended even to behavioral changes with a different interaction partner and even when participants were unaware of being observed. It appears that the self-concept change produced in these studies was genuine, at least to the extent of being able to produce consistent behavior with a different interaction partner in a new setting.

A second explanation would hold that interpersonal concerns motivate a more thorough and hence more impactful job of biased scanning. In private, perhaps, it does not matter what the subject does, says, or thinks, and so people may respond in a careless or lazy fashion (see Tetlock, 1983). When one's public identity and reputation are implicated, however, one is more careful and thorough about preparing, analyzing, and executing one's actions. Thus, in the present research, subjects may have engaged in more extensive biased scanning in the public condition than in the private condition. If this explanation were correct, one might have expected subjects' answers to the stimulus questions to be longer, more detailed, or more polarized in the public circumstances. No such effect was found, but possibly these measures were not sensitive to subtle differences in scanning. Thus, this explanation is only weakly contradicted by the present results and deserves further study

A third explanation is that public circumstances magnified the impact of biased scanning. This one is similar to the second explanation, but it emphasizes the power of the scanning's result rather than the scanning itself. That is, perhaps people in private circumstances did the same amount of biased scanning as did the subjects in public circumstances, but the others' presence and awareness increased the salience of the results of the scanning. Metaphorically, people in the public condition may have felt as if someone were looking over their shoulder while they scanned their self-concepts. What they scanned may have been accentuated by the realization that it was to be seen not only in one's own mind but also by another person, and this increased salience may have intensified the material's impact on the self-concept.

This "magnified scanning" hypothesis is consistent with the general view that people carefully consider the information others have about them (e.g., Baumeister, 1982; Schlenker, 1980, 1986). After all, when one is privately scanning information about oneself, there is little reason to be deeply struck or surprised or impressed by anything one finds, because one is merely reviewing self-knowledge. When revealing information to another, however, one is constructing one's public image, because that information becomes part of how one will be perceived by that person. In a sense, the self-presenter is choosing from among all of his or her self-knowledge (which will all still be there later) to share some selected information with other people. What the self-presenter chooses will be the core and essence of how these people will later perceive the self-presenter. Thus, by virtue of the audience's relative lack of knowledge about the self-presenter, these few facts become magnified in importance, whereas they may not have stood out for any particular reason among the self-presenter's own great mass of self-knowledge.

Finally, public circumstances may impair rather than facilitate the processing of information about the self, thereby preserving bias from being rectified. In this view, people have a large mass of potentially contradictory information about themselves, including knowledge that in different situations they have behaved differently (e.g., Jones & Nisbett, 1971). In private, people may scan for particular information, but extensive scanning would also reveal contradictory memories. People can furnish the requested information, but they simultaneously recognize conflicting evidence, which prevents them from being swayed or biased by the requested information. In Study 2, for example, when asked questions designed to elicit introverted behavior, subjects in the private condition may have also recalled instances of extraverted behavior (which they did not verbalize), and so the net effect was unbiased (or debiased) scanning, which would explain why no self-concept change resulted. In public, however, people may have devoted some of their attention to the interactive and self-presentational demands of the situation. This reduction in available cognitive resources might conceivably have suppressed their capacity for finding contradictory information, whereas the dominant response of scanning for confirmatory instances went on unimpaired.

This explanation would be consistent with emerging evidence about how self-presentation consumes cognitive resources (Baumeister et al., 1989; Paulhus & Levitt, 1987) and how the expectation of future interaction channels attention into thinking about the other person (Devine, Sedikides, & Fuhrman, 1989). It would also be consistent with evidence that cognitive load (or "cognitive busyness") increases correspondence bias (Gilbert, Krull, & Pelham, 1988; Gilbert & Osborne, 1989; Gilbert, Pelham, & Krull, 1988). Gilbert and his colleagues have shown that under cognitive load, people tend to discount situational causes and overattribute behavior of other people to personality traits, and one could plausibly extend that argument to say that self-presentation produces cognitive load that results in overattribution of one's own behavior to one's own traits.

Like the second explanation, the cognitive load hypothesis predicts differences in how people responded to the questions, and again no differences were found, but the absence of such differences is inadequate to rule this explanation out. Another minor problem with the cognitive load hypothesis is that it posits that people engage in more thorough cognitive processing in private situations, when they do not have to do so, in contrast to the "cognitive miser" pattern, suggesting that people engage in the least amount of cognitive effort required (Fiske & Taylor, 1984). Indeed, Tetlock (1983) showed that people engage in the most thorough and complex cognitive processing in response to the demands of public situations, and so it seems somewhat implausible to propose that subjects in the private condition went to all the trouble of searching their memories for counterexamples. The cognitive load explanation would also seemingly predict that high self-monitors would be less affected than low self-monitors (because high self-monitors presumably are more skilled at monitoring their own behavior and presumably have a wider, more discrepant range of past behaviors to review), contrary to the present findings, but this too is only a weak contradiction.[2] Because it invokes multiple unsubstantiated assumptions, it must be considered tentative or even doubtful unless further research can provide more direct support for it.

Results emerging from another laboratory provide additional help in discriminating between these explanations. Schlenker, Dlugolecki, and Doherty (1992) showed that the internalizing effects of self-presentation were not undone by inducing corrective (opposite) biased scanning. That is, their subjects presented themselves in one fashion and then scanned their self-concepts for evidence of the opposite trait, but they still internalized their self-presentations. Moreover, self-presentationally magnified scanning without actual self-presentation (which they accomplished by telling subjects at the last minute that the anticipated interview was canceled) failed to produce internalization. These results contradict the view that biased scanning mediates the effect of public behavior on the self-concept (my second explanation). They also further weaken the case for the fourth (cognitive load) explanation, because that explanation is based on a lack of corrective cognition, whereas Schlenker et al.'s subjects showed internalization even after being specifically induced to engage in precisely such a corrective scanning process. Their results are most consistent with the "magnified scanning" explanation, which holds

that public behavior intensifies the impact of biased scanning.

## Temporary or Permanent Change?

One important issue in research on self-concept change is whether the observed changes are permanent or temporary. Consistent with previous findings (e.g., Fazio et al., 1981), the present research indicates only that the changes are not so completely temporary that they evaporate once the person leaves the immediate situation. As Experiment 2 showed, these changes are sufficiently enduring to be able to elicit consistent behavior in a subsequent situation with new interaction partners. In the present research, of course, subjects were carefully debriefed at the end, and so no lasting self-concept changes would likely be found in a delayed follow-up measure, but it is instructive to speculate whether (in the absence of debriefing) induced self-concept shifts could have persisted indefinitely.

At first blush, it seems implausible and even absurd to suggest that a few loaded questions could potentially change someone's self-concept for life. On the other hand, if such questions help crystallize and articulate a particular view of self, it could have a lasting influence. Persistence of such change could well be aided by several other processes. As noted earlier, researchers have argued and shown that multiple processes operate to maintain the self-concept and insulate it from change (e.g., Swann, 1987). If a change does occur, however small or brief it may be initially, it may then benefit from these processes, which in effect would defend the new self-concept from reverting to the previous one.

The present investigation's findings about the crucial role of interpersonal context suggest additional implications about the possibilities for enduring self-concept change. If the awareness of others is indeed crucial for fostering self-concept change, then the subsequent interpersonal context may be equally decisive in determining which changes endure and which ones evaporate. If a person changes his or her self-view in one context, such as during an encounter group or retreat, and then returns to the preexisting network of relationships, the altered view of self may be quickly dispelled. Opportunities for genuine, lasting change in the self-concept would therefore tend to be linked to entry into new social networks, such

[2]Thus, one might even propose that high self-monitors actually monitor the external situation, rather than themselves, and so they might have fewer attentional resources to devote to scanning their self-concepts for contradictory material.

as moving to a new neighborhood, starting or ending college, entering or leaving military service, and changing jobs. In this connection, it is useful to examine brainwashing, which is aimed at bringing about lasting and fundamental changes in identity, self-concept, and attitudes. The most effective techniques for achieving such changes have relied on separating the individual from the old network of relationships, enmeshing the person briefly in a new network designed to foster the change, and then putting the suitably changed person into a new, permanent setting where the altered identity can become the firm, stable basis for long-term role performance (e.g., Lifton, 1957).

## Conclusion

The present investigation began with the question of whether self-concept change through internalization was influenced by the interpersonal context, and the answer appears to be an emphatic yes. In fact, the present results cast doubt on whether people will internalize their behavior (i.e., alter their self-concepts to fit their recent behavior) in the absence of an interpersonal context and self-presentational concerns. In the public conditions, internalization effects were strong and consistent, and they extended to behavioral effects. The same behaviors performed in private conditions produced only weak and inconsistent patterns of reported self-concept change and no effects on behavioral measures. The present results suggest that biased scanning theory needs to be extended to accommodate interpersonal factors. Only when biased scanning is magnified by the presence, interest, and surveillance of other people does it produce significant and lasting change in the self-concept.

In 1902, Cooley proposed the "looking glass self" as a metaphor for how the self-concept is determined by the views of others, and many subsequent theorists and researchers have reconfirmed that other people's perceptions constitute an important part of the self and exert a strong influence on individuals' conceptions of themselves (e.g., Goffman, 1959; Mead, 1934; Schlenker, 1980; Sullivan, 1953; see also Baumeister, 1986, and Schlenker, 1986, for compilations). Wicklund and Gollwitzer (1982) have even asserted that people seemingly feel that their identity claims require validation by others to give them social

reality. The present results show yet another way in which other people can influence the self-concept: Identical behaviors are internalized much more strongly when observed by others than when private or secret. The looking glass self may function as a magnifying glass during self-perception, so that what one sees in oneself while others are present has an extra powerful impact on the self-concept.

## REFERENCES

Baumeister, R. F. (1982). A self-presentational view of social phenomena. *Psychological Bulletin, 91,* 3–26.

Baumeister, R. F. (1986). *Identity: Cultural change and the struggle for self.* New York: Oxford University Press.

Baumeister, R. F., Hutton, D. G., & Tice, D. M. (1989). Cognitive processes during deliberate self-presentation: How self-presenters alter and misinterpret the behavior of their interaction partners. *Journal of Experimental Social Psychology, 256,* 59–78.

Baumeister, R. F., & Ilko, S. (1991). *Shallow gratitude: Public and private acknowledgment of external help in accounts of success.* Manuscript submitted for publication.

Baumeister, R. F., & Jones, E. E. (1978). When self-presentation is constrained by the target's knowledge: Consistency and compensation. *Journal of Personality and Social Psychology, 36,* 608–618.

Baumeister, R. F., & Tice, D. M. (1984). Role of self-presentation and choice in cognitive dissonance under forced compliance: Necessary or sufficient causes? *Journal of Personality and Social Psychology, 46,* 5–13.

Carlsmith, J. M., Collins, B. E., & Helmreich, R. E. (1966). Studies in forced compliance. I: The effect of pressure for compliance on attitude change produced by face-to-face role playing and anonymous essay writing. *Journal of Personality and Social Psychology, 4,* 1–13.

Carver, C. S., & Scheier, M. F. (1981). *Attention and self-regulation: A control theory approach to human behavior.* New York: Springer-Verlag.

Collins, B. E., & Hoyt, M. F. (1972). Personal responsibility-for-consequences: An integration and extension of the "forced compliance" literature. *Journal of Experimental Social Psychology, 8,* 558–593.

Cooley, C. H. (1902). *Human nature and the social order.* New York: Scribner.

Cooper, J., & Fazio, R. H. (1984). A new look at dissonance theory. In L. Berkowitz (Ed.), *Advances in experimental social psychology* (Vol. 17, pp. 229–266). San Diego, CA: Academic Press.

Devine, P. G., Sedikides, C., & Fuhrman, R. W. (1989). Goals in social information processing: The case of anticipated interaction. *Journal of Personality and Social Psychology, 56,* 680–690.

Duval, S., & Wicklund, R. A. (1972). *A theory of objective self-awareness.* San Diego, CA: Academic Press.

Fazio, R. H., Effrein, E. A., & Falender, V. J. (1981). Self-perceptions following social interaction. *Journal of Personality and Social Psychology, 41,* 232–242.

Festinger, L., & Carlsmith, J. M. (1959). Cognitive consequences of forced compliance. *Journal of Abnormal and Social Psychology, 58,* 203–210.

Fiske, S. T., & Taylor, S. E. (1984). *Social cognition.* Reading, MA: Addison-Wesley.

Gergen, K. J. (1965). Interaction goals and personalistic feedback as factors affecting the presentation of self. *Journal of Personality and Social Psychology, 1,* 413–424.

Gilbert, D. T., Krull, D. S., & Pelham, B. W. (1988). Of thoughts unspoken: Social inference and the self-regulation of behavior. *Journal of Personality and Social Psychology, 55,* 685–694.

Gilbert, D. T., & Osborne, R. E. (1989). Thinking backward: Some curable and incurable consequences of cognitive busyness. *Journal of Personality and Social Psychology, 57,* 940–949.

Gilbert, D. T., Pelham, B. W., & Krull, D. S. (1988). On cognitive busyness: When person perceivers meet persons perceived. *Journal of Personality and Social Psychology, 54,* 733–740.

Goffman, E. (1959). *The presentation of self in everyday life.* New York: Anchor Books.

Gollwitzer, P. M. (1986). Striving for specific identities: The social reality of self-symbolizing. In R. F. Baumeister (Ed.), *Public self and private self* (pp. 143–159). New York: Springer-Verlag.

Greenberg, J., & Pyszczynski, T. (1985). Compensatory self-inflation: A response to the threat to self-regard of public failure. *Journal of Personality and Social Psychology, 49,* 273–280.

Helmreich, R., & Collins, B. E. (1968). Studies in forced compliance: Commitment and magnitude of inducement to comply as determinants of opinion change. *Journal of Personality and Social Psychology, 10,* 75–81.

James, W. (1890). *The principles of psychology.* New York: Holt.

Jones, E. E., & Nisbett, R. E. (1971). *The actor and observer: Divergent perceptions of the causes of behavior.* Morristown, NJ: General Learning Press.

Jones, E. E., Rhodewalt, F., Berglas, S., & Skelton, J. A. (1981). Effects of strategic self-presentation on subsequent self-esteem. *Journal of Personality and Social Psychology, 41,* 407–421.

Kelley, H. H. (1971). *Attribution in social interaction.* Morristown, NJ: General Learning Press.

Kiesler, C. A. (1971). *The psychology of commitment.* San Diego, CA: Academic Press.

Kulik, J. A., Sledge, P., & Mahler, H. I. M. (1986). Self-confirmatory attribution, egocentrism, and the perpetuation of self-beliefs. *Journal of Personality and Social Psychology, 50,* 587–594.

Langer, E. J., & Abelson, R. P. (1972). The semantics of asking a favor: How to succeed in getting help without really dying. *Journal of Personality and Social Psychology, 24,* 26–32.

Lifton, R. J. (1957). *Methods of forceful indoctrination: Observations and interviews.* New York: Group for the Advancement of Psychiatry.

Maracek, J., & Mettee, D. R. (1972). Avoidance of continued success as a function of self-esteem level of esteem certainty, and responsibility for success. *Journal of Personality and Social Psychology, 22,* 90–107.

Markus, H., & Kunda, Z. (1986). Stability and malleability

of the self-concept. *Journal of Personality and Social Psychology, 51,* 858–866.

McFarlin, D. B., & Blascovich, J. (1981). Effects of self-esteem and performance feedback on future affective preferences and cognitive expectations. *Journal of Personality and Social Psychology, 40,* 521–531.

Mead, G. H. (1934). *Mind, self, and society.* Chicago, IL: University of Chicago Press.

Paulhus, D. (1982). Individual differences, self-presentation, and cognitive dissonance: Their concurrent operation in forced compliance. *Journal of Personality and Social Psychology, 43,* 838–852.

Paulhus, D. L., & Levitt, K. (1987). Desirable responding triggered by affect: Automatic egotism? *Journal of Personality and Social Psychology, 52,* 245–259.

Rhodewalt, F. (1986). Self-presentation and the phenomenal self On the stability and malleability of the self-concept. In R. F. Baumeister (Ed.), *Public self and private self* (pp. 117–142). New York: Springer-Verlag.

Rhodewalt, F., & Agustsdottir, S. (1986). Effects on self-presentation on the phenomenal self. *Journal of Personality and Social Psychology, 50,* 47-55.

Riess, M., & Schlenker, B. R. (1977). Attitude change and responsibility avoidance as modes of dilemma resolution in forced compliance settings. *Journal of Personality and Social Psychology, 35,* 21–30.

Ross, L., Lepper, M., & Hubbard, M. (1975). Perseverance in self-perception and social perception: Biased attributional processes in the debriefing paradigm. *Journal of Personality and Social Psychology, 32,* 880–892.

Schlenker, B. R. (1980). *Impression management: The self-concept, social identity, and interpersonal relationships.* Monterey, CA: Brooks/Cole.

Schlenker, B. R. (1982). Translating actions into attitudes: An identity-analytic approach to the explanation of social conduct. In L. Berkowitz (Ed.), *Advances in Experimental Social Psychology* (Vol. 15, pp. 193–247)· San Diego, CA: Academic Press.

Schlenker, B. R. (1986). Self-identification: Toward an integration of the public and private self. In R. F. Baumeister (Ed.), *Public self and private self* (pp. 21–62). New York: Springer-Verlag.

Schlenker, B. R., Dlugolecki, D. W., & Doherty, K. (1992). *The impact of self-presentations on self-appraisals and behavior: The roles of commitment and biased scanning.* Unpublished manuscript, University of Florida.

Schlenker, B. R., & Goldman, H. J. (1982). Attitude change as a self-presentation tactic following attitude consistent behavior: Effects of role and choice. *Social Psychology Quarterly, 45,* 92–99.

Schlenker, B. R., & Schlenker, P. A. (1975). Reactions following counterattitudinal behavior which produces positive consequences. *Journal of Personality and Social Psychology, 31,* 962–971.

Schlenker, B. R., & Trudeau, J. V. (1990). Impacts of self-presentations on private self-beliefs: Effects of prior self-beliefs and misattribution. *Journal of Personality and Social Psychology, 58,* 22–32.

Snyder, M. (1974). Self-monitoring of expressive behavior. *Journal of Personality and Social Psychology, 30,* 526–537.

Snyder, M., & Gangestad, S. (1986). On the nature of self-monitoring: Matters of assessment, matters of validity.

*Journal of Personality and Social Psychology, 51,* 125–139.

Sullivan, H. S. (1953). *The interpersonal theory of psychiatry.* New York: Norton.

Swann, W. B., Jr. (1983). Self-verification: Bringing social reality into harmony with the self. In J. Suls & A. G. Greenwald (Eds.), *Social psychological perspectives on the self* (Vol. 2, pp. 33–66). Hillsdale, NJ: Erlbaum.

Swann, W. B., Jr. (1987). Identity negotiation: When two roads meet. *Journal of Personality and Social Psychology, 53,* 1038–1051.

Swann, W. B., Jr., & Ely, R. J. (1984). A battle of wills: Self-verification versus behavioral confirmation. *Journal of Personality and Social Psychology, 46,* 1287–1302.

Swann, W. B., Jr., & Hill, C. A. (1982). When our identities are mistaken: Reaffirming self-conceptions through social interaction. *Journal of Personality and Social Psychology, 43,* 59–66.

Swann, W. B., Jr., & Predmore, S. C. (1985). Intimates as agents of social support: Sources of consolation or despair?

*Journal of Personality and Social Psychology, 49,* 1609–1617.

Swann, W. B., Jr., & Read, S. J. (1981). Self-verification processes: How we sustain our self-conceptions. *Journal of Experimental Social Psychology, 17,* 351–372.

Tetlock, P. E. (1983). Accountability and complexity of thought. *Journal of Personality and Social Psychology, 8,* 74–83.

Tetlock, P. E., & Manstead, A. S. R. (1985). Impressive management versus intrapsychic explanations in social psychology: A useful dichotomy? *Psychological Review, 92,* 59–77.

Tice, D. M. (1987). *Similarity of others and dispositional versus situational attributions.* Unpublished dissertation, Princeton University.

Wicklund, R. A., & Brehm, J. W. (1976). *Perspectives on cognitive dissonance.* Hillsdale, NJ: Erlbaum.

Wicklund, R. A., & Gollwitzer, P. M. (1982). *Symbolic self-completion.* Hillsdale, NJ: Erlbaum.

# Self-Esteem

Self-esteem has been one of the most durable topics in the broader domain of self-research. As interest in many other topics has waxed and waned, interest in self-esteem has remained strong, and each new generation has brought a new set of findings to contribute. Each of the last four decades has seen important works on self-esteem, and the next few are likely to see further developments.

Yet, despite this steady stream of research, the meaning, importance, and power of self-esteem remain less than fully understood. We know that people differ reliably and consistently in their levels of self-esteem—but what do these differences entail? What is the best way to characterize the differences between people with high vs. low self-esteem?

An important part of the answer to that question is presented in the first paper in this section. Campbell (1990) shows that people with low self-esteem lack a clear, stable, consistent understanding of themselves. Low self-esteem is, thus, not a firm conviction that the self is worthless or despicable. It is rather simply the lack of a clear idea that the self is worthy and wonderful. Many of the laboratory findings that show that people with low self-esteem perform worse at this or that task can be explained on the basis of Campbell's work: People with low self-esteem simply do not manage themselves effectively because they do not understand themselves in a consistent, usable fashion.

This new view should replace the standard, traditional assumption that there are two kinds of people, one of which is convinced that they are great and the other being convinced that they are terrible. Instead, one group of people is convinced that they are great, but the other simply lacks firm convictions about themselves.

The enduring puzzle about the meaning of individual differences in self-esteem is accompanied by a second puzzle, namely about the value of these differences. In the 1980s, our society seemingly became convinced that high self-esteem has considerable value and many practices, especially in connection with raising and teaching children, were modified in the effort to boost and sustain self-esteem. Yet the research findings have not provided much evidence that high self-esteem helps people be more successful in work or love; perform better at school or work; avoid problems such as drug addiction, poverty, venereal disease, and unwanted pregnancy; or be better citizens, such as in higher moral or altruistic behavior.

Several recent works have begun to question the value of boosting self-esteem, one of which is reproduced here. Baumeister, Smart, and Boden (1996) searched the literature for evidence in support of the widespread view that low self-esteem causes violence, but what they found contradicted that view. It appears that perpetrators of violence tend to have favorable opinions of themselves and, in fact, violence often stems from having these favorable views of self attacked.

The opposite conclusion, namely that high self-esteem causes violence, does not fit the data either. My understanding is that high self-esteem is actually a mixed bag that contains several very different sorts of people. Some of these have quiet self-confidence and an accurate appreciation of their abilities. Others are simply conceited. After all, having high self-esteem simply means holding a favorable opinion of oneself, and this favorable view can be haughty arrogance just as well as it can signify a comfortable acceptance of self. Consistent with this view, Kernis, Granneman, and Barclay (1989; Kernis, 1993) found that the category of high self-esteem contains both some exceptionally hostile and some exceptionally non-hostile people.

Several recent works are relevant. Colvin, Block, and Funder (1995) searched specifically for people with inflated self-esteem by comparing people's self-ratings with how other people rated them. In a laboratory study, these people with inflated high self-esteem emerged as conceited, self-centered people who did not care a great deal for others. They interrupted other people in conversation, expressed hostility toward anyone who disagreed with them, talked *at* instead of *with* other people, and did a variety of other things that irritated others. Long-range data linked this inflated self-esteem to maladjustment patterns and interpersonal problems.

Laboratory experiments by Bushman and Baumeister (1998) sought to provide direct tests of the threatened egotism model from the Baumeister et al. (1996) paper that is reproduced here. People were provoked (or not, in a control condition) by being given a bad evaluation of an essay they had written, and they then had the opportunity to aggress against the person who had offended them. Low self-esteem failed to predict aggression; in fact, in two studies, two different measures of self-esteem yielded nothing. But in both studies, a measure of narcissism did yield significant effects. People scoring high in narcissism were more aggressive toward people who had provoked and offended them.

Narcissism may thus capture an important segment of people with high self-esteem—indeed, the more nasty, conceited sort. Narcissism refers to a tendency to regard oneself as superior to others and to expect other people to treat one as special. Narcissism is associated with instability of self-esteem (see Kernis, 1993; Rhodewalt, Madrian, & Cheney, 1998), in the sense that narcissists have high opinions of themselves that do fluctuate from day to day in response to events.

In the coming years, the study of narcissism is likely to

expand. Because narcissists are more similar to each other than are people in the broad category of high self-esteem, research findings may be clearer and more consistent. Moreover, the negative connotation of narcissism may serve as a valuable complement to the generally favorable connotation of high self-esteem. By studying both self-esteem and narcissism, researchers may gradually move toward a more balanced understanding of the benefits and costs of holding a favorable opinion of yourself.

## REFERENCES

Baumeister, R. F., Smart, L., & Boden, J. M. (1996). Relation of threatened egotism to violence and aggression: The dark side of high self-esteem. *Psychological Review, 103,* 5–33.

Bushman, B. J., & Baumeister, R. F. (1998). Threatened egotism, narcissism, self-esteem, and direct and displaced aggression: Does self-love or self-hate lead to violence? *Journal of Personality and Social Psychology, 75,* 219–229.

Campbell, J. D. (1990). Self-esteem and clarity of the self-concept. *Journal of Personality and Social Psychology, 59,* 538–549.

Colvin, C. R., Block, J., & Funder, D. C. (1995). Overly positive evaluations and personality: Negative implications for mental health. *Journal of Personality and Social Psychology, 68,* 1152–1162.

Kernis, M. H. (1993). The roles of stability and level of self-esteem in psychological functioning. In R. Baumeister (Ed.), *Self-esteem: The puzzle of low self-regard* (pp. 167–182). New York: Plenum.

Kernis, M. H., Granneman, B. D., & Barclay, L. C. (1989). Stability and level of self-esteem as predictors of anger arousal and hostility. *Journal of Personality and Social Psychology, 56,* 1013–1022.

Rhodewalt, F., Madrian, J. C., & Cheney, S. (1998). Narcissism, self-knowledge, organization, and emotional reactivity: The effects of daily experiences on self-esteem and affect. *Personality and Social Psychology Bulletin, 24,* 75–86.

# Discussion Questions

1. Why might people with high self-esteem have clearer, more definite concepts of themselves than people with low self-esteem?
2. What is the difference between narcissism and high self-esteem?
3. Describe the most violent, hostile, aggressive people you have known. Did they have high or low self-esteem?
4. Is loving oneself a prerequisite for loving others? Or could it be an obstacle (i.e., can self-love make one less able to love other people)?
5. What advantages or benefits are likely to flow from having a clear, definite self-concept (such as people with high self-esteem typically have)? How might their lives be better?
6. Do you think high self-esteem causes self-concept clarity or vice versa? Or could some third factor be at work, underlying both?
7. Can you think of any other possible drawbacks to having very high self-esteem?

# Suggested Readings

McFarlin, D. B., & Blascovich, J. (1981). Effects of self-esteem and performance feedback on future affective preferences and cognitive expectations. *Journal of Personality and Social Psychology, 40,* 521–531. This important paper clarifies the basic cognitive and motivational properties of self-esteem. People with low self-esteem want to succeed just as much as people with high self-esteem—they simply are less confident that they can accomplish it. Meanwhile, people with low self-esteem respond to failure by reducing their aspirations and expectations, whereas people with high self-esteem paradoxically show the opposite result.

Crocker, J., & Major, B. (1989). Social stigma and self-esteem: The self-protective properties of stigma. *Psychological Review, 96,* 608–630. This award-winning paper tackled one of the standard social science questions, namely the relation between race and self-esteem. Contrary to the prevailing view that African-Americans suffer from low self-esteem, these authors have compiled statistics from published studies to yield the opposite conclusion: African-Americans have higher self-esteem than others. The authors then explore how this may have come about.

Baumeister, R. F. (1993). (Ed.). *Self-esteem: The puzzle of low self-regard.* New York: Plenum. This volume contains chapters by most of the leading psychological researchers on self-esteem, each of whom describes his or her research program and general conclusions.

California Task Force to Promote Self-esteem and Personal and Social Responsibility (1990). *Toward a state of self-esteem.* Sacramento, CA: California State Department of Education. This book was the manifesto of California's task force. It expresses the optimistic hope that raising self-esteem solves a multitude of personal and social problems.

Baumeister, R. F., Tice, D. M., & Hutton, D. G. (1989). Self-presentational motivations and personality differences in self-esteem. *Journal of Personality, 57,* 547–579. This article summarizes evidence from many studies to show that self-esteem scores typically range from the top to the middle of the scale, with very few people scoring at the low end of possible scores. It further argues that people with low self-esteem seek to avoid risk and protect themselves against failure—in contrast to people with high self-esteem, who seek to enhance the self with successes and are willing to take risks to accomplish that.

Brockner, J. (1984). Low self-esteem and behavioral plasticity: Some implications for personality and social psychology. In L. Wheeler (Ed.), *Review of personality and social psychology* (Vol. 4, pp. 237–271). Beverly Hills, CA: Sage. This review article presents the broad conclusion that people with low self-esteem are more affected by social influence and other persuasive aspects of the situation than other people.

# Self-Esteem and Clarity of the Self-Concept

Jennifer D. Campbell • University of British Columbia

This article examines the association between evaluative and knowledge components of the self. Four studies tested the hypothesis that the self-concepts of low-self-esteem (LSE) people are characterized by less clarity or certainty than those of high-self-esteem (HSE) people. LSE subjects exhibited less extremity and self-reported confidence when rating themselves on bipolar trait adjectives (Study 1), less temporal stability in their trait ratings over a 2-month interval (Study 2), less congruence between their self-concepts and their subsequent perceptions of situation-specific behavior and memory for prior behavior (Study 3), and less internal consistency, lower self-rated confidence, and longer reaction times when making me/not me responses to pairs of opposite traits (Study 4). Alternative accounts of the results and the implications of self-concept clarity for understanding the pervasive impact of self-esteem on behavior are discussed.

Research on individual differences in self-esteem has a long, prolific history in psychology. Empirical studies now number in the thousands, and the number continues to expand at a remarkable rate. Although several reasons could be cited for the topic's popularity, perhaps the most important is that self-esteem has been shown to have a pervasive impact on human behavior. Research has demonstrated, for example, that individual differences in self-esteem affect behavior in diverse content areas such as competition, conformity, attraction, causal attribution, achievement, and helping (see Wells & Marwell, 1976; Wylie, 1974, 1979, for reviews).

One area in which self-esteem appears to exert especially powerful effects is with respect to people's reactions to self-relevant feedback or information (e.g., Jones, 1973). Affective reactions to such feedback adhere to a self-enhancement formulation; because people lower in self-esteem have greater enhancement needs, they experience more pain in response to negative feedback and more pleasure in response to positive feedback. However, cognitive reactions—acceptance or rejection of the feedback as a veridical reflection of the self—generally conform to a consistency formulation (Shrauger, 1975; Swann, Griffin, Predmore, & Gaines, 1987). When measures such as perceived accuracy, attributions, or diagnosticity are examined, the data typically yield a main effect for feedback (positive feedback is generally more accepted than negative feedback) and a Self-Esteem × Feedback interaction; low self-esteem (LSE) subjects are relatively more accepting of unfavorable feedback and less accepting of favorable feedback than are high self-esteem (HSE) subjects (McFarlin & Blascovich, 1981; Moreland & Sweeney, 1984; Shrauger, 1975; Swann et al., 1987).

self- enhancement vs. consistency formulation

223

Although most studies obtain the consistency interaction, there usually is an asymmetry between the positive and negative feedback conditions; self-esteem differences are more consistently obtained or are more pronounced under negative conditions than under positive conditions. In his review of self-serving biases in attributions, Zuckerman (1979) concluded that "self-esteem effects are obtained primarily after failure" (p. 261). Investigators who examined the effects of success or failure on subsequent expectancies and performance also reported asymmetric consistency effects. Simple effects analyses of the interaction yield substantial self-esteem differences in expectancies and performance under failure conditions, but the differences are small and not reliable under success conditions (Brockner, 1979; DePaulo, Brown, Ishii, & Fisher, 1981; Shrauger & Sorman, 1977).

When the asymmetry is combined with the greater overall acceptance of positive feedback, the data suggest that HSE people accept only positive (consistent) information, whereas LSE people accept (and are affected by) both types of information. This pattern was clearly demonstrated by Campbell and Fairey (1985), who included a control group, allowing for the impact of success and failure to be assessed separately. Experimental subjects wrote an explanation for either a hypothetical success or a hypothetical failure outcome on an upcoming anagram test; control subjects neither considered an outcome nor wrote an explanation. Self-esteem differences in subsequent expectations and performance within the success and failure conditions yielded the asymmetry noted earlier. Under success conditions, self-esteem differences were negligible, but under failure conditions, LSE subjects exhibited substantially lower expectations and performance than did HSE subjects. More importantly, comparisons with control subjects indicated that explaining a hypothetical success increased the expectations and performance of both LSE and HSE subjects, whereas explaining a hypothetical failure decreased the expectations and performance of only LSE subjects.

Brockner (1984) reviewed the reactions-to-feedback literature and other research showing, for example, that LSE people are also more susceptible to influence attempts, the effects of self-focusing stimuli, and anxiety-provoking stimuli. He advanced the concept of LSE *plasticity*: LSE people are generally more susceptible to the effects of self-relevant social cues than are HSE people. Whereas HSE people only accept or are affected by external cues that are consistent with their self-concept (positive cues), LSE people appear to be susceptible to a broad range of self-relevant stimuli.

LSE plasticity provides a good description or summary of the relevant data, but does not constitute an explanation for the phenomenon of why more negative self-evaluations (LSE) are associated with greater overall susceptibility to social cues. Although negative self-regard provides a reasonable account for the greater susceptibility to unfavorable cues, the more general susceptibility of LSE people is difficult to account for simply in terms of negativity.

In considering this issue, note that self-esteem is not an isolated trait, but one that is correlated with a number of other personality traits. For example, Watson and Clark (1984) showed that a number of personality scales, including trait anxiety, neuroticism, ego strength, and repression–sensitization, are indicators of a stable and pervasive trait that they label negative affectivity (NA). They define NA as the disposition to experience aversive emotional states and note that high-NA people tend to be "distressed and upset and have a negative view of self" (p. 465). Because self-esteem is intertwined with a number of other dispositions, LSE plasticity is possibly not a reflection of negative evaluations per se, but of some correlate thereof.

The present article attempts to demonstrate that an important concomitant of self-esteem is the degree of certainty or clarity in the self-concept. Specifically, I suggest that LSE people have more poorly articulated notions of who or what they are. Although this suggestion is not a new one, it has not been subjected to rigorous empirical examination and, perhaps more importantly, has been largely ignored in the self-esteem literature. This neglect is unfortunate because an established association between self-esteem and self-concept clarity could serve as an important theoretical function in providing an integrative explanation for a diverse set of research findings. In particular, it seems reasonable that if LSE people do have more uncertain self-concepts, they should be more dependent on, susceptible to, and influenced by external self-relevant stimuli.

The remainder of this introductory section focuses on the definitional status of self-esteem and self-concept clarity and the general research strategies used here to examine the association between them. The implications of a relation between self-esteem and self-concept clarity will be discussed more fully after the studies and their results have been presented.

## Self-Esteem and Self-Concept Clarity

In many current theories, the self-concept is viewed as a cognitive schema that organizes abstract and concrete memories about the self and controls the processing of self-relevant information (e.g., Kihlstrom & Cantor, 1983; Markus, 1980). Viewing the self as a cognitive structure has yielded many new and provocative insights (Kihlstrom, Cantor, Albright, Chew, Klein, & Neidenthal, 1988), but theorists have also recognized that affect or evaluation (self-esteem) may play a critical role both in the structure of the self-concept and in its interface with external information (e.g., Rogers, 1981; Tesser & Campbell, 1983).

The self is explicitly viewed here as having both an evaluative and a knowledge component. I conceptualize the evaluative component as trait self-esteem, a global self-reflexive attitude addressing how one feels about the self when it is viewed as an object of evaluation. This conceptualization does not deny the fact that feelings of self-worth can vary over time and roles, and that different roles are differentially important in affecting self-regard (e.g., Burke, 1980; Campbell & Tesser, 1985; Wells & Marwell, 1976). However, it is important to distinguish (a) outer self-esteem (Rosenberg, 1979) or self-evaluation (Tesser & Campbell, 1983)—temporary feelings of self-regard that vary over situations, roles, feedback, events, and the reflected appraisals of others (Cooley, 1912; Coopersmith, 1967; Rosenberg, 1979; Tesser & Campbell, 1983)—from (b) inner or trait self-esteem—a global personal judgment of worthiness that appears to form relatively early in the course of development, remains fairly constant over time, and is resistant to change (Epstein, 1983). Measures of trait self-esteem, the construct of interest here, have been shown to exhibit high temporal stability coefficients, even over long periods of time (e.g., Mortimer, Finch, & Kumka, 1982; O'Malley & Bachman, 1983).

The knowledge component consists of beliefs about one's attributes. Self-esteem differences in the contents of the knowledge component are not at issue here. The fact that HSE people describe themselves with more positive attributes is well-known, and indeed, the positivity of self-descriptions is sometimes used to measure self-esteem (e.g., Sherwood, 1962, reprinted in Robinson & Shaver, 1973). The hypothesis focuses on the clarity or certainty of the knowledge structure: the extent to which the contents or self-beliefs are clearly and confidently defined.

Because self-concept clarity has some overlap with the broader construct of identity, the suggestion that there is a positive relation between self-esteem and clarity is not a new one. Classical (e.g., Adler, 1959; Allport, 1961; Erikson, 1959) and contemporary (e.g., Marcia, 1980) personality theorists have typically assumed that higher levels of identity (achievement, integration, status) are associated with higher levels of self-esteem. However, tests of this assumption have usually been limited to correlating two self-report measures of the constructs (e.g., correlating a self-esteem scale with an identity diffusion or ego strength scale). Although these correlations are usually substantial (e.g., Block, 1961; O'Brien & Epstein, 1988), this type of evidence is weak in that it is subject to problems of common method variance and social desirability.

## Present Research

The present research relies on self-reports but does not use the contents of self-reports for measuring clarity. The general research strategy is (a) to use either structural characteristics of the self-descriptions or unobtrusive measures (e.g., reaction times) to measure clarity, or (b) to conduct indirect tests of the general hypothesis that are less subject to self-presentational motives.

Four studies are reported. Study 1 examined the hypothesis that self-esteem would be positively associated with the extremity and confidence of self-ratings on bipolar trait adjectives. Study 2 examined the hypothesis that self-esteem would be positively associated with the temporal stability of self-reports over a 2-month interval. Study 3 examined the hypothesis that the congruence between the self-concept and subsequent perceptions of situation-specific behavior and memory for previous behavior would be greater for HSE than LSE people. Study 4 examined the association between self-esteem and the internal consistency of self-reports and provided a replication of the relation between self-esteem and confidence (Study 1) by including self-reported confidence and reaction time measures.

Within the studies, some variables were operationalized with multiple measures that differed only slightly from one another. This was done because these variables have been operationalized in somewhat different ways and there is no consensus on a single best measure. However, multiple measures of the same variable should not be construed as providing convergent validity for the hypothesis; only measures of different variables and results of different tests are relevant to the issue of convergent validity.

Subjects were selected from students in undergraduate psychology courses who completed the Revised Janis-Field Feelings of Inadequacy Scale (JF scale; Eagly, 1967) at the beginning of the academic year (a minimum of 4 weeks prior to the study). The JF scale is a 20-item Likert scale with a possible range of 20 to 100, which has been widely used to measure self-esteem; its reliability and validity have been demonstrated elsewhere (Church, Truss & Velicer, 1980; Eagly, 1967; Robinson & Shaver, 1973). Split-half reliabilities have ranged from .72 to .83 (Robinson & Shaver, 1973). Temporal stability of the scale is particularly important, given the present lag between the JF measure and participation in a study; Campbell, Chew, and Scratchley (1999) obtained a 3-month test/retest coefficient of .92 for the JF scale.

On the basis of a median split of JF scores, students were classified as either LSE or HSE and then were recruited to participate in a study. Because the studies were conducted over a 2-year period, subjects were recruited from one of two pretest samples ($N$s = 380 and 187). Subjects whose scores were within 2 points of the median (*Mdns* = 68.5 and 67.5) were not recruited. I include the JF means and standard deviations of selected LSE and HSE subjects in the description of each study.[1] No mention was made of the pretest

instrument at the time of recruitment and no subject participated in more than one study. All subjects either received extra course credit or were paid $4.00 for participation.

## Study 1

Study 1 was based on the notion that self-concept certainty should be reflected in the extremity and confidence of self-descriptions. Specifically, I expected that when LSE and HSE subjects were asked to describe themselves on scales anchored by pairs of bipolar adjectives, LSE subjects would give ratings nearer the midpoint of the scale and indicate lower subjective confidence in their ratings. To interpret extremity as reflecting certainty or clarity, as opposed to reflecting positivity, an attempt was made to select bipolar pairs in which the poles did not differ greatly in terms of social desirability. For example, if pairs such as warm/cold and shy/outgoing were used, higher extremity on the part of HSE subjects could simply reflect their tendency to more strongly endorse positive attributes or to more strongly reject negative attributes. On the other hand, if pairs such as conventional/unconventional and competitive/cooperative were used and no self-esteem differences in mean ratings were obtained, greater extremity would appear to indicate more clarity of self-definition on these dimensions.

### Method

Ninety-two LSE (*M* = 56.34, *SD* = 7.36) and 92 HSE (*M* = 76.02, *SD* = 6.10) subjects were given a set of 15 bipolar adjectives and were asked to indicate how they viewed themselves on each pair (7-point scales), then to rate how confident or sure they felt about their self-rating on 5-point scales anchored by *not at all confident* and *very confident*. The 15 pairs consisted of the adjectives predictable/unpredictable, silly/serious, tactful/candid, unconventional/conventional, assertive/soft-spoken, solemn/lighthearted, gentle/boisterous, deliberate/spontaneous, competitive/cooperative, quiet/outspoken, independent/dependent, cautious/risky, ambitious/laid-back, extravagant/thrifty, and yielding/dominant. Data from 2 subjects (1 LSE, 1 HSE) were deleted because of incomplete responses.

---

[1]Although the Revised Janis-Field Feelings of Inadequacy Scale (JF Scale) was used to select subjects, another measure of self-esteem, the Texas Social Behavior Inventory (TSBI; Helmreich, Stapp, & Ervin, 1974), was also administered in one of the pretest samples. The correlation between TSBI and JF scores was $r(378)$ = .79 and the results of Studies 1 and 4 (the two studies that used this sample) were highly similar when TSBI scores were substituted for JF scores in the analyses.

## Results

Three measures of extremity were calculated for each subject: the average absolute deviation from the scale midpoint, the standard deviation of their 15 responses, and the number of extreme responses (e.g., responses 1, 2, 6, 7 as opposed to 3, 4, 5). Each subject's mean response and average confidence rating for the 15 items were also computed. The three extremity measures were highly correlated with one another (avg. $r = .93$), moderately correlated with self-reported confidence (avg. $r = .24$), and not correlated with the mean response (avg. $r = -.07$).

The five measures were first analyzed with single-variable (self-esteem) analyses of variance (ANOVAs). The mean responses of LSE subjects ($M = 3.80$) and HSE subjects ($M = 3.82$) were almost identical, $F < 1$. However, as anticipated, the two groups differed on the three measures of extremity and the confidence measure. LSE subjects gave responses that were, on the average, closer to the midpoint of the scale ($M = 1.20$) than did HSE subjects ($M = 1.31$), $F(1, 180) = 4.27$, $p < .04$. The average standard deviation of LSE subjects' responses ($SD = 1.43$) was smaller than that of HSE subjects ($SD = 1.58$), $F(1, 180) = 8.22$, $p < .01$. LSE subjects gave fewer extreme responses ($M = 5.44$) than did HSE subjects ($M = 6.46$), $F(1, 180) = 5.46$, $p < .03$. Finally, LSE subjects exhibited lower confidence in their ratings ($M = 3.62$) than did HSE subjects ($M = 3.95$), $F(1, 180) = 23.87$, $p < .001$. Correlational analyses yielded a similar pattern. Although JF scores were not related to subjects' mean responses ($r = .01$), they were moderately, but significantly, correlated with the absolute deviation from the midpoint ($r = .23$), the standard deviation ($r = .27$), the number of extreme responses ($r = .22$), and the average confidence of those responses ($r = .45$; all), all $ps < .01$.

Although subjects' average response to the 15 items was unrelated to self-esteem, analyses of the individual items revealed that HSE subjects rated themselves as more assertive, lighthearted, outspoken, independent, ambitious, and dominant than did LSE subjects, $Fs(1, 174) > 5.61$, $ps < .02$. Because the desirability differences in these items may have contributed to the extremity effects, a second set of analyses using only the 9 items with no self-esteem differences in mean responses (all $Fs < 1.2$) was conducted. The analyses yielded comparable results: LSE subjects exhibited smaller

deviations from the midpoint ($r = .19$), smaller standard deviations ($r = .22$), fewer extreme responses ($r = .18$), and lower confidence ($r = .38$) than did HSE subjects, $ps < .02$.

## Study 2

Study 2 examined the hypothesis that LSE subjects would exhibit less temporal stability in their self-descriptions than HSE subjects. To the extent that subjects are uncertain or lack clear definitions of their attributes, their self-descriptions should exhibit more change over time.

### Method

Twenty LSE ($M = 58.00$, $SD = 8.13$) and 20 HSE ($M = 76.45$, $SD = 6.21$) subjects were selected from a pretest sample that had completed the JF self-esteem scale and had rated their traits on a set of 20 unipolar social adjectives at the beginning of the academic term. Subjects had rated each of the adjectives with respect to how they generally behaved in social interactions on 7-point scales anchored by *not at all descriptive of me* and *very descriptive of me*. Ten of the adjectives were positive (intelligent, articulate, warm, considerate, talkative, confident, assertive, friendly, socially competent, likable) and 10 were negative (cold, obnoxious, defensive, shy, boring, awkward, rude, arrogant, embarrassed, nervous). Subjects were contacted 8–9 weeks later to participate in a study concerned with self-perceptions. When subjects reported for the study, they were placed in individual cubicles and asked to rate themselves on the same adjectives used in the pretest session.

### Results

Four measures of temporal stability were calculated for each subject: (a) the absolute difference (ABS DIFF) between each of the 20 ratings, the average of which provided an overall measure of the extent to which subjects changed their ratings between the two testing occasions, (b) the average adjusted difference score (ADJ DIFF), indexing the amount of change exhibited as a percentage of the change possible given the initial ratings (e.g., an initial rating of 1 or 7 allows a possible change of 6 points, whereas an initial rating of 4 allows a possible change of only 3 points), (c) the number of adjectives that exhibited any change in ratings between the two testing occasions, and (d) the within-subject correlation coefficient (Fisher's $r$-to-$z$ transformation) between the two sets of ratings (ZCORR), which assesses the extent to which the items were ranked similarly on both occasions. The three change measures were highly correlated with one another (avg. $r = .89$) and change was negatively correlated with ZCORR, the similarity in rank orders (avg. $r = -.78$).

Single-factor ANOVAs revealed that, compared with HSE subjects, LSE subjects had higher ABS DIFF scores (.91 vs. .64), $F(1, 38) = 10.86$, $p < .01$, had higher ADJ DIFF scores (22% vs. 15%), $F(1, 38) = 17.45$, $p < .001$, changed their ratings on more of the adjectives (12.20 vs. 10.25), $F(1, 38) = 5.85$, $p < .03$, and exhibited lower correlations between the two sets of ratings (ZCORR = .85 vs. 1.40, $r$ transformation of ZCORR = .65 vs. .86), $F(1, 38) = 22.35$, $p < .001$. Correlational analyses yielded a similar pattern. All four stability measures were reliably correlated with JF scores; subjects lower in self-esteem exhibited more absolute change ($r = -.43$), more adjusted change ($r = -.49$), more changed adjectives ($r = -.32$), and lower within-subject correlations ($r = .51$), all $ps < .05$.

Although the change measure results are straightforward, the ZCORR measure must be interpreted with caution because within-subject correlations, like all correlations, are sensitive to differences in range or variability. Consistent with the established positivity bias of HSE subjects, subjects higher in self-esteem more strongly endorsed the 10 positive adjectives ($rs = .61$ and .49 at Time 1 and Time 2) and more strongly rejected the 10 negative adjectives ($rs = -.77$ and $-.65$). However, LSE subjects exhibited more evaluative inconsistency in their responses (see also Campbell & Fehr, 1990). The correlations between the JF scale and the within-subject standard deviations on the positive and negative adjectives were $-.60$ and $-.56$ at Time 1 and $-.42$ and $-.60$ at Time 2. This combination resulted in JF scores being moderately, but not significantly, correlated with the within-subject standard deviation of the 20 ratings at Time 1 ($r = .23$), but not at Time 2 ($r = .04$). To determine if this variability advantage on the part of HSE subjects contributed to their higher temporal stability coefficients, the partial correlation between JF and ZCORR, controlling for the standard deviations of Time 1 and Time 2 ratings, was calculated. The correlation remained highly reliable ($r = .50$, $p < .01$).[2]

## Study 3

Study 2 suggested that the self-concepts of HSE subjects were more stable over time; when asked on two occasions to rate their traits, HSE subjects gave ratings that changed less and the traits were rank ordered more similarly over time. Study 3 examined another type of stability: the correspondence between beliefs about one's behavior in general (traits) and beliefs about one's behavior in a specific situation. To the extent that generalized beliefs about the self (the self-concept) are clearly defined and confidently held, they should correspond more closely with beliefs about situation-specific behavior. To test the hypothesis that HSE people would show greater congruence between the self-concept and beliefs about situation-specific behavior, I had subjects who provided self-concept (trait) ratings in a pretest session participate in a dyadic interaction 2–3 months later, rating the same adjectives for how they believed they behaved during the interaction.

The prediction of greater congruence between the self-concept and situation-specific beliefs on the part of HSE subjects was partially based on the concept that schemas exert pull or bias on current beliefs and perceptions, and that better articulated schemas exert more pull (Markus, 1977; Millar & Tesser, 1986; Taylor & Crocker, 1981; Tesser, 1978). If HSE subjects do exhibit greater congruence, one might ask whether this congruence is achieved at the expense of reality. That is, high congruence could derive from perceptions of current behavior that are highly distorted by the

---

[2]Another possible solution to the differential variance problem was to reverse the scoring on the negative adjectives before calculating the correlations. However, when this was done, Revised Janis-Field Feelings of Inadequacy Scale (JF) scores strongly, but negatively, correlated with the within-subject standard deviations of the ratings at Time 1 ($r = -.64$) and Time 2 ($r = -.61$). In this case, (when differences in variance strongly favored low-self-esteem [LSE] correlations), LSE subjects still exhibited lower within-subject correlations (ZCORR = .75) than did high-self-esteem (HSE) subjects (ZCORR = .84), and the partial correlation between JF and ZCORR (controlling for the standard deviation of Time 1 and Time 2 ratings) was in the expected direction ($r = .25$), but neither result was significant.

well-articulated schema, or high congruence could derive from the fact that the better articulated schemas either direct or reflect greater actual consistency in behavior over situations. Assessing the accuracy of social perceptions involves a number of complex methodological issues that are beyond the scope of the present article (see Campbell & Fehr, 1990; Funder, 1987; Kenny & Albright, 1987, for discussions of accuracy issues). However, a more tractable issue was addressed by collecting partner's ratings of the subject's behavior during the interactions. Although partner's ratings do not necessarily represent reality, they do allow one to ascertain the extent to which congruence with the self-concept is attained at the cost of congruence with the partner's perceptions.

A secondary goal of Study 3 was to examine self-esteem differences in the extent to which the self-concept biases memory for previous behavior. Approximately 2 weeks after the interaction, subjects were contacted and asked to recall how they had rated their own behavior during the interaction. Although there was no reason to expect that self-esteem would be associated with the overall accuracy of recall, one would expect it to be associated with the type of errors made. Because schemas are used to fill in unknown or forgotten information (Kihlstrom & Canter, 1983), subjects with better articulated self-concepts (HSE subjects) should exhibit recall errors that are more biased in the direction of the self-concept.

## Method

### SUBJECTS

Thirty-seven LSE ($M$ = 56.94, $SD$ = 7.40) and 39 HSE ($M$ = 77.05, $SD$ = 5.11) subjects were selected from a pretest sample that completed the JF scale and rated themselves on the same set of 20 adjectives used in Study 2 (self-concept ratings) at the beginning of the academic year. Data from 5 subjects were deleted, 4 (2 LSE, 2 HSE) because they failed to complete the memory ratings and 1 (LSE) because of missing data on the self-ratings during the interaction.

### PROCEDURE

Pairs of same-sex subjects were recruited for a getting acquainted study approximately 2–3 months after completing the JF scale and the self-concept measure. Half of the subjects from each

esteem group were paired with an LSE partner; half were paired with an HSE partner. After determining that the pair was unacquainted, the experimenter told the subjects that they would engage in a 15-minute conversation. During the first 5 minutes, they would become acquainted by talking about their backgrounds, hobbies, and interests. During the other two 5-minute segments, they would discuss an opinion issue on which they agreed and an opinion issue on which they disagreed. Following the conversation, they would complete a questionnaire giving their impressions of the interaction.

After completing a brief opinion survey (used to select the two opinion topics), subjects were left alone to begin the first segment. The experimenter returned after 5 minutes to announce the first topic and again 5 minutes later to announce the second topic (topic order was counterbalanced). Subjects were then taken to separate rooms to complete the impression questionnaire. They were assured that their responses were confidential and would not be shown to their partner. The experimenter first gave the subjects the list of 20 adjectives and asked the subjects to rate each adjective with respect to how they thought they behaved or felt during the conversation. Subjects were then asked to rate the same adjectives with respect to how their partner behaved or felt during the conversation. Subjects were subsequently thanked for their participation and told that in 2 weeks they would be contacted to complete an additional questionnaire.

Two weeks later, subjects were mailed a questionnaire asking them to rate the adjectives with respect to how they believed they behaved or felt during the conversation. Reminder calls were made to subjects who had not returned the ratings within a week. Because some subjects required multiple phone calls or the mailing of replacement questionnaires, or both, the number of days that elapsed between the interaction and the memory ratings was quite variable ($M$ = 20.34, $SD$ = 8.90). However, elapsed time was not reliably associated with any of the dependent measures ($r$s < .18) and partial correlations revealed that, when elapsed time was controlled for, the associations between self-esteem and these measures were virtually unchanged.

## Results

Four sets of ratings were available for each subject. The 20 adjectives were rated with respect to (a) the subject's self-concept (SC; the trait ratings

**TABLE 12.1. Congruence Between Self-Concept, Self-Ratings, Partner's Ratings, and Remembered Self-Ratings by Self-Esteem: Average Absolute Differences**

| Congruence between | Low self-esteem | High self-esteem | ANOVA $F(1, 69)$ | $p <$ | Correlation JF, congruence |
|---|---|---|---|---|---|
| SC/SR | 1.27 | 1.04 | 3.40 | .07 | −.40* |
| SR/PR | 1.20 | 1.10 | 1.40 | ns | −.17 |
| SC/REM.SR | 1.24 | 0.95 | 5.54 | .05 | −.42* |
| SR/REM.SR | 0.69 | 0.68 | <1 | ns | −.05 |

Note. $N$ = 71. ANOVA = analysis of variance; JF = Janis-Field Self-Esteem Scale; SC = self-concept (general behavior ratings); SR = self-ratings of behavior during interaction; PR = partner's ratings of subject during interactions; REM.SR = recall of self-ratings.
*$p$ < .01, two-tailed.

given in the pretest), (b) the subject's self-ratings (SR) of his or her behavior during the interaction, (c) the partner's ratings (PR) of the subject's behavior during the interaction, and (d) the subject's remembered self-ratings (REM.SR) of how he or she behaved during the interaction. All ratings were made on 7-point scales anchored by *not at all* and *very descriptive*.

The first hypothesis was concerned with self-esteem differences in the congruence between the self-concept (SC) and perceptions of subsequent situation-specific behavior (SR). Two measures of SC/SR congruence were calculated: the average absolute difference (ABS DIFF) and the within-subject correlation (ZCORR)[3] between the two sets of ratings (see Study 2 for details). The same two measures were also calculated to assess the congruence between self-ratings and partner ratings (SR/PR), self-ratings and remembered self-ratings (SR/REM.SR), and the self-concept and remembered self-ratings (SC/REM.SR).

The measures were analyzed with single-factor ANOVAs (preliminary analyses indicated that topic order and self-esteem of the partner had no main or interactive effects); each measure was also correlated with the JF scale. The ABS DIFF results are given in Table 12.1, and the ZCORR results are given in Table 12.2.

The hypothesis that HSE subjects would exhibit greater correspondence between the self-concept and perceptions of situation-specific behavior (SC/SR) was supported (Row 1, Tables 12.1–2). The difference between the two sets of ratings (ABS DIFF) was smaller and the correlation between them (ZCORR) was higher for HSE than LSE subjects. In addition, both measures were substantially correlated with the JF scale in the expected direction.

The comparison of self-ratings with partner's ratings (SR/PR) indicated that the higher SC/SR correspondence exhibited by HSE subjects was not achieved at the cost of reduced congruence with the partner (Row 2, Tables 12.1–2). There were no significant self-esteem differences in the extent to which subjects' self-ratings agreed with those given by their partners.

The second hypothesis was that HSE subjects would exhibit memory errors that were more biased in the direction of their self-concepts than would LSE subjects. Before directly examining this hypothesis, note that the SC/REM.SR congruence measures (Row 3, Tables 12.1–2) yielded significant self-esteem differences; HSE subjects' recall of their behavior during the interaction was closer to their self-concept ratings than the recalled ratings given by LSE subjects. Also note that self-esteem was unrelated to the overall accuracy of recall. The SR/REM.SR congruence measures (Row 4, Tables 12.1–2) indicated that subjects recalled their previous ratings quite accurately and that self-esteem was not associated with recall accuracy, $F$s < 1.

If the memory errors that were made were biased towards the self-concept, the congruence between remembered self-ratings and the self-concept (SC/REM.SR) should be greater than the congruence between ratings given during the interaction and the self-concept (SC/SR). The second hypothesis suggested that this difference (SC/SR vs. SC/REM.SR) should be more pronounced for HSE than for LSE subjects.

Analyses comparing the SC/REM.SR and SC/

[3]Self-esteem differences in the ZCORR measures here are not subject to the problem of differential variance noted in Study 2. Self-esteem was only slightly correlated with the within-subject standard deviations (unreversed scoring) on the four sets of ratings (all $r$s < .08).

SR congruence measures (Rows 1 and 3 of the tables) as a function of self-esteem (Self-Esteem × Type of Congruence ANOVAs) yielded only some support for the hypothesis. The ABS DIFF measure did reveal a marginal bias for HSE subjects, $F(1, 36) = 3.94$, $p < .06$ and no bias for LSE subjects, $F < 1$, but the anticipated interaction was not significant, $F < 1$. The ZCORR measure did yield a reliable Self-Esteem × Type of Congruence interaction, $F(1, 69) = 4.39$, $p < .04$; HSE subjects exhibited memory errors that were biased toward the self-concept, $F(1, 36) = 8.69$, $p < .01$, whereas LSE subjects did not, $F < 1$. Therefore, despite the high levels of overall accuracy exhibited by both groups, the memory errors made by HSE subjects were quite systematically biased toward the self-concept, whereas the memory errors made by LSE subjects were more or less random with respect to the self-concept.

## Study 4

The primary purpose of Study 4 was to examine the hypothesis that LSE subjects would exhibit less internal consistency in their self-descriptions than would HSE subjects. Internal consistency was operationalized by asking subjects to make "me"/"not me" decisions for a long list of adjectives, within which were embedded pairs of opposites (e.g., careless/careful). Internal consistency was simply the number of opposite pairs that elicited consistent responses ("me" to one and "not me" to its opposite). The study also provided an opportunity to reexamine self-esteem differences in the subjective confidence of self-descriptions. The time subjects took to make their "me"/"not me"

decisions was recorded and, after each decision, subjects were asked to rate how confident they felt about their response.

### Method

Eighteen LSE ($M = 54.76$, $SD = 7.96$) and 18 HSE ($M = 79.61$, $SD = 6.08$) subjects were recruited for a study examining self-descriptions. Subjects reported individually and were informed that a microcomputer would present them with a list of adjectives. For each adjective, they were to press y if they believed the adjective described them and press n if it did not. They were told that although they had to make a decision for every adjective, the computer would subsequently prompt them to indicate how confident they felt about that response by presenting a 7-point scale ranging from *not at all* to *extremely confident.* After demonstrating a couple of practice trials, the experimenter left the subject alone in the room to complete the task.

Subjects were presented with 56 adjectives, 50 of which represented 25 pairs of opposites (e.g., timid/bold, lazy/hardworking, proud/humble, conventional/unconventional, and calm/nervous). Presentation order was randomized for each subject. The computer recorded "me"/"not me" decisions, reaction times (RT), and confidence ratings for the 50 target adjectives. Data from one LSE subject were lost because of a computer malfunction.

### Results

The results were generally consistent with the hypotheses. LSE subjects gave consistent responses to fewer of the 25 pairs (17.22 or 69%) than did HSE Subjects (20.18 or 81%), $F(1, 33) = 9.27$, $p$

**TABLE 12.2. Congruence Between Self-Concept, Self-Ratings, Partner's Ratings, and Remembered Self-Ratings by Self-Esteem: Average Within-Subject Correlations**

| Congruence between | Low self-esteem | High self-esteem | ANOVA $F(1, 69)$ | Correlation JF, congruence |
|---|---|---|---|---|
| SC/SR | .57 | .74 | 6.98* | .41* |
| SR/PR | .69 | .75 | 1.48 | .10 |
| SC/REM.SR | .57 | .79 | 13.02* | .47* |
| SR/REM.SR | .85 | .87 | <1 | .15 |

*Note.* $N = 71$. Table entries are $r$ transformations of the ZCORR measures. ANOVA = analysis of variance; JF = Janis-Field Self-Esteem Scale; SC = self-concept (general behavior ratings); SR = self-ratings of behavior during interaction; PR = partner's ratings of subject during interactions; REM.SR = recall of self-ratings.
*$p < .01$, two-tailed.

SUMMARY ↓

< .01. LSE Subjects took marginally longer (M = 4.50 s) to make response decisions than did HSE subjects (M = 3.81 s), F(1, 33) = 2.90, p < .10. LSE subjects gave lower confidence ratings (M = 5.07) than did HSE subjects (M = 5.40), F(1, 33) = 4. 38, p < .05. JF scores were significantly correlated with all three measures: the number of consistent responses (r = .42), average RT (r = −.34), and average confidence ratings (r = .43), ps < .05.

One might argue that inconsistent responses in this study did not necessarily reflect lack of clarity or certainty about the self. That is, when subjects responded "me" or "not me" to both members of opposite pairs, it was not because they were uncertain of their standing on the dimension, but because they held clear, confident views that they were either consistently moderate on the dimension or were flexible in their ability to display both types of behavior.

To ascertain if an inconsistent response pattern was associated with lower confidence, the average RT and confidence rating for the adjective pairs that had elicited consistent and inconsistent responses was calculated for each subject. Self-Esteem × Type of Response ANOVAs on the measures yielded substantial main effects for type of response, F(1, 33) = 9.88 for RT and F(1, 33) = 46.52 for confidence, ps < .01. The adjective pairs on which subjects had made inconsistent responses were associated with longer RTs (4.72 s vs. 4.02 s) and lower confidence ratings (4.77 vs. 5.38) than adjective pairs on which consistent responses had been given.

These main effects did not interact with self-esteem; both LSE and HSE subjects took longer and indicated lower confidence for adjective pairs on which they had responded inconsistently. Indeed, the two groups exhibited highly similar RTs and confidence for inconsistent adjective pairs, Fs < 1. The main effects of self-esteem on overall RT and confidence reported in the first paragraph of this section derived from the fact that (a) LSE subjects made more inconsistent responses and (b) on the adjective pairs associated with consistent responses, LSE subjects had marginally longer RTs (4.34 s vs. 3.66 s) and lower confidence (5.27 vs. 5.51) than HSE subjects, Fs > 2.95, ps <.10.

## Discussion

The four studies reported here generally support the hypothesis that LSE people have less clearly

defined concepts of who or what they are in terms of their personality attributes. When asked to describe themselves on bipolar adjectives (Study 1), LSE subjects tended to give responses nearer the midpoint of the scales and to indicate that they were less confident of their ratings. When asked to rate their personality traits on two occasions (Study 2), LSE subjects exhibited less temporal stability in terms of the amount of change and the extent to which the traits were ranked similarly on both occasions. Study 3 indicated that the self-concepts of LSE subjects were less congruent with their subsequent perceptions of current behavior and their memory for prior behavior. The study also provided some (mixed) evidence that HSE subjects exhibited memory errors that were more biased toward the self-concept than did LSE subjects. Finally, when asked to make "me"/"not me" responses to pairs of opposite traits, LSE subjects in Study 4 exhibited less internal consistency, lower self-rated confidence, and marginally longer RTS than did HSE subjects.

### Alternative Explanations

Each study has a number of potential methodological problems or alternative explanations. Consider, for example, the extremity results of Study 1. Although these results were interpreted as reflecting self-esteem differences in self-concept clarity, one could argue that extremity simply reflects differences in positivity or response styles. An attempt was made to discount the positivity explanation by conducting an analysis using only adjectives with no self-esteem differences in mean responses, but the response style interpretation was not addressed. With samples such as the present one, people who are classified as LSE are low only in a relative sense. Because the large majority of responses to items in self-esteem scales indicate favorable self-esteem (Bachman & O'Malley, 1984), the modal response of a subject classified as LSE is in fact near the theoretical midpoint of the scale, neither strongly accepting the positive items nor strongly rejecting the negative items. Therefore, one could argue that the present association between self-esteem and extremity simply represents a congruence of conservative response styles to the self-esteem scale and to the bipolar rating task. A conceptually similar alternative was advanced by Baumeister, Tice, and Hutton (1989), who argued that LSE may simply reflect a more cautious self-presentational style.

Although response style is a viable alternative explanation for the extremity (and confidence) results, it does not provide a reasonable account of self-esteem differences in the temporal stability or internal consistency of self-descriptions. A tendency to respond conservatively or cautiously should not, in itself, have led to less consistent responses over time (Study 2); less congruence between the self-concept and subsequent perceptions of situation-specific behavior (Study 3); or less consistent responses within a testing occasion, particularly on a consistency measure that forced subjects to make binary decisions (Study 4). These results do not, of course, contradict the notion that LSE people may adopt more cautious self-presentational styles, but they do suggest that there is something more at stake than just differences in self-presentation style. The relative instability and inconsistency of LSE subjects' self-descriptions implies that their self-definitions are more confused or uncertain, an intrapsychic uncertainty that could easily lead them to adopt a more cautious self-presentational style.

One could also argue that the extremity effect in Study 1 was not replicated in Study 2 and Study 3; self-esteem was not reliably or consistently correlated with the within-subject standard deviation of subjects' responses in those studies. However, Study 2 and Study 3 used ratings on evaluative unipolar adjectives, responses to which are ambiguous with respect to clarity. For example, people who are uncertain where they lie along an unassertive–assertive dimension could rate themselves *not at all* (1) or *moderate* (4) when presented with one of the two anchors. And although the established positivity bias of HSE subjects (stronger endorsements of positive adjectives and stronger rejections of negative adjectives) would lead to more HSE variability, this difference is attenuated by the fact that LSE subjects exhibit more evaluative inconsistency or variability within sets of positive and negative adjectives (Campbell &

Fehr, 1990). Therefore, these studies do not, and were not intended to, provide an appropriate test of the extremity hypothesis.

A similar set of points could be made about the results of Studies 2–4. That is, each study or measure associated with a potential set of alternative explanations, only some of which were addressed within a given study. Therefore, the present research can be considered to provide good support for the self-esteem/clarity hypothesis only when the studies are considered as a package: a pattern of convergent evidence derived from testing different specific hypotheses with different procedures and measures.

### Self-Esteem, Complexity, and Flexibility

One important alternative interpretation of the present data is conceptual in nature and is not limited to the results of any particular study. The results arguably do not reflect self-esteem differences in self-concept clarity, but differences in self-complexity or flexibility. That is, in relation to LSE subjects, HSE subjects' self-concepts are simple and rigid; their simplicity is reflected in the extremity and internal consistency of self-descriptions, and their rigidity is reflected in high temporal stability and in the fact that they exert a strong impact on current perceptions and memory.

This alternative is very difficult to address because the point at which a clearly defined, confident schema shades into one that is simplistic and rigid is highly ambiguous. This conceptual ambiguity is reflected in the fact that very similar measures have been used to operationalize complexity–flexibility and uncertainty of the self-concept. For example, Sande, Goethals, and Radloff (1988) recently interpreted lower extremity on ratings of bipolar adjectives and endorsement of both pairs of opposite traits as empirical indicators of a more multifaceted (flexible, complex) self-concept. Given that both interpretations are plausible, one must rely on supplementary evidence in attempting to distinguish whether the self-concepts of LSE people are more uncertain, more complex–flexible, or perhaps both.

The self-reported confidence and temporal stability measures in the present studies suggest that, even if the self-concepts of LSE people are more complex–flexible, they are also characterized by

link to complexity of self - Notes

less confidence and stability. LSE subjects claimed to be less certain of their self-descriptions (Studies 1 and 4). In addition, the measures that could be interpreted as reflecting either complexity–flexibility or uncertainty (extremity and internal consistency) were inversely correlated with self-reported confidence. For example, the pairs of opposite traits that subjects responded to inconsistently were associated with lower confidence ratings and longer RTs for both LSE and HSE subjects (Study 4). Finally, LSE subjects exhibited less stability in their trait ratings over time and less correspondence between their trait ratings and subsequent perceptions of situation-specific behavior.

More importantly, some studies have directly addressed the relation between self-esteem and complexity–flexibility. The results suggest that self-esteem is positively associated with the complexity and flexibility of the self-concept. Campbell, Chew, and Scratchley (1991) measured self-complexity with a trait-sorting task used by Linville to assess the complexity of group and self-schemas (Linville, 1982a; Linville & Jones, 1980). Subjects sorted 27 traits into groups according to which ones they thought belonged together when thinking about the self; they could form as few or as many groups as they wished, could put a trait in more than one group, and did not have to use all the traits. Two measures of complexity were calculated from the trait sort; the number of groups and a statistic, $H$, which reflects the number of independent binary dimensions needed to reproduce the sort (see Linville, 1982b; Scott, Osgood, & Peterson, 1979, for descriptions of this measure). Self-esteem was positively correlated with both measures ($rs = .32$).

With respect to flexibility, Paulhus and Martin (1988) distinguished between *functional flexibility*, which they defined as the capability of performing a range of social behaviors when required by the situation, and *situationality*, which they defined as the tendency to view one's behavior as being dependent on the situation. Consistent with the general concept of LSE plasticity, they reported that self-esteem was negatively correlated with situationality; LSE subjects claimed that their behavior depended more on the situation. However, self-esteem was positively correlated with functional flexibility; HSE people claimed that they were capable of performing a wider range of behaviors when required by the situation. Although

the self-report nature of these data dictates that they be viewed with some caution, the distinction between dependent (situationality) and controlled (flexibility) variation of behavior over situations may be theoretically useful in separating uncertainty from flexibility. The fact that LSE people perceive that they change more, but are less able to control that change, suggests a self-concept that is susceptible, not flexible, in responding to the social environment.

## Magnitude, Form, and Direction of the Self-Esteem/Clarity Relation

### MAGNITUDE OF THE RELATION

The correlations between self-esteem and the clarity measures used here were not large; they ranged from approximately .20 to .50. However, the present measures were selected because of their indirect or unobtrusive nature. Although such measures have strong benefits in terms of reduced reactivity (demand), social desirability, self-presentation, and common method variance, they are also weak in that variability can result from a variety of factors unrelated to the construct of interest (e.g., Webb, Campbell, Schwartz, & Sechrest, 1966). As noted earlier, correlations between self-esteem and self-report scales of identity are typically much higher than the correlations obtained here. For example, O'Brien and Epstein (1988) report correlations of .67 and .71 between their identity integration scale and the Rosenberg (1965) and JF (Eagly, 1967) self-esteem scales, respectively. Therefore, the utility of this research lies in providing independent, converging evidence for the presence of an association between self-esteem and self-concept clarity, not in estimating its strength.

### FORM OF THE RELATION

The relation between self-esteem and self-concept certainty could be curvilinear; that is, people with very low self-esteem may have more negative, but better defined, self-schemas than people with only moderately low self-esteem. The present data were examined for evidence of a curvilinear relation, but no such evidence emerged, despite the fact that at least some subjects in each study had self-esteem scores well below the theoretical midpoint of the scale. Given the nature of the present sample, one cannot exclude the possibility of extreme or clinical groups that hold highly negative views of the self with great certainty. However, even if the linear relation obtained here is limited to "normal" subjects, it is important to recall that, within such samples, variations in self-esteem have been shown to have substantial effects on a large variety of behaviors (Brockner, 1984; Wylie, 1979).

## DIRECTION OF THE RELATION

This research provides no evidence with respect to the causal direction of the relation, but plausible accounts can be given for both directions. For example, the notion of cognitive-affective crossfire (e.g., Swann et al., 1987) would suggest that LSE could lead to self-concept uncertainty. The basic premise is that although people are more cognitively accepting of information that is consistent with their self-views, all people affectively prefer positive information. For HSE people, there is no conflict; they cognitively accept the preferred positive feedback. However, LSE people are caught in a crossfire; negative feedback is accepted because it is consistent with their self-views, but it is also affectively abhorrent. Conflicting cognitive and emotional reactions to self-relevant information could result in self-concepts characterized by high levels of uncertainty.

On the other hand, it is also plausible that self-concept uncertainty could lead to lower self-esteem. If one assumes that all social environments produce some share of potentially negative or threatening information, uncertainty would render one more susceptible to this information and result in lowered self-esteem.

Both causal processes are reasonable; it seems likely that, at least among adults, the relation is reciprocal and confounded. Uncertainty increases susceptibility to negative information, which leads to LSE, and LSE results in a cognitive–affective conflict that increases uncertainty. To the extent that this is true, the cycle is self-perpetuating and may help to account for the high temporal stability of global self-esteem and the difficulty clinicians have in bringing about long-term improvements in self-esteem.

## Negative Affectivity (NA) and Realism

The argument that the self-concepts of LSE people are characterized by more confusion or uncertainty is seemingly inconsistent with some aspects of the depressive realism literature (see Alloy & Abramson, 1988, for a recent review). The depressive realism hypothesis has a weak version and a strong version (Ackermann & DeRubeis, 1989). The present argument is not inconsistent with the claim that people high in NA (e.g., depressed, LSE) lack a number of optimistic biases—biases that are, in the long run, adaptive and contribute to a sense of well-being (Taylor & Brown, 1988). However, the present argument does appear inconsistent with the strong version of the hypothesis, which contends that high NA people are, in fact, more accurate in their perceptions and judgments. In particular, the claim that negative affect people are more accurate in their self-perceptions (e.g., Lewinsohn, Mischel, Chaplin, & Barton, 1980) seems to contradict the argument that the self-concepts of such people lack clarity. Lewinsohn et al. showed that following a group interaction, (a) depressed subjects gave self-ratings that were less positive than those of nondepressed subjects and (b) when these self-ratings were compared with those of objective observers, depressed subjects' ratings were quite accurate, whereas nondepressed subjects' ratings were overly positive. However, observers' ratings are not necessarily a measure of objective reality and a number of authors have suggested that, because trained judges are prone to be especially harsh in their ratings (Gotlib & Meltzer, 1987), the low self-ratings of depressed subjects possibly just happened to coincide better with the relatively critical observer ratings (Coyne & Gotlib, 1983; Gotlib & Meltzer, 1987).

Campbell and Fehr (1990) recently provided support for this view. They assessed, for LSE and HSE people, the congruence between self–other ratings and assessed the accuracy of perceived conveyed impressions (congruence between beliefs about the others' impressions and others' actual impressions) for both interaction partners and observers. Observers rated subjects much more harshly than did interaction partners. However, neither observers nor interaction partners differed in their ratings of LSE and HSE subjects. Therefore, although LSE subjects did appear more accurate when their perceptions were compared to the observer criterion, they also appeared less accurate when their perceptions were compared with the interaction partner criterion. This result and others (e.g., Dykman, Abramson, Alloy, &

Hartlage, 1989) suggest that dysphoric people differ in the contents of their self-concepts, but either group can appear more realistic or accurate depending on the relative match between their schemas and the reality criterion (Ackermann & DeRubeis, 1989). If dysphoric people are not necessarily wiser, the notion that their self-concepts are relatively confused and uncertain is highly congruent with their other cognitive, emotional, and behavioral characteristics.

## Implications

People who suspect that they might possess negative attributes or lack positive attributes evidently prefer continued certainty to the possibility of acquiring certain knowledge that this is true (e.g., Berglas & Jones, 1978). This preference can be expressed by failing to seek comparison information (Flett, Vredenburg, Pliner, & Krames, 1987) or by selectively attending to comparison information that is less diagnostic (Campbell, Fairey, & Fehr, 1986), among other ways.

Holding negative beliefs with certainty may be more detrimental to mental health than maintaining some degree of uncertainty. Garber, Miller, and Abramson (1980) suggested that it is the certainty of expectancies about being unable to avoid negative outcomes (or obtain positive ones) that is critical in depression. In support of this suggestion, Andersen and Lyon (1987) reported a sharp increase in depressive affect when subjects were led to believe that an aversive event was certain to occur (100% likelihood) in relation to anticipated likelihoods of 75%, 50%, 25%, and 0%.

Despite the fact that uncertainty may be preferred and may have less deleterious consequences than holding negative beliefs with certainty, it is also costly. The present data simply suggest that it is associated with lower self-esteem. However, because the self-concept performs a number of important social and personal functions, such as processing self-relevant information, providing goals to direct behavior, and conveying a consistent image to others, people with identity confusion can experience a variety of social, emotional, and motivational deficits (Baumeister, 1986). A recent study by Brown and Smart (1989) also suggested that self-concept uncertainty may be a health risk; people with uncertain self-concepts were more vulnerable to stress-induced deteriora-

tions in health than those with a strong sense of identity.

When self-esteem is considered within the higher order construct of NA (Watson & Clark, 1984), its relation with self-concept clarity may have broader theoretical implications. NA (the disposition to experience aversive emotional states) is a diffuse trait, reflecting stable, pervasive differences in negative mood and self-concept. Positive affectivity (PA, the disposition to experience positive emotional states) is not simply the opposite of NA, but is viewed as reflecting extraversion and high levels of enthusiasm and energy (Watson, 1988; Watson & Tellegen, 1985). Watson and Pennebaker (1989) reported an average correlation of –.30 between scales measuring NA and PA, indicating that these traits are somewhat independent of each other. Self-concept certainty may be useful in accounting for the relative independence of NA and PA in much the same way that it was used here to help account for the fact that self-esteem is highly related to reactions to negative feedback, but not to positive feedback. That is, self-concept uncertainty may be an important component of NA in that, if potentially threatening environmental events were encountered, it would render one more susceptible to aversive emotional states but would not necessarily affect a proclivity to (also) experience positive emotional states.

## Summary

When the present studies are considered in conjunction with other research, the assumption that identity is closely linked with self-esteem (e.g., Adler, 1959) appears to be well-founded. Current evidence suggests that the evaluative and knowledge components of the self may be associated in several ways. This article provides evidence that people lower in self-esteem have self-knowledge structures that are less clearly defined in terms of the extremity and confidence of self-descriptions, less temporally stable, and less internally consistent. Other studies noted here indicated that LSE self-schemas may also be less complex (Campbell et al., 1991) and less functionally flexible (Paulhus & Martin, 1988). In addition, a recent study by Greenwald, Bellezza, and Banaji (1988) suggested that LSE may be associated with less extensiveness in the self-knowledge structure, especially for more positive aspects of the self. Finally, Campbell and Fehr (1990) provided some evidence that LSE people exhibit less evaluative consistency in their self-descriptions and are less likely to believe that others see them as they see themselves.

The self-esteem/identity relation has been largely neglected in the self-esteem literature, in which the self-concepts of LSE and HSE people are typically assumed to differ only about the positivity of their contents. However, many of the striking differences in behaviors, thoughts, and feelings that have been viewed as deriving from differences in positivity can be explained equally well, if not better, by attributing them to differences in self-concept certainty. These include not only self-esteem differences in reactions to feedback, but also a number of self-esteem phenomena within the areas of social influence, achievement, interpersonal attraction, and attribution.

Finally, it is possible that self-concept certainty may play a role in understanding the processes that underlie the more general trait of NA. Although a systematic investigation of the relations between NA, PA, self-concept certainty, self-esteem, and the various affective, cognitive, and behavioral concomitants of these traits has yet to be undertaken, self-concept certainty could be a crucial component in a generic disposition to experience aversive emotional states.

## REFERENCES

Ackermann, R., & DeRubeis, R. J. (1989). *Is depressive realism real?* Unpublished manuscript, Department of Psychology, University of Pennsylvania, Philadelphia.

Adler, A. (1959). *The practice and theory of individual psychology.* Totowa, NJ: Littlefield, Adams.

Alloy, L. B., & Abramson, L. Y. (1988). Depressive realism: Four theoretical perspectives. In L. B. Alloy (Ed.), *Cognitive processes in depression* (pp. 223–265). New York: Guilford Press.

Allport, G. (1961). *Pattern and growth in personality.* New York: Holt, Rinehart & Winston.

Andersen, S. M., &, Lyon, J. E. (1987). Anticipating undesired outcomes: The role of outcome certainty in the onset of depressive affect. *Journal of Experimental Social Psychology, 23,* 428–443.

Bachman, J. G., & O'Malley, P. M. (1984). Black–White differences in self-esteem: Are they affected by response styles? *American Journal of Sociology 90,* 624–639.

Baumeister, R. F. (1986). *Identity.* New York: Oxford University Press.

Baumeister, R. F., Tice, D. M, & Hutton, D. G. (1989). Self-presentational motivation and personality differences in self-esteem. *Journal of Personality, 57,* 547–579.

Berglas, S., & Jones, E. E. (1978). Drug choice as a self-handicapping strategy in response to noncontingent success. *Jour-*

*nal of Personality and Social Psychology, 36,* 405–417.

Block, J. (1961). Ego identity, role variability, and adjustment. *Journal of Consulting Psychology, 25,* 392–397.

Brockner, J. (1979). The effects of self-esteem, success–failure, and self-consciousness on task performance. *Journal of Personality and Social Psychology, 37,* 1732–1741.

Brockner, J. (1984). Low self-esteem and behavioral plasticity: Some implications for personality and social psychology. In L. Wheeler (Ed.), *Review of personality and social psychology* (Vol. 4, pp 237–271). Beverly Hills, CA: Sage.

Brown, J. D., & Smart, S. A. (1989). *Role of self-concept certainty in buffering the adverse impact of stressful life events.* Unpublished manuscript, University of Washington, Department of Psychology, Seattle.

Burke, P. J. (1980). The self: Measurement requirements from an interactionist perspective. *Social Psychology Quarterly, 43,* 18–29.

Campbell, J. D., Chew, B., & Scratchley, L. S. (1991). Cognitive and emotional reactions to daily events: The effects of self-esteem and self-complexity. *Journal of Personality, 59,* 473–505.

Campbell, J. D., & Fairey, P. J. (1985). Effects of self-esteem, hypothetical explanations, and verbalization of expectancies on future performance. *Journal of Personality and Social Psychology, 48,* 1097–1111.

Campbell, J. D., Fairey, P. J., & Fehr, B. (1986). Better than me or better than thee? Reactions to intrapersonal and interpersonal performance feedback. *Journal of Personality, 54,* 479–493.

Campbell, J. D., & Fehr, B. (1990). Self-esteem and perceptions of conveyed impressions: Is negative affectivity associated with greater realism? *Journal of Personality and Social Psychology, 58,* 122–133.

Campbell, J. D., & Tesser, A. (1985). Self-evaluation maintenance processes in relationships. In S. Duck & D. Perlman (Eds.), *Understanding personal relationships: An interdisciplinary approach* (Vol. 1, pp. 107–135). Beverly Hills, CA: Sage.

Church, M. A., Truss, C. Y., & Velicer, W. F. (1980). Structure of the Janis-Field Feelings of Inadequacy Scale. *Perceptual and Motor Skills, 50,* 935–939.

Cooley, C. (1912). *Human nature and the social order.* New York: Scribner's.

Coopersmith, S. (1967). *The antecedents of self-esteem.* San Francisco: Freeman.

Coyne, J. C., & Gotlib, I. H. (1983). The role of cognition in depression: A critical appraisal. *Psychological Bulletin, 94,* 472–505.

DePaulo, B., Brown, P., Ishii, S., & Fisher, J. (1981). Help that works: The effects of aid on subsequent task performance. *Journal of Personality and Social Psychology, 41,* 478–487.

Dykman, B. S., Abramson, L. Y., Alloy, L. G., & Hartlage, S. (1989). Processing ambiguous and unambiguous feedback by depressed and nondepressed college students: Schematic biases and their implications for depressive realism. *Journal of Personality and Social Psychology, 56,* 431–445.

Eagly, A. H. (1967). Involvement as a determinant of response to favorable and unfavorable information. *Journal of Personality and Social Psychology Monograph, 7,* (3, Pt. 2, Whole No. 643).

Epstein, S. (1983). The unconscious, the preconscious, and

the self-concept. In J. Suls & A. Greenwald (Eds.), *Psychological perspectives on the self* (Vol. 2, pp. 219–247). Hillsdale, NJ: Erlbaum.

Erikson, E. (1959). Identity and the life cycle: Selected papers. *Psychological Issues, 1*, 1–171.

Flett, G. L., Vredenburg, K., Pliner, P., & Krames, L. (1987). Depression and social comparison information-seeking. *Journal of Social Behavior and Personality, 2*, 473–484.

Funder, D. C. (1987). Errors and mistakes: Evaluating the accuracy of social judgment. *Psychological Bulletin, 101*, 75–90.

Garber, J., Miller, S. M., & Abramson, L. Y. (1980). On the distinction between anxiety and depression: Perceived control, certainty, and probability of goal attainment. In J. Garber & M. E. P. Seligman (Eds.), *Human helplessness: Theory and applications* (pp. 131–169). San Diego, CA: Academic Press.

Gotlib, I. H., & Meltzer, S. J. (1987). Depression and the perception of social skill in dyadic interaction. *Cognitive Therapy and Research, 11*, 41–54.

Greenwald, A. G., Bellezza, F. S., & Banaji, M. R. (1988). Is self-esteem a central ingredient of the self-concept? *Personality and Social Psychology Bulletin, 14*, 34–45.

Helmreich, R., Stapp, J., & Ervin, C. (1974). The Texas Social Behavior Inventory (TSBI): An objective measure of self-esteem or social competence. *JSAS Catalog of Selected Documents in Psychology, 4*, 79 (Ms. No. 681).

Jones, S. C. (1973). Self and interpersonal evaluations: Esteem theories versus consistency theories. *Psychological Bulletin, 79*, 185–199.

Kenny, D. A., & Albright, L. (1987). Accuracy in interpersonal perception: A social relations analysis. *Psychological Bulletin, 102*, 390–402.

Kihlstrom, J. F., & Cantor, N. (1983). Mental representations of the self. In L. Berkowitz (Ed.), *Advances in experimental social psychology* (Vol. 17, pp 1–47). San Diego, CA: Academic Press.

Kihlstrom, J. F., Cantor, N., Albright, J. S., Chew, B. R., Klein, S. B., & Neidenthal, P. M. (1988). Information processing and the study of the self. In L. Berkowitz (Ed.), *Advances in experimental social psychology* (Vol. 21, pp. 159–187). San Diego, CA: Academic Press.

Lewinsohn, P. M., Mischel, W., Chaplin, W., & Barton, R. (1980). Social competence and depression: The role of illusory self-perceptions. *Journal of Abnormal Psychology, 89*, 203–212.

Linville, P. W. (1982a). Affective consequences of complexity regarding the self and others. In M. S. Clark & S. T. Fiske (Eds.), *Affect and cognition* (pp. 79–109). Hillsdale, NJ: Erlbaum.

Linville, P. W. (1982b). The complexity–extremity effect and age-based stereotyping. *Journal of Personality and Social Psychology, 42*, 193–211.

Linville, P. W., & Jones, E. E. (1980). Polarized appraisals of outgroup members. *Journal of Personality and Social Psychology, 38*, 689–703.

Marcia, J. E. (1980). Identity in adolescence. In J. Adelson (Ed.), *Handbook of adolescent psychology* (pp. 159–187). New York: Wiley.

Markus, H. (1977). Self-schemata and processing information about the self. *Journal of Personality and Social Psychology, 35*, 63–78.

Markus, H. (1980). The self in thought and memory. In D. M.

Wegner & R. R. Vallacher (Eds.), *The self in social psychology* (pp. 102–130). New York: Oxford University Press.

McFarlin, D. B., & Blascovich, J. (1981). Effects of self-esteem and performance on future affective preferences and cognitive expectations. *Journal of Personality and Social Psychology, 40*, 521–531.

Millar, M. G., & Tesser, A. (1986). Thought-induced attitude change: The effects of schema structure and commitment. *Journal of Personality and Social Psychology, 51*, 259–269.

Moreland, R. L., & Sweeney, P. D. (1984). Self-expectancies and reactions to evaluations of personal performance. *Journal of Personality, 52*, 156–176.

Mortimer, J. T., Finch, M. D., & Kumka, D. (1982). Persistence and change in development: The multidimensional self-concept. In P. B. Baltes & O. G. Brim, Jr. (Eds.), *Life-span development and behavior* (Vol. 4, pp. 263–313). Orlando, FL: Academic Press.

O'Brien, E. J., & Epstein, S. (1988). *MSEI: The multidimensional self-esteem inventory*. Odessa, FL: Psychological Assessment Resources.

O'Malley, P. M., & Bachman, J. G. (1983). Self-esteem: Change and stability between ages 13 and 23. *Developmental Psychology, 19*, 257–268.

Paulhus, D. L., & Martin, C. L. (1988). Functional flexibility: A new conception of interpersonal flexibility. *Journal of Personality and Social Psychology, 55*, 88–101.

Robinson, J. P., & Shaver, P. R. (1973). *Measures of social psychological attitudes*. Ann Arbor, MI: Institute for Social Research.

Rogers, T. B. (1981). A model of the self as an aspect of the human information-processing system. In N. Cantor & J. F. Kihlstrom (Eds.), *Personality cognition, and social interaction* (pp. 193–214). Hillsdale, NJ: Erlbaum.

Rosenberg, M. (1965). *Society and the adolescent self-image*. Princeton, NJ: Princeton University Press.

Rosenberg, M. (1979). *Conceiving the self*. New York: Basic Books.

Sande, G. N., Goethals, G. R., & Radloff, C. E. (1988). Perceiving one's own traits and others': The multifaceted self. *Journal of Personality and Social Psychology, 54*, 13–20.

Scott, W. A., Osgood, D. W., & Peterson, C. (1979). *Cognitive structure: Theory and measurement of individual differences*. Washington, DC: V. H. Winston.

Sherwood, J. J. (1962). *Self-identity and self-actualization: A theory and research*. Unpublished doctoral dissertation, University of Michigan, Ann Arbor.

Shrauger, J. S. (1975). Responses to evaluation as a function of initial self-perceptions. *Psychological Bulletin, 82*, 581–596.

Shrauger, J. S., & Sorman, P. B. (1977). Self-evaluations, initial success and failure, and improvement as determinants of persistence. *Journal of Consulting and Clinical Psychology, 45*, 784–795.

Swann, W. B., Jr., Griffin, J. J., Jr., Predmore, S. C., & Gaines, B. (1987). The cognitive–affective crossfire: When self-consistency confronts self-enhancement. *Journal of Personality and Social Psychology, 52*, 881–889.

Taylor, S. E., & Brown, J. D. (1988). Illusion and well-being: A social psychological perspective on mental health. *Psychological Bulletin, 103*, 193–210.

Taylor, S. E., & Crocker, J. (1981). Schematic bases of social information processing. In E. T. Higgins, C. P. Herman, & M. P. Zanna (Eds.), *Social cognition: The Ontario Symposium* (pp. 89–134). Hillsdale, NJ: Erlbaum.

Tesser, A. (1978). Self-generated attitude change. In L. Berkowitz (Ed.), *Advances in experimental social psychology* (Vol. 11, pp. 289–338). San Diego, CA: Academic Press.

Tesser, A., & Campbell, J. (1983). Self-definition and self-evaluation maintenance. In J. Suls & A. Greenwald (Eds.), *Psychological perspectives on the self* (Vol. 2, pp. 1–31). Hillsdale, NJ: Erlbaum.

Watson, D. (1988). Intraindividual and interindividual analyses of positive and negative affect: Their relation to health complaints, perceived stress, and daily activities. *Journal of Personality and Social Psychology, 54,* 1020–1030.

Watson, D., & Clark, L. A. (1984). Negative affectivity: The disposition to experience aversive emotional states. *Psychological Bulletin, 96,* 465–490.

Watson, D., & Pennebaker, J. W. (1989). Health complaints, stress and distress: Exploring the central role of negative affectivity. *Psychological Review, 96,* 234–254.

Watson, D., & Tellegen, A. (1985). Toward a consensual structure of mood. *Psychological Bulletin, 98,* 219-235.

Webb, E. B., Campbell, D. T., Schwartz, R. D., & Sechrest, L. (1966). *Unobstrusive measures: Nonreactive research in the social sciences.* Chicago: Rand McNally.

Wells, L. E., & Marwell, G. (1976). *Self-esteem.* Beverly Hills, CA: Sage.

Wylie, R. (1974). *The self-concept* (Vol. 1). Lincoln: University of Nebraska Press.

Wylie, R. (1979). *The self-concept* (Vol. 2). Lincoln: University of Nebraska Press.

Zuckerman, M. (1979). Attribution of success and failure revisited, or: The motivational bias is alive and well in attribution theory. *Journal of Personality, 47,* 245–287.

# Relation of Threatened Egotism to Violence and Aggression: The Dark Side of High Self-Esteem

Roy F. Baumeister • Case Western Reserve University
Laura Smart • University of Virginia
Joseph M. Boden • Case Western Reserve University

Conventional wisdom has regarded low self-esteem as an important cause of violence, but the opposite view is theoretically viable. An interdisciplinary review of evidence about aggression, crime, and violence contradicted the view that low self-esteem is an important cause. Instead, violence appears to be most commonly a result of threatened egotism—that is, highly favorable views of self that are disputed by some person or circumstance. Inflated, unstable, or tentative beliefs in the self's superiority may be most prone to encountering threats, and hence, to causing violence. The mediating process may involve directing anger outward as a way of avoiding a downward revision of the self-concept.

Only a minority of human violence can be understood as rational instrumental behavior aimed at securing or protecting material rewards The pragmatic futility of most violence has been widely recognized: Wars harm both sides, most crimes yield little financial gain, terrorism and assassination almost never bring about the desired political changes, most rapes fail to bring sexual pleasure, torture rarely elicits accurate or useful information, and most murderers soon regret their actions as pointless and self-defeating (Ford, 1985; Gottfredson & Hirschi, 1990; Groth, 1979; Keegan, 1993; Sampson & Laub, 1993; Scarry, 1985). What drives people to commit violent and oppressive actions that so often are tangential or even contrary to the rational pursuit of material self-interest? This article reviews literature relevant to the hypothesis that one main source of such violence is threatened egotism, particularly when it consists of favorable self-appraisals that may be inflated or ill-founded and are confronted with an external evaluation that disputes them.

The focus on egotism (i.e., favorable self-appraisals) as one cause of violent aggression runs contrary to an entrenched body of wisdom that has long pointed to low self-esteem as the root of violence and other antisocial behavior. We shall examine the arguments for the low self-esteem view and treat it as a rival hypothesis to our emphasis on high self-esteem. Clearly, there are abundant theoretical and practical implications that attend the question of which level of self-esteem is associated with greater violence. The widely publicized popular efforts to bolster the self-esteem of various segments of the American population in recent decades (e.g., see California Task Force, 1990) may be valuable aids for reducing violence if low self-esteem is the culprit—or they may be making the problems worse.

Indeed, if high self-esteem is a cause of violence, then the implications may go beyond the direct concern with interpersonal harm. Many researchers share the opinion that high self-esteem is desirable and adaptive and can even be used as one indicator of good adjustment (e.g., Heilbrun, 1981; Kahle, Kulka, & Klingel, 1980; Taylor, 1989; Taylor & Brown, 1988; Whitley, 1983), but this one-sidedly favorable view of egotism would have to be qualified and revised: Favorable impressions of oneself may not be an unmitigated good from the perspective of society if they lead to violence. In our view, the benefits of favorable self-opinions accrue primarily to the self and they are, if anything, a burden and potential problem to everyone else. Hence the widespread norms condemning conceit and arrogance, as well as the tendency to shift toward modesty when in the company of friends (Tice, Muraven, Butler, & Stillwell, 1994). E. Anderson (1994) recently even suggested that self-esteem among youth gangs and similar groups conforms to a zero-sum pattern, which means that any increment in status, respect, or prestige of one person detracts from what is available for everyone else.

Although some researchers favor narrow and precise concepts of self-esteem, we shall use the term in a broad and inclusive sense. By *self-esteem* we mean simply a favorable global evaluation of oneself. The term *self-esteem* has acquired highly positive connotations, but it has ample synonyms, the connotations of which are more mixed, including pride, egotism, arrogance, honor, conceitedness, narcissism, and sense of superiority, which share the fundamental meaning of favorable self-evaluation. A related set of concepts refers to favorable evaluations of the self by others, including prestige, admiration, public esteem, and respect. Favorable evaluations are also implicit in liking and loving, although those terms have additional meanings. Of particular importance for the present review is that our deliberately broad usage of the term *self-esteem* is not limited to the direct results of validated trait measures of self-esteem, although we pay close attention to such

measures when available. To reduce confusion, we shall favor the term egotism to refer both to favorable appraisals of self and to the motivated preference for such favorable appraisals, regardless of whether they are valid or inflated. Any assumption or belief that one is a superior being, or any broadly favorable assessment of self (especially in comparison with other people), is relevant.

Thus, in brief, the purpose of this article is to understand how self-appraisals are related to interpersonal violence. We hasten to add that we are not proposing a general theory of violence or aggression, and we assume that many aggressive acts may have little or no relation to self-esteem. Moreover, when self-appraisals are involved, they may be only one of several factors, so we are not asserting that other causes become irrelevant or secondary. The intent is merely to understand how self-appraisals affect violence in those cases in which they are involved. There do seem to be many such cases.

## Traditional View: Low Self-Esteem Causes Violence

A long tradition has regarded low self-esteem as a powerful and dangerous cause of violence. This view seems to be so widely and uncritically accepted that it is often casually asserted in the absence of evidence and even in the presence of apparently contrary evidence. When reading the literature for this review, we repeatedly found cases in which researchers summarized observations that depicted aggressors as egotistical and arrogant, but then added the conventional supposition that these individuals must be suffering from low self-esteem. (Hence we shall, in some cases, cite authors in this section as arguing in favor of low self-esteem but shall then later cite their empirical observations as contradicting it.)

One does not have to look far to find examples of the assertion that low self-esteem causes violence. E. Anderson (1994) recently cited low self-esteem as a persistent cause of the violence among youth gangs. Similarly, Jankowski (1991) referred to "self-contempt" of gang members as a cause of violence. Renzetti (1992) said that the jealousy and possessiveness that lead to domestic violence have generally been understood as resulting from low self-esteem. Staub (1989) cited as traditional the view that low self-esteem generally causes all manner of violence, although he was careful not to endorse that conclusion himself and in fact supplied some contrary evidence. Gondolf (1985) noted that wife beaters have usually been characterized as having low self-esteem, although he pointed out that the evidence for this is largely indirect, namely from clinical case studies of their victims (Walker, 1979). Long (1990) asserted that low self-esteem and feelings of inadequacy are prominent characteristics of most terrorists. MacDonald (1975) said that armed robbers "lack self-esteem" (p. 263). Wiehe (1991) said that a possible motive for sibling violence is "as a way to bolster or increase their low self-esteem" (p. 17). Kirschner (1992) claimed that several murderers (in this case, adoptees who had killed their adoptive fathers) suffered from low self-esteem and viewed themselves as bad. Levin and McDevitt (1993) casually mentioned low self-esteem as if it were commonly known to be an important cause of hate crimes.

In other cases, the weaknesses and fallacies in the low self-esteem view are readily apparent. Thus, in one of the classic works on the psychology of violence, Toch (1969/1993) referred to a "compensatory relationship between low self-esteem and violence" (pp. 133–134), and he suggested that people with low self-esteem turn violent as a way of gaining esteem. Yet Toch did not have any direct evidence of low self-esteem; he merely inferred that these men must suspect themselves of weakness because they seemed so concerned with refuting that impression. Alternative interpretations, particularly that they have highly favorable views of self that are threatened by disrespectful others, are equally possible. Indeed, in the same passage in which Toch referred to the self-doubts and "sense of inadequacy" of violent men, he also proposed that these same offenders had "exaggerated self-esteem" (p. 136), which is obviously the opposite assertion. He also said that such an individual "demands unwarranted respect" (p. 136), which is close to our own argument of an inflated sense of deservingness (e.g., excessively high self-esteem). In short, Toch's explanation is internally inconsistent.

In another example, Oates and Forrest (1985) asserted that abusive mothers had low self-esteem. They based this conclusion on a purported measure of self-esteem that was actually a single item

asking the mother whether she wished her child would grow up like herself abusive mothers tended to give self-deprecating answers to this question. At the time of data collection the mothers had all recently been referred for child abuse. Under those circumstances, it would seem almost mandatory to show some self-deprecation and to be hesitant about expressing the wish that one's child would follow in one's footsteps. To label that response as low self-esteem seems potentially misleading.

Likewise, Schoenfeld (1988) proposed that the high crime rate among American Black people is due to their low self-esteem. In his analysis, Blacks were reduced by slavery to a state of extremely low self-esteem. When slavery ended, this low self-regard was perpetuated by Jim Crow laws and, more recently, by the modern welfare system, which fosters helplessness and dependency. Thus, in Schoenfeld's view, low self-esteem is responsible for the high crime rate. Unfortunately this analysis suffers from several flaws. First, it does not fit the temporal shifts in crime rate among Blacks, which is now reaching its highest levels as slavery recedes farther and farther into the background. Second, as Crocker and Major's (1989) review showed, self-esteem levels among Blacks are now equal to or higher than the self-esteem levels of Whites. Third, it is far from certain that slaves had low self-esteem; Patterson (1982) insisted that slaves did not simply internalize the unflattering views society held of them.

Our review did not uncover any one definitive or authoritative statement of the theory that low self-esteem causes violence, so it is necessary for us to consider several possible versions of that theory. One view (and one that seems implicit in many writings) is that people who lack self-esteem hope to gain it by violent means, such as by aggressively dominating others. In this view, violence would be a technique of self-enhancement, in the sense that it is used as a means of increasing one's esteem. A long tradition has assumed that people with low self-esteem must be strongly oriented toward self-enhancement, because they want to gain more of what they lack.

The self-enhancement version of the low self-esteem view is internally plausible, but the accumulation of research findings has now rendered it untenable. The motivation to seek self-enhancement has been shown to be characteristic of people high (rather than low) in self-esteem and, in fact, it appears to be weak or absent among people with

*self-enhancement*

low self-esteem (Baumeister, Tice, & Hutton, 1989; Tice, 1991, 1993). Indeed, people with low self-esteem appear to be ambivalent about rising in esteem and they often avoid circumstances that might raise their self-esteem (De La Ronde & Swann, 1993; Swann, 1987; Swann, Griffin, Predmore, & Gaines, 1987).

A similar contradiction can be found in recent work on the psychology of terrorism. Long (1990) summarized what various writers have concluded about the most common personality traits of terrorist individuals as including "low self-esteem and a predilection for risk-taking" (p. 18). Long's explication of the nature of this low self-esteem seemed, however, to fit very closely what is known about high self-esteem. In Long's account, these individuals "tend to place unrealistically high demands on themselves and, when confronted with failure, to raise rather than lower their aspirations" (p. 18). High self-esteem is associated with higher aspirations than low self-esteem in general (e.g., Baumeister & Tice, 1985). The particular, ironic pattern of responding to failure by raising one's aspirations further was shown by McFarlin and Blascovich (1981) to be characteristic of people with high self-esteem; Baumeister, Heatherton, and Tice (1993) replicated that pattern and showed that it extended to increased risk-taking after failure or other ego threat. It may once have been plausible to think that people with low self-esteem would be prone to take risks and raise their aspirations after failure, but those patterns have now been linked to high rather than low self-esteem. Thus, Long's purported evidence for low self-esteem among terrorists in fact seems to indicate a pattern of high self-esteem.

Another variation of the low self-esteem theory is based on the notion of a subculture of violence. This notion emerged in the late 1960s as one explanation for violence among stigmatized minority populations. According to this view, members of these minority groups lacked access to the traditional or mainstream sources of self-esteem, so they formed communities in which aggressive behavior was an alternative source. The subculture of violence hypothesis has lost ground, however, as researchers have been unable to identify any community or subculture that places a positive value on violent acts (see Tedeschi & Felson, 1994).

Yet another version would propose that all people desire to regard themselves favorably;

people with high self-esteem have satisfied this need and can ignore it, whereas it remains a focal concern of those with low self-esteem. In this view, high self-esteem ought to confer a kind of immunity to ego threats, because the person is so secure in his or her self-appraisal that nothing can diminish it. However, researchers have not found that most people with high self-esteem are so cheerfully indifferent to insults, criticism, or disrespect. Indeed, the strong and sometimes irrational reactions of people with high self-esteem to negative feedback have been abundantly documented (Baumeister et al., 1989, 1993; Baumeister & Tice, 1985; Blaine & Crocker, 1993; McFarlin & Blascovich, 1981). Some studies suggest that people with high self-esteem are, if anything, more sensitive to criticism than people with low self-esteem (e.g., Schlenker, Soraci, & McCarthy, 1976; Shrauger & Lund, 1975).

Toch (1969/1993) observed that many violent men seek out or manufacture situations in which their self-worth is challenged, with the result being a violent confrontation. Because Toch espoused the low self-esteem view, we infer that he thought low self-esteem would be a factor that dictated such efforts. Possibly Toch thought that people who lack self-esteem seek out such challenges as a way of gaining esteem. To us,[1] however, it seems implausible that people who hold low opinions of themselves will seek out situations that will provide tests or other feedback. Low self-esteem would favor an avoidance of such feedback, for several reasons: These people want to protect themselves from bad feedback (Baumeister et al., 1989); they dislike and distrust flattering, enhancing feedback (Swann, 1987); and they are not strongly motivated to gain accurate feedback (Sedikides, 1993). Only the person with a highly favorable opinion of self will be inclined to seek out risky situations to prove his or her merit. Picking fights with dangerous individuals strikes us as a dubious strategy for gaining esteem, and it seems likely to appeal mainly to individuals with irrationally high confidence.

There is one final and limited variation on the self-esteem view that appears to be more plausible than the others. Some causes of violence may have little to do with self-esteem and, as a result, some

---

[1] In fairness to Toch, we have the benefit of several decades of research on self-esteem that was not available to him in 1969.

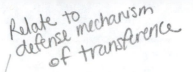
*Relate to mechanism of defense mechanism of transference*

people at any level of self-esteem may become aggressive. The combination of violent tendencies and low self-esteem might then exert an influence on choice of target. As we said, it would seemingly require high confidence to attack a powerful person, but when the target is seemingly weak and helpless the odds of success may seem quite high. Accordingly, people with low self-esteem may channel their violent tendencies into attacks on such weak and helpless targets. Men who attack women and adults who attack children might well have low self-esteem, not because low self-esteem causes violence, but because low self-esteem causes them to seek a victim who is unlikely to retaliate. On a priori basis, therefore, domestic violence seems like the most promising milieu in which to find evidence of aggression by people who lack self-esteem.

*Summary*

In summary, the view that low self-esteem causes violence has been widely asserted but rarely elaborated. Our efforts to reconstruct the theorizing behind the low self-esteem hypothesis have resulted in several versions, none of which is broadly satisfactory. Some are internally inconsistent, whereas others seem internally plausible on a priori grounds but run contrary to the accumulated evidence about self-esteem. The most viable view in our version saw low self-esteem not as a cause of violence but as causing a preference for safe, helpless targets, suggesting that any violent tendencies that exist among people with low self-esteem will most likely be expressed in situations in which fear of retaliation is minimal.

## High Self-Esteem and Violence

In contrast to the low self-esteem view, we propose that highly favorable self-appraisals are the ones most likely to lead to violence. As noted in the previous section, the traditional theories linking low self-esteem to violence suffer from ambiguities, inconsistencies, and contradictory empirical evidence. The opposite view therefore deserves consideration.

There are some bases for suggesting that egotism could lead directly to violence. People who regard themselves as superior beings might feel entitled to help themselves to the resources of other, seemingly lesser beings, and indeed they might even aggress against these lesser beings

without compunction, just as people kill insects or mice without remorse (Myers, 1980). Also, many violent episodes involve a substantial element of risk, and a favorable self-appraisal might furnish the requisite confidence to take such a chance. In plain terms, egotists might be more likely to assume that they will win a fight, so they would be more willing to start it.

Our main argument, however, does not depict self-esteem as an independent and direct cause of violence. Rather, we propose that the major cause of violence is high self-esteem combined with an ego threat. When favorable views about oneself are questioned, contradicted, impugned, mocked, challenged, or otherwise put in jeopardy, people may aggress. In particular, they will aggress against the source of the threat.

In this view, then, aggression emerges from a particular discrepancy between two views of self: a favorable self-appraisal and an external appraisal that is much less favorable. That is, people turn aggressive when they receive feedback that contradicts their favorable views of themselves and implies that they should adapt less favorable views. More to the point it is mainly the people who refuse to layer their self-appraisals who become violent.

One major reason to suggest that violence may result from threatened egotism is that people are extremely reluctant to raise their self-appraisals in a downward direction. This assertion must be understood in the context of the research literature concerning the motivations that surround self-appraisals. This literature has been dominated by two somewhat conflicting hypotheses. One holds that people wish to hold maximally positive views of themselves and so seek to enhance their self-appraisals whenever possible (e.g., Darley & Goethals, 1980; Greenwald, 1980; Schlenker, 1980; Taylor & Brown, 1988). The other is that people seek to maintain consistent self-appraisals and therefore seek to avoid changing their self-concepts at all (e.g., De La Ronde & Swann, 1993; Swann, 1987). Although these two views make contradictory predictions in some settings, they agree emphatically that people are reluctant to change toward more unflattering views of themselves. The avoidance of loss of esteem is thus the dearest and presumably strongest pattern of self-concept motivation (Baumeister, 1993). Decreases in self-esteem are aversive for nearly everyone.

The relevance of level of trait self-esteem to these two motives (enhancement and consistency) requires elaboration. First, consider the self-enhancement motive. People with favorable opinions of themselves have been shown to exceed those with low self-esteem in desire for self-enhancement (Baumeister et al., 1989; Tice, 1991, 1993). The quest for opportunities to prove oneself or to raise one's standing should therefore appeal mainly to people with high self-esteem. For example, a pattern of seeking out situations in which one's worth is challenged or disputed might strike a very confident person as a good chance to refute such threats and show oneself off to be a winner. In contrast, people with low self-esteem will probably tend to avoid such situations.

Meanwhile, the orientation toward self-protection (against losing self-esteem) has been shown to be more characteristic of people with low, rather than high, self-esteem. On the surface, this seems to suggest a contradiction to our portrayal of aggression as resulting from threatened egotism because low, rather than high, self-esteem is associated with broad, chronic concern with avoiding loss of esteem. Yet this is misleading. Self-protection characterizes the habitual orientation of people with low self-esteem because they are constantly concerned with avoiding situations that could result in a loss of esteem. People with high self-esteem do not show a strong self-protective orientation habitually because they do not anticipate that they will fail or lose esteem. When threats to esteem do arise, however, people with high self-esteem respond in ways that are often drastic and irrational (see Blaine & Crocker, 1993, for review; see also Baumeister et al., 1993; Baumeister & Tice, 1985; McFarlin & Blascovich, 1981). Thus, people with high self-esteem do indeed hate to lose esteem. Most of the time they scarcely think about the possibility that they will lose esteem, so it is only when a threat emerges that they become extremely defensive.

Self-verification theory (Swann, 1987) is based on the notion that people resist changes to their self-concepts. This motive to maintain consistent self-appraisals means that people who think somewhat poorly of themselves may resist favorable feedback. People who think well of themselves, on the other hand, may be broadly receptive to favorable feedback because it largely confirms their self-appraisals. However, they will react quite strongly against unfavorable feedback.

Thus, the self-enhancement and self-verification motives both predict that the strongest negative reactions to external feedback will arise when people who think well of themselves receive unflattering feedback. In our view, that is precisely the discrepancy most likely to lead to violence—when favorable views of self are met with external, less favorable appraisals.

To elaborate this basic theoretical position, we shall proceed as follows. First, we shall examine some likely moderators of the link between egotism and violence. These moderators are based on the assumption that anything that increases either the frequency or the subjective impact of discrepancies between favorable self-appraisals and external ego threats will increase the likelihood of violence. Second, we shall examine the role of affect as mediating between threatened egotism and aggressive behavior. Last, we shall examine the interpersonal context of threatened egotism.

## Favorable and Inflated Self-Appraisals

If threatened egotism causes aggression, then whatever views of self encounter the greatest number of threats should be the ones most commonly associated with violence. On an a priori basis, it would seem that the higher the self-esteem, the greater the range of feedback that would be seen as threatening. Thus, for example, people who believe themselves to be among the top 10% on any dimension may be insulted and threatened whenever anyone asserts that they are in the 80th, 50th, or 25th percentile. In contrast, someone with lower self-esteem who regards himself or herself as being merely among the top 60% would only be threatened by the feedback that puts him or her at the 25th percentile; indeed, feedback that puts him or her at the 80th percentile, which was threatening and insulting to the person with very high self-esteem, might even be received as praise by someone with much lower self-esteem.

In short, the more favorable one's view of oneself, the greater the range of external feedback that will be perceived as unacceptably low. To the extent that violence arises from threats to self-esteem (in the sense of receiving external feedback that evaluates one less favorably than one's self-evaluation), violence should be more common among people with high self-esteem.

One could dispute the aforementioned reasoning by arguing that feedback is actually very selectively distributed. That is, maybe the person who regards himself or herself as at the 90th percentile

self-enhancement vs. self-verification

is in fact so competent that he or she will almost never receive the 25th percentile feedback. To the extent that feedback tends to cluster around accurate appraisal of one's true abilities (including social feedback, i.e., being seen accurately by others), there might be no difference in the frequency of threatening feedback received by people at any level of self-appraisal.

There would, however, be one major exception to the argument that the general accuracy of feedback would counteract the excess vulnerability of high self-esteem to threat. Favorable views of self that are unwarranted, exaggerated, or ill-founded would be especially prone to disconfirmation by accurate feedback. Whenever people's self-appraisals are more favorable than their objective qualities would warrant, the result may be a pervasive vulnerability to threatening feedback. And how often does that happen? Evidence suggests that people with favorable self-opinions frequently benefit from distortion, selective perception, or exaggeration. The pervasiveness of such inflated views of self, particularly among people with high self-esteem, has been well documented (Taylor & Brown, 1988).

Thus, to the extent that feedback tends to be accurate instead of random, its subjective impact will depend on whether the recipient's self-appraisals are accurate or inflated. Accurate feedback will tend to confirm self-appraisals, including favorable ones, if they were realistic to begin with. Accurate feedback will, however, tend to disconfirm self-appraisals that are unrealistically positive. The implication is that unrealistically positive self-appraisals will increase the frequency with which external ego threats are encountered. Inflated views of self should therefore increase the frequency of violence.

## Instability, Uncertainty, and Evaluative Dependency

In the section on low self-esteem, we mentioned the hypothesis that people with favorable self-appraisals would be indifferent to bad feedback because it would not threaten them. As we said, researchers have not generally found many people who are immune to criticism, but there may be a kernel of truth in that reasoning. Undoubtedly there are individual differences and situational variations in the degree to which people care about the opinions of others. Such variations would presumably alter the subjective impact of bad feedback and ego threats and, as a result, they would moderate the degree of aggressive response. Unlike inflated self-appraisals, which increase the frequency with which one encounters ego threats, these variables increase the importance of ego threats and hence magnify the hostile response.

One factor that seems likely to moderate the impact of external appraisals is the degree of certainty of the relevant self-appraisal. Someone who is certain of having a particularly good trait may be relatively less affected by contradictory feedback as compared with someone who is less certain. Accordingly, those people with uncertain but positive views of self may also be the ones most prone to elicit defensive responses to ego threats.

Many views of identity formation have emphasized that people require the validation of others (e.g., Baumeister, 1986; Cooley, 1902/1964; James, 1890/1950; Mead, 1934; Schlenker, 1980, 1986). Probably the most thorough explication of how uncertainty of self-appraisal is linked to reliance on external validation was provided in the work of Wicklund and Gollwitzer (1982). In multiple studies, they showed that people vary in the degree to which they are motivated to have others confirm their identity claims. Although nearly everyone requires some social validation, some people become heavily dependent on it, whereas others require much less, and these variations can be partly explained on the basis of having acquired a stock of symbolic affirmations of the self (which boost certainty and what Wicklund and Gollwitzer called "completeness"). Once a person has accumulated abundant trappings of success, for example, he or she may not feel any urgent need to acquire more, and a stray pejorative remark can be easily shrugged off. In contrast, a person whose claim to the desired identity is tentative or incomplete may feel a frequent need to gain validation by others and may be acutely sensitive to slighting remarks. Thus, people who feel incomplete and who consequently feel a pervasive need for social validation of their favorable self-conceptions are more susceptible to ego threats.

Another relevant pattern would be stability of self-appraisal. Some self-appraisals are relatively stable over time, which suggests that they are not greatly affected by daily events. In contrast, other self-appraisals fluctuate more widely from day to day. Kernis (1993) and his colleagues showed that global levels of self-esteem fluctuate more widely in some people than in others. It seems likely that people who have unstable self-appraisals will tend to become sensitive and defensive, so bad feedback will produce a quicker and stronger reaction in them than in people with stable self-appraisals. Shifts toward more negative self-appraisals generally bring anxiety, depression, anger, and other forms of negative affect (Heatherton & Polivy, 1991; Higgins, 1987). People wish to avoid these unpleasant states, so people with unstable self-esteem should be strongly motivated to ward off any event that might potentially lower their self-esteem. To such an individual, bad feedback or criticism from other people would almost certainly contain the risk of bringing one's self-esteem down, so one may react strongly to any hint of such ego threats. In contrast, people whose self-esteem remains the same regardless of what happens would have much less reason to fear criticism or other bad feedback. The result would be that people with unstable high self-esteem might well become violent in response to even seemingly minor or trivial threats to self-esteem. Consistent with this reasoning Kernis, Cornell, Sun, Berry, and Harlow (1993) found that people with high but unstable self-esteem were most prone to respond defensively to unfavorable feedback.

This section has reviewed several factors that would likely increase the magnitude and subjective impact of ego threats—instability, certainty, and evaluative dependency on others. The common theme appears to be that favorable self-appraisals that are insecurely held may be most vulnerable to ego threats. Although we have said that these self-appraisals will lead to violence by increasing the magnitude rather than the frequency of ego threats, there could be an apparent increase in frequency too: Instances of minor, slight, or minimal bad feedback could elicit strong reactions from such insecure egotists, whereas secure egotists would dismiss such events as too trivial to be worth a response.

## The Mediating Role of Affect

Thus far we have proposed that violence tends to follow from a certain pattern of discrepant appraisals (i.e., favorable self-appraisals and unfavorable external appraisals) and that whatever increases the frequency or subjective impact of such discrepancies will increase aggression. Yet it is a long step from inconsistent appraisals to violent action. One

crucial intervening variable may be affect. Hence it may be helpful to expand our position to say that encountering a discrepancy between public and private self-appraisals will engender aversive arousal states, which in turn foster aggression.

Is negative affect an adequate explanation for aggression? For many years, theorizing was influenced, if not dominated by, the view that frustration was an essential cause (Dollard, Doob, Miller, Mowrer, & Sears, 1939). Although it was undeniable that many frustrated people become aggressive, contrary findings did gradually accumulate. Some aggression did not seem to follow from frustration, and some frustrations did not result in aggression. In a sweeping reformulation of this research, Berkowitz (1989) concluded broadly that aggression results from negative affective states in general, proposing that frustration and anger had been overemphasized. Any negative affect could cause aggression.

Although Berkowitz (1989) made a compelling case for expanding aggression theory beyond a narrow focus on feelings of anger and frustration, there is not yet sufficient evidence available to conclude that all states of negative affect can cause aggression (as he noted). Indeed, Baron (1976) showed that exposing participants to a pitiable injury victim reduced subsequent aggressiveness. He concluded that empathic pity is incompatible with aggressive impulses. Likewise, guilt may often inhibit aggressive acts (e.g., Baumeister, Stillwell, & Heatherton, 1994). Meanwhile, there is little to suggest that sadness leads to aggression. The most appropriate conclusion at present seems to be that some forms of negative affect can produce or increase aggressive tendencies.

Meanwhile, it is relatively straightforward to suggest that ego threats can produce negative affect. Decreases in state self-esteem often lead to negative affect (Heatherton & Polivy, 1991). Discovering that one falls short of ideals or violates one's proper standards of behavior produces various negative affect states (Higgins, 1987). Leary, Tambor, Terdal, and Downs (1995) recently provided evidence linking self-esteem to interpersonal appeal and status, and interpersonal rejection or exclusion is a central cause of anxiety (Baumeister & Tice, 1990), so it seems fair to expect that decreases in self-esteem will bring anxiety too.

Despite this seemingly straightforward pathway from ego threats to lowered self-esteem to negative affect to aggression, however, careful inspection suggests several potential problems and inconsistencies. Higgins (1987) proposed that perceiving oneself as falling short of ideals should engender low-arousal emotions such as dejection and sadness, and there is little evidence that such emotions lead to aggression. Moreover, if drops in self-esteem were responsible for the negative affect that resulted in aggression, then one would have to make the strong prediction that low self-esteem (if only as a temporary state) was a crucial factor. Last, the view that people revise their self-appraisals readily in response to external threats runs contrary to considerable evidence that people resist such downward revisions (Greenwald, 1980; Swann, 1987; Taylor & Brown, 1988).

We propose, instead, that when favorable views of self are confronted with unflattering external feedback, the person faces a choice point. The affective response will depend on which path is chosen. One path is to accept the external appraisal and revise one's self-esteem in a downward direction. Sadness, anxiety, and dejection might well result from such a course. In contrast, the other path is to reject the external appraisal and uphold one's more favorable self-appraisal. The confluence of self-consistency and self-enhancement motives would suggest that this is generally the preferred response. In such a case, the person would infer that the external evaluation is mistaken and undeserved, and he or she may well develop anger or other negative affect toward the source of that evaluation.

The hypothesis of a choice point was anticipated to some extent by Berkowitz's (1989) observation that many bad experiences lead to a choice between fight or flight reactions—that is, between a self-assertive, aggressive response and one of defeated withdrawal. It also suggests how some seemingly contradictory findings and implications can be integrated. Thus, research on shame suggests, on the one hand, that this global feeling of being a despicable person often leaps to a tendency to withdraw or hide from others (Lewis, 1971; Tangney, 1991, 1992). On the other hand, there is evidence that shame-prone people tend to externalize blame and become angry and aggressive toward others (Tangney, Wagner, Barlow, Marschall, & Gramzow, 1994; Tangney, Wagner, Fletcher, & Gramzow, 1992), and clearly angry aggression is a very different response that seems incompatible with social withdrawal. It may be, however, that a potentially shame-inducing experience causes some people to accept the unflattering evaluation and withdraw, whereas others respond by refusing to accept the evaluation and by becoming angry toward the evaluator.

A similar choice point is suggested by recent research findings about envy. Envy arises when someone else has what the envious person wanted, which can imply that oneself is less worthy and less deserving than the other (Salovey, 1991; Salovey & Rodin, 1984). Smith, Parrott, Ozer, and Moniz (1994) found that envy leads to hostility only if the person retains a favorable view of self as deserving the positive outcome, in which case the envied person's advantage is seen as unjust and unfair. In contrast, if the person accepts the implication and feels inferior to the envied person, then hostility does not ensue. Once again, then, the affective response to an ego threat depends on the self-appraisal, and the response that maintains a favorable self-appraisal leads to aggression.

By this reasoning, then, aggression can be regarded as a crude technique of affect regulation. Meloy (1988) made this argument in explicit detail for psychopaths, who engage in predatory violence to avoid a broad range of unwanted emotions. To avoid certain negative emotional states, such as shame, dejection, sadness, and disappointment with oneself, the person refuses to contemplate information that reflects unfavorably about the self. When others attempt to provide such unfavorable feedback, the person becomes agitated and directs unpleasant emotions at them. By focusing on his or her hostility toward the evaluators, the person avoids the dismal cycle of accepting the feedback, revising his or her self-concept, and experiencing the dejected feelings about the self.

This affective view dovetails well with the previous analysis of possible moderators. People whose favorable self-conceptions are inflated, uncertain, or unstable may become quite sensitive to unflattering feedback and may react with hostility. Indeed, this analysis has one further implication, which is that the hostile response may often seem wildly disproportionate to the actual informational power of the external evaluation or even to any contemplated reduction in self-esteem. Because the angry, hostile response is essentially a means of preventing oneself from having to suffer through a depressing revision of self-appraisal, its function is largely anticipatory. Hence highly sensitive individuals may react with considerable hostility to seemingly minor ego threats. In other words, once a person becomes familiar with the emotional distress of losing self-esteem, he or she may become watchful for potential or incipient threats and may react strongly to what observers would regard as slight or trivial offenses.

## Interpersonal Context

The last issue to consider is the interpersonal dimension. In most cases, violence is not a random eruption of intrapsychic forces, but rather is directed toward a particular target in the context of some meaningful communications.

Two interpersonal aspects stand out. First, aggression may be a meaningful and coercive response to the unflattering evaluation. We have proposed that aggression results from a discrepancy between a favorable self-appraisal and an unfavorable external appraisal. The matter is not concluded simply because the recipient decides not to accept the unfavorable evaluation. Even after that decision is made, the person remains confronted by someone who is expressing a negative view (which is now seen as undeserved and unjust). By aggressing against the evaluator, the person may accomplish several things, including punishing the evaluator for the bad feedback, impugning the other's right to criticize, and discouraging that person (and others) from expressing similar evaluations in the future. Tedeschi and Felson (1994) recently argued that aggression should be reconceptualized as coercive behavior. In this context, a violent response may coerce the other person into withdrawing the bad evaluation.

Second, a successful violent attack achieves a symbolic dominance over the other person, so it affirms one's esteem to the extent of being superior to the victim. Violence may therefore be one form of self-affirmation, which is a common response to ego threats (Steele, 1988). This response may help explain two otherwise puzzling patterns of aggression. One is the seeming logical irrelevance of violence to most ego threats. For example, someone who beats up someone who has insulted his intelligence does not provide any positive proof of intelligence, but self-affirmation theory emphasizes that people who feel their esteem threatened in one sphere often respond by asserting positive qualities in another sphere (Steele, 1988; see also Baumeister & Jones, 1978; Greenberg & Pyszczynski, 1985). The other puzzling pattern concerns displaced aggression. If

aggression is understood as a communicative response to unfavorable feedback, then it would be illogical to aggress against a third person. But such displacement may become comprehensible as a way of asserting superiority over someone else, especially if the evaluator is an unsuitable target for aggression.

The link between aggression and superiority may have evolutionary roots. Certain pack animals develop status hierarchies in which one's position in the hierarchy depends on which others one can defeat in a fight. Human history has certainly contained abundant episodes consistent with that pattern; indeed, in the transition from nomadic, barbarian life to civilization, the most common pattern was for the warriors to become the aristocracy, with the foremost fighters or battlefield leaders becoming the individual rulers (e.g., McNeill, 1982, 1991).[2] Thus, in both evolutionary and cultural history, high status has been linked to fighting. It is plausible that some aggressive responses derive from this deeply rooted impulse to achieve physical dominance over rivals, rather than from some calculated response to discrepant self-appraisals.

Although the analogy to pack hierarchies is clearly speculative, there is one relevant implication that deserves mention. In any small group hierarchy, the amount of prestige available is limited. (Other limited resources, such as material rewards, may also be involved, insofar as these are distributed in proportion to status.) One can only gain at the expense of another.

Hence, under conditions of scarcity, the negotiation of esteem may take on a zero-sum aspect. E. Anderson (1994) proposed that, in poor communities in America, self-esteem does indeed conform to zero-sum patterns. Gaining esteem requires taking it away from others. This analysis greatly expands the range of acts that can constitute an ego threat. If the amount of self-esteem is fixed, then positive claims by one person are sufficient to constitute a threat to others. Thus, one does not have to criticize a person to threaten his or her self-esteem; merely making favorable claims about oneself is enough.

---

[2]This is a slight oversimplification of McNeill's argument. The hunt leader tended to rule in hunting societies, and warriors soon emerged as rulers in early civilizations, but in between there may have been an interval during which peasant farmers lived in peace under near anarchy or loose social structures dominated by priests. Still, kingship and aristocracy were closely linked to leadership in war, which is the relevant point.

Violence as a self-affirmation tool

This zero-sum aspect of esteem should mainly apply to small, fixed hierarchies, but some forms of it may be apparent even in a broad society in which the amount of available esteem is less obviously limited. Feather (1994) recently reviewed research on the "tall poppy" phenomenon, namely the seeming pleasure that people may derive from witnessing the downfall of highly successful people. That pleasure could well be linked to such a zero-sum esteem pattern, especially if highly successful people are perceived as unfairly hogging or hoarding esteem that would otherwise be available to many others.

Still, it must be noted that Feather (1994) did not find the tall poppy effect to be widespread or robust. The zero-sum aspect of esteem-related violence may be limited to highly particular, circumscribed patterns, such as those in which there is some explicit sense of competition for a limited amount of status.

## Summary of High Self-Esteem Theory

In summary, we propose that one major cause of violent response is threatened egotism, that is, a favorable self-appraisal that encounters an external, unfavorable evaluation. Factors that increase the frequency or impact of such encounters will increase violence. In particular, unrealistically positive or inflated views of self, and favorable self-appraisals that are uncertain, unstable, or heavily dependent on external validation, will be especially vulnerable to encountering such threats. Such threats often elicit anger and other negative affects when the person refuses to accept and internalize the unflattering evaluation. (If the person accepts the evaluation and revises his or her self-esteem downward, aggression will be less likely.) The anger and the aggressive response typically occur in an interpersonal framework: They are most commonly directed at the source of the bad evaluation. Aggression serves to refute and prevent bad evaluations as well as to constitute a means of achieving symbolic dominance and superiority over the other person. Figure 1 summarizes this theory.

## Review of Empirical Findings

If reliable data on self-esteem levels of violent and nonviolent citizens were available, it would be rela-

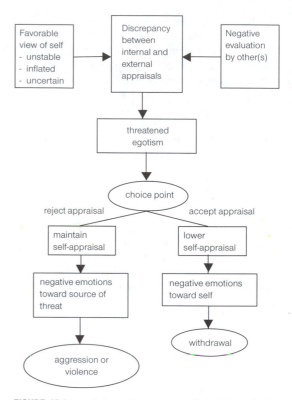

**FIGURE 13.1.** ■ Schematic representation of the relation of threatened egotism to violent behavior.

tively easy to resolve the question of who is most violent, although some theoretical questions would remain. Alternatively, if self-esteem had been routinely measured in laboratory studies of aggression, there would be at least one methodologically solid source of evidence. Unfortunately, neither of these is the case. Accordingly, it is necessary to look at a broad range of evidence about aggression, violence, oppression, and other forms of evil behavior and to consider carefully how self-esteem might be involved. In particular, claims about the self made during violent incidents, or assumptions about the self that make violence possible, deserve close attention.

The present review will survey literature on violence, encompassing both traditional laboratory studies of aggression and prejudice by experimental psychologists and data from outside psychology, most notably criminology. Tedeschi and Felson (1994) noted the irony that aggression psychologists and criminologists rarely read each other's literatures, despite common interests and despite the obvious value of converging evidence.

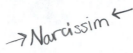
→ Narcissim ←

Widom (1991) cited broad "agreement" that scholars "need to look beyond disciplinary boundaries" (p. 130) for problems such as family violence and child abuse. No single discipline in the social sciences can claim a monopoly on insights into violence.

We shall begin by looking at efforts to predict violent, aggressive behavior from measures of egotism, including self-esteem and narcissism. Then we shall turn to the complementary strategy of looking at violent criminals, groups, and other aggressive individuals to ascertain how favorably they appraise themselves.

## Self-Reported Hostile Tendencies

We begin with survey studies that include both measures of self-esteem and of self-reported angry, violent, or hostile tendencies. Several studies have sought links between standard measures of self-appraisal and reports of aggressive actions. In particular, Kernis, Grannemann, and Barclay (1989) gave self-esteem measures to their participants on multiple occasions, which allowed the researchers to assess both the (mean) level of each participant's self-esteem and the degree of fluctuation in self-esteem scores. Kernis et al. used the fluctuation index as a measure of stability of self-esteem. These scores were then used to predict responses on an inventory of anger and hostility.

Kernis, Grannemann, et al. (1989) found that the highest levels of self-reported angry and hostile responses were associated with participants who had high but unstable self-esteem scores. Efforts to predict aggressive tendencies from self-esteem scores alone were inconclusive and, in fact, people with high but stable scores in self-esteem showed the lowest rates of anger and hostility. In our view, this is profoundly important evidence about the psychology of bullies and other aggressors: Their opinions of themselves are very favorable but vulnerable to fluctuations. Another way of describing this response pattern is that these hostile individuals were mostly quite high in their self-ratings but they did occasionally drop to substantially lower levels, which indicates that they were familiar with the distress and other aversive aspects of losing esteem.

One must assume that people whose self-esteem occasionally drops will be sensitive and vulnerable to ego threats in a way that people who show

consistent, stable, impervious high self-esteem are not. Kernis, Grannemann, et al.'s (1989) results thus seem quite compatible with the view that aggression ensues when people with very favorable views of themselves encounter an ego threat that evokes the possibility of losing esteem, although that conclusion requires some inferences beyond their data. Their findings do clearly link self-reported aggressive tendencies with unstable high self-esteem.

Similar studies have also been conducted with narcissism. The term *narcissism* is based on the Greek myth about the young man who fell in love with his own reflection, and is commonly used to refer to self-love; however, psychological (especially clinical) usages of the term have added the implication of artificially inflated egotism. Wink (1991) analyzed narcissism as having several components. All of them were correlated with disregard for others, which we have suggested is one factor that contributes to willingness to behave violently.

More important, the component that Wink (1991) defined as grandiosity or exhibitionism was particularly correlated with aggressiveness. That aspect suggests that wishing to show off to others, particularly to convince them to hold an unrealistically positive view of oneself, has an important link to aggression. Similar findings were reported by Raskin, Novacek, and Hogan (1991). They found positive intercorrelations among grandiosity, dominance, narcissism, and hostility, thus again suggesting that these wildly favorable views of self are involved in aggressive behavior.[3]

## CRITIQUE

These studies may be criticized as subject to various biases of self-report, but they have the advantage that they can include good, psychometrically sound measures, and so the information about self-appraisals is good. These are in some ways the first substitute for having data that include direct measures of self-esteem and subsequent measures of violent behavior. The step from self-reported hostility questionnaires to actual violent action

---

[3]They found, oddly, that if one takes the narcissism, grandiosity, and dominance out of hostility, the residual hostility is negatively related to self-esteem. It is not clear what this means; perhaps there is some aspect of violence that is associated with low self-esteem. Or perhaps this is an overcorrection.

requires several inferences, however. The main risk would be that reluctance to admit hostility would be unequally distributed along the range of self-appraisal responses; presumably, people who wish to present themselves favorably would score high on self-esteem but low on hostility. Such a tendency would work against the obtained findings, however, and so it seems appropriate to accept these findings unless further work contributes contrary evidence.

## CONCLUSION

Self-reported hostility does not correlate simply or directly with self-esteem scores, but the most hostile people seem to be a subset of people having favorable self-appraisals. Inflated self-appraisals and unstable high self-esteem have been linked to hostility, consistent with two of the hypothesized moderators.

### Group Differences

An indirect strategy is to look at groups that are known to differ in self-esteem or egotism and then compare their rates of aggressive actions. Obviously, these are correlational patterns and any one of them is inevitably subject to multiple alternative explanations. Only if there is broad agreement from multiple comparisons could one even begin to draw a tentative conclusion. Still, in an interdisciplinary literature review it seems desirable to examine as many sources of evidence as possible.

Gender differences can be considered relevant. Men have higher self-esteem than women (e.g., Harter, 1993; Veroff, Douvan, & Kulka, 1981), although the difference is not large and may be diminishing in the modern world (see also Crocker & Major, 1989). Men are also more aggressive than women, although the size of the difference depends on what measure is used. In laboratory studies of aggressive behavior, the difference is about one third of a standard deviation (Eagly, 1985). In violent crime, the difference is much larger. Although the precise figure varies according to crime and nation, men are between 5 and 50 times as likely to be arrested as women (Wilson & Herrnstein, 1985). The crime rate for women has risen in the United States since the 1960s, but most of that is due to property crimes, and women commit only about 10% of violent crimes (Wilson & Hermstein, 1985). Victimization surveys, which avoid possible

biases in the arresting system, point to similar differences. The only domain of violence in which women have been found to equal men is domestic violence, to which we shall return.

In general, then, men are more violent than women, and they also have higher self-esteem. This finding is most consistent with our hypothesis that high self-esteem is a cause of violence. One qualification is that the size of the self-esteem difference seems too small to account for the large difference in violent crime rates. It is also worth noting that the only realm in which women are more violent than men is child abuse, which could fit the view that attacking a safe, weak target may be a strategy among people with low self-esteem.

Another group known to have low self-esteem is depressed people (e.g., Allgood-Merton, Lewinsohn, & Hops, 1990; Altman & Wittenborn, 1980; Brown, Andrews, Harris, Adler, & Bridge, 1986; Brown & Harris, 1978; Cofer & Wittenborn, 1980; Tennen & Affleck, 1993; Tennen & Herzberger, 1987). The National Research Council's (1993) report on violence noted that many types of mental illness have been linked to violence, but depression had only been found in connection with family violence. Even those findings were subject to multiple ambiguities, including the possibility that depression was the result rather than the cause of violence and the possibility that depression was the result of one's own prior victimizations (given the often reciprocal and generational nature of family violence). More generally, it does not appear that depression is a major cause of violence.[4] That finding is consistent with the high self-esteem hypothesis, although the operative factor in depression could be unrelated to self-esteem (e.g., apathy or lack of energy is the aspect of depression that prevents violence).

Psychopaths constitute another relevant group on the fringes of normality. Although mental illness as a cause of crime is beyond the scope of this review, psychopaths are not mentally ill in the usual sense because they are well in touch with reality and their actions are apparently freely chosen, as opposed to being driven by compulsions or irresistible impulses (Hare, 1993). Hare described them as "social predators" and, although they are not inherently or even normally crimi-

---

[4]Another qualification is that depressed people do have elevated rates of suicide. Still, outwardly directed violence is low.

nals, they do commit a disproportionately high rate of violent crimes (in fact, he estimated that they are responsible for 50% of serious crimes). As to their self-views, Hare characterized them as having a "narcissistic and grossly inflated view of their self-worth and importance [and] a truly astounding egocentricity and sense of entitlement, and [as] see[ing] themselves as the center of the universe, as superior beings" (p. 38). They have grandiose conceptions of their abilities and potentialities, which have also been discussed by Meloy (1988). These observations support the link between inflated self-appraisals and aggression. Hare also noted that psychopaths' sense of superiority is accompanied by a tendency to regard other people as simply objects to be exploited.

Thus, psychopaths seem to fit the view of highly favorable opinions of self as a source of violence. Hare (1993) also observed them to be "highly reactive to perceived insults or slights" (p. 59). We propose that such hypersensitivity might reflect the use of violence to ward off emotional distress, and Meloy (1988) proposed that link as central to the psychopathic mentality. Although they are not socially sensitive in the sense of having high empathy or concern for others, they are sensitive in the sense of understanding how to manipulate other people and are certainly sensitive to any blows to their egotism. Hare's observations are thus consistent with the view that threatened egotism is a main cause of violence, although they also support the view that egotism can cause violence directly because one disregards the other's interests and point of view.

Comparing self-esteem across racial or ethnic groups is complicated by several factors, such as measurement issues and temporal changes, but the very possibility of temporal shifts presents an appealing chance to look for covariation in self-esteem and violence levels. In the 19th and early 20th centuries, American White men presumably were fairly securely convinced of their superior status. This confidence is generally assumed to have eroded in recent decades, and indeed research now indicates that Black people have self-esteem levels equal to or higher than those of White people (see Crocker & Major, 1989, for review). Concerted efforts to boost racial pride and dignity among Black Americans in the 1960s and 1970s may have contributed to this shift.

Meanwhile, violence levels also appear to have changed, directly contradicting the view that low self-esteem promotes violence. During the period when White men had the highest self-esteem, they were also apparently the most violent group. Historians believe that rapes of White women by Black men were quite rare, whereas the reverse was relatively common (e.g., Brownmiller, 1975). Likewise, the majority of interracial murders involved White men killing Blacks, a pattern that is still reasonably well documented into the 1920s (e.g., Brearly, 1932; Hoffman, 1925; Von Hentig, 1948). These patterns have been reversed in recent decades as Black self-esteem has risen relative to White self-esteem. According to Scully (1990), Black men now rape White women approximately 10 times as often as White men rape Black women. The timing of this reversal appears to coincide with the concerted cultural efforts to boost self-esteem among Blacks: LaFree's (1976) review of multiple studies of interracial rape concluded that researchers found approximately equal numbers of Black-on-White and White-on-Black rape in the 1950s, but since 1960 all studies have found a preponderance of Black-on-White rape (see also Brownmiller, 1975). Similarly, recent murder statistics indicate that the strong majority (80%–90%) of interracial murders now consist of Blacks murdering Whites (Adler, 1994). Clearly, both races have committed far too many horrible crimes, and neither race can find much claim to any moral high ground in these statistics, but the shifting patterns on both sides repeatedly link higher or rising esteem with increasing criminal violence toward the other.[5]

To seek converging evidence regarding cross-temporal shifts in self-appraisals and aggression, we examined research on manic–depressive

[5] To forestall the drawing of unintended implications from these data, we hasten to add that we are not advocating that any particular group or category should be denied a basis for pride or self-esteem. We do think that a diverse society such as the United States is likely to function best if all groups cultivate an attitude of respect and appreciation toward all others and seek a severely judicious balance between humility and pride regarding their own group's accomplishments. Efforts to impose humility on others are likely to backfire, and indeed some of America's racial problems can probably be traced to past policies of deliberate subjugation that were based on one race's ill-founded assumptions of innate superiority. It is hoped that both races have had enough opportunity to learn that respect ought to be earned as an individual rather than claimed as a member of a racial group. The apparent link between racial egotism and violence toward others may be one of the more unsavory demonstrations of the cross-racial universality of human nature.

(bipolar) disorders. Although these individuals are mentally ill and therefore fall outside the main scope of our review, they do provide an appealing chance to examine intraindividual fluctuations in self-esteem. Inflated, grandiose self-esteem occurs in the manic phase and presumably disappears or inverts during the depressive phase (American Psychiatric Association, 1994). Evidence suggests that aggressive actions and general patterns of hostility or irritability coincide mainly with the manic state (Goodwin & Jamison, 1990), which is again consistent with the view that favorable and inflated self-appraisals are linked to violence.

Another variation on the group-differences strategy is to look at groups who are defined by particular states rather than permanent traits. Indeed, although state self-esteem is strongly correlated with trait self-esteem, it does fluctuate around the chronic level (Heatherton & Polivy, 1991; Kernis, 1993). One particularly relevant group would be people who consume alcohol. It is well documented that alcohol consumption increases aggression (Bushman & Cooper, 1990). This conclusion has been well supported by laboratory studies on aggression, although the usual conclusion is that alcohol does not so much create aggression as increase aggressive responding once aggression is elicited by other causes. Moreover, it is well established that the majority of violent crimes are committed by people who have consumed alcohol, and indeed this point has been established repeatedly and separately for murder, rape, and assault (National Research Council, 1993; see also Gottfredson & Hirschi, 1990; Groth, 1979; Norris, 1988).

What, then, is the self-esteem level of people who consume alcohol? Evidence indicates that alcohol raises the favorability of self-appraisals. Intoxicated people rate themselves more favorably than they would otherwise (Banaji & Steele, 1989; Diamond & Wilsnack, 1978; Hurley, 1990; Konovsky & Wilsnack, 1982; Orford & Keddie, 1985). Apparently, then, alcohol generally helps create a state of high self-esteem. Thus, again, a group that shows elevated egotism also shows unusually high rates of violence.

## CRITIQUE

Data on large groups can furnish quite accurate indexes of rates of violence with high external validity. The drawback is that each group differ-

ence is subject to multiple possible explanations. For example, it is difficult to be certain that the favorable self-assessments of intoxicated people are a mediating factor in their violence; it is plausible that there are direct links from alcohol to violence, without self-esteem being involved. Moreover, it is possible that the violence is perpetrated by a minority portion of the group who may be atypical in self-appraisals. For example, men are both more violent and more egotistical than women, but it is possible that most of the violence is perpetrated by men who do not share the egotism common to their gender. Therefore, none of the findings in this section permits a strong conclusion about the link between self-appraisals and violence. On the other hand, the convergence across multiple comparisons is impressive in its contradiction to the low self-esteem view. To put this another way: Although each of the results covered in this section could be explained with reference to other factors, it would require considerable explaining and an abandonment of parsimony to continue asserting that low self-esteem causes violence.

## CONCLUSION

If low self-esteem did cause violence, one would expect that, in general, groups with lower self-esteem would be more violent, but the evidence reviewed in this section repeatedly found the opposite. It is difficult to maintain belief in the low self-esteem view after seeing that the more violent groups are generally the ones with higher self-esteem; at best, one would have to assume that the effect is weak enough to be overridden by many other variables. The effort to invoke alternative explanations is especially difficult in light of evidence that, over time, shifts in self-esteem are accompanied by shifts in aggression, such that the periods of higher self-esteem are the ones linked to greater violence.

Moreover, several findings suggest that inflated or unstable views of self are linked to violence. The grandiose self-appraisals of psychopaths and manics, and the inflation of self-appraisal during alcoholic intoxication, provide support for this view.

## Murder and Assault

We turn now to considering violent crimes by individuals. Studies have examined various samples of offenders, and our goal is to ascertain what direct observations of offenders have suggested about their self-appraisals. A general methodological problem is that offenders are most available for study after arrest and imprisonment, but the humiliating process could well have an effect on self-esteem. Being captured for a crime is a prominent failure experience and, moreover, the assertion of humble remorse is often perceived as a prerequisite for parole and early release. As a result, superficial evidence of low self-esteem should be especially easy to find in studies of convicted offenders.

Despite any methodological bias toward low self-esteem, however, studies of violent offenders have typically suggested strong tendencies toward egotism and narcissism, and any signs of low self-esteem are at best ambiguous. Thus, the classic study of violent men by Toch (1969/1993) sought to classify them into types. His taxonomy was weakened by the fact that the two most common types could not be reliably distinguished, and the third largest was related to the second, so in a sense what Toch produced was one very large category and an assortment of small exceptions. The large category (the majority) consisted of men for whom threatened egotism was behind the violence. Although, as noted earlier, Toch's remarks were inconsistent as to whether these men secretly had high or low self-esteem, he was clear that these men generally became violent as a means of proving positive self-worth and refuting perceived insults. These individuals often seemed to seek out or manufacture situations in which their image was challenged and they could bolster it by aggressive action. As we have said, this pattern suggests confidence and possibly arrogance.

Berkowitz (1978) studied a sample of British men imprisoned for assault. The investigation sought evidence for the hypothesis of a subculture of violence. More precisely, Berkowitz tried to show that these men were motivated by the desire to look good by showing off through aggressive behavior that would be admired by others. But he was unable to find evidence to support that hypothesis. Instead, most of the fights had begun when one man thought another had insulted or belittled him. "Our impression is that their egos were fragile indeed" (p. 158), said Berkowitz, which could mean low self-esteem or could mean a defensive pattern of high self-esteem. He said that these men seemed excessively prone to regard

another's remarks as insulting or belittling, which seems consistent with the unstable high self-esteem suggested by Kernis, Grannemann, et al. (1989) and with the hypersensitivity Hare (1993) observed among psychopaths. The impression of egotism is further supported by Berkowitz's finding that most of the men said they had had high confidence that they would win the fight. Thus, in general, Berkowitz was unable to confirm his initial hypothesis that aggression was a means of making a good impression on others or of adhering to subcultural values or securing material rewards: "If anything, pride appears to be far more significant than direct external benefits. Wounded pride certainly seems to enrage them" (1978, p. 160). Wounded pride is essentially the same as threatened egotism, as we have proposed.

A recent study of homicide by Polk (1993) confirmed these conclusions. Polk noted that nowadays many homicides occur in connection with other crimes such as robbery, but in the remaining cases the homicide is often the result of an altercation that begins with challenges and insults. The person who feels he (or, less often, she) is losing face in the argument may resort to violence and murder.

Several studies have used the Minnesota Multiphasic Personality Inventory (MMPI) on various populations of offenders (see Wilson & Herrnstein, 1985, for review). Three of the 10 MMPI scales are relevant to low self-esteem: Depression (2), which includes self-deprecation; Psychasthenia (7), which includes anxiety and indecision; and Social Introversion (0), which includes insecurity and shyness. The weight of the evidence, including some prospective longitudinal studies, as reviewed by Wilson and Herrnstein, has not consistently shown any relationship between psychasthenia and criminality, but the other two scales are both negatively related to criminality: Depressed, self-deprecating, insecure, and shy people are underrepresented among criminals. These findings are difficult to reconcile with the view that links low self-esteem to violent and antisocial tendencies. Wilson and Herrnstein concluded that the "lack of criminal tendencies among those whose highest scores are on scales 2, 5, and 0 are by now commonplace in the empirical literature on crime" (p. 188). By this measure, then, the patterns that suggest low self-esteem produce remarkably few criminals.

Even within samples of offenders, it appears that

indicators of egotism can discriminate violent and troublesome tendencies, and it is the favorable views of self that are linked to the worse actions. Gough, Wenk, and Rozynko (1965) administered the California Psychological Inventory to young men (in their late teens) on parole. The researchers were able to predict future parole violations (recidivism) with some success, the sort of predictive success that had eluded previous researchers. Among the traits that predicted high recidivism were being egotistical and outspoken (as well as "touchy," which suggests being easily offended); meanwhile, being modest and unassuming were among the traits associated with men who were least likely to violate parole. These results all seem to fit the view linking favorable views of self to violent tendencies.

Similar tendencies are evident even earlier in life. Studies of aggressiveness in children are of special interest because aggressive children show substantially higher rates of adult aggression and criminal violence (e.g., Huesmann, Eron, Lefkowitz, & Walder, 1984). Olweus (1994) recently summarized his own program of research on bullies, who have been shown in follow-up studies to have four times the level of serious criminality during adult life that nonbullies show. In contrast to victims of bullying, who show multiple indications of low self-esteem, the bullies themselves seemed relatively secure and free from anxiety. "In contrast to a fairly common assumption among psychologists and psychiatrists, we have found no indicators that the aggressive bullies (boys) are anxious and insecure under a tough surface" (p. 100), said Olweus, adding that multiple samples and methods had confirmed this conclusion, and concluding that bullies "do not suffer from poor self-esteem" (p. 100).

One of the most earnest and empathic efforts to understand the subjective experience of committing crimes was that of Katz (1988). Homicide as well as assault emerged in his study as typically caused by threats to the offender's public image. In Katz's view, the offender privately holds a positive view of self, but the eventual victim impugns that view and implicitly humiliates the offender, often in front of an audience. The response is unplanned violence resulting in injury or death. Katz insisted that feelings of being humiliated are quickly transformed into rage. Katz argued that many men feel that almost anyone can judge them and impugn their esteem, whereas for women self-

esteem is most heavily invested in their intimate relationships—with the result that men will attack strangers, whereas women mainly just murder their intimate partners, because only the partners can threaten their self-esteem to a sufficient degree to provoke such a violent response.

Furthermore, Katz (1988) argued that many youthful circles and street subcultures extend substantial respect to the "badass" sort of person who transcends the pressures to conform to societal norms, rationality, and ideals. This prized identity is cultivated in part by creating the impression of being unpredictably prone to chaos and irrational violence. More generally, street violence, whether by individuals or gangs, often revolves around competing claims to hold a special, elite identity.

Concern over respect is hardly limited to modern lower-class youths. Upper classes often have had just as much appetite for egotistical gratifications. Wyatt-Brown (1982) said that the slave codes and other racial practices of the antebellum South all had the fundamental theme that Black people should show sincere respect for all Whites. Moreover, he said that in the Northeast, given the open industrial economy and abundant universities, self-worth could be established through scholarly erudition or financial success, but such means were largely unavailable to Southern men, who therefore resorted to violence instead. Accordingly, murder rates in the South were many times higher than property crimes and many times higher than the corresponding murder rates in the Northeast.

The violence proneness of the American South has been elaborated by Nisbett (1993). His work emphasized the point that Southern Americans are more inclined than Northerners to endorse violence in response to insults. In laboratory and other studies reported by Nisbett, Southern participants were more angry in response to insults than were Northerners, and they advocated more severe and violent solutions to scenarios involving conflicts and insults. The Southern "culture of honor" is an important cause of this tendency toward violence. A similar conclusion was reached by Ellison (1991), who found that Southerners are more likely than others to condone defensive or retaliatory forms of violence. Violence is therefore instrumental in enhancing one's honor or reputation.

Dueling is a traditional and widely disseminated pattern of violence that is similar to the way Nisbett (1993) and others have portrayed the violent honor culture of the South. Dueling provides a ritualized form of aggression that can be regarded simply as a formalized, systematic form of ordinary fighting. According to Kiernan's (1989) account of dueling in European history, dueling was intimately tied to highly favorable views of self and to threats to this esteem. Dueling was mainly practiced by the upper classes, who (back when no egalitarian ideologies diminished their sense of being innately superior people) cultivated their inflated notions of honor, virtue, and entitlement to respect. Minor acts could be construed as insults, prompting the offended person to insist on fighting on the so-called field of honor. Thus, this visible and durable form of violence sprang directly from inflated notions of personal (and familial) superiority and from ego threats.

Indeed, Wyatt-Brown's (1982) history of the culture of honor in the American antebellum South noted that dueling was common and was felt by many to be an obligatory response whenever one was insulted. However, Wyatt-Brown's comments could be construed to fit either the high self-esteem or the low self-esteem theory. In favor of the latter, he said that winners and sometimes even losers of duels gained esteem in the eyes of others. He speculated that some duelists suffered from an "inner sense of worthlessness" (p. 360) that prompted them to fight as a way of gaining public esteem. Still, that remark was overtly speculative and may be a concession to the conventional wisdom that low self-esteem causes violence. In contrast, Wyatt-Brown's fundamental analysis of honor began with "the inner conviction of self-worth" (p. 14), to which public validation must be added, so fighting duels was a means of publicly defending one's claims to a positive identity against external doubts or slights.

In our view, the weight of evidence presented by Wyatt-Brown (1982) supports the view that upper-class Southern men generally held favorable, rather than humble or unfavorable, views of themselves, even if there might be some uncertainty or instability attending their egotism. The role of ego threat is clear, in any case, insofar as duels were nearly always initiated in response to derogatory comments by another, about oneself or one's family.

## CRITIQUE

Again, the convergence across many studies is far more conclusive than the individual results themselves. In all studies of violent populations and samples of offenders, it must be acknowledged that they may be atypical of the broader population. Hence, although studies have consistently characterized offenders as egotistical, one cannot assume that all egotists have violent tendencies.

## CONCLUSION

Multiple studies of murder and assault have found threatened egotism to be a significant factor. In some spheres, such as dueling, the link is explicit and formal, whereas in most others it emerges as a common factor. The view that low self-esteem leads to violence appears contradicted by studies on offenders, ranging from childhood bullies to convicted murderers.

Many of the studies reviewed here included observations as to how seemingly trivial the provocation was. This is consistent with the view that such aggression has an anticipatory nature, designed to head off possible losses of esteem. The pattern of responding violently to slight or incipient threats suggests a hypersensitivity to bad feedback, which could well signify anticipatory emotional responses and some tentativeness about the favorable self-appraisals that are questioned.

We can thus see a consistent pattern across cultural, historical, situational, and class boundaries. Many violent acts by individuals occur in response to derogatory remarks or acts by others, including ones that seem minor or trivial to observers. In most cases, the perpetrators appear to be men who privately believe in their own superior worth, but who encounter others who impugn or dispute that belief. Violence may be especially likely when the individual lacks alternative means to prove or establish his superiority.

## Rape

Rape is a complex crime, and there is considerable controversy about its definition, causes, and meanings. Some apparent causes, such as displaced revenge for prior mistreatment and belief in rape myths, seemingly have little relevance to self-esteem, but there is some evidence that self-esteem can be involved in rape.

An eminent book on rape by Groth (1979) reported that in one major pattern, rapes were often preceded by various blows to the rapist's self-esteem, causing him to feel that he "had been wronged, hurt, put down, or treated unjustly" (p. 16), usually by some woman. In the other major pattern Groth identified, either a woman or a man does something to the rapist that "undermines his sense of competency and self-esteem" (p. 30), and raping is a means of "restor[ing] his sense of power, control, identity, and worth" (p. 31).[6] Although Groth did reiterate the standard line of interpreting the rape as reflecting low self-esteem, his argument that the rape "restores" positive views of self contradicted that analysis, because it implies that positive views of self exist to be restored. It would perhaps have been more precise to say that rape tends to result from a favorable view of self that has recently been impugned by another person or situation. Groth's observations generally seem most consistent with the view that high but unstable self-esteem is the cause of sexual violence. Groth insisted further that the appeal of rape is not sexual release but rather enjoyment of the victim's helplessness and thus of one's own superior power (the rapist "thrives on a feeling of omnipotence," p. 47). He added that participation in gang rape is often motivated by "an effort to retain status" (p. 80), and that the leader of a gang rape enjoys both control over the victim and over his cohorts.

Over 100 convicted rapists were interviewed by Scully and Marolla (1985) to ascertain their motives and rewards. The enjoyment of power over one's victim was cited by many. A number of respondents made the comment, also found in Groth's (1979) interviews, that one raped a particular woman to disabuse her of her sense of superiority. That is, the woman gave the man the impression she thought she was better than he was, so he raped her as a way of proving her wrong. The implications for self-esteem are quite apparent: Rape is motivated by the man's belief in his own superiority, which has been challenged or disputed by the woman (or occasionally by someone else). The selection of victim on the basis of her own apparent self-esteem is consistent with the zero-sum view of self-esteem, in which one can only gain esteem at the expense of others.

In a later work, Scully (1990) reported ample signs of egotism among many of the convicted rapists, especially those who denied their guilt. She said many of these men spontaneously bragged to her about their sexual prowess and about their other attributes and accomplishments, even claiming to be "multitalented superachievers" (p. 112). It

seems fair to regard these as inflated self-appraisals, especially when one considers that all the men were in prison at the time. A large minority even thought their victims would regard them favorably afterward. She too found evidence of selecting a victim on the basis of the victim's perceived high self-esteem, such as the case of the rapist who described his motivation and satisfaction by saying "I felt like I had put her [the victim] in her place" (Scully, 1990, p. 134).

Marital rape is likewise a controversial issue (even to define), and its causes are poorly understood, but again there is some evidence of issues of self-esteem and control. Finkelhor and Yllo (1985) cited a common masculine belief in entitlement as a cause of marital rape. Husbands rape their wives to prove their sexual ownership and rights over their wives, as well as to demonstrate superior power and achieve a victory over the wife. The surprisingly high rates of anal intercourse (which is linked to dominance; see Baumeister, 1989) and forced sex in front of witnesses both suggest that marital rape often is essentially an effort to achieve symbolic proof of the husband's superior status. This brings up the broader issue of domestic violence, to which we turn in the next section.

### CRITIQUE

The studies reviewed in this section suffer from limitations in sampling measurement, quantification, and basis for comparison. Research into the psychology of rapists remains in a preliminary state, partly because researchers have focused mainly on victims, and in many cases strong ideological commitments may have complicated the development of empirically based theory. The studies cited here are valuable sources of observations and impressions, but the evidence is not strong enough to justify sweeping generalizations or firm causal conclusions.

### CONCLUSION

Preliminary evidence portrays rapists as having firm beliefs in male superiority and often elaborate beliefs in their own individual superiority, all

---

[6]Groth did identify a third type of rape, based on sadism, but he said that was statistically a very small and rare pattern. It is irrelevant to our hypothesis.

of which is contrary to the low self-esteem view. Some observations support the view that ego threats figure prominently in the events leading up to rape. In many cases, however, the victim was not the source of the ego threat. Additional observations by several researchers did, however, fit the pattern we noted based on the zero-sum view of esteem, namely that some offenders choose a victim simply because her own apparent self-esteem somehow constitutes a threat to the rapist's belief in his superiority, even though she never evaluated him directly.

## Domestic Violence Between Partners

We proposed that domestic violence was the one sphere in which there would be extra reasons to expect that low self-esteem might predict violence, insofar as unconfident people might select safe, relatively helpless targets for their aggressive impulses. As it happens, researchers have devoted more effort to measuring and studying the effects of self-esteem on domestic than on other forms of violence.

Despite frequent portrayals of wife beaters as having low self-esteem (e.g., Walker, 1979), the evidence has not provided much support for this view. Stets (1991) found no link between self-esteem and inflicting violence among men; among women, there were weak correlations between inflicting violence, being the victim of partner violence, and having low self-esteem. Burke, Stets, and Pirog-Good (1988) found "that self-esteem was not related directly to either physical or sexual abuse for men or for women" (p. 283), although there were some "spurious" correlations as a result of shared variance with gender identity measures. This conclusion seems consistent with Kernis's (1993) position that measuring self-esteem alone (as opposed to looking for the pattern of high but unstable, or variable, self-esteem) may be of little help in determining the causes of violence.

Even studies that have found low self-esteem correlated with inflicting violence suffer from ambiguities that have caused the researchers to question the traditional view that low self-esteem causes violence. Goldstein and Rosenbaum (1985) found significantly lower levels of self-esteem among physically abusive husbands than among happily married husbands or among unhappily married but nonviolent husbands. They observed,

however, that the correlational findings were inconclusive and that it is "probable" that "abusing one's wife is self-esteem damaging" (p. 427); thus, low self-esteem may be the effect rather than the cause. Their sampling method may also have contributed to this, because it consisted of men who had referred themselves for therapy as wife abusers. As Holtzworth-Munroe (1992) has noted, studies of domestic violence typically find severe differences between the minority of abusers who admit to being abusers and the majority of them who tend to minimize or deny their violence and who lay blame for violent incidents on external factors, such as the victim's provocations. It does seem that voluntarily identifying oneself as a wife batterer and reporting for therapy would be incompatible with furnishing a highly favorable rating of self on a self-esteem scale.

One other study that found correlations was done by Russell and Hulson (1992). They used a nonstandard self-esteem measure that they thought would be especially relevant to domestic violence and an unorthodox sample to find several correlations suggesting that low self-esteem among wives was linked to both perpetrating and receiving both psychological and physical abuse and that low self-esteem among husbands was correlated with inflicting psychological abuse (e.g., insulting the partner) but not physical abuse. A multiple regression analysis eliminated most of their effects, although they did find that wives low in self-esteem were still more likely to physically attack their husbands.

Thus, repeated efforts to link measures of low self-esteem to self-reported physical violence have not yielded much. Possibly clearer evidence comes from studies concerned with understanding the motives and circumstances that lead to wife beating. Gelles and Straus (1988) summarized a common provocation to domestic violence by saying that people tended to hit their spouses and children "after they felt that their self-worth had been attacked or threatened" (p. 35). They noted that the threat to self-worth may be external, such as at work, or it may originate in the family itself. In the latter case, family members know what others are sensitive and vulnerable about and may say cruel or disparaging things, which elicit physically violent responses. This pattern was found "over and over again" (p. 79) in interviews. Similarly, Gondolf (1985) characterized wife beaters in his sample as men who strongly endorsed traditional views about family and gender roles, particularly the "male expectation of privilege" (p. 82) and an exaggerated sense of responsibility for the family. When family events failed to follow their expectations or jeopardized their sense of privilege, they turned violent.

A historical study of physically abusive husbands around the turn of the century by Peterson (1991) is typical and relevant. Peterson characterized the typical wife beater in his sample as "not an all-powerful patriarch but rather a husband with but marginal resources" (p. 12) insofar as these husbands tended to lack money, education, and other signs of status, especially in comparison with their wives. Peterson inferred that the lack of status would translate into low self-esteem and was consequently quite puzzled by the signs that these men believed strongly in male superiority. Indeed, in discussing the findings, Peterson cited what he regarded as an inconsistency in the literature, namely evidence that wife beaters were men who lacked status and power but who nonetheless held traditional views about male dominance in marriage. To Peterson, these findings seemed to suggest contradictory conclusions about the role of self-esteem.

Such findings are only conflicting, however, if one subscribes to the theory that low self-esteem is the cause of family violence. To us, the findings aptly capture the prototypical cause of violent aggression: threatened egotism, or in this case the man's firm belief in his own superiority coupled with the threat (due to some status superiority enjoyed by the wife) that others may not share that belief. Men who regarded themselves as superior but who saw that their wives had surpassed them on some important dimensions seemed quite likely to feel this insecure, threatened egotism, which may have led them to strike out against their wives. From our perspective, this pattern confirms that a crucial cause of the violence was the men's beleaguered belief in their own superiority.

Similar findings have been reported by Gelles and Straus (1988), who noted that "status inconsistency is an important component of the profile of the battering husband" (p. 88). They said the typical wife beater feels obliged to hold down the traditional male role of superiority and family dominance but feels undermined by having less economic or social resources than his neighbors and often even his wife. Claes and Rosenthal (1990) likewise found that wife abuse was positively correlated with the husband's perception of the wife as having high reward power. Gelles and Straus reported that many wife beaters spoke to them of "needing" to strike their wives to show them who was the boss (e.g., p. 92). Once again, this view precisely fits the formula we have proposed: The man regards himself as superior but fears that others do not sufficiently endorse that view.

Another methodologically strong and often cited study of spouse abuse was done by Hornung, McCullough, and Sugimoto (1981). They found that, contrary to conventional wisdom, working wives are attacked by their husbands more than wives who stay at home, presumably because of status inconsistency: The wife who remains at home does not implicitly threaten her husband's superior status in the family. Thus, again, it is the pattern of beliefs in one's (the husband's) superiority, coupled with circumstances that seem to contradict or undermine that superiority, which is most conducive to violence.

Indeed, many of Hornung et al.'s (1981) findings support the view that a threatened sense of male superiority is an important cause of domestic violence by men. Hornung et al. studied only reports by wives and emphasized violence by husbands. Some of their specific findings seem internally inconsistent unless one assumes that educational level sets expectations and occupational level is perceived as the actual achievement outcome. In that view, domestic violence was most common when men held high but frustrated expectations. Highly educated men with relatively uneducated wives were violent, which is consistent with the view that seeing oneself as superior is a cause of violence. Yet when the woman's occupational level was higher than the man's, the man tended to become violent. Wives in the top occupational stratum were subjected to high violence; men in the top stratum were relatively nonviolent. Indeed, when the woman's job was higher in status than her husband's, the likelihood of life-threatening violence was six times higher than when the pair's occupations were similar or compatible.

Above all, men who had been highly educated but had not attained high-status occupations were particularly violent, and this was intensified if the wife had achieved high status. Men who were overachievers, however, in the sense of enjoying occupational status and success above and beyond what their educational level would normally predict, were significantly less violent than control participants. In other words, when men's expectations exceeded their outcomes, they were highly violent, but when their outcomes exceeded their expectations, they were exceptionally nonviolent. This finding shows that not all status inconsistencies are equally likely to lead to violence. Threatened egotism increases the risk of violence, whereas the opposite form of inconsistency (success despite humility) reduces it.

All of these findings suggest that men beat their wives to maintain the superiority of the husband role that has been threatened or jeopardized. When the man's outcomes fall short of his expectations, he is vulnerable to feeling that his wife will not respect him and he may be especially prone to reassert his superiority with physical violence. When the wife has reached a level of occupational success that is higher than her husband's, he is again more likely to beat her, presumably as away of enforcing his sense of superiority.

Related to this is a finding by Goldstein and Rosenbaum (1985), which suggests that abusive husbands are more likely than others to interpret a wife's behavior as threatening or damaging to the man's favorable image of self. A man who feels his superior status is tenuous, possibly because his occupational success has not measured up to his or his wife's expectations, may be extra sensitive to comments or actions by her that might imply a disparaging or disrespectful attitude.

To be sure, not all domestic violence is perpetrated by men. Straus (1980) and others have noted that most researchers began with the assumption that spouse abuse is mainly perpetrated by men, yet often objective data fail to confirm that. Two reasons that have been suggested are that men tend to not report being physically abused by their wives (because they would be ashamed of being physically bested by a woman) and that the superior size and strength of men typically mean that they inflict greater harm on their wives than wives can inflict on husbands. Straus's own data found approximately equal rates of domestic violence by both genders, which surprised him and his colleagues, leading to a series of supplementary analyses aimed at finding the ballyhooed preponderance of male violence. Several analyses (e.g., analyzing frequency rather than mere incidence and restricting analyses to severe violence) failed to yield any difference, but finally one pattern emerged in which men were more violent: In cases in which there was mutual, escalating violence, husbands escalated to higher levels of violence than their wives.

This lone finding may be suspect because so many analyses were done before something could be found to fit the researchers' preconceptions, but if we assume that it is nonetheless correct and valid, it seems to fit very well the notion of threatened egotism as a cause of violence. Mutual violence presumably means that the couple is prone to engage in physical fighting. Assuming, again, that the majority of men are physically superior at fighting and that they would regard being beaten by a woman as a disgrace, it may simply be that when a man finds himself in a physical battle with his wife, he escalates to a level of brutality at which he is sure to win the fight. In other words, the inclination to beat one's spouse may be equally distributed across men and women, and men are only more violent toward their spouses when their egotism (i.e., their sense of superiority and immunity to embarrassment) is jeopardized.

Renzetti (1992) studied partner abuse in lesbian relationships, which provides a valuable complement to the studies that have focused on male perpetrators of domestic violence. Her data, along with several other studies she cited, confirmed the contribution of status inconsistency to domestic violence. Batterers wanted to be the decision makers, but the victims tended to have more money and other resources, according to victims' reports, which were Renzetti's sole source of data.

The two largest direct causes of violence in Renzetti's (1992) data, however, were dependency and jealousy. She noted that equality and independence are particularly strong ideals in lesbian communities because of feminist ideology and other reasons; the more one woman felt dependent on the other, the more violent she was likely to be, and her violence seemed to signify power and autonomy that contradicted the implication of her apparent dependency. Meanwhile, Renzetti noted that jealousy is strongly blended with envy in homosexual relationships, thus adding a significant element of ego threat, because the outside person who pursues one's partner would also be an eligible partner for oneself, and so apparently the person has chosen one's partner over oneself, suggesting that the interloper has judged oneself as somehow less attractive than one's partner. Thus, the ego threat of partner infidelity is doubled in homosexual as compared with heterosexual triangles.

## CRITIQUE

Consistent with our prediction that the low self-esteem view would fare best in studies of domestic violence, there have been some findings supporting that theory. However, these effects are weak and small and have often failed to replicate. Several of the studies contained multiple and fundamental flaws. Problems of sampling are crucial because the most conveniently available sample usually consists of people who identify and reproach themselves as violent spouses (such as those who have sought therapy), but these are a seriously atypical minority (Holtzworth-Munroe, 1992). The possibility that low self-esteem was a result of abuse, or especially that low self-esteem causes women to stay in mutually abusive relationships, has been advanced as a likely explanation even when findings have found low self-esteem to correlate with violence. Indeed, one ought to expect considerable self-deprecation among people who have acknowledged beating their wives or partners, given the stigma. The findings that women with low self-esteem aggress against their partners are complicated by the reciprocal nature of much marital violence: If a battered woman strikes her husband in self-defense, as many researchers propose is common, it is misleading to depict her act as a result of her low self-esteem. Larger, more careful, and more systematic studies have found no direct link between self-esteem and domestic violence, and presumably for that reason researchers have recently shifted emphasis to status inconsistency. The link between status inconsistency and domestic violence appears to be reasonably well supported, although not all inconsistencies are equally productive of violence.

## CONCLUSION

Much research on domestic violence has been shaped by the traditional belief that low self-esteem is a major cause, but repeated efforts have yielded, at best, weak and ambiguous findings consistent with that view. When preliminary findings have linked low self-esteem with violence, the evidence has usually disappeared under the influence of statistical controls, rigorous sampling, or prospective methods. It does not appear that low self-esteem causes domestic violence. Meanwhile, evidence of egotism among physically abusive husbands is abundant. Studies of these men repeatedly portray them as believing strongly in male superiority, especially in the face of circumstances that might question their own superiority over their female partners.

Research has shown strong support for the hypothesis that status inconsistency is a major cause of domestic violence, especially violence against women. Male perpetrators apparently believe themselves as being entitled to superior regard but find that circumstances fail to confirm these inflated notions of self, and so they attack their partners. Often the attack is a direct effort to reassert the superiority they believed themselves entitled to enjoy, such as the men who beat their wives to show them "who's the boss," in their common phrase. Still, it is important to note that not all forms of inconsistency produce violence, and so it is slightly misleading to assert status inconsistency as a cause. Violence seems to arise when circumstances question favorable assumptions about the self; in contrast, when circumstances provide equally inconsistent but highly favorable implications about the self, violence is low. Thus, only some forms of inconsistency are relevant. So the evidence points to threatened egotism as the decisive cause of domestic violence between adult partners.

## Other Domestic Violence: Parents and Children

As we suggested, child abuse may be the form of violence most likely to yield evidence of low self-esteem, because people who happen to feel violent while lacking self-esteem would be most likely to choose relatively helpless targets such as children. A series of studies has indeed suggested that child abusers have low self-esteem (S. C. Anderson & Lauderdale, 1982; Evans, 1980; Melnich & Hurley, 1969). More recent work has begun to question that conclusion, however. Shorkey and Armendariz (1985) replicated the lower self-esteem found among child abusers (from a sample in counseling) but concluded that it is not the main causal factor.

One of the most important studies, however, was done by Christensen, Brayden, Dietrich, McLaughlin, Sherrod, and Altemeier (1994). They suggested that previous studies may have been misled by reliance on samples of incarcerated abusers or abusers in therapy because being publicly identified as a child abuser may well lower self-esteem, especially on measures that emphasize getting along well with others. They therefore conducted a prospective study and found no difference in self-esteem between the eventual abusers and the comparison group. They concluded that low self-esteem is not a risk factor for potential physical abuse.

One other prospective study, by Altemeier, O'Conner, Vietze, Sandler, and Sherrod (1983), also provided relevant evidence. They found that abusive mothers differed mainly in that they were more likely to endorse the statement "I'm usually unsuccessful in life" than others. This statement could indicate low self-esteem, but it could also indicate experiences that threaten high self-esteem. A more recent study by Dutton and Hart (1992) found that high levels of narcissism, particularly narcissistic personality disorders, were associated with violence against family members. Thus, there is evidence to support the view that excessively favorable but threatened views of self lead to violence.

Elder abuse is another form of domestic violence that is often perpetrated by women, although both genders are well represented among such batterers. Pillemer's (1985) findings contradicted the traditional stereotype of elder abuse as caused by helpless dependency of the victims and by the perpetrator's resentment of the victim's neediness. Pillemer found that the victims of elder abuse tended to be more independent than control participants. The abusers, however, tended to be dependent on the victims for money, transportation, or other resources. The abusers apparently were embarrassed by and resented their own dependency. Thus, the refusal to accept an inferior or dependent role appears to be a major cause of elder abuse, which fits the pattern of high but threatened self-esteem.

The most common but, ironically, least studied form of domestic violence is between siblings. Wiehe (1991) conducted a victim survey but noted that almost nothing is known about perpetrators, except for the cases in which victims become perpetrators. The systematic selection of weaker, vulnerable targets was confirmed in their findings, according to a general pattern in which abusers tended to be older, stronger, and male, and victims tended to be younger, weaker, and female. Whether low self-esteem dictated the preference for weaker victims is quite unclear, however. All that was clear was that the most common situa-

tion to produce sibling violence was when older siblings were left in charge of younger ones who then defied their authority in some way, so the older siblings used violence to assert their authority, gain compliance, or simply intimidate the younger ones. This finding seems most consistent with the pattern we have already seen multiple times of threatened but favorable ( in this case situational) views of self. The older, abusive sibling presumably feels entitled to superior status and authority, as conferred by the parents, and feels this superior status is threatened when the younger sibling fails to obey or comply.

Still, this pattern is merely situational, and one cannot draw any clear conclusions about the trait levels of self-esteem among abusers. It is plausible that abusers regard themselves as superior and hence entitled to hit or hurt their weaker, supposedly inferior siblings. It seems less plausible a priori to suggest that older siblings left in charge by their parents feel inferior to their younger siblings, as the low self-esteem view might suggest, but it cannot be ruled out empirically.

## CRITIQUE

Many studies of intergenerational domestic violence are methodologically weak, and very little evidence of any sort exists with regard to sibling violence. Still, some fairly rigorous work has been done, particularly with regard to parents who abuse children. These studies have found no link between self-esteem and violence.

## CONCLUSION

Early studies found occasional support for the traditional hypothesis of low self-esteem as a cause of domestic violence, but that support has eroded in recent years as methodologically better studies have examined the issue. More recent evidence seems to be moving toward a status inconsistency explanation instead of a low self-esteem explanation, which would parallel the evolution of empirically based theory with regard to domestic violence between adult partners. People become violent because they refuse to accept a dependent role or because they feel that their superior role has been challenged or questioned. Some evidence has begun pointing to narcissism (i.e., inflated love of self) as a cause of violence against family members. All these findings seem best characterized as indicating that domestic violence arises when privately favorable views of self are impugned by external circumstances or by other people's particular, disrespectful actions but, given the present state of the literature on intergenerational abuse, that conclusion must be regarded as quite tentative.

## Violent Youth Gangs and Juvenile Delinquency

The classic study of juvenile delinquency by Glueck and Glueck (1950) compared juvenile delinquents against a matched sample of nondelinquent boys. Although the study was an early one and has been criticized on methodological grounds, it benefited from a large sample and extensive work and, according to the focused review by Wilson and Herrnstein (1985) nearly all of their findings have been replicated by subsequent studies. The Glueck and Glueck study did not measure self-esteem directly, indeed it antedated most modern self-esteem scales, but there were plenty of related variables. The pattern of findings offers little to support the hypothesis that low self-esteem causes delinquency. Delinquent boys were more likely than control boys to be characterized as self-assertive, socially assertive, defiant, and narcissistic, none of which seems compatible with low self-esteem. Meanwhile, the delinquents were less likely than the comparison group to be marked by the factors that do indicate low self-esteem, including severe insecurity, feelings of helplessness, feelings of being unloved, general anxiety (a frequent correlate of low self-esteem), submissiveness, and fear of failure. Thus, the thoughts and actions of juvenile delinquents suggested that they held quite favorable opinions of themselves.

As Sampson and Laub (1993) noted, it is useful to look for convergences between the Glueck and Glueck (1950) study and more recent studies of youthful violence, not only because of the seminal nature of the Gluecks' work, but also because their data were collected several decades ago and on an almost entirely White sample, unlike more recent studies. Converging findings thus confer especially high confidence in conclusions that can be supported across time and ethnicity.

One of the most thorough research projects on youth gangs was that of Jankowski (1991), whose work involved 10 years, several cities, and 37 gangs. Although as a sociologist he was disinclined

to use self-esteem or personality factors as explanatory constructs, his study did furnish several important observations. Jankowski specifically rejected the notion that acting tough is a result of low self-esteem or feelings of inadequacy. In his words, "There have been some studies of gangs that suggest that many gang members have tough exteriors but are insecure on the inside. This is a mistaken observation" (p. 27). He said that, for many members, the appeal of the gang is the positive respect it enjoys in the community, as well as the respectful treatment from other gang members, which he found to be an important norm in nearly all gangs he studied. He said most gang members "expressed a strong sense of self-competence and a drive to compete with others" (p. 102). When they failed, they always blamed something external rather than personal inadequacy or error. This last observation is especially relevant because several controlled studies have shown that such behavior is characteristic of high self-esteem and contrary to the typical responses of people with low self-esteem (Fitch, 1970; Ickes & Layden, 1978; Tennen & Herzberger, 1987; see also Kernis, Brockner, & Frankel, 1989).

Jankowski's (1991) characterization of the personal attitudes and worldviews of gang members likewise contains indicators of egotism. He said gang members tended to believe that their parents had capitulated to accept a humble life of poverty and failure, which they refused to do themselves. Mainly, he found, gang members were violent toward people "whom they perceived to show a lack of respect or to challenge their honor" (p. 142). Another main cause of gang violence is personal ambition: People behave violently to enhance their status in the organization, and to harm or discredit their rivals. The conclusion that the more ambitious people become the more violent ones is difficult to reconcile with the view that violence arises from low self-esteem.

Another sociologist, E. Anderson (1994), summarized his observations on Black street gangs by noting that the code of the streets centers around "respect," which gangs regard as an external quality involving being "granted the deference one deserves" (p. 82). Thus, his analysis indicates that gang members believe they deserve to be treated as superior beings—that is, their self-esteem is high—but they are constantly vulnerable to external circumstances that may dispute or fail to recognize their superiority. He said that gang members learn early in life that humility (which is one of the concepts linked to modesty and low self-esteem) is not a virtue, whereas people who win fights also gain the admiration of others. In fact, gang members have often been socialized with lessons that underscore the necessity of correcting someone who shows disrespect.

The high level of violence among modern youth gangs is partly due to what E. Anderson (1994) described as a zero-sum aspect, in which prestige and respect are gained by depriving others of them, so people may look for fights or conflicts as a way to assert their superiority over others. Anderson also said that respect is enhanced by what he calls "nerve," which is essentially a matter of acting as if oneself is above the rules that apply to others and as if one disregards the rights of others. In our view, both of these elements of nerve imply a view of one's own superiority and thus should be linked to high self-esteem. In a similar vein, Katz (1988) noted that many youthful circles and street subcultures afford respect mainly to the "badass" sort of person who transcends the pressures to conform to societal norms, rationality, and ideals. This prized identity is cultivated in part by creating the impression of being unpredictably prone to chaos and irrational violence.

The zero-sum hypothesis may help explain the frequent provocations that lead to violence; after all, if showing disrespect often elicits violence, why would people ever show disrespect to youthful gang members? Yet it is clear that many people do and, in particular, gang members insult members of other gangs. According to Horowitz and Schwartz (1974), most of what passes for gang violence is actually a matter of conflicts between individuals, while full-scale gang battles are quite rare (see also Jankowski, 1991). Still, the group is the operative unit in many cases. Violence is typically precipitated when one person impugns the honor or dignity of the other, most commonly by an insult, but also by any violation of etiquette. The code of honor is central to gang life, and gang members regard their own group as superior; the insults are often spoken as a way of asserting the superiority of one's own group, to which the insulted party must respond by defending the esteem of his (or sometimes her) group. If the zero-sum view is correct, then derogating rival groups would be perceived as an effective way of asserting and boosting the esteem of one's own group.

Indeed, one of Katz's (1988) most provocative

arguments is that youth gangs, which bring early deaths to so many of their members, actually have a positive investment in sustaining community violence because that violence offers them a respectable justification for existence, as protection against the dangerous urban environment, without which the gang would seem a mere childish association. The pervasiveness of violence thus helps support the gang members' egotism by transforming them from a club of trouble-making boys into a prestigious corps of warriors defending their community.

In any case, intergang violence comes to revolve around competing claims to be members of a privileged elite, and the occasion for violence is often a merely symbolic aspersion that the rival group's claims are unfounded, such as by making a humorous verbal insult or writing the name of one's gang in the home territory of the other gang. The gang members' preoccupation with respect (as in the common neologism *dissing*) reflects the ongoing tension between private, exalted views of self, which are shared and supported by the gang, and public perception of themselves as potentially falling short. McCall's (1994) recent firsthand account of his own violent youth emphasizes the concern with maintaining respect by putting down others and violently preventing others from showing disrespect to oneself. Other accounts make similar points (Bing, 1991; Currie, 1991).

Studies of adult gangs show similar patterns. Members of organized crime tend to regard themselves as superior beings and command deferential, respectful treatment from others (Anastasia, 1991; Arlacchi, 1992). Likewise, studies of prison gangs have observed that they form along racial and ethnic lines and hold explicit ideologies of their own racial or ethnic superiority, which is intensified as they come to operate as an elite group within the prison (Camp & Camp, 1985; Lyman, 1989).

## CRITIQUE

Studies of juvenile delinquents and youth gangs have generally lacked the rigor of experimental studies, but they have used a variety of observational and occasionally quantitative measures. Researchers from different disciplines concur in depicting these young men as egotistical in several ways, and they concur emphatically on the apparent preoccupation with respect and self-assertion. They also agree that insults or other disrespectful treatment tends to lead to violence. In view of this convergence, it seems reasonable to accept these conclusions, until or unless contradictory evidence can be marshaled. The evidence about organized crime and prison gangs is largely exploratory and impressionistic and should be regarded as preliminary.

## CONCLUSION

Although standardized measures of self-esteem have generally been lacking from studies of juvenile delinquents and gang members, there are ample indications of egotism from those studies. Gang members apparently think, talk, and act like people with high self-esteem and there is little to support the view that they are humble or self-deprecating, or even that they are privately full of insecurities and self-doubts. Violent youths seem sincerely to believe that they are better than other people, but they frequently find themselves in circumstances that threaten or challenge these beliefs. In those circumstances they tend to attack other people. It also appears that they sometimes manipulate or seek out such challenges to their esteem, in order to enhance their esteem by prevailing in a violent contest. Similar patterns have been observed in adult criminal gangs, but more research is needed.

## Political Terror (Government Repression, Terrorism, and War)

Political organizations perpetrate a great deal of violence. In this section we shall examine terrorism, government repression, assassination, and war. Genocidal activities may also be considered as political violence, but they will be covered in the following section.

An immense amount of suffering has resulted from internal repressive campaigns mounted by tyrannical governments. Chirot (1994) provided an authoritative global survey of 20th-century tyrannies. As a political scientist, his primary interest was in political structures and developments as causes of tyranny, but he concluded that threatened collective egotism was often an important factor in leading to tyranny. In case after case he examined, nations or national groups developed a strong ideology that emphasized their own superiority to other nations and groups. Tyrannies typi-

cally emerged when the ideology of superiority was accompanied by the perception that they did not receive the respect that was due them. As a fairly extreme example, prior to the Communist takeover, Russians felt themselves culturally and morally superior to the decadent nations of Western Europe, but they believed that accidental advantages of material wealth and military innovation had given the Westerners the edge and prevented Russia from taking its rightful place of leadership. This made Russians receptive to the emergence of a strong government that took the form of the Communist tyranny and whose internal terrors and purges still hold the record for the most killing by any government. Similar conclusions have been suggested by Staub (1985, 1989) and Ford (1985).

It is also useful to examine the motives and beliefs of the individuals who carry out repressive policies, although such information is relatively difficult to obtain. In particular, the psychology of the individuals who administer torture for repressive regimes has received only intermittent study for various obvious reasons, including the secrecy surrounding the activities and the reluctance of former torturers to participate in research or tell their stories after the regime has been discredited.

The methods used to train torturers should have considerable theoretical interest for the present debate. If low self-esteem leads to violence, then one would presumably train torturers by instilling feelings of inferiority and humility in them; in contrast, if high self-esteem facilitates violence, then the most effective training would instill attitudes of elitist superiority. The evidence appears to favor the latter. Gibson and Haritos-Fatouros (1986; see also Peters, 1985) described procedures used to train torturers during the military regime in Greece in the late 1960s and early 1970s. Relevant aspects of training included telling the trainees that they were special and fortunate to be included in this elite corps.[7] The sense of superiority was buttressed after the training by conferring

---

[7]To be sure, during the training phase, there was a period during which the initiates received humiliating treatment, but this appears to be standard for many military training regimens and indeed has been proposed by Aronson and Mills (1959) as an effective aid toward building strong emotional ties to the group. It is perhaps most precise to say that a preparatory phase of humility during training is followed by a more permanent phase of belonging to a superior elite. In any case,

many special privileges and marks of status on these men, such as allowing them to wear their hair long (unlike most soldiers) and wear civilian clothes, lending them military cars for personal use, and allowing them to eat free meals in good restaurants instead of dining on military fare. The authors noted that this instilling a sense of elitism and privilege was not unique to these groups, because other programs designed to train especially violent individuals, such as the U.S. Green Berets, do the same.

In particular, torturers are apparently strongly indoctrinated with the view that the superior culture, as embodied in their nation with its current regime, is threatened by evil forces, of whom the torture victims are representatives. Thus, the ideology of inherent but jeopardized superiority is acutely emphasized among the people who must carry out the violence. Conquest's (1986, 1990) observations about Russian terror and repression present a similar picture, although no systematic or quantitative study was involved.

Whereas repressive governments have all the forces of laws, police, and state bureaucracy on their side, terrorist groups typically lack all of these. Most commonly, terrorists are campaigning for radical political change and thus must live outside the law and in opposition to state institutions. Despite the opposite situation, they seem to share some important characteristics with tyrannical governments. In particular, they seem to cultivate the same attitude of moral superiority over their victims and enemies (e.g., Reich, 1990). Hee's (1993) detailed account indicated that her training as a terrorist in North Korea emphasized the pervasive belief in the moral superiority of North Korea in all nonmaterial aspects, over everyone else in the world. The backwardness, poverty, and other disadvantages of North Korea may have constituted some ego threat and, indeed, Hee reported how much dissonance she suffered during her espionage and terrorist missions abroad, which showed her how much better off the citizens of other countries were than North Koreans. Still, she and her peers were quite willing to perform violent acts even against unsuspecting, noncombatant citizens because of their belief in their own moral superiority. Post (1990) made a simi-

lar argument, which he exemplified with a story in which a new recruit objected to innocent people being killed if the terrorist group carried out its plan to bomb a department store; the group leader patiently explained that anyone shopping in such a store must be a capitalist and hence was not innocent.

We already mentioned that Long (1990) said that terrorists had low self-esteem but then provided evidence suggestive of high self-esteem (e.g., terrorists raise aspirations after failure, as do people high in self-esteem). Later in his book, Long partly contradicted his own assertion about low self-esteem by describing terrorist leaders as narcissistic (p. 18). If the leaders—those who are most responsible for the terrorist violence—hold the grandiose and inflated views of self that are the hallmark of narcissism, it is hard to regard terrorism as deriving from low self-esteem.

Two additional forms of political violence, namely assassination and warfare, deserve brief mention. Assassination has always been quite unusual, but its importance makes it worth considering despite its rarity. Ford's (1985) history does not, however, provide much indication of either high or low self-esteem as a prominent characteristic of assassins. This form of violence may well be a product of concerns and causes that do not include self-esteem.

Unlike assassination, war has been extremely common; indeed, Sluka (1992) summarized various estimates that there have been approximately 14,000 wars since 3600 B.C., and the four decades following World War II contained only 26 days of world peace.[8] Generalization is therefore quite hazardous. Still, recent and salient evidence seems hard to reconcile with the view that low self-esteem, as in lack of national pride, prompts nations to go to war. It is difficult to characterize imperial Japan, Nazi Germany, or Hussein's Iraq, for example, as suffering from low self-esteem; rather, such cases seem to fit the pattern of excessively favorable views of self that produce dreams of glory and anger that the rest of the world fails to pay sufficient respect. Staub (1985) concluded that cultural attitudes of superiority are important causes of warfare and other violence.

If we examine war from the perspective of the

---

what matters is that by the time these men began their duties as torturers they had been led to regard themselves as special, superior individuals.

[8]Even that estimate is high, because it is based on only international wars. If civil wars were counted too, there probably would be no days of peace at all.

individuals who carry it out, rather than from the perspective of national ideology, once again there seems ample evidence of egotism. Keegan (1993) has concluded that professional soldiers, from the Romans to the present, were not generally attracted and sustained in military life by financial gain, but rather by pride in belonging to a valued group, concern over winning admiration and fellowship of colleagues, accumulation of honor, and largely symbolic recognitions of success.

Recent efforts to understand the attitudes that make people favorably inclined toward war have been summarized by Feshbach (1994). In his research program, two sets of attitudes stood out (see Kosterman & Feshbach, 1989). He called the first of these *patriotism,* which he explained chiefly in terms of attachment feelings, although some element of pride is involved. The second attitude he referred to as *nationalism,* which he explicitly defined in terms of belief in the superiority of one's nation over others. Both of these attitudes are positively related to militaristic attitudes, but nationalism shows much stronger relationships to prewar and pronuclear attitudes. Nationalism is also positively correlated with individual aggressive tendencies. These results indicate that feelings of collective superiority are linked to violent, militaristic inclinations, ranging from personal conflicts to nuclear war.

## CRITIQUE

Most of the work reviewed in this section was done by historians, sociologists, and political scientists. When judged by psychologists' standards of methodological rigor, this work is relatively weak, but when judged on its own terms it fares better. Moreover, the convergence of evidence across different disciplines helps rule out the danger that disciplinary biases or methodological artifacts have shaped the conclusions.

## CONCLUSION

Except for assassination, it appears that political violence is often correlated with, and preceded by, strongly favorable self-regard and the perception that these views are threatened or disputed by others. In most cases it is the collective self-perception of superiority that is involved. Some signs indicate that individuals who carry out political violence are either indoctrinated with the view of

their own superiority or marked by narcissistic traits. Psychologists may question the methodological rigor of these studies, but the conclusion does seem consistent with the general patterns we have already seen in other spheres, and interdisciplinary convergence is itself a persuasive indicator. The only contrary view was Long's (1990) characterization of terrorists as having low self-esteem, but as we noted his elaboration seemed to indicate high self-esteem after all.

## Prejudice, Oppression, and Genocide

It would seem that the argument in favor of high self-esteem would be relatively easy to make in the case of prejudice and oppression. Thus, in the United States, there was until recently a long tradition of general discrimination and oppression against Black citizens; it would be difficult to argue that these things occurred because White people believed they were inferior to Blacks. By the same token, the most discussed and sensational pattern of genocide in the modern era was the extensive murder of Jews by Nazi-dominated, traditionally Christian Germany. It would require some rather severe stretches of the imagination to contend that the Nazis believed themselves inferior to the Jews, whom they denounced as "vermin". Indeed, the Nazis styled themselves the "master race," a label that seems hard to reconcile with a theory that they held a low opinion of themselves.

Racist prejudice in the United States appears to have had its major origin in the period during which the majority of Black Americans were slaves. In nearly all societies that have practiced slavery, slaves ranked at the bottom of the social hierarchy of self-worth, and the lowest ranking free people (including freed slaves) were often very concerned to establish their superiority to slaves (Patterson, 1982). Indeed, in America's Civil War, a problem faced by the southern aristocrats was how to enlist the support of the poor White population for a war that offered it little in terms of economic or political benefits; the main solution was to appeal to these people's sense of self-esteem by pointing out that if the South were to lose the war, the Black slaves would be freed and would become the equals of these poor Whites (McPherson, 1988). Apparently, the poor Whites agreed with that argument sufficiently to enroll and fight in the Civil War.

The loss of the Civil War constituted a double

blow to the immense pride of the southern aristocrats: First, they had been unthinkably defeated by the despised Yankees, and second, the Reconstruction governments sought to make the Blacks fully equal to all other citizens. The infamous Ku Klux Klan was founded and spread in response to these ego threats, stimulated by the perception that "insolent" Blacks now refused to treat Whites as inherently superior beings (e.g., by stepping out of the way on the sidewalk). Initially, Klan activities were designed to play humiliating but otherwise harmless pranks on Blacks, as if simply to prove White superiority. Soon, however, the Klan began to become violent against two groups of targets: Black people who seemed upwardly mobile, thereby refuting White supremacy, and White people who helped Blacks or otherwise treated them as equals. Although leadership and initiative came from the upper classes, most Klan violence over the years was perpetrated by lower-class White men who presumably had the most to fear in terms of loss of status from the notion of Black equality (Wade, 1987). Thus, the emergence and history of the Ku Klux Klan seem consistent with the notion that threatened egotism, in this case firm beliefs in White supremacy that were undermined by political and socioeconomic changes, is a powerful cause of prejudice and related violence. Indeed, at the congressional hearings on the Klan in 1921, the Imperial Wizard testified that the doctrine of White supremacy was not intended as a matter of "race hatred" but rather of "race pride" (Wade, 1987, p. 164).

Although the Klan has been largely discredited and driven underground, the 1980s witnessed a resurgence of racially motivated group activity, most notably among disaffected young White men who formed neo-Nazi groups ("skinheads"). Hamm (1993) noted the irony of such groups emerging during the 1980s, since that era was marked by high graduation rates and low unemployment rates among young White men. Moreover, Hamm found that, even within such groups, the members who participated in violent activities had higher career aspirations and higher levels of education than the nonviolent members. The members did, however, frequently express that they resented the advances by and preferential treatment of minorities. To integrate these observations, we would suggest that the high aspirations and sense of entitlement reflected favorable views of self, which increased the vulnerability to disconfirmation and threat, as symbolized by the perceived gains by non-White minorities. Levin and McDevitt's (1993) recent work on hate crimes paints a similar portrait of young White men as disaffected by their own eroding entitlements and resenting the gains made (presumably at their expense) by minorities.

Slavery itself was a major form of oppression and, indeed, it probably exceeded most other forms of prejudice and discrimination. Although there were often economic motives for slavery, Patterson (1982) concluded that slavery in the American South was atypical of most slave systems in several respects, including the relatively high financial rewards it brought to slave owners. In the history of the world, Patterson said, slave-owning was neither vital nor particularly helpful for the accumulation of wealth. Instead, the major appeal of slavery was that it increased the honor and prestige of the owners. (Indeed, he said that whenever the practice was allowed, slaves liked to own slaves themselves, because to do so conferred prestige on them—and slaves generally had few means of gaining such prestige.) Thus egotism rather than greed may often have been the major force behind the institution of slavery.

Imperialism has been a major form of international oppression for many centuries, although it reached a peak late in the 19th century as most of the main Western industrial nations sought overseas colonies. Although there were clearly economic motives for imperialism, motives of national pride and self-esteem were also relevant. We assume it will not be controversial to point out that the nationalistic attitudes supporting imperialism were essentially those of high collective self-esteem and even narcissism. One place to look for evidence would be in the so-called scramble for Africa during the 19th century, which formed a kind of climax to European imperialistic projects and, indeed, the subsequent decolonization of Africa signified the end of the imperialistic era. Pakenham (1991) provided a detailed account of this conquest of Africa. On the one hand, economic greed was undoubtedly a factor; but the economic promise of many colonies was never entirely spelled out and, in retrospect, it is clear that most colonies brought net financial losses (often severe) rather than gains. Pakenham concluded that national prestige was often associated with size of empire, and people wanted their nation's empire to expand regardless of financial prospects. Several of the military confrontations over obscure swamps or disease-infested wastelands can hardly be explained on any basis except national pride. In particular, territorial acquisitions by one of the principal rivals, especially France and England, often produced consternation among the others, who felt that their collective self-esteem was in jeopardy unless they could match or surpass them.

Dower (1986) provided considerable historical evidence that the Pacific segment of World War II was seen by both sides as a race war. This racial dimension to the conflict led to more extreme derogation of enemies and much higher levels of atrocity (on both sides) than were seen in the European war. A parallel pattern can be found in the European war, however, insofar as the Germans treated captured British and American soldiers, whom they regarded as fellow Aryans, much better than the Russians and other soldiers, whom they regarded as inferior races. The role of collective self-esteem in the Pacific war was quite clear: Both sides (i.e., the United States and Japan) regarded themselves as racially superior, but as threatened by the successes and evil intentions of the others. As evidence that the collective superiority went deeper than mere rhetoric, Dower cited multiple examples of strategic errors that were based in underestimating the enemy because of the assumption that the enemy, as an inferior race, would be militarily stupid and incompetent. For example, the United States did not believe the inferior Japanese capable of the strike on Pearl Harbor and, even after the fact, it was often assumed that the Germans must have planned the attack for the Japanese! On the other side, the Japanese thought that the decadent Westerners would not be willing to endure the hardship of a protracted war and so would give up easily, perhaps even right after Pearl Harbor.

Genocide is undoubtedly the most sinister form or manifestation of prejudice. Staub's (1989) psychological analysis of four major genocides repeatedly referred to the aggressor's sense of being superior and being better, which is often aggravated by threatening conditions. In each of the four cases, the genocides were perpetrated by nationalities and regimes with strong beliefs in their own innate superiority, but had suffered some threat or blow to their sense of superiority. Moreover, within the society, those responsible for the killing, such as Hitler's SS in Germany and the military in Argentina, constituted a privileged, respected elite. Large-scale mass murder emerged as a means of cleansing the body politic of impure, evil, decadent influences as well as a means of satisfying the wish to blame one's misfortunes on a scapegoat who could then be punished. Indeed, Staub's general conclusions point directly to threatened egotism: "When a sense of superiority combines with an underlying (and often unacknowledged) self-doubt, their contribution to the potential for genocide and mass killing can be especially high" (p. 19). The combination of high collective self-esteem (and the resulting "sense of entitlement") with the recent threats, blows, or losses provides a "belief in unfulfilled greatness" (p. 234), which constitutes an important precondition and motivation for genocide.

There have been some controlled studies of the relation of self-esteem to prejudice. The traditional theory was, as usual, that low self-esteem causes prejudice, and so it was assumed that people who lack self-esteem would be the most prejudiced against others. Preliminary work seemed to fit this pattern (e.g., Stephan & Rosenfield, 1978; see Wills, 1981, for review), although the evidence was limited, indirect, or ambiguous. Crocker and Schwartz (1985) showed, however, that this semblance of derogating others reflects the general negativity of people with low self-esteem: Although they may rate out-groups negatively, they rate other people and themselves negatively too, and so it is misleading to say that they are prejudiced against out-groups.

A more precise picture of the role of self-esteem in prejudice has emerged from more recent work by Crocker and her colleagues. Crocker, Thompson, McGraw, and Ingerman (1987) showed a pattern of responding to ego threats by showing more in-group bias (i.e., rating one's own group more favorably in comparison to other groups). Only people with high self-esteem showed this pattern. Likewise, Crocker and Luhtanen (1990) showed that people who scored high in collective self-esteem (i.e., favorable self-evaluation based on one's memberships and affiliations, as opposed to individual self-esteem) showed the same pattern of derogating out-groups in response to threats to their egotism (in this case, being told that the group to which they belonged had performed poorly on a test and was therefore insensitive, immature, and suffered some cognitive and affective deficits). Although the effects in these studies were not uniform across all measures and conditions, the bulk of their findings suggests that prejudicial responses may be strongest among people with high self-esteem and particularly when such people are subjected to ego threats.

## CRITIQUE

As already noted, early studies suggested that low self-esteem was linked to prejudice, but more recent and careful studies have reached the opposite conclusion, and the early work appears to have suffered from methodological and interpretive flaws. The studies on prejudice and violence come from multiple fields and point to similar conclusions.

## CONCLUSION

Current research has suggested that racial and ethnic prejudice accompany favorable views of self. Meanwhile, abundant evidence from across several disciplines confirms the view that intergroup violence is often linked to prejudiced views that typically depict the in-group as superior to the out-group. Furthermore, some evidence suggests that the most severe violence occurs when a group perceives that its superior position is being eroded or threatened by the rise of a rival group.

## General Discussion

Several main conclusions can be drawn from our survey of relevant empirical evidence. It must be noted that direct, prospective studies linking sophisticated measures of self-appraisal to real violence have been quite rare, and so it has been necessary to look for converging evidence from diverse sources and multiple methods. The volume and diversity of the evidence are necessary to compensate for the lack of unambiguous, rigorous work focused on the hypotheses. With a topic as full of ethical, practical, and theoretical complexities as violence, this problem may be inevitable.

The traditional view that low self-esteem is a cause of violence and aggression is not tenable in light of the present evidence. Most studies failed to find any support for it, and many provided clear and direct contradictory findings. Aggressors seem to believe that they are superior, capable beings. Signs of low self-esteem such as self-deprecation, humility, modesty, and self-effacing mannerisms,

seem to be rare (underrepresented) among violent criminals and other aggressors. The typical, self-defining statements by both groups and individuals who aggress indicate a belief in their superiority, not inferiority. Violent and criminal individuals have been repeatedly characterized as arrogant, confident, narcissistic, egotistical, assertive, proud, and the like. By the same token, violent, aggressive, and criminal groups tend to share beliefs in their own superiority, ranging from the "man of honor" designation of Mafia initiates to the "master race" ideology of the Nazis. Also, from individual hate crimes to genocidal projects, violence that is linked to prejudice is generally associated with strong views that one's own group is superior and the out-group is inferior, even subhuman.

We suggested that domestic violence might be the one sphere in which the low self-esteem view would fare best. That sphere was indeed the only one in which supportive findings (i.e., linking low self-esteem to violence) were reported, but even those tended to be weak, exceptional, and contradicted by the findings of more careful and systematic studies. The possibility that people with low self-esteem may sometimes choose relatively weak and helpless targets as victims remains plausible, although even it cannot be asserted as correct at present.

The rejection of the low self-esteem view does not mean, however, that high self-esteem is a cause of violence. Most bullies, violent criminals, and other aggressors seem to think highly of themselves, but it is not true that most people who think highly of themselves are violent. The most precise conclusion appears to be that violence is perpetrated by a small subset of people with favorable views of themselves. Or, to put it another way, violence is produced by a combination of favorable self-appraisals with situational and other factors.

The most important situational factor that interacts with favorable self-appraisals to cause violence is an ego threat. The evidence conformed broadly to the view that violence is often caused by an encounter in which a favorable self-appraisal is confronted with an external, less favorable evaluation. In all spheres we examined, we found that violence emerged from threatened egotism, whether this was labeled as wounded pride, disrespect, verbal abuse, insults, anger manipulations, status inconsistency, or something else. For huge nationalities, medium and small groups, and lone individuals, the same pattern was found: Violence resulted most commonly from feeling that one's superiority was somehow being undermined, jeopardized, or contradicted by current circumstances.

We do not wish to claim that threatened egotism is the sole cause of aggression and, indeed, there is ample room to discuss biochemical or genetic causes, modeling effects, instrumental aggression, and other factors. But in terms of the potent link between self-appraisals and violence, the discrepancy between favorable self-views and external threats is the most important cause.

The theory that the discrepancy between self-appraisals and external evaluations causes violence led to the further prediction that violence would be increased by anything that raised the frequency or impact of such discrepancies. We proposed that inflated or unrealistically positive self-appraisals would tend to lead to violent responses because, to the extent that feedback clusters around accurate, realistic appraisals, it will tend to contradict such unrealistically favorable opinions of self. There was moderate support for that view, including evidence about tyrants, career criminals, psychopaths, and convicted rapists. Also, some of the most effective direct predictors of violence were narcissism scales, particularly subscales for grandiosity and exhibitionism. It remains to be determined how these self-enhancing illusions compare with the positive illusions of nonviolent people and how widely disseminated they are. For the present, however, it seems reasonable to accept the view that inflated, overly positive self-appraisals are associated with violence.

Another moderator we proposed was that unstable or uncertain beliefs about the self's good qualities should be especially vulnerable and sensitive to external ego threats. Again, a broad assortment of evidence fit this view, but further work is needed. There was direct evidence that unstable, high self-esteem is most closely linked with hostility (Kernis, Grannemann, et al., 1989).

The affective component of the theory is relatively straightforward. It is clear that ego threats elicit negative affect and that negative affect can lead to violence. The evidence is less clear as to whether anger represents a defensive effort to ward off other forms of negative affect that might follow from accepting the bad feedback, but that hypothesis remains plausible. Meanwhile, we predicted from the affect theory that severely violent reactions would sometimes follow from seemingly minor or trivial ego threats; this prediction was confirmed by multiple observations in various investigations.

The interpersonal framework offers relevant insights. It would be misleading to suggest that the experience of discrepant self-appraisals causes an aimless eruption of aggressive impulses. Rather, aggression is most commonly directed at the source of the unflattering evaluation, so it makes sense to regard many aggressive acts as communicative responses to unwelcome, disputed appraisals. Also, some sources provided direct confirmation of the view that aggression is a means of dominating another person, hence symbolizing one's superiority over that person.

On the basis of the zero-sum view of self-esteem, we predicted that one person's positive self-assertions could constitute a threat to, and elicit a violent response from, others. There was some evidence consistent with that view, especially in the selection of targets based on their presumptive feelings of superiority. Still, this seems to be an unusual pattern rather than the norm. The view that zero-sum esteem pressures are exceptional and circumscribed phenomena would be consistent with Feather's (1994) conclusion about the "tall poppy" effect, namely that it too only occurs under specific, limited, and unusual circumstances.

## Is It Really High Self-Esteem?

A reevaluation of the relationship between self-appraisals and violence is clearly warranted. Indeed, it seems overdue: It is surprising that the low self-esteem view has survived so long, and one wonders if there were not something correct about it to allow it to endure with so little direct support. Is there any way to salvage the view that low self-esteem contributes to violence? And do narcissistic, inflated, arrogant self-appraisals really constitute high self-esteem?

To be sure, definitions of self-esteem may vary. We have used the term in a broad and inclusive sense to encompass all favorable self-appraisals, including confidence and self-respect as well as arrogance and narcissism. In contrast, some might prefer to define self-esteem in a way that would eliminate all distasteful and problematic forms; if this were possible then it might be plausible to deny that high self-esteem leads to violence. It is difficult to see, however, what basis other than the mere value judgment itself might be used to differentiate benign from malignant self-esteem.

Obviously, if high self-esteem is defined in a way that stipulates that it can only produce positive, desirable consequences, then it cannot lead to violence or aggression, but this is circular. In our view, the heavily positive connotation that self-esteem has acquired in recent American thought is partly a result of biased and wishful thinking that simply refuses to acknowledge the darker side. If one remains with the simple, literal definition of self-esteem as a favorable appraisal of oneself, than arrogant narcissists and conceited, egotistical bullies do indeed have high self-esteem.

A more subtle line of reasoning might propose that the superficially favorable self-views of conceited and other violent individuals are actually defensive reactions that are designed to conceal unfavorable self-appraisals. Possibly these are defensive versions of high self-esteem, underneath which lies a hidden but truly low self-esteem. Theorists wishing to make this argument might be encouraged by the evidence we have reviewed suggesting that not all people with high self-esteem are violent. If only a subset of people with high self-esteem are violent, might this subset consist of people for whom high self-esteem is a false veneer to cover up low self-esteem? If so, then one might yet find a way to argue that low self-esteem is a cause of violence. In other words, perhaps some people who regard themselves unfavorably become self-assertive and violent as a result, possibly as a way of compensating for this sense of inferiority. Because this theory enjoys the luxury of being able to interpret contrary evidence as meaning the opposite of what it literally signifies, it is difficult to disprove. In other words, if favorable self-assertions are taken as signs of low self-esteem, then the hypothesis of low self-esteem is difficult to falsify.

Still, there is some relevant evidence. The pattern of responding to bad feedback with defensively positive assertions about the self, which Long (1990) observed among terrorists and Jankowski (1991) mentioned with violent gangs, has been shown in laboratory studies; but is characteristic of high rather than low self-esteem (Baumeister, 1982; Baumeister et al., 1993; McFarlin & Blascovich, 1981). A method of distinguishing high from merely defensive high self-esteem was published in 1975 (Schneider & Turkat, 1975), but researchers have not identified very many patterns in which the two groups differ. The lack of such findings seems to indicate

that the pattern of positive self-assertion, despite privately low self-appraisal, is relatively rare.

Moreover, as we noted, a number of researchers specifically contradicted the view that the violent individuals they studied were secretly suffering from inferiority complexes or self-loathing (e.g., Jankowski, 1991; Olweus, 1994). The basis for these conclusions was not reported, but then again one wonders what sort of basis might be fully satisfactory, given the difficulty of falsifying such a hypothesis. Still, one researcher who made such an assertion (Jankowski, 1991) had spent over a decade living among gangs and getting to know hundreds of gang members, so it seems fair to assume that he would have seen ample evidence of their inner low self-esteem if it existed.

There is also a fundamental conceptual problem with the approach of saying that low self-esteem is often concealed beneath a veneer of high self-esteem. Even if one believes that some people who assert high self-esteem actually have low self-esteem, low self-esteem cannot be regarded as the true cause of violence. There are plenty of people who do clearly have low self-esteem and, as we have shown, they are generally less violent than others. It is quixotic to assert that egotists are actually self-doubters as a way of salvaging the hypothesis that self-doubters are the violent ones, given the nonviolence of most self-doubters.

At best, one would have to concede that individuals with overt low self-esteem are nonviolent and, therefore, only those with covert low self-esteem are violent. But if one accepts that only the covert version of low self-esteem leads to violence, then seemingly one has already conceded the role of high self-esteem as decisive. In other words, the crucial distinction is between people who admit to having low self-esteem and those whose (putative) low self-esteem is concealed by some veneer of high self-esteem. Insofar as only the latter group are violent, then the decisive factor would be the veneer of high self-esteem. The favorable self-appraisal would thus still be the cause of violence, even if it did coexist with some hidden, unfavorable self-appraisal.

We have seen that violence is most common when favorable self-appraisals are threatened and such episodes might cause the individual to entertain doubts, at least temporarily, about the favorable self-appraisals. We have proposed that violence is a means of evading such doubts and affirming the favorable views of self, but it is plau-

↑ Interesting

→ Relate to derogation of partner

sible that the aggressors did suffer doubts at least momentarily and some might propose that the doubts were the impetus for the violence. If one can refer to these self-doubts as low self-esteem, then perhaps a very watered-down version of the low self-esteem theory might be upheld after all.

Yet that conclusion would be seriously misleading. The operative, indeed decisive beliefs, about the self are the highly favorable ones. Self-doubts only lead to violence in the context of some commitment to highly favorable self-appraisals. The self-doubt point is perhaps best understood in the context of the repeated evidence that inflated or uncertain views about the self were the views most strongly linked to violent action. The composite prototype of the aggressor that emerged from our review of the literature is a man whose self-appraisal is unrealistically positive. His exaggerated impression of his superiority is prone to encounter contrary feedback, which may cause him to doubt himself momentarily, but to which he soon responds with violence. It would be quite appropriate for him to feel such doubts because, after all, the self-view in question is inaccurate. In the end, however, he preserves the unrealistically favorable self-appraisal by attacking the source of the ego threat. To say that he was violent because of low self-esteem is a serious distortion of the episode. Indeed, his momentary doubts seem better described as the disturbing voice of reality than as low self-esteem.

On both empirical and theoretical grounds, therefore, we must reject the view that low self-esteem causes violence. Aggressive, violent, and hostile people consistently express favorable views of themselves. And even if one could document hidden low self-esteem beneath the surface of apparently high self-esteem, for which empirical support is scant, it would still be necessary to regard the surface egotism rather than the hidden self-doubts as causally crucial.

Why, then, has the low self-esteem theory persisted? One likely answer is that social scientists have failed to distinguish adequately between internal and external appraisals. Violence does ensue on receipt of bad evaluations from other people; it is only the negative self-evaluations that fail to lead to violence. Symbolic interactionism (e.g., Mead, 1934) proposed that self-views are principally derived from the feedback one receives from others. This style of thought may have encouraged many thinkers to ignore the distinction

and assume that people who are criticized by others must consequently have low self-esteem. It has taken decades for the accumulation of evidence to show that self-appraisals are only weakly related to external appraisals and that, in many cases, people overtly resist revising their self-appraisals in the face of external feedback (Crocker & Major, 1989; Shrauger & Schoeneman, 1979; Swann & Hill, 1982). For present purposes, the crucial point is that threatened egotism is something quite different than low self-esteem. Another possible reason for the persistence of the low self-esteem view is that a broad reaction against blaming the victim, dating back to Ryan's 1971 critique, may have encouraged writers to phrase the causes of violence in terms of self-evaluation, rather than in terms of provocative, evaluative acts by the future victim.

It may seem that confusing public esteem with self-esteem is a small error or technicality. However, the result of this error has been to promote a view that is precisely the opposite of the correct one. The reason that disrespectful treatment sometimes leads to violence is that the aggrieved individual regards himself or herself quite favorably and hence is unwilling to tolerate being treated in a way that fails to confirm this favorable self-regard. It is thus the favorable views of self that foster violence.

## Implication for Future Work

Several suggestions for further work emerge from this review. Most pressing is the need for direct and careful study of the ways in which egotism leads to aggression and violence. We recommend that laboratory researchers turn some attention to the role of views about the self in producing retaliation. In particular, the mediating roles of emotional states and particular interpersonal contexts deserve further study.

As we noted, it is simplistic to assume a direct and unmoderated link between self-esteem and aggression, so further experimentation may need more than a self-esteem scale and a bogus shock generator. The causal power of ego threats has been well established, although rarely discussed as such, in laboratory work as well as in nonlaboratory research into violence. What is needed, therefore, is systematic exploration of how particular views about the self interact with ego threats to increase aggression. Both situational factors and individual differences may moderate the tendency of ego threats to produce aggression. Regarding the latter, it may be desirable to give careful thought to how views about the self are to be assessed. As already noted, self-esteem measures alone may be less successful than measures of narcissism (e.g., Raskin et al., 1991; Wink, 1991), stability of self-esteem (Kernis, 1993), or defensive self-esteem (Schneider & Turkat, 1975).

Another potential problem may lie in the fact that most standard self-esteem measures were designed with the assumption that high self-esteem indicates healthy adjustment and good adaptation to life; indeed high self-esteem scores are sometimes used as a criterion measure of adjustment (e.g., Heilbrun, 1981; Kahle et al., 1980; Whitley, 1983). In our view, self-esteem should be a relatively value-neutral construct referring to positive evaluation of self, so an effective and valid scale would identify the arrogant, conceited narcissist just as well as the person who holds an unbiased appreciation of his or her own well-recognized good qualities. Not all scales may be effective in this regard, however. One apt approach may be to focus on variance shared between measures of high self-esteem and narcissism: Both concepts imply favorable self-appraisals, but the underlying evaluative bias about the desirability of these self-appraisals pushes in opposite directions, so the shared variance might be what remains after these opposing biases are removed. [. . .]

Although we are not clinicians, it seems necessary to point out that the theoretical understanding of the causes of violence does have implications for interventions as well. If low self-esteem were really the cause of violence, then it would be therapeutically prudent to make every effort to convince rapists, murderers, wife beaters, professional hit men, tyrants, torturers, and others that they are superior beings. From our reading of the empirical literature, however, these people are often violent precisely because they already believe themselves to be superior beings. It would therefore be more effective to direct therapeutic efforts elsewhere (e.g., at cultivating self-control) and, if any modifications to self-appraisals were to be attempted, then perhaps it would be better to try instilling modesty and humility.

## Conclusion

As compared with other cultures and other historical eras, modern America has been unusually fond of the notion that elevating the self-esteem of each individual will be best for society (e.g., see Huber, 1971). America is also, perhaps not coincidentally, one of the world's most violent societies, with rates of violent crime that far exceed even those of other modern, industrialized nations. The hope that raising everyone's self-esteem will prove to be a panacea for both individual and societal problems continues unabated today (e.g., California Task Force, 1990) and, indeed, the allusions in the mass media to the desirability of self-esteem suggest that it may even be gaining in force. In this context, the notion that low self-esteem causes violence may have been widely appealing as one more reason to raise self-esteem.

Our review has indicated, however, that it is threatened egotism rather than low self-esteem that leads to violence. Moreover, certain forms of high self-esteem seem to increase one's proneness to violence. An uncritical endorsement of the cultural value of high self-esteem may therefore be counterproductive and even dangerous. In principle, it might become possible to inflate everyone's self-esteem, but it will almost certainly be impossible to insulate everyone against ego threats. In fact, as we have suggested, the higher (and especially the more inflated) the self-esteem, the greater the vulnerability to ego threats. Viewed in this light, the societal pursuit of high self-esteem for everyone may literally end up doing considerable harm.

REFERENCES

Adler, J. (1994, August 15). Murder: A week in the death of America. *Newsweek, 124,* 24–43.

Allgood-Merton, B., Lewinsohn, P. M., & Hops, H. (1990). Sex differences and adolescent depression. *Journal of Abnormal Psychology, 99,* 55–63.

Altemeier, W. A., O'Conner, S., Vietze, P. M., Sandler, H. M., & Sherrod, K. B. (1983). Antecedents of child abuse. *Journal of Pediatrics, 100,* 823–829.

Altman, J. H., & Wittenborn, J. R. (1980). Depression-prone personality in women. *Journal of Abnormal Psychology, 89,* 303–308.

American Psychiatric Association. (1994). *Diagnostic and statistical manual of the mental disorders* (4th ed.). Washington, DC: Author.

Anastasia, G. (1991). *Blood and honor: Inside the Scarfo mob—The Mafia's most violent family.* New York: Morrow.

Anderson, E. (1994, May). The code of the streets. *Atlantic Monthly, 273,* 81–94.

Anderson, S. C., & Lauderdale, M. L. (1982). Characteristics of abusive parents: A look at self-esteem. *Child Abuse and Neglect, 6,* 285–293.

Arlacchi, P. (1992). *Men of dishonor: Inside the Sicilian Mafia* (M. Romano, Trans.). New York: Morrow.

Aronson, E., & Mills, J. (1959). The effect of severity of initiation on liking for a group. *Journal of Abnormal and Social Psychology, 59,* 177–181.

Banaji, M. R., & Steele, C. M. (1989). Alcohol and self-evaluation: Is a social cognition approach beneficial? *Social Cognition, 7,* 137–151.

Baron, R. A. (1976). The reduction of human aggression: A field study on the influence of incompatible responses. *Journal of Applied Social Psychology, 6,* 95–104.

Baumeister, R. F. (1982). Self-esteem, self-presentation, and future interaction: A dilemma of reputation. *Journal of Personality, 50,* 29–45.

Baumeister, R. F. (1986). *Identity: Cultural change and the struggle for self.* New York: Oxford University Press.

Baumeister, R. F. (1989). *Masochism and the self.* Hillsdale, NJ: Erlbaum.

Baumeister, R. F. (1993). Understanding the inner nature of low self-esteem: Uncertain, fragile, protective, and conflicted. In R. Baumeister (Ed.), *Self-esteem: The puzzle of low self-regard* (pp. 201–218). New York: Plenum Press.

Baumeister, R. E., Heatherton, T. F., & Tice, D. M. (1993). When ego threats lead to self-regulation failure: Negative consequences of high self-esteem. *Journal of Personality and Social Psychology, 64,* 141–156.

Baumeister, R. F., & Jones, E. E. (1978). When self-presentation is constrained by the target's knowledge: Consistency and compensation. *Journal of Personality and Social Psychology, 36,* 608–618.

Baumeister, R. F., Stillwell, A. M., & Heatherton, T. F. (1994). Guilt: An interpersonal approach. *Psychological Bulletin, 115,* 243–267.

Baumeister, R. F., & Tice, D. M. (1985). Self-esteem and responses to success and failure: Subsequent performance and intrinsic motivation. *Journal of Personality, 53,* 450–467.

Baumeister, R. F., & Tice, D. M. (1990). Anxiety and social exclusion. *Journal of Social and Clinical Psychology, 9,* 165–195.

Baumeister, R. F., Tice, D. M., & Hutton, D. G. (1989). Self-presentational motivations and personality differences in self-esteem. *Journal of Personality, 57,* 547–579.

Berkowitz, L. (1978). Is criminal violence normative behavior? Hostile and instrumental aggression in violent incidents. *Journal of Research in Crime and Delinquency, 15,* 148–161.

Berkowitz, L. (1989). Frustration–aggression hypothesis: Examination and reformulation. *Psychological Bulletin, 106,* 59–73.

Bing, L. (1991). *Do or die.* New York: HarperCollins.

Blaine, B., & Crocker, J. (1993). Self-esteem and self-serving biases in reactions to positive and negative events: An integrative review. In R. Baumeister ( Ed.), *Self-esteem: The puzzle of low self-regard* (pp. 55–85). New York: Plenum Press.

Brearly. H. C. (1932). *Homicide in the United States.* Chapel Hill: University of North Carolina Press.

Brown, G. W., Andrews, B., Harris, T., Adler, Z., & Bridge, L. (1986). Social support, self-esteem, and depression. *Psychological Medicine, 16,* 813–831.

Brown, G. W., & Harris, T. (1978). *The social origins of depression: A study of psychiatric disorder in women.* London: Tavistock.

Brownmiller, S. (1975). *Against our will: Men, women, and rape.* New York: Simon & Schuster.

Burke, P. J., Stets, J. E., & Pirog-Good, M. A. (1988). Gender identity, self-esteem, and physical and sexual abuse in dating relationships. *Social Psychology Quarterly, 51,* 272–285.

Bushman, B. J., & Cooper, H. M. (1990). Effects of alcohol on human aggression: An integrative research review. *Psychological Bulletin, 107,* 341–354.

California Task Force to Promote Self-esteem and Personal and Social Responsibility. (1990). *Toward a state of self-esteem.* Sacramento: California State Department of Education.

Camp, G. M., & Camp, C. G. (1985). *Prison gangs: Their extent, nature, and impact on prisons.* Washington, DC: U.S. Department of Justice.

Chirot, D. (1994). *Modern tyrants: The power and prevalence of evil in our age.* New York: Free Press.

Christensen, M. J., Brayden, R. M., Dietrich, M. S., McLaughlin, F. J., Sherrod, K. B., & Altemeier, W. A. (1994). The prospective assessment of self-concept in neglectful and physically abusive low-income mothers. *Child Abuse and Neglect, 18,* 225–232.

Claes, J. A., & Rosenthal, D. M. (1990). Men who batter women: A study in power. *Journal of Family Violence, 5,* 215–224.

Cofer, D. H., & Wittenborn, J. R. (1980). Personality characteristics of formerly depressed women. *Journal of Abnormal Psychology, 89,* 309–314.

Conquest, R. (1986). *The harvest of sorrow: Soviet collectivization and the terror-famine.* New York: Oxford University Press.

Conquest, R. (1990). *The great terror: A reassessment.* New York: Oxford University Press.

Cooley, C. H. (1964). *Human nature and the social order.* New York: Schocken. (Original work published 1902)

Crocker, J., & Luhtanen, R. (1990). Collective self-esteem and ingroup bias. *Journal of Personality and Social Psychology, 58,* 60–67.

Crocker, J., & Major, B. (1989). Social stigma and self-esteem: The self-protective properties of stigma. *Psychological Review, 96,* 608–630.

Crocker, J., & Schwartz, I. (1985). Prejudice and ingroup favoritism in a minimal intergroup situation: Effects of self-esteem. *Personality of Social Psychology Bulletin, 11,* 379–386.

Crocker, J., Thompson, L. L., McGraw, K. M., & Ingerman, C. (1987). Downward comparison, prejudice, and evaluations of others: Effects of self-esteem and threat. *Journal of Personality and Social Psychology, 52,* 907–916.

Currie, E. (1991). *Dope and trouble: Portraits of delinquent youth.* New York: Pantheon Books.

Darley, J. M., & Goethals, G. R. (1980). People's analyses of the causes of ability-linked performances. In L. Berkowitz (Ed.), *Advances in experimental social psychology* (Vol. 13, pp. 1–37). New York: Academic Press.

De La Ronde, C., & Swann, W. B. (1993). Caught in the crossfire: Positivity and self-verification strivings among people with low self-esteem. In R. Baumeister (Ed.), *Self-esteem: The puzzle of low self-regard* (pp. 147–165). New York: Plenum Press.

Diamond, D. L., & Wilsnack, S. C. (1978). Alcohol abuse among lesbians: A descriptive study. *Journal of Homosexuality, 4,* 205–216.

Dollard, J., Doob, L., Miller, N., Mowrer, O., & Sears, R. (1939). *Frustration and aggression.* New Haven, CT: Yale University Press.

Dower, J. W. (1986). *War without mercy: Race and power in the Pacific war.* New York: Pantheon Books.

Dutton, D. G., & Hart, S. D. (1992). Risk markers for family violence in a federally incarcerated population. *International Journal of Law and Psychiatry, 15,* 101–112.

Eagly, A. H. (1985). *Sex differences in social behavior: A social-role interpretation.* Hillsdale, NJ: Erlbaum.

Ellison, C. (1991). An eye for an eye? A note on the southern subculture of violence thesis. *Social Forces, 69,* 1223–1239.

Evans, A. L. (1980). Personality characteristics and disciplinary attitudes of child-abusing mothers. *Child Abuse and Neglect, 6,* 285–293.

Feather, N. T. (1994). Attitudes toward high achievers and reactions to their fall: Theory and research concerning tall poppies. In M. Zanna (Ed.), *Advances in experimental social psychology* (Vol. 26, pp. 1–73). San Diego, CA: Academic Press.

Feshbach, S. (1994). Nationalism, patriotism, and aggression: A clarification of functional differences. In L. R. Huesmann (Ed.), *Aggressive behavior: Current perspectives* (pp. 275–291). New York: Plenum Press.

Finkelhor, D., & Yllo, K. (1985). *License to rape: Sexual abuse of wives.* New York: Free Press.

Fitch, G. (1970). Effects of self-esteem, perceived performance, and choice on causal attributions. *Journal of Personality and Social Psychology, 16,* 311–315.

Ford, F. L. (1985). *Political murder: From tyrannicide to terrorism.* Cambridge, MA: Harvard University Press.

Gelles, R. J., & Straus, M. A. (1988). *Intimate violence: The causes and consequences of abuse in the American family.* New York: Simon & Schuster/Touchstone.

Gibson, J. T., & Haritos-Fatouros, M. (1986, November). The education of a torturer. *Psychology Today, 20,* 50–58.

Glueck, S., & Glueck, E. T. (1950). *Unraveling juvenile delinquency.* Cambridge, MA: Harvard University Press.

Goldstein, D., & Rosenbaum, A. (1985). An evaluation of the self-esteem of maritally violent men. *Family Relations, 34,* 425–428.

Gondolf, E. W. (1985). *Men who batter.* Holmes Beach, FL: Learning Publications.

Goodwin, F. K., & Jamison, K. R. (1990). *Manic-depressive illness.* New York: Oxford University Press.

Gottfredson, M. R., & Hirschi, T. (1990). *A general theory of crime.* Stanford, CA: Stanford University Press.

Gough, H. G., Wenk, E. A., & Rozynko, V. V. (1965). Parole outcome as predicted from the CPI, the MMPI, and a base expectancy table. *Journal of Abnormal Psychology, 70,* 432–441.

Greenberg, J., & Pyszczynski, T. (1985). Compensatory self-inflation: A response to the threat to self-regard of public failure. *Journal of Personality and Social Psychology, 49,* 273–280.

Greenwald, A. G. (1980). The totalitarian ego: Fabrication and revision of personal history. *American Psychologist, 35,* 603–618.

Groth, A. N. (1979). *Men who rape: The psychology of the offender.* New York: Plenum Press.

Hamm, M. S. (1993). *American skinheads: The criminology and control of hate crime.* Westport, CT: Praeger.

Hare, R. D. (1993). *Without conscience: The disturbing world of the psychopaths among us.* New York: Simon & Schuster/Pocket.

Harter, S. (1993). Causes and consequences of low self-esteem in children and adolescents. In R. Baumeister (Ed.), *Self-esteem: The puzzle of low self-regard* (pp. 87–116). New York: Plenum Press.

Heatherton, T. F., & Polivy, J. (1991). Development and validation of a scale for measuring state self-esteem. *Journal of Personality and Social Psychology, 60,* 895–910.

Hee, K. H. (1993). *The tears of my soul.* New York: Morrow.

Heilbrun, A. B. (1981). Gender differences in the functional linkage between androgyny, social cognition, and competence. *Journal of Personality and Social Psychology, 41,* 1106–1118.

Higgins, E. T. (1987) . Self-discrepancy: A theory relating self and affect. *Psychological Review, 94,* 319–340.

Hoffman, F. L. (1925). *The homicide problem.* Newark, NJ: Prudential Press.

Holtzworth-Munroe, A. (1992). Attributions and maritally violent men: The role of cognitions in marital violence. In J. Harvey, T. Orbuch, & A. Weber (Eds.), *Attributions, accounts, and close relationships* (pp. 165–175). New York: Springer-Verlag.

Hornung, C. A., McCullough, B. C., & Sugimoto, T. (1981). Status relationships in marriage: Risk factors in spouse abuse. *Journal of Marriage and the Family, 43,* 675–692.

Horowitz, R., & Schwartz, G. (1974). Honor, normative ambiguity, and gang violence. *American Sociological Review, 39,* 238–251.

Huber, R. M. (1971). *The American idea of success.* New York: McGraw-Hill.

Huesmann, L. R., Eron, L. D., Lefkowitz, M. M., & Walder, L. O. (1984). The stability of aggression over time and generations. *Developmental Psychology, 20,* 1120–1134.

Hurley, D. L. (1990). Incest and the development of alcoholism in female survivors. *Alcoholism Treatment Quarterly, 7,* 41–56.

Ickes, W., & Layden, M. A. (1978). Attributional styles. In J. Harvey (Ed.), *New directions in attribution research* (Vol. 2, pp. 119–152). Hillsdale, NJ: Erlbaum.

James, W. (1950). *The principles of psychology* (Vol. 2). New York: Dover Publications. (Original work published 1890)

Jankowski, M. S. (1991). *Islands in the street: Gangs and American urban society.* Berkeley: University of California Press.

Kahle, L. R., Kulka, R. A., & Klingel, D. M. (1980). Low adolescent self-esteem leads to multiple interpersonal problems: A test of social adaptation theory. *Journal of Personality and Social Psychology, 39,* 496–502.

Katz, J. (1988). *Seductions of crime: Moral and sensual attractions in doing evil.* New York: Basic Books.

Keegan, J. (1993). *A history of warfare.* New York: Knopf.

Kernis, M. H. (1993). The roles of stability and level of self-esteem in psychological functioning. In R. Baumeister (Ed.), *Self-esteem: The puzzle of low self-regard* (pp. 167–182). New York: Plenum Press.

Kernis, M. H., Brockner, J., & Frankel, B. S. (1989). Self-esteem and reactions to failure: The mediating role of overgeneralization. *Journal of Personality and Social Psychology, 57,* 707–714.

Kernis, M. H., Cornell, D. P., Sun, C. R., Berry, A., & Harlow, T. (1993). There's more to self-esteem than whether it is high or low: The importance of stability of self-esteem. *Journal of Personality and Social Psychology, 65,* 1190–1204.

Kernis, M. H., Grannemann, B. D., & Barclay, L. C. (1989). Stability and level of self-esteem as predictors of anger arousal and hostility. *Journal of Personality and Social Psychology, 56,* 1013–1022.

Kiernan, V G. (1989). *The duel in European history.* Oxford, England: Oxford University Press.

Kirschner, D. (1992). Understanding adoptees who kill: Dissociation, patricide, and the psychodynamic of adoption. *International Journal of Offender Therapy and Comparative Criminology, 36,* 323–333.

Konovsky, M., & Wilsnack, S. C. (1982). Social drinking and self-esteem in married couples. *Journal of Studies on Alcohol, 43,* 319–333.

Kosterman, R., & Feshbach, S. (1989). Toward a measure of patriotic and nationalistic attitudes. *Political Psychology, 10,* 257–274.

LaFree, G. D. (1976). Male power and female victimization: Towards a theory of interracial rape. *American Journal of Sociology, 88,* 311–328.

Leary, M. R., Tambor, E. S., Terdal, S. K., & Downs, D. L. (1995). Self-esteem as an interpersonal monitor: The sociometer hypothesis. *Journal of Personality and Social Psychology, 68,* 518–530.

Levin, J., & McDevitt, J. (1993). *Hate crimes: The rising tide of bigotry and bloodshed.* New York: Plenum Press.

Lewis, H. B. (1971). *Shame and guilt in neurosis.* New York: International Universities Press.

Long, D. E. (1990). *The anatomy of terrorism.* New York: Free Press.

Lyman, M. D. (1989). *Gangland: Drug trafficking by organized criminals.* Springfield, IL: Charles C Thomas.

MacDonald, J. M. (1975). *Armed robbery: Offenders and their victims.* Springfield, IL: Charles C Thomas.

McCall, N. (1994). *Makes me wanna holler: A young black man in America.* New York: Random House.

McFarlin, D. B., & Blascovich, J. (1981). Effects of self-esteem and performance feedback on future affective preferences and cognitive expectations. *Journal of Personality and Social Psychology, 40,* 521–531.

McNeill, W. H. (1982). *The pursuit of power.* Chicago: University of Chicago Press.

McNeill, W. H. (1991). *The rise of the West.* Chicago: University of Chicago Press.

McPherson, J. M. (1988). *Battle cry of freedom: The Civil War era.* New York: Oxford University Press.

Mead, G. H. (1934). *Mind, self, and society.* Chicago: University Chicago Press.

Melnich, B., & Hurley, J. R. (1969). Distinctive personality attributes of child-abusing mothers. *Journal of Consulting and Clinical Psychology, 33,* 746–749.

Meloy, J. R. (1988). *The psychopathic mind: Origins, dynamics, and treatment.* Northvale, NJ: Aronson.

Myers, D. (1980). *The inflated self.* New York: Seabury Press.

National Research Council. (1993). *Understanding and preventing violence.* Washington, DC: National Academy Press.

Nisbett, R. E. (1993). Violence and U.S. regional culture. *American Psychologist, 48,* 441–449.

Norris, J. (1988). *Serial killers: The growing menace.* New York: Doubleday.

Oates, R. K., & Forrest, D. (1985). Self-esteem and early background of abusive mothers. *Child Abuse and Neglect, 9,* 89–93.

Olweus, D. (1994). Bullying at school: Long-term outcomes for the victims and an effective school-based intervention program. In R. Huesmann (Ed.), *Aggressive behavior: Current perspectives* (pp. 97–130). New York: Plenum Press.

Orford, J., & Keddie, A. (1985). Gender differences in the functions and effects of moderate and excessive drinking. *British Journal of Clinical Psychology, 24,* 265–279.

Pakenham, T. (1991). *The scramble for Africa: White man's conquest of the Dark Continent from 1876 to 1912.* New York: Avon/Random House.

Patterson, O. (1982). *Slavery and social death.* Cambridge, MA: Harvard University Press.

Peters, E. (1985). *Torture.* Oxford, England: Blackwell.

Peterson, D. (1991). Physically violent husbands of the 1890s and their resources. *Journal of Family Violence, 6,* 1–15.

Pillemer, K. (1985). The dangers of dependency: New findings on domestic violence against the elderly. *Social Problems, 33,* 146–158.

Polk, K. (1993). Observations on stranger homicide. *Journal of Criminal Justice, 21,* 573–582.

Post, J. M. (1990). Terrorist psycho-logic: Terrorist behavior as a product of psychological forces. In W Reich (Ed.), *Origins of terrorism: Psychologies, ideologies, theologies, and states of mind* (pp. 25–40). Cambridge, England: Cambridge University Press.

Raskin, R., Novacek, J., & Hogan, R. (1991). Narcissistic self-esteem management. *Journal of Personality and Social Psychology, 60,* 911–918.

Reich, W. (Ed.). (1990). *Origins of terrorism: Psychologies, ideologies, theologies, and states of mind.* Cambridge, England: Cambridge University Press.

Renzetti, C. M. (1992). *Violent betrayal: Partner abuse in lesbian relationships.* Newbury Park, CA: Sage.

Russell, R. J., & Hulson, B. (1992). Physical and psychological abuse of heterosexual partners. *Personality and Individual Differences, 13,* 457–473.

Ryan, W. (1971). *Blaming the victim.* New York: Vintage.

Salovey, P. (1991). Social comparison processes in envy and jealousy. In J. Suls & T. A. Wills (Eds.), *Social comparison: Contemporary theory and research* (pp. 261–285). Hillsdale, NJ: Erlbaum.

Salovey, P., & Rodin, J. (1984). Some antecedents and consequences of social-comparison jealousy. *Journal of Personality and Social Psychology, 41,* 780–792.

Sampson, R. J., & Laub, J. H. (1993). *Crime in the making: Pathways and turning points through life.* Cambridge, MA: Harvard University Press.

Scarry, E. (1985). *The body in pain: The making and unmaking of the world.* New York: Oxford University Press.

Schlenker, B. R. (1980). *Impression management: The self-concept, social identity and interpersonal relations.* Monterey, CA: Brooks/Cole.

Schlenker, B. R. (1986). Self-identification: Toward an integration of the private and public self. In R. Baumeister (Ed.), *Public self and private self* (pp. 21–62). New York: Springer-Verlag.

Schlenker, B. R., Soraci, S., & McCarthy, B. (1976). Self-esteem and group performance as determinants of egocentric perceptions in cooperative groups. *Human Relations, 29,* 1163–1176.

Schneider, D. J., & Turkat, D. (1975). Self-presentation following success or failure: Defensive self-esteem models. *Journal of Personality, 43,* 127–135.

Schoenfeld, C. G. (1988). Blacks and violent crime: A psychoanalytically oriented analysis. *Journal of Psychiatry and Law, 16,* 269–301.

Scully, D. (1990). *Understanding sexual violence: A study of convicted rapists.* New York: HarperCollins.

Scully, D., & Marolla, J. (1985). "Riding the bull at Gilley's". Convicted rapists describe the rewards of rape. *Social Problems, 32,* 251–263.

Sedikides, C. (1993). Assessment, enhancement, and verification determinants of the self-evaluation process. *Journal of Personality and Social Psychology, 65,* 317–338.

Shorkey, C. T., & Armendariz, J. (1985). Personal worth, self-esteem, anemia, hostility and irrational thinking of abusive mothers: A multivariate approach. *Journal of Clinical Psychology, 41,* 414–421.

Shrauger, J. S., & Lund, A. K. (1975). Self-evaluation and reactions to evaluations from others. *Journal of Personality, 43,* 94–108.

Shrauger, J. S., & Schoeneman, T. J. (1979). Symbolic interactionist view of self-concept: Through the looking glass darkly. *Psychological Bulletin, 86,* 549–573.

Sluka, J. A. (1992). The anthropology of conflict. In C. Nordstrom & J. Martin (Eds.), *The paths to domination, resistance, and terror* (pp. 18–36). Berkeley: University of California Press.

Smith, R. H., Parrott, W. G., Ozer, D., & Moniz. A. (1994). Subjective injustice and inferiority as predictors of hostile and depressive feelings in envy. *Personality and Social Psychology Bulletin, 20,* 717–723.

Staub, E. (1985). The psychology of perpetrators and bystanders. *Political Psychology, 6,* 61–85.

Staub, E. (1989). *The roots of evil: The origins of genocide and other group violence.* New York and Cambridge, England: Cambridge University Press.

Steele, C. M. (1988). The psychology of self-affirmation: Sustaining the integrity of the self. In L. Berkowitz (Ed.), *Advances in experimental social psychology* (Vol. 21, pp. 261–302). New York: Academic Press.

Stephan, W. G., & Rosenfield, D. (1978). Effects of desegregation on racial attitudes. *Journal of Personality and Social Psychology, 36,* 795–804.

Stets, J. E. (1991). Psychological aggression in dating relationships: The role of interpersonal control. *Journal of Family Violence, 6,* 97–114.

Straus, M. (1980). Victims and aggressors in marital violence. *American Behavioral Scientist, 23,* 681–704.

Swann, W. B. (1987). Identity negotiation: Where two roads meet. *Journal of Personality and Social Psychology, 53,* 1038–1051.

Swann, W. B., Griffin, J. J., Predmore, S. C., & Gaines. B. (1987). The cognitive–affective crossfire: When self-consistency confronts self-enhancement. *Journal of Personality and Social Psychology, 52,* 881–889.

Swann, W B., & Hill, C. A. (1982). When our identities are mistaken: Reaffirming self-conceptions through social interaction. *Journal of Personality and Social Psychology, 43,* 59–66.

Tangney, J. P. (1991). Moral affect: The good, the bad, and the ugly. *Journal of Personality and Social Psychology, 61,* 598–607.

Tangney, J. P. (1992). Situational determinants of shame and guilt in young adulthood. *Personality and Social Psychology Bulletin, 18,* 199–206.

Tangney, J. P., Wagner, P. E., Barlow, D. H., Marschall, D. E., & Gramzow, R. (1994). *The relation of shame and guilt to constructive vs. destructive responses to anger across the lifespan.* Manuscript submitted for publication.

Tangney, J. P., Wagner, P. E., Fletcher, C., & Gramzow, R. (1992). Shamed into anger? The relation of shame and guilt to anger and self-reported aggression. *Journal of Personality and Social Psychology, 62,* 669–675.

Taylor, S. E. (1989). *Positive illusions: Creative self-deception and the healthy mind.* New York: Basic Books.

Taylor, S. E., & Brown, J. D. (1988). Illusion and well-being: A social psychological perspective on mental health. *Psychological Bulletin, 103,* 193–210.

Tedeschi, J. T., & Felson, R. B. (1994). *Violence, aggression, and coercive actions.* Washington, DC: American Psychological Association.

Tennen, H., & Affleck, G. (1993). The puzzles of self-esteem: A clinical perspective. In R. Baumeister (Ed.), *Self-esteem: The puzzle of low self-regard* (pp. 241–262). New York: Plenum Press.

Tennen, H., & Herzberger, S. (1987). Depression, self-esteem, and the absence of self-protective attributional biases. *Journal of Personality and Social Psychology, 52,* 72–80.

Tice, D. M. (1991). Esteem protection or enhancement? Self-handicapping motives and attributions differ by trait self-esteem. *Journal of Personality and Social Psychology, 60,* 711–725.

Tice, D. M. (1993). The social motivations of people with low self-esteem. In R. Baumeister (Ed.), *Self-esteem: The puzzle of low self-regard* (pp. 55–85). New York: Plenum Press.

Tice, D. M., Muraven, M., Butler, J., & Stillwell, A. M. (1994). *Self presentations to friends and strangers.* Manuscript submitted for publication.

Toch, H. (1993). *Violent men: An inquiry into the psychology of violence.* Washington, DC: American Psychological Association. (Original work published 1969)

Veroff, J., Douvan, E., & Kulka, R. A. (1981). *The inner American: A self-portrait from 1957 to 1976.* New York: Basic Books.

Von Hentig, H. (1948). *The criminal and his victim.* New Haven, CT: Yale University Press.

Wade, W. C. (1987). *The fiery cross: The Ku Klux Klan in America.* New York: Touchstone/Simon & Schuster.

Walker, L. E. (1979). *The battered woman.* New York: Harper & Row.

Whitley, B. E. (1983). Sex role orientation and self-esteem: A critical meta-analytic review. *Journal of Personality and Social Psychology, 44,* 765–778.

Wicklund, R. A., & Gollwitzer, P. M. (1982). *Symbolic self-completion.* Hillsdale, NJ: Erlbaum.

Widom, C. S. (1991). A tail on an untold tale: Response to "biological and genetic contributors to violence—Widom's untold tale." *Psychological Bulletin, 109,* 130–132.

Wiehe, V. R. (1991). *Perilous rivalry: When siblings become abusive.* Lexington, MA: Heath/Lexington Books.

Wills, T. A. (1981). Downward comparison principles in social psychology. *Psychological Bulletin, 90,* 245–271.

Wilson, J. Q., & Herrnstein, R. J. (1985). *Crime and human nature.* New York: Simon & Schuster.

Wink, P. (1991). Two faces of narcissism. *Journal of Personality and Social Psychology, 61,* 590–597.

Wyatt-Brown, B. (1982). *Southern honor: Ethics and behavior in the old South.* New York: Oxford University Press.

# Self-Regulation

The study of how the self regulates itself has been a relative latecomer among social psychology's subtopics in the study of self. Although a handful of researchers had addressed the topic in the 1960s and 1970s, it was not until late in the 1980s that the area gained broad attention in the field.

The early pioneers included Walter Mischel, whose work on delay of gratification explicated and highlighted the inner struggle to resist temptation and make oneself pursue long-term goals at the expense of immediate rewards. Fred Kanfer analyzed self-control processes in clinical phenomena and called attention to the need to incorporate client self-regulatory processes into therapeutic interventions aimed at changing behavior. These men and Albert Bandura signaled the field that behaviorist theory would never be adequate for explaining human behavior unless, at the very least, researchers allowed for how people could regulate themselves by administering rewards and punishments to themselves.

The first paper in this section is Bandura's (1977) landmark article on self-efficacy. This work, backed up by many subsequent empirical papers, helped persuade the field that a positive sense of self-efficacy is vitally conducive to successful performance and general well-being. In an important sense, efficacy is the complement to high self-esteem. Self-esteem is an assessment of being, whereas self-efficacy refers to doing: It is a belief that one can accomplish tasks successfully. The complementarity of the two is perhaps best shown by their interactive effects on happiness. Campbell (1981) noted that, even though self-esteem and self-efficacy each produces a main effect that increases happiness, the

281

two interact to produce exceptionally high levels of subjective well-being among people who score high on both (see also Campbell, Converse, & Rodgers, 1976). Bandura was himself a clinical psychologist, and his paper here draws on clinical phenomena as well as laboratory findings to argue that achieving a sense of mastery is often a vital step forward toward a healthier, more successful self.

Bandura's later thinking elaborated the simple notion of self-efficacy into a broader set of ideas regarding human agency in general. The expectation of being able to perform some action is an important step toward actually performing it, and he has even proposed that this helps bridge the metaphysical gap between thinking and doing, thus addressing the age-old problem of how action is initiated (Bandura, 1989).

One of the first books to use the term "self-regulation" in the title was Carver and Scheier's (1981) important book, which has influenced almost all subsequent thinking about self-regulation. Their background had been in the study of self-awareness and, indeed, when the book was published it was widely recognized as the definitive book on self-awareness—even though self-awareness did not appear in the title. In their thinking, however, the core function of self-awareness is to enable the self to appraise where it is in relation to where it wants to be, so as to facilitate progress toward personal goals. They signaled in their book that the state of self-awareness itself was less important than the regulation of self in approaching its goals.

This section contains Carver & Scheier's 1982 article on self-regulation, which covers some of the key ideas in their book. The central point is the application of feedback-loop theory to self-awareness and self-regulation. In this article, they elaborate the simple loop into a hierarchy of loops and explain how people's attention moves up and down the hierarchy during self-regulation. Subsequent work has had difficulty getting firm tests of the hierarchy hypothesis, but many studies have found the simple feedback-loop concepts very useful.

The final article in this section is a series of laboratory experiments exploring the idea that self-regulation operates like a strength or energy, as in the traditional notion of "willpower." The focus here is on the "operate" phase of Carver and Scheier's test-operate-test-exit model of self-regulation: How do people actually alter themselves in order to reach their standards? Baumeister, Bratslavsky, Muraven, and Tice (1998) found that acts of self-control seemed to consume some energy or strength, insofar as subsequent self-control was impaired. Their results also suggested that the self's other acts of volition, such as making choices and responding actively instead of passively, also draw on this same energy or strength. Thus, apparently the self has a limited resource that it uses for a broad range of acts of volition and self-control.

## REFERENCES

Bandura, A. (1977). Self-efficacy: Toward a unifying theory of behavior change. *Psychological Review, 84,* 191–215.

Bandura, A. (1989). Human agency in social cognitive theory. *American Psychologist, 44,* 1175–1184.

Baumeister, R. F., Bratslavsky, E., Muraven, M., & Tice, D. M. (1998). Ego depletion: Is the active self a limited resource? *Journal of Personality and Social Psychology, 74,* 1252–1265.

Campbell, A. (1981). *The sense of well-being in America.* New York: McGraw-Hill.

Campbell, A., Converse, P. E., & Rodgers, W. L. (1976). *The quality of American life: Perceptions, evaluations, and satisfactions.* New York: Russell Sage.

Carver, C. S., & Scheier, M. F. (1981). *Attention and self-regulation: A control theory approach to human behavior.* New York: Springer-Verlag.

Carver, C. S. & Scheier, M. F. (1982). Control theory: A useful conceptual framework for personality-social, clinical and health psychology. *Psychological Bulletin, 92,* 111–135.

# Discussion Questions

1. What might the authors of these three papers offer someone as advice about how to embark on a diet to lose weight or an exercise program to increase fitness?
2. How does self-efficacy differ from high self-esteem?
3. What can each of these three theories of self-regulation offer to explain how some celebrities come to ruin by way of drug and alcohol addiction?
4. Suppose you were a behavior therapist confronted with a patient suffering from poor control and impulsive, addictive patterns. What exercises might you design to increase someone's self-efficacy, improve the operation of feedback-loop cycles, or increase regulatory strength?
5. Where does regulatory strength fit into the feedback loop model? Are these different theories of self-regulation compatible or are they contradictory?
6. Some people call self-control "the master virtue" because it seems to be implicit in most conceptions of moral, virtuous behavior, just as failed self-control is central to many vices. What do each of these three theories have to contribute to understanding moral, virtuous behavior?
7. Alcohol is known to impair self-regulation in many different contexts. How exactly might alcohol have this effect? What aspects or processes of self-control does it undermine?

# Suggested Readings

Baumeister, R. F., Heatherton, T. F., & Tice, D. M. (1994). *Losing control: How and why people fail at self-regulation.* San Diego, CA: Academic Press. An easy-to-read summary of what research has learned about self-control failure. It includes specific chapters devoted to many spheres of self-regulation, such as eating, smoking, alcohol, controlling emotions, and task performance. Or, for a brief overview of the book's main conclusions, see Baumeister, R. F., & Heatherton, T. F. (1996). Self-regulation failure: An overview. *Psychological Inquiry, 7,* 1–15.

Bandura, A. (1989). Human agency in social cognitive theory. *American Psychologist, 44,* 1175–1184. This offers an overview of Bandura's subsequent thinking, including a rephrasing of the self-efficacy theory in cognitive rather than behavioral terms. Recommended for advanced students.

Carver, C. S., & Scheier, M. F. (1981). *Attention and self-regulation: A control theory approach to human behavior.* New York: Springer-Verlag. This book was one of social psychology's most important and influential works of the 1980s. It offers an inclusive overview of published research on self-awareness as well as explaining the feedback-loop model.

Gottfredson, M. R., & Hirschi, T. (1990). *A general theory of crime.* Stanford, CA: Stanford University Press. This excellent, informative book by two leading criminologists states that deficient self-control is the most important theoretical key to understanding crime and criminals.

Mischel, W. (1996). From good intentions to willpower. In P. Gollwitzer & J. Bargh (Eds.), *The psychology of action* (pp. 197–218). New York: Guilford. Or Mischel, W. (1974). Processes in delay of gratification. In L. Berkowitz (Ed.), *Advances in experimental social psychology* (Vol. 7, pp. 249–292). San Diego, CA: Academic Press. Mischel's work on delay of gratification in children was one of the foundations of modern theories about self-regulation. Delaying gratification requires the child to resist immediate temptation for long-term outcomes, so impulses must be controlled with various cognitive and emotional strategies.

Peele, S. (1989). *The diseasing of America.* Boston, MA: Houghton Mifflin Co. A thought-provoking, controversial, and highly readable attack on prevailing theories about addiction.

Wegner, D. M., Schneider, D. J., Carter, S. R., & White, T. L. (1987). Paradoxical effects of thought suppression. *Journal of Personality and Social Psychology, 53,* 5–13. This popular paper opened up a line of research on thought control. Now why can't you get that annoying song out of your head?

# Self-Efficacy: Toward a Unifying Theory of Behavioral Change

Albert Bandura • Stanford University

The present article presents an integrative theoretical framework to explain and predict psychological changes achieved by different modes of treatment. This theory states that psychological procedures, whatever their term, alter the level and strength of *self-efficacy*. It is hypothesized that expectations of personal efficacy determine whether coping behavior will be initiated, how much effort will be expended, and how long it will be sustained in the face of obstacles and aversive experiences. Persistence in activities that are subjectively threatening but in fact relatively safe produces, through experiences of mastery, further enhancement of self-efficacy and corresponding reductions in defensive behavior. In the proposed model, expectations of personal efficacy are derived from four principal sources of information: performance accomplishments, vicarious experience, verbal persuasion, and physiological states. The more dependable the experiential sources, the greater are the changes in perceived self-efficacy. A number of factors are identified as influencing the cognitive processing of efficacy information arising from enactive, vicarious, exhortative, and emotive sources. The differential power of diverse therapeutic procedures is analyzed in terms of the postulated cognitive mechanism of operation. Findings are reported from microanalyses of enactive, vicarious, and emotive modes of treatment that support the hypothesized relationship between perceived self-efficacy and behavioral changes. Possible directions for further research are discussed.

Current developments in the field of behavioral change reflect two major divergent trends. The difference is especially evident in the treatment of dysfunctional inhibitions and defensive behavior. On the one hand, the mechanisms by which human behavior is acquired and regulated are increasingly formulated in terms of cognitive processes. On the other hand, it is performance-based procedures that are proving to be most powerful for effecting psychological changes. As a consequence, successful performance is replacing symbolically based experiences as the principle vehicle of change.

The present article presents the view that changes achieved by different methods derive from a common cognitive mechanism. The apparent divergence of theory and practice can be reconciled by postulating that cognitive processes mediate change, but cognitive events are induced and altered most readily by experience of mastery arising from effective performance. The distinction between process and means is underscored because it is often assumed that a cognitive mode of operation requires a symbolic means of induction. Psychological changes can be produced through

285

means other than performance accomplishments. Therefore, the explanatory mechanism developed in this article is designed to account for changes in behavior resulting from diverse modes of treatment.

## Cognitive Locus of Operation

Psychological treatments based on learning principles were originally conceptualized to operate through peripheral mechanisms. New behavior was presumably shaped automatically by its effects. Contingency learning through paired stimulation was construed in connectionist terms as a process in which responses were linked directly to stimuli. Altering the rate of preexisting behavior by reinforcement was portrayed as a process wherein responses were regulated by their immediate consequences without requiring any conscious involvement of the responders.

Growing evidence from several lines of research altered theoretical perspectives on how behavior is acquired and regulated. Theoretical formulations emphasizing peripheral mechanisms began to give way to cognitively oriented theories that explained behavior in terms of central processing of direct, vicarious, and symbolic sources of information. [. . . ] To summarize briefly, it has now been amply documented that cognitive processes play a prominent role in the acquisition and retention of new behavior patterns. Transitory experiences leave lasting effects by being coded and retained in symbols for memory representation. Because acquisition of response information is a major aspect of learning, much human behavior is developed through modeling. From observing others, one forms a conception of how new behavior patterns are performed and, on later occasions the symbolic construction serves as a guide for action (Bandura, 1971). The initial approximations of response patterns learned observationally are further refined through self-corrective adjustments based on informative feedback from performance.

Learning from response consequences is also conceived of largely as a cognitive process. Consequences serve as an unarticulated way of informing performers what they must do to gain beneficial outcomes and to avoid punishing ones. [. . .]

Motivation, which is primarily concerned with activation and persistence of behavior, also is partly rooted in cognitive activities. The capacity to represent future consequences in thought provides one cognitively based source of motivation. Through cognitive representation of future outcomes, individuals can generate current motivators of behavior. Seen from this perspective, reinforcement operations affect behavior largely by creating expectations that behaving in a certain way will produce anticipated benefits or avert future difficulties (Bolles, 1972). In the enhancement of previously learned behavior, reinforcement is conceived of mainly as a motivational device, rather than as an automatic response strengthener.

A second cognitively based source of motivation operates through the intervening influences of goal setting and self-evaluative reactions (Bandura, 1976b, 1977). Self-motivation involves standards against which to evaluate performance. By making self-rewarding reactions conditional on attaining a certain level of behavior, individuals create self-inducements to persist in their efforts until their performances match self-prescribed standards. Perceived negative discrepancies between performance and standards create dissatisfactions that motivate corrective changes in behavior. Thus, both the anticipated satisfactions of desired accomplishments and the negative appraisals of insufficient performance provide incentives for action. Having accomplished a given level of performance, individuals often are no longer satisfied with it and make further self-reward contingent on higher attainments.

The reconceptualization of human learning and motivation in terms of cognitive processes has major implications for the mechanisms through which therapeutic procedures alter behavioral functioning. [. . .] The present article outlines a theoretical framework in which the concept of self-efficacy is assigned a central role for analyzing changes achieved in fearful and avoidant behavior. The explanatory value of this conceptual system is then evaluated by its ability to predict behavioral changes produced through different methods of treatment.

## Efficacy Expectations as a Mechanism of Operation

The present theory is based on the principal assumption that psychological procedures, whatever their form, serve as means for creating and strengthening expectations for personal efficacy.

Within this analysis, efficacy expectations are distinguished from response-outcome expectancies. The difference is presented schematically in Figure 14.1.

An outcome expectancy is defined as a person's estimate that a given behavior will lead to certain outcomes. An efficacy expectation is the conviction that one can successfully execute the behavior required to produce the outcomes. Outcome and efficacy expectations are differentiated because individuals can believe that a particular course of action will produce certain outcomes but, if they entertain serious doubts about whether they can perform the necessary activities, such information does not influence their behavior.

In this conceptual system, expectations of personal mastery affect both initiation and persistence of coping behavior. The strength of people's convictions in their own effectiveness is likely to affect whether they will even try to cope with given situations. At this initial level, perceived self-efficacy influences choice of behavioral settings. People fear and tend to avoid threatening situations they believe exceed their coping skills, although they get involved in activities and behave assuredly when they judge themselves capable of handling situations that would otherwise be intimidating.

Not only can perceived self-efficacy have directive influence on choice of activities and settings, but, through expectations of eventual success, it can affect coping efforts once they are initiated. Efficacy expectations determine how much effort people will expend and how long they will persist in the face of obstacles and aversive experiences. The stronger the perceived self-efficacy, the more active the efforts. Those who persist in subjectively threatening activities that are in fact relatively safe will gain corrective experiences that reinforce their sense of efficacy, thereby eventually eliminating their defensive behavior. Those who cease their coping efforts prematurely will retain their self-debilitating expectations and fears for a long time.

The preceding analysis of how perceived self-efficacy influences performance is not meant to imply that expectation is the sole determinant of behavior. Expectation alone will not produce desired performance if the component capabilities are lacking. Moreover, there are many things that people can do with certainty of success that they do not perform because they have no incentives to

**FIGURE 14.1.** ■ Diagrammatic representation of the difference between efficacy expectations and outcome expectations.

do so. Given appropriate skills and adequate incentives, however, efficacy expectations are a major determinant of people's choice of activities, how much effort they will expend, and of how long they will sustain effort in dealing with stressful situations.

## Dimensions of Efficacy Expectations

Empirical tests of the relationship between expectancy and performance of threatening activities have been hampered by inadequate expectancy analysis. In most studies, the measures of expectations are mainly concerned with people's hopes for favorable outcomes, rather than with their sense of personal mastery. Moreover, expectations are usually assessed globally only at a single point in a change process, as though they represent a static, unidimensional factor. Participants in experiments of this type are simply asked to judge how much they expect to benefit from a given procedure. When asked to make such estimates, participants assume, more often than not, that the benefits will be produced by the external ministrations, rather than gained through the development of self-efficacy. Such global measures reflect a mixture of, among other things, hope, wishful thinking, belief in the potency of the procedures, and faith in the therapist. It therefore comes as no surprise that outcome expectations of this type have little relation to magnitude of behavioral change (Davison & Wilson, 1973; Lick & Bootzin, 1975).

Efficacy expectations vary on several dimensions which have important performance implications. They differ in *magnitude*. Thus, when tasks are ordered in level of difficulty, the efficacy expectations of different individuals may be limited to the simpler tasks, extend to moderately difficult ones, or include even the most taxing performances. Efficacy expectations also differ in *generality*. Some experiences create circumscribed mastery expectations, while others instill a more generalized sense of efficacy that extends well beyond the specific treatment situation. In addition, expectancies vary in *strength*. Weak expectations are easily extinguished by disconfirming experiences, whereas individuals who possess strong expectations of mastery will persevere in their coping efforts despite disconfirming experiences.

An adequate expectancy analysis, therefore, requires detailed assessment of the magnitude, generality, and strength of efficacy expectations commensurate with the precision with which behavioral processes are measured. Both efficacy expectations and performance should be assessed at significant junctures in the change process to clarify their reciprocal effects on each other. Mastery expectations influence performance and are, in turn, altered by the cumulative effects of one's efforts.

## Sources of Efficacy Expectations

In this social learning analysis, expectations of personal efficacy are based on four major sources of information: performance accomplishments, vicarious experience, verbal persuasion, and physiological states. Figure 14.2 presents the diverse influence procedures commonly used to reduce defensive behavior, as well as the principal source through which each treatment operates to create expectations of mastery. Any given method, depending on how it is applied, may of course draw, to a lesser extent, on one or more other sources of efficacy information. For example, as we shall see shortly, performance-based treatments not only promote behavioral accomplishments, but also extinguish fear arousal, thus authenticating self-efficacy through enactive and arousal sources of information. Other methods, however, provide fewer ways of acquiring information about one's capability for coping with threatening situations. By postulating a common mechanism of operation, this analysis provides a conceptual framework within which to study behavioral changes achieved by different modes of treatment.

## PERFORMANCE ACCOMPLISHMENTS

This source of efficacy information is especially influential because it is based on personal mastery experiences. Successes raise mastery expectations while repeated failures lower them, particularly if the mishaps occur early in the course of events. After strong efficacy expectations are developed through repeated success, the negative impact of occasional failures is likely to be reduced. Indeed, occasional failures that are later overcome by determined effort can strengthen self-motivated persistence if one finds, through experience, that even the most difficult obstacles can be mastered by sustained effort. The effects of fail-

EFFICACY EXPECTATIONS

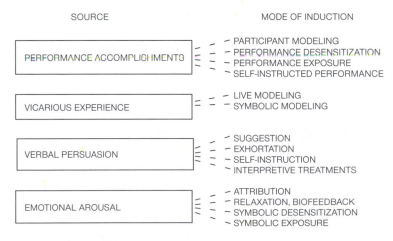

**FIGURE 14.2.** ■ Major sources of efficacy information and the principal sources through which different modes of treatment operate.

ure on personal efficacy therefore partly depend on the timing and the total pattern of experiences in which the failures occur.

Once established, enhanced self-efficacy tends to generalize to other situations in which performance was self-debilitated by preoccupation with personal inadequacies (Bandura, Adams, & Beyer, 1977; Bandura, Jeffery, & Gajdos, 1975). As a result, improvements in behavioral functioning transfer not only to similar situations, but to activities that are substantially different from those on which the treatment was focused. Thus, for example, increased self-efficacy gained through rapid mastery of a specific animal phobia can increase coping efforts in social situations, as well as reduce fears of other animals. However, the generalization effects occur most predictably to the activities that are most similar to those in which self-efficacy was restored by treatment (Bandura, Blanchard, & Ritter, 1969).

Methods of change that operate on the basis of performance accomplishments convey efficacy information in more ways than simply through the evidence of performance improvements. In the course of treatments employing modeling with guided performance, participants acquire a generalizable skill for dealing successfully with stressful situations, which they use to overcome a variety of dysfunctional fears and inhibitions in their everyday life (Bandura et al., 1977; Bandura et al., 1975). Having a serviceable coping skill at one's disposal undoubtedly contributes to one's sense of personal efficacy. Behavioral capabilities can also be enhanced through modeling alone (Bandura, 1971; Flanders, 1968). However, participant modeling provides additional opportunities for translating behavioral conceptions to appropriate actions and for making corrective refinements toward the perfection of skills.

Most of the treatment procedures that have been developed in recent years to eliminate fearful and defensive behavior have been implemented through either performance or symbolic procedures. Regardless of the methods involved, results of comparative studies attest to the superiority of performance-based treatments. In the desensitization approach devised by Wolpe (1974), clients receive graduated exposure to aversive events in conjunction with anxiety reducing activities, usually in the form of muscular relaxation. A number of experiments have been reported in which relaxation is paired with scenes in which phobics

visualize themselves engaging in progressively more threatening activities or enacting the same hierarchy of activities with the actual threats. Findings based on different types of phobias consistently reveal that performance desensitization produces substantially greater behavioral change than does symbolic desensitization (LoPiccolo, 1970; Sherman, 1972; Strahley, 1966). Physiological measures yield similar results. Symbolic desensitization reduces autonomic responses to imagined but not actual threats, whereas performance desensitization eliminates autonomic responses to both imagined and actual threats (Barlow, Leitenberg, Agras, & Wincze, 1969). The substantial benefits of successful performance are typically achieved in less time than is required to extinguish arousal to symbolic representations of threats.

More recently, avoidance behavior has been treated by procedures involving massive exposure to aversive events. In this approach, intense anxiety is elicited by prolonged exposure to the most threatening situations and is sustained at high levels, without relief, until emotional reactions are extinguished. Several investigators have compared the relative success of prolonged exposure to aversive situations in imagery and actual encounters with them in ameliorating chronic agoraphobias. Real encounters with threats produce results decidedly superior to imagined exposure, which has weak, variable effects (Emmelkamp & Wessels, 1975; Stern & Marks, 1973; Watson, Mullett, & Pillay, 1973). Prolonged encounters that ensure behavioral improvements are more effective than distributed brief encounters that are likely to end before successful performance of the activity is achieved (Rabavilas, Boulougouris, & Stefanis, 1976).

The participant modeling approach to the elimination of defensive behavior utilizes successful performance as the primary vehicle of psychological change. People displaying intractable fears and inhibitions are not about to do what they dread. Therefore, in implementing participant modeling, therapists structure the environment so that clients can perform successfully despite their incapacities. This is achieved by enlisting a variety of response induction aids, including preliminary modeling of threatening activities, graduated tasks, enactment over graduated temporal intervals, joint performance with the therapist, protective aids to reduce the likelihood of feared consequences, and variation in the severity of the threat itself (Bandura, Jeffery, & Wright, 1974). As treatment progresses, the supplementary aids are withdrawn so that clients effectively cope unassisted. Self-directed mastery experiences are then arranged to reinforce a sense of personal efficacy. Through this form of treatment, incapacitated people rapidly lose their fears, are able to engage in activities they formerly inhibited, and display generalized reductions of fears toward threats beyond the specifically treated conditions (Bandura, 1976a).

Participant modeling has been compared with various symbolically based treatments. These studies corroborate the superiority of successful performance facilitated by modeling as compared to vicarious experience alone (Bandura et al., 1969; Blanchard, 1970b; Lewis, 1974; Ritter, 1969; Roper, Rachman, & Marks, 1975), to symbolic desensitization (Bandura et al., 1969; Litvak, 1969), and to imaginal modeling in which clients visualize themselves or others coping successfully with threats (Thase & Moss, 1976). When participant modeling is subsequently administered to those who benefit only partially from the symbolic procedures, avoidance behavior is thoroughly eliminated within a brief period.

The findings summarized above are consistent with self-efficacy theory, but they do not shed much light on the mechanism by which specific mastery experiences produce generalized and enduring changes in behavior. Verification of the operative mechanism requires experimental evidence that experienced mastery does in fact alter the level and strength of self-efficacy and that self-efficacy is, in turn, linked to behavior. We shall return later to research which addresses itself specifically to the linkages between treatment procedures, perceived self-efficacy, and behavior.

## VICARIOUS EXPERIENCE

People do not rely on experienced mastery as the sole source of information concerning their level of self-efficacy. Many expectations are derived from vicarious experience. Seeing others perform threatening activities without adverse consequences can generate expectations in observers that they, too, will improve if they intensify and persist in their efforts. They persuade themselves that if others can do it, they should be able to achieve at least some improvement in performance (Bandura & Barab, 1973). Vicarious experience, relying as it does an inferences from social comparison, is a less dependable source of information about one's capabilities than is direct evidence of personal accomplishments. Consequently, the efficacy expectations induced by modeling alone are likely to be weaker and more vulnerable to change.

A number of modeling variables that are apt to affect expectations of personal efficacy have been shown to enhance the disinhibiting influence of modeling procedures. Phobics benefit more from seeing models overcome their difficulties by determined effort than from observing facile performances by adept models (Kazdin, 1973; Meichenbaum, 1971). Showing the gains achieved by effortful coping behavior to observers not only minimizes the negative impact of temporary distress, but demonstrates that even the most anxious can eventually succeed through perseverance. Similarity to the model in other characteristics, which increases the personal relevance of vicariously derived information, can likewise enhance the effectiveness of symbolic modeling (Kazdin, 1974b).

Modeled behavior with clear outcomes conveys more efficacy information than if the effects of the modeled actions remain ambiguous. In investigations of vicarious processes, observing one perform activities that meet with success does, indeed, produce greater behavioral improvements than witnessing the same performances modeled without any evident consequences (Kazdin, 1974c, 1975). Diversified modeling, in which the activities observers regard as hazardous are repeatedly shown to be safe by a variety of models, is superior to exposure to the same performances by a single model (Bandura & Menlove, 1968; Kazdin, 1974a, 1975, 1976). If people of widely differing characteristics can succeed, then observers have a reasonable basis for increasing their own sense of self-efficacy.

The pattern of results reported above offers at least suggestive support for the view that exemplifications of success through sustained effort with substantiating comparative information can enhance observers' perceptions of their own performance capabilities. Research will be presented below that bears more directly on the proposition that modeling procedures alter avoidance behavior through the intervening influence of efficacy expectations.

## VERBAL PERSUASION

In attempts to influence human behavior, verbal persuasion is widely used due to its ease and ready availability. People are led, through suggestion, into believing they can cope successfully with what has overwhelmed them in the past. Efficacy expectations induced in this manner are also likely to be weaker than those arising from one's own accomplishments because they do not provide an authentic experiential base for them. In the face of distressing threats and a long history of failure in coping with them, whatever mastery expectations are induced by suggestion can be readily extinguished by disconfirming experiences.

Results of several lines of research attest to the limitation of procedures that attempt to instill outcome expectations in people simply by telling them what to expect. In laboratory studies, "placebo" conditions designed suggestively to raise expectations of improvement produce little change in refractory behavior (Lick & Bootzin, 1975; Moore, 1965; Paul, 1966). Whether this is due either to the low credibility of the suggestions or to the weakness of the induced expectations cannot be determined from these studies because the expectations were not measured.

Numerous experiments have been conducted in which phobics receive desensitization treatment either without any expectancy information or with suggestions that it is either highly efficacious or ineffective. The differential outcome expectations are verbally induced prior to, during, or immediately after treatment in the various studies. The findings generally show that desensitization reduces phobic behavior, but the outcome expectancy manipulations have either no effect or weak, inconsistent ones (Howlett & Nawas, 1971; McGlynn & Mapp, 1970; McGlynn, Mealiea, & Nawas, 1969; McGlynn, Reynolds, & Linder, 1971). As in the "placebo" studies, it is difficult to make conclusive interpretations because the outcome expectations induced suggestively are not measured prior to the assessment of behavior changes, if at all. Simply informing participants that they will or will not benefit from treatment does not mean that they necessarily believe what they are told, especially when it contradicts their other personal experiences. Moreover, in the studies just cited, the verbal influence is aimed mainly at raising outcome expectations rather than at enhancing self-efficacy. It is changes on the latter

dimension that are most relevant to the theory under discussion.

Although social persuasion alone may have definite limitations as a means of creating an enduring sense of personal efficacy, it can contribute to the successes achieved through corrective performance. That is, people who are socially persuaded that they possess the capabilities to master difficult situations and are provided with provisional aids for effective action are likely to mobilize greater effort than those who receive only the performance aids. However, to raise expectations of personal competence by persuasion, without arranging conditions to facilitate effective performance, will most likely lead to failures that discredit the persuaders and further undermine the recipients' perceived self-efficacy. It is therefore the interactive, as well as the independent, effects of social persuasion on self-efficacy that merit experimental consideration.

## EMOTIONAL AROUSAL

Stressful and taxing situations generally elicit emotional arousal that, depending on the circumstances, might have informative value concerning personal competency. Therefore, emotional arousal is another constituent source of information that can affect perceived self-efficacy in coping with threatening situations. People rely partly on their state of physiological arousal in judging their anxiety and vulnerability to stress. Because high arousal usually debilitates performance, individuals are more likely to expect success when they are not beset by aversive arousal than if they are tense and viscerally agitated. Fear reactions generate further fear of impending stressful situations through anticipatory self-arousal. By conjuring up fear-provoking thoughts about their ineptitude, individuals can rouse themselves to elevated levels of anxiety that far exceed the fear experienced during the actual threatening situation.

As will be recalled from the earlier discussion, desensitization and massive exposure treatments aimed at extinguishing anxiety arousal produce some reductions in avoidance behavior. Anxiety arousal to threats is likewise diminished by modeling, and is even more thoroughly eliminated by experienced mastery achieved through participant modeling (Bandura & Barab, 1973; Bandura et al., 1969; Blanchard, 1970a). Modeling approaches have other advantages for enhancing self-efficacy, thereby removing dysfunctional fears. In addition to diminishing proneness to aversive arousal, such approaches also teach effective coping skills by demonstrating proficient ways of handling threatening situations. The latter contribution is especially important when fear arousal partly results from behavioral deficits. It is often the case that fears and deficits are interdependent. Avoidance of stressful activities impedes development of coping skills and results in the lack of competency that provides a realistic basis for fear. Acquiring behavioral means for controlling potential threats attenuates or eliminates fear arousal (Averill, 1973; Notterman, Schoenfeld, & Bersh, 1952; Szpiler & Epstein, 1976). Behavioral control not only allows one to manage the aversive aspects of an environment; it also affects how the environment is likely to be perceived. Potentially stressful situations that can be controlled are construed as less threatening; such cognitive appraisals further reduce anticipatory emotional arousal (Averill, 1973).

Diminishing emotional arousal can reduce avoidance behavior, but different theories posit different explanatory mechanisms for the observed effects. In the theory from which the emotive treatments are derived, emotional arousal is conceived of as a drive that activates avoidance behavior. This view stresses the energizing and reinforcing functions of arousal reduction. Social learning theory, on the other hand, emphasizes the informative function of physiological arousal. Simply acknowledging that arousal is both informative and motivating by no means resolves the issue in dispute, because these are not necessarily two separate effects that somehow jointly produce behavior. Rather, the cognitive appraisal of arousal, to a large extent, determines the level and direction of motivational inducements to action. Certain cognitive appraisals of one's physiological state might be energizing, whereas other appraisals of the same state might not (Weiner, 1972). Moreover, many forms of physiological arousal are generated cognitively by arousing trains of thought. When motivation is conceptualized in terms of cognitive processes (Bandura, 1977; Weiner, 1972), the informational and motivational effects of arousal are treated as interdependent, rather than as separate, events. We shall return to this issue later when we consider the differential predictions made from social learning theory and the dual-process theory

of avoidance behavior concerning the behavioral effects of extinguishing anxiety arousal.

Researchers working within the attributional framework have attempted to modify avoidance behavior by directly manipulating the cognitive labeling of emotional arousal (Valins & Nisbett, 1971). The presumption is that if phobics are led to *believe* that the things they have previously feared no longer affect them internally, the cognitive reevaluation alone will reduce avoidance behavior. In treatment analogues of this approach, phobics receive false physiological feedback suggesting that they are no longer emotionally upset by threatening events. Results of this procedure are essentially negative. Early claims that erroneous arousal feedback reduces avoidance behavior (Valins & Ray, 1967) are disputed by methodologically superior studies showing that false feedback of physiological tranquility in the presence of threats has either no appreciable effect on subsequent fearful behavior (Gaupp, Stern, & Galbraith, 1972; Howlett & Nawas, 1971; Kent, Wilson, & Nelson, 1972; Rosen, Rosen, & Reid, 1972; Sushinsky & Bootzin, 1970) or produces minor changes under limited conditions such as to be of little practical consequence (Borkovec, 1973).

Misattribution of emotional arousal is another variant of the attributional approach to modification of fearful behavior. The strategy here is to lead fearful people into believing that their emotional arousal is caused by a nonemotional source. To the extent that they no longer label their agitated state as anxiety, they will behave more boldly. It may be possible to reduce mild fears by this means (Ross, Rodin, & Zimbardo, 1969), but the highly anxious are not easily led into misattributing their anxiety to irrelevant sources (Nisbett & Schachter, 1966). When evaluated systematically, misattribution treatments do not produce significant changes in chronic anxiety conditions (Singerman, Borkovec, & Baron, 1976) and some of the benefits reported with other dysfunctions cannot be replicated (Bootzin, Herman, & Nicassio, 1976; Kellogg & Baron, 1975). There is also some suggestive evidence that, in laboratory studies, the attenuation of fear may be due more to the veridicality of arousal information than to misattribution of fear arousal to an innocuous source (Calvert-Boyanowsky & Leventhal, 1975).

Any reduction in fear resulting from deceptive feedback is apt to be short-lived because illusory assurances are not an especially reliable way of creating durable self-expectations. However, more veritable experiences that reduce the level of emotional arousal can set a reciprocal process of change in motion. In the social learning view, potential threats activate fear largely through cognitive self-arousal (Bandura, 1969, 1977). Perceived self-competence can therefore affect susceptibility to self-arousal. Individuals who come to believe that they are less vulnerable than they previously assumed are less prone to generate frightening thoughts in threatening situations. Those whose fears are relatively weak may reduce their self-doubts and debilitating self-arousal to the point where they perform successfully. Performance successes, in turn, strengthen self-efficacy. Such changes can, of course, be reliably achieved without resort to ruses. Moreover, mislabeling arousal or attributing it to erroneous sources is unlikely to be of much help to the highly anxious. Severe acrophobics, for example, may be temporarily misled into believing that they no longer fear high elevations, but they will reexperience unnerving internal feedback when confronted with dreaded heights. It should also be noted that, in attributional explanations of the success of behavioral treatments, the heavy emphasis on physiological arousal derives more from speculations about the nature of emotion (Schachter, 1964) than from evidence that arousal is a major determinant of defensive behavior.

## Cognitive Processing of Efficacy Information

The discussion thus far has centered primarily on the many sources of information—enactive, vicarious, exhortative, and emotive—that people use to judge their level of self-efficacy. At this point, a distinction must be drawn between information contained in environmental events and information as processed and transformed by the individual. The impact of information on efficacy expectations will depend on how it is cognitively appraised. A number of contextual factors, including the social, situational, and temporal circumstances under which events occur, enter into such appraisals. For this reason, even success experiences do not necessarily create strong generalized expectations of personal efficacy. Expectations that have served self-protective functions for years are

not quickly discarded. When experience contradicts firmly established expectations of self-efficacy, they may undergo little change if the conditions of performance are such as to lead one to discount the import of the experience.

The corrective value of information derived from successful performance can be attenuated in several ways. The first involves discrimination processes, the consequences individuals anticipate were they to perform feared activities differ in circumstances that vary in safeguards. As a result, they may behave boldly in situations signifying safety, but retain their unchanged self-doubts under less secure conditions. Such mitigative discriminations can extend to the treatments themselves, as well as to the situational circumstances in which behavioral attainments occur. This is especially true of treatments relying solely on symbolic and vicarious experience. Achieving reductions in fear to threats presented symbolically is unlikely to enhance perceived self-efficacy, to any great extent, in people who believe that success in imagery does not portend accomplishments in reality. Information conveyed by facilely modeled performances might likewise be minimized by anxious observers on the grounds that the models possess special expertise, enabling them to prevent injurious consequences that might otherwise befall the unskilled. Because such discriminations, even though objectively mistaken, impede change in self-efficacy, observers will be reluctant to attempt feared activities and will be easily dissuaded by negative experience.

Cognitive appraisals of the causes of one's behavior, which have been examined extensively in investigations of self-attributional processes (Bem, 1972), can similarly delimit gains in self-efficacy from behavioral attainments. It was previously shown that attributions of affect and actions to illusory competence have little, if any, effect on refractory behavior. This does not, of course, mean that causal appraisals are of limited importance in the process of behavior change. Quite the contrary, performance attainment is a prominent source of efficacy information, but is by no means unambiguous. As already mentioned briefly, people can gain competence through authentic means but, because of faulty appraisals of the circumstances under which they improve, will credit their achievements to external factors, rather than to their own capabilities. Here, the problem is one of inaccurate ascription of personal competency to situational factors. Successes are more likely to enhance self-efficacy if performances are perceived as resulting from skill than from fortuitous or special external aids. Conversely, failures would be expected to produce greater reductions in self-efficacy when attributed to ability, rather than to unusual situational circumstances. The more extensive the situational aids for performance, the greater are the chances that behavior will be ascribed to external factors (Bem, 1972; Weiner, 1972).

*attribution*

Even under conditions of perceived self-determination of outcomes, the impact of performance attainments on self-efficacy will vary depending on whether one's accomplishments are ascribed mainly to ability or to effort. Success with minimal effort fosters ability ascriptions that reinforce a strong sense of self-efficacy. By contrast, analogous successes achieved through high expenditure of effort connote a lesser ability and are thus likely to have a weaker effect on perceived self-efficacy. Cognitive appraisals of the difficulty level of the tasks will further affect the impact of performance accomplishments on perceived self-efficacy. To succeed at easy tasks provides no new information for altering one's sense of self-efficacy, whereas mastery of challenging tasks conveys salient evidence of enhanced competence. The rate and pattern of attainments furnish additional information for judging personal efficacy. Thus, people who experience setbacks but detect relative progress will raise their perceived efficacy more than those who succeed but see their performances leveling off compared to their prior rate of improvement.

Extrapolations from theories about attribution and self-perception to the field of behavioral change often imply that people must labor unaided or under inconspicuously arranged influences if they are to convince themselves of their personal competence (Kopel & Arkowitz, 1975). Such prescriptions are open to question on both conceptual and empirical grounds. Cognitive misappraisals that attenuate the impact of disconfirming experiences can be minimized without sacrificing the substantial benefits of powerful induction procedures. This is achieved by providing opportunities for self-directed accomplishments after the desired behavior has been established. Any lingering doubts people might have, either about their capabilities or about prob-

able response consequences under unprotected conditions, are dispelled easily in this manner (Bandura et al., 1975). The more varied the circumstances in which threats are mastered independently, the more likely are success experiences to authenticate personal efficacy and impede formation of discriminations that insulate self-perceptions from disconfirming evidence.

Results of recent studies support the thesis that generalized, lasting changes in self-efficacy and behavior can best be achieved by participant methods using powerful induction procedures initially to develop capabilities, then removing external aids to verify personal efficacy, then finally using self-directed mastery to strengthen and generalize expectations of personal efficacy (Bandura et al., 1975). Independent performance can enhance efficacy expectations in several ways: (a) It creates additional exposure to former threats, which provides participants with further evidence that they are no longer aversively aroused by what they previously feared. Reduced emotional arousal confirms increased coping capabilities. (b) Self-directed mastery provides opportunities to perfect coping skills, which lessen personal vulnerability to stress. (c) Independent performance, if well executed, produces success experiences, which further reinforce expectations of self-competency.

Extensive self-directed performance of formerly threatening activities under progressively challenging conditions at a time when treatments are usually terminated could also serve to reduce susceptibility to relearning of defensive patterns of behavior. A few negative encounters among many successful experiences that have instilled a strong sense of self-efficacy will, at most, establish discriminative avoidance of realistic threats, an effect that has adaptive value. In contrast, if people have limited contact with previously feared objects after treatment, whatever expectations of self-efficacy were instated would be weaker and more vulnerable to change. Consequently, a few unfavorable experiences are likely to reestablish defensive behavior that generalizes inappropriately.

We have already examined how cognitive processing of information conveyed by modeling might influence the extent to which vicarious experience effects changes in self-efficacy. Among the especially informative elements are the models' characteristics (e.g., adeptness, perseverance, age, expertness), similarity between models and observers, difficulty of the performance tasks, situational arrangements under which the modeled achievements occur, and diversity of modeled attainments.

Just as the value of efficacy information generated enactively and vicariously depends on cognitive appraisal, so does the information arising from exhortative and emotive sources. The impact of verbal persuasion on self-efficacy may vary substantially depending on the perceived credibility of the persuaders' prestige, trustworthiness, expertise, and assuredness. The more believable the source of the information, the more likely are efficacy expectations to change. The influence of credibility on attitudinal change has, of course, received intensive study. But its effects on perceived self-efficacy remain to be investigated.

People judge their physiological arousal largely on the basis of their appraisal of the instigating conditions. Thus, visceral arousal occurring in situations perceived to be threatening is interpreted as fear, arousal in thwarting situations is experienced as anger, and that resulting from irretrievable loss of valued objects as sorrow (Hunt, Cole, & Reis, 1958). Even the same source of physiological arousal may be interpreted differently in ambiguous situations, depending on the emotional reactions of others in the same setting (Mandler, 1975; Schachter & Singer, 1962).

When tasks are performed in ambiguous or complex situations in which there is a variety of evocative stimuli, the informational value of the resultant arousal will depend on the meaning imposed upon it. People who perceive their arousal as stemming from personal inadequacies are more likely to lower their efficacy expectations than those who attribute their arousal to certain situational factors. Given a proneness to ascribe arousal to personal deficiencies, the heightened attention to internal events can result in reciprocally escalating arousal. Indeed, as Sarason (1976) has amply documented, individuals who are especially susceptible to anxiety arousal readily become self-preoccupied with their perceived inadequacies in the face of difficulties, rather than with the task at hand. [. . .]

## Microanalysis of Self-efficacy and Behavioral Change

To test derivations from the social learning analysis of the process of change, an experiment was conducted in which severe phobics received treatments designed to create differential levels of efficacy expectations. The relationship between self-efficacy and behavioral change was then analyzed in detail (Bandura et al., 1977). Adult snake phobics, whose phobias affected their lives adversely, were administered for equivalent periods, either participant modeling, modeling alone, or no treatment. In participant modeling, which operates through direct mastery experiences, subjects were assisted, by whatever induction aids were needed, to engage in progressively more threatening interactions with a boa constrictor, which included holding the snake, placing open hands in front of its head as it moved about the room, holding the snake in front of their faces, and allowing it to crawl freely in their laps. [. . .]

Subjects receiving the modeling treatment merely observed the therapist perform the same activities for an equivalent period. [. . .] Subjects assigned to the control condition participated in the assessment procedures without receiving any intervening treatment. [. . .]

Consistent with the social learning analysis of the sources of self-efficacy, experiences based on performance accomplishments produced higher, more generalized, and stronger efficacy expectations than did vicarious experience, which in turn exceeded those in the control condition. [. . .] Performance change corresponds closely to the magnitude of expectancy change. The greater the increments in self-perceived efficacy the greater the changes in behavior. [. . .] Participant modeling produced the more generalized increases in efficacy expectations and the more generalized behavioral changes.

Although the enactive and vicarious treatments differed in their power to enhance self-efficacy, the efficacy expectations were equally predictive of subsequent performance, irrespective of how they were instated. The higher the level of perceived self-efficacy at the completion of treatment, the higher was the level of approach behavior for efficacy expectations instated enactively ($r = .83$) and vicariously ($r = .84$). [. . .]

To test the theory that desensitization changes behavior through its intervening effects on efficacy expectations, severe snake phobics were administered the standard desensitization treatment until their emotional reactions were completely extinguished to imaginal representations of the most aversive scenes (Bandura & Adams, 1977). The assessment procedures were identical to those used in the preceding experiment. Subjects' approach behavior was tested on the series of performance tasks before and after the desensitization treatment. The level, strength, and generality of their efficacy expectations were similarly measured before treatment, upon completion of treatment but prior to the posttest, and following the posttest.

The findings show that phobics whose anxiety reactions to visualized threats have been thoroughly extinguished emerge from the desensitization treatment with widely differing efficacy expectations. Performance corresponds closely to level of self-efficacy. The higher the subjects' level of perceived self-efficacy at the end of treatment, the more approach behavior they subsequently performed in the posttest assessment ($r = .74$).

Results of the microanalysis of congruence between self-efficacy at the end of treatment and performance on each of the tasks administered in the posttest are consistent with the findings obtained from enactive and vicarious treatment. Self-efficacy was an accurate predictor of subsequent performance on 85% for all the tasks and 83% for the subset of tasks that subjects were unable to perform in the pretest assessment. Subjects successfully executed tasks within the range of their perceived self-efficacy produced by the desensitization treatment, whereas they failed at tasks they perceived to be beyond their capabilities. [. . .]

## Concluding Remarks

[. . .] Cognitive processing of efficacy information, which is an important component function in the proposed theory, is an especially relevant area for research. A number of factors were identified as influencing the cognitive appraisal of efficacy information conveyed by each of the major sources of self-efficacy. Previous research from a number of different perspectives, demonstrating that some of these factors affect attitudinal and behavioral changes, has suggestive value. But it is investigations that include assessment of the intervening self-efficacy link that can best provide validity for the present theory.

The operative process involved in the relationship between efficacy expectations and action also requires further investigation. It will be recalled that efficacy expectations are presumed to influence level of performance by enhancing intensity

and persistence of effort. [. . .] Further research on the processes postulated in the present theoretical formulation should increase our understanding of the relationship between cognitive and behavioral change.

## REFERENCES

Averill, J. R. (1973). Personal control over aversive stimuli and its relationship to stress. *Psychological Bulletin, 80,* 286–303.

Bandura, A. (1969). *Principles of behavior modification.* New York: Holt, Rinehart & Winston.

Bandura, A. (Ed.). (1971). *Psychological modeling: Conflicting theories.* Chicago: Aldine-Atherton.

Bandura, A. (1976a). Effecting change through participant modeling. In J. D. Krumboltz & C. E. Thoresen (Eds.), *Counseling methods.* New York: Holt, Rinehart & Winston.

Bandura, A. (1976b). Self-reinforcement: Theoretical and methodological considerations. *Behaviorism, 4,* 135–155.

Bandura, A. (1977). *Social learning theory.* Englewood Cliffs, NJ: Prentice-Hall.

Bandura, A., & Adams, N. E. (1977). Analysis of self-efficacy theory of behavioral change. *Cognitive Therapy and Research, 1,* 287–310.

Bandura, A., Adams, N. E., & Beyer, J. (1977). Cognitive processes mediating behavioral changes. *Journal of Personality and Social Psychology, 35,* 125–139.

Bandura, A., & Barab, P. G. (1973). Processes governing disinhibitory effects through symbolic modeling. *Journal of Abnormal Psychology, 82,* 1–9.

Bandura, A., Blanchard, E. B., & Bitter, B. (1969). The relative efficacy of desensitization and modeling approaches for inducing behavioral, affective, and attitudinal changes. *Journal of Personality and Social Psychology, 13,* 173–199.

Bandura, A., Jeffery, R. W., & Gajdos, E. (1975). Generalizing change through participant modeling with self-directed mastery. *Behaviour Research and Therapy, 13,* 141–152.

Bandura, A., Jeffery, R. W., & Wright, C. L. (1974). Efficacy of participant modeling as a function of response induction aids. *Journal of Abnormal Psychology, 83,* 56–64.

Bandura, A., & Menlove, F. L. (1968). Factors determining vicarious extinction of avoidance behavior through symbolic modeling. *Journal of Personality and Social Psychology, 8,* 99–108.

Barlow, D. H., Leitenberg, H., Agras, W. S., & Wincze, J. P. (1969). The transfer gap in systematic desensitization: An analogue study. *Behaviour Research and Therapy, 7,* 191–196.

Bem, D. J. (1972). Self-perception theory. In L. Berkowitz (Ed.), *Advances in experimental social psychology* (Vol. 6). New York: Academic Press.

Blanchard, E. B. (1970a). The generalization of vicarious extinction effects. *Behaviour Research and Therapy, 7,* 323–330.

Blanchard, E. B. (1970b). Relative contributions of modeling, informational influences, and physical contact in extinction of phobic behavior. *Journal of Abnormal Psychology, 76,* 55–61.

Bolles, R. C. (1972). Reinforcement, expectancy, and learning. *Psychological Review, 79,* 394–409.

Borkovec, T. D. (1973). The role of expectancy and physiological feedback in fear research: A review with special reference to subject characteristics. *Behavior Therapy, 4,* 491–505.

Bootzin, R. R., Herman, C. P., & Nicassio, P. (1976). The power of suggestion: Another examination of misattribution and insomnia. *Journal of Personality and Social Psychology, 34,* 673–679.

Calvert-Boyanowsky, J., & Leventhal, H. (1975). The role of information in attenuating behavioral responses to stress: A reinterpretation of the misattribution phenomenon. *Journal of Personality and Social Psychology, 32,* 214–221.

Davison, G. C., & Wilson, G. T. (1973). Processes of fear reduction in systematic desensitization: Cognitive and social reinforcement factors in humans. *Behavior Therapy, 4,* 1–21.

Emmelkamp, P. M. G., & Wessels, H. (1975). Flooding in imagination vs. flooding *in vivo*: A comparison with agoraphobics. *Behaviour Research and Therapy, 13,* 7–15.

Flanders, J. P. (1968). A review of research on imitative behavior. *Psychological Bulletin, 69,* 316–337.

Gaupp, L. A., Stern, R. M., & Galbraith, G. G. (1972). False heart-rate feedback and reciprocal inhibition by aversion relief in the treatment of snake avoidance behavior. *Behavior Therapy, 3,* 7–20.

Howlett, S. C., & Nawas, M. M. (1971). Exposure to aversive imagery and suggestion in systematic desensitization. In R. D. Rubin, A. A. Lazarus, H. Fensterheim, & C. M. Franks (Eds.), *Advances in behavior therapy.* New York: Academic Press.

Hunt, J. McV., Cole, M. W., & Reis, E. E. S. (1958). Situational cues distinguishing anger, fear, and sorrow. *American Journal of Psychology, 71,* 136–151.

Kazdin, A. E. (1973). Covert modeling and the reduction of avoidance behavior. *Journal of Abnormal Psychology, 81,* 87–95.

Kazdin, A. E., (1974), Comparative effects of some variations of covert modeling. *Journal of Behavior Therapy and Experimental Psychiatry, 5,* 225–232.

Kazdin, A. E. (1974). Covert modeling, model similarity, and reduction of avoidance behavior. *Behavior Therapy, 5,* 325–340.

Kazdin, A. E. (1974). Effects of covert modeling and reinforcement on assertive behavior. *Journal of Abnormal Psychology, 83,* 240–252.

Kazdin, A. E. (1975). Covert modeling, imagery assessment, and assertive behavior. *Journal of Consulting and Clinical Psychology, 43,* 716–724.

Kazdin, A. E. (1976). Effects of covert modeling, multiple models, and model reinforcement on assertive behavior. *Behavior Therapy, 7,* 211–222.

Kellogg, R., & Baron, R. S. (1975). Attribution theory, insomnia, and the reverse placebo effect: A reversal of Storms and Nisbett's findings. *Journal of Personality and Social Psychology, 32,* 231–236.

Kent, R. N., Wilson, G. T., & Nelson, R. (1972). Effects of false heart-rate feedback on avoidance behavior: An investigation of "cognitive desensitization." *Behavior Therapy, 3,* 1–6.

Kopel, S., & Arkowitz, H. (1975). The role of attribution and self-perception in behavior change: Implications for behavior therapy. *Genetic Psychology Monographs, 92,* 175–212.

Lewis, S. (1974). A comparison of behavior therapy techniques in the reduction of fearful avoidance behavior. *Behavior Therapy, 5,* 648–655.

Lick, J., & Bootzin, R. (1975). Expectancy factors in the treatment of fear: Methodological and theoretical issues. *Psychological Bulletin, 82,* 917–931.

Litvak, S. B. (1969). A comparison of two brief group behavior therapy techniques on the reduction of avoidance behavior. *The Psychological Record, 19,* 329–334.

LoPiccolo, J. (1970). Effective components of systematic desensitization (Doctoral dissertation, Yale University, 1969). *Dissertation Abstracts International, 31,* 1543B. (University Microfilms No. 70-16300).

Mandler, G. (1975). *Mind and emotion.* New York: Wiley, 1975.

McGlynn, F. D., & Mapp, R. H. (1970). Systematic desensitization of snake-avoidance following three types of suggestion. *Behaviour Research Therapy, 8,* 197–201.

McGlynn, F. D., Mealiea, W. L., & Nawas, M. M. (1969). Systematic desensitization of snake-avoidance under two conditions of suggestion. *Psychological Reports, 25,* 220–222.

McGlynn, F. D., Reynolds, E. J., & Linder, L. H. (1971). Systematic desensitization with pre-treatment and intra-treatment therapeutic instructions. *Behaviour Research and Therapy, 9,* 57–63.

Meichenbaum, D. H. (1971). Examination of model characteristics in reducing avoidance behavior. *Journal of Personality and Social Psychology, 17,* 298–307.

Moore, N. (1965). Behaviour therapy in bronchial asthma: A controlled study. *Journal of Psychosomatic Research, 9,* 257–276.

Nisbett, R. E., & Schachter, S. (1966). Cognitive manipulation of pain. *Journal of Experimental Social Psychology, 2,* 221–236.

Notterman, J. M., Schoenfeld, W. N., & Bersh, P. J. (1952). A comparison of three extinction procedures following heart rate conditioning. *Journal of Abnormal and Social Psychology, 47,* 674–677.

Paul, G. L. (1966). *Insight vs. desensitization in psychotherapy.* Stanford, CA: Stanford University Press.

Rabavilas, A. D., Boulougouris, J. C., & Stefanis, C. (1976). Duration of flooding sessions in the treatment of obsessive-compulsive patients. *Behaviour Research and Therapy, 14,* 349–355.

Ritter, B. (1969). The use of contact desensitization, demonstration-plus-participation, and demonstration alone in the treatment of acrophobia. *Behaviour Research and Therapy, 7,* 157–164.

Röper, G., Rachman, S., & Marks, I. (1975). Passive and participant modelling in exposure treatment of obsessive-compulsive neurotics. *Behaviour Research and Therapy, 13,* 271–279.

Rosen, G. M., Rosen, E., & Reid, J. B. (1972). Cognitive desensitization and avoidance behavior: A reevaluation. *Journal of Abnormal Psychology, 80,* 176–182.

Ross, L., Rodin, J., & Zimbardo, P. T. (1969). Toward an attribution therapy: The reduction of fear through induced cognitive-emotional misattribution. *Journal of Personality and Social Psychology, 12,* 279–288.

Sarason, I. G. (1976). Anxiety and self-preoccupation. In I. G. Sarason & C. D. Spielberger (Eds.), *Stress and anxiety* (Vol. 2). Washington, DC: Hemisphere.

Schachter, S. (1964). The interaction of cognitive and physiological determinants of emotional state. In L. Berkowitz (Ed.), *Advances in experimental social psychology.* New York: Academic Press.

Schachter, S., & Singer, J. E. (1962). Cognitive, social, and physiological determinants of emotional state. *Psychological Review, 69,* 379–399.

Sherman, A. R. (1972). Real-life exposure as a primary therapeutic factor in the desensitization treatment of fear. *Journal of Abnormal Psychology, 79,* 19–28.

Singerman, K. J., Borkovec, T. D., & Baron, R. S. (1976). Failure of a "misattribution therapy" manipulation with a clinically relevant target behavior. *Behavior Therapy, 7,* 306–313.

Stern, R., & Marks, I. (1973). Brief and prolonged flooding: A comparison in agoraphobic patients. *Archives of General Psychiatry, 28,* 270–276.

Strahley, D. F. (1966). Systematic desensitization and counterphobic treatment of an irrational fear of snakes (Doctoral dissertation, University of Tennessee, 1965). *Dissertation Abstracts, 27,* 973B. (University Microfilms No. 66-5366).

Sushinsky, L. W., & Bootzin, R. R. (1970). Cognitive desensitization as a model of systematic desensitization. *Behaviour Research and Therapy, 8,* 29–33.

Szpiler, J. A., & Epstein, S. (1976). Availability of an avoidance response as related to autonomic arousal. *Journal of Abnormal Psychology, 85,* 73–82.

Thase, M. E., & Moss, M. K. (1976). The relative efficacy of covert modeling procedures and guided participant modeling in the reduction of avoidance behavior. *Journal of Behavior Therapy and Experimental Psychiatry, 7,* 7–12.

Valins, S., & Nisbett, R. E. (1971). *Attribution processes in the development and treatment of emotional disorders.* Morristown, NJ: General Learning Press.

Valins, S., & Ray, A. (1967). Effects of cognitive desensitization on avoidance behaviour. *Journal of Personality and Social Psychology, 7,* 345–350.

Watson, J. P., Mullett, G. E., & Pillay, H. (1973). The effects of prolonged exposure to phobic situations upon agoraphobic patients treated in groups. *Behaviour Research and Therapy, 11,* 531–545.

Weiner, B. (1972). *Theories of motivation.* Chicago: Markham.

Wolpe, J. (1974). *The practice of behavior therapy.* New York: Pergamon Press.

# Control Theory: A Useful Conceptual Framework for Personality-Social, Clinical, and Health Psychology

Charles S. Carver • University of Miami
Michael F. Scheier • Carnegie-Mellon University

Control theory provides a model of self-regulation that we believe is useful in the analysis of human behavior. As an illustration of the breadth of its applicability, we present the basic construct of control theory—the discrepancy-reducing feedback loop—and discuss certain of its implications for theory in three separate areas of human psychology. In personality-social, clinical, and health psychology, the construct proves to fit well with known phenomena and with the theories most recently developed to account for the phenomena. Moreover, in each case, control theory appears to make a distinct and unique contribution to the state of the area. We conclude by noting the integrative potential that is suggested by these illustrations and by noting some issues that should receive attention in future work.

Cybernetic or control theory is a general approach to the understanding of self-regulating systems. Its central ideas have been around for a long time (see, for example, Cannon's 1929, 1932, discussion of homeostatic physiological mechanisms), but its birth as a distinct body of thought is usually traced to the publication of Wiener's (1948) book, *Cybernetics: Control and Communication in the Animal and the Machine.* Since then, control theory (in various forms) has had a major impact on areas of work as diverse as engineering (e.g., Dransfield, 1968; Ogata, 1970), applied mathematics (e.g., Berkovitz, 1974; Davis, 1977), economics (e.g., Balakrishnan, 1973; Pindyck, 1973), and medicine (e.g., Guyton, 1976). Indeed, this breadth of application has led some people to argue that control processes are ubiquitous, identifiable in virtually any sort of self-regulating system, a point of view termed general systems theory (e.g., Buckley, 1968; Miller, 1978; von Bertalanffy, 1968).

Despite the integrative promise held out by such arguments, psychologists (with a few exceptions such as Miller, Galanter, & Pribram, 1960) have generally been disinclined to examine in detail the control-theory perspective on self-regulation. This seems particularly true with regard to areas of psychology that focus on the behavior of the whole person (e.g., personality psychology) as opposed to focusing on more circumscribed processes (e.g., physiological regulation). In part, this lack of interest probably stems from the fact that alternative approaches—largely deriving from learning theories—have fully occupied theorists' attention during this period. In part, reluctance to think seriously about these ideas may stem from the fact that cybernetic concepts are "outsiders," ideas that evolved in a context other than the study of human or animal behavior.

In any case, we suggest that these ideas have a great deal to recommend them as a model of human functioning. Describing our basis for that assertion is the purpose of this article. We focus here on three areas of work. The first is the area of our own research: a set of problems in personality and social psychology that concern how people's moment-to-moment actions are determined. The second area is a facet of clinical psychology: recent accounts of cognitive bases by which therapeutic behavior change is effected. The third area is the newly emerging field of health psychology, or behavioral medicine: analyses of ways in which people attempt to maintain their physical well being. In each case, we argue that control theory, as represented by the feedback processes outlined just below, makes a substantial contribution to the problem area under examination.

## Control Processes: The Feedback Loop

The basic unit of cybernetic control is the—negative feedback loop (see Figure 15.1)—termed *negative* because its function is to negate, or reduce, sensed deviations from a comparison value. Though it may look abstract at first, the component processes of this system are really quite simple. The *input function* is the sensing of a present condition. That perception is then compared against a point of reference via a mechanism called a *comparator*. If a discrepancy is perceived between the present state and the reference value, a behavior is performed (*output function*), the goal of which is to reduce the discrepancy. The behavior does not counter the discrepancy directly, but by having an impact on the system's environment (i.e., anything external to the system). Such an impact creates a change in the present condition, leading to a different perception, which in turn is compared anew with the reference value. This arrangement thus constitutes a closed loop of control, the overall purpose of which is to minimize deviations from the standard of comparison.

As a concrete example of how these notions can be applied to behavior, imagine a person driving a car down an otherwise empty road. What exactly

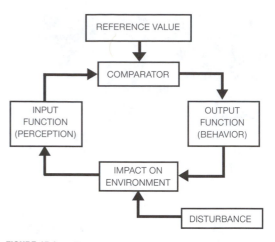

**FIGURE 15.1** ■ The negative feedback loop—the basic unit of cybernetic control.

are people doing when they are driving? Once on the road, driving (for most people) is partly a process of maintaining a visual image of the road sweeping past the fenders and hood of the car. One attempts to keep just the proper proportion of the road visible on one's left while the right edge of the road's image intersects the hood at just the proper place. But what happens if this image is not maintained? If, for example, the road begins to curve to the left, the driver will eventually notice that more of the road is becoming visible on the left-hand side of the car. This perception differs discriminably from the idealized perception (the standard of comparison). For the well-practiced driver, this discrepancy is quickly countered by a slight turn of the steering wheel. This action brings the image of the road back into the appropriate configuration vis-à-vis the image of the hood. Indeed, well-practiced drivers make the adjustments so smoothly that discrepancies are consistently kept quite small.

All of the component processes of Figure 15.1 are used in this example: perception, comparison of the perception with a standard behavioral output, and the effect of the behavior on the environment. Two elements of Figure 15.1, however, have not yet been addressed in any detail. These are the two influences that originate outside the loop: reference value and what is labeled *disturbance*. Let us consider the latter influence first. Forces from outside occasionally impinge on any system that does not exist in a complete vacuum. In our example, movements of the driver's hands are not the influences on the orientation of the car with respect to the image of the road. Moving forward (which driving entails) inevitably introduces a variety of disturbances, as the road curves to the left or the right, as air turbulence buffets the car, and so on. If a crosswind shifts the car's orientation or if one enters a curve, the visual image of hood and road departs from the desired image, requiring compensatory behavior.

Note, however, that the essence of the disturbance is simply that it influences the present state separately from the system's own action. Though it is most intuitive to construe the disturbance as discrepancy *creating,* that is not its defining quality. Indeed, an environmental disturbance may actually be discrepancy *reducing.* Suppose, for example, that our driver enters a slight curve to the right. A second later a sharp gust of wind sweeps in from the left. In this case, the second disturbance counters the effects of the first disturbance on the driver's perception, and the driver need not behave at all. The correct perception is induced by the action of the second disturbance.

This example allows us to emphasize the central function of a feedback system. Its purpose is not to create "behavior," but to create and maintain the perception of a specific desired condition: that is, whatever condition constitutes its reference value or standard of comparison.

Where does the standard of comparison come from? This is a trickier question. To address it usefully, we must introduce one more bit of complexity—the notion of hierarchical organization. Powers (1973a; see also Powers, 1973b) explicitly considers the possibility that control systems can be interconnected hierarchically and argues that such an organization underlies the self-regulation of behavior in living systems. It is on his reasoning that we now build.[1]

A hierarchically organized system by definition has both superordinate and subordinate goals. Attainment of the latter are requisite to—and intimately involved in—attainment of the former. Powers (1973a, 1973b) argues that a superordinate system "behaves" by providing reference values to feedback systems at the next lower level of the hierarchy. That is, the behavioral output of the superordinate system constitutes the setting of standards for the next lower level. That lower level, in turn, behaves by providing reference values to the next lower level, and so on. At the very lowest level of the behavioral hierarchy in an animal sys-

tem, the behavior is more obviously behavior: changes in muscle tensions.

At each level of the hierarchy, the results of the behavior are presumably assessed by monitoring perceptual input information at the appropriate level of abstraction and by comparing it with the reference values provided from the level above (cf. Norman, 1981; Reason, 1979). At the lowest level, there are sensors that indicate the present level of muscle tension and a comparator that assesses whether the desired muscle tensions are being created (although such perceptions and comparisons may not be represented in conscious awareness). Similar processes presumably occur at successively superordinate levels as perceptual input, which integrated to the level of abstraction that is appropriate to that level (cf. Hubel & Wiesel, 1963, 1965; Palmer, 1977) is compared with the reference values at each level.

This description of a hierarchical organization is abstract and written strictly in terms of control processes. Powers is much more specific, however, about what qualities he believes are controlled at each level of his proposed hierarchy. To illustrate his reasoning, let us return to our example. This time we will not limit ourselves to the processes by which a driver stays on the road and out of the ditches. Instead, let us acknowledge that people drive for specific reasons, reasons that vary from wanting to be somewhere in particular, to wanting to get some fresh air and see the countryside, to wanting to hear the sounds and feel the surge of a powerful engine.

Our driver is a college student, who is headed across town to deliver a set of class notes to a friend. He had borrowed the notes earlier to catch up on lectures missed because of illness. Now the friend needs the notes back. As the young man makes a right turn at a stop sign, precisely what goal is guiding his behavior? To illustrate the levels of this hierarchy, we will invest him with a goal at the highest level of abstraction that Powers postulates and work our way downward. (This exercise is illustrated graphically in Figure 15.2.)

The young man in our example has an image of

---

[1]The Powers model is one example of a broader class of possibilities (cf. discussions of "production systems" by Newell, 1973; Newell & Simon, 1972; and by Bower, 1978; and of levels of "action identification" by Vallacher & Wegner, 1981). We focus on the Powers hierarchy here in part because we find that aspects of his nomenclature nicely capture the essence of certain qualities of human action.

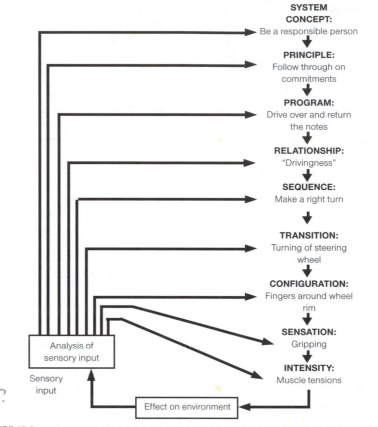

SYSTEM
CONCEPT:
Be a responsible person

PRINCIPLE:
Follow through on
commitments

PROGRAM:
Drive over and return
the notes

RELATIONSHIP:
"Drivingness"

SEQUENCE:
Make a right turn

TRANSITION:
Turning of steering
wheel

CONFIGURATION:
Fingers around wheel
rim

SENSATION:
Gripping

INTENSITY:
Muscle tensions

Analysis of
sensory input

Sensory
input

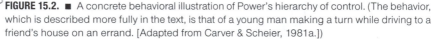

Effect on environment

*upper level → competence/integrity?*

*actual/ ought*

*ideals*

**FIGURE 15.2.** ■ A concrete behavioral illustration of Power's hierarchy of control. (The behavior, which is described more fully in the text, is that of a young man making a turn while driving to a friend's house on an errand. [Adapted from Carver & Scheier, 1981a.])

himself as a good, responsible, and thoughtful person. This idealized self-image of the personal characteristics that he wants to embody is one example of the type of reference value that Powers terms a *system concept.* Periodically, though not necessarily always, this young man attempts to behave in such a way that his perception of his present self (which presumably represents an abstracted integration of a variety of available information) is as congruent as possible with that image of who he thinks he should be. This attempt represents self-regulation at the level of system concepts, the highest level of control that Powers postulates.

But how does one go about living up to one's ideal self? What are the behavioral outputs that allow people to minimize sensed discrepancies between how they are and how they want to be? One plausible argument is that system concepts

imply very general guiding principles that can be used in self-regulation. For example, one becomes (or stays) a good and responsible person partly by adhering to the principle that one should follow through on one's commitments. In accord with this reasoning, Powers suggests that directly subordinate to control of system concepts is a level of self-regulation that he termed *principle control.* Structures at the level of system concepts behave by specifying principles for use as reference values at this next lower level of abstraction.

Guiding principles represent a starting point in the attempt to describe how people self-regulate with respect to system concepts. But principles are, in a sense, content free. That is, the essential characteristic of a principle is that it is applicable to many kinds of behavior. To return to our student, "following through on one's commitments" could easily mean a hundred different things, at different times and places. Honoring one's commitments is not a *behavior,* but rather a *quality* of behavior, which could be realized in a wide range of overt actions.

How, then, are principles put into operation? How do people self-regulate with regard to such a standard? To answer this question, we move to the next lower level of control in this hierarchy: program control. What Powers terms a program is similar to what Schank and Abelson (1977) termed a *script.* It specifies a general course of action, but is more than a simple list of acts. Instead, it incorporates a series of implicit if–then decisions because what is done at any given point of the program depends in part on what circumstances are encountered at that point. The young man in our example has entered into a program that we might call "drive over to Joe's house and return his notes." Its if–then character is illustrated by the fact that not all of its actions are specified beforehand. Our student may ordinarily take the most direct route to his friend's house. But if he is low on gas, he may stop at a service station; if traffic is heavy, he may choose a more indirect route; and if he encounters a barricade in the road, he will make a detour. All of these decisions are made, however, in the service of matching behavior to the goal of returning the notes. (Note also that the variations in behavior that may occur within the program implicitly occur in order to promote conformity to other goals, i.e., to avoid being stranded, delayed by traffic, or driving into a hazardous area.)

Programs can be entered for a variety of reasons; we believe that control at this level is particularly important in human self-regulation (cf. Schank & Abelson, 1977). What is most important in the present context, however, is the notion that self-regulation with respect to a principle takes place either by determining which programs are undertaken or by influencing decisions that are made in the course of executing a program. Said differently, the specification of some sort of program represents the behavioral output required for successful self-regulation at the principle level. Programs, in effect, provide some behavioral content in which a principle can be reflected.

This content, however, is still fairly abstract. What does it really mean to "drive over to Joe's house and deliver the notes"? For one thing, doing this requires the creation of a type of relationship between oneself, a motor vehicle, and the rest of the environment—a complex relationship

termed driving. Doing that, in turn, requires combinations of acts done in the appropriate sequences. The student opens the car door before sitting down and inserts the key into the ignition before turning the key. Preparing to turn right at a stop sign, he stops, starts rolling again, and then begins to turn the steering wheel. Consistent with this description, Powers postulates relationship and sequence control as the next two levels that are (successively) subordinate to program control.[2]

Specifying particular event sequences to be matched, however, does not end the process of producing overt behavioral acts. Actually producing behavior entails control of more and more concrete behavioral qualities (see Figure 15.3). For example, making a right turn ultimately depends on the creation of transitions from one orientation to another as the person turns the steering wheel. Being able to do this depends on the successive creation of appropriate configurations between the wheel and the person's hands and fingers and, at the very core, the creation of appropriate levels of muscle tensions in several parts of the body.

All of these qualities of behavior represent lower and lower levels of control in the Powers hierarchy. Each superordinate level acts by specifying reference values to the next subordinate level. Each level monitors its progress by comparisons with sensory input of the relevant type and at the appropriate level of abstraction. As the driver turns the wheel, his behavior is simultaneously matching reference values throughout the range of the hierarchy. He is creating muscle tensions, turning the wheel, delivering the notes to his friend, following through on his commitment, and buttressing his self-image as a responsible person.[3]

---

[2]One might dispute the way that Powers defines specific levels or determines that a specific level is subordinate to another; indeed, we have done so elsewhere. One might even argue that hierarchical control should have different constituents altogether (set Broadbent, 1977; Newell, 1973). In our view, however, such arguments do not render the central concept of a hierarchy of control processes less compelling or interesting.

[3]For clarity, we have chosen an example that seems intuitively accessible for a reader who is not accustomed to thinking in terms of the hierarchy that Powers proposes. There is no conceptual difference, however, between the sort of behavioral goal we are discussing and other goals that might seem a bit more amorphous (e.g., keeping close to nature). The only difference is in the specific behaviors called for. The latter goal might dictate that the person systematically choose scenic byways over superhighways whenever possible. Additional illustrations are described elsewhere (Carver & Scheier. 1981a, 1981b, 1982a, 1983; Scheier & Carver, 1982).

Reference values in this hierarchy are being matched, and new values being substituted, more quickly at lower levels than at higher levels. That is, many changes in muscle tensions are involved in making a single turn; it takes many turns to get to the friend's house and it takes more than one act of responsibility to sustain one's self-esteem. This difference in time scales is directly implied by the logic of a hierarchy of control (see Carver & Scheier, 1981a, Chapter 2). But it also fits nicely with the common observation that abstract goals are normally attained more gradually, over longer periods of time, than are concrete ones.

In the welter of details, it is easy to lose track of one of the important benefits conferred by this hierarchical sort of approach: It allows one to account successfully for the fact that exceedingly restricted and concrete behavioral acts (i.e., changes in levels of muscle tensions) are used to create behavioral events that are often so abstract as to seem completely unrelated to those concrete acts (e.g., writing an article, winning a tennis tournament, faithfully executing the office of president). Indeed, to the best of our knowledge, it seems to be the *only* approach that claims to provide such an account.

Now that we have described the hierarchy proposed by Powers (1973a, 1973b), let us return to the question that prompted us to address it in the first place: Where does the reference value for behavior come from? One portion of the answer should now be apparent. In a hierarchically organized system, the standard of comparison for the behavior of a subordinate loop is specified as the output of a loop at the next higher level of analysis. (It should also be obvious that the terms *standard* and *reference value* have dramatically different referents at different levels of the hierarchy.)

We are still left, however, with a need to account for the presence of a reference value at whatever level is at the top of the hierarchy. The argument that it is supplied from above is specious here because there is no higher level of control in the organization of the system.

Moreover, the preceding discussion may have induced some readers to conclude mistakenly that we see every level of control—from system concepts downward—as involved in all acts of behavioral self-regulation. We do not (see also Vallacher & Wegner, 1981). We suggest that people often function at the level of program control with little or no reference to higher order goals. (All levels

below whatever level is functionally superordinate would continue to operate, of course, because their operation occurs in the service of the functionally superordinate level.) Indeed, there is no reason in principle why yet a lower level might not be functionally superordinate for long periods of time. For example, imagine an assembly-line worker repeating the same sequence of acts over and over, oblivious to the fact that the sequence may also be relevant to goals at higher levels of abstraction. These considerations require that the question raised above be made more general: Specifically, where does the reference value come from at whatever level is *functionally superordinate* at the present time?

The attempt to answer this question takes us from a general discussion of control theory and the Powers hierarchy to a more specific discussion of how such ideas may be applied to the domain of personality and social psychology. Accordingly, let us state our position briefly here and elaborate on it in the following section. In short, we assume that, when people enter a new behavioral situation, they implicitly categorize that situation, based partly on the situation's observable elements and partly on the person's previously organized knowledge about physical and social environments (see Neisser, 1976). We suggest further that how-to-behave information is stored in memory, along with more perceptual or conceptual information, as a function of prior associations between behavior and categories of settings. The process of perceiving or construing the new setting may also cause this behavior-specifying information to be retrieved. If so, this information then constitutes the functionally superordinate behavioral standard. Depending on what level of self-regulation is temporarily superordinate, the standard may be quite abstract (e.g., enhance your reputation as a scientist) or much more concrete (e.g., transcribe these raw data onto a ledger sheet).

What determines what level of control is functionally superordinate? Our answer is only a partial one and is more descriptive than explanatory. We suggest that the highest level of control operating at any given moment corresponds to the level to which the person is focally attentive at that moment (cf. Shallice's, 1978, discussion of the "dominant action system"). In adults, this most often means control at the program level, although self-regulation is sometimes governed by principles and system concepts.

It is relatively easy to provide a rationale for why attention is so often fixed at the level of program control. Program control consists of a maze of implicit decisions. If one condition exists at a choice point, one behavior occurs; if other conditions are encountered, a different behavior occurs. Although such courses of action can become so ritualized that they require little attention and are executed all-at-a-piece (see, e.g., Langer, 1978; Norman, 1981), many are not. The unpredictability of the flow of events requires that they be attended to (cf. Norman & Shallice, 1980).

It also is relatively easy to see how attention can be drawn to lower levels of control, rendering them temporarily superordinate. For example, when the matching of a reference value is temporarily impeded at a lower level, higher level self-regulation is suspended as the person attempts to remedy the lower level problem (cf. Kimble & Perlmuter, 1970; Mancuso, 1977).

It is harder, however, to specify what causes attention to shift to higher levels of control. Why should people *ever* use principles or system concepts? One way to begin to account for an upward shift in control would be to assume that the organism has a built-in tendency toward an increase in organization as it adapts continuously to its environment. Piaget, of course, postulates just such a "developmental equilibration process," involving organization and adaptation as the two functional invariants that characterize psychological growth (see, e.g., Flavell, 1963). What should cause this tendency to exist is less clear. Most explanations reduce to the argument that greater organization— and greater abstraction of organization— facilitates functioning in ever more diverse circumstances. Despite this uncertainty about its source, any pressure toward development of higher order control structures would seem to imply a tendency to, at least periodically, attend to and self-regulate at the level that is emerging or that constitutes the highest level accessible. Thus, even though most human activity can probably proceed with nothing more complex than programs at work, it is undeniable that people do, on occasion, self-regulate at the levels of principles and system concepts.

## Personality-Social Psychology

Thus far we have presented the logic of control theory's basic concept—the feedback loop—and suggested how that construct can be applied to the self-regulation of behavior. But we have not yet offered concrete support for our reasoning, nor have we applied the reasoning to issues that are being addressed by research psychologists. We do so now, beginning with the area of our own greatest interest: personality and social psychology.

Let us start by examining several of the assertions made just above and the data that support them. First, we made the assumption that knowledge about objects and events becomes organized over time in schematic fashion and that these organized structures are used to interpret and recognize new objects and events. This line of reasoning has led to an active area of theory and research in cognitive psychology (see Anderson, 1980, for a review). Furthermore, on the basis of the reasonable assumption that people and the physical and social settings in which they interact represent an important set of objects and events, researchers have also obtained considerable support for this reasoning in personality-social psychology. Work in this area, often termed "social cognition," has produced evidence that we impose schematic organization on our knowledge about environments (e.g., Brewer & Treyens, 1981), about other people (e.g., Cantor & Mischel, 1977), and about ourselves (e.g., Rogers, Rogers, & Kuiper, 1979). The principles underlying these knowledge structures appear to be the same as those underlying the organization that is imposed on more arbitrary stimuli in the cognitive laboratory.

Our second assumption was that behavior specifying information is encoded as part of, or in association with, some of the knowledge structures that are used to recognize and construe events. This notion is consonant with a variety of approaches to category development and use (see, e.g., Neumann, 1975; Rosch, 1978; Rosch & Mervis, 1975; Rosch, Mervis, Gray, Johnson, & Boyes-Braem, 1976), although few theorists have emphasized it. One major exception is Schank and Abelson's (1977) argument that "scripts" are dual-purpose structures: that is, they help a person to understand and interpret what is going on, and they also specify information about how to behave.

There also is research evidence of associations between descriptive knowledge and behavioral specifications. Rosch and Mervis (1975) reported that subjects who were instructed to list attributes of specific items often listed behaviors commonly applied to the items. "Apples," for example, might elicit a list of attributes that would include "you can eat them." In a different domain, Price (1974) found that people see classes of behavior as differing in their appropriateness to different settings, a finding that supports Barker's (1968) long-held position that behavior settings are integrated systems of physical and behavioral elements. The findings of both of these projects are one step removed from our argument in that the data consisted of spontaneous mentions of behavior, and ratings of its appropriateness, rather than acting or preparing to act. The data do, however, suggest mental associations between objects and settings on the one hand and behavior on the other.

Studies in the domain of person perception may be less equivocal on this point. For example, making a particular stereotype salient as applicable to a target person influences the kinds of information that subjects later seek out about the person (Snyder & Swann, 1978; Carver & de la Garza, 1981; see Hamilton, 1979, or Brewer, Dull, & Lui, 1981, for evidence that stereotypes are organized schematically). A similar effect results from the arbitrary division of subjects into an ingroup and an outgroup (Wilder & Allen, 1978). Although information seeking may not seem terribly "behavioral," all of these effects did go beyond the simple inference of a second attribute, from the knowledge of a first attribute. All represent active attempts to obtain additional information.

Similar biases in behavior as a function of an initial categorization have also been found in other domains. Subjects allocate more resources to ingroup than to outgroup members (Allen & Wilder, 1975; Billig & Tajfel, 1973), presumably reflecting behavioral biases induced by such categorizations. Racial categorizations also influence perceivers' actions toward stimulus persons (Rubovits & Maehr, 1973; Word, Zanna, & Cooper, 1974), as do categorizations based on physical attractiveness (Snyder, Tanke, & Berscheid, 1977). Indeed, construing a person in terms of his or her present role has been found to lead to actions that are quite different from those that occur when construing the same person as a unique individual (Carles & Carver, 1979). Taken together, these findings seem to render quite plausible the notion that the certain knowledge structures that are used to identify and categorize persons also incorporate information specifying how to behave toward those persons.

One recent study (Carver, Ganellen, Froming, & Chambers, 1981) has even directly tested the assumption that the behavioral information associated with a knowledge structure can be rendered more accessible, and thus more likely to be used, by "priming" the interpretive structure with which it is associated. Srull and Wyer (1979) found that exposing subjects to a series of items that contained words pertaining to aggressiveness and hostility caused the interpretive schema for hostility to be more accessible later on, thus to be used to a greater extent in perceiving an ambiguous stimulus person. Carver et al. (1981) found that this effect of priming also generalizes to behavior: Exposure to the aggression-related items led to enhanced aggression in a completely separate context.

## Attention and Self-Regulation

Despite the evidence that behavioral specifications are stored in association with other elements of knowledge structures, we do not believe that simply accessing such information inevitably ensures that it will be reflected (as a superordinate reference value) in the person's behavior. There still must be some mechanism to account for the fitting of behavior to that value. Consistent with our position that the execution of behavior reflects a hierarchy of self-regulatory feedback loops, we have proposed that the engagement of the loop, at whatever level of control is superordinate, partially depends on the person's focus of attention (Carver, 1979; Carver & Scheier, 1981a, 1981b, 1982a). More specifically, we suggest that directing attention to the *self*, when a behavioral standard has been evoked by the nature of one's role or the setting, engages the comparator at the level of control that is superordinate. The result is a tendency to compare one's perceptions of one's present state or behavior against the standard, leading (when possible) to a reduction of perceptible discrepancies between the two.

We should note that our use of terms such as self-directed attention, self-focus, and self-awareness does not necessarily connote a lengthy examination of the self or the attainment of a dramatic insight into one's motives or character. In the present context, these terms mean little more than the momentary shifting of attention to the salient standard and the standard-relevant aspect of one's present behavior (see Carver & Scheier, 1981a, Chapter 3, for detail). We should also note that we assume the discrepancy-reduction process to be relatively automatic; we do not assume that the person necessarily thinks the matter through in verbal or near-verbal terms. Nor do we assume that people necessarily will be able to recollect or reconstruct, with a high degree of accuracy what they did or why (cf. Broadbent, 1977, pp. 192–194). We assume only that the reference value and the perception of present behavior are temporarily focal and that the one is used to guide the other. Nonetheless, it is incontrovertible that people do sometimes think their behavior through and analyze their reasons for doing one thing or another. Sometimes—though not always—people who are behaving according to a logical principle can spontaneously verbalize the principle and state that they are consciously using it. How to conceptualize the difference between these two conditions is a difficult question. Consciousness of use represents a kind of recursiveness of the process of attention, removing one from the self-regulation process per se, stepping outside it for a moment as if to examine it. This recursiveness is not necessary for self-regulation to occur. But it does happen and, presumably, has a function. It may be that this process is involved in the shaping and smoothing of the self-regulatory functions (see Broadbent, 1977; LaBerge & Samuels, 1974; Mandler, 1975; Powers 1980) and represents a way in which reference values are encoded with sufficient redundancy for future automatic use.

Our characterization of the self-regulatory events that follow from self-focus has two aspects. The first is the assumption that self-directed attention results in an increased tendency to compare one's present state with relevant and salient reference values. There is indirect evidence that such active comparisons do follow from self-focus. In a series of studies (Scheier & Carver, 1983a), subjects with high levels of self-focus were more likely than subjects with lower levels to seek out concrete information that would facilitate the comparison process that was assumed to be occurring mentally at a more abstract level. Operationally, in two studies, this meant reexamining a geometric figure that the subjects were attempting to copy accurately. In two other studies, it meant seeking out information about performance norms on test items. In all cases, self-focus was positively associated with the seeking of such information. This, in turn, suggests a more active comparison against relevant performance standards as a function of increased attending to the self.

The second aspect of the above characterization is that self-focus promotes enhanced self-regulation. If the comparator's functioning reveals a discrepancy between perceived state and reference value, the relatively automatic result is behavioral output aimed at countering the deviation. There is abundant evidence that self-focus does result in increased conformity to salient behavioral standards.[4] The behavioral domains sampled in this research range from aggression (Carver, 1974, 1975; Scheier, Fenigstein, & Buss, 1974), to letter copying (Carver & Scheier, 1981c; Wicklund & Duval, 1971), to the use of the equity norm in resource allocation (Greenberg, 1980), and beyond (see Carver & Scheier, 1981a, for a more thorough review). Furthermore, the standards in question have ranged from personal attitudes (Carver, 1975; Gibbons, 1978), to commonly internalized norms (Scheier et al., 1974) to information contained in experimental instructions (Wicklund & Duval, 1971). In all of these cases, manipulations increasing self-directed attention resulted in closer behavioral conformity to the standard, which was situationally salient.[5]

The superordinate behavioral standards in these studies typically stood at the program or principle level of the Powers hierarchy. As one illustration, unprovoked subjects in the Scheier et al. (1974) study shocked women less intensely in the context of a presumed learning experiment when self-focus was high than when it was low, presumably because they were adhering more closely to a principle resembling chivalry (Buss, 1966), having shown that men deliver less shock to women than to other men. Subjects in other studies, using the same paradigm (Carver, 1975), chose their levels of punishment on the basis of preexisting opin-

---

[4]Though these findings are often interpreted as reflecting a self-attention-induced increase in "drive" (see Duval & Wicklund, 1972), results of a recent study (Carver & Scheier, 1981c) appear to cast doubt on the adequacy of a drive-based analysis.

[5]One important distinction among behavioral standards would seem to be between the relatively private and personal standards that people have (e.g., their attitudes and moral beliefs) and standards that are evoked by means such as acts of social comparison. The latter would seem to be more temporary and situation-specific than the former, although both clearly are used to guide behavior at various times. Our position is that the two are similar in serving as reference values for self-regulation, but they differ in terms of what superordinate reference values they follow from. This issue is discussed at length elsewhere (Carver & Scheier, 1981a; Scheier & Carver, 1981, 1983b).

*tie to last week*

ions about whether using punishment was an effective and justifiable way to produce learning. These attitudes were reflected in behavior only when self-focus was relatively high.

It is also worthy of some note that the behavior of interest in these specific studies—aggression or punishment—was executed in a very artificial manner; that is, by pressing one of 10 buttons on a given trial, they chose from among 10 intensities of shock to deliver. This illustrates how research subjects display abstract qualities of behavior in very concrete physical acts. As we indicated earlier, the notion of a hierarchy of control structures accounts nicely for such a capability, whereas it seems difficult to do so without such a hierarchy.

## Expectancy

Our approach to self-regulation incorporates one additional facet that is less obviously related to control theory than the processes discussed thus far. Specifically, we have argued that discrepancy reduction normally follows the comparison between present state and behavioral standard, although an impulse to withdraw or disengage from the attempt may occur if the person's expectancy of being able to reduce the discrepancy is sufficiently unfavorable. We assume an expectancy-assessment process, which may be either momentary or prolonged, that is separate and distinct from the discrepancy-reduction process. It may occur either before or during a discrepancy-reduction attempt and, presumably, involves an integration of information from several potential sources. These include a consideration of physical or social constraints on one's behavior and the depth and breadth of one's resources (cf. Lewin, Dembo, Festinger, & Sears, 1944).

We assume a dichotomy among people's responses to this assessment process. In a real sense, responses ultimately reduce to two classes: further attempts and disengagement from the attempt (see Figure 15.3). People's further attempts may well vary in intensity or enthusiasm as a function of variations in expectancy, when expectancies are sufficiently favorable as to ensure further attempts (cf. Miller & Dollard, 1941). Also, the subjective probability at which further efforts give way to resignation and disengagement will certainly vary with the importance of the behavioral goal. But we see some merit in emphasizing that a sort of

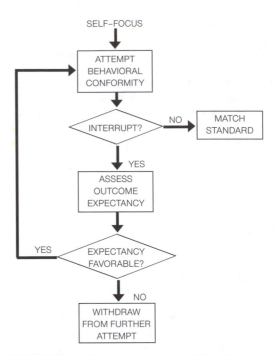

**FIGURE 15.3.** ■ A flow-chart description of the expectancy-assessment process and the behavioral responses that follow when impediments are encountered in a discrepancy-reduction attempt. (Adapted from Carver, 1979.)

"watershed" exists among responses, separating further efforts from the abandonment of effort.

One reason for this emphasis stems from the fact that, although expectancy constructs have had a long history in psychology (see Feather, 1982), rarely, if ever, have they been construed as reflecting control processes. It is easy to do so, however, provided one is willing to assume the dichotomy outlined above among the forms of behavior to which they lead. Said differently, the expectancy assessment process can be construed, at least in part, as constituting a binary, yes-or-no decision: Either continue to try or withdraw from the attempt. Although it may not be immediately obvious, the comparator of a feedback loop is also making such a decision: The values being compared either are or are not the same. This decision-making character is much more apparent in Miller et al.'s (1960) Test-Operate-Test-Exit (TOTE) construct, which is a sequential description of the behavior of a feedback system. More specifically, the "test" of the TOTE, which constitutes the behavior of the system's comparator, yields a yes-or-no judgment. This determines whether control is transferred to "operate" or to "exit." Although there is some disagreement as to how widely discrete and sequential decision-making processes do occur in behavioral self-regulation (see Cooper & Shepard, 1973; Grossberg, 1980; Powers, 1973a), we believe that something very much like this occurs in what we are referring to as an outcome-expectancy assessment. Thus, the assessment process itself can be viewed in control-theory terms without too much difficulty.

This watershed aspect of our model has received empirical support in a variety of studies. For example, chronic expectancies of being able to cope successfully with a specific strong fear were found to interact with self-focus in a situation in which the fear was induced. Favorable expectancies produced enhanced efforts when self-focus was high, and unfavorable expectancies produced early withdrawal when self-focus was high (Carver, Blaney, & Scheier, 1979a). Expectancies did not predict behavior, however, when self-focus was lower. In other research, situationally manipulated expectancies of being able to make up for a poor performance interacted with self-focus in a fashion similar, influencing subjects' persistence on a second task (Carver, Blaney, & Scheier, 1979b; Scheier & Carver, 1982). These effects have also been replicated conceptually with a measure of performance, rather than persistence (Carver & Scheier, 1982b). Finally, yet other studies have implicated the interaction between unfavorable expectancies and self-focus in the performance impairments associated with low self-esteem (Brockner, 1979) and test anxiety (Carver, Peterson, Follansbee, & Scheier, 1981). [. . .]

## Two Other Applications

We now turn to two other areas of theory and research on human behavior, which cybernetic concepts either use explicitly or implicitly. Our primary interest will be in noting similarities to the ideas already discussed and indicating some of the issues that emerge in applying the ideas to these different areas of work.

### Clinical Psychology:
### Cognitive Models of Behavior Change

Several theorists in the cognitive-behavioral camp of clinical psychology have made an energetic and thoughtful attempt to specify accurate and comprehensive models of the parameters of behavior change (e.g., Bandura, 1977; Kanfer, 1977; Kanfer & Hagerman, 1981). We see these efforts as important and agree with much of what the theorists have said. These accounts share one implicit problem, however, which may not be obvious at first glance. Although they historically derive from learning theory, they have moved steadily farther and farther away from the assumptions of the learning-theory paradigm. In order to gain sharper predictive accuracy, these theorists are, in effect, abandoning their conceptual heritage. We suggest, however, that while leaving the old heritage behind, they are moving inexorably toward a new one. Without having fully realized it, these theorists have been developing descriptions of the processes of cybernetic control.

The most explicit statements in this area are probably those of Kanfer (1977; Kanfer & Hagerman, 1981) and Bandura (1977). Both discuss the process of self-regulation as involving self-imposition of behavioral standards, observation of one's own actions, and evaluation of these actions by comparing them with the standards (see also Mischel, 1973). In addition, both discuss the importance of the person's expectancies of being either able or unable to alter behavior in the direction of the standard, viewing them as critical determinants of whether the person continues to strive or gives up the attempt (cf. Rotter, 1954). The importance of expectancies in the behavior change process has also been verified empirically (e.g., Bandura, Adams, & Beyer, 1977; Bandura, Adams, Hardy, & Howells, 1980).

The resemblance between these ideas and the concepts that we have used in our own work (described above) is striking. Our focus has been on the moment-to-moment regulation of behavior, whereas the theoretical statements by Kanfer and Bandura have emphasized the longer term regulation of behavior *change*. Despite the difference in time scales, however, the processes themselves seem nearly identical: the existence of a reference value, the self-reflective comparison between that value and one's present state, and the attempt (unless countermanded by an unfavorable expectancy) to match the one with the other. These processes also map directly onto the component processes of the feedback loop introduced in Figure 15.1.

Other than the difference in time scales, apparently the only major difference between our approach and these approaches concerns reliance on a self-reinforcement construct to account for behavior change. We do not invoke the concept, but the social learning approach to behavior and behavior change typically does. Even Kanfer, who has long recognized the similarity between his ideas and the cybernetic approach to self-regulation (see Kanfer & Phillips, 1970), and has even adopted some of the language of control theory (see Kanfer & Hagerman, 1981), ultimately rests his analysis on the postulate that there is self-reinforcement for goal attainment and self-punishment for failure to attain goals.

This postulate, which has come to seem like something of an afterthought, seems to be retained in these theories, at least partly, because it binds them to the learning paradigm from which they evolved. It thus provides a sense of continuity and stability—far from a trivial goal. But is the self-reinforcement postulate really effective in that regard? The answer is not clear. The concept of self-reinforcement has always been a fuzzy one. It is appealing when it accounts for behavior for which there are no obvious external reinforcers. But it is also disturbing because it could potentially be applied everywhere, thus obviating the need to discuss external reinforcement at all.

This problem, in turn, raises more general questions about the need to assume rewards as the universal controls over behavior. There *are* other possibilities (see Powers, 1973b). For example, informational feedback—knowledge of the effects of one's behavior—is commonly treated as a special type of reinforcer. It could as easily be argued, however, that the information regarding the outcome of one's action, and the subsequent guidance that it provides, are what is truly basic to self-regulation (cf. Locke, Shaw, Saari, & Latham, 1981, especially pp. 135–136). We give the term *reinforcer* to events that impart such information only because that term seems to give the events greater substance. This argument is certainly not new (see Adams, 1968; Annett, 1969; Brewer, 1974; Locke, Cartledge, & Koeppel, 1968), but it is often disregarded by psychologists with social-learning orientations.

Interestingly enough, difficulties with the reinforcement concept once prompted Bandura (1976) to suggest that it may be useful to abandon the term altogether and, instead, talk simply about self-regulation. In effect, such a change in constructs would place theorists such as Bandura squarely in the midst of control theory. We have argued elsewhere (Carver & Scheier, 1981a) that the past reluctance to seriously consider this step is based in part on a misunderstanding of cybernetic concepts. The time may be right to reexamine the issue.

Before leaving this section, let us draw one more connection between the processes of therapeutic behavior change and control-theory concepts. In particular, we wish to note the relevance of the hierarchy of control processes suggested by Powers (1973a) for the task of conceptualizing behavior change. It seems likely that, in adult self-regulation, reference values for behavior at low levels of control are normally specified easily and automatically. The behavioral qualities that are being specified at those levels, regardless of the behavior, are typically well learned because they are component elements of a great many kinds of action. Thus, it should be no surprise that having component skills makes observational learning easier because it allows persons to focus on behavioral qualities at high levels of abstraction. Nor is it surprising that muscle coordinations generalize across different domains of activity.

It seems likely, however, that a good deal of behavioral disruption that is viewed as neurotic or maladaptive stems from an inability to specify reference values from the level of system concepts (or principles) down to—and through—the level of program control. Thus, for example, many people want to be "fulfilled," or "likable," or "successful," but have no idea what actions will move them in the direction of those superordinate goals. Indeed, they often do not know where to begin in *determining* what concrete steps will provide such superordinate discrepancy reduction.

Focusing on the discrepancies between their salient reference values and present self-perceptions has the added consequence of repeatedly (and painfully) reminding these people of their inability to reduce the discrepancies. This awareness may lead to withdrawal or disengagement from the attempt to match the higher order reference values. Because the social environment often does not allow a permanent disengagement, the cycle continues: inability to attain higher order goals, awareness of that inability, and negative feelings following from that awareness (see also Carver & Scheier, 1985). All of this is further exacerbated by the fact that continued failure causes the expectancies of future failure to become more stable (see Weiner, 1974), leading to even lower likelihood of exerting sustained efforts toward the higher order goals.

Such difficulties are very distressing, particularly when they involve central aspects of one's life. How are they to be resolved? It seems sensible that the process of dealing effectively with this sort of problem would not differ in principle from the process of resolving other sorts of problems. That is, the issues inherent in dealing with problems in one's own psychological self-management may be essentially the same issues as are inherent in dealing with problems of an intellectual sort (e.g., physics problems). Perhaps examining research on the evolution and use of problem-solving strategies in intellectual areas can provide information that is useful in conceptualizing the process of successful behavior change.

A cursory examination of such research yields two conclusions, one simple, the other more complex. First, effective handling of a novel problem requires that it is broken down into concrete components, each of which is manageable by itself. To generalize this point to the therapy process, a useful way for a person to approach a psychological problem would be to analyze the abstract complaint in terms of the concrete acts of ineffective self-regulation that are associated with it (indeed, that may constitute it) and to re-specify those component acts in more effective ways. This line of argument is consistent with the reasoning underlying cognitive therapies (see, e.g., Beck, 1976; Meichenbaum, 1977).

The more complex conclusion stems from the fact that recent research on intellectual problem solving typically finds evidence of a sort of "bootstrapping" effect (see, e.g., Anzai & Simon, 1979; Larkin, McDermott, Simon, & Simon, 1980). That is, the way in which an initial problem is approached differs markedly from the way problems are approached after gaining some experience (see also related discussions of how perceptions are organized differently as a function of experience; Chase & Simon, 1973; Rosch et al., 1976). The initial attempt involves generating small components of behavioral strategy. Once a component structure is incorporated into the behavioral stream, it then is used as a vehicle for generating higher order structures. Indeed, once a sophisticated understanding of the task has been developed, the initial component behavior—which led to the development of the more abstract behavior in the first place—may be abandoned as less efficient than a previously unconsidered alternative. The long-term result of this process is that the person is not simply capable of solving a specific problem, but has learned a general approach to a *class* of problems. This sort of finding also has implications for therapy. If the bootstrapping effect generalizes to solving problems in one's own behavioral self-management, a properly focused therapy should induce in clients a greater ability to analyze and resolve their problems in new domains (cf. Belmont, 1978).

Let us add one final note, which stems from the hierarchy of control but constitutes quite a different point. Specifically, as discussed earlier, Powers (1973a, 1973b) proposed a hierarchy of control structures in which all levels, from the superordinate on down, are functioning simultaneously. This conceptualization suggests an interesting conclusion: The process of specifying and executing effective programs of action is not just a step that *enables* one to attain higher order goals. Rather, specifying and executing effective programs is precisely the *process* of attaining the higher order goals. More concretely, self-satisfaction in goal attainment can often be expected to accrue from the doing, rather than from the having done.

To summarize the points made in this section, cognitively oriented theorists attempting to conceptualize the process of behavior change have reached a degree of consensus as to the importance of self-imposed behavioral standards and the self-monitoring of one's progress in comparison with those standards. There has also been a renewed emphasis on the role played by expectancies about effective discrepancy reduction. In its evolution, however, this approach has increasingly become a theory without a metatheory. Cybernetics provides a metatheory that fits well with the developing models.

## Health Psychology

We now address the relatively new domain of health psychology, where several theorists have already begun to make explicit use of cybernetic constructs to describe how people attempt to keep themselves healthy. Good health—however it is defined—constitutes a reference value just like any other. Furthermore, self-regulation with regard to that value has all the earmarks of self-regulation in other domains.

For example, merely checking one's temperature, taking one's pulse or blood pressure, or trying out the flexibility of one's hand and fingers is an intelligible activity only when viewed in control-theory terms (Schwartz, 1978, 1979). That is, whatever information is obtained by any of these actions is meaningful only when compared with some reference value. Indeed, when people do such things, it is usually for the express purpose of determining whether there is a discrepancy between the present and "normal" state. A discrepancy implies a state of less-than-ideal health (see Leventhal, Meyer, & Nerenz, 1980; Leventhal, Nerenz, & Straus, 1980). The result usually is the taking of some action in an attempt to shift reality back toward the standard of comparison (e.g., taking medication for an elevated temperature or rubbing liniment on aching fingers).

Seeking out a physician for a checkup is conceptually the same process. The physician is able to use esoteric devices to obtain otherwise inaccessible information about one's present state and can prescribe a broader range of potential behaviors to aid in discrepancy reduction if a discrepancy is perceived. But in all these cases people as "health care systems" (Schwartz, 1978, 1979)—whether they use the physician as a perceptual-behavioral adjunct or use only the perceptual channels and behavioral options that are normally available to them—can be seen as constituting discrepancy-reducing feedback loops.

Schwartz (e.g., 1978, 1979) discussed the use of techniques such as biofeedback in precisely the same terms. A biofeedback device provides one with a perceptual input that is more accessible than is usually the case, for whatever physiological state is being monitored. In effect, two feedback loops are linked hierarchically. The subject's goal is, for example, to light a light on the face of an apparatus. Doing this, however, requires regulating some physiological system with respect to some specific reference value as well.

Earlier in the article, we discussed the mediating role of self-attention in behavioral self-regulation. It is of some interest, then, that attention appears to play a role in self-regulation of health-relevant behavior, as well as the kinds of behavior addressed earlier. There is, for example, evidence that levels of chronic self-focus help to determine the degree to which people take steps to counter the stresses caused by life events (Mullen & Suls, 1982). In addition, Schwartz (1980) recently reported the finding that self-attention—as defined by attending to natural internal biofeedback—promotes an increased regularity in the functioning of the system being attended to.

The notion of a hierarchy of control has additional implications in the field of health psychology, most obviously in connection with ineffective self-regulation, as was also true in the preceding section. One straightforward problem stems from the fact that certain physical disorders (e.g., hypertension) have no known symptoms. Despite this, people with the disorder often persist in attempting to ascertain their present conditions by means of easily monitored (internal) perceptual events. In effect, they define for themselves some symptom to observe. Of greater importance, they then proceed to regulate their behavior *on the basis of the presence or absence of that symptom* (Leventhal, Meyer et al., 1980).

This tendency leads to either of two kinds of problems. If the symptom goes away, people may stop taking their medication, believing that their blood pressure is down when it is not. If the symptom persists, on the other hand, people may become despondent, believing (incorrectly) that their blood pressure is remaining elevated despite their faithful following of the doctor's orders. Feeling that the medication is not helping may lead these people to discontinue it. In either case, the long-term result is that the person ceases taking the medication that is actually effective in keeping blood pressure low.[6]

This example makes two noteworthy points. First, the case under scrutiny involves two hierarchically ordered levels of self-regulation. The more obvious level is the monitoring of a symptom and the attempt to stay symptom free. But this attempt is occurring in the service of a higher order goal: staying healthy by reducing blood pressure. The person in this example has developed a faulty behavioral specification from the higher order loop to the lower one. That is, the behavior that the higher order loop is calling for in order to reduce blood pressure—symptom monitoring—is actually irrelevant to that goal. This disjunction is an example of what we have referred to elsewhere as

---

[6]This should not necessarily be read as an endorsement of medication per se. Schwartz (1978, 1979) argued persuasively that an overreliance on medication results in an artificial regulation of the physical state, which can have unfortunate consequences of its own.

"misregulation" (Carver & Scheier, 1981a). In misregulation, the person is actively regulating behavior at one level, but doing so is failing to reduce discrepancies—and may even be enlarging them—at a higher level.[7]

The second point made by this example is that the how of self-regulation at the lower level of control is partially dependent on the person's expectancy of successfully matching the reference value (i.e., eliminating the symptom) by means of the behavior being undertaken (i.e., taking medication). A person who sees that continued pill taking is not influencing the symptom that is being monitored is beginning to develop an unfavorable expectancy concerning the effectiveness of that behavior. This can lead to disengagement from the attempt to eliminate the symptom by use of the drug (i.e., to discontinuation of compliance with the prescribed medical regimen).

To summarize the points made in this section, the cybernetic model appears to provide a good accounting of health-related behavior ranging from symptom monitoring to the use of biofeedback techniques and compliance or noncompliance with medical regimens. This brief discussion does not exhaust the ways in which health psychologists are using information-processing and control-theory ideas (see, e.g., Leventhal, Nerenz et al., 1980). But it does give some idea of the success that this general approach has enjoyed there. [. . .]

## Conclusion

We have attempted to indicate here how the principles of cybernetics are of value to three rather separate areas of human psychology. In each of these areas of research and thought, control theory seems to be a useful tool in the conceptualization

and analysis of human behavior. In each case that was addressed, the application of such ideas is relatively recent. But, in each case, there also is a remarkable fit between research findings (and the specific theories with which they are associated) and the feedback model with which we began. When combined across the three cases we have examined, there is a good deal of integrative promise. Given this promise, we suggest that it is time for more of us to take a closer look at the concepts of control theory.

## REFERENCES

Adams, J. A. (1968). Response feedback and learning. *Psychological Bulletin, 70,* 486–504.

Alien, V. L., & Wilder, D. A. (1975). Categorization, belief similarity, and intergroup discrimination. *Journal of Personality and Social Psychology, 32,* 971–977.

Anderson, J. R. (1980). *Cognitive psychology and its implications.* San Francisco: Freeman.

Annett, J. (1969). *Feedback and human behavior.* Baltimore, MD: Penguin Books.

Anzai, Y., & Simon, H. A. (1979). The theory of learning by doing. *Psychological Review, 86,* 124–140.

Balakrishnan, A. V. (1973). *Stochastic differential systems.* New York: Springer-Verlag.

Bandura, A. (1976). Self-reinforcement: Theoretical and methodological considerations. *Behaviorism, 4,* 135–155.

Bandura, A. (1977). Self-efficacy: Toward a unifying theory of behavior change. *Psychological Review, 84,* 191–215.

Bandura, A., Adams, N. E., & Beyer, J. (1977). Cognitive processes mediating behavioral change. *Journal of Personality and Social Psychology, 35,* 125–139.

Bandura, A., Adams, N. E., Hardy, A. B., & Howells, G. N. (1980). Tests of the generality of self-efficacy theory. *Cognitive Therapy and Research, 4,* 39–66.

Bandura, A., & Simon, K. M. (1977). The role of proximal intentions in self-regulation of refractory behavior. *Cognitive Therapy and Research, 1,* 177–193.

Barker, R. G. (1968). *Ecological psychology: Concepts and methods for studying the environment of human behavior.* Stanford, CA: Stanford University Press.

Beck, A. T. (1976). *Cognitive therapy and the emotional disorders.* New York: International Universities Press.

Belmont, J. (1978). Individual differences in memory: The cases of normal and retarded development. In M. Greenberg & P. Morris (Eds.), *Aspects of memory.* London: Methuen.

Berkovitz, L. D. (1974). *Optimal control theory.* New York: Springer-Verlag.

Billig, M., & Tajfel, H. (1973). Social categorization and similarity in intergroup behavior. *European Journal of Social Psychology, 3,* 27–52.

Bower, G. H. (1978). Contacts of cognitive psychology with social learning theory. *Cognitive Therapy and Research, 2,* 123–146.

Bower, G. H., & Cohen, P. R. (1982). Emotional influences in memory and thinking: Data and theory. In M. S. Clark & S. T. Fiske (Eds.), *Affect and cognition: The 17th annual Carnegie symposium on cognition.* Hillsdale, NJ: Erlbaum.

---

[7]Although this example makes our point concerning hierarchical organization fairly clearly, we would also like to draw some attention to the more general issue here, which is the importance of knowing how a superordinate goal such as good health is defined by the person and, thus, what strategies are specified for goal attainment. Consider another illustration (suggested to us by Karen Matthews). To one person, good health is the absence of perceptible symptoms of disease; to a second, it implies a state of better-than-average physical fitness, a balanced dirt, and so on. This difference has obvious implications for behavior. Consider, for example, which person is more likely to be systematic about taking a prescribed medication even after symptoms are no longer salient, or which is more likely to engage in preventive medicine.

Brewer, M. B., Dull, V., & Lui, L. (1981). Perceptions of the elderly: Stereotypes as prototypes. *Journal of Personality and Social Psychology, 41*, 656–670.

Brewer, W. F. (1974). There is no convincing evidence for operant or classical conditioning in adult humans. In W. B. Weimer & D. S. Palermo (Eds.), *Cognition and the symbolic processes*. Hillsdale, NJ: Erlbaum.

Brewer, W. F., & Treyens, J. C. (1981). Role of schemata in memory for places. *Cognitive Psychology, 13*, 207–230.

Broadbent, D. E. (1977). Levels, hierarchies, and the locus of control. *Quarterly Journal of Experimental Psychology, 29*, 181–201.

Brockner, J. (1979). The effects of self-esteem, success-failure, and self-consciousness on task performance. *Journal of Personality and Social Psychology, 37*, 1732–1741.

Buckley, W. (1968). *Modern systems research for the behavioral scientist*. Chicago: Aldine.

Buss, A. H. (1966). The effect of harm on subsequent aggression. *Journal of Experimental Research in Personality, 1*, 249–255.

Cannon, W. B. (1929). Organization for physiological homeostasis. *Physiological Review, 9*, 399–431.

Cannon, W. B. (1932). *The wisdom of the body*. New York: Norton.

Cantor, N., & Mischel, W. (1977). Traits as prototypes: Effects on recognition memory. *Journal of Personality and Social Psychology, 35*, 38–48.

Carles, E. M., & Carver, C. S. (1979). Effects of person salience versus role salience on reward allocation in a dyad. *Journal of Personality and Social Psychology, 37*, 2071–2080.

Carver, C. S. (1974). Facilitation of physical aggression through objective self-awareness. *Journal of Experimental Social Psychology, 10*, 365–370.

Carver, C. S. (1975). Physical aggression as a function of objective self-awareness and attitudes toward punishment. *Journal of Experimental Social Psychology, 11*, 510–519.

Carver, C. S. (1979). A cybernetic model of self-attention processes. *Journal of Personality and Social Psychology, 37*, 1251–1281.

Carver, C. S., Blaney, P. H., & Scheier, M. F. (1979). Focus of attention, chronic expectancy, and responses to a feared stimulus. *Journal of Personality and Social Psychology, 37*, 1186–1195.

Carver, C. S., Blaney, P. H., & Scheier, M. F. (1979). Reassertion and giving up: The interactive role of self-directed attention and outcome expectancy. *Journal of Personality and Social Psychology, 37*, 1859–1870.

Carver, C. S., & de la Garza, N. H. (1981). *Schema-guided information search in stereotyping of the elderly*. Manuscript submitted for publication.

Carver, C. S., Ganellen, R., Froming, W. J., & Chambers, W. (1981). *Are many acts of modeling "accessibility" phenomena?* Manuscript submitted for publication.

Carver, C. S., Peterson, L. M., Follansbee, D. J., & Scheier, M. F. (1981). *Effects of self-directed attention on performance and persistence among persons high and low in test anxiety*. Manuscript submitted for publication.

Carver, C. S., & Scheier, M. F. (1981a). *Attention and self-regulation: A control-theory approach to human behavior*. New York: Springer Verlag.

Carver, C. S., & Scheier, M. F. (1981b). A control-systems approach to behavioral self-regulation. In L. Wheeler (Ed.), *Review of personality and social psychology* (Vol. 2). Beverly Hills, CA: Sage.

Carver, C. S., & Scheier, M. F. (1981c). The self-attention-induced feedback loop and social facilitation. *Journal of Experimental Social Psychology, 17*, 545–568.

Carver, C. S., & Scheier, M. F. (1982a). An information-processing perspective on self-management. In P. Karoly & F. Kanfer (Eds.), *Self-management and behavior change*. New York: Pergamon.

Carver, C. S., & Scheier, M. F. (1982b). Outcome expectancy, locus of attributions for expectancy, and self-directed attention as determinants of evaluations and performance. *Journal of Experimental Social Psychology, 18*, 184–200.

Carver, C. S., & Scheier, M. F. (1985). A control-theory approach to human behavior and implications for problems in self-management. In P. C. Kendall (Ed.), *Advances in cognitive-behavioral research and therapy* (Vol. 4). Orlando, FL: Academic Press.

Chase, W. G., & Simon, H. A. Perception in chess. *Cognitive Psychology, 4*, 55–81.

Cooper, L. A., & Shepard, R. N. (1973). Chronometric studies of the rotation of mental images. In W. G. Chase (Ed.), *Visual information processing*. New York: Academic Press.

Davis, M. H. A. (1977). *Linear estimation and stochastic control*. New York: Wiley.

Dransfield, P. (1968). *Engineering systems and control*. Englewood Cliffs, NJ: Prentice-Hall.

Duval, S., & Wicklund, R. A. (1972). *A theory of objective self-awareness*. New York: Academic Press.

Feather, N. T. (1982). *Expectations and actions: Expectancy value models in psychology*. Hillsdale, NJ: Erlbaum.

Flavell, J. H. (1963). *The developmental psychology of Jean Piaget*. New York: Van Nostrand Reinhold.

Gibbons, F. X. (1978). Sexual standards and reactions to pornography: Enhancing behavioral consistency through self-focused attention. *Journal of Personality and Social Psychology, 36*, 976–987.

Greenberg, J. (1980). Attentional focus and locus of performance causality as determinants of equity behavior. *Journal of Personality and Social Psychology, 38*, 579–585.

Grossberg, S. (1980). Human and computer rules and representation are not equivalent. *Behavioral and Brain Sciences, 3*, 111–169.

Guyton, A. C. (1976). *Textbook of medical physiology*. Philadelphia: W. B. Saunders.

Hamilton, D. L. (1979). A cognitive-attributional analysis of stereotyping. In L. Berkowitz (Ed.), *Advances in experimental social psychology* (Vol. 12). New York: Academic Press.

Hubel, D. H., & Wiesel, T. N. (1963). Shape and arrangement of columns in cat's striatal cortex. *Journal of Physiology* (London), *165*, 559–568.

Hubel, D. H., & Wiesel, T. N. (1965). Receptive fields and functional architecture in two non-striate visual areas (18 and 19) of the cat. *Journal of Neurophysiology, 28*, 229–289.

Kanfer, F. H. (1977). The many faces of self-control, or behavior modification changes its focus. In R. B. Stuart (Ed.), *Behavioral self-management: Strategies, techniques, and outcomes*. New York: Brunner/Mazel.

Kanfer, F. H., & Hagerman, S. (1981). The role of self-regulation. In L. P. Rehm (Ed.), *Behavior therapy for depression: Present status and future direction*. New York: Academic Press.

Kanfer, F. H., & Phillips, J. S. (1970). *Learning foundations of behavior therapy.* New York: Wiley.

Kimble, G. A., & Perlmuter, L. C. (1970). The problem of volition. *Psychological Review, 77,* 361–384.

LaBerge, D., & Samuels, S. (1974). Toward a theory of automatic information processing in reading. *Cognitive Psychology, 6,* 293–323.

Langer, E. J. (1978). Rethinking the role of thought in social interaction. In J. H. Harvey, W. Ickes, & R. F. Kidd (Eds.), *New directions in attribution research* (Vol. 2). Hillsdale, NJ: Erlbaum.

Larkin, J., McDermott, J., Simon, D. P., & Simon, H. A. (1980). Expert and novice performance in solving physics problems. *Science, 208,* 1335–1342.

Leventhal, H. (1980). Toward a comprehensive theory of emotion. In L. Berkowitz (Ed.), *Advances in experimental social psychology* (Vol. 13). New York: Academic Press.

Leventhal, H., Meyer, D., & Nerenz, D. (1980). The common sense representation of illness danger. In S. Rachman (Ed.), *Medical psychology* (Vol. 2). New York: Pergamon.

Leventhal, H., Nerenz, D., & Straus, A. (1980). Self-regulation and the mechanisms for symptom appraisal. In D. Mechanic (Ed.), *Psychosocial epidemiology.* New York: Neale Watson.

Lewin, K., Dembo, T., Festinger, L., & Sears, P. S. (1944). Level of aspiration. In J. McV. Hunt (Ed.), *Personality and the behavior disorders.* New York: Ronald Press.

Locke, E. A., Cartledge, V., & Koeppel, J. (1968). Motivational effects of knowledge of results: A goal-setting phenomenon? *Psychological Bulletin, 70,* 474–485.

Locke, E. A., Shaw, K. N., Saari, L. M., & Latham, G. P. (1981). Goal setting and task performance: 1969–1980. *Psychological Bulletin, 90,* 125–152.

Mancuso, J. C. (1977). Current motivational models in the elaboration of personal construct theory. In J. Cole (Ed.), *Nebraska Symposium on Motivation* (Vol. 24). Lincoln: University of Nebraska Press.

Mandler, G. (1975). Consciousness: Respectable, useful, and probably necessary. In R. L. Solso (Ed.), *Information processing and cognition: The Loyola symposium.* Hillsdale, NJ: Erlbaum.

Meichenbaum, D. (1977). *Cognitive behavior modification: An integrative approach.* New York: Plenum.

Miller, G. A., Galanter, E., & Pribram, K. H. (1960). *Plans and the structure of behavior.* New York: Holt, Rinehart & Winston.

Miller, J. G. (1978). *Living systems.* New York: McGraw-Hill.

Miller, N. E., & Dollard, J. (1941). *Social learning and imitation.* New Haven, CT: Yale University Press.

Mischel, W. (1973). Toward a cognitive social learning reconceptualization of personality. *Psychological Review, 80,* 252–283.

Mullen, B., & Suls, J. (1982). "Know thyself": Stressful life changes and the ameliorative effect of private self-consciousness. *Journal of Experimental Social Psychology, 18,* 43–55.

Neisser, U. (1976). *Cognition and reality.* San Francisco: Freeman.

Neumann, P. G. (1975). Visual prototype formation with discontinuous representation of dimensions of variability (Doctoral dissertation, University of Colorado, 1975). *Dissertation Abstracts International, 36,* 4209B. (University Microfilms No. 76-3933)

Newell, A. (1973). Production systems: Models of control structures. In W. G. Chase (Ed.), *Visual information processing.* New York: Academic Press.

Newell, A., & Simon, H. A. (1972). *Human problem solving.* Englewood Cliffs, NJ: Prentice-Hall.

Norman, D. A. (1981). Categorization of action slips. *Psychological Review, 88,* 1–15.

Norman, D. A., & Shallice, T. (1980). *Attention to action: Willed and automatic control of behavior.* Unpublished manuscript, 1980. (Available from Donald A. Norman, Center for Human Information Processing, University of California at San Diego, La Jolla, California 92037.)

Ogata, K. (1970). *Modern control engineering.* Englewood Cliffs, NJ: Prentice-Hall.

Palmer, S. E. (1977). Hierarchical structure in perceptual representation. *Cognitive Psychology, 9,* 441–474.

Pindyck, R. S. (1973). *Optimal planning for economic stabilization. The application of control theory to stabilization policy.* Amsterdam: North-Holland.

Powers, W. T. (1973a). *Behavior: The control of perception.* Chicago: Aldine.

Powers, W. T. (1973b). Feedback: Beyond behaviorism. *Science, 179,* 351–356.

Powers, W. T. (1973b). A systems approach to consciousness. In J. M. Davidson & R. J. Davidson (Eds.), *Psychobiology consciousness.* New York: Plenum.

Price, R. H. (1974). The taxonomic classification of behaviors and situations and the problem of behavior-environment congruence. *Human Relations, 27,* 567–585.

Reason, J. (1979). Actions not as planned: The price of automatization. In G. Underwood & R. Stevens (Eds.), *Aspects of consciousness: I. Psychological issues.* London: Academic Press.

Rogers, T. B., Rogers, P. J., & Kuiper, N. A. (1979). Evidence for the self as a cognitive prototype: The "false alarms effect." *Personality and Social Psychology Bulletin, 5,* 53–56.

Rosch, E. (1978). Principles of categorization. In E. Rosch & B. B. Lloyd (Eds.), *Cognition and categorization.* Hillsdale, NJ: Erlbaum.

Rosch, E., & Mervis, C. (1975). Family resemblances: Studies in the internal structure of categories. *Cognitive Psychology, 7,* 573–605.

Rosch, E., Mervis, C., Gray, W., Johnson, D., a Boyes-Braem, P. (1976). Basic objects in natural categories. *Cognitive Psychology, 8,* 382–439.

Rotter, J. B. (1954). *Social learning and clinical psychology.* New York: Prentice-Hall.

Rubovits, P. C., & Maehr, M. L. (1973). Pygmalion black and white. *Journal of Personality and Social Psychology, 25,* 210–218.

Schank, R. C., & Abelson, R. P. (1977). *Scripts, plans, goals, and understanding.* Hillsdale, NJ: Erlbaum.

Scheier, M. F., & Carver, C. S. (1981). Private and public aspects of the self. In L. Wheeler (Ed.), *Review of personality and social psychology* (Vol. 2). Beverly Hills, CA: Sage.

Scheier, M. F., & Carver, C. S. Cognition, affect, and self-regulation. In M. S. Clark & S. T. Fiske (Eds.), *Affect and cognition: The 17th annual Carnegie symposium on cognition.* Hillsdale, NJ: Erlbaum.

Scheier, M. F., & Carver, C. S. (1982). Self-consciousness, outcome expectancy, and persistence. *Journal of Research in Personality, 16*(4), 409–418.

Scheier, M. F., & Carver, C. S. (1983a). Self-directed attention and the comparison of self with standards. *Journal of Experimental Social Psychology, 19,* 205–222.

Scheier, M. F., & Carver, C. S. (1983). Two sides of the self: One for you and one for me. In J. Suls & A. G. Greenwald (Eds.), *Psychological perspectives on the self* (Vol. 2, pp. 123–157). Hillsdale, NJ: Erlbaum.

Scheier, M. F., Fenigstein, A., & Buss, A. H. (1974). Self-awareness and physical aggression. *Journal of Experimental Social Psychology, 10,* 264–273.

Schwartz, G. E. (1978). Psychobiological foundations of psychotherapy and behavior change. In S. L. Garfield & A. E. Bergin (Eds.), *Handbook of psychotherapy and behavior change* (2nd ed.). New York: Wiley.

Schwartz, G. E. (1979). The brain as a health care system. In G. C. Stone, F. Cohen, & N. E. Adler (Eds.), *Health psychology—A handbook.* San Francisco: Jossey-Bass.

Schwartz, G. E. (1980). *Self-attention and automatic psychophysiological self-regulation: A cybernetic analysis.* Paper presented at the meeting of the American Psychological Association, Montreal, September.

Shallice, T. (1978). The dominant action system: An information-processing approach to consciousness. In K. S. Pope & J. L. Singer (Eds.), *The stream of consciousness: Scientific investigations into the flow of human experience.* New York: Wiley.

Snyder, M., & Swann, W. B., Jr. (1978). Hypothesis-testing in social interaction. *Journal of Personality and Social Psychology, 36,* 1202–1212.

Snyder, M., Tanke, E. D., & Berscheid, E. (1977). Social perception and interpersonal behavior: On the self-fulfilling nature of social stereotypes. *Journal of Personality and Social Psychology, 35,* 656–666.

Srull, T. K., & Wyer, R. S., Jr. (1979). The role of category accessibility in the interpretation of information about persons: Some determinants and implications. *Journal of Personality and Social Psychology, 37,* 1660–1672.

Vallacher, R. R., & Wegner, D. M. (1981). *A theory of action identification.* Monograph in preparation.

von Bertalanffy, L. (1968). *General systems theory.* New York: Braziller.

Weiner, B. (1974). An attributional interpretation of expectancy-value theory. In B. Weiner (Ed.), *Cognitive views of human motivation.* New York: Academic Press.

Wicklund, R. A., &, Duval, S. (1971). Opinion change and performance facilitation as a result of objective self-awareness. *Journal of Experimental Social Psychology, 7,* 319–342.

Wiener, N. (1948). *Cybernetics: Control and communication in the animal and the machine.* Cambridge, MA: M.I.T. Press.

Wilder, D. A., & Allen, V. L. (1978). Group membership and preference for information about others. *Personality and Social Psychology Bulletin, 4,* 106–110.

Word, C. O., Zanna, M. P., & Cooper, J. (1974). The nonverbal mediation of self-fulfilling prophecies in interracial interaction. *Journal of Experimental Social Psychology, 10,* 109–120.

# Ego Depletion: Is the Active Self a Limited Resource?

Roy F. Baumeister, Ellen Bratslavsky, Mark Muraven, and Dianne M. Tice • Case Western Reserve University

Choice, active response, self-regulation, and other volition may all draw on a common inner resource. In Experiment 1, people who forced themselves to eat radishes instead of tempting chocolates subsequently quit faster on unsolvable puzzles than people who had not had to exert self-control over eating. In Experiment 2, making a meaningful personal choice to perform attitude-relevant behavior caused a similar decrement in persistence. In Experiment 3, suppressing emotion led to a subsequent drop in performance of solvable anagrams. In Experiment 4, an initial task requiring high self-regulation made people more passive (i.e., more prone to favor the passive-response option). These results suggest that the self's capacity for active volition is limited and that a range of seemingly different, unrelated acts share a common resource.

Many crucial functions of the self involve volition: making choices and decisions, taking responsibility, initiating and inhibiting behavior, and making plans of action and carrying out those plans. The self exerts control over itself and the external world. To be sure, not all human behavior involves planned or deliberate control by the self, and, in fact, recent work has shown that a great deal of human behavior is influenced by automatic or nonconscious processes (see Bargh, 1994, 1997). But, undoubtedly, some portion involves deliberate, conscious, controlled responses by the self, a portion that may be disproportionately important to the long-term health, happiness, and success of the individual. Even if it were shown that 95% of behavior consisted of lawful, predictable responses to situational stimuli by automatic processes, psychology could not afford to ignore the remaining 5%. As an analogy, cars are probably driven straight ahead at least 95% of the time, but ignoring the other 5% (such as by building cars without steering wheels) would seriously compromise the car's ability to reach most destinations. By the same token, the relatively few active, controlling choices by the self greatly increase its chances of achieving its goals. And, if those few "steering" choices by the self are important, then so is whatever internal structure of the self is responsible for it.

In the present investigation, we were concerned with this controlling aspect of the self. Specifically, we tested hypotheses of ego depletion as a way of learning about the self's executive function. The core idea behind ego depletion is that the self's acts of volition draw on some limited resource, akin to strength or energy; therefore, one act of volition will have a detrimental impact on subsequent volition. We sought to show that a preliminary act of self-control in the form of resisting temptation (Experiment 1) or a preliminary act of choice and responsibility (Experiment 2) would undermine self-regulation in a subsequent, unrelated domain, namely persistence at a difficult and frustrating task. We then sought to verify that the effects of ego depletion are indeed maladaptive and detrimental to performance (Experiment 3). Lastly, we undertook to show that ego depletion resulting from acts of self-control would interfere with subsequent decision making by making people more passive (Experiment 4).

Our research strategy was to look at effects that would carry over across wide gaps of seeming irrelevance. If resisting the temptation to eat chocolate can leave a person prone to give up faster on a difficult, frustrating puzzle, that would suggest that those two very different acts of self-control draw on the same limited resource. And if making a choice about whether to make a speech contrary to one's opinions were to have the same effect, it would suggest that this very same resource is also the one used in general for deliberate, responsible decision making. This resource would presumably be one of the most important features of the self.

## Executive Function

The term *agency* has been used by various writers to refer to the self's exertion of volition, but this term has misleading connotations: An agent is quintessentially someone who acts on behalf of someone else, whereas the phenomenon under discussion involves the self acting autonomously on its own behalf. The term *executive function* has been used in various contexts to refer to this aspect of self and may be preferable (e.g., Epstein, 1973; see Baumeister, 1998). Meanwhile, we use the term *ego depletion* to refer to a temporary reduction in the self's capacity or willingness to engage in volitional action, (including controlling the environment, controlling the self, making choices, and initiating action) caused by prior exercise of volition.

The psychological theory that volition is one of the self's crucial functions can be traced back, at least, to Freud (1923/1961a, 1933/1961b), who described the ego as the part of the psyche that must deal with the reality of the external world by mediating between conflicting inner and outer pressures. In his scheme, for example, a Victorian gentleman standing on the street might feel urged by his id to head for the brothel and by his superego to go to church, but it ultimately is left up to his ego to start his feet walking in one direction or the other. Freud also seems to have believed that the ego needed to use some energy in making such a decision.

Recent research has convincingly illuminated the self's nearly relentless quest for control (Brehm, 1966; Burger, 1989; DeCharms, 1968; Deci & Ryan, 1991, 1995; Langer, 1975; Rothbaum, Weisz, & Snyder, 1982; Taylor, 1983, 1989; White, 1959). It is also known that, when the self feels highly responsible (accountable) for its actions, its cognitive and behavioral processes change (Cooper & Scher, 1994; Linder, Cooper, & Jones, 1967; Tetlock, 1983, 1985; Tetlock & Boettger, 1989). Active responses also have more powerful effects on the self and its subsequent responses than do passive ones (Allison & Messick, 1988; Cioffi & Garner, 1996; Fazio, Sherman, & Herr, 1982). The processes by which the self monitors itself, in order to approach standards of desired behavior, have also been studied (Carver & Scheier, 1981; Duval & Wicklund, 1972; Wegner, 1994; Wegner & Pennebaker, 1993).

Despite these efforts, it is hard to dispute that an understanding of the executive function remains far more vague and rudimentary than other aspects of self-theory. Researchers investigating cognitive representations of self have made enormous progress in recent decades (for reviews, see Banaji & Prentice, 1994; Fiske & Taylor, 1991). Likewise, there has been considerable progress on interpersonal aspects of selfhood (e.g., Leary, 1995; Leary & Kowalski, 1990; Schlenker, 1980; Tesser, 1988). In comparison, understanding of the self's executive function lags behind at a fairly primitive level.

## Ego Depletion

The notion that volition depends on the self's expenditure of some limited resource was anticipated by Freud (1923/1961a, 1933/1961b). He thought the ego needed some form of energy to accomplish its tasks and to resist the energetic promptings of id and superego. Freud was fond of the analogy of horse and rider because, as he said, the rider (analogous to the ego) is generally in charge of steering but is sometimes unable to prevent the horse from going where it wants to go. Freud was rather vague and inconsistent about where the ego's energy came from, but he recognized the conceptual value of postulating that the ego operated on an energy model.

Several modern research findings suggest that some form of energy or strength may be involved in acts of volition, Most of these have been concerned with self-regulation. Indeed, Mischel (1996) has recently proposed that the colloquial notion of will-power be revived for self-regulation theory and a literature review by Baumeister, Heatherton, and Tice (1994) concluded that much evidence about self-regulatory failure fits a model of strength depletion.

An important early study by Glass, Singer, and Friedman (1969) found that participants exposed to unpredictable noise stress subsequently showed decrements in frustration tolerance, as measured by persistence on unsolvable problems.[1] Glass et al. concluded that adapting to unpredictable stress involves a "psychic cost," which implies an expenditure or depletion of some valuable resource. They left the nature of this resource to future research, which has not made much further progress.

Additional evidence for a strength model was provided by Muraven, Tice, and Baumeister (1998), whose research strategy influenced the present investigation. Muraven et al. sought to show that consecutive exertions of self-regulation were characterized by deteriorating performance, even though the exertions involved seemingly unrelated spheres. In one study, they showed that trying not to think about a white bear (a thought-control task borrowed from Wegner, 1989; Wegner, Schneider, Carter, & White, 1987) caused people to give up more quickly on a subsequent anagram task. In another study, an affect-regulation exercise caused subsequent decrements in endurance at squeezing a handgrip. These findings suggest that exertions of self-control do carry a psychic cost and deplete some scarce resource.

To integrate these scattered findings and implications, we suggest the following. One important part of the self is a limited resource that is used for all acts of volition, such as controlled (as opposed to automatic) processing, active (as opposed to passive) choice, initiating behavior, and overriding responses. Because much of self-regulation involves resisting temptation and, hence, overriding motivated responses, this self-resource must be able to affect behavior in the same fashion that motivation does. Motivations can be strong or weak, and stronger impulses are presumably more difficult to restrain; therefore, the executive function of the self presumably also operates in a strong or weak fashion, which implies that it has a dimension of strength. An exertion of this strength in self-control draws on this strength and temporarily exhausts it (Muraven et al., 1998), but it also presumably recovers after a period of rest. Other acts of volition should have similar effects, which is the hypothesis of the present investigation.

## Experiment 1

Experiment 1 provided evidence for ego depletion by examining consecutive acts of self-control. The study was originally designed to test competing hypotheses about the nature of self-control, also known as self-regulation. Clearly, the control over self is one of the most important and adaptive applications of its executive function. Research on monitoring processes and feedback loops has illuminated the cognitive structure that processes relevant information (e.g., Carver & Scheier, 1981; Wegner, 1994), but the actual process by which an organism alters its own responses or subjective states is far less well understood. At least three different models of the nature of self-regulation can be proposed. Moreover these three models make quite different predictions about the effectiveness of self-control immediately after an exertion of self-control in some unrelated sphere. Experiment 1 provided a test of these three competing predictions by requiring participants to engage in two seemingly unrelated acts of self-control.

One model views self-regulation as essentially a skill. In this model, people gradually develop the skill to regulate themselves over long periods of time. On any given occasion, however, skill remains roughly constant across repeated trials, except for small and gradual learning effects, so there should be little or no change in effectiveness of self-control on two successive exertions within a short time.

---

[1]These researchers also showed that an illusion of controllability eliminated this effect. From our perspective, this implies that part of the stress involves the threat or anticipation of continued aversive stimulation, which the illusion of controllability dispelled. In any case, it is plausible that the psychic cost was paid in terms of affect regulation, that is, making oneself submit and accept the aversive, unpredictable stimulation.

Another model portrays self-regulation as essentially a knowledge structure. In this view, self-control operates like a master schema that makes use of information about how to alter one's own responses or states. On the basis of this model, an initial act of self-regulation should prime the schema, thereby facilitating subsequent self-control. Another version of this view would be that the self-regulatory system is normally in a standby or depowered mode until it is pressed into action by one act of self-control. Once activated, the system would remain in operation ( "on") for a time, making further acts of self-control easier.

A third model states that self-regulation resembles energy In this view, acts of self-regulation involve some kind of exertion that expends energy, therefore depleting the supply available. Unless the supply is very large, initial acts of self-regulation should deplete it, thereby impairing subsequent self-control.

Thus, the three models respectively predict either no change, an increase, or a decrease in effectiveness of self-control following an initial act of self-control. Other models are possible, such as the possibility that self-regulation involves a collection of domain-specific but unrelated knowledge structures. An initial act of self-control should prime and therefore facilitate self-control in the same sphere but produce no change in other, unrelated spheres. Still, these three models provide sufficiently conflicting predictions about the sequence of unrelated acts of self-control to make it worth conducting an initial test.

In the present research, we used impulse control which, to many people, is the classic or paradigmatic form of self-control. More precisely, we manipulated self-control by instructing some hungry individuals to eat only radishes while they were faced with the tempting sight and aroma of chocolate. Thus, they had to resist the temptation to perform one action while making themselves perform a similar, but much less desirable, action. We then sought to measure self-control in an unrelated sphere by persistence at a frustrating puzzle-solving task. A series of frustrating failures may often make people want to stop doing the task, so self-control is needed to force oneself to continue working.

If resisting temptation depends on skill, then this skill would predict no change in persistence under frustration. If resisting temptation involves activating a knowledge structure or master

schema,, then priming this schema should facilitate self-control, and people should persist longer on the puzzles. Finally, if resisting temptation uses some kind of strength or energy, then this will be depleted afterward, decreasing subsequent persistence.

## Method

### PARTICIPANTS

Data were collected in individual sessions from 67 introductory psychology students (31 male, 36 female) who received course credit for taking part.

### PROCEDURE

Participants signed up for a study on taste perception. Each participant was contacted to schedule an individual session. At that time, the experimenter requested the participant to skip one meal before the experiment and make sure not to have eaten anything for at least 3 hours.

The laboratory room was carefully set up before participants in the food conditions arrived. Chocolate chip cookies were baked in the room in a small oven and, as a result, the laboratory was filled with the delicious aroma of fresh chocolate and baking. Two foods were displayed on the table at which the participant was seated. One display consisted of a stack of chocolate chip cookies, augmented by some chocolate candies. The other consisted of a bowl of red and white radishes.

The experimenter provided an overview of the procedures, secured an informed consent, and then elaborated the cover story. She explained that chocolates and radishes had been selected for the taste perception study because they were highly distinctive foods familiar to most people. She said that there would be a follow-up measure for sensation memory the next day, so she asked the participant to agree not to eat any chocolates or radishes (other than in the experiment) for 24 hours after the session.

Participants in the chocolate and radish conditions were then asked to take about 5 minutes to taste the assigned food while the experimenter was out of the room. In the radish condition, the experimenter asked the participant to eat at least two or three radishes and, in the chocolate condition, the participant was asked to eat at least two or three cookies or a handful of the small candies. Participants were reminded to eat only the food that had been assigned to them. The experimenter left the room and surreptitiously observed the participant through a one-way mirror recording the amount of food eaten and verifying that the participant ate only the assigned food. (To minimize self-aware-ness, the mirror was almost completely covered with a curtain.)

After about 5 minutes, the experimenter returned and asked the participant to fill out two question-naires. One was the Brief Mood Introspection Scale (BMI; Mayer & Gaschke, 1988), and the other was the Restraint Scale (Herman & Polivy, 1975). Then the experimenter said that it was nec-essary to wait at least 15 minutes to allow the sen-sory memory of the food to fade. During that time, she said, the participant would be asked to pro-vide some preliminary data that would help the researchers learn whether college students differed from high school students in their problem-solv-ing ability. The experimenter said that the partici-pant would therefore be asked to work on a test of problem solving. The problem solving was pre-sented as if it were unrelated to the eating, but in fact it constituted the main dependent measure.

There was also a no-food control condition. Participants assigned to this condition skipped the food part of the experiment and went directly to the problem-solving part.

The problem-solving task was adapted from a task used by Glass et al. (1969), adapted from Feather (1961). The puzzle requires the person to trace a geometric figure without retracing any lines and without lifting his or her pencil from the pa-per. Multiple slips of paper were provided for each figure, so the person could try over and over. Each participant was initially given several practice fig-ures to learn how the puzzles worked and how to solve them, with the experimenter present to an-swer any questions. After the practice period, the experimenter gave the participant the two main test figures with the instructions:

You can take as much time and as many trials as you want. You will not be judged on the number of trials or the time you will take. You will be judged on whether or not you finish tracing the figure. If you wish to stop before you finish [i.e., solve the puzzle], ring the bell on the table.

Unbeknownst to the participant, both these test figures had been prepared so as to be impossible to solve.

The experimenter then left the room and timed how long the participant worked on the task be-fore giving up (signified by ringing the bell). Fol-lowing an a priori decision, 30 minites was set as the maximum time; the 4 participants who were still working after 30 minutes were stopped by the experimenter at that point. For the rest, when the experimenter heard the bell, she reentered the room and administered a manipulation check question-naire. When the participants finished, the experi-menter debriefed, thanked, and dismissed them.

## Results

### MANIPULATION CHECK

The experimenter surreptitiously observed all par-ticipants during the eating phase to ascertain that they ate the stipulated food and avoided the other. All participants complied with the instructions. In particular none of the participants in the radish condition violated the rule against eating choco-lates. Several of them did exhibit clear interest in the chocolates, to the point of looking longingly at the chocolate display and in a few cases even picking up the cookies to sniff at them. But no participant actually bit into the wrong food.

The difficulty of the eating task was assessed on the final questionnaire. Participants in the rad-ish condition said that they forced themselves in an effortful fashion to eat the assigned food more than participants in the chocolate condition, $F(1, 44) = 16.10, p < .001$. They also rated resisting the nonassigned food as marginally significantly more difficult, $F(1, 44) = 3.41, p < .07$. During the de-briefing, many participants in the radish condition spontaneously mentioned the difficulty of resist-ing the temptation to eat the chocolates.

### PERSISTENCE

The main dependent measure was the amount of time participants spent on the unsolvable puzzles. A one-way analysis of variance (ANOVA) indi-cated significant variation among the three condi-tions, $F(2, 64) = 26.88, p < .001$. The means are presented in Table 16.1. Paired comparisons among the groups indicated that participants in the radish condition quit sooner on the frustrating task than did participants in either the chocolate condition, $t(44) = 6.03, p < .001$, or the no-food (control) condition, $t(44) = 6.88, p < .001$. The chocolate

**TABLE 16.1. Persistence on Unsolvable Puzzles (Experiment 1)**

| Condition | Time (min) | Attempts |
|---|---|---|
| Radish | 8.35 | 19.40 |
| Chocolate | 18.90 | 34.29 |
| No food control | 20.86 | 32.81 |

*Note.* Standard deviations for Column 1, top to bottom, are 4.67, 6.86, and 7.30. For Column 2, SDs = 8.12, 20.16, and 13.38.

condition did not differ from the no-food control condition, $t < 1$, *ns.*

It is conceivable that the time measure was affected by something other than persistence, such as speed. That is, the interpretation would be altered if the participants in the radish condition tried just as many times as those in the chocolate condition and merely did so much faster. Hence, we also analyzed the number of attempts that participants made before giving up. A one-way ANOVA on these tallies again yielded significant variation among the three conditions, $F(2, 64) = 7.61$, $p = .001$. The pattern of results was essentially the same as with duration of persistence, as can be seen in Table 16.1. Paired comparisons again showed that participants in the radish condition gave up earlier than participants in the other two conditions, which did not differ from each other.[2]

## MOODS

The mood measure contains two subscales, and we conducted a one-way ANOVA on each, using only the radish and chocolate conditions (because this measure was not administered in the no-food control condition). The two conditions did not differ in valence (i.e., pleasant vs. unpleasant) of mood, $F(1, 44) = 2.62$, *ns*, nor in arousal, $F < 1$, *ns.*

## DIETING

The analyses on persistence were repeated using dieting status (from the Restraint Scale) as an independent variable. Dieting status did not show either a main effect or an interaction with condition on either the duration of persistence or the number of attempts.

## FATIGUE AND DESIRE TO QUIT

The final questionnaire provided some additional evidence beyond the manipulation checks. One item asked the participant how tired he or she felt after the tracing task. An ANOVA yielded significant variation among the conditions, $F(2, 64) = 5.74$, $p < .01$. Participants in the radish condition were more tired ($M = 17.96$) than those in the chocolate ($M = 11.85$) or no-food ($M = 12.29$) conditions (the latter two did not differ). Participants in the radish condition also reported that their fatigue level had changed more toward increased tiredness ($M = 6.28$) than participants in either the chocolate ($M = -0.90$) or no-food ($M = 1.76$) conditions, $F(2, 64) = 5.13$, $p < .01$.

Participants in the radish condition reported that they had felt less strong a desire to stop working on the tracing task than had participants in the other two conditions, $F(2, 64) = 4.71$, $p < .01$. Yet they also reported forcing themselves to work on the tracing task more than participants in the other two conditions, $F(2, 64) = 3.20$, $p < .05$. The latter may have been an attempt to justify their relatively rapid quitting on that task. The former may indicate that they quit as soon as they felt the urge to do so, in contrast to the chocolate and no-food participants who made themselves continue for a while after they first felt like quitting.

## Discussion

These results provide initial support for the hypothesis of ego depletion. Resisting temptation seems to have produced a psychic cost, in the sense that afterward participants were more inclined to give up easily in the face of frustration. It was not that eating chocolate improved performance. Rather, wanting chocolate but eating radishes instead, especially under circumstances in which it would seemingly be easy and safe to snitch some chocolates, seems to have consumed some resource and therefore left people less able to persist at the puzzles.

Earlier, we proposed three rival models of the nature of self-regulation. These results fit a strength model better than a skill or schema model. If self-

---

[2]As this article went to press, we were notified that this experiment had been independently replicated by Timothy J. Howe, of Cole Junior High School in East Greenwich, Rhode Island, for his science fair project. His results conformed almost exactly to ours, with the exception that mean persistence in the chocolate condition was slightly (but not significantly) higher than in the control condition. These converging results strengthen confidence in the present findings.

regulation were essentially a knowledge structure, then an initial act of self-regulation should have primed the schema, thereby facilitating subsequent self-regulation. The present results were directly opposite to that prediction. A skill model would predict no change across consecutive acts of self-regulation, but we did find significant change. In contrast, a strength or energy model predicted that some vital resource would be depleted by an initial act of self-regulation, leading to subsequent decrements, which corresponds to what we found.

It is noteworthy that the depletion manipulation in this study required both resisting one impulse (to eat chocolate) and making oneself perform an undesired act (eating radishes). Both may have contributed to ego depletion. Still, the two are not independent. Based on a priori assumptions and comments made by participants during the debriefing, it seems likely that people would have found it easier to make themselves eat the radishes if they were not simultaneously struggling with resisting the more tempting chocolates.

Combined with other evidence (especially Muraven et al., 1998), therefore, it seems reasonable to infer that self-regulation draws on some limited resource akin to strength or energy and that this resource may be common for many forms of self-regulation. In Experiment 1, we found that an initial act of resisting temptation (i.e., an act of impulse control) impaired the subsequent persistence at a spatial puzzle task. Muraven et al. found that an act of affect regulation (i.e., trying either to stifle or amplify one's emotional response) lowered subsequent stamina on a physical task, that an initial act of thought suppression reduced persistence at unsolvable anagrams, and that thought suppression impaired the subsequent ability to hide one's emotions. These various carryovers between thought control, emotion control, impulse control, and task performance indicate that these four main spheres of self-regulation all share the same resource. Therefore, the question for Experiment 2 was whether that same resource would also be involved in other acts of choice and volition beyond self-regulation.

# Experiment 2

Experiment 2 addressed the question of whether the same resource that was depleted by not eating chocolate (in Experiment 1) would be depleted by an act of choice. For this, we used one of social psychology's classic manipulations: High choice versus low choice to engage in counterattitudinal behavior. Festinger and Carlsmith (1959) showed that people change their attitudes to make them consistent with behavior when they have been induced to act in ways contrary to their attitudes. Linder et al. (1967) showed that this effect occurs only when people have been led to see their own (counterattitudinal) behavior as freely chosen; many studies have replicated these effects.

Our interest was not in the attitudinal consequences of counterattitudinal behavior, however. Rather, our hypothesis was that the act of making the choice to engage in counterattitudinal behavior would involve the self and deplete its volitional resource. As an index of this ego depletion, we measured frustration tolerance using the same task that we used in Experiment 1, namely persistence at unsolvable puzzles. The puzzles, of course, had nothing to do with our independent variable (next year's tuition), so, in all direct ways, the two behaviors were irrelevant.

Dissonance research has provided some evidence consistent with the view that making a choice involves an exertion by the self. The original article by Linder et al. (1967) reported that participants in the high-choice (free-decision, low-incentive) condition spent about half a minute deciding whether to engage in the counterattitudinal behavior, even though all consented to do it, whereas low-choice participants did not spend any such time. This is consistent with the view that the self was engaging in some effortful activity during the choice exercise. More generally, Cooper and Scher (1994; see also Cooper & Fazio, 1984; Scher & Cooper, 1989) concluded that personal responsibility for aversive consequences is the core cause of cognitive dissonance. This conclusion puts emphasis on the taking or accepting of personal responsibility for one's actions—thus an active response by the self.

The design of Experiment 2 thus involved having people make a counterattitudinal speech (favoring a large tuition increase, to which most students were opposed) under high- or low-choice conditions. Because our focus was on the active choice making by the self, we also included a condition in which people chose to make a proattitudinal speech opposing the increase. Choosing to engage in a proattitudinal behavior should not cause dissonance (see Cooper & Scher,

1994; Cooper & Fazio, 1984; Festinger, 1957; Linder et al., 1967), but it should still deplete the self to some degree because it still involves an act of choice and taking responsibility. We did not have any basis for predicting whether choosing to engage in counterattitudinal behavior would deplete the self more than choosing to engage in proattitudinal behavior but we expected that there should still be some depletion.

## Method

### PARTICIPANTS

Participants were 39 undergraduate psychology students (25 male, 14 female), who participated in individual sessions. They were randomly assigned among four experimental treatment conditions: counterattitudinal choice, counterattitudinal no choice, proattitudinal choice, and no speech (control). To ensure that the issue was personally relevant to all participants, we excluded 8 additional potential participants who were either graduating seniors or who were on full scholarship because preliminary testing revealed that next year's tuition did not matter to students in these categories.

### PROCEDURE

The experimenter greeted each participant and explained that the purpose of the study was to see how people respond to persuasion. They were told that they would be making stimuli that would be played to other people to alter their attitudes. In particular they would be making an audiotape recording of a persuasive speech regarding projected tuition increases for the following academic year. The topic of tuition raises was selected on the basis of a pilot test: A survey had found that students rated the tuition increase as the most important issue to them.

The experimenter said that all participants would record speeches that had been prepared in advance. The importance of the tuition increase issue was highlighted. The experimenter also said that the university's Board of Trustees had agreed to listen to the speeches to see how much impact the messages would have on their decisions about raising tuition.

The experimenter showed the participant two folders, labeled *prostuition raise* and *anti-tuition*

**TABLE 16.2. Persistence on Unsolvable Puzzles (Experiment 2)**

| Condition | Time (min) | Attempts |
|---|---|---|
| Counterattitudinal speech | | |
| High choice | 14.30 | 26.10 |
| No choice | 23.11 | 42.44 |
| Proattitudinal speech | | |
| High choice | 13.80 | 24.70 |
| No speech control | 25.30 | 35.50 |

*Note.* Standard deviations (SP5) for Column 1, top to bottom, are 6.91, 7.08, 6.49, and 5.06. For Column 2, SDs = 14.83, 22.26, 7.13, and 9.14.

*raise.* Participants in the no-choice (counterattitudinal) condition were told that they had been assigned to make the pro-tuition raise speech. The experimenter said that the researchers already had enough people making the speech against the tuition raise, so it would not be possible to give the participant a choice as to which speech to make. In contrast, participants in the high-choice conditions were told that the decision of which speech to make was entirely up to them. The experimenter explained that, because there were already enough participants in one of the groups, it would help the study a great deal if they chose to read one folder rather than the other. The experimenter then again stressed that the final decision would remain entirely up to the participant. All participants agreed to make the speech that they had been assigned.

Participants in the no-speech control condition did not do this part of the experiment. The issue of tuition increase was not raised with them.

At this point, all participants completed the same mood measure used in Experiment 1. The experimenter then began explaining the task for the second part of the experiment. She said there was some evidence of a link between problem-solving abilities and persuasiveness. Accordingly, the next part of the experiment would contain a measure of problem-solving ability. For participants in the speech-making conditions, the experimenter said that the problem-solving task would precede the recording of the speech.

The problem-solving task was precisely the same one used in Experiment 1, involving tracing geometric figures without retracing lines or lifting the pen from the paper. As in Experiment 1, the participant's persistence at the frustrating puzzles was the main dependent measure. After signaling the experimenter that they wished to stop working on the task, participants completed a brief questionnaire that included manipulation checks. They were then completely debriefed, thanked, and sent home.

## Results

### MANIPULATION CHECK

The final questionnaire asked participants (except in the control condition) how much they felt that which speech they chose to make was up to them. A one-way ANOVA confirmed that there was significant variation among the conditions, $F(2, 31) = 15.46$, $p < .001$. Participants in the no-choice condition indicated that it was not up to them which speech to make ($M = 27.10$), whereas participants in the counterattitudinal– ($M = 10.21$) and proattitudinal–choice conditions ($M = 6.60$) both indicated high degrees of choice. Another item asked how much the participant considered reading an alternative to the speech suggested by the experimenter. On this too there was significant variation among the three conditions, $F(2, 31) = 11.53$, $p < .001$, indicating that high-choice participants considered the alternative much more than participants in the no-choice condition.

### PERSISTENCE

The main dependent measure was the duration of persistence on the unsolvable puzzles. The results are presented in Table 16.2. A one-way ANOVA on persistence times indicated that there was significant variation among conditions, $F(3, 35) = 8.42$, $p < .001$. Paired comparisons confirmed that the counterattitudinal– and the proattitudinal–choice conditions each differed significantly from both the control and the counterattitudinal–no-choice conditions. Perhaps surprisingly, the two choice conditions did not differ significantly from each other.

Similar results were found using the number of attempts, rather than time, as the dependent measure of persistence. The ANOVA indicated significant variation among the four conditions, $F(3, 35) = 3.24$, $p < .05$. The same pattern of paired cell differences was found: Both conditions involving high choice led to a reduction in persistence, as compared with the no-speech control condition and the no-choice counterattitudinal speech condition.[3]

### MOOD STATE

One-way ANOVAs were conducted on each of the two subscales of the BMI Scale. There was no evidence of significant variation among the four conditions in reported valence of mood (i.e., pleasant vs. unpleasant), $F(3, 35) < 1$, *ns*. There was also no evidence of variation in arousal, $F(3, 35) < 1$, *ns*. These results suggest that the differences in persistence were not due to differential moods engendered by the manipulations.

## Discussion

The results supported the ego depletion hypothesis and suggest that acts of choice draw on the same limited resource used for self-control. Participants who agreed to make a counterattitudinal speech under high choice showed a subsequent drop in their persistence on a difficult, frustrating task, as compared with participants who expected to make the same speech under low choice (and as compared with no-speech control participants). Thus, taking responsibility for a counterattitudinal behavior seems to have consumed a resource of the self, leaving it with less of that resource available to prolong persistence at the unsolvable puzzles.

Of particular further interest was the high-choice proattitudinal behavior condition. These people should not have experienced any dissonance, yet they showed significant reductions in persistence on unsolvable problems. Dissonance is marked by an aversive arousal state (Cooper, Zanna, & Taves, 1978; Zanna & Cooper, 1974; Zanna, Higgins, & Taves, 1976), but this arousal or negative affect apparently is not what is responsible for ego depletion; we found almost identical evidence of ego depletion among people who chose to make the nondissonant, proattitudinal speech.

---

[3]The differences between the control condition and the two high-choice conditions failed to reach significance if we used the error term from the ANOVA as the pooled variance estimate. The proattitudinal–choice condition did differ from the control condition in a standard *t* test using only the variance in those two cells, $t(18) = 2.94$, $p < .01$. The counterattitudinal–choice condition differed marginally from the no-speech control using this latter method, $t(18) = 1.71$, $p = .105$. The high variance in the counterattitudinal–no-choice condition also entailed that it differed only marginally from the counterattitudina–choice condition if the actual variance in those cells was used, rather than the error term, $t(17) = 1.90$, $p = .07$.

Thus, it is not the counterattitudinal behavior that depletes the self. Indeed, people who expected to perform the counterattitudinal behavior under low choice persisted just as long as no-speech control participants. Making a speech contrary to one's beliefs does not necessarily deplete the self in any way that our measure detected. Meanwhile, making a speech that supports one's beliefs did deplete the self, provided that the person made the deliberate, free decision to do so.

The implication is that it is the exercise of choice, regardless of the behavior, that depletes the self. Whatever motivational, affective, or volitional resource is needed to force oneself to keep trying in the face of discouraging failure apparently is the same resource that is used to make responsible decisions about one's own behavior and is fairly limited.

## Experiment 3

Experiments 1 and 2 suggested that self-regulation is weakened by prior exercise of volition, either in the form of resisting temptation (Experiment 1) or making a responsible choice (Experiment 2). In both studies, the dependent variable involved persistence on unsolvable problems. It is reasonable to treat such persistence as a challenge for self-regulation because people undoubtedly would feel inclined to give up when their efforts are met with frustration and discouraging failure. Overcoming that impulse (in order to persist) would require an act of self-control.

An alternative view, however, might suggest that it is adaptive to give up early on unsolvable problems. Persistence is, after all, only adaptive and productive when it leads to eventual success. Squandering time and effort on a lost cause is thus wasteful, and optimal self-management would involve avoiding such waste (e.g., McFarlin, 1985). It is true that such an argument would require one to assume that our participants actually recognized the task as unsolvable, although there was no sign that they did. In fact, most participants expressed surprise during the debriefing when they were told that the puzzles were in fact unsolvable. Yet, for us to contend that ego depletion has a negative effect, it seemed necessary to show some decrement in task performance. Unsolvable puzzles cannot show such a decrement because no amount of persistence leads to success. Study 3, therefore,

was designed to show that ego depletion can impair performance on solvable tasks.

Because broad conclusions about ego depletion are difficult to draw from any single procedure, it seemed desirable to use very different procedures for Study 3. Accordingly, the manipulation of ego depletion involved affect regulation (i.e., controlling one's emotions). Affect regulation is one important sphere of self-regulation (e.g., Baumeister et al., 1994). In this study, some participants were asked to watch an emotionally evocative videotape and stifle any emotional reaction they might have. To ensure that the effects were due to self-regulation, rather than the particular emotional response, we used both positive (humorous) and negative (sad and distressing) stimuli.

For the measure of task performance, we selected anagram solving. This widely used performance measure has elements of both skill and effort. More to the point, we suspected that success at anagrams would require some degree of self-regulation. One must keep breaking and altering the tentative combinations of letters one has formed and must make oneself keep trying despite multiple initial failures. In the latter respect, anagram solving resembles the dependent measure used in the first two studies, except that persistence can actually help lead to success. The prediction was that participants who had tried to control their emotional responses to the videotape would suffer from ego depletion and, as a result, would perform more poorly at anagrams.

### Method

#### PARTICIPANTS

Participants were 30 (11 male and 19 female) undergraduates who took part in connection with introductory psychology requirements. They participated in individual sessions and were randomly assigned among the conditions.

#### PROCEDURE

The experimenter explained that the purpose of the study was to see which personality traits would make people more responsive to experiencing emotions. They were told that the first part of the procedure would involve watching a movie.

In the suppress-emotion condition, participants were instructed to try not to show or feel any emotions during the movie. The experimenter said that the participant would be videotaped while watching the film, so it was essential to try to conceal and suppress any emotional reaction. Meanwhile, participants in the no-regulation condition were instructed to let their emotions flow while watching the movie, without any attempt to hide or deny these feelings. They were also told that their reactions would be videotaped.

Following these instructions, each participant saw a 10-minute videotape. Half of the participants in each condition saw a humorous video featuring the comedian Robin Williams. The others saw an excerpt from the film *Terms of Endearment*, portraying a young mother dying from cancer. At the end of the video clip, participants completed the BMI Scale.

Then the experimenter extended the cover story to say that they would have to wait at least 10 minutes after the film to allow their sensory memory of the movie to fade. During that time, they were asked to help the experimenter collect some preliminary data for future research by completing an anagram task. Participants received 13 sets of letters that they were to unscramble to make English words during a 6-minute period. The participant was left alone to do this task. After 6 minutes, the experimenter returned and administered a postexperimental questionnaire. After the participant completed that, he or she was debriefed and thanked.

## Results

### MANIPULATION CHECK

The final questionnaire asked participants to rate how much effort it had required to comply with the instructions for watching the video clip. Participants in the suppress-emotion condition reported that they found it required much more effort ($M = 13.88$) than participants in the no-regulation condition ($M = 5.64$), $t(28) = 2.88$, $p < .01$. Similar effects were found on an item asking people how difficult it was to follow the instructions while following the video, $t(28) = 4.95$, $p < .001$, and on an item asking how much they had to concentrate in complying with the instructions, $t(28) = 5.42$, $p < .001$. These findings confirm that it required a greater exertion to suppress one's emotional response than to let it go.

In addition, the films were perceived quite dif-

**TABLE 16.3. Success at Solvable Puzzles (Experiment 3)**

| Condition | Solved | SD |
|---|---|---|
| Suppress | 4.94 | 2.59 |
| No regulation | 7.29 | 3.52 |

ferently. On the item asking participants to rate the movie on a scale ranging from 1 (*sad*) to 25 (*funny*), participants rated the comedy video as much funnier ($M = 21.94$) than the sad video clip ($M = 4.54$), $t(29) = 4.62$, $p < .001$. There were no differences as a function of ego depiction condition in how the movie was perceived.

### ANAGRAM PERFORMANCE

The main dependent variable was performance on the anagram task. Table 16.3 shows the results. Participants in the suppress-emotion condition performed significantly worse than participants in the no-regulation condition in terms of the number of anagrams correctly solved, $t(28) = 2.12$, $p < .05$. There was no effect for type of movie.

### MOOD

There was no difference in either mood valence or arousal between participants who tried to suppress their emotional reactions and those who let their emotions go. Hence, any differences in performance between these conditions should not be attributed to differential mood or arousal responses.

## Discussion

The results confirm the view that ego depletion can be detrimental to subsequent performance. The alternative view, that Experiments 1 and 2 showed improved self-regulation because it is adaptive to give up early on unsolvable tasks, cannot seemingly account for the results of Experiment 3. In this study, an act of self-regulation—stifling one's emotional response to a funny or sad video clip—was followed by poorer performance at solving anagrams. Hence, it seems appropriate to suggest that some valuable resource of the self was actually depleted by the initial act of volition, as opposed to merely suggesting that initial acts of volition alter subsequent decision making.

## Experiment 4

The first three experiments provided support for the hypothesis of ego depletion. Experiment 4 was designed to provide converging evidence using quite different procedures. Also, Experiment 4 was designed to complement Experiment 2 by reversing the direction of influence: Experiment 2 showed that an initial act of responsible decision making could undermine subsequent self-regulation, whereas Experiment 4 was designed to show that an initial act of self-regulation could undermine subsequent decision making.

Experiment 4 used procedures that contrasted active and passive responding. In many situations, people face a choice between one course of action that requires an active response and another course that will occur automatically if the person does nothing (also called a *default option*). In an important study, Brockner, Shaw, and Rubin (1979) measured persistence in a futile endeavor under two contrasting situations. In one, the person had to make a positive move to continue, but the procedure would stop automatically if he or she did nothing (i.e., confirming was active and quitting was passive). The other situation was the reverse, in which a positive move was required to terminate, whereas continuing was automatic unless the person signaled to quit. Brockner et al. found greater persistence when persistence was passive than when it was active.

In our view, the findings of Brockner et al. (1979) may reflect a broader pattern that can be called a *passive-option effect*. The passive-option effect can be defined by saying that, in any choice situation, the likelihood of any option being chosen is increased if choosing involves a passive rather than active response. Sales organizations such as music, book, and film clubs, for example, find that their sales are higher if they can make the customer's purchasing response passive rather than active; they prefer to operate on the basis that each month's selection will automatically be mailed to the customer and billed unless the customer actively refuses it.

For present purposes, the passive-option effect is an important possible consequence of the limited resources that the self has for volitional response. Our assumption is that active responding requires the self to expend some of its resources, whereas passive responses do not. The notion that the self is more involved and implicated by active

responding than by passive responding helps explain evidence that active responses leave more lasting behavioral consequences. For example, Cioffi and Garner (1996) showed that people were more likely to follow through when they had actively than passively volunteered for the same act.

The passive-option effect thus provides a valuable forum for examining ego depletion. Active responses differ from passive ones in that they require the expenditure of limited resources. If the self's resources have already been exhausted (i.e., under ego depletion), the self should therefore be all the more inclined to favor the passive option.

To forestall confusion, we hasten to point out that the term *choice* can be used in two different ways, so a passive option may or may not be understood as involving a choice, depending on which meaning is used. Passive choice is a choice in the sense that the situation presents the person with multiple options, the outcome of which is contingent on the person's behavior (or nonbehavior). It is, however, not a choice in the volitional sense, because the person may not perform an intrapsychic act of volition. For example, a married couple who sleeps together on a given night may be said to have made a choice that night insofar as they could, in principle, have opted to sleep alone or with other sleeping partners. Most likely, though, they did not go through an active-choice process that evening, but rather they simply did what they always did. The essence of passive options, in our understanding, is that the person does not engage in an inner process of choosing or deciding, even though alternative options are available. Passive choices, therefore, should not deplete the self's resources.

In Experiment 4, we showed participants a very boring movie and gave them a temptation to stop watching it. For some participants, quitting was passive, whereas, for others, quitting required an active response. The dependent variable was how long people persisted at the movie. According to the passive-option effect, they should persist longer when persisting was passive than when persisting required active responses. We predicted that ego depletion would intensify this pattern.

Prior ego depletion was manipulated by altering the instructions for a task in a way that varied in how much the person had to regulate his or her responses. The basic task involved crossing out all instances of the letter *e* in a text. People can learn to do this easily and quickly; they become accustomed to scanning for every *e* and then crossing it out. To raise the self-regulatory difficulty, we told people not to cross out the letter *e* if any of several other criteria were met, such as if there was another vowel adjacent to the *e* or one letter removed. These people would, presumably, then scan for each *e* but would have to override the response of crossing it out whenever any of those criteria were met. Their responses thus had to be regulated according to multiple rules, unlike the others who could simply respond every time they found an *e*. Our assumption was that consulting the complex decision rules and overriding the simple response would deplete the ego, unlike the simpler version of the task.

## Method

### PARTICIPANTS

Eighty-four undergraduate students (47 males, 37 females) participated for partial fulfillment of a course requirement. Each individual testing session lasted about 30 minutes.

### PROCEDURE

The experimenter told participants that the experiment was designed to look at "whether personality influences how people perceive movies." After signing an informed consent form, participants completed several personality questionnaires to help maintain the cover story. (Except for an item measuring tiredness, the questionnaires are not relevant to the current study and will not be discussed further.)

Participants then completed the regulatory-depletion task. Each was given a typewritten sheet of paper with meaningless text on it (a page from an advanced statistics book with a highly technical style) and told to cross off all instances of the letter *e*. For the participants assigned to the ego-depletion condition, the task was made quite difficult, requiring them to consult multiple rules and monitor their decisions carefully. They were told that they should only cross off an *e* if it was not adjacent to another vowel or one extra letter away from another vowel (thus, one would not cross off the *e* in *vowel*). Also, the photocopy of the stimulus page had been lightened, making it relatively difficult to read, thus further requiring close attention. In contrast, participants in the no-deple-

tion condition were given an easily legible photocopy with good contrast and resolution and were told to cross off every single *e* with no further rules or stipulations.

The experimenter then told participants that they were going to watch two movies and that, after each movie, they would answer a few simple questions about it. He explained that the videos were rather long and the participant did not have time to watch the complete movie. It would be up to the participant when to stop. The participant was, however, cautioned to "watch the video long enough so that you can understand what happened and answer a few questions about the video."

The experimenter next gave the participant a small box with a button attached. Participants were told to ring the buzzer when they were done watching the movie, at which point the experimenter would reenter the room and give them a few questions to answer. Half of the participants were told to press the button down when they wanted to stop (active quit condition). The others were told to hold down the button as long as they wanted to watch more of the movie; releasing the button would cause the movie to stop (passive quit condition). The buzzer was wired to signal the experimenter when the button was pressed (active quit condition) or released (passive quit condition). In other words, half of the participants stopped the movie by pressing down on a button, whereas the other half of the participants stopped the movie by taking their hand off of a button.

Participants were then shown a film that had been deliberately made to be dull and boring. The entire film consisted of an unchanging scene of a blank white wall with a table and a computer junction box in the foreground. The movie is just a picture of a wall and nothing ever happens, although participants were unaware of this fact and were motivated to keep watching to make sure that nothing did actually occur. Participants were told that after they stopped watching this video, they would see another video of highlights from a popular, humorous television program (*Saturday Night Live*). Participants therefore believed that after they finished watching the aversive, boring picture of a wall they would get to watch a pleasant, amusing video. This was done to give participants an added incentive to stop watching the boring video and also to remove the possibility that stopping the movie would immediately allow them to leave the experiment; although, to be sure, terminating the first movie would in fact bring them closer to their presumed goal of completing the experiment and being able to leave.[4]

The experimenter left the room, surreptitiously timing how long participants watched the video. When participants rang the buzzer (either by pressing or releasing the button, depending on the condition), the experimenter noted the time and reentered the room. At this point, participants completed a brief questionnaire about their thoughts while watching the movie and their level of tiredness. Participants were then completely debriefed, thanked, and sent home.

## Results

### MANIPULATION CHECK

On a 25-point scale, participants assigned to the difficult-rules condition reported having to concentrate on the task of crossing off the *e*s more than participants assigned to the easy-rules condition, $t(63) = 2.30, p < .025$. Participants in the ego-depletion condition needed to concentrate more than participants in the no-depletion condition, which should have resulted in participants in the ego-depletion condition using more ego strength than participants in the no-depletion condition.

Further evidence was supplied by having participants rate their level of tiredness at the beginning and end of the experiment. Participants in the ego-depletion condition became more tired as the experiment progressed, compared with participants in the no-depletion condition, $t(83) = 2.79, p < .01$. Changes in level of tiredness can serve as a rough index of changes in effort exerted and therefore regulatory capacity (see Johnson, Saccuzzo, & Larson, 1995), suggesting that participants in the ego-depletion condition indeed used more regulatory strength than participants in the no-depletion condition.

### MOVIE WATCHING

The main dependent measure was how long participants watched the boring movie. These results are presented in Table 16.4. The total time participants spent watching the boring movie was analyzed in a 2 (rules) × 2 (button position) ANOVA. Consistent with the hypothesis, the two-way interaction between depletion task rules (depletion vs. no depletion) and what participants did to quit

watching the movie (active quit vs, passive quit) was significant, $F(1, 80) = 5.64, p < .025$. A planned comparison confirmed that participants under ego depletion watched more of the movie when quitting required an active response than when quitting involved a passive response, $F(1, 80) = 7.21, p < .01$. The corresponding contrast in the no-depletion condition found no difference in movie duration as a function of which response was active versus passive, $F(1, 80) = 0.46, ns$. Thus, participants who were depleted were more likely to take the passive route, compared with participants who were not as depleted.

Additionally, there was a strong trend among participants who had to make an active response in order to quit: They watched the movie longer when they were in the ego-depletion condition than in the no-depletion condition, $F(1, 80) = 3.35, p < .07$. In other words, when participants had to initiate an action to quit, they tended to watch the movie longer when they were depleted than when they were not. Participants who had to release the button to quit tended to stop watching the movie sooner when they were depleted than when they were not depleted, although this was not statistically significant, $F(1, 80) = 2.33, p < .15$. Participants who had to do less work to quit tended to quit sooner when they were depleted than when they were not depleted.

## Discussion

The results of Experiment 4 provide further support for the hypothesis of ego depletion, insofar as ego depletion increased subsequent passivity. We noted that previous studies have found a passive-option effect, according to which a given option is chosen more when it requires a passive response than when it requires an active response. In the present study, ego depletion mediated the passive-option effect.

Experiment 4 manipulated ego depletion by having people complete a complex task that required careful monitoring of multiple rules and frequent altering of one's responses—more specifically, they were instructed to cross out every instance of the letter *e* in a text except when vari-

---

[4]Of course, participants were informed that they wee free to leave at any time. Still, most participants preferred to complete the procedure and leave the experiment having accomplished something, as opposed to leaving in the middle of the procedure.

**TABLE 16.4. Boredom Tolerance (Experiment 4)**

| Condition | No depletion | Depletion |
|---|---|---|
| Active quit | 88 | 125 |
| Passive quit | 102 | 71 |
| Difference | −14 | 54 |

*Note.* Numbers are mean durations, in seconds, that participants watched the boring movie. Bottom row (difference) refers to size of passive–option effect (the passive quit mean subtracted from the active quit mean).

ous other conditions were met, in which case they had to override the simple response of crossing out the *e*. These people subsequently showed greater passivity in terms of how long they watched a boring movie. They watched it longer when continuing was passive (and stopping required an active response) than when continuing required active responses (and stopping would be passive). Without ego depletion, we found no evidence of the passive-option effect: People watched the movie for about the same length of time regardless of whether stopping or continuing required the active response.

Thus, Experiment 4 found the passive-option effect only under ego depletion. That is, only when people had completed an initial task requiring concentration and careful monitoring of one's own responses in relation to rules did they favor the passive option (regardless of which option was passive). These findings suggest that people are less inclined to make active responses following ego depletion. Instead, depleted people are more prone to continue doing what is easiest, as if carried along by inertia.

Earlier, we suggested that the results of Experiment 2 indicated that choice depleted the ego. It might seem contradictory to suggest that passive choice does not draw on the same resource, but in fact we think the results of the two studies are quite parallel. The procedures of Experiment 2 involved active choice, insofar as the person thought about and consented to a particular behavior. The no-choice condition corresponded to passive choice in an important sense because people did implicitly have the option of refusing to make the assigned counterattitudinal speech, but they were not prompted by the experimenter to go through an inner debate and decision process. The active choices in Experiment 4 required the self to abandon the path of least resistance and override any inertia that was based on how the situation was set

up, so it required the self to do something. Thus, the high- and low-choice conditions of Experiment 2 correspond to the active and passive options of Experiment 4. Only active choice draws on the self's volitional resource.

## General Discussion

The present investigation began with the idea that the self expends some limited resource, akin to energy or strength, when it engages in acts of volition. To explore this possibility, we tested the hypothesis that acts of choice and self-control would cause ego depletion: Specifically, after one initial act of volition, there would be less of this resource available for subsequent ones. The four experiments reported in this article provided support for this view.

Experiment 1 examined self-regulation in two seemingly unrelated spheres. In the key condition, people resisted the impulse to eat tempting chocolates and made themselves eat radishes instead. These people subsequently gave up much faster on a difficult, frustrating puzzle task than did people who had been able to indulge the same impulse to eat chocolate. (They also gave up earlier than people who had not been tempted.) It takes self-control to resist temptation, and it takes self-control to make oneself keep trying at a frustrating task. Apparently, both forms of self-control draw on the same limited resource, because doing one interferes with subsequent efforts at the other.

Experiment 2 examined whether an act of personal, responsible choice would have the same effect. It did. People who freely, deliberately consented to make a counterattitudinal speech gave up quickly on the same frustrating task used in Experiment 1. Perhaps surprisingly, people who freely and deliberately consented to make a proattitudinal speech likewise gave up quickly, which is consistent with the pattern of ego depletion. In contrast, people who expected to make the counterattitudinal speech under low-choice conditions showed no drop in persistence, as compared with no-speech controls.

Thus, it was the act of responsible choice, not the particular behavior chosen, that depleted the self and reduced subsequent persistence. Regardless of whether the speech was consistent with their beliefs (to hold tuition down) or contrary to them (to raise tuition), what mattered was whether they made a deliberate act of choice to perform the behavior. Making either choice used up some resource, leaving them subsequently with less of whatever they needed to persist at a difficult, frustrating task. The effects of making a responsible choice were quite similar to those of resisting temptation in Experiment 1.

Experiment 3 was designed to address the alternative explanation that ego depletion actually improved subsequent self-regulation, insofar as giving up early on unsolvable problems could be considered as an adaptive response. In this experiment the dependent variable was task performance on solvable puzzles. Ego depiction resulting from an exercise in affect regulation impaired performance on that task.

We had shown (in Experiment 2) that ego-depletion effects carried over from responsible decision making have an impact on self-regulation. Experiment 4 was designed to show the effect in the opposite direction, namely that prior exertion of self-regulation would have an impact on decision making. To do this, we measured the degree of predominance of the passive option. People were presented with a choice situation in which they could respond either actively or passively. We varied the response format so that the meaning of the passive versus active response was exchanged in a counterbalanced fashion. Prior ego depletion (created by having people do a task that required monitoring their own behavior and multiple, overriding rules) increased people's tendency to use the passive response.

The assumption underlying Experiment 4 was that active responding draws on the same resource that the self uses to make responsible decisions and exert self-control. When that resource is depleted, people apparently have less of it available to make active responses. Therefore, they become more passive.

Taken together these four studies point toward a broad pattern of ego depletion. In each of them, an initial act of volition was followed by a decrement in some other sphere of volition. We found that an initial act of self-control impaired subsequent self-control (Experiment 1), that making a responsible decision impaired subsequent self-control (Experiment 2), that self-control lowered performance on a task that required self-control (Experiment 3), and that an initial act of self-control led to increased passivity (Experiment 4).

The procedures used in these four studies were deliberately made to be quite different. We have no way of directly measuring the internal resource that the self uses for making decisions or regulating itself. Hence, it seemed important to demonstrate ego depletion in circumstances as diverse as possible, in order to rule out the possibility that results could be artifacts of a particular method or sphere of volition. Our view is that the convergence of findings across the four studies is more persuasive evidence than any of the individual findings.

## Alternative Explanations

It must be acknowledged that the present studies provided no direct measures of the limited resource, hence no direct evidence that some inner quantity is diminished by acts of volition. The view that the active self involves some limited resource is thus an inference based on behavioral observations. It is therefore especially necessary to consider possible alternative interpretations of the effects we have shown.

One alternative view is that some form of negative affect caused participants in this research to give up early on the frustrating task. The task was, after all, designed to be frustrating or discouraging, insofar as it was unsolvable. It seems plausible that depression or other negative emotions might cause people to stop working at a task.

Although negative affect can undoubtedly affect persistence, the present pattern of results does not seem susceptible to an explanation on the basis of negative affect for several reasons. We measured negative affect repeatedly and did not find it to differ significantly among the conditions in the various experiments. Moreover, in Experiment 3, we found identical effects, regardless of whether the person was trying to stifle a positive or negative emotion. Our work converges with other evidence that mood effects cannot explain aftereffects of stress (Cohen, 1980).

A second alternative explanation would be that the results were due to cognitive dissonance, especially insofar as several of the procedures required counterattitudinal behavior, such as eating radishes instead of chocolate or refusing to laugh at a funny movie. Indeed, Experiment 2 included a condition that used a dissonance procedure, namely having people consent (under high choice) to record a speech in favor of a big tuition increase, contrary to the private beliefs of nearly all participants. Still, dissonance does not seem to provide a full explanation of the present effects. There is no apparent reason that dissonance should reduce persistence on an unrelated, subsequent task. Moreover, Experiment 2 found nearly identical effects of choosing a proattitudinal behavior as for choosing a counterattitudinal behavior whereas dissonance should only arise in the latter condition.

A variation on the first two alternate explanations is that arousal might have mediated the results. For example, cognitive dissonance has been shown to be arousing (Zanna & Cooper, 1974) and some participants possibly felt simply too aroused to sit there and keep struggling with the unsolvable problems. Given the variations and nonlinearities as to how arousal affects task performance, the decrement in anagram performance in Experiment 3 might also be attributed to arousal. Our data do, however, contradict the arousal explanation in two ways. First, self-report measures of arousal repeatedly failed to show any effects. Second, high arousal should presumably produce more activity rather than passivity, but the effects of ego depletion in Experiment 4 indicated an increase in passivity. If participants were more aroused, they should not have also become more passive as a result.

As already noted, the first two experiments were susceptible to a third alternative explanation, that quitting the unsolvable problems was actually an adaptive, rational act of good self-regulation instead of a sign of self-regulation failure. This interpretation assumes that participants recognized that the problems were unsolvable and so chose rationally not to waste any more time on them. This conclusion was contradicted by the evidence from the debriefing sessions, in which participants consistently expressed surprise when they learned that the problems had been unsolvable. More importantly, Experiment 3 countered that alternative explanation by showing that ego depletion produced decrements in performance of solvable problems.

Another explanation, based on equity considerations, would suggest that experimental participants arrive with an implicit sense of the degree of obligation they owe to the researchers and are unwilling to do more. In this view, for example, a person might feel that she has done enough by making herself eat radishes instead of chocolates and therefore feels that she does not owe the ex-

perimenter maximal exertion on subsequent tasks. Although there is no evidence for such a view, it could reasonably cover Experiments 1 and 3. It has more difficulty with Experiment 4 because someone who felt he had already done enough during the highly difficult version of the initial task would presumably be less willing to sit longer during a boring movie, which is the opposite of what happened in the active-quit condition. Experiment 2 also is difficult to reconcile with this alternative explanation because the participants did not actually complete any initial task. (They merely agreed to one.) Moreover, in that study, the effects of agreeing to make a proattitudinal speech were the same as making a counterattitudinal speech, whereas an equity calculation would almost surely assume that agreeing to make the counterattitudinal speech would be a much greater sacrifice.

## Implications

The present results could potentially have implications for self-theory. The pattern of ego depletion suggests that some internal resource is used by the self to make decisions, respond actively, and exert self-control. It appears, moreover, that the same resource is used for all of these, as indicated by the carryover patterns we found (i.e., exertion in one sphere leads to decrements in others). Given the pervasive importance of choice, responsibility, and self-control, this resource might well be an important aspect of the self. Most recent research on the self has featured cognitive representations and interpersonal roles. The present research does not in any way question the value of that work, but it does suggest augmenting the cognitive and interpersonal aspects of self with an appreciation of this volitional resource. The operation of this volitional, agentic, controlling aspect of the self may require an energy model.

Moreover, this resource appears to be quite surprisingly limited. In Study 1, for example, a mere 5 minutes of resisting temptation in the form of chocolate caused a reduction by half in how long people made themselves keep trying at unsolvable puzzles. It seems surprising to suggest that a few minutes of a laboratory task, especially one that was not described as excessively noxious or strenuous, would seriously deplete some important aspect of the self. Thus, these studies suggest that whatever is involved in choice and self-control is both an important and very limited resource. The activities of the self should perhaps be understood in general as having to make the most of a scarce and precious resource.

The limited nature of this resource might conceivably help explain several surprising phenomena that have been studied in recent years. A classic article by Burger (1989) documented a broad range of exceptions to the familiar, intuitively appealing notion that people generally seek and desire control. Under many circumstances, Burger found that people relinquish or avoid control, and moreover, even under ordinary circumstances, there is often a substantial minority of people who do not want control. The ego-depletion findings of the present investigation suggest that exerting control uses a scarce and precious resource, and the self may learn early on to conserve that resource. Avoiding control under some circumstances may be a strategy for conservation.

Bargh (1997) has recently shown that the scope of automatic responses is far wider than many theories have assumed and, indeed, that even when people seem to be consciously making controlled responses, they may in fact be responding automatically to subtle cues (see also Bargh, 1982, 1994). Assuming that the self is the controller of controlled processes, it is not surprising that controlled processes should be confined to a relatively small part of everyday functioning because they are costly. Responding in a controlled (as opposed to automatic) fashion would cause ego depletion, leaving the self potentially unable to respond to a subsequent emergency or to regulate itself. Hence, staying in the automatic realm would help conserve this resource.

It is also conceivable that ego depletion is central to various patterns of psychological difficulties that people experience, especially ones that require unusual exertions of affect regulation, choice, or other volition. Burnout, learned helplessness, and similar patterns of pathological passivity might have some element of ego depletion. Coping with trauma may be difficult precisely because the self's volitional resources were depleted by the trauma, but are needed for recovery. Indeed, it is well established that social support helps people recover from trauma, so it could be that the value of social support lies partly in the way other people take over the victim's volitional tasks (ranging from affect regulation to making dinner), thus conserving the victim's resources or allowing them time to replenish. On the darker

side, it may be that highly controlled people who seem to snap, abruptly perpetrating acts of violence or outrage, may be suffering from some abrupt depletion that has undermined the control they have maintained, possibly for years, over these destructive impulses. These possible implications lie far beyond the present data, however.

We acknowledge that we do not have a clear understanding of the nature of this resource. We can say this much: The resource functions to connect abstract principles, standards, and intentions to overt behavior. It has some link to physical tiredness, but is not the same. The resource seems to have a quantitative continuum, like a strength. We find it implausible that ego depletion would have no physiological aspect or correlates at all, but we are reluctant to speculate about what physiological changes would be involved. The ease with which we have been able to produce ego depletion using small laboratory manipulations suggests that the extent of the resource is quite limited. This implies that it would be seriously inadequate for directing all of a person's behavior, so conscious, free choice must remain at best restricted to a very small proportion of human behavior. By the same token, most behavior would have to be automatic instead of controlled, assuming that controlled processes depend on this limited resource. Still, as we noted at the outset, even a small amount of this resource would be extremely adaptive in enabling human behavior to become flexible, varied, and able to transcend the pattern of simply responding to immediate stimuli.

## Concluding Remarks

Our results suggest that a broad assortment of actions make use of the same resource. Acts of self-control, responsible decision making, and active choice seem to interfere with similar acts that follow soon after. The implication is that some vital resource of the self becomes depleted by such acts of volition. To be sure, we assume that this resource is commonly replenished, although the factors that might hasten or delay the replenishment remain unknown, along with the precise nature of this resource. If further work can answer such questions, it promises to shed considerable light on human agency and the mechanisms of control over self and world.

For now, however, two final implications of the present evidence about ego depletion patterns deserve reiterating. On the negative side, these results point to a potentially serious constraint on the human capacity for control (including self-control) and deliberate decision making. On the positive side, they point toward a valuable and powerful feature of human selfhood.

## REFERENCES

Allison, S. T., & Messick, D. M. (1988). The feature-positive effect, attitude strength, and degree of perceived consensus. *Personality and Social Psychology Bulletin, 14,* 231–241.

Banaji, M. R., & Prentice, D. A. (1994). The self in social contexts. In L. Porter & M. Rosenzweig (Eds.), *Annual review of psychology* (Vol. 45, pp. 297–332). Palo Alto, CA: Annual Reviews.

Bargh, J. A. (1982). Attention and automaticity in the processing of self-relevant information. *Journal of Personality and Social Psychology, 43,* 425–436.

Bargh, J. A. (1994). The four horsemen of automaticity: Awareness, intention, efficiency, and control in social cognition. In R. S. Wyer, Jr., & T. K. Srull (Eds.), *Handbook of social cognition* (pp. 1–40). Hillsdale, NJ: Erlbaum.

Bargh, J. A. (1997). The automaticity of everyday life. In R. S. Wyer (Ed.), *Advances in social cognition* (Vol. 10, pp. 1–61). Mahwah, NJ: Erlbaum.

Baumeister, R. F. (1998). The self. In D. T. Gilbert, S. T. Fiske, & G. Lindzey (Eds.), *Handbook of social psychology* (4th ed., pp. 680–740). New York: McGraw-Hill.

Baumeister, R. F., Heatherton, T. F., & Tice, D. M. (1994). *Losing control: How and why people fail at self-regulation.* San Diego, CA: Academic Press.

Brehm, J. (1966). *A theory of psychological reactance.* New York: Academic Press.

Brockner. J., Shaw, M. C., & Rubin, J. Z. (1979). Factors affecting withdrawal from an escalating conflict: Quitting before it's too late. *Journal of Experimental Social Psychology, 11,* 492–503.

Burger, J. M. (1989). Negative reactions to increases in perceived personal control. *Journal of Personality and Social Psychology, 56,* 246–256.

Carver, C. S., & Scheier, M. F. (1981). *Attention and self-regulation: A control theory approach to human behavior.* New York: Springer-Verlag.

Cioffi, D., & Garner, R. (1996). On doing the decision: The effects of active vs. passive choice on commitment and self-perception. *Personality and Social Psychology Bulletin, 22,* 133–147.

Cohen, S. (1980). Aftereffects of stress on human performance and social behavior: A review of research and theory. *Psychological Bulletin, 88,* 82–108.

Cooper, J., & Fazio, R. H. (1984). A new look at dissonance theory. In L. Berkowitz (Ed.), *Advances in experimental social psychology* (Vol. 17, pp. 229–266). New York: Academic Press.

Cooper, J., & Scher, S. J. (1994). Actions and attitudes: The role of responsibility and aversive consequences in persuasion. In T. Brock & S. Shavitt (Eds.), *The psychology of persuasion* (pp. 95–111). San Francisco: Freeman.

Cooper, J., Zanna, M. P., & Taves, P. A. (1978). Arousal as a necessary condition for attitude change following induced compliance. *Journal of Personality and Social Psychology, 36,* 1101–1106.

DeCharms, R. (1968). *Personal causation.* New York: Academic Press.

Deci, E. L., & Ryan, R. M. (1991). A motivational approach to self: Integration in personality. In R Dienstbier (Ed.), *Nebraska Symposium on Motivation: Vol. 38. Perspectives on motivation* (pp. 237–288). Lincoln: University of Nebraska Press.

Deci, E. L., & Ryan, R. M. (1995). Human autonomy: The basis for true self-esteem. In M. Kernis (Ed.), *Efficacy, agency and self-esteem* (pp. 31–49). New York: Plenum.

Duval S., & Wicklund, R. A. (1972). *A theory of objective self-awareness.* New York: Academic Press.

Epstein, S. (1973). The self-concept revisited: Or a theory of a theory. *American Psychologist, 28,* 404–416.

Fazio, R. H., Sherman, S. J., & Herr, P. M. (1982). The feature-positive effect in the self-perception process: Does not doing matter as much as doing? *Journal of Personality and Social Psychology, 42,* 404–411.

Feather, N. T. (1961). The relationship of persistence at a task to expectation of success and achievement related motives. *Journal of Abnormal and Social Psychology, 63,* 552–561.

Festinger, L. (1957). *A theory of cognitive dissonance.* Stanford, CA: Stanford University Press.

Festinger, L., & Carlsmith, J. M. (1959). Cognitive consequences of forced compliance. *Journal of Abnormal and Social Psychology, 58,* 203–210.

Fiske, S., & Taylor, S. E. (1991). *Social cognition* (2nd ed.). New York: McGraw-Hill.

Freud, S. (1961a). The ego and the id. In J. Strachey (Ed. and Trans.), *The standard edition of the complete psychological works of Sigmund Freud* (Vol. 19, pp. 12–66). London: Hogarth Press. (Original work published 1923)

Freud, S. (1961b). New introductory lectures on psycho-analysis. In J. Strachey (Ed. and Trans.), *The standard edition of the complete psychological works of Sigmund Freud* (Vol. 22, pp. 7–182). London: Hogarth Press. (Original work published 1933)

Glass, D. C., Singer, J. E., & Friedman, L. N. (1969). Psychic cost of adaptation to an environmental stressor. *Journal of Personality and Social Psychology, 12,* 200–210.

Herman, C. P., & Polivy, J. (1975). Anxiety, restraint, and eating behavior. *Journal of Abnormal Psychology, 84,* 666–672.

Johnson. N. E., Saccuzzo, D. P., & Larson, G. E. (1995). Self-report effort versus actual performance in information processing paradigms. *Journal of General Psychology, 122,* 195–210.

Langer, E. J. (1975). The illusion of control. *Journal of Personality and Social Psychology, 32,* 311–328.

Leary, M. R. (1995). *Self-presentation: Impression management and interpersonal behavior.* Madison, WI: Brown & Benchmark.

Leary, M. R., & Kowalski, R. M. (1990). Impression management: A literature review and two-component model. *Psychological Bulletin, 107,* 34–47.

Linder, D. E., Cooper, J., & Jones, E. E. (1967). Decision freedom as a determinant of the role of incentive magnitude in attitude change. *Journal of Personality and Social Psychology, 6,* 245–254.

Mayer, J. D., & Gaschke, Y. N. (1988). The experience and meta-experience of mood. *Journal of Personality and Social Psychology, 55,* 102–111.

McFarlin, D. B. (1985). Persistence in the face of failure: The impact of self-esteem and contingency information. *Personality and Social Psychology Bulletin, 11,* 152–163.

Mischel, W. (1996). From good intentions to willpower. In P. Gollwitzer & J. Bargh (Eds.), *The psychology of action* (pp. 197–218). New York: Guilford Press.

Muraven, M., Tice, D. M., & Baumeister, R. F. (1998). Self-control as limited resource: Regulatory depletion patterns. *Journal of Personality and Social Psychology, 74,* 774–789.

Rothbaum, F., Weisz, J. R., & Snyder, S. S. (1982). Changing the world and changing the self: A two-process model of perceived control. *Journal of Personality and Social Psychology, 42,* 5–37.

Scher, S. J., & Cooper, J. (1989). The motivational basis of dissonance: The singular role of behavioral consequences. *Journal of Personality and Social Psychology, 56,* 899–906.

Schlenker, B. R. (1980). *Impression management: The self-concept, social identity, and interpersonal relations.* Monterey, CA: Brooks/Cole.

Taylor, S. E. (1983). Adjustment to threatening events: A theory of cognitive adaptation. *American Psychologist, 38,* 1161–1173.

Taylor, S. E. (1989). *Positive illusions: Creative self-deception and the healthy mind.* New York: Basic Books.

Tesser, A. (1988). Toward a self-evaluation maintenance model of social behavior. In L. Berkowitz (Ed.), *Advances in experimental social psychology* (Vol. 21, pp. 181–227). San Diego, CA: Academic Press.

Tetlock, P. E. (1983). Accountability and complexity of thought. *Journal of Personality and Social Psychology, 45,* 74–83.

Tetlock, P. E. (1985). Accountability: A social check on the fundamental attribution error. *Social Psychology Quarterly, 48,* 227–236.

Tetlock, P. E., & Boettger, R. (1989). Accountability: A social magnifier of the dilution effect. *Journal of Personality and Social Psychology, 57,* 388–398.

Wegner, D. M. (1989). *White bears and other unwanted thoughts.* New York: Vintage.

Wegner, D. M. (1994). Ironic processes of mental control. *Psychological Review, 101,* 34–52.

Wegner. D. M., & Pennebaker, J. W. (Eds.). (1993). *Handbook of mental control.* Englewood Cliffs, NJ: Prentice Hall.

Wegner, D. M., Schneider. D. J., Carter. S. R., & White, T. L. (1987). Paradoxical effects of thought suppression. *Journal of Personality and Social Psychology, 53,* 5–13.

White, R. (1959). Motivation reconsidered: The concept of competence. *Psychological Review, 66,* 297–333.

Zanna. M. P., & Cooper, J. (1974). Dissonance and the pill: An attribution approach to studying the arousal properties of dissonance. *Journal of Personality and Social Psychology, 29,* 703–709.

Zanna, M. P., Higgins, E. T., & Taves, P. A. (1976). Is dissonance phenomenologically aversive? *Journal of Experimental Social Psychology, 12,* 530–538.

# Self and Culture

The massive amount of research on self has struck some readers as disturbingly out of balance, because most of it is based on studies of modern American college students. Even in our own Western culture, the nature of selfhood has changed dramatically over the past ten centuries (Baumeister, 1987). Do our contemporaries in other cultures have different kinds of selves?

An influential paper by Triandis (1989) proposed multiple ways that cultures and selves can vary—and co-vary. Some societies pressure individuals to conform to standard values and behavior patterns, whereas others permit a broad range of diversity and deviance. Some societies embed the self in a complex web of multiple relationships so that a single person performs many different roles, while others keep each individual in one or two well-defined groups, which he or she can ill afford to alienate. Some societies place paramount value on sincerity and authenticity, which means that the person is expected to be true to his or her inner convictions, but in other societies the important thing is that publicly visible behavior be proper and appropriate to prevailing norms, regardless of what beliefs the person may privately entertain.

The article reproduced here is an influential successor to Triandis's groundbreaking work. Markus and Kitayama (1991) focus on one crucial dimension on which selves differ across cultures, namely independence vs. interdependence. That is, in cultures such as North America, the self is understood as a distinct, autonomous entity that stands out from its surroundings and can move from one context to another intact—but in Asian cultures the self is conceptualized as irrevocably embedded in its group and network of social relations. The clarity and elegance of Markus and Kitayama's theorizing have helped this article become

337

extremely influential to researchers interested in cross-cultural research on the self.

Markus and Kitayama's subsequent work has turned to the question of the cross-cultural universality in the desire to think well of oneself. Heine, Lehman, Markus, and Kitayama (in press) contend that Japanese do not share the American pattern of self-esteem motivation. While Americans might try to cover up or ignore their failures to preserve a flattering view of self, Japanese will direct their attention to their shortcomings to try to improve. The argument that some cultures shape selves that lack the motive to think well of self is likely to provide an important challenge to a central aspect of self theory and to be a productive focus of empirical controversy.

### REFERENCES

Baumeister, R. F. (1987) How the self became a problem: A psychological review of historical research. *Journal of Personality and Social Psychology, 52,* 163–176.

Heine, S. J., Lehman, D. R., Markus, H. R., & Kitayama, S. (in press). Is there a universal need for positive self-regard? *Psychological Review.*

Markus, H. R., & Kitayama, S. (1991). Culture and the self: Implications for cognition, emotion, and motivation. *Psychological Review, 98,* 224–253.

Triandis, H. C. (1989). The self and social behavior in differing cultural contexts. *Psychological Review, 96,* 506–520.

# Discussion Questions

1. Give examples of how independent and interdependent people might differ in the ways that they spend their leisure time.
2. Are differences between Americans and Japanese merely small variations in emphasis or do they reflect a radically and basically different way of being human?
3. In the broad sweep of human evolution and history, which form of self-concept (the independent or the interdependent) has been more common?
4. What differences in American versus Asian cultures might have caused these differences in self-concept?

# Suggested Readings

Triandis, H. C. (1989). The self and social behavior in differing cultural contexts. *Psychological Review, 96,* 506–520. This article preceded and influenced the Markus and Kitayama work reproduced here. Triandis casts a wider net and offers many valuable, fascinating ideas about how cultures vary and how selves vary along with them.

Baumeister, R. F. (1987). How the self became a problem: A psychological review of historical research. *Journal of Personality and Social Psychology, 52,* 163–176. This paper offers a summary of how Western concepts of selfhood have evolved over the centuries to reach their current, confused state.

Cross, S. E., & Madson, L. (1997). Models of the self: Self-construals and gender. *Psychological Bulletin, 122,* 5–37. Also Baumeister, R. F., & Sommer, K. L. (1997). What do men want? Gender differences and two spheres of belongingness: Comment on Cross & Madson (1997). *Psychological Bulletin, 122,* 38–44. Cross and Madson borrow the independent-interdependent taxonomy from Markus and Kitayama and use it to discuss gender differences. They contend that women favor interdependence whereas men strive for independence. In response, Baumeister and Sommer propose that Cross and Madson have caricatured male psychology and overlooked social, interdependent strivings that do not conform to dyadic intimacy.

# Culture and the Self: Implications for Cognition, Emotion, and Motivation

Hazel Rose Markus • University of Michigan
Shinobu Kitayama • University of Oregon

People in different cultures have strikingly different construals of the self, of others, and of the interdependence of the two. These construals can influence, and in many cases determine, the very nature of individual experience, including cognition, emotion, and motivation. Many Asian cultures have distinct conceptions of individuality that insist on the fundamental relatedness of individuals to each other. The emphasis is on attending to others, fitting in, and harmonious interdependence with them. American culture neither assumes nor values such an overt connectedness among individuals. In contrast, individuals seek to maintain their independence from others by attending to the self and by discovering and expressing their unique inner attributes. As proposed herein, these construals are even more powerful than previously imagined. Theories of the self from both psychology and anthropology are integrated to define in detail the difference between a construal of the self as independent and a construal of the self as interdependent. Each of these divergent construals should have a set of specific consequences for cognition, emotion, and motivation; these consequences are proposed and relevant empirical literature is reviewed. Focusing on differences in self-construals enables apparently inconsistent empirical findings to be reconciled and raises questions about what have been thought to be culture-free aspects of cognition, emotion, and motivation.

In America, "the squeaky wheel gets the grease." In Japan, "the nail that stands out gets pounded down." American parents who are trying to induce their children to eat their suppers are fond of saying "think of the starving kids in Ethiopia, and appreciate how lucky you are to be different from them." Japanese parents are likely to say "think about the farmer who worked so hard to produce this rice for you; if you don't eat it, he will feel bad, for his efforts will have been in vain" (H.

Yamada, personal communication). A small Texas corporation seeking to elevate productivity told its employees to look in the mirror and say "I am beautiful" 100 times before coming to work each day. Employees of a Japanese supermarket that was recently opened in New Jersey were instructed to begin the day by holding hands and telling each other that "he" or "she is beautiful" ("A Japanese Supermarket," 1989).

Such anecdotes suggest that people in Japan and

America may hold strikingly divergent construals of the self, others, and the interdependence of the two. The American examples stress attending to the self, the appreciation of one's difference from others, and the importance of asserting the self. The Japanese examples emphasize attending to and fitting in with others and the importance of harmonious interdependence with them. These construals of the self and others are tied to the implicit, normative tasks that various cultures hold for what people should be doing in their lives (cf. Cantor & Kihlstrom, 1987; Erikson, 1950; Veroff, 1983). Anthropologists and psychologists assume that such construals can influence, and in many cases determine, the very nature of individual experience (Chodorow, 1978; Dumont, 1970; Geertz, 1975; Gergen, 1968; Gilligan, 1982; Holland & Quinn, 1987; Lykes, 1985; Marsella, De Vos, & Hsu, 1985; Sampson, 1985, 1988, 1989; Shweder & LeVine, 1984; Smith, 1985; Triandis, 1989; Weisz, Rothbaum, & Blackburn, 1984; White & Kirkpatrick, 1985).

Despite the growing body of psychological and anthropological evidence that people hold divergent views about the self, most of what psychologists currently know about human nature is based on one particular view—the so-called Western view of the individual as an independent, self-contained, autonomous entity who (a) comprises a unique configuration of internal attributes (e.g., traits, abilities, motives, and values) and (b) behaves primarily as a consequence of these internal attributes (Geertz, 1975; Sampson, 1988, 1989; Shweder & LeVine, 1984). As a result of this monocultural approach to the self (see Kennedy, Scheier, & Rogers, 1984), psychologists' understanding of those phenomena that are linked in one way or another to the self may be unnecessarily restricted (for some important exceptions, see Bond, 1986, 1988; Cousins, 1989; Fiske, 1991; Maehr & Nicholls, 1980; Stevenson, Azuma, & Hakuta, 1986; Triandis, 1989; Triandis, Bontempo, Villareal, Asai, & Lucca, 1988). In this article, we suggest that construals of the self, of others, and of the relationship between the self and others may be even more powerful than previously suggested and that their influence is clearly reflected in differences among cultures. In particular, we compare an *independent* view of the self with one other, very different view, an *interdependent* view. The independent view is most clearly exemplified in some sizable segment of American culture, as well as in many Western European cultures. The interdependent view is exemplified in Japanese culture as well as in other Asian cultures. But it is also characteristic of African, Latin-American, and many southern European cultures. We delineate how these divergent views of the self—the independent and the interdependent—can have a systematic influence on various aspects of cognition, emotion, and motivation.

We suggest that, for many cultures of the world, the Western notion of the self as an entity containing significant dispositional attributes, and as detached from context, is simply not an adequate description of selfhood. Rather, in many construals, the self is viewed as *inter*dependent with the surrounding context, and it is the "other" or the "self-in-relation-to-other" that is focal in individual experience. One general consequence of this divergence in self-construal is that when psychological processes (e.g., cognition, emotion, and motivation) explicitly, or even quite implicitly, implicate the self as a target or as a referent, the nature of these processes will vary according to the exact form or organization of self inherent in a given construal. With respect to cognition, for example, for those with interdependent selves, in contrast to those with independent selves, some aspects of knowledge representation and some of the processes involved in social and nonsocial thinking alike are influenced by a pervasive attentiveness to the relevant *others* in the social context. Thus, one's actions are more likely to be seen as situationally bound, and characterizations of the individual will include this context. Furthermore, for those with interdependent construals of the self, both the expression and the experience of emotions and motives may be significantly shaped and governed by a consideration of the reactions of others. Specifically, some emotions, like anger, which derive from and promote an independent view of the self, may be less prevalent among those with interdependent selves, and self-serving motives may be replaced by what appear as other-serving motives. An examination of cultural variation in some aspects of cognition, emotion, and motivation will allow psychologists to ask what exactly is universal in these processes, which has the potential to provide some new insights for theories of these psychological processes.

In this analysis, we draw on recent research efforts devoted to characterizing the general differences between American or Western views of personhood and Eastern or Asian perspectives (e.g., Heelas & Lock, 1981; Hofstede, 1980; Marsella et al., 1985; Roland, 1988; Schwartz & Bilsky, 1990; Shweder, 1990; Shweder & LeVine, 1984; Stigler, Shweder, & Herdt, 1990; Triandis, 1989; Triandis & Brislin, 1980; Weisz et al., 1984). We extract from these descriptions many important differences that may exist in the specific content, structure, and functioning of the self-systems of people of different cultural backgrounds. The distinctions that we make between independent and interdependent construals must be regarded as general tendencies that may emerge when the members of the culture are considered as a whole. The prototypical American view of the self, for example, may prove to be most characteristic of White, middle-class men with a Western European ethnic background. It may be somewhat less descriptive of women in general, or of men and women from other ethnic groups or social classes. Moreover, we realize that there may well be important distinctions among those views we discuss as similar and that there may be views of the self and others that cannot easily be classified as either independent or interdependent.

Our intention is not to catalog all types of self-construals, but rather to highlight a view of the self that is often assumed to be universal but which may be quite specific to some segments of Western culture. We argue that self-construals play a major role in regulating various psychological processes. Understanding the nature of divergent self-construals has two important consequences. On the one hand, it allows us to organize several apparently inconsistent empirical findings and to pose questions about the assumed universality for many aspects of cognition, emotion, and motivation (see Shweder, 1990). On the other hand, it permits us to better specify the precise role of the self in mediating and regulating behavior.

## The Self: A Delicate Category

### Universal Aspects of the Self

In exploring the possibility of different types of self-construals, we begin with Hallowell's (1955) notion that people everywhere are likely to develop an understanding of themselves as physically distinct and separable from others. Head (1920), for example, claimed the existence of a universal

schema of the body that provided one with an anchor in time and space. Similarly, Allport (1937) suggested that there must exist an aspect of personality that allows one, when awakening each morning, to be sure that he or she is the same person who went to sleep the night before. Most recently, Neisser (1988) referred to this aspect of self as the *ecological self,* which he defined as "the self as perceived with respect to the physical environment: 'I' am the person here in this place, engaged in this particular activity" (p. 3). Beyond a physical or ecological sense of self, each person probably has some awareness of internal activity, such as dreams, and of the continuous now of thoughts and feelings, which are private to the extent that they cannot be directly known by others. The awareness of this unshared experience will lead the person to some sense of an inner, private self.

### Divergent Aspects of the Self

Some understanding and representation of the private, inner aspects of the self may well be universal, but many other aspects of the self may be quite specific to particular cultures. People are capable of believing an astonishing variety of things about themselves (cf. Heelas & Lock, 1981; Marsella et al., 1985; Shweder & LeVine, 1984; Triandis, 1989). The self can be construed, framed, or conceptually represented in multiple ways. A cross-cultural survey of the self lends support to Durkheim's (1912/1968) early notion that the category of the self is primarily the product of social factors and, to Mauss's (1938/1985) claim that, as a social category, the self is a "delicate" one, subject to quite substantial, if not infinite, variation.

The exact content and structure of the inner self may differ considerably by culture. Furthermore, the nature of the outer or public self that derives from one's relations with other people and social institutions may also vary markedly by culture. And, as suggested by Triandis (1989), the significance assigned to the private, inner aspects versus the public, relational aspects in regulating behavior will vary accordingly. In fact, it may not be unreasonable to suppose, as did numerous earlier anthropologists (see Allen, 1985), that in some cultures, on certain occasions, the *individual,* in the sense of a set of significant inner attributes of the person, may cease to be the primary unit of consciousness. Instead, the sense of belonging to a social relation may become so strong that it makes better sense to think of the *relationship* as the functional unit of conscious reflection.

The current analysis focuses on just one variation in what people in different cultures can come to believe about themselves. This one variation concerns what they believe about the relationship between the self and *others* and, especially, the degree to which they see themselves as *separate* from others or as *connected* with others. We suggest that the significance and exact functional role that the person assigns to the other when defining the self depend on the culturally shared assumptions about the separation or connectedness between the self and others.

## Two Construals of the Self: Independent and Interdependent

### The Independent Construal

In many Western cultures, there is a faith in the inherent separateness of distinct persons. The normative imperative of this culture is to become independent from others and to discover and express one's unique attributes (Johnson, 1985; Marsella et al., 1985; J. G. Miller, 1988; Shweder & Bourne, 1984). Achieving the cultural goal of independence requires construing oneself as an individual whose behavior is organized and made meaningful primarily by reference to one's own internal repertoire of thoughts, feelings, and actions, rather than by reference to the thoughts, feelings, and actions of others. According to this construal of self, to borrow Geertz's (1975) often quoted phrase, the person is viewed as "a bounded, unique, more or less integrated motivational and cognitive universe, a dynamic center of awareness, emotion, judgment, and action organized into a distinctive whole and set contrastively both against other such wholes and against a social and natural background" (p. 48).

This view of the self derives from a belief in the wholeness and uniqueness of each person's configuration of internal attributes (Johnson, 1985; Sampson, 1985, 1988, 1989; Waterman, 1981). It gives rise to processes like "self-actualization," "realizing oneself," "expressing one's unique configuration of needs, rights, and capacities," or "developing one's distinct potential." The essential aspect of this view involves a conception of the self as an autonomous, independent person; we thus refer to it as the *independent construal of the self.* Other similar labels include *individualist, egocentric, separate autonomous, idiocentric,* and *self-contained.* We assume that, on average, relatively more individuals in Western cultures will hold this view than will individuals in non-Western cultures. Within a given culture, however, individuals will vary in the extent to which they are good cultural representatives and construe the self in the mandated way.

The independent self must, of course, be responsive to the social environment (Fiske, 1991). This responsiveness, however, is fostered not so much for the sake of the responsiveness itself. Rather, social responsiveness often, if not always, derives from the need to strategically determine the best way to express or assert the internal attributes of the self. Others, or the social situation in general, are important but, primarily as standards of reflected appraisal or as sources that can verify and affirm the inner core of the self. [. . .]

### The Interdependent Construal

In contrast, many non-Western cultures insist, in Kondo's (1982) terms, on the fundamental connectedness of human beings to each other. A normative imperative of these cultures is to maintain this interdependence among individuals (De Vos, 1985; Hsu, 1985; Miller, 1988; Shweder & Bourne, 1984). Experiencing interdependence entails seeing oneself as part of an encompassing social relationship and recognizing that one's behavior is determined by, contingent on, and, to a large extent, organized by what the actor perceives to be the thoughts, feelings, and actions of others in the relationship. The Japanese experience of the self, therefore, includes a sense of interdependence and of one's status as a participant in a larger social unit (Sampson, 1988). Within such a construal, the self becomes most meaningful and complete when it is cast in the appropriate social relationship. According to Lebra (1976), the Japanese are most fully human in the context of others.

This view of the self and the relationship between the self and others features the person, not as separate from the social context, but as more connected and less differentiated from others. People are motivated to find a way to fit in with relevant others, to fulfill and create obligation, and in general to become part of various interpersonal relationships. Unlike the independent self, the significant features of the self according to this construal are to be found in the interdependent and, thus, in the more public components of the self. We therefore call this view the *interdependent construal of the self.* The same notion has been variously referred to, with somewhat different connotations, as *sociocentric, holistic, collective, allocentric, ensembled, constitutive, contextualist, connected,* and *relational.* As with the independent self, others are critical for social comparison and self-validation yet, in an interdependent formulation of the self, these others become an integral part of the setting, situation, or context to which the self is connected, fitted, and assimilated. The exact manner in which one achieves the task of connection, therefore, depends crucially on the nature of the context, particularly the others present in the context. Others thus participate actively and continuously in the definition of the interdependent self.

The interdependent self also possesses and expresses a set of internal attributes, such as abilities, opinions, judgments, and personality characteristics. However, these internal attributes are understood as situation specific, and thus as sometimes elusive and unreliable. And, as such, they are unlikely to assume a powerful role in regulating overt behavior, especially if this behavior implicates significant others. In many domains of social life, one's opinions, abilities, and characteristics are assigned only secondary roles—they must instead be constantly controlled and regulated to come to terms with the primary task of interdependence. Such voluntary control of the inner attributes constitutes the core of the cultural ideal of becoming mature. The understanding of one's autonomy as secondary to, and constrained by, the primary task of interdependence distinguishes interdependent selves from independent selves, for whom autonomy and its expression is often afforded primary significance. An independent behavior (e.g., asserting an opinion) exhibited by a person in an interdependent culture is likely to be based on the premise of underlying interdependence and thus may have a somewhat different significance than it has for a person from an independent culture. [. . .]

Interdependent selves certainly include representations of invariant personal attributes and abilities, and these representations can become phenomenologically quite salient. In many circumstances, they are less important in regulating observable behavior and are not assumed to be particularly diagnostic of the self. Instead, the self-knowledge that guides behavior is of the self-in-relation to specific others in particular contexts. The fundamental units of the self-system, core conceptions, or self-schemata are thus predicated on significant interpersonal relationships.

An interdependent self cannot be properly characterized as a bounded whole, for it changes structure with the nature of the particular social context. Within each particular social situation, the self can be differently instantiated. The uniqueness of such a self derives from the specific configuration of relationships that each person has developed. What is focal and objectified in an interdependent self, then, is not the inner self, but the *relationships* of the person to other actors (Hamaguchi, 1985).

The notion of an interdependent self is linked with a monistic philosophical tradition in which the person is thought to be of the same substance as the rest of nature (see Bond, 1986; Phillips, 1976; Roland, 1988; Sass, 1988). As a consequence, the relationship between the self and other, or between subject and object, is assumed to be much closer. Thus, many non-Western cultures insist on the inseparability of basic elements (Galtung, 1981), including self and other, and person and situation. In Chinese culture, for instance, there is an emphasis on synthesizing the constituent parts of any problem or situation into an integrated or harmonious whole (Moore, 1967; Northrop, 1946). Thus, persons are only parts that, when separated from the larger social whole, cannot be fully understood (Phillips, 1976; Shweder, 1984). Such a holistic view is in opposition to the Cartesian, dualistic tradition that characterizes Western thinking, in which the self is separated from the object and from the natural world. [. . .]

In Japan, the word for self, *jibun*, refers to "one's share of the shared life space" (Hamaguchi, 1985). The self, Kimura (cited in Hamaguchi, 1985) claimed, is "neither a substance nor an attribute having a constant oneness" (p 302). According to Hamaguchi (1985), for the Japanese, "a sense of identification with others (sometimes including conflict) pre-exists and selfness is confirmed only through interpersonal relationships. . . . Selfness is not a constant like the ego but denotes a fluid concept which changes through time and situations according to interpersonal relationships" (p. 302).

The Japanese anthropologist Lebra (1976) defined the essence of Japanese culture as an "ethos of social relativism." This translates into a constant concern for belongingness, reliance, dependency, empathy, occupying one's proper place, and reciprocity. She claimed the Japanese nightmare is exclusion, meaning that one is failing at the normative goal of connecting to others. This is in sharp contrast to the American nightmare, which is to fail at separating from others, as can occur when one is unduly influenced by others, does not stand up for what one believes, or goes unnoticed or undistinguished.

An interdependent view of self does not result in a merging of self and other, nor does it imply that one must always be in the company of others to function effectively, or that people do not have a sense of themselves as agents who are the origins of their own actions. On the contrary, it takes a high degree of self-control and agency to effectively adjust oneself to various interpersonal contingencies. Agentic exercise of control, however, is directed primarily to the inside and to those inner attributes, such as desires, personal goals, and private emotions, which can disturb the harmonious equilibrium of interpersonal transaction. This can be contrasted with the Western notion of control, which primarily implies an assertion of the inner attributes and a consequent attempt to change the outer aspects, such as one's public behaviors and the social situation (see also Weisz et al., 1984).

Given the Japanese notion of control that is inwardly directed, the ability to effectively adjust in the interpersonal domain may form an important basis of self-esteem, and individualized styles of such adjustment to social contingencies may contribute to the sense of self-uniqueness. Thus, Hamaguchi (1985), for example, reported that, for the Japanese, "the straightforward claim of the naked ego" (p. 303) is experienced as childish. Self-assertion is not viewed as being authentic, but instead as being immature. This point is echoed in M. White and LeVine's (1986) description of the meaning of *sunao*, a term used by Japanese parents to characterize what they value in their children:

A child that is *sunao* has not yielded his or her personal autonomy for the sake of cooperation; cooperation does not suggest giving up the self, as it may in the West; it implies that working with others is the appropriate way of expressing and

enhancing the self. Engagement and harmony with others is, then, a positively valued goal and the bridge—to open-hearted cooperation, as in *sunao*—is through sensitivity, reiterated by the mother's example and encouragement. (p. 58)

Kumagai (1981) said *sunao* "assumes cooperation to be an act of affirmation of the self" (p 261). Giving in is not a sign of weakness; rather, it reflects tolerance, self-control, flexibility, and maturity.

## THE ROLE OF THE OTHER IN THE INTERDEPENDENT SELF

In an interdependent view, in contrast to an independent view, others will be assigned much more importance, will carry more weight, and will be relatively focal in one's own behavior. There are several direct consequences of an interdependent construal of the self. First, relationships, rather than being means for realizing various individual goals, will often be ends in and of themselves. Although people everywhere must maintain some relatedness with others, an appreciation and a need for people will be more important for those with an interdependent self than for those with an independent self. Second, maintaining a connection to others will mean being constantly aware of others and focusing on their needs, desires, and goals. In some cases, the goals of others may become so focal in consciousness that the goals of others may be experienced as personal goals. In other cases, fulfilling one's own goals may be quite distinct from those of others, but meeting another's goals, needs, and desires will be a necessary requirement for satisfying one's own goals, needs, and desires. The assumption is that, while promoting the goals of others, one's own goals will be attended to by the person with whom one is interdependent. Hence, people may actively work to fulfill the others' goals while passively monitoring the reciprocal contributions from these others for one's own goal-fulfillment. Yamagishi (1988), in fact, suggested that the Japanese feel extremely uncomfortable, much more so than Americans, when the opportunity for such passive monitoring of others' actions is denied.

From the standpoint of an independent, "selfish" self, one might be led to romanticize the interdependent self, who is ever attuned to the concerns of others. Yet, in many cases, responsive and cooperative actions are exercised only when there is a reasonable assurance of the "good-intentions" of others, namely their commitment to continue to engage in reciprocal interaction and mutual support. Clearly, interdependent selves do not attend to the needs, desires, and goals of *all* others. Attention to others is not indiscriminate, it is highly selective and will be most characteristic of relationships with "in-group" members. These are others with whom one shares a common fate, such as family members or members of the same lasting social group, such as the work group. Out-group members are typically treated quite differently and are unlikely to experience either the advantages or disadvantages of interdependence. Independent selves are also selective in their association with others, but not to the extent of interdependent selves because much less of their behavior is directly contingent on the actions of others. Given the importance of others in constructing reality and regulating behavior, the in-group–out-group distinction is a vital one for interdependent selves; the subjective boundary of one's "in-group" may tend to be narrower for the interdependent selves than for the independent selves (Triandis, 1989).

To illustrate the reciprocal nature of interaction among those with interdependent views, imagine that one has a friend over for lunch and has decided to make a sandwich for him. The conversation might be: "Hey, Tom, what do you want in your sandwich? I have turkey, salami, and cheese." Tom responds, "Oh, I like turkey." Note that the friend is given a choice because the host assumes that friend has a right, if not a duty, to make a choice reflecting his inner attributes, such as preferences or desires. And the friend makes his choice exactly because of the belief in the same assumption. This script is "natural," however, only within the independent view of self. What would happen if the friend were a visitor from Japan? A likely response to the question "Hey, Tomio, what do you want?" would be a little moment of bewilderment and then a noncommital utterance like "I don't know." This happens because, under the assumptions of an interdependent self, it is the responsibility of the host to be able to "read" the mind of the friend and offer what the host perceives to be the best for the friend. And the duty of the guest, on the other hand, is to receive the favor with grace and to be prepared to return the favor in the near future, if not right at the next moment. A likely, interdependent script for the same situation would be: "Hey, Tomio, I made you a turkey sandwich

because I remember that last week you said you like turkey more than beef." And Tomio will respond, "Oh, thank you, I really like turkey."

The reciprocal interdependence with others, which is the sign of the interdependent self, seems to require constant engagement of what Mead (1934) meant by taking the role of the other. It involves the willingness and ability to feel and think what others are feeling and thinking, to absorb this information without being told, and then to help others satisfy their wishes and realize their goals. Maintaining connection requires inhibiting the "I" perspective and processing instead from the "thou" perspective (Hsu, 1981). The requirement is to "read" the other's mind and thus to know what the other is thinking or feeling. In contrast, with an independent self, it is the individual's responsibility to "say what's on one's mind" if one expects to be attended to or understood.

## Consequences of an Independent or an Interdependent View of the Self

Table 17.1 presents a brief, highly simplified summary of some of the hypothesized differences between independent and interdependent construals of the self. These construals of self and other are conceptualized as part of a repertoire of self-relevant schemata used to evaluate, organize, and regulate one's experience and action. As schemata, they are patterns of one's past behaviors as well as patterns for one's current and future behaviors (Neisser, 1976). Markus and Wurf (1987) called this assortment of self-regulatory schemata the *self-system*. Whenever a task, an event, or a situation is self-relevant, the ensuing processes and consequences are likely to be influenced by the nature of the self-system. The self-system has been shown to be instrumental in the regulation of intrapersonal processes such as self-relevant information processing, affect regulation, and motivation and in the regulation of interpersonal processes such as person perception, social comparison, and the seeking and shaping of social interaction (see Cantor & Kihlstrom, 1987; Greenwald & Pratkanis, 1984; Markus & Wurf, 1987, for reviews). The goal of this article is to further specify the role of the self-system in behavior by examining how these divergent cultural self-schemata influence individual experience.

In the current analysis, we hypothesize that the

**TABLE 17.1. Summary of Key Differences Between an Independent and an Interdependent Construal of Self**

| Feature compared | Independent | Interdependent |
|---|---|---|
| Definition | Separate from social context | Connected with social context |
| Structure | Bounded, unitary, stable | Flexible, variable |
| Important features | Internal, private (abilities, thoughts, feelings) | External, public (statuses, roles, relationships) |
| Tasks | Be unique | Belong, fit-in |
| | Express self | Occupy one's proper place |
| | Realize internal attributes | Engage in appropriate action |
| | Promote own goals | Promote others' goals |
| | Be direct; "say what's on your mind" | Be indirect; "read other's mind" |
| Role of others | *Self-evaluation:* others important for social comparison, reflected appraisal | *Self-definition:* relationships with others in specific contexts define the self |
| Basis of self-esteem[a] | Ability to express self, validate internal attributes | Ability to adjust, restrain self, maintain harmony with social context |

[a]Esteeming the self may be primarily a Western phenomenon, and the concept of self-esteem should perhaps be replaced by self-satisfaction, or by a term that reflects the realization that one is fulfilling the culturally mandated task.

independent versus interdependent construals of self are among the most general and overarching schemata of the individual's self-system. These construals recruit and organize the more specific self-regulatory schemata. We are suggesting here, therefore, that the exact organization of many self-relevant processes and their outcomes depends crucially on whether these processes are rooted in an independent construal of the self or they are based primarily on an interdependent construal of the self. For example, in the process of lending meaning and coherence to the social world, we know that people will show a heightened sensitivity to self-relevant stimuli. For those with an independent view of self, this includes information relevant to one's self-defining attributes. For one with an interdependent view of self, such stimuli would include information about significant others with whom the person has a relationship or information about the self in relation to another person. [. . .]

A third important function of the self-concept suggested by Markus and Wurf (1987) is that of motivating persons, of moving them to action. The person with an independent view of self should be motivated to those actions that allow expression of one's important self-defining, inner attributes (e.g., hardworking, caring, independent, and powerful), whereas the person with an interdependent view of self should be motivated to those actions that enhance or foster one's relatedness or connection to others. On the surface, such actions could look remarkably similar (e.g., working in-

credibly hard to gain admission to a desirable college), but the exact source, or etiology, of the energizing motivation may be powerfully different (De Vos, 1973; Maehr & Nicholls, 1980).

In the following sections, we discuss these ideas in further detail and review the empirical literature, which suggests that there are significant cognitive, emotional, and motivational consequences of holdings an independent or an interdependent view of the self.

## Consequences for Cognition

If a cognitive activity implicates the self, the outcome of this activity will depend on the nature of the self-system. Specifically, there are three important consequences of these divergent self-systems for cognition. First, we may expect those with interdependent selves to be more attentive and sensitive to others than those with independent selves. The attentiveness and sensitivity to others, characterizing the interdependent selves, will result in a relatively greater cognitive elaboration of the other or of the self-in-relation-to-other. Second, among those with interdependent selves, the unit of representation of both the self and the other will include a relatively specific social context in which the self and the other are embedded. This means that knowledge about persons, either the self or others, will not be abstract and generalized across contexts, but instead will remain specific to the focal context. Third, a consideration of the social context and reactions of others may also shape some basic, nonsocial cognitive activities such as categorizing and counterfactual thinking. [. . .]

## MORE INTERPERSONAL KNOWLEDGE

If the most significant elements of the interdependent self are the self-in-relation-to-others elements, there will be a need, as well as a strong normative demand, for knowing and understanding the social surrounding, particularly others in direct interaction with the self. That is, if people conceive of themselves as interdependent parts of larger social wholes, it is important for them to be sensitive to and knowledgeable about the others who are the coparticipants in various relationships, and about the social situations that enable these relationships. Maintaining one's relationships and ensuring a harmonious social interaction requires a full understanding of these others; that is, knowing how they are feeling, thinking, and likely to act in the context of one's relationships to them. It follows that those with interdependent selves may develop a dense and richly elaborated store of information about others or of the self in relation.

Kitayama, Markus, Tummala, Kurokawa, and Kato (1990) examined this idea in a study requiring similarity judgments between self and other. A typical American finding is that the self is judged to be more dissimilar to other than other is to the self (Holyoak & Gordon, 1983; Srull & Gaelick, 1983). This finding has been interpreted to indicate that, for the typical American subject, the representation of the self is more elaborated and distinctive in memory than the representation of another person. As a result, the similarity between self and other is judged to be less when the question is posed about a more distinctive object (Is *self* similar to other?) than when the question is posed about a less distinctive object (Is *other* similar to self?). If, however, those with interdependent selves have at least as much knowledge about some others as they have about themselves, this American pattern of findings may not be found.

To test these predictions, Kitayama et al. (1990) compared students from Eastern cultural backgrounds (students from India) with those from Western cultural backgrounds (American students). As shown in Figure 17.1, for the Western subjects, Kitayama et al. replicated the prior findings in which the self is perceived as significantly more dissimilar to the other than is the other to the self. Such a finding is consistent with a broad

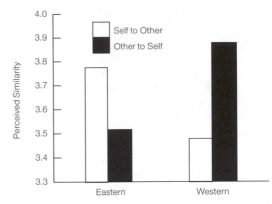

**FIGURE 17.1** ■ Mean perceived similarity of self to other and other to self by subjects with Eastern and Western cultural backgrounds.

range of studies showing that, for individuals with a Western background, supposedly those with independent selves, self-knowledge is more distinctive and densely elaborated than knowledge about other people (e.g., Greenwald & Pratkanis, 1984). This pattern, however, was nonsignificantly reversed for the Indian subjects, who judged the self to be somewhat more similar to the other than is the other to the self. It appears, then, that for the latter, more interdependent subjects, knowledge about others is relatively more elaborated and distinctive than knowledge about the self. Asymmetry in similarity judgments is an indirect way to evaluate knowledge accessibility, but a more direct measure of cross-cultural differences in knowledge of the other should reveal that those with interdependent selves have more readily accessible knowledge of the other.

## CONTEXT-SPECIFIC KNOWLEDGE OF SELF AND OTHER

A second consequence of having an interdependent self, as opposed to an independent self, concerns the ways in which knowledge about self and other is processed, organized, and retrieved from memory. For example, given an interdependent self, knowledge about the self may not be organized into a hierarchical structure with the person's characteristic attributes (e.g., intelligent, competent, and athletic) as the superordinate nodes, as is often assumed in characterizations of the independent self. In other words, those with interdependent selves are less likely to organize knowledge about the "self in general" or about the "other in general." Specific social situations are more likely to serve as the unit of representation than are attributes of separate persons. One learns about the self with respect to a specific other in a particular context and, conversely, about the other with respect to the self in a particular context.

In exploring variations in the nature of person knowledge, Shweder and Bourne (1984) asked respondents in India and America to describe several close acquaintances. The descriptions provided by the Indians were more situationally specific and more relational than those of Americans. Indian descriptions focused on behavior; they described what was done, where it was done, and to whom or with whom it was done. The Indian respondents said, "He has no land to cultivate but likes to cultivate the land of others," or "When a quarrel arises, he cannot resist the temptation of saying a word," or "He behaves properly with guests but feels sorry if money is spent on them." It is the behavior itself that is focal and significant rather than the inner attribute that supposedly underlies it. Notably, this tendency to provide the specific situational or interpersonal context when providing a description was reported to characterize the free descriptions of Indians regardless of social class, education, or literacy level. It appears, then, that the concreteness in person description is not due to a lack of skill in abstracting concrete instances to form a general proposition, but rather a consequence of the fact that global inferences about persons are typically regarded as not meaningful or informative.

Americans also describe other people in terms of the specifics of their behavior, but typically this occurs only at the beginning of relationships when the other is relatively unknown, or if the behavior is somehow distinctive and does not readily lend itself to a trait characterization. Rather than saying "He does not disclose secrets," Americans are more likely to say "He is discreet or principled." Rather than "He is hesitant to give his money away" Americans say "He is tight or selfish." Shweder and Bourne (1984) found that 46% of American descriptions were of the context-free variety, whereas this was true of only 20% from the Indian sample.

A study by J. G. Miller (1984) on patterns of explanation among Indian Hindus and Americans revealed the same tendency for contextual and relational descriptions of behavior among Indian respondents. In the first phase of her study, respondents generated two prosocial behaviors and two deviant behaviors and then explained why each behavior was undertaken. For example, in the prosocial case, respondents were asked to "describe something a person you know well did recently that you considered good for someone else." Miller coded the explanations for reference to dispositional explanations; for reference to social, spatial, temporal location and for reference to specific acts or occurrences. Like Shweder and Bourne (1984), she found that, on average, 40% of the reasons given by American respondents referred to the general dispositions of the actor. For the Hindu respondents, dispositional explanations constituted less than 20% of their responses.

In a second phase of the study, Miller (1984) asked both American and Indian respondents to explain several accounts of the deviant behaviors generated by the Indian respondents. For example, a Hindu subject narrated the following incident:

> This concerns a motorcycle accident. The back wheel burst on the motorcycle. The passenger sitting in the rear jumped. The moment the passenger fell, he struck his head on the pavement. The driver of the motorcycle—who is an attorney—as he was on his way to court for some work, just took the passenger to a local hospital and went on and attended to his court work. I personally feel the motorcycle driver did a wrong thing. The driver left the passenger there without consulting the doctor concerning the seriousness of the injury—the gravity of the situation—whether the passenger should be shifted immediately—and he went on to the court. So ultimately the passenger died. (p. 972)

Respondents were asked why the driver left the passenger at the hospital without staying to consult about the seriousness of the passenger's injury. On average, Americans made 36% of their attributions to dispositions of the actors (e.g., irresponsible; pursuing success) and 17% of their attributions to contextual factors (driver's duty to be in court). In comparison, only 15% of the attributions of the Indians referred to dispositions, whereas 32% referred to contextual reasons. Both the American and the Indian subjects focused on the state of the driver at the time of the accident but, in the Indian accounts, the social role of the driver appears to be very important to understand-

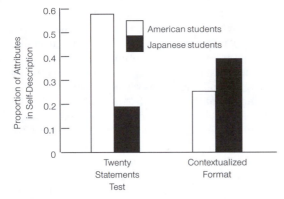

**FIGURE 17.2** ■ Mean proportion of psychological attributes endorsed by American and Japanese students in two self-description tasks.

ing the events. He is obligated to his role, he has a job to perform. Actions are viewed as arising from relations or interactions with others; they are a product of obligations, responsibilities, or commitments to others and are thus best understood with respect to these interpersonal relations. This preference for contextual explanations has also been documented by Dalal, Sharma, and Bisht (1983).

These results call into question the exact nature of the fundamental attribution error (Ross, 1977). In this error, people, in their efforts to understand the causes of behavior, suffer from an inescapable tendency to perceive behavior as a consequence of the internal, personal attributes of the person. Miller's (1984) Indian respondents also explained events in terms of properties or features of the person, yet these properties were their role relationships—their socially determined relations to specific others or groups. Because role relationships necessarily implicate the social situation that embeds the actor, it is unclear whether the explanations of the Indian respondents can be viewed as instances of the fundamental attribution error. It may be that the fundamental attribution error is only characteristic of those with an independent view of the self.

The tendency to describe a person in terms of his or her specific behavior and to specify the context for a given behavior is also evidenced when those with interdependent selves provide self-descriptions. Cousins (1989) compared the self-descriptions of American high school and college students with the self-descriptions of Japanese high

school and college students. He used two types of free-response formats, the original Twenty Statements Test (TST; Kuhn & McPartland, 1954), which simply asks "Who Am I?" 20 consecutive times, and a modified TST, which asks subjects to describe themselves in several specific situations (me at home, me with friends, and me at school). When responding to the original TST, the Japanese self-descriptions were like those of the Indians in the Shweder and Bourne (1984) study. They were more concrete and role specific ("I play tennis on the weekend"). In contrast, the American descriptions included more psychological trait or attribute characterizations ("I am optimistic" and "I am friendly"). However, in the modified TST, where a specific interpersonal context was provided so that respondents could envision the situation (e.g., me at home) and presumably who was there and what was being done to whom or by whom, this pattern of results was reversed. As shown in Figure 17.2, the Japanese showed a stronger tendency to characterize themselves in psychological trait or attribute terms than did Americans. In contrast, Americans tended to qualify their self-descriptions, claiming, for example, "I am sometimes lazy at home."

Cousins (1989) argued that the original TST essentially isolates or disembeds the "I" from the relational or situational context and, thus, self-description becomes artificial for the Japanese respondents, who are more accustomed to thinking about themselves within specific social situations. For these respondents, the contextualized format "Describe yourself as you are with your family" was more "natural" because it locates the self in a habitual unit of representation, namely in a particular interpersonal situation. Once a defining context was specified, the Japanese respondents were decidedly more willing to make generalizations about their behavior and describe themselves abstractly using trait or attribute characterizations.

American students, in contrast to their Japanese counterparts, were more at home with the original TST because this test elicits the type of abstract, situation-free self-descriptions that form the core of the American, independent self-concept. Such abstract or global characterizations, according to Cousins (1989), reflect a claim of being a separate individual whose nature is not bound by a specific situation. When responding to the contextualized self-description questions, the American students qualified their descriptions as if to say "This is how I am at home, but don't assume this is the way I am everywhere." For American respondents, selfness, pure and simple, seems to transcend any particular interpersonal relationships.

## BASIC COGNITION
## IN AN INTERPERSONAL CONTEXT

One's view of self can have an impact even on some evidently nonsocial cognitive activities. I. Liu (1986) described the emphasis that the Chinese place on being loyal, obedient, and pious to their superiors, whether they are parents, employers, or government officials. He claimed that most Chinese adhere to a specific rule that states "If your superiors are present, or indirectly involved, in any situation, then you are to respect and obey them" (I. Liu, 1986, p 78). The power and influence of this rule appear to go considerably beyond that provided by the American admonition to "respect one's elders." I. Liu (1986) argued that the standard of self-regulation, which involves the attention and consideration of others, is so pervasive that it may actually constrain verbal and ideational fluency. He reasoned that taking account of others in every situation is often at odds with individual assertion or with attempts at innovation or unique expression. This means, for example, that in an unstructured creativity task in which the goal is to generate as many ideas as possible, Chinese subjects may be at a relative disadvantage. In a similar vein, T. Y. Liu and Hsu (1974) suggested that consideration of the rule "respect and obey others" uses up cognitive capacity that might otherwise be devoted to a task, which may be the reason that Chinese norms for some creativity tasks fall below American norms.

Charting the differences between an independent and interdependent self may also illuminate the controversy surrounding the debate between Bloom (1981, 1984) and Au (1983, 1984) over whether the Chinese can reason counterfactually (for a thorough review of this debate, see Moser, 1989). Bloom's studies (1981) on the counterfactual began when he asked Chinese-speaking subjects questions like "If the Hong Kong government were to pass a law requiring that all citizens born outside of Hong Kong make weekly reports of their activities to the police, how would you react?" Bloom noted that his respondents con-

sistently answered "But the government hasn't," "It can't," or "It won't." Pressed to think about it anyway, the respondents became frustrated, claiming that it was unnatural or un-Chinese to think in this way. American and French respondents answered similar questions readily and without complaint. From this and subsequent studies, Bloom (1981, 1984) concluded that Chinese speakers "might be expected typically to encounter difficulty in maintaining a counterfactual perspective as an active point of orientation for guiding their cognitive activities" (1984, p. 21).

Au (1983) challenged Bloom's conclusions. Using different stimulus materials and different translations of the same stimulus materials, she reported that Chinese subjects performed no differently from their Western counterparts. The controversy continues, however, and many investigators remain unconvinced that the differences Bloom and others have observed in a large number of studies on counterfactual reasoning are solely a function of awkward or improper translations of stimulus materials.

Moser (1989), for example, discussed several of Bloom's (1981, 1984) findings that are not easily explained away. He described the following question that Bloom (1981, pp. 53–54) gave to Taiwanese, Hong Kong, and American subjects in their native language.

Everyone has his or her own method for teaching children to respect morality. Some people punish the child for immoral behavior, thereby leading him to fear the consequences of such behavior. Others reward the child for moral behavior, thereby leading him to want to behave morally. Even though both of these methods lead the child to respect morality, the first method can lead to some negative psychological consequences—it may lower the child's self-esteem.

According to the above paragraph, what do the two methods have in common? Please select only one answer.

A. Both methods are useless.
B. They have nothing in common, because the first leads to negative psychological consequences.
C. Both can reach the goal of leading the child to respect morality.
D. It is better to use the second.
E. None of the above answers makes sense. (If you choose this answer, please explain.)

Bloom (1984) reported that 97% of American subjects responded C, but that only 55% of the Taiwanese and 65% of the Hong Kong respondents answered C. In explaining his results, he wrote:

Most of the remaining Chinese-speaking subjects chose D or E and then went on to explain, based on their own experience and often at great length and evidently after much reflection, why, for instance, the second method might be better, or why neither method works, or why both methods have to be used in conjunction with each other, or perhaps, why some other specified means is preferable. For the majority of these subjects, as was evident from later interviewing, it was not that they did not see the paragraph as stating that both methods lead the child to respect morality, but they felt that choosing that alternative and leaving it at that would be misleading since in their experience that response was untrue. As they saw it, what was expected, desired, must be at a minimum an answer reflecting their personal considered opinion, if not a more elaborated explanation of their own experiences relevant to the matter at hand. Why else would anyone ask the question? American subjects, by contrast, readily accepted the question as a purely "theoretical" exercise to be responded to according to the assumptions of the world it creates rather than in terms of their own experiences with the actual world. (Bloom, 1981, p. 54)

It is our view that differences in response between the Americans and the Chinese may be related to whether the respondent has an independent or interdependent construal of the self. If one's actions are contingent on, determined by, or made meaningful by one's relationships and social situations, it is reasonable to expect that respondents with interdependent selves might focus on the motivation of the person administering the question and on the nature of their current relationship with this person. Consequently, in the process of responding, they might ask themselves, "What is being asked of me here? What does this question expect of me or require from me? What are potential ramifications of answering in one way or another in respect to my relationship with this person?" In Lebra's (1976) terms, what is "my proper place?" in this social interaction [i.e., me and the interviewer], and what are the "obligations attached to [it?]" (p. 67). To immediately respond to the question as a purely abstract or theoretical exercise would require ignoring the currently con-

stituted social situation and the nature of one's relationship with the other. This, of course, can be done, but it does not mean that it will be easily, effortlessly, or automatically done. And this is especially true when the pragmatics of a given context appears to require just the opposite. It requires ignoring the other's perspective and a lack of attention to what the other must be thinking or feeling to ask such a question. One's actions are made meaningful by reference to a particular set of contextual factors. If these are ignored or changed, then the self that is determined by them changes also. Those with relatively unencumbered, self-contained, independent selves can readily, and without hesitation, entertain any of a thousand fanciful possible worlds because there are fewer personal consequences—the bounded, autonomous self remains essentially inviolate.

One important implication of this analysis is that people with interdependent selves should have no disadvantage in counterfactual reasoning if the intent of the questioner and the demand of the situation is simply to test the theoretical reasoning capacities of the person. One such situation would involve an aptitude test such as the Scholastic Aptitude Test (SAT). Indeed, on the quantitative portion of the SAT, which requires substantial hypothetical and counterfactual reasoning (e.g., "If Tom walked 2 miles per hour, then how far will he have walked in 4 hours?"), both Taiwanese and Japanese children perform considerably better than their American peers (Stevenson et al., 1986).

It would appear important, therefore, to distinguish between competence and performance or between the presence of particular inference skills and the application of these skills in a particular pragmatic context (see also Laboratory of Comparative Human Cognition, 1982). The discussion thus far implies that, regardless of the nature of the self-system, most people with an adequate level of education possess the skills of hypothetical reasoning and the ability to think in a counterfactual fashion. Yet, the application of these skills in a particular situation varies considerably with the nature of the self-system. Some people may invoke these skills much more selectively. For those with interdependent selves, in contrast to those with independent selves, a relatively greater proportion of all inferences will be contingent on the pragmatic implications of a given situation, such as the perceived demands of the interviewer, the convention of the situation, and the rules of conversation.

Do styles of thinking and inference vary above and beyond those that derive from the pragmatic considerations of particular social situations? This question has yet to be more carefully addressed. However, given the tendency to see people, events, and objects as embedded within particular situations and relationships, the possibility seems genuine. Chiu (1972), for example, claimed that the reasoning of American children is characterized by an inferential–categorical style, whereas the reasoning of Taiwanese Chinese subjects displays a relational contextual style. When American children described why two objects of a set of three objects went together, they were likely to say "because they both live on a farm." In contrast, Chinese children were more likely to display a relational–contextual style, putting two human figures together and claiming the two go together "because the mother takes care of the baby." In the latter case, the emphasis is on synthesizing features into an organized whole. Bruner (1986) referred to such differences as arising from a paradigmatic versus a narrative mode of thought. In the former, the goal is abstraction and analyzing common features; in the latter, establishing a connection or an interdependence among the elements.

## Consequences for Emotion

In psychology, emotion is often viewed as a universal set of largely prewired internal processes of self-maintenance and self-regulation (Buck, 1988; Darwin, 1896; Ekman, 1972; LeDoux, 1987). This does not mean, though, that emotional experience is also universal. On the contrary, as suggested by anthropologists Rosaldo (1984), Lutz (1988), and Solomon (1984), culture can play a central role in shaping emotional experience. As with cognition, if an emotional activity or reaction implicates the self, the outcome of this activity will depend on the nature of the self-system. And apart from the fear induced by bright lights and loud sounds, or the pleasure produced by a sweet taste, there are likely to be few emotions that do not directly implicate one's view of the self. Thus, Rosaldo (1984) contended "feelings are not substances to be discovered in our blood but social practices organized by stories that we both enact and tell. They are structured by our forms of understanding" (p. 143) and, we would add, specifically, by one's construal of the self. In an extension of these ideas, Lutz (1988) argued that, although most emotions are viewed as universally experienced "natural" human phenomena, emotions are anything but natural. Emotion, she contended, "can be viewed as cultural and interpersonal products of naming, justifying, and persuading by people in relationship to each other. Emotional meaning is then a social rather than an individual achievement—an emergent product of social life" (Lutz, 1988, p. 5).

Among psychologists, several cognitively oriented theorists of emotion have suggested that emotion is importantly implicated and embedded in an actual social situation as construed by the person (e.g., De Riviera, 1984; Roseman, 1984; Scherer, 1984). Accordingly, not only does the experience of an emotion depend on the current construal of the social situation (e.g., Frijda, Kuipers, & ter Schure, 1989; Shaver, Schwartz, Kirson, & O'Connor, 1987; C. Smith & Ellsworth, 1987), but the experienced emotion in turn plays a pivotal role in changing and transforming the very nature of the social situation by allowing a new construal of the situation to emerge and, furthermore, by instigating the person to engage in certain actions. From the current perspective, construals of the social situation are constrained by, and largely derived from, construals of the self, others, and the relationship between the two. Thus, emotional experience should vary systematically with the construal of the self.

The present analysis suggests several ways in which emotional processes may differ with the nature of the self-system. First, the predominant eliciting conditions of many emotions may differ markedly according to one's construal of the self. Second, and more importantly, which emotions will be expressed or experienced, and with what intensity and frequency, may also vary dramatically.

## EGO-FOCUSED VERSUS OTHER-FOCUSED EMOTIONS

The emotions systematically vary according to the extent to which they follow from, and also foster and reinforce, an independent or interdependent construal of the self. This is a dimension that has largely been ignored in the literature. Some emotions, such as anger, frustration, and pride, have the individual's internal attributes (his or her own needs, goals, desires, or abilities) as the primary referent. Such emotions may be called *ego focused*. They result most typically from the blocking (e.g., "I was treated unfairly"), the satisfaction, or the confirmation (e.g., "I performed better than others") of one's internal attributes. Experiencing and expressing these emotions further highlights these self-defining, internal attributes and leads to additional attempts to assert them in public and confirm them in private. As a consequence, for those with independent selves to operate effectively, they have to be "experts" in the expression and experience of these emotions. They will manage the expression, and even the experience, of these emotions so that they maintain, affirm, and bolster the construal of the self as an autonomous entity. The public display of one's own internal attributes can be at odds with the maintenance of interdependent, cooperative social interaction, and when unchecked can result in interpersonal confrontation, conflict, and possibly even overt aggression. These negative consequences, however, are not as severe as they might be for interdependent selves because the expression of one's internal attributes is the culturally sanctioned task of the independent self. In short, the current analysis suggests that, in contrast to those with more interdependent selves, the ego-focused emotions will be more frequently expressed, and perhaps experienced, by those with independent selves.

In contrast to the ego-focused emotions, some other emotions, such as sympathy, feelings of interpersonal communion, and shame, have another person, rather than one's internal attributes, as the primary referent. Such emotions may be called *other focused*. They typically result from being sensitive to the other, taking the perspective of the other, and attempting to promote interdependence. Experiencing these emotions highlights one's interdependence, facilitates the reciprocal exchanges of well-intended actions, leads to further cooperative social behavior, and thus provides a significant form of self-validation for interdependent selves. As a consequence, for those with interdependent selves to operate effectively, they will have to be "experts" in the expression and experience of these emotions. They will manage the expression, and even the experience, of these emotions so that they maintain, affirm, and reinforce the construal of the self as an interdependent entity. The other-focused emotions often discourage the autonomous expression of one's internal attributes

and may lead to inhibition and ambivalence. Although among independent selves these consequences are experienced negatively (e.g., as timidity) and can, in fact, have a negative impact, they are tolerated, among interdependent selves, as the "business of living" (Kakar, 1978, p. 34). Creating and maintaining a connection to others is the primary task of the interdependent self. In short, this analysis suggests that, in contrast to those with more independent selves, these other-focused emotions will be more frequently expressed and perhaps even experienced among those with interdependent selves.

## EGO-FOCUSED EMOTIONS—EMOTIONS THAT FOSTER AND CREATE INDEPENDENCE

In a comparison of American and Japanese undergraduates, Matsumoto, Kudoh, Scherer, and Wallbott (1988) found that American subjects reported experiencing their emotions *longer* than did Japanese subjects, even though the two groups agreed in their ordering of which emotions were experienced longest (i.e., joy = sad > anger = guilt > fear = shame = disgust). Americans also reported feeling these emotions more intensely than the Japanese and reported more bodily symptoms (e.g., lump in throat, change in breathing, more expressive reactions, and more verbal reactions) than did the Japanese. Finally, when asked what they would do to cope with the consequences of various emotional events, significantly more of the Japanese students reported that no action was necessary.

One interpretation of this pattern of findings may assume that most of the emotions examined, with the exception of shame and possibly guilt, are what we have called ego-focused emotions. Thus, people with independent selves will attend more to these feelings and act on the basis of them, because these feelings are regarded as diagnostic of the independent self. Not to attend to one's inner feelings is often viewed as being inauthentic or even as denying the "real" self. In contrast, among those with more interdependent selves, one's inner feelings may be less important in determining one's consequent actions. Ego-focused feelings may be regarded as by-products of interpersonal relationships, but they may not be accorded privileged status as regulators of behavior. For those with interdependent selves, it is the interpersonal context that assumes priority over the inner attributes, such as private feelings. The latter may need to be controlled or de-emphasized so as to effectively fit into the interpersonal context.

Given these differences in emotional processes, people with divergent selves may develop very different assumptions about the etiology of emotional expressions for ego-focused emotions. For those with independent selves, emotional expressions may literally "express" or reveal the inner feelings such as anger, sadness, and fear. For those with interdependent selves, however, an emotional expression may be more often regarded as a public instrumental action that may or may not be related directly to the inner feelings. Consistent with this analysis, Matsumoto (1989), using data from 15 cultures, reported that individuals from hierarchical cultures (that we would classify as being generally interdependent; see Hofstede, 1980), when asked to rate the intensity of an angry, sad, or fearful emotion displayed by an individual in a photograph, gave lower intensity ratings than those from less hierarchical cultures. Notably, although the degree of hierarchy inherent in one's cultures was strongly related to the intensity ratings given to those emotions, it was not related to the correct identification of these emotions. The one exception to this finding was that people from more hierarchical cultures (those with more interdependent selves) were less likely to correctly identify emotional expressions of happiness. Among those with interdependent selves, often those from hierarchical cultures, positive emotional expressions are most frequently used as public actions in the service of maintaining interpersonal harmony and, thus, are not regarded as particularly diagnostic of the actor's inner feelings or happiness.

For those with interdependent selves, which are composed primarily of relationships with others instead of inner attributes, it may be very important not to have intense experiences of ego-focused emotions. This may be particularly true for negative emotions like anger. Anger may seriously threaten an interdependent self and thus may be highly dysfunctional. In fact, some anthropologists explicitly challenge the universalist view that all people experience the same negative emotions. Thus, in Tahiti, anger is highly feared, and various anthropological accounts claim that there is no expression of anger in this culture (see Levy, 1973; Solomon, 1984). It is not that these people have learned to inhibit or suppress their "real" anger, but that they have learned the importance of attending to others, considering others, and being gentle in all situations and, as a consequence, very little anger is elicited. In other words, the social reality is construed and actually constructed in such a way that it does not lend itself to the strong experience, let alone the outburst, of negative ego-focused emotions such as anger. The same is claimed for Ukta Eskimos (Briggs, 1970). They are said not to feel, express, or even to talk about anger. The claim is that they do not show anger even in those circumstances that would certainly produce complete outrage in Americans. These Eskimos use a word that means "childish" to label angry behavior when it is observed in foreigners.

Among the Japanese, there is a similar concern with averting anger and avoiding a disruption of the harmony of the social situation. As a consequence, experiencing anger or receiving anger signals may be relatively rare events. A study by Miyake, Campos, Kagan, and Bradshaw (1986), which compared Japanese and American infants of 11 months of age, provides suggestive evidence for this claim. These investigators showed each infant an interesting toy and paired it with a mother's vocal expression of joy, anger, or fear. Then they measured the child's latency to resume locomotion toward the toy after the mother's utterance. The two groups of infants did not differ in their reactions to expressions of joy or fear. But, after an angry vocal expression of the mother, there was a striking difference between the two groups. The Japanese children resumed locomotion toward the toy after 48 seconds, American children after only 18 seconds. It may be that the Japanese children are relatively more traumatized by their mother's anger expressions because these are such rare events.

Notably, in the West, a controversy exists about the need, desirability, and importance of expressing one's anger. Assuming a hydraulic model of anger, some argue that it is necessary to express anger so as to avoid boiling over or blowing up at a later point (Pennebaker, 1982). Others argue for the importance of controlling one's anger so as not to risk losing control. No such controversy appears to exist among those in predominantly interdependent cultures, where a seemingly unchallenged norm directs individuals to restrain their inner feelings and, particularly, the overt expression of these feelings. Indeed, many interdependent cultures have well-developed strategies that render them expert at avoiding the expression of negative emotions. For example, Bond (1986) reported that, in China, discussions have a clear structure that is explicitly designed to prevent conflict from erupting. To begin with, discussants present their common problems and identify all the constraints that all the participants must meet. Only then do they state their own views. To Westerners, such a pattern appears as vague, beating around the bush, and not getting to the heart of the matter. However it is part of a carefully executed strategy of avoiding conflict, and thus perhaps the experience of negative emotions. Bond, in fact, noted that, among school children in Hong Kong and Taiwan, there is a tendency to cooperate with opponents even in a competitive reward structure and to rate future opponents more positively than others who will not be opponents (Li, Cheung, & Kau, 1979, 1982).

In a recent cross-cultural comparison of the eliciting conditions of several emotions, Matsumoto et al. (1988) also found that Japanese respondents appear to be avoiding anger in close relations. Specifically, for the Japanese, closely related others were rarely implicated in the experience of anger. The Japanese reported feeling anger primarily in the presence of strangers. It thus appears that not only the expression, but also the experience of such an ego-focused emotion as anger, is effectively averted within an interdependent structure of relation. When anger arises, it happens outside of the existing interdependence, as in confrontation with out-groups (e.g., Samurai warfare in feudal Japan). In contrast, Americans and Western Europeans report experiencing anger primarily in the presence of closely related others. This is not surprising, given that expressing and experiencing ego-focused, even negative emotions, is one viable way to assert and affirm the status of the self as an independent entity. Consistent with this analysis, Stipek, Weiner, and Li (1989) found that when describing situations that produce anger, Chinese subjects were much more likely than American subjects to describe a situation that happened to someone else ("a guy on a bus did not give up a seat to an old woman"). For Americans, the major stimulus to anger was the situation where the individual was the victim ("a friend broke a promise to me").

Other emotions, such as pride or guilt, may also differ according to the nature of the mediating self-system. As with anger, these expressions may be avoided or they will assume a somewhat different form. For example, if defined as being proud of one's own individual attributes, *pride* may mean hubris, and its expression may need to be avoided for those with interdependent selves. Consistent with the idea that pride in one's own performance may be inhibited among those with interdependent selves, Stipek et al. (1989) found that the Chinese were decidedly less likely to claim their own successful efforts as a source of pride than were Americans. These investigators also reported that the emotion of guilt takes on somewhat different connotations as well. Among those with independent selves, who are more likely to hold stable, cross-situational beliefs and to consider them self-definitional, "violating a law or a moral principle" was the most frequently mentioned cause of guilt. Among Chinese, however, the most commonly reported source of guilt was "hurting others psychologically."

## OTHER-FOCUSED EMOTIONS—EMOTIONS THAT CREATE AND FOSTER INTERDEPENDENCE

Those with interdependent selves may inhibit the experience, or at least the expression, of some ego-focused emotions, but they may have a heightened capacity for the experience and expression of those emotions that derive primarily from focusing on the other. In Japan and China, for example, there is a much greater incidence of cosleeping, cobathing, and physical contact between mother and child than is typically true in most Western countries. The traditional Japanese mother carries the child on her back for a large part of the first 2 years. Lebra (1976) claimed that Japanese mothers teach their children to fear the pain of loneliness, whereas Westerners teach children how to be alone. Japanese and Chinese socialization practices may help the child develop an interdependent self in the first place and, at the same time, the capacity for the experience of a relatively greater variety of other-focused emotions.

The greater interdependence that results between mothers and their children in Japan is reflected in the finding that the classification of infants according to the nature of their attachments to their mothers (i.e., secure, ambivalent, and avoidant) departs markedly from the pattern typically observed in Western data. Specifically, many more Japanese infants are classified as "ambivalently attached" because they seem to experience decidedly more stress following a brief separation from the mother than do American infants (Ainsworth, Bell, & Stayton, 1974; Miyake, Chen, & Campos, 1985). This finding also indicates that a paradigm like the typical stranger situation is inherently linked to an independent view of self and, thus, may not be appropriate for gauging attachment in non-Western cultures.

In Japan, socialization practices that foster an intense closeness between mother and child give rise to the feeling of *amae. Amae* is typically defined as the sense of, or the accompanying hope for, being lovingly cared for and involves depending on and presuming another's indulgence. Although, as detailed by Kumagai and Kumagai (1985), the exact meaning of *amae* is open to some debate, it is clear that "the other" is essential. When a person experiences *amae,* she or he "feels the freedom to do whatever he or she wills" while being accepted and cared for by others with few strings attached. Some say *amae* is a type of complete acceptance, a phenomenal replication of the ideal mother-infant bond (L. T. Doi, 1973). From our point of view, experiencing *amae* with respect to another person may be inherent in the formation and maintenance of a mutually reciprocal, interdependent relationship with another person. If the other person accepts one's *amae,* the reciprocal relationship is symbolically completed, leading to a significant form of self-validation. If, however, the other person rejects one's *amae,* the relationship will be in jeopardy. [. . .]

## Consequences for Motivation

The study of motivation centers on the question of why people initiate, terminate, and persist in specific actions in particular circumstances (e.g., Atkinson, 1958; Mook, 1986). The answer given to this question in the West usually involves some type of internal, individually rooted need or motive—the motive to enhance one's self-esteem, the motive to achieve, the motive to affiliate, the motive to avoid cognitive conflict, or the motive to self-actualize. These motives are assumed to be part of the unique, internal core of a person's self-system. But what is the nature of motivation for those with interdependent self-systems? What form does it take? How does the ever-present need to attend to others and to gain their acceptance influence the form of these internal, individual motives? Are the motives identified in Western psychology the universal instigators of behavior?

As with cognition and emotion, motivational processes that implicate the self depend on the nature of the self-system. If we assume that *others* will be relatively more focal in the motivation of those with interdependent selves, various implications follow. First, those with interdependent selves should express, and perhaps experience, more of those motives that are social or that have the other as referent. Second, as we have noted previously, for those with independent selves, agency will be experienced as an effort to express one's internal needs, rights, and capacities and to withstand undue social pressure. However, among those with interdependent selves, agency will be experienced as an effort to be receptive to others, to adjust to their needs and demands, and to restrain one's own inner needs or desires. Motives related to the need to express one's agency or competency (e.g., the achievement motive) are typically assumed to be common to all individuals. Yet, among those with interdependent selves, striving to excel or accomplish challenging tasks may not be in the service of achieving separateness and autonomy, as is usually assumed for those with independent selves, but instead in the service of more fully realizing one's connectedness or interdependence. Third, motives that are linked to the self, such as self-enhancement, self-consistency, self-verification, self-affirmation, and self-actualization, may assume a very different form depending on the nature of the self that is being enhanced, verified, or actualized.

### MORE INTERDEPENDENT MOTIVES?

Murray (1938) assembled what he believed to be a comprehensive list of human motivations (see also Hilgard, 1953, 1987). Many of these motives seem most relevant for those with independent selves, but the list also includes some motives that should have particular salience for those with interdependent selves. These include *deference,* the need to admire and willingly follow a superior, to serve gladly; *similance,* the need to imitate or emulate others, to agree and believe; *affiliation,* the need to form friendships and associations; *nurturance,* the need to nourish, aid, or protect another; *succorance,* the need to seek aid, projection, or sympathy and to be dependent; *avoidance of blame*, the need to avoid blame, ostracism, or punishment by inhibiting unconventional impulses and to be well behaved and obey the law; and *abasement,* the need to comply and accept punishment or self-deprecation. Many of the social motives suggested by Murray seem to capture the types of strivings that should characterize those with interdependent selves. When the cultural imperative is to seek connectedness, social integration, and interpersonal harmony, most of these motives should be typically experienced by the individual as positive and desirable. In contrast, when the cultural task centers on maintaining independence and separateness, holding any of these motives too strongly (e.g., similance and succorance) often indicates a weak or troubled personality. Thus, Murray, for example, gave the need to comply the pejorative label of *need for abasement.*

The limited evidence for the idea that those with interdependent selves will experience more of the social or interdependent motives comes from Bond (1986), who summarized several studies exploring the motive patterns of the Chinese (see also McClelland, 1961). He found that the level of various motives are a fairly direct reflection of the collectivist or group-oriented tradition of the Chinese. Thus, Chinese respondents show relatively high levels of need for abasement, socially oriented achievement, change, endurance, intraception, nurturance, and order; moderate levels of autonomy, deference, dominance, and succorance; and low levels of individually oriented achievement, affiliation, aggression, exhibition, heterosexuality, and power. The socially oriented achievement motive has, as its ultimate goal, a desire to meet expectations of significant others, whereas the individually oriented achievement motive implies a striving for achievement for its own sake (discussed later). Hwang (1976) found, however, that with continuing rapid social change in China, there is an increase in levels of exhibition, autonomy, intraception, and heterosexuality and a decrease in levels of deference, order, nurturance, and endurance. Interestingly, it appears that those with interdependent selves do not show a greater need for affiliation, as might at first be thought, but instead they exhibit higher levels of those motives that reflect a concern with adjusting oneself so as to occupy a proper place with respect to others.

## THE MOTIVE FOR COGNITIVE CONSISTENCY

Another powerful motive assumed to fuel the behavior of Westerners is the need to avoid or reduce cognitive conflict or dissonance. Classic dissonance occurs when one says one thing publicly and feels another, quite contrasting thing privately (Festinger & Carlsmith, 1959). And such a configuration produces particular difficulty when the private attitude is a self-defining one (Greenwald, 1980). One might argue, however, that the state of cognitive dissonance arising from counterattitudinal behavior is not likely to be experienced by those with interdependent selves. First, it is the individuals' roles, statuses, or positions, and the commitments, obligations, and responsibilities they confer, that are the constituents of the self, and in that sense they are self-defining. One's internal attributes (e.g., private attitudes or opinions) are not regarded as the significant attributes of the self. Furthermore, one's private feelings are to be regulated in accordance with the requirements of the situation. Restraint over the inner self is assigned a much higher value than is expression of the inner self. Thus, Kiefer (1976) wrote:

> Although Japanese are often acutely aware of discrepancies between inner feelings and outward role demands, they think of the latter . . . as the really important center of the self. Regarding feelings as highly idiosyncratic and hard to control, and therefore less reliable as sources of self-respect than statuses and roles, the Japanese tends to include within the boundaries of the concept of self much of the quality of the intimate social group of which he is a member. (R. J. Smith, 1985, p. 28)

More recently, T. Doi (1986) has argued that Americans are decidedly more concerned with consistency between feelings and actions than are the Japanese. In Japan, there is a virtue in controlling the expression of one's innermost feelings; no virtue accrues from expressing them. Triandis (1989), for example, reported a study by Iwao (1988), gave respondents a series of scenarios and asked them to judge which responses would be appropriate for the person described in the scenario. In one scenario, the daughter brings home a person from another race. One of the possible responses given was "thought that he would never allow them to marry but told him he was in favor of their marriage." This answer was rated as best by only 2% of Americans. In sharp contrast, however, it was rated as best by 44% of the Japanese. Among the Americans, 48% thought it was the worst response, whereas only 7% of the Japanese rated it as the worst.

## COMMON MOTIVES
## IN AN INTERDEPENDENT CONTEXT

Of those motives assumed by Murray (1938) and Hilgard (1987) to be universally significant, the achievement motive is the most well-documented example. Variously defined as the desire to overcome obstacles, exert power, do something as well as possible, or to master, manipulate, or organize physical objects, human beings, or ideas (Hall & Lindzey, 1957; Hilgard, 1987), the achievement motive is thought to be a fundamental human characteristic. However, the drive for achievement in an interdependent context may have some very different aspects from the motive for achievement in an independent cultural context. In a recent analysis of the content and structure of values in seven cultures (i.e., Australia, United States, Spain, Finland, Germany, Israel, and Hong Kong), S. H. Schwartz and Bilsky (1990) found a conflict between values that emphasize independent thought and action and those that emphasize restraining of one's own impulses in all samples except Hong Kong. In the Hong Kong sample, self-restraint appeared to be quite compatible with independent thought and action.

Although all individuals may have some desire for agency or control over their own actions, this agency can be accomplished in various ways (Maehr, 1974). Pushing oneself ahead of others and actively seeking success does not appear to be universally valued. An illuminating analysis of control motivation by Weisz et al. (1984) suggests that acting on and altering the world may not be the control strategy of choice for all people. Instead, people in many Asian cultures appear to use what is termed *secondary control.* This involves accommodating to existing realities "sometimes via acts that limit individualism and personal autonomy but that enhance perceived alignment or goodness of fit with people, objects, or circumstances" (Weisz et al., 1984, p. 956).

The American notion of achievement involves breaking away, pushing ahead, and gaining control over surroundings. How do selves concerned with fitting in and accommodating to existing realities achieve? The question of achievement motive in an interdependent context is all the more compelling because many of the most collective societies of the world currently appear extremely preoccupied with achievement. In an analysis of Chinese children's stories, for example,

Blumenthal (1977) found that the most common behavior was achievement-oriented in nature, the second most frequent was altruism, and the third was social and personal responsibility. Among junior high school students in Japan, the motto "pass with four, fail with five" is now common. This refers to the fact that if one is sleeping 5 hours a night, he or she is probably not studying hard enough to pass exams. It appears, however, that this strong emphasis on achievement motivation is, in part, other motivated. It is motivated by a desire to fit into and meet the expectations of the group. In the child's case, the group is the family, and the child's mission is to enhance the social standing of the family by gaining admission to one of the top universities. The motive to achieve need not necessarily reflect a motive to achieve for "me" personally (Maehr & Nicholls, 1980). It can have social or collective origins. Children are striving to achieve the goals of others, such as family and teachers, with whom they are reciprocally interdependent. Consistent with this notion, Yu (1974) reported that the strength of achievement motivation was correlated positively with familism and filial piety. Striving for excellence necessarily involves some distancing or separating from some others, but the separation allows the child to properly accomplish the task of the student and thus to fulfill his or her role within the family.

Several studies by Yang (Yang, 1982/1985; Yang & Liang, 1973) have sought to distinguish between two types of achievement motivation: individually oriented and socially oriented. Individually oriented achievement motivation is viewed as a functionally autonomous desire in which the individual strives to achieve some internalized standards of excellence. In contrast, socially oriented achievement motivation is not functionally autonomous; rather, individuals persevere to fulfill the expectations of significant others, typically the family (Bond, 1986). With socially oriented achievement, when the specific achievement goal is met, the intense, formerly evident achievement motivation may appear to vanish. This analysis indeed fits many anecdotal reports indicating that, once admitted into the college of their choice or hired by their preferred company, Japanese high school and college students are no longer particularly interested in achievement.

Once a new goal is established, of course, the socially oriented achievement motive may be easily reengaged by any figure who can serve as a symbolic substitute for family members. A longitudinal survey conducted in Japan over the last 30 years (Hayashi, 1988) has repeatedly shown that approximately 80% of the Japanese, regardless of sex, age, education, and social class, prefer a manager with a fatherlike character (who demands a lot more than officially required in the work, yet extends his care for the person's personal matters even outside of work) over a more Western-type, task-oriented manager (who separates personal matters from work and demands as much as, yet no more than, officially required). In a large number of surveys and experiments, Misumi and his colleagues (summarized in Misumi, 1985) have demonstrated that, in Japan, a leader who is both demanding and personally caring is most effective regardless of the task or the population examined (e.g., college students, white-collar workers, and blue-collar workers). This is in marked contrast to the major conclusion reached in the leadership literature in the United States, which suggests that leadership effectiveness depends on a complex interaction between characteristics of leaders, characteristics of followers, and, most importantly, on the nature of the task (Fiedler, 1978; Hollander, 1985). According to our analysis, in Japan as well as in other interdependent cultures, it is the personal attachment to the leader, and the ensuing obligation to him or her, that most strongly motivate people to do their work. Motivation mediated by a strong personal relationship, then, is unlikely to be contingent on factors associated with the specific task or environment.

## THE SELF-RELATED MOTIVES

The motive to maintain a positive view of the self is one motive that psychologists since James (1890) through Greenwald (1980), Harter (1983), Steele (1988), and Tesser (1986) have assumed to be universally true. What constitutes a positive view of self depends, however, on one's construal of the self. For those with independent selves, feeling good about oneself typically requires fulfilling the tasks associated with being an independent self; that is, being unique, expressing one's inner attributes, and asserting oneself (see Table 17.1). Although not uncontested, a reasonable empirical generalization from the research on self-related motives is that Westerners, particularly those with high self-esteem, try to enhance themselves whenever possible, a tendency that results in a pervasive self-serving bias. Studies with American subjects demonstrate that they take credit for their successes, explain away their failures, and try to aggrandize themselves in various ways (e.g., Gilovich, 1983; Lau, 1984; J. B. Miller, 1986; Whitley & Frieze, 1985; Zuckerman, 1979). Maintaining self-esteem requires separating oneself from others and seeing oneself as different from and better than others. At 4 years old, children already show a clear self-favorability bias (Harter, 1990). When asked to compare themselves with others with respect to intelligence, friendliness, or any skill, most children think they are better than most others. Wylie (1979) reported that American adults also consider themselves to be more intelligent and more attractive than average, and Myers (1987), in a national survey of American students, found that 70% of students believe they are above average in leadership ability and, with respect to the "ability to get along with others," 0% thought they were below average, 60% thought they were in the top 10%, and 25% thought they were in the top 1%. Moreover, as documented by Taylor and Brown (1988), among Americans, most people feel that they are more in control and have more positive expectations for themselves and their future than they have for other people. This tendency toward false uniqueness presumably derives from efforts of those with independent selves to maintain a positive view of themselves.

The motive of maintaining a positive view of the self may assume a somewhat different form, however, for those with interdependent selves. Feeling good about one's interdependent self may not be achieved through enhancement of the value attached to one's internal attributes and the attendant self-serving bias. Instead, positive feelings about the self should derive from fulfilling the tasks associated with being interdependent with relevant others: belonging, fitting in, occupying one's proper place, engaging in appropriate action, promoting others' goals, and maintaining harmony (see Table 17.1). This follows for at least two reasons. First, people with interdependent selves are likely to be motivated by other-focused emotions, such as empathy and *oime* (i.e., the feeling of psychological indebtedness) and to act in accordance with the perceived needs and desires of their partners in social relations, may produce a social dynamic where individuals strive to enhance each other's self-esteem. In such reciprocal relationships, *other* enhancement could be more instrumental to self-enhancement than direct attempts at self-enhancement because the latter are likely to isolate the individual from the network of reciprocal relationships. Second, self-esteem among those with interdependent selves may be based in some large measure on their capacity to exert control over their own desires and needs so that they can indeed belong and fit in. As noted earlier (see also Weisz et al., 1984), such self-control and self-restraint are instrumental to the ability to flexibly adjust to social contingencies and thus are highly valued in interdependent cultures. Indeed, self-restraint together with flexible adjustment is often regarded as an important sign of the moral maturity of the person.

A developmental study by Yoshida, Kojo and Kaku (1982, Study 1) has documented that self-enhancement or self-promotion are perceived quite negatively in Japanese culture. Second (7–8 years old), third (8–9 years old), and fifth graders (10–11 years old) at a Japanese elementary school were asked how their classmates (including themselves) would evaluate a hypothetical peer who commented on his own superb athletic performance either in a modest, self-restrained way or in a self-enhancing way. The evaluation was solicited on the dimension of personality ("Is he a good person?") and on the dimension of ability ("Is he good at [the relevant athletic domain]?"). As shown in Figure 17.3A, the personality of the modest peer was perceived much more positively than was that of the self-enhancing peer. Furthermore, this difference became more pronounced as the age (grade) of the respondents increased. A similar finding also has been reported for Chinese college students in Hong Kong by Bond, Leung, and Wan (1982), who found that individuals giving humble or self-effacing attributions following success were liked better than those giving self-enhancing attribution. The most intriguing aspect of the Yoshida et al. (1982) study, however, is their finding for the ability evaluation, which showed a complete crossover interaction (see Figure 17.3B). Whereas the second graders took the comment of the peer at face value, perceiving the self-enhancing peer to be more competent than the modest peer, this trend disappeared for the third graders, and then completely reversed for the fifth graders. Thus, the fifth graders perceived that the modest peer was more competent than the self-enhancing peer. These findings indicate that, as children are so-

cialized in an interdependent cultural context, they begin to appreciate the cultural value of self-restraint and, furthermore, to believe in a positive association between self-restraint and other favorable attributes of the person not only in the social, emotional domains but also in the domains of ability and competence. Although it is certainly possible for those with independent selves to overdo their self-enhancement (see Schlenker & Leary, 1982), for the most part, the American prescription is to confidently display and express one's strengths; those who do so are evaluated positively (e.g., Greenwald, 1980; Mullen & Riordan, 1988).

## SELF- OR OTHER-SERVING BIAS

Given the appreciation that those with interdependent selves have for self-restraint and self-control, the various self-enhancing biases that are common in Western culture may not be prevalent in many Asian cultures. In an initial examination of potential cultural variation in the tendency to see oneself as different from others, Markus and Kitayama (1992) administered questionnaires containing a series of false-uniqueness items to large classes of Japanese college students in Japan and to large classes of American college students in the United States. In both cases, the classes were chosen to be representative of university students as a whole. They asked a series of questions of the form "What proportion of students in this university have higher intellectual abilities than yourself?" There were marked differences between the Japanese and the American students in their estimations of their own uniqueness; the Americans displayed significantly more false uniqueness than the Japanese. American students assumed that only 30% of people on average would be better than themselves on various traits and abilities (e.g., memory, athletic ability, independence, and sympathy), whereas the Japanese students showed almost no evidence of this false uniqueness. In most cases, the Japanese estimated that about 50% of students would be better than they were or have more of a given trait or ability. This is, of course, the expected finding if a representative sample of college students were evaluating themselves in a relatively nonbiased manner.

In a recent series of studies conducted in Japan with Japanese college students, Takata (1987) showed that there is no self-enhancing bias in so-

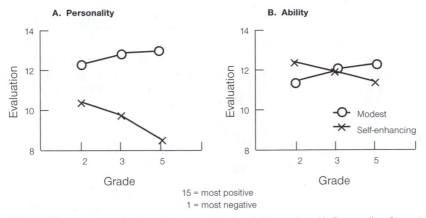

**FIGURE 17.3.** ■ Mean evaluations by second, third, and fifth graders. (A: Personality of target person. B: Ability of target person. Drawn from results by Yoshida, Kojo, and Kaku, 1982.)

cial comparison. In fact, he found just the opposite—a strong bias in the self-effacing direction. Participants performed several anagram problems that were alleged to measure memory ability. After completion of the task, the participants were presented with their actual performance on some of the trials and also the performance of another person picked at random from the pool of subjects who had allegedly completed the study. The direction of the self–other difference was manipulated to be either favorable or unfavorable to the subject. The dependent measures were collected in a private situation to minimize self-presentational concerns. Furthermore, because it was considered possible that the subjects might still believe they had a chance of seeing the other person afterward, in a followup study the "other person" was replaced with a computer program that allegedly simulated the task performance of the average college student.

Several studies (e.g., Goethals, 1989; Marks, 1984; Wylie, 1979) reveal that, with respect to abilities, Americans typically give themselves higher ratings than they give to others. Thus, when a comparison with another is unfavorable to the self, the self-enhancement hypothesis predicts that Americans should show little confidence in this estimate of their ability and seek further information. This, in fact, was the case in an American study by J. M. Schwartz and Smith (1976), which used a procedure very similar to Takata's (1987). When subjects performed poorly relative to another person, they had very little confidence in their

own score. These American data contrast sharply with the Japanese data. Takata's study shows a tendency exactly the opposite of self-enhancement. Furthermore, the pattern did not depend on whether the comparison was made with another person or with the computer program. The Japanese subjects felt greater confidence in their self-evaluation and were less interested in seeking further information when they had unfavorable self-evaluations than when they had favorable ones. Similarly, Wada (1988) also reported that Japanese college students were convinced of their level of ability on a novel, information integration task after failure feedback, but not after success feedback. These data suggest what might be called a modesty bias or an other-enhancement bias in social comparison.

A similar modesty bias among those with interdependent selves has also been suggested by Shikanai (1978), who studied the causal attribution for one's own success or failure in an ability task. Typically, American subjects believe that their internal attributes such as ability or competence are extremely important to their performance; this is particularly the case when they have succeeded (e.g., Davis & Stephan, 1980; Gilmor & Reid, 1979; Greenberg, Pyszczynski, & Solomon, 1982; Weiner, 1986). In the Shikanai study, Japanese college students performed an anagram task. Half of them were subsequently led to believe that they scored better than the average and thus "succeeded," whereas the other half were led to believe that they scored worse than the average and

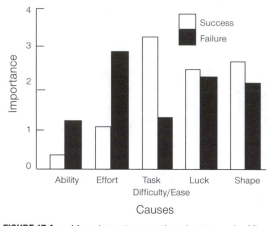

**FIGURE 17.4** ■ Mean importance rating given to each of five causes following success and failure. (Drawn from results by Shikanai, 1978.)

thus "failed." Subjects were then asked to choose the most important factor in explaining the success or the failure for each of 10 pairs made from the 5 possible causes for performance (i.e., ability, effort, task difficulty [or ease], luck, and mental–physical "shape" of the day). Shikanai analyzed the average number of times each cause was picked as most important (possible minimum of 0 and maximum of 4). As shown in Figure 17.4, a modesty bias was again obtained, especially after success. Whereas failure was attributed mainly to the lack of effort, success was attributed primarily to the ease of the task. Furthermore, the potential role of ability in explaining success was very much downplayed. Indeed, ability was perceived to be more important after a failure than after a success, whereas task difficulty (or its ease) was regarded to be more important after a success than after a failure. Subsequent studies by Shikanai that examined attribution of success and failure of others did not find this pattern (Shikanai, 1983, 1984). Thus, the pattern of "modest" appraisal seems to be specific to the perception and the presentation of the self and does not derive from a more general causal schema applicable to both self and others. For others, ability is important in explaining success. Yoshida et al. (1982, Studies 2 and 3), who studied explanations of performance in a Japanese elementary school, found the tendency to deemphasize the role of ability in explaining success as early as the second grade.

Observations of a tendency to self-efface, not to reveal the typical American pattern of blaming

others or the situation when explaining failure, have been made outside of the experimental laboratory as well. In a study by Hess et al. (1986), Japanese mothers explained poor performance among their fifth graders by claiming a lack of effort. In marked contrast, American mothers implicated effort in their explanations but viewed ability and the quality of the training in the school as equally important. This study also required the children to explain their own poor performance by assigning 10 points to each of five alternatives (ability, effort, training at school, bad luck, and difficulty of math). Japanese children gave 5.6 points to lack of effort, but American children gave 1.98 points. H. Stevenson (personal communication, September 19, 1989) noted that, in observations of elementary school classrooms, Japanese teachers, in contrast to American teachers, rarely refer to differences in ability among their students as an explanation for performance differences, even though the range of ability as assessed by standardized tests is approximately the same. Those with interdependent selves thus seem more likely to view intellectual achievement not as a fixed attribute that one has a certain amount of, but instead as a product that can be produced by individual effort in a given social context. [. . .]

## Conclusions

We have described two divergent construals of the self—an *independent* and an *interdependent* view. The most significant differences between these two construals is in the role that is assigned to the other in self-definition. Others and the surrounding social context are important in both construals but, for the interdependent self, others are included *within* the boundaries of the self because relations with others in specific contexts are the defining features of the self. In the words of Lebra (1976), the individual is in some respects "a fraction" and becomes whole when fitting into or occupying one's proper place in a social unit. The sense of individuality that accompanies an interdependent self includes an attentiveness and responsiveness to others that one either explicitly or implicitly assumes will be reciprocated by these others, as well as the willful management of one's other-focused feelings and desires so as to maintain and further the reciprocal interpersonal relationship. One is conscious of where one belongs with re-

*communal vs. exchange relationships*

spect to others and assumes a receptive stance toward these others, continually adjusting and accommodating to these others in many aspects of behavior (Azuma, 1984; Weisz et al., 1984). Such acts of fitting in and accommodating are often intrinsically rewarding because they give rise to pleasant, other-focused emotions (e.g., feeling of connection) while diminishing unpleasant ones (e.g., shame) and, furthermore, because the self-restraint required in doing so forms an important basis of self-esteem. Typically, then, it is others rather than the self that serve as the referent for organizing one's experiences.

With an independent construal of the self, others are less centrally implicated in one's current self-definition or identity. Certainly, others are important for social comparison, for reflected appraisal and in their role as the targets of one's actions, yet at any given moment, the self is assumed to be a complete, whole, autonomous entity, without the others. The defining features of an independent self are attributes, abilities, traits, desires, and motives that may have been social products but have become the "property" of the self-contained individual (see Sampson, 1989) and are assumed to be the source of the individual's behavior. The sense of individuality that accompanies this construal of the self includes a sense of oneself as an agent, as a producer of one's actions. One is conscious of being in control over the surrounding situation and of the need to express one's own thoughts, feelings, and actions to others and is relatively less conscious of the need to receive the thoughts, feelings, and actions of others. Such acts of standing out are often intrinsically rewarding because they elicit pleasant, ego-focused emotions (e.g., pride) and also reduce unpleasant ones (e.g., frustration). Furthermore, the acts of standing out, themselves, form an important basis of self-esteem. [. . .]

Self-esteem for those with an independent construal of the self depends on one's abilities, attributes, and achievements. The most widely used measure of self-esteem, the Rosenberg Self-Esteem Scale, requires the endorsement of items like "I am a person of worth" or "I am proud of my abilities." Self-esteem associated with an interdependent self could include endorsement of similar items, although what it means to be, for example, a person of worth could well have a different meaning. Or high self-esteem may be more strongly associated with an endorsement of items that gauge one's ability to read the situation and to respond as required. If this is the case, a threat or challenge to the self may not come in the form of feedback that one is unlike a cherished conception of the inner or dispositional self (dumb instead of smart; submissive rather than dominant) but instead in terms of a threat of a disruption of, or a disconnection from, the relation or set of relations with which one forms an interdependent whole. [. . .]

In sum, we have argued that the view one holds of the self is critical in understanding individual behavior and also the full nature of those phenomena that implicate the self. A failure to replicate certain findings in different cultural contexts should not lead to immediate despair over the lack of generality of various psychological principles or to the conclusion of some anthropologists that culturally divergent individuals inhabit incomparably different worlds. Instead, it is necessary to identify the theoretical elements or processes that explain these differences. We suggest that how the self is construed may be one such powerful theoretical element.

## REFERENCES

Ainsworth, M. D. S., Bell, S. M., & Stayton, D. (1974). Infant–mother attachment and social development. In M. P. Richards (Eds.), *The introduction of the child into a social world* (pp. 95–135). London: Cambridge University Press.

Allen, N. J. (1985). The category of the person: A reading of Mauss's last essay. In M. Carrithers, S. Collins, & S. Lukes (Eds.), *The category of the person: Anthropology, philosophy, history* (pp. 26–35). Cambridge, England: Cambridge University Press.

Allport, G. W. (1937). *Personality: A Psychological interpretation.* New York: Holt.

Atkinson, J. (Ed.). (1958). *Motives in fantasy, action and society.* New York: Van Nostrand.

Au, T. K. (1983). Chinese and English counterfactuals: The Sapir-Whorf hypothesis revisited. *Cognition, 15,* 162–163.

Au, T. K. (1984). Counterfactuals: In reply to Alfred Bloom. *Cognition, 17,* 289–302.

Azuma, H. (1984). Secondary control as a heterogeneous category. *American Psychologist, 39,* 970–971.

Bloom, A. (1981). *The linguistic shaping of thought.* Hillsdale, NJ: Erlbaum.

Bloom, A. (1984). Caution—the words you use may effect what you say: A response to Au. *Cognition, 17,* 281.

Blumenthal, E. P. (1977). Models in Chinese moral education: Perspectives from children's books. *Dissertation Abstracts International, 37*(10-A), 6357–6358.

Bond, M. H. (1986). *The psychology of the Chinese people.* New York: Oxford University Press.

Bond, M. H. (Ed.). (1988). *The cross-cultural challenge to social psychology.* Beverly Hills, CA: Sage.

Bond, M., Leung, K., & Wan, K.-C. (1982). The social impact of self-effacing attributions: The Chinese case. *Journal of Social Psychology, 118,* 157–166.

Briggs, J. (1970). *Never in anger.* Cambridge, MA: Harvard University Press.

Bruner, J. (1986). *Actual minds, possible worlds.* New York: Plenum Press.

Buck, R. (1988). *Human motivation and emotion* (2nd ed.). New York: Wiley.

Cantor, N, & Kihlstrom, J. (1987). *Personality and social intelligence.* Englewood Cliffs, NJ: Prentice-Hall.

Chiu, L. H. (1972). A cross-cultural comparison of cognitive styles in Chinese and American children. *International Journal of Psychology, 7,* 235–242.

Chodorow, N. (1978). *The reproduction of mothering: Psychoanalysis and the sociology of gender.* Berkeley, CA: University of California Press.

Cousins, S. (1989). Culture and selfhood in Japan and the U.S. *Journal of Personality and Social Psychology, 56,* 124–131.

Dalal, A. K., Sharma, R., & Bisht, S. (1983). Causal attributions of ex-criminal tribal and urban children in India. *Journal of Social Psychology, 119,* 163–171.

Darwin, C. R. (1896). *The expression of emotions in man and animals.* New York: Philosophical Library.

Davis, M. H., & Stephan, W. G. (1980). Attributions for exam performance. *Journal of Applied Social Psychology, 10,* 235–248.

De Riviera, J. (1984). The structure of emotional relationships. In P. Shaver (Ed.), *Review of personality and social psychology: Emotions, relationships, and health* (pp. 116–145). Beverly Hills, CA: Sage.

De Vos, G. A. (1973). *Socialization for achievement: Essays on the cultural psychology of the Japanese.* Berkeley: University of California Press.

De Vos, G. (1985). Dimensions of the self in Japanese culture. In A. Marsella, G. De Vos, & F. L. K. Hsu (Eds.), *Culture and self* (pp. 149–184). London: Tavistock.

Doi, L. T. (1973). *The anatomy of dependence.* Tokyo: Kodansha.

Doi, T. (1986). *The anatomy of self: The individual versus society.* Tokyo: Kodansha.

Dumont, L. (1970). *Homo hierarchicus.* Chicago: University of Chicago Press.

Durkheim, E. (1968). *Les formes elementaires de la vie religieuse* [Basic forms of religious belief] (6th ed.). Paris: Presses Universitarires de France. (Original work published 1912)

Ekman, P. (1972). Universals and cultural differences in facial expression of emotion. In J. K. Cole (Eds.), *Nebraska symposium on motivation* (pp. 207–283). Lincoln: University of Nebraska Press.

Erikson, E. (1950). Identification as the basis for a theory of motivation. *American Psychological Review, 26,* 14–21.

Festinger, L., & Carlsmith, J. M. (1959). Cognitive consequences of forced compliance. *Journal of Abnormal and Social Psychology, 58,* 203–210.

Fiedler, F. E. (1978). Recent development in research on the contingency model. In L. Berkowitz (Ed.), *Group processes* (pp. 209–225). New York: Academic Press.

Fiske, A. P. (1991). *Structures of social life: The four elementary forms of human relations: Communal sharing, authority ranking, equality matching, market pricing.* New York: Free Press.

Fiske, S. T, & Taylor, S. E. (1984). *Social cognition.* Reading, MA: Addison-Wesley.

Frijda, N. H., Kuipers, P, & ter Schure, E. (1989). Relations among emotion appraisal and emotional action readiness. *Journal of Personality and Social Psychology, 57,* 212–228.

Galtung, J. (1981). Structure, culture, and intellectual style: An essay comparing Saxonic, Teutonic, Gallic and Nipponic approaches. *Social Science Information, 20,* 817–856.

Geertz, C. (1975). On the nature of anthropological understanding. *American Scientist, 63,* 47–53.

Gergen, K. J. (1968). Personal consistency and the presentation of self. In C. Gordon & K. J. Gergen (Eds.), *The self in social interaction: Classic and contemporary perspectives* (Vol. 1, pp. 299–308). New York: Wiley.

Gilligan, C. (1982). *In a different voice: Psychological theory and women's development.* Cambridge, MA: Harvard University Press.

Gilmor, T. M., & Reid, D. W. (1979). Locus of control and causal attribution for positive and negative outcomes on university examinations. *Journal of Research in Personality, 13,* 154–160.

Gilovich, T. (1983). Biased evaluation and persistence in gambling. *Journal of Personality and Social Psychology, 40,* 797–808.

Goethals, A. (1989, April). *Studies of false uniqueness.* Paper presented at the Research Center for Group Dynamics Seminar, Institute for Social Research, University of Michigan, Ann Arbor, MI.

Greenberg, J., Pyszczynski, T., & Solomon, S. (1982). The self-serving attributional bias: Beyond self-presentation. *Journal of Experimental Social Psychology, 18,* 56–67.

Greenwald, A. G. (1980). The totalitarian ego: Fabrication and revision of personal history. *American Psychologist, 35,* 603–618.

Greenwald, A. G, & Pratkanis, A. R. (1984). The self. In R. S. Wyer & T. K. Srull (Eds.), *Handbook of social cognition* (Vol. 3, pp. 129–178). Hillsdale, NJ: Erlbaum.

Hall, C. S., & Lindzey, G. (1957). *Theories of personality.* New York: Wiley.

Hallowell, A. I. (1955). *Culture and experience.* Philadelphia: University of Pennsylvania Press.

Hamaguchi, E. (1985). A contextual model of the Japanese: Toward a methodological innovation in Japan studies. *Journal of Japanese Studies, 11,* 289–321.

Harter, S. (1983). The development of the self-system. In E. M. Hetherington (Eds.), *Handbook of child psychology: Vol. 4. Socialization, personality, and social development* (4th ed.). New York: Wiley.

Harter, S. (1990). Causes, correlates and the functional role of global self-worth: A life span perspective. In R. J. Sternberg & J. Kolligian, Jr. (Eds.), *Competence considered* (pp. 67–97). New Haven, CT: Yale University Press.

Hayashi, C. (1988). *National character of the Japanese.* Tokyo: Statistical Bureau, Japan.

Head, H. (1920). *Studies in neurology.* London: Oxford University Press.

Heelas, P. L. F., & Lock, A. J. (Eds.). (1981). *Indigenous psychologies: The anthropology of the self.* London: Academic Press.

Hess, R., Azuma, H., Kashiwagi, K., Dickson, W. P., Nagano, S., Holloway, S., Miyake, K., Price, G., Hatano, G., & McDevitt, T. (1986). Family influences on school readiness and achievement in Japan and the United States: An overview of a longitudinal study. In H. Stevenson, H. Azuma, & K. Hakuta (Eds.), *Child development and education in Japan* (pp. 147–166). New York: Freeman.

Hilgard, E. R. (1953). *Introduction to psychology.* New York: Harcourt, Brace.

Hilgard, E. R. (1987). *Psychology in American: A historical survey.* New York: Harcourt Brace Jovanovich.

Hofstede, G. (1980). *Culture's consequences: International differences in work-related values.* Beverly Hills, CA: Sage.

Hogan, R. (1975). Theoretical egocentrism and the problem of compliance. *American Psychologist, 30,* 533–540.

Holland, D., & Quinn, N. (1987). *Cultural models in language and thought.* Cambridge, England: Cambridge University Press.

Hollander, E. P. (1985). Leadership and power. In G. Lindzey & E. Aronson (Eds.), *Handbook of social psychology* (Vol. 2, pp. 485–537). New York: Random House.

Holyoak, K. J., & Gordon, P. C. (1983). Social reference points. *Journal of Personality and Social Psychology, 44,* 881–887.

Hsu, E. L. K. (1981). *American and Chinese: Passage to differences.* Honolulu: University of Hawaii Press.

Hsu, E. L. K. (1985). The self in cross-cultural perspective. In A. J. Marsella, G. De Vos, & E. L. K. Hsu (Eds.), *Culture and self* (pp. 24–55). London: Tavistock.

Hwang, C. H. (1976). Change of psychological needs over thirteen years. *Bulletin of Educational Psychology* (Taipei), *9,* 85–94.

Iwao, S. (1988, August). *Social psychology's models of man: Isn't it time for East to meet West?* Invited address to the International Congress of Scientific Psychology, Sydney, Australia.

James, W. (1890). *Principles of psychology.* New York: Holt.

A Japanese supermarket in New Jersey. (1989, April 6). *New York Times,* p. 4.

Johnson, F. (1985). The Western concept of self. In A. Marsella, G. De Vos, & E. L. K. Hsu (Eds.), *Culture and self.* London: Tavistock.

Kakar, S. (1978). *The inner world: A psychoanalytic study of childhood and society in India.* Delhi, India: Oxford University Press.

Kennedy, S., Scheier, I., & Rogers, A. (1984). The price of success: Our monocultural science. *American Psychologist, 39,* 996–997.

Kiefer, C. W. (1976). The *danchi zoku* and the evolution of metropolitan mind. In L. Austin (Ed.), *The paradox of progress* (pp. 279–300). New Haven, CT: Yale University Press.

Kitayama, S., Markus, H., Tummala, P., Kurokawa, M., & Kato, K. (1990). *Culture and self-cognition.* Unpublished manuscript.

Kondo, D. (1982). *Work, family and the self: A cultural analysis of Japanese family enterprise.* Unpublished doctoral dissertation, Harvard University.

Kuhn, M. H., & McPartland, T. S. (1954). An empirical investigation of self-attitudes. *American Sociological Review, 19,* 68–76.

Kumagai, H. A. (1981). A dissection of intimacy: A study of "bipolar posturing" in Japanese social interaction—*amaeru* and *amayakasu,* indulgence and deference. *Culture, Medicine, and Psychiatry, 5,* 249–272.

Kumagai, H. A., & Kumagai, A. K. (1985). The hidden "I" in *amae:* "Passive love" and Japanese social perception. *Ethos, 14,* 305–321.

Laboratory of Comparative Human Cognition. (1982). Culture and intelligence. In R. J. Sternberg (Ed.), *Handbook of human intelligence* (pp. 642–719). London: Cambridge University Press.

Lau, R. R. (1984). Dynamics of the attribution process. *Journal of Personality and Social Psychology, 46,* 1017–1028.

Lebra, T. S. (1976). *Japanese patterns of behavior.* Honolulu: University of Hawaii Press.

LeDoux, J. E. (1987). Emotion. In V. Mount Castle (Ed.), *Handbook of physiology: Vol. I. The nervous system* (pp. 419–459). Bethesda, MD: American Physiological Society.

Levy, R. (1973). *The Tahitians.* Chicago: University of Chicago Press.

Li, M.-C., Cheung, S.-F., & Kau, S.-M. (1979). Competitive and cooperative behavior of Chinese children in Taiwan and Hong Kong. *Acta Psychologica Taiwanica, 21,* 27–33. (From *Psychological Abstracts,* 1982, *67,* Abstract No. 11922)

Liu, I. (1986). Chinese cognition. In M. H. Bond (Ed.), *The psychology of the Chinese people* (pp. 73–105). New York: Oxford University Press.

Liu, T. Y., & Hsu, M. (1974). Measuring creative thinking in Taiwan by the Torrance test. *Testing and Guidance, 2,* 108–109.

Lutz, C. (1988). *Unnatural emotions: Everyday sentiments on a Micronesian atoll and their challenge to Western theory.* Chicago: University of Chicago Press.

Lykes, M. B. (1985). Gender and individualistic vs. collectivist bases for notions about the self. In A. J. Stewart & M. B. Lykes (Eds.), *Gender and personality: Current perspectives on theory and research* (pp. 268–295). Durham, NC: Duke University Press.

Maehr, M. (1974). Culture and achievement motivation. *American Psychologist, 29,* 887–896.

Maehr, M., & Nicholls, J. (1980). Culture and achievement motivation: A second look. In N. Warren (Ed.), *Studies in cross-cultural psychology* (Vol. 2, pp. 221–267). New York: Academic Press.

Marks, G. (1984). Thinking one's abilities are unique and one's opinions are common. *Personality and Social Psychology Bulletin, 10,* 203–208.

Markus, H. (1977). Self-schemas and processing information about the self. *Journal of Personality and Social Psychology, 35,* 63–78.

Markus, H., & Kitayama, S. (1992). Cultural variation in the self-concept. In G. R. Goethals & J. Strauss (Eds.), *Multidisciplinary perspectives on the self.* New York: Springer-Verlag.

Markus, H., & Wurf, E. (1987). The dynamic self-concept: A social psychological perspective. *Annual Review of Psychology, 38,* 299–337.

Marsella, A., De Vos, G., & Hsu, F. L. K. (1985). *Culture and self.* London: Tavistock.

Matsumoto, D. (1989). Cultural influences on the perception of emotion. *Journal of Cross-Cultural Psychology, 20,* 92–105.

Matsumoto, D., Kudoh, T., Scherer, K., & Wallbott, H. (1988). Antecedents of and reactions to emotions in the United States and Japan. *Journal of Cross-Cultural Psychology, 19,* 267–286.

Mauss, M. (1985). A category of the human mind: The notion of person; the notion of self [W. D. Halls, Trans.]. In M. Carrithers, S. Collins, & S. Lukes (Eds.), *The category of the person: Anthropology, philosophy, history* (pp. 1–25). Cambridge, England: Cambridge University Press. (Original work published 1938)

McClelland, D. C. (1961). *The achieving society.* New York: Free Press.

Mead, G. H. (1934). *Mind, self, and society.* Chicago: University of Chicago Press.

Miller, J. B. (1986). *Towards a new psychology of women* (2nd ed.). Boston: Beacon Press.

Miller, J. G. (1984). Culture and the development of everyday social explanation. *Journal of Personality and Social Psychology, 46,* 961–978.

Miller, J. G. (1988). Bridging the content–structure dichotomy: Culture and the self. In M. H. Bond (Ed.), *The cross-cultural challenge to social psychology* (pp. 266–281). Beverly Hills, CA: Sage.

Misumi, J. (1985). *The behavioral science of leadership: An interdisciplinary Japanese research program.* Ann Arbor, MI: University of Michigan Press.

Miyake, K., Campos, J., Kagan, J., & Bradshaw, D. L. (1986). Issues in socioemotional development. In H. Stevenson, H. Azuma, & K. Hakuta (Eds.), *Child development and education in Japan* (pp. 239–261). New York: Freeman.

Miyake, K., Chen, S., & Campos, J. J. (1985). Infant temperament, mother's mode of interaction, and attachment in Japan: An interim report. In I. Bretherton & E. Waters (Eds.), *Growing points of attachment theory and research. Monographs of the Society for Research in Child Development* (Vol. 50(1–2), pp. 276–297). Chicago: University of Chicago Press.

Mook, D. G. (1986). *Motivation: The organization of action.* New York: Norton.

Moore, C. A. (Ed.). (1967). Introduction: The humanistic Chinese mind. In *The Chinese mind: Essentials of Chinese philosophy and culture* (pp. 1–10). Honolulu: University of Hawaii Press.

Moser, D. (1989). *If this paper were in Chinese, would Chinese people understand the title?* Unpublished manuscript, Indiana University.

Mullen, B., & Riordan, C. A. (1988). Self-serving attributions in naturalistic settings: A meta-analytic review. *Journal of Applied Social Psychology, 18,* 3–22.

Murray, H. A. (1938). *Explorations in personality.* New York: Oxford University Press.

Myers, D. (1987). *Social psychology* (2nd ed.). New York: McGraw-Hill.

Neisser, U. (1976). *Cognition and reality: Principles and implications of cognitive psychology.* San Francisco: Freeman.

Neisser, U. (1988). Five kinds of self-knowledge. *Philosophical Psychology, 1,* 35–59.

Northrop, E. S. C. (1946). *The meeting of East and West.* New York: Macmillan.

Pennebaker, J. W. (1982). *The psychology of physical symptoms.* New York: Springer-Verlag.

Phillips, D. C. (1976). *Holistic thought in social science.* Stanford, CA: Stanford University Press.

Roland, A. (1988). *In search of self in India and Japan: Toward a cross-cultural psychology.* Princeton, NJ: Princeton University Press.

Rosaldo, M. Z. (1984). Toward an anthropology of self and feeling. In R. A. Shweder & R. A. LeVine (Eds.), *Culture*

*theory: Essays on mind, self, and emotion* (pp. 137–157). Cambridge, England: Cambridge University Press.

Roseman, I. J. (1984). Cognitive determinants of emotion: A structural theory. In P. Shaver (Ed.), *Review of personality in social psychology* (Vol. 5, pp. 11–36). Beverly Hills, CA: Sage.

Ross, L. D. (1977). The intuitive psychologist and his shortcomings: Distortions in the attribution process. In L. Berkowitz (Ed.), *Advances in experimental social psychology* (Vol. 10, pp. 173–220). New York: Academic Press.

Sampson, E. E. (1985). The decentralization of identity: Toward a revised concept of personal and social order. *American Psychologist, 40,* 1203–1211.

Sampson, E. E. (1988). The debate on individualism: Indigenous psychologies of the individual and their role in personal and societal functioning. *American Psychologist, 43,* 15–22.

Sampson, E. E. (1989). The challenge of social change for psychology: Globalization and psychology's theory of the person. *American Psychologist, 44,* 914–921.

Sass, L. A. (1988). The self and its vicissitudes: An "archaeological" study of the psychoanalytic avant-garde. *Social Research, 55,* 551–607.

Scherer, K. R. (1984). Emotions as a multi-component process: A model and some cross-cultural data. In P. Shaver (Ed.), *Review of personality and social psychology: Emotions, relationships, and health* (pp. 37–63). Beverly Hills, CA: Sage.

Schlenker, B. R., & Leary, M. R. (1982). Social anxiety and self-presentation: A conceptualization and model. *Psychological Bulletin, 92,* 641–669.

Schwartz, J. M., & Smith, W. P. (1976). Social comparison and the inference of ability difference. *Journal of Personality and Social Psychology, 34,* 1268–1275.

Schwartz, S. H., & Bilsky, W. (1990). Toward a theory of the universal content and structure of values: Extensions and cross-cultural replications. *Journal of Personality and Social Psychology, 58,* 878–891.

Shaver, P., Schwartz, J., Kirson, D., & O'Connor, C. (1987). Emotion knowledge: Further exploration of a prototype approach. *Journal of Personality and Social Psychology, 52,* 1061–1086.

Shikanai, K. (1978). Effects of self-esteem on attribution of success–failure. *Japanese Journal of Experimental Social Psychology, 18,* 47–55.

Shikanai, K. (1983). Effects of self-esteem on attributions of others' success or failure. *Japanese Journal of Experimental Social Psychology, 23,* 27–37.

Shikanai, K. (1984). Effects of self-esteem and one's own performance on attribution of others' success and failure. *Japanese Journal of Experimental Social Psychology, 24,* 37-46.

Shweder, R. A. (1984). Preview: A colloquy of culture theorists. In R. A. Shweder & R. A. LeVine (Eds.), *Culture theory: Essays on mind, self, and emotion* (pp. 1–24). Cambridge, England: Cambridge University Press.

Shweder, R. A. (1990). Cultural psychology: What is it? In J. W. Stigler, R. A. Shweder, & G. Herdt (Eds.), *Cultural psychology: Essays on comparative human development* (pp. 1–46). Cambridge, England: Cambridge University Press.

Shweder, R. A., & Bourne, E. J. (1984). Does the concept of the person vary cross-culturally? In R. A. Shweder & R. A. LeVine (Eds.), *Culture theory: Essays on mind, self and emotion* (pp. 158–199). Cambridge, England: Cambridge University Press.

Shweder, R. A, & LeVine, R. A. (Eds.). (1984). *Culture theory: Essays on mind, self, and emotion.* Cambridge, England: Cambridge University Press.

Smith, C., & Ellsworth, P. C. (1987). Patterns of appraisal and emotion related to taking an exam. *Journal of Personality and Social Psychology, 52,* 475–488.

Smith, R. J. (1985). A pattern of Japanese society: In society or knowledgement of interdependence? *Journal of Japanese Studies, 11,* 29–45.

Solomon, R. C. (1984). Getting angry: The Jamesian theory of emotion in anthropology. In R. A. Shweder & R. A. LeVine (Eds.), *Culture theory: Essays on mind, self, and emotion* (pp. 238–254). Cambridge, England: Cambridge University Press.

Srull, T. K., & Gaelick, L. (1983). General principles and individual differences in the self as a habitual reference point: An examination of self-other judgments of similarity. *Social Cognition, 2,* 108–121.

Steele, C. (1988). The psychology of self-affirmation: Sustaining the integrity of the self. In L. Berkowitz (Ed.), *Advances in experimental social psychology* (Vol. 21, pp. 181–227). San Diego, CA: Academic Press.

Stevenson, H., Azuma, H., & Hakuta, K. (1986). *Child development and education in Japan.* New York: Freeman.

Stigler, J. W., Shweder, R. A., & Herdt, G. (Eds.). (1990). *Cultural psychology: Essays on comparative human development.* Cambridge, England: Cambridge University Press.

Stipek, D., Weiner, B., & Li, K. (1989). Testing some attribution-emotion relations in the People's Republic of China. *Journal of Personality and Social Psychology, 56,* 109–116.

Stryker, S. (1986). Identity theory: Developments and extensions. In K. Yardley & T. Honess (Eds.), *Self and identity* (pp. 89–104). New York: Wiley.

Takata, T. (1987). Self-deprecative tendencies in self-evaluation through social comparison. *Japanese Journal of Experimental Social Psychology, 27,* 27–36.

Taylor, S. E., & Brown, J. D. (1988). Illusion and well-being: A social psychological perspective on mental health. *Psychological Bulletin, 103,* 193–210.

Tesser, A. (1986). Some effects of self-evaluation maintenance on cognition and action. In R. M. Sorrentino & E. T. Higgins (Eds.), *Handbook of motivation and cognition: Foundations of social behavior* (pp. 435–464). New York: Guilford Press.

Triandis, H. C. (1989). The self and social behavior in differing cultural contexts. *Psychological Review, 96,* 506–520.

Triandis, H. C., Bontempo, R., Villareal, M. J., Asai, M., & Lucca, N. (1988). Individualism and collectivism: Cross-cultural perspectives on self-ingroup relationships. *Journal of Personality and Social Psychology, 54,* 323–338.

Triandis, H. C., & Brislin, R. W. (Eds.). (1980). *Handbook of cross-cultural social psychology* (Vol. 5). Boston: Allyn & Bacon.

Veroff, J. (1983). Contextual determinants of personality. *Personality and Social Psychology Bulletin, 9,* 331–344.

Wada, M. (1988). Information seeking in self-evaluation of ability [Abstract]. In *Proceedings of Japanese Psychological Association Meeting, 52,* 222.

Waterman, A. S. (1981). Individualism and interdependence. *American Psychologist, 36,* 762–773.

Weber, M. (1958). *The Protestant ethic and the spirit of capitalism* (T. Parsons, Trans.). New York: Scribner.

Weiner, B. (1986). *An attributional theory of emotion and motivation.* New York: Springer-Verlag.

Weisz, J. R., Rothbaum, F. M., & Blackburn, T. C. (1984). Standing out and standing in: The psychology of control in America and Japan. *American Psychologist, 39,* 955–969.

White, G. M., & Kirkpatrick, J. (Eds.). (1985). *Person, self and experience: Exploring Pacific ethnopsychologies.* Los Angeles: University of California Press.

White, M., & LeVine, R. A. (1986). What is an *Ii ko* (good child)? In H. Stevenson, H. Azuma, & K. Hakuta (Eds.), *Child development and education in Japan* (pp. 55–62). New York: Freeman.

Whitley, B. E., Jr., & Frieze, I. H. (1985). Children's causal attributions for success and failure in achievement settings: A meta-analysis. *Journal of Educational Psychology, 77,* 608–616.

Wylie, R. C. (1979). *The self-concept: Vol. 2. Theory and research on selected topics.* Lincoln: University of Nebraska Press.

Yamagishi, T. (1988). Exit from the group as an individualistic solution to the free-rider problem in the United States and Japan. *Journal of Experimental Social Psychology, 24,* 530–542.

Yang, K. S. (1981a). The formation of change of Chinese personality: A cultural-ecological perspective [In Chinese]. *Acta Psychologica Taiwanica, 23,* 39–56.

Yang, K. S. (1982). Causal attributions of academic success and failure and their affective consequences. *Acta Psychologica Taiwanica, 24,* 65–83. (From *Psychological Abstracts,* 1985, *72,* Abstract No. 13126)

Yang, K. S. (1986). Chinese personality and its change. In M. H. Bond (Ed.), *The psychology of the Chinese people* (pp. 106–170). New York: Oxford University Press.

Yang, K. S., & Liang, W. H. (1973). Some correlates of achievement motivation among Chinese high school boys [In Chinese]. *Acta Psychologica Taiwanica, 15,* 59–67.

Yoshida, T., Kojo, K., & Kaku, H. (1982). A study on the development of self-presentation in children. *Japanese Journal of Educational Psychology, 30,* 30–37.

Yu, E. S. H. (1974). Achievement motive, familism, and *hsiao*: A replication of McClelland-Winterbottom studies. *Dissertation Abstracts International, 32,* 593A. (University Microfilms No. 74-14, 942)

Zuckerman, M. (1979). Attribution of success and failure revisited, or: The motivational bias is alive and well in attribution theory. *Journal of Personality, 47,* 245–287.

# Motivation and Self-Knowledge

Motivation and cognition are the two eternal themes in psychological theories. At the height of the cognitive revolution, it was fashionable to try to explain everything with as purely cognitive theories as possible, resorting to motivational explanations only as a last resort. In self theory, however, the motivations never disappeared entirely. It is obvious that (1) people desire (i.e., are motivated to seek) information about themselves and (2) they prefer some answers over others. Who can remain indifferent to finding out that you are sexy, smart, or talented?

As the introductory chapter in this book makes clear, three main motives have dominated social psychology's theories about self-knowledge. These are the desires for favorable information (self-enhancement), for consistency (self-verification), and for accurate information (diagnosticity). Much research has debated how these motives compete and compromise. The first two papers in this section address those questions.

Swann, Griffin, Predmore, and Gaines (1987) focus on the interplay between enhancement and verification motives. Following influential theorizing by Shrauger (1975) and initial findings by McFarlin and Blascovich (1981), these authors provide elegant data suggesting that people's preferences differ, depending on whether the measures are based on emotion or cognition. People may emotionally prefer favorable feedback, regardless of what they think of themselves, but they are less likely to believe highly favorable feedback, especially when it exceeds their current beliefs. Thus, self-enhancement rules by emotion, but cognition is guided by the consistency motive.

Swann's later work seeks other ways to reconcile these competing motives. In subsequent papers, he proposes that people have an immediate, automatic response to favorable feedback, whereas it is a slower, controlled response that emphasizes consistency. Thus, hearing excessive praise, one's first reaction might be "Terrific!"—but, after having some time to think it over, one may recognize the praise as excessive and begin to question and reject it (Swann, Hixon, Stein-Seroussi, & Gilbert, 1990).

Sedikides (1993) accepts that all three motives for self-knowledge are valid and focuses his work on estimating their relative power. By pitting them against each other in various experimental settings, he was able to draw conclusions about which motive is generally the strongest. One might assume that the desire for accurate information would be the strongest because it is most adaptive. After all, accurate information is, almost by definition, the

most useful because acting on the basis of wrong ideas seems a prescription for trouble. Yet, ironically, Sedikides found that the motivation to obtain accurate information was the weakest of the three motives.

The third paper in this set takes a different approach to the theme of motivation and self-knowledge. Steele (1988) proposes that people have a basic need to affirm their views of themselves, to express and validate their favorable opinions of themselves. He proposes that this motivation is a crucial but hidden factor in a broad range of psychological phenomena. Much of what people do is actually driven by this urge to affirm the self, so when people are permitted to affirm themselves, they fail to exhibit many of the standard patterns that researchers have shown, such as cognitive dissonance and attitude change.

## REFERENCES

McFarlin, D. B., & Blascovich, J. (1981). Effects of self-esteem and performance feedback on future affective preferences and cognitive expectations. *Journal of Personality and Social Psychology, 40,* 521–531.

Sedikides, C. (1993). Assessment, enhancement, and verification determinants of the self-evaluation process. *Journal of Personality and Social Psychology, 65,* 317–338.

Shrauger, J. S. (1975) Responses to evaluation as a function of initial self-perceptions. *Psychological Bulletin, 82,* 581–596.

Steele, C. M. (1988). The psychology of self-affirmation: Sustaining the integrity of the self. In L. Berkowitz (Ed.), *Advances in experimental social psychology* (Vol. 21, pp. 261–302). New York: Academic Press.

Swann, W. B., Griffin, J. J., Predmore, S. C., & Gaines, B. (1987). The cognitive-affective crossfire: When self-consistency confronts self-enhancement. *Journal of Personality and Social Psychology, 52,* 881–889.

Swann, W. B., Hixon, J. G., Stein-Seroussi, A., & Gilbert, D. T. (1990). The fleeting gleam of praise: Cognitive processes underlying behavioral reactions to self-relevant feedback. *Journal of Personality and Social Psychology, 59,* 17–26.

# Discussion Questions

1. When your friends ask for your opinion of their work, appearance, or personality, do you give a blunt, critical answer or a supportive, positive one?

2. What situations might make people desire diagnostic information (putting accuracy above other motives) most strongly?

3. Would you want your spouse to either recognize all your faults and flaws or have an idealized impression of you? Is complete honesty about each other's weak points the best policy when dating or when pursuing a long-term relationship?

4. Self-affirmation theory seems to hold that different aspects or activities of the self are largely interchangeable—affirming that one can overcome setbacks with respect to another. What are likely to be the limits to this generality?
5. How might these various self-knowledge motivations differ between people with high vs. low self-esteem?

# Suggested Readings

Kunda, Z. (1990). The case for motivated reasoning. *Psychological Bulletin, 108,* 480–498. This recent review discusses how motivations can bias and distort mental processes. Many, but not all, of the motivations are linked to the self.

Dunning, D. (1999). A newer look: Motivated social cognition and the schematic representation of social concepts. *Psychological Inquiry, 10,* 1–11. This article provides a recent and captivating overview of progress in the study of motivated cognition, with emphasis on the author's own contributions (which are important and creative). The article is followed by two other articles on motivated cognition (by Kunda and Murray), which also are good, and then a series of brief comments written by many other experts in the field, offering an exchange of debate among scholars.

Swann, W. B. (1987). Identity negotiation: Where two roads meet. *Journal of Personality and Social Psychology, 53,* 1038–1051. In this paper, Swann offers an overview of his research program and his views about self-enhancement vs. self-verification.

Baumeister, R. F., Dale, K., & Sommer, K. L. (1998). Freudian defense mechanisms and empirical findings in modern social psychology: Reaction formation, projection, displacement, undoing, isolation, sublimation, and denial. *Journal of Personality, 66,* 1081–1124. Freud's defense mechanism theory was perhaps the first major psychological theory about how self-knowledge is affected by preferences and motivations. This article reviews published studies relevant to many of these defense mechanisms.

# The Psychology of Self-Affirmation: Sustaining the Integrity of the Self

Claude M. Steele • Department of Psychology, University of Washington

*Sam*: Why is it what you just said strikes me as a mass of rationalizations?

*Michael*: Don't knock rationalization. Where would we be without it? I don't know anyone who could get through the day without two or three juicy rationalizations. They're more important than sex.

*Sam*: Ah, come on. Nothin's more important than sex.

*Michael*: Oh Yeah? You ever gone a week without a rationalization?

(*The Big Chill*, 1982)

In 1957, Leon Festinger relied heavily on the rationalizations of cigarette smokers to illustrate the nature of dissonance processes. The smoker's dilemma was ideal for this purpose; smoking cigarettes stands in dissonant relationship to evidence that cigarettes harm health, an inconsistency clearly in need of resolution. Means of reducing dissonance were illustrated as possible resolutions of the dilemma: the smoker could quit, deny or diminish the health risks, rationalize that the benefits of smoking (e.g., relaxation) outweighed its risks, and so on. Importantly, from the standpoint of the reasoning presented in this article, Festinger's description of these resolutions included only changes (cognitive or behavioral) related to the provoking inconsistency; the elements of the inconsistency—the habit of smoking and the belief that smoking causes disease—had to be changed, rationalized, or diminished in importance. In 1957, this restriction surely seemed reasonable. Society was not saturated with information linking smoking to lung cancer, heart disease, and emphysema. Nor was social disapproval of smoking prevalent. Thus, the smoker might well have escaped his dilemma through denial of the smoking–health link or another of Festinger's remedies.

These remedies, however, should be less effective in the world of the contemporary smoker. Evidence that smoking causes serious disease is virtually unassailable and widely disseminated. Social disapproval of smoking borders on the zealous; laws even restrict it to isolated areas. Aside from quitting, contemporary society has made it difficult for the smoker to resolve the dilemma through any of the remedies outlined by Festinger. Still, of course, people continue to smoke, which raises an interesting question: Is the battery of cognitive strategies and rationalizations that Festinger granted to the smoker sufficient to explain how he copes with his dilemma in these times, or does the smoker have an extra degree of psychological resilience not captured by dissonance theory?

In this article, I will argue that the latter of these possibilities is closer to fact and attempt a general analysis of the processes through which this "resilience" is achieved. At the basis of this analysis, I propose the existence of a self-system that essentially explains ourselves, and the world at large, to ourselves. The purpose of these constant explanations and rationalizations is to maintain a phenomenal experience of the self (self-conceptions and images) as adaptively and morally adequate—that is, as competent, good, coherent, unitary, stable, capable of free choice, capable of controlling important outcomes, and so on. I view these self-affirmation processes as being activated by information that threatens the perceived adequacy or integrity of the self and as running their course until this perception is restored through explanation, rationalization, and/or action.

From the standpoint of these processes, what is disturbing about the inconsistency of smoking cigarettes (aside from fear of the actual effects of smoking) is not the inconsistency itself, as Festinger had argued, but the threat the inconsistency poses to the perception of self-integrity, its implication that one is foolish or unable to control important behavior. Thus, to reduce the disturbing impact of his dilemma, the smoker need not, in contrast to Festinger's view, resolve the provoking inconsistency. He need only engage in some affirmation of general self-integrity, even when that affirmation bears no relationship to either smoking or the inconsistency that smoking produces. He might, for example, join a valued cause, spend more time with his children, or try to accomplish more at the office and, in these ways, affirm a larger sense of being an adequate person. The inconsistency would remain, of course. However, in the context of other valued self-concepts, it should pose less threat to global self-integrity and thus be more tolerable. Herein may lie the smoker's resilience—a resilience that, I hope to demonstrate, has been underestimated in many areas of social psychological research, including research on dissonance and attributional processes, the focus of this article.

The smoker's dilemma can illustrate another point as well, one primarily of orientation: the research reported in this article focuses on how people cope with the implications of threat to their self-regard, rather than on how they cope with the threat itself. Smoking cigarettes, and the possibility of ill effects that go with it, obviously constitute a physical threat to the smoker's welfare and outcome. The smoker must, in some way, cope with this threat; he can quit, deny the risks, smoke less, and so on. Considerable research and theory in psychology have examined how people cope with threats per se (e.g., Lazarus, 1968, 1983). Indeed, nearly all theory concerning how people respond to environmental and interpersonal demands can pertain to how people cope with actual threat. In addition to constituting a threat to physical health, however, smoking cigarettes can threaten the perceived integrity of the self, one's sense of adaptive and moral adequacy. In general, threats of this sort can arise in many ways: from our own behavior, as in the case of smoking or personal failure; from the judgments of others, as in the case of prejudicial judgments; from catastrophic events, as in the case of serious illness that threatens our sense of control over important outcomes; and so on.

In making this point, several additional considerations should be emphasized. Threats can differ in how much they threaten one's welfare versus one's self-regard. An earthquake, for example, may pose considerable threat to one's actual life outcomes, but relatively little threat to one's self-regard. In contrast, faculty raise reviews may pose relatively little threat to life outcomes, but might pose considerable threat to self-regard. It also is clear that adaptation to one of these aspects of threat can constitute adaptation to the other. Surely if the smoker successfully stops smoking, he will have coped effectively with its threat to both health and self-regard. Likewise, if the smoker develops strong self-conceptions of efficacy with regard to quitting, he should find it easier to quit, as efficacy expectations foster strong behavior motivation (cf. Bandura, 1977, 1982). Adaptations to these different aspects of a threat can be interrelated, even interchangeable. This article, however, analyzes how coping processes restore self-regard, rather than how they address the provoking threat itself.

## Name-Calling and Compliance: A Demonstrational Study

The idea that people might try to cope with one kind of self-threat by affirming an unrelated aspect of the self—an idea central to our later reasoning about self-affirmation—was first suggested in our research by the results of an experiment on the effect of name-calling on compliance (Steele, 1975). The important elements of this study were as follows.

In the first part of this experiment, the part in which self-threat was manipulated, women in Salt Lake City who were at home during the day were telephoned on a Wednesday afternoon by a male experimenter posing as a pollster. After introducing himself and inquiring about their interest in participating in a future poll on women's issues, he told women randomly assigned to a relevant negative name condition that it was pretty much common knowledge that, as members of their community, they were uncooperative with community projects. That was the name-calling. He ended his calls by asking each subject whether she would like to see a future poll on women's issues conducted in her community. Because of the unusually strong ethic for community cooperation in this heavily Mormon city (approximately 50% of the population), especially among women who work at home, we presumed that this name-calling would threaten a reasonably important self-concept of these women. The experiment included several other conditions as well. In a positive name condition, the pollster in the first telephone contact told the women that it was common knowledge that, as members of their community, they were cooperative with community projects. In an irrelevant negative name condition, again based on their community membership, the pollster impugned their concern for driving safety and the carefulness of their driving. Finally, there was a base rate control condition in which subjects did not receive any initial telephone contact.

Two days later, on Friday, the women in all conditions (in the control condition these women had not received an initial call) were contacted by a female experimenter posing as a community member ostensibly unrelated to the first caller. She asked each woman to help with a community project—the development of a food co-op—by listing everything in her kitchen to help guide the wholesale buying for the co-op. She told the women that she would call them back the following Monday to collect the information. (Subjects who agreed to help were recontacted and their information was passed on to a real food co-op.)

The predictions for this experiment were guided by a general cognitive consistency theory framework. The relevant negative name condition, we assumed, would establish an inconsistency between the implications of the name—that as a member of her community the subject was perceived as uncooperative—and the subject's self-concept of being a cooperative person. Furthermore, we expected more subjects in this condition to help with the food co-op to bolster their self-concept of being cooperative, thereby refuting the provoking inconsistency. Following this logic, we expected less helping in the other conditions, in the positive name and control conditions, because no motivating inconsistency had been established and in the irrelevant negative name condition, because, presumably, the driving safety inconsistency could not be discounted by helping with a food co-op. In fact, as a point to which I shall return, the irrelevant negative name condition was included only at the last moment as a control for the role of consistency processes in mediating the predicted effects.

The mean percentages in Figure 18.1 show that, as expected, the relevant negative name condition caused more helping than either the base rate or positive name conditions—virtually twice as much. The figure, however, reveals a surprise: the irrelevant negative name condition also caused twice as much helping as other conditions. Regardless of whether subjects were called uncooperative with community projects or bad drivers, more of them helped in negative name conditions than

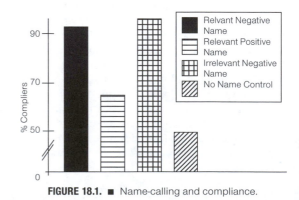

**FIGURE 18.1.** ■ Name-calling and compliance.

in other conditions, and dramatically so. These same condition effects were also reflected in the actual amount of compliance, as measured by the amount of information subjects provided during final phone contact. These results bring to light several issues that have directed our research in the years since and comprise the major themes of this article.

## Self-Affirmation Processes and Their Implications

### THE IMPORTANCE OF SELF-AFFIRMATION PROCESSES

Clearly, consistency-maintaining processes did not mediate the effects of name-calling in this study. Helping with the establishment of a community food co-op could not refute, in the irrelevant negative name condition, the specific inconsistency stemming from the bad driver name. Thus, the greater helping of women in this condition had to be mediated by some process other than the need for psychological consistency. The simplest explanation seems to be that women in the negative name conditions helped more in order to reaffirm their general goodness and worth after their goodness had been threatened. While helping with a food co-op could not disprove the bad driver label, it could help in proving that they were good, worthy people. We argued, then, that name-calling induced helping in this study by arousing a general ego-protective system, one function of which is to affirm an overall self-concept of worth after it has been threatened.

In doing so, we suggest the importance of such a self-system in mediating many social psychological phenomena; in particular, responses to self-threat. In different terms, virtually all self-theorists have described this aspect of the self. William James (1915) used the terms "self-seeking" or "self-preservation" to describe the seeking of things, including relationships and beliefs, that benefit and protect our welfare and self-esteem. Allport (1943) described the same aspect of the self with the term "ego-enhancement" and (Epstein (1973) asserted that there is a basic need to enhance and protect the self to which "all other needs are subordinate." Greenwald (1980) more recently proposed a "totalitarian ego" that biases information processing to affirm the goodness, strength, and stability of the self. The function of this ego-

protective system is generally assumed to be that of sustaining self-concepts that facilitate effective behavior. This view is most explicit, perhaps, in Bandura's theory of self-efficacy (cf. Bandura, 1977, 1982), which assumes that expected efficacy with regard to a behavior is critical to motivating performance of the behavior. Other research, as well, has demonstrated that expectations of efficacy, even when illusory, are critical to the undertaking and persistence of effective action (cf. Greenwald, 1980; Silver & Wortman, 1980; Taylor, 1983). [. . .]

My work assumes the existence of a self-esteem system that explains ourselves, a system that persistently explains our behavior and the world at large, sustaining a phenomenal experience of the self as adaptively and morally adequate. This self-affirmation system, we assume, is activated whenever information threatens the perceived integrity of the self and pressures for adaptation, either behavioral or cognitive, until this perception is restored. Our research suggests that these processes have more systematic influence on social psychological phenomena than has yet been recognized. This article describes this research and then presents a model of these processes.

### THE FLUIDITY OF SELF-AFFIRMATION PROCESSES

That some women responded to an impugnment of their driving by helping more with a food co-op suggests that people respond to self-threat more fluidly than is typically recognized. Like the smoker described earlier in the article, people can apparently adapt to self-threat through actions that affirm the general integrity of the self even when these adaptations do nothing to resolve the provoking threat itself. Indeed, this may be the only adaptation possible for some threats. Taylor (1983) has found, for example, that breast cancer victims, unable to eliminate the threat they are under, adapt by changing their lives to affirm their basic values, such as quitting a boring job to write short stories.

As important, this fluidity of adaptation suggests the existence of a larger, ego-protective self-system that is not geared to resolving specific self-concept threats, but to maintaining an overall conception of self-integrity. Allport (1943) made a similar point in reacting to educator John E. Anderson's remark that a student's "success in one area may more than compensate for failure in many areas" (1942, p. 349):

> Only in terms of ego psychology can we account for such fluid compensation. Mental health and happiness, it seems, does not depend upon the satisfaction of this drive or that drive, it depends rather upon the person finding some area of success somewhere. (Allport, 1943, p. 466)

Thus, perhaps more than any other effect attributable to ego protection, this "fluid compensation" implies the existence of a system for maintaining perceived integrity of the self, rather than for resolving particular self-threats.

## SELF-AFFIRMATION PROCESSES AND SOCIAL PSYCHOLOGICAL THEORY

If this reasoning can be granted for the moment, it has implications for an important class of theories in social psychology—theories constructed around distinct motives such as for consistency, equity, self-completion, control, and freedom. In tests of these motives, they are invariably aroused by some form of self-threat; for example, in reactance research (Brehm, 1966) by threatening a personal freedom, in self-completion research (e.g., Wicklund & Gollwitzer, 1983) by threatening the achievement of an important self-goal, in equity research (e.g., Walster, Walster, & Berscheid, 1978) by threatening a self-conception of fairness, in learned helplessness research (Seligman, 1975) by threatening one's environmental control, and so on. Self-affirmation logic suggests that the actual goal of subjects following these manipulations may be to affirm the integrity of the self—like the women called a negative name in the name-calling experiment or like our modern smoker—rather than to resolve particular motive states tied to particular threats.

This possibility may have been obscured by a paradigmatic problem in testing of these models. Specifically, subjects are usually given only one means of responding to the threat, a means that invariably counters the particular threat itself. For example, following an equity manipulation, subjects are only allowed to restore equity; following a dissonance manipulation, subjects are only allowed to restore consistency; and, following a reactance manipulation, subjects are only allowed to reassert the threatened freedom. Subjects' use of the "forced" options in these experiments—the

only available means of reaffirming self-integrity after it has been threatened—is then taken as evidence of a distinct motivational process. If other self-affirming responses were available in these experiments, subjects might have used them and, having done so, they might even have foregone attempts to resolve the provoking threats. Taylor (1983) made a similar point in describing some women's adaptations to contracting breast cancer; ". . . the specific [adaptive] response . . . has no fixed meaning independent of the goals or functions it serves. The specific form matters little or not at all" (p. 1169). This fact, I shall argue, clouds the interpretation of much of the research testing specific motivational processes in social psychology.

The logic underlying these themes can be summarized in two working assumptions. First, after an important self-concept is threatened, an individual's primary self-defensive goal is to affirm the general integrity of the self, not to resolve the particular threat. Second, because of this overriding goal, the motivation to adapt to a specific self-threat of one sort may be overcome by affirmation of the broader self-concept or of an equally important, yet different, aspect of the self-concept, without resolving the provoking threat.

Over the years, we have tested this reasoning in several contexts, particularly those that would allow us to pit these arguments against specific motive theories in social psychology. I turn first to our research examining these ideas as an alternative account of dissonance processes.

## Dissonance as Self-Affirmation

> Some affirmation of our worth seems to stem for the very nature of life. To live is to act; to act (without whim) is to act for reasons; to view our actions as based on good reasons is to see them as endowed with some degree of worth; and to identify ourselves with such acts is tacitly to regard ourselves as having worth. (Martin, 1985, p. 6)

What disturbed the women in the name-calling experiment about being called uncooperative with community projects apparently was not the inconsistency established by the name, but the name's threat to their sense of being good people. Could the same thing be true for psychological inconsistency in general? Could the motivation to reduce inconsistency stem more from a need to affirm the integrity of the self than from a need to resolve important inconsistencies per se? To examine this possibility, we turned to the largest body of findings attributable to a consistency motive: dissonance phenomena.

For nearly 30 years, dissonance researchers have tricked subjects into "volunteering" self-contradictory actions such as writing public essays against their beliefs, expending effort on meaningless tasks, and delivering embarrassing speeches in front of prestigious audiences. Lacking any better means of reducing their distress over these actions, subjects typically attempt to justify them by changing their beliefs or attitudes to be more consistent with their actions. For example, they state that their beliefs were not really so different from the essay they wrote or that the meaningless task they worked so hard at was not really so meaningless. Most versions of dissonance theory (e.g., Cooper & Fazio, 1984; Festinger, 1957; Wicklund & Brehm, 1976) assume that the sheer inconsistency of these relatively important cognitions implores some resolution.

Our interest in dissonance was piqued by another fact as well. Almost from the inception of the theory, there has been ambiguity over the role of self-based processes in mediating dissonance effects (e.g., Aronson, 1969; Brehm & Cohen, 1962; Wicklund & Brehm, 1976). While keeping the consistency principle as the basic framework of the theory, revisionists have argued that conditions unrelated to consistency are necessary for dissonance arousal: the dissonant act has to be freely chosen; its negative consequences have to be foreseeable; it has to contradict an important, firmly held expectancy; and so on. Clearly, these conditions have as much to do with ensuring that the dissonant act will threaten one's goodness, competence, and worth as with activating consistency motives. Greenwald and Ronis (1978) offered the following analysis of the counterattitudinal role-playing experiment, which highlights this point:

It becomes possible to hypothesize that the pair of cognitions that produces the tension toward cognitive change [i.e., dissonance motivation] is not the AB pair . . . A (*I believe X*, where X is the initial opinion) and B (*I agreed to advocate not X*) . . . but rather a somewhat different pair, that is, C (*I caused [undesired] consequence Y*) and a self-concept cognition, D (*I am a good [or intelligent] person who does not do such evil [or stu-*

*pid] things*) . . . . The motivation for cognitive change in contemporary versions of dissonance theory is indistinguishable from ego defense. (pp. 54–55)

Although the contending interpretations of dissonance phenomena became increasingly distinct at the conceptual level, research achieved little empirical separation. Invariably, the conditions tested by the revisionists confounded both sources of change. Consider, for example, the foreseeability variable. Research has shown that subjects must be able to foresee the negative consequences of a dissonant act for it to arouse dissonance (e.g., Cooper, 1971; Goethals & Cooper, 1975). Such foreseeability, however, establishes both an inconsistency (i.e., "I believe x, yet knowingly did not x") and impugns the self (i.e., "having done x in the face of its negative consequences, I am bad or stupid"). Which of these effects, then, causes dissonance?

These accounts of dissonance processes, we recognized, paralleled the accounts of the name-calling results. Greater compliance following the uncooperative label, like the changes following dissonant acts, could stem from a need to reestablish psychological consistency or to reaffirm a threatened self. In the name-calling experiment, the irrelevant negative name condition unconfounded these processes, preventing the operation of consistency processes while allowing self-affirmation processes.

The logic of this condition suggested how the explanations of dissonance could be unconfounded: simply allow subjects to do something after a dissonant act, leaving the provoking inconsistency intact but affirming their larger self-worth. We expressed this logic as follows:

If dissonance stems from the threat to the self (ego) inherent in a given inconsistency, then after dissonance has been aroused, thoughts and actions that affirm an important aspect of the self-concept should reduce dissonance by casting the self in a positive light. This should occur even when the self-affirming thoughts have no relevance to the provoking inconsistency (in the sense of being able to resolve it or reduce its objective importance). For example, though specific inconsistencies happen to them all, the resulting dissonance may be reduced in the idealist by defense of a good cause, in the religious person by worship, or in the aesthetic by appreciation of a good painting. When considered along with value-affirming images of the self, specific, self-threat-ening inconsistencies may become tolerable. On the other hand, if dissonance is rooted in a need for psychological consistency, then self-affirma-tion—being unable to resolve or dismiss the still important inconsistency—should not reduce dis-sonance. (Steele & Liu, 1983, p. 6)

The results of an earlier experiment by Steele and Liu (1981) fit this reasoning. Prior to writing dissonant essays opposing state funding for handi-cap facilities, some subjects were told that they could help blind students by recording exams onto casettes after writing the essay. Other subjects were given no such expectation. Dissonance-reducing attitude change occurred only among subjects not expecting the later, value-affirming response. Ex-pecting to help may have allowed these subjects to affirm an image of themselves as helpful people (e.g., "Although I am writing the essay, I may still help the blind, showing that I am a concerned per-son.") Expectations of affirming their image may have reduced dissonance by minimizing the self-concept threat inherent in the dissonant act. Un-fortunately, a consistency interpretation cannot be ruled out. Resolving to help the blind could make the provoking inconsistency seem less important (e.g., "Although I wrote the essay, my helping the blind will undo some of the harm.") which is a standard means of dissonance reduction.

If our reasoning is sound, however, the affirma-tion of any important self-concept—to the extent that it counters the self-threat inherent in the dis-sonant act—should reduce dissonance.

## Reducing Dissonance through Value Affirmation

Our first test of this reasoning used the following version of the standard forced-compliance disso-nance paradigm. Subjects were selected for strongly opposing a tuition hike at the University of Washington (as identified through classroom questionnaires and contacted by phone). When they arrived for their individual session, they were told that the experiment examined the effects of attitudes on social perception. To "activate" their attitudes, ostensibly for the social-perception task, they were asked to participate in a "legislative sur-vey" of student views on tuition increases. Then, because of an ostensible oversupply of essays op-posing the hike, they were asked to support a sub-stantial tuition increase in their essays. High dis-

sonance was established by giving subjects ample choice to write this essay; low dissonance was es-tablished by giving subjects no choice to write this essay. Dissonance reduction was measured as the amount subjects changed their postessay attitudes to fit their essay position. Typically, of course, subjects with choice change their attitudes in this paradigm, while subjects without choice do not.

To test our reasoning about self-affirmation, we had to somehow allow subjects to affirm an im-portant self-concept between the dissonant essay and postattitude measure. To provide such a test, we first identified two groups of tuition-opposing subjects, one with a strong economic–political value orientation and another without this orien-tation. (This was done by administering Schorr's Test of Values along with the tuition-hike ques-tionnaires described above.) Then, in a high-choice condition of the experiment, between the essay and attitude measure, both groups of subjects com-pleted the Economic–Political subscale of the Allport–Vernon Study of Values (20 items). Com-pleting this subscale, we assumed, would affirm a valued self-concept for subjects with a strong eco-nomic–political value orientation, but not for sub-jects without this value orientation. If self-affir-mation reduces dissonance, this subscale should eliminate dissonance-reducing attitude change among subjects who hold this value, but not among those who do not.

This experiment also included conditions to rep-licate the standard effect of dissonance on attitude change. These replication conditions followed the above procedures except that the attitude measure immediately followed the dissonant essay, preced-ing the value scale. In one of these conditions sub-jects had a choice in writing the essay and, in the other, they did not. We expected significant disso-nance-reducing attitude change in the former, but not in the latter. Both subject groups were run in each replication condition. The total design of this experiment took the form of a 2 × 3 factorial, which arose from crossing two levels of the subject vari-able (i.e., whether or not subjects were economic–politically oriented) with three treatment condi-tions: a high choice-affirmation first condition, a high choice-attitude measure first condition, and a low choice-attitude measure first condition.

Figure 18.2 presents subjects' postattitudes. (There were no condition differences in subjects' preattitudes.) Larger numbers indicate greater at-titude change, away from the most extreme oppo-

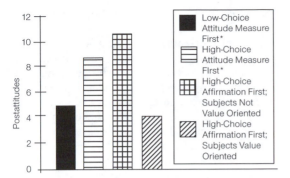

**FIGURE 18.2** ■ Dissonance as self-affirmation. In this figure, the 31-point scale has been inverted. An asterisk indicates data from both value- and non-value-oriented subjects

sition to the hike. For the conditions replicating the standard dissonance effect—labeled High Choice-Attitude Measure First and Low Choice-Attitude Measure First in the figure—the results are collapsed over both subject groups, as this factor made no difference in these conditions. These conditions replicated the standard effect of dissonance on attitude change: subjects given a choice to write the essay were significantly more favorable toward the tuition hike than those given little choice.

The central question of this experiment is whether affirmation of a valued, but unrelated, self-concept can eliminate dissonance and its accompanying changes. If this is possible, completion of the economic–political scale should cause less dissonance–reducing attitude among subjects who hold this value than among those who do not. Figure 18.2 shows that this is precisely what happened. Economic–political subjects who could affirm this value immediately after writing a dissonant essay changed their attitudes significantly less than non-economic–political subjects in the same condition. A self-affirming experience, even one so brief as the completion of a 20-item value scale, eliminated dissonance in this paradigm.

## Affirmation or Distraction?

We assumed that the value scale eliminated dissonance among like-valued subjects in the above study by allowing them to affirm a valued self-concept. Arguably, however, the scale might have reduced dissonance among these subjects by distracting them from thinking about the dissonant essay. Both the passage of time and distracting

activity have been shown to reduce dissonance (e.g., Crane & Messe, 1970; Zanna & Azziza, 1976). Clearly, neither the time delay nor distraction from completing the scale had this effect alone, or in combination, since the same scale did not reduce dissonance among non-economic–political subjects who also completed it. Nonetheless, another version of the distraction explanation remained possible. The high self-relevance of the value scale for economic–political subjects may have caused them to be more absorbed in it, more distracted from dissonant thoughts, and thus less in need of dissonance-reducing change than non-economic–political subjects.

To test this possibility, we designed an experiment based on the principle that dissonance, once dissipated through misattribution or distraction, can be reinstated. [. . .] The critical condition in this experiment replicated the self-affirmation condition in the earlier study—economic–political subjects wrote dissonant essays followed by a value scale and a postattitude measure—with one exception: just after the value scale and before the postattitude measure, these subjects wrote down three "key" words from their dissonant essays. The results of this experiment, which also included conditions replicating the basic effect of dissonance on attitude change and the dissonance-reducing effect of value affirmation, clearly showed that distraction did not mediate the self-affirmation effect in the earlier study. Economic–political subjects in the "affirmation first/reinstatement" condition did not change their attitudes to reduce dissonance, despite evidence (from the dissonance-replication condition) that dissonance had been aroused in this study. This occurred even though they were forced to recall their dissonant essays after the value scale and before the attitude measure, eliminating whatever distracting effect the value scale might have had. [. . .]

## Dissonance and the Lab Coat

One criticism of our position has been that it ". . . has not addressed sufficient data to be a complete theory of the causes of cognitive dissonance" (Cooper and Fazio, 1984, p. 232). Although pinched by this statement, we acknowledge that it has some validity. Dissonance has not lived by forced compliance alone; whether affirming self-worth can reduce dissonance in other dissonance paradigms is, after all, an empirical question. It might be argued, in fact, that the forced-compliance paradigm is especially favorable to the self-affirmation effect. Writing a public essay against one's beliefs may be more self-threatening than dissonant acts in other dissonance paradigms and therefore more mediated by self-protective processes.

To address this issue, we examined the effect of self-affirmation on dissonance reducing change in the free-choice paradigm, in which subjects simply chose between two moderately valued alternatives—for example, two record albums. The positive features of the nonchosen alternative and the negative features of the chosen alternative are then inconsistent with the choice itself, establishing a dissonance-provoking inconsistency This inconsistency is reduced by upgrading one's evaluation of the chosen alternative and downgrading one's evaluation of the nonchosen alternative in what is called a "spread of alternatives" or, more simply, a rationalization. As they typically are not between highly important alternatives, the choices in these experiments cannot be deemed highly self-threatening—yet a self-affirmation interpretation is possible. Whatever dissonance is aroused in this paradigm may stem less from the inconsistency it establishes than from the choice's threat to the subject's self-competence, goodness, and other self-concepts.

We conducted a free-choice experiment (Steele, Hopp, & Gonzales, 1986) in which, as part of an ostensible "marketing survey," subjects rated their liking of 10 popular record albums and then ranked them in order of preference. The critical dissonance-provoking choice was produced by giving the subjects a choice to keep either the fifth- or sixth-ranked album. As part of the self-affirmation procedure, half of the subjects had been selected for holding a strong scientific value orientation and having indicated on a selection questionnaire that a lab coat symbolized their personal values and professional goals. The other subjects were selected for holding a strong business orientation as symbolized by a business suit. After choosing a record album to keep, half of the subjects in each group were asked to put on lab coats in preparation for another experiment involving messy laboratory tasks. For the other half, this instruction was omitted. After waiting 10 minutes, all subjects rerated the albums, providing the critical dependent measure whether subjects rationalized their choice by changing their evaluations.

Putting on a lab coat after the choice and before rerating the albums, we reasoned, would affirm a central value orientation for the science subjects, but not for the business subjects. These procedures formed a 2 × 2 design in which one factor was whether or not subjects wore lab coats after their choice. The second factor was whether they held a strong science or business value orientation. If dissonance-reducing change in this paradigm stems from the threat to the self inherent in the choice, the lab coat should eliminate this change among science subjects, for whom it affirms a valued self-concept, but not among business subjects, for whom it affirms nothing. If this change stems from the inconsistency inherent in this choice, the lab coat should not reduce dissonance for either group.

Figure 18.3 presents the condition means for the "spread of alternatives" index, computed for each subject by adding the increase in rating for the chosen alternative to the decrease in rating for the nonchosen alternative. The larger the rating, the more dissonance reduction; the closer it is to zero, the less dissonance reduction. As the figure shows, the self-affirmation prediction was strongly supported. For science-oriented subjects, the simple act of putting on a white lab coat significantly reduced their dissonance over the choice of record albums. For business-oriented subjects, the coat had no effect. Science subjects wearing a lab coat showed virtually no spread of alternatives, significantly less than subjects in any other condition. The lab coat eliminated their dissonance completely. This result has been replicated (cf. Steele et al., 1986). Clearly, then, the effect of self-affirmation on dissonance generalizes to paradigms other than the forced-compliance.

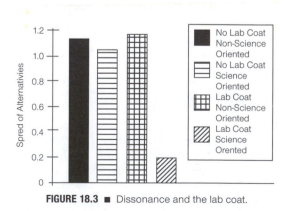

**FIGURE 18.3** ■ Dissonance and the lab coat.

## The Nature of Dissonance Motivation

Taken together, the results of this series of studies provide strong support for the reasoning derived from the name-calling experiment. Whether psychological inconsistency emanates from a name or one's own dissonant behavior, the disturbing thing about it, the thing that motivates behavior and cognitive changes, is its inherent threat to self-adequacy, not the fact of the inconsistency. In all these experiments, once subjects were allowed to affirm integrity-restoring images of the self, they tolerated specific inconsistencies with no attempt at resolution. I might add that the effect of the self-affirmation procedures in these experiments did not stem from their enhancement of subjects' moods, a condition that has been shown to eliminate dissonance effects (cf. Cooper, Zanna, & Taves, 1978; Steele, Southwick, & Critchlow, 1981). Nonetheless, Steele and Liu (1983) measured the effect of the value scales used in these procedures on subjects' moods. Even among subjects holding the same value, the scale had no mood-enhancing effect. Over these studies, self-affirmation appears to have eliminated dissonance by somehow reducing the "sting-to-the-self" inherent in dissonance-provoking inconsistencies.

### WHAT DISSONANCE IS NOT

As Wicklund and Brehm (1976) have noted, early versions of dissonance theory ". . . did not reduce the tension state of dissonance to more molecular elements in an attempt to explain why inconsistency should be motivating" (p. 283). Revisions of the theory detailed conditions needed for dissonance arousal that, as noted earlier, confounded inconsistency and self threat. For example, Aronson (1969) argued, in essence, that an inconsistency had to implicate the self to arouse dissonance. Although Aronson's view essentially limits dissonance-provoking inconsistencies to those that involve the self (a position identical to our own) Aronson retained the idea that dissonance reduction is motivated by a need for psychological consistency among the provoking cognitions, rather than a need to affirm the larger self, as we have argued. Aronson, for example, would not predict that affirming an aspect of the self unrelated to a dissonance-provoking inconsistency could reduce the pressure to resolve the inconsistency.

The present studies unconfounded self-threat and inconsistency; they found that an otherwise dissonant-provoking inconsistency does not motivate cognitive change once the self is affirmed.

Other research has further shown that dissonant inconsistency does not motivate change once the unpleasant affect associated with it is eliminated through drugs (e.g., Cooper et al., 1978; Steele et al., 1981) or misattributed to another source, such as an ingested pill or poor lighting (e.g., Zanna & Cooper, 1976). Cognitive inconsistency may be a part of dissonance arousal in that any self-threatening cognitions may be necessarily inconsistent with self-images of adequacy and integrity. Psychological inconsistency may be a necessary form that self-threat takes. Indeed, a perceived "inconsistency" of the self—in the sense of one's actions contradicting one's important beliefs, for example—should arouse dissonance. However, our findings show that the inconsistency of such a threat has no motivational significance in its own right and is not the aspect of these threats that stirs dissonance motivation.

### WHAT DISSONANCE IS

Rather, dissonance motivation is stirred by the implication of the inconsistency that one is not adaptively or morally adequate. Doing something that meets all of the requirements of a dissonant act (e.g., "choosing" to write an essay against one's beliefs) makes one feel foolish; raises doubts about one's competence, adaptive coherence, self-control, and other self-concepts; and, as a consequence, motivates one to reaffirm one's adequacy. At a very important level, dissonance appears to be no more complicated than this.

This analysis does away with the revisions of dissonance theory that to arouse dissonance the inconsistent action must be chosen, its consequences must be foreseeable, the person must feel personally responsible for the action, and so on (cf. Cooper & Fazio, 1984). In light of our findings, we view these revisions as simply clarifying the circumstances under which an inconsistent action will be self-threatening. More to our point here, these restrictions exclude several examples of the dissonance-provoking inconsistencies with which Festinger originally defined the theory (cf. Greenwald & Ronis, 1978). One of these is that "if a person were standing dry in the rain and yet could see no evidence that he was getting wet, these two cognitions would be dissonant with one another" (Festinger, 1957, p. 14). We would agree with Festinger. Standing dry in the rain should certainly threaten the self—drawing one's right-mindedness into question—and, in our view, arouse "dissonance." This "dissonance," in turn, should press one toward some understanding, even though it involved no element of personal responsibility, choice, or foreseeability of consequences. Thus, the self-affirmation analysis of dissonance would not incorporate these conditions as requirements of dissonance arousal. Whenever an inconsistency threatens the integrity of the self, we argue that it should arouse dissonance motivation. We differ from Festinger, of course, in believing that the motivating aspect of such inconsistency is not inconsistency itself, but its threat to the self.

## REDUCING DISSONANCE

Our findings also suggest that dissonance can be reduced in ways not captured by dissonance theory in any of its past versions, but in ways that may be quite characteristic of real life. As noted earlier, dissonance can be soothed away; that is, factors that directly diminish the negative affect of dissonance (such as phenobarbital and alcohol) or cause this affect to be misattributed to other sources have all been shown to reduce dissonance. To this list of non-consistency-restoring remedies, we add activities that affirm valued self-concepts. Herein may lie the comforting power of activities such as therapy, prayer, conversation with supportive friends, and reading which frequently do not resolve or dismiss the specific causes of our stresses but nonetheless diminish their effects. Apparently, dissonance can be reduced without altering or adding to the cognitions involved in the provoking inconsistency; it is the image of the self that is at issue, not the inconsistency of cognitions. [. . .]

# A Psychology of Experimental Embarrassments: A Paradigm Problem

The long and short of it may be that the dissonance literature chiefly concerns the psychology of what people do to recover from experimentally engineered major embarrassments. (Abelson, 1983, p. 43)

Abelson's complaint, I suggest, can be taken a step further. If the motivational effects of cognitive dissonance stem from the self-threat inherent in provoking manipulation (i.e., the inconsistency manipulation), the same may be true of other motivational effects in social psychology. Consider the example of equity research (e.g., Walster et al., 1978). To arouse a motive for psychological equity, subjects in these experiments are put into an inequitable relationship with another person; for example, they are induced to cheat or harm the person or are rewarded more than another person for the same task. Afterward, subjects are given just one means of setting things right: they are allowed to give actual compensation to their victim or their attempts to psychologically justify their inequitable behavior are measured. That subjects usually restore equity, actually or psychologically, is then taken as evidence of an underlying motive for equity. The present reasoning, however, suggests that subjects may restore equity in these experiments simply because it is the only means of self-affirmation available after the self-threatening inequity manipulation. Had they been allowed to do something that reaffirmed their worth without restoring equity, they may well have done so and foregone equity restoration. Evidence to this effect would not argue against the existence of equity restoration effects; rather, it would mean 1) that such effects do not stem from a distinct motivation for equity, but from a general motive to affirm the self after it has been threatened and 2) that responses other than equity-restoring ones may reduce this motivation.

The same paradigmatic limitation clouds the interpretation of other social psychological motives as well, including reactance (Brehm, 1966), self-completion (Wicklund & Gollwitzer, 1983), learned helplessness (e.g., Abramson, Seligman, & Teasdale, 1978), uniqueness (Fromkin, 1970), and guilt. In each of these cases, after self-threatening operations are used to arouse the specific motive, subjects are given only one response with which to cope with the threat, a response ostensibly capable of reducing the aroused motive, but also capable of affirming the self. When subjects use this response, it is taken as evidence of the existence of a specific motivational process. Were these subjects allowed other coping responses—in particular, responses capable of affirming the self, but not capable of resolving the motive presumed to be aroused—a very different picture of the motivational basis of effects in these paradigms would probably emerge.

Whether a self-affirmation interpretation of any of these processes is correct must be verified, of course, by research. Nevertheless, the findings we have presented raise the unsettling possibility that research in these paradigms is not tapping distinctive motivational processes, but is tapping how subjects respond to a variety of experimental embarrassments, as Abelson suggested for dissonance research.

## Attribution as Self-Affirmation

To examine this critique of motivational research, we selected a motivational relationship of central importance in social psychology: the hypothesized relationship between control motivation and attributional analysis. An important fact about attributions has come to light, which places this relationship in the forefront of attribution research. Although less obvious from the perspective of most attribution theory (which focuses on how people make attributions) than from the perspective of everyday experience, people apparently do not always make attributions about the events and actions they notice. Sometimes they attribute things to causes; sometimes they don't bother. This fact raises the important question of what causes or motivates people to engage in attributional analysis, to go to the trouble of assigning cause.

The longstanding working hypothesis has been that people assign cause due to a distinctive motivation to gain and maintain control over the environment. In Kelley's (1971) words:

> The purpose of causal analysis—the function it serves for the species and the individual—is effective control. The attributor is not simply an attributor, a seeker after knowledge. His latent goal in gaining knowledge is that of effective management of himself and his environment. He is not a pure "scientist" then, but an applied one. (p. 22)

Indeed, the factors that have been shown to increase attributional analysis can be viewed as those arousing a distinctive motive for environmental control: unexpected information (e.g., Clary & Tesser, 1983; Hastie, 1984), negative outcomes for oneself and others (e.g., Harvey, Yarkin, Lightner, & Town, 1980), expectations of future interactions

with a target person (e.g., Harvey et al., 1980; Miller, Norman, & Wright, 1978), and increased personal involvement with the issue under consideration (Pittman, Scherrer, & Wright, 1977).

Perhaps the clearest support for the control-motivation hypothesis comes from experiments by Pittman and his colleagues (Pittman & D'Agostino, 1985; Pittman & Pittman, 1980) in which control deprivation was manipulated directly through learned helplessness training (Seligman, 1972, 1975). (This procedure involves varying the amount of noncontingent feedback, which subjects receive on a concept-formation task.) Following this manipulation, subjects read about an author who wrote an essay opposing nuclear power. Attributional analysis was measured as the extent to which their attributions about the author's motives reflected relevant information they were provided; the more extreme their attributions in the direction of this information, the more attributional analysis they were presumed to have engaged in. Deprivation of control (under both low and high helplessness training) significantly increased attributional analysis on this measure. Control group subjects who experienced no control deprivation (no helplessness training) showed virtually no attributional analysis. These findings fit the view that the act of making attributions serves a distinctive control motive, a view most compatible with Kelley (1971) and Heider's (1958) discussions of control motivation in attribution processes.

The present critique of motivational research, however, suggests another interpretation. Independent of any motive for actual environmental control, the control-deprivation procedures in these experiments may arouse a simple self-affirmation motive, a motive to affirm an image of oneself as competent and able to control important outcomes. This motive could increase attributional analysis in several ways, most obviously, perhaps, by increasing self-serving attributions that protect or enhance the self. The attribution of success to the self and of failure to circumstance is an example. Perhaps, less obviously, a self-affirmation motive may increase attributional analysis of events unrelated to the threat or even the self. Merely explaining an event implies that one can recognize and understand its causes; thus, one is a more or less efficacious person. Conceivably, then, after the control threat in the Pittman research, subjects may have made more extreme attributions about the author's behavior only to enhance an efficacious self-image, to appear as if they "knew it all."

Liu and Steele (1986) conducted two experiments to test which motive—one for actual control or one for a self-image of being able to control—mediates the effects of control deprivation on attribution in the Pittman and Pittman paradigm. If, after a control threat, people make more extreme attributions from available information to affirm a self-image of efficacy, then this effect should be reduced by thoughts and actions following the threat that affirms a valued self-concept. This should occur even when the thoughts contribute nothing to actual environmental control. On the other hand, if, after a control threat, people make more extreme attributions to regain actual environmental control, intervening self-affirming thoughts should do little to reduce this effect.

Our first experiment attempted to (1) replicate the pattern of effects reported by Pittman and Pittman (1980) and (2) test whether a self-affirming experience could eliminate the increase in attributional analysis that follows control deprivation. In the interest of replication, we used the basic paradigm developed by Pittman and Pittman (1980) in which the attribution measure followed the manipulation of control deprivation through learned helplessness training. The attribution measure asked subjects to rate the strength of external and internal factors in causing an author to write an essay favoring nuclear power plants. As one factor, half of the subjects were told that the author wrote the essay for payment, while half were told that he wrote it for his private journal only. The more that subjects analyzed this information following control deprivation, the more extreme their attributions should be in the direction of the given information. The second factor was three levels of learned helplessness training: no, low, and

high. Based on the Pittman and Pittman findings, we expected more extreme attributions (reflecting more attributional analysis) in the high, and especially in the low, helplessness treatments.[1] A fourth level of this factor was included to test the effects of a self-affirming experience on the control deprivation–attribution relationship. Modeled after the self-affirmation procedure developed by Steele and Liu (1983), this condition allowed subjects to affirm a valued self-concept (again, by completing an economic–political value scale; all subjects in the experiment strongly held this value orientation) immediately after the low helplessness training (the condition that had produced the strongest effects in Pittman and Pittman, 1980) and before the attribution measure. If more extreme attributions following control deprivation stem from a motive to affirm an efficacious self-image, then attributions in this condition should be less extreme than in other helplessness conditions.

This experiment also included mood and task performance measures. The original Pittman and Pittman study showed that greater control deprivation generally led to worse moods and task performance. We reasoned that if self-affirmation eliminated the effect of control deprivation on attributions, it should do the same for mood and performance.

To summarize, this experiment took the form of a 2 × 4 factorial design with two levels of the information factor (external and internal attributional information) and four levels of control deprivation (no, low, and high helplessness training, and a self-affirmation condition).

Figure 18.4 presents subjects' ratings of how much external influence the essayist was under. Larger numbers indicate stronger attributions to external factors (7-point scale). On this measure, the more attributional analysis that subjects engaged in, the more the attributions made by external attribution subjects (who were told that the protagonist wrote the essay for payment) should exceed those made by internal attribution subjects (who were told that the essay was a journal entry). These results clearly replicate those of Pittman and Pittman. Unlike no helplessness training, both low and high helplessness training caused stronger external attributions among subjects given "payment" information than among subjects given "private journal" information. In support of the self-affirmation prediction, the self-relevant value scale in the self-affirmation condition eliminated the

---

[1] Although both treatments led to more extreme attributions, Pittman and Pittman found somewhat stronger attributions among low than high helplessness subjects. They discuss a number of interpretations of this result—for example, that the materials used in this paradigm obscure the monotonic relationship between deprivation and attribution, that the two treatments "represented points equally high on the 'control-deprivation-attributional-activity curve,' but were on opposite sides of the inflection point" (p. 385), and so on—but none have been established. Thus, to maximize the strength of the control deprivation manipulation in our research, we simply used the helplessness procedure (low helplessness training) that showed the strongest relationship to attribution.

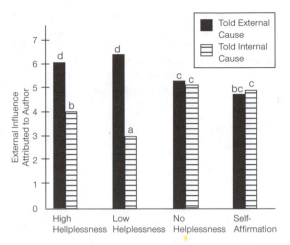

**FIGURE 18.4** ■ Attribution as affirmation: Study 1. The 7 on the vertical axis indicates greatest aggreement with the statement that "external influences probably caused the author to write the essay." Conditions not sharing letters differ at *p* < .05.

effect of low helplessness training on attributions. After this scale, subjects who underwent low helplessness training made attributions as though they had received no helplessness training at all. This pattern of effects (supported by a significant information-condition-by-helplessness-condition interaction) was mirrored on all other attributional measures as well. Finally, the self-affirmation procedure also eliminated the detrimental effect of low helplessness training on subjects' mood and task performance. These findings suggest that, in this paradigm, greater attributional analysis following control deprivation reflects an effort to regain an efficacious self-image, rather than actual environmental control, and lends generality to our critique of motivational paradigms in social psychology.

Still, an alternative explanation had to be considered. Completion of any value scale, even one not self-relevant, might have eliminated the effects of helplessness training on attribution and mood. The first experiment did not include a control condition to show that completion of the scale would not eliminate these effects for subjects who did not hold the value represented on the scale. To test this possibility, and to replicate the self-affirmation effect in this paradigm, we conducted a second experiment, which replicated the low helplessness and self-affirmation conditions described above. However, to reduce design complexity, all

subjects were given external attribution information, that the author wrote the essay for payment. The primary dependent measure was attribution of external influence. In addition, half the subjects in each of these conditions were selected for strongly holding the economic–political value orientation, while half were selected for not holding it. Completion of the economic–political subscale of the Allport–Vernon Study of Values in the self-affirmation condition should be self-affirming for subjects holding this value orientation, but not for subjects not holding it.

Figure 18.5 presents the condition means for subjects' ratings of external influence. The self-affirmation interpretation was clearly supported. The value scale in the self-affirmation condition eliminated the effects of helplessness training on external attributions only among subjects for whom the scale was self-relevant: economic–political subjects. The same pattern of effects held for related attribution measures and mood measure as well. To eliminate the effects of helplessness training on attributions and mood, the value scale had to allow an affirmation of the self. After learned helplessness training, attributional analysis apparently has the goal of affirming one's self-image of efficacy, not of regaining one's actual control of the environment—at least in these experiments.

A note of qualification is in order, however. Although the present findings may be mediated by a self-affirmation motive, a motive for actual control could be equally, or even more, important

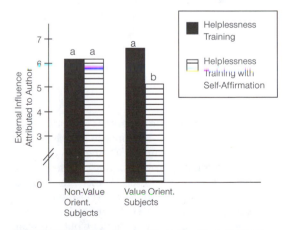

**FIGURE 18.5** ■ Attribution as affirmation: Study 2. The 7 on the vertical axis indicates greatest attributed external influence. Conditions not sharing letters differ at *p* < .05.

under different circumstances; for example, when the control threat is ongoing. A student's analysis of the reasons for having failed his first chemistry exam (e.g., due to lack of ability, motivation, preparation, etc.) may be motivated as much by a need to gain control of the outcomes in that situation as a need for self-affirmation. Even so, our research shows rather convincingly that a motive for self-affirmation is one of the motives that control deprivation can arouse and that, in this paradigm, it is the motive that mediates the effects of control deprivation.

The results of these studies also bring to light an undiscovered effect of ego-based motives on attributional processes: these motives can motivate the sheer act of making attributions—of assigning cause—even when the resulting attributions do not pertain to the self. Being able to assign a cause to events and actions—to explain why my friend is an avid sailor, why rock musicians tend to be thin, why people climb mountains, and so on—implies that I have the ability to understand and, perhaps, control important outcomes. This ability affirms the adaptive adequacy of the self. The findings in our research extend the domain of recognized ego influences on attribution. In addition to influencing the type of attributions made— that is, pressuring attributions to be self-serving— these motives also influence the tendency to make attributions in the first place.

Finally, in conjunction with the dissonance experiments, the present experiments make it clear that to establish a distinctive motivational process in social psychology it must be shown that the motive state in question cannot be reduced by responses that only affirm the self.

## Toward a Model of Self-Affirmation Processes

Although models of one or another aspect of what I have been calling self-affirmation have begun to emerge—[. . .] for example, Greenwald's description of "totalitarian ego" biases and ego-task functions (e.g., Greenwald, 1980, 1982)—there have been few efforts predicated on experimental evidence to develop a comprehensive model of these processes. No doubt, such a model would go well beyond the scope of our present findings as well. Nonetheless, these findings do enable several gen-

eralizations, some of which are conclusions about the general nature of these processes based on our research, while others are propositions supported or suggested by this evidence that take our reasoning toward a model of self-affirmation processes. I begin with the conclusions.

## Conclusions: The Nature of Self-Affirmation

### THE GOAL OF SELF-AFFIRMATION: GLOBAL SELF-INTEGRITY

Our findings support the existence of a self-system that functions to sustain a phenomenal experience of the self—that is, self-concepts and images of the self, past, present and future—as having adaptive and moral adequacy, as being competent, good, stable, integrated, capable of choice and control, and so forth. As noted at the outset of this article, a system of this sort is presumed in all comprehensive models of the self. Our findings provide further evidence of its existence but, most importantly, they bring to light an important fact about the system: its goal is to maintain global conceptions of self-adequacy, not necessarily to resist specific self-threats that arise from self-threatening circumstances and events. In all of our experiments, subjects eliminated the effect of specific self-threats by affirming central, valued aspects of the self. In a dissonance experiment, for example, aesthetically-oriented subjects eliminated the dissonance arising from public opposition to funding for the handicapped through self-affirming thoughts of beautiful concerts and paintings (the item content on the aesthetic value scale). [. . .]

### THE FLEXIBILITY OF SELF-AFFIRMATION

Based on this fact, people have considerable flexibility in coping with threats to self-integrity, perhaps more than has been commonly recognized. They can try to adapt to the threat itself by either trying to directly diminish or eliminate, diminish the perception of threat, or by diminishing the perception that the threat threatens self-integrity. Most theories relevant to self-threat (e.g., dissonance, learned helplessness) have focused on these avenues of adaptation. In addition, however, our evidence shows that people can adapt to a threat with behavioral and cognitive changes not directed

relate to prejudice

toward the threat itself, but toward affirming the perception of global self-integrity. This last category of adaptations adds an extra degree of coping flexibility and resilience that, as I argued at the outset of this article, may explain how an individual continues to smoke despite the inescapable reasons not to. Any adaptation, cognitive or behavioral, that affirms self-integrity can reduce the impact of specific threats to that integrity. These adaptations can vary widely and are widely interchangeable, allowing "fluid compensation."

## SELF-AFFIRMATION AS A SOURCE OF SELF-OBJECTIVITY

Although self-affirmation processes are generally thought of as a source of distortion in information processing, our findings show another side, one that has a quite different effect. Specifically, the pressure for self-affirming thoughts about one topic can be reduced by salient, self-affirming thoughts about another, even unrelated, topic. In all of our dissonance experiments, for example, when subjects were allowed self-affirming thoughts after their dissonant actions, they gave up trying to rationalize them. Generalizing salient, self-affirming thoughts should make it easier to be objective about other, self-threatening information and should reduce the pressure to diminish the threat inherent in this information. In this way, self-affirming thoughts may be an effective means of reducing thought-distorting defense mechanisms such as denial and rationalization. At any rate, our ability to think objectively about particular self-threatening information may depend, at least partially, on what other thoughts about the self are salient at the time the information is processed.

## Propositions:
## The Mechanisms of Self-Affirmation

In this section, to summarize and make our reasoning explicit, I present three propositions about self-affirmation processes.

### AROUSAL OF A SELF-AFFIRMATION MOTIVE

*Proposition I:* Cognitions that threaten the perceived integrity of the self—i.e., its adaptive and moral adequacy—arouse a motive to reaffirm the self, to reestablish a perception of global self-in-

tegrity. Threatening cognitions arise from a number of sources: information in the environment, the behavior of others toward us, the judgments of others (e.g., the impugning judgments of the pollster in our name-calling experiments), our own behavior (e.g., dissonant actions or failure at a learned helplessness task), and cognitions that we invoke in response to particular situations or events. In each case, these cognitions threaten the perceived integrity of the self and, in each case, they lead to behaviors that, we argue, reflect an underlying motivation to reaffirm that integrity. In Allport's (1943) words, the "ego-system" is engaged by any ". . . frustration of goal-seeking behavior or any kind of threat to the individual . . ." (p. 470).

### THE REDUCTION OF THE SELF-AFFIRMATION MOTIVE

*Proposition II:* The motive for self-affirmation can be reduced by behavioral or cognitive changes that 1) reduce the threat or the perception of threat, and/or 2) do not address the threat, but restore the perceived integrity of the self, its overall adaptive, and moral adequacy. This last goal can be accomplished by affirming and sustaining valued self-images. To be effective, these images must be at least as important to the individual's perception of self-adequacy as are the negative images inherent in the threat. As noted earlier, the focus of self-affirmation is on maintenance of general conceptions and images of the self, rather than on coping with specific self-threats. Thus, the motive for self-affirmation should foster resolution of the provoking threat only to maintain the perception of self-integrity. Moreover, as noted, it is this fact which enables flexibility in our coping with self-threat.

*The Importance of Self-Affirmation.* This proposition addresses another issue as well, one nicely illustrated by a student who, after hearing our ideas in class, asked me if I believed that a brief value scale could counteract the self-threat of being abandoned in divorce. Although I was never sure whether the question reflected intellectual skepticism or personal hope, it touched on a more basic question not addressed in our research that had to be addressed in our model; namely, what degree of self-affirmation is sufficient to reduce the impact of a given self-threat?

In addressing this issue, the present proposition makes explicit an assumption that has been an implicit part of our reasoning and research designs: we have assumed that, to effectively reduce the impact of a self-threat through self-affirmation, the affirmed self-images must be at least as important to perceived self-adequacy as the self-images that are threatened. The goal of self-affirmation, as we have defined it, is to maintain an overall perception of self-adequacy. Thus, to restore this perception after it has been threatened, the affirmed adequacy must be able to offset, in importance to overall adequacy, the adequacy that has been threatened. This has been the case in each of our experiments. The value scale in the dissonant experiments, for example, allowed subjects holding the same value to affirm self-images that were presumably more important to their perceptions of self-adequacy than the negative images stemming from the dissonant act. These experiments, of course, do not constitute a test of this assumption (this would require varying the relative importance of threatening and affirming self-images to the perception of adequacy), so the present proposition goes beyond our current data. Still, based on the assumption that the goal of self-affirmation is the perception of global self-adequacy, it is implied by our logic; to offset a threat to self-adequacy, one must affirm a self-image that supports this adequacy, as much as the threat threatens it. In answer to the student's question, then, the sense of adequacy gained from a self-relevant value scale is likely to counteract the self-threat of a dissonant essay, as a penance would absolve a venial sin, but is unlikely to counteract the broader threat of abandonment in divorce. In this instance, self-affirmation is likely to become a preoccupying effort, persisting over time until the many threatened self-images become less accessible in thought and memory, and alternative self-affirming images become well established.

*The Threat-Relevance of Self-Affirmation.* Finally, I will note that the relatedness of a self-affirmation to the provoking threat is not included in Proposition II as a determinant of an affirmation's effectiveness, that is, its ability to reduce the self-affirmation motive. However, it might be argued that self-affirming changes addressed to the threat should be more effective than changes that affirm unrelated, valued aspects of the self. Unless the provoking threat is defused, actually or psychologically, the argument goes, its recall over the normal course of events will rearouse the affirmation motive, causing residual self-affirmation tension. Our research has shown, however, that both immediate and delayed arousal of this motive can be reduced as effectively by affirmation of unrelated, valued self-concepts as by changes that address the threat directly. If a professor loses at tennis, for example, affirmations that refute the implications of the loss—such as that it resulted from a sore ankle—do not appear to reduce self-affirmation pressure more definitively than affirmation of unrelated self-images— such as that one is a good lecturer and that tennis is therefore not so important. The effectiveness of a self-affirming adaptation, as Proposition II suggests, seems to depend less on its being related to the provoking threat than its being able to restore a sense of overall adequacy against which the threat is less important.

Interestingly, however, Proposition II does suggest a circumstance under which relatedness should matter. When the very most important aspects of the self are threatened, so there are no equally important alternative self-images, self-affirmations that address the provoking threat should be more effective than affirmations of these less important, alternative self-concepts. Consider, for example, the young tennis professional whose most important self-concepts involve tennis playing. Losing at tennis, for this person, would threaten self-images for which there are no equally important, alternative self-images that can be affirmed. Thus, adaptations that address the implications of losing itself—more practice, rationalizations, a rematch with the same opponent, and so on—may be the only route to self-affirmation. Such may be the cost of a highly focused personality whose sense of adequacy is lodged in only one domain of life.

## DETERMINING THE MEANS OF SELF-AFFIRMATION

Thus far, I have discussed what can affirm the self, but have been mute as to how these adaptations are determined, an explanation of which has been attempted only rarely. Abelson (1959) argued that, in resolving belief dilemmas, people tend to use the easiest modes of resolution first; Gotz-Marehand, Gotz, and Irle (1974) showed that subjects tend to reduce dissonance through the first means available; Walster et al. (1978) reasoned that, in restoring equity, people choose the means that is most effective relative to its costs. Beyond these occasional discussions, the question of how adaptations are determined has received little attention. Our research to date provides no definitive picture of this process, but suggests the importance of some determining factors.

In affirming themselves, dissonance subjects used attitude change or value affirmation, depending only on which came first; the same held for control-deprived subjects in the choice between attribution and value affirmation; and subjects called "bad drivers" were willing to seek affirmation through an available opportunity to help with a food co-op. In determining which means of self-affirmation was used, availability was more important in these experiments than either an adaptation's ability to reduce a particular threat (e.g., inconsistency or learned helplessness) or particular social psychological motives (i.e., dissonance and control motives). Based on this reasoning, the following proposition is offered.

*Proposition III:* The means of self-affirmation will be determined by availability, that is, the degree to which a given adaptation is accessible in the individual's perception, memory, or imagination (cf. Nisbett & Ross, 1976; Tversky & Kahneman, 1973) and, among equally available adaptations, by perceptions of their relative effectiveness-to-cost ratios. An adaptation can be made available by cues related to the threat, the immediate situation that suggests a means of adaptation, individual differences that make a given means of adaptation accessible (as prayer may be for the devout), prior experiences that "prime" a given means of adaptation, memory associations, and so on.

This is not to argue that we are slaves to availability, locked into seeking affirmation through whatever presents itself. Even when highly available, a given adaptation may be rejected because it is seen as ineffective or too costly in time or resources. Although I may experience a highly available, compensatory impulse to help with the dishes after arriving late at the Fathers-and-Sons banquet, because of the perceived costs, I might wind up seeking an easier route to affirmation, perhaps donating more to the benefit drive. More likely, once a given adaptation is available, effectiveness-to-cost judgments will influence whether it is used. Still, our findings suggest that availability is a powerful, if not all powerful, determinant of how we go about affirming the self. [. . .]

## REFERENCES

Abelson, R. P. (1959). Modes of resolution of belief dilemmas. *Journal of Conflict Resolution, 3,* 343–352.

Abelson, R. P. (1983). Whatever became of consistency theory? *Personality and Social Psychology Bulletin, 9,* 37–54.

Abramson, L. Y., Seligman, M. E. P., & Teasdale, J. (1978). Learned helplessness in humans: Critique and reformulation. *Journal of Abnormal Psychology, 87,* 49–74.

Allport, G. W. (1943). The ego in contemporary psychology. *Psychological Review, 50,* 451–478.

Anderson, J. E. (1942). National Society for the Study of Education. *The psychology of learning.* Forty-first Yearbook, Pt. 2. Bloomington, IL: Public Schools Publ.

Aronson, E. (1969). The theory of cognitive dissonance: A current perspective. In L. Berkowitz (Ed.), *Advances in experimental social psychology* (Vol. 4) (pp. 1–34). New York: Academic Press.

Bandura, A. (1977). Self efficacy: Toward a unifying theory of behavior change. *Psychological Review, 84,* 191–215.

Bandura, A. (1982). Self-efficacy mechanism in human agency. *American Psychologist, 37,* 122-147.

Bower, G. H., & Gilligan, S. G. (1979). Remembering information related to one's self. *Journal of Research in Personality, 3,* 420–432.

Brehm, J. W. (1966). *A theory of psychological reactance.* New York: Academic Press.

Brehm, J. W., & Cohen, A. R. (1962). *Explorations in cognitive dissonance.* New York: Wiley.

Clary, E. G., & Tesser, A. (1983). Reactions to unexpected events: The naive scientist and interpretive activity. *Personality and Social Psychology Bulletin, 9,* 609–620.

Cooper, J. (1971). Personal responsibility and dissonance: The role of foreseen consequences. *Journal of Personality and Social Psychology, 18,* 354–363.

Cooper, J., & Fazio, R. H. (1984). A new look and dissonance theory. In L. Berkowitz (Ed.), *Advances in experimental social psychology,* (Vol. 17) (pp. 229–262). New York: Academic Press.

Cooper, J., Zanna, M. P., & Taves, P. A. (1978). Arousal as a necessary condition for attitude change following induced compliance. *Journal of Personality and Social Psychology, 36,* 1101–1106.

Crano, W. D., & Meese, L. A. (1970). When does dissonance fail? The time dimension in attitude measurement. *Journal of Personality, 38,* 493–508.

Epstein, S. (1973). The self-concept revisited: Or a theory of a theory. *American Psychologist, 28,* 404–416.

Festinger, L. (1957). *A theory of cognitive dissonance.* Evanston, IL: Row Peterson.

Fromkin, R. L. (1970). Effects of experimentally aroused feelings of undistinctiveness upon evaluation of scarce and novel experiences. *Journal of Personality and Social Psychology, 16,* 521-530.

Goethals, G. R., & Cooper, J. (1975). When dissonance is reduced: The timing of self-justificatory attitude change. *Journal of Personality and Social Psychology, 32,* 361–367.

Gotz-Marehand, B., Gotz, J., & Irle, M. (1974). Reference of dissonance reduction modes as a function of their order, familiarity and reversibility. *European Journal of Social Psychology, 4,* 201–228.

Greenwald, A. G. (1980). The totalitarian ego: Fabrication and revision of personal history. *American Psychologist, 35,* 603–618.

Greenwald, A. G. (1982). Ego task analysis: An integration of research on ego-involvement and self-awareness. In A. Hastorf & A. Isen (Eds.), *Cognitive social psychology.* New York: Elsevier.

Greenwald, A. G., & Ronis, D. L. (1978). Twenty years of cognitive dissonance: Case study of the evolution of a theory. *Psychological Review, 85,* 53–57.

Harvey, J. H., Yarkin, K. L., Lightner, J. M., & Town, J. P. (1980). Unsolicited attribution and recall of interpersonal events. *Journal of Personality and Social Psychology, 38,* 551–568.

Hastie, R. (1984). Causes and effects of causal attribution. *Journal of Personality and Social Psychology, 46,* 44–56.

Heider, F. (1958). *The psychology of interpersonal relations.* New York: Wiley.

James, W. (1915). *Psychology, briefer course.* New York: Holt.

Kelley, H. H. (1971). Attribution theory in social interaction. In E. E. Jones et al. (Eds.), *Attribution: Perceiving the causes of behavior.* New York: General Learning Press.

Lazarus, R. S. (1968). Emotions and adaptation: Conceptual and empirical relations. In W. J. Arnold (Ed.), *Nebraska symposium on motivation.* Lincoln, NE: University of Nebraska Press.

Lazarus, R. S. (1983). The costs and benefits of denial. In S. Breznitz (Ed.), *Denial of stress.* New York: International Universities Press.

Liu, T. J., & Steele, C. M. (1986). Attribution as self-affirmation. *Journal of Personality and Social Psychology, 51,* 531–540.

Martin, M. (1985). General introduction. In M. Martin (Ed.), *Self-deception and self-understanding.* Lawrence, Kansas: University of Kansas Press.

Miller, D. T., Norman, S. A., & Wright, E. (1978). Distortion in person perception as a consequence of the need for effective control. *Journal of Personality and Social Psychology, 36,* 598–607.

Nisbett, R. E., & Ross, L. (1976). *Human inference: Strategies and shortcomings of social judgement.* Englewood Cliffs, NJ: Prentice Hall.

Pittman, T. S., & D'Agostino, P. R. (1985). Motivation and attribution: The effects of control deprivation and subsequent information processing. In J. Harvey & G. Weary (Eds.), *Current perspectives on attribution research* (Vol. 1). New York: Academic Press.

Pittman, T. S., & Pittman, N. L. (1980). Deprivation of control and the attribution process. *Journal of Personality and Social Psychology, 39,* 377–389.

Pittman, T. S., Scherrer, F. W., & Wright, J. B. (1977). The effect of commitment on information utilization in the attribution process. *Personality and Social Psychology Bulletin, 3,* 276–279.

Seligman, M. E. P. (1972). Learned helplessness. *Annual Review of Medicine, 23,* 407–412.

Seligman, M. E. P. (1975). *Helplessness: On depression, development, and death.* San Francisco: Freeman.

Silver, R. I., & Wortman, C. B. (1980). Coping with undesirable life events. In J. Garber & M. E. P. Seligman (Eds.), *Human helplessness: Theory and applications.* New York: Academic Press.

Steele, C. M. (1975). Name-calling and compliance. *Journal of Personality and Social Psychology, 31,* 361–369.

Steele, C. M., Hopp, H., & Gonzales, J. (1986). *Dissonance and the lab coat: Self-affirmation and the free choice paradigm.* Unpublished manuscript, University of Washington.

Steele, C. M., & Liu, T. J. (1981). Making the dissonance act unreflective of the self: Dissonance avoidance and the expectancy of a value-affirming response. *Personality and Social Psychology Bulletin, 7,* 363–387.

Steele, C. M., & Liu, T. J. (1983). Dissonance processes as self-affirmation. *Journal of Personality and Social Psychology, 45,* 5–19.

Steele, C. M., Southwick, L., & Critchlow, B. (1981). Dissonance and alcohol: Drinking your troubles away. *Journal of Personality and Social Psychology, 41,* 831–846.

Taylor, S. E. (1983). Adjustment to threatening events: A theory of cognitive adaptation. *American Psychologist, 38,* 1161–1173.

Tversky, A., & Kahneman, D. (1973). Availability: A heuristic for judging frequency and probability. *Cognitive Psychology, 5,* 207–232.

Walster, E., Walster, W. G., & Berscheid, E. (1978). *Equity: Theory and research.* Boston: Allyn & Bacon.

Wicklund, R. A., & Brehm, J. W. (1976). *Perspectives on cognitive dissonance.* Hillsdale, NJ: Erlbaum.

Wicklund, R. A., & Gollwitzer, P. M. (1983). A motivational factor in self-report validity. In J. Suls (Ed.), *Psychological perspectives on the self* (Vol. 1). Hillsdale, NJ: Erlbaum.

Zanna, M. P., & Azziza, C. (1976). On the interaction of repression-sensitization and attention in resolving cognitive dissonance. *Journal of Personality, 44,* 577-593.

# The Cognitive-Affective Crossfire: When Self-Consistency Confronts Self-Enhancement

William B. Swann, Jr., John J. Griffin, Jr., Steven C. Predmore, and Bebe Gaines • University of Texas at Austin

*link to preferences:*

*HSE – enhancing*

*LSE – verifying*

Self-consistency theory assumes that people want others to treat them in a predictable manner. Self-enhancement theory contends that people want others to treat them in a positive manner. We attempted to help reconcile the two theories by testing the hypothesis that people's cognitive responses conform to self-consistency theory and their affective responses conform to self-enhancement theory. We presented individuals who possessed either positive or negative self-concepts with either favorable or unfavorable social feedback. We then measured cognitive reactions to the feedback (e.g., perceived self-descriptiveness) and affective reactions to the feedback (e.g., mood states). Cognitive responses were primarily driven by the consistency of the feedback, while affective responses were controlled by how enhancing it was. We propose that conceptualizing cognition and affect as partially independent mental systems helps to resolve some long-standing paradoxes regarding people's responses to self relevant social feedback.

When we undertake to cure a patient, to free him from the symptoms of his malady, he confronts us with a vigorous, tenacious resistance that lasts during the whole time of the treatment. This is so peculiar a fact that we cannot expect much credence for it. . . . Just consider, this patient suffers from his symptoms and causes those about him to suffer with him . . . and yet he struggles, in the very interests of the malady, against one who would help him. How improbable this assertion must sound! (Freud, 1921, p. 248)

Improbable perhaps, yet Freud's assertion has fared well over the years. *Self-consistency* theo-

rists, for example, contend that, much like Freud's patients, people with negative self-concepts undermine opportunities to better themselves by engaging in cognitive and behavioral activities that perpetuate their self-views. Yet, as Freud feared, such contentions have raised a fair number of eyebrows. *Self-enhancement* theorists, for example, have rejected self-consistency theory by arguing that, in fact, people with negative self-concepts are highly motivated to improve their self-views. This raises an important question: Does either self-consistency or self-enhancement theory offer a more compelling characterization of human nature?

*Links to SE (lo vs. hi)? relationships – Sandra*

## Self-Consistency Versus Self-Enhancement

Self-consistency theory can be traced to the writings of Prescott Lecky (1945). His central assumption was that self-conceptions are critical for survival because they enable people to predict and control the nature of social reality (e.g., Epstein, 1973; Mead, 1934). People therefore are motivated to preserve their self-views, which is accomplished by thinking and behaving in ways that perpetuate their conceptions of self.

Since Lecky's (1945) initial statement, several theorists have extended his formulation by identifying several specific cognitive and behavioral strategies through which people stabilize their self-views (e.g., Secord & Backman, 1965; Swann, 1983). Furthermore, some (e.g., Epstein, 1983; Swann, 1983) have suggested that these activities are mediated by a highly general, cognitively based preference for stimuli that are predictable, familiar, stable, and uncertainty reducing. From this vantage point, people strive to acquire information that confirms their self-conceptions because their thought processes are structured so that confirmatory information seems especially trustworthy, diagnostic, and accurate.

Self-enhancement theory is based loosely on various personality theories (e.g., Horney, 1937; Rogers, 1961) and learning theory. Its central assumption is that people are motivated to increase their feelings of personal worth (e.g., Epstein, 1973; Tesser, 1985). In addition, self-enhancement theory (at least in its most logically consistent and popular form) assumes that, because people with negative self-concepts lack self-esteem more than their counterparts, they will compensate for this lack by trying to enhance their self-views more than will their high self-esteem counterparts (e.g., Jones, 1973).

Both theoretical formulations predict that people with positive self-views work to maintain such views, albeit for different reasons. However, the two theories make competing predictions regarding people with negative self-views. That is, self-consistency theorists assume that individuals with negative self-concepts prefer negative feedback because it is predictable; self-enhancement theorists assume that such individuals prefer positive feedback because they want to think well of themselves.

Given that self-consistency and self-enhancement theory make very different predictions re-

garding responses of individuals who possess negative self-views, it appears that one theory could be discounted by simply examining the relevant responses of such individuals. This is not so. Several decades of research have produced mixed results, with some studies favoring self-consistency theory and others favoring self-enhancement theory (for reviews, see Jones, 1973; Shrauger, 1975; Swann, 1985).

Shrauger (1975) attempted to bring order to this confusing state of affairs by suggesting that some dependent variables tended to produce consistency effects, while others tended to produce enhancement effects. In particular, measures of certain cognitive processes (e.g., recall, perceptions of the self-descriptiveness of feedback)[1] seemed to support self-consistency theory. In contrast, measures that had a more affective flavor (e.g., pleasure or disappointment with feedback) seemed to support the self-enhancement position. An intriguing implication of Shrauger's proposal was that people with negative self-concepts would have rather ambivalent reactions to unfavorable feedback. Although such individuals might value such feedback on a cognitive level, they would also find it affectively abhorrent.

Although Shrauger's (1975) hypothesis was reasonably consistent with the existing data, workers in the area were slow to accept it. One problem was that Shrauger provided little theoretical justification for his notion that cognitive and affective responses were independent. In addition, he was unable to marshal direct empirical evidence for his hypothesis. We shall focus on these two shortcomings in this article, but we will deal first with the empirical issues and leave the conceptual issues for the General Discussion.

## Evidence for the Cognitive–Affective Independence Hypothesis

The major problem with the evidence Shrauger (1975) cited in support of his cognitive–affective

---

[1] After Shrauger (1975), we use the term *cognitive processes* in a limited sense to refer to the relatively analytical, controlled processes that are presumably indexed by ratings of self-descriptiveness. As a result, when we use the term *cognitive-affective crossfire,* we are referring to a conflict between the products of these analytical processes and the affective system, rather than to a conflict between the entire cognitive system and the entire affective system.

independence hypothesis was that researchers had examined either cognitive or affective reactions; no one had examined both types of reactions in the context of a single study. This introduced the possibility that procedural differences other than the nature of the dependent variable could have accounted for the conflicting results of those who examined cognitive versus affective reactions.

Since Shrauger's review, two published investigations have attempted to test his hypothesis directly, but neither has offered strong support for his position. McFarlin and Blascovich (1981) tapped cognitive responses by asking people (a) to indicate their ability to perform a task and (b) to predict how well they would perform. The measure of affect was problematic, however. Instead of providing participants with feedback and measuring their affective reactions, the researchers asked them to indicate their preferences regarding future performances.

Given the absence of a direct measure of affective reactions to feedback, the McFarland and Blascovich (1981) study is, at best, tangentially relevant to the hypothesis that people with negative self-views value unfavorable feedback on a cognitive level, yet find it affectively abhorrent. Therefore, it may not be telling that some of their results contradicted Shrauger's hypothesis. Most importantly, contrary to the cognitive–affective independence notion, the affective measure was as closely associated with one of the measures of cognition ($r = .62$) as the two measures of cognition were to one another ($r = .67$).

The results of a field investigation by Moreland and Sweeney (1984) are potentially more relevant to Shrauger's hypothesis. These investigators assessed the relation between scores on a midterm exam and students' subsequent affective states and cognitive appraisals of the exam. The findings were complex, but it is fairly clear that both the cognitive and affective responses supported the self-enhancement position. Contrary to Shrauger's hypothesis and consistency theory, participants with low self-esteem generally regarded positive feedback as more self-descriptive than negative feedback.

Nevertheless there is a good reason why Moreland and Sweeney's (1984) measures of cognitive reactions may have failed to support self-consistency theory. Consider that most college students possess relatively high self-esteem. Given this, Moreland and Sweeney's procedure of iden-

tifying low-self-esteem individuals by performing a median split may have classified people who were in reality high in self-esteem as low in self-esteem. Such misclassified high-self-esteem individuals would reject the negative feedback as being nondescriptive of self: not in the service of self-enhancement strivings, as the authors concluded, but in the service of self-consistency tendencies. For this reason, the pattern of cognitive responses that Moreland and Sweeney interpreted as supportive of self-enhancement theory may have supported self-consistency theory in reality.

In short, more than a decade has passed since Shrauger (1975) presented his important hypothesis, and the verdict is still out. What is needed is a study in which (a) people who possess negative or positive self-views receive feedback that is clearly consistent or inconsistent with their self views and (b) cognitive and affective reactions are measured by instruments capable of discriminating the two. Toward this end, we recruited individuals who scored in the upper or lower 20th percentile of a large sample on a measure of self-esteem. We presented favorable feedback to some individuals and unfavorable feedback to others. We then measured, in counterbalanced order, cognitive and affective reactions to the feedback.

Cognitive reactions included participants' perceptions of the accuracy of the feedback, competence of the evaluator, diagnosticity of the evaluation technique, and attributions regarding the cause of the feedback. We used a mood measure to tap affect because we believed that such a measure would provide us with a relatively pure index of affect. We also measured attraction to the rater so that we would be able to compare our findings to those of earlier investigators who assessed this variable. As have previous workers (e.g., Shrauger, 1975), we believed that this measure might tap both cognitive and affective reactions because attraction to a rater might be influenced by one's perception of that rater's credibility as well as the mood induced by that rater.

Our major prediction was that cognitive reactions to the feedback would be relatively independent of affective reactions. Specifically, we anticipated that cognitive reactions would be based on the degree to which the feedback confirmed participants' self-views, with confirmatory feedback regarded as more accurate, diagnostic, and so on. In contrast, we expected that affective reactions would be based on the favorability of the feedback, with favorable feedback producing more positive mood states than unfavorable feedback.

## Method

### Participants and Measure of Self-Concept

Participants were 48 male and 58 female undergraduates who took part in the investigation for credit in their introductory psychology course. Five participants were deleted because they were suspicious of the experimental procedure.

Participants were drawn from a large sample of students who completed Helmreich, Spence, and Stapp's (1974) Team Social Behavior Inventory (TSBI) during a pretest session at the beginning of the semester. This scale emphasizes social self-esteem (e.g., "I have no doubts about my social competence," "I am not likely to speak to people until they speak to me.") Scores on the TSBI could range from 16 to 80; the actual range was 25 to 80. We classified individuals who scored below the 20th percentile (51) as negative-self-concept individuals and those who scored above the 80th (66) percentile as positive-self-concept individuals. Experimenters remained unaware of participants' TSBI scores throughout the experimental procedure. We also measured the certainty of participants' self-views. This variable had no effects on the dependent variables and will not be discussed further.

### Procedure

#### COVER STORY AND SPEECH

A female experimenter introduced the experiment as an investigation of the accuracy of first impressions formed on the basis of nonverbal information only. She explained that two people would be involved in the experiment, the participant and an evaluator. The first step would be for the participant to deliver a speech. The evaluator would watch the participant deliver the speech through a soundproof, one-way mirror, allegedly to prevent the evaluation from being influenced by what the participant said. The evaluator would then assess the participant. Shortly thereafter, the participant would examine the evaluator's assessment and judge its accuracy. Comments made by participants during debriefing revealed that they found this cover story entirely plausible.

The speech consisted of several unremarkable excerpts from Desmond Morris's novel *The Naked Ape*. After giving the speech, the participant waited for 5 minutes while the evaluator ostensibly prepared his or her evaluation (evaluators were always alleged to have the same sex as the participant). The experimenter then entered with a handwritten evaluation that had been prepared in advance. In the favorable feedback condition, the feedback asserted that the participant was socially skilled:

> From the way he (she) looked reading this speech this person seems socially self-confident. I'd say he (she) probably feels comfortable and at ease around other people he (she) doesn't know very well. He (she) seems to have little doubt of his (her) social competence. That's about all I could tell about him (her).

In the unfavorable feedback condition, the feedback was simply the negation of that used in the favorable feedback condition:

> From the way he (she) looked reading this speech this person doesn't seem real socially self-confident. I'd say he (she) probably feels somewhat uncomfortable and anxious around other people he (she) doesn't know too well. He (she) seems to have some doubts about his (her) social competence. That's about all I could tell about him (her).

#### COGNITIVE AND AFFECTIVE REACTIONS TO THE FEEDBACK

Immediately after reading the feedback participants completed two series of questionnaires in counterbalanced order. One set of questionnaires tapped their cognitive reactions to the feedback and another assessed their affective reactions to the feedback. Three additional items measured attraction to the evaluator.

We assessed four distinct cognitive reactions. Five items indexed perceived accuracy of the feedback, five items tapped perceived competence of the evaluator, three items tapped perceived diagnosticity of the rating technique, and two items measured participants' attributions regarding the feedback.

We assessed affective reactions with a measure of mood, Zuckerman and Lubin's (1965) Multiple Affect Adjective Checklist (MAACL). This instrument is designed to measure depression, anxiety, and hostility.

After participants completed all measures of cognition and affect, they were thoroughly debriefed, thanked, and dismissed.

## ITEM ANALYSIS

Items were deleted from our measures if including them in a given scale diminished the internal consistency of that scale. According to this criterion, we deleted single items from the perceived competence, perceived diagnosticity, and liking for the evaluator scales. The reliability analyses reported in the Appendix indicate that all of our scales displayed high levels of internal consistency. The precise wording of all measures included in the analyses can also be found in the Appendix.

## OBSERVER RATINGS

To obtain a rough index of the veridicality of our participants' self-ratings, we had two observers watch participants give their speech and rate them on the following bipolar trait scales: unsociable–sociable, socially confident–unconfident, socially awkward–poised, shy–outgoing, self-doubting–self assured, socially competent–incompetent, cold–warm, nervous–at ease. Observers also attempted to guess whether participants had high or low self-esteem.

## Results and Discussion

We examined the impact of the self-concept, feedback, and order of presentation variables on participants' cognitive and affective reactions. We then assessed covariation between the cognitive and affective measures by submitting them to a factor analysis. Finally, we examined the impact of self-concept on the ratings of observers. The effects of sex of participant are not discussed as this variable did not qualify any of the findings reported here.

### Impact of Feedback, Self-Concept, and Order on Cognitive Reactions

All measures of cognitive reactions were entered into 2 (feedback: favorable, unfavorable) × 2 (self-concept; positive, negative) × 2 (order: cognitive first, affective first) least squares analyses of variance (ANOVAS). Our primary prediction was that there would be an interaction between self-concept and feedback, such that those with positive self-concepts would regard favorable feedback as especially self-descriptive (i.e., accurate, diagnostic, delivered by a competent rater, reflective of self) and those with negative self-concepts would regard unfavorable feedback as especially self-descriptive.

The means displayed in Table 19.1 support our predictions. The Self-Concept × Feedback interaction was reliable for all five cognitive measures, including accuracy, $F(1, 90) = 75.28$, $p < .001$; competence of the evaluator, $F(1, 89) = 55.36$, $p < .001$; diagnosticity of the evaluation technique, $F(1, 90) = 15.33$, $p < .001$; self-attribution, $F(1, 90) = 20.66$, $p < .001$; and other attribution, $F(1, 90) = 14.85$, $p < .001$.[2]

Simple effects analyses revealed that positive-self-concept individuals who received favorable feedback regarded it as more accurate, $F(1, 39) = 122.60$, $p < .001$; the rater as more competent, $F(1, 38) = 93.77$, $p < .001$; and the technique as more diagnostic, $F(1, 38) = 21.56$, $p < .001$. These individuals were also inclined to attribute the favorable feedback to themselves, $F(1, 39) = 21.56$, $p < .001$, and not to characteristics of the evaluator, $F(1, 39) = 5.48$, $p < .03$. Negative-self-concept individuals displayed precisely the opposite tendency. That is, negative-self-concept individuals who received unfavorable feedback regarded it as particularly accurate, $F(1, 56) = 12.77$, $p < .001$, and the evaluator as particularly competent, $F(1, 56) = 6.26$, $p < .02$. They were not inclined to attribute the feedback to characteristics of the evaluator, $F(1, 56) = 14.46$, $p < .001$. Relative to positive-self-concept individuals, these individuals also displayed nonreliable tendencies to regard the technique as more diagnostic and to attribute the feedback to themselves.

These data support the notion that people's cognitive reactions to feedback are driven by a concern with its consistency with their self-conceptions. Closer examination indicated that cognitive reactions were also influenced by the sheer positivity of the feedback. That is, ignoring the self-concept variable, there was an overall tendency

---

[2]The degrees of freedom for different dependent measures vary slightly because participants occasionally failed to complete measures.

**TABLE 19.1. Cognitive Reaction as a Function of Self-Esteem and Feedback**

| Cognitive measure | Positive self-concept | | Negative self-concept | |
|---|---|---|---|---|
| | Favorable feedback ($n = 22$) | Unfavorable feedback ($n = 18$) | Favorable feedback ($n = 26$) | Unfavorable feedback ($n = 32$) |
| Accuracy | 32.45 | 10.50 | 20.62 | 29.22 |
| Competence | 26.29 | 12.11 | 18.19 | 22.47 |
| Evaluation of technique | 13.71 | 8.22 | 10.92 | 12.15 |
| Self-attribution | 6.86 | 3.39 | 6.12 | 6.63 |
| Other-attribution | 4.91 | 6.06 | 6.13 | 4.50 |

*Note.* The higher the mean, the greater the perceived accuracy of the feedback (range = 5–45); the greater the perceived competence of the rater (range = 4–36), the more diagnostic the technique (range = 2–18); and the greater the attribution to self (range = 1–9) or other (range = 1–9).

for participants to believe that the favorable feedback was more accurate, diagnostic, and so forth, than the unfavorable feedback. The main effect of feedback was reliable for all the measures, save the measure of other attribution: accuracy, $F(1, 90) = 17.85$, $p < .001$; competence of the evaluator, $F(1, 89) = 16.50$, $p < .001$; diagnosticity of the evaluation technique, $F(1, 90) = 7.15$, $p < .001$; and self-attribution, $F(1, 90) = 11.48$, $p < .001$.

To assess the relative importance of the consistency and favorability of the feedback, we compared the percentage of variance accounted for by the Self-Concept × Feedback interaction versus the main effect of feedback. The interaction effect accounted for 88, 85, 76, 56, and 74% of the systematic variance on the measures of accuracy, competence, diagnosticity, self-attribution, and evaluator attribution, respectively. The feedback effect accounted for only 5, 10, 18, 18, and 10% of the systematic variance on these same measures. Of course, one must be careful in generalizing the results of this analysis, because characteristics of our experiment or subject population may have influenced the outcome.

Yet, if cognitive responses are only sensitive to the consistency of the feedback, why should there have been any main effect of feedback at all? One possibility is that the self-views of positive, as compared to negative, self-concept individuals were more closely matched to the consistent feedback. That is, despite the fact that our negative-self-concept participants scored in the lower 20% of our pretest sample, their average score was 46: just 2 points below the theoretical midpoint of the scale (range = 16–80). The self-views of negative-self-concept participants therefore were negative

in a relative sense only. In contrast, the average score of our positive-self-concept individuals was 70. Clearly, the self-views of these individuals were positive in an absolute, as well as a relative sense.

There were no main or interactive effects of the order variable on any of the cognitive measures.

## Affective Reactions to the Feedback

All measures of affective reactions were entered into 2 (feedback: favorable, unfavorable) × 2 (self-concept: positive, negative) × 2 (order: cognitive first, affective first) least squares analyses of variance (ANOVAs). Our major prediction was that positive- and negative-self-concept individuals alike would feel better after receiving favorable feedback, as compared to unfavorable feedback. This was the case. The data in Table 19.2 indicate that participants who received unfavorable, as compared to favorable, feedback were more depressed, $F(1, 92) = 15.41$, $p < .001$; hostile, $F(1, 92) = 8.81$, $p < .004$; anxious, $F(1, 92) = 11.97$, $p < .001$; and experienced less negative affect overall, $F(1, 92) = 15.92$, $p < .001$ (the last index was a composite measure comprised of the depression, hostility, and anxiety scores). Participants also were more attracted to the evaluator in the favorable feedback condition, $F(1, 86) = 43.86$, $p < .001$.

We also expected that the consistency of the feedback would not influence affective reactions. The measures of mood supported this prediction. That is, none of the mood measures showed an interaction between self-concept and feedback, all $F$s *ns*. There was, however, a reliable Self-Concept × Feedback interaction on the attraction variable, $F(1, 86) = 7.19$, $p < .01$. Although everyone

**TABLE 19.2. Affective Reaction as a Function of Self-Esteem and Feedback**

| | Positive self-concept | | Negative self-concept | |
| | Favorable feedback ($n = 21$) | Unfavorable feedback ($n = 19$) | Favorable feedback ($n = 26$) | Unfavorable feedback ($n = 33$) |
| Affective measure | | | | |
|---|---|---|---|---|
| Overall negative affect | 67.09 | 55.05 | 59.85 | 51.97 |
| Depression | 29.41 | 24.21 | 26.85 | 22.70 |
| Hostility | 21.59 | 17.37 | 19.92 | 18.94 |
| Anxiety | 16.09 | 13.47 | 13.08 | 10.33 |
| Attraction | 12.90 | 7.00 | 12.92 | 10.07 |

Note. The higher the mean, the more positive the overall affective state (range = 0–89); the less depressed (range = 0–40); the less hostile (range = 0–28), the less anxious (range = 0–21); and the greater the attrraction to the rater.

preferred favorable evaluators to unfavorable ones, this tendency was stronger among positive-self-concept individuals, $F(1, 38) = 41.5$, $p < .001$, as compared with negative-self-concept individuals, $F(1, 53) = 10.93$, $p < .001$. Even so, the interaction effect on the attraction variable accounted for only 9% of the systematic variance; in contrast, the feedback effect accounted for 67% of the systematic variance.

The analyses also revealed that participants' emotional reactions to the feedback were more polarized when the measures of affect were collected before, rather than after, the measures of cognition. The means in Table 19.3 indicate that order interacted with feedback on the measure of depression, $F(1, 92) = 4.90$, $p < .03$; hostility, $F(1, 92) = 4.68$, $p < .04$; overall negative affect, $F(1, 92) = 4.90$, $p < .03$; and attraction to the evaluator, $F(1, 86) = 10.68$, $p < .002$. A similar but nonreliable pattern characterized the measure of anxiety ($p < .16$).

Simple effects analyses revealed that, when the affective measures occurred first, participants displayed a clear preference for the favorable evaluation and evaluator on all five measures of affect (all $ps < .001$). In contrast, when the affective measures were collected second, the preference for favorable feedback was consistently weaker. In fact, this preference was only reliable in the case of the measure of attraction ($p < .01$).

Why did affective responses to the feedback vanish when they were measured after cognition? One possibility is that the simple passage of time diminished affective responses. Alternatively, the act of completing the cognitive measures may have been critical. Although this is plausible, it was not that completing the cognitive measures focused attention on the discrepancy between affect and cognition, because even positive-self-concept individuals (for whom there was no such discrepancy) displayed weaker affective reactions to the feedback after completing the cognitive measures.

**TABLE 19.3. Affective Reaction as a Function of Order and Feedback**

| | Affective first | | Cognitive first | |
| | Favorable feedback ($n = 19$) | Unfavorable feedback ($n = 31$) | Favorable feedback ($n = 29$) | Unfavorable feedback ($n = 21$) |
| Affective measure | | | | |
|---|---|---|---|---|
| Negative affect | 65.16 | 50.48 | 61.86 | 56.85 |
| Depression | 29.05 | 22.10 | 27.34 | 24.95 |
| Hostility | 21.16 | 17.42 | 20.38 | 19.76 |
| Anxiety | 14.95 | 10.97 | 14.14 | 12.24 |
| Attraction | 13.68 | 8.10 | 12.39 | 10.20 |

Note. The higher the mean, the more positive the overall affective state—less depressed, less hostile, less anxious—and the greater the attraction to the rater.

## Covariation Between the Measures of Cognition and Affect

To determine if the measures of cognition and affect were orthogonal, we entered the measures of cognitive and affective reactions into a principle components factor analysis with oblique rotation (Nie, Hull, Jenkins, Steinbrenner, & Bent, 1975). Two factors emerged from the initial oblique solution: the first accounted for 47% of the variance and had an eigenvalue of 4.24, while the second accounted for 24.4% of the variance and had an eigenvalue of 2.19. The eigenvalues for all other factors were less than 1.

The loadings for the first two factors after rotation can be seen in Table 19.4. All of the cognitive measures loaded heavily on the first factor only, while all of the mood measures loaded heavily on the second factor only. The sole measure that loaded on both factors was the index of attraction to the evaluator. It is, therefore, not surprising that the correlation between the first and second factors was a modest −.24. This evidence of cognitive–affective independence is especially striking when one considers that the cognitive and affective measures shared some method variance because we used self-reports to tap affective states.

In summary, the factor analysis indicated that (a) the cognitive measures were closely related to one another but were relatively independent of the affective measures, (b) the affective measures were closely related to one another but were relatively independent of the cognitive measures, and (c) the attraction measure was a hybrid measure related to both the cognitive and affective measures.

## Observer Ratings

Observers were able to discriminate positive-self-concept individuals from their counterparts. One way ANOVAs revealed that observers rated positive-self-concept participants as more sociable and self-confident than negative-self-concept individuals, $F(1, 92) = 7.01$, $p < .01$, $Ms = 95.9$ and 85.1, respectively. Observers were also able to guess whether participants were high or low in self-esteem at an above-chance level, $F(1, 92) = 5.66$, $p < .02$.

## General Discussion

Our findings suggest that both self-consistency and self-enhancement theory offer valuable insights into people's reactions to social feedback. For example, as self-consistency theory suggests, participants with negative self-concepts indicated that unfavorable feedback was more self-descriptive than favorable feedback. As self-enhancement theory suggests, even though those with negative self-concepts regarded unfavorable feedback to be quite accurate and self-descriptive, they were more depressed, anxious, and hostile after they received it. Our data, therefore, provide strong support for Shrauger's (1975) hypothesis that cognitive reactions to social feedback conform to self-consistency theory and affective reactions conform to self-enhancement theory.

Even so, our data raise questions regarding the assumptions underlying both self-consistency and self-enhancement theory. One relatively minor question, which is specific to self-enhancement theory, concerns the fact that the affective reactions of participants with positive and negative self-conceptions did not differ. This is inconsistent with the strong form of self-enhancement theory, which stipulates that, relative to individuals with positive self-concepts, those with negative self-concepts should be more pleased by positive feedback and more displeased by negative feedback. Our data, together with the fact that there is little definitive support for the strong version (see Shrauger, 1975), suggest that it may be time to

**TABLE 19.4. Oblique Factor Pattern Matrix After Rotation With Kaiser Normalization**

| Measure | Factor 1 | Factor 2 |
|---|---|---|
| Cognitive measures | | |
| Perceived accuracy of the feedback | .99 | .05 |
| Perceived competence of evaluator | .94 | −.06 |
| Perceived diagnosticity of the technique | .71 | .03 |
| Attribution to self | .70 | −.01 |
| Attribution to other | .65 | .08 |
| | | |
| Affective measures | | |
| Depression | .01 | .93 |
| Hostility | −.12 | .74 |
| Anxiety | .13 | .82 |
| | | |
| Attraction to evaluator | .49 | −.34 |

*Note.* Δ = 0.

opt for a weak form of self-enhancement theory in which people with positive self-views prefer favorable feedback just as much as those with negative self-views.

A more fundamental problem with both self-consistency and self-enhancement theory is raised by our evidence that cognitive and affective reactions seemed relatively independent. This finding is problematic for both theories because both subscribe to the assumption of psychological unity, which holds that a superordinate cognitive system oversees all mental activity and resolves inconsistencies between thoughts, feelings, and actions. Our findings clearly clash with the unity assumption in that our participants' cognitive and affective reactions seemed independent. That is, both the factor analysis and the fact that cognitive reactions were more likely to persist over time than affective reactions suggest that cognitive and affective responses are independent. More importantly, the overall pattern of data indicate that cognitive responses were based on the subjective veridicality of the stimuli, such as the extent to which the feedback was consistent with the person's self-views, and affective responses were simply based on whether or not the feedback was threatening.

One implication of our findings, then, is that both self-consistency and self-enhancement theorists should drop the unity assumption. Some have already begun to do this. Swann (1987), for example, has suggested that the self-verification formulation (a variant of self-consistency theory) applies to cognitive and behavioral responses, but not affective responses. In light of the wide range of responses that fall into these response classes, it may be necessary for theorists to become even more specific regarding the type of responses covered by their theories.

Our evidence that cognitive and affective responses are independent raises questions concerning why this might be the case. More recent work by dual- and multiple-systems theorists (e.g., Epstein, 1983; Gazzaniga, 1985; Greenwald, 1982; Izard, 1984; Tomkins, 1981; Wilson, 1985; Zajonc, 1980) may be relevant here. This work suggests that the cognitive and affective systems are designed to perform very different tasks. The cognitive system is presumably designed to classify stimuli and analyze their logical properties and subjective veridicality. For example, when social feedback is received it is first classified (e.g., favorable or unfavorable to self). Then the feedback is compared to information about the self that is stored in memory. If the feedback concurs with the information in memory, it is accepted as self-descriptive; if not, it is rejected.

Two characteristics of the decision process that the cognitive system uses are especially noteworthy. First, analysis of the subjective veridicality of stimuli is relatively time consuming because it entails searching memory and comparing the stimulus with stored information. Second, decisions reached by the cognitive system are only incidentally sensitive to the valence of feedback. That is, because the cognitive system is concerned with how incoming feedback compares with existing knowledge of self, the valence of the feedback matters only in that it determines whether it is classified as either consistent or inconsistent with the self.

In contrast, the affective system enables the organism to respond quickly to events that pose an immediate threat to personal safety. This rather primitive system reacts on the basis of relatively gross discriminations (i.e., threatening vs. not threatening, favorable to self vs. unfavorable to self) and little or no analysis of the subjective veridicality of stimuli. This system, then, trades precision for speed. It may not perform highly sophisticated analyses of stimuli, but it reacts quickly.

The major difference between the cognitive and affective systems, then, is how they improve the organism's chances of survival. The cognitive system achieves this end through a systematic analysis of the subjective veridicality of stimuli; the affective system does so by quickly recognizing threats to safety and spurring the organism to action. To be sure, the distinction between the two systems is not clear-cut (e.g., Epstein, 1983). For example, affective responses are dependent on some rudimentary cognitive analyses of stimuli, enough to allow the organism to recognize the stimuli (e.g., Lazarus, 1984; see also discussions by Birnbaum, 1981; Mellers, 1981; Zajonc, 1980, 1984). In our opinion, however, the fact that some interaction may occur between the cognitive and affective systems does not diminish the utility of conceptualizing them as relatively independent systems with distinct capabilities and agendas.

An important implication of the cognitive–affective independence notion, of course, is that it

*shallow vs. deep processing*

suggests the possibility that people may be caught in crossfires between the two systems. In our study, for example, participants with negative self-views who received unfavorable feedback found such feedback cognitively acceptable, yet affectively abhorrent. This prompts one to ask how people escape from such crossfires.

One possibility is that the cognitive system resolves such crossfires by muting or transforming the affective response. Indeed, the structure of the cognitive and affective systems might favor such an outcome: Insofar as the affective system is adapted for rapid decision-making processes and the cognitive system is adapted for more reflective processes (e.g., Epstein, 1983; Zajonc, 1980), the cognitive system should become increasingly dominant over time.

Our findings offer some support for the notion that cognitive responses eventually encroach upon affective responses. That is, our participants' affective responses to feedback faded over time, while their cognitive responses persisted. Other investigators have offered additional evidence of a tendency for cognitions to modify affective experiences. For example, recent evidence indicates that when people's behavioral predispositions toward some target person are based largely on affect (e.g., when they have just met a target), inducing them to think about that target can systematically alter their subsequent behavior toward him or her (e.g., Millar & Tesser, 1986; Wilson, Dunn, Bybee, Hyman, & Rotondo, 1984). Similarly, there is evidence that people "manage" their emotions by altering or juggling cognitions related to those emotions (e.g., Hochschild, 1983). For example, to cope with a drunk and unruly passenger, a flight attendant might transform his or her anger into sympathy by supposing that the passenger is grieving the death of a spouse. A somewhat similar strategy is used by cognitive therapists (e.g., Beck, 1967; Ellis, 1962) who often treat emotional disturbances by encouraging clients to develop interpretations of negative events that are highly adaptive.

From this perspective, the cognitive system is remarkably facile at fashioning ways of avoiding or eliminating cognitive–affective crossfires. Note, however, that such improvisations are not universally effective. At times, the source of the affect may be so powerful that no amount of cognitive gymnastics can defy it. In some cases, this may be

for the best, particularly when the ability of the cognitive system to mute affective states might encourage people to make behavioral choices that actually increase affective distress in the future. For example, to the extent that people with negative self-views convince themselves that unfavorable feedback is desirable because it is trustworthy and predictable, they may be tempted to seek out intimates who are apt to provide them with such feedback (e.g., Swann & Fisher, 1986). These intimates may then supply them with unfavorable feedback that fuels future bouts of depression (e.g., Swann & Predmore, 1985).

## Implications and Conclusions

Much of the history of social and personality psychology can be understood as an unsuccessful quest for evidence of psychological unity. Part of this history, which involves efforts to find unity in people's reactions to feedback, has been discussed in this report. But researchers interested in responses to feedback have not been the only ones to venture into their laboratories in search of unity and emerge with evidence of disunity. For example, disunity and lack of consistency has been a major theme in research on the relation of attitudes to behavior (e.g., Fazio & Zanna, 1981; Wicker, 1969) and in treatments of the "trait-situation controversy" (e.g., Magnusson & Endler, 1977). Similarly, research on emotion and misattribution of arousal has suggested that two separate psychological systems contribute to the experience of emotion: one that controls arousal and another that interprets it (e.g., Zillman, 1983). Furthermore, investigations of people's introspective powers have suggested that the psychological system that explains overt behavior has no access to the system that generates behavior (e.g., Nisbett & Wilson, 1977; Wilson, 1985).

To be sure, the assumption of psychological unity is appealing in many ways. It is simple, elegant, and phenomenologically compelling. And it is pragmatic; were it not for the assumption of psychological unity, holding people responsible for their actions might be a rather awkward affair. Yet our data suggest that, at least with respect to reactions to social feedback, people are not nearly as single minded as the unity assumption would lead us to believe.

# REFERENCES

Beck, A. T. (1967). *Depression: Causes and treatment.* Philadelphia: University of Pennsylvania Press.

Birnbaum, M. H. (1981). Thinking and feeling: A skeptical review. *American Psychologist, 37,* 99–101.

Ellis, A. (1962). *Reason and emotion in psychotherapy.* New York: Lyle Stuart.

Epstein, S. (1973). The self-concept revisited: Or a theory of a theory. *American Psychologist, 28,* 404–416.

Epstein, S. (1983). The unconcious, the preconcious, and the self-concept. In J. Suls & A. G. Greenwald (Eds.), *Psychological perspectives on the self* (Vol. 2, pp. 219–247). Hillsdale, NJ: Erlbaum.

Fazio, R. H., & Zanna, M. P. (1981). Direct experience and attitude-behavior consistency. In L. Berkowitz (Ed.), *Advances in experimental social psychology* (Vol. 14, pp. 162–202). New York: Academic Press.

Freud, S. (1921). *A general introduction to psychoanalysis.* New York: Boni & Liverwright.

Gazzaniga, M. S. (1985). *The social brain.* New York: Basic Books.

Greenwald, A. G. (1982). Is any*one* in charge? Personalysis versus the principle of personal unity. In J. Suls (Ed.), *Psychological perspectives on the self* (Vol. 1, 151–181). Hillsdale, NJ: Erlbaum.

Helmreich, R., Spence, J. T., & Stapp, J. (1974). Short form of the Texas social behavior inventory, an objective measure of self-esteem. *Bulletin of the Psychonomic Society, 4,* 473–475.

Hochschild, A. (1983). *The managed heart.* Berkeley, CA: University of California Press.

Horney, K. (1937). *The neurotic personality of our time.* New York: Norton.

Izard, C. E. (1984). Emotion–cognition relationships and human development. In C. E. Izard, J. Kagan, & R. B. Zajonc (Eds.), *Emotions, cognition, and behavior* (pp. 17–37). New York: Cambridge University Press.

Jones, S. C. (1973). Self and interpersonal evaluations: Esteem theories versus consistency theories. *Psychological Bulletin, 79,* 185–199.

Lazarus, R. S. (1984). On the primacy of cognition. *American Psychologist, 39,* 124–129.

Lecky, P. (1945). *Self-consistency: A theory of personality.* New York: Island Press.

Losco-Szpiler, J. P., & Epstein, S. (1978, April), *Reactions to favorable and unfavorable evaluations in everyday life as a function of level of self-esteem.* Paper presented at the meeting of the Eastern Psychological Association, Washington, DC.

Magnusson, D., & Endler, N. S. (1977). *Personality at the crossroads: Current issues in interactional psychology.* Hillsdale, NJ: Erlbaum.

McFarlin, D. B., and Blascovich, J. (1981). Effects of self-esteem and performance on future affective preferences and cognitive expectations. *Journal of Personality and Social Psychology, 40,* 521–531.

Mead, G. H. (1934). *Mind, self and society.* Chicago: University of Chicago Press.

Mellers, B. A. (1981). Feeling more than thinking. *American Psychologist, 36,* 802–803.

Millar, M. G., & Tesser, A. ( 1986). Effects of affective and cognitive focus on the attitude–behavior relation. *Journal of Personality and Social Psychology, 51,* 270–276.

Moreland, R. L., & Sweeney, P. D. (1984). Self-expectancies and reactions to evaluations of personal performance. *Journal of Personality, 52,* 156–176.

Nie, N. H., Hull, C. H., Jenkins, J. G., Steinbrenner, K., & Bent, D. H. (1975). *Statistical package for the social sciences.* New York: McGraw-Hill.

Nisbett, R. E., & Wilson, T. D. (1977). Telling more than we can know: Verbal reports on mental processes. *Psychological Review, 84,* 231–259.

Rogers, C. R. (1961). *On becoming a person: A therapists' view* of *psychotherapy.* Boston: Houghton Mifflin.

Secord, P. F., & Backman, C. W. (1965). An interpersonal approach to personality. In B. Maher (Ed.), *Progress in experimental personality research* (Vol. 2, pp. 91–125) New York: Academic Press.

Shrauger, J. S. (1975). Responses to evaluation as a function of initial self-perceptions. *Psychological Bulletin, 82,* 581–596.

Swann, W. B., Jr. (1983). Self-verification: Bringing social reality into harmony with the self. In J. Suls & A. G. Greenwald (Eds.), *Social psychological perspectives on the self* (Vol. 2, pp. 33–66). Hillsdale, NJ: Erlbaum.

Swann, W. B., Jr. (1985). The self as architect of social reality. In B. Schlenker (Ed.), *The self and social life* (pp. 100–125). New York: McGraw-Hill.

Swann, W. B., Jr. (1987). *Identity negotiation: Where two roads meet.* Unpublished manuscript, University of Texas at Austin.

Swann, W. B., Jr., & Fisher, D. A. (1986). *Male selection and the self-concept.* Unpublished manuscript, University of Texas at Austin.

Swann, W. B., Jr., & Predmore, S. C. (1985). Intimates as agents of social support: Sources of consolation or despair. *Journal of Personality and Social Psychology, 49,* 1609–1617.

Tesser, A. (1985, August). *Toward a self-evaluation maintenance model of social behavior.* Paper presented at the annual convention of the American Psychological Association, Los Angeles.

Tomkins S. S. (1981). The quest for primary motives: Biography and autobiography of an idea. *Journal of Personality and Social Psychology, 41,* 306–329.

Wicker, A. W. (1969). Attitudes versus actions: The relationship of verbal and overt behavioral responses to attitude objects. *Journal of Social Issues, 25,* 41–78.

Wilson, T. D. (1985). Strangers to ourselves: The origins and accuracy of beliefs about one's own mental states. In J. H. Harvey & G. Weary (Eds.), *Attribution in contemporary psychology* (pp. 9–36). New York: Academic Press.

Wilson, T. D., Dunn, D. S., Bybee, J. A., Hymen, D. B., & Rotondo, J. A. (1984). Effects of analyzing reasons on attitude-behavior consistency. *Journal of Personality and Social Psychology, 47,* 5–16.

Zajonc, R. B. (1980). Feeling and thinking: Preferences need no inferences. *American Psychologist, 35,* 151–175.

Zajonc, R. B. (1984). On the primacy of affect. *American Psychologist, 39,* 117–123.

Zillman, D. (1983). Transfer of excitation in emotional behavior. In J. T. Cacioppo & R. Petty (Eds.), *Social psychophysiology: A sourcebook* (pp. 215–240). New York: Guilford.

Zuckerman, M., & Lubin, B. (1965). *Manual for the multiple affect adjective checklist.* San Diego, CA: Educational and Industrial Testing Service.

# Assessment, Enhancement, and Verification Determinants of the Self-Evaluation Process

Constantine Sedikides • University of North Carolina at Chapel Hill

The 3 major self-evaluation motives were compared: self-assessment (people pursue accurate self-knowledge), self-enhancement (people pursue favorable self-knowledge), and self-verification (people pursue highly certain self-knowledge). Subjects considered the possession of personality traits that were either positive or negative and either central or peripheral by asking themselves questions that varied in diagnosticity (the extent to which the questions could discriminate between a trait and its alternative) and in confirmation value (the extent to which the questions confirmed possession of a trait). Subjects selected higher diagnosticity questions when evaluating themselves on central positive rather than central negative traits and confirmed possession of their central positive rather than central negative traits. The self-enhancement motive emerged as the most powerful determinant of the self-evaluation process, followed by the self-verification motive.

Self-understanding is a major concern for people across the life span (Breytspraak, 1984; Damon, 1983). Increased self-understanding carries several positive implications for the individual. Self-understanding is likely to lead to a well-defined (i.e., structurally sound, stable, and certain) self-concept. A well-defined self-concept facilitates self-regulation (Carver & Scheier, 1981), provides a sense of self-continuity (Dennett, 1982; Gergen & Gergen, 1988), accelerates processing of self-relevant information (Bargh, 1982), is associated with positive affect about the self (Baumgardner, 1990), is a key to goal setting (Markus & Nurius, 1986; Schlenker, 1985), influences social perception (Markus, Smith, & Moreland, 1985; Srull & Gaelick, 1983), determines choice of partner as well as behavior in personal relationships (Cantor, Mackie, & Lord, 1984; Snyder, Gangestad, & Simpson, 1983), and contributes to the projection of a consistent and desirable self-image to others (Harris & Snyder, 1986; Tice & Baumeister, 1990).

People can take several avenues in their quest for self-understanding. For example, they may evaluate themselves by comparing themselves with socially significant others (Kruglanski & Mayseless, 1990; Wood, 1989), engaging in attributional thinking (Bradley, 1978; Nisbett & Valins, 1972), using consensus information (Krosnick & Sedikides, 1990; Kulik & Taylor, 1981), or remembering their past (Ross, 1989; Ross & Conway, 1986). Regardless of its exact form, however, the self-evaluation process is likely to be motivated. Next, I discuss the motivational determinants of the self-evaluation process.

## Motivational Determinants of the Self-Evaluation Process

Self-evaluation can be accomplished through any of three primary routes: (a) the objective and accurate gathering and appraisal of self-relevant information, (b) the positive coloring of self-relevant information, or (c) the affirmation of preexisting self-conceptions. These three routes manifest the influence of three respective motives: self-assessment, self-enhancement, and self-verification. Discussion of these motives follows.

### Accurate Self-Assessment

According to the self-assessment view, people are motivated to reduce uncertainty about their abilities or personality characteristics. Uncertainty is reduced by obtaining an objective and accurate picture of the self in self-evaluative settings. An accurate picture of the self is obtained through maximally diagnostic tests or tasks. Diagnostic tasks are high informational value tasks; more specifically, they are tasks that can clearly distinguish between people high versus people low in ability level or between people having a given personality trait versus having its alternative. According to the self-assessment perspective, people will tend to prefer high diagnosticity tasks when evaluating the self, regardless of the potentially negative implications for the self of task outcome. Valence of task outcome (i.e., success vs. failure), valence of personality characteristics evaluated (i.e., positive vs. negative), and level of ability uncovered (i.e., high vs. low) are inconsequential to diagnosticity preferences (for reviews, see Trope, 1983, 1986).

### Biased Self-Enhancement

According to the self-enhancement view, individuals involved in self-evaluation desire to enhance the positivity of their self-conceptions or protect the self from negative information. To this end, people will selectively process self-relevant information. For example, people will focus on infor-

mation that has favorable implications for the self, avoiding information that has unfavorable implications. People will be mainly concerned not with task diagnosticity, but with the valence of the task outcome or personality characteristic evaluated and the implications of this evaluation for the self. People can tolerate some inferential ambiguity in exchange for positive implications. As a result, people will regard tasks diagnostic of success, high ability, or positive personality attributes as more attractive and preferable than tasks diagnostic of failure, low ability, or negative personality attributes, respectively (for reviews, see Kunda, 1990, and Taylor & Brown, 1988).

### Conservative Self-Verification

According to the self-verification view, people are motivated to verify their preexisting self-conceptions. For example, people will verify their positive self-conceptions by seeking out favorable feedback, but will also verify their negative self-conceptions by soliciting unfavorable feedback about their abilities or personalities. Stated somewhat differently, people will seek verification for their certain self-conceptions to a greater degree than their uncertain self-conceptions. What matters is consistency between self-conceptions and feedback, rather than self-conception or feedback valence (for reviews, see Swann, 1983, 1990).

## Toward Comparative Testing

Each of the three views just discussed has received ample empirical support when tested independently. Comparative tests of the three views, however, are relatively infrequent (Sedikides & Strube, 1993). It is comparative, rather than independent, testing that can provide unequivocal evidence regarding the strength of each motive's influence on the self-evaluation process. Next, I describe a task that has the potential to afford comparative testing of the three views and derive task-specific predictions of each view.

### Self-Reflection Task

The task used in the present investigation involved self-reflection on the part of the subjects. Self-reflection is defined as the consideration of whether one possesses certain personality traits. Personality traits contain, of course, information about a variety of personal domains, such as one's social behavior, relationships, moral values, work habits, and performance quality. When inquiring about the possession of particular personality traits, people can ask themselves hypothetical questions pertaining to their attitudes, preferences, intentions, or behaviors. People can ask themselves at least two types of questions: (a) high versus low diagnosticity and (b) hypothesis-true versus alternative-true.

Question diagnosticity is defined in terms of the probability that the behavior, intention, or attitude alluded to by the question is present or absent, provided that the relevant trait is present or absent. A high diagnosticity question will ask about a behavior that is highly probable when a person possesses a trait (e.g., extraversion) and highly improbable when the person possesses the alternative trait (e.g., introversion; see Trope & Bassok, 1982). For instance, if a person wonders whether he or she is introverted, a diagnostic question might be "In my leisure time, do I like to stay home alone?" A desire to be alone is highly likely in introverted people and highly unlikely in extroverted people. Thus, either a yes or no answer would deliver useful information about this person's relative position on the introversion–extraversion trait dimension.

Self-reflection can also take the form of asking either hypothesis-true or alternative-true questions. Hypothesis-true questions confirm possession of the relevant trait when answered yes and deny possession of the trait when answered no. Alternative-true questions confirm possession of the relevant trait when answered no and deny possession of the trait when answered yes (see Devine, Hirt, & Gehrke, 1990). An example of a hypothesis-true question for the trait *friendly* is "Do I greet acquaintances by name when I meet them?" A yes answer to this question confirms possession of the trait *friendly,* whereas a no answer disconfirms possession of the trait. An example of an alternative-true question is "Would I avoid talking to people I don't know at a party?" In this case, a yes answer disconfirms possession of the trait *friendly,* whereas a no answer confirms possession of the trait.

Class of question (hypothesis-true vs. alternative-true) can be combined with the answer to the

question (yes vs. no) to form a new variable, namely response type. Answering yes to a hypothesis-true question or no to an alternative-true question is a confirmatory response type. Answering no to a hypothesis-true question or yes to an alternative-true question is a disconfirmatory response type. In conclusion, the self-reflection process is accomplished by asking the self questions that can vary in terms of diagnosticity and response type.

The self-reflection task sufficiently simulates the process of self-evaluation. This task is likely to instigate cognitive mechanisms that are consistent with major accounts of the information-gathering process (Kruglanski, 1990; Snyder, 1981; Trope & Bassok, 1982). As epitomized by Kruglanski's (1990) theory of lay epistemics, these accounts accept that the knowledge acquisition process is twofold: The first stage involves hypothesis generation and the second entails hypothesis evaluation. Another advantage of the self-reflection task is that it provides a useful framework for comparative testing of the self-assessment, self-enhancement, and self-verification perspectives. I now turn to specific predictions that the three perspectives make with regard to this task.

## Predictions

The three perspectives make contrasting predictions concerning the self-evaluation process and, particularly, the self-reflection task. In the following sections, I state the predictions for each pair of perspectives in reference to standard features of experimental design.

To set up the context for the ensuing discussion, the reader should be reminded briefly of the general procedure of the reported experiments and informed of the experimental design. Subjects selected or generated questions of varying diagnosticity to self-reflect on traits that were either central or peripheral to their self-concept (*trait centrality*) and were either positive or negative (*trait valence*). Subsequently, subjects either confirmed or disconfirmed the selected questions. The question diagnosticity procedure (i.e., selecting questions of varying diagnosticity) is directly relevant to comparatively testing all three pairs of views. The response type procedure (i.e., confirmation or disconfirmation of questions) is only relevant to comparing the self-enhancement and self-verification views.

## SELF-ASSESSMENT VERSUS SELF-ENHANCEMENT

As implied in the preceding paragraph, the discussion on self-assessment and self-enhancement refers exclusively to question diagnosticity. These two views make conflicting predictions regarding the trait centrality main effect, the trait valence main effect, and the interaction.

*Trait Centrality Main Effect.* The self-assessment view asserts that self-evaluation is primarily motivated by the need for uncertainty reduction. It follows that people will be interested predominantly in gathering knowledge about relatively unknown ability or personality characteristics, but will be rather unconcerned with accumulating knowledge about well-known ability or personality characteristics. The self-enhancement view is mute with regard to this issue.

Subjects in the present investigation self-reflected on traits that were either central or peripheral by asking themselves questions of varying diagnosticity. Central traits (or self-schematic traits[1]; see Markus, 1977) are high in self-descriptiveness and personal importance, whereas peripheral traits (or non-self-schematic traits) are low in self-descriptiveness and personal importance. Central traits are, by definition, traits on which subjects have considerable self-knowledge (Catrambone & Markus, 1987; Markus, 1977). Central traits are the

> reflection of the invariances people have discovered in their own social behavior. They represent patterns of behavior that have been observed repeatedly, to the point where a framework is generated that allows one to make inferences from scant information or to quickly streamline and interpret complex sequences of events. (Markus, 1977, p. 64)

In contrast, peripheral traits are those about which subjects have little self-knowledge or certainty. It follows that, according to the self-assessment view, subjects will choose higher diagnosticity questions when self-reflecting on peripheral, rather than central, traits (trait centrality main effect). The self-enhancement view is mute with regard to this effect.

*Trait Valence Main Effect.* According to the self-enhancement view, people are more likely to accept successful outcomes or inferences about positive self-conceptions than failure outcomes or inferences about negative self-conceptions. The self-assessment view is rather mute with regard to this issue. Nevertheless, this view would have some difficulty explaining why people prefer success outcomes or positive feedback over failure outcomes or negative feedback in cases of equal outcome or feedback diagnosticity.

The present investigation expressed its concern with outcome valence or feedback valence by implicating the variable trait valence, namely whether the traits on which subjects self-reflected were positive or negative. According to the self-enhancement view, subjects will choose high diagnosticity questions when self-reflecting on positive traits because they desire to gain credible validation of their positive characteristics, but will choose low diagnosticity questions when self-reflecting on negative traits in an effort to avoid high credence information, which is damaging to the self (trait valence main effect). The self-assessment view would have some difficulty accounting for this main effect.

*Trait Centrality × Trait Valence Interaction.* A crucial variable for distinguishing between the two views is diagnosticity of performance outcome (i.e., success vs. failure). The self-assessment view predicts that individuals will be equally likely to prefer tasks of high success and failure diagnosticity because the discovery of capabilities and liabilities are equally attractive and conducive to uncertainty reduction. In contrast, the self-enhancement view predicts that individuals will find high success diagnosticity tasks attractive and preferable because these are likely to unveil their talents. However, they will find diagnosticity tasks unattractive and worth avoiding because these tasks are likely to expose their limitations.

In the context of the present investigation, asking the self high diagnosticity questions about positive central traits is assumed to be conceptually equivalent to high success diagnosticity, whereas asking about negative central traits is taken as conceptually equivalent to high failure diagnosticity. Conversely, asking the self low

---

[1]Markus (1977) used the terms *self-schematic* and *non-self-schematic* idiographically, whereas I am using the terms *central* and *peripheral* to refer both to subjects' collective self-concept (Experiments 1, 2, 3, 5, and 6) and to their idiographic self-concept (Experiment 4).

diagnosticity questions about positive peripheral traits is assumed to be analogous to low success diagnosticity, whereas asking questions about negative peripheral traits is taken as comparable to low failure diagnosticity.

The self-assessment view predicts that subjects will prefer high diagnosticity questions when self-reflecting on peripheral, as opposed to central traits, regardless of trait valence (i.e., trait centrality main effect). Consequently, a reliable interaction would be incompatible with this view. The self-enhancement view, however, makes a strong interaction prediction. Subjects will select questions of much higher diagnosticity when self-reflecting on central positive, compared with central negative, traits but they will prefer either slightly higher or equally high diagnosticity questions when self-reflecting on peripheral positive traits relative to peripheral negative traits. The interaction prediction can be stated in an alternative manner. Subjects will choose higher diagnosticity questions to self-reflect on central positive, compared with peripheral positive, traits, and they will choose lower diagnosticity questions to self-reflect on central negative, compared with peripheral negative, traits. The interaction prediction is based on the notion that individuals are more heavily invested in the enhancement and protection of their central, not peripheral, self-conceptions (Frey & Stahlberg, 1987; Gruder, 1977; Miller, 1976; Sherman, Presson, & Chassin, 1984; for a review, see Greenwald, 1981).

## SELF-ASSESSMENT VERSUS SELF-VERIFICATION

As a reminder, the discussion contrasting predictions of the self-assessment and self-verification views pertains exclusively to question diagnosticity. This discussion involves the trait centrality main effect.

The self-assessment view predicts that people will be more likely to seek knowledge about their uncertain, as opposed to certain, self-conceptions. In contrast, the self-verification view predicts that people will seek knowledge about their certain, as opposed to their uncertain, self-conceptions. In the language of the present experimental design, both views predict a trait centrality main effect, but they predict a different direction for this effect. In particular, the self-assessment view predicts that people will select higher diagnosticity questions when self-reflecting on peripheral, rather than cen-

tral, traits whereas the self-verification view predicts that people will select higher diagnosticity questions when self-reflecting on central, rather than peripheral, traits.

## SELF-ENHANCEMENT VERSUS SELF-VERIFICATION

The discussion involving the contrast between the self-enhancement and self-verification perspectives pertains to both question diagnosticity and response type.

*Question Diagnosticity.* The two perspectives make conflicting predictions concerning the trait valence main effect and the interaction.

*Trait valence main effect.* The self-enhancement perspective predicts that people will want to learn more about their assets than their liabilities. It follows that subjects will select higher diagnosticity questions to find out about their positive, rather than negative, traits (trait valence main effect). The self-verification view is mute with regard to this effect.

*Train Centrality × Valence interaction.* Both perspectives predict a significant interaction, but of a different pattern. According to the self-enhancement perspective, people will prefer more accurate information about their central positive self-conceptions than their central negative self-conceptions. Furthermore, people will prefer less accurate information about their central negative self-conceptions than about their peripheral negative self-conceptions. In the context of the present investigation, subjects will choose higher diagnosticity questions to self-reflect on central positive, rather than central negative, traits and they will choose lower diagnosticity questions to self-reflect on central negative, rather than peripheral negative, traits.

According to the self-verification perspective, however, people will want equally accurate information about their central positive and central negative self-conceptions (given that they are presumably held with equal certainty) and will want more accurate information about their central negative, as opposed to peripheral negative, self-conceptions. In the context of this investigation, subjects will select equal diagnosticity questions when self-reflecting on central positive and central negative traits, but will select higher diagnosticity questions when self-reflecting on central negative, as opposed to peripheral negative, traits.

*Response Type.* The two perspectives make conflicting predictions with regard to the trait centrality main effect, the trait valence main effect, and the interaction.

*Trait centrality main effect.* Will subjects be more likely to confirm their central, rather than peripheral, self-conceptions? In the absence of information about self-conception valence, the self-enhancement view is mute concerning this issue. However, the self-verification view predicts that subjects will be more likely to verify their central, rather than peripheral, self-conceptions (or traits) because the central self-conceptions are, by definition, a more integral and permanent part of their self-concept. Thus, the self-verification view predicts a trait centrality main effect.

*Trait valence main effect.* Will subjects be more likely to confirm their positive, as opposed to negative, self-conceptions? The self-enhancement perspective predicts that subjects will strongly prefer to confirm their positive over their negative self-conceptions or traits. Thus, this perspective predicts a trait valence main effect. The self-verification perspective is mute regarding this effect.

*Trait Centrality × Trait Valence interaction.* According to the self-enhancement view, subjects will confirm possession of central positive self-conceptions or traits to a higher extent than possession of central negative self-conceptions or traits; however, subjects will evidence either a slight or no tendency at all to confirm their peripheral positive self-conceptions to a greater extent than their peripheral negative self-conceptions. Alternatively, subjects will confirm their central positive self-conceptions to a larger degree than their peripheral positive self-conceptions, and they will disconfirm their central negative self-conceptions to a larger degree than their peripheral negative self-conceptions. Thus, the self-enhancement view predicts a significant Trait Centrality × Trait Valence interaction. An interaction of this form, however, would be unanticipated by the self-verification view, which (as stated earlier) predicts that subjects will confirm their central self-conceptions, regardless of valence (i.e., trait centrality main effect).

## Overview of the Investigation

This investigation consisted of five pilot studies and six experiments. The pilot studies accomplished two major objectives. First, they established traits that the population under consideration regarded as central and peripheral to their collective self-concept. These collective traits were used in all experiments except Experiment 4. The function of collective (as opposed to idiographic) traits was to create a state of "unknowingness" about the traits during the self-reflection process. The second objective attained by the pilot studies was to generate behavioral questions of varying diagnosticity for each trait.

The experiments tested the relative strength of the three perspectives in regulating the self-evaluation process. In all experiments, subjects self-reflected on traits that were either central or peripheral and either positive or negative. In Experiment 1, subjects selected from a list of three questions to ask themselves; in Experiment 2, they selected six questions; in Experiment 3, subjects generated their own questions; and, in Experiment 4, they generated both their own traits and their own questions. Experiment 5 replicated Experiment 1 and extended it by introducing a new manipulation: Some of the subjects were instructed to be accurate and objective in the question selection procedure. Finally, in Experiment 6, subjects selected questions to reflect either on themselves or on an acquaintance.

## Pilot Testing

### Pilot Study 1

The purpose of Pilot Study 1 was to derive personality traits that the population of University of Wisconsin (UW) introductory psychology students regarded as either central or peripheral to their collective self-concept. In this and all subsequent pilot studies, subjects were UW introductory psychology students run in small groups ranging in size from 4 to 10.

One hundred thirty subjects were instructed to list six traits that described them well and were important to them (i.e., central traits) and six traits that did not describe them well and were not important to them (i.e., peripheral traits). Subsequently, the experimenter and helpful colleagues compiled a list of central and peripheral traits under the stipulation that each trait was mentioned by at least 75% of the subjects. The central traits (and synonyms) were *kind* (considerate, gentle, sensitive, and thoughtful), *friendly* (cheerful, co-operative, happy, and pleasant), and *trustworthy* (dependable, faithful, reliable, and sincere). The peripheral traits (and synonyms) were *modest* (down-to-earth, humble, unassuming, and unpretentious), *predictable* (structured, organized, and planned), and *uncomplaining* (carefree, easygoing, and laid-back). Synonyms were determined by consulting the following sources: *Allen's Synonyms and Antonyms* (Allen, 1972), *The New Roget's Thesaurus in Dictionary Form* (Lewis, 1978), *and Webster's Ninth New Collegiate Dictionary* (1989).

Although the traits just described were mentioned by a decisive majority of subjects (i.e., 75%), it is always possible that the traits were, in part, a result of procedural peculiarities or sampling error. To offset this possibility, another list of traits was compiled: central and peripheral traits mentioned by at least one third of the subjects. This conservative procedure could afford a more convincing account of the collectively held central and peripheral traits when tested in a new study along with the traits mentioned by 75% of the subjects. The resulting additional "central" traits were clean, honest, independent, intelligent, open-minded, patriotic, and self-confident. The resulting additional "peripheral" traits were extroverted, funny, gossipy, hardworking, greedy, optimistic, romantic, and selfish. Thus, Pilot Study 1 produced a total of 21 traits, 10 central and 11 peripheral.

## Pilot Study 2

The purpose of Pilot Study 2 was to cross-validate the results of Pilot Study 1 by having subjects rate the self-descriptiveness and personal importance of each trait. Each of 130 subjects received a booklet containing the 21 personality traits chosen in Pilot Study 1. Subjects rated each trait as to how well it described them on a scale ranging from *does not describe me at all* (1) to *describes me very well* (11); also, they rated how important the trait was to them on a scale ranging from *not very important to me* (1) to *very important to me* (11). The average rating for each trait dimension across subjects constituted the trait's self-descriptiveness and importance scores. The average self-descriptiveness and importance score constituted the trait's centrality score. Self-descriptiveness and importance scores were highly cor-

related, with correlations for the 21 traits ranging from .78 to .93, all $p$s < .0001.

Three central and three peripheral traits were selected according to the following two rules. First, the central traits should have scores falling above the 90th percentile of the distribution, whereas peripheral trait scores should hover near the 50th percentile. Second, the traits should not be synonymous. The central traits selected were kind ($M$ = 9.78), friendly ($M$ = 9.76), and trustworthy ($M$ = 9.76). The peripheral traits selected were modest ($M$ = 6.23), predictable ($M$ = 6.32), and uncomplaining ($M$ = 6.64). The mean rating for the central traits ($M$ = 9.77) was significantly higher than the mean rating for the peripheral traits ($M$ = 6.40), $t(129)$ = 44.74, $p$ <.0001. In conclusion, the results of Pilot Study 2 validated the results of Pilot Study 1.

The traits just described were all positive (see Anderson, 1968). Next, the negative pole of each trait was derived. The negative poles (hereafter referred to as negative traits) were unkind, unfriendly, untrustworthy, immodest, unpredictable, and complaining. Thus, the final trait list contained 12 traits: 3 central positive (kind, friendly, and trustworthy), 3 central negative (unkind, unfriendly, and untrustworthy), 3 peripheral positive (modest, predictable, and uncomplaining), and 3 peripheral negative (immodest, unpredictable, and complaining).

## Pilot Study 3

The aim of Pilot Study 3 was to obtain high and low diagnosticity behaviors for each of the 12 selected traits. Eighty subjects participated. Forty were provided with the six positive traits and 40 were provided with the six negative traits. Half of the subjects in each condition generated three high diagnosticity behaviors for each trait; the remaining half generated three low diagnosticity behaviors for each trait. Diagnosticity was defined in terms of the probability of distinguishing between a trait and its polar opposite. Thus, a high diagnosticity behavior was defined as one that would be highly likely to reveal whether the person performing the behavior would possess a given trait or its polar opposite.

The experimenter and helpful colleagues edited the behaviors, generated a few new ones, and also used additional behaviors from Fuhrman,

Bodenhausen, and Lichtenstein's (1989) list. Twenty-four behaviors resulted for each trait. Twelve of the 24 behaviors were considered highly diagnostic of each trait, while the remaining 12 questions were considered low diagnostic of each trait.

## Pilot Study 4

The goal of Pilot Study 4 was to cross-validate the results of Pilot Study 3. A list containing the traits and questions was administered in booklet form to 120 subjects. Each page of the booklet contained a trait listed at the top with its dictionary definition following. Definitions were derived from *Webster's Ninth New Collegiate Dictionary* (1989). The questions followed on the same page. The traits and questions on each page were randomly ordered. Subjects were instructed to rate the diagnosticity of each question on a 9-point scale. Specifically, subjects rated how well the question would help them discriminate between the polar ends of the trait dimension under consideration. The scales ranged from *does not discriminate at all* (1) to *discriminates very well* (9). On the basis of subjects' ratings, three high diagnosticity and three low diagnosticity questions were selected for each trait.

## Experiment 1

This experiment represents the first attempt of the present investigation to examine the relative influence of self-assessment, self-enhancement, and self-verification on the self-evaluation process.

### Method

#### SUBJECTS

Subjects were 120 UW students. In this and all subsequent experiments, (a) subjects were introductory psychology students participating for extra course credit, (b) subjects were run in small groups of 2 to 9, and (c) dividers set in the experimental room prevented subjects from seeing one another when seated.

#### EXPERIMENTAL DESIGN

The experimental design involved a 2 (trait centrality: central traits vs. peripheral traits) × 2 (trait valence: positive traits vs. negative traits) × 3 (trait presentation order) between-subjects factorial. Thus, each subject self-reflected on three traits from one of the four following categories: central positive, central negative, peripheral positive, and peripheral negative. Subjects were randomly assigned to the experimental conditions.

#### PROCEDURE

Each subject received a booklet. Subjects were informed on the cover page that the experiment was concerned with self-understanding and that a good way for people to understand themselves is by asking questions to find out whether they have various (three in this instance) personality traits. The next three pages contained the three personality traits, one on each page. Each trait was listed at the top of the page, followed by its dictionary definition. Each trait was accompanied by a list of 12 questions. Half of the questions were hypothesis-true and half were hypothesis-false.[2] Furthermore, half of the questions were relatively high, and half relatively low, in diagnosticity. The 12 questions within each list were presented to subjects in a fixed random order. Subjects selected the 3 questions they would most likely ask themselves to find out whether they possessed the trait under consideration. After completing the question selection procedure for all traits, subjects answered the nine questions they had selected with a yes or a no.

### Results and Discussion

#### QUESTION DIAGNOSTICITY

A mean diagnosticity score was calculated for the nine questions chosen by each subject. The diagnosticity scores were entered in a 2 (trait centrality) × 2 (trait valence) × 3 (trait presentation order) analysis of variance (ANOVA).[3]

The trait centrality main effect was significant.

---

[2]The within-subjects variable class of question (hypothesis-true vs. alternative-true) was used in this investigation for counterbalancing purposes.

[3]In all six experiments, separate analyses were conducted for each of the three traits. The analyses yielded results consistent for all traits and identical to the ones reported, although weaker. Thus, the presented analyses collapse across the three traits.

Contrary to the self-assessment view, and in support of the self-verification view, subjects chose higher diagnosticity questions when self-reflecting on central traits ($M = 7.30$), rather than peripheral, traits (M = 6.53), $F(1, 108) = 40.79$, $p <.0001$. The trait valence main effect was not significant: Subjects did not reliably choose higher diagnosticity questions when self-reflecting on positive ($M = 6.94$), as opposed to negative ($M = 6.89$), traits, $F(1, 108) = 0.14$, $p < .71$. This finding fails to lend support to the self-enhancement view.

The Trait Centrality × Trait Valence interaction was significant, $F(1, 108) = 12.45$, $p < .001$ (Table 20.1). Subjects selected higher diagnosticity questions while self-reflecting on central positive, as opposed to central negative, traits, $t(58) = 3.88$, $p < .0001$. It appeared that subjects wished to discover that they possessed central positive traits to a greater extent than central negative traits. This pattern was not evident in the case of peripheral traits. In fact, a marginally significant reversal of the preceding pattern was obtained. Subjects manifested a tendency for selecting higher diagnosticity questions while self-reflecting on peripheral negative, as opposed to peripheral positive traits, $t(58) = -1.83$, $p < .07$. This interaction is consistent with the self-enhancement perspective. However, the interaction can be looked at somewhat differently: Subjects selected higher diagnosticity questions when self-reflecting on central positive, rather than peripheral positive, traits, $t(58) = 6.91$, $p < .0001$ and selected higher diagnosticity questions when self-reflecting on central negative, rather than peripheral negative, traits, $t(58) = 2.06$, $p < .04$. From this angle, the interaction is in line with the self-verification perspective.

## RESPONSE TYPE

The total number of confirmatory and disconfirmatory responses was computed for each subject. For presentational simplicity reasons, a new index was created by subtracting the disconfirmatory responses from the confirmatory responses. Thus, positive difference scores indicate confirmation or acceptance of possessing a trait, whereas negative difference scores indicate disconfirmation or denial of possessing a trait.

The difference scores were entered in a 2 (trait centrality) × 2 (trait valence) × 3 (trait presentation order) ANOVA. The trait centrality main effect was not significant: Subjects were equally likely to confirm central ($M = 0.22$) and peripheral ($M = -0.03$) traits, $F(1, 108) = 0.21$, $p < .65$. The self-verification perspective was not supported. In contrast, the trait valence main effect was significant, $F(1, 108) = 188.35$, $p < .0001$. Subjects confirmed possession of positive traits ($M = 3.84$) and disconfirmed possession of negative traits ($M = -3.65$), a pattern consistent with the self-enhancement view.

The trait valence main effect was qualified by a significant interaction between trait valence and trait centrality, $F(1, 108) = 124.47$, $p < .0001$ (Table 20.1). Subjects strongly confirmed the possession of central positive traits and disconfirmed the possession of central negative traits, $t(58) = 19.86$, $p < .0001$. At the same time, subjects were somewhat likely to confirm the possession of peripheral positive traits and disconfirm the possession of peripheral negative traits, $t(58) = 1.69$, $p < .09$. The interaction can be viewed in a different way: Subjects were more likely to confirm positive traits when these traits were central, rather than peripheral, $t(58) = 8.25$, $p < .0001$, and were more likely to disconfirm negative traits when these traits were central, rather than peripheral, $t(58) = -7.75$, $p < .0001$. The results of the interaction bolster the self-enhancement view and fail to support the self-verification view.

## Experiment 2

One could argue that the partial support for self-enhancement obtained in Experiment 1 may be a

**Table 20.1. Mean Diagnosticity Scores and Response Type (Confirmatory Minus Disconfirmatory Responses) as a Function of Trait Centrality and Trait Valence in Experiment 1**

| Dependent measure | Central traits | | Peripheral traits | |
| --- | --- | --- | --- | --- |
| | Positive | Negative | Positive | Negative |
| Diagnosticity scores | 7.53 | 7.06 | 6.34 | 6.72 |
| Response type | 7.00 | -6.57 | 0.67 | -0.73 |

methodological artifact. Subjects in Experiment 1 were asked to select only 3 of 12 questions: It is possible that subjects tended to self-enhance because the prospect for self-assessment or self-verification was unduly restrictive. An opportunity for thorough self-reflection might yield different results. If subjects had the opportunity to select a larger set of questions (i.e., more than 3), they could be more attuned to self-assessing or self-verifying concerns. The purpose of Experiment 2 was to address this possibility.

## Method

The experimental design and procedure were similar to those in Experiment 1, with one noteworthy exception: 120 subjects self-reflected on each trait by selecting six, rather than three, questions.

## Results and Discussion

### QUESTION DIAGNOSTICITY

The trait centrality main effect was significant. Subjects chose higher diagnosticity questions to self-reflect on central ($M = 7.02$), rather than peripheral ($M = 6.56$), traits, $F(1, 108) = 35.91, p < .0001$. This finding runs contrary to the self-assessment perspective and is in agreement with the self-verification perspective. The trait valence main effect was also significant. Subjects chose higher diagnosticity questions in self-reflecting on positive ($M = 6.89$), as opposed to negative ($M = 6.69$), traits, $F(1, 108) = 7.00, p < .009$. That is, subjects preferred high diagnosticity information when they wanted to examine possession of positive traits, but avoided high diagnosticity information when they were confronted with the possibility of learning about their negative traits. This finding is congruent with the self-enhancement perspective.

The main effects just described were qualified by a significant Trait Centrality × Trait Valence interaction, $F(1, 108) = 33.26, p < .0001$ (Table 20.2). Subjects selected higher diagnosticity questions to self-reflect on central positive, rather than central negative, traits, $t(58) = 6.75, p < .0001$, and also selected higher diagnosticity questions to self-reflect on peripheral negative, rather than peripheral positive, traits, $t(58) = -2.03, p < .05$. Viewing the interaction from a different angle, subjects chose higher diagnosticity questions when self-reflecting on central positive, rather than peripheral positive, traits, $t(58) = 9.08, p < .0001$, but chose equally diagnostic questions when self-reflecting on central negative and peripheral negative traits, $t(58) = 0.15, p < .88$. Regardless of the viewing angle, the interaction pattern is partially supportive of the self-enhancement view and certainly incompatible with the self-verification view.

### RESPONSE TYPE

The trait centrality main effect was significant: Subjects confirmed central traits ($M = 1.10$) and disconfirmed peripheral traits ($M = -1.40$), $F(1, 108) = 7.76, p < .006$, a finding that supports the self-verification view. The trait valence main effect also reached significance: Subjects confirmed possession of positive traits ($M = 8.17$) and disconfirmed possession of negative traits ($M = -8.47$), $F(1, 108) = 343.45, p < .0001$. This finding is in agreement with the self-enhancement view.

The two main effects just described were qualified by a significant interaction between trait valence and trait centrality, $F(1, 108) = 104.31, p < .0001$ (Table 20.2). Subjects confirmed possession of central positive and disconfirmed possession of central negative traits, $t(58) = 23.84, p < .0001$. Subjects also confirmed possession of peripheral positive and disconfirmed possession of peripheral negative traits, $t(58) = 5.36, p < .0001$. Viewed somewhat differently, subjects confirmed possession of positive traits when these traits were central, rather than peripheral, $t(58) = 9.53, p < .0001$,

Table 20.2. Mean Diagnosticity Scores and Response Type (Confirmatory Minus Disconfirmatory Responses) as a Function of Trait Centrality and Trait Valence in Experiment 2

| Dependent measure | Central traits | | Peripheral traits | |
|---|---|---|---|---|
| | Positive | Negative | Positive | Negative |
| Diagnosticity scores | 7.34 | 6.70 | 6.44 | 6.68 |
| Response type | 14.00 | −11.80 | 2.33 | −5.13 |

and disconfirmed possession of negative traits when these traits were central rather than peripheral, $t(58) = -5.26$, $p < .0001$. The results obtained support the self-enhancement, but not the self-verification view.

## Experiment 3

The preceding experiments suggested that, in the context of the self-reflection task, the self-evaluation process is guided predominantly by self-enhancing concerns. One potential limitation of these experiments, however, might be that they used an arguably impoverished simulation of the self-reflection process. The objective of Experiment 3 was to examine the self-reflection process in a situation of presumably higher ecological validity. Subjects were allowed to generate their own questions, as they would in a self-reflection period initiated on their own.

### Method

#### SUBJECTS, EXPERIMENTAL DESIGN, AND PROCEDURE

The design was identical to that of Experiment 1. The procedure was also identical to that of Experiment 1, with one notable alteration: Instead of selecting questions from an experimenter-provided list, 120 subjects generated their own questions. Thus, subjects generated three questions to self-reflect on each of three traits.

#### CODING

Two judges, who were unaware of the purpose and design of the experiment, independently rated the questions that subjects had generated for degree of diagnosticity. Judges were told to decide how well each question discriminated between the relevant trait and its alternative: "Knowing the answer to a given question (affirmative or negative), how well would you be able to tell whether the person having the trait under consideration is kind versus unkind (or friendly vs. unfriendly, trustworthy vs. untrustworthy, modest vs. immodest, predictable vs. unpredictable, and uncomplaining vs. complaining)?" Judges rated each question on a 9-point scale ranging from *not at all diagnostic* (1) *to extremely diagnostic* (9). Intercorrelations

of judges' ratings for the nine questions ranged from .54 to .85, all $p$s < .0001. The mean judge diagnosticity rating was used in the analyses to follow. (Additional separate analyses for each ratings produced similar results).

The judges also coded subjects' responses to each question as either confirmatory or disconfirmatory. Interjudge agreement was considerably high ($k = .94$). Judges resolved their few disagreements through discussion. (Again, additional separate analyses for each judge yielded identical results.)

### Results and Discussion

#### QUESTION DIAGNOSTICITY

A significant trait centrality main effect revealed that subjects generated higher diagnosticity questions to self-reflect on central ($M = 7.30$), as opposed to peripheral ($M = 6.76$), traits, $F(1, 108) = 22.64$, $p < .0001$. This result supports the self-verification view and runs contrary to the self-assessment view. The trait valence main effect was significant and consistent with the self-enhancement perspective: Subjects generated higher diagnosticity questions when self-reflecting on positive ($M = 7.27$), as opposed to negative ($M = 6.79$), traits, $F(1, 108) = 18.08$, $p < .0001$.

These main effects were qualified by a significant interaction, $F(1, 108) = 37.22$, $p < .0001$ (Table 20.3). As far as the central traits were concerned, subjects generated higher diagnosticity questions to self-reflect on positive, as opposed to negative, ones, $t(58) = 10.63$, $p < .0001$; however, with regard to peripheral traits, subjects generated equally diagnostic questions to self-reflect on both positive and negative ones, $t(58) = -1.07$, $p < .29$. Alternatively, subjects generated higher diagnosticity questions when self-reflecting on central positive, as opposed to peripheral positive, traits, $t(58) = 7.70$, $p < .0001$, but generated equally diagnostic questions when self-reflecting on central negative and peripheral negative traits, $t(58) = -0.96$, $p < .34$. The interaction pattern is consistent with the self-enhancement view, but fails to support the self-verification view.

#### RESPONSE TYPE

The trait centrality main effect was not significant: Subjects were not more likely to confirm central

**Table 20.3. Mean Diagnosticity Scores and Response Type (Confirmatory Minus Disconfirmatory Responses) as a Function of Trait Centrality and Trait Valence in Experiment 3**

| Dependent measure | Central traits | | Peripheral traits | |
|---|---|---|---|---|
| | Positive | Negative | Positive | Negative |
| Diagnosticity scores | 7.88 | 6.71 | 6.65 | 6.87 |
| Response type | 6.23 | −6.20 | 0.60 | −1.07 |

($M = 0.02$), as opposed to peripheral ($M = -0.24$), traits, $F(1, 108) = .22, p < .64$, thus failing to support the self-verification perspective. The trait valence main effect was significant: Subjects confirmed possession of positive traits ($M = 3.42$) and disconfirmed possession of negative traits ($M = -3.64$), $F(1, 108) = 146.49, p < .0001$. This finding is congruent with the self-enhancement perspective.

Paralleling the earlier findings, the trait valence main effect was qualified by a significant interaction, $F(1, 108) = 84.09, p < .0001$ (Table 20.3). Subjects confirmed the possession of central positive, and disconfirmed the possession of central negative traits, $t(58) = 16.77, p < .0001$. Subjects also manifested a tendency toward confirming the possession of peripheral positive, and disconfirming the possession of peripheral negative traits, $t(58) = 1.74, p < .09$. Viewed somewhat differently, subjects were more likely to confirm positive traits when these were central rather than peripheral, $t(58) = 6.35, p < .0001$, and more likely to disconfirm negative traits when these were central, rather than peripheral, $t(58) = -6.22, p < .0001$. These results lend support to the self-enhancement, but not the self-verification view.

## Experiment 4

Arguably, the procedures of the preceding three experiments did not pay full justice to the self-verification perspective. An adequate testing of this perspective would require that subjects' preexisting self-conceptions (both positive and negative) be at stake during the self-evaluation process. Experiments 1–3 assumed that subjects' collective central traits satisfied this requirement. However, a more rigorous test would demand that subjects self-evaluate in reference to idiographically defined preexisting (i.e., central) self-conceptions.

Experiment 4 was designed to provide such a test.

Experiment 4 fulfilled another objective: It tested the assumption made in the previous three experiments that central traits are held with higher certainty than peripheral traits. This assumption was the basis for pitting the self-verification perspective against the self-assessment perspective. Thus, submitting this assumption to empirical scrutiny would also afford a more valid examination of the self-verification and self-assessment perspectives.

The third purpose of Experiment 4 was to eliminate a rival hypothesis. Specifically, it is possible that the findings of the previous experiments were due partially to the three subject-generated central positive traits (i.e., kind, friendly, and trustworthy) being more positive than the three subject-generated peripheral positive traits (i.e., modest, predictable, and uncomplaining). Stated otherwise, trait centrality may have been confounded with trait valence. To examine this possibility, an additional pilot study was conducted (Pilot Study 5). Eighty undergraduates rated all six traits on a scale ranging from *least positive, desirable, or favorable* (0) to *most positive, desirable, or favorable* (6). Presentation of the traits was randomized for each subject. Central positive traits ($M = 5.60$) were rated as more desirable than peripheral positive traits ($M = 3.96$), $t(79) = 20.65, p < .0001$. [Analogously, the experimenter-generated central negative traits ($M = 0.60$) were rated as more undesirable than the experimenter-generated peripheral negative traits ($M = 3.24$), $t(79) = -26.07, p < .0001$.] The results of Pilot Study 5 leave open the likelihood of confounding between trait centrality and trait valence. This likelihood can be reduced by using idiographic traits.

Finally, Experiment 4 was designed to control for an additional possible weakness of Experiments

1–3, namely the artificiality with which negative traits were created. It was assumed that the experimenter-derived negative traits (i.e., unkind, unfriendly, untrustworthy, immodest, unpredictable, and complaining) were as central or peripheral to the subjects' collective self as were the subject-generated positive traits (i.e., kind, friendly, trustworthy, modest, predictable, and complaining). Obviously, this assumption needs validation.

## Method

### SUBJECTS, EXPERIMENTAL DESIGN, AND PROCEDURE

Three hundred fourteen UW undergraduates, run in large groups, filled out a brief questionnaire during the second week of an academic semester (first session). The questionnaire asked subjects to list (a) four traits that they thought were as positive as possible, described them very well, and were as important to them as possible (i.e., central positive traits); (b) four traits that they thought were as negative as possible, described them very well, and were as important to them as possible (i.e., central negative traits); (c) four traits that they thought were as positive as possible, did not describe them well, and were not important to them (i.e., peripheral positive traits); and (d) four traits that they thought were as negative as possible, did not describe them well, and were not important to them (i.e., peripheral negative traits). Subjects were instructed to make every attempt to list four traits in each of the categories. Next, subjects rated each trait they had listed on a 9-point scale, ranging from *extremely uncertain about having this trait* (1) to *extremely certain about having this trait* (11), assessing the certainty with which the trait was held. Finally, subjects recorded their names and phone numbers.

Three experimental assistants telephoned 149 subjects between the 7th and 14th week of the same academic semester. The assistants telephoned only subjects who had complied with the request to list four traits in each category (257 subjects, or 82%, did so). The assistants scheduled an individual appointment with subjects for a "study on self-perception" (second session). Six subjects refused to participate and 23 did not report to the laboratory at the scheduled time. The remaining 120 subjects were used in the experiment.

Each of the 120 subjects was randomly assigned to one of the conditions of the 2 (trait centrality) × 2 (trait valence) between-subjects design of the experiment. Assignment to a given condition carried the implication that the subject would be asked to self-reflect exclusively on traits pertaining to this condition. That is, subjects self-reflected on only 3 of the 16 traits that they had listed in the first experimental session. This procedure was followed in an effort to conceal the relation between the first and second experimental sessions. Alternatively, this procedure was intended to create a state of "unknowingness" regarding the self-reflection task.

To summarize, subjects generated three questions for each of three traits from among the 16 they had listed in the first session. In addition, subjects generated three questions for each of three traits that they had not listed in the first session. Data pertaining to these additional questions were not used in analyses. This extra precaution was taken in an attempt to further disguise the relation between the two experimental sessions.

The order of the six traits was randomly determined for each subject. Before being dismissed, subjects were asked to guess the purpose of the experiment. They also were specifically probed regarding whether they thought that "any prior experience with studies in the Psychology Department this semester affected their responses in the present study." No subject guessed the purpose of the experiment or the relation between the two experimental sessions.

### CODING

As in Experiment 3, two judges rated each question for degree of diagnosticity on a 9-point scale ranging from *not at all diagnostic* (1) to *extremely diagnostic* (9). Intercorrelations of judges' ratings for the nine questions ranged from .72 to .87, all $ps < .0001$. The mean judge diagnosticity rating was used in the analyses to follow. (Separate analyses for the ratings of individual judges yielded identical results.)

The judges also coded subjects' responses to each question as either confirmatory or disconfirmatory. Interjudge agreement was high ($k = .89$). Judges resolved their disagreements through deliberation. (Again, separate analyses for individual judges produced identical results.)

## Results and Discussion

### QUESTION DIAGNOSTICITY

Pitting the self-verification against the self-assessment perspective required validation of the assumption that trait centrality implies trait certainty. The results indeed validated this assumption: Central traits ($M = 6.96$) were held with higher certainty than peripheral traits ($M = 6.05$), $F(1, 119) = 44.10, p < .0001$.

The trait centrality main effect was significant. Subjects generated higher diagnosticity questions while self-reflecting on central ($M = 7.13$), as opposed to peripheral ($M = 6.55$), traits, $F(1, 116) = 55.80, p < .0001$. This result is consistent with the self-verification perspective and inconsistent with the self-assessment perspective. The trait valence main effect also reached significance in support of the self-enhancement perspective: Subjects generated higher diagnosticity questions while self-reflecting on positive ($M = 7.05$), as opposed to negative (M = 6.63), traits, $F(1, 116) = 28.91, p < .0001$.

The two main effects just described were qualified by a significant interaction, $F(1, 116) = 68.14, p < .0001$ (Table 20.4). Subjects generated higher diagnosticity questions to self-reflect on central positive relative to central negative traits, $t(58) = 10.35, p < .0001$, but tended to generate higher diagnosticity questions to self-reflect on peripheral negative relative to peripheral positive traits, $t(58) = -1.91, p < .06$. Stated otherwise, subjects generated higher diagnosticity questions when self-reflecting on central positive, as opposed to peripheral positive, traits, $t(58) = 12.12, p < .0001$, but generated equally diagnostic questions when self-reflecting on central negative and peripheral negative traits, $t(58) = -0.52, p < .34$. This interaction is generally supportive of the self-enhancement perspective and nonsupportive of the self-verification perspective.

### RESPONSE TYPE

The trait centrality main effect was significant: Subjects combined their central traits ($M = 5.40$) to a higher extent than their peripheral traits ($M = 0.07$), $F(1, 16) = 83.34, p < .0001$, thus supporting the self-verification perspective. The trait valence main effect was also significant: Subjects confirmed possession of positive traits ($M = 4.14$) and disconfirmed possession of negative traits ($M = -1.34$), $F(1, 1116) = 22.97, p < .0001$. This result is compatible with the self-enhancement perspective.

Interaction is most crucial for the issue of relative support for the self-enhancement versus self-verification views. The interaction was significant, $F(1, 116) = 4.22, p < .042$ (Table 20.4). Subjects confirmed the possession of central positive traits to a greater extent than the possession of central negative traits, $t(58) = 6.30, p < .0001$, a finding that supports the self-enhancement view at the expense of the self-verification view. Furthermore, subjects were somewhat more likely to confirm possession of peripheral positive than peripheral negative traits, $t(58) = 1.63, p < .10$. The interaction can be stated in an alternative manner. Subjects were more likely to confirm possession of central positive than peripheral positive traits, $t(58) = 11.00, p < .0001$, a result predicted by the self-enhancement view, but also were more likely to confirm possession of central negative than peripheral negative traits, $t(58) = 4.11, p < .0001$. This latter finding (i.e., confirmation of central negative traits to a larger degree than peripheral negative traits) is discrepant from the findings of the previous three experiments and is predicted by the

**Table 20.4. Mean Diagnosticity Scores and Response Type (Confirmatory Minus Disconfirmatory Responses) as a Function of Trait Centrality and Trait Valence in Experiment 4**

| Dependent measure | Central traits | | Peripheral traits | |
|---|---|---|---|---|
| | Positive | Negative | Positive | Negative |
| Diagnosticity scores | 7.66 | 6.60 | 6.44 | 6.60 |
| Response type | 7.40 | 4.73 | 2.00 | −1.27 |

self-verification, but not the self-enhancement, perspective.

## Experiment 5

It is possible that Experiments 1–4 were biased against the self-assessment perspective. Specifically, instructions in these experiments did not provide subjects with any clues on how to engage in self-reflection. Subjects were informed that the experiments were studies of self-understanding and that one way to gain self-understanding is through self-questioning. However, subjects were not supplied with any pertinent criteria that could guide them in the question selection or question generation process.

The design of Experiment 5 was identical to that of Experiment 1, with one important exception. Experiment 5 included a condition in which subjects were instructed to conduct the self-reflection process as a scientist would. Subjects were encouraged to be as objective and accurate as possible in selecting questions and were explicitly told that they should ask themselves questions that would be most informative in detecting the trait under examination (for a similar manipulation, see Zukier & Pepitone, 1984). Thus, the major purpose of Experiment 5 was to explore whether an emphasis on objectivity, accuracy and question informativeness would amplify the influence of self-assessment concerns on the self-reflection process.

### Method

Two hundred forty subjects participated in this experiment. The design was identical to that of Experiment 1, with the addition of a mode of thinking (nonscientific vs. scientific) variable. After

selecting and answering three questions per trait under either a nonscientific or scientific mode of thinking, subjects completed a manipulation check. The manipulation check consisted of the following question: "In selecting the questions, how hard did you try to be objective, accurate, and scientifically minded?" Subjects responded on a single-item scale ranging from *not at all hard* (1) to *extremely hard* (9).

### Results and Discussion

#### MANIPULATION CHECK

Manipulating the mode of thinking was effective: Subjects in a scientific mode reported striving harder toward accuracy ($M = 7.01$) than subjects in a nonscientific mode ($M = 6.35$), $F(1, 216) = 22.41$, $p < .0001$. Two matters require additional consideration. First, the manipulation, although effective, was not as powerful as expected. Second, the absolute means indicate that subjects generally tended toward the belief that they were being accurate.

#### QUESTION DIAGNOSTICITY

Replicating previous findings, subjects selected higher diagnosticity questions while self-reflecting on central ($M = 6.98$), as opposed to peripheral ($M = 6.41$), traits, $F(1, 216) = 34.11$, $p < .0001$, a finding that fails to support the self-assessment view but is in line with the self-verification view. Furthermore, subjects chose higher diagnosticity questions when self-reflecting on positive ($M = 6.92$), as opposed to negative ($M = 6.45$), traits, $F(1, 216) = 21.37$, $p < .0001$, a finding that is consistent with the self-enhancement view. More pertinent to the objectives of this experiment, the mode of thinking main effect was not significant,

Table 20.5. Mean Diagnosticity Scores and Response Type (Confirmatory Minus Disconfirmatory Responses) as a Function of Trait Centrality and Trait Valence in Experiment 5

| Dependent measure | Central traits | | Peripheral traits | |
|---|---|---|---|---|
| | Positive | Negative | Positive | Negative |
| Diagnosticity scores | 7.49 | 6.47 | 6.35 | 6.46 |
| Response type | 6.87 | −5.97 | 0.33 | −0.57 |

$F(1, 216) = 0.05, p < .82$. Subjects tended to select equally diagnostic questions, regardless of being in a scientific or nonscientific mode.

The Trait Centrality × Trait Valence interaction was significant, $F(1, 216) = 33.55, p < .0001$ (Table 20.5). Subjects selected higher diagnosticity questions when self-reflecting on central positive, rather than central negative, traits, $t(118) = 7.55, p < .0001$, but selected equal diagnosticity questions when self-reflecting on peripheral positive and peripheral negative traits, $t(118) = -0.83, p < .41$. The interaction can be inspected in an alternative way. Subjects were more likely to choose higher diagnosticity questions when self-reflecting on central positive, as opposed to peripheral positive, traits, $t(118) = 10.30, p < .0001$, but likely to choose equal diagnosticity questions when self-reflecting on central negative and peripheral negative traits, $t(118) = 0.30, p < .98$. These patterns are generally consistent with the self-enhancement, but not the self-verification, view.

Most importantly, none of the interactions involving mode of thinking was significant: Mode of Thinking × Trait Centrality, $F(1, 216) = 0.06, p < .82$; Mode of Thinking × Trait Valence, $F(1, 216) = 1.33, p < .25$; and Mode of Thinking × Trait Centrality × Trait Valence, $F(1, 216) = 0.67, p < .42$. Instructions to subjects to be objective and accurate did not alter the strength of the influence of self-enhancement concerns on self-reflection.

RESPONSE TYPE

The trait centrality main effect was marginally significant: Subjects evidenced a tendency to confirm central traits ($M = 0.45$) and disconfirm peripheral traits ($M = -0.12$), $F(1, 216) = 3.08, p < .08$, thus providing weak support for the self-verification perspective. Paralleling previous findings, subjects confirmed possession of positive traits ($M = 3.60$) and disconfirmed possession of negative traits ($M = -3.27$), $F(1, 216) = 452.25, p < .0001$, thus lending support to the self-enhancement view. Furthermore, subjects were equally likely to confirm or disconfirm the traits, regardless of mode of thinking, main effect $F(1, 216) = 2.73, p < .11$.

The Trait Valence × Trait Centrality interaction reached significance, $F(1, 216) = 341.47, p < .0001$ (Table 20.5). Subjects confirmed the possession of central positive traits and disconfirmed the possession of central negative traits, $t(118) = 33.14, p < .0001$. Subjects also manifested a tendency toward confirming the possession of peripheral positive traits and disconfirming the possession of peripheral negative traits, $t(118) = 1.73, p < .08$. The interaction pattern can be viewed differently: Subjects were more likely to confirm positive traits when they were central, rather than peripheral, $t(118) = 16.49, p < .0001$, and more likely to disconfirm negative traits when they were central, rather than peripheral, $t(118) = -10.57, p < .001$. These results are in agreement with the self-enhancement, but not the self-verification, view.

Most importantly, mode of thinking did not interact with trait centrality or trait valence: Mode of Thinking × Trait Centrality, $F(1, 216) = 0.52, p < .47$; Mode of Thinking x Trait Valence, $F(1, 216) = 1.54, p < .22$; and Mode of Thinking × Trait Centrality × Trait Valence, $F(1, 216) = 0.27, p < .61$. Again, it appears that instructions attempting to sensitize subjects to accuracy concerns did not reduce people's inclination to self-enhance while self-reflecting.

## Experiment 6

Arguing in favor of the operation of self-enhancement concerns during self-reflection requires additional validation. Specifically, for this argument to be plausible, one should demonstrate that self-enhancement concerns are operative when thinking about the self, but inoperative when thinking about a nonsignificant other. The purpose of Experiment 6 was to provide such validational data.

### Method

Two hundred forty subjects participated in this experiment. The experimental design was the same as in previous experiments, with the addition of the referent (self vs. other) variable. Specifically, half of the subjects reflected on traits pertinent to the self, whereas the remaining half reflected on traits pertinent to an acquaintance of theirs, a "person they had met only once or twice."

### Results and Discussion

QUESTION DIAGNOSTICITY

Significant trait centrality and trait valence main effects replicated previous results. Subjects selected higher diagnosticity questions when self-reflecting on central ($M$ = 7.15), as opposed to peripheral ($M$ = 6.77), traits, $F(1, 216)$ = 35.56, $p$ < .0001 (support for self-verification), and selected higher diagnosticity questions when self-reflecting on positive ($M$ = 7.04), rather than negative ($M$ = 6.88), traits, $F(1, 216)$ = 6.81, $p$ < .0001 (support for self-enhancement). However, the referent main effect did not approach significance, $F(1, 216)$ = 1.75, $p$ <. 19.

The Trait Centrality × Trait Valence interaction reached significance, $F(1, 216)$ = 12.63, $p$ < .0001 (Table 20.6). Subjects selected higher diagnosticity questions when self-reflecting on central positive as opposed to central negative traits, $t(118)$ = 4.12, $p$ <.0001, but selected equal diagnosticity questions when self-reflecting on peripheral positive and peripheral negative traits, $t(118)$ = –0.58, $p$ < .56. Viewed somewhat differently, subjects were more likely to choose higher diagnosticity questions when self-reflecting on central positive, as opposed to peripheral positive traits, $t(118)$ = 5.74, $p$ < .0001, but likely to choose equal diagnosticity questions when self-reflecting on central negative and peripheral negative traits, $t(118)$ = 1.59, $p$ < .12. The pattern of means generally is in line with the self-enhancement, but not the self-verification perspective.

The interaction just described was qualified by a reliable triple interaction among trait centrality, trait valence, and referent, $F(1, 216)$ = 15.48, $p$ < .0001. Simple Trait Centrality × Trait Valence ANOVAs conducted within each referent condition disclosed a significant interaction when the referent was the self, $F(1, 108)$ = 23.05, $p$ < .0001, but not when the referent was the other, $F(1, 108)$ = 0.09, $p$ < .76 (Figure 20.1). These findings demonstrated that self-enhancement concerns were present when subjects reflected on themselves, but absent when subjects reflected on an acquaintance.

## RESPONSE TYPE

The trait centrality main effect was not significant: Subjects were equally likely to confirm their central ($M$ = 0.44) and peripheral ($M$ = 0.50) traits, $F(1, 216)$ = 0.03, $p$ < .87, thus failing to support the self-verification view. A significant trait valence main effect, $F(1, 216)$ = 116.94, $p$ < .0001, which revealed that subjects confirmed possession of positive traits ($M$ = 2.67) and disconfirmed possession of negative traits ($M$ = –1.74), thus advocating self-enhancement. More pertinent to the objectives of this experiment, the referent main effect was not significant, $F(1, 216)$ = 0.24, $p$ < .63.

The Trait Valence × Trait Centrality interaction was significant, $F(1, 216)$ = 64.46, $p$ < .0001 (Table 20.6). Subjects confirmed the possession of central positive traits and disconfirmed the possession of central negative traits, $t(118)$ = 9.57, $p$ < .0001. Subjects also manifested an inclination toward confirming the possession of peripheral positive traits and disconfirming the possession of peripheral negative traits, $t(118)$ = 1.86, $p$ < .07. Alternatively, subjects were more likely to confirm positive traits when they were central, as opposed to peripheral, $t(118)$ = 4.49, $p$ < .0001, and were more likely to disconfirm negative traits when they were central, as opposed to peripheral, $t(118)$ = –4.69, $p$ < .0001. The interaction pattern is in line with the self-enhancement, but not the self-verification, view.

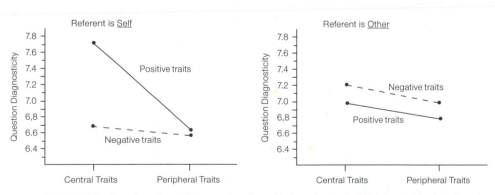

FIGURE 20.1 Question dianosticity as a function of trait centrality, trait valence, and referent.

**Table 20.6. Mean Diagnosticity Scores and Response Type (Confirmatory Minus Disconfirmatory Responses) as a Function of Trait Centrality and Trait Valence in Experiment 6**

| Dependent measure | Central traits | | Peripheral traits | |
| --- | --- | --- | --- | --- |
| | Positive | Negative | Positive | Negative |
| Diagnosticity scores | 7.34 | 6.95 | 6.73 | 6.80 |
| Response type | 4.27 | −3.40 | 1.07 | −0.07 |

Most importantly, the three-way interaction among trait centrality, trait valence, and referent was significant, $F(1, 216) = 59.30$, $p < .0001$. Simple Trait Centrality × Trait Valence ANOVAs conducted within each referent condition revealed a significant interaction when the referent was the self, $F(1, 108) = 175.54$, $p < .0001$, but not when the referent was the other, $F(1, 108) = 0.04$, $p < .84$ (Figure 20.2). Again, it appeared that the motive to self-enhance was evoked when subjects reflected on the self, but not when they reflected on an acquaintance.

## General Discussion

This investigation used a new paradigm, the self-reflection task, in an effort to understand the motivational antecedents of the self-evaluation process. Six experiments tested a total of 960 subjects to comparatively gauge the strength of the self-assessment, self-enhancement, and self-verification motives in regulating the self-evaluation process. The obtained results and their contribution to existing literature are highlighted next.

Relative Strength of the Self-Assessment and Self-Enhancement Motives

Past literature favored the thesis of the self-assessment perspective, that the self-evaluation process aims at uncertainty reduction. People seek diagnostic information primarily in reference to relatively little-known characteristics (Sorrentino & Hewitt, 1984; Trope, 1979). The evidence favorable to the self-assessment perspective was gathered in independent tests. However, no evidence was obtained in the comparative tests used in the present investigation. To begin with, these tests (five experiments) demonstrated that people prefer higher diagnosticity information when evaluating themselves on positive, as opposed to negative, traits, a finding congruent with the self-enhancement view (see also Alicke, 1985; Bradley, 1978; Greenwald, 1980).

Past literature is mixed on whether people are equally likely to prefer tasks of high success and high failure diagnosticity (self-assessment view) or whether people find high success diagnosticity tasks more attractive than high failure diagnosticity tasks (self-enhancement view). Trope (1980)

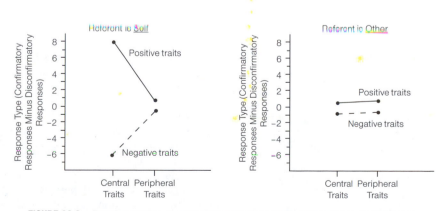

**FIGURE 20.2** Response type as a function of trait centrality, trait valence, and referent.

showed that task attractiveness increases both with diagnosticity of success and failure, a finding congruent with the self-assessment perspective. Similarly, Strube, Lott, Le-Xuan-Hy, Oxenberg, and Deichmann (1986, Experiment 1) found that task choice was a function of both success and failure diagnosticity. However, Strube et al. (1986, Experiment 1) reported an increase in task preference as a function of both success and failure diagnosticity, but did not fully replicate this finding in Experiment 2: Only a marginally significant preference was found for high, compared with low, failure diagnosticity tasks. It should be noted, nonetheless, that Strube et al. (1986, Experiments 1 and 2) obtained an interaction between diagnosticity of success and of failure, such that the most desired task was high in both forms of diagnosticity. In another investigation, Strube and Roemmele (1985) reported that subjects preferred high over low diagnosticity of success tasks, but manifested no preference for higher over lower diagnosticity of failure tasks, a finding favoring the self-enhancement perspective (the Diagnosticity of Success × Diagnosticity of Failure interaction was also present in this case). Finally, Brown (1990, Experiment 2) found that subjects were eager to seek more knowledge about their abilities after success, as test validity (a variable conceptually similar to test diagnosticity) increased, but were not concerned with additional opportunities for ability evaluation following failure, especially in the case of high test validity. These findings are compatible with the self-enhancement perspective.

The present results provided unequivocal support for the self-enhancement view. In all six experiments, subjects preferred higher diagnosticity questions when evaluating themselves on central positive, as opposed to either central negative or peripheral negative, traits.

In conclusion, the self-enhancement motive was found to be more influential than the self-assessment motive in guiding the self-evaluation process. Note that the self-enhancement motive predominated even when subjects were explicitly instructed to be self-assessing (Experiment 5).

## Relative Strength of the Self-Enhancement and Self-Verification Motives

The present investigation afforded comparative testing of several aspects of the self-enhancement and self-verification views. A recapitulation of the main predictions and findings follows.

The self-enhancement view predicts that people will prefer more accurate (i.e., higher diagnosticity) information about their central positive than central negative traits, whereas the self-verification perspective predicts that people will prefer equally accurate information about their central positive and central negative traits. All six experiments favored the self-enhancement view, including Experiment 4, which examined idiographically subjects' preexisting central positive and central negative traits.

Furthermore, the self-enhancement view predicts that people will confirm their central positive traits and disconfirm their central negative traits, whereas the self-verification view predicts that people will be equally likely to confirm their central positive and central negative traits. The results of all six experiments favored the self-enhancement view, including Experiment 4.

The self-enhancement perspective also predicts that people will prefer less accurate (i.e., lower diagnosticity) information about their central negative relative to their peripheral negative traits, whereas the self-verification perspective predicts that people will prefer more accurate information about their central negative relative to their peripheral negative traits. The self-enhancement perspective was not supported in any of the experiments: People generally preferred equal diagnosticity information pertaining to both their central negative and peripheral negative traits. The self-verification perspective was not supported in five of six experiments. The sixth experiment (Experiment 1) yielded results consistent with this perspective, but these should be considered spurious due to lack of replicability.

Furthermore, the self-enhancement view predicts that people will disconfirm their central negative traits to a greater extent than their peripheral negative traits. In contrast, the self-verification view predicts that people will confirm their central negative traits to a greater extent than their peripheral negative traits. Five experiments (i.e., the ones that used subjects' collectively preexisting self-conceptions) supported the self-enhancement view. However, Experiment 4, which used subjects' idiographically preexisting self-conceptions furnished support for the self-verification view. Thus, it is likely that the relative lack of strong support for the self-verification perspective in this instance is due to the particular methodological procedures used.

In conclusion, the general trend of the comparative tests was to support the notion that the self-enhancement motive is more influential than the self-verification in steering the self-evaluation process. Additional findings of the investigation (i.e., subjects selecting higher diagnosticity questions to self-reflect on positive, as opposed to negative, traits and subjects tending to confirm their peripheral positive traits to a greater degree than their peripheral negative traits) were consistent with this notion.

However, an important qualification is necessary. Arguably, a most stringent test of the self-enhancement versus self-verification perspectives would require that two additional conditions are met. First, subjects' central negative traits should be as important to them as their central positive traits. Second, subjects should be as certain of their central negative traits as they are of their central positive traits. None of the present experiments collected data directly relevant to the first condition; Experiment 4 assumed importance equivalence, but did not test this assumption. Furthermore, only Experiment 4 gathered data pertaining to the second condition, which was not met: Subjects were less certain of their central negative traits ($M = 6.70$) than their central positive traits ($M = 7.22$), $F(1, 119) = 9.17$, $p < .003$.

These qualifications, however, are tempered by rather formidable methodological difficulties. Is it possible to find people who have central negative self-conceptions that are equally important to them as are their central positive self-conceptions? Is it possible to find people who hold central negative self-conceptions with equal certainty as central positive self-conceptions? Stated otherwise, is it possible to equalize within individuals for importance and certainty of central negative versus central positive self-conceptions, controlling at the same time for valence? The present investigation (especially Experiment 4) represented a first attempt to address these issues, an attempt that ought to be followed up by future comparative tests.

## Relative Strength of the Self-Assessment and Self-Verification Motives

The self-assessment perspective predicts that people will prefer knowledge about their poorly known, rather than well-known, attributes, whereas the self-verification perspective predicts the opposite. The present comparative tests (all six experiments) demonstrated that people prefer higher diagnosticity information when evaluating themselves on well-known or certain characteristics (i.e., central traits) relative to little-known or uncertain characteristics (i.e., peripheral traits), a finding that bolsters the self-verification view at the expense of the self-assessment view (see also Maracek & Mettee, 1972; Swann & Ely, 1984).

## A Final Note on Relative Strength

The present results provided converging evidence in support of the self-enhancement perspective. The self-reflection process appears to be regulated predominantly by self-enhancement concerns. People are likely to form inferences favorable to the self, even when pondering the self in the absence of external feedback.

These findings represent an addition to the recent wave of empirical evidence for, and theoretical emphasis on, the role of self-enhancement on self-perception. Self-enhancement biases have been shown to affect speed of processing of self-relevant information (among others) (Kuiper, Olinger, MacDonald, & Shaw, 1985; Kunda, 1987), memory for self-relevant information (Crary, 1966; Silverman, 1964), judgments regarding the self (Alicke, 1985; Brown, 1986; Weinstein, 1980), causal attributions implicating the self (Green & Gross, 1979; Taylor & Koivumaki, 1976), social comparison processes (Brickman & Bulman, 1977; Tesser, 1988; Wills, 1981), and strategic self-presentation (Baumeister & Jones, 1978; Cialdini & Richardson, 1980; Godfrey, Jones, & Lord, 1986; Schlenker, 1975; for thorough discussions of mechanisms responsible for maintenance of self-enhancement biases, see Brown, 1991, and Taylor & Brown, 1988).

## Implications and Limitations

Implications and potential limitations of the present investigation are considered next.

### IMPLICATION: THE QUESTION OF AWARENESS

Are people aware of their self-enhancing shading of the self-evaluation process? The manipulation check data of Experiment 5 suggest that they are not. People subjectively believe that they are being accurate when, objectively, they are self-enhancing. This implies that enhancing self-evaluative thinking may be quite difficult to eradicate. At the very least, simple instructions attempting to increase people's awareness of their self-enhancing appear to be ineffective. This may be due to people either lacking access to their own cognitive processes (Nisbett & Wilson, 1977) or, being unable to modify their chronic and habitual self-enhancing thinking (Bargh, 1982; Lewicki, 1985; Paulhus & Levitt, 1987), which attests to the strength and pervasiveness of the self-enhancing motive.

The preceding discussion does not necessarily assume that it is desirable to eradicate self-enhancing tendencies. In fact, such tendencies are arguably functional for people and contribute to their mental health (Brown, 1991; Taylor & Brown, 1988).

## POTENTIAL LIMITATIONS

Two potential limitations of the present investigation are considered: whether the diagnosticity questions were equivalent across experimental conditions and whether there is a need for an exclusive focus on people with chronically low self-esteem or negative self-concept.

### WERE THE DIAGNOSTICITY QUESTIONS EQUIVALENT ACROSS EXPERIMENTAL CONDITIONS?

One potential limitation concerns a methodological procedure: more specifically, the problem of equivalence of the diagnosticity questions. Were the questions pertaining to central traits equivalent, in terms of their preratings, to the questions pertaining to peripheral traits? Also were the questions referring to positive traits equivalent to those referring to negative traits?

It is unlikely that the equivalence problem affected the results of the present investigation for at least two reasons. First, prerating differences in questions were very small. Second, and most important, two of the six experiments (i.e., Experiments 3 and 4) did not use the prerated questions, but used questions that subjects generated. The results of these two experiments were generally in agreement with the findings of the four experiments that used the prerated questions.

### IS THERE A NEED FOR AN EXCLUSIVE FOCUS ON PEOPLE WITH CHRONICALLY LOW SELF-ESTEEM OR NEGATIVE SELF-CONCEPT?

The methodology of the present research may raise another concern: Can self-enhancement and self-verification be unequivocally distinguished if the experimental focus is not exclusively on people with chronically low self-esteem or negative self-concept? Using exclusively low self-esteem or negative self-concept subjects would allow one to draw and test clear-cut predictions regarding the two perspectives: The self-enhancement perspective predicts that subjects will prefer to learn or confirm favorable information about themselves, whereas the self-verification perspective predicts that subjects will prefer to learn or confirm unfavorable information about themselves.

First, as an aside, the variable of self-esteem was not used in the present investigation because it is not clear exactly how to conceptualize global self-esteem and its relation with the self-concept. In fact, this may be one reason why research involving global self-esteem sometimes fails to produce informative results even within the domain of the self-enhancement versus self-verification controversy (e.g., Swann, Pelham, & Krull, 1989; see also Krosnick & Sedikides, 1990). Thus, it is preferable to focus on the self-concept (i.e., a person's cognitive representation of his or her attributes) rather than self-esteem. Indeed, the results of the present investigation illustrated that focusing on properties of people's self-conceptions (i.e., their centrality and valence) can afford a sufficiently rigorous comparative test of the two perspectives.

Second, given that subjects were randomly assigned to the experimental conditions, it is reasonable to assume that an equal proportion of negative self-concept and positive self-concept subjects were represented in the experimental cells. Hence, the obtained results qualify as a general law of human self-evaluation: People, in general, favor and subsequently confirm the discovery of positive, rather than negative, characteristics.

Nevertheless, self-concept valence (as well as self-esteem valence) is an individual differences variable; as such, it is certainly likely to moderate aspects of the self-evaluation process. Still, however, the viability of a given theoretical conclusion does not necessarily depend on moderator variables. In the present case, the right to draw general theoretical conclusions about the relative strength of the self-enhancement versus self-verification motive does not necessitate the presence or absence of moderator variables. Only the "when" question demands discussion of moderator variables, which I now discuss.

## The When Question

A profitable approach for future research is the "when" question (Brown, 1990); namely, "What are the circumstances under which one motive is likely to be more effective than another in influencing the self-evaluation process?" Recent empirical and theoretical contributions have identified several moderators of the self-evaluation process (Sedikides & Strube, 1993; Swan, 1990). For example, task or attribute ambiguity may qualify as such (Brown, 1986). In cases of self-evaluation on unambiguous tasks or attributes, as in research reported by Trope and his colleagues, assessment concerns should predominate, whereas in instances of self-evaluation on ambiguous tasks or self-attributes, enhancement concerns should be prevalent (Dunning, Meyerowitz, & Holzberg, 1989). Attribute modifiability or controllability may also be a determinant of the emergence of self-assessment versus self-enhancement concerns (Brown, 1990). People may seek accurate feedback when evaluating modifiable attributes (e.g., skills), but seek self-flattering feedback when evaluating relatively fixed attributes (e.g., aptitudes). Finally, mood may also qualify as a moderator. A sad mood is likely to lead to negative self-perception and evaluation, whereas a happy mood is likely to produce positive self-perception and evaluation (Sedikides, 1992). Thus, people in a sad mood may be prone to self-assessment, whereas people in a happy mood may be prone to self-enhancement.

## Concluding Remarks

The results of the present investigation show that the self-enhancement motive is relatively the most powerful determinant of the self-evaluation process, followed by self-verification. However, in acknowledgment of people's ability to draw flexibly on alternative motives, given different settings, tasks, prior experiences, and personal orientations, future research will need to concentrate not only on the "when" question, but also on an attempt to integrate the existing literature. An integrational model could be either at a microlevel (e.g., Are the three motives implicated in different stages of the self-evaluative sequence?) or at a macrolevel (e.g., Are the three motives involved in different developmental stages?). Regardless, research on the three self-evaluation motives has a promising future.

## REFERENCES

Alicke, M. D. (1985). Global self-evaluation as determined by the desirability and controllability of trait adjectives. *Journal of Personality and Social Psychology, 49*, 1621–1630.

Allen, F. S. (1972). *Allen's synonyms and antonyms.* New York: Barnes & Noble.

Anderson, N. H. (1968). Likableness ratings of 555 personality trait words. *Journal of Personality and Social Psychology, 9*, 272–279.

Bargh, J. A. (1982). Attention and automaticity in the processing of self-relevant information. *Journal of Personality and Social Psychology, 43*, 425–436.

Baumeister, R. F., & Jones, E. E. (1978). When self-presentation is constrained by the target's knowledge: Consistency and compensation. *Journal of Personality and Social Psychology, 36*, 608–618.

Baumgardner, A. H. (1990). To know oneself is to like oneself: Self-certainty and self-affect. *Journal of Personality and Social Psychology, 58*, 1062–1072.

Bradley, G. W. (1978). Self-serving biases in the attribution process: A reexamination of the fact or fiction question. *Journal of Personality and Social Psychology, 36*, 56–71.

Breytspraak, L. M. (1984). *The development of self in later life.* Boston: Little, Brown.

Brickman, P., & Bulman, R. J. (1977). Pleasure and pain in social comparison. In J. M. Suls & R. L. Miller (Eds.), *Social comparison processes: Theoretical and empirical perspectives* (pp. 149–186). Washington, DC: Hemisphere.

Brown, J. D. (1986). Evaluations of self and others: Self-enhancement biases in social judgments. *Social Cognition, 4*, 353–376.

Brown, J. D. (1990). Evaluating one's abilities: Shortcuts and stumbling blocks on the road to self-knowledge. *Journal of Experimental Social Psychology, 26*, 149–167.

Brown, J. D. (1991). Accuracy and bias in self-knowledge. In C. R. Snyder & D. F. Forsyth (Eds.), *Handbook of social and clinical psychology. The health perspective* (pp. 158-178). Elmsford, NY: Pergamon Press.

Cantor, N., Mackie, D., & Lord, C. G. (1984). Choosing partners and activities: The social perceiver decides to mix it up. *Social Cognition, 3*, 256–272.

Carver, C. S., & Scheier, M. F. (1981). *Attention and self-regulation: A control-theory approach to human behavior.* New York: Springer-Verlag.

Catrambone, R., & Markus, H. (1987). The role of self-schemas in going beyond the information given. *Social Cognition, 5*, 349–368.

Cialdini, R. B., & Richardson, K. D. (1980). Two indirect tactics of impression management: Basking and blasting. *Journal of Personality and Social Psychology, 39*, 406–415.

Crary, W. G. (1966). Reactions to incongruent self-experiences. *Journal of Consulting Psychology, 30,* 246–252.

Damon, W. (1983). *Social and personality development: Infancy through adolescence.* New York: Norton.

Dennett, D. (1982). Why do we think what we do about why we think what we do? *Cognition, 12,* 219–237.

Devine, P., Hirt, E., & Gehrke, E. (1990). Diagnostic and confirmation strategies in trait hypothesis testing. *Journal of Personality and Social Psychology, 58,* 952–963.

Dunning, D., Meyerowitz, J. A., & Holzberg, A. D. (1989). Ambiguity and self-evaluation: The role of idiosyncratic trait definitions in self-serving assessments of ability. *Journal of Personality and Social Psychology, 57,* 1082–1090.

Frey, D., & Stahlberg, D. (1987). Selection of information after receiving more or less reliable self-threatening information. *Personality and Social Psychology Bulletin, 12,* 434–441.

Fuhrman, R. W., Bodenhausen, G. V., & Lichtenstein, M. (1989). On the trait implications of social behaviors: Kindness, intelligence, goodness, and normality ratings for 400 behavior statements. *Behavior Research Methods, Instruments, and Computers, 21,* 587–597.

Gergen, K. J., & Gergen, M. M. (1988). Narrative and the self as relationship. In L. Berkowitz (Ed.), *Advances in experimental social psychology* (Vol. 21, pp 17–56). San Diego, CA: Academic Press.

Godfrey, D. K., Jones, E. E., & Lord, C. G (1986). Self-promotion is not ingratiating. *Journal of Personality and Social Psychology, 50,* 106–115.

Green, S. K., & Gross, A. E. (1979). Self-serving biases in implicit evaluations. *Personality and Social Psychology Bulletin, 5,* 214–217.

Greenwald, A. G. (1980). The totalitarian ego: Fabrication and revision of personal history. *American Psychologist, 35.* 603–618.

Greenwald, A. G. (1981). Self and memory. In G. H. Bower (Ed.), *The psychology of learning and motivation* (Vol. 15, pp 201–236). San Diego, CA: Academic Press.

Gruder, C. L. (1977). Choice of comparison persons in evaluating oneself. In J. M. Suls & R. L. Miller (Eds.), *Social comparison processes: Theoretical and empirical perspectives* (pp. 21–41). Washington, DC: Hemisphere.

Harris, R. N., & Snyder, C. R. (1986). The role of uncertain self-esteem in self-handicapping. *Journal of Personality and Social Psychology, 51,* 451–458.

Krosnick, J. A., & Sedikides, C. (1990). Self-monitoring and self-protective biases in use of consensus information to predict one's own behavior. *Journal of Personality and Social Psychology, 58,* 718–728.

Kruglanski, A. W. (1990). Motivations for judging and knowing: Implications for causal attribution. In E. T. Higgins & R. M. Sorrentino (Eds.), *Handbook of motivation and cognition* (Vol. 2, pp. 333–368). New York: Guilford Press.

Kruglanski, A. W. & Mayseless, 0. (1990). Classic and current social comparison research: Expanding the perspective. *Psychological Bulletin, 108,* 195–208.

Kuiper, N. A., Olinger, L. J., MacDonald, M. R., & Shaw, B. F. (1985). Self-schema processing of depressed and nondepressed content: The effects of vulnerability on depression. *Social Cognition, 3,* 77–93.

Kulik, J. A., & Taylor, S. E. (1981). Self-monitoring and the use of consensus information. *Journal of Personality, 49,* 75–84.

Kunda, Z. (1987). Motivated inference: Self-serving generation and evaluation of causal theories. *Journal of Personality and Social Psychology, 53,* 636–647.

Kunda, Z. (1990). The case for motivated reasoning. *Psychological Bulletin, 108,* 480–498.

Lewicki, P. (1985). Nonconscious biasing effects of single instances on subsequent judgments. *Journal of Personality and Social Psychology, 48,* 563–574.

Lewis, N. (1978). *The new Roget's thesaurus in dictionary form* (Rev. ed.). New York: Berkley.

Maracek, J., & Mettee, D. R. (1972). Avoidance of continued success as a function of self-esteem, level of esteem certainty, and responsibility for success. *Journal of Personality and Social Psychology, 22,* 90–107.

Markus, H. (1977). Self-schemas and processing information about the self. *Journal of Personality and Social Psychology, 35,* 63–78.

Markus, H., & Nurius, P. (1986). Possible selves. *American Psychologist, 41,* 954–969.

Markus, H., Smith, J., & Moreland, R. L. (1985). Role of the self-concept in the perception of others. *Journal of Personality and Social Psychology 49,* 1494–1512.

Miller, D. T. (1976). Ego involvement and attributions for success and failure. *Journal of Personality and Social Psychology, 34,* 901–906.

Nisbett, R. E., & Valins, S. (1972). Perceiving the causes of one's own behavior. In E. E. Jones, D. E. Kanouse, H. H. Kelley, R. E. Nisbett, S. Valins, & B. Weiner (Eds.), *Attribution: Perceiving the causes of behavior* (pp. 63–78). Morristown, NJ: General Learning Press.

Nisbett, R. E., & Wilson, T. D. (1977). Telling more than we can know: Verbal reports on mental processes. *Psychological Review, 84,* 231–259.

Paulhus, D. L., & Levitt, K. (1987). Desirable responding triggered by affect: Automatic egotism? *Journal of Personality and Social Psychology, 52,* 245-259.

Ross, M. (1989). Relation of implicit theories to the construction of personal histories. *Psychological Review, 96,* 341–357.

Ross, M., & Conway, M. (1986). Remembering one's own past: The construction of personal histories. In R. M. Sorrentino & E. T. Higgins (Eds.), *Handbook of motivation and cognition* (pp. 122–144). New York: Guilford Press.

Schlenker, B. R. (1975). Self-presentation: Managing the impression of consistency when reality interferes with self-enhancement. *Journal of Personality and Social Psychology, 32,* 1030–1037.

Schlenker, B. R. (1985). Identity and self-identification. In B. R. Schlenker (Ed.), *The self and social life* (pp. 65–99). New York: McGraw-Hill.

Sedikides, C. (1992). Changes in the valence of the self as a function of mood. *Review of Personality and Social Psychology, 14,* 271–311.

Sedikides, C., & Strube, M. J. (1997). Self-evaluation: To thine own self be good, to thine own self be sure, and to thine own self be true, and to thine own self be better. In M. P. Zanna (Ed.), *Advances in experimental social psychology* (Vol. 29, 209–269). New York: Academic Press.

Sherman, S. J., Presson, C. C., & Chassin, L. (1984). Mechanisms underlying the false consensus effect: The special role of threats to the self. *Personality and Social Psychology Bulletin, 10,* 127–138.

Silverman, I. (1964). Self-esteem and differential responsiveness to success and failure. *Journal of Abnormal and Social Psychology, 69*, 115–119.

Snyder, M. (1981). Seek, and ye shall find: Testing hypotheses about other people. In E. T. Higgins, C. P. Herman, & M. P. Zanna (Eds.), *Social cognition: The Ontario Symposium* (Vol. 1, pp. 277–303). Hillsdale, NJ: Erlbaum.

Snyder, M., Gangestad, S., & Simpson, J. A. (1983). Choosing friends as activity partners: The role of self-monitoring. *Journal of Personality and Social Psychology, 45*, 1061–1072.

Sorrentino, R. M., & Hewitt, E. C. (1984). The uncertainty-reducing properties of achievement tasks revisited. *Journal of Personality and Social Psychology, 47*, 884–889.

Srull, T. K., & Gaelick, L. (1983). General principles and individual differences in the self as a habitual reference point: An examination of self-other judgments of similarity. *Social Cognition, 2*, 108–121.

Strube, M. J., Lott, C. L., Le-Xuan-Hy, G. M., Oxenberg, J., & Deichmann, A. K. (1986). Self-evaluation of abilities: Accurate self-assessment versus biased self-enhancement. *Journal of Personality and Social Psychology, 51*, 16–25.

Strube, M. J., & Roemmele, L. A. (1985). Self-enhancement, self-assessment, and self-evaluative task choice. *Journal of Personality and Social Psychology, 49*, 981–993.

Swann, W. B., Jr. (1983). Self-verification: Bringing social reality into harmony with the self. In J. Suls & A. G. Greenwald (Eds.), *Psychological perspectives on the self* (Vol. 2, pp 33–66). Hillsdale, NJ: Erlbaum.

Swann, W. B., Jr. (1990). To be adored or to be known? The interplay of self-enhancement and self-verification. In E. T. Higgins & R. M. Sorrentino (Eds.), *Handbook of motivation and cognition: Foundations of social behavior* (Vol. 2, pp. 408–448). New York: Guilford Press.

Swann, W. B., Jr., & Ely, R. J. (1984). A battle of wills: Self-verification versus behavioral confirmation. *Journal of Personality and Social Psychology, 46*, 1287–1302.

Swann, W. B., Jr., Pelham, B., & Krull, D. S. (1989). Agreeable fancy or disagreeable truth? Reconciling self-enhancement and self-verification. *Journal of Personality and Social Psychology, 57*, 782–791.

Taylor, S. E., & Brown, J. D. (1988). Illusion and well-being: A social psychological perspective on mental health. *Psychological Bulletin, 103*, 193–210.

Taylor, S. E., & Koivumaki, J. H. (1976). The perception of self and others: Acquaintanceship, affect, and actor-observer differences. *Journal of Personality and Social Psychology, 46*, 489–502.

Tesser, A. (1988). Toward a self-evaluation maintenance model of social behavior. In L. Berkowitz (Ed.), *Advances in experimental social psychology* (Vol. 21, pp. 181–227). San Diego CA: Academic Press.

Tice, D. M., & Baumeister, R. F. (1990). Self-esteem, self-handicapping, and self-presentation: The strategy of inadequate practice. *Journal of Personality, 58*, 443–464.

Trope, Y. (1979). Uncertainty-reducing properties of achievement tasks. *Journal of Personality and Social Psychology, 37*, 1505–1518.

Trope, Y. (1980). Self-assessment and task performance. *Journal of Personality and Social Psychology, 18*, 201–215.

Trope, Y. (1983). Self-assessment in achievement behavior. In J. M. Suls & A. G. Greenwald (Eds.), *Psychological perspectives on the self* (Vol. 2, pp. 93–121). Hillsdale, NJ: Erlbaum.

Trope, Y. (1986). Self-enhancement and self-assessment in achievement behavior. In R. M. Sorrentino & E. T. Higgins (Eds.), *Handbook of motivation and cognition: Foundations of social behavior* (Vol. 2, pp. 350–378). New York: Guilford Press.

Trope, Y., & Bassok, M. (1982). Confirmatory and diagnosing strategies in social information gathering. *Journal of Personality and Social Psychology, 43*, 22–34.

*Webster's Ninth New Collegiate Dictionary* (1989). Springfield, MA: Merriam-Webster.

Weinstein, N. D. (1980). Unrealistic optimism about future life events. *Journal of Personality and Social Psychology, 39*, 806–820.

Wills, T. A. (1981). Downward comparison principles in social psychology. *Psychological Bulletin, 90*, 245–271.

Wood, J. V. (1989). Theory and research concerning social comparisons of personal attributes. *Psychological Bulletin, 106*, 231–248.

Zukier, H., & Pepitone, A. (1984). Social roles and strategies in prediction: Some determinants of the use of base rate information. *Journal of Personality and Social Psychology, 47*, 349–360.

# Strategies

In this section, we examine some patterns of behavior that arise as people seek to maintain their favorable views of themselves and occasionally improve them. Undoubtedly people have many such strategies, and these should be regarded as important illustrations rather than as a complete roster.

Self-handicapping was an important means of manipulating attributions, and the article by Jones and Berglas (1978) has been an influential first presentation of the theory. That same year, Berglas and Jones (1978) published a pair of experiments showing that people would choose performance-impairing drugs when they had received initial success and doubted they could repeat that success (and hence needed an excuse for potential failure). Self-handicapping captured the imagination of many social psychologists because it offered a seemingly logical, seductive path into what was ultimately self-destructive behavior.

Subsequent work expanded on this phenomenon. Kolditz and Arkin (1982) showed that the motive for self-handicapping is strongly self-presentational: People are much less likely to self-handicap in private circumstances than when someone is watching them and making judgments about their ability. Tice (1991) showed that people may self-handicap either to provide an excuse for failure or to enhance their credit for success (i.e., by overcoming obstacles), and trait self-esteem predicts which motive people use. Tucker, Vuchinich, and Sobell (1981) returned to the original interest in alcohol abuse and showed that people do actually consume alcohol to give themselves an excuse for failure. Harris and Snyder (1986) showed that uncertain self-esteem led to self-handicapping, thus showing that self-handicapping is most likely when you want to believe something good about yourself but are not sure.

The second paper in this section, by Cialdini and his colleagues, is the classic demonstration of a pattern called "basking in reflected glory": People identify themselves ever more with winners and successful people than with losers. In this work, the link remained constant (i.e., between the student and his or her university), but people would prominently display this link after a football victory—whereas after a loss they would distance themselves from their school. These effects are especially strong when people are motivated to think well of themselves.

A subsequent study (Cialdini & Richardson, 1980) extended the "basking" idea to show "blasting" as well. When people want to shore up their images of themselves, they can either raise the stock of their own institution (such as by boasting about how great their school is) or bad-mouth a rival institution.

An elegant and broad theory about these patterns is described in the article by Tesser (1988). He said that being linked to a very successful person can be either a blessing or a curse. There is of course the "reflection" process, by which the other person's successes bring added credit and luster to those who are associated with them, which is why successful people attract fans and groupies. On the other hand, there is sometimes a "comparison" process, in which the other person's successes make you look bad. The impact of another's performance on the self will depend on how close the link is between you and whether you perform in that same sphere. Ideally, then, you want a spouse who is terrifically successful at something far removed from your own career!

## REFERENCES

Berglas, S., & Jones, E. E. (1978). Drug choice as a self-handicapping strategy in response to non-contingent success. *Journal of Personality and Social Psychology, 36,* 405–417.

Cialdini, R. B., Borden, R. J., Thorne, A., Walker, M. R., Freeman, S., & Sloan, L. R. (1976). Basking in reflected glory: Three (football) field studies. *Journal of Personality and Social Psychology, 34,* 366–375.

Cialdini, R. B., & Richardson, K. D. (1980). Two indirect tactics of image management: Basking and blasting. *Journal of Personality and Social Psychology, 39,* 406–415.

Harris, R. N., & Snyder, C. R. (1986). The role of uncertain self-esteem in self-handicapping. *Journal of Personality and Social Psychology, 51,* 451–458.

Jones, E. E., & Berglas, S. C. (1978). Control of attributions about the self through self-handicapping strategies: The appeal of alcohol and the role of underachievement. *Personality and Social Psychology Bulletin, 4,* 200–206.

Kolditz, T. A., & Arkin, R. M. (1982). An impression management interpretation of the self-handicapping strategy. *Journal of Personality and Social Psychology, 43,* 492–502.

Tesser, A. (1988). Toward a self-evaluation maintenance model of social behavior. In L. Berkowitz (Ed.), *Advances in experimental social psychology* (Vol. 21, pp. 181–227). San Diego, CA: Academic Press.

Tice, D. M. (1991). Esteem protection or enhancement? Self-handicapping motives and attributions differ by trait self-esteem. *Journal of Personality and Social Psychology, 60,* 711–725.

Tucker, J. A., Vuchinich, R. E., & Sobell, M. B. (1981). Alcohol consumption as a self-handicapping strategy. *Journal of Abnormal Psychology, 90,* 220–230.

# Discussion Questions

1. What other patterns of self-handicapping can you identify beyond those discussed by Jones and Berglas (i.e., alcohol abuse and underachievement)?
2. Is there a difference between self-handicapping and simply making excuses for oneself?

3. Suppose you married someone who worked in the same field as yourself. What problems lie in store for your marriage, according to Tesser's theory? How might you counteract these problems?

4. What right do sports fans have to claim that they are "number 1" after their team wins? How does the fan become linked with the team's success?

5. Do students show the "basking" effect more with men's or women's teams? Why the difference? Is this likely to change over the next few decades?

6. Self-handicapping theory suggests that sometimes people seek to avoid valid information. What other patterns reflect the effort to avoid or invalidate information about the self?

# Suggested Readings

Berglas, S., & Jones, E. E. (1978). Drug choice as a self-handicapping strategy in response to non-contingent success. *Journal of Personality and Social Psychology, 36,* 405–417. This is the original set of experiments on self-handicapping (before the term was even coined). As in the "impostor phenomenon," people were led to experience great success while privately believing that it was just luck and they would not be able to repeat their feats or live up to newly inflated expectations. They responded by choosing to take drugs resembling alcohol.

Tice, D. M. (1991). Esteem protection or enhancement? Self-handicapping motives and attributions differ by trait self-esteem. *Journal of Personality and Social Psychology, 60,* 711–725. Self-handicapping offers two benefits: Blame for failure is reduced, while credit for success is increased. Tice shows that people with low self-esteem, who are mainly oriented toward self-protection, self-handicap to ward off blame for failure, whereas people with high self-esteem (oriented toward enhancement rather than protection) do it to enhance success.

Baumeister, R. F. (1990). Suicide as escape from self. *Psychological Review, 97,* 90–113. (OR) Heatherton, T. F., & Baumeister, R. F. (1991). Binge eating as escape from self-awareness. *Psychological Bulletin, 110,* 86–108. (OR) Baumeister, R. F. (1991). *Escaping the self.* New York: Basic Books. These works show people's efforts to escape and avoid awareness of themselves. Suicide, binge eating, masochistic sexuality, meditations, and other practices often revolve around how to lose awareness of oneself.

Higgins, R. L., Snyder, C. R., & Berglas, S. (1990). *Self-handicapping: The paradox that isn't.* New York: Plenum. This book offers a good, although slightly dated, overview of self-handicapping research, with contributions by many important researchers.

# Control of Attributions about the Self Through Self-handicapping Strategies: The Appeal of Alcohol and the Role of Underachievement

Edward F. Jones • Princeton University
Steven Berglas • Harvard Medical School

This article explores the hypothesis that alcohol use and underachievement may serve as strategies to externalize the causation of poor performance and to internalize the causation of good performance. Such a strategy may be prominently used especially by those who have a precarious but not entirely negative sense of self-competence. The etiology of this strategic preference may follow either of two scenarios. The child may attach desperate importance to this competence image because competence is the condition for deserving parental love. Or the child may have been rewarded for accidental attributes or performances that do not predict future success, thus leaving him in a position of one who has reached a status he fears he cannot maintain through his own control. The linkage of alcohol appeal to underachievement strategies is stressed; both are seen as expressions of the same overconcern with competence.

Let us proceed from the premise that people use attributional principles in the service of self-image protection. We believe that people actively try to arrange the circumstances of their behavior so as to protect their conceptions of themselves as competent, intelligent persons. This is part of a general pattern of self-presentation that goes beyond the verbal claims and disclosures that are usually considered under that heading. We shall explore the hypothesis that the appeal of alcohol can be understood with reference to its strategic role in obscuring the meaning of performance feedback. We shall try to relate this discussion of strategic alcohol use to the similarly obscurant possibilities of underachievement and overachievement, here seen as strategies for controlling self-attributions by withdrawing or augmenting one's effort.

If there is any novelty in our premise, perhaps it lies in the suggestion that we sometimes do things to *avoid* diagnostic information about our own characteristics and capacities. Social comparison theory (Festinger, 1954) posits a fundamental motive to gain an accurate view of reality and a discriminating appraisal of our abilities to cope with it. Indeed, attribution theory itself is typically couched in terms of stabilizing the distal features of the environment and accurately penetrating the causal structure of the social world. Harold Kelley (1971) makes this very explicit in his emphasis on the relationship between accurate or stable attributions and control through understanding. But do people always want to know precisely who they are and exactly what they are capable of accomplishing at their best? We doubt it, and we suggest that social psychologists have overlooked each person's need for certain kinds of ambiguity to allow room for self-sustaining and self-embellishing fantasies.

To illustrate the dangers of too much self-knowledge, we offer this brief excerpt from the musings of Denison Andrews (1975) upon learning from his old grade school principal that his measured IQ is only 125:

> Keep cool. Control wobbly knees. 125. Not brilliant. Not undiscovered genius. Ordinary bright. Everyday bright like everyone else . . . No brighter than my stockbroker. No brighter than insurance agent. Did they laugh when I applied to medical school? . . . IQ has no meaning. Totally discredited. No one takes it seriously . . . Who was Otis anyway? I test badly. IQ doesn't measure creativity. Winston Churchill. Maybe I was depressed. Maybe I had an earache. A bad night's sleep. Maybe I lost time daydreaming. Creatively . . . "

Here we see the tortured efforts of posterior defensive attribution, but our present argument is that people actively select those settings for action that render performance feedback ambiguous, thus anticipating the kinds of excuses Andrews is forced to lamely offer.

The hypothesis, specifically, is that an important reason why some people turn to alcohol is to avoid the implications of negative feedback for failure and to enhance the impact of positive feedback for success. This is part of the more general notion that people drink to escape from responsibility for their actions, but it is more specific than that notion, and it trades on the public assumption that alcohol generally interferes with or disrupts performance. This assumption paves the way for what we shall call self-handicapping strategies. By finding or creating impediments that make good performance less likely, the strategist nicely protects his sense of self-competence. If the person does poorly, the source of the failure is externalized in the impediment; perhaps in the glass or the

bottle. In the terms of Jones and Davis (1965), it is difficult for the strategist and for others to make a "correspondent inference" about competence. If the person does well, then he or she has done well in spite of less than optimum conditions. According to Kelley's (1971) augmentation principle, the person's competence should receive a boost. Alcohol is what Kelley refers to as an inhibitory cause of a successful performance effect, whereas ability is a facilitative cause. The presence of ability as an inferred potential cause of a given performance level is augmented by the presence of alcohol. Regardless of what the outcome is, the self-handicapping strategist cannot lose, at least in those settings where the attributional implications of performance are more important than the success of the performance itself.

Before going any further, it might be helpful to run through some other examples of self-handicapping to show that alcohol appeal is only one subset of a variety of strategic instances. The high school senior who gets but two hours of sleep before taking his SAT exams may be a self-handicapper. The ingratiator who avoids disclosing his true preferences or opinions protects himself from the ultimate implications of rejection as a person. Even, if he gets rejected, this isn't so bad if he was "just trying to he nice," if he held his true self in reserve. Similarly, the professional actor may build a career around the externalization aspect of self-handicapping by constantly retreating to roles so that failure is never attached to the real self. We have all seen the occasional talk show guest who, actor or comedian by profession, is petrified by the assigned "role" of being himself. Self-handicappers are legion in the sports world, from the tennis player who externalizes a bad shot by adjusting his racket strings, to the avid golfer who systematically avoids taking lessons or even practicing on the driving range.

Therapists have long been aware of the appeal of the "sick" role to those who wish temporarily to drop out of life's competition. This is a form of self-handicapping where the body is seen as outside the system of personal responsibility. Many clinicians have noted that even the roles of "neurotic" or "mental" patients may be partly strategic in nature. Carson (1969), for example, points out that "acquisition of the label 'mentally ill' is not invariably treated as a major disaster by the person so labeled . . . it is an excellent 'cover story' for various types of rulebreaking ('it's not me who is doing this—it's my illness')" (p. 228).

The self-handicapper, we are suggesting, reaches out for impediments, exaggerates handicaps, embraces any factor reducing personal responsibility for mediocrity and enhancing personal responsibility for success. One does this to shape the implications of performance feedback both in one's own eyes and in the eyes of others. Handicapping is a self-defending maneuver whose significance is probably augmented by the presence of an audience, but we emphasize that the public value of the strategy is not its original impetus. This lies in the exaggerated importance of one's own private conception of self-competence and the need to protect that conception from unequivocal negative feedback even in the absence of others.

## Underachievement as a Strategy to Protect Self-esteem

The same defensive dynamic may underly the strategy of underachievement, a strategy that involves the subtraction of facilitative effort rather than the imposition of inhibitory performance barriers. The underachiever, like the impediment-seeking externalizer, wishes to avoid the most drastic implications of possible failure. If one is excessively worried about his basic competence and simply cannot face the prospect of being judged incompetent, it is better to exert less than total effort, thus inviting probable (but not inevitable) failure, than to try and risk a possible failure that would implicate the self more irrevocably. In the unlikely event of successful achievement the performer who has only casually or half-heartedly involved himself gains the added esteem award of ability-relevant positive feedback.

At this point, there are two broad questions that must be confronted. The first is whence derives this intense concern with the maintenance of a competence image? The second is what determines the choice of alcohol or underachievement over other strategic alternatives within the self-handicapping family?

## The Choice of the Alcohol Strategy

Considering the latter question first, it must be clearly understood that the appeal of alcohol is a function of many things beside the personality of the drinker or the stresses inherent in his life. Jessor and his colleagues (1973), for example, have noted that drug abuse and problem drinking may be (1) a learned way of coping with personal frustrations and anticipated failure, (2) an expression of opposition to or rejection of conventional society—including the very norms that define the behavior as a problem, (3) a negotiation for or claim on status transformation or development transition, or (4) a manifestation of solidarity with the peer subculture. So we are interested at best in one set of factors that predispose individuals to alcohol use, though it may well be the set that is most likely to lead to serious problem drinking.

The path from use to abuse to addiction involves many complexities that take us beyond our present concern. What interests us at this point are the factors that predispose a person toward alcohol use and which enhance the reinforcement value of such an agent. Our basic proposition rests on the fact that alcohol has the reputation of reducing one's responsibility for good performance. But it has other properties that undoubtedly enhance its attractiveness to the self-handicapper. Here the relationship between alcohol appeal and underachievement must be specifically stressed. Beckett (1974) notes that alcohol and drug addicts are almost distinct underachievers. Jessor and his colleagues (1973) also stress the negative relationship between achievement value and the appeal of drugs and alcohol. While the conventional interpretation would emphasize the direct effects of problem drinking on performance capability, our present view suggests that both alcohol appeal and underachievement may be symptoms of the same self-protective strategy. For reasons that we shall explore below, the problem drinker and the underachiever are fearful of receiving the unequivocal message that they are unworthy and incompetent. They perhaps suspect this might be true and are very afraid of being "discovered." So much follows directly from the original hypothesis of self-handicapping: such a person would be motivated to get equivocal or biased information from the environment about self-worth.

Another aspect of the appeal of alcohol is that it lends itself to a subjectively temporary strategic commitment. The drinker does not set out to achieve addiction. He believes that he can control the agent that temporarily lowers his performance capacity. This belief fits nicely into *mañana* fantasies that are so common in alcohol use. These fantasies involve thoughts about how successful one will be *when* he breaks the drinking habit or could be *if* he did. The problem drinker tells himself that he will report for meaningful social measurement when he's good and ready, but typically he never is. The suspected truth is too horrible to risk, and in the meantime he may prosper in fantasies of glorified competence.

There is no question that alcohol has direct physiological effects on nervous system functioning. The appeal of alcohol has been commonly attributed to its euphoric and anxiety reducing effects (Cappell & Herman, 1972; Kingham, 1958). Our present line of argument adds a psychological dimension to the anxiety-reduction phenomenon. It suggests that anxiety is typically centered around one's competence or respectworthiness and that it is reduced when the alcohol provides an excuse for marginal performance. This oversimplifies the complex interactive effects of alcohol and mood, since there are legendary as well as vividly real examples of drink-induced morosity (e.g., the "crying jag"). But the euphoric effects of alcohol are certainly more commonly observed and therefore built into the expectations of the drinker himself. Self-handicapping agents, like alcohol, may in fact enhance performance for those with an inordinate fear of the competence implications of failure. Weiner and Sierad (1975), in a fascinating study, examined the digit symbol performance of subjects high in need for achievement and those low in need for achievement (but high in fear of failure). Half of these subjects ingested a placebo under the impression that it would interfere with visuo-motor performance. All subjects were given periodic failure feedback and their performance was measured. The high fear-of-failure subjects actually performed better after taking the performance-inhibiting placebo than those in the control condition. The subjects high in need for achievement performed better in the control condition in line with their normal tendency to attribute failure to low effort and to try harder. When the pill obscured this attributional line they did not perform as well. Although this is not Weiner and Sierad's exact interpretation, we would suggest that the high fear-of-failure subjects do better in the pill condition because the placebo removes the competence implications of failure and this reduction in anxiety actually releases energy for attention, motivation and, therefore, improved performance.

## The Competence Image

But now let us return to the question of etiology and consider the special reasons why strategies to protect one's competence image are necessary. Why is it so important for the potential alcoholic to avoid information implying that he is unworthy and incompetent? Imagine the following developmental scenario. The potential problem drinker, like the rest of us, early realizes that reward follows good behavior. However, social rewards have either or both of two meanings. The first of these is the *exchange* implication, reward rendered for costs incurred. The child who receives thanks for wiping the dishes may accept this merely as a quid pro quo, rather than drawing any deep inferences about his or her basic worthiness. On the other hand, there may be something about the "thanks" that does carry a self-esteem increment. The reward may have *signifying* implications as an exchange value (cf. Jones, 1964).

The potentially dual meaning of reward introduces a complexity that the developing child may find difficult to penetrate. A part of this complexity is the difficulty of establishing whether the love of significant others is unconditional. The child may reflect on whether the parental rewards received are solely contingent on performance (exchange) or whether they are signals of parental love and esteem (signification). We can imagine the child attempting to separate these implications, these parental messages, by experimental tests to find out whether there is love in the absence of performance. One· source of the "competence complex" that we theoretically attribute to the potential problem drinker may be the tentative discovery that he or she is not unconditionally loved. The very unpleasantness of this experimental outcome may support the disinclination to conduct similar unconfounded experiments in the future.

## Reactions to Conditional Love

Here there is a crucial choice point. The child can confound subsequent experimental tests of parental love by oversufficient effort and application. Such a child is driven to zeal by an overdetermined fear of failure, for failure may invite further evidence that love is conditional on performances. The vicious circularity of this strategic course is apparent in the attributional implications of overachievement. The more one tries, the more essential it is that one avoids failure, for failure under conditions of high effort carries unequivocal implications about ability. In this way, perhaps, trying can lead only to more trying. The overachievement strategy is a precarious one, but with sufficient talent, appropriate choice of performance setting, and luck, it may effectively propel the person into relative emotional security. Even the overachiever may be periodically attracted to alcohol and to nonperformance settings in which he may escape the burdens of being tested while competence is fully engaged.

The other path is more self-destructive and involved. The feedback from the child's conditional love experiments goes beyond the simple exchange implication to carry a more complicated message. The child reads the message as saying "You can do it if you try, and that's why we love you." And if the child does occasionally succeed, the only reward is a "We knew it all along," which vindicates the parents more than it reinforces the child. These messages create the bind of the underachiever. He who fails without trying maintains a precarious hold on the illusion of love and admiration. The resulting strategy of lowered motivation may be buttressed by a culturally derived competence elitism. We live in a world in which people are (sometimes secretly) admired for their talent and intelligence regardless of the quality of actual performances. This may be a residual of the many myths stressing the inevitable genetic superiority of the aristocracy and the nobly born (going back at least to Oedipus). It may also be a not unreasonable interpretation of Calvinist predestination doctrines. The vital importance of underlying competence may be stressed by the parents who are motivated to see their children as the carriers of their own superior genetic potential.

This line of argument seems to fly in the face of the results of Weiner and his colleagues (1971) who have shown that the low ability person who tries hard is rewarded more than the able slacker by subjects playing a teacher role. In such a teacher-student context the exchange model may emphasize the importance of doing one's best. However, it is another matter when we ask whether the average person would rather be a highly motivated dummy or a highly competent low achiever. Theoretically, the competent person has more potential control over performance outcomes than the incompetent person. Motivation can be turned on at some later time: competence is more irrevoca-

bly fixed. Some results by Nicholls (1975) support this notion that performance linked to ability is more gratifying than performance linked to effect.

Thus the self-handicapper, whether seeking to impose external performance impediments or to withdraw effect, may in many ways be similar to the overachiever. Each is fearful that failure will implicate competence. Each has an abnormal investment in the question of self-worth. One succeeds in avoiding failure through persistent effort; the other embraces failure as an alternative to self-implicating feedback. We have suggested that each strategy originates in a conditional love experiment in which the child draws different conclusions from the evidence that the signs of love are actually or potentially absent after failure.

## The Role of Reinforcement Contingency

An alternative scenario points to the contingency of rewards and performance as more crucial than the signification value of parental messages. Perhaps the self-handicapping path is followed by those whose reinforcement history has been capricious or chaotic. It is not that they have been unrewarded: it is that they have not been able to determine consistently what the reward was for, or they suspect that they have been rewarded for extraneous reasons such as beauty or the ascribed status of simply being a family member. We are reminded here of Seligman's (1975) theory of depression as a condition growing out of noncontingent reward histories. Of particular interest is the "success depression" where rewards have been ample, but uninformative regarding one's competence image.

The notion of self-protecting strategies implies, after all, that the strategist has something to protect. There has to have been some experience of success, something in the person's history that has created a fragile and ambiguous, but not a wholly negative, self-concept. The perpetual loser may not be the prime candidate for alcohol abuse. He may be more likely to handle his problems by drastically lowering his aspirations to fit realistically his meagre talents.

No doubt success-avoidance has other motivational origins as well. For one thing, success often incurs a future obligation to perform at a high level (cf. Jones, 1973). A performance Peter Principle often operates such that success propels a person into new and more demanding challenges where the risk of failure increases. This would seem to amplify further the appeal of self-handicapping strategies for both the failure-avoider and the success depressive.

These alternative etiologies describe different reinforcement histories. In the first version the potential problem drinker responds to what he fears might happen if he were to commit himself to maximal effort or establish ideal conditions for a performance. In the second version, the emphasis is more on the protection of ill-gotten gains. Both etiological versions, however, emphasize the potential addicts' vital concern with the signifying implications of performance for his self-image of competence. Both assume that this image has become a deep and over-riding consideration. Both further assume that the individual is willing to settle for confounded performance feedback rather than taking the chance on repeated tests of the conditional love hypothesis under maximally informative conditions. The problem drinker and the underachiever are willing to forego success to protect the illusion that they have the competence to be consistently successful.

From the viewpoint of advice to parents, however, the implications of the two scenarios appear antithetical. On the one hand we imply that parents should avoid tying rewards exclusively to performance. On the other hand we inveigh against non-contingent reinforcement schedules. What is the poor parent to do in this ostensible no-win situation? Somehow, the parent must segregate his or her signifying response from those which provide informative feedback about performance. Interest and affection should not be withdrawn in the absence of achievement, but contingent tutelage is essential to give the child a sense of adaptive control or effectance. Often, we suspect, the parents divide their roles so that the cross-sex parent emphasizes non-contingent, signifying love, whereas the same-sex parent emphasizes feedback contingent on performance (in part through serving as a performance model). The two roles combine in the ideal case to provide emotional security and a sense of mastery of the environment. To the extent that signification and exchange feedback are inextricably tangled in the family setting, there is potential for the kind of competence concern that leads to disturbances in achievement strivings and/or the subsequent appeal of such performance inhibitors as alcohol.

REFERENCES

Andrews, D. (1975). Stupid. *Harvard Magazine, 78,* 6–8.

Beckett, H. D. (1974). Hypotheses concerning the etiology of heroin addiction. In P. G. Bourne (Ed.), *Addiction.* New York: Academic Press.

Cappell, H., & Herman, C. P. (1972). Alcohol and tension reduction: A review. *Quarterly Journal of Studies on Alcohol, 33,* 33–64.

Carson, R. C. (1969). *Interaction concepts of personality.* Chicago: Aldine.

Festinger, L. (1954). A theory of social comparison processes. *Human Relations, 7,* 117–140.

Jessor, R., Jessor, L. S., & Finney, J. (1973). A social psychology of marijuana use: Longitudinal studies of high school and college youth. *Journal of Personality and Social Psychology, 26,* 1–15.

Jones, E. E. (1964). *Ingratiation.* New York: Appleton-Century-Crofts.

Jones, E. E., & Davis, K. E. (1965). From acts to disposition: The attribution process in person perception. In L. Berkowitz (Ed.), *Advances in experimental social psychology*, Vol. 2; New York: Academic Press.

Jones. S. C. (1973). Self- and interpersonal evaluations: Esteem theories versus consistency theories. *Psychological Bulletin, 79,* 185–199.

Kelley, H. H. (1971). *Attribution in social interaction.* Morristown, NJ: General Learning Press.

Kingham, R. J. (1958). Alcoholism and the reinforcement theory of learning. *Quarterly Journal of Studies on Alcohol, 19,* 320–330.

Nicholls, J. G. (1975). Causal attributions and other achievement-related cognitions: Effects of task outcome attainment value, and sex. *Journal of Personality and Social Psychology, 31,* 379–389.

Seligman, M. E. P. (1975). *Helplessness.* San Francisco: W. H. Freeman.

Weiner, B., Frieze. I., Kukla, A., Reed, L., Rest, S., Rosenbaum, R. M. (1971) *Perceiving the causes of success and failure.* Morristown, NJ: General Learning Press.

Weiner, B., & Sierad, J. (1975). Misattribution for failure and enhancement of achievement strivings. *Journal of Personality and Social Psychology, 31,* 415–421.

# Basking in Reflected Glory: Three (Football) Field Studies

Robert B. Cialdini • Arizona State University

Richard J. Borden • Purdue University

Avril Thorne • Arizona State University

Marcus Randall Walker • Ohio State University

Stephen Freeman • Ohio State University

Lloyd Reynolds Sloan • University of Notre Dame

The tendency to "bask in reflected glory" (BIRG) by publicly announcing one's associations with successful others was investigated in three field experiments. All three studies showed this effect to occur even though the person striving to bask In the glory of a successful source was not involved in the cause of the source's success. Experiment 1 demonstrated the BIRG phenomenon by showing a greater tendency for university students to wear school-identifying apparel after their school's football team had been victorious than nonvictorious. Experiments 2 and 3 replicated this effect by showing that students used the pronoun *we* more when describing a victory than a nonvictory of their school's football team. A model was developed asserting that the BIRG response represents an attempt to enhance one's public image. Experiments 2 and 3 indicated, in support of this assertion, that the tendency to proclaim a connection with a positive source was strongest when one's public image was threatened.

I t is a common and understandable tendency for people who have been successful in some positive way to make others aware of their connection with that accomplishment. However, there also appears to be a seemingly less rational but perhaps more interesting tendency for people to publicize a connection with *another person* who has been successful. This latter inclination might be called the tendency to bask in reflected glory (BIRG). That is, people appear to feel that they can share in the glory of a successful other with whom they are in some way associated; one manifestation of this feeling is the public trumpeting of the association. Such a phenomenon is not hard to under-

stand when the one wishing to share in another's success has been instrumental to that success. However, the more intriguing form of the phenomenon occurs when the one who basks in the glory of another has done nothing to bring about the other's success. Here, a simple case of affiliation or membership is sufficient to stimulate a public announcement of the critical connection.

There does seem to be abundant anecdotal evidence that people try to make us cognizant of their connections with highly positive or successful others. The forms of these connections are varied. For example, they may imply similarity of residence, past or present. States and cities like to list the names of famous entertainers, statesmen, beauty contest winners, etc., who live or were born within their boundaries; the state of Indiana has even gone so far as to brag that more vice-presidents of the United States have come from Indiana than any other state. Other such connections involve ethnic or religious affiliation: Italians speak proudly of the ethnic background of Marconi, and Jews refer to Einstein's heritage. Still other connections reflect physical similarities: "Napoleon was short, too." Sexual identity may also give rise to the BIRG phenomenon: At one women's movement forum attended by one of the authors, there was a round of feminine applause when it was announced that Madame Curie was a woman and Lee Harvey Oswald was not. Finally, connections suitable for BIRGing may be as tenuous as an incidental contact: We all know people who delight in recounting the time they were in the same theater, airplane, or restroom with a famous movie star.

While there appears to be rich informal support of the sort described above for the existence of a BIRG phenomenon, there seem to be no experimental investigations of the effect. Thus, it was the purpose of this series of studies to examine this tendency to bask in the reflected glory of another or group of others. In so doing, it was hoped to: (a) reliably demonstrate the existence of the phenomenon, (b) establish its generality over experimental contexts and measures, (c) determine a mediating process for its occurrence, and (d) discover some of its limiting conditions and thereby gain further information as to its nature.

One of the most obvious arenas for the working of BIRG effects in our society is the athletic arena. Fans of championship teams gloat over their team's accomplishments and proclaim their affiliation with buttons on their clothes, bumper stickers on their cars, and banners on their public buildings. Despite the fact that they have never caught a ball or thrown a block in support of their team's success, the tendency of such fans is to claim for themselves part of the team's glory; it is perhaps informative that the chant is always "*We're* number one," never "*They're* number one."

It was our view that a sports context would be ideal for a test of some of our notions concerning BIRG effects. Our expectation was that an individual would attempt to bask in the glory of an associated, successful source by publicly announcing his or her affiliation with the source and that this effect would be obtained even when the affiliation was clearly irrelevant (i.e., noninstrumental) to the success of the source. In order to gather data relevant to the above hypothesis, an experiment was simultaneously conducted at seven universities with powerful intercollegiate football teams during part of the 1973 football season. It was predicted that students at these schools would be more likely to announce publicly their connection with their universities after the varsity football teams had been successful than after the teams had not been successful. We decided to measure students' tendency to announce their university affiliation by means of an examination of clothing. The frequency with which students wore apparel that clearly identified the university that they attended was hoped to be a subtle yet sensitive measure of the willingness to declare publicly a university affiliation.

## Experiment 1

### Method

#### PROCEDURE

From the third week of the 1973 collegiate football season through the last week of regular play, the apparel of students enrolled in sections of introductory psychology courses at seven large universities was covertly monitored. At each school, three types of data were recorded in the same classes every Monday during the season: (a) the number of students present in the class, (b) the number of students with apparel identifying the school of attendance, and (c) the number of students with apparel identifying a school other than the school of attendance. Data recorders at each place received the following definitions prior to data collection:

> Apparel identifying the school of attendance is identified as apparel which unambiguously identifies your school through names, insignia, or emblems. Examples would be buttons, jackets, sweatshirts, tee shirts, etc., which display the school name, team nickname or mascot, or university insignia. Apparel which appears school-related *solely* through the use of colors would not qualify. Also excluded are utilitarian objects which

announce a university affiliation such as brief-cases, notebooks, or bookcovers. Apparel identifying a school other than the school of attendance are those which meet the same criteria for inclusion as above but which identify a school other than your own.

The data recorders were not members of the classes they monitored.

## Results

Over all schools and across all weeks, an average of 176.8 students were present in the monitored classes; an average of 8.4% of these students wore apparel identifying the university of attendance, while 2% of them wore apparel identifying a school other than the university of attendance. Because of huge differences among the schools in absolute amounts of these two kinds of apparel wearing and in order to make comparisons between the universities as well as between the types of apparel wearing, standardized indexes of relevant apparel wearing were considered necessary. The standard we decided on was the highest percentage of relevant apparel wearing that occurred on any Monday during the season; this standard was simply computed as the number of students wearing relevant apparel that day divided by the number of students in class that day. The percentages of apparel wearing on all other Mondays of the season were scored as proportions of the highest percentage. So, the Monday with the largest percentage of relevant apparel wearing was scored as 1.00, and any other Monday percentage was scored as a fraction (proportion) of that standard. This procedure was performed on the data from each school for the two relevant categories of apparel wearing: school-of-attendance apparel wearing and schools-nonattendance apparel wearing. A mean proportion for each category was obtained for Mondays following a team's wins and nonwins; these are the mean proportions presented in Table 22.1. As can be seen from Table 22.1, these indexes showed a generally consistent tendency for students to wear school-of-attendance apparel more after victories than nonvictories; but this was not the case for school-of-nonattendance apparel. Because of the non-normality of the proportion data, the scores were converted to ranks, and Wilcoxon matched-pairs signed-ranks tests were performed using school as the unit of analysis.[1] Despite the conservativeness of such an approach

(for this mode of analysis, $n$ is only 7), the Wilcoxon $T$ reflected a conventionally significant difference on the school-of-attendance measure ($T = 2$, $p < .05$, two-tailed). This result indicated, as predicted, that Mondays following football victories ranked significantly higher in school-of-attendance apparel wearing than Mondays following nonvictories.[2] The mean rank for victories was 3.2, while that for nonvictories was 4.9. A similar test for school-of-nonattendance apparel did not show any effect; the victory and nonvictory mean ranks for this measure were 3.4 and 3.7, respectively. This latter result suggests that the obtained effect on the school-of-attendance measure is not attributable to a simple tendency to wear clothing of a certain type (e.g., athletic team jackets, sweat shirts, tee shirts, etc.) after an athletic team victory.

## Discussion

In all, we found support for our expectations concerning the BIRG phenomenon. Students chose to display more apparel indicators of their academic affiliation after their university's varsity football team had recently been successful. It appears, then, from these data and from numerous anecdotal reports that people desire to make others aware of what seem to be their causally meaningless associations with positive sources.[3] Why? what do they intend to get from it? Perhaps, the answer has to

---

[1]In any conversion of parametric data to ranks, the possibility exists that the ranked scores will not fully reflect the character of the parametric data. In order to examine such a possibility with respect to our results, a correlational analysis was performed on the standardized index scores and their derived rank scores. A highly similar relationship ($r = -.83$) between the two forms of scores was found; the negativity of this correlation is simply due to the fact that the better ranks of those of lower numerical value.

[2]It may be instructive to note that the single exception from this pattern in Table 22.1 occurred at the University of Michigan as a direct result of a 10–10 tie with Ohio State University in a game for the Big Ten Conference Championship. Most observers, especially the Michigan supporters, felt that the Michigan team had outplayed Ohio State that day and that the game demonstrated Michigan's superiority. However, that tie game constituted Michigan's only entry in our nonwin resulting in the only reversal in our data.

[3]It might be argued that some subjects felt that their presence in the stands on the day of a game *directly* contributed to their team's success. This seems an unlikely explanation for the obtained results, as an analysis of the data of Experiment 1 showed an equally strong BIRG effect for home and away games.

**TABLE 22.1. Indexes of Relevant Apparel Wearnng at the Seven Monitored Universities**

| School | School-of-attendance apparel wearing | | | | School-of-nonattendance apparel wearing | | | |
|---|---|---|---|---|---|---|---|---|
| | Wins | | Nonwins | | Wins | | Nonwins | |
| Arizona State | .63 | (5) | .61 | (1) | .58 | (5) | .68 | (1) |
| Louisiana State | .80 | (5) | .33 | (3) | .58 | (5) | .51 | (3) |
| Ohio State | .69 | (4) | .30 | (1) | .56 | (4) | .94 | (1) |
| Notre Dame | .67 | (7) | .49 | (1) | .62 | (7) | .52 | (1) |
| Michigan | .52 | (5) | .83 | (1) | .20 | (5) | .00 | (1) |
| Pittsburgh | .76 | (4) | .27 | (2) | .31 | (4) | .50 | (2) |
| Southern California | .36 | (6) | .26 | (1) | .17 | (6) | .00 | (1) |
| M | .63 | | .44 | | .43 | | .45 | |

*Note.* Numbers in parentheses represent the number of games that fell into wins and nonwins categories for each school.

do with Heider's balance formulation (1958). Heider discussed two types of perceived relations between things: sentiment relations, which imply a feeling state between stimuli, and unit relations, which merely imply that things are connected in some manner. It is the unit relationship that seems akin to the noninstrumental connection that people tend to publicize between themselves and a successful or otherwise positive source. The results of the present experiment could well be seen as consistent with balance theory. For example, if observers perceive a positive unit relationship (e.g., university affiliation) between a student and a successful football team and if observers generally evaluate successful teams positively, then in order to keep their cognitive systems in balance, the observers would have to evaluate the student positively as well. Hence, we might expect the student to want to make the unit connection evident to as many observers as possible, in this case, through the wearing of university-identifying clothing. The process whereby one publicly seeks to associate himself or herself with a successful other, then, may be reinforced by the tendency of observers to respond in a similar fashion to associated stimuli.

Indirect evidence that tends to support this hypothesis comes from research concerning the transmission of positive and negative information. Manis, Cornell, and Moore (1974) have shown that one who transmits information that the recipient favors is liked more by the recipient than one who transmits information that the recipient disfavors. This liking occurred even though it was understood that the transmitters did not necessarily endorse the communicated information. Like the royal messengers of old Persia who were feted when they brought news of military victory but killed when they brought news of defeat, the transmitters in the Manis et al. (1974) study acquired the valence of the message with which they were simply paired. Moreover, there is evidence that people recognize this generalization effect and tend to take actions that connect them, in the eyes of observers, with positive rather than negative news. For example, Rosen and Tesser have repeatedly shown (e.g., Rosen & Tesser, 1970; Tesser, Rosen, & Batchelor, 1972; Teeser, Rosen, & Tesser, 1971) that people prefer to be connected with the communication of good news to another than with the communication of bad news. Investigating the basic effect, Johnson, Conlee, and Tesser (1974) found their subjects reluctant to communicate negative information not because they felt guilty about transmitting bad news but because they feared that they would be negatively evaluated by the recipient of such news; again, this was true even though all concerned knew that the communicators had in no way caused the bad news. Thus, it appears from these data that: first, individuals who are merely associated with a positive or negative stimulus (in this case, favorable or unfavorable information) will tend to share, in an observer's eyes, the affective quality of the stimulus; and second, at some level individuals seem to understand the workings of this phenomenon and make use of it in the ways they present themselves to others. We wish to interpret the results of Experiment 1 in terms of this formulation. Students at our seven monitored universities chose to wear school-of-attendance apparel after football team victories in order to *display* their connection with the successful team and thereby to enhance their esteem in the eyes of observers to the connection. However, another explanation of our findings exists as well. Perhaps the tendency to wear university-related clothing following team wins had nothing to do with an attempt to proclaim the favorable connection to others but only reflected an increased positivity toward the university as a consequence of team success. That is, it is possible that a football victory caused students to like their school more, and this heightened attraction manifested itself in the tendency to wear school-identified apparel. To test these alternative explanations and to establish the generality of the tendency to BIRG in a different experimental situation than that of Experiment 1, a second experiment was conducted.

## Experiment 2

The major distinction between the competing interpretations described above is the contention of the BIRG model that students wore school-of-attendance clothing after victories in order to publicize their university affiliations and hence increase their prestige in the view of *others*. The "heightened attraction" formulation makes no such claim: One is simply seen to like the school more following victories, and this, rather than the possibility of increased interpersonal prestige, is said to stimulate the wearing of relevant apparel. We decided to test these explanations by way of an examination of the pronoun usage of university students describing the outcome of one of their school's football contests. Earlier in this article we alluded to the tendency of athletic fans to crowd in front of television cameras, wave their index fingers high, and shout, "*We*'re number one!" The choice of this pronoun seemed to us a very good measure of the tendency to BIRG. By employing the pronoun *we*, one is publicly able to associate oneself with another person or group of persons. Through the use of some other designation, for example, *they*, one is able to distance oneself from (i.e., to weaken the perceived association with) another person or persons. It was our feeling that in order to BIRG a successful football team, students would be more likely to describe the outcome of a team victory using the pronoun *we* than they would a team nonvictory. Thus, it was our expectation that this tendency to connect oneself with a positive source but distance oneself from a negative source would influence subjects to use the term, "We won," to describe a team win but use the third person (e.g., "They lost") to describe a loss.[4] Further, in line with our BIRG model it was expected that this differential use of language would be most pronounced when the subject's esteem in the eyes of an observer had been recently lowered. That is, if we are correct in proposing that one proclaims a connection with a positive source in an attempt to raise one's esteem in the view of others, then one should be most likely to declare such a connection when that esteem has recently been jeopardized. Thus, if we were to create experimentally in subjects a need to bolster esteem in the eyes of an observer, subjects should be most likely to announce publicly (through use of the pronoun *we*) a connection with a successful team and be least likely to publicize a connection with an unsuccessful team. On the other hand, subjects who have less need to elevate an observer's evaluations of themselves should show a lesser effect. The simple "heightened attraction" model would not make such a prediction, since one's prestige in the eyes of others is not a critical variable in that formulation.

### Method

#### SUBJECTS

The subjects were 173 undergraduates at a large state university with a nationally ranked football team. Subjects were randomly selected from student listings in the university phone directory. The sample included approximately equal distribution of males and females.

#### PROCEDURE

During a 3-day period midway through the 1974 football season, subjects were contacted on the phone by one of 16 experimenters (eight males and eight females) identified as an employee of a "Regional Survey Center" with headquarters in an out-of-state city. The caller explained that he (she) was conducting a survey of college students'

---

[4]It should be evident to the reader that the general statement of the BIRG formation includes not only the tendency to bask in reflected glory but also the tendency to distance unattractive sources.

knowledge of campus issues and was in town that day calling students at the subject's university. Subjects agreeing to participate (93%) were then asked a series of six factually oriented forced-choice questions about aspects of campus life (e.g., "What percent of students at your school are married? Would you say it's closer to 20% or 35%?"). Following the subject's sixth response, the caller administered the first manipulation. Half of the subjects were told that they had done well on the test, and half were told that they had done poorly. Specifically, subjects were told:

> That completes the first part of the questions. The average student gets three out of six correct. You got [five; one] out of six correct. That means you [did really well; didn't do so well] compared to the average student.

Subjects were then told that there were a few more questions and that the first concerned students' knowledge of campus athletic events. At this point the second experimental manipulation occurred. Half of the subjects were asked to describe the outcome of a specific football game; their school's football team had won this game. The other half were asked to describe the outcome of a different game; this was a game that their team had lost. The question was phrased as follows:

> In the [first; third] game of the season, your school's football team played the University of [Houston, Missouri]. Can you tell me the outcome of that game?

If a subject did not know the results of the game, a new subject was called. Otherwise the subject's verbatim description of the game outcome was recorded. At the end of the interview, all subjects were fully debriefed.

## INDEPENDENT VARIABLES

Two factors were manipulated; a subject's personal outcome on the survey task (success or failure) and the affiliated football team's outcome in the game described (win or nonwin). These factors combined to produce a 2 × 2 factorial design.

## DEPENDENT VARIABLES

Subjects' tendency to use a *we* or *non-we* response in describing a team outcome constituted our dependent measure. Descriptions such as "We won," "We got beat," etc., were considered *we* responses.

All other descriptions (e.g., "The score was 14–6, Missouri." "They lost.") were classified as *non-we* responses.

## PREDICTIONS

Two predictions were made. First, it was hypothesized that subjects would emit more *we* responses in describing a team victory than a team defeat. Second, it was expected that the effect of Hypothesis 1 would be greatest for subjects who had "failed" the survey test. The latter hypothesis was based on the assumption that subjects in the personal failure conditions would attempt to associate themselves publicly with a positive event or distance themselves from a negative event through language usage in order to bolster or salvage their damaged image, in the eyes of the caller. Subjects in the personal success conditions were not expected to show a similar sized effect, as their prestige had already been ensured via their successful task performance. Evidence that public success and failure on an experimental task leads to differential tendencies for social approval has been offered by Schneider (1969). He manipulated success and failure and found failure subjects to present themselves more favorably to an observer who could provide an evaluation. Thus, if the BIRG phenomenon is indeed an attempt to gain social approval, we should see our failure subjects BIRG more than our success subjects.

## Results

Of the 173 subjects, the data of 5 were discarded because they clearly reported the game results incorrectly. For example, the description "We won" was not counted if in fact the subject's team had lost the game in question. The percentages of *we* responses emitted in the four experimental conditions are presented in Table 22.2. The first prediction, that *we* usage would be greater in the descriptions of team victories than team defeats, was tested by comparing the team win conditions against the team nonwin conditions. A significant effect was obtained, $\chi^2(1) = 4.20$, $p < .05$, confirming Hypothesis 1. The second prediction, that the tendency for *we* responses to attend victory rather than defeat descriptions would be strongest after a personal failure, was tested as an interaction of the two major independent variables. The resultant statistic, suggested by Langer and

**TABLE 22.2. Percentage of Subjects Using "We", Experiment 2**

| Team outcome | % Personal outcome | | Mean % |
| | Success | Failure | |
| --- | --- | --- | --- |
| Win | 24 (11/45) | 40 (16/40) | 32 (27/85) |
| Nonwin | 22 (9/41) | 14 (6/42) | 18 (15/83) |

Abelson (1972) for testing interactions within a 2 × 2 contingency table, just missed conventional significance levels, $Z = 1.75$, $p < .08$, two-tailed. Tests of the simple main effects of the interaction strongly supported Hypothesis 2. The difference in we responding between the team success and team failure cells of the personal failure condition was highly significant, $\chi^2(1) = 6.90$, $p < .01$. The comparable test within the personal success condition did not approach significance, $\chi^2(1) = .07$, *ns*. There were no significant sex effects in the data.

## Discussion

The data of Experiment 2 seem clearly to support the general BIRG formulation. Subjects used the pronoun *we* to associate themselves more with a positive than a negative source, and this effect was most pronounced when their public prestige was in jeopardy. We interpret these results as evidence for our contention that people display even the most noninstrumental connections between themselves and the success of others so as to receive positive evaluations from the observers of those connections.

It should be evident that the observer's tendency to assign positivity to one who is associated with positive things is crucial to our hypothesizing about the BIRG phenomenon. It follows from our previously stated assumption that if a person understood that a given observer did not value the success of a specific source, that person would be less likely to try to BIRG that source to the observer. So, if one of our subjects knew that an observer abhorred successful college athletic programs, we would predict that there would be little likelihood of the subject attempting to make visible a connection with a winning football team. But this is a fairly

obvious example; few people would predict otherwise. A more subtle and perhaps more informative demonstration might be obtained through a somewhat different manipulation of the observer's relationship to the connection. When an observer to a highly positive association can also lay claim to the association, the prestige of the connection is diffused and, consequently, reduced for anyone attempting to bask in its glory. It is when one's bond to a positive source is not shared by an audience that its prestige value is optimal. Thus, when everyone has a similar positive characteristic, there is no special prestige involved in possessing it, and the likelihood that any one person will boast about that quality should be reduced. For example, a resident of California is less likely to brag to fellow Californians about the favorable climate than to geographically distant others, especially those who cannot claim similarly pleasant weather. It is our hypothesis, then, that the tendency to BIRG a positive source should occur most often when one's connection with the source is stronger than the observer's.[5] A third study was conducted to test this contention.

## Experiment 3

In Experiment 2, it was shown that a personal failure experience increased our subjects' tendency to associate themselves with a positive source and decreased their tendency to associate themselves with a negative source. We have argued that this result occurred because the failure experience lowered perceived prestige and motivated subjects to try to either bolster their images in the eyes of others or prevent them from being further degraded. Central to this argument is the assumption that one's simple, noninstrumental connections are seen to influence observers' personal evaluations. If so, it should be the case that in addition to their use as dependent measures, such connections could be used as effective independent variables. That is, it should be possible to influence subjects' behavior

[5]We do not wish to suggest that the tendency to BIRG a positive source never takes place when the observer's association to a successful other is as strong as one's own but only that the prestige to be derived from a unique (vis-à-vis the observer) connection is relatively more desirable.

by publicly connecting them with either positive or negative events. In fact, if we are correct in our assumption, manipulating one's public connections with good or bad things should have the same effect as manipulating one's personal success or failure experiences. For example, just as Experiment 2 showed that subjects who failed a task increased the tendency to affiliate themselves with a winner and decreased the tendency to affiliate themselves with a loser in the eyes of an observer to their failure, it follows from our formulation that subjects who are merely publicly connected with a negative event should emit comparable BIRG responses in the presence of an observer to that connection. Experiment 3 was designed to test this possibility and represented a conceptual replication and extension of Experiment 2.

## Method

### SUBJECTS

The subjects were 170 undergraduates at a large state university with a powerful football team. The university was not the same as that of Experiment 2; however, subjects were selected for participation in a fashion identical to that of Experiment 2.

### PROCEDURE

Following the completion of play for the university's football team, subjects were called on the phone by 1 of 18 experimenters (11 males and 7 females) identified as an employee of either the "university's Survey Center" located on campus or the "Regional Survey Center" located in an out-of-state city. Subjects were told that a survey was being conducted of "undergraduates' knowledge of university athletic events." Those agreeing to participate (96%) were asked to describe the outcome of first one, then another of their football team's last games of the year. One of the games constituted an important victory, and the other an important nonvictory in the team's season. Half of the subjects were first requested to describe the nonvictory game and, having responded, to describe the victory game. The other subjects had the requests put to them in reverse order. The subjects' verbatim descriptions of the game results were recorded.

### INDEPENDENT VARIABLES

Two factors were orthogonally varied: the strength of the subject's affiliation to the university team compared with that of the observer (same as observer's or stronger than observer's) and order of presentation of the games to be described (victory game description requested first or nonvictory game description requested first).

### DEPENDABLE VARIABLES

The dependent measure was the pattern of *we* and *non-we* usage employed by subjects to describe the combination of the victory and nonvictory games. Three combinations were possible. A subject could have used the same *we* or *non-we* term to describe both the victory and the nonvictory, could have used *we* to describe the non-victory, and *non-we* to describe the victory, or finally, could have used *we* for a victory and *non-we* for a nonvictory.

### PREDICTIONS

It was predicted, first, that there would be an overall tendency for subjects to use *we* in their descriptions of a team victory and *non-we* in their descriptions of a team nonvictory. Such a finding would replicate the basic BIRG effect obtained in Studies 1 and 2. A second hypothesis was that the tendency to use *we* for victory and *non-we* for nonvictory descriptions would be greater in the nonvictory-description-requested-first conditions. Such a result would constitute a conceptual replication of the second finding of Experiment 2. On the basis of the BIRG model, we expected that the effect of publicly describing a negative event with which one is connected would be equivalent in nature to publicly failing on a task. Both operations were thought to reduce subjects perceptions of their prestige as seen by an observer and, hence, to increase the likelihood of subjects' attempts to ensure the positivity of subsequent evaluations. The third prediction was that Hypothesis 2 would hold most strongly when the observer was identified with an off-campus organization. This expectation was based on the belief that felt prestige to be gained from one's connections to a source is greater and, thus more sought after, when one's connections to that source are stronger than an observer's. Confirmation of this prediction would appear as an interaction of the independent variables of the study.[6]

## Results

As expected and consistent with the results of Experiments 1 and 2, the basic BIRG effect occurred in Experiment 3 to support our first hypothesis. That is, subjects used the term *we* nearly twice as often to describe a victory than a nonvictory (26% vs. 13.5%). This effect is further confirmed when the data are examined in terms of individual subjects' *we/non-we* usage patterns. The majority of subjects were constant in their pattern of responding to the two requests for descriptions; they consistently used either *we* or *non-we* to describe both game outcomes. Thus, there was a strong tendency for our subjects to be consistent in their verbal usage patterns for the two descriptions. However, in 23 instances subjects provided an inconsistent *we/non-we* pattern. In 22 of those instances, the pattern supported the BIRG model; the pronoun *we* was used for the victory description and a *non-we* term was used for the nonvictory description. Using McNemar's test for the significance of changes (Siegel, 1956, pp. 63–67) and correcting for continuity, the data are highly significant, $\chi^2(1) = 17.39$, $p < .001$. The tests of Hypotheses 2 and 3 were conducted by considering the distribution (across the cells of our design) of the instances of *we/non-we* usage fitting the pattern predicted by the BIRG model. Table 22.3 presents these data.

TABLE 22.3. Percentage of Subjects Using both "We" for Victory Descriptions and "Non-We" for Nonvictory Descriptions, Experiment 3

| | Order of request[a] | |
|---|---|---|
| Strength of subject's connection to team relative to observer's | Victory description requested first | Nonvictory description requested first |
| Stronger than observer's | 3 (1/39) | 21 (10/47) |
| Same as observer's | 11 (4/36) | 14 ( 7/48) |
| Mean % | 7 (5/75) | 18 (17/95) |

[a]Numbers given are percentages.

Hypothesis 2 stated that more subjects would use *we* to describe the victory and *non-we* to describe the nonvictory when they were asked to describe the nonvictory first. As expected, subjects were significantly more likely to so respond in the nonvictory-description-requested-first conditions, $\chi^2(1) = 4.69$, $p < .05$. Hypothesis 3 stated that Hypothesis 2 would hold most clearly when the subjects were more strongly connected with the university team than was the observer. As predicted, Hypothesis 2 was supported to a greater extent when the observer was affiliated with an off-campus rather than a campus agency. However, this tendency did not quite reach conventional levels of significance, $Z = 1.72$, $p < .085$. As in Experiment 2, there were no significant effects for sex of subject.

## General Discussion

Overall, Experiments 1, 2, and 3 provided strong support for the BIRG formulation. All three experiments showed a significant tendency for students to strive to associate themselves publicly with their university's football team more after the team had been successful. A striking aspect of the phenomenon is that subjects sought to proclaim their affiliation with a successful source even when they in no way caused the source's success. This component of the effect suggests a mediator consistent with balance theory. It is our contention that people make known their noninstrumental connections with positive sources because they understand that observers to these connections tend to evaluate connected objects similarly. It appears that the tendency to BIRG is an attempt to secure esteem

---

[6]The experimenters, undergraduate students in a laboratory social psychology course, were not fully aware of these predictions. In order to test the influence of conscious or unconscious experimenter bias on the results of this study, the experimenters were informed of the nature of Hypothesis 1. However, they were blind to the more subtle Hypotheses 2 and 3. If only Hypothesis 1 were confirmed, the data would likely have to be interpreted as potentially influenced by the experimenter bias artifact.

The investigation of such a possibility was deemed an important one, since in the prior experiments, experimenters had knowledge of the experimental hypothesis. In Experiment 1, some data recorders were unintentionally informed of the major hypothesis, while others were not. An analysis of the data from these two groups found only a minimal difference in the data patterns, with the uninformed group's data actually more favorable to prediction than the informed group. However, in Experiment 2, all experimenters had knowledge of the prediction.

from those who can perceive the connection. Studies 2 and 3 provided support for such an interpretation. Both showed that experimental operations designed to threaten a subject's esteem in the eyes of an observer caused subjects to be more likely to try publicly to associate themselves with positive sources. Intriguingly, it was possible to increase the tendency to BIRG in these experiments either by initially causing the subject to experience personal failure in an observer's eyes or by initially causing the subject to be noninstrumentally connected with a negative event in an observer's eyes. These manipulations proved functionally equivalent in modifying subject pronoun usage. Thus, in support of our basic argument, being merely associated with someone else's success and failure had much the same effect as personal success and failure. Experiment 3 provided evidence in a different way as well that the desire for prestige is the mediator of the BIRG response. It demonstrated that when subjects' affiliation with a positive source was stronger than an observer's (and therefore carried a greater amount of prestige), they were most likely to BIRG that source in the presence of the observer.

These studies suggest a way to understand how the fortunes of affiliated sports teams can cause lavish displays of civic gratitude and pride in American cities, or "sports riots" in Europe, or murders in South America of players and referees whose actions had caused a home-team defeat. Through their simple connections with sports teams, the personal images of fans are at stake when their teams take the field. The team's victories and defeats are reacted to as personal successes and failures.

Throughout this article we have stressed an interpersonal mediator of the BIRG phenomenon—the perceived esteem of others. We do not wish, however, to preclude the possibility of the tendency to BIRG privately. That is, for wholly intrapersonal reasons, people may draw connections between themselves and positive sources. For example, one may well feel an enhancement of self-esteem that is unrelated to the assessments of others when one is associated with success or positivity. Such an effect could also be interpreted in terms of a ten-

dency to respond similarly to associated objects. It might be that the results of our experiments are, in some degree at least, due to a desire to bolster or maintain one's self-concept. The tendency to employ appropriate apparel or language in a way that connects oneself to something good may involve an attempt to remind oneself of such connections and, thereby, positively affect self-esteem. The fact that in Experiment 2 we were able to influence the BIRG response simply by manipulating the characteristics of the observer suggests that the BIRG phenomenon is not mediated solely by intrapersonal phenomena. Nonetheless, it remains possible that the tendency to BIRG has its basis in a desire to affect self-image as well as social image. In fact, since there is evidence that how we regard ourselves is influenced by how we perceive that others regard us (e.g., Harvey, Kelley, & Shapiro, 1957), these two mediators are not mutually exclusive.

## REFERENCES

Harvey, O. J., Kelley, H. H., & Shapiro, M. M. (1957). Reactions to unfavorable evaluations of self made by other persons. *Journal of Personality, 25,* 393–411.

Heider, F. (1958). *The psychology of interpersonal relations.* New York: Wiley.

Johnson, R., Conlee, M., & Tesser, A. (1974). Effects of similarity of fate on bad news transmission: A reexamination. *Journal of Personality and Social Psychology, 29,* 644–648.

Langer, E. J., & Abelson, R. P. (1972). The semantics of asking a favor: How to succeed in getting help without really dying. *Journal of Personality and Social Psychology, 24,* 26–32.

Manis, M., Cornell, S. D., & Moore, J. C. (1974). Transmission of attitude-relevant information through a communication chain. *Journal of Personality and Social Psychology, 30,* 81–94.

Rosen, S., & Tesser, A. (1970). On the reluctance to communicate undesirable information. The MUM effect. *Sociometry, 33,* 253–263.

Schneider, D. J. (1969). Tactical self-presentation after success and failure. *Journal of Personality and Social Psychology, 13,* 262–268.

Siegel, S. (1956), *Nonparametric statistics for the behavioral sciences.* New York: McGraw-Hill.

Tesser, A., Rosen, S., & Batchelor, T. (1972). On the reluctance to communicate bad news (the MUM effect): A role play extension. *Journal of Personality, 40,* 88–103.

Tesser, A., Rosen, S., & Tesser, M. (1971). On the reluctance to communicate undesirable messages (the MUM effect): A field study. *Psychological Reports, 29,* 651–654.

# Toward a Self-Evaluation Maintenance Model of Social Behavior

Abraham Tesser • University of Georgia

This article describes some of the research that has kept me preoccupied over the last six to eight years. The research explores social behavior through something called a Self-Evaluation Maintenance (SEM) model. In the space alloted I briefly describe that model; describe several studies to provide a feel for the kind of research that has been completed in an attempt to explore the predictions of the model; and take a bird's eye view of the research and the model to establish the comprehensiveness of the research, the systemic nature of the model, and the interactive quality of its predictions. Next, the SEM model is fit into the perspective of related work including self-theories, social comparison theory, and Cialdini's BIRGing research. Then I review the epistemological status of the model. Here I hope to show that by focusing more on mediating processes there is something to be learned about emotion and affect. Finally, I conclude by pointing out some of the implications of the research for a variety of areas in psychology.

## The Self-Evaluation Maintenance Model

The SEM model assumes

1. persons behave in a manner that will maintain or increase self-evaluation
2. one's relationships with others have a substantial impact on self-evaluation. The SEM model is composed of two dynamic processes. Both the *reflection process* and the *comparison process* have as component variables the closeness of another and the quality of that other's performance. These two variables interact in affecting self-evaluation but do so in quite opposite ways in each of the processes.

One's self-evaluation may be raised to the extent that a close other performs very well on some activity, that is, one can bask in the reflected glory of the close other's good performance. For example, one can point out her close relationship with her friend "the concert pianist" and thereby increase her own self-evaluation. The better the other's performance and the closer the psychological relationship, the more one can gain in self-evaluation through the reflection process. The intellectual parent of the reflection process is Cialdini's work on BIRGing (Cialdini, Borden, Thorne, Walker, Freeman, & Sloan, 1976; Cialdini & Richardson, 1980).

The outstanding performance of a close other can, however, cause one's own performance to pale by comparison and decrease self-evaluation. Being close to a high-performing other invites comparison and results in one's own performance looking bad, thereby adversely affecting self-evaluation. Again, the better the other's performance and the closer the psychological relationship, the greater the loss in self-evaluation through the comparison process. The intellectual parent of the comparison process comes from social comparison theory (e.g., Festinger, 1954; Goethals, 1984; Suls & Miller, 1977) and is most closely compatible with Wills' (1981) idea of downward comparison.

In both the reflection process and the comparison process, if closeness or the level of the other's performance decreases, the effects of the reflection and comparison processes are attenuated or perhaps even reversed. For example, if the other person has little to do with oneself (i.e., is psychologically distant), one cannot bask in the reflected glory of his/her accomplishments nor is one as likely to engage in comparison processes. Psychological closeness is like unit relatedness (Heider, 1958): friends are closer than strangers, persons with more characteristics in common are closer than persons with fewer characteristics in common, and so on. (See Campbell & Tesser, 1985, for a more complete discussion of the closeness variable.) Similarly, if the performance of the other is mediocre, one cannot increase self-evaluation by reflection nor is one as likely to suffer decreases in self-evaluation by comparison.

It should be apparent from the description that both the reflection and comparison processes depend on the same two variables but have opposite effects on self-evaluation: when closeness and performance are high there is a potential gain in self-evaluation through the reflection process but there is a potential loss through the comparison process. That being the case, the question arises: when will a close other's outstanding performance raise self-evaluation (via reflection) or lower self-evaluation (via comparison)? To answer this question, the *relevance* variable is introduced.

Individuals can recognize, value, and attend to the performance of others on a large variety of dimensions. However, any individual has a personal stake in doing well on only a small subset of performance dimensions. For example, being a good football player may be important to an individual's self-definition, but being a good speller may be inconsequential. A dimension is important to an individual's self-definition to the extent that he strives for competence on the dimension, describes himself in terms of the dimension, or freely chooses to engage in tasks that are related to the dimension. Another's performance is *relevant* to an individual's self-definition to the extent that the performance is on a dimension that is important to the individual's self-definition and to the extent that the other's performance is not so much better or worse than the individual's own performance that comparisons are rendered difficult.

According to the SEM model the relevance of another's performance to one's self-definition determines the relative importance of the reflection and comparison process. If the other's performance is highly relevant, then the comparison process will be relatively important and one will suffer by comparison to the close other's better performance. If the other's performance is minimally relevant, the reflection process will be relatively important and one can enhance self-evaluation by basking in the reflected glory of a close other's better performance.

Perhaps the best way to illustrate the operation of the model is through an example. Suppose Alice and her good friend Barbara try out for the high school symphonic band and only Barbara is selected. Suppose further that doing well in music is an important part of Alice's self-definition. Relevance is high, so the comparison process should be more important than the reflection process: since Barbara is close and performs better than Alice, there is a potential loss in self-evaluation for Alice. To prevent this loss, Alice can do a variety of things. She can alter the closeness of her relationship with Barbara. She can spend less time around her or focus on ways in which the two of them are different. By reducing the closeness, the impact of Barbara's better performance is reduced. Alice can also change her self-definition. She can spend less time studying music or decide that butterfly collecting is much more interesting. By reducing the importance of music to her self-definition, the relevance of Barbara's performance is reduced. The reflection process becomes relatively more important with the consequence that Alice may actually gain in self-evaluation through her close friend Barbara's good performance. Finally, Alice can attempt to affect Barbara's performance. By reducing Barbara's performance she also reduces the threat of comparison. She can break Barbara's reed or hide her music for the next tryout or she can come to believe that Barbara's good performance was based on luck. Or, she can attempt to alter her own performance by practicing more.

## Some Research Examples

We have completed a number of studies now that tend to corroborate each of these strategies. Below I will review several of these studies to give you a feel for the kind of research that has been done. The studies look at changes in relative performance as a function of the relevance and closeness of the other person, changes in closeness as a function of the relevance and performance of the other, and changes in relevance or self-definition as a function of the other's closeness and performance.

### The Effects of Closeness and Relevance on Performance

AFFECTING ANOTHER'S PERFORMANCE

Suppose an individual is able to facilitate or hinder another's performance. Under what conditions will she facilitate the other's performance? Under what conditions will she hinder the other's performance? The SEM model suggests that the answers to these questions are conditional. That is, helping or hurting another depends on an interactive combination of the relevance of the performance dimension and the closeness of the other. When relevance is high the comparison process is more important than the reflection process. Thus, one will suffer by the other's good performance particularly if the other is close. Therefore, in order to avoid this threat to self-evaluation, when relevance is high the closer the other the less help one would expect the other to be given. On the other hand, when relevance is low, the reflection process is more important than the comparison process. One may bask in the reflection of the other's good performance, particularly if the other is close. In order to enjoy that reflection, then, when relevance is low the closer the other the more help should be given to the other.

To test this set of hypotheses, Jon Smith and I (Tesser & Smith, 1980) designed a laboratory experiment. Male subjects were recruited and asked to bring a friend to the lab with them. Each session was composed of two pairs of friends. The four subjects were individually seated in booths around the experimenter. They were told that they would participate in a verbal task. For half the subjects, the task was described as measuring important verbal skills, leadership, et cetera (high relevance). The remaining subjects were told that the task was not related to verbal intelligence or leadership or anything of importance that we could determine (low relevance). The task was actually based on the game *Password*. Each of the subjects, in turn, was given an opportunity to guess a target word from a set of clues. The clues ostensibly came from the other three participants who chose them from a list. Since the clues were graded in difficulty, the other participant could give clues that would make it easier or more difficult to guess the target word. The first two persons to guess the target word came from each of the two friendship pairs. By experimental arrangement, these two persons were made to perform poorly. It is the subsequent behavior of these two that we keep track of. If they want to help the other perform well (i.e., better than themselves), they could give clues that are easy; if they want to "hurt" the other (i.e., make him perform less well), they could give him difficult clues. The next two persons to perform were both friend and stranger to the former participants.

Common sense suggests (as well as a number of psychological theories) that one should help one's friend. However, the SEM model prediction is not that simple. When relevance is low and one can bask in the reflected glory of another's good performance, then, certainly one should help one's friend more than a stranger. However, this relationship should be attenuated and perhaps even reversed when relevance is high.

We looked at the number of experimental sessions in which the friend was helped more than the stranger and the number of sessions in which the stranger was helped more than the friend. The prediction from the SEM model was strongly upheld. When relevance was low the friend was helped more than the stranger in 10 of the 13 sessions. When relevance was high, the stranger was helped more than the friend in 10 of the 13 sessions.

Now I would like to turn to another laboratory study. This one, conducted with Jennifer Campbell (Tesser & Campbell, 1982), tested the same hypotheses. However, instead of examining a behavioral criterion, it examined cognitions or beliefs about the other's performance as a dependent variable. I think this study is particularly interesting because it has some very definite implications for psychological projection (e.g., Holmes, 1978; Sherwood, 1981). In most studies of projection, an individual is given information that he possesses an undesirable trait or attribute which he previously believed he did not possess. The extent to and conditions under which he attributes that trait to target others, that is, projects it, is then examined. From the present point of view, the feedback can be seen as a manipulation which lowers an individual's performance on a relevant dimension, thus increasing the target's relative performance. Given high relevance, the model predicts that individuals should tend to distort the target's performance downward (i.e., project the negative trait onto the target other). Further, the model predicts that this effect should be more pronounced given a psychologically close target than given a more distant target.

There is some evidence that such a pattern does occur with the projection of negative attributes (Secord, Backman, & Eachus, 1964; Bramel, 1963; Edlow & Kiesler, 1966). However, the obtained pattern can be explained by assuming that projection is a simple, nonmotivated information-processing strategy. If a person learns something new about himself, he will, to the extent that the other is similar, simply assume that it is also true of the other (Holmes, 1978). This "information-processing" interpretation can be made to confront the SEM interpretation. The information-processing model implies that projection should increase with closeness regardless of the valence of the feedback: if one learns something positive about himself, he should be just as likely to project that as something negative. Furthermore, the information-processing model is mute with respect to the relevance of the feedback for the individual's self-definition. The SEM model makes different predictions. First, it does not necessarily predict any general tendency to project more onto close versus distant targets. Projection should be conditioned by the relevance and valence of the feedback. More positive and less negative feedback (i.e., positivity) should be projected onto a close target when the feedback is on a low-relevance dimension than when it is on a high-relevance dimension. Further, this difference in positivity in projection should be attenuated for a distant target. To explore the information-processing and

self-evaluation maintenance explanations of social patterning in projection the following procedure was used.

Two pairs of female friends reported for each session. They were told that the study concerned personality and impression formation. Each subject was given an opportunity to describe herself to the others so that they might form impressions of one another. Then each of the participants was individually seated before a microcomputer which administered a number of items purportedly measuring social sensitivity and esthetic judgment ability. For each item, the subject was given two choices. After she chose what she thought was the correct answer and received feedback regarding that answer, she was asked to guess what answer her friend had given to the item or what answer one of the other participants, a stranger, had given to the item. The computer was programmed to provide feedback that the subject was right on half the items and wrong on half the items. Finally, subjects filled out a variety of questionnaires including items which measured the importance or relevance of social sensitivity and esthetic judgment to their own self-definition. In sum, each subject was given an opportunity to estimate the performance of a close (friend) or distant (stranger) other on both more or less relevant performance dimensions.

Recall the SEM prediction. Closeness and relevance should interact in affecting one's beliefs about the other's performance. When relevance is low one should be more charitable toward one's friend than toward a stranger. When relevance is high this effect should be attenuated, perhaps even reversed. Contrast this prediction with one which might be derived from a straightforward information-processing model. An information processing model might suggest that one simply projects one's own answers onto one's friend. Since one's friend is more similar to the self that would be the best guess one could make.

We looked first at projection (i.e., the number of answers that the subject said that the other gave that was similar to her own answers). There was not an overall difference as a function of closeness, as predicted by the information-processing model. Let us now consider positivity in perception, or the number of answers the subject guessed the other would get right. On this form of the dependent variable the SEM prediction is upheld. As can be seen in Figure 23.1, when the task is irrel-

*Lisa's friend study*

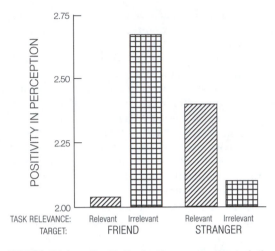

**FIGURE 23.1** ■ Positivity in the perception of the performance of friends (close others) and strangers (distant others) on tasks which are relevant or irrelevant to one's self-definition. From Abraham Tesser and Jennifer Campbell, Self-evaluation Maintenance and the Perception of Friends and Strangers. *The Journal of Personality, 50:3,* pp. 261–279. Copyright ©1982 by Duke University Press.

evant, subjects are more charitable toward the friend than toward the stranger. When the task is relevant, however, just the opposite is the case. Subjects are more charitable toward the stranger than toward the friend. Thus, the data appear to support the SEM model's predictions regarding defensive projection rather than predictions derived from the information-processing model.[1]

Some recent work on the false consensus effect (Marks & Miller, 1986; Ross, Green, & House, 1977) seems to support the "projection" aspects of these findings. According to the false consensus hypothesis people have a tendency to assume falsely that others will exhibit the same behaviors, attributes, and values as themselves. There has been a substantial amount of research on this bias and the general finding tends to substantiate the hypothesis (Mullen, Atkins, Champion, Edwards, Hardy, Story, & Vanderklok, 1985). However, the SEM model suggests that when it comes to performance, particularly performance on a relevant dimension, one should not see others as similar but rather as performing less well. In a recent theoretical review, Marks and Miller (1986) conclude that this is the case. For example, Gary Marks (1984) found that when dealing with performance dimensions or ability dimensions rather than a false

consensus effect, one obtains a false uniqueness effect. Jennifer Campbell (1986), in a very sophisticated analysis of the accuracy issue in projection and the false consensus effect, similarly found a false uniqueness effect when dealing with performance or ability dimensions. Further, this false uniqueness effect becomes even more pronounced as the performance dimension becomes more self-relevant. Finally, Suls and Wan (1987) found false uniqueness effects on estimates of fear when such estimates could bolster one's perceived self-competence. I think the cross-fertilization among these approaches (psychological projection, false consensus, and the SEM model) will turn out to be a good thing.

## AFFECTING OWN PERFORMANCE

If one conceptualizes performance in relative terms, then comparison and reflection processes can be affected not only by changing another's performance but by changing one's own performance as well. Let us focus first on relevant performance. When a close other's performance is relevant to one's self-identification there is a potential for one to suffer lowered self-evaluation via the comparison process. One way to reduce this potential is to increase one's own efforts (behavioral) or facilitatively distort the perception of one's own performance (cognitive).

There is some preliminary evidence consistent with both of these resolutions. Tesser, Campbell, and Campbell (reported in Tesser & Campbell, 1986) looked at own actual performance among high school students. Relevance of school was defined in terms of interest in having additional education. It follows from the model that, given high relevance of school:

1. The better another's performance, the more one will try and, hence, the better one's own performance.
2. This will be particularly true if the other is close (i.e., a friend).

---

[1]The SEM hypothesis can also be contrasted with a balance theory hypothesis (Heider, 1958). Since one likes or is in a unit relationship with a friend but not necessarily with a stranger, one should, according to balance theory, attribute good things to one's friend. As noted in the text, this general difference was not obtained. Only in the low-relevance condition was one more charitable to one's friend.

On the other hand, given low relevance:

3. The overall impact of others' performance on one's own should be attenuated.
4. The difference between friends and nonfriends should also be attenuated.

The effects of socioeconomic status, sex, and race were statistically removed from each respondent's own grade point average (GPA). Respondents were divided in terms of high or low interest in school. Within these groups, respondent's own "residualized" GPA was correlated with the GPA of a classmate that the respondent nominated as a friend and a classmate that the respondent did not nominate as a friend. The pattern of correlations conformed to theoretical expectations. The only correlation which was significantly more positive than zero is that among high-relevance respondents and their friends. When school is relevant, i.e., respondents want more education, the difference between the correlations for friends and nonfriends is significant. When school is not relevant, the corresponding difference in correlations is not significant. None of the other differences in correlation are significant.

There is also evidence for the distortion of one's own performance. Tesser, Campbell, and Smith (1984) compared performance ratings that fifth and sixth graders made of their own performance, on a relevant activity and on an irrelevant activity, with the ratings made by their teacher. If the teachers' ratings are interpreted as an "objective" benchmark then the students distorted their performance upward on the relevant activity and downward on the irrelevant activity.

Although these studies are consistent with the present viewpoint, they are correlational and there are a number of plausible alternative explanations of the results. What is needed is a more detailed theoretical analysis and more focused research. Generally, I would expect that performance which is important to one's self-definition is well practiced and actually difficult to improve. So it becomes important to specify the conditions under which threat from the comparison process will affect increased efforts to improve own performance. Since it is difficult to improve performance, attempts at actual improvement should be more likely when another's performance is unambiguously better than one's own performance (and difficult to distort) and it is difficult or costly to re-

duce the level of that close other's performance. Further, if one believes that effort will result in better performance, then increased task effort might be more likely as a result of the threat of comparison.

The good performance of a close other could result in increasing own effort because the other's performance is "inspirational." That is, the good performance of a close other may redefine the possibilities for the self: "If he/she can do it so can I." My guess is that the inspirational effect is most likely when the close other has not outperformed the self in the past and/or the other's better performance relies on a new (to the self) instrumentality. Both conditions define a *possibility* for self-improvement: in the first instance, when someone who has not been better than the actor becomes better than the actor it may suggest that the actor can also improve. The introduction of a new instrumentality, the second condition, also suggests that the actor can improve himself, this time by doing things differently.

To this point we have focused on the conditions under which persons may attempt to increase their own efforts to make their performance better. The SEM model suggests that there are also circumstances under which one may actually perform at a less-than-optimal level. In dealing with the maximization of own performance we focused on the comparison process of the SEM model. People can maintain a positive self-evaluation by the reflection process as well. One can bask in the reflected glory of a close other's outstanding performance if that performance has little relevance to one's self-definition. One way of making another's performance look good is to make one's own (relative) performance look bad. This leads to the prediction that when the performance of another is low in relevance to the self the closer the other the greater the possibility that one will actually perform poorer than he/she would when that other's performance is self-relevant.

Since there is a general tendency for people to want to do well, the prediction of self-handicapping may not seem plausible. Therefore, qualifications of this prediction may be in order. For example, from an intuitive perspective the relevance of the activity to the other person should play a role. If the performance is highly relevant to the other (but low in relevance to the self), there is an added inducement to handicap one's own performance. Under high relevance to the other, one's own poorer performances provide something for the other. That is, while the self is basking in the other's (relative) accomplishment, the other is not threatened by comparison. The closer the relationship with the other person is the greater the impact of relevance-to-other on self's own performance.

Clearly, this line of thinking is speculative. A better understanding of the determinant of own effort on own self-handicapping is important from both a practical and a theoretical perspective. It would seem then that this would be a productive line of research to pursue.

## The Effects of Relevance and Performance on Closeness

Now we focus on some research dealing with the effects of relevance and performance on closeness. How should relevance, or self-definition, interact with another's performance to affect closeness? Let's go back to the basic dynamics of the SEM model to make a prediction. When relevance is high the comparison process is more important than the reflection process and one will suffer by the other's good performance, particularly if the other is close. In order to avoid this potential threat to self-evaluation we would expect that when relevance is high the better the other's performance the less close or the more distance one will put between one's self and the other. On the other hand, when relevance is low and the reflection process is important there is the possibility of basking in the reflected glory of another's good performance, particularly if that other is close. Therefore, in order to experience that potential gain, when relevance is low, the better the other's performance the closer one should put oneself to another.

To test this hypothesis, we (Pleban & Tesser, 1981) returned to the laboratory. When our male subjects showed up they found one other subject already there. Both participants filled out a questionnaire which asked them to indicate how important various areas were to their self-definition. The areas consisted of things like rock music, current events, hunting and fishing, and so on. After finishing the questionnaire, the two subjects competed in a kind of college bowl competition. The experimenter, on a random basis, selected a topic that was either high or low in relevance to the subject's self-definition. The other subject, actually a confederate, had previously memorized the

answers to all the questions. When the questioning began, the confederate varied his performance so that he either clearly outperformed the real subject, performed about the same, or was outperformed by the real subject. Following the question-and-answer period the subjects were given feedback about how they did. The subject learned that he had performed about average, near the 50th centile. The subject also learned that the confederate was clearly better (performing at the 80th percentile), slightly better (performing at the 60th percentile), slightly worse (performing at the 40th percentile), or much worse (performing at the 20th percentile). Thus, we had manipulated relevance to the subject's self-definition and the relative performance of the other.

In order to measure closeness, we asked the subjects to go into an adjoining room. The confederate sat down first and we simply measured how close or far the subject sat from the confederate. After they were seated, a questionnaire containing alternative, paper and pencil, measures of closeness was administered. Recall our expectations: when relevance is high, the better the other's performance the less close the subject should put himself to the other. When relevance is low, the better the other's performance the closer the subject should put himself to the other.

It should be noted at the outset that level of performance made no difference when the subject outperformed the confederate. However, when the confederate outperformed the subject, each of the expectations from the SEM model was sustained. Let us look first at the behavioral index (see Figure 23.2), the distance the individual sat from the confederate. As can be seen, as the confederate's performance improved from the 60th percentile to the 80th percentile, the subject's distance increased when the topic was one of high relevance; the subject's distance decreased or closeness increased when the topic was of low relevance. Similar effects were obtained with the behavioroid index (Aronson & Carlsmith, 1968), "Would you want to work with this (confederate) again?" and with the cognitive index, "How much are you and this confederate alike?" There were no reliable effects on the affect index, "How attracted are you to this confederate?" Taken together these results offer some nice support for the hypotheses and also suggest that the closeness variable be defined in unit-formation terms rather than affect terms. Both the behavioral and the cognitive indices of close-

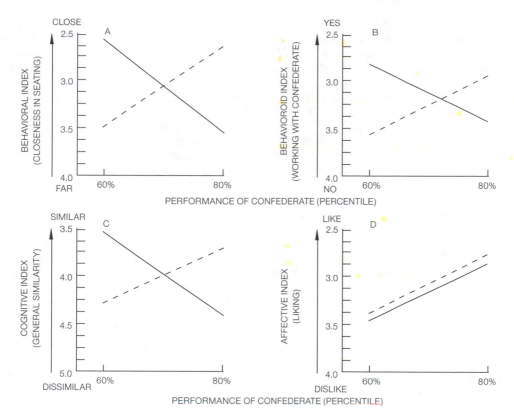

**FIGURE 23.2** ■ The effects of relative performance and relevance on closeness to other as indexed by behavioral, behavioroid, cognitive, and affective indices. Solid lines indicate high relevance; broken lines indicate low relevance. From Pleban and Tesser (1981).

ness showed the predicted effect, while the affective index did not.

Before we take this conclusion too seriously, however, I would like to describe a study by Toni Giuliano and Dan Wegner (personal communication, May, 1985). The study was done for another purpose but seems to have some clear implications for the self-evaluation maintenance model and its predictions about closeness. The model predicts that we should be close to others who do not outperform us on things that are self-definitional and thereby do not threaten us by comparison, but do outperform us on things that are not self-definitional so that we can bask in their reflected glory. Giuliano and Wegner gave 50 couples a list of topics, including things like restaurants, movies, money and business, phone numbers, famous sculptures, and so on. For each topic, each member of the couple had to indicate which of them was an expert, that they were both experts, or that neither was an expert. Let us assume that areas in

which one claims expertise are more relevant than areas in which one does not claim expertise. If one's partner acknowledges one's expertise there is no threat by comparison as a result of closeness. Further, to acknowledge another's expertise in an area in which one does not claim personal expertise (low relevance) is to provide for the opportunity to bask in the reflected glory of that other, particularly if the other is close.

Giuliano and Wegner computed what they call a differentiation score (i.e., the number of items on which one member of the couple claims expertise and the other member corroborates that claim). The SEM model leads us to expect that the greater the number of such items; that is, the higher the differentiation score, the closer the couple. Giuliano and Wegner correlated the differentiation score with the couple's rated satisfaction with the relationship. The correlation was in the predicted direction and it was substantial, $r = .60$.

Although there are undoubtedly alternative ex-

*Close Relationships*

✗

planations, the Giuliano and Wegner data seem to be consistent with the SEM model. They are also consistent with the notion of complementarity in interpersonal attraction. Couples that show a large number of areas in which there are acknowledged *differences* in expertise are more satisfied with the relationship. The prominent finding in the interpersonal attraction literature is that persons who are *similar* to one another tend to be more satisfied (e.g., Byrne, 1969). Elsewhere (Campbell & Tesser, 1985; Tesser, 1984) we have argued that much of the evidence for similarity leading to attraction concerns similarity on what might be called emotional dimensions. That is, values, opinions, and the like. As noted above, patterns of complementarity or uniqueness are more likely to be associated with closeness on things like ability domains or performance domains.

*Explain husbands/ wives who work together*

## The Effects of Performance and Closeness on Relevance

Now let us turn to some examples of research on the determinants of self-definition or the relevance parameter. Again, the model makes some very specific predictions. Recall that the relevance parameter directly weights the comparison process and inversely weights the reflection process. Thus, the relevance of an activity increases the importance of the comparison process relative to the reflection process. When another's performance is better than one's own, one should reduce the relevance of that performance dimension. This would permit one to bask in reflected glory rather than suffer by comparison. Further, one's tendency to reduce relevance should be greater the closer the other person. In short, the better another's performance in an activity the less relevant should that activity be to one's self-definition, particularly if the other person is close.

The study to be described here has both behavioral and cognitive measures of relevance or self-definition. The laboratory study was completed in collaboration with Del Paulhus (Tesser & Paulhus, 1983). Pairs of male subjects were told that the experiment concerned the validation of a personality inventory. Half the subjects were led to believe that the two of them were scheduled at the same time because they were very much alike in a number of different ways (the close condition). The remaining subjects were led to believe that they were scheduled at the same time because they were

very different from one another (the distant condition). The subjects were then seated before a microcomputer and worked on a task which they were told measured cognitive–perceptual integration. After working on the task for some time, they were given feedback. Subjects learned that they had outperformed the other subject or that the other subject had outperformed them at cognitive–perceptual integration. Thus, we had manipulated closeness and performance. (The study was actually more involved than this and dealt with the issue of public versus private self-evaluation maintenance. This issue, however, is beyond the scope of this article. See Tesser & Barbee, 1985; Tesser & Moore, 1987; and Tesser & Paulhus, 1983, for discussion.) There were three measures of relevance: an interview measure in which the subjects were asked how important cognitive–perceptual integration was to them; a questionnaire measure, again asking how important cognitive–perceptual integration was; and a behavioral measure. The behavioral measure involved surreptitiously observing the amount of time the subjects spent reading biographies of persons they believed were high in cognitive–perceptual integration versus low in cognitive–perceptual integration.

Each of the measures produced the same pattern of results. They were therefore combined and are displayed in Figure 23.3. Recall our prediction: the better another does relative to the self, the less relevant should be the performance dimension, particularly when that other is close. This is precisely the pattern that was found and the interaction is significant.

Now we leave the laboratory and look at data from a "real world" setting, that of the family. These data have been collected by William Owens, who has over the last several years collected biographical data on a large number of undergraduates at the University of Georgia (e.g., Owens & Schoenfeldt, 1979). One of the questions that he has asked these freshmen is "During the time you spent at home, how successful were your brothers and/or sisters in such things as popularity, skills, possessions, and appearance?" They were able to respond, "The other was more successful," "We were equally successful," or "I was more successful." Thus, there was a measure of relative performance among siblings. But what about a measure of closeness? Certainly siblings are close. While this is true, we (Tesser, 1980) took difference in age as an index of relative closeness. That is, we

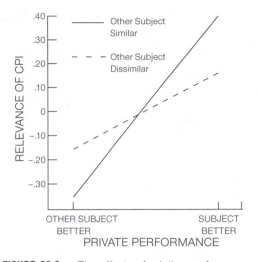

**FIGURE 23.3** ■ The effects of relative performance on cognitive–perceptual integration (CPI) and similarity (i.e., closeness) of other on the relevance of CPI to one's self-definition. Relevance is averaged over behavioral, interview, and questionnaire measures. From "The definition of self: Private and public self-evaluation management strategies" by A. Tesser and D. Paulhus, 1983, *Journal of Personality and Social Psychology, 44,* 672–682. Copyright 1983 by the American Psychological Association. Adapted by permission.

assumed that siblings separated by less than three years of age were closer than siblings separated by more than three years of age. Now we had measures of relative performance and closeness. What about relevance? Recall that relevance has to do with self-identity. Fortunately, Owens included a couple of items which dealt with identification with the sibling: "How much were you like your brother or sister in skills and ability . . . ways of acting in social situations?" Now we had, if not direct measures, at least proxies for each of the items we needed to test the hypothesis. We are interested in the interactive effects of closeness and performance on relevance or, in this case, identification with the sibling.

We focused only on the respondents from two sibling families. The data displayed in Figure 23.4 are the effect of closeness. That is, a positive number means more identification when the sibling is close (less than three years apart in age) than when the sibling is distant (more than three years apart in age). A negative number means less identification when the sibling is close than when the sibling is distant.

There were no effects for females.[2] It is the data for males that are displayed, and these data are quite consistent with the model. When the respondent believes he is outperformed by his sibling, then the closer (in age) the sibling the less the identification with the sibling. On the other hand, when the respondent believes he outperforms his sibling this closeness effect is reversed: greater closeness (in age) leads to greater identification. Thus, the model appears to have some nontrivial implications for self-identity and for intrafamily relationships.

The implications of the SEM model for family relationships have only begun to be explored. For example, there has been some discussion of the use and development of SEM processes in a family context (Tesser, 1984). And there are some preliminary, archival data bearing on the dynamics of father–son relationships (Tesser, 1980, Study 3). In spite of these beginnings, however, some of the fascinating and fundamental questions about the applicability of comparison and reflection processes in parent–child relationships have yet to be dealt with in any definitive way. [. . .]

## The Model in Perspective

To this point I have given a broad-brush description of the SEM and reviewed a sample of the available evidence to evaluate it. The SEM model draws on a number of research traditions in psychology and sociology. The model is generally related to what might loosely be called self-theory. Its more specific antecedents include social comparison

---

[2]Although SEM predictions have been supported in several studies including females, on the few occasions on which gender effects have been found the SEM effects have been stronger for males than for females. This may mean a variety of things. Perhaps the tasks used had differential relevance for males and females; perhaps the comparison process (competition) is less important for females than for males (Bond & Vinacke, 1961; Gilligan, 1982). It is worth noting in this context that the differences between males and females may also characterize differences between cultures which may make the model more or less applicable. For example, when the comparison process is presumed to be important, the formulation may work best for people with a desire to enhance their self-evaluation *individualistically,* such as Western or even American society. Societies with a more collectivist orientation, in which individual value is presumably less prized (such as Soviet Russia in theory), might not show the same kind of effects.

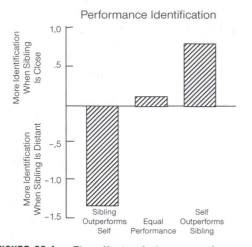

**FIGURE 23.4 ■** The effects of closeness of age and perceived relative performance of sibling on performance identification with sibling. Data for male subjects only. Data from "Self-esteem maintenance in family dynamics" by A. Tesser, 1980, *Journal of Personality and Social Psychology, 39*, 77–91. Copyright 1980 by the American Psychological Association. Adapted by permission.

theory and Cialdini's research and theorizing on "BIRGing" phenomena. Below I deal with each of these.

## Self-Theory

The self-evaluation model has at its core the assumption that persons behave so as to maintain a positive self-evaluation. Such a notion is not new. William James (1907) discussed it at the turn of the century. While most contemporary psychologists agree that persons tend to see themselves in a positive light (cf. Greenwald, 1980; Taylor & Brown, 1986), whether such positive self-perception is motivated or a cold information-processing strategy is still debatable. Thus, some investigators see self-serving attribution biases as motivated (Bowerman, 1978; Bradley, 1978; Zuckerman, 1979) while others see them as the result of information-processing strategies and biases (Nisbett & Ross, 1980; Miller & Ross, 1975). There is even an emerging literature to suggest that self-serving biases/distortions may be associated with positive mental health (Taylor & Brown, 1986). For example, compared to normals, mildly depressed/low self-esteem individuals are less vulnerable to an illusion of control (e.g.,

Greenberg & Alloy, 1987) and more accurate (and less optimistic) in estimating future task performance (e.g., Campbell & Fairey, 1985). This is not to say that even nondepressed/high self-esteem persons do not have some negative self-conceptions (e.g., shy, fat; Wurf & Markus, 1983, 1986). The general thrust, however, is toward positivity. Obviously maintenance of positive self-evaluation is central to the SEM model and, therefore, so are these issues.

The relevance parameter of the model deals specifically with the substance of one's self-definition and there are a number of self-theories that address this question as well (cf. Gordon & Gergen, 1968). McGuire (e.g., McGuire, 1987; McGuire, Child, & Fujioka, 1978; McGuire & Padawer-Singer, 1976) has noted that psychological investigations of self-concept have focused very narrowly on self-evaluation or self-esteem. However, when persons are allowed to choose the dimensions that are salient or significant to them, fewer than 10% of their choices deal with self-evaluative dimensions (McGuire & Padawer-Singer, 1976). Although self-evaluation dimensions per se may constitute only a small fraction of spontaneous choices, the large majority of the dimensions chosen are subject to evaluation. For example, attributes such as actor, jogger, bridge player, gardener, expert on baseball, and mother are not in themselves self-evaluative, but performance on these attributes is certainly subject to evaluation. The SEM model suggests that the relevance of these "nonevaluative" attributes for one's self-definition is determined to a large extent by attempts to maintain a positive self-evaluation.

Hazel Markus (1977) has suggested that the substance of one's self inheres in relatively enduring self-schemas. These schemas serve to make pertinent areas of the individual's functioning more salient, easier to remember, and easier to organize. Persons who are self-schematic with respect to a particular attribute in Markus's terms are, in the terminology of the present model, persons for whom that attribute is relevant.[3] Thus, the two bodies of research appear to be complementary.

---

[3] In the present approach relevant dimensions are dimensions on which persons strive for excellence. According to Markus, people can have self-schemas on nonperformance dimensions—some people have a fat self-schema (Markus, Sentis, & Hammill, 1979). Even here, however, it is possible to think of someone striving to become thin.

Markus's work details the effects of relevance on information processing (e.g., Markus & Wurf, 1987) and the present work makes some suggestions about the conditions under which self-schemata will change.

From a symbolic interactionist position (Mead, 1934), the self emerges from social interaction (Stryker & Statham, 1985). Thus, Cooley (1902) developed the notion of the looking-glass self. One's view of one's self comes from what one imagines others think of him/her. The present thesis also suggests that others play a crucial role in determining the substance of self but that the actor himself is a more active ingredient in the genesis of imagined (and real) consensus. I have already detailed how others' closeness and performance affect one's self-view. Perhaps the interpersonal aspects of these dynamics lead persons to share the same view of one another. That is, it is to each actor's advantage, especially if they are in a close relationship, to agree on how they see one another. It is to Actor A's advantage to see Actor B as the kind of person who is good at "X" if Actor A is good at "Y," just as it is to Actor B's advantage to see himself as good at "X" if Actor A is good at "Y." By doing this both can take joy in and promote the accomplishments of the other without being threatened by those accomplishments. Thus, one might speculate that persons negotiate their self-identity with those around them (Secord & Backman, 1965; Swann, 1983; Swann & Predmore, 1985). The result of such a process would be a kind of bargain in which the participants agree on a set of complementary identities. The agreement would serve to validate one another's view of self while enhancing one's own view of self.

## Social Comparison Theory

[. . .] Social comparison theory is predicated on the notion that persons want to understand their world. They come together, communicate, and influence one another to gain cognitive clarity, to validate their opinions and to evaluate their skills. The theory does prominently include the notion that there is a unidirectional drive upward with respect to abilities, and a number of subsequent workers have focused on the role of self-evaluation maintenance (e.g., Gruder, 1977; Hakmiller, 1966; Thornton & Arrowood, 1966; Wheeler, 1966; Friend & Gilbert, 1973; Wills, 1981, 1985;

Wood, Taylor, & Lichtman, 1985). However, the emphasis of the original theory is clearly on gaining cognitive clarity rather than on self-enhancement. In contrast, the present approach starts at the point at which the person already knows how to evaluate his abilities (and opinions) and deals with the consequences of such knowledge.[4] The motivational emphasis is not on reducing uncertainty but rather on maintaining or enhancing self-evaluation.

Much of the classical research generated by the theory of social comparison processes is only tangentially relevant to the present formulation. The rank-order choice experimental paradigm is an example. In this paradigm, an individual is given feedback (i.e., a score on a particular attribute) and is then asked which other scores in the distribution he would like to examine. A typical finding with this paradigm is that subjects tend to want to see scores of others slightly higher than themselves (e.g., Wheeler, 1966). These findings can be interpreted as supporting both cognitive clarity and self-evaluation maintenance motives (e.g., Gruder, 1977). However, desire for private information about score distributions is not equivalent to affecting the public psychological distance to another. Indeed, these two variables behave quite differently (Wheeler, Shaver, Jones, Goethals, Cooper, Robinson, Bruou, & Butzine, 1969; Wilson & Benner, 1971). The latter is more nearly what is meant by closeness in the present model. Furthermore, none of the studies, to this writer's knowledge, varies the relevance of the performance dimension. Thus, interpretation of the outcomes in terms of the SEM model is only possible if one is willing to make some assumption about relevance. The rank-order choice paradigm is typical of the kind of research generated by social comparison theory. [. . .]

The models are also quite different in their specifics. The "comparison component" of the SEM model comes formally closest to social comparison theory. Recall, however, that the comparison component is only half of the SEM model. The SEM model also includes a "reflection compo-

---

[4]Brickman and his colleagues (Brickman & Bulman, 1977; Perloff & Brickman, 1980) have dealt with social comparison-like situations in which persons know where they stand with respect to some ability. The questions they raise and sensitively deal with are as follows: When will an individual avoid or seek comparison? When will he display or withhold information about his own performance?

nent," the notion that persons can gain in self-evaluation by being close to a high-performing other on a low-relevance dimension. There is no analogous component in the theory of social comparison processes.

## Cialdini's BIRGing Research

The reflection component of the model comes closest to Cialdini's research on "Basking in Reflected Glory," or BIRGing (Cialdini et al., 1976). Cialdini and his co-workers have found that persons tend to put themselves into close association with "winners." For example, college students are more likely to wear clothing that identifies their own school following a winning football weekend than following a losing football weekend. Students are more likely to use the pronoun "we" when describing a football game that their school team won than when describing a football game that their school lost. Furthermore, the latter tendency is more pronounced after the students have undergone a failure experience than after they have undergone a success experience. This finding suggests that BIRGing is in the service of self-evaluation maintenance.

Cialdini and Richardson (1980) explain BIRGing in terms of Heider's (1958) balance theory. The argument is that if a person is in a positive unit relation with a positively evaluated entity, then balance forces will lead the person to be positively evaluated. As a further test of this explanation, they reasoned that if a person is in a negative relation with another entity, to the extent that the entity was negatively evaluated, balance forces would cause the person to be positively evaluated. In an experiment designed to test this idea subjects were given either a success or failure experience and were then given an opportunity to rate (compliment or "blast") their own university (positive association) or a rival university (negative association). Consistent with the balance theory prediction, the tendency to compliment one's own university and blast the rival university increased with prior threat to self-evaluation.

The BIRGing research and theorizing is quite consistent with the SEM model. However, the BIRGing research is more generally interpreted in terms of self-presentation rather than private self-evaluation. Further, there is no relevance parameter in the BIRGing approach and it deals only with the reflection half of the SEM model. On the basis of the research reviewed here, I would argue that a more complete picture must include both reflection and comparison processes and a way of weighting these processes, i.e., a relevance parameter. [. . .]

## Conclusion

It should be clear that the SEM approach has implications for a variety of areas of concern to psychologists. It has implications for prosocial behavior, the helping and hurting of others to affect their performance. It has implications for one's own personal performance as well. There are implications for interpersonal relationships, attraction, unit formation, and the like (See Campbell & Tesser, 1985, for discussion). It also raises some developmental questions: What is the origin of the self-evaluation maintenance processes? How do they play themselves out in families? (See Tesser, 1984, for discussion.) Lowered self-evaluation and negative affect are the hallmarks of depression. The SEM model provides a social psychological perspective for understanding these symptoms. Each of these implications is worth pursuing, but they are beyond the present discussion.

### REFERENCES

Aronson, E., & J. M. Carlsmith. (1968). Experimentation in social psychology. In G. Lindzey & E. Aronson (Eds.), *Handbook of social psychology, social edition* (Vol. 2). Reading, MA: Addison-Wesley.

Bond, J. R., & Vinacke, W. E. (1961). Coalitions in mixed-sex triads. *Sociometry, 24,* 61–75.

Bowerman, W. R. (1978). Subjective competence: The structure, process and functions of self-referent causal attributions. *Journal of the Theory of Social Behavior, 8,* 45–75.

Bramel, D. (1963). Selection of target for defensive projection. *Journal of Abnormal and Social Psychology, 66,* 318–324.

Byrne, D. (1969). Attitudes and attraction. In L. Berkowitz (Ed.), *Advances in experimental social psychology* (Vol. 4) (pp. 36–90). New York: Academic Press.

Campbell, J. D. (1986). Similarity and uniqueness: The effects of attribute type, relevance, and individual differences in self-esteem and depression. *Journal of Personality and Social Psychology, 50,* 281–294.

Campbell, J. D., & Fairey, P. J. (1985). Effects of self-esteem, hypothetical explanations, and verbalization of expectancies on future performance. *Journal of Personality and Social Psychology, 48,* 1097–1111.

Campbell, J. D., & Tesser, A. (1985), Self evaluation maintenance processes in relationships. In S. Duck & D. Perlman (Eds.), *Personal Relationships* (Vol. 1). London: Sage.

Cialdini, R. B., Borden, R. J., Thorne, A., Walker, M. R., Freeman, S., & Sloan, L. R. (1976). Basking in reflected glory: Three (football) field studies. *Journal of Personality and Social Psychology, 34,* 366–375.

Cialdini, R. B., & Richardson, K. D. (1980). Two indirect tactics of image management: Basking and blasting. *Journal of Personality and Social Psychology, 39,* 406–415.

Cooley, C. H. (1902). *Human nature and the social order.* New York: Scribner.

Edlow, D. W., & Kiesler, C. A. (1966). Ease of denial and defensive projection. *Journal of Experimental Social Psychology, 2,* 56–59.

Festinger, L. (1954). A theory of social comparison processes. *Human Relations, 7,* 117–140.

Friend, R. M., & Gilbert, J. (1973). Threat and fear of negative evaluation as determinants of locus of social comparison. *Journal of Personality, 41,* 328–340.

Gilligan, C. (1982). *In a different voice.* Cambridge, MA: Harvard University Press.

Goethals, G. B. (1984). *Social comparison theory: Psychology from the lost and found.* Paper presented at the American Psychological Association, Toronto.

Gordon, C., & Gergen, K. J. (1968). (Eds.), *The self in social interaction* (Vol. 1). New York: Wiley.

Greenberg, M. S., & Alloy, L. B. (1987). Depression versus anxiety: Differences in self and other schemata. In L. B. Alloy (Ed.), *Cognitive processes in depression.* New York: Guilford.

Greenwald, A. G. (1980). The totalitarian ego: Fabrication and revision of personal history. *American Psychologist, 35,* 603–618.

Gruder, C. L. (1977). Choice of comparison persons in evaluating one's self. In J. Suls & R. L. Miller (Eds.), *Social comparison process: Theoretical and empirical perspectives.* Washington, DC: Hemisphere.

Hakmiller, K. L. (1966). Threat as a determinant of downward comparison. *Journal of Experimental Social Psychology, 2* (Suppl. 1), 32–39.

Heider, F. (1958). *The psychology of interpersonal relations.* New York: Wiley.

Holmes, D. S. (1978). Projection as a defense mechanism. *Psychological Bulletin, 85,* 677–688.

James, W. (1907). *The principles of psychology* (Vol. 1). New York: Holt.

Marks, G. (1984). Thinking one's abilities are unique and one's opinions are common. *Personality and Social Psychology Bulletin, 10,* 203–208.

Marks, G., & Miller, N. (1986). Ten years of research on the "False Consensus Effect": An empirical and theoretical review. *Psychological Bulletin, 102,* 72–90.

Markus, H. (1977). Self-schemata and processing information about the self. *Journal of Personality and Social Psychology, 35,* 63–78.

Markus, H., Sentis, K., & Hamill, R. (1979). *Thinking fat: Self-schemas for body weight and the processing of weight relevant information.* Unpublished manuscript, University of Michigan.

Markus, H., & Wurf, E. (1987). The dynamic self-concept: A social psychological perspective. *Annual Review of Psychology, 38,* 300–333.

McGuire, W. J. (1987). Content and process in the experience of self. In L. Berkowitz (Ed.), *Advances in experimental social psychology* (Vol. 20). New York: Academic Press.

McGuire, W. J., McGuire, C. V., Child, P., & Fujioka, T. (1978). Salience of ethnicity in the spontaneous self-concept as a function of one's ethnic distinctiveness in the social environment. *Journal of Personality and Social Psychology, 36,* 511–520.

McGuire, W. J., & Padawer-Singer, A. (1976). Trait salience in the spontaneous self-concept. *Journal of Personality and Social Psychology, 33,* 743–754.

Mead, G. H. (1934). *Mind, self and society.* Chicago: University of Chicago Press.

Miller, D. T., & Ross, M. (1975). Self-serving biases in the attribution of causality: Fact or fiction? *Psychological Bulletin, 82,* 213–225.

Mullen, B., Atkins, J. L., Champion, D. S., Edwards, C., Hardy, D., Story, J. E., & Vanderklok, M. (1985). The false consensus of 155 hypothesis tests: A metananalysis. *Journal of Experimental Social Psychology, 22,* 262–283.

Nisbett, R., & Ross, L. (1980). *Human inferences: Strategies and shortcomings of social judgment.* Englewood Cliffs, NJ: Prentice-Hall.

Owens, W. A., & Schoenfeldt, L. F. (1979). Toward a classification of persons. *Journal of Applied Psychology, (Monograph), 64,* 569–607.

Pleban, R., & Tesser, A. (1981). The effects of relevance and quality of another's performance on interpersonal closeness. *Social Psychology Quarterly, 44,* 278–285.

Ross, L., Green, D., & House, P. (1977). The false consensus phenomenon: An attributional bias in self-perception. *Journal of Experimental Social Psychology, 13,* 279–301.

Secord, P. F., & Backman, C. W. (1965). An interpersonal approach to personality. In B. A. Maher (Ed.). *Progress in experimental personality research* (Vol. 2) (pp. 91–125). New York: Academic Press.

Secord, P. F., Backman, C. W., & Eachus, H. T. (1964). Effects of imbalance in the self-concept on the perception of persons. *Journal of Abnormal and Social Psychology, 68,* 442–446.

Sherwood, G. G. (1981). Self-serving biases in person perception: A reexamination of defense. *Psychological Bulletin, 90,* 445–459.

Stryker, S., & Statham, A. (1985). Symbolic interaction and role theory. In G. Lindzey & E. Aronson (Eds.), *Handbook of social psychology* (Vol. I) (3rd ed.) (pp. 311–378). New York: Random House.

Suls, J. & Wan, C. K. (1987). In search of the false uniqueness phenomenon: Fear and estimates of social consensus. *Journal of Personality and Social Psychology, 52,* 211–217.

Swann, W. B., Jr. (1983). Self-verification: Bringing social reality into harmony with the self. In J. Suls & A. G. Greenwald (Eds.), *Psychological perspectives on the self* (Vol. 2). Hillsdale, NJ: Erlbaum.

Swann, W. B., & Predmore, S. C. (1985). Intimates as agents of social support: Sources of consolation or despair? *Journal of Personality and Social Psychology, 49,* 1609–1617.

Taylor, S. E., & Brown, J. D. (1986). Illusion and well-being: Some social psychological contributions to a theory of mental health. Submitted to *American Psychologist.*

Tesser, A. (1980). Self-esteem maintenance in family dynamics. *Journal of Personality and Social Psychology, 39,* 77–91.

Tesser, A. (1984). Self-evaluation maintenance processes: Implications for relationships and development. In J. Masters & K. Yarkin (Eds.), *Boundary areas of psychology: Social and development.* New York: Academic Press.

Tesser, A., & Barbee, A. (1985). *Appearing competent: Self-evaluation maintenance processes.* Unpublished manuscript, University of Georgia.

Tesser, A., & Campbell, J. (1980). Self-definition: The impact of the relative performance and similarity of others. *Social Psychology Quarterly, 43*, 341–347.

Tesser, A., & Campbell, J. (1982). Self-evaluation maintenance and the perception of friends and strangers. *Journal of Personality, 59*, 261–279.

Tesser, A., & Campbell, J. (1983). Self-definition and self-evaluation maintenance. In J. Suls & A. Greenwald (Eds.), *Social psychological perspectives on the self* (Vol. 2).

Tesser, A., & Campbell, J. (1986). A self-evaluation maintenance model of student motivation. In C. Ames & R. Ames (Eds.), *Research on motivation in education: The classroom milieu.* Orlando, FL: Academic Press.

Tesser, A., Campbell, J., & Smith, M. (1984). Friendship choice and performance: Self-evaluation maintenance in children. *Journal of Personality and Social Psychology, 46*, 561–574.

Tesser, A., & Moore, J. (1987). On the convergence of public and private aspect of self. In R. Baumeister (Ed.), *Public self and private self.* Berlin: Springer-Verlag.

Tesser, A., & Paulhus, D. (1983). The definition of self: Private and public self-evaluation management strategies. *Journal of Personality and Social Psychology, 44*, 672–682.

Tesser, A., & Smith, J. (1980). Some effects of friendship and task relevance on helping: You don't always help the one you like. *Journal of Experimental Social Psychology, 16*, 582–590.

Thibaut, J. W., & Kelley, H. H. (1959). *The social psychology of groups.* New York: Wiley.

Thornton, D. A., & Arrowood, A. J. (1966). Self-evaluation, self-enhancement, and the locus of social comparison. *Journal of Experimental Social Psychology, 2* (Suppl. 1), 40–48.

Wheeler, L. (1966). Motivation as a determinant of upward comparison. *Journal of Experimental Social Psychology, 2* (Suppl. 1), 27–31.

Wheeler, L., Shaver, K. G., Jones, R. A., Goethals, G. R., Cooper, J., Robinson, J. E., Gruder, C. L., & Butzine, K. W. (1969). Factors determining choice of a comparison other. *Journal of Experimental Social Psychology, 5*, 219–232.

Wills, T. A. (1981). Downward comparison principles in social psychology. *Psychological Bulletin, 90*, 245–271.

Wills, T. A. (1985). Downward comparison as a coping mechanism. In C. R. Snyder & C. Ford (Eds.), *Clinical and social-psychological perspectives on negative life events.* New York: Academic Press.

Wilson, S. R., & Benner, L. A. (1971). The effects of self-esteem and situation upon comparison choices during ability evaluation. *Sociometry, 34*, 381–397.

Wood, J. V., Taylor, S. E., & Lichtman, R. R. (1985). Social comparison in adjustment to breast cancer. *Journal of Personality and Social Psychology, 49*, 1169–1183.

Wurf, E., & Markus, H. (1983). *Cognitive consequences of the negative self.* Paper presented at 91st annual meeting of the American Psychological Association, Anaheim, CA.

Zuckerman, M. (1979). Attribution of success and failure revisited, or: The motivational bias is alive and well in attribution theory. *Journal of Personality, 47*, 245–287.

# Appendix: How to Read
# a Journal Article in Social Psychology

Christian H. Jordan and Mark P. Zanna • University of Waterloo

## How to Read a Journal Article in Social Psychology

When approaching a journal article for the first time, and often on subsequent occasions, most people try to digest it as they would any piece of prose. They start at the beginning and read word for word, until eventually they arrive at the end, perhaps a little bewildered, but with a vague sense of relief. This is not an altogether terrible strategy; journal articles do have a logical structure that lends itself to this sort of reading. There are, however, more efficient approaches–approaches that enable you, a student of social psychology, to cut through peripheral details, avoid sophisticated statistics with which you may not be familiar, and focus on the central ideas in an article. Arming yourself with a little foreknowledge of what is contained in journal articles, as well as some practical advice on how to read them, should help you read journal articles more effectively. If this sounds tempting, read on.

Journal articles offer a window into the inner workings of social psychology. They document how social psychologists formulate hypotheses, design empirical studies, analyze the observations they collect, and interpret their results. Journal articles also serve an invaluable archival function: They contain the full store of common and cumulative knowledge of social psychology. Having documentation of past research allows researchers to build on past findings and advance our understanding of social behavior, without pursuing avenues of investigation that have already been explored. Perhaps most importantly, a research study is never complete until its results have been shared with others, colleagues and students alike. Journal articles are a primary means of communicating research findings. As such, they can be genuinely exciting and interesting to read.

That last claim may have caught you off guard. For beginning readers, journal articles may seem anything but interesting and exciting. They may, on the contrary, appear daunting and esoteric, laden with jargon and obscured by menacing statistics. Recognizing this fact, we hope to arm you, through this paper, with the basic information you will need to read journal articles with a greater sense of comfort and perspective.

Social psychologists study many fascinating topics, ranging from prejudice and discrimination, to culture, persuasion, liking and love, conformity and obedience, aggres-

461

sion, and the self. In our daily lives, these are issues we often struggle to understand. Social psychologists present systematic observations of, as well as a wealth of ideas about, such issues in journal articles. It would be a shame if the fascination and intrigue these topics have were lost in their translation into journal publications. We don't think they are, and by the end of this paper, hopefully you won't either.

Journal articles come in a variety of forms, including research reports, review articles, and theoretical articles. Put briefly, a *research report* is a formal presentation of an original research study, or series of studies. A *review article* is an evaluative survey of previously published work, usually organized by a guiding theory or point of view. The author of a review article summarizes previous investigations of a circumscribed problem, comments on what progress has been made toward its resolution, and suggests areas of the problem that require further study. A *theoretical article* also evaluates past research, but focuses on the development of theories used to explain empirical findings. Here, the author may present a new theory to explain a set of findings, or may compare and contrast a set of competing theories, suggesting why one theory might be the superior one.

This paper focuses primarily on how to read research reports, for several reasons. First, the bulk of published literature in social psychology consists of research reports. Second, the summaries presented in review articles, and the ideas set forth in theoretical articles, are built on findings presented in research reports. To get a deep understanding of how research is done in social psychology, fluency in reading original research reports is essential. Moreover, theoretical articles frequently report new studies that pit one theory against another, or test a novel prediction derived from a new theory. In order to appraise the validity of such theoretical contentions, a grounded understanding of basic findings is invaluable. Finally, most research reports are written in a standard format that is likely unfamiliar to new readers. The format of review and theoretical articles is less standardized, and more like that of textbooks and other scholarly writings, with which most readers are familiar. This is not to suggest that such articles are easier to read and comprehend than research reports; they can be quite challenging indeed. It is simply the case that, because more rules apply to the writing of research reports, more guidelines can be offered on how to read them.

## The Anatomy of Research Reports

Most research reports in social psychology, and in psychology in general, are written in a standard format prescribed by the American Psychological Association (1994). This is a great boon to both readers and writers. It allows writers to present their ideas and findings in a clear, systematic manner. Consequently, as a reader, once you understand this format, you will not be on completely foreign ground when you approach a new research report—regardless of its specific content. You will know where in the paper particular information is found, making it easier to locate. No matter what your reasons for reading a research report, a firm understanding of the format in which they are written will ease your task. We discuss the format of research reports next, with some practical suggestions on how to read them. Later, we discuss how this format reflects the process of scientific investigation, illustrating how research reports have a coherent narrative structure.

### TITLE AND ABSTRACT.

Though you can't judge a book by its cover, you can learn a lot about a research report simply by reading its title. The title presents a concise statement of the theoretical issues investigated, and/or the variables that were studied. For example, the following title was taken almost at random from a prestigious journal in social psychology: "Sad and guilty? Affective influences on the explanation of conflict in close relationships" (Forgas, 1994, p.

56). Just by reading the title, it can be inferred that the study investigated how emotional states change the way people explain conflict in close relationships. It also suggests that when feeling sad, people accept more personal blame for such conflicts (i.e., feel more guilty).

The abstract is also an invaluable source of information. It is a brief synopsis of the study, and packs a lot of information into 150 words or less. The abstract contains information about the problem that was investigated, how it was investigated, the major findings of the study, and hints at the theoretical and practical implications of the findings. Thus, the abstract is a useful summary of the research that provides the gist of the investigation. Reading this outline first can be very helpful, because it tells you where the report is going, and gives you a useful framework for organizing information contained in the article.

The title and abstract of a research report are like a movie preview. A movie preview highlights the important aspects of a movie's plot, and provides just enough information for one to decide whether to watch the whole movie. Just so with titles and abstracts; they highlight the key features of a research report to allow you to decide if you want to read the whole paper. And just as with movie previews, they do not give the whole story. Reading just the title and abstract is never enough to fully understand a research report.

## INTRODUCTION

A research report has four main sections: introduction, method, results, and discussion. Though it is not explicitly labeled, the introduction begins the main body of a research report. Here, the researchers set the stage for the study. They present the problem under investigation, and state why it was important to study. By providing a brief review of past research and theory relevant to the central issue of investigation, the researchers place the study in an historical context and suggest how the study advances knowledge of the problem. Beginning with broad theoretical and practical considerations, the researchers delineate the rationale that led them to the specific set of hypotheses tested in the study. They also describe how they decided on their research strategy (e.g., why they chose an experiment or a correlational study).

The introduction generally begins with a broad consideration of the problem investigated. Here, the researchers want to illustrate that the problem they studied is a real problem about which people should care. If the researchers are studying prejudice, they may cite statistics that suggest discrimination is prevalent, or describe specific cases of discrimination. Such information helps illustrate why the research is both practically and theoretically meaningful, and why you should bother reading about it. Such discussions are often quite interesting and useful. They can help you decide for yourself if the research has merit. But they may not be essential for understanding the study at hand. Read the introduction carefully, but choose judiciously what to focus on and remember. To understand a study, what you really need to understand is what the researchers' hypotheses were, and how they were derived from theory, informal observation, or intuition. Other background information may be intriguing, but may not be critical to understand what the researchers did and why they did it.

While reading the introduction, try answering these questions: What problem was studied, and why? How does this study relate to, and go beyond, past investigations of the problem? How did the researchers derive their hypotheses? What questions do the researchers hope to answer with this study?

## METHOD

In the method section, the researchers translate their hypotheses into a set of specific, testable questions. Here, the researchers introduce the main characters of the study—the subjects or participants—describing their characteristics (gender, age, etc.) and how many of them were involved. Then, they describe the materials (or apparatus), such as any questionnaires or special equipment, used in the study. Finally, they describe chronologically the procedures of the study; that is, how the study was conducted. Often, an overview of the research design will begin the method section. This overview provides a broad outline of the design, alerting you to what you should attend.

The method is presented in great detail so that other researchers can recreate the study to confirm (or question) its results. This degree of detail is normally not necessary to understand a study, so don't get bogged down trying to memorize the particulars of the procedures. Focus on how the independent variables were manipulated (or measured) and how the dependent variables were measured.

Measuring variables adequately is not always an easy matter. Many of the variables psychologists are interested in cannot be directly observed, so they must be inferred from participants' behavior. Happiness, for example, cannot be directly observed. Thus, researchers interested in how being happy influences people's judgments must infer happiness (or its absence) from their behavior—perhaps by asking people how happy they are, and judging their degree of happiness from their responses; perhaps by studying people's facial expressions for signs of happiness, such as smiling. Think about the measures researchers use while reading the method section. Do they adequately reflect or capture the concepts they are meant to measure? If a measure seems odd, consider carefully how the researchers justify its use.

Oftentimes in social psychology, getting there is half the fun. In other words, how a result is obtained can be just as interesting as the result itself. Social psychologists often strive to have participants behave in a natural, spontaneous manner, while controlling enough of their environment to pinpoint the causes of their behavior. Sometimes, the major contribution of a research report is its presentation of a novel method of investigation. When this is the case, the method will be discussed in some detail in the introduction.

Participants in social psychology studies are intelligent and inquisitive people who are responsive to what happens around them. Because of this, they are not always initially told the true purpose of a study. If they were told, they might not act naturally. Thus, researchers frequently need to be creative, presenting a credible rationale for complying with procedures, without revealing the study's purpose. This rationale is known as a *cover story,* and is often an elaborate scenario. While reading the method section, try putting yourself in the shoes of a participant in the study, and ask yourself if the instructions given to participants seem sensible, realistic, and engaging. Imagining what it was like to be in the study will also help you remember the study's procedure, and aid you in interpreting the study's results.

While reading the method section, try answering these questions: How were the hypotheses translated into testable questions? How were the variables of interest manipulated and/or measured? Did the measures used adequately reflect the variables of interest? For example, is self-reported income an adequate measure of social class? Why or why not?

## RESULTS

The results section describes how the observations collected were analyzed to determine whether the original hypotheses were supported. Here, the data (observations of behavior) are described, and statistical tests are presented. Because of this, the results section is often intimidating to readers who have little or no training in statistics. Wading through complex and unfamiliar statistical analyses is understandably confusing and frustrating. As a result, many students are tempted to skip over reading this section. We advise you not to do so. Empirical findings are the foundation of any science and results sections are where such findings are presented.

Take heart. Even the most prestigious researchers were once in your shoes and sympathize with you. Though space in psychology journals is limited, researchers try to strike a balance between the need to be clear and the need to be brief in describing their results. In an influential paper on how to write good research reports, Bem (1987) offered this advice to researchers:

> No matter how technical or abstruse your article is in its particulars, intelligent nonpsychologists with no expertise in statistics or experimental design should be able to comprehend the broad outlines of what you did and why. They should understand in general terms what was learned. (p. 74)

Generally speaking, social psychologists try to practice this advice.

Most statistical analyses presented in research reports test specific hypotheses. Often, each analysis presented is preceded by a reminder of the hypothesis it is meant to test. After an analysis is presented, researchers usually provide a narrative description of the result in plain English. When the hypothesis tested by a statistical analysis is not explicitly stated, you can usually determine the hypothesis that was tested by reading this narrative description of the result, and referring back to the introduction to locate an hypothesis that corresponds to that result. After even the most complex statistical analysis, there will be a written description of what the result means conceptually. Turn your attention to these descriptions. Focus on the conceptual meaning of research findings, not on the mechanics of how they were obtained (unless you're comfortable with statistics).

Aside from statistical tests and narrative descriptions of results, results sections also frequently contain tables and graphs. These are efficient summaries of data. Even if you are not familiar with statistics, look closely at tables and graphs, and pay attention to the means or correlations presented in them. Researchers always include written descriptions of the pertinent aspects of tables and graphs. While reading these descriptions, check the tables and graphs to make sure what the researchers say accurately reflects their data. If they say there was a difference between two groups on a particular dependent measure, look at the means in the table that correspond to those two groups, and see if the means do differ as described. Occasionally, results seem to become stronger in their narrative description than an examination of the data would warrant.

Statistics *can* be misused. When they are, results are difficult to interpret. Having said this, a lack of statistical knowledge should not make you overly cautious while reading results sections. Though not a perfect antidote, journal articles undergo extensive review by professional researchers before publication. Thus, most misapplications of statistics are caught and corrected before an article is published. So, if you are unfamiliar with statistics, you can be reasonably confident that findings are accurately reported.

While reading the results section, try answering these questions: Did the researchers provide evidence that any independent variable manipulations were effective? For example, if testing for behavioral differences between happy and sad participants, did the researchers demonstrate that one group was in fact happier than the other? What were the major findings of the study? Were the researchers' original hypotheses supported by their observations? If not, look in the discussion section for how the researchers explain the findings that were obtained.

## DISCUSSION

The discussion section frequently opens with a summary of what the study found, and an evaluation of whether the findings supported the original hypotheses. Here, the researchers evaluate the theoretical and practical implications of their results. This can be particularly interesting when the results did not work out exactly as the researchers anticipated. When such is the case, consider the researchers' explanations carefully, and see if they seem plausible to you. Often, researchers will also report any aspects of their study that limit their interpretation of its results, and suggest further research that could overcome these limitations to provide a better understanding of the problem under investigation.

Some readers find it useful to read the first few paragraphs of the discussion section before reading any other part of a research report. Like the abstract, these few paragraphs usually contain all of the main ideas of a research report: What the hypotheses were, the major findings and whether they supported the original hypotheses, and how the findings relate to past research and theory. Having this information before reading a research report can guide your reading, allowing you to focus on the specific details you need to complete your understanding of a study. The description of the results, for example, will alert you to the major variables that were studied. If they are unfamiliar to you, you can pay special attention to how they are defined in the introduction, and how they are operationalized in the method section.

After you have finished reading an article, it can also be helpful to reread the first few paragraphs of the discussion and the abstract. As noted, these two passages present highly distilled summaries of the major ideas in a research report. Just as they can help guide your reading of a report, they can also help you consolidate your understanding of a report once you have finished reading it. They provide a check on whether you have understood the main points of a report, and offer a succinct digest of the research in the authors' own words.

While reading the discussion section, try answering these questions: What conclusions can be drawn from the study? What new information does the study provide about the problem under investigation? Does the study help resolve the problem? What are the practical and theoretical implications of the study's findings? Did the results contradict past research findings? If so, how do the researchers explain this discrepancy?

## Some Notes on Reports of Multiple Studies

Up to this point, we have implicitly assumed that a research report describes just one study. It is also quite common, however, for a research report to describe a series of studies of the same problem in a single article. When such is the case, each study reported will have the same basic structure (introduction, method, results, and discussion sections) that we have outlined, with the notable exception that sometimes the results and discussion section for each study are combined. Combined "results and discussion" sections contain the same information that separate results and discussion sections normally contain. Sometimes, the authors present all their results first, and only then discuss the implications of these results, just as they would in separate results and discussion sections. Other times, however, the authors alternate between describing results and discussing their implications, as each result is presented. In either case, you should be on the lookout for the same information, as outlined above in our consideration of separate results and discussion sections.

Reports including multiple studies also differ from single study reports in that they include more general introduction and discussion sections. The general introduction, which begins the main body of a research report, is similar in essence to the introduction of a single study report. In both cases, the researchers describe the problem investigated and its practical and theoretical significance. They also demonstrate how they derived their hypotheses, and explain how their research relates to past investigations of the problem. In contrast, the separate introductions to each individual study in reports of multiple studies are usually quite brief, and focus more specifically on the logic and rationale of each particular study presented. Such introductions generally describe the methods used in the particular study, outlining how they answer questions that have not been adequately addressed by past research, including studies reported earlier in the same article.

General discussion sections parallel discussions of single studies, except on a somewhat grander scale. They present all of the information contained in discussions of single studies, but consider the implications of all the studies presented together. A general discussion section brings the main ideas of a research program into bold relief. It typically begins with a concise summary of a research program's main findings, their relation to the original hypotheses, and their practical and theoretical implications. Thus, the summaries that begin general discussion sections are counterparts of the summaries that begin discussion sections of single study reports. Each presents a digest of the research presented in an article that can serve as both an organizing framework (when read first), and as a check on how well you have understood the main points of an article (when read last).

## Research Reporting as Story Telling

A research report tells the story of how a researcher or group of researchers investigated a specific problem. Thus, a research report has a linear, narrative structure with a beginning, middle, and end. In his paper on writing research reports, Bem noted that a research report:

> ...is shaped like an hourglass. It begins with broad general statements, progressively narrows down to the specifics of [the] study, and then broadens out again to more general considerations. (1987, p. 175)

This format roughly mirrors the process of scientific investigation, wherein researchers do the following: (1) start with a broad idea from which they formulate a narrower set of hypotheses, informed by past empirical findings (introduction); (2) design a specific set of concrete operations to test these hypotheses (method); (3) analyze the observations collected in this way, and decide if they support the original hypotheses (results); and (4) explore the broader theoretical and practical implications of the findings, and consider how they contribute to an understanding of the problem under investigation (discussion). Though these stages are somewhat arbitrary distinctions—research actually proceeds in a number of different ways—they help elucidate the inner logic of research reports.

While reading a research report, keep this linear structure in mind. Though it is difficult to remember a series of seemingly disjointed facts, when these facts are joined together in a logical, narrative structure, they become easier to comprehend and recall. Thus, always remember that a research report tells a story. It will help you to organize the information you read, and remember it later.

Describing research reports as stories is not just a convenient metaphor. Research reports are stories. Stories can be said to consist of two components: A telling of what happened, and an explanation of why it happened. It is tempting to view science as an endeavor that simply catalogues facts, but nothing is further from the truth. The goal of science, social psychology included, is to *explain* facts, to explain *why* what happened happened. Social psychology is built on the dynamic interplay of discovery and justification, the dialogue between systematic observation of relations and their theoretical explanation. Though research reports do present novel facts based on systematic observation, these facts are presented in the service of ideas. Facts in isolation are trivia. Facts tied together by an explanatory theory are science. Therein lies the story. To really understand what researchers have to say, you need consider how their explanations relate to their findings.

## The Rest of the Story

> There is really no such thing as research. There is only search, more search, keep on searching. (Bowering, 1988, p. 95)

Once you have read through a research report, and understand the researchers' findings and their explanations of them, the story does not end there. There is more than one interpretation for any set of findings. Different researchers often explain the same set of facts in different ways.

Let's take a moment to dispel a nasty rumor. The rumor is this: Researchers present their studies in a dispassionate manner, intending only to inform readers of their findings and their interpretation of those findings. In truth, researchers aim not only to inform readers, but also to *persuade* them (Sternberg, 1995). Researchers want to convince you their ideas are right. There is never only one explanation for a set of findings. Certainly, some explanations are better than others; some fit the available data better, are more parsimonious, or require fewer questionable assumptions. The point here is that researchers are very passionate about their ideas, and want you to believe them. It's up to you to decide if you want to buy their ideas or not.

Let's compare social psychologists to salesclerks. Both social psychologists and salesclerks want to sell you something; either their ideas, or their wares. You need to decide if you want to buy what they're selling or not—and there are potentially negative consequences for either decision. If you let a sales clerk dazzle you with a sales pitch, without thinking about it carefully, you might end up buying a substandard product that you don't really need. After having done this a few times, people tend to become cynical, steeling themselves against any and all sales pitches. This too is dangerous. If you are overly critical of sales pitches, you could end up foregoing genuinely useful products. Thus, by analogy, when you are too critical in your reading of research reports, you might dismiss, out of hand, some genuinely useful ideas—ideas that can help shed light on why people behave the way they do.

This discussion raises the important question of how critical one should be while reading a research report. In part, this will depend on why one is reading the report. If you are reading it simply to learn what the researchers have to say about a particular issue, for example, then there is usually no need to be overly critical. If you want to use the research as a basis for planning a new study, then you should be more critical. As you develop an understanding of psychological theory and research methods, you will also develop an ability to criticize research on many different levels. And *any* piece of research can be criticized at some level. As Jacob Cohen put it, "A successful piece of research doesn't conclusively settle an issue, it just makes some theoretical proposition to some degree more likely" (1990, p. 1311). Thus, as a consumer of research reports, you have to strike a delicate balance between being overly critical and overly accepting.

While reading a research report, at least initially, try to suspend your disbelief. Try to understand the researchers' story; that is, try to understand the facts—the findings and how they were obtained—and the suggested explanation of those facts—the researchers' interpretation of the findings and what they mean. Take the research to task only after you feel you understand what the authors are trying to say.

Research reports serve not only an important archival function, documenting research and its findings, but also an invaluable stimulus function. They can excite other researchers to join the investigation of a particular issue, or to apply new methods or theory to a different, perhaps novel, issue. It is this stimulus function that Elliot Aronson, an eminent social psychologist, referred to when he admitted that, in publishing a study, he hopes his colleagues will "look at it, be stimulated by it, be provoked by it, annoyed by it, and then go ahead and do it better.... That's the exciting thing about science; it progresses by people taking off on one another's work" (1995, p. 5). Science is indeed a cumulative enterprise, and each new study builds on what has (or, sometimes, has not) gone before it. In this way, research articles keep social psychology vibrant.

A study can inspire new research in a number of different ways, such as: (1) it can lead one to conduct a better test of the hypotheses, trying to rule out alternative explanations of the findings; (2) it can lead one to explore the limits of the findings, to see how widely applicable they are, perhaps exploring situations to which they do not apply; (3) it can lead one to test the implications of the findings, furthering scientific investigation of the phenomenon; (4) it can inspire one to apply the findings, or a novel methodology, to a different area of investigation; and (5) it can provoke one to test the findings in the context of a specific real world problem, to see if they can shed light on it. All of these are excellent extensions of the original research, and there are, undoubtedly, other ways that research findings can spur new investigations.

The problem with being too critical, too soon, while reading research reports is that the only further research one may be willing to attempt is research of the first type: Redoing a study better. Sometimes this is desirable, particularly in the early stages of investigating a particular issue, when the findings are novel and perhaps unexpected. But redoing a reasonably compelling study, without extending it in any way, does little to advance our understanding of human behavior. Although the new study might be "better," it will not be "perfect," so *it* would have to be run again, and again, likely never reaching a stage where it is beyond criticism. At some point, researchers have to decide that the evidence is compelling enough to warrant investigation of the last four types. It is these types of studies that most advance our knowledge of social behavior. As you read more research reports, you will become more comfortable deciding when a study is "good enough" to move beyond it. This is a somewhat subjective judgment, and should be made carefully.

When social psychologists write up a research report for publication, it is because they believe they have something new and exciting to communicate about social behavior. Most research reports that are submitted for publication are rejected. Thus, the reports that are eventually published are deemed pertinent not only by the researchers who wrote them, but also by the reviewers and editors of the journals in which they are published. These people, at least, believe the research reports they write and publish have something important and interesting to say. Sometimes, you'll disagree; not all journal articles are created equal, after all. But we recommend that you, at least initially, give these well-meaning social psychologists the benefit of the doubt. Look for what they're excited about. Try to understand the authors' story, and see where it leads you.

## Author Notes

Preparation of this paper was facilitated by a Natural Sciences and Engineering Research Council of Canada doctoral fellowship to Christian H. Jordan. Thanks to Roy Baumeister, Arie Kruglanski, Ziva Kunda, John Levine, Geoff MacDonald, Richard Moreland, Ian Newby-Clark, Steve Spencer, and Adam Zanna for their insightful comments on, and appraisals of, various drafts of this paper. Thanks also to Arie Kruglanski and four anonymous editors of volumes in the series, Key Readings in Social Psychology for their helpful critiques of an initial outline of this paper. Correspondence concerning this article should be addressed to Christian H. Jordan, Department of Psychology, University of Waterloo, Waterloo, Ontario, Canada N2L 3G1. Electronic mail can be sent to chjordan@watarts.uwaterloo.ca.

## REFERENCES

American Psychological Association (1994). *Publication manual* (4th ed.). Washington, D.C.

Aronson, E. (1995). Research in social psychology as a leap of faith. In E. Aronson (Ed.), *Readings about the social animal* (7th ed., pp. 3–9). New York: W. H. Freeman and Company.

Bem, D. J. (1987). Writing the empirical journal article. In M. P. Zanna & J. M. Darley (Eds.), *The compleat academic: A practical guide for the beginning social scientist* (pp. 171–201). New York: Random House.

Bowering, G. (1988). *Errata.* Red Deer, Alta.: Red Deer College Press. Cohen, J. (1990). Things I have learned (so far). *American Psychologist, 45,* 1304–1312.

Forgas, J. P. (1994). Sad and guilty? Affective influences on the explanation of conflict in close relationships. *Journal of Personality and Social Psychology, 66,* 56–68.

Sternberg, R. J. (1995). *The psychologist's companion: A guide to scientific writing for students and researchers* (3rd ed.). Cambridge: Cambridge University Press.

# Author Index

# Subject Index